The Writer's Craft

ANNOTATED TEACHER'S EDITION

SENIOR AUTHOR
SHERIDAN BLAU
University of California at Santa Barbara

CONSULTING AUTHOR
PETER ELBOW
University of Massachusetts at Amherst

SPECIAL CONTRIBUTING AUTHOR
DON KILLGALLON
Baltimore County Public Schools

SENIOR CONSULTANTS
Arthur Applebee
State University of New York at Albany

Judith Langer
State University of New York at Albany

ML *McDougal, Littell & Company*
Evanston, Illinois

Dallas • Phoenix • Columbia, SC

ISBN 0-8123-8669-8
Copyright © 1995 by McDougal, Littell & Company
Box 1667, Evanston, Illinois 60204

1 2 3 4 5 6 7 8 9 10–VJM–99 98 97 96 95 94

Contents of the Teacher's Edition

The Writer's Workshops

The authors of *The Writer's Craft* believe that writing is an exciting journey of discovery where students explore ideas, examine options, problem-solve, and share what they have done with others. Every assignment in each Writer's Workshop builds upon these ideas.

Guided ASSIGNMENT

Cause and Effect

FROM THE WATER IS WIDE

BY PAT CONROY

When something important happens in life, we usually want to know why. By analyzing causes and effects, we can understand the world better, learn from mistakes, and even make improvements.

In the following excerpt, Pat Conroy analyzes what went wrong to destroy life on the island of Yamacraw, off the coast of South Carolina. As you read, notice how one primary cause sets off a chain of effects that leads to the end of a way of life.

[Yamacraw] is not a large island, nor an important one, but it represents an era and a segment of history that is rapidly dying in America. The people of the island have changed very little since the Emancipation Proclamation. Indeed, many of them have never heard of this proclamation. They love their island with genuine affection but have watched the young people move to the city, to the lands far away and far removed from Yamacraw. The island is dying, and the people know it.

In the parable of Yamacraw there was a time when the black people supported themselves well. . . . Each morning the strong young men would take to their bateaux and search the shores and inlets for the large clusters of oysters, which the women and old men in the factory shucked into large jars. Yamacraw oysters were world famous . . . and the oyster factories operating on the island provided a substantial living for all the people. Everyone worked and everyone made money. Then a villain appeared. It was an industrial factory situated on a knoll above the Savannah River many miles away from Yamacraw. The villain spewed its excrement into the river, infected the creeks, and as silently as the pull of the tides, the filth crept to the shores of Yamacraw. As every good health inspector knows, the unfortunate consumer who lets an infected oyster slide down his throat is flirting with hepatitis. . . . Soon after this, little white signs were placed by the oyster banks forbidding anyone to gather the oysters. Ten thousand oysters were now as worthless as grains of sand. . . .

Since a factory is soulless and faceless, it could not be moved to understand the destruction its coming had wrought. When the oysters became contaminated, the island's only industry folded almost immediately. The great migration began. A steady flow of people faced with starvation moved toward the cities. They left in search of jobs. . . . Over 300 people left the island. They left reluctantly, but left permanently and returned only on sporadic visits to pay homage to the relatives too old or too stubborn to leave. As the oysters died, so did the people.

Think and Respond

What does Pat Conroy say caused the waters around Yamacraw to become polluted? According to Conroy's analysis, what effects did the pollution have on the island's way of life? What do you think was Conroy's goal in analyzing the chain of events on Yamacraw? How could you use a cause-and-effect analysis to explore a problem or situation?

148

Starting from Literature

Each Guided and Related Assignment begins with a model that focuses on a specific writing type or strategy.

• **The Introduction** presents the writing type to be covered, previews the model, and sets a purpose for reading.

• **Models** cover a wide range of writing types, from traditional and contemporary literature, to newspaper and magazine articles, to TV story boards. Students gain a sense of how writing functions in the real world.

• **Think and Respond** questions allow students to respond to what they have read and prepare them to begin writing a piece of their own.

Related ASSIGNMENT

Responding to Media

Oil potential spawns fears in Alaska tribe

Every day you are bombarded with information from radio, television, magazines, newspapers, movies, billboards, and books. To make sense of all these messages, which sometimes are confusing and contradictory, you must learn to respond to them personally and critically. As you read the newspaper article on this page, think carefully about the information you are being given. Are both sides of the issue being presented fairly?

From USA TODAY

Trimble Gilbert's people have lived in Arctic Village, Alaska, in the barren prairie of the Arctic Circle, for 1,000 years. From the world beyond, they want only privacy.

But Gilbert, and about 300 Gwich'in Indians holding a tribal meeting in Arctic Village this week, now find themselves caught up in an environmental drama that stretches for miles away.

Arctic Village lies in the shadow of the ghostly, frozen Arctic National Wildlife Refuge, home to a 1.5-million-acre coastal plain some think could be a mother lode of oil.

"North America's Saudi Arabia," is what some have called the ANWR; others report the smell of oil in the snow.

Congressional interest in exploring the ANWR—opposed by the Gwich'in who fear it would disrupt the caribou they depend on for subsistence and culture—was put on hold after [recent] . . . oil spills.

But [tension in the Middle East] has scrambled the picture. Some Congress members are now eyeing the ANWR as well as offshore sites in Florida, California and the Northwest.

"We're proud to be in the United States, to be American Indians. But we can see the future," says Gilbert, the chief, spokesman and pastor for the Gwich'in—pronounced GWI-chin—of Arctic Village. "If we lose the caribou, we don't know how we're going to live here."

To environmentalists, renewed interest in ANWR—as well as calls to lift [the] . . . ban on drilling in coastal areas in the Lower 48—is both an overreaction and a symptom of a nonexistent national energy policy. . . .

264

Teaching Strategies

Teacher's notes provide you with all the help you need:

• Prereading suggestions to help motivate and focus your students

• Follow-up ideas to help students respond to the reading and to tie the literature to the writing assignment that follows.

Suggestions on the Teaching Preview page (see T12) provide other ideas for springing into writing from literature.

Moving to Writing

After discussing the model, your students are invited to write on their own. The detailed Guided Assignments lead students through each stage of the writing process, where they are presented with different strategies and encouraged to experiment, problem solve, and collaborate with others.

INVITATION TO *Write*

Russell Baker provided comical instructions for carving a turkey. Now write your own description of a process—one that shows how to do something, tells how something works, or explains how an event takes place.

Does everyone know how to play Monopoly, or how Joe Montana scored a touchdown with just seconds to go? Of course not. That's why process explanations are so useful. They help people learn from each other about how to do something, how something works, or how an event happened. To help others learn about processes you understand, you need to analyze what goes into the process—what steps are involved and sometimes what skills and materials are needed. In the assignment that follows, you will analyze a process and share information by explaining the process to others.

P REWRITE AND EXPLORE

1. Look for Ideas. You complete, observe, or are part of different processes every day. Think about which of these processes most interest you, or try one or more of the following activities to help you identify a process you would like to explain.

Exploratory Activities

- **Observing** Watch favorite performers or athletes in motion and make notes or sketches of the steps they use to complete an action. You may also want to study photos or videotapes.
- **Brainstorming about science and history** Complete the sentence "I wonder how . . ." in as many ways as possible. Perhaps you've always wondered how volcanoes erupt, how a microwave oven works, or how the Statue of Liberty was designed and installed. Let your mind roam free to think of ideas that intrigue you.

HANDBOOKS
FOR HELP & PRACTICE
Sharing Techniques, pp. 323–325
Appropriate Details, p. 355
Solving Problems, pp. 456–458
Sources of Information, pp. 476–478
Interviewing Skills, pp. 481–482

- **Inventing** Think of games or machines you might like to invent and how they might work. You might enjoy brainstorming ideas with a partner and trying them out together.
- **Interviewing** Think of something you wish you knew how to do, such as the Heimlich maneuver, and interview someone in your community who is familiar with the process.
- **Reading literature** Think of fictional works you've read, such as Jack London's "To Build a Fire," in which an explanation of a process adds reality to a scene. Consider a process you might explain as part of a realistic narrative of your own.

One student, Danny, decided to observe his favorite athletes—professional baseball players. He videotaped a baseball game and observed the tape in slow motion, making sketches and notes about pitching and batting. His sketches and notes about pitching follow.

PROBLEM
S O L V I N G
How can I find a process that is interesting or important to me?

ONE STUDENT'S PROCESS

1. stands on mound, leaning toward home plate
2. watches catcher for a sign
3. shifts his weight to his back leg and goes into a windup
4. brings his front leg up waist high, rotates his body away from home plate
5. reaches pitching hand back toward second, swings his raised leg, and pushes off his back leg
6. brings pitching arm around, elbow first, and releases the ball about a foot in front of his head

150   Workshop 5

Informative Writing   151

- **The Invitation to Write** refers back to the literary model and describes the assignment students are to complete.

- Creative **Exploratory Activities** help students find topics they can care about.

- Throughout the lesson, cross-references to the **Handbooks** provide you with ideas for mini-lessons and show your students where they can look for additional help.

- **One Student's Process** follows a student writer through every stage of the assignment.

Also consider whether there is any background information your readers will need before you begin explaining the process. If you are explaining something that readers can do themselves, are there any materials they need to gather or skills they must have before they can do the process? Plan to give this information at the beginning of your explanation, as Russell Baker did.

DRAFT AND DISCOVER

1. Begin your draft. Begin your draft by explaining why the process is important, useful, or worth understanding. Then, with your writing goals in mind, try to describe the process in a lively way that will engage the reader's interest. One of the best ways to accomplish this is to concentrate on telling or showing why this process is important or interesting to you. If you have trouble making your writing lively, try one or more of the following techniques.

HANDBOOKS

Writing Introductions, pp. 341–342
Using Diagrams, pp. 357–358

Strategies

- **Description** Provide enough details so that readers can understand the process exactly or, if appropriate, repeat the steps themselves. Use precise, vivid words to describe the process. In "Slice of Life," for example, Russell Baker used the words *torso, posterior, thigh, drumstick,* and *gristle* to identify parts of a turkey. He used the vivid words *skewered, sawing,* and *sever* to describe the carver's motions.
- **Definition** To keep your readers from becoming confused, define any special terms they might not understand.
- **Illustrations** Look for places where illustrations might help your readers understand the process you are explaining. Often a simple diagram can show an action that is difficult to explain in words. A flowchart can help readers understand at a glance how all the steps in a process are related. See the Related Assignment on page 168 for help in creating a flow chart.
- **Ways to begin** Use your introduction to establish clearly for your readers what you will be explaining. Think of ways to make your readers recognize why

PROBLEM SOLVING

How can I make my writing lively?

- **Drafting Strategies** demonstrate how modes and purposes can be woven together.
- **Problem-Solving notes** show students that writing is a series of questions and decisions.

- **Writer's Choice** options remind students that there is no one right way to complete any piece of writing.
- **Review questions** for both the writer and the peer reader make revision a rich, interactive process.
- **The Standards for Evaluation** feature shares assessment secrets with the students.
- **Revisions in progress** show peer response at work.
- **Writing Tips, Computer Tips, and Grammar Tips** provide helpful advice where students need it.

Writer's Choice Do you want to maintain your original position or reevaluate it in light of your responses?

5. Take a break. Give your draft a rest. Then return to it by asking yourself—and your peer readers—challenging questions such as the following.

COMPUTER TIP

Invite another writer to type in comments and questions in a different font. Answer them, and then erase the reader's comments.

REVIEW YOUR WRITING

Questions for Yourself

- Does my paper help me understand the issue more completely?
- Do I clearly state the nature of the issue and my position on it?
- Do I recognize possible objections to my views? Do I answer them?
- Have I included facts and details to support my position?
- Have I included a strong conclusion?

Questions for Your Peer Readers

- Is my paper interesting to read?
- Does the opening make the issue clear?
- Where do you think my position is strongest? Where do you think my position is weakest?
- Does my paper sound as if I respect you as a reader? Does my paper sound as if I respect those who disagree with me?
- Can you think of other points to support my view? To oppose it?

HANDBOOKS

FOR HELP & PRACTICE

Peer Response, pp. 378–382
Grammatical Voice, pp. 417–418
Evaluating Ideas, pp. 452–453
Faulty Reasoning, pp. 453–455

REVISE YOUR WRITING

1. Evaluate your responses. Think about your own and your readers' reactions to your paper. Which ones have hit on points that you ought to change? Also keep in mind these guidelines for evaluating persuasive writing.

Standards for Evaluation

Effective persuasive writing . . .

- states the topic clearly in an effective introduction.
- supports a clearly stated opinion with facts or reasons, and elaborates on each reason.
- maintains a reasonable tone.
- takes opposing views into account and answers them.
- uses language effectively and avoids faulty logic.
- includes a conclusion that sums up reasons or provides a call to action.

2. Problem-solve. Rework your draft to fix the problems you have identified. Helen made the changes below after a peer reader wrote suggestions on her first draft.

ONE STUDENT'S PROCESS

Most of us go through our entire lives without ever seeing an animal dying in a laboratory cage. Its easy for us not to think about the suffering thats involved, because we don't see it.

More than 100 million animals die each year in the labatories of the world.

For a moment, however, try to imagine an island populated by 100 million sick, injured, and dying animals—mice lumpy with tumors, cats writhing in pain after surgery, rabbits blinded by irritating chemicals, pregnant baboons injured in staged automobile accidents, dogs with stomachs weighed down by lethal doses of shoe polish or floor wax.

According to veterinarian and animal-rights advocate Dr. Michael W. Fox,

I agree that it's a terrible situation. Perhaps more details could make it seem more real.

The figure 100 million is impressive. Where did you get it?

Writing **TIP**

To give your writing a lively, personal tone, imagine that your reader is sitting across the table from you.

T5

- **An annotated student model** shows how a completed piece of writing meets the standards presented in the lesson. ▶

- **Linking Grammar and Writing** provides a springboard to language instruction.
- **Creative publishing ideas** make sure students have a real audience for their writing. ▶

- **Learning from Your Writing Process** encourages students to reflect on what they've learned.
- **Writer to Writer** lets students know that professional writers face the same concerns they do.
▼

ONE STUDENT'S PROCESS

Product Testing on Animals is Wrong!

Helen Tanaka

Most of us go through our entire lives without ever seeing an animal dying in a laboratory cage. It's easy for us not to think about the suffering that's involved, because we don't see it. For a moment, however, try to imagine an island populated by 100 million sick, injured, and dying animals—mice lumpy with tumors, cats writhing in pain after surgery, rabbits blinded by irritating chemicals, pregnant baboons injured in staged

| Appeals to audience in an appropriate voice |
| States the topic clearly in an effective introduction |
| Supports opinion with detailed reasons |
| Cites facts to support opinions |

Persuasion **219**

---

3. Proofread your work. Make a clean copy of your paper and then check it for errors in grammar, usage, and mechanics. If you've used statistics to support your argument, make sure they're accurate.

LINKING GRAMMAR AND WRITING

Active Versus Passive Voice

Good persuasive writing usually uses the active voice to make readers feel involved.

PROBLEM: The same reactions are not always shared by people and animals.

CORRECTED: People and other animals don't always share the same reactions.

See Grammar Handbook 33, pages 590–592, for additional help with this problem.

HANDBOOKS FOR HELP & PRACTICE

Publishing Your Work, pp. 402–403
Discussion Skills, pp. 479–480

PUBLISH AND PRESENT

- **Create a leaflet or brochure** out of your persuasive paper. Illustrate it and distribute copies.
- **Give an oral report based on your paper.** Instead of just reading your report aloud, adapt it for a more informal presentation. You might give a brief introduction to your report and then hold a question-and-answer session to involve your classmates.
- **Form a readers' circle.** Get together with peers who have written on the same topic or related topics. Use your discussion as a launching pad for exploration of related topics.
- **Keep your paper in your writing portfolio.** Refer to it whenever you write another persuasive piece.

LEARNING FROM YOUR WRITING PROCESS

WRITER TO WRITER

It is a great mistake to regard a dictionary definition as "telling us all about" a word.

S. I. Hayakawa, U.S. Senator and author

1. Reflect on your writing. Now that you have completed your composition that defines and have read several others, think about the process you followed. Ask yourself the questions below and record your answers in your writing log or attach the page you record your answers on to your definition.

- What did you learn from writing this composition that you might use in the future? In particular, what ways of defining ideas can you use in other pieces of writing?
- Of all the definitions you've read (Didion's, the student's, any of your classmates', and your own), which ones did you like the most? Why did you like them? What made these good definitions? What do you think made them good pieces of writing?

2. Apply your skills. Try your hand at one or more of the following activities.

- **Cross curricular** Choose a key term from a math or science book. Write a brief definition of the term. Then do some thinking and reading about the subject in preparation for writing a longer, extended definition.
- **Literature** Read a poem that defines an abstract term, such as "Spring is like a perhaps hand" by e.e. cummings. Then try writing your own poem. Choose an abstract term like *beauty, justice, friendship,* or *love.* Write a series of vivid, concrete images—thing you can see, touch, taste, hear, or smell—that define the term for you.
- **Related assignments** Follow the suggestions on pages 134–142 to write an extended metaphor or a comparison and contrast composition.

The streamlined **Related Assignments** provide general guidelines for students but allow them the freedom to problem-solve within motivating, less-traditional formats.

Oral Histories	Flow Charts	Learning Logs
Advertisements	Tall Tales	Advice Columns
Song Lyrics	Editorials	Family Histories

The Writing Handbook

When do you want to teach your students about transitional devices? When they write a story? Before they explain a process? Perhaps you want to review the concept with each lesson. With the unique Writing Handbook, *you* decide what your students need to learn and when they need to learn it.

The Writing Handbook is divided into three sections, each with a wealth of mini-lessons:
- Writing Process
- Style
- Academic Skills

Use the cross-references in the Writer's Workshops to decide when to present lessons, or teach them whenever *you* see the need. You can also encourage your students to use the lessons independently.

Using Graphic Devices

At various points during the writing process you may find it difficult to sort out your ideas because you cannot clearly "see" what you are thinking. Using graphic devices—making pictures of what's on your mind—is a good way to help organize your ideas and generate new ones. Some of the graphic devices shown in this lesson can help you find ideas. Others will be more helpful in later stages of the writing process, when you begin elaborating and organizing your ideas, or when you are drafting and revising.

WRITING HANDBOOK 9

Writing **TIP**

Graphic devices can be helpful in both generating and developing ideas.

USING DIAGRAMS

Clustering is a way of showing the relationships among ideas. It is a particularly good way to generate ideas because it allows related ideas to "grow" freely from one another. In a **cluster,** a number of related ideas are grouped together using circles and lines. Two similar ways to show related ideas are **idea trees** and **spider maps.** In an idea tree, the main ideas are shown as "branches" and related ideas as "twigs" on the branches. In a spider map, related ideas are connected like the legs on a spider. Study the examples below.

Cluster—Threatened and Endangered Species

Using Graphic Devices **357**

USING TOPIC SENTENCES

A paragraph is often built on a **topic sentence,** a sentence that states the main idea, or topic, of the paragraph. Sometimes the topic sentence establishes what will be said in the paragraph. Other times the topic sentence summarizes what has been said. A topic sentence can be found anywhere in a paragraph—at the beginning, at the end, or in the middle.

Beginning with the Topic Sentence As you read the following paragraph, notice how the main idea is stated in its first sentence. All the other sentences illustrate or "prove" the main idea with specific details. This is one of the most common ways to develop a paragraph.

The town was dead. Its beds were empty and cold. The only sound was the power hum of electric lines and dynamos, still alive, all by themselves. Water ran in forgotten bathtubs, poured out into living rooms, onto porches, and down through little garden plots to feed neglected flowers. In dark theaters, gum under the many seats began to harden with tooth impressions still in it.

Ray Bradbury, *The Martian Chronicles*

LITERARY **MODEL**

Moon Rise, Hernandez, New Mexico, 1941. Photograph by Ansel Adams

Drafting Paragraphs **347**

- **Each mini-lesson** focuses on a key concept or skill.

- **Literary, professional, and student models** provide examples of different techniques and strategies.

- **Abundant practice** enables students to practice their new skills or hone abilities they already have.

- **Teaching suggestions** in the Teacher's Edition show how mini-lessons can be used for reference, preteaching or reteaching.

Grammar and Usage Handbook

Research has shown that grammar and usage lessons, taught in isolation, do not improve student writing. Indeed, they can sometimes have a negative effect. *The Writer's Craft* solves this problem with its innovative Grammar and Usage Handbook. Every lesson provides instruction and practice in the context of writing, revision, and literature. Students learn not only the *what*, but also the *why* and *how* of language skills.

MISPLACED AND DANGLING MODIFIERS

Place a verbal or verbal phrase as close as possible to the word it modifies.

I saw an alligator at the other side of that pond looking through my binoculars.

Did you find the sentence above unclear or perhaps humorous? If a verbal or verbal phrase is misplaced, it may appear to modify the wrong word and can confuse the reader. In addition, poorly placed modifiers distract the reader from what is actually being said. A word that modifies the wrong word or group of words is called a **misplaced modifier.**

Unclear The three Simpson children attempted to wash the family dog, *giggling wildly*. (Is the dog *giggling wildly*?)

You can easily correct this sentence by bringing the participial phrase and the word it modifies closer together.

Clear *Giggling wildly*, the three Simpson children attempted to wash the family dog. (The participial phrase *Giggling wildly* now clearly modifies *children*.)

Another kind of error is the **dangling modifier.** This error occurs when the word that the verbal phrase should logically relate to is not in the sentence.

Unclear *To mow the lawn*, the grass must be dry. (Who will mow the lawn? The grass?)

One way to correct a dangling modifier is to add the word that ~~relates to. Sometimes additional rewording is~~ ~~sentence clear.~~

~~lawn,~~ you should make sure the grass is dry. ~~w~~ the wording of this sentence has been ~~the phrase~~ *To mow the lawn* now modifies *you*.)

Using Verbals and Appositives   **691**

• Each lesson begins with a thorough introduction to the concept. Numerous charts and examples clarify the explanation.

INDEFINITE PRONOUNS

Indefinite pronouns do not refer to a definite person or thing. An indefinite pronoun usually does not have an antecedent.

Several of the cars were over ten years old.

Occasionally an indefinite pronoun has an antecedent.

The chess players began the game. *Both* were concentrating.

Some indefinite pronouns are singular, and some are plural. Others can be singular or plural, depending on the context.

	Indefinite Pronouns			
Singular	another	each	everything	one
	anybody	either	neither	somebody
	anyone	everybody	nobody	someone
	anything	everyone	no one	something
Plural	both	few	many	others
	several			
Singular or Plural	all	any	most	none
	some			

Practice Your Skills

A. CONCEPT CHECK

Indefinite Pronouns Write the indefinite pronouns in each sentence. Identify each pronoun as *Singular* or *Plural*.

1. No one knows exactly how many people live in the United States, but the Bureau of the Census does its best to find out.
2. The census begins with a list of all of the households in the country.
3. Many people are hired, and some go from door-to-door.
4. Each of the apartments in a building is a separate entry.
5. Then the Bureau sends a form to everyone on the list.
6. Most of the households receive a short form to fill out.
7. Others receive a form with very detailed questions.
8. A difficulty arises when someone does not have a permanent home.
9. Special personnel try to contact anyone without a home.
10. If the census is to succeed, everybody must cooperate.

Writing Theme
The Census

• **Thematic exercises** center around a subject that can be used as a springboard to writing.

Using Pronouns   **561**

- **A variety of exercises** provide meaningful application of each concept.

Concept Checks review the basic idea of the lesson in a simple format.

Drafting and Revision Skills exercises put the concept to work through such activities as sentence combining and elaboration.

Application in Writing allows students to experiment with different formats while applying new skills.

Application in Literature activities show the concept at work in professional writing.

Proofreading activities provide opportunities to sharpen editing skills.

Practice Your Skills

A. CONCEPT CHECK

Adverbs Write the adverbs in this paragraph and the word each modifies. Also tell that word's part of speech.

Writing Theme
Sailing

(1) At dawn the wind fell away, and the ship cruised slowly in the deceptively calm sea. (2) The crew had just finished its morning chores. (3) Suddenly the rain came down in torrents. (4) It soon filled the empty water drums. (5) Then the clouds lifted and the sun broke through. (6) Steam rose from the soaked decks and gradually drifted away. (7) By dark, however, the boat was pitching wildly. (8) Finally, the captain headed the ship south, and it eventually sailed beyond the squall.

B. DRAFTING SKILL

Choosing Adverbs The novelist Henry James once wrote to a friend, "I'm glad you like adverbs—I adore them; they are the only qualifications I really much respect." Write the following passage twice, each time using different adverbs to fill each blank.

(1) Cheryl walked _____ down the block. (2) In the east, the sun had _____ risen. (3) She looked around _____ . (4) As she reached the end of the dock, a board creaked _____ under her foot. (5) The sound was _____ audible. (6) Cheryl breathed _____ . (7) Then she leaned _____ against a piling. (8) Above her, a bird called out _____ , exactly mirroring her own feelings. (9) The sound of voices talking _____ came to her from one of the boats. (10) She turned and walked _____ toward the source of the sounds.

C. APPLICATION IN WRITING

Describing a scene. Adverbs help a writer describe action precisely. Imagine that you want to describe the scene below in a story. Use adverbs to recreate the i

---

sisters. Alcott's faithful readers had no idea that she was also the author of dozens of stories of a very different kind. Including adventure stories and popular thrillers.

C. APPLICATION IN LITERATURE

Using Fragments Effectively As you have learned, professional writers sometimes use fragments for special purposes. Find the fragments in the following passage. Write them on your paper and then add words to make them complete sentences. Compare the two versions and suggest why Saroyan used the fragments in his writing.

(1) [Homer McCauley] got out of bed and brought out his body-building course from New York and began reading the instructions for the day. (2) His brother Ulysses watched, as he always did . . . . (3) After some ordinary preliminary exercises, including deep breathing, Homer lay flat on his back and lifted his legs stiffly from the floor.
(4) "What's that?" Ulysses said.
(5) "Exercises."
(6) "What for?"
(7) "Muscle."
(8) "Going to be the strongest man in the world?"
(9) "Naah."
(10) "What then?"
(11) "You go back to sleep," Homer said.
(12) Ulysses got back in bed but sat up, watching.
(13) At last Homer began to get dressed.
(14) "Where you going?"
(15) "School."

William Saroyan, The Human Comedy

C. PROOFREADING SKILL

Correcting Errors with Modifiers Proofread the following paragraphs. Then rewrite them, correcting all of the errors, including errors in spelling, punctuation, and grammar. Pay special attention to the use of adjectives and adverbs.

Scientists divide whales into two main groups according to there methods of feeding. The largest group is call toothed whales. These kind of whales do not feed on nothing smaller than fish. Among these toothed whales are dolphins porpoises, and killer whales.

The second group, called baleen whales, is more larger in size than toothed whales, baleen whales feed on tiny shrimp-like animales known as plankton. The blue whale, part of this second group, is larger than any animal. Oddly, the group of larger whales' eat the more smaller-sized food.

Scrimshaw on a whale tooth shows whalers towing a dead whale to their ship.

Complete Sentences **527**

Review and Assessment

How can you check your students' progress? The Pupil's Edition and Resource File for *The Writer's Craft* offer a wide variety of assessment tools.

Writing Assessments

• **Writing Prompts** Based on state assessments used by many states and colleges, these prompts allow you to check student writing progress.

• **Guides to Analytic and Holistic Scoring** Guidelines help you check achievement on any writing assignment.

• **Portfolio Assessment Suggestions** in the Pupil Book and guidelines in this Teacher's Edition (see T-28) will help you use this effective evaluative technique.

Grammar and Usage Assessment

• **Checkpoints**
These provide a mixed review after every two or three sections.

• **Section Reviews**
Application and Review Sets allow you to evaluate student progress after every main Handbook section.

• **Skills Assessment**
Structured like many state and college assessments, these items allow a mixed review of dozens of language concepts.

• **Pretests and Mastery Tests**
The standardized format of these tests provide you with a quick way to evaluate student understanding.

T10

Test Prompts
Writing Prompts: Persuasion

A. In many cities and towns across the country, street performers have made a comeback. They play instruments, juggle, or even tell jokes, hoping to earn money for their efforts. Some people feel that these performers enliven a town; others are annoyed by the noise and crowds they attract. *What do you think your community's policy toward these people should be? Write an article to be submitted to your local government defending your point of view.*

B. Jan, who exercises regularly, claims that her workouts relax her and increase her energy. Marc, a fan of spectator rather than participant sports, believes that physical activity for its own sake can become compulsive, leading to injury and to a distorted sense of values. *Write an article for a youth fitness newsletter supporting your opinions on this issue.*

C. Some people would argue that working students are in a good position today. These people might point out that part-time employment opportunities enable students to earn money while still in school and that minimum wage laws ensure that they are paid reasonably for their work. Others might argue that working distracts students from their studies. *Write a letter to the editor of your local newspaper explaining your views on student employment and offering suggestions for action.*

D. *Write a movie review that you will present to the members of your school Teen Screen Club. Choose a movie you have seen recently and be sure to support your recommendation with details about specific aspects of the film, such as plot, characterization, and action.*

E. Experimentation using animals is a major source of scientific knowledge. Many people oppose animal experimentation, however, on the grounds that animal life is as important as human life and that laboratory procedures cause animals unnecessary pain and suffering. On the other hand, proponents may say that laboratory animals are treated with respect and that experiments provide knowledge that will benefit all living things. *In a letter to the editor of your local newspaper, present and support your stand on animal experimentation.*

From Teacher's Resource File

CHECK POINT
PAGES 663–669

Writing Theme
Overcoming Difficulties

A. Write the conjunctions and interjections in the following sentences. Identify each as a *Coordinating Conjunction, Correlative Conjunction, Subordinating Conjunction, Conjunctive Adverb,* or *Interjection.*

1. Elvis Presley was born on January 8, 1935, in a shack in Tupelo, Mississippi, but he rose to wealth and fame unrivaled in the history of rock music.
2. Oh, how his father Vernon worked to provide for his wife and son.
3. At about ten years of age, Elvis asked his parents if he could have a bicycle.
4. They had neither the money nor any way of obtaining it.

APPLICATION AND REVIEW

A. Application in Literature Write the italicized words or phrases in the following passage. Tell whether each verbal is a *Gerund, Participle,* or *Infinitive.*

(1) The dragon Smaug approached the village. . . . *Roaring,* he swept back over the town. (2) A hail of dark arrows leaped up and snapped and rattled on his scales and jewels; and their shafts fell back, *kindled by his breath* burning and hissing into the lake. No fireworks you ever imagined equalled the sights that night. (3) At the *twanging of the bows* and the *shrilling of the trumpets,* the dragon's wrath blazed to its height, till he was blind and mad with it. (4) No one had dared *to give battle to him* for many an age; nor would they have dared now, if it had not been for the grim-voiced man (Bard was his name), wh[...] and urging the M[...] arrow.

(5) Fire leape[...] while high in the[...] trees by the shore[...] *leaping* shadows[...] swooped, straight[...] taking no heed *to*[...] seeking only to se[...]

GRAMMAR
HANDBOOK
37

Writing Theme
Myth and Legend

670

B. Sentence Combining ing the instruction in[...] and make any other nec[...]

1. The dragon appears[...] *It is* a mythical beas[...] an appositive.)
2. In the Orient, drag[...] supernatural wisdom[...] luck. (Use two partic[...]

Skills
ASSESSMENT

TEST 1 *Grammar Handbooks 29–32*

Directions One or more of the underlined sections in the following sentences may contain errors of grammar, usage, punctuation, spelling, or capitalization. Write the letter of each incorrect item, then rewrite the item correctly. If there is no error in an item, write E.

Example Edith Hamiltons' book Mythology makes it clear. That
 A   B
Zeus' power was not unlimited. No error
 C   D   E
Answer A—Edith Hamilton's; B—clear that

1. Although it is commonly accepted by astronomers and other scientists that the Universe

Special Features

Throughout the pupil's editions, special features provide opportunities for students to enjoy themselves as they learn.

- **Sketchbooks**
Sometimes funny, sometimes thought-provoking, the Sketchbooks let students experiment with "no-risk writing."

- **Sentence Composing**
By imitating the sentences of professional writers, students develop their own more sophisticated style.

- **On the Lightside**
Your students will learn that language study can be fun.

Sketchbook

It was at ten o'clock to-day that the first of all Time Machines began its career. I gave it a last tap, tried all the screws again, put one more drop of oil on the quartz rod, and sat myself in the saddle. . . .

H. G. Wells
THE TIME MACHINE

What if a time machine took you to another era? What age would you like to have lived in? How would your life have been different then? How would it have been the same? What could you learn from the people living in that time period? What could you teach them?

Additional Sketches
How do they do that? How does it work?

Write a recipe. It could be directions for cooking something, but it doesn't have to be. It could be a recipe for success, for happiness, or for anything else you can think of.

146

Sentence
COMPOSING

Delayed Modifiers

Experienced writers sometimes place adjectives after (rather than before) the person, place, or thing they describe to add interest, variety, and style to their sentences. Notice how the author, instead of writing "The somber and dull forests," adds power to the model sentence by delaying the adjectives that describe the forest.

MODEL
The forests, <u>somber and dull</u>, stood motionless and silent on each side of the broad stream.
Joseph Conrad, "The Lagoon"

A. Combining Sentences Combine the two sentences by placing the adjectives from the second sentence in the place indicated by a caret ($_\wedge$).

Example
The forests,$_\wedge$, stood motionless and silent on each side of the broad stream. The forests were somber and dull.

Combined Sentence
The forests, <u>somber and dull</u>, stood motionless and silent on each side of the broad stream.

1. A bird somewhere, $_\wedge$, called for its friends. The bird was lonely and lost.
Robert Lipsyte, The Contender

2. The red fearless eyes still looked at him, $_\wedge$. The eyes were impersonal, unafraid and detached.
John Steinbeck, Th

3. The old house was the same, $_\wedge$, but as we stared down the street thought we saw an inside shutter move. The house was droopy ar
Harper Lee, To Kill a Moc

4. The screen glowed silver, and soon life began to unfold, $_\wedge$. Life w beautiful and passionate and sad.
William Faulkner, "Dry Sep

5. The diggers gathered about the rim of the pit, $_\wedge$. The diggers wer staring.
Edmund Ware, "An Underground E

6. A sigh, $_\wedge$, marked an almost imperceptible pause, and then his word flowed on, without a stir, without a gesture. The sigh was short and
Joseph Conrad, Tales of

Sentence

On the Lightside

SPEAKING CAJUN

Perhaps you have tasted gumbo, or jambalaya, or creole, or other Cajun dishes. These complex recipes are reflections of the culture of the Cajuns, who have lived for more than two hundred years in the bayous of southern Louisiana. During this time, however, the Cajuns have contributed more than food; they have also created a rich and hearty language called the Cajun dialect. Like their food, the Cajun language is a spicy mixture. It is basi-

Canada. When the British captured the colony, they forced out everyone who would not swear allegiance to the British. Many of the Acadians moved to Louisiana. There they established their own communities and maintained a separate culture. Their French language did not have the words to describe some of the things they encountered in this frontier land, so they borrowed words from the English settlers, Native Americans, and slaves they encountered in this new homeland. Over time, they even changed

Using The Teacher's Edition

The Teacher's Edition of *The Writer's Craft* provides you with all the help you will need to prepare comprehensive, exciting lessons.

1

Personal and Expressive Writing

Overview

Personal and expressive writing is writing that grows out of the writer's responses to events in his or her own life. Such writing offers individuals a way to reflect on the value and impact of their experiences. Most students find it among the most accessible and inviting forms of writing because, in preparation for it, they need little more than their memories and their powers of reflection. This kind of writing is recommended for early in the year for several reasons. Because it is comfortable and familiar, it allows students to develop skills within a nonthreatening context. In addition, it shows students the value of becoming invested in their own writing, an important notion that will serve them well in all other writing they do. The Workshop includes the following Guided and Related Assignments:

1. **Guided: Reflective Essay** helps students develop techniques and strategies for exploring the significance of experiences and for narrating those experiences.

2. **Related: Autobiographical Incident** develops reflective and narrative skills introduced in the reflective essay by having students explore and recount a specific incident from their own lives and explain its deeper meaning.

3. **Related: Monologue** provides an objective approach to expressive writing by having students examine the inner workings of characters' minds.

Teaching Preview

Preparation Guide

1. Use the Overview on this page and the Teacher's Choice descriptions on page 21 as a basis for deciding which assignment(s) to teach.

2. Preview the assignments and the teacher's notes and identify concerns that may require preteaching or extra support given your class's abilities. The handbook

3. Preview the chart below for support materials in the Teacher's Resource File that may be used with this Workshop. Resources are for use with the Guided Assignment unless otherwise noted.

mini-lessons suggested within the lesson may also provide guidance.

Support Materials

WRITER'S CRAFT RESOURCES

Prewrite and Explore
Thinking Skills Transparencies, pp. 13–14
Thinking Skills Worksheets, p. 9

Draft and Discover
Elaboration, Revision, and Proofreading Worksheets, p. 1

Revise Your Writing
Guidelines for Writing Assessment and Portfolio Use, pp. 8, 19–22
Peer Response Guides, pp. 5–6
Student Revision Model Transparencies, pp. 5–8
Elaboration, Revision, and Proofreading Worksheets, p. 2

Assessment
Tests and Writing Assessment Prompts, p. 1

Extension Activities
Writing Prompts for Fine Art Transparencies, pp. 7, 8, 14, 17, 20
Writing from Literature, pp. 1–44
Standardized Test Practice

Educational Technology
(available separately)
Writer's DataBank
Electronic English Handbook
Multimedia Workshop
Your Personal Trainer for the New SAT
In Perspective (videodisc)

OTHER RESOURCES

Books and Journals
Moffett, James. Active Voice. Portsmouth: Boynton, 1992.
Welty, Eudora. One Writer's Beginnings. Cambridge: Harvard UP, 1984.

Films and Videos
Narration and Description. Films Incorp. Educ. (30 min.).
Writing with Both Sides of Your Brain. Charles Clark Co., Inc.

Computer Software
"Finding a Writing Style." Write On: Secondary Collection. Humanities Software, Inc. Apple family, Macintosh, PC/MS-DOS.
"Writer's Helper Stage II," The IBM Process Writing Package. EduQuest. PC/MS-DOS.

Workshop Management Guidelines

The chart below indicates the number of days recommended for each phase of the Guided and Related Assignments. Stars indicate portions of the assignment that may be completed outside the classroom if time is limited or if teachers wish the activity to be completed by students independently.

REFLECTIVE ESSAY
Starting from Literature	1 day
Prewrite	1–2 days*
Draft	1–2 days*
Revise	1–2 days*
Publish	open
Learning	1 day*
Reteaching	open
Extension/Enrichment	open
Sentence Composing	1 day*

AUTOBIOGRAPHICAL INCIDENT
Starting from Literature	1 day
Exploring	1–2 days*
Drafting	1–2 days*
Reviewing	1–2 days
Publishing	open
Reteaching	open
Extension/Enrichment	open

MONOLOGUE
Starting from Literature	1 day
Preparing	1–2 days*
Creating	1–2 days*
Reviewing	1–2 days
Publishing	open
Reteaching	open
Extension/Enrichment	open

Linking Literature, Writing, and Grammar

The following options may be used to provide students with an integrated language experience. Begin by assigning and discussing any of the recommended pieces of literature. Use the suggested strategy to provide a link to the Guided Assignment.

LINKING LITERATURE AND WRITING

Option 1
Starting Point: excerpt from *Hunger of Memory* by Richard Rodriguez on pages 22–23 of *The Writer's Craft*
Strategy: Use the teaching suggestions on pages 22–23 to lead students into the Guided Assignment.

Option 2
Starting Point: "Lines Composed a Few Miles Above Tintern Abbey" by William Wordsworth
Strategy: Point out that Wordsworth wrote this reflective poem while revisiting the ruins of Tintern Abbey after an absence of five years. As students respond to the poem, help them recognize that the scene — as well as the time that had passed since he had last seen it — made the speaker in the poem aware of a sense of loss as well as a sense of new maturity and insight that increasing years brought. Encourage students to think of places or objects that might trigger important reflections and insights for them on which they might base a reflective essay.

Option 3
Starting Point: "The Marx Brothers" by J.B. Priestley
Strategy: As students respond to this essay, ask them to evaluate its structure. What made Priestley think about the Marx Brothers? Where in his essay does he narrate events? Where in his essay does he reflect on his experiences? What conclusions does he draw about the Marx Brothers from his personal experience? Encourage students to consider ways in which they might apply the kind of structure Priestley has used as they write their own essays.

LINKING WRITING AND GRAMMAR

Before the drafting or revision stage of this assignment, caution students to watch carefully the way they use verb tenses. Remind students that if they describe experiences from the past and then discuss their current reflections about them, they should keep verb tenses consistent: past tense to describe past events and present tense to describe current feelings. Ask students to check their work for consistent use of verb tenses as you write the following examples on the board:

Past Tense: A huge wave *welled* up and seemed about to engulf me. I *screamed* in terror.

Present Tense: When I *look* back and *think* about that wave, I still *feel* that same terror.

Go over the rules about the consistent use of verb tenses on pages 641–653 of the Grammar and Usage Handbook. If problems with verb tense usage still appear in student papers, assign the exercises on those pages for reteaching. Additional practice can be found in the Grammar and Usage Practice Book on pages 41–44.

Teaching Preview Pages

These pages appear before every Writer's Workshop and contain the following information:

• Workshop Overview
Introduces the focus of the workshop and explains the relationships among the Guided and Related Assignments.

• Preparation Guide
Guides your planning decisions and provides a chart of available support materials in the Teacher's Resource File.

• Linking Literature, Writing, and Grammar
Presents three options for basing each writing assignment on literature. Shows how to link any option with a grammar and usage mini-lesson.

• Workshop Management Guidelines
Indicates recommended number of days for each assignment, with suggestions for independent study.

Informative
Exposition:
Classification

Related Assignment
EXTENDED METAPHOR

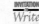

Workshop Introduction

In the Pupil's Edition, this page allows both students and teachers to see — at a glance — the focus of the workshop and the writing types they will be exploring.

• Workshop Objectives

Lists general objectives for the Workshop as a whole.

• Teacher's Choice

Helps the teachers choose assignments by describing each one, suggesting which students might benefit most, and recommending when it might best be taught.

Lesson Notes

The Teacher's Edition continues to help the teacher throughout the lesson. In addition to the literature notes shown on page T3, each lesson contains the following material:

• Objectives

Specific goals for each part of the lesson.

• Preteaching Suggestions

Ideas for using mini-lessons from the Writing Handbook.

• Teaching Strategies

Point-of-Use notes that truly make this one book for all students. Included are suggestions for

Modeling
Speaking and Listening Opportunities
Teaching Tips
Individualizing Instruction Tips for teaching LEP, LD, cultural diversity, and different ability levels
Collaborative Opportunities
Spot Checks
Stumbling Blocks Potential problems and tips to avoid them
Personal Touch Suggestions for making yourself into a co-writer in the classroom
Managing the Paper Load Ideas for cutting down on grading and review

---

Writer's Workshop 4:
Informative Exposition: Classification

Objectives

Guided Assignment: DEFINITION
To recognize examples of extended definition and to plan, draft, revise, proofread, and share an extended definition

Related Assignment: EXTENDED METAPHOR
To identify the characteristics of extended metaphor and to write, review, and share an extended metaphor

Related Assignment: COMPARISON AND CONTRAST
To identify the characteristics of comparison and to write, review, and share a comparison of two people or things

Teacher's Choice

Guided Assignment
Definition This assignment is appropriate for most students because it can accommodate a wide range of topics and skill levels, and it draws on students' particular interests. The assignment also reinforces students' ability to classify and analyze information—prerequisites to the process of synthesis, which students will explore in Workshop 5. This assignment may be most useful after students have had experience with writing descriptions.

Related Assignments
Extended Metaphor This assignment is especially appropriate for advanced students and those keenly interested in literature. Visual learners may find photographs or other works of art useful springboards to writing.

Comparison and Contrast This assignment may be useful with students who are interested in the natural and social sciences. Ties to literature are also evident.

Workshop 4   **117**

Reproduced pupil page:

Prewrite and Explore

Objectives

1. To use prewriting activities to generate ideas for a description of a process
2. To select a topic and explore goals and audience for a process description
3. To gather and organize information for a process description

Preteaching

Preview the Prewrite and Explore section. If there are skills or concepts that your students may need help with, present them at this point. The following mini-lesson references may help you in your selection and instruction. The cross-references in the pupil text will give students access to the same lessons for independent study.

Handbook Mini-Lessons
• Sharing Techniques, pp. 323–325
• Appropriate Details, p. 335
• Solving Problems, pp. 456–458
• Sources of Information, pp. 476–478
• Interviewing Skills, pp. 481–482

Teaching Strategies

Modeling

Show a videotape of a professional football or basketball player in action. If possible, show the action in slow motion. Encourage students to identify the steps followed and list them on the board. If videotapes are unavailable, you might have a student athlete pantomime the steps used to complete an action and list them on the board.

Individualizing Instruction

LEP Students Encourage students to identify processes with which they are familiar and to dramatize or sketch the steps for a peer who can help supply English words.

INVITATION to Write

Russell Baker provided comical instructions for carving a turkey. Now write your own description of a process—one that shows how to do something, tells how something works, or explains how an event takes place.

Does everyone know how to play Monopoly, or how Joe Montana scored a touchdown with just seconds to go? Of course not. That's why process explanations are so useful. They help people learn from each other about how to do something, how something works, or how an event happened. To help others learn about processes you understand, you need to analyze what goes into the process—what steps are involved and sometimes what skills and materials are needed. In the assignment that follows, you will analyze a process and share information by explaining the process to others.

PREWRITE AND EXPLORE

HANDBOOKS FOR HELP & PRACTICE
Sharing Techniques, pp. 323–325
Appropriate Details, p. 335
Solving Problems, pp. 456–458
Sources of Information, pp. 476–478
Interviewing Skills, pp. 481–482

1. Look for ideas. You complete, observe, or are part of different processes every day. Think about which of these processes most interest you, or try one or more of the following activities to help you identify a process you would like to explore.

Exploratory Activities

• **Observing** Watch favorite performers or athletes in motion and make notes or sketches of the steps they use to complete an action. You may also want to study photos or videotapes.

• **Brainstorming about science and history** Complete the sentence "I wonder how . . ." in as many ways as possible. Perhaps you've always wondered how volcanoes erupt, how a microwave oven works, or how the Statue of Liberty was designed and installed. Let your mind roam free to think of ideas that intrigue you.

150   Workshop 5

---

150   Workshop 5

Springboard

Present as a warmup exercise a rapid association of ideas. Begin by mentioning a person, place, thing, or idea. Students should then supply as many "how-to" topics as they can that are related to that idea. For example, the first word mentioned might be school. The students may suggest topics, such as how to use the computers in the computer lab or how to study for a test. Continue supplying topics until all ideas have been exhausted. Then have a student offer another word or phrase that will suggest other how-to topics.

• **Brainstorming** Write the heading "If I Ruled the World" at the top of a sheet of paper. With two or three classmates, make a list of issues that are important to you and what you would do about them.

• **Reading literature** Think about the conflicts in works you've read. For example, the barber in "Lather and Nothing Else" by Hernando Téllez had to decide whether or not to kill his enemy. If you had to choose sides in such a conflict, which side would you be on?

2. Share promising ideas. Look over the ideas you've generated, and narrow your choices down to the most promising issues. Then share them with classmates, listening for their responses to your ideas and also listening for issues mentioned by other students that you might like to pursue.

3. Select and define an issue. Select the issue that seems most promising to you and freewrite for ten minutes presenting your view of it. Don't hesitate to present arguments against your position; you will want to consider and perhaps deal with opposing positions as you write. If you have trouble defining your issue, try listing the basic ideas or positions involved. Here is the list one student, Helen, made of the positions on the issue of product-testing on animals.

Writing **TIP**
Look for issues that have a personal meaning to you.

ONE STUDENT'S PROCESS

animals are subjected to testing for consumer products

some manufacturers conduct cruel experiments that ignore animal rights

some animal rights advocates want tests on animals stopped even when helpful to humans

some scientists feel other testing methods can be used

I Stand Here—I love animals, think unnecessary testing should be stopped

---

Individualizing Instruction

Learning Styles Help visual learners choose an issue by bringing in current news magazines and allowing students to browse through the photographs. Visual and auditory learners might also watch or listen to a news analysis program on television or radio for ideas on current or controversial issues.

Spot Check

As students work through the exploratory activities to select a topic, make sure they are looking at controversial issues and not just matters of personal preference.

Stumbling Block

As students identify and explore their topics for persuasive writing, encourage them to analyze their feelings about the issue carefully. If after defining the issue they are still unsure about how they feel about it, encourage them to look for another topic. (You might refer students to the Data Sheets and the Ideas for Writing Booklet as other sources of ideas for topics.) Emphasize that it is very difficult to persuade someone else about something you are not sure of yourself.

Teacher's Edition *continued*

- **Guidelines for Evaluation** Rubrics for evaluating final student papers.

- **Reteaching** Suggestions for providing additional instruction in areas where students were not successful.

- **Extension and Enrichment Ideas** Moves students beyond the assignment.

- **Learning from Your Writing Process** Helps students learn from each assignment and build writing portfolios.

- **Summary and Closure** Reviews the key points of the lesson.

- **Other Features**

  Connections
  Links to Literature, Science, Social Studies, and the Fine Arts

  Springboards
  Motivating quotes and activities

  Off the Record
  Humor for you—just because you need it sometimes!

Linking Grammar and Writing

As students revise their drafts, suggest that they pay attention to the use of adjectives and adverbs and other modifiers such as the prepositional and participial phrase. You might use or direct students to Handbook 34, Using the Correct Modifier, pages 628–629; Handbook 35, Prepositional Phrases as Modifiers, pages 657–658; and Handbook 37, The Participial Phrase, page 684.

Guidelines for Evaluation

The following guidelines may be used for a close evaluation of a personal narrative. See The Guidelines for Evaluating Writing in the Teacher's Resource File for additional help with holistic or analytic scoring.

Ideas and Content
- relates a meaningful experience
- includes details that fully develop character, setting, and plot
- includes descriptive details and effective dialogue
- demonstrates the importance of the event to the writer
- reflects an awareness of audience in word choice and detail

Structure and Plot
- consistently uses the first-person point of view
- includes a beginning, middle, and end
- uses transition words and phrases
- uses chronological order effectively
- groups related ideas into paragraphs
- uses clear, varied sentences

Grammar, Usage, and Mechanics
- uses standard grammar and usage
- uses correct spelling, punctuation, and capitalization

Managing the Paper Load

Remember that you need not grade all of the points listed above. For grammar and mechanics in particular, limit your focus when grading. Before students finish revising, explain the criteria that you will use for evaluation.

96 Workshop 3

---

2. Problem solve. Rework your draft, taking into consideration your own review of your narrative and the responses of your peer readers. Think about the comments your peer readers have made, but don't feel bound by them. As you revise, keep in mind your own goals for your writing.

Charles made these changes to the beginning of his draft as he responded to the suggestions of a peer reader.

ONE STUDENT'S PROCESS

"I have an announcement to make," Dad said. We were just beginning dinner. My mother looked up while I continued to eat. I was in a hurry. The guys were waiting. Dad asked, "May I have your attention too, Chuck?" I was surprised at his question. Dad knew I always ate dinner quickly so I could play basketball. Then Dad told us that things hadn't been going very well at the factory. Well last week he heard from Jack who moved to Florida and found a job there. Jack said his plant is looking for more people. My dad decides he's going to try it.

I like your beginning, but can you do more to set the scene?

I can't picture what's happening. How about using dialogue here?

I'm confused about when this is happening.

3. Proofread your work. Make a clean copy that includes all your changes. Then check for errors in grammar, usage, and mechanics because these kinds of errors can distract a reader. Remember that verb tense and the punctuation of dialogue are particularly important in narrative writing.

96 Workshop 3

Social Studies Connection

Autobiographies Point out that well-known leaders often write their memoirs or autobiographies in personal narrative form. Suggest that students find and read the memoirs or autobiographies of figures they admire such as Winston Churchill or Gandhi. Tell students to look for the characteristics of an effective personal narrative as they read.

Then something happened. On my way out the door to basketball one afternoon, I yelled, "Mom, I won't be home for dinner." She didn't answer, so I went to look for her. She had her back to me, kneeling beside a carton and carefully wrapping the family photographs she had taken off the wall. When I said, "Mom," she didn't turn around. I walked around the box and said, "Mom, I won't be . . ." I broke off my words in mid-sentence. My mother was crying.

"I guess you caught me," she said, trying to smile. "But, why . . .?"

"Oh, I guess I was just feeling sentimental—you know, old pictures and everything." Then she looked at me, and the smile disappeared. "No, Chuck, it's really more than that."

"You mean you don't want to move either! That's great! When Dad realizes how we both feel, he'll agree to stay here." I was on a roll again, already planning what I was going to tell the guys.

My mother looked at me a little sadly. "I wish it were that simple, Chuck. You're right. I don't want to move, but then neither does your father. We've lived in this city all our lives."

"Then, let's stay! I could hardly believe that maybe things would go my way after all.

"Chuck, think about it. What will happen if we stay? I don't have a job. You know your father's plant is in danger of closing. How can we afford a place to live, food to eat, or even basketball shoes for you if we don't have jobs?" The smile returned for a moment as she mentioned the shoes.

I went back to my room and tentatively fingered one of the empty cartons. "How was I to know?" I protested, half to myself and half to the cartons. For once in my life, I didn't have a quick answer. I needed time to digest what Mom had said. Basketball would have to wait today.

Middle of narrative is well-developed. Descriptive details help reader picture the scene between mother and son.

Narrative is told in chronological order.

Ending shows the significance of the narrative.

Personal Narrative **99**

Reteaching

Assess the needs of students who were not successful in developing an effective personal narrative and identify two or three areas in which additional practice is needed. Assign the appropriate Handbook Mini-Lessons, along with the support materials listed for each lesson. A concept commonly requiring reteaching for this assignment is

Chronological Order: Handbook 4
The following suggestions and resources may also be useful.

1. Dialogue Remind students that a successful narrative contains natural-sounding dialogue. To help students achieve better dialogue, suggest that pairs of students act out scenes from their narratives in which two or more characters interact. Have students develop and record dialogue for the scenes. Students can then use this dialogue to replace some of the narration in their drafts.

2. Characterization To help students develop their characters, suggest that they select one or more characters from their narratives and do five minutes of focused freewriting about each character. Tell students to include as many descriptive details as possible. Circulate and help students as they weave some of these details into their personal narrative.

3. Grammar and Usage: Shifts in Tense In a small group, review with students rules of verb tense. Ask students to find examples of sentences with errors of this type in their drafts. As a group revise the sentences.

Extension and Enrichment

- Suggest that students use the techniques of dialogue and description in their diaries or journals.
- Some students might enjoy using their personal narratives to develop a play. Suggest that students work in small groups to select a narrative, identify one or more scenes, develop a script with dialogue and stage directions, and create props.

LEARNING FROM YOUR WRITING PROCESS

WRITER TO WRITER

There is only one trait that marks the writer. He is always watching. It's a kind of trick of mind and he is born with it.
Morley Callaghan, Canadian novelist and short-story writer

...your writing. Ask yourself the following questions, ...y useful thoughts or ideas in your own writing log:

...hniques did I find helpful in writing my process ...on?
...s most difficult about writing this piece?
...cessful was I in analyzing all the steps in the

...skills. Try one or more writing activities in the fol...

...ricular Visit a science class and observe an experiment in progress. Ask questions about the experiment and ...n on it. Then submit an explanation of the process to ...n you observed and ask how well you explained the

... Read a biographical or autobiographical selection, "A Christmas Memory," "These Were the Sioux," or "I ...y the Caged Bird Sings." Describe a process that ...on in the time and place described in the selection ...sual in your own time and place.
...Call a representative of a local organization, such ...ling group, the police department, the fire depart... ...your local Red Cross. Ask if there are any health- or ...ured processes you can help the organization to edu...ublic about. Prepare pamphlets or posters about the ...d distribute and display them at your local shopping

...signments Follow the suggestions on pages 162– ...ite a cause-effect analysis or create a flowchart.

Informative Writing **161**

Learning from Your Writing Process

Objective
To analyze and reflect upon what has been learned about the writing process and the writing of a description of a process

Teaching Strategies

Reflecting on the Process

Encourage students to share their thoughts as well as to suggest any other questions that might be useful in thinking about the writing experience. Suggest that students think about and try to recognize the things that went especially well, not just those that were not successful.

Writing Portfolio

Suggest that students save their evaluations with their final process descriptions in their writing portfolios. Encourage students to review their self-evaluations from the Guided Assignment in Workshop 4, in which they explored another kind of informative writing. How do their assessments differ? Do they see any common strengths or weaknesses?

Summary and Closure

Before proceeding to the next lesson, be sure students have internalized the following key ideas:

1. A process description explains how to do something, how something works, or how an event happened.
2. An effective process description includes a clear explanation of the steps, logical order, and appropriate transitions.
3. Many informational books are based entirely on descriptions of process. However, this type of writing is also found in short stories and novels.

Give students time to summarize what they have learned by describing the characteristics of an effective description of a process and by explaining how the skill of writing effective process descriptions can help them in other school subjects, particularly science and social studies.

Informative Writing **161**

Off the Record

"Writing is so difficult that I often feel that writers, having had their hell on earth, will escape all punishment hereafter."
Jessamyn West
To See the Dream

Teacher's Resource File

Motivation, reinforcement, creative approaches to writing, and practical teaching support are the hallmarks of the Teacher's Resource File.

Transparency Pack

A wealth of transparencies enhances all of your writing lessons.

- **Fine Art Transparencies** Classic and contemporary art reproductions offer springboards to writing. Worksheets provide writing prompts for a variety of modes.

- **Thinking Skills Transparencies** These graphic organizers can be used to help students find or develop ideas. Worksheets provide practice with each device.

- **Student Revision Model Transparencies** Ideal for modeling purposes, these transparencies provide practice in analyzing and responding to the writing of others.

Guidelines for Writing Assessment and Portfolio Use

This booklet includes evaluation guidelines; models of strong, average, and weak student responses; and materials to aid in portfolio building.

T15

Teacher's Resource File *continued*

Elaboration, Revision, and Proofreading Worksheets

Practice activities give students extra experience with three key writing skills.

Peer Response Guides

Students are given prompts to guide them through peer response sessions for each Guided Assignment.

Writing Resource Book

Practice and reteaching exercises for each section of the Writing Handbook strengthen important skills.

Grammar and Usage Practice Book

Practice and reteaching exercises reinforce concepts taught in every Grammar Handbook section. A special section of Proofreading exercises helps students increase their proofreading skills.

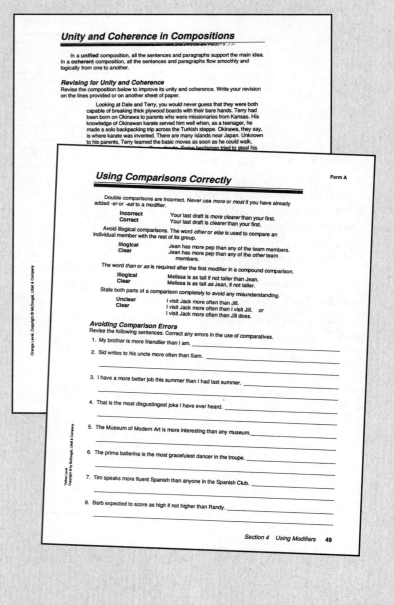

Vocabulary Development

Thirty-six lessons improve student vocabulary through a variety of activities and word lists based on SAT and ACT examinations.

Tests and Assessment

This complete testing and assessment package offers Pretests, Skills Assessment, and Mastery Tests for all grammar, usage, and mechanics concepts. Writing Prompts for Assessment are provided for each Guided Assignment in the text to help prepare students for evaluation situations.

Writing from Literature

Writing prompts designed to accompany twenty-two frequently taught literary selections provide students opportunities to practice the types of writing covered in the Guided Assignments.

Standardized Test Practice

Helpful exercises provide practice and teach students strategies for a variety of standardized test question formats covering vocabulary, error identification, revision in context, and critical reading.

Writing Research Papers

This resource provides complete information on all aspects of writing a research paper, from choosing a topic to preparing final manuscript in correct MLA style.

Lesson Plans

Covering all the Guided and Related Assignments plus the Writing Handbook, the Lesson Plans help teachers make effective use of the Teacher's Edition and ancillary materials.

Educational Technology
(available separately)

- *Writer's DataBank*
- *Grammar Test Generator*
- *Your Personal Trainer for the New SAT*
- *Multimedia Workshop*
- *In Perspective* (videodisc)

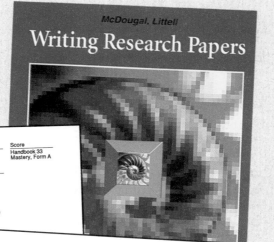

McDougal, Littell
Writing Research Papers

Name _____ Date _____ Score _____
Handbook 33
Mastery, Form A

Using Verbs

A. Identifying Kinds of Verbs
Choose the answer that identifies the boldfaced verb in each sentence. (2 points each)

1. Our largest and second-newest state *is* Alaska.
   O A. action verb   O B. linking verb
2. The FBI *traced* the spy's phone call to an address on Kirkland Str
   O A. action verb   O B. linking verb
3. The mummy room in the museum *smelled* musty.
   O A. action verb   O B. linking verb
4. The bus passengers *were complaining* about the loud volume
   O A. action verb   O B. linking verb
5. Rita *looked* skeptically at the picture of the unicorn on the circus
   O A. action verb   O B. linking verb
6. Milton *seemed* frustrated by the diagramless crossword puzzle
   O A. action verb   O B. linking verb

B. Identifying Transitive and Intransitive Verbs
Choose the answer that identifies the boldfaced verb in each sente

7. The librarian *showed* some of the classic films starring Shirle
   O A. transitive verb   O B. intransitive
8. Barbara *became* a physical therapist to help children with mu
   O A. transitive verb   O B. intransitive
9. Newspaper reporters *must meet* strict deadlines.
   O A. transitive verb   O B. intransitive
10. The founders of the colony of Georgia *named* it for George
    O A. transitive verb   O B. intransitiv
11. All the runners *trained* with weights attached to their shoes
    O A. transitive verb   O B. intransitiv

C. Identifying Active and Passive Voice Verbs
Choose the name of the voice of each boldfaced verb.

12. The mural *The Last Supper was painted* by Leonardo da
    O A. active   O B. passive

Orange Level, Copyright © McDougal, Littell & Company

Critical Reading

Critical-reading questions test your ability to comprehend written material and to draw inferences from what you read. The following strategies can help you answer these types of questions:

- Skim the entire passage quickly.
- Read the questions that follow the passage.
- Reread the passage carefully, keeping the questions you will have to answer in mind.

Passage I
The following passage is from the short story "Louisa, Please Come Home" by the American author Shirley Jackson. The story is narrated by Louisa Tether, a young woman who ran away from home three years ago. She is now returning with her old next-door neighbor, Paul, to confront her family.

I wondered if they were watching us from the window. It was hard for me to imagine how my mother and father would behave in a situation like this, because they always made such a point of being quiet and dignified and proper; . . . the front door ahead was still tight shut. I
5 wondered if we would have to ring the doorbell; I had never had to ring this doorbell before. I was still wondering when Carol opened the door for us. "Carol!" I said. I was shocked because she looked so old, and then I thought that of course it had been three years since I had seen her, and she probably thought that I looked older, too. "Carol," I said, "Oh,
10 Carol!" I was honestly glad to see her.

1. Who is the "I" in this passage?
   (A) Carol
   (B) Louisa's father
   (C) Louisa
   (D) a girl pretending to be Louisa

Is there a better way to teach writing?

Philosophy and Rationale

Authors:
Peter Elbow, Professor of English, University of Massachusetts at Amherst
Sheridan Blau, Senior Lecturer in English and Education, University of California at Santa Barbara

Teachers are constantly bombarded with confident pronouncements from experts and textbooks about the teaching of writing. But tidy theories don't usually hold up in the complex realities of the high school classroom. This book, therefore, is based on the classroom experience of many teachers teaching in many different circumstances: experiences of success and of frustration and of puzzlement.

The truth is, writing is not a body of theoretical knowledge or precepts. Writing, rather, is a body of practices and strategies and activities—above all, a *craft.* Therefore if we truly want to teach writing, we must engage students in the activities of craftspersons. We must ask them to be writers and see themselves as writers. The premise of the book, then, is that we can and should treat our students as writers—putting strong faith in them yet also making strong demands on them.

The best way to explain what this book is about is to list some of the important things we know about writers:

Writers are not all alike. Therefore, there is no single "writing process" or lock-step set of procedures that works for all writers or is appropriate for all students. Indeed, even the same person needs different processes on different occasions and for different kinds of writing. *The Writer's Craft* is based on the premise that students are no more like each other than other writers are, and that it is counterproductive to try to impose one alleged "writing process" on all students for all writing.

Writers make choices. Since writers are *not* alike, it follows, then, that they encounter different problems as they work and employ different strategies. Therefore this book is not organized in a linear fashion where every student follows the same path. Rather, it assumes that students will blaze their own trails. As each assignment is presented in the book, students are given numerous important but necessary decisions to make. (For example, "Do you want to start out by making an outline before you have done any writing, or wait until you've explored your ideas on paper or written a discovery draft? Good writers proceed in both ways.") Some assignments offer a great deal of guidance to the student and others offer very little. In short, the assignments as a whole follow a coherent path, yet there are many opportunities for choice.

Writers learn to write by writing. This book, therefore, does not require a lot of reading *about* writing. Instead it constantly invites the student to write: to write often, in many different forms and contexts, and for different audiences.

Writers learn by reflecting. Writers think about what they do. They observe themselves, learn from practice, think about the choices they make. They talk to others who are engaged in the same business, sharing problems and successes, and comparing the writing choices each of them made. So this book asks students to look not only at *what* they write but at *how* they write, to reflect for themselves on the complicated vagaries of their own writing processes, and to talk with other students and with teachers about how things went.

Writers learn by reading. Thus the book puts a big emphasis on reading the writing of others: the writing of fellow students in the class, the writing of well-known published writers, and some writing by students in other parts of the country (which is included in the book). The readings by published writers in the wider world are not just literary pieces: they also represent a wide range of other types of writing—from magazine articles to scripts to workaday on-the-job writing. The book reprints these writings as chances for students to see what other writers have done: not as pieces to revere—to put under glass like paintings in a museum—but rather as opportunities for students to come at them as fellow writers and questioners. Always, throughout the book, the question is, "Let's see: what choices was the writer making here?"

There is a community of writers. A few writers may squirrel themselves away from others and write entirely on their own, but, as the last two points above illustrate, most writers have important connections with other writers and with a larger community. The teachers behind this book have consciously emphasized this connected model of the writer. The book asks students to work with the smaller community of other writers in the class: to talk about writing and compare notes and drafts and discuss the writing process and give responses to each other. And it also asks students to work with and see themselves as part of the larger community of writers and readers in the world.

Writers must care about what they write. If they just do exercises, if they just find ideas and transmit them *like telegraph operators,* they will have no personal investment in what they write. This book shows students how to find writing ideas that matter to them. It encourages them to take responsibility for what they write, take ownership, take pride.

Writers have a lot to say. Because students are young and inexperienced—because they sometimes even tell us, "I have nothing to write about"—it is tempting to think of them as empty vessels that must be filled. But the teachers behind this book have found that their best teaching comes when they emphasize not what students *don't* know and can't do, but what they *do* know and can do. When we build on the considerable knowledge and language skills that students already have, they learn new things much faster. Experienced writers trust their own thinking, and students, too, must be given some confidence in themselves to function at their best.

Good writers explore and discover as they write. The book helps students to learn how to start from what they *don't* know as well as from what they do know—and then write their way to understanding. In short, writing is thinking, not just recording what is already worked out in some book or in one's mind. To write is to observe, to analyze, to solve problems, to make decisions. This book gives students continual practice in various forms of thinking.

Writers should experiment. The teachers behind this book made a conscious choice to push for a variety of writing experiences. Students should write in diverse modes. They should push at the edges of their experience and develop skills that come from trying various kinds of writing—from learning logs to narratives to essays to visual "story boards." And not all writing need be earnest and heavy. Writers and students need low-stakes writing, too, in order to learn to take some of the risks and have some of the fun that is necessary if a writer is to develop. So while the book asks that most major assignments go through multiple drafts and be carefully revised, it also asks students in the "sketchbook" and journal sections to make quick sketches and learn to play with writing.

Teachers have a unique opportunity with this program. The perspective that writing is a craft, and that students learn most from writing, provides teachers with an exciting role. Instead of feeling compelled to lecture or provide ready-made advice that fits all students and all situations, a teacher can instead be a coach, guide, responder, and nudger—one who will encourage those students who are too timid or fearful, and yes, push those who need a push.

How do I set up my classroom?

Establishing a Writing Workshop Classroom

Author:
Linda Lewis, Writing Specialist, Ft. Worth Independent School District

How can a teacher organize a classroom for effective writing instruction? Perhaps predictably, there is no one best way. Outstanding writing classrooms take many different forms, each reflecting the preferences and personalities of the teacher and students who form that particular writing community. All effective classrooms, however, provide a caring, supportive environment that encourages even the most reluctant students to grow as writers. This environment is based on certain expectations:

- Everyone writes
- Everyone shares
- Everyone responds

If these expectations are met, a fourth goal is achieved:

- Everyone succeeds

Creating a Favorable Atmosphere

An effective writing classroom is actually a social place — an interactive community of writers. In such a classroom, the students are responsible for their own learning and committed to their own growth as writers; however, they are equally responsible for the learning and development of others.

Establishing Expectations. The teacher's approach to writing can have a tremendous impact on the classroom. Therefore, the following attitudes should be evident in every day's activities.

- **Writing is a meaningful activity** To help students realize that writing has purpose, they should be encouraged to read as much as possible and to become aware of the power of the written word. Magazine excerpts, speeches, business proposals, and newspaper articles are all excellent vehicles for making this point. To reinforce this understanding, the students' own writing must be done for real purposes and real audiences. *The Writer's Craft* can be used to give students opportunities to apply their skills in activities as diverse as oral histories and storyboards.

- **Everyone can write** The basic assumption that underlies an effective writing classroom is that everyone has both something to say and the basic tools with which to say it. Even reluctant writers should be engaged in producing whole texts, not just sentences or paragraphs. The teacher can reinforce this expectation by emphasizing and evaluating not only the student's final writing product, but also his or her individual process and progress.

- **Writing involves sharing and responding** The purpose of almost all writing is communication. Therefore, students should be encouraged to share their writing at every stage of the writing process and to solicit the types of responses that they need from their peers. See pages T24 – T27 for more information on peer response and collaborative learning.

Setting Up the Classroom. The arrangement and content of the classroom itself can dynamically reinforce and enhance the feeling of a writing community.

- **The furniture** Student desks or tables can be arranged in many different configurations to facilitate various aspects of the writing activity. For example, some teachers prefer to have the class carry out individual and large-group activities with desks in traditional rows, rearranging them in clusters for collaborative work or peer-response sessions and in a large circle for sharing finished work. Others designate specific areas of the room for various writing activities, perhaps providing an editing corner, a conference table, tables for group response activities, and an area with student desks for private writing.

- **Displays of illustrative materials** Writing — by the students, the teacher, and professional writers — should be profusely displayed in the classroom, and changed as the teacher or students discover exciting new models. Several drafts of a given piece of writing, quotations by published authors about their writing process and products, and favorite writing samples can be included in these displays. A special motivational display, for example, could include brief autobiographical blurbs and pictures that students compile for their hypothetical future books.

- **Reference sources** In addition to providing an appropriate arrangement of furniture and motivational displays, an effective writing classroom should include a reference area stocked with various dictionaries, thesauruses, handbooks, and other reference books.

Some teachers also provide files of writing done by students in previous classes.

Roles of Teacher and Students

To promote the individual and collaborative goals of effective writing instruction, both the teacher and the students must be aware of the different roles they can play in the classroom.

The teacher's roles. There is no one writing process that will work for all students in all writing situations. Therefore, an effective writing teacher is a co-writer, collaborator, coach, and facilitator, rather than a lecturer.

- **The teacher as co-writer and collaborator** Probably one of the best ways for a teacher to advance the expectations of a writing classroom is to become a writer along with the students. In sharing not only finished writing products, but also work in progress, the teacher can instruct students through direct involvement and interaction.

- **The teacher as coach and facilitator** In addition to writing with students, the teacher can facilitate their learning in many ways. For example, during exploratory activities the teacher can help students find topics in which they can become invested; during drafting, support and problem-solve with individual students as needed; and during revision, provide guidance and individual or small-group instruction.

Monitoring writing groups is another way the teacher can help writers to grow.

The students' roles. Like the teacher, the students in an interactive writing classroom play many different roles.

- **The student as writer** It is important that students view themselves as writers with ideas to communicate to others, not as students completing an assignment for the teacher. The kinds of "real world" writing assignments included in *The Writer's Craft* can help create this attitude in the classroom. So can the use of peer response groups and an emphasis on other actual audiences. Probably the most important way to make students feel like writers, however, is to *treat* them as writers, to respect their ability as craftpersons and encourage them to analyze writing problems, explore options, and experiment with techniques.

- **The student as collaborator** In a writing workshop classroom, students are encouraged to share work in progress, help each other problem solve, and contribute ideas to the work of peers, if asked. Students who are not used to such an arrangement may at first have difficulty with this more open approach to writing, and should be allowed to work independently. However, teachers can encourage interaction by having writers work with single partners initially, and then combine to form groups as they become conversant and comfortable with sharing.

- **The student as responder** Student writing improves dramatically when students share their writing with each other. (See Peer Sharing and Peer Response on page T24.) There are several specific ways that teachers can help students become effective peer responders: (1) have students evaluate "training papers" by students from other classes before addressing the writing of classmates, (2) have them role-play successful and unsuccessful response groups and critique the interactions, (3) model appropriate comments using transparencies such as those available in the Teacher's Resource File.

Ensuring Success

The success of a writing classroom depends largely on three factors: (1) clarity of goals, (2) commitment to working toward them, and (3) criteria for assessing progress and achievement. The teacher who is able to establish a favorable atmosphere for writing and clear goals for writers as described above, is well on the way to success. Developing concrete standards of evaluation and making students aware of them is another important factor.

Standards of evaluation Students are more apt to become successful writers if they understand the specific criteria by which their writing will be judged before they undertake an assignment. The Standards for Evaluation in the Guided Assignments, as well as the Guidelines for Evaluating Writing in the Teacher's Resource File, can help students become familiar with and learn to identify the qualities of good writing and develop strategies for effecting them as they write.

In addition, students should be encouraged to reflect on their writing process as they complete each piece. They should also examine their writing portfolios from time to time and note their consistent strengths and weaknesses as well as specific aspects of their development as writers.

A writing workshop classroom can be a lively and stimulating place. And when it is successful, the teacher's expectations and those of the students become reality: everyone writes, everyone shares, everyone responds, and everyone succeeds.

How can I combine literature, writing, and grammar?

Integrating the Language Arts

Authors:

Arthur N. Applebee, Professor of Education, State University of New York at Albany

Judith A. Langer, Professor of Education, State University of New York at Albany

The English language arts curriculum has always been compartmentalized into a variety of special topics, including literature, writing, and grammar. Thought of as separate subjects, they have competed for time and attention in the classroom and in instructional materials. In this view, if we give more time to writing, then we must give less time to literature or grammar. This compartmentalization reflects a "building block" approach to student learning, implying that the various aspects of the language arts can be taught separately and yet can still be put together by the student into some meaningful whole. This approach lends itself well to neatly organized segments of curriculum planning, presented in elaborate scope and sequence charts meant to coordinate the teaching of particular skills within each particular segment of the English curriculum.

Yet this building block approach does not fit very well with the ways in which human beings learn and use language. Rather than learning skills in isolation, we learn them best in the context of experiences. Young children learn to talk because they want to communicate their needs and share their interests with those around them. Older students similarly learn to read and write most effectively when they are reading, writing, and talking about things that interest and matter to them — and when they have a purpose for reading and writing about these things. An integrated approach to the language arts is much more effective in promoting "higher literacy" in students than the building block approach.

The workshops in *The Writer's Craft* reflect the importance of an integrated approach to student language learning, and offer a variety of ways in which teachers can foster the integration of writing with literature and grammar. Some general suggestions follow.

Integrating Writing with Literature

The primary emphasis in many English classrooms is on the teaching of literature. The following suggestions provide ideas for integrating literature with the kinds of writing activities suggested in *The Writer's Craft*:

1. Let students think through writing. Use the students' responses to the literature — their developing understandings and interpretations — as the prompt for a writing activity. As students discuss and debate their responses, the motivation and opportunity to work out their ideas in writing can develop naturally out of their discussions. This is particularly true with the selections in McDougal, Littell's *Responding to Literature* series, which places a similar emphasis on a process-oriented approach to the teaching of English language arts.

2. Use literary selections as springboards. The literature students read may suggest similar situations they want to explore, or concepts they want to analyze, or it may prompt them to create their own contribution to a particular genre.

3. Use selections as examples of how other writers have gone about the craft of writing. Students can profitably spend some time discussing their responses to the selections, sorting out their differing evaluations and interpretations, before examining the ways in which the selections have been shaped and crafted.

4. Let students explore their understandings of and reactions to other students' writing. Examples of student work can be discussed in the same ways that you discuss published selections. If drafts are available, student work may be particularly useful in highlighting the choices a writer makes, and the effects those choices have on readers.

Integrating Grammar Instruction

Students gain effective control of the conventions of written English when they are given many opportunities to use them in the context of their own writing. Isolated exercises in punctuating dialogue, for example, are likely to mean very little to students; learning how to punctuate dialogue because they want to incorporate it into a narrative of their own is much more likely to lead to long-term learning. Similarly, practice in the use of conjunctions in subordinate clauses will be little more than game playing; addressing subordination in the context of developing a complex argument is much more likely to lead to a real mastery of the thinking strategies that underlie such grammatical devices.

To integrate grammar with writing and literature:

1. Encourage students to examine unusual features of the literature they read. Discuss how those features influence students' reactions. For example, students may become aware of the effect of Hemingway's short, simple sentences or of James Joyce's complex syntactical arrangements.

2. Emphasize specific writing conventions that may help while students are drafting or revising particular types of writing. Information about how to punctuate dialogue is likely to be particularly relevant when writing a story or reporting on an interview, for example. Information about formal versus informal usage is likely to be most relevant in writing to unknown or distant audiences.

3. Use opportunities for publication to provide instruction in grammar and usage tailored to individual students. Problems with the conventions of written English are usually highly individualized. In any given class, one student may have trouble with pronoun referents, another with managing the subjunctive, and still another with semicolons. Instruction to deal with such problems will be most effective as each student is revising a work to share with others. At that point, they will usually have a fairly clear idea of what they want to say, and are likely to be ready for help in saying it as clearly and effectively as they can. The Mini-lessons in the Grammar and Usage Handbook are particularly useful in this context.

4. Let students teach one another. Some of the most effective instruction in grammar can come from peer responses to student writing. Because different students have different strengths, they can provide very effective help in "polishing" one another's drafts for publication — and the process of explaining the suggestions they make will strengthen each student's understanding of effective grammar and usage. For example, student pairs can help by reading each others' work and marking a "check" on any portion of the paper that doesn't "sound right" to them. The "check" can highlight questions about spelling, mechanics, grammar, or word choice and can signal useful places the writer can rethink when polishing the piece.

Each of the workshops in *The Writer's Craft* highlights one or another aspect of grammar and usage in the context of the particular types of writing that students are being asked to do. Rather than isolated skill and drill, this grammar content is designed to highlight the relationship between knowledge of the conventions of language and the craft of writing. Each workshop encourages students to experiment with language to make their own writing more effective.

The Language Arts Trio: Literature, Writing, and Grammar

Approached in these ways as interrelated segments of larger activities, the language arts "building blocks" can be taught just as systematically as the old scope-and-sequence charts implied — but much more effectively. When teachers integrate literature, writing, and grammar in their instructional program, the language arts will build upon and support each other. Instead of completing isolated lessons that assume the students will later be able to transfer the separate language arts skills to real literacy situations, students will learn language skills in complete and meaning-laden contexts in the first place. Thus, students' reading, writing, and language skills will develop in concert, in ways both students and their teachers recognize as meaningful, purposeful, and useful.

Is there a way to get students more involved?

Peer Sharing and Peer Response

Author:
Peter Elbow, Professor of English, University of Massachusetts at Amherst

Paul Goodman once said, "If we learned to speak the way we learn to write, there'd be lots more people who can't speak." Why? Because in many classrooms the context for writing is inexorable: the student writes, the teacher grades, and the teacher is the only audience. Imagine what speaking would be like if we spoke only to one person, and if every time we ever spoke, we were evaluated. Is this really the best way for students to learn to write? Does this diet of nothing but teacher grades and "corrected" papers really provide students with the nourishment they need to be better writers? *And* do tall stacks of papers only for teachers' eyes make for sane writing teachers?

There is another alternative: peers as audience and peers as responders. Peers are not a substitute for teachers as audience and responders, but a supplement or addition. Classmates are not asked to evaluate or correct each others' papers but rather to do what they are best at: to function as an audience, and provide an honest account of how they understand the text, how they reacted, and what was going on in their minds as they read. More and more teachers are finding peer responding a crucially helpful strand in their teaching.

Why Use Peer Response?

The use of peer response groups helps teachers to create a powerful change in their classrooms. Why is peer response so effective?

Students need audiences. One of the greatest weaknesses in student writing is a lack of awareness and connection with audience. When students write only for the teacher (which usually means for a grade), they often fall into certain bad habits — treating writing as an empty school exercise, and attempting simply to just "get it right" or "give teachers what they want." Yet surprisingly, students often care less about what they turn in to

teachers than they do about what they read to or share with each other. They often hand writing to teachers that they don't really believe in.

When students write for their peers, however, they become very concerned about what they say and how they say it. In fact, the most powerful thing about the regular use of peer sharing and response groups is that students naturally and easily begin to learn that writing is not so much a matter of "figuring out what the teacher wants" but rather of discovering what they themselves have to say and then seeing whether they have gotten it across effectively to readers.

Just as this textbook tries to teach students that not everyone writes in the same way, so too does it teach students that not everyone reads in the same way. Peer response introduces students to the complex but ultimately empowering truth that the same text often produces different responses in different readers. The writer is then left in the position of having to evaluate those different responses and make writerly decisions about how to revise.

Teachers need relief. Another powerful reason teachers are making more and more use of peer response groups is brutally practical: the paper load for teachers. Students don't learn to write well unless they write a great deal — which means writing more papers than teachers have time to read carefully and comment on. Peer sharing and response groups provide a way to increase the amount of writing that students do while assuring them of a response. For even though students may not be skilled at providing evaluation and advice, they are excellent at providing the one thing that writers need most — *an audience.*

Types of Response

Most students have never written words that they didn't turn in to a teacher for evaluation and criticism. Yet limiting feedback to this kind of response can cripple students' writing. Student writing almost always takes a big turn for the better when this traditional audience-relation is balanced by use of the other relationships described below. Indeed, this variety of types is crucial, for it provides the ideal "balanced audience diet" that students need — a balance among different relations to readers.

Private writing. Students need opportunities to write privately — to do some writing that they don't show to anyone. This provides a crucial foundation of safety and comfort in writing and an arena for risk-taking.

Pure sharing. Students need opportunities to share their writing with readers — but sometimes just for the sake of sharing with no response at all. This increases the risk ("going public"), and yet still provides a strong degree of safety since there is no feedback. The emphasis is placed on *communicating* rather than *feedback*. Sharing heightens the social dimension of writing, and there is also an enormous amount of extremely efficient learning that goes on, especially when the sharing is oral. Nothing teaches us so much about writing as the feel of our own sentences in our mouths and the sound of them in our ears. The process also gives students experience in working in groups before having to learn feedback techniques.

Limited feedback. Students sometimes need opportunities to share writing and get responses — but not get criticism. By holding off the question of "how good is the writing?" students discover what is probably the most useful kind of feedback — learning how readers *understand* their words. Limited feedback, therefore, involves more risk, more feedback, and more learning. But because there is no criticism or advice, students find it a rewarding way to share, and can listen nondefensively to responses from readers.

Full feedback. By working in peer groups in the two ways previously described, students heighten their reading and responding skills. Now they are ready to give and receive responses to the more demanding writerly questions like these: "What worked well and not so well? What suggestions do you have?"

This textbook provides a rich range of specific suggestions, prompts, and examples to enable students to learn how to become good peer responders to each other. By taking advantage of these techniques, students will find an audience, their teacher will gain time to teach, and writing will remain the exciting exchange of ideas and opinions it should always be.

Is there a way to get students more involved?

Collaborative and Cooperative Learning

Author:
David Wallace, Researcher with the Center for the Study of Writing at Carnegie-Mellon University

Learning to use one's knowledge in collaboration with others is essential for success in and out of school. Consequently, group learning is becoming central to classrooms across the curriculum.

Collaborative learning is defined as any group activity that asks students to work together on a task. Advocates of collaborative learning assert that it motivates students to learn, improves social skills, and promotes self-esteem in students of all abilities. The students work together, and the teacher focuses on the different groups, carefully listening, watching, suggesting, and being prepared to work through any problems that naturally arise in the context of group work.

In **cooperative learning,** a more structured type of collaborative work, the success of one individual is linked to that of others. Each group member is responsible for helping other members to learn and for contributing a piece to a whole. Cooperative learning might be used, for example, if students were directed to stage a play, create an advertising campaign, complete a complex report, or produce a book of oral histories. Each student is held accountable for his or her own contributions and each student's mastery is assessed.

The following is a list of strategies for using collaborative and cooperative learning with your students.

Getting Started

Divide the class into groups. Group students of differing abilities or talents together; assure students that creativity, problem-solving abilities, listening skills, empathy, and writing skills share equal importance in group work. Also, remind students that while they are responsible for their own learning, they are also responsible for helping others in the group to learn. Students should work together in an atmosphere of care, acceptance, trust, and support. Competi-

tion has no role in collaborative learning. The size of groups depends on the purpose of the collaborative effort. Small groups of two or three students each are most appropriate when students are sharing personal writing and will benefit most from the individual attention one or two peers can offer. Larger groups of no more than six members can be effective too, particularly if the assignment is large or complex.

Specify objectives and purpose. Set clear, specific goals and objectives for each collaborative learning session. Also make sure students understand on what criteria they will be assessed.

Provide a structure. Assign specific responsibilities to students working in groups, or have the students do so themselves. For example, students working in a discussion group can take on specific roles, such as facilitator or discussion leader, recorder, reporter, and materials manager. If students are working cooperatively on a larger project, such as a research report, the assignment itself may be divided into parts and assigned; each student is responsible for completing his or her share of the work and for helping to join the pieces into a cohesive whole.

Monitor progress and achievement. The teacher's role during cooperative learning is that of facilitator or consultant. As group members work together, the teacher should circulate among them, mentally noting behavior and participation for future performance assessment. If necessary, the teacher should enter a group to clear up any misunderstandings or to ask questions that will direct students' thinking. If more than one group is having difficulty, the teacher may interrupt to reteach or clarify a point with the entire class.

Address assessment. Certain informal collaborative situations, such as peer response, require no evaluation procedure. Some situations, however, require assessment and grading to keep students account-

able for successful group process, for their own learning, and for that of other group members. Options for using grades to reward students for group learning include:
• averaging individual scores within each group;
• giving a single score to all group members who have worked cooperatively on a single product;
• giving all group members the lowest score;
• choosing at random one group member's paper or exam to grade;
• giving individual scores plus bonus points for successful group performance and the development of social skills

Students should share in the assessment process by evaluating their own performance and that of their group. Students may judge that they've been successful if they have met the designated goals of the collaborative learning session. In evaluating group process, they might consider such questions as, "Did I feel supported? challenged? confronted? Were feelings hurt or were ideas shared and feedback given in an encouraging, supportive way? How might we improve the process next time?" Teachers and students should discuss what works and what doesn't work in group process and brainstorm together on ways of improving collaborative learning skills.

Ideas for Collaborative Learning

The Writer's Craft encourages students to work together in groups to explore concepts and ideas, problem-solve, brainstorm, and collaborate during all phases of the writing process. The collaborative learning activities that follow can be effectively adapted for use in the English classroom.

Collaborative planning. While students working alone during the planning stage rarely go beyond deciding what information to include in their texts, students planning in pairs or small groups consider the full range of writing variables and keep them in mind throughout the writing process. Developed at the Center for the Study of Writing at Berkeley and Carnegie-Mellon University under co-director Linda Flower, collaborative planning helps students become more aware of their writing process; students learn to evaluate and think critically about their writing options, and through dialogue with teachers and peers, they learn to monitor their own learning about writing.

Before students begin to draft a writing assignment, divide the class into pairs or groups of three; have them take turns in the roles of writer and partner, talking through their writing ideas. While the writer talks about his or her plan, partners help the writer by acting as a sounding board, listening carefully, asking for clarification or elaboration, and suggesting alternatives. For collaborative planning to be successful, writers should be prepared to discuss their ideas about content, audience, purpose, and form; partners should be prepared to support the writer, help elaborate writing plans, and explore new possibilities.

Jigsaw projects. Students may choose to work collaboratively on any large or complex project, dividing the assignment into "pieces" and assigning each student to a piece. Students creating a video, for example, could divide the project into such "pieces" as research, scriptwriting, direction, and production. Students would then work together to meld the pieces into a coherent whole.

Learning partners. After presenting new information on a topic or giving an assignment to the entire class, have students review the material out loud with a peer, using their notes as necessary to summarize or explain. For example, students could meet in small groups after grammar instruction. They could take turns paraphrasing the new rules out loud, presenting examples of the concept at work, or finding examples in their reading. The whole group can then complete or review the answers to the practice activities together, make necessary corrections, and submit a single set of answers for grading.

Research groups. Students may conduct research on a topic and pool information into a written or oral report. Students will need to divide the work load equally, with each person responsible for researching a particular aspect of their outline. Students will join the pieces of information into a cohesive whole; one grade can be assigned to the entire group.

Problem solving. Have small groups of students work together to address a problem of mutual concern in the school or community. Students should first brainstorm a list of ideas and issues, select and narrow a single topic, develop and then execute a plan of action, such as a letter-writing campaign, petition drives, community interviews, editorial writing, and so on. Groups should periodically report the status of their efforts to the entire class.

Are tests the only way to check progress?

Assessment and Response to Student Writing

Authors:
Arthur N. Applebee, Professor of Education, State University of New York at Albany
Judith A. Langer, Professor of Education, State University of New York at Albany

Traditionally, much of the work in the teaching of writing has occurred in the process of responding to and assessing what students write. Teachers have given students topics to write about, and then have spent a great deal of time marking the papers that result — giving grades, making suggestions for ways the writing could have been improved, and correcting errors.

Such an approach is exhausting for teachers — the paperload quickly becomes overwhelming — and discouraging for students — whose papers "bleed" with the teachers' red penciling. Such an approach also works against what we know about the writing process. When students write about topics that have substance and depth, we can expect their work to be characterized by growth and change over time. They will try out and abandon ideas. They will reorganize sections. Beginnings and endings will drift out of alignment with the rest of the text and need to be redrafted. This is the "normal" state of affairs among the best of writers, and characterizes the *process* of crafting a text.

For students to engage in the kinds of thoughtful exploration described above, evaluation — judgments about how well the work has been done — needs to be separated from response — reactions to the paper and ideas for further development that come from an interested reader. This is because evaluation, although well-intentioned, can become too much a focus of ongoing instruction, and therefore inhibiting to students; it teaches them not to take risks, not to try new forms, not to draft and redraft, but to concentrate on letter-perfect work that says little and goes nowhere.

Response is the critical feature in writing instruction; it helps students know what works, what doesn't, and how to go about improving what they have written. The ideal writing environment invites students to engage in exploratory writing and offers response to work-in-process.

Evaluation and grades are postponed until later.

Providing Effective Response

Teachers can use a number of strategies to ensure that students receive sufficient and helpful response to their work. The most powerful is the use of peer readers and peer response groups (see pages T24–T25). The following suggestions should also be kept in mind:

1) Limit the amount of writing to which you, the teacher, respond.

Writers need frequent responses from interested readers, but that does not mean that the teacher needs to read everything that is written. Instead students may be asked to share with each other initial brainstorming about a topic, to reflect upon one another's notes and journals, and to respond to early drafts.

These early drafts and explorations have served their purpose once they have been discussed with an interested reader, or mined for the nuggets that will become part of later drafts. Therefore, there is no reason for the teacher to read them, too: indeed, the teacher can become a bottleneck and may inadvertently turn students back toward thoughts already abandoned.

2) Respond to work in progress as a collaborator rather than an evaluator.

Teachers can, of course, be very helpful while students are working on their drafts. They can show new ways to solve writing problems, suggest other issues to consider, and offer their own responses as readers about what parts are clear, what parts are interesting, and what parts fail to convince. These kinds of responses are instructional in the best sense: the teacher's suggestions about work in progress can become part of the developing writer's repertoire of strategies and models, available for use in other contexts.

Exploring Assessment

Reader response is certainly the most productive way to respond to student writing, but evaluation is, of course, necessary. Report cards demand grades, and students want to know how they are doing. But there are a number of ways in which evaluation can be managed so it supports rather than subverts the processes of teaching and learning.

Choose criteria carefully. Since writing should be considered a process for exploring ideas and sharing them with others, it follows that conventions of writing should be treated as part of this process rather than as the focus of instruction. It is easy, however, for both writers and teacher to get bogged down in usage and mechanics.

Therefore, to prevent both writers and evaluators from losing track of the key issues of writing, it is important to have clear, consistent standards about what "writing well" will mean in your class. If "writing well" is to mean exploring ideas and experimenting with ways to share them effectively, then students who try to do this should be rewarded with higher grades — even if their experiments lead them to make mistakes. A new and difficult task, completed with some uncertainty, may reflect much more growth in writing achievement than a simple task completed with little thought and no "error."

Use a variety of evaluation methods. In recent years, teachers have developed a number of different ways to formalize their evaluations of student writing. Most of these have been used in the context of large-group assessment, where the concern is with how well students are doing *relative to* one another or to some external criterion. Using such procedures (for example, general impression [or holistic] scoring, analytic scoring, or primary trait scoring) is generally inappropriate within a classroom when used in a formal sense, but can be extremely helpful when used informally to guide teachers' and students' mutual understandings of the goals of the writing task. These methods, however, should be used sparingly and combined with more flexible techniques such as peer response and portfolio assessment.

For those occasions when holistic or analytic evaluations are desired, the Writing Workshops in *The Writer's Craft* include specific criteria for evaluation of various types of writing, as does the booklet *Evaluating Student Writing* in the Teacher's Resource File. Underlying these criteria are a few, broad questions that can be used in assessing how well the writing succeeds:
• Is the writer's purpose clear? Has it caught my interest?
• Is there enough detail for me to accept or reject what the writer has said?
• Does the writing carry me through clearly from beginning to end, or are there places where I get lost or miss the point?
• Do the drafts indicate the student is learning to use the responses of readers effectively, or are successive drafts little more than neater versions of the same text?
• Has the writer taken care in the final draft to avoid distracting, careless errors in presentation?

Using Portfolios

Writers vary in how well they write from topic to topic and day to day. Again, this is normal and natural, but we often forget about it when judging how well a writer writes. To offer a well-grounded evaluation of a student's writing skills, we need to examine a broad sample of that student's work.

Portfolios of student work offer one of the best vehicles for classroom-based assessment, for two reasons: 1) They typically contain a variety of different samples of student work; and 2) they make it easy to separate evaluation from the process of instruction. Evaluation can be based on the diverse samples of work in the portfolio rather than on the day-to-day progress of an individual piece of classroom work.

Portfolios take almost as many forms as there are teachers, and can be tailored to virtually any classroom situation. The major options involve the form that portfolios take, what is included in them, and how they are evaluated.   *continued*

Portfolio Options

Form. Portfolios are a cumulative collection of the work students have done. The most popular forms include

- a traditional "writing folder" in which students keep their work
- a bound notebook with separate sections kept for work in progress and final drafts
- a looseleaf notebook in which students keep their drafts and revisions
- a published collection of carefully selected and hand-bound work.

Content. Portfolios provide an ideal way to illustrate how a student's work has developed over time, and will give students, parents, administrators, and other teachers a much stronger sense of what students can do. Portfolios may contain

- everything a student writes for a particular class
- a selection of "best work" representing the diverse kinds of writing that a student has done
- selections chosen to represent each of the types of writing a student has done during a grading period
- a diverse collection of a student's performance including drawings and illustrations, tape recordings or videotapes of group work, and readings or dramatic presentations of the student's writing
- drafts and revisions
- a selection of finished work, chosen by the student, the teacher, or the student and teacher working together

Students can also be encouraged to reflect further upon their own progress as writers, providing an introductory essay summarizing their work as they see it in the portfolio. Like the reflective activities included at the end of each workshop in this textbook, such reflection can help students become aware of and take control over their own growth as writers.

Evaluating Content. Just as teachers vary in the form and content of the portfolios they ask their students to build, they also vary in how they use portfolios to determine students' grades.

An approach that many teachers have found to be particularly effective is to base grade a selection of work from the portfolio — chosen to reflect the range of types of writing that students have done during the grading period. Students can be asked to select the pieces to be graded, making the choice themselves or in conjunction with the teacher. With this approach, they should be given guidelines for what to choose: a narrative, a synthesis, and a persuasive essay, perhaps, plus an additional piece of their own choosing. The particular guidelines should reflect the goals and assignments in the writing program during the grading period.

The ability to choose works to be graded — rather than being graded on everything — can be a powerful motivational device as well. Many teachers give their students the opportunity to work further on the selections they want to have graded. Returning to these writings at a later point, students often recognize for themselves ways to make their writing more effective, and may reshape them substantially before offering them for evaluation.

Weaning students from excessive evaluation. Many teachers who are new to such a workshop approach, postponing evaluation rather than interjecting it into the writing process, worry that students want quicker grades. If they aren't graded, will they do the work? One transitional device that works well in many classrooms is to give points when students have completed each separate part of the work. Everyone who completes a first draft, for example, might get a point, with another for doing a revision. These points can be totaled across the marking period to become part of the final grade.

If evaluation is separated from instruction, if criteria for evaluation are kept consistent with those stressed during instruction, and if response becomes a responsibility shared with students as well as the teacher, assessment can become an effective complement to the process of learning to write.

How do I meet the needs of different students?

Teaching Writing to Language Minority Students

Authors:
Marguerite Calderone, Associate Professor of Education in Psychology, University of Texas, El Paso
Sheridan Blau, Senior Lecturer in English and Education, University of California, Santa Barbara

Increases in the immigrant population during the past two decades have dramatically transformed the cultural makeup of many American classrooms. Not since the great wave of immigrations around the turn of the last century have English teachers in American schools been so challenged to meet the special language needs of their students.

Few veteran English teachers are likely to feel professionally prepared to operate successfully in a multi-cultural, multi-lingual classroom. What follows here are some strategies for teaching writing to language-minority students — strategies that research has shown are especially effective with non-English speaking students but which are equally applicable to all students.

Developing Prior Knowledge

The more experience a writer has with the concepts and terms associated with a topic for writing, the easier it will be to write about that topic. Similarly, the more knowledge a teacher has of the culture and background of minority students, the easier it will be to adapt teaching strategies and writing assignments to meet their needs.

Hold class discussions. Clarify cultural references and provide general information to the entire class. Encourage language minority students to comment on similarities to and differences from their own cultures.

Explore teaching alternatives. The use of visual aids and hands-on experiences are effective strategies for building prior knowledge and student confidence.

Encourage students to write about their native customs, holidays, geography, and foods. Such topics will be more comfortable for language-minority students. Additionally, the felt-pride from sharing their native culture will act as strong motivation for writing.

Provide opportunities for reading popular American magazines and newspapers. These activities will familiarize language-minority students with American people, places, and events. Television, movies, theater, and similar cultural activities will have the same impact.

Developing Vocabulary and Genre Knowledge

Mastering English vocabulary and patterns of discourse is essential to building writing proficiency among language-minority students. Students who are asked to write about a school or government election, for example, must be familiar with the terms and concepts of the subject, such as *parties, platform, campaign, run-off, running mate,* and so on. Ideally, preteaching vocabulary would become a regular part of each assignment. *continued*

Similarly, students who are asked to write a mock political campaign speech will feel entirely unable to do so unless they know what one looks and sounds like. All students should be given the opportunity to read a number of models of whatever type of writing they are being asked to produce.

Peer Interaction

Through group discussion, students with limited English proficiency can build a repertoire of concepts, phrases, and rhetorical strategies by trial-and-error, questioning, and modeling. Whenever possible, divide the class into small discussion groups. Each group should include at least one language-minority student. Establish a protocol that requires all students to speak within the group. In this way language-minority students will be exposed to vocabulary and rhetorical strategies they can model and be encouraged to try out their developing English proficiency.

Writing in the Primary Language

There is strong research evidence showing that limited-English proficiency students in American schools can make significant progress toward literacy in English by reading and writing for some time in their primary language, making the transition to writing exclusively in English as they acquire English fluency. Allowing students to write in their primary language during the early stages of English acquisition offers the following advantages:

• It establishes a firm basis for acquiring universal reading and writing skills that are easily transferred from one language to another.

• It promotes success, enhances self-esteem, and builds students' confidence in their abilities as readers and writers.

• It enables students to function at the highest levels of their cognitive abilities,

unhampered by their limited English proficiency.

How can writing in languages other than English become a realistic instructional strategy in classes where teachers don't speak the primary language or languages of their non-English speaking students? Following are some strategies for implementing this instructional strategy:

• Encourage students to write in their primary language whenever they encounter a particularly demanding or complex writing assignment. This will enable them to clarify their thinking about the topic even if no one else can read what they've written.

• Have students write in their primary language only during the prewriting stage. Allowing them to focus their topic, generate ideas, and organize their material in a familiar language will lead to enhanced comprehension and increased motivation.

• Seek out individuals fluent in the student's primary language to act as responders. Such individuals might be teacher aides, parents, or classmates who speak the student's primary language but who are also fluent in English. Of course, if there are several students who share the same primary language, they can act as peer reviewers for one another.

• Invite students to translate their own primary language essays. Such translations should not be treated as final drafts, however, but as rough draft translations produced for the benefit of the teacher. Teachers who receive these translations can respond to the ideas contained in the translated essay rather than on problems in English language usage.

Additional Strategies

Following are some additional strategies for working with language minority students.

• Preview the assignment to spot potential areas of difficulty — with cul-

tural concepts, language requirements, research needs, and so on. Provide preteaching as necessary.

• Read aloud difficult parts of the assignment or lesson, allowing time for questions and clarification.

• Precede writing activities with similar oral activities to allow students to separate the task of clarifying ideas from that of translating them into written form.

• Provide guided practice, especially with prewriting and revising techniques.

• Increased, individualized feedback and monitoring will enhance student comprehension and offer support — both of which lead to more successful writing experiences.

References

California State Department of Education (1981). *Schooling and Language Minority Students: A Theoretical Framework.* California State University, Los Angeles, EDAC.

Cummins, J. (1986). *Empowering Minority Students.* Sacramento, CA: California Association for Bi-Lingual Education.

Damon, W. (1984). "Peer Education: The Untapped Potential." *Journal of Applied Developmental Psychology:* 5, 331-343.

Stevens, R. J.; Madden, N. A.; Slavin, R. E.; & Farnish, A. M. (1987). Cooperative Integrated Reading and Composition (CIRC). Baltimore, MD: Center for Research on Elementary and Middle Schools, Johns Hopkins University.

Calderone, M.; Tinajero, J.; & Hertz-Lazarowitz, R. (1990). "Effective Transition into English Reading Through CIRC." Baltimore, MD: Center for Research on Effective Education for Disadvantaged Students, Johns Hopkins University.

How do I meet the needs of different students?

Addressing Different Learning Styles

People of all ages perceive and process information in different ways. A familiarity with learning styles can help educators develop teaching strategies to meet the needs of all students in the classroom.

The Types of Learners

Research on left and right brain functions has led to a variety of theories about preferred learning styles. The left brain is thought to be the center for analytical, logical, verbal, sequential, and convergent thinking, while the right brain is thought to be the center for emotion and visual, spatial, creative, experiential, and divergent cognitive styles. Left-brain students, who have traditionally been rewarded by the educational system, tend to excel in such school subjects as reading, mathematics, and computer programming. Right-brain dominant students tend to excel in art, dance, music, and geometry.

In addition to left/right brain classification, students are often categorized according to three learning styles: visual, auditory, and kinesthetic.

Visual learners best comprehend and retain information presented in the form of graphs, charts, diagrams, and other visual images, such as fine art and photographs. Often, they benefit from a multimedia approach to learning.

Auditory learners, like visual learners, often benefit from a multi-media approach to learning. They need not only to read it and see it, but to hear it and discuss it.

Kinesthetic learners process information through tactile sensations, learning from activities that enable them to work with their hands or create meaning through movement and physical expression.

Harvard psychologist Howard Gardner has taken the analysis of learning styles and left and right brain dominance to yet another level in his theory of multiple intelligences.

The Seven Types of Intelligence

Linguistic	Verbal excellence, reading and writing skills
Logical-Mathematical	Conceptual, logical, abstract thinking
Spatial	Interest in visual images and pictures; designing, building, and inventing
Musical	Sensitivity to rhythm, singing, moving to and playing music
Bodily-Kinesthetic	Communicating with body language; processing information through bodily sensations
Interpersonal	Organizing, communicating, socializing, understanding others
Intrapersonal	Preferring to work alone and being independent, private, and self-motivated

Everyone has multiple intelligences and different styles of learning. However teachers, who tend to be left-brain oriented and strong in linguistic and logical-mathematical intelligences, often teach primarily in the modes most comfortable for them. They may therefore be unconsciously leaving a number of students out of the learning process. Yet how can any teacher adequately address the bewildering array of learning styles that may be present in any one classroom?

With its integrated approach to the development of writing, *The Writer's Craft* helps solve this problem by providing students with opportunities to work in a variety of learning modes. Teachers need only encourage students to take advantage of various learning strategies to maximize their intellectual and creative potential.

Applications in
The Writer's Craft

Teacher's notes throughout the text point out the following learning opportunities:

Fine Art and Illustrations The art program throughout *The Writer's Craft* provides visual or spatial learners with an engaging and entertaining way into the material. Invite students to consider how the art enhances and reflects concepts in the text, and use the illustrations as springboards to creative writing.

Workshops and Related Assignments At each grade level, Workshops and Related Assignments include a broad range of activities, not all of which are writing based. Visual and spatial learners, for example, will particularly enjoy creating story boards, pictorial essays, flow charts and organizational charts, and interpreting art. Auditory and musical learners will especially like creating videos, writing choral poems and song lyrics, and making oral presentations and rebuttals.

Exploratory Activities Workshops begin with a wide range of Exploratory Activities, providing students with options for entering writing assignments comfortably and naturally. The teacher can encourage students to experiment with the options until they find those that work best.

Graphic Organizers Graphic devices

such as spider maps, tree diagrams, flow charts, and pie graphs can be a tremendous boon to visual and kinesthetic students who learn from the physical act of writing ideas, organizing them spatially, and seeing and making the connections between them. Left-brain dominant students can organize their information with time lines, charts, and analysis frames.

Publishing Options The wide variety of publishing options offered throughout the Workshops allows students to tailor their work to their own learning styles. In different assignments, for example, students may be encouraged to include photographs or drawings, build models, incorporate music, or use videotapes, recordings, slides, or photos in a multimedia presentation.

Collaborative and Independent Learning Auditory and interpersonal learners may enjoy working collaboratively to brainstorm solutions to problems, discuss ideas, and share their writing. (See pages T26 to T27.) Peer response sessions are also ideal for these kinds of learners. However, each lesson is so complete that the intrapersonal, or solitary, learner can succeed with little help from others.

Special Help with
Learning Disabilities

Learning disabled students typically have average or above-average potential; however, specific areas of deficiency (which vary from student to student) make the processing of information and the acquisition of skills more difficult. Students with learning disabilities often display some or all of the following characteristics.

- Low reading level
- Low motivation
- Difficulty organizing work or ideas
- Poor memory
- Difficulty sequencing and processing information
- Difficulty following directions and

completing assignments
- Difficulty thinking, reasoning, and generalizing
- Hyperactivity and distractability
- Poor fine-motor coordination and handwriting

It is essential to remember that learning disabilities are often physiologically based and beyond the student's control. What can appear to be inattentiveness or an uncooperative attitude may, in fact, reflect an inability to learn through conventional channels.

Whenever possible, teachers should provide opportunities for LD students to process information in their own preferred learning style. This approach will allow them to maximize their intellectual and creative potential in school. The following general strategies, along with any of the alternative strategies described in the section on Learning Styles, will help students get the most from classroom experiences.

- Seat students toward the front of the classroom where there are no obstructions to seeing or hearing.

- Present essential directions or material from the text both orally and in writing.

- Supply visual aids whenever possible to reinforce material from the text.

- To help students compensate for poor short- and long-term memory, repeat important ideas frequently and begin each lesson with a summary of material covered the previous day.

- When giving an assignment, model sample problems on the board, breaking the process down into clearly ordered steps.

- Encourage collaborative learning. Carefully monitor sessions to make sure they take place in an atmosphere of care, empathy, and support.

- Occasionally pair students according to ability for special peer-review sessions. For example, pair an LD student who has difficulties with sequencing and ordering events with a student who is particularly strong in those areas.

I've got a computer... Now what?

Teaching English in The Electronic Age

Author:
Dawn Rodrigues, Associate Professor of English, Colorado State University

New technology brings exciting changes to the curriculum. In the English classroom, the most visible of these changes has been the arrival of the computer, with all of its attendant software. The sheer volume of available material has proven to be occasionally intimidating, but teachers *can* take control of the technology by selectively integrating computer programs and strategies into their teaching.

Benefits of the Computer

Although research on the use of the computer in English classrooms is still somewhat limited, many studies have revealed some significant benefits of using a word processor:

• Students enjoy composing on a computer, tending to write more and work harder at their writing.

• Students do not resist revision, since changes can be more easily executed.

• Collaboration among students increases.

Computers have also proven to be especially helpful with low-ability students or those with handicaps and learning disabilities. First, the actual *physical* act of writing becomes easier, and the process as a whole becomes less intimidating—when words on a screen can be instantly deleted, writing anxiety diminishes. Second, the process of using the computer forces special needs students to focus more directly on their task. Finally, the clean, printed text eliminates some students' embarrassment over poor handwriting—for the first time in their lives, they can be proud of their writing.

In another important benefit, students using computers start to *understand* more about the writing process. As they watch words appear and disappear, as they see chunks of text move from one section of their essay to another, they see the process of thinking and writing in action.

New Strategies for Writing Instruction

With the increasing availability of computers, teachers can recommend that students use composing and collaborative strategies that were not possible before. Many of these strategies, such as invisible writing, listmaking, and the development of a writer's file, can be found in *The Writer's Craft* in the feature labeled Computer Tip. Some other strategies follow:

• Students can leave gaps in their paper where they need to add material or where they want to invite response from others. Notes such as the following, to themselves or their peer readers, can provide the cues: CAN YOU HELP ME THINK OF A BETTER EXAMPLE HERE? or MAYBE THIS WOULD WORK AS THE INTRO—TRY LATER.

• Students can work on portions of the draft that they are most comfortable with, and then electronically paste the pieces together as their ideas take shape.

• Teachers and peer readers can read drafts on screen and leave notes to the writer at the appropriate points.

Making It Work

Making students comfortable with computers does not require that the entire class meet regularly in a lab. At many schools, a teacher can reserve a computer lab on occasion for the entire class. On those days, the teacher can introduce valuable computer-writing techniques, such as the use of an "alternate screen" to store outlines or notes while composing in the other window. Spell-checkers, on-line thesauruses, and specialized software programs can also be introduced. If a lab is not available, the teacher can occasionally bring a computer into the classroom to demonstrate various techniques, run through software programs, or allow students to demonstrate favorite word-processing strategies.

No matter how the computer is used, however, it is important to remember that not all students adapt to word processing in the same way. Therefore, the teacher must be prepared to provide plenty of individual instruction. For example, freed from the restrictions of pen and paper, some students may overwrite. These individuals must be shown how to evaluate content and delete unnecessary material. Other students may have trouble adapting pen-and-paper planning or revision to the screen. These writers could be encouraged to use print-outs in combination with composing on screen until they become more comfortable with the computer.

Conclusion

Computers, when used creatively, can be a powerful addition to a writing class. The computer has the amazing ability to transform itself into whatever the teacher or writer wants it to be—a magic slate for writing, an electronic window to an audience, or an endless resource for ideas and strategies. It allows teachers to create an almost unlimited set of instructional techniques, and a chance to re-envision writing instruction.

What do I do each day?

Planning the Curriculum

The Writer's Craft provides teachers with a unique resource for developing an English program that can be tailored to individual classrooms, teaching styles, and curriculum needs. The flexible Workshop/Handbook format of the books is ideally suited to the demands of the modern classroom, where state, district, and school requirements must all be met even as teachers work to address the specific needs of their students.

Targeting Objectives

State and District Objectives The assignments and lessons in The Writer's Craft cover all of the concepts most commonly listed in state and district guidelines. By referring to the objectives listed with every Writer's Workshop and Handbook mini-lesson, teachers can choose those assignments that best allow them to meet the requirements of their own states and districts.

Classroom Objectives Specific classroom needs can be identified through the use of diagnostic materials provided in the Teacher's Resource File. Grammar Pretests and Writing Assessment Prompts

allow teachers to pinpoint areas where students need extra help. Writing Assignments and Mini-lessons can then be chosen accordingly.

Literature-Based Objectives English teachers increasingly are being asked to formally integrate the language arts: literature, writing, and grammar. A feature called Linking Literature, Grammar, and Writing, which appears on the Teaching Preview Pages of this Teacher's Edition, provides guidance in linking writing and grammar logically to a piece of literature.

Planning the Lesson

The Writer's Craft provides teachers with a clear, detailed resource for planning lessons.

Teaching Preview Pages The Teaching Preview pages that precede each Writer's Workshop include the following:

• An overview of the Workshop

• A chart of useful support materials from the Teacher's Resource File

• Suggestions for linking literature, grammar, and writing

• Workshop Management Guidelines, detailing the number of days needed for each writing assignment and noting which steps can be completed outside the classroom as independent study

Lesson Plans The Teacher's Resource File includes a booklet of Lesson Plans that help teachers structure each lesson according to the suggested Lesson Cycle on the following page. Included on the Lesson Plans are a review of Objectives and Resources, and suggestions for breaking a long-term writing assignment over several days.

Teacher's Notes Each lesson in The Writer's Craft is accompanied by detailed notes that provide helpful advice and teaching strategies. Used during the Teaching Preview, they can help teachers choose approaches and select appropriate

support materials from the Teacher's Resource File.

Addressing Different Ability Levels

One of the key problems teachers face centers around the necessity of preparing multiple lesson plans for students of different ability levels. Often, time does not allow such meticulous preparation, or the diversity of student abilities requires a prohibitive number of alternatives. Additionally, pigeonholing students into "ability levels" often ignores the fact that weaker students may excel with some kinds of assignments, while stronger students may flounder on others. The result of this apparently unmanageable situation is often guilt for the teacher and frustration for students.

The Writer's Craft has solved this problem through the structure of its lessons. Built-in options throughout each assignment allow students to choose approaches that best suit their abilities or learning styles. The Writing Handbook and Grammar and Usage Handbook allow students — of any ability level or background — who are having problems to find additional help. Each student, therefore, can proceed as quickly or methodically as he or she likes, without disturbing the rest of the class.

So that students receive the full benefit of these options, the teacher may want to preview the following options within the writing assignments and be prepared to point them out to students during the lesson:

Writer's Choice
Exploratory Activities
Strategies
Publishing Options
Handbook Mini-lessons (cross-references)

The article Addressing Different Learning Styles on pages T33–T34 provides additional useful information.

What do I do each day?

Suggested Lesson Cycle

The lesson cycle presented at right has been proven to be an effective teaching strategy. *Writer's Craft* resources appropriate to each phase of the lesson are listed on the right. The lesson cycle may be applied in two basic ways:

1. As the structure of complete, self-contained daily lessons
2. As the overall structure of a multi-day assignment with the central section (in squares) repeated as often as necessary.

- Pupil Text
- Teacher's Edition
- Resource File

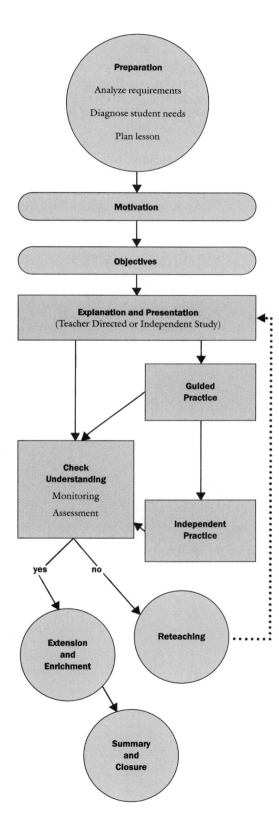

The Writer's Craft

Preparation
State and District Curricula
- Writing Resource Book
- Grammar and Usage Practice Book
- Grammar Pretests
- *The Writer's Craft* Lesson Plans
- Teaching Preview
- Teacher's Choice

Motivation
- Starting from Literature
- Motivate
- Think and Respond
- Springboard

Objectives
- Assignment Rationale
- Objectives
- Set a Purpose

Explanation and Presentation
- Preteaching
- Writer's Workshops
- Handbook Mini-Lessons
- Teaching Strategies
  Teaching Tips
  Individualizing Instruction
  Collaborative Opportunities

Guided and Independent Practice
- Teaching Strategies
- Guided and Related Assignments
- Mini-Lesson Activities and Exercises
- Teacher's Resource File
  Ideas for Writing
  Thinking Skills Transparencies
  Fine Art Transparencies
  Student Revision Model Transparencies
  Peer Response Guides

Check Understanding
- Spot Check
- Teacher's Resource File
  Writing Assessment Prompts
  Guidelines for Evaluating Writing
  Grammar Post-Tests
- Writing Portfolio
- Managing the Paper Load

Reteaching
- Reteaching Notes
- Handbook Mini-Lessons
- Teacher's Resource File
  Writing Resource Book
  Grammar and Usage Practice Book
  Elaboration, Revision, and
    Proofreading Worksheets

Extension and Enrichment
- On the Lightside
- Sketchbooks
- Connections
- Extension and Enrichment

Summary and Closure
- Learning from Your Writing Process
- Summary and Closure

Assignment Chart

Concept Development in *The Writer's Craft*

The Writer's Craft grows in sophistication as your students do, providing a rich variety of writing assignments that become more challenging in every grade. **Guided Assignments** are listed in bold, followed by Related Assignments, in each strand below.

Writing Strands	Grade 9	Grade 10	Grade 11	Grade 12
Personal and Expressive Writing	**Journal Writing to Public Writing** Personal Letter Learning Log	**Autobiographical Incident** Family History Tall Tale	**Memoir** College Application Song Lyric	**Reflective Essay** Autobiographical Incident Monologue
Observation and Description	**Focused Description** Field Notes Haiku	**Observing Situations and Settings** Interview Character Sketch	**Interview Profile** Eyewitness Report Oral History	**Journalistic Narrative** Personality Profile Video
Narrative and Literary Writing	**Personal Narrative** Oral History Storyboard	**Poetry** Story Monologue	**The Short Story** Dramatic Scene Narrative Poem	**Dramatic Writing** Story Choral Poem
Informative Exposition: Classification	**Definition** Extended Metaphor Comparison and Contrast	**Comparison and Contrast** Definition Analogy	**Classification** Comparison and Contrast Organizational Chart	**Explaining Concepts and Ideas** Science Report Collaborative Writing
Informative Exposition: Analysis	**Describing a Process** Cause-and-Effect Analysis Flowchart	**Cause and Effect** Myth Hypothesis	**Examining Changes** Science Fiction Pictorial Essay	**Subject Analysis** Graphic Aid Project Evaluation
Informative Exposition: Synthesis	**Essay of Advice** Consumer Report Problems and Solutions	**Problem and Solution** Advice Essay Group Discussion	**Drawing Conclusions** Lab Report Opinion Poll	**Making Proposals** Rebuttal Oral Presentation
Persuasion	**Supporting Opinions** Letter to the Editor Critical Review	**Controversial Issue** Persuasive Speech Editorial	**Persuasive Essay** Satire Ad Copy	**Argument Analysis** Establishing Conflict Debate
Writing about Literature	**Personal Response to Literature** Point of View Responding to Media	**Interpretative Essay** Interpreting Art Director's Notes	**Critical Analysis** Personal Response Parody	**Literary Analysis** Exploring a Proverb Critical Review
Reports	**The Short Research Paper** I-Search Paper	**Research Report** Saturation Report	**Research Report** Genealogical Research	**Research Paper** Career Search
Writing for Assessment	**Responding to Essay Questions** Responding to a Writing Prompt	**Essays in Other Subjects**	**Written Exams**	**Responding to Readings**

The Writer's Craft

SENIOR AUTHOR
SHERIDAN BLAU
University of California at Santa Barbara

CONSULTING AUTHOR
PETER ELBOW
University of Massachusetts at Amherst

SPECIAL CONTRIBUTING AUTHOR
DON KILLGALLON
Baltimore County Public Schools

SENIOR CONSULTANTS
Arthur Applebee
State University of New York at Albany

Judith Langer
State University of New York at Albany

ML McDougal, Littell & Company
Evanston, Illinois

Dallas • Phoenix • Columbia, SC

SENIOR AUTHOR

Sheridan Blau, Senior Lecturer in English and Education and former Director of Composition, University of California at Santa Barbara; Director, South Coast Writing Project; Director, Literature Institute for Teachers

The Senior Author, in collaboration with the Consulting Author, helped establish the theoretical framework of the program and the pedagogical design of the Workshop prototypes. In addition, he guided the development of the spiral of writing assignments, served as author of the Literary Workshops, and directed the Contributing Authors in the completion of Guided Assignments.

CONSULTING AUTHOR

Peter Elbow, Professor of English, University of Massachusetts at Amherst; Fellow, Bard Center for Writing and Thinking

The Consulting Author, in collaboration with the Senior Author, helped establish the theoretical framework for the series and the pedagogical design of the Writer's Workshops. He also provided material for use in the Writing Handbooks and reviewed selected units for consistency with current research and the philosophy of the series.

SENIOR CONSULTANTS

These consultants reviewed lesson prototypes to ensure consistency with current research. In addition, they reviewed and provided editorial advice on the completed Writer's Workshops.

Arthur N. Applebee, Professor of Education, State University of New York at Albany; Director, Center for the Learning and Teaching of Literature; Senior Fellow, Center for Writing and Literacy

Judith A. Langer, Professor of Education, State University of New York at Albany; Co-director, Center for the Learning and Teaching of Literature; Senior Fellow, Center for Writing and Literacy

SPECIAL CONTRIBUTING AUTHOR

Don Killgallon, English Chairman, Educational Consultant, Baltimore County Public Schools. Mr. Killgallon conceptualized, designed, and wrote all of the features on sentence composing.

ACADEMIC CONSULTANTS

In collaboration with the Consulting Author and Senior Author, the Academic Consultants helped shape the design of the Workshops. They also reviewed selected Workshops and mini-lessons to ensure appropriateness for the writing classroom.

Linda Lewis, Writing Specialist, Fort Worth Independent School District

John Parker, Professor of English, Vancouver Community College

CONTRIBUTING AUTHORS

C. Beth Burch, Assistant Professor in English Education, Purdue University; formerly English Teacher with Lafayette High School

Sandra Robertson, English Teacher, Santa Barbara Junior High School in California; Fellow and teacher-consultant of the South Coast Writing Project and the Literature Institute for Teachers, both at the University of California, Santa Barbara

Linda Smoucha, formerly English Teacher, Mother Theodore Guerin High School, River Grove, IL

Carol Toomer Boysen, English Teacher, Williams School, Oxnard, California; Fellow and teacher-consultant of the South Coast Writing Project and the Literature Institute for Teachers

Richard Barth-Johnson, English Teacher, Scattergood Friends School, West Branch, Iowa; National Writing Project Fellow

Robert and Marilyn Shepherd, education consultants and writers, Rockport, MA

John Phreaner, formerly Chairman of the English Department at San Marcos High School, Santa Barbara; Co-director of the South Coast Writing Project and the Literature Institute for Teachers

Wayne Swanson, Educational Materials Specialist, Chicago, IL

Joan Worley, Assistant Professor of English and Director of the Writing Center at the University of Alaska, Fairbanks; National Writing Project Fellow

Cherryl Armstrong, Assistant Professor of English at California State University, Sacramento; National Writing Project Fellow

Valerie Hobbs, Co-director of the Program in Intensive English, University of California, Santa Barbara; Fellow of the South Coast Writing Project and the Literature Institute for Teachers

STUDENT CONTRIBUTORS

Amy Adams, DeSoto, TX; Tom Adams, Sam Marcos, CA; Ryan Bevington, Seattle, WA; Mike Blacksome, Cedar Rapids, IA; Jason Boettcher, Seattle, WA; Diane Ciesel, Northfield, IL; Rita Colafella, Watertown, MA; Shirley DeVaun, Northfield, IL; Sean Ellars, Cedar Rapids, IA; Erika Garcia, Des Plaines, IL; Leslie Gewin, Birmingham, AL; Beth Hill, Tuscaloosa, AL; Tamara Huffstutter, Birmingham, AL; Wayne Jarmon, Birmingham, AL; Lisa Korpan, Northfield, IL;, Brad A. Mullin, Cedar Rapids, IA; Karen Munn, Jackson, MS; Adalberto Pina, Boston, MA; Scott Robicheaux, Tuscaloosa, AL; Hilda Rodney, Roxbury, MA; Tahnit Sakakeeny, Watertown, MA; Jason Sofie, Seattle, WA; Emily Wilson, Seattle, WA.

TEACHER REVIEWERS

Dr. Joanne Bergman, English Teacher, Countryside High School, Clearwater, FL

Regina Dalicandro, English Department Chairperson, Mather High School, Chicago, IL

Becky Ebner, Trainer for the New Jersey Writing Project in Texas; English Teacher, Clark High School, San Antonio, TX

Sister Sheila Holly, S.S.J., M.A., English Department Chairperson, Saint Maria Goretti High School, Philadelphia, PA

Dr. William J. Hunter, Assistant Principal, English Department, John Jay High School, Brooklyn, NY

Rene Bufo Miles, English Teacher, Academic Magnet Program at Burke High School, Charleston, SC

Margaret N. Miller, Language Arts Consultant (6-12); Library Coordinator (K-12), Birdville I.S.D., Fort Worth, TX

Janet Rodriguez, English Teacher, Clayton Valley High School, Concord, CA

Mark Rougeux, English and Journalism Teacher; Newspaper Advisor, Glenville High School, Cleveland, OH

Bennie Malroy Sheppard, English Teacher, High School for Law Enforcement and Criminal Justice, Houston, TX

Sue Wilson, English Department Chairperson, Wade Hampton High School, Greenville, SC

Beverly Zimmerman, English Department Chairperson, English High School, Jamaica Plain, MA

ISBN 0-8123-8668-X
Copyright © 1995 by McDougal, Littell & Company
Box 1667, Evanston, Illinois 60204
All rights reserved. Printed in the United States of America.

1 2 3 4 5 6 7 8 9 10 – VJM – 99 98 97 96 95 94

Contents Overview

Writer's Workshops

Guided Assignments

Related Assignments

Writing Handbook

Mini-lessons in
- Writing Process
- Style
- Academic Skills

Grammar and Usage Handbook

Mini-lessons in
- Grammar
- Usage
- Mechanics

You are an individual. You think and act in ways that are uniquely your own. This book recognizes that individuality. On every page you will be encouraged to discover techniques best suited to your own personal writing style. Just as important, you will learn to think your way through every writing task.

In each of the Writer's Workshops, you will experiment with ideas and approaches as you are guided through a complete piece of writing. Cross-references to the Handbooks will allow you to find additional help when you need it. Then, as you write, you will discover what you think about yourself—and about the world around you.

v

Table of Contents

Starting Points

For more in-depth treatment of each stage of the writing process, see the Writing Handbook, pages 308–490.

Writer's Workshops

In the *Writer's Workshops*, students learn to write by writing, not by reading about writing.

Each Workshop explores a particular type of writing through three different writing assignments.

WRITER'S WORKSHOP 1

Personal and Expressive Writing

Creative *Sketchbooks* encourage students to experiment through no-risk writing activities.

Each assignment begins with literature and other professional writing—some traditional, some as contemporary as today's newspaper.

Throughout each Guided Assignment, students follow the progress of one student's writing process, culminating in the successful *Student Model*.

In the *Sentence Composing* activities, students analyze and imitate the syntax of professional writers, thus adding variety and sophistication to the structure of their own sentences.

Observation and Description

Narrative and Literary Writing

Exploratory Activities in each Guided Assignment help students find topics they can care about.

Assignments such as the storyboard take writing into the real world.

Questions for both the writer and the peer reader foster self-assessment and peer response.

Standards for Evaluation provides a checklist that enables students to decide how effectively their writing meets the general criteria for a specific writing type.

Informative Exposition: Analysis

Suggestions for publishing and presenting offer a variety of formats for sharing writing with different audiences.

Learning from Your Writing Process helps students grow as writers with learning log activities and new writing applications.

Assignments such as the flowchart allow students with different learning styles to shine.

Informative Exposition: Synthesis

In every assignment, students are encouraged to develop a unique writing process that fits their own topics and writing styles.

Linking Grammar and Writing demonstrates the connections between effective writing and grammar, usage, and mechanics.

Persuasion

All key modes and purposes are covered
in both traditional and non-traditional formats.

Multiple drafting and revising strategies
enable students to suit the writing process
to their particular writing task.

On the Lightside highlights the humor and
idiosyncrasies of our language.

Students combine responses to literature with expression in writing.

Collaborative planning activities foster an atmosphere of mutual cooperation and support.

The importance of the media is addressed throughout the book.

Writing About Literature

xiv

Reports

The research paper affords practice in gathering, organizing, synthesizing, and documenting information.

Students learn MLA style for research reports.

Problem-solving activities and questions help students work through the stages of the writing process.

Nontraditional report formats are also explored.

Students gain practice in an increasingly important skill—writing for assessment.

Writing for Assessment

xvi

Writing Handbook Mini-lessons

WRITING PROCESS

Prewriting

Drafting

The *Writing Handbook* allows students to find extra help when they need it. Cross-referenced in the Writer's Workshops, the Handbook also enables teachers to prepare mini-lessons that meet the needs of each classroom or individual student.

Detailed lessons on the writing process may be used for preteaching or to help students problem-solve during the composing process.

Each mini-lesson contains activities for practice and reinforcement.

Key topics such as elaboration are given comprehensive coverage.

xvii

Practical approaches to peer response are provided in Handbook 13.

Graphic devices are presented as invaluable tools to writing.

Literary, professional, and student models enhance the teaching.

The *Style* section helps developing writers increase the sophistication of their writing.

STYLE

The levels and variety of language are covered in Handbook 18.

The *Academic Skills* section covers topics necessary for success in any classroom.

Handbooks 19 and 20 include strategies to help students improve the rhythm and variety of their sentences.

Critical thinking skills are presented as the cornerstone of all effective writing.

xix

Oral communication skills are introduced in Handbook 27 and built on throughout the writing workshops.

Practical test-taking strategies are presented for both classroom and standardized tests.

Grammar and Usage Handbook Mini-lessons

The *Grammar and Usage* mini-lessons present grammar in the context of writing.

Skills Assessment pages—including a pretest, a post-test, and four proficiency tests—provide teachers with the instruments to gauge student learning.

Lessons include a wide variety of exercises: Concept Checks, Drafting and Revision activities, Applications in Literature, Applications in Writing, and Proofreading activities.

Application and Review can be used for review purposes, for extra practice, or as a check of student mastery of a topic.

xxiii

The *Appendix* provides resources most commonly used by writers.

A detailed *Glossary for Writers* provides definitions of all key writing terms.

Getting Ready to Write

Emblems, by Roger de la Fresnaye, 1913. ©The Phillips Collection, Washington, D.C.

WHY WRITE?

Every time you sit down to write, something extraordinary happens. You stare at a blank piece of paper for a period of time, and eventually the words begin to flow. Those words can take you in many different directions. You may not end up where you originally wanted to be; or you may end up somewhere you never dreamed of going. That's because writing is a process, a journey of discovery in which you can explore your thoughts, experiment with ideas, and search for connections. Writing is basically nothing more or less than thinking on paper.

Why think on paper, though, when you can do it in your head? One reason is that you can only remember a limited amount of material at one time. Like the memory of a computer, writing provides a storage-and-retrieval bin for your ideas. The recording of those ideas frees your mind from having to remember and allows you to keep on thinking. Wherever your mind wants to go, your pencil or other writing tool can follow.

Writing can help you work through something you don't understand, record your learning process, and extend your knowledge. In addition, writing can make it possible to relive an experience you had long ago or create ideas, characters, and events that no one ever thought of before. Through writing, you can explore and record your thoughts, feelings, ideas, and imaginings for yourself alone, or you can communicate them to others—to an audience.

> **Writing provides a storage-and-retrieval bin for your ideas that frees you to keep on thinking.**

Getting Ready
to Write   **1**

Writing for Personal Reasons

There are as many personal reasons for writing as there are people. Several high school students shared their reasons:

"Writing is my 'camera' when I want to preserve a moment."
Tahnit Sakakeeny—Watertown, Massachusetts

"I believe writing is a wonderful escape from reality."
Karen Munn—Jackson, Mississippi

"I express things that I can't tell to someone by talking personally."
Erika Garcia—Des Plaines, Illinois

"I understand myself better when I write because I can see the way I am thinking."
Emily Wilson—Seattle, Washington

"I write when I feel 'share-ful'."
Mike Blocksome—Cedar Rapids, Iowa

"I write because it makes me feel good."
Hilda Rodney—Roxbury, Massachusetts

"I write to remember things."
Scott Robicheaux—Tuscaloosa, Alabama

"If a picture is worth a thousand words, why not write a few words to create a picture?"
Amy Adams—De Soto, Texas

You can write to remind yourself to do something or to record a thought that just occurred to you; to share a secret with a friend or to lock the secret away in your journal; to take notes on a book you're reading or to write a story; to fulfill a class assignment or to submit an article to the school newspaper stating that your teachers assign too much writing. You can write to express your feelings or to influence other people; to describe and remember what you have experienced or to imagine life in another time, place, or body; to explain what you know to someone else or to discover what you believe.

Writing to Learn

Elie Wiesel, a writer and survivor of the Nazi concentration camps who won the 1986 Nobel Peace Prize, said, "I write to understand as much as to be understood." No matter what personal reasons you have for writing, and whether or not you are aware of it, you, too, increase your understanding every time you write.

Writing is not a mysterious activity. It is a natural process that everyone can learn and adapt to fit his or her own needs. You can use it to explore a concept in science, review a lesson in social studies, or analyze a piece of literature. It can also help you understand your own feelings and behavior and other people's points of view. In helping you learn to write, this book provides a powerful tool for learning—a tool that you can use throughout your life.

HOW TO USE THIS BOOK

How did you learn to walk? Not by reading a book on locomotion or human anatomy, but by doing it—by practicing until your muscles responded automatically. That's how you learn to write, too—by writing, not only by reading about it. In this book you will do just that.

The book is divided into three major sections—**Writer's Workshops** and two **Handbooks.** You will begin writing immediately by following specific guidelines provided in the Workshops and by referring to the Handbooks for additional help as you need it. The graphic illustration on this page indicates how this process works. The individual parts of the book will be explained in more detail on the pages that follow.

Writer's Workshops

Guided Assignments

Related Assignments

Writing Handbook

Mini-lessons in
- Writing Process
- Style
- Academic Skills

Grammar and Usage Handbook

Mini-lessons in
- Grammar
- Usage
- Mechanics

Getting Ready to Write **3**

Writer's Workshops

As an example of the kinds of writing in the **Writer's Workshops**, have students turn to page 57, which provides an introduction and rationale for the descriptive writing assignments done in Writer's Workshop 2.

Guided Assignments

Suggest that students turn to the **Guided Assignment** on Focused Description beginning on page 58 to preview the kinds of suggestions for writing that are provided in this feature of the book. Here students will find suggestions for starting from literature, prewriting and exploring, drafting and discovering, revising and proofreading, and publishing and presenting their work.

Related Assignments

To show students an example of the kinds of **Related Assignments** offered in the text, have them turn to page 76 for additional applications of the writing skills introduced in the Guided Assignment. These Related Assignments provide students with tips for starting from literature, prewriting, writing, reviewing, and publishing and presenting their work.

Additional Writing Opportunities

Have students turn to page 56 for an example of one of the **Sketchbooks** presented in the text. This page provides students with opportunities for ungraded writing that may be useful in the chapters that follow. The **Sentence Composing** feature beginning on page 81 can be used to illustrate the professional models and accompanying sentence-combining and sentence-imitation exercises that students can use to improve their writing technique and style.

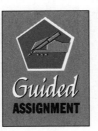

Writer's Workshops

Each writer's workshop focuses on a specific writing type, purpose, or skill. You will have an opportunity to explore this aspect of writing in several different settings—a guided assignment and two related assignments.

Guided Assignments The guided assignments offer detailed suggestions for doing a specific piece of writing. As you write, you will decide which, if any, of these suggestions will help you accomplish your purpose and enable you to complete the assignment to your satisfaction. If you have questions that are not answered in the guided assignment itself or if you need more help, explanation, or practice, you can turn to the handbooks at the back of the book. At each step in your writing process, however, you are encouraged to explore alternate approaches and to discover a way of writing that works for you.

Related Assignments Each guided assignment is accompanied by two related writing applications that can be done instead of, or in addition to, the main assignment. The related assignments build on and extend the skills presented in the guided assignments. While the guided assignments offer many suggestions for completing your writing, the related assignments allow you greater freedom to explore the process on your own, make your own decisions, and solve your own problems. Like the guided assignments, the related assignments refer you to specific handbook sections for additional help and encourage you to explore your personal writing process. You may refer to the handbooks at any time and for any reason. You may also refer to the guided assignment in the workshop for help with skills specifically related to that type of writing.

Additional Writing Opportunities At regular intervals throughout the book, you will find the **Sketchbooks** and **Sentence Composing** features, which provide additional opportunities to practice your writing skills.

The Sketchbooks give you a chance to just try out and have fun with your ideas without worrying about presenting them in finished form or even sharing them with anyone if you would rather not do so.

The Sentence Composing feature provides sentences excerpted from the works of professional writers. You can use these expertly crafted sentences as models to improve your own writing technique and style.

Handbooks

Just as everyone learns to walk at a different rate, everyone learns to write differently and needs different kinds of help along the way. This text offers that help in the form of two handbooks—the **Writing Handbook,** which covers specific aspects of the writing process, style, and academic skills, and the **Grammar and Usage Handbook,** which covers grammar, usage, and mechanics. The guided assignments include cross-references to appropriate handbook sections, and you can consult these or any other sections at any point in your writing process. You can use the handbooks in two basic ways as you complete a particular writing activity:

- for quick reference to answer a technical question—for example, "How do I punctuate quotations?"
- for in-depth practice of a skill—for example, writing a conclusion.

How the Parts Work Together

As you explore many different ways of writing, you will probably find that you use this book in different ways at different times. You will probably also find that you use the book somewhat differently from your classmates. That's as it should be. No two writers and no two writing activities are the same.

For example, one writer may already know the characteristics of a good narrative and understand how to write it. This writer probably would need very little of the help provided in the guided assignment to produce a good piece of narrative writing. In fact, under the direction of the teacher, that writer might even skip the guided assignment entirely and do one of the related assignments in that workshop instead.

However, this same writer may not be as familiar with the elements of persuasive writing and would need a great deal of practice in learning how to support opinions effectively. He or she might need to follow that guided assignment quite closely and work through all the exercises in several handbook sections to learn the material thoroughly and produce a finished piece of writing to be proud of.

This book provides all the help any writer might need and encourages each individual to decide exactly what, how, and when that help is needed. You are like no other writer who ever existed; and this book will enable you to develop into the best writer you can possibly be.

Getting Ready
to Write   **5**

Handbooks

As an example of how students can use the **Writing Handbook** to help them during the writing of a Guided Assignment, have them turn to page 330, "How Do I Plan and Organize My Writing?" and look at the types of organizational strategies suggested in this handbook. Then have students turn to "The Sentence and Its Parts" beginning on page 497 as an example of how they can refer to the **Grammar and Usage Handbook** to solve problems in grammar, usage, and mechanics as they proofread assignments in the Writer's Workshops or any other work in progress.

Writing is your personal triumph over the blank page, your successful expression of your own ideas. No matter how many resources you consult or how many people you ask for advice in doing a piece of writing, in the end you alone are responsible for the words that appear on your paper.

However, writing is also a social activity. You generally write to someone—whether that person is real or imagined, and whether or not he or she will actually ever read your words. In addition, because a good deal of your writing will be done in or for school, you often will be writing with other people.

Your Teacher as Co-Writer

You probably are used to thinking of your teacher as someone you write *for,* not *with*. However, your teacher is not only your most experienced reader, but a writer as well, and can work with you in a variety of ways as you write.

Modeling and Evaluating Your teacher can provide examples of good writing and can offer general guidelines that work for many writers. He or she also can help you evaluate problems you are having and offer suggestions for finding solutions.

Coaching and Editing Like a coach who works with athletes to help them develop their skills and achieve their potential, your teacher can serve as a "test reader" for your work. His or her reactions can help you discover if your writing will be effective for your audience. Your teacher also can evaluate your work at any stage of the writing process and can comment on what is especially effective and why (or offer specific suggestions on how to improve it).

The Classroom—A Community of Writers

Not only your teacher, but also your classmates and the entire classroom offer many opportunities for working together during the writing process. Your classmates can be a source of much helpful support and response.

Providing an Audience Often you and your classmates will be working individually on the same writing assignment. If your teacher so directs, you can provide an audience for each other—

listening to ideas, discussing various approaches to the writing task, or brainstorming solutions to individual or common problems.

Asking for and Giving Peer Response   Your classmates are a good source of specific responses to your writing. You may be nervous about sharing your writing with your peers if you haven't done it before, but remember that you are all in the same situation and that they probably are as apprehensive as you are. In a spirit of understanding, you will be able both to ask for and to give helpful responses. These responses can range from a general reaction—for example, "How did you feel as you read my writing: bored, interested, confused, enthusiastic, angry?"—to a specific comment such as, "What did you want to know more about?"

Writing Collaboratively   You also may have a chance to work collaboratively with one or more classmates at various stages of the writing process. Collaborative writing can offer several advantages over working alone. It can provide a rich source of different ideas and points of view; a supportive, helpful atmosphere; and a safe testing ground for new reflections and approaches.

In fact, much writing in the world outside the classroom is done collaboratively. This textbook, for example, was produced by many people working together in a variety of ways—planning the contents and actually doing the writing as a joint effort, writing separate parts of the book, working with others in fitting the parts together, or just responding to each others' work.

One way to get experience in writing with others is to do **collaborative planning,** in which you explore and develop your initial plans for writing by explaining those plans to a supporter. The supporter listens, asks questions, and encourages you to develop your plans. The two of you then switch roles and repeat the process.

There are many ways of collaborating later on in the writing process as well. For example, after doing collaborative planning for a report, individual students may research and write separate subsections, and then discuss plans for revision and publication as a group. In writing a collaborative story, on the other hand, everyone might want to work through the entire writing process together, perhaps with individuals taking responsibility for developing outlines for specific characters, incidents, or dialogue.

There is no right or wrong way to write with others—the choice depends on the writing activity and on the personalities and writing styles of the individuals involved. The choice is yours.

> **Collaborative writing . . . can provide a rich source of different ideas and points of view; a supportive, helpful atmosphere; and a safe testing ground for new reflections and approaches.**

Getting Ready
to Write   **7**

LEARNING LOGS, JOURNALS, AND WRITING PORTFOLIOS

As you learn to write, you probably will find that you are learning from the process of writing and that you want to write more. A good way to keep track of what you have learned from your writing and what you want to think about for your future writing is to keep a journal.

Many people—not only writers—keep journals or logs. When a radio announcer teased Dodgers pitcher Orel Hershiser about his log, Hershiser replied that he cared too much about what he did and was too mistrustful of human memory not to keep a written record of what made him pitch well one day and poorly another. As Hershiser learned, practice alone is not enough to improve a skill. You also have to monitor your progress to determine what effect the practice is having. Likewise, to become a better writer, you must not only write frequently, but you must also learn how to evaluate carefully your writing process and progress.

Learning Logs

Keeping track of what you are learning is important no matter what the specific area of knowledge is—throwing a fastball, solving quadratic equations, using a microscope, writing a play, or giving a speech. A **learning log** is a place for you to record and reflect on the knowledge you have gained—from living in the world, from studying in your classes, and from your own thinking. A learning log actually can be an aid to learning. As you record information and your thoughts about it in a learning log, you may find that you more thoroughly understand what you learn and see connections that you otherwise might not have noticed.

Journals

A **journal,** or **writer's file,** is a place of your own, an informal way you can get extensive writing practice and also collect ideas for future writing projects.

A journal can:

- provide enjoyment;
- help clear your mind;
- free your imagination;

- offer the privacy, freedom, and safety to experiment and to develop as a writer;
- let you try out writing ideas and approaches that are not fully formed and that you might be afraid to show to a reader;
- provide a sourcebook for clippings, photos, bits of conversation, or observations that you find interesting and that may provide writing ideas.

You can use a writer's journal to collect a wide array of items. Some entries may be unformed ideas or impressions that will never be developed; others may be personal experiences or feelings that you may later turn into a story or poem. You also might decide to include completed pieces of imaginative writing, such as science fiction stories, humorous essays, or poems, that you create just for your own pleasure. There are no rules for keeping a journal—it is a highly individualized process—however, if you'd like some help in getting started, Guided Assignment 1 on pages 30–41 offers specific suggestions on beginning a journal and using it effectively.

Writing Portfolios

A good way to showcase and share what you have written as well as to track your writing progress is to keep a **writing portfolio,** a collection of finished pieces of writing and selected notes and drafts that went into their creation. You also can keep a separate **working folder** of your writing in progress and later transfer the finished piece to your portfolio. You may want to attach a note to your work reflecting on your writing process and evaluating the results. Keeping a writing portfolio can help you and your teacher trace the development of a specific piece of writing; analyze how your writing process has changed—or stayed the same; discover how your personal writing voice and style have developed; and identify the writing skills you have mastered and those that you still need to work on.

Specific opportunities for using your portfolio are offered throughout this book. A writing portfolio is like a family picture album, in which you can clearly see how you have changed. Understanding that process of development can help you continue to grow.

THINKING THROUGH YOUR WRITING PROCESS

Objectives

- To become familiar with the stages of the writing process
- To understand the flexible and recursive nature of the writing process
- To view writing as a process of exploration and discovery

Teaching Strategies

You may want to use this section before beginning the Writer's Workshops if any of the following situations is true:

1. Students are not familiar with the idea of a writing process.

2. Students need to review the terms or techniques associated with the writing process.

3. Students are not used to viewing the writing process as a flexible, recursive activity that can be shaped to fit different writing tasks and individual writing styles.

The belief that "writing is thinking made visible" is central to the instructional approach of this textbook. In every activity, students are shown that writing is a process of examining options, making choices and decisions, and solving problems. It is essential, therefore, that students not view the writing process as a lockstep procedure with one right approach.

To help teachers communicate this idea, this section follows two students through the completion of the same writing assignment. Each student makes different decisions and uses different techniques, *all of which are valid*. As you discuss the material with your students be sure to ask them what decision they might have made on the same assignment.

Thinking Through Your Writing Process

Writing is a process through which you discover what you think about yourself and the world around you. It does not require new and unfamiliar skills, but rather, uses skills you already have mastered. Writing is an extension of the processes of thinking and speaking, and it provides you with new strategies for understanding, creating, and communicating ideas.

THE STAGES OF THE WRITING PROCESS

How do you get started on a writing project? Do you make a detailed outline? Write notes on little scraps of paper? Take a walk and think things over? Talk to a friend about your ideas? Do you rewrite several times or do you tend to stick with your first ideas? There is no one right way to write. The right one is the one that works best for you and your particular writing activity.

There are four basic stages, however, that most writers go through at some point in the process:

- prewriting
- drafting and discovery
- revising and proofreading
- publishing and presenting

Prewriting

Prewriting is a time for exploring ideas and collecting material from many different sources. It is a time for "priming the pump," for getting your creative juices flowing. You also examine what you know about your writing task and what you need to find out.

Drafting and Discovery

This stage involves just "getting it down on paper" without worrying about getting it right. Writing truly can be a process of discovery, in which you learn what you want to say and try one or several ways of saying it. Often at this stage you decide on a precise topic, purpose, and audience for your writing.

Revising and Proofreading

During this stage you review your personal goals for writing and determine if you have met them. Sharing your writing with others as you proceed may help you. As you revise, you may need to loop back through several of the stages of the writing process, or you may decide to start all over. Once you are satisfied with the content of your writing, you begin to **proofread** the material, locating and correcting errors in grammar, usage, and mechanics.

Publishing and Presenting

In this stage you formally share your finished piece of writing with others. This sharing may take the form of an oral presentation, a dramatic performance, or a visual production as well as the traditional publication in print. However, sharing also can take place throughout your writing process.

The stages of the writing process outlined above are not separate steps that you complete one at a time. They often overlap. Some writers may begin drafting immediately, combining that stage with prewriting. Others may revise continuously during the drafting stage and even after a piece is published. The following diagram illustrates the flexible nature of the writing process:

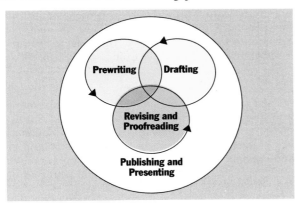

Writing well is more than just completing a series of stages. It is also a way of discovering and understanding what you think. Like any other activity in which you encounter new ideas, writing requires that you examine an idea from different angles, follow it to its logical conclusion, and reshape it if necessary. Remember: just as no two people think alike, no two people write alike.

Thinking Through
Your Writing Process **11**

Prewriting: Choosing a Topic

As students read this section, have them note the categories and techniques mentioned in the text for generating topics (*personal experiences, interests, knowledge about flying, one's journal, brainstorming with friends*). Then have students list other sources and ways to generate ideas for topics having to do with flying. Each time they cite a general category of source (''people you know''; ''magazines'') urge them to think of a more specific example (''my uncle who flies a cropduster''; ''Aviation Weekly''). Use the discussion to help students appreciate the wide variety of sources and techniques a writer can use to think of a topic for writing.

The Albatros, German fighter plane used in World War I

THE WRITING PROCESS IN ACTION

To see the flexible nature of the writing process in action, consider how two students, Dan and Sara, approached a history assignment to write about flying and what it means to them. Notice the various techniques they used and how they adapted the process to suit their individual interests and learning styles.

Prewriting

As they began working on their writing assignment, Dan and Sara took different approaches to several important aspects of their task: **choosing a topic, establishing a purpose and personal goals, identifying an audience, choosing a form,** and **gathering and developing information.**

Choosing a Topic In considering what they would write about, both Dan and Sara started with their personal experiences, interests, and knowledge about flying.

Dan had always been fascinated by airplanes and flying and had made several entries related to aviation in his writing journal during the past year. "My journal could be a good source of ideas," he thought. As he leafed through the pages, the following entry caught his eye:

There was a story in the newspaper today about a ten-year-old boy who flew a small plane across the United States. Of course, his flight instructor went with him, but the boy was at the controls the whole time. What a great adventure that must have been! I wonder what flying lessons are like. Maybe someday I'll find out.

Reading this entry reminded Dan of how excited he was about learning to fly. He decided to write a paper describing what a flying lesson would be like.

Sara, who knew very little about flying, used another approach to thinking about her writing assignment. She and some friends brainstormed and came up with the following topics: *stunt flying, the Wright brothers, hot-air balloons, famous pilots,* and *the Concorde.* Because she was very interested in people, Sara was intrigued by the topic of famous pilots. She realized, however, that she would need to learn more about individual aviators before choosing a specific topic.

In looking through books in the library, Sara discovered that most of the famous pilots were men. She wondered if there were any famous women flyers. More research led her to a book about women pilots and to a picture that caught her attention. The picture was of a jet plane diving toward the desert, and its caption read, "The fastest woman in the world, Jackie Cochran, breaks another record—the sound barrier." Sara thought that Jackie Cochran must have been an extraordinary person, and she decided to do research to learn more about her and to write about her life and accomplishments.

Establishing a Purpose and Personal Goals There are a variety of purposes for writing. Some of the most common are **to express yourself, to inform, to entertain, to analyze,** and **to persuade.** A piece of writing may have one or several purposes. For example, the purpose of a humorous story about a flying machine that didn't get off the ground would be to entertain. On the other hand, a letter to your state representative about your opposition to the expansion of

Prewriting: Purpose/Personal Goals

After students read the five common purposes for writing, have them discuss items from Sara's brainstorming list in terms of these purposes. For example, what might they write about stunt-flying if their purpose were to entertain? To analyze? To inform? *(Possible responses: to entertain: a suspenseful story about the competition between two stunt flyers; to analyze and inform: an explanation of exactly how a certain stunt is performed)* Use the discussion to point out that two writers can address the same topic but for completely different purposes. Also lead students to recognize that a piece of writing about a given topic can fulfill more than one purpose, even though one purpose may be predominant.

the local airport might have two purposes: to inform the representative of your views and to persuade him or her to vote against funds to expand the airport.

In addition to deciding on the general purpose of a piece of writing, writers at some point must determine the specific **personal goals** they want to accomplish. For example, a personal goal could be to communicate the excitement of a flying lesson or to discover what motivated one woman aviator to break speed records. Many writers determine their purpose and personal goals for doing a particular piece of writing in the early stages of the writing process. It is not necessary to determine these variables initially, however. They often become clear later in the process as you consider the other aspects of your writing.

Whenever you choose to determine your personal goals, asking yourself the following questions can guide your decision.

- What do I really want to accomplish in writing this piece?
- How do I want my audience to respond to it?

Because Dan was already familiar with his topic, he was able to answer these questions and state the purpose of his paper clearly before he began writing:

ONE STUDENT'S PROCESS — DAN

I am excited about learning to fly and want to express this excitement so that my readers can share it. My paper should be entertaining, too, because flying lessons would be fun.

What experience can I describe that would both express my excitement and also be entertaining? Probably the first time up in a plane with an instructor is the most thrilling, so that would be a good topic for my paper.

On the other hand, Sara was not sure what direction her paper would take when she began it. She, therefore, decided to continue learning about her topic and to clarify her purpose later in her writing process.

Identifying an Audience It is important to ask yourself who will read your writing, because the answer will determine not only what information you include in your paper, but also how you present your material. Writing is saying something to someone, and unless you know who that someone is, you cannot be sure that you have gotten your message across. Sometimes your audience is chosen for you. For example, if you are writing a speech about the job of an air traffic controller for a Career Day assembly, your audience is your fellow students. At other times, you can choose who your readers will be, or even if you want to share your writing at all.

You do not have to determine your audience before you start your writing, but you *will* have to decide whom you are writing for at some point in your writing process. Occasionally, you may decide to write just for yourself and look for an audience later. In general, however, identifying your audience will help you tailor your writing to meet your readers' needs and so best communicate your ideas. Asking yourself questions such as the following may be helpful:

- What aspects of my subject will my readers find most interesting?
- What do my readers already know about the subject? What do they need to know?
- What approach and language will make my presentation most effective?

Prewriting: Identifying an Audience

Ask students to identify a variety of possible audiences for Dan, from general ones ("ninth-graders") to specific ones (the student in the next seat). Then discuss the idea of a "provisional audience," in cases where the writer doesn't know or does not want to spend time specifying an actual audience: the writer can imagine addressing some particular person while writing his or her piece. Dan, for example, could provisionally write his piece for his best friend, someone with whom he might be motivated to share his excitement about flying. Keeping this reader in mind may help Dan think of things to say, even though the finished piece might be presented not just to his best friend but to some larger audience he decides upon later.

Although Dan and Sara's assignment was for a history class, their teacher had asked them to find an additional place to submit their papers and to write for that audience.

Dan knew exactly what he wanted to write about, but he wasn't sure who his readers would be.

ONE STUDENT'S PROCESS
DAN

I don't know yet who the audience for this piece will be. I'd like to submit it to a magazine for flying buffs, but I don't know if any of those magazines accept articles like this. I'll have to do some research to find out.

However, I don't want to take time to do that research now, because I'm really excited about the subject and want to start collecting information and getting it down on paper.

Sara, on the other hand, knew the audience she wanted to address.

ONE STUDENT'S PROCESS
SARA

I will submit my paper to the essay contest on the theme of "Achievers" sponsored by our local newspaper. My audience will be the editors and readers of the newspaper. Because my readers may not have heard of Jackie Cochran, I'll be sure to include background information about her. Because the contest deals with achievers, I'll focus on what Jackie Cochran contributed to aviation and how she was able to accomplish what she did.

Choosing a Form The **form** is the type of writing in which you express your ideas, such as a story, a poem, a play, a letter, an essay, an article, a report, or a speech. Like the purpose and audience of your writing, the form may or may not be clear before you begin writing. It may, however, emerge from a consideration of your topic, purpose, and audience.

Because Sara had decided to enter her work in an essay contest, the choice of form was already made. On the other hand, Dan was free to choose a form. He could write an article about what happens during the first flying lesson or make up a story about a young pilot's first flight. Because Dan wasn't sure what audience he would be writing for, he decided not to choose a form at this time.

Gathering and Developing Information Although Dan and Sara approached their writing task differently, they both gathered more information on their topics before proceeding.

Dan decided that a flight instructor at the county airport would be a good source of information. Here are some of Dan's questions and notes he took during his interview of the instructor.

ONE STUDENT'S PROCESS   DAN

Question: What happens during a flying lesson?
Answer: The flight instructor demonstrates a maneuver—such as a turn, climb or glide—then talks the student through the same maneuver.

Question: Are flying lessons dangerous?
Answer: An experienced instructor knows when to let a student continue and when to take over the controls. There are few accidents.

Question: What happens if a student panics?
Answer: Actually, that happens to almost everyone at some time. The instructor provides support and encouragement and generally can talk the student through the difficulty.

Question: What skill is the hardest to learn?
Answer: Landings are the hardest to master. New pilots tend to come in either too high, so they glide over the field without landing, or too low, so they have to add power to clear the trees.

Prewriting: Choosing a Form

Ask students how the course of Dan's writing might be affected if he makes a decision about his form at this time. Would his next step differ, if he were writing a story, from the step he would take if he were writing an essay? How? Point out that while Dan can put off his decision about form at this point, he will have to make a decision eventually. At what stage will Dan have to make a decision and what might he do now to make his decision easier later? Suggest to students that a decision does not have to be all-or-nothing. Dan could make a decision at this point to treat his topic in some fictional form without deciding yet whether to write a short story, a novel, or a narrative poem.

Prewriting: Gathering/ Developing Information

Ask students whether Sara should interview the same flight instructor Dan talked to and if so, what she should ask him. Help students recognize that since the flight instructor is a professional in the same field as Jackie Cochran, he might have relevant information and valuable opinions, and might be able to point Sara toward further sources or suggest fruitful angles and insights. Use the whole discussion to emphasize that gathering information is not a one-track process: writers have to keep their minds open, explore a variety of sources, let new information affect them and, if appropriate, dislodge them from the security of fixed ideas and intentions they had at the outset of the writing process.

Drafting and Discovery

Point out that at this stage, Sara's purpose and personal goal are beginning to take shape and ask students to formulate a statement of each. *(Purpose: to present an informative portrait of Jackie Cochran; personal goal: to find out as much as she can about a person she now realizes she finds inspiring)* Have students compare Sara's purpose and goal with the ones Dan formulated much earlier in his writing process. Lead students to see that the two have formulated equally valid and useful purposes and goals, even though they arrived at their formulations by different routes.

Sara decided to continue her library research to help her better understand Jackie Cochran. She listed the following specific questions to help guide her reading:

ONE STUDENT'S PROCESS
SARA

Background information
What was Jackie Cochran's family history?
Why did she become so interested in aviation?
How did she become a pilot?
What difficulties did she have to overcome?
Achievements as a pilot
What records did she set?
How did she break the sound barrier?
How did she set a precedent for other women pilots?

Sara realized that these questions were only a tool to help her organize her search for information and that she might go off in other directions or change direction entirely as she learned more about her topic.

Drafting and Discovery

The next step in the writing process is getting your ideas down on paper. This is the discovery stage of writing. It is the time to follow your thoughts wherever they lead you, to try different ways of expressing your ideas, and to change direction, jump ahead, or backtrack and start over. It is the time when you make meaning from your ideas and the information you have gathered.

As Sara began to draft her report, she realized that she had become fascinated with Jackie Cochran as a person. As Sara thought about and began to identify with the pilot, she discovered many questions that had not been answered in her initial research.

Because Sara was eager to learn the answers to these questions, she decided to do even more research. She also realized at this point that she wanted to present her report as a personal portrait of Jackie Cochran.

I wonder why Jackie felt so strongly about flying. How did her dedication affect her family and friends? Why was she able to accomplish something that no other woman had been able to do? My ice skating means a lot to me, but I wonder if I would be able to dedicate myself to it as completely as Jackie Cochran dedicated herself to flying. I wish I could talk to her and find out about her firsthand.

At this stage the main thing to concentrate on is getting something down on paper. Like Sara, let yourself become involved with your topic and pursue an approach that is meaningful to you. Don't get bogged down worrying about mistakes in grammar, usage, and mechanics or about neatness, logical progression, and word choice. You will have time to deal with all of those issues after you have completed your draft.

However, because drafting is a discovery process, it usually involves evaluation, rethinking, and change. In fact, you may find you need to do things wrong and make a mess before you finally get it all right. For this reason, drafting and revision often occur simultaneously. In fact, some people extensively rework and shape their writing as they draft. Feel free to revise your writing as much or as little as you like during this stage of your writing process.

Whatever drafting process you use, keep the following points in mind.

Ideas   As you draft you should pay attention to where your writing is taking you. Are you developing the idea you initially had in mind, concentrating on one aspect of it, or dealing with something else entirely? If you are going in a different direction, how do you want to proceed from there?

Organization   As you think about the main focus of your writing, you might also consider the relationships among the ideas that support it. Begin to experiment with various ways to organize the material. Are your main ideas related logically in terms of time, space, importance, or a combination of these? How can you best organize your paper to express these relationships?

Drafting: Organization

After students have read the list of different ways to organize a piece, ask them which system would be best, in their opinion, for the piece that Sara is writing. Encourage a variety of responses. For example, one student might think Sara should give a chronological account of Cochran's career and let the portrait of her personality emerge from her actions; another might think she should begin with Cochran's most striking achievements and then fill in the pertinent background. Discuss the advantages of each system, and use the discussion to emphasize the fact that no one answer is correct when a writer is looking for a way to organize material in writing: the method must suit both the material and the writer's own approach.

Drafting: Peer Response

Have students study and discuss the comments in the margins of the paper—do they agree with the comments and do they think the comments are expressed in a useful way? Why or why not? Have students put themselves in Sara's place and consider how they would respond to the comments. Lead them to recognize that a writer can respond to comments in a whole range of ways. Sara, for example, could make an inference from a comment that was not intended by the person who commented; she could decide she doesn't agree with a comment and therefore just ignore it; or she could accept a reader's recommendation in part but not in full. For example, she might agree with the third comment on her paper and decide to give further details about Jackie's character, but not necessarily *here* as the responder suggests.

Peer Response Although the actual composing of a piece of writing is usually a solitary project, discussion with your peers can help you at any stage of the process. Other people bring fresh eyes and unique experiences to their reading, so their responses can help you see your own writing more objectively.

After finishing her first draft, Sara set it aside for a few days. When she reread it, she knew it wasn't quite right and asked several peers the following questions about her writing.

- What parts did you like best? Least?
- What message do you think I am trying to get across?
- Why do you think I chose to write about this topic?
- What did you want to know more about? What parts went on too long?
- Did the beginning work for you? Did the ending?
- Did you have any trouble following my ideas?

Here are some responses Sara's peer readers gave after reading a paragraph from her first draft:

ONE STUDENT'S PROCESS

SARA

> I had trouble following this

> I'm not sure what your point is here.

> I'd like to know more about her character here.

Jackie Cochran got her pilot's license in three weeks. She got the idea for flying lessons from a man that she would later marry. She met Floyd Odlum at a party. Odlum was a successful Lawyer and Investor. He was the son of a minister from Ohio. Jackie told him about her cosmetic business. He told her she would "almost need wings" to stay ahead of the competition. Jackie used her vacation to take flying lessons and took the written exam orally because she could barely read.

Revising and Proofreading

Sara was now ready to revise her essay. She had already laid the groundwork for this important stage of the writing process by evaluating her own work and asking peer readers for opinions.

Like Sara, after finishing a draft, you should put it aside for a few hours—or even a day or two if you have time. Your most important task in revision is to review your personal goals in writing the particular piece and to assess whether you have achieved them. Your ideas should be communicated clearly, leaving the reader with no confusion about what you are trying to say.

Consider your peer readers' comments carefully, but remember that you do not have to use all, or even any, of their suggestions. Before incorporating a suggested change, consider if it would help you fulfill your purpose and improve your writing. If you do decide to make a change, decide what type of revision it involves: **rethinking content**—changing your basic message because of new information you learned or problems your peer readers found; **reworking structure**—reorganizing your material because your message was not communicated clearly; or **refining mechanics and usage**—proofreading for mechanical errors.

The following checklists will help you revise your work:

Checklist for Rethinking Content

- Have I discovered what's important about my topic and expressed this focus or main idea clearly in my draft?
- Can I add any ideas to help my readers better understand my message?
- Can I delete any unnecessary ideas?
- Are my ideas presented so they can be easily understood?

Have students look for changes they would make in Sara's piece in each of the categories mentioned here—rethinking content, reworking structure, and refining mechanics and usage. Have students use the comments in the margins as points of departure: what kind of change does each comment call for?

Checklist for Reworking Structure

- Do the details I present relate directly to my focus or main idea?

- Is my material organized effectively and logically and are the relationships between my ideas clear?

- Do my sentences and paragraphs flow smoothly and logically?

- Does each paragraph focus clearly a single main idea?

- Can I use lists or devices such as charts, tables, or graphs to make my structure clearer?

- Can I combine sentences to make my writing more graceful and clear?

Checklist for Refining Mechanics and Usage

- Have I used punctuation marks and capitalization correctly?

- Have I checked the spellings of all unfamiliar words in the dictionary?

- Have I corrected all run-on sentences and sentence fragments?

- Have I used all strong verbs, vivid adjectives, and precise nouns?

The standard set of symbols called **revising and proofreading marks** will make it easy for you to indicate and for a reader to understand how you want to revise your draft. These marks can be used to indicate any type of revision—in content, structure, or mechanics and usage—and can be incorporated at any stage of your writing process. The most important and most frequently used of these marks are shown in the chart on the following page.

Revising and Proofreading Marks

∧	Insert letters or words.	⌒	Close up.
⊙	Add a period.	¶	Begin a new paragraph.
≡	Capitalize a letter.	∧	Add a comma.
/	Make a capital letter lower case.	∼	Switch the positions of letters or words.
— or ⌿	Take out letters or words.		

Sara used several of these marks in revising the paragraph of her first draft shown on page 20. Notice that she incorporated all the suggestions made by her peer readers and found some additional defects in structure and mechanics, which she also corrected.

SARA

~~Jackie Cochran got her pilot's license in three weeks.~~

Jackie Cochran
She got the idea for flying lessons from a man ~~that~~ *whom* she would later marry. She met Floyd Odlum at a party. Odlum was a successful ~~Lawyer~~ lawyer and ~~Investor~~ investor. ~~He was the son of a minister from Ohio.~~ *When* Jackie told him about her cosmetics business, ~~He told her~~ *replied that* she would "almost need wings" to stay ahead of the competition. *That summer* Jackie used her vacation to take flying lessons and took the written exam orally because she *She paid for them out of her savings. She had to take* ~~could~~ *was* barely ~~read~~ *able to* read.

> This sentence is confusing my readers. It doesn't belong here.

> I need a transition here.

> I need details here.

Revising: Proofreading

Have students read the corrected paper aloud and see if they can read smoothly and easily enough to hear how it flows. Then discuss the importance of using proofreading marks in such a way as to facilitate a smooth reading: if a paper gets too messy and illegible to follow easily, the writer may have trouble knowing whether his or her corrections are improving the piece. Discuss how to mark up a piece of writing so it is readable.

Publishing

Point out that different pieces of writing fit different publishing formats. Given what students know about the pieces Dan and Sara have written, what format would they suggest to each one for publishing his or her piece? Have them think of several outlets for each one and discuss the possibility of tailoring a piece slightly for different publishing outlets.

Publishing and Presenting

The last stage in the writing process is sharing your final product. Not all of the writing you do, however, will be shared. You may write just for your journal or do samples of work for your portfolio that you do not complete at the time. You also may continue revising your work even after you have shared it. Although you often will be writing for your teachers and peers, there are many opportunities for you to share your work with a wider audience in a variety of formats. Several options are listed here. Consider trying any or all of them and adding your own ideas to the list.

Readers' Circles Form a readers' circle with three classmates. Read one anothers' writing and discuss the thoughts and feelings evoked in you.

Writing Exchange Groups As a class, share your writing with students in another class or school.

Booklets Publish a booklet of student writing on a particular topic or of a particular type, such as poetry.

Newspapers and Magazines Submit your writing to your local or school newspaper or to a local or national magazine that accepts student writing.

Performances Dramatize a story or poem and present it to your class or school assembly.

Videos or Multimedia Presentations Create a video or multimedia presentation using music, slides, mime, or dance to illustrate or accompany an oral reading of your writing.

Writing Portfolios Keep your writing in a writing portfolio and reread it in a month or two. You will have a different personal response to your work at that time and may decide to continue revising it and to share it with your original or a different audience.

Learning from Your Writing Process

After you have completed a piece of writing, think about your own personal approach to writing. Asking yourself questions such as the following will help you evaluate and learn from that process and develop your skills.

- Did I become involved in my topic and learn something from writing about it?
- Which aspects of the writing were easiest for me? Which were most difficult?
- What part of my writing process is getting easier?
- What was the biggest problem I had during my writing process? What solution did I find? How can I improve my writing process next time?
- Can I see any changes in my writing style?
- Did I notice any features in my peers' writing or in the reading I have done that I would like to try myself? How could I apply these ideas?
- What new ideas did I discover?
- How can I apply the skills I have learned?

Record your answers to these questions and attach them to the finished piece in your working folder or portfolio. This evaluation will help you become aware of your writing process and will serve as a permanent record of your progress as a writer.

1

Personal and Expressive Writing

Overview

Personal and expressive writing calls on students to communicate personal feelings, ideas, and goals. It is both the most direct kind of writing and the most familiar—students have done it from an early age and will continue to do so all their lives. Through experimentation with personal and expressive writing, student writers can tap into and further develop their own voice and style. It is an excellent first assignment because each writer is the ultimate authority for the accuracy of the material, and, for this reason, it is suggested that these assignments not be graded. Workshop 1 includes the following Guided and Related Assignments:

1. **Guided: Journal Writing to Public Writing** introduces the journal and offers guidelines for moving from a journal entry to a finished piece of writing.

2. **Related: Personal Letter** demonstrates how the material that makes up a journal entry can be shared in a letter.

3. **Related: Learning Log** translates the concept of a journal into a learning tool, showing students how to write their way to the understanding of a concept.

Teaching Preview

Preparation Guide

1. Use the Overview on this page and the Teacher's Choice descriptions on page 27 as a basis for deciding which assignment(s) to teach.

2. Preview the assignments and the teacher's notes and identify concerns that may require preteaching or extra support given your class's abilities. The handbook mini-lessons suggested within the lesson may also provide guidance.

3. Preview the chart below for support materials in the Teacher's Resource File that may be used with this Workshop. Resources are for use with the Guided Assignment unless otherwise noted.

Support Materials

WRITER'S CRAFT RESOURCES

Prewrite and Explore
Thinking Skills Transparencies, pp. 1–2
Thinking Skills Worksheets, p. 1

Draft and Discover
Elaboration, Revision, and Proofreading Worksheets, p. 1

Revise Your Writing
Guidelines for Writing Assessment and Portfolio Use, pp. 8, 19–21
Peer Response Guides, pp. 7–8
Student Revision Model Transparencies, pp. 5–6
Elaboration, Revision, and Proofreading Worksheets, p. 2

Assessment
Tests and Writing Assessment Prompts, p. 1

Extension Activities
Writing Prompts for Fine Art Transparencies, pp. 10, 11, 15, 17
Writing from Literature, pp. 1–44
Standardized Test Practice

Educational Technology
(available separately)
Writer's DataBank
Electronic English Handbook
Multimedia Workshop
Your Personal Trainer for the New SAT
In Perspective (videodisc)

• •

OTHER RESOURCES

Books and Journals
Ditmer, Alan E. "Letters: The Personal Touch in Writing." *English Journal.* 80.1 (1991): 18–24.
Fulwiler, Toby, ed. *The Journal Book.* Portsmouth: Boynton, 1987.
Latta, Dawn B. "In-Process and Retrospect Journals: Putting Writers Back in Writing Processes." *English Journal.* 80.1 (1991): 60–66.

 Film and Videos
A Certain Age (Smithsonian World Series). PBS Video. (60 min.)

 Computer Software
"The Me Disk II." *Write On: Intermediate Collection.* Humanities Software. Apple family, Macintosh, PC/MS-DOS.
PreWrite, Level 2. Mindscape. Apple family.

Workshop Management Guidelines

The chart below indicates the number of days recommended for each phase of the Guided and Related Assignments. Stars indicate portions of the assignment that may be completed outside the classroom if time is limited or if teachers wish the activity to be completed by students independently.

JOURNAL WRITING TO PUBLIC WRITING

Starting from Literature ....1 day
Prewrite ....2 days*
Draft ....2–3 days
Revise ....1 day
Publish ....1–2 days
Learning ....1 day*
Reteaching ....open
Sentence Composing ....1 day*

PERSONAL LETTER

Starting from Literature ....1 day
Writing ....1 day*
Reviewing ....1 day
Publishing ....1 day

LEARNING LOG

Starting from Literature ....1 day
Choosing Subject/Creating Log
　　Entry ....1 day
Reviewing ....1 day
Publishing ....1 day

Linking Literature, Writing, and Grammar

The following options may be used to provide students with an integrated language experience. Begin by assigning and discussing any of the recommended pieces of literature. Use the suggested strategy to provide a link to the Guided Assignment.

LINKING LITERATURE AND WRITING

Option 1

Starting Point: Bob Greene's journal entries on pages 28–29 of *The Writer's Craft*

Strategy: Use the teaching suggestions on pages 28–29 to lead students into the Guided Assignment.

Option 2

Starting Point: "I Wandered Lonely as a Cloud" by William Wordsworth

Strategy: As students respond to this poem, elicit from them that the descriptions in the poem are the result of careful observations that the author wove into a lyrical response. Encourage students to begin recording observations of natural phenomena in their journals. Explain that these might prove useful as they work on the Guided Assignment.

Option 3

Starting Point: "Obituary of a Bone Hunter" by Loren Eiseley

Strategy: As you discuss this nonfiction piece, have students point out examples of introspection. Use this opportunity to discuss with students how writing about oneself often leads to new insights or a clarification of ideas and feelings. Point out the value of journal writing; have students read the selections from Bob Greene's journal on page 28 and lead them into the Guided Assignment.

LINKING WRITING AND GRAMMAR

Before the drafting or revision stage of this assignment, tell students that as they go from their private journal writing to a finished piece of public writing, they should be alert to the presence of sentence fragments. Although fragments are fine for journal writing and often acceptable in dialogue, they can confuse a reader in more formal situations. Ask students to assess their use of fragments in their papers as you write the following examples on the board.

Incorrect: I changed my final answer. Although I still think I was right.

Correct: I changed my final answer although I still think I was right.

Incorrect: Emily Dickinson is my favorite poet. A recluse with little formal schooling who turned to the life of the imagination.

Correct: Emily Dickinson is my favorite poet. A recluse with little formal schooling, she turned to the life of the imagination.

Review sentence fragments and sentence structure on pages 524–532 of the Grammar and Usage Handbook. If inappropriate sentence fragments still appear on student papers, assign the exercises on those pages for reteaching. Additional practice can be found in the *Grammar and Usage Practice Book* on pages 19–20.

Sketchbook

Objective

To use names and nicknames as a springboard to informal writing

Using the Prompt

Tell students that the sketches they will be writing will not be graded. Point out that these sketches are a means of self-discovery. Encourage students to be as frank as possible in their writing, emphasizing that the sketches need not be shared with anyone.

To help students get started, you might bring in a book of "names for babies" that gives an alphabetical list of common names and their meanings. Allow students time to locate their names in the book. Share your first and middle names and discuss what they mean to you and whether you like or dislike them. Tell students what name you would like to have and why.

Ask volunteers to share nicknames they had as children that they have since outgrown. Have them explain how they acquired their nicknames.

Students can use the ideas in the Additional Sketches section as alternative springboards for writing.

Encourage students to begin a writing portfolio. Suggest that they keep this sketch in the portfolio for possible use in the workshop that follows.

Sketchbook

Just as artists fill their sketchpads with doodles and rough drawings, writers fill their notebooks with thoughts and rough drafts. The Sketchbooks presented throughout this book give you a chance to sketch out your ideas. Use the words and images on these pages as starting points; feel free to change them or adapt them in any way you please. Just try something out and have fun with it. See where your writing takes you.

Your name is one of your most personal possessions. Tell everything you know about your name. Are there different forms of it? Do you have nicknames? Do you know why you were given your first name and your nicknames? Do you know where your first or last name came from or what either one means? How do you feel about each of your names? If you were to give yourself a new name, what would it be?

Additional Sketches

What's on your mind today?
Who are you?

26

WRITER'S **1** WORKSHOP

Personal and Expressive Writing

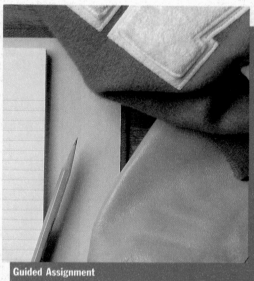

Guided Assignment
JOURNAL WRITING TO PUBLIC WRITING

Related Assignment
PERSONAL LETTER

Related Assignment
LEARNING LOG

You take a phone message. You send an invitation. You write an essay for school. These are just a few of the everyday ways you use writing to communicate with others. Sometimes, however, you write just for yourself—to express your thoughts, to clarify your ideas and feelings, or to capture a meaningful experience.

In this workshop you will focus on personal writing. The guided assignment will show you how you can use a journal to record your thoughts and then polish them to share with others. The related assignments will give you additional strategies you can use to experiment with diary entries and a learning log.

27

Writer's Workshop 1:
Personal and Expressive Writing

Objectives

Guided Assignment:
FROM JOURNAL WRITING TO PUBLIC WRITING
To learn techniques for journal writing and to choose a journal entry to develop as public writing and to draft, revise, proofread, and share a piece of writing

Related Assignment:
PERSONAL LETTER
To write, review, proofread, and share a personal letter

Related Assignment:
LEARNING LOG
To select a subject and to write, review, and share a learning log entry

Teacher's Choice

Guided Assignment
From Journal Writing to Public Writing
The personal writing required in this Guided Assignment will appeal to most students and will help them form the habit of regularly expressing themselves in writing. The Guided Assignment is an excellent first assignment because it teaches students how to generate public writing from a journal.

Related Assignments
Personal Letter LEP students may be more comfortable with this assignment, which allows them to express themselves informally in a personal letter to a real or imaginary friend.

Learning Log This assignment is especially appropriate for crosscurricular use. You may wish to collaborate with teachers of other subjects by sharing ideas from the learning logs. Adapt the assignment for auditory learners by having them tape-record ideas about their subjects before writing.

FROM JOURNAL WRITING TO PUBLIC WRITING

Assignment Rationale

Journal writing has been given prominent placement in this textbook because it appeals to most students and is one of the most common and useful forms of personal writing. Journals give us insight into ourselves as we are now and as we were in the past. The act of writing about an experience helps us understand that experience and its significance in our lives. Making daily journal entries is excellent writing—and thinking—practice, helping to hone writing skills and to increase powers of observation. Journals also provide a rich source of ideas for other writing.

Starting from Literature

Objective

To respond to journal entries of a professional writer as a springboard for writing

Teaching Strategies

Motivate

With the class brainstorm some topics that teenagers of the 1950's or 1960's might have written about. What topics might be the same as those that concern teens today?

Tap Prior Knowledge

Ask students if they have ever had an encounter with a parent that they wish they had handled differently or if they are aware of any new fads in music or dress. Explain that in this excerpt Bob Greene makes these and other everyday events the subjects of his journal entries.

Guided ASSIGNMENT

Journal Writing to Public Writing

A journal entry is a record of your own experiences written by the person who understands them best—you! Journal writing is a way to clarify your thoughts and feelings, to record observations, and to explore the meaning of events. When writer Bob Greene was a high school student in 1964, he began a journal in response to a recommendation from his teacher. As you read his journal entries, think about how he must have felt as he wrote these entries.

28

from
BE TRUE TO YOUR SCHOOL
by Bob Greene

January 15

We took a quiz in Algebra class today and for once I knew what I was doing. I got 100. Not that it will count for much, but it put me in a good mood. Those quizzes that we hand across the desk to someone else and grade right away in class are sort of like Polaroid pictures; you find out how you did immediately, but there's no suspense.

My good mood only lasted for one period. Our chemistry test came back and I got a 40 on it. I've flunked them before, but 40 is really bad....

February 1

I was in my room playing my guitar tonight when Dad tried to walk in. I had the door locked. He started shaking the door, and when I opened it he said, "Why do you always lock this? What are you trying to hide?"

I don't know why I do it. It seems to be the only privacy I have in the world — Timmy's room is right across the hall from me, and Debby's is right next door, and Mom and Dad's is right across from hers. It's like we're right on top of each other all the time, and the only way I can have a place that's mine is to lock the door.

I don't think that's such an irrational idea. I guess if I had tried to explain it that way to Dad, he might have understood. But I just said, "I'm not trying to hide anything."

He looked around the room and shook his head. Then he walked out; he left the door open a few inches....

February 10

Right before the bell to start home-room, I went into the boy's locker room. About twelve guys were standing in front of the big mirror, trying to comb the front of their hair down on their foreheads.

The only thing people are talking about is the Beatles. All during last month there have been some of us who have liked their music, but the Ed Sullivan appearance changed everything. Now virtually everyone in the school is Beatles-crazy. It was funny to see guys with crew cuts and flattops standing in front of the mirror, trying to make their hair look like Paul McCartney's.

Think AND Respond

What kinds of thoughts and events did Bob Greene write about in his journal? How are the events similar to happenings in your own life or in the lives of your friends? Do his entries give you any suggestions for things to include in your own journal?

29

Literature Connection

Author Note   Award winning columnist and author Robert Bernard Greene, Jr., was born in 1947 and still refers to himself as being from Columbus, Ohio. Greene kept the diary on which *Be True to Your School* is based when he was 17 and was attempting to improve his ability to write and report.

Set a Purpose

Before students read the excerpt, discuss the side-column notes. Ask how writing in a journal might help a writer clarify thoughts and feelings or understand the meaning of events. Then have students read the excerpt, keeping in mind the purpose-setting statement given at the end of the side column.

Think and Respond

Elicit Personal Responses

Have students write and then discuss their responses to Greene's journal entries. Focus the discussion on how Greene's experiences might be similar to their own experiences at home and at school.

Explore the Author's Techniques

To help students use the excerpt as a model for their journal entries, encourage students to examine some techniques Greene uses. Point out how he records a specific event and how he feels about the event. (Page 28, paragraph 1: We took . . . doing. Not . . . mood.) Greene describes his encounter with his father (Page 28, paragraph 3: I . . . in.), then explores his feelings about why he keeps his door locked. In the process, Greene reaches the conclusion that it is not irrational to want privacy. (Page 28, paragraphs 4 and 5: It's . . . door. I don't think . . . idea.) Greene also uses specific descriptive details that help a reader visualize a scene. (Page 29, paragraph 7: About twelve . . . foreheads.)

Point out that because Greene includes descriptive details and his feelings about events, he would be able to develop any one of these journal entries into a short story or essay.

Link Literature to Writing

Greene used everyday events at home and at school as the subjects of his journal entries. He made them interesting by including his thoughts and feelings and details about the events. Suggest that as students make their journal entries, they include their thoughts and feelings as well as descriptive details about events in their lives.

The Journal

Teaching Strategies

Personal Touch

Consider sharing a few of your own journal entries with students. Discuss how journal writing helps a writer reflect on the events in his or her life. Emphasize that journals can also be used for writing practice, for recording new information, and for monitoring one's own learning. Invite students who already keep a journal to share their thoughts on journal writing. Focus the discussion on individual approaches to the use of a journal.

Teaching Tip: Subjects for Journal Entries

During discussion make clear that journal entries do not have to be about exotic or unusual events. Common everyday occurrences often make the most interesting journal entries.

Keep a journal as Bob Greene did. Write in it for at least ten minutes each day. Later, you can use some of your entries for public writing ideas. This Workshop may provide you with ideas to get started.

A journal is a writer's private, personal account of events, thoughts, ideas, feelings, reactions, and responses. Journals may take several forms. Some of the more common types are diaries, which detail the day's events; learning logs, which record ideas and responses to lessons or educational activities; and sketchbooks, which provide a place for regular practice for writers, artists, and musicians.

In keeping a journal for yourself, you will be participating in a long tradition of writers and thinkers who believe they can learn more about themselves and their world by writing each day. Through the daily reflection that occurs as you write, you, too, can learn more about yourself and your world. In addition, writing in a journal each day can help improve your writing by making writing a natural task, part of your daily routine—not something you do only when a paper is due!

Here is what several student writers have to say about journal writing:

> "I keep a journal of all my spontaneous thoughts so that when I get a chance I can put these thoughts into writing."
>
> **Tamara Huffstutter**
> **Birmingham, Alabama**

> "My journal contains poems, doodles, and short stories. It also contains observations that I felt like writing."   **Shirley DeVaun**
> **Northfield, Illinois**

> "Journal writing can expand your thought horizon, which is a great deal of my satisfaction in writing."   **Jason Sofie**
> **Seattle, Washington**

30   Workshop 1

KEEP A JOURNAL

1. Begin your daily journal now. What you write about each day is up to you. The important element is to write daily. Writing for at least ten to twenty minutes each day is a good way to begin to reap the benefits of journal writing.

2. Find a format that works for you. Whether you write in a spiral-bound notebook, a black artbook, a composition book with a drawing on the cover, or a loose-leaf notebook, your journal should feel comfortable and inviting. Your journal should be like a room of your own, with your favorite posters on the walls and your own kind of music playing.

3. Date every entry. Doing so may later help you remember the importance of the experiences in your life. You might also want to include the time you write every day. Patterns may eventually emerge that you will find interesting.

4. Create sections, if you like. You might like to have a section for a writer's log, in which you record ideas for future writing. Another section might be for reader response, in which you record insights you attain from your reading.

5. Write for yourself. Journal writing can be playful and experimental. Jokes, poems, descriptions of people, clippings, and all manner of observations and ideas may find their way into your journal. Assume that no one else will be reading what you write. Remember, though, that you are writing not only for the person you are today but also for the person you will be in the future. Therefore, you should give sufficient details so that when you reread your entries at a future date, you can capture a sense of the unique person you were and what you were experiencing at the time you wrote. For example, Bob Greene was writing only for himself in his journal, but reading his thoughts now gives us insights into Greene as a teenager and the time in which he grew up. Although a journal is a place to feel free and to experiment without having to worry about dotting every *i* and crossing every *t,* you will probably be pleased later that you gave some thought to the future audience of you!

PROBLEM SOLVING

How can I use my journal?

Modeling

Help students get started by modeling a journal entry on the board. Choose an event that occurred in the classroom or at school with which all students are familiar. Describe the event and how you felt at the time or what you learned from the event.

Teaching Tip: Writing Ideas

Encourage students to keep a section of their journals for writing ideas. In this section they might write a few words or phrases about an idea as it occurs to them. They might also write brief quotations that appeal to them or make notes about some interesting incident that they heard on the news. Point out that this section should not contain full-fledged journal entries but snippets of information that contain a germ of an idea for later writing.

Teaching Tip: Audience

Emphasize that journal writing is a very personal kind of writing. Stress that even though students themselves are the only audience for their journal writing, they should describe events thoroughly so that they will have a full sense of their experiences when they review their entries. Just as teenagers and adults are fascinated by stories of their childhoods, students will be interested in remembering exactly what they were thinking and feeling at the time they made their entries.

Springboard

Encourage students to write about themselves and their ideas by quoting Henry David Thoreau: "I should not talk so much about myself if there were anybody else whom I knew as well." Tell students that Thoreau's famous book *Walden* is based on journal notes he kept about his activities during the two years he spent living alone on Walden Pond.

As students make journal entries, you might encourage them to make a check mark next to the entries they may wish to use later for public writing.

Prewrite and Explore

Objectives

1. To use prewriting techniques to generate ideas for journal entries
2. To select a journal entry to develop for public writing
3. To identify goals and audience for a piece of public writing

Preteaching

Preview the Prewrite and Explore section. If there are skills or concepts students may need help with before prewriting, present them at this time. The mini-lesson references below may help you in your selection and instruction. The cross-references in the pupil text will give students access to the same lessons for independent study.

> *Handbook Mini-Lessons*
> - Writing Variables, pp. 311–316
> - Personal Techniques, pp. 317–320
> - Writing Techniques, pp. 320–323
> - Brainstorming, pp. 323–324

Teaching Strategies

Management Tip

Allow a few minutes at the beginning of each class for students to make journal entries. Encourage students who are "stuck" for ideas simply to freewrite. Do not assign topics for journal entries. Allow students to be responsible for their own topics.

Writer's Choice   Rather than writing on every page of your journal, you might consider writing on only the left-hand pages. Then when you reread, you can use the right-hand pages to make comments or observations.

PREWRITE AND EXPLORE

1. Look for writing ideas.   Remember that your own experiences are the best sources for journal writing. If you are having trouble getting started, one or more of the following activities may inspire you.

Exploratory Activities

- **Recalling**   Close your eyes and picture a meaningful event that happened to you today. Recall the sounds, smells, and sensations as well as the sights. Quickly sketch out the event on paper.
- **Observing**   Look out the window to see if you can spot a scene or object that stirs a response in you.
- **Freewriting**   Set a timer for ten minutes and start writing with any word that comes to mind. Keep writing for the full time, without worrying about mechanics or neatness.
- **Sketchbook**   Reread what you wrote about your name in the activity on page 26. Do you have further thoughts on how your name might influence who you are?
- **Memoir**   Look back over the course of your life, and jot down the events that have most affected the person you are today. Beginning a journal with a short life history is a good way to establish who you were when you began to write.
- **Predicting**   Think about ten years from now. How old will you be? What will you be doing? Where will you be living? Who will be your friends? Describe a day in your life ten years from now.
- **Reading Literature**   In small groups, share experiences similar to those of Bob Greene or other people you have read about to spark writing ideas. For example, Loren Eiseley shares his fear in "Obituary of a Bone Hunter" and Agnes de Mille shares her experiences with dance in *Dance to the Piper*.

HANDBOOKS
FOR HELP & PRACTICE

Writing Variables, pp. 311–316
Personal Techniques, pp. 317–320
Writing Techniques, pp. 320–323
Brainstorming, pp. 323–324

Writing
—**TIP**—

When you free-write, do not try to edit your ideas. Just keep writing.

Visual Learners Visual learners may want to include drawings with their journal entries. However, make sure students include enough text to make their ideas clear. Such students may also want to include photographs or pictures cut from magazines or other sources. Students can then write responses to these visual prompts.

Collaborative Opportunity

Encourage interested students to meet in small groups to discuss the journal entries that they are considering for public writing. Group members may provide one another with feedback by discussing how interesting the entries are and how they might be expanded or transformed into something new.

Look over the ideas you came up with by doing the Exploratory Activities. In the days and weeks ahead, use these ideas as starting points for journal writing. In addition to these Exploratory Activities, check the ideas in the "Apply Your Skills" section under "Learning from Your Writing Process" on page 41.

2. Select a writing idea for public writing. One of the most common uses for a journal is as a source for future writing ideas. After you have written in your journal for a week or more, choose one idea that you can use as the basis for writing that you will share with others. Before settling on one entry, consider the following points:

- Which entry has at least the kernel of an idea that someone else might find interesting?
- Does the entry suggest a possible writing format to you? Is it already a little bit like a poem, letter, essay, or story?
- Is this entry one that you like well enough to expand or revise?
- If this entry deals with something very personal, can you change it enough so that you will feel comfortable about sharing it with others?

As one student, Jessica, went through her journal, she came across the following entry she had written as she looked out her bedroom window one evening.

PROBLEM
S O L V I N G

What thoughts do I want to share with others?

Science Connection

To help students develop their powers of observation, bring in an object such as a mechanism from a watch or a prism or an object from the natural world, such as a crystal or a fossil. Suggest that students write a journal entry describing the object and noting details that would be of interest to scientists.

Critical Thinking

Evaluating Encourage students to examine One Student's Process and to note how Jessica's journal entry includes her reflections about a simple phenomenon—moonlight shining through fog—that she observed. Ask students if they think Jessica's journal entry is a suitable basis for a piece of public writing. Make sure students offer reasons for their answers. *(Students may answer that the entry is suitable because it includes an insight that might interest others.)*

Managing the Paper Load

After students have selected a journal entry and identified a goal and an audience, have them work in pairs to explain their approaches to each other. As students are working together, you might confer with pairs that need additional guidance.

Spotcheck

Quickly check to be certain students' journal entries are suitable for public writing and not too private to be shared.

ONE STUDENT'S PROCESS

A dog barked. As the night moved on fog and darkness. Fog so thick over the town like a blanket. You saw just thick clustered fog — no bright stars, but just the moon shining its bright light through the fog. The fog was helpless against the light.

This goes to show you that all things and all people have their own weaknesses and strengths, and they should not be intimidated by their weakness, but rather by their weakness a new strength may be awaiting to burst out like the great moon. The fog may part to give room for the new found strength. And in time if you concentrate on your own bright moon your weakness or fog may go away. Although most of the time if you don't concentrate on your moon your fog will creep right back in.

Jessica decided to use this entry as a basis for public writing because she felt her ideas about the moon and the fog were worth sharing with others. She also felt that she would enjoy expanding this entry because she could further clarify her own insights.

 Writer's Choice Decide whether you want to revise your journal entry so that it is a more fully developed version of itself, or whether you would prefer to revise it into something almost entirely new.

3. List your goals. Think about what you want to accomplish with your writing. At this time, you might also decide what form you want your writing to take. Some possibilities are an essay, a short story, or a letter.

4. Identify your audience. Think about who will read what you are writing. You can shape your writing to that audience. Do you want to write for peers or for people younger or older? Sometimes who your audience is won't become clear until you have begun writing.

Off the Record   CALVIN AND HOBBES / By Bill Watterson

DRAFT AND DISCOVER

1. Begin your draft. As you begin, write freely, using your journal entry for ideas. Try not to copy your entry, but use it as a source of ideas instead. Don't worry about making mistakes of any kind because you can make changes later. The important thing is to put your ideas down on paper. The following shows the beginnings of Jessica's first draft, which she based on her journal entry.

ONE STUDENT'S PROCESS

A dog barked its last bark and then lay down to rest. Darkness moved in, and fog crept along the old country road. The fog was like a blanket. It drifted over the town very slowly. It covered the country world of the town.

This goes to show you that all things and all people have their own weaknesses and strengths and they should not be intimidated by their weakness, but rather by their weakness a new strength may be awaiting to burst out like the great moon. The fog may part to give room for the new found strength. And in time if you concentrate on your own bright moon your weakness or fog may go away. Although most of the time if you don't concentrate on your moon your fog will creep right back in.

2. Take a break. After you complete your draft, put it aside for at least a few hours. Most writers find that working intently on personal material, like that from a journal entry, can be so engrossing that they can lose perspective. Time away from it will enable you to take a fresh look at it later.

3. Review your writing. Reread your draft or ask a peer to respond to it. The answers to the following questions may help you discover some strengths and weaknesses in your draft.

HANDBOOKS
FOR HELP & PRACTICE

Getting Started,
pp. 340–344

Peer Response,
pp. 378–382

Sharing During Writing,
pp. 401–402

Writing Voice,
pp. 405–408

Complete Sentences,
pp. 524–532

COMPUTER TIP

You might want to enter the journal entry you've chosen onto the computer, adding and deleting ideas as they occur to you.

Draft and Discover

Objectives

1. To draft a piece of writing using an idea from a journal entry
2. To respond to one's own writing and that of one's peers

Preteaching

Preview the content of the Draft and Discover section for skills or strategies with which students may need special help. The mini-lessons listed below may be useful in providing this instruction.

> ### Handbook Mini-Lessons
> - Getting Started, pp. 340–344
> - Peer Response, pp. 378–382
> - Sharing During Writing, pp. 401–402
> - Writing Voice, pp. 405–408
> - Complete Sentences, pp. 524–532

Teaching Strategies

 Individualizing Instruction

LD and LEP Students To help these students formulate their ideas without undue concern about form, you might suggest that they tape-record their first drafts, then write what they have reworked.

Managing the Paper Load

To help fix problems before they become too difficult for you and students to remedy easily, confer briefly with students as needed during drafting. Focus on students' goals and the form they have chosen for their writing. Call attention to any especially descriptive passages, and point out any areas that lack specific, interesting details.

Modeling

You might model the process of reviewing a draft by answering the "Questions for Yourself" about your own draft. You might also read aloud a draft offered by a volunteer and answer the "Questions for Your Peer Readers." Emphasize the importance of offering specific comments ("I'd like to know how you felt about the event you described in the second paragraph.") instead of general ones ("I like your writing.").

Peer Response

Because this is the first of the Guided Assignments, you might suggest that students exchange papers with partners and write their answers to "Questions for Your Peer Readers." After comments have been returned to writers, invite students to read aloud any comments that seem especially useful and to explain *why* they are helpful.

Revise Your Writing

Objectives

1. To evaluate the responses to a draft
2. To use the responses to revise a draft
3. To proofread a draft for errors in spelling, grammar, and punctuation

Preteaching

Preview the Revise Your Writing section. Use this section and any problems you have noted in students' drafts to identify the skills and strategies you want to review. The mini-lessons listed below may be helpful.

> **Handbook Mini-Lessons**
> • Revising for Ideas, pp. 375–376
> • Proofreading, pp. 376–377
> • Adding Detail, pp. 386–388

Grammar
—TIP—

Check that each sentence ends with the appropriate punctuation mark.

HANDBOOKS
FOR HELP & PRACTICE

Revising for Ideas, pp. 375–376
Proofreading, pp. 376–377
Adding Detail, pp. 386–388

REVIEW YOUR WRITING

Questions for Yourself

• Do I like the form my writing has taken?

• Is it necessary to read the journal entry in order for someone to understand this piece of writing?

• Does my entry make a point or convey a central idea?

• What do I like about what I've written so far? How can I build on that?

• Does this piece of writing fulfill the goals I set?

Questions for Your Peer Readers

• Was this piece of writing easy to follow, or did you find yourself getting lost?

• What point do you think I was trying to make?

• Did my first few sentences make you want to read more?

• Which part of my writing worked best for you? Can you tell me which words or phrases you found striking or interesting?

• What would you like to hear more about?

REVISE YOUR WRITING

1. Evaluate the responses to your draft. Review your own thoughts and the responses of your peer readers. Which ones do you think would make your writing better? If you do not understand a peer reader's comments, be sure to ask that person for clarification.

2. Problem-solve. Rework your draft, incorporating the revisions you have decided to make. Work to strengthen the good points and to eliminate the weaknesses. On the next page, see the changes that Jessica made in response to suggestions from a classmate.

3. Proofread your work. Make a clean copy that incorporates all your changes. Then look for errors in grammar, punctuation, and spelling. These kinds of errors can be distracting to a reader and can spoil the effect of a well-developed piece of writing.

Springboard

Students might enjoy discussing portions of *The Diary of Anne Frank*. Read aloud or invite volunteers to read aloud one or two brief excerpts from the book. Discuss the events Anne describes. Does she include her reflections on the events? How does she make her writing interesting?

ONE STUDENT'S PROCESS

Have you ever   you might be like   ?
  I thought about how the moonlight and the fog act.
If   are like most   you
This goes to show you that all things and all people
    both
have their own weaknesses and strengths. It is impor-
                        let   intimidate you
tant not to be intimidated by any of your weaknesses.
Instead,
  By recognizing a weakness, you may be able to develop
                        a strength that is just
or discover a new strength, waiting to burst out like

the great moon and shine out in delight!

I like the way you make the point that people can overcome their weaknesses.

This sounds a little weak.

This is a great comparison, but do you really need to mention the moon again?

Teaching Strategies

Critical Thinking

Analyzing   Discuss Jessica's revision with students, pointing out the specificity of the peer reader's comments and Jessica's responses to them. Help students realize that revising involves more than just correcting errors. During revising, a writer works to find solutions to problems he or she and a peer reader have discovered. If you wish to provide other examples of revision, you might use the Student Revision Model Transparency for this assignment.

Individualizing Instruction

Basic Students   You might pair each of these students with an advanced student during the revision process. The advanced student can assist his or her partner in evaluating peer responses and determining an approach to revision.

Linking Grammar and Writing

Before students complete their revisions, briefly review run-on sentences. Offer several examples ("I like to write in a journal every day even though I'm busy with other things, and I write about things that bother me and things that happen, and sometimes I even write stories, and once in a while I let somebody read something.") and work with students as a group to revise the sentences, emphasizing the importance of communicating ideas and information clearly. You might also refer students to page 528 in the Grammar and Usage Handbook for additional help with run-on sentences.

Managing the Paper Load

To protect students' privacy yet verify that they are writing in their journals, you might have students show you their journals and select one or two entries for you to read.

After students have completed their revisions and before they make a final clean copy, have them meet in small groups to share and evaluate their revisions. Students can refer again to the Questions for Your Peer Readers on page 36. They may also offer one another help in locating grammar and spelling errors. This will save you time when evaluating final revisions.

GRAMMAR AND WRITING

SENTENCE FRAGMENTS

Journal entries are often random jottings and therefore full of sentence fragments and partial ideas. As you go from journal writing to a more formal public writing, be careful to use complete sentences.

PROBLEM: As the night moved on fog and darkness. Fog so thick over the town like a blanket.

CORRECTED: As the night moved on, the fog and darkness came in. The fog was so thick that it was like a blanket covering the town.

See Grammar Handbook 30, pages 524–527 for additional help with this problem.

Publish and Present

Objective

To publish and present a piece of writing developed from a journal entry

Teaching Strategies

Management Tip

If you create a classroom display, you might provide one class period for students to read one another's writing. Have students discuss which pieces they liked best and why.

Teaching Tip: Self-evaluation

Encourage students to keep a writing portfolio that includes their first drafts and revisions along with finished work. Students will be able to evaluate not only how their writing changes, but how their process of writing changes as well.

HANDBOOKS
FOR HELP & PRACTICE
Publishing Your Work,
pp. 402–403

PUBLISH AND PRESENT

- **Make a classroom display.** With your classmates, choose a place to display your writing. Give the display a title such as "From Me to You." You might want to include your original journal entry and a note to the reader in which you explain the relationship between the two items.
- **Tape record your writing.** Then send it to a relative or friend who would enjoy hearing it.
- **Put out a newsletter.** As a class, issue a weekly newsletter that features interesting insights and observations from journal writings.
- **Begin a book of essays and other writings.** As a class, use a scrapbook or other large book for writing that you and your classmates want to share with one another. Add to the book throughout the school year.
- **Start a writing portfolio.** Use a folder to save your work. One advantage of keeping a portfolio is that you can see how your writing style changes through the school year.
- **Create a time capsule.** Collect journal writing that could give future generations a "slice of life" in the 1990's.

Discovering the Moon

Jessica Vasquez

A dog barked its last bark before lying down for the night. As darkness moved in, fog quietly crept along into the small country town. The fog was a blanket, slowly drifting over and down, covering the silent country world.

The fog was very thick that night, the thickest anyone in the small town had ever seen. If you had been in the town that evening, you would have seen the thickly clustered fog hiding the bright stars the country people had grown up with and had come to expect.

Suddenly, the moon began to shine its bright beams of light. The fog grew helpless and weak against the bright beams of moonlight. The light of the moon gradually emerged through the now defenseless and vulnerable fog.

Have you ever thought about how you might be like the moonlight and the fog? If you are like most people, you have both strengths and weaknesses. It is important not to let any of your weaknesses intimidate you. Instead, by recognizing a weakness, you may be able to develop or discover a new strength, a strength that is just waiting to burst out in delight!

Your strength becomes like the great and powerful moon, shining brightly and ready to break through a weakness, until that weakness, like the fog, eventually may part to give room to the newly found strength so that it may grow and prosper. In time, if you concentrate on your own bright moon, your weakness, or fog, may eventually seem to disappear. Remember, though, if you forget to concentrate on your powerful moon, your fog might just take a chance and quietly creep, creep, creep toward your moon.

Journal entry provides starting point for public writing

Uses description to establish a mood

Engages reader interest with a question

Makes its point with a clever comparison

Journal Writing **39**

Using the Model

You might have students work in small groups to compare Jessica's journal entry on page 34 with her final essay on pages 39–40. Suggest that groups discuss these questions: How did Jessica expand her journal entry? Did she meet her goal of sharing her insight and motivating her readers to apply it? Is her final essay interesting? Why? Invite groups to summarize their discussions for the class.

Reteaching

Assess the needs of students who were not successful in developing an effective piece of writing from a journal entry and identify two or three areas in which additional practice is needed. Assign the appropriate Handbook Mini-lessons, along with the support materials listed for each lesson. Concepts commonly requiring reteaching for this assignment are

Adding Detail: Handbook 14
Developing your Writing Voice: Handbook 17

The following suggestions and resources may also be useful.

1. Selecting a Journal Entry Work with students who had difficulty choosing a journal entry to develop into a piece of public writing. Have each student identify a few journal entries for you to read. Discuss the entries with students, pointing out those that contain interesting ideas or insights. Brainstorm a few ideas about the form a particular entry might take.

2. Grammar and Usage: Sentence Fragments Remind your students that whereas fragments are acceptable in journal writing, they usually are not acceptable in more formal writing. Write one or two sentence fragments on the chalkboard. Then work with students to revise them into complete sentences. To reinforce students' ability to recognize and correct sentence fragments, suggest that students review several of their journal entries and locate sentence fragments. Have students work with partners to correct the fragments.

Learning from Your Writing Process

Objective

To analyze and reflect upon what students have learned about their writing process and about journal writing and public writing

Teaching Strategies

Critical Thinking

Interpreting Joan Didion interprets and remembers experiences through her notebooks. Have students discuss why she talks about "keeping lines open." What does she mean? Why are her notebooks useful only to herself?

Reflecting on the Process

As students answer the questions, have them pay special attention to the question about the biggest problem they encountered in moving from journal to public writing. Encourage students to discuss the problems as well as some of their solutions. You may also direct the class discussion to the kinds of peer responses students found especially helpful.

WRITER TO WRITER

We forget all too soon the things we thought we could never forget. We forget the loves and the betrayals alike, forget what we whispered and what we screamed, forget who we were . . .

It is a good idea, then, to keep in touch, and I suppose that keeping in touch is what notebooks are all about. And we are all on our own when it comes to keeping those lines open to ourselves: your notebooks will never help me, nor mine you.

Joan Didion, novelist, journalist, and screenwriter

1. Reflect on your writing. Think about the process you used to move from your private journal writing to a piece of public writing to be shared with others. Ask yourself the following questions and record your thoughts in your writing log.

Social Studies Connection

History Journals kept by people in the past are some of the most important sources of historical knowledge. (You might mention *The Original Journals of the Lewis and Clark Expedition*, edited by Reuben Gold Thwaites, as an example.) Suggest that students choose a historical figure they have studied and write two or three journal entries as if they were that person. Encourage students to include details about major events or about everyday life that historians would fine useful.

- How did I choose my journal entry for public writing? If I had to begin again, would I choose the same entry?
- What was my biggest problem in going from private writing to public writing?
- Did I choose a topic that continued to interest me or did I begin to lose enthusiasm for the subject?
- What was the easiest part in going from a journal entry to a polished product?
- What kinds of responses to my writing did I find particularly helpful in revising my work?
- In what ways were Bob Greene's journal entries and Jessica's student writing helpful to me? What did I learn from the writing of other students in this class?
- If I had to base another piece of writing on a journal entry, what would I do differently next time?

2. Apply your skills. Use what you have learned in this Workshop to try one or more of the following activities.

- **General** Interview older family members to find out how they feel about the value of journal writing. Make a list of questions before you begin the interviews. Take notes or record their answers. Then summarize their remarks in your journal. Later, you can use your journal entry to write an essay in which you compare and contrast their attitudes about keeping a journal with yours.
- **Literature** Choose a character from a literary work you are studying and for a week write journal entries that the character might write. Try to capture the way the character would talk and think.
- **Cross curricular** Keep a log for one week recording the difficulties and triumphs you encounter in one course, such as science or math. Use your log to review what you've learned and identify where you need more help.
- **History** Invent journal entries that could have been written during a critical period in the career of a historical figure you are studying.
- **Related assignments** Follow the suggestions on pages 42–52 for writing a letter and creating a learning log.

Literature Connection

Nonfiction to Read Students may enjoy reading examples of writing that stem from the life experiences of the author. You might suggest "The Washwoman" by Isaac Bashevis Singer and excerpts from *I Know Why the Caged Bird Sings* by Maya Angelou.

Writing Portfolio

Have students keep their answers to the questions in their writing portfolios. Explain that as students complete other writing assignments, they will be able to review their self-evaluations and note how they, as writers, have changed. Point out that in addition to answering the questions, students may want to make note of strategies that worked especially well for them in this writing assignment.

Application

Students who are interested in the second activity might enjoy working in pairs. Partners can select a character, write their own individual journal entries, then collaborate to devise a scene, using as a resource ideas from both journal entries.

Summary and Closure

Before proceeding to the next lesson be sure students have internalized the following concepts:

1. Ideas for journal entries can come from everyday experiences and can be generated by a variety of techniques.

2. Journal entries can serve as the basis for public writing.

3. To develop a piece of public writing from a journal entry, a writer must identify goals, form, and audience, and organize and clarify the material.

Allow students time to summarize what they learned by describing techniques for generating ideas for journal entries and by explaining how a journal entry can be developed into a piece of public writing. Students should also summarize how keeping a journal might help them in other school subjects.

Starting from Literature

Objective

To respond to a model of a personal letter as a springboard to writing

Teaching Strategies

Motivate

Ask students who they would most like to receive a letter from, and why. Encourage volunteers to share their answers with the class.

Tap Prior Knowledge

Ask students to think about the phone calls they make to and receive from friends. What kinds of things do they talk about? What are some of the problems with phone calls? How might a letter be more effective?

Set a Purpose

Before students read the letter, discuss the side-column notes. Ask students to think about people with whom they might correspond. What would they write about in their letters? As students read the letter, encourage them to keep in mind the purpose stated at the end of the side column.

Related
ASSIGNMENT

Personal Letter

Suppose you went to your mailbox tomorrow and found it jammed with letters. There would be letters from friends who had moved away, from relatives in other states, and from your favorite TV stars, musicians, authors, and politicians. Sound impossible? It isn't. All you have to do is write them first.

Writing a letter is a way to share your thoughts, feelings, and experiences. Like friendship, corresponding lets you learn more about yourself and about people who are important to you.

The writer of this letter describes her new job as a circus clown. Note how she allows her friend to picture her exciting experiences.

42

> March 12
>
> Dear Karen,
> Thanks for your letter and your note to us all in Japan. We've been here almost three weeks (feels like two years), but we didn't work for the first few days—they had trouble getting the tent up. Even so, my body feels like it did the first two weeks of clown college—OUCH !!
> Being in the show is very different from clown college. For instance, we have to be here at 9 a.m. to work on production numbers and build props all day, and it isn't until 9 p.m. that we really get time to rehearse our material. At the same time, it is incredibly exciting. I have elephants and camels living in my backyard, and I know people who can hang by their hair or

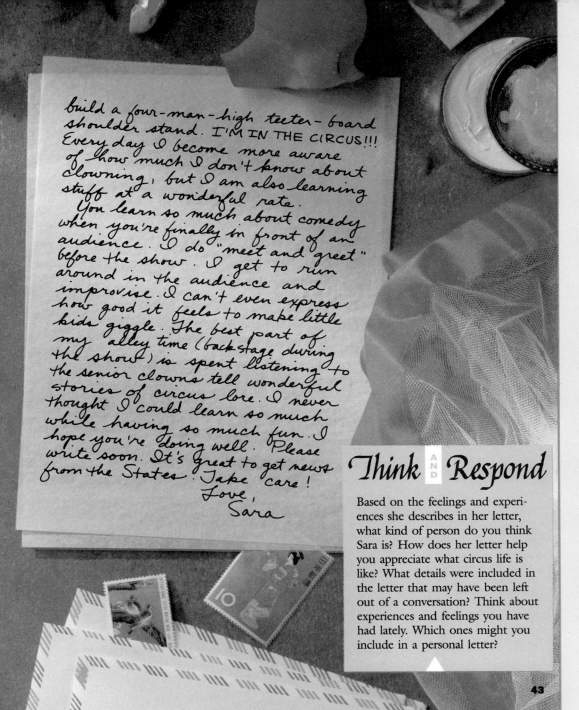

build a four-man-high teeter-board shoulder stand. I'M IN THE CIRCUS!!! Every day I become more aware of how much I don't know about clowning, but I am also learning stuff at a wonderful rate.

You learn so much about comedy when you're finally in front of an audience. I do "meet and greet" before the show. I get to run around in the audience and improvise. I can't even express how good it feels to make little kids giggle. The best part of my alley time (backstage during the show) is spent listening to the senior clowns tell wonderful stories of circus lore. I never thought I could learn so much while having so much fun. I hope you're doing well. Please write soon. It's great to get news from the States. Take care!
Love,
Sara

Think AND Respond

Based on the feelings and experiences she describes in her letter, what kind of person do you think Sara is? How does her letter help you appreciate what circus life is like? What details were included in the letter that may have been left out of a conversation? Think about experiences and feelings you have had lately. Which ones might you include in a personal letter?

Elicit Personal Responses

Have students record their personal responses to Sara's letter in their journals or learning logs. Students can answer some or all of the questions on this page and add any other reactions they may have had. Then discuss the responses as a class. Focus on the details Sara uses to help her friend learn about her new life. Ask students if they were able to imagine Sara's experiences.

Explore the Author's Techniques

To help students use the example as a model for a personal letter, review the letter as a class, focusing on the techniques Sara uses. Point out the informal, friendly, conversational tone of the letter. (Page 42, paragraph 1: We've . . . up. Even so . . . OUCH!!!) Note also how the writer uses jargon, then explains it for her reader. (Page 43, paragraph 2: I do ''meet and greet'' . . . show. I get . . . improvise. The best part . . . lore.) Point out how Sara describes in detail some aspect of her activity, then tells how she feels about it. (Page 43, paragraph 2: I get . . . improvise. I can't . . . giggle.) Encourage students to use descriptive details and to share their feelings when they write personal letters.

Link Literature to Writing

Point out that Sara clearly is enjoying her experiences in the circus and is enthusiastic about sharing them with her friend. To interest students in writing their own letters, have them consider people they care about and events or experiences that they feel enthusiastic about.

Guiding Your Writers

Objectives

1. To choose an audience and purpose for a personal letter
2. To write a personal letter describing specific experiences and expressing interest in the other person
3. To review, proofread, and share a personal letter

Preteaching

Look through the remainder of the assignment for any skills or concepts with which students may need help. The mini-lessons listed below may be useful in your selection and instruction. The cross-references in the pupil text will give students access to the same lessons for independent study.

Handbook Mini-Lessons
- Personal Techniques, pp. 317–320
- Appropriate Details, pp. 355–356
- Self-Assessment, p. 378
- Commas in Letters, p. 782

Teaching Strategies

Teaching Tip: Material for Letters

Encourage students to review their journals for interesting experiences, thoughts, and feelings that they might want to share in a letter.

INVITATION TO Write

In Sara's letter, she described her experiences and feelings in a new job. Now write a letter to a friend or relative in which you share something interesting that has happened to you.

Like journal entries, letters are personal writings that record your observations, feelings, and experiences. But unlike other forms of personal writing, letters are almost always written to be shared with other people.

Despite the ease of communicating by telephone, there are still benefits to writing letters. For example, often you can share ideas and feelings in letters that you might not feel comfortable expressing face to face. Letter writing can also give you the time to share your ideas and feelings in a more considered and carefully worded way than is usually possible in conversation. In addition, through letters you can communicate with people you might not otherwise meet, such as rock musicians, movie stars, authors, and Presidents. Finally, a letter is like a gift. While a phone call is quickly forgotten, a letter is permanent. Read and reread, it will strengthen your bonds with other people.

HANDBOOKS
FOR HELP & PRACTICE

Personal Techniques, pp. 317–320
Appropriate Details, pp. 355–356
Self-Assessment, p. 378
Commas in Letters, p. 782

WRITING A PERSONAL LETTER

1. Choose someone to write to. Usually you write a letter to contact an old friend or share some news with a relative. Perhaps you'd like to offer sympathy or support someone whom you've read about in the newspaper.

Writer's Choice If you would like to write a letter to a famous person, ask your librarian to point out reference books that might contain the name and address of the person's publisher or agent. For inspiration for your letter, try reading some of the published letters of this person.

44   Workshop 1

Social Studies Connection

Students might enjoy writing letters to a class of ninth graders in another state or country. (Your local library should be able to supply you with the addresses of some pen-pal organizations.) Before students write, they might do research to learn about the particular country or state, and then brainstorm a list of questions they might ask in their letters.

2. Think about the "look" of your letter. You may be writing to someone who wouldn't mind if your letter were written on a napkin. Sometimes, however, the look of a letter may make a difference. A word processed letter, for example, might seem impersonal. On the other hand, humorous or colorful stationery could add a note of interest.

3. Relax and start "talking." Remember, you don't have to join the circus to write interesting letters. Almost anything can be good material for a personal letter—people you've met, places you've gone, and your own unique observations of the world around you.

To get the ideas rolling, think of letter writing as "talking" on paper. Try to relate information in interesting or humorous ways. Use vivid examples, colorful details, imaginative language. As topics come to mind, also think about how you can best describe them. Is there a funny angle? There's no need to be tongue-tied because you have plenty of time and privacy to say exactly what you want.

4. Keep your audience in mind. You would probably share different things with a good friend than you would with a person you'd never met. Think about topics that will interest the person to whom you are writing. Some audiences will need more details and explanations than others. People's senses of humor can be very different, too.

5. Describe specific experiences. In her letter to Karen, Sara doesn't just write: "I like being in the circus." Rather, she provides details and examples that show why she enjoys circus life: "I have elephants and camels living in my backyard, and I know people who can hang by their hair or build a four-man-high teeter-board shoulder stand. . . ." Good details and examples like this make her reader feel included in her life.

6. Express your interest in the other person. Your letter is like one side of a conversation. You won't hear the other side until your correspondent writes back to you. Asking questions is a good way to show interest in the other person and to keep a correspondence going. Like conversations, correspondences are sometimes hard to get started but well worth the effort once they do.

THE FAR SIDE   By GARY LARSON

Reprinted with permission.

"Oh my God! It's from Connie! She's written me a 'John deer' letter!"

Personal Letter **45**

Literature Connection

Students might enjoy locating and reading the letters of some well-known authors, such as Mark Twain or Charles Dickens. You might also encourage students to write letters to their favorite authors. Students might include in their letter questions about the particular author's writing process. They might also share their thoughts about certain of the author's works.

Teaching Tip: Expressing Interest

Point out that specific questions such as "How are you getting along in algebra class?" or "What kinds of flowers are you going to plant in the garden this year?" show more genuine interest than the overused "How are you?" or "What's new?" Remind students that they can also express interest by requesting a response to the letter. Such a request lets the person know the writer of the letter values hearing from him or her.

Reteaching

Assess the needs of students who did not develop an effective personal letter and identify two or three areas in which additional practice is needed. Assign the appropriate Handbook Mini-Lessons, along with the support materials listed for each lesson. Concepts commonly requiring reteaching for this assignment are

Personal Techniques: Handbook 2
Self-Assessment: Handbook 13

The following suggestions and resources may also be useful.

1. Vivid Details Point out to students that vivid details will make their letters more interesting to readers. To help students focus on details, you might assign Thinking Skills Worksheet: Describing. Then have pairs of students write each other letters about the same school event. Each student should read and respond to the letter he or she has received, indicating any interesting details about the event that might be added.

2. Conversational Tone Sometimes students' letters have a stilted tone. To help students achieve a natural, conversational tone, have students tape-record their letters. Encourage students to imagine that they are speaking directly to the person. Then have students transcribe their letters.

Extension and Enrichment

• Have students experiment with writing a personal letter from another viewpoint. Students might relate the activity to other subject areas such as literature or history. For example, a student might take on a particular character from a novel or short story and write a letter to another character, or he or she might select a certain historical period and write a letter as a person of that time. For example, a student might imagine he or she is a resident of ancient Sparta and write a letter to a friend describing the latest athletic competition.

Universal Alphabet,
by Jan Baker

REVIEWING YOUR WRITING

1. Read the letter to yourself. Imagine someone sent the letter you have just written to you. Is it clear and interesting? Is it newsy and entertaining? Is it personal and sincere?

2. Don't be too critical. Your purpose is to communicate with someone you feel close to or are interested in. A beautifully crafted letter is, of course, a fine thing. More important, however, is the quality of the feelings that your letter expresses.

3. Proofread your work for clarity. Personal letters can be informal. You can use contractions, run-on sentences, and fragments which you would not use in more formal types of writing. However, check to see that your letter contains no mistakes that would make its meaning unclear.

PUBLISHING AND PRESENTING

• **Mail the letter.** This is doubtlessly the easiest type of writing to publish. All you have to do is put it in a stamped envelope and the post office does the rest. Before you mail your letter, however, you may want to add an additional personal touch by illustrating an event or experience in the letter with a simple cartoon or drawing.

• **Create a book of correspondence.** Save the letters from a person who writes to you often. Read through the letters before you write your next letter, and think about how the letters have changed over time. Consider, too, how your letters to this person might also have changed.

46   Workshop 1

Humanities Connection

Art Note Since early childhood, Jan Baker, the artist who created *Universal Alphabet,* has been fascinated with the shapes that are the letters of the alphabet. As an artist, she uses letters and words in nearly every work, believing not only in their aesthetic beauty, but in their communicative power, as well. In *Universal Alphabet,* a book of handmade paper that unfolds into a three-dimensional screen, Baker created an alphabet composed of letters from many different alphabets, including Greek, Hebrew, and Japanese. What effect would such a universal alphabet have on international communication? How would the world be different if all people spoke and wrote the same language?

On the Lightside

SURNAMES

What's in a name? Family names, or *surnames,* contain clues about ancestry, family relationships, occupations, and more.

Until the twelfth century, many people got along with just their first names. But as society became more sophisticated, more information was needed. Some people came to be identified with where they lived, giving us such general surnames as Brooks, Hill, and Green (for village green), and such specific ones as Washington and Cleveland.

Others were identified by family relationships. Johnson was obviously the son of John, and Williams was a shortening of William's son. The Scots contributed *Mc* or *Mac,* which means "son of," so McPherson was the son of the parson. In Scandinavia the surname changed from generation to generation. A Carl Svenssen would be Sven's son, but Carl's daughter (*dóttir*) Helga would be Helga Carlsdóttir, not Helga Svenssen.

Many names can be traced to occupations. Butcher, Carpenter, and Weaver are obvious examples. One of the most common is the metalworker tending the forge—the Smith. The equivalent in Germany was the Schmidt, in Poland the Kowalczyk, in Hungary the Kovács, in Syria the Haddad,

and in Spain the Herrera. The person who ran the mill became the English Miller, the German Müller, the Italian Molinari, and the Greek Mylonas. The *-ster* in Brewster and Webster showed that the brewer and the weaver were women. Names, which may seem to be our most personal possessions, in fact have rich histories of their own.

Remind students of the Sketchbook activity that they completed at the beginning of Workshop 1. You might have students briefly review their writing from that activity and share their thoughts about their names.

Read and discuss *Surnames* with students. You might then encourage students to find other sources that provide information about the origins of names. Suggest that students use the sources to research their own surnames. Additional information about names might be supplied by family members.

Suggest that students use their journals to write about their research experience and the information they found.

Starting from Literature

Objective

To respond to a student model of a learning log entry as a springboard to writing

Teaching Strategies

Motivate

Ask students if they would like a device that would help them learn faster, memorize better, and pass tests with ease. Explain that this lesson will help them learn to use such a device—a learning log.

Tap Prior Knowledge

Ask students if they have used memorization techniques that were especially helpful. For example, have they ever created a trigger for recalling the parts of a system by making a sentence out of words that start with the same letter as each part in the system? Or have they found that reciting material out loud helps them remember it? Have they discovered other techniques that help them learn?

Set a Purpose

Before students read the sample learning log entry, ask them if they can recall instances where writing about something helped them learn more about it. Then have students read the learning log entry, keeping in mind the purpose-setting statement and questions at the end of the side column.

Related
ASSIGNMENT

Learning Log

Have you ever written to a friend about an event and been surprised as you wrote at the number of details you could recall and the revealing new thoughts you had? One wonderful thing about the physical act of writing is that it can help you remember specific information more easily and accurately. Also, the thoughts you put in writing often clarify what you are trying to understand. So writing, like reading, can be a powerful learning tool.

Examine this entry from a learning log. As you read, look for the different kinds of information that the student has recorded. What does she include in addition to the facts? Where does she make connections between subjects?

48

April 22, Thatcher Woods

Bog: noun, wet or spongy ground; marsh; *verb,* to sink or stick in a bog. Sounded boring when I looked the word up. Today we took a biology field trip to a bog near Thatcher Woods, and it was great. We found an old deck that we could walk onto from solid ground and just sit floating on this bog. We identified all the trees and plants in the bog area. Then we made a stab at naming some of the insects and animals we observed. (Note: Ask Mr. Packen about those "water walkers.") Tim remembered the word *boggy* from a line of an Emily Dickinson poem we read in English class. The poem was about a snake. The line was something like "He likes a *boggy* acre." (Check to find out the title of the poem.) Mr. Packen explained how a bog gets formed. He told about the glaciers melting and some hollows having water but not many minerals. Sphagnum colonies would grow from the top down and the bottom up at the same time. (I'm not sure I get this point—check later.) A layer of very fine stuff would float down and form a false bottom. A bog may look solid, but you may have a few layers of moss and stuff before you fall all the way through. I liked thinking about how the bog had been kind of percolating there all these years. The story of bogs might make a good report topic for later.

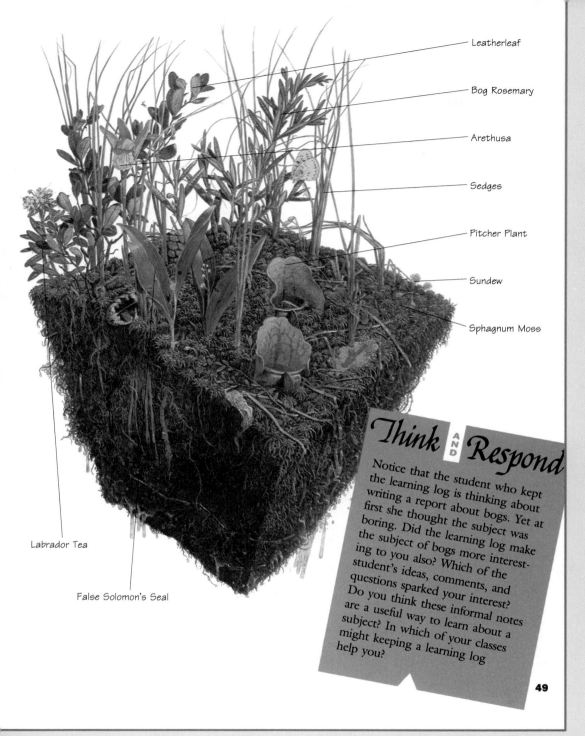

Leatherleaf

Bog Rosemary

Arethusa

Sedges

Pitcher Plant

Sundew

Sphagnum Moss

Labrador Tea

False Solomon's Seal

Think AND Respond

Notice that the student who kept the learning log is thinking about writing a report about bogs. Yet at first she thought the subject was boring. Did the learning log make the subject of bogs more interesting to you also? Which of the student's ideas, comments, and questions sparked your interest? Do you think these informal notes are a useful way to learn about a subject? In which of your classes might keeping a learning log help you?

49

Elicit Personal Responses

After students have read the entry, invite them to share their reactions to it. Focus the discussion on how students might use a learning log, encouraging them to give specific examples.

Explore the Author's Techniques

To make students aware of some of the ways in which a learning log might be used, point out some of the techniques the writer of the model entry used. Call attention to the fact that the writer included a dictionary definition of *bog*, her personal observation of the bog, (Page 48, paragraph 1: We found . . . bog. We identified . . . area. Then . . . observed.) and information she learned from her teacher. (Page 48, paragraph 1: He told . . . minerals. Sphagnum . . . time. A layer . . . bottom.) Point out also that the writer included her personal response to the experience, (Page 48, paragraph 1: I liked . . . years.) questions she had, (Page 48, paragraph 1: Note: . . . ''water walkers.'') and notes about links to other subject areas. (Page 48, paragraph 1: Check . . . poem.)

Link Literature to Writing

Emphasize that the writer of the learning log entry was surprised to find her subject more interesting than she had anticipated. She discovered that the subject stretched her imagination and that she might even want to investigate it further. As students begin their own learning logs in the assignment that follows, encourage them to approach subjects with an open mind and to think about ways they can use what they learn, just as the student who wrote about bogs did.

Springboard

You might check your local television listings and suggest that students watch a particular news program, documentary, or some other educational program. Encourage students to make notes about elements of the program that might make interesting learning log entries. Have students compare and discuss their notes in class.

Guiding Your Writers

Objectives

1. To select a subject for a learning log entry
2. To write, review, and share a learning log entry

Preteaching

Preview the rest of the assignment. Review any skills or concepts with which students may need help. Use the Thinking Skills Transparencies as well as the mini-lesson references below to help in your selection and instruction. The cross-references in the pupil text will give students access to the same lessons for independent study.

> **Handbook Mini-Lessons**
> - Graphic Devices, pp. 357–360
> - Evaluating Ideas, p. 452–453
> - Taking Notes, pp. 459–460
> - Reading Skills, pp. 462–463

Teaching Strategies

Teaching Tip: Learning Tools

Briefly review the uses of a journal, which students learned about in the first Guided Assignment. Remind students that journals provide a place for them to record their thoughts and feelings as well as ideas for writing. Emphasize that a learning log can be another useful, personal tool. Stress that learning logs help students monitor and "take charge" of their own learning.

Teaching Tip: Subjects for Learning Logs

As students consider possible subjects for a learning log entry, encourage them to think about material they will be tested on or classes in which they have difficulty. You might have students brainstorm a list of possible topics.

INVITATION TO Write

The excerpt from a learning log shows what one student recorded during a biology field trip. Write an entry for your own learning log, explaining something interesting that you learned recently.

A learning log is a type of personal journal that helps you make sense of new information. In a learning log you can record information in your own words from your classes, labs, or field trips. Also, you can write down your feelings, reactions, and questions.

Writing down your thoughts in the informal way of a learning log helps you to understand your subject more thoroughly, and also helps you to see when you need more information. You may even want to keep learning logs for activities outside of your schoolwork. What did you discover about the environment, for example, by reading a newspaper or magazine article on recycling? Did watching a new building go up in your neighborhood teach you something about construction? Did you also learn something about the jobs of construction workers?

CHOOSING A SUBJECT

HANDBOOKS
FOR HELP & PRACTICE

Graphic Devices,
pp. 357–360
Evaluating Ideas,
pp. 452–453
Taking Notes,
pp. 459–460
Reading Skills,
pp. 462–463

1. Select a learning situation. Choose a learning situation in which you are comfortable and where you expect to learn something of interest or importance to you. Do not be put off if you find information on your subject confusing the first time you come across it. Writing about an interesting but complex subject will help you identify gaps in your knowledge, as the writer of the learning log about bogs discovered.

2. Be selective about what you record. Don't write down every bit of information that is offered on your subject. Remember that one purpose of a learning log is to help you remember related ideas clearly and accurately. Making a cluster diagram or idea chart can help you see relationships. For example, the writer of the excerpt

50 Workshop 1

Science Connection

Students who were particularly interested in the model entry may enjoy writing their own scientific learning log entries. Suggest possible subjects such as another kind of ecosystem (ponds, swamps, and so on), a system of the human body, or the habitat of a certain animal. You might confer with a ninth-grade science teacher who can suggest pertinent subjects.

you read recorded information on how a bog is formed and also included an association she made to a line from a poem about a "boggy acre."

3. Remember your audience. Since a learning log is a tool for you, you are your own audience. Be natural and say what you want in a way that will be useful to you. Notice that the writer of the excerpt was not afraid to admit that she did not fully understand some of the facts. She made a note to check with her teacher later.

CREATING YOUR LOG ENTRY

1. Tell *when* and *why* you are writing. Record the date and the place where you gathered the information. Also, explain the significance or usefulness to you of the material you are recording. Will you be tested on it, for example? Is it a possible report topic? Might the material be useful in another class?

2. React and respond. Begin to digest and organize your information. Express your ideas. Questions like the following can help you process your thoughts: *What have I learned about this subject? What is another way of expressing this idea? What don't I understand? What resources would help me learn more about this subject? What is especially interesting about this topic?* Copy dictionary definitions into the log if useful. Also note any statistics, or precise numbers, if they are important. If you don't fully understand something, do not hesitate to say so: "I'm not sure I get this point." If an idea or experience was fun, say so: "I liked thinking about how the bog had been kind of percolating. . . ."

3. Make connections among ideas. One very important learning skill is the ability to connect one idea with another. Questions like these may help you: *How does this idea connect with other concepts I already understand? What is a related word or idea? How can I apply this idea to my everyday life? What would happen if . . . ?* If a comment by one of your classmates suggests an interesting connection, include it in your learning log entry.

4. Write freely but clearly. Be relaxed about style and structure in your entry. Abbreviations and sentence fragments are acceptable. Remember, however, that you should write clearly enough so that when you review your material later you don't have to waste time trying to decipher what you have written.

Writing
TIP
Record new information in your learning log while facts and details are fresh in your mind.

Modeling

You might model a learning log entry on the board, using as your subject a new story, an article, or some other selection that you and your class have just read. In your entry, be sure to include your personal reactions and observations to the selection, and encourage students to contribute their ideas. If possible, brainstorm with students several related ideas and show the relationship among ideas by drawing a cluster diagram on the board.

Learning Log **51**

Guidelines for Reviewing Learning Log Entries

Because a learning log is a device that helps students monitor and improve their own learning, the learning log entries should not be graded. You will probably want to review the entries, keeping in mind the following characteristics of a useful entry:

- includes a date and a purpose
- has a clear focus
- includes material related to the focus
- lists questions raised for further investigation
- indicates new or related ideas that have been generated
- includes personal responses to the material

Reteaching

Assess the needs of students who were not successful in developing an effective learning log entry and identify two or three areas in which additional practice is needed. Assign the appropriate Handbook Mini-Lessons, along with the support materials listed for each lesson. Concepts commonly requiring reteaching are

Taking Notes: Handbook 25
Reading Skills: Handbook 25

The following suggestions may also be useful.

1. Finding a Focus In a small group, work with students who had difficulty finding a subject for a learning log entry. Have students briefly describe what they studied in each class that day or the day before, and work with them to make a list of topics. Have each student choose one of the topics and describe some of the information he or she remembers about it. Demonstrate how it might be made into a learning log entry.

2. Making Connections To help students who had difficulty making connections have them create charts with a column for main ideas from their learning log entries. Other columns in the chart should be labeled with subject headings such as history, literature, science, or mathematics. For each main idea, elicit suggestions for a related idea to go under each of the subject headings.

REVIEWING YOUR WRITING

1. Read your log entry. Have you recorded important information that is clearly related to your focus? Has the material you have written clarified your thinking? Have you indicated any gaps in your knowledge that need to be investigated more fully? Has the information in your entry led you to new or related ideas?

2. Organize your entry. You might introduce order by crossing out duplicate material, numbering bits of information in sequence, and marking the most important points with a highlighter.

3. Follow up on what you have learned. After reviewing your entry, make a list of questions for which you would like answers and a list of things you could do to answer these questions. Such activities might include doing library research, conducting an interview, taking a poll, or writing a report.

PUBLISHING AND PRESENTING

- **Share your log.** Find a classmate who has written on the same topic as the one you chose. Since no two people have exactly the same thoughts and observations, your logs will no doubt be different. Make a new learning log entry that contains information about something you learned by reading your classmate's log.

- **Record material covered in your school classes.** Form a study group with other members of your class. Discuss what you learn each day and share your ideas and insights, using your learning logs as a handy reference.
- **Write answers to questions.** Use your log to write down questions as you learn; then find and record the answers.
- **Record ideas.** Keep your log as a sourcebook of ideas, using your observations, reactions, and responses as material for other writing projects. What you have entered in your log can be adapted to many forms or styles of writing. Your log notes may also be useful in preparing an illustrated report or multimedia presentation.

Sentence
COMPOSING

Analyzing Sentences

In the Writer's Workshops, you learn ways to compose and structure different types of writing. You can also learn ways to compose and structure individual sentences. The Sentence Composing lessons presented after each Writer's Workshop show you how professional writers structure their sentences.

Notice the variety in the sentences that make up this description.

MODELS

1. Dicey looked out over the tall marsh grasses, blowing in the wind.
2. Dust motes danced lazily up and down in the light.
3. Dicey stood, pulling the scraper across the curved planks.

Cynthia Voight, *Dicey's Song*

By breaking down each sentence into its parts, you can see the impact the parts have on one another and on the sentence as a whole.

1. Dicey looked out / over the tall marsh grasses, / blowing in the wind.
2. Dust motes danced lazily / up and down / in the light.
3. Dicey stood, / pulling the scraper / across the curved planks.

A. Identifying Imitations Break the sentences that follow each model sentence into their logical parts. Then identify the sentence that has the same structure as the model.

Model: Dicey looked out over the tall marsh grasses, blowing in the wind.

1. a. Marie was showing us the photographs, yellowed with age.
   b. The children stared down at the honeybees, careening from flower to flower.

Model: Dust motes danced lazily up and down in the light.

2. a. From the torn seams, cotton stuffing poked out here and there.
   b. The guards marched smartly back and forth before the gate.

Objectives

1. To analyze professional models of various sentence structures
2. To identify imitations of professional models
3. To imitate various sentence structures

Preteaching

This lesson focuses on analyzing professional models of various sentence structures and writing original sentences that imitate those structures. You might review or refer students to Grammar Handbook 29, The Sentence and Its Parts: The Complete Sentence, page 497; Complete Subjects and Predicates, page 502; Grammar Handbook 35, Using Prepositions, Conjunctions, and Interjections: Prepositional Phrases as Modifiers, page 657; Grammar Handbook 37, Using Verbals and Appositives: The Participial Phrase, page 684.

Model: Dicey stood, pulling the scraper across the curved planks.

3. a. The champion smiled, recalling the roar of the crowd.
   b. Sharon reached down and retrieved the note from the wastebasket.

B. Unscrambling Sentences The sentence parts below are similar to each model sentence. Unscramble the parts and write a sentence that has the same structure as the model. Include proper punctuation.

Model: Dicey looked out over the tall marsh grasses, blowing in the wind.

1. a. at the glassy sea
   b. the sailor gazed out
   c. sparkling in the dawn

2. a. the lion crept on
   b. grazing by the river
   c. toward the two young antelope

3. a. shimmering in the sunlight
   b. into the clear blue water
   c. Denise dived down

4. a. into the old haywagon
   b. the children climbed up
   c. weathering by the barn

Model: Dust motes danced lazily up and down in the light.

5. a. to and fro
   b. in the breeze
   c. bright balloons drifted aimlessly

6. a. on the ice
   b. two skaters glided smoothly
   c. around and around

7. a. deeper and deeper
   b. into the rocky soil
   c. the drill bored relentlessly

8. a. fireflies flashed fleetingly
   b. in the night sky
   c. here and there

Model: Dicey stood, pulling the scraper across the curved planks.

9. a. catching the bar
   b. the trapeze artist soared
   c. at the last minute

10. a. in the dugout
    b. slapping hands
    c. the players celebrated

11. a. tapping her foot
    b. his mother waited
    c. on the hardwood floor

12. a. the soloist bowed
    b. of the audience
    c. acknowledging the applause

C. Imitating Sentences Write a sentence that imitates the structure of each example sentence below. The parts of each sentence are indicated by slash marks (/). Examine each part and see how it relates to the other sentence parts.

Example	Dicey looked out over the tall marsh grasses, blowing in the wind.
Student Sentence	Sam spread out under the umbrella, blocking the sun.

1. Dust motes danced lazily / up and down / in the light.

2. Dicey stood, / pulling the scraper / across the curved planks.

3. The boy looked at them, / big black ugly insects.
   Doris Lessing, *African Stories*

4. There were five of us, / my two brothers, / two pals, / and myself.
   Christy Brown, *My Left Foot*

5. Six months later, / we pulled into Seattle, / leaving a track / across the United States / as erratic as a mouse's track / in snow.
   E.B. White, "From Sea to Shining Sea"

6. At first / the sound of the boy / dragging brush / annoyed me.
   Marjorie Kinnan Rawlings, "A Mother in Mannville"

7. Captain Bentick was a family man, / a lover of dogs / and pink children / and Christmas.
   John Steinbeck, *The Moon Is Down*

8. Behind a billboard, / on an empty lot, / he opened the purse / and saw a pile / of silver and copper coins.
   Charles Chaplin, *My Autobiography*

9. The magician patted the hand, / holding it quietly / with a thumb on its blue veins, / waiting for life to revive.
   T.H. White, *The Book of Merlyn*

10. The monster was a whale shark, / the largest shark / and the largest fish / known in the world today.
    Thor Heyerdahl, *Kon-Tiki*

Application Write a paragraph that describes an object or narrates an incident. Include sentences that imitate one or more of the model sentences in this lesson. Notice how these sentences add variety to your writing.

Grammar Refresher The model sentences above contain phrases used as modifiers. To learn more about using phrases as modifiers, see Handbook 35, pages 657–658 and Handbook 37, pages 691-692.

Teaching Preview

Overview

Observation and description, writing that stems from sensory perceptions, can have many purposes. Students will use observation and description to inform, explain, and entertain. They will also extend their personal and expressive writing skills, introduced in Workshop 1, as they focus on information they derive from their senses. Workshop 2 includes the following Guided and Related Assignments:

1. **Guided: Focused Description** introduces students to the concept that a description should form one general impression; it also shows students how to organize descriptive details logically to create that impression.

2. **Related: Field Notes** builds on skills introduced in the Guided Assignment by demonstrating how to take observation notes in a controlled situation and how to present these notes effectively.

3. **Related: Haiku** extends skills of observation and description by introducing traditional haiku form and instructing students how to use their sensory perceptions to write a haiku.

Preparation Guide

1. Use the Overview on this page and the Teacher's Choice descriptions on page 57 as a basis for deciding which assignment(s) to teach.

2. Preview the assignments and the teacher's notes and identify concerns that may require preteaching or extra support given your class's abilities. The handbook mini-lessons suggested within the lesson may also provide guidance.

3. Preview the chart below for support materials in the Teacher's Resource File that may be used with this Workshop. Resources are for use with the Guided Assignment unless otherwise noted.

Support Materials

WRITER'S CRAFT RESOURCES

Prewrite and Explore
Thinking Skills Transparencies, pp. 5–6
Thinking Skills Worksheets, p. 3

Draft and Discover
Elaboration, Revision, and Proofreading Worksheets, p. 3

Revise Your Writing
Guidelines for Writing Assessment and Portfolio Use, pp. 9, 22–24
Peer Response Guides, pp. 9–10
Student Revision Model Transparencies, pp. 7–10
Elaboration, Revision, and Proofreading Worksheets, p. 4

Assessment
Tests and Writing Assessment Prompts, p. 2

Extension Activities
Writing Prompts for Fine Art Transparencies, pp. 7, 9, 14, 21
Writing from Literature, pp. 1–12, 17–20, 23–28, 35–38, 41–42
Standardized Test Practice

 Educational Technology
(available separately)
Writer's DataBank
Electronic English Handbook
Multimedia Workshop
Your Personal Trainer for the New SAT
In Perspective (videodisc)

• •

OTHER RESOURCES

Books and Journals
Moffett, James. *Active Voice: A Writing Program Across the Curriculum.* Portsmouth: Boynton, 1992.
Zinsser, William. "Writing About a Place." *On Writing Well.* New York: Harper, 1988, 96–109.

 Films and Videos
Creative Writing: A Way of Seeing. Charles Clark Co. (31 min.)

Haiku. AIMS Media, Inc. (18 min.)
Haiku: Short Poetry of Japan. Wombat Film & Video. (28 min.)

 Computer Software
"Haiku to Free Verse." *Write On: Secondary Poetry Series.* Humanities Software. Apple family, Macintosh, PC/MS-DOS.
Poetry Express. Mindscape. Apple family.

Workshop Management Guidelines

The chart below indicates the number of days recommended for each phase of the Guided and Related Assignments. Stars indicate portions of the assignment that may be completed outside the classroom if time is limited or if teachers wish the activity to be completed by students independently.

FOCUSED DESCRIPTION

Starting from Literature ....1 day
Prewrite ....1 day*
Draft ....1–2 days*
Revise ....1 day
Publish ....1–2 days
Learning ....1 day*
Reteaching ....open
Extension/Enrichment......................open
Sentence Composing......................1 day*

FIELD NOTES

Starting from Literature ....1 day
Taking Notes.....................................1 day*
Reworking Notes............................1 day*
Publishing ....1 day

HAIKU

Starting from Literature ....1 day
Finding a Subject/Writing ....1 day
Reviewing...1 day
Publishing ....1 day

Linking Literature, Writing, and Grammar

The following options may be used to provide students with an integrated language experience. Begin by assigning and discussing any of the recommended pieces of literature. Use the suggested strategy to provide a link to the Guided Assignment.

LINKING LITERATURE AND WRITING

Option 1

Starting Point: Excerpt from *Dragondrums* by Anne McCaffrey on pages 58–59 of *The Writer's Craft*

Strategy: Use the teaching suggestions on pages 58–59 to lead students into the Guided Assignment.

Option 2

Starting Point: "The Cask of Amontillado" by Edgar Allan Poe

Strategy: As you discuss the short story, have students focus on Poe's use of sensory details as the two men proceed deeper into the catacombs. As a group, create an observation chart of the details and determine the one general impression made. Conclude your discussion by generalizing about the importance of creating a unified impression in a description and then lead into the Guided Assignment.

Option 3

Starting Point: "Birches" by Robert Frost

Strategy: As students discuss the poem, have them point out descriptive details that help them to experience the movement of the trees. Remind students that vivid images may also be found in prose. As an example, have them read the excerpt from *Dragondrums* on pages 58–59. Discuss the descriptive detail and then proceed with the Guided Assignment.

LINKING WRITING AND GRAMMAR

Before the drafting or revision stage of this assignment, tell students that modifiers are often used to provide descriptive detail. Remind students to be sure that the modifiers are placed in the correct position in a sentence. Have students look for examples of the use of modifiers in their papers and then put these examples on the board.

Incorrect: Freshly cut and in delicate shades of pink and peach, I placed the flowers into the sparkling crystal vase.

Correct: I placed the flowers, freshly cut and in delicate shades of pink and peach, into the sparkling crystal vase.

Incorrect: Having lost the first round, more practice was needed.

Correct: Having lost the first round, the team decided to practice more.

Go over the rules for using modifiers on pages 691–692 of the Grammar and Usage Handbook. If problems with modifiers still appear on student papers, assign the exercises on those pages for reteaching. Additional practice can be found in the *Grammar and Usage Practice Book* on page 129.

Objective

To use a literary excerpt as a springboard to informal writing

Using the Prompt

Explain that the writing activities in the Sketchbook are informal and will not be graded. Emphasize that students should feel free to experiment as they write.

Show students some postcards or magazine pictures of scenes that are rich in detail. Choose one and model for students how you would describe the scene to someone who could not see it. Include many sensory details in your description.

Sketchbook

The magpies were drawn to construction. There was something piratical in their black eyes and intent, lilting flight. Perhaps they liked the glitter of tenpenny nails driven into red tarpaper, or flaxen sawdust billowing from the blade of the table saw, or the bolts buried like coins in the pickup's muddy tire tracks. Perhaps they simply liked the mess—the stray work glove stranded in the innermost coil of a bale of chicken wire, the shavings swept into heaps, the heaps left to unravel in the wind, the oil drums brimming with junk.

Elizabeth Tallent
"GRANT OF EASEMENT"

You are a magpie gliding along with the breeze. You look below at the changing scenery. Then one scene catches your eye. You perch on a tree limb and take a closer look. What do you see? Concentrate on making your description vivid.

Additional Sketches

Close your eyes and tell everything you hear, smell, taste, and feel. Feel with both your sense of touch and your emotions.

Choose an object that has been important to you or that means a lot to you. It might be some toy or piece of clothing or picture. Describe it in as much loving detail as you can.

WRITER'S **2** WORKSHOP

Observation and Description

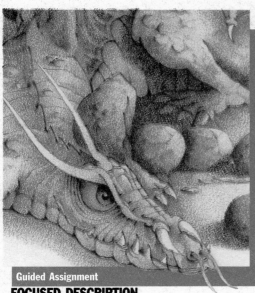

Guided Assignment
FOCUSED DESCRIPTION

Related Assignment
FIELD NOTES

Related Assignment
HAIKU

Detail from pg. 76/77

When you read good descriptive writing, the page turns into a window that allows you to see all the things the writer describes. If the description is particularly strong, you can open the window and step through it into the world on the other side of the page. In this workshop you will explore ways of writing vivid descriptions to convey your impressions of people, places, and things. You will also have a chance to use your descriptive powers out in the field and to write a descriptive form of poetry called haiku.

57

Writer's Workshop 2:
Observation and Description

Objectives

Guided Assignment:
FOCUSED DESCRIPTION
To recognize a focused description and to use prewriting activities to plan a focused description and to draft, revise, proofread, and share a focused description

Related Assignment:
FIELD NOTES
To identify the format and content of field notes and to take field notes of an event in a natural or controlled setting

Related Assignment:
HAIKU
To identify the structure and elements of a haiku and to write an original haiku

Teacher's Choice

Guided Assignment
Focused Description Detailed, accurate description is the basis of clear writing in all areas. For this reason, you will probably want to use the assignment with all students early in the year.

Related Assignments
Field Notes This assignment gives students the opportunity to go out into the "field" to observe an event and to take notes. Cross-curricular ties will depend on the kind of activity students choose to observe, but it is likely that a tie can be made to either the natural or social sciences. You might check with teachers of those subjects to see when students might most benefit from this assignment.
Haiku This assignment might be used as enrichment for those students who want to experiment with mood, imagery, vocabulary, and tone. You might also use the assignment in conjunction with a poetry unit.

Assignment Rationale

A focused description uses sensory details to re-create a person, place, object, or event. In this assignment students learn to observe, record, develop, and organize to create a strong, clear impression. Vivid description is an essential part of most good writing. Knowing how to write effective descriptions will prove useful to students as they explore narrative, imaginative, informative, and persuasive writing. Students will also be able to apply their new skills in other subject areas, particularly the natural and social sciences.

Starting from Literature

Objective

To respond to a professional model of a focused description as a springboard to writing

Teaching Strategies

Motivate

Provide a sketchy description of a familiar object. (For example, the Statue of Liberty might be described as a "tall, somewhat greenish statue.") Ask students if they can identify the object from your description. Discuss the importance of describing items accurately and in detail.

Tap Prior Knowledge

Discuss with students some fantasy worlds with which they are familiar—from those of fairy tales to those of science-fiction stories. Have students explain why such worlds are appealing. Then tell students that as they read the excerpt, they will be transported to Anne McCaffrey's imaginary world of the planet Pern.

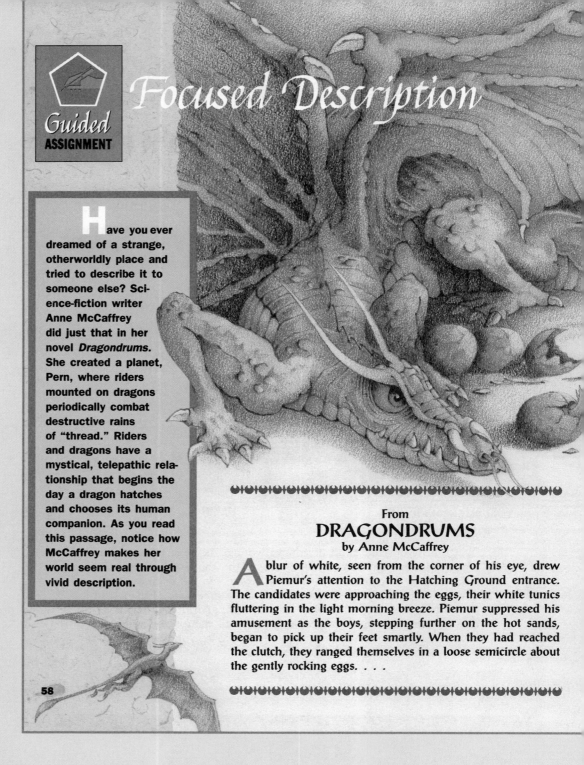

Guided ASSIGNMENT
Focused Description

Have you ever dreamed of a strange, otherworldly place and tried to describe it to someone else? Science-fiction writer Anne McCaffrey did just that in her novel *Dragondrums*. She created a planet, Pern, where riders mounted on dragons periodically combat destructive rains of "thread." Riders and dragons have a mystical, telepathic relationship that begins the day a dragon hatches and chooses its human companion. As you read this passage, notice how McCaffrey makes her world seem real through vivid description.

From
DRAGONDRUMS
by Anne McCaffrey

A blur of white, seen from the corner of his eye, drew Piemur's attention to the Hatching Ground entrance. The candidates were approaching the eggs, their white tunics fluttering in the light morning breeze. Piemur suppressed his amusement as the boys, stepping further on the hot sands, began to pick up their feet smartly. When they had reached the clutch, they ranged themselves in a loose semicircle about the gently rocking eggs. . . .

58

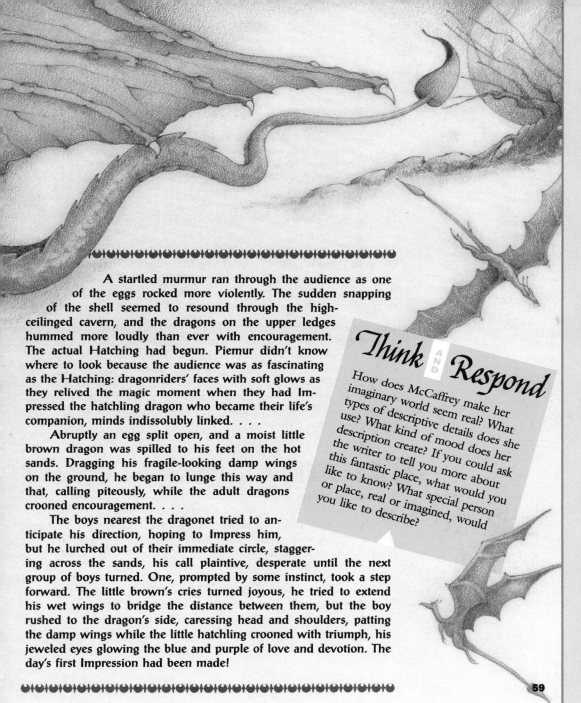

A startled murmur ran through the audience as one of the eggs rocked more violently. The sudden snapping of the shell seemed to resound through the high-ceilinged cavern, and the dragons on the upper ledges hummed more loudly than ever with encouragement. The actual Hatching had begun. Piemur didn't know where to look because the audience was as fascinating as the Hatching: dragonriders' faces with soft glows as they relived the magic moment when they had Impressed the hatchling dragon who became their life's companion, minds indissolubly linked. . . .

Abruptly an egg split open, and a moist little brown dragon was spilled to his feet on the hot sands. Dragging his fragile-looking damp wings on the ground, he began to lunge this way and that, calling piteously, while the adult dragons crooned encouragement. . . .

The boys nearest the dragonet tried to anticipate his direction, hoping to Impress him, but he lurched out of their immediate circle, staggering across the sands, his call plaintive, desperate until the next group of boys turned. One, prompted by some instinct, took a step forward. The little brown's cries turned joyous, he tried to extend his wet wings to bridge the distance between them, but the boy rushed to the dragon's side, caressing head and shoulders, patting the damp wings while the little hatchling crooned with triumph, his jeweled eyes glowing the blue and purple of love and devotion. The day's first Impression had been made!

Think AND Respond

How does McCaffrey make her imaginary world seem real? What types of descriptive details does she use? What kind of mood does her description create? If you could ask the writer to tell you more about this fantastic place, what would you like to know? What special person or place, real or imagined, would you like to describe?

59

Literature Connection

Author Note Anne McCaffrey was born in the United States but now lives at Dragonhold in County Wicklow, Ireland. She is an award-winning writer of science fiction. *Dragondrums*, from which this excerpt is taken, is the final novel in the Harper Hall Trilogy.

Set a Purpose

Before students read the excerpt, discuss the side notes, focusing on the elements of McCaffrey's imaginary world. To stress the importance of description in all writing, point out that this excerpt is from a science fiction novel, not from a descriptive essay. Then have students read the excerpt, keeping in mind the purpose stated at the end of the side column.

Think and Respond

Elicit Personal Responses

Encourage students to share their responses to the excerpt. As you discuss the selection, focus on the impression or mood that McCaffrey created with descriptive details.

Explore the Author's Techniques

To help students use the excerpt as a model, discuss some of the techniques McCaffrey uses. For example, reread with students the section where the little brown dragon hatches. Point out how McCaffrey uses details that appeal to the senses of sight, hearing, and touch (Page 59, paragraph 2: Abruptly an egg . . . hot sands. Dragging . . . crooned encouragement. Paragraph 3: The boys nearest . . . turned. The little brown's . . . and devotion.) to make the event seem real. Point out also how the details create a mood of wonder.

Link Literature to Writing

Explain that McCaffrey's description makes a strong impression on the reader because she provides a variety of sensory details that help the reader fully experience the dragon hatching ceremony as well as the *feeling* of the event. Challenge students to think about ways in which they might describe a special place or person so that their readers can clearly imagine the person or place.

Prewrite and Explore

Objectives

1. To use prewriting techniques to generate ideas for a focused description
2. To use freewriting to list ideas and details on several topics
3. To choose a topic and identify goals, audience, sensory information, emotions, mood, and physical vantage point for a focused description

Preteaching

Preview the Prewrite and Explore section. If there are skills or concepts that students may need help with before prewriting, present them at this time. The Thinking Skills transparencies as well as the mini-lesson references below may help you in your selection and instruction. The cross-references in the pupil text will give students access to the same lessons for independent study.

> **Handbook Mini-Lessons**
> - Personal Techniques, pp. 317–320
> - Creating Charts, pp. 358–359
> - Adding Detail, pp. 386–388

Teaching Strategies

Modeling

Use the second Exploratory Activity to model one way to find a topic for a focused description. Select a place you have visited, and tell students what it looks like as you picture it in your mind. If you like, freewrite about the place on the board. Include details that appeal to several senses.

INVITATION TO Write

Anne McCaffrey made an imaginary place seem real by writing a vivid description of it. Using as many sensory details as possible, write a description of a person, place, or object that you have observed or imagined.

Like an intriguing photograph, good descriptive writing can stimulate your curiosity and transport you to a new world. Yet descriptive writing can go a step beyond photography, which is limited to visual imagery. Effective description can re-create *all* of the senses, and it can evoke moods and emotions as well.

Description can enhance virtually any kind of writing. You can use it in a short story to create an unforgettable character, setting, or mood. In a biology report, description allows you to record accurately the physical characteristics of a specimen. In an editorial, you can graphically describe conditions to which you want to draw attention. In fact, whether it is the focus of an entire essay, a paragraph, or just a few words and phrases, description can be found in almost every piece of writing.

PREWRITE AND EXPLORE

HANDBOOKS
FOR HELP & PRACTICE

Personal Techniques, pp. 317–320
Creating Charts, pp. 358–359
Adding Detail, pp. 386–388

1. Look for ideas. Can you think of an occasion when you found something so interesting you couldn't wait to describe it to your friends? Is there someone or something that has a special meaning to you? If you want help finding a subject for your description, try one or more of these activities.

Exploratory Activities

- **Daydreaming** If there were such a place as a perfect world, what would it be like? Daydream alone or brainstorm with a partner, jotting down as many details as you can.

- **Postcards** Recall a few places you have traveled to. Which of them seem most unusual or interesting? What local sights were most arresting? Try to picture these places as they might appear on a postcard. With images of one or two of these places in mind, freewrite your recollection of them.
- **Tuning In** Describe the sounds you hear in your neighborhood. You might hear water running, an air conditioner humming, a dog barking, cars or buses rumbling by. See how much detail you can add to your description.
- **Exploring science** Think about a plant, animal, or natural phenomenon you find intriguing. Freewrite about its unique characteristics.
- **Reading literature** In *I Know Why the Caged Bird Sings,* Maya Angelou described a special place from her childhood. In "A Christmas Memory" and "The Night the Bed Fell," Truman Capote and James Thurber described special people from their childhoods. After reading these descriptions, or others like them, recall special people and places from your own childhood and freewrite about several of them.

2. Select a writing topic. Look over the ideas you have generated and take some time to freewrite about the ones you find most interesting. Think about which ones you can observe, remember, or imagine clearly and that would be most likely to interest others. For other possible ideas, look at the suggestions in the "Apply Your Skills" section on page 71 or consider the ideas you experimented with in a Sketchbook on page 56. Then choose one idea to write about.

Writer's Choice Your description can stand on its own, or it can be part of a longer piece of writing, such as a news report or a personal narrative.

3. List your goals. What can you accomplish with your description? Can you show why something is important to you or why it affects you in a certain way? Can you make a character in a story more vivid or the setting more memorable? Can you record the details of your subject in order to make an explanation of it clearer? You may wish to freewrite about your goals.

What do I want to accomplish with my description?

Observation and Description **61**

 Individualizing Instruction

Learning Styles Auditory learners might enjoy the "Tuning In" activity. You might consider gathering some objects for the "Exploring Science" activity that kinesthetic learners can handle and describe.

Cultural Differences Students who are from another country might like to describe a place in that country or a person or object from the country.

Teaching Tip: Goals

Students sometimes have difficulty understanding that they should have specific goals for their writing. To illustrate the process of identifying a goal, remind students of the place you described for them. (page 60, Modeling) Discuss goals you might have for a description of the place, such as encouraging others to visit the place or explaining why you would like to live there. Encourage students to suggest other goals a writer might have for describing a particular place. Briefly discuss how particular goals affect a piece of writing. For example, if you intend to persuade others to visit a place, you might focus on describing the most attractive characteristics of the place.

Literature Connection

Descriptive Passage to Read You might read aloud the following excerpt from "You Need to Go Upstairs" by Rumer Godden: "Now you are in the house. At first, it is curiously still; and then always out of the stillness you find it. This is the hall and in it are the smells and sounds of all the rooms: furniture cream and hot pipes, carpet and dried roses from the drawing room, tobacco and a little of pickles from the dining room, mint and hot cakes from the kitchen, and down the stairs comes soap from the bathroom." Discuss the kinds of details Godden included that help the reader envision the setting.

To save time later, you might confer briefly with individual students during the prewriting stage. Check to see that each student has selected a topic that is appropriate for a focused description. Ask each student to briefly explain his or her goal(s).

Teaching Tip: Sensory Details

To help students focus on the sensory details in the excerpt by Thomas Wolfe, you may want to read or have a volunteer read it aloud. Then discuss with students the language that Wolfe uses to appeal to the senses. During discussion you might create several spider maps or webs on the board, writing the particular sense in the center of each web and recording words that appeal to that sense around it.

One student, Michael, began freewriting about places that were special to him. That got him thinking about the tree in his backyard, which would soon be cut down. He chose to focus on that tree. But he wanted to write more than just a physical description. Here are some of his notes as he got started.

ONE STUDENT'S PROCESS

That tree has been around so long. I remember the treehouse I built in it, all the years of picking up its leaves. The way it changes with the seasons. It may be just a tree, but it means a lot to me. I can already hear the sound the chainsaws will make tomorrow. I think I'll describe the tree, so I remember what it was like. But I also want to explain why something as simple as a tree can make me feel such strong emotions.

PROBLEM
S O L V I N G

How does my subject look, sound, taste, smell, and feel?

4. Identify your audience. Your selection and arrangement of details will also depend on your audience. How familiar will they be with your subject? What information do your readers need? What part of your description will they find most interesting?

5. Gather information through your senses. Whether you have chosen a subject you can observe directly or you need to recall or imagine the sensory details, a powerful description will generally include the use of several of your senses. If you were describing the ocean, you might recall its sharp, fishy aroma (smell) and the feeling of sand being sucked from beneath your feet as the waves lapped against you (touch). You might picture the sea gulls held motionless by the wind above the water's jagged green surface (sight). What about the clanking of the metal fittings on beached sailboats (sound) or the saltiness of the spray (taste)?

Notice how writer Thomas Wolfe uses the senses of touch, sight, hearing, and smell to describe his boyhood experience of watching a circus train arrive in his town at dawn.

62   Workshop 2

City Interior,
by Charles Sheeler,
1936

M O D E L

I would rush madly through my [paper] route in the cool and thrilling darkness that comes just before break of day, and then I would go back home and get my brother out of bed.
. . . My brother and I would "catch" the first street car of the day bound for the "depot" where the circus was. . . .

Then, having reached the dingy, grimy, and rickety depot section, we would get out, and walk rapidly across the tracks of the station yard, where we could see great flares and steamings from the engines, and hear the crash and bump of shifting freight cars, the swift sporadic thunders of a shifting engine, the tolling of bells, the sounds of great trains on the rails.

And to all these familiar sounds, . . . to all the sharp and thrilling odors of the trains—the smell of cinders, acrid smoke, of musty, rusty freight cars, the clean pine-board of crated produce, and the smells of fresh stored food . . . there would be added now, with an unforgettable magic and familiarity, all the strange sounds and smells of the coming circus.

The gay yellow sumptuous-looking cars in which the star performers lived and slept, still dark and silent, heavily and powerfully still, would be drawn up in long strings upon the tracks. And all around them the sounds of the unloading circus would go on furiously in the darkness.

Thomas Wolfe, _From Death to Morning_

Observation and
Description   **63**

Critical Thinking

Analyzing Encourage students to identify and discuss the mood that Thomas Wolfe creates in the excerpt from _Death to Morning_. Discuss how Wolfe's vivid description of the sights (Page 63, paragraph 1: . . . thrilling darkness . . . bed. Paragraph 3: Then, having . . . great flares), sounds (Page 63, paragraph 3: . . . and hear the crash . . . on the rails. Page 63, paragraph 5: . . . still dark . . . the tracks.), and smells (Page 63, paragraph 4: . . . the smell of cinders . . . coming circus.) build a sense of excitement and anticipation.

Collaborative Opportunity

Suggest that students meet with partners or in small groups to discuss plans for their descriptions. Suggest that each writer share his or her ideas, focusing particularly on sensory details, mood, and physical vantage point. Partners or group members should offer feedback in each area. Emphasize that specific comments or suggestions ("Will you include details about the sounds you might hear?") are the most helpful to a writer. In addition, point out that students can work together to identify strategies that might help them flesh out their ideas. For example, students might decide to brainstorm together to further develop lists of sensory details.

Humanities Connection

Art Note Charles Sheeler (1883–1965) was a member of the Precisionists, a group of painters who painted real scenes using carefully composed geometrical shapes. In _City Interior,_ note the precise, strong lines of the buildings, the train tracks, and the pipes. The geometric boundaries of this detached, self-contained landscape serve to draw the observer into imagined spaces beyond— through the open windows, up the stairway, through the tunnel on the train tracks, across the sky on the steel catwalk. Place yourself in _City Interior._ What sensory details can you see, hear, feel, smell, and taste?

Draft and Discover

Objectives

1. To draft a focused description, using sensory and figurative language
2. To respond to one's own writing and the writing of peers

Preteaching

Skim the Draft and Discover section for skills or strategies that students may need special help with before drafting. The Elaboration Worksheets from the Revision, Proofreading, and Elaboration booklet as well as the mini-lesson references listed below may help you in your selection and instruction.

> **Handbook Mini-Lessons**
> - Types of Organization, pp. 331–335
> - Getting Started, pp. 340–343
> - Peer Response, pp. 378–382
> - Sound Devices, p. 412
> - Literal/Figurative Language, pp. 413–414

Teaching Strategies

Teaching Tip: Finding a Focus

Suggest that students review their prewriting notes and ask themselves the following questions to determine a focus for their descriptions: What part of my subject means the most to me? What aspect of my subject affects me the most? How do the details I have listed indicate the most important part of my subject?

Writing
—TIP—

You may want to record and classify the details you observe in a graphic organizer like the ones shown in Handbook 9, Using Graphic Devices, pp. 357–360.

HANDBOOKS
FOR HELP & PRACTICE

Types of Organization, pp. 331–335

Getting Started, pp. 340–343

Peer Response, pp. 378–382

Sound Devices, p. 412

Literal/Figurative Language, pp. 413–414

Study your subject closely to sharpen your sensory awareness. Freewrite about your subject's unique characteristics, involving all your senses. How does it look, feel, taste, smell, and sound? Be specific.

6. Consider your emotions. You can also use sensory details to convey what your subject means to you or what emotions you associate with it. For instance, if you want to convey the love you have for your grandfather, you might talk about the wrinkles that radiate from his eyes and near the corners of his mouth, adding character to his face and warmth to his smile.

7. Consider the mood you want to create. Mood is the feeling a writer creates about his or her subject. You can use sensory words to create a mood such as tension, excitement, or fear. Notice how Anne McCaffrey changed the mood in her description by first describing the hatchling as *staggering* and *plaintive* and then describing the boy's *caressing* it until it *crooned with triumph.*

8. Experiment with physical vantage point. You can present a close-up view, describe a vast scene, or choose a vantage point that is somewhere in between. How would it look from an ant's perspective or from the top of a tall building? To explore what vantage point works best with your subject, you can try freewriting from several different points of view.

 Writer's Choice You can observe your subject at different times of day or only at one particular time. Also, you can choose to present a close-up perspective or a wide-angle view.

DRAFT AND DISCOVER

1. Choose a focus. Your prewriting notes should give you a rich array of details to use as you build your description. But how do you put them all together? You need to find a focus for your description. Your main idea should be presented in sharpest focus, with background details supporting the subject and contributing to the overall effect. Find the center—the most important aspect—of your subject and make it the focus of your description.

2. Enrich your description. As you write, look for details that will achieve the effect you want. The following strategies can help you add richness to your description.

64   Workshop 2

Art Connection

Vantage Points You might select one of the Fine Art transparencies for this grade level, such as *Christina's World* by Andrew Wyeth, to spark student discussion of vantage point. As an alternative, you might allow students to choose a work of art whose vantage point particularly interests them. Some suggestions include a painting by Georgia O'Keeffe or a photograph by Ansel Adams or Galen Rowell. Encourage students to identify the vantage point in each work and to discuss why the artist might have chosen to present his or her subject in that way.

Strategies

- **Sensory language** Choose your words carefully to convey sensations vividly and suggest a mood clearly. Notice how Anne McCaffrey used words such as *murmur, croon, moist,* and *glowing* to capture the wonder of the ritual she described.
- **Figurative language** Use imaginative comparisons to help readers see things in new ways. Similes such as "his hands were like cracked, old leather" and metaphors such as "her eyes were beacons of hope" convey vivid pictures. Another type of metaphor, personification, gives human qualities to non-human objects. "The tree shivered in the wind," is one example.

3. Organize your draft. Some writers organize their details before they even begin their first draft. Other writers draft their thoughts as they occur. Then they order and rearrange their ideas in a later draft. Use whichever method works best for you. You must, however, organize your description in order to create a clear, well-ordered impression of your subject. Here are three common methods of organization.

- **Spatial order** Arrange details from bottom to top, left to right, inside to outside, back to front, near to far, and so on. This method works well when your purpose is to present an objective description, as you would in a report.
- **Order of impression** Arrange details according to what first catches your attention. Then describe details that you notice later. This type of organization can give a "you are there" quality to your description. Anne McCaffrey organized her description this way. What details struck you first in the costumes pictured above?
- **Order of importance** Present the most significant detail first. Other less important details follow. Or begin with less important details and work up to the most significant detail.

4. Take a break. When you finish the first draft, put it aside for awhile. Then take a fresh look at it, trying to imagine that you are experiencing for the first time the person or thing described. You may also want to ask a peer to respond to your draft.

PROBLEM SOLVING

What words and phrases can I use to make my description come alive?

Sardinians wear lavish native costumes to welcome spring.

Observation and Description   **65**

Individualizing Instruction

Basic Students These students may need some guidance in developing figurative language for their descriptions. You might confer briefly with them as they draft, modeling the thinking process by asking such questions as, "What is this (person, place, object) like? What other things are like that in some way?"

Critical Thinking

Analyzing After you have discussed the various methods of organization, refer students again to the excerpt by Thomas Wolfe on page 63. Encourage students to identify Wolfe's method of organization (order of impression) and to comment on its effects. Point out how Wolfe's arrangement of details contributes to the mood of excitement and anticipation.

Individualizing Instruction

LD Students These students may have some difficulty in determining a method of organization for their descriptions. You might confer briefly with them, reviewing their prewriting notes and discussing options. Discuss their writing goals, helping them understand the connection between organization and purpose. If possible, you might work with them to order their details in a short list that they might follow as they draft. As an alternative, you might suggest that they confer with writing partners, who can assist them in determining an appropriate arrangement of details.

Managing the Paper Load

To help you detect major problems before the revision stage, consider offering students the option of scheduling a time to confer briefly with you during drafting. At that time you might skim their descriptions, offering feedback on focus, sensory details, and organizational method.

Peer Response

After students have reviewed their drafts and are ready for peer response, you might suggest that they choose questions from this page for their peer readers. Make sure students understand that they can add other questions as well. You might also suggest that students read their descriptions aloud so that their peer readers can focus on the descriptive details. Students who wish might use the Peer Response Guides for this assignment.

Revise Your Writing

Objectives

1. To evaluate the responses to a draft of a focused description
2. To use the responses and a set of standards to revise a draft
3. To proofread for errors in grammar, spelling, and punctuation

Preteaching

Preview the Revise Your Writing section. Use the information from this section and any problems you have noted in students' drafts to identify skills or concepts that you want to review. The Student Revision Model Transparencies and the Revision and Proofreading Worksheets from the Revision, Proofreading, and Elaboration booklet as well as the mini-lesson references listed below may help you in your selection and instruction.

Handbook Mini-Lessons
- Unity in Compositions, pp. 363–364
- Peer Response, pp. 378–382
- Using Specific Words, pp. 383–385
- Misplaced Modifiers, p. 691

REVIEW YOUR WRITING

Questions for Yourself
- Does my description have a clear focus?
- Does my description convey the feelings I want to express about my subject?
- Have I used vivid language or figures of speech to create a clear picture?
- Have I used details that appeal to the senses?
- Can I create a stronger impression by moving or deleting some details?

Questions for Your Peer Reader
- Can you picture in your mind the person, place, or object I am describing?
- Can you tell how I feel about this subject?
- Which details did you especially like? Are there any details you think I should leave out? Why?
- Does the order of the details help give you a clear impression of the subject? Do you think a different order or vantage point would work better?

REVISE YOUR WRITING

HANDBOOKS
FOR HELP & PRACTICE

Unity in Compositions, pp. 363–364
Peer Response, pp. 378–382
Using Specific Words, pp. 383–385
Misplaced Modifiers, pp. 691–692

1. Evaluate your responses. Review your own thoughts and the responses of your peer reader. Also keep in mind that an effective description generally displays these characteristics:

Standards for Evaluation

An effective description . . .

- has a specific focus and a clear sense of purpose.
- uses sensory details and precise words to create a vivid picture, establish a mood, or express emotion.
- uses figurative language when appropriate.
- uses a logical organizational strategy.

Springboard

Before students begin revising, discuss these words of James Baldwin: "I do a lot of rewriting. It's very painful. You know it's finished when you can't do anything more to it, though it's never exactly the way you want it." Ask students how this quote relates to their writing experiences.

2. Problem-solve. Decide what changes you will make, taking care to revise only what will strengthen your composition. Then rework your draft accordingly.

Here is an excerpt from Michael's draft as well as the comments he received from a peer reader. Notice the changes he made after reviewing the comments.

ONE STUDENT'S PROCESS

Towering 50 feet into the air, it looks majestic and strong. But this tree will be felled tomorrow. It has withstood summers of drought and floods, and more than one severe windstorm, only to be cut down tomorrow to clear the yard for an aluminum-sided garage. A team of woodcutters, their chainsaws buzzing, squirting sawdust into the air, will make short work of the tree.

                    sever   sturdy
They will remove the maple's branches from the trunk
          hack at stout   mighty
one by one, and cut its base until finally the tree falls,
will topple, crashing to the ground,
      guided by the ropes of the woodcutters.

This seems a little repetitious.

Great details!

Maybe some stronger words will show your feelings.

3. Proofread your work. Make a clean copy that incorporates all the changes you decided on. Then check your work for errors in grammar, punctuation, and spelling. Correct these mistakes so that readers will not be distracted from your description by them. Don't be surprised if you discover new problems to solve or have new ideas to add during proofing. You can easily return to an earlier stage of revision.

Grammar
── **TIP** ──
Make sure that each verb you use agrees in number with its subject.

Observation and Description **67**

Stumbling Block

Some students may have difficulty evaluating the responses of peer readers. You may want to discuss the marginal comments in One Student's Process, focusing on how each comment offers specific information to which the writer can respond. Encourage students to look for these kinds of specific comments as they review the responses of their peer readers.

Teaching Tip: Self-Evaluation

Encourage students to use the Standards for Evaluation to evaluate their drafts. Students might jot down on their drafts key words from the standards (*specific focus, clear sense of purpose,* and so on), and then indicate with a plus or minus sign their evaluation of that element of the description.

Guidelines for Evaluation

The following guidelines may be used for a close evaluation of a focused description. See the Guidelines for Evaluating Writing in the Teacher's Resource File for additional help with holistic or analytic scoring.

Ideas and Content
- demonstrates a clear purpose
- describes a person, place, or object
- uses sensory details and precise words to create an impression, mood, or feeling
- includes figurative language, as appropriate

Structure and Form
- focuses on one subject
- uses an appropriate method of organization: spatial order, order of impression, or order of importance
- groups related ideas into paragraphs

Grammar, Usage, and Mechanics
- uses standard grammar and usage
- uses capitalization and punctuation correctly
- uses correct spelling

Managing the Paper Load

You may want to use the Writing Evaluation Guidelines checklist for this assignment to evaluate students' descriptions. If students themselves have completed the checklist, you might compare and briefly discuss the two evaluations.

Publish and Present

Objective

To publish and present a focused description

Teaching Strategies

Cooperative Learning

You might suggest that students work in small groups with each group publishing a booklet of descriptions. Each group member should be responsible for some aspect of the booklet, such as the cover, the table of contents, page layout, or art. Groups might display their booklets in the classroom or school library.

HANDBOOKS
FOR HELP & PRACTICE

Publishing Your Work,
pp. 402–403

LINKING
GRAMMAR AND WRITING
MISPLACED MODIFIERS

Modifiers such as adjectives, adverbs, and prepositional phrases can be important in a description, but misplaced modifiers can result in confusing, strange, or even humorous statements. As you write, place your modifiers as close as possible to the nouns they modify. Read your work aloud to help catch such errors.

PROBLEM: The man spoke *loudly* with the red *hat*. (Was he having a conversation with the hat? Was the hat helping him speak loudly?)

CORRECTED: The man *with the red hat* spoke loudly.

See Grammar Handbook 37, pages 691–692 for additional help with this problem.

PUBLISH AND PRESENT

- **Booklets**   As a class project, publish a travel guide about places both real and imaginary, using your classmembers' descriptions. Illustrate the written descriptions with photographs or drawings.
- **Portrait gallery**   Make a bulletin board of photos or sketches of people that have been described. Display each written description and its visual counterpart, but in mixed order. Have students from another writing class match the photos and sketches with their correct descriptions. (You could do the same thing using postcards or photos of the places described.)
- **Newspapers and magazines**   Submit your writing to your school or local newspaper, or send it to a magazine that accepts student writing.
- **Writing exchange groups**   Your class could circulate writing within an exchange group or between your group and one at another school.
- **Oral reading**   If you have written a description of a familiar item or well-known place from an unusual vantage point, read your description aloud without specifically naming what you are describing. Have your audience guess what it is.

ONE STUDENT'S PROCESS

The Silver Maple

Michael Clayfeld

It is sometime between late afternoon and early evening in August. The bright orange ball of the sun, though low in the sky, has not yet set. The air is thick and heavy and still. I can taste its wetness. Although evening is approaching, it promises little relief from the humid heat of midday. My skin feels clammy all over, and my damp hair clings to the skin at the nape of my neck.

Outside my door, I sit sprawled on the worn cement stoop that still holds the heat of noon. Through the screen door, my mother signals me to come in for dinner, but I am not hungry. From the stoop, I contemplate the forty-year-old silver maple tree in my backyard. Towering 50 feet into the air, it looks majestic and strong. It has withstood summers of drought and floods, and more than one severe windstorm. But this tree will be felled tomorrow to clear the yard for an aluminum-sided garage. A team of woodcutters, their chainsaws buzzing, squirting sawdust into the air, will make short work of the tree. They will sever the maple's sturdy branches from the trunk one by one and hack at its stout base. Finally, the mighty tree will topple, crashing to the ground, guided by the ropes of the woodcutters. I have seen trees cut down before, even watched with interest at their destruction, but this time I will not watch.

I shuffle over to the tree and circle its weather-beaten trunk. I guess it must be about three feet in diameter. Then I run my fingers over the coarse bark. It feels dry and cracked and jagged. In some places I can easily peel back the bark and, with the tip of my finger, flick off its skin as I often did on lazy summer afternoons.

About five feet up the trunk, I notice that the tree forks off into four stout limbs, making it look like a

Uses sensory details to establish a mood

Vivid verbs convey emotion.

Observation and Description **69**

Description in Nature Writing To provide other examples of description, you might read or suggest that students read excerpts from the nature writings of Annie Dillard *(Pilgrim at Tinker Creek, Teaching a Stone to Talk)* or Loren Eiseley *(The Invisible Pyramid)*. Ask students to identify techniques the authors use to describe their subjects.

Using the Model

Consider asking a volunteer to read aloud Michael's final description. Remind students that Michael wanted to explain why an ordinary tree could arouse such strong feelings. Ask students if they think Michael met his goal and have them offer reasons for their answers. Focus further discussion on the sensory details Michael included and the mood his description evoked.

Reteaching

Assess the needs of students who were not successful in developing an effective description and identify two or three areas in which additional practice is needed. Assign the appropriate Handbook Mini-Lessons, along with the support materials listed for each lesson. Concepts commonly requiring reteaching are

Literal and Figurative Language: Handbook 18
Using Specific Words: Handbook 14

The following suggestions may also be helpful.

1. Sensory Details Remind students that a successful description embodies details that appeal to the senses. Then suggest several places such as an old house, a forest, and a busy city street. Tell students to picture one of the places in their minds and then quickly list details about the place that appeal to each of the senses. Then, as a group, use a chart similar to that on Thinking Skills Worksheet: Observing to map the details, adding more as students think of them.

2. Methods of Organization Briefly review spatial order, order of impression, and order of importance. Refer students to Handbook 10, pp. 364–368 for transitional devices that can be used with each of these organizational patterns. Then have students use each method to describe the street on which they live.

Extension and Enrichment

• Suggest that students find examples of description in their favorite books or stories. Invite students to read the passages to the class or to include them as professional examples in a classroom display.

• Suggest that students choose a historical event, imagine that they were present at the time, and write a firsthand account of the event.

• Students might also enjoy writing a character sketch of a famous person.

Specific details support close observation.

Uses figurative language

Details arranged by order of importance

Conclusion expresses the writer's feelings about his subject.

four-fingered hand about to clutch an object. It is there that I can see knots of wood scarring the surface of the bark where branches had been trimmed away years ago. Like a spider's web, spokes radiate toward the center of each knot. Just above these knots, tiny mushrooms no larger than beads of water sprout on the bark.

From these four main limbs, a myriad of smaller branches stretch heavenward. What seems like millions of leaves, hunter green on top and silver on their underside, spill into the deepening blue sky. They form a gigantic umbrella that has often sheltered my skin from the blistering summer sun.

I reach up for one of these leaves and quickly snap it from the tree, causing the rest of the leaves on that branch to rustle. As I hold the leaf in my hand, I know this autumn it will not change color. This thought stirs memories of previous autumns, and I am in my yard again, grumbling as I rake endless piles of crisp golden leaves into mounds to be bagged and dragged to the curb. Then, too, I am a child again, diving into huge piles of crunchy leaves and scattering them to the wind. I skid across the entire yard on the slippery floor of these leaves.

I remember, too, the decayed leaves of early spring, the leaves that had not been picked up in autumn. They had fallen into the white stones surrounding the bushes that line our fence. When I finally collected these leaves in early spring, their sogginess repulsed me. They discolored my fingers, turning them a rusty brown, and they left a thin coat of dirty brown color upon the white stones.

Most of all, I remember the rickety treehouse I once built with scraps of lumber. Perched between the branches of my castle like a king on his throne, I would sit up there for hours, doing nothing in particular.

Nightfall now eases upon me and calls me back to the reality of the present. I still hold in my clenched hand the leaf I had picked. I amble into the house and walk upstairs to my room. Smoothing the leaf, I place it between the pages of my history book. I will miss that tree.

70   Workshop 2

Literature Connection

Poems to Read   Remind students that poets frequently use figurative and sensory language in their poems. Suggest that students read several poems, noting how the poets describe people, places, and things. Some poems students might consider are ''Macavity: The Mystery Cat'' by T. S. Eliot, ''Rhinoceros'' by Adrien Stoutenberg, and ''The Fish'' by Elizabeth Bishop.

LEARNING FROM YOUR WRITING PROCESS

W R I T E R   T O   W R I T E R

If a writer stops observing, he is finished. But he does not have to observe consciously nor think how it will be useful.

Ernest Hemingway

1. Reflect on your writing. Ask yourself the following questions and record any useful thoughts or ideas in your own writing log.

- Was I able to observe, recall, or imagine vivid sensory details? How can I improve my abilities in these areas?
- Did the order in which I presented details help draw a clearer picture of my subject?
- Was I able to express my ideas in both exact language and imaginative figures of speech?
- Did I enjoy sharing my impressions of a person, place, or thing with other people? Why or why not?
- How is my description similar to the one written by Anne McCaffrey and the description in One Student's Process? How is it different? What parts of mine do I prefer?

2. Apply your skills. Try one or more writing activities in the following areas:

- **Cross curricular** Sketch or photograph leaves or wildflowers from your community and write a brief description of each specimen. Publish your work as a booklet for your school library.
- **Literature** Read the science-fiction stories "The Feeling of Power" by Isaac Asimov, "All Cats Are Gray" by Andre Norton, and "There Will Come Soft Rains" by Ray Bradbury. Notice how the authors use sensory details to make the settings seem real. Write your own short science-fiction story set in an imaginary place. Use vivid details of setting.
- **General** Look through a magazine to find a product or fashion you could describe vividly. Use sensory words to describe the product vividly to likely customers.

▶ FOR YOUR **PORTFOLIO**

Observation and Description **71**

Learning from Your Writing Process

Objective

To analyze and reflect upon what has been learned about the writing process and the writing of a focused description.

Teaching Strategies

Reflecting on the Process

Suggest that in addition to answering the questions on page 71, students might jot down any strategies or techniques that they found especially useful as well as any that did not prove successful. For example, some students may have discovered that brainstorming sensory details with a partner worked particularly well while others may have found the construction of a chart of details to be helpful.

Writing Portfolio

Encourage students to keep their responses in their writing portfolios. Suggest that students review their self-evaluations from the first Guided Assignment. Ask them to compare the process of writing a description with that of developing a piece of writing from a journal entry. Did they use any of the same strategies? Did they experiment with any new techniques?

Summary and Closure

Before proceeding to the next lesson, be sure that students have internalized the following key concepts:

1. Description can be used in other kinds of writing.

2. Sensory details and figurative language are important elements in a focused description.

3. An effective description is organized logically and creates a vivid impression, mood, or feeling.

Have students summarize what they have learned about writing a focused description; ask them why knowing how to write a focused description might be useful in other school subjects.

Starting from Literature

Objective

To respond to professional models of field notes as a springboard to writing

Teaching Strategies

Motivate

Ask students to imagine what it might have been like to be present when astronaut Neil Armstrong walked on the moon or when Edmund Hillary and Tenzing Norgay reached the summit of Mount Everest. Encourage students to suggest other major events and to comment on the kinds of things they might have observed at such events.

Tap Prior Knowledge

Ask students what they know about the scientific method, or the way scientists work. Elicit that scientists observe carefully, describe their observations, draw conclusions, and sometimes determine the need for further observation or experimentation. Ask students how they think making notes during observation, as scientists do, compares with writing a description, as students did in the last assignment.

Set a Purpose

Before students read the excerpts, discuss the side-column notes. Make sure students understand that they are about to read the first-hand accounts of two scientists who were actually present when the world's first atomic bomb was detonated. Ask students what they think the scientists might have seen, heard, and felt. Then have students read the excerpts, and tell them to keep in mind the purpose given at the end of the side column.

Related
ASSIGNMENT

Field Notes

from
THE MAKING OF THE ATOMIC BOMB
RICHARD RHODES

The date was July 16, 1945; the place, near Alamogordo, New Mexico. The first atomic bomb had just been detonated, and the world would never be the same. Two scientists who helped create the bomb took field notes, recording their observations of and reactions to that historic event.

Can you imagine how they felt as they witnessed that epic explosion? As you read these excerpts from their field notes, think about how differently each scientist responded to it.

We were lying there, very tense in the early dawn, and there were just a few streaks of gold in the east; you could see your neighbor very dimly. Those ten seconds were the longest ten seconds I ever experienced. Suddenly there was an enormous flash of light, the brightest light I have ever seen or that I think anyone has ever seen. It blasted; it pounced; it bored its way right through you. It was a vision that was seen with more than the

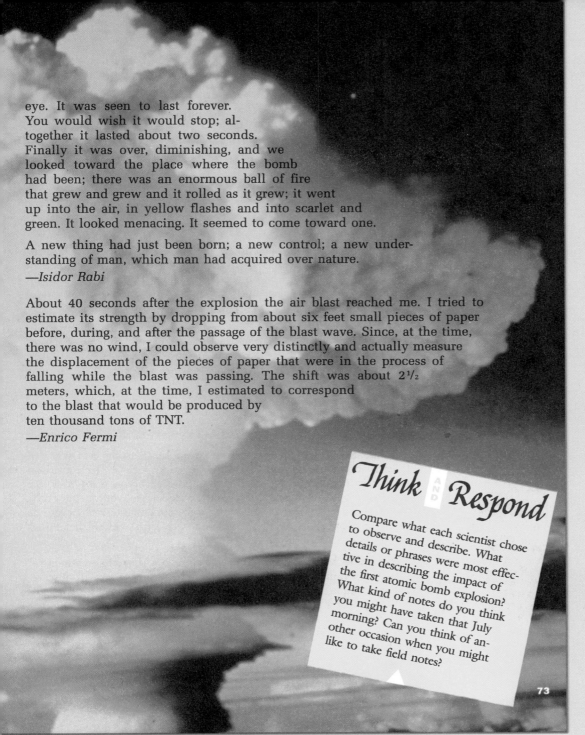

eye. It was seen to last forever.
You would wish it would stop; altogether it lasted about two seconds.
Finally it was over, diminishing, and we
looked toward the place where the bomb
had been; there was an enormous ball of fire
that grew and grew and it rolled as it grew; it went
up into the air, in yellow flashes and into scarlet and
green. It looked menacing. It seemed to come toward one.

A new thing had just been born; a new control; a new understanding of man, which man had acquired over nature.

—*Isidor Rabi*

About 40 seconds after the explosion the air blast reached me. I tried to
estimate its strength by dropping from about six feet small pieces of paper
before, during, and after the passage of the blast wave. Since, at the time,
there was no wind, I could observe very distinctly and actually measure
the displacement of the pieces of paper that were in the process of
falling while the blast was passing. The shift was about $2\frac{1}{2}$
meters, which, at the time, I estimated to correspond
to the blast that would be produced by
ten thousand tons of TNT.

—*Enrico Fermi*

Think AND Respond

Compare what each scientist chose to observe and describe. What details or phrases were most effective in describing the impact of the first atomic bomb explosion? What kind of notes do you think you might have taken that July morning? Can you think of another occasion when you might like to take field notes?

73

Literature Connection

Author Note   Enrico Fermi (1901–1954), the 1938 Nobel Prize winner in physics, was an Italian-born American physicist who worked on nuclear processes and became involved in the atomic bomb project at Los Alamos, New Mexico.

Isidor Rabi (1898–1988), another Nobel Prize winner in physics, was born in what is now Poland. Rabi also became involved with the atomic bomb,

consulting with its creators. Both Fermi and Rabi later advocated nuclear arms limitation.

Think and Respond

Elicit Personal Responses

Discuss the excerpts, asking volunteers to point out passages that they found particularly descriptive or moving. Ask students to comment on possible reasons for the two scientists' diverse responses to this monumental event.

Explore the Authors' Techniques

To help students use the excerpt as a model for their writing, examine some of the techniques the authors used in making their field notes. Both scientists made careful observations of the event. Rabi, however, focused on visual details as he described the event. (Page 72, paragraph 1: . . . just a few streaks of gold . . . very dimly. Page 73, paragraph 1: Finally it was . . . scarlet and green.) In addition, he used vivid, precise verbs to describe the light's effect. (Page 72, paragraph 1: It blasted . . . you.) Point out too that Rabi included some subjective statements, or observations, about how the experience affected him personally. (Page 72, paragraph 1: Those ten seconds . . . experienced. . . . the brightest light . . . seen. It was . . . eye. It was seen . . . forever. You would wish . . . stop;)

Fermi, on the other hand, focused on the feel, or strength, of the blast and reported objectively the results of a simple experiment that he conducted immediately after the bomb exploded. (Page 73, paragraph 3: I tried . . . wave. The shift . . . TNT.)

Link Literature to Writing

Like many scientists who learn more about subjects through observation, Fermi and Rabi observed and made notes about an event that they witnessed. Point out to students that they witness dozens of events each day (students buying lunch in the school cafeteria, sporting activities in a neighborhood park, and so on). Ask students to brainstorm quickly a list of such events, and write their responses on the board. Point out that, like Fermi and Rabi, students can learn more about an event or situation by observing it carefully and by accurately recording their observations.

Guiding Your Writers

Objectives

1. To identify an event and develop a plan for making observations
2. To take field notes of an event in a natural or controlled setting
3. To interpret, organize, and share field notes

Preteaching

Preview the remainder of the assignment. If there are skills or concepts students may need help with, present them at this time. The mini-lesson references below may help you in your selection and instruction. The cross-references in the pupil text will give students access to the same lessons for independent study.

Handbook Mini-Lessons

- Types of Organization, pp. 331–334
- Types of Elaboration, pp. 351–354
- Using Specific Words, pp. 383–385
- Taking Notes, pp. 459–460

Teaching Strategies

 Individualizing Instruction

Learning Styles Visual learners may want to make sketches or take pictures during their observations. Some learning disabled students and auditory learners will find a tape-recorder particularly useful. Students who benefit from structure and direction may want to approach their "in the field" experience with a chart or some other device for recording observations. Other students may prefer to jot down notes freely as they observe an event.

Writing TIP

You may want to use a small tape recorder instead of pencil and paper to record your observations.

HANDBOOKS
FOR HELP & PRACTICE

Types of Organization, pp. 331–335

Types of Elaboration, pp. 351–354

Using Specific Words, pp. 383–385

Taking Notes, pp. 459–460

INVITATION TO Write

The field notes of the two scientists reveal careful observation of a dramatic event. Now make your own field notes, carefully describing your observations and reactions.

Originally, the term "field notes" designated the notes natural scientists made while observing land formations, plants, and animals in their natural settings or "in the field." Now, however, the term can refer to any notes taken during a controlled period of observation.

Taking field notes requires the same careful focusing, observation, and recording necessary for any descriptive writing. Earth-shattering events, like the one described in the excerpt, and aspects of nature are not the only subjects worth observing. Field notes can be taken anywhere—in your backyard, on a bus, in a grocery store, at your school, at a sports event.

TAKING FIELD NOTES

1. Identify a subject to observe. Choose anything that you can learn about through observation. Also, make sure you have a reason for conducting the observation. Suppose that you want to know more about the eating habits of the people in your community. You could take field notes at the local supermarket, observing as young people, the elderly, and those with large and small families buy their groceries.

2. Decide when and how you will carry out your observations. Also, set limits on how long and how many times you will observe. For example, you could observe a dog's reactions to different individuals to try to determine what behaviors have a positive or negative influence on animals. You might choose a brief time period and a specific location where you can find the behaviors you want to observe.

74   Workshop 2

Springboard

As a warm-up exercise, spend a few minutes of class time in concentrated observation. You might display a group of similar objects, such as three or four books or several potatoes or a collection of leaves. Suggest that each student focus on one object, without revealing his or her choice. As they observe, students should jot down descriptive details that would make it possible for another student to identify the particular object from the description alone. Suggest that volunteers read their details aloud and have other students identify the objects.

3. Use all your senses. If you are observing a controlled event such as a scientific experiment, you will probably want to focus on measurable characteristics such as temperature, size, density, and weight. In more natural settings, you can observe colors, sounds, smells, and movement. You may also want to jot down any associations that help you describe the experience. For example, in taking notes on a chemistry experiment, you might write, "The gas smells like rotten eggs." In observing people, you might want to compare their behavior in one situation to their behavior in another setting. Or you might compare the behavior of two species in similar situations.

 Writer's Choice You can record your notes in an objective manner, or you can choose a more personal, subjective approach.

REWORKING YOUR NOTES

1. Select the notes that best describe the subject you have observed. You do not need to use all of your rough notes in the final draft of your field notes. In selecting from your notes, you may find it helpful to add brief explanations of why you think a detail or an observation is important or interesting.

2. Organize your notes in an order that suits your material. Most field notes are organized in chronological order—that is, in the order in which events happened. However, other types of organization you might consider are cause-effect and organization by degree.

3. Draw a conclusion. If appropriate, tell what you have learned or inferred from your observation.

PUBLISHING AND PRESENTING

- **Share your field notes with classmates.** If several of you took notes on the same event, compare your observations. What did some of you notice that others did not?
- **Develop your field notes into a complete piece of writing.** For example, notes for a lab report could become the basis for a full-scale science project or for a science fiction story.

Writing
—TIP—
Use whatever abbreviations or personal shorthand you need to keep pace with your observations.

Field Notes **75**

Collaborative Opportunity

To help students recognize whether they have included an adequate interpretation of their field notes, suggest that students exchange drafts with partners and underline the sentences that explain the significance of the field notes.

Guidelines for Evaluation
Good field notes:
- include accurate observations of a subject or event
- reflect the use of several senses
- include an interpretation of the details, if appropriate
- are organized logically
- display standard grammar and usage
- use correct spelling, capitalization, and punctuation

Reteaching

Assess the needs of students who were not successful in developing effective field notes and identify two or three areas in which additional practice is needed. Assign the appropriate Handbook Mini-Lessons, along with the support materials listed for each lesson. Concepts commonly requiring reteaching are

Types of Organization: Handbook 4
Using Specific Words: Handbook 14

The following suggestions and resources may also be useful.

1. Variety of Sensory Details Remind students that sensory details are necessary for strong field notes. Suggest students use Thinking Skills Worksheet: Observing to practice recording appropriate details. Then have students work with partners to observe a school event. Have students who omitted details that appeal to certain senses (hearing and smell, for example) from their field notes note only those details. Partners should record details that appeal to the other senses.

2. Logical Order For those students who had difficulty maintaining chronological order assign Thinking Skills Worksheet: Chronological Order. Have students list in order all the steps in a simple activity such as putting air in the tires of a bicycle or making a grilled cheese sandwich.

Starting from Literature

Objective

To respond to professional examples of haiku as a springboard to writing

Teaching Strategies

Motivate

Ask students to cite examples of great art, and discuss the works they mention. Suggest that it is possible to create a work of art by writing three short lines. Explain that haiku poetry depends on just such brevity, not on extended description or explanation, to convey a message.

Tap Prior Knowledge

Ask students to think about the nature of a telegram. How are telegram messages constructed? What are some advantages of using a telegram to communicate?

Emphasize that just a few words can communicate a powerful message. But haiku poetry, unlike a telegram, conveys contact with nature and tries to evoke the insight that such contact can bring.

Set a Purpose

To enhance discussion of the side-column notes, have students think about the contact they had with ordinary objects during their morning routines (pillow, toothbrush, chair, spoon, shoe, and so on). Have them jot down a personal list of such items. Point out that their experience with any of these items can provide fertile ground for a haiku poem.

Call attention to the purpose-setting statement at the end of the side column, and have students read the poems.

(Author pronunciation: José Juan Tablada —hō sä' wän' täb lä' də; Ryota—rē ō' tə; Issa—ē' sə; Matsuo Bashō—mat sōō' ō bä shō')

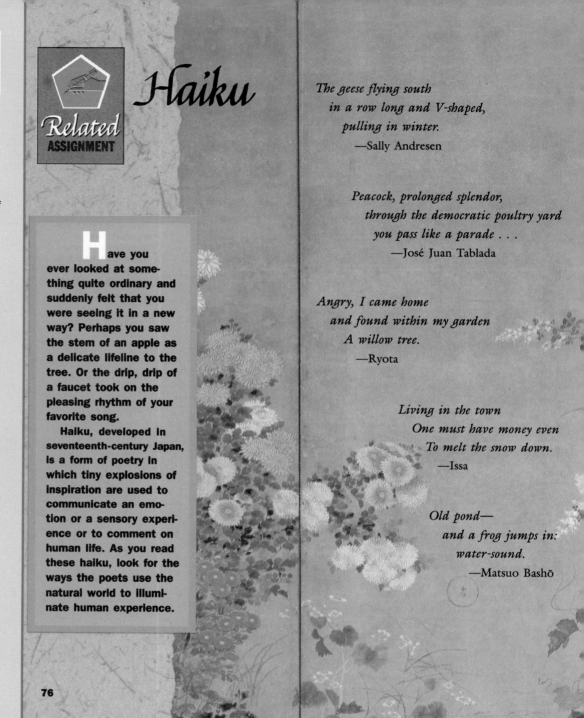

Related ASSIGNMENT

Haiku

Have you ever looked at something quite ordinary and suddenly felt that you were seeing it in a new way? Perhaps you saw the stem of an apple as a delicate lifeline to the tree. Or the drip, drip of a faucet took on the pleasing rhythm of your favorite song.

Haiku, developed in seventeenth-century Japan, is a form of poetry in which tiny explosions of inspiration are used to communicate an emotion or a sensory experience or to comment on human life. As you read these haiku, look for the ways the poets use the natural world to illuminate human experience.

The geese flying south
in a row long and V-shaped,
pulling in winter.
—Sally Andresen

Peacock, prolonged splendor,
through the democratic poultry yard
you pass like a parade . . .
—José Juan Tablada

Angry, I came home
and found within my garden
A willow tree.
—Ryota

Living in the town
One must have money even
To melt the snow down.
—Issa

Old pond—
and a frog jumps in:
water-sound.
—Matsuo Bashō

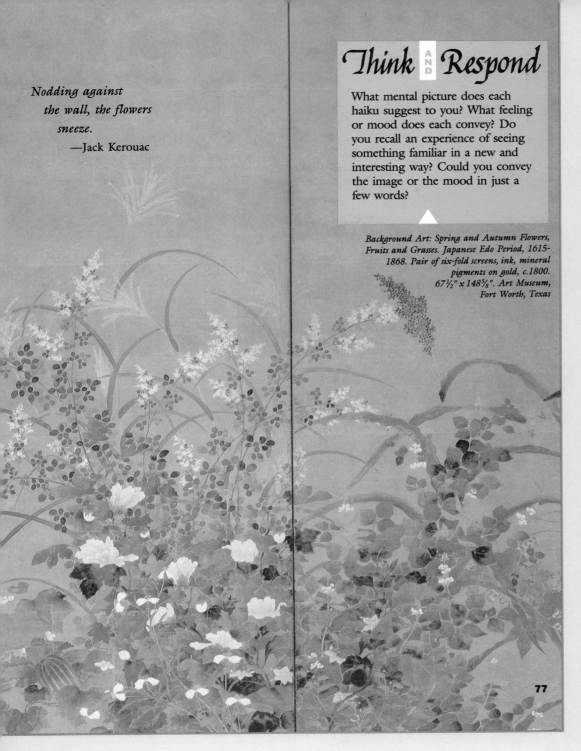

Nodding against
the wall, the flowers
sneeze.

—Jack Kerouac

Think AND Respond

What mental picture does each haiku suggest to you? What feeling or mood does each convey? Do you recall an experience of seeing something familiar in a new and interesting way? Could you convey the image or the mood in just a few words?

Background Art: Spring and Autumn Flowers, Fruits and Grasses. Japanese Edo Period, 1615-1868. Pair of six-fold screens, ink, mineral pigments on gold, c.1800. 67½" x 148⅝". Art Museum, Fort Worth, Texas

77

Think and Respond

Elicit Personal Responses

Suggest that students freewrite their personal responses to the image in any one of the poems. Then compare and discuss students' responses, using the Think and Respond questions as a guide.

Explore the Authors' Techniques

To prepare students to write their own haiku, review some of the poets' techniques. For example, call attention to Bashō's use of stark description and concrete words (''old pond,'' ''jumps in'') and Ryota's connection between an emotion and an object in nature (''Angry,'' ''a willow tree''). Point out how each poet has depicted one main image and focused on ordinary objects found in nature. Suggest that students may wish to use some of these techniques in their own work.

Link Literature to Writing

Point out that the haiku that students read were effective because the poets were able to convey the meaning and emotion that can be found in ordinary events and objects. Suggest that as they look for topics, students might think about all the events in a day that they may take for granted—things they look at without really seeing or things they do ''without thinking.'' Explain that the following assignment will help students view everyday experiences as material for poetic expression.

Literature Connection

Author Note Matsuo Bashō (1644–1694), the most renowned Japanese haiku poet, was once a samurai. Bashō (his pen name) elevated what had been merely a popular, ''gossipy'' pastime to a literary recording of eternal beauty and universal truth. He did so by infusing his poetry with Zen philosophy.

Issa (1763–1827), another Japanese haiku poet, lived a tragic life but captured the spiritual loneliness of the common people with his simple yet lyrical language.

Guiding Your Writers

Objectives

1. To identify the structure and elements of a haiku
2. To choose a subject for a haiku
3. To write, review, and share an original haiku

Preteaching

Preview the rest of the assignment. If there are skills or concepts students may need help with, present them at this time. The mini-lesson references below may help you in your selection and instruction. The cross-references in the pupil text will give students access to the same lessons for independent study.

> **Handbook Mini-Lessons**
> - Personal Techniques, pp. 317–320
> - Adding Detail, pp. 386–388
> - Sound Devices, p. 412
> - Literal/Figurative Language, pp. 413–414

Teaching Strategies

Stumbling Block

Some students may try to fill their poems with adjectives. Remind them of the directness of haiku by pointing to Bashō's simple description of the pond (''old'') or the absence of adjectives in Ryota's description of the willow tree.

Teaching Tip: Imagery

Briefly review some of the devices that help writers create strong images—sensory words, similes, metaphors, personification. Ask for examples of each, and discuss those that students offer. You might write them on the board for student reference during drafting. Encourage students to experiment with these devices to help them create fresh, vivid images.

INVITATION TO Write

> The haiku you just read use images from nature to suggest a truth about the human world. Now write a haiku of your own that creates a strong image and communicates a particular mood or theme.

The traditional haiku form has three lines with a pattern of five syllables in the first line, seven in the second, and five in the third. Modern poets have varied the syllable count but still use a single, strong image to capture a moment or mood. Like all good descriptive writing, creating haiku relies on careful observation of the world around you.

FINDING A SUBJECT

HANDBOOKS
FOR HELP & PRACTICE

Personal Techniques, pp. 317–320

Adding Detail, pp. 386–388

Sound Devices, p. 412

Literal/Figurative Language, pp. 413–414

1. Be open to inspiration. Haiku may start from an image, a mood, or an idea. Notice connections between the natural world and your emotions. Think about your favorite time of year. How does snow or summer sun make you feel? Consider the sky at night or leaves dripping onto a rainy city street. If you find that your surroundings do not spark your imagination, try starting with a particular mood or idea, such as peace or tranquility. Describe the images that come to your mind.

2. Select the idea that creates the strongest image in your mind. Jot down the words that come to you as you visualize the scene or imagine the mood you want to describe. Use your five senses to gather the details that will make your haiku come alive for readers. Notice that each haiku you read concentrated on only one image or sound or feeling at a time. An exercise that can help you to sharpen your senses is to stand on the sidewalk at a busy intersection with your eyes closed. Can you concentrate on only one sound? Open your eyes and take notes on your sensations.

78 Workshop 2

Social Studies Connection

Haiku has significant connections with philosophical themes in Japanese culture. Zen Buddhism, for example, affirms that through meditation one can attain a flash of insight about the nature of reality—a feeling of ''ah''ness, or the ''haiku moment.'' Ask students to read an encyclopedia article about Zen and to look for connections to haiku.

3. Elaborate on the image or idea that you have selected. If possible, observe your image and then freewrite about your feelings. How does hearing, seeing, tasting, or smelling your subject, for example, make you feel? Jot down the words and phrases that come to your mind.

4. Seek simplicity. After freewriting, consider ways to simplify until you reach a single timeless idea or image. Because a haiku is very brief, a single focus is essential.

WRITING HAIKU

1. Put your thoughts into haiku form.
Begin by using the key words suggested by your image or mood. Also, you might write a single sentence, as if you were describing your image or mood in a letter to one of your friends. Then proceed to shape your sentence into haiku form.

 Writer's Choice Your haiku may follow the traditional 5–7–5 syllable pattern, or you may use a more flexible form that does not follow the traditional strict syllable count.

2. Experiment with language. Explore various word choices, forms of figurative language, and other writing techniques to convey your image or mood. Note that there are different ways of suggesting an image, mood, or idea. Spare, evocative language encourages the reader to complete the meaning of Matsuo Bashō's image. José Juan Tablada suggests his meaning by contrasting the shimmer and lordliness of the peacock with the "democratic henyard." Ryota contrasts human anger with home and garden and graceful tree to suggest the effect of nature on human emotion.

3. Play with the sound and rhythm of your lines. Notice how the soft rhythm of the first two lines in Jack Kerouac's haiku is broken by the harsh sound of the word *sneeze,* making the poem funny and lively. You may want to use alliteration, simile, or metaphor to enhance the sound and rhythm of your own haiku, or to introduce the element of surprise.

Haiku   **79**

Consider composing your own haiku and write it on the board for students to analyze. Ask volunteers to respond to the image in your poem and to comment on the mood the poem evokes. Discuss the limits people encounter when trying to evaluate another person's sharing of a meaningful event or idea through poetry.

Guidelines for Evaluation
Good haiku poetry:
- creates a single, strong image
- conveys a mood or emotion
- focuses on nature and ordinary experience
- uses direct, expressive language
- may make use of a three-line 5-7-5 syllable pattern

Reteaching

Assess the needs of students who were not successful in developing an effective haiku and identify two or three areas in which additional practice is needed. Assign the appropriate Handbook Mini-Lessons, along with the support materials listed for each lesson. Concepts commonly requiring reteaching are

Sound Devices: Handbook 18
Literal/Figurative Language: Handbook 18

The following suggestions may also be helpful.

1. Image Some students may have had difficulty coming up with appropriate material for a haiku. Use a word-association exercise to help these students find an image that might serve as a basis for a haiku. Call out a word and have students immediately write the first word that comes into their minds, along with your word. Ask students to review carefully the list of paired words and discuss with them any ideas that emerge as potential haiku material.

2. Mood and Emotion Remind students that a successful haiku evokes a particular mood or emotion. To help students understand this concept, discuss with them the mood or feeling evoked by certain images. Begin by suggesting an image such as a storm cloud. Then ask questions such as, "What does the cloud look like?" "How do you feel or what do you think of as you imagine it?" Encourage group members to offer answers. You might then continue the activity, having other group members offer images and ask questions about moods and feelings.

Extension and Enrichment

• Have students find and read several "non-haiku" poems. Suggest that as students read each poem they consider the following questions: What is the subject of the poem? What images does the poet describe? Does the poem evoke a mood or feeling? Does the poem have a pattern or scheme? How is the poem different from the haiku poems in this assignment? How is it the same? Ask students to share what they find with the class.

REVIEWING YOUR WRITING

1. Read your haiku aloud to yourself or a friend. Another possibility is to record the poem on tape so that you can listen to it more than once, evaluating its rhythm, flow, and word choice.

2. Evaluate the form of the haiku. Is the rhythm of your haiku right for the theme you are trying to convey? If you used the traditional 5–7–5 form, do the lines break in appropriate or sensible places? If you used a more flexible form, do the line breaks contribute to the rhythm and uphold the sense of the poem?

PUBLISHING AND PRESENTING

• **Publish a booklet.** Compile your own and your classmates' haiku. You may wish to make enough copies to distribute to classmates, teachers, and your parents.

• **Illustrate your haiku.** Use traditional Japanese style for your drawings. Japanese illustrations are deceptively simple—often they are line drawings with, perhaps, a wash of color.

• **Make a haiku banner.** Some computer software programs are designed to print large banners.

• **Enter a poetry contest.** Contact your local or state arts council. Find out if there are any poetry contests for which your haiku may be eligible.

• **Present a reading.** Together with several classmates, plan to read your haiku aloud. Practice so your reading style reveals the simplicity and clarity of the poems. Evoke a mood by playing appropriate music and by displaying photographs or posters associated with the poems.

Black Sun,
by Isamu Noguchi

Humanities Connection

Art Note Born of an American mother and a Japanese father, Noguchi, the sculptor of *Black Sun,* studied art in New York and Paris before returning to Japan to explore his Japanese cultural heritage. He used his knowledge of the Japanese tradition of garden design to create gardens and outdoor environments in which his sculptures became part of the complete whole.

Black Sun, made of black Brazilian granite and measuring 108 inches in diameter, resides outside the Seattle Art Museum. Ask: How is the outdoor setting appropriate for this sculpture?

Sentence
COMPOSING

Introductory Modifiers

One way experienced writers add variety to their writing is by occasionally beginning a sentence with a modifier. Placing the modifier as the first word of the sentence calls attention to it, raises the reader's interest in what will follow, and provides an interesting change from the usual sentence structure.

MODEL

Curious, they gathered at the cab window.

Glendon Swarthout, *Bless the Beasts and the Children*

A. Identifying Imitations Some of the sentences below imitate the model—in sentence structure but not in content. Identify the sentences that have the same structure as the model.

1. Jack ran toward the gaudy billboard, slipped, and fell.
2. Tired, we stopped to rest by the edge of the lake.
3. Down the rocky incline the horses stampeded.
4. Confident, she stepped up to the microphone.
5. After the game, the players signed autographs.
6. As the rocket rose, it trailed a plume of smoke and fire.
7. Exhausted, the hikers collapsed near the shore of the lake.
8. Refusing to answer the question, the witness began crying.
9. Sensing the approach of the lioness, the wildebeest fled.
10. Victorious, the players celebrated on the sideline.
11. While we waited, the sun broke through the clouds.
12. Screaming, the unruly child ran through the restaurant.

B. Unscrambling Sentences The sentence parts below are similar to the ones in the model sentence. Unscramble the parts and write a sentence that imitates the model, including punctuation.

1. a. the sergeant
   b. frustrated
   c. stared at the blank wall

2. a. looked back at the accident
   b. the police officer
   c. hesitating

Sentence Composing: Introductory Modifiers

Objectives

1. To identify sentences that contain introductory modifiers
2. To combine pair of sentences by using introductory modifiers
3. To expand sentences by adding introductory modifiers
4. To write original sentences with introductory modifiers

Preteaching

These exercises focus on the use of introductory modifiers to achieve variety in writing. You might review or refer students to Grammar Handbook 34, Using Modifiers: Adjectives, pages 620–625; Grammar Handbook 37, Using Verbals and Appositives: Participles, pages 683–686.

ANSWER KEY

A. Identifying Imitations
2, 4, 7, 10, 12

B. Unscrambling Sentences
1. Frustrated, the sergeant stared at the blank wall.
2. Hesitating, the police officer looked back at the accident.

3. Limping, the quarterback walked toward the sidelines.
4. Stunned, the driver sat frozen behind the wheel.
5. Enchanted, the fan gazed at the singer.
6. Sniffling, the child sat alone.
7. Relieved, the nervous student closed her test booklet.
8. Fearful, the crowd retreated.
9. Trembling, the puppy licked the boy's hand.
10. Chuckling, my aunt closed the door.
11. Enraged, the bull charged the matador.
12. Honking, the geese raced across the sky.

C. Combining Sentences

1. Growling, the dog tugged at the garbage can lid.
2. Furious, Jack stormed out of the meeting.
3. Exhausted, Mr. Billings collapsed on the sofa.
4. Overjoyed, Sandy reached for her trophy.
5. Smiling, the jogger easily ran the course.
6. Gasping, the audience saw the aerialist fall.
7. Roaring, the jet buzzed the airfield.
8. Livid, the coach called a timeout.
9. Silent, the mourners left the cemetery.
10. Stammering, the boy told his story.

---

3. a. limping
   b. walked toward the sidelines
   c. the quarterback

4. a. sat frozen behind the wheel
   b. the driver
   c. stunned

5. a. the fan
   b. enchanted
   c. gazed at the singer

6. a. sat alone
   b. the child
   c. sniffling

7. a. closed her test booklet
   b. relieved
   c. the nervous student

8. a. retreated
   b. fearful
   c. the crowd

9. a. the puppy
   b. trembling
   c. licked the boy's hand

10. a. closed the door
    b. my aunt
    c. chuckling

11. a. enraged
    b. charged the matador
    c. the bull

12. a. raced across the sky
    b. the geese
    c. honking

C. Combining Sentences Combine each pair of sentences to match the model sentence. To do this, find the key modifier in one sentence and place it at the beginning of the other sentence.

1. The dog was growling. The dog tugged at the garbage can lid.

2. Jack stormed out of the meeting. Jack was furious.

3. Mr. Billings was exhausted. Mr. Billings collapsed on the sofa.

4. Sandy looked overjoyed. Sandy reached for her trophy.

5. The jogger easily ran the course. The jogger was smiling.

6. The audience was gasping. The audience saw the aerialist fall.

7. The jet buzzed the airfield. The jet was roaring.

8. The coach was livid. The coach called a timeout.

9. The mourners left the cemetery. The mourners were silent.

10. The boy was stammering. The boy told his story.

D. Expanding Sentences Begin each sentence with a single word followed by a comma to make the sentence match the model. In this exercise, use at least one word that ends in –ed and one that ends in –ing. (**Hint:** Your word must describe whatever comes immediately after the comma.)

1. Simon peered through the dirty window.

2. The dolphin leaped into the air and rang the bell.

3. The hitter swung with all her might.

4. Cranston slept soundly through the night.

5. Albert whirled around the dance floor.

6. The crowd cheered the racers on.

7. The hungry lion returned to the pride.

8. The dragster shot from the staging lights.

9. The tomcat licked its wounds.

10. Mary retired for the night.

E. Imitating Sentences Now that you are familiar with the sentence parts and their arrangement in the model sentence, write three sentences of your own that imitate the structure of the model.

> *Example*   Flattened, the tin can lay on the road.

Application Write a short paragraph that includes one of the sentences you wrote in Exercise E. In the rest of the paragraph, write sentences that blend well with this sentence. Notice how the structure of your sentence adds variety to the paragraph.

> *Example*   Rounding the corner at Greenway Avenue, the garbage truck hit a series of bumps, and the junk inside made a racket that sounded like the rattling of a skeleton. A single tin can, however, was all that fell onto the street. Instantly, a car hit it. <u>Flattened, the tin can lay on the road.</u> A stray dog gingerly looked for oncoming traffic, then darted toward the can, sniffed it, but quickly abandoned it when a car pulled around the corner.

Grammar Refresher The model sentences above are *simple sentences*. They contain just one independent clause. Each one, however, begins with a modifier that describes the subject. To learn more about modifiers, see Handbook 34.

D. Expanding Sentences
Answers will vary.

E. Imitating Sentences
Answers will vary.

Application
Answers will vary.

Sentence Composing   **83**

3

Narrative and Literary Writing

Overview

Narrative writing recounts how real or imagined events unfold through time. It constitutes the main ingredient in all forms of storytelling and is, therefore, closely linked with literary writing. Students will apply the personal, expressive, and sensory writing skills introduced in Workshops 1 and 2 as they shape their own experiences and observations into compelling narratives. The Workshop makes a good bridge from purely personal, expressive writing to more disciplined expository forms because students draw on their experience but must organize it into a tight, narrative structure. Workshop 3 includes the following Guided and Related Assignments:

1. **Guided: Personal Narrative** shows students how to identify potential narratives in their experiences, and develop these into accounts of historical interest.

2. **Related: Oral History** helps students build on the skills from the Guided Assignment as they interview other people, identify potential narratives in their experiences, and develop these into accounts of historical interest.

3. **Related: Storyboard** further builds on narrative skills developed in the Guided Assignment by helping students represent real or imagined events in an annotated sequence of visual panels.

Teaching Preview

Preparation Guide

1. Use the Overview on this page and the Teacher's Choice descriptions on page 85 as a basis for deciding which assignment(s) to teach.

2. Preview the assignments and the teacher's notes and identify concerns that may require preteaching or extra support given your class's abilities. The handbook mini-lessons suggested within the lesson may also provide guidance.

3. Preview the chart below for support materials in the Teacher's Resource File that may be used with this Workshop. Resources are for use with the Guided Assignment unless otherwise noted.

Support Materials

WRITER'S CRAFT RESOURCES

Prewrite and Explore
Thinking Skills Transparencies, pp. 13–14
Thinking Skills Worksheets, p. 8

Draft and Discover
Elaboration, Revision, and Proofreading Worksheets, p. 5

Revise Your Writing
Guidelines for Writing Assessment and Portfolio Use, pp. 10, 25–27
Peer Response Guides, pp. 11–13
Student Revision Model Transparencies, pp. 11–14
Elaboration, Revision, and Proofreading Worksheets, p. 6

Assessment
Tests and Writing Assessment Prompts, p. 3

Extension Activities
Writing Prompts for Fine Art Transparencies, pp. 7, 8, 12, 14, 21, 22
Writing from Literature, pp. 1–2, 5–6, 11–12, 19–20, 23–24, 29–30, 33–36, 39–40, 43–44
Standardized Test Practice

 Educational Technology
(available separately)
Writer's DataBank
Electronic English Handbook
Multimedia Workshop
Your Personal Trainer for the New SAT
In Perspective (videodisc)

● ●

OTHER RESOURCES

Books and Journals
Brown, Cynthia. *Like It Was: A Complete Guide to Writing Oral History*. New York: Teachers & Writers Collaborative, 1988.
Rule, Rebecca and Susan Wheeler. *Creating the Story: Guides for New Writers*. Portsmouth: Heinemann, 1992.

 Films and Videos
Choosing Specific Words. Phoenix/BFA Films & Video, Inc. (18 min.)

Narration and Description. Films Incorp. Educ. (30 min.)

◆ **Computer Software**
Student Writing Center. The Learning Company. PC/MS-DOS, Windows 3.1, 386 or better, 2MB RAM (4MB recommended), hard disk (with 8MB free); VGA or better.
Start-A-Story. I/CT. PC/MS-DOS, 256K.

Linking Literature, Writing, and Grammar

The following options may be used to provide students with an integrated language experience. Begin by assigning and discussing any of the recommended pieces of literature. Use the suggested strategy to provide a link to the Guided Assignment.

LINKING LITERATURE AND WRITING

Option 1

Starting Point: Excerpt from *Act One* by Moss Hart on pages 86–88 of *The Writer's Craft*

Strategy: Use the teaching suggestions on pages 86–88 to lead students into the Guided Assignment.

Option 2

Starting Point: "Mrs. Flowers" from *I Know Why the Caged Bird Sings* by Maya Angelou on pages 571–576 of McDougal, Littell's *Literature and Language,* Grade 9.

Strategy: Ask students to discuss Mrs. Flowers' impact on Marguerite and then to think of similarly impressive people in their own experience. Have students recount a significant interaction with one such person and help them see they may be able to use this interaction as the basis for their personal narrative in the Guided Assignment.

Option 3

Starting Point: "The Raven" by Edgar Allan Poe

Strategy: After students have read Poe's poem, point out that he recounts strange and surprising events. Discuss what gives these events their peculiar quality. Then have students jot down or relate an event in which they were involved that had similar qualities or twists. Conclude the discussion by leading into the Guided Assignment.

LINKING WRITING AND GRAMMAR

Before the drafting or revision stage of this assignment, explain to students that consistent use of verb tenses is crucial in narrative writing. Emphasize that there is nothing inconsistent about shifting tenses as such: A narrative may refer to events in different times, and the writer must shift tense to place each event in its proper time frame. Writers err when they shift tense needlessly. Discuss why the use of different tenses is correct in the first example that follows, but not in the second one.

Correct: I *remember* the time I *went* to Sally's house for New Year's. I *had been looking* forward to the holiday for weeks. At last the big day *dawned*.

Faulty: I remember the time I *went* to Sally's house for New Year's. I *am looking* forward to the holiday for weeks. At last the big day *had dawned!*

Ask students to look through their own papers for examples of faulty tense shifts. Then go over the functions and uses of different verb tenses on pages 603–610 of the Grammar and Usage Handbook. If students continue to use verb tenses inaccurately, assign the exercises on those pages for reteaching. Additional practice can be found in the *Grammar and Usage Practice Book* on pages 81–86.

Workshop Management Guidelines

The chart below indicates the number of days recommended for each phase of the Guided and Related Assignments. Stars indicate portions of the assignment that may be completed outside the classroom if time is limited or if teachers wish the activity to be completed by students independently.

PERSONAL NARRATIVE

Starting from Literature ....1 day
Prewrite ....2 days*
Draft ....3 days*
Revise ....1–2 days*
Publish ....1 day
Learning ....1 day*
Reteaching ....open
Extension/Enrichment......................open
Sentence Composing......................1 day*

ORAL HISTORY

Starting from Literature ....1 day
Interview/Tape to Paper ....1–2 days*
Reviewing..1 day
Publishing ....1 day

STORYBOARD

Starting from Literature/Planning/
    Preparing.....................................1 day*
Reviewing/Publishing ....1 day

Sketchbook

Objective

To use a literary excerpt as a springboard to informal writing

Using the Prompt

The writing activities suggested in the Sketchbook are designed to be informal in order to allow risk-taking and discovery. Students' writing should not be graded.

Share a humorous or memorable family event with the class. Explain why the event made a lasting impression on you.

When introducing the excerpt, explain that James Thurber was an American humorist and cartoonist. After reading and discussing the excerpt, ask students what memorable family event they might use as a writing topic. Suggest that students work in pairs, telling their stories to partners as a form of oral rehearsal before writing. Explain to students that they can use the ideas in the Additional Sketches section as alternatives.

Encourage students to keep their writing in their writing portfolios for possible use in the workshop that follows.

Sketchbook

I suppose that the high-water mark of my youth in Columbus, Ohio, was the night the bed fell on my father. It makes a better recitation (unless, as some friends of mine have said, one has heard it five or six times) than it does a piece of writing, for it is almost necessary to throw furniture around, shake doors, and bark like a dog, to lend the proper atmosphere and verisimilitude to what is admittedly a somewhat incredible tale. Still, it did take place.

Some Nights She Threw Them All

James Thurber
"THE NIGHT THE BED FELL"

Tell a story about a memorable family incident.

Additional Sketches

Tell the story of the time in your life when you were most frightened or most amused.

Write an eyewitness account of a historical event.

84

WRITER'S **3** WORKSHOP

Narrative and Literary Writing

Guided Assignment
PERSONAL NARRATIVE

Related Assignment
ORAL HISTORY

Related Assignment
STORYBOARD

Have you ever laughed at a friend's account of a funny or embarrassing moment? Have you ever been moved by a family member's story about a sad or touching event? We hear people recount their experiences every day, and these stories often remind us of joyous, tragic, silly, or important events in our own lives. Many writers will tell you that their story ideas come from their own experiences—something that has happened to them, something they have observed, or something they have seen others experience. In this workshop you will study ways you can use your experiences to write a personal narrative. Using these skills, you can also create an oral history or a storyboard.

85

Objectives

Guided Assignment:
PERSONAL NARRATIVE
    To recognize examples of personal narrative and to use prewriting activities to plan, draft, revise, proofread, and share a personal narrative

Related Assignment:
ORAL HISTORY
    To conduct an interview and to draft, revise, and share an oral history

Related Assignment:
STORYBOARD
    To identify the format and elements of a storyboard and to plan, create, review, and share a storyboard

Teacher's Choice

Guided Assignment
    Personal Narrative   This Guided Assignment is appropriate for most students because it draws on personal experience and serves as an introduction to other types of narrative writing. The assignment also offers opportunities to relate students' narratives to stories or autobiographies being read in literature.

Related Assignments
    Oral History This assignment takes students into the community to interview people. As a result, the assignment offers cross-curricular ties to Social Studies. Because of the emphasis on speaking and listening, the assignment is ideally suited to auditory learners.
    Storyboard Because storyboards are used most often for programs and advertisements that appear on film, this assignment is especially appropriate for visual learners and for students interested in the broadcast media.

Assignment Rationale

A personal narrative is the telling of a story of everyday life. To write personal narratives, students must reflect on the meaning of their own experiences and tell their stories in a coherent fashion. This highly individual focus prepares students for the study of other kinds of narrative writing. In addition, it reinforces students' appreciation of the literary elements of character, plot, and setting.

Starting from Literature

Objective

To respond to a professional model of a personal narrative as a springboard to writing

Teaching Strategies

Motivate

Ask students how people show that they care about others without saying so. Through discussion, elicit some of the ways people show love or concern without using words.

Tap Prior Knowledge

Ask students if they have ever discovered something about their relationship with another person that was surprising, pleasant, or disappointing. Invite volunteers to explain what they discovered and how. Explain that in the excerpt students will read, Moss Hart describes how a surprise outing leads to an important discovery about his relationship with his father.

Personal Narrative

from

ACT
ONE

by Moss Hart

When you read a personal narrative, you will usually enjoy it more if it in some way reminds you of your own experiences or emotions. In the same way, when you write a personal narrative, you want to make the experience meaningful to others. As you read this personal narrative from playwright Moss Hart's autobiography, think about how he makes his experience significant to you.

Obviously Christmas was out of the question—we were barely staying alive. On Christmas Eve my father was very silent during the evening meal. Then he surprised and startled me by turning to me and saying, "Let's take a walk." He had never suggested such a thing before, and moreover it was a very cold winter's night. I was even more surprised when he said as we left the house, "Let's go down to a Hundred Forty-ninth Street and Westchester Avenue." My heart leapt within me. That was the section where all the big stores were, where at Christmastime open pushcarts full of toys stood packed end-to-end for blocks at a stretch. On other Christmas Eves I had often gone there with my aunt, and from our tour of the carts she had gathered what I wanted the most. My father had known this, of course, and I joyously concluded that this walk could mean only one thing—he was going to buy me a Christmas present.

On the walk down I was beside myself with delight and an inner relief. . . . I wanted a Christmas present terribly—not a present merely, but a symbol, a token of some sort. I needed some sign from my father or mother that they knew what I was going through and cared for me. . . .

Set a Purpose

Before students read the excerpt, discuss the side-column notes, encouraging students to speculate about how a writer makes an experience significant to the reader. Explain that the excerpt from *Act One* is an example of a personal narrative. Then have students read the excerpt to find out what Moss Hart discovers and how he makes his experience meaningful for the reader.

87

Literature Connection

Author Note   Born in New York City in 1904, Moss Hart became famous during the 1930's for the witty comedies about American life that he wrote with George S. Kaufman. One play, *You Can't Take It With You,* won the 1937 Pulitzer Prize in drama. Hart's autobiography, *Act One,* was published in 1959 and became a bestseller; it was made into a film in 1965.

Think and Respond

Elicit Personal Responses

Have students write in their journals or learning logs their personal responses to the excerpt. Then, as a class, discuss the responses. Focus the discussion on Hart's discovery and why he might have chosen to write about it.

Explore the Author's Techniques

To help students use the excerpt as a model for their writing, work through the selection with students, examining the author's techniques. For example, point out that throughout the piece Hart uses strong visual images (Page 86, paragraph 1: That was . . . stretch. Page 88, paragraph 3: We hurried . . . seen.) and couples this with ongoing revelations of his feelings. (Page 86, paragraph 1: Then he . . . walk. My heart . . . me. Page 86, paragraph 2: On the walk . . . relief.) Also, Hart lets the reader know early on the importance of the gift (Page 86, paragraph 2: I wanted . . . sort.) and at the end reflects on the experience, telling the reader the conclusion he has drawn. (Page 88, paragraph 2: Nor did . . . each other.) Suggest that students may want to use some of these techniques in their personal narratives.

Link Literature to Writing

An effective narrative reminds readers of their own experiences and emotions. Many students will be able to identify with the topic of Moss Hart's excerpt—a relationship with a parent. Suggest that experiences of this kind might serve as a basis for students' writing. Explain that the Guided Assignment that follows will help students develop their experiences into moving personal narratives that convey the significance of everyday events.

We hurried on, our heads bent against the wind, to the cluster of lights ahead that was 149th Street and Westchester Avenue, and those lights seemed to me the brightest lights I had ever seen. Tugging at my father's coat, I started down the line of pushcarts. There were all kinds of things that I wanted, but since nothing had been said by my father about buying a present, I would merely pause before a pushcart to say, with as much control as I could muster, "Look at that chemistry set!" or, "There's a stamp album!" or, "Look at the printing press!" Each time my father would pause and ask the pushcart man the price. Then without a word we would move on to the next pushcart. Once or twice he would pick up a toy of some kind and look at it and then at me, as if to suggest this might be something I might like, but I was ten years old and a good deal beyond just a toy; my heart was set on a chemistry set or a printing press. There they were on every pushcart we stopped at, but the price was always the same and soon I looked up and saw we were nearing the end of the line. Only two or three more pushcarts remained. My father looked up, too, and I heard him jingle some coins in his pocket. In a flash I knew it all. He'd gotten together about seventy-five cents to buy me a Christmas present, and he hadn't dared say so in case there was nothing to be had for so small a sum.

As I looked up at him I saw a look of despair and disappointment in his eyes that brought me closer to him than I had ever been in my life. I wanted to throw my arms around him and say, "It doesn't matter . . . I understand . . . this is better than a chemistry set or a printing press . . . I love you." But instead we stood shivering beside each other for a moment—then turned away from the last two pushcarts and started silently back home. I don't know why the words remained choked up within me. I didn't even take his hand on the way home nor did he take mine. We were not on that basis. Nor did I ever tell him how close to him I felt that night—that for a little while the concrete wall between father and son had crumbled away and I knew that we were two lonely people struggling to reach each other.

Think AND Respond

Why do you think the author chose to share this particular event? Can you understand the feelings the young Moss Hart experienced? Does the episode remind you of events in your own life that you might like to write about?

INVITATION TO Write

Moss Hart's narrative told about an event that was important to him. Now it's your turn to write a personal narrative based on an experience that happened to you or to someone you know.

Events happen in everyone's life that leave a lasting impact. These can be times when you discover something about yourself or someone else, experience something new, or have a strong emotional reaction. Writing a personal narrative is one way that you can explore discoveries, experiences, and feelings that, like Moss Hart's, are both personal and universal.

PREWRITE AND EXPLORE

1. Look for ideas. Do you ever feel that you have no ideas for writing? Often the best ideas are those closest to you. When writing a narrative, you can draw on many personal sources for ideas. To begin to focus your thoughts, try one or more of the following activities.

Exploratory Activities

- **Recalling** Look through your pockets, a junk drawer, or a photo album to see if the objects you find might stir memories that could make a good narrative.
- **Listing** Look in your journal for events to write about. List them on a piece of paper. Next to each item, write some interesting details that you remember about the event.
- **Storytelling** In pairs or small groups, share some family stories. Think about the stories that the other students tell. Do they remind you of events in your own life that you might like to write about?

HANDBOOKS
FOR HELP & PRACTICE

Writing Variables, pp. 311–316
Personal Techniques, pp. 317–320
Creating Charts, pp. 358–359

Personal Narrative   **89**

Prewrite and Explore

Objectives

1. To use prewriting activities to generate ideas for a personal narrative
2. To use freewriting to explore potential topics
3. To choose a topic and explore goals, audience, characters, setting, and plot for a personal narrative

Preteaching

Preview the Prewrite and Explore section. If there are skills or concepts students may need help with before prewriting, present them at this time. The Thinking Skills Transparencies and the mini-lessons listed below may help you in your selection and instruction. The cross references in the pupil text will give students access to the same lessons for independent study.

Handbook Mini-Lessons
- Writing Variables, pp. 311–316
- Personal Techniques, pp. 317–320
- Creating Charts, pp. 358–359

Teaching Strategies

Modeling

Consider using the first Exploratory Activity to model one way to generate ideas for a personal narrative. Bring in a few photographs of yourself from different periods of your life. Share with students the memories associated with each picture.

 Individualizing Instruction

Cultural Differences If students use the Storytelling Activity, be aware that in some cultures and in some families sharing personal experiences is not an acceptable practice. Help students who are uncomfortable with such a focus to choose topics based on events outside the home, such as those associated with school.

Individualizing Instruction

Learning Styles Encourage visual learners to use time lines, idea trees, cluster diagrams, or other graphic devices to help them choose and organize ideas for a personal narrative. You might use the Thinking Skills Transparencies or refer students to Handbook 9, Using Graphic Devices, pp. 357–360. Students who benefit from structure and direction may find a detailed story plan or map helpful in the planning stage.

Stumbling Block

Some students may complain that their experiences seem too insignificant to write about. Point out that most personal narratives do not deal with major life or death issues but with quiet, telling moments that reveal some truth about a person, time, or place. You might direct students who are having difficulty finding a topic to the Data Sheets or the Ideas for Writing booklet.

Writing
—TIP—

An idea tree or cluster may help you find material.

- **Constructing a time line** Create a time line of some important events in your life. Record positive events above the line and negative ones below it. If you like, compare your time line with those of other students to see if you can come up with additional ideas.
- **Reading literature** Personal narratives can spark many emotions. For example, Moss Hart tells of a moving incident in his autobiography, and James Thurber tells of a humorous one in "The Night the Bed Fell." What emotions have other narratives stirred in you? You might like to write a narrative that will stir a similar emotion in your audience.

2. Select a writing topic. Look over the ideas that you have come up with by doing the Exploratory Activities. List two or three especially promising ideas. Then freewrite on one or more of them to discover how much you have to say. If you are still having trouble coming up with an idea, check your writing portfolio for other suggestions and unfinished sketches. Also look for ideas in interesting scenes, people, or situations like the one below. Check the ideas you experimented with in the Sketchbook on page 84. The "Apply Your Skills" section on page 101 may give you additional ideas.

A strange person in an equally strange place. Why?

Writer's Choice Do you want to make a plan for your whole narrative first, or do you want just to start writing and see where your idea takes you? Good writers work both ways.

One student writer, Charles, decided to construct a time line, using events that were important to him. He wanted to see if he could make a narrative out of any of them. In this lesson you will follow Charles's writing process, beginning with the time line below.

ONE STUDENT'S PROCESS

POSITIVE

| started school | learned to skate | got first basketball | played on school basketball team | had to move |

5 | | | | 10 | | | | 15

broke arm — snowbound for week — dog died — had to move

NEGATIVE

As Charles studied his completed time line, he asked himself questions such as the following:

- Which of these incidents had a lasting effect on me?
- Which would I change if I could?
- Which one made me feel an emotion I could share?
- Which incident taught me something important?

Charles decided to write about the time the family was moving two thousand miles away because it taught him something important about both himself and his parents.

3. List your goals. Now that you have selected a topic, begin to think about what you want your writing to accomplish. Charles had the following goals:

- to describe an important personal experience
- to describe an insight into his parents' feelings
- to get others to think about their own parents

Although writers sometimes decide on their goals ahead of time, sometimes they just start writing to see where ideas lead them.

4. Identify your audience. Who do you want your readers to be? Having an audience in mind may help you shape your writing. For example, your readers for this narrative might be your friends, your

PROBLEM

S O L V I N G

How can I evaluate the ideas I've generated?

Use examples from stories students are currently reading to model how writers describe setting, show character, or develop plot. You might also have students note how Moss Hart reveals the setting in the excerpt from *Act One*. Also note the Literature Connection below.

Managing the Paper Load

To minimize teacher review time during the planning stage, suggest that students work in pairs or small groups to respond to one another's topics and goals. Encourage students to share their plans for character, plot, and setting as well. If you wish, you might confer briefly with groups that request additional feedback.

Draft and Discover

Objectives

1. To draft a personal narrative, using description and dialogue to reveal characters and events
2. To respond to one's own writing and the writing of peers

Preteaching

Preview the Draft and Discover section. If there are skills or strategies that students may need help with before drafting, present them at this time. The Elaboration Worksheets from the Revision, Proofreading, and Elaboration booklet as well as the mini-lessons listed below may help you in your selection and instruction.

> ### Handbook Mini-Lessons
> - Types of Organization, pp. 331–335
> - Writing Introductions, p. 341
> - Types of Elaboration, pp. 351–354
> - Types of Conclusions, pp. 371–373
> - Dialogue in Fiction, pp. 434–435

PROBLEM SOLVING

What narrative elements do I want to include in my story?

HANDBOOKS
FOR HELP & PRACTICE

Types of Organization, pp. 331–335

Writing Introductions, pp. 341–342

Types of Elaboration, pp. 351–354

Types of Conclusions, pp. 371–373

Dialogue in Fiction, pp. 434–435

92   Workshop 3

---

family, or even your own children someday! Identifying your audience can help you make appropriate word choices. Remember, however, that your audience might not suggest itself until you are well into the drafting stage.

5. Explore your story.   Before you begin drafting, you might want to review the elements of a narrative.

- **Characters**   Think about the people who are part of your narrative. Try to recall as many details about them as you can. You might want to jot down a brief description of each one to keep them clear in your mind. For example, think about how old your characters were at the time the incident occurred as well as how they dressed and what they looked like. How did they act and react to others? Show some of these characteristics. Don't just tell about them.
- **Setting**   Think about the time and place of your narrative. Be sure to describe the setting in detail if it is important to the action of the narrative. For example, if your narrative is about being caught in a blizzard, you will need to use descriptive details to show the reader why the situation was a dangerous one. If your narrative takes place in more than one setting, consider how to make the transition smooth from scene to scene.
- **Plot**   You will know what your basic plot—or related sequence of events—is before you start drafting, because you are telling about something that really happened. Remember that in many narratives the speaker often faces and relates some sort of conflict. Moss Hart built his conflict on his expectation of receiving a Christmas present. Will your narrative deal with a conflict? What is it? You already know how the events ended because you experienced them, but do you know what final words you will use to close your narrative? Sometimes as you write, wording that you hadn't considered will suggest itself, so try not to feel locked into a particular conclusion.

DRAFT AND DISCOVER

1. Begin your draft.   Remember that this is just a draft. You shouldn't try to make it perfect yet. You'll have time to make changes later. As you begin drafting, think about using some of the following strategies to make your narrative a strong one.

Literature Connection

Literary Elements   You might use the following fictional stories to provide other examples of literary elements: "A Mother in Mannville" by Marjorie Kinnan Rawlings (character), "Through the Tunnel" by Doris Lessing (setting), and "The Open Window" by Saki (plot).

Strategies

- **Description** Descriptive details that appeal to the senses can make your narrative more real for a reader.
- **Dialogue** Using dialogue can help you recreate events, reveal what characters are like, and present information in a dramatic manner. Notice how Moss Hart's use of dialogue helps to reveal the feelings of a son toward his father. Keep in mind that your narrative will be more effective if you clearly convey to readers why the incident is important to you.

2. Organize your draft. One common way to organize a narrative is according to chronological order. However, you can try other organizational patterns as well. For example, you may wish to try beginning your draft with an exciting event or some dialogue. You may even want to start in the middle of the narrative and fill in earlier events with a flashback. Then, tell the remainder of your narrative in chronological order, using transitional devices to cue your reader to changes in the time sequence.

The following is the beginning of Charles's unrevised first draft. Notice how Charles began his draft by using dialogue. Then he continued to relate his story in chronological order.

ONE STUDENT'S PROCESS

"Time for dinner!" my mother called out, and I hurried to the table. My dad was already sitting in his usual place. My mom entered the room carrying a dish, and we were soon all three seated around the table.

"I have an announcement to make," Dad said. My mother looked up while I gobbled down my dinner. I was in a hurry. The guys were waiting.

Dad asked, "May I have your attention too, Chuck?" I was surprised at his question. Dad knew I always ate dinner quickly so I could play basketball.

Writing
TIP

To help your readers form mental pictures of what is happening, *show* events; don't just *tell* about them.

COMPUTER
TIP

If you are having trouble starting, turn down the screen and begin typing. In this way, your words will not distract you.

Teaching Strategies

Speaking and Listening

Explain that writers often have to reconstruct dialogue that they cannot remember word for word. Encourage students to read dialogue aloud to partners to determine whether it sounds "real" or "authentic."

 Individualizing Instruction

LEP Students Students for whom English is a second language or students who speak in a dialect may need special help with writing dialogue. Explain that in some instances foreign words or dialect help to make the narrative authentic.

LD Students Before these students begin their drafts, review the events they plan to include in their personal narratives. If possible, help them arrange the events in chronological order, making a numbered list that they might follow when drafting. Review transition words that show time (Handbook 10, p. 364) and write the words on the board. Encourage students to refer to this list of words as they draft.

Personal Touch

Using a topic you have chosen for a personal narrative, discuss ways you might organize it and how you will use description and dialogue.

Individualizing Instruction

Advanced Students You might encourage these students to develop their plots fully by building the action towards a climax. Point out the climax in the Hart excerpt. (Page 88, paragraph 1: In a flash . . . all. He'd . . . sum.) Suggest that students experiment with an arrangement of events that leads to a dramatic turning point in the narrative.

Springboard

If students are having difficulty creating good dialogue, ask them to take a break from writing and "eavesdrop" on the conversations of friends and family. They might record actual snatches of dialogue in their logs. By listening carefully, students should learn to re-create the characteristic speech patterns of the people they know well.

Managing the Paper Load

To avoid major problems in the revision stage, conduct brief problem-solving conferences with students during the drafting stage. Focus particularly on the development of character, plot, and setting and the use of description and dialogue.

Peer Response

Help students choose the type of peer response they want. Students might select specific questions from the list that they want their peer readers to answer. Those students whose narratives hinge on character may be concerned about the vividness of their portrayals. Those who are writing about an exciting series of events may want to focus on the question, "Did you have any trouble following the narrative?" Students who want a broad range of responses might use the Peer Response Sheet for this assignment.

PROBLEM
S O L V I N G

How well does my draft say what I want it to say?

Writing
— TIP —

Reading your dialogue aloud can help you write realistic passages.

3. Take a break. After you complete your draft, put it aside for a few hours or a day. Then reread it when your mind is fresh, or ask your peer readers to respond to it. Questions such as the following can help you and your peers respond to your draft.

R E V I E W   Y O U R   W R I T I N G

Questions for Yourself
- Does what I've written match the story in my head? Do I like the direction my draft is taking?
- Have I found a focus for my story, or does it just wander?
- Have I set the story in a place and time that helps my reader understand more about the events?
- Am I close to achieving any of the goals I set for myself? Have my goals developed or changed?
- Why is this narrative meaningful to me? Does this come through in the story?

Questions for Your Peer Readers
- What do you think the narrative is about? Summarize it for me.
- Did you have any trouble following the events in my story? If so, where?
- Why do you think I chose to tell this narrative?
- What did you want to know more about?
- What words or phrases were most effective?
- Which characters or events were most vivid?
- What were some of the things you were thinking about as you were reading?
- Did the beginning capture your interest? Did the ending bring the narration to a satisfying conclusion?

 Writer's Choice Would your narrative be more effective if you started it earlier or later in the sequence of events? Do you want to continue to work with this draft, or do you want to change the direction of the narrative? At this point, you may even decide to start over with a totally new idea.

REVISE YOUR WRITING

1. Evaluate your responses. As you prepare to revise your narrative, think about your own reactions and the comments of your peer readers. Keep in mind that while your peers can give you valuable feedback, you are not bound by their comments or suggestions. It is up to you to decide what changes to make to your narrative, if any. However, you should consider the following guidelines, which are often used to evaluate personal narratives.

Standards for Evaluation

An effective personal narrative . . .

- includes such elements as character, setting, and plot and develops these elements with appropriate details.
- uses description and dialogue as appropriate to enhance the narrative.
- shows events rather than tells about them.
- establishes and maintains a consistent tone and point of view.
- shows what the significance of the narrative is to the writer.
- contains a well-developed beginning, middle, and end and uses chronological order effectively.
- demonstrates a clear sense of audience through the use of appropriate language and the choice of details.

HANDBOOKS
FOR HELP & PRACTICE

Coherence in Compositions, pp. 368–370

Peer Response, pp. 378–382

Shifts in Tense, pp. 608–609

Quotation Marks, pp. 795–801

Grammar ─ TIP ─

Make sure that each pronoun you use refers clearly to the noun or pronoun it replaces.

The pieces of your story should fit together like these puzzle pieces.

Personal Narrative **95**

Revise Your Writing

Objectives

1. To evaluate the responses to a draft of a personal narrative
2. To use the responses and a set of standards to revise the draft
3. To proofread for errors in spelling, grammar, usage, and mechanics

Preteaching

Based on any problems you have noted in students' drafts and on a preview of the Revise Your Writing section, identify the skills or strategies that you want to review before students revise. The Student Revision Model Transparency for this assignment, the Revision and Proofreading Worksheets from the Revision, Proofreading, and Elaboration booklet, as well as the mini-lessons listed below may help you in your selection and instruction.

> **Handbook Mini-Lessons**
> - Coherence in Compositions, pp. 368–370
> - Peer Response, pp. 378–382
> - Shifts in Tense, pp. 608–609
> - Quotation Marks, pp. 795–801

Teaching Strategies

Critical Thinking

Evaluating After discussing the Standards for Evaluation with students, suggest that they consider each characteristic of an effective narrative as they revise their drafts. Some students may want to use the Guidelines for Evaluating Writing checklist for this assignment to evaluate their drafts and to focus their revision efforts.

◇ Individualizing Instruction

Learning Styles Students with a strong visual sense might like to sketch the events, characters, and scenes of their personal narratives in order to find ways to revise them. Auditory learners might make and listen to tape recordings of their drafts to find areas to improve.

Linking Grammar and Writing

As students revise their drafts, suggest that they pay attention to the use of adjectives and adverbs and other modifiers such as the prepositional and participial phrase. You might use or direct students to Handbook 34, Using the Correct Modifier, pages 628–629; Handbook 35, Prepositional Phrases as Modifiers, pages 657–658; and Handbook 37, The Participial Phrase, page 684.

Guidelines for Evaluation

The following guidelines may be used for a close evaluation of a personal narrative. See the Guidelines for Evaluating Writing in the Teacher's Resource File for additional help with holistic or analytic scoring.

Ideas and Content
- relates a meaningful experience
- includes details that fully develop character, setting, and plot
- includes descriptive details and effective dialogue
- demonstrates the importance of the event to the writer
- reflects an awareness of audience in word choice and detail

Structure and Plot
- consistently uses the first-person point of view
- includes a beginning, middle, and end
- uses transition words and phrases
- uses chronological order effectively
- groups related ideas into paragraphs
- uses clear, varied sentences

Grammar, Usage, and Mechanics
- uses standard grammar and usage
- uses correct spelling, punctuation, and capitalization

Managing the Paper Load

Remember that you need not grade all of the points listed above. For grammar and mechanics in particular, limit your focus when grading. Before students finish revising, explain the criteria that you will use for evaluation.

2. Problem solve. Rework your draft, taking into consideration your own review of your narrative and the responses of your peer readers. Think about the comments your peer readers have made, but don't feel bound by them. As you revise, keep in mind your own goals for your writing.

Charles made these changes to the beginning of his draft as he responded to the suggestions of a peer reader.

ONE STUDENT'S PROCESS

I like your beginning, but can you do more to set the scene?

I can't picture what's happening. How about using dialogue here?

I'm confused about when this is happening.

> "I have an announcement to make," Dad said. ~one evening as~ We were just beginning dinner. My ~Mom~ mother looked up ~expectantly~ while ~wolf down my mashed potatoes.~ I continued to eat. I was in a hurry. The guys were ~for me to play basketball~ waiting. Dad asked, "May I have your attention too, ~Your mashed potatoes can wait."~ ~I looked up in surprise.~ Chuck?" I was surprised at his question. Dad knew I al- ~get out to the court.~ ways ate dinner quickly so I could play basketball. Then ~" You know~ ~haven't~ Dad told us that things hadn't been going very well at the factory. Well last week he heard from Jack who ~—you remember him—he~ ~He~ moved to Florida and found a job there. Jack said his ~d~ ~I'm~ plant is looking for more people. My dad decides he's going to try it."

3. Proofread your work. Make a clean copy that includes all your changes. Then check for errors in grammar, usage, and mechanics because these kinds of errors can distract a reader. Remember that verb tense and the punctuation of dialogue are particularly important in narrative writing.

Social Studies Connection

Autobiographies Point out that well-known leaders often write their memoirs or autobiographies in personal narrative form. Suggest that students find and read the memoirs or autobiographies of figures they admire such as Winston Churchill or Gandhi. Tell students to look for the characteristics of an effective personal narrative as they read.

LINKING
GRAMMAR **AND** WRITING
SHIFTS IN TENSE

Pay special attention to verb tenses in your writing. Unnecessary shifts in tense can be confusing or distracting to your reader.

PROBLEM: Mom looks up while I continued to eat.
CORRECTED: Mom looked up while I continued to eat.

See Grammar Handbook 33, pages 608–609, for additional help with this problem.

PUBLISH AND PRESENT

- **Form a readers' circle with three other writers.**   Read each narrative and discuss your responses to it. This should not be an editing session. Just describe your thoughts and feelings.
- **Submit your narrative to a local paper or national magazine.** A book like *Young Writer's Market* will help you find publications that welcome submissions.
- **Read the narrative aloud to your class.**   Add music or photographs to make it a multimedia experience.
- **Keep your narratives in a special book.**   Give it to your parents or save it for your children.
- **Keep your narrative in your writing portfolio.**   Read it again in a month or two. At that time, you will have a clearer personal response to your writing.

HANDBOOKS
FOR HELP & PRACTICE

**Publishing Your Work,
pp. 402–403**

LEP Students   These students may have difficulty recognizing shifts in tense. If problems are evident, use Handbook 33, pp. 608–609 to provide extra practice.

Publish and Present

Objective

To publish and present a personal narrative

Teaching Strategies

Personal Touch

If you have written a personal narrative along with your students, consider reading it aloud to the class or sharing it with a small group in a reader's circle.

Cooperative Learning

If desktop publishing equipment is available in your school, allow a group of interested students to publish a book of class narratives. Work with the group to establish specific responsibilities for each group member. One student might input the stories, another provide art direction, and so on. Share the finished product with other classes.

Using the Model

Suggest that students use the Questions for Your Peer Readers on page 94, as well as the marginal annotations on pages 98–99, to discuss their reactions to "The Change." During discussion, call attention to Charles's use of dialogue (paragraphs 5 and 9–15). Ask students what Charles reveals about his characters' thoughts and feelings through this dialogue. In addition, you might suggest that students use the model to evaluate their personal narratives in a similar fashion. If students spot weaknesses, encourage them to revise further.

Effective introduction: Word choice and dialogue help to show rather than just tell what is happening.

Characters, setting, and basic plot have all been introduced in the beginning of the narrative.

Dialogue reveals what the main character is like.

ONE STUDENT'S PROCESS

The Change

Charles Malta

"I have an announcement to make," Dad said one evening as we were just beginning dinner. Mom looked up expectantly while I continued to wolf down my mashed potatoes. I was in a hurry. The guys were waiting for me to play basketball.

"May I have your attention too, Chuck? Your mashed potatoes can wait a minute."

I looked up in surprise. Dad knew I always ate dinner quickly so I could get out to the court.

"You know things haven't been going very well at the factory. Well last week, I heard from Jack—you remember him—he moved to Florida and found a job there. He said his plant is looking for more people. I decided I'm going to try it. I gave my two-weeks' notice to my boss today; I figure we can be out of the apartment and on the way to Florida by the end of the month." Dad looked around with a wary smile on his face.

I said the first thing that popped into my head (I usually do). "Are you crazy? Florida is two thousand miles from here. What about my basketball? What about my friends? What about school?" I was on such a roll that I hardly noticed when Mom got up and left the table.

The next few days passed in a blur. I vaguely remember telling my friends the news, but I refused to believe that it would ever come to pass.

Our apartment became very quiet although Mom was home. She had lost her job when the car dealership she was working for had filed for bankruptcy. I pretty well ignored both her and Dad—after all, they were turning my whole life upside down.

When Dad brought home cartons so that I could pack up my room, I just let them sit in a corner. No one could force me to do something I didn't want to do!

Literature Connection

Narrative to Read   Students might enjoy reading Beryl Markham's autobiography, *West With the Night,* which relates her experiences as a bush pilot in Africa.

Then something happened. On my way out the door to basketball one afternoon, I yelled, "Mom, I won't be home for dinner." She didn't answer, so I went to look for her. She had her back to me, kneeling beside a carton and carefully wrapping the family photographs she had taken off the wall. When I said, "Mom," she didn't turn around. I walked around the box and said, "Mom, I won't be. . . ." I broke off my words in mid-sentence. My mother was crying.

"I guess you caught me," she said, trying to smile.

"But, why . . .?"

"Oh, I guess I was just feeling sentimental—you know, old pictures and everything." Then she looked at me, and the smile disappeared. "No, Chuck, it's really more than that."

"You mean you don't want to move either! That's great! When Dad realizes how we both feel, he'll agree to stay here." I was on a roll again, already planning what I was going to tell the guys.

My mother looked at me a little sadly. "I wish it were that simple, Chuck. You're right. I don't want to move, but then neither does your father. We've lived in this city all our lives."

"Then, let's stay!" I could hardly believe that maybe things would go my way after all.

"Chuck, think about it. What will happen if we stay? I don't have a job. You know your father's plant is in danger of closing. How can we afford a place to live, food to eat, or even basketball shoes for you if we don't have jobs?" The smile returned for a moment as she mentioned the shoes.

I went back to my room and tentatively fingered one of the empty cartons. "How was I to know?" I protested, half to myself and half to the cartons. For once in my life, I didn't have a quick answer. I needed time to digest what Mom had said. Basketball would have to wait today.

Middle of narrative is well-developed. Descriptive details help reader picture the scene between mother and son.

Narrative is told in chronological order.

Ending shows the significance of the narrative.

Personal Narrative **99**

Reteaching

Assess the needs of students who were not successful in developing an effective personal narrative and identify two or three areas in which additional practice is needed. Assign the appropriate Handbook Mini-Lessons, along with the support materials listed for each lesson. A concept commonly requiring reteaching for this assignment is

Chronological Order: Handbook 4

The following suggestions and resources may also be useful.

1. Dialogue Remind students that a successful narrative contains natural-sounding dialogue. To help students achieve better dialogue, suggest that pairs of students act out scenes from their narratives in which two or more characters interact. Have students develop and record dialogue for the scenes. Students can then use this dialogue to replace some of the narration in their drafts.

2. Characterization To help students develop their characters, suggest that they select one or more characters from their narratives and do five minutes of focused freewriting about each character. Tell students to include as many descriptive details as possible. Circulate and help students as they weave some of these details into their personal narrative.

3. Grammar and Usage: Shifts in Tense In a small group, review with students rules of verb tense. Ask students to find examples of sentences with errors of this type in their drafts. As a group revise the sentences.

Extension and Enrichment

• Suggest that students use the techniques of dialogue and description in their diaries or journals.

• Some students might enjoy using their personal narratives to develop a play. Suggest that students work in small groups to select a narrative, identify one or more scenes, develop a script with dialogue and stage directions, and create props.

Learning from Your Writing Process

Objective

To analyze and reflect upon what has been learned about the writing process and the writing of a personal narrative

Teaching Strategies

Critical Thinking

Expressing Opinions Ask students if they think other writers would agree or disagree with Porter's comment about where ideas come from. Invite discussion. Use the Literature Connection at the bottom of this page if you wish to use a specific example from the works of Katherine Anne Porter.

Reflecting on the Process

You may want to model the procedure by answering some of the questions about your own writing experience. Encourage students to record any other responses, in addition to those generated by the questions on this page, that they might have about the experience of writing a personal narrative.

WRITER TO WRITER

The truth is, I have never written a story in my life that didn't have a very firm foundation in actual experience— somebody else's experience quite often, but an experience that became my own by hearing the story, by witnessing the thing, by hearing just a word perhaps. It doesn't matter, it just takes a little—a tiny seed. Then it takes root, and it grows. It's an organic thing.

Katherine Anne Porter, novelist and short story writer

▶ FOR YOUR **PORTFOLIO**

1. Reflect on your writing. Now that you have completed your narrative and read several others, think about the process you used. Ask yourself the following questions, and record any useful thoughts or ideas in your writing log or attach them to your finished paper.

- What parts of the narrative did I find easy to write? What parts were the most difficult? Why did I find these parts difficult to write?
- What parts of my writing process are getting easier? Are ideas coming more easily?
- Am I finding peer response comments useful? How do they make me a better writer? Do I feel more comfortable giving others comments about their work?

100 Workshop 3

Literature Connection

Story to Read You may wish to have students read Katherine Anne Porter's "He." Referring back to her quote about where writing ideas come from, ask students to speculate about where Porter might have gotten the idea for the story.

- Did I do the right amount of planning before I began drafting? Would my work have benefitted from more—or less—planning?
- What was the biggest problem I encountered during this writing process? What solution did I find? How can I improve my writing process next time?
- If I had to give one piece of advice to someone who was just beginning to write a narrative, what would I say that might be helpful?
- When I compare my narrative to other pieces of writing in my writing portfolio, what are some changes I see in my style?
- How is narrative writing different from other kinds of writing I have done? Which kind of writing do I enjoy doing most?
- After reading several narratives and trying one of my own, how would I describe the most important features of a good narrative? For example, did I notice anything in the writing of Moss Hart that I would like to try myself? Was there something in the writing of one of my classmates that I particularly liked?

2. Apply your skills.   Use your knowledge to develop one of the following activities.

- **Cross curricular**   Write a narrative that describes an event in the life of a person from history. Choose someone who fascinates you.
- **Literature**   Become a favorite character from a favorite short story. For example, you might choose to be Rainsford in "The Most Dangerous Game." From that character's point of view, retell an incident in the story.
- **General**   Interview a person who works at a store or some other business in your neighborhood. Ask that person to describe an unusual work-related incident that he or she remembers. Recreate the incident in a narrative.
- **Creative**   Imagine that it is fifteen years in the future, and you are now a teacher in this very school. Describe the typical school day in the twenty-first century through the eyes of you, the teacher.
- **Related assignments**   Follow the suggestions on pages 102–112 to write an oral history or a storyboard.

Writing Portfolio

Suggest that students keep their prewriting notes, their finished narratives, and their final reflections in their writing portfolios. You might suggest that students refer to their self-evaluations of the process of writing a focused description (Guided Assignment, Workshop 2) and consider the following questions: In writing a personal narrative, how did I use what I learned about sensory details in a focused description? Did I learn any new techniques from writing a personal narrative that I might use in writing a description?

Application

The Apply Your Skills activities show the wide variety of situations in which personal narrative can be used. Encourage students to select at least one activity with which to experiment.

Summary and Closure

Before proceeding to the next assignment, be sure students have internalized the following key concepts:

1. A personal narrative is the story of a meaningful experience that is written in the first person.

2. Description and dialogue are important elements in a personal narrative.

3. An effective personal narrative is meaningful not only to the writer but to the reader as well.

Allow students time to summarize what they have learned by describing the characteristics of an effective personal narrative and by telling why knowing how to write a personal narrative might help them in other school subjects.

Social Studies Connection

Reported Events   You might suggest that students who wish to experiment further with narrative writing scan the newspaper for ideas for narratives. Point out that journalists typically report events in a straightforward fashion without embellishment—telling the who, what, when, where, why, and how of a story. Encourage students to elaborate on the facts of a story, providing elements of character, plot, and setting. The narrative can be written from the first person to create a fictitious "personal narrative" based on a reported event.

Starting from Literature

Objective

To respond to a professional model of an oral history as a springboard to writing

Teaching Strategies

Motivate

Ask students what they have learned about the past by listening to the stories of older family members or neighbors. What skills have they learned from their parents, who in turn learned from their parents?

Tap Prior Knowledge

Ask students if they have ever conducted an interview, perhaps for an assignment in another class or when gathering information for a report. Invite volunteers to describe the interviews and to tell what they learned. Students who have never conducted a formal interview should think about times when they asked questions as an older person told a story. What kinds of questions did they ask? What did they discover? Did they repeat the story to anyone else?

Set a Purpose

Discuss the side-column notes. Emphasize the fact that this excerpt from the *Foxfire* collection is the result of an interview. Point out that the excerpt includes two major sections: the writer's introduction and the actual words of Doug Sheppard. Suggest that as students read the account they think about the purpose of the introduction and the kinds of information Doug Sheppard shares.

Oral History

An oral history is a very old, rich form of literature. It is the story of a person's experiences told by that person in his or her own words. An oral history may tell the effect of major historical events on a person's life. Or, like the following excerpt, it may have a more personal subject.

The story of bird carver Doug Sheppard is one of a collection of oral histories published in a magazine called *Foxfire*. These histories are based on interviews conducted by some Georgia students under the guidance of their teacher. As you read, notice how the students set the scene and allow Doug Sheppard to tell his own story.

102

BIRD CARVER

BY DOUG SHEPPARD
as told to Bit Carver,
Shelley Pace, and Susie Nichols

*I*magine a place where the only sounds are a creek in the distance tumbling over rocks and birds of all kinds singing around a peaceful three-room cottage. It seems that someone would be able to carve birds effortlessly in such surroundings. And thirty-two-year-old Doug Sheppard does make it look easy. He talked to us about how he started carving birds and what his dreams and plans are as he shaped a wren from a chunk of basswood.

MAY 10

I've been carving birds like this about five years, but I've been around it all my life. . . . One time, years ago, I carved a bird out and that was a pretty good bird. . . . I believe my mother's still got that bird somewhere.

My dad showed me ways to do things when I started carving. I really didn't learn much from him. He'd tell me something and I wouldn't listen to him. I was determined to do it my own way. A wood carver's going to do it their own way—no matter what, everybody's going to be different.

When I started out I wasn't any good at all, . . . but I keep learning more about it. As small as it is, there's a whole lot to learn, believe it or not. . . .

I do watch the birds when I can, and I feed them through the winter. . . . I've got a good pair of binoculars and I have several books on bird identification and use them for reference and as models sometimes for my carvings.

I'm starting to really understand paint now. I understand how to mix the colors and the blending and what you've got to do to make it look good. . . . I'm thinking about going to Western Carolina University this fall and taking a year of art. . . .

I want to carve one to where it's like a real bird of some kind and be just as good as these [famous] wildlife artists. . . . I know I can do it now, or think I can. I can do real fine work.

Think AND Respond

What details of Doug Sheppard's narrative made you want to know more about him? Are there questions you would like to ask him? Consider what Doug Sheppard reveals about being a wood carver and about his own character. What did you learn from the oral narrative that you would not have known if the writer had chosen a more traditional form?

103

Elicit Personal Responses

After students have finished reading, have them write in their journals or learning logs their responses to the oral history. Then discuss reactions as a class, referring to the Think and Respond questions. Ask students to consider the kinds of questions the writer might have asked Doug Sheppard.

Explore the Author's Techniques

A directed close reading and discussion will help students discover some of the author's techniques. For example, point out that the opening sentence issues a friendly invitation to the reader and describes the setting in vivid and specific language. (Page 102, paragraph 1: Imagine . . . cottage.) After introducing the setting and the subject of the oral history, the writer arranges the woodcarver's words in logical order: the first quoted segment describes how Doug Sheppard got started (Page 103, paragraphs 1 and 2), subsequent segments tell how he improved his craft (Page 103, paragraphs 3 and 4), and the concluding part speaks of his ambitions for the future (Page 103, paragraphs 5 and 6).

Link Literature to Writing

Like other pieces of effective writing, an oral history includes an introduction that engages the interest of the reader and prepares the reader for what is to come. The words of the person being interviewed tell his or her own story, but the writer must structure the questions and select the parts of the answers that best communicate the subject of the oral history. Suggest that students keep these ideas in mind as they do the Related Assignment.

Guiding Your Writers

Objectives

1. To choose a person to interview and to write open-ended interview questions
2. To conduct and record the interview
3. To transcribe the interview and organize the material
4. To draft an oral history, including an appropriate introduction and an accurate recounting of the person's exact words
5. To revise, proofread, and share an oral history

Preteaching

Read through the lesson, noting any skills and concepts for which the students may need preparation. The Thinking Skills Transparencies as well as the mini-lessons listed below may be useful. The cross references in the pupil text will give students access to the same lessons for independent practice.

Handbook Mini-Lessons

- Types of Organization, pp. 331–334
- Varieties of Language, pp. 409–411
- Dialogue in Nonfiction, p. 435
- Taking Notes, pp. 459–461
- Interviewing Skills, pp. 481–482

Teaching Strategies

Collaborative Opportunity

Students might work in small groups to brainstorm lists of possible subjects, interviewees, and interview questions. After individual students have identified who they will interview and have written their questions, allow them to role-play their interviews, practicing with partners in class.

Management Tip

You may want to collaborate with a ninth-grade social studies teacher to identify a relevant theme for the oral histories. You may find the following resource helpful: *Like It Was: A Complete Guide to Writing Oral History* by Cynthia Stokes Brown.

INVITATION TO Write

Doug Sheppard's oral history is a narrative about the life of a wood carver in rural Georgia. Now interview someone in your own community with an interesting story to tell and write up the interview as an oral history.

Like any narrative, an oral history tells a story and uses well-chosen details to bring an incident or person to life. However, your role in creating an oral history is very different from your role in writing other kinds of narratives. For most narratives, you choose the story you want to tell and the details that will help you tell it. In presenting an oral history, you choose a person to interview and the questions to ask, but the person you interview tells the story.

CONDUCTING THE INTERVIEW

HANDBOOKS
FOR HELP & PRACTICE

Types of Organization, pp. 331–335

Varieties of Language, pp. 409–411

Dialogue in Nonfiction, p. 435

Taking Notes, pp. 459–460

Interviewing Skills, pp. 481–482

1. Choose someone to interview. Pick an individual with an interesting job or trade, an intriguing family history, or simply a good story to tell. Think about what you want to learn from that person. Then set a date, time, and place for the interview.

2. Compose open-ended questions. Questions that require more than a yes or no answer will get the person talking. For example, you might have asked Doug Sheppard, "How did you get started carving birds?"

3. Think as you listen. Although you probably will want to tape-record the interview, it might be helpful to jot down important points, questions that occur to you, or ideas on how to organize the material as the interview progresses.

4. Ask follow-up questions. The best time to get more information is while you are still conducting the interview. Don't forget, however, that the person you are interviewing should do most of the talking.

Social Studies Connection

You might read aloud or suggest that students read portions of *The Good War* or *Working*, two collections of oral histories by Studs Terkel. Ask students to share with the class their favorite excerpts from the books and to explain why they found the particular stories interesting.

ADVANCING FROM TAPE TO PAPER

1. Choose a focus. Decide what mood you want to create and which details or events you want to highlight.

2. Listen to the tape. On individual index cards, take notes on the important information you want to include in your oral history. Be sure to present enough facts and details to make the person you interviewed come alive for the reader.

3. Organize your index cards. A coherent narrative is based on logically ordered details. It may help to group details under headings. Try different organizations to see which works best.

4. Draft an introduction. Include any necessary background information. For example, the introduction to the oral history of Doug Sheppard establishes the setting, tells his age, and briefly states the subject.

5. Use the words of the person you interviewed. If the person speaks a dialect or nonstandard English, you may wish to capture the sound of that speech using special spellings. For example:

> You didn't see no little 'uns. That's th' reason we had s' much better dances. They'd just sit back. They didn't git in there t' bother nothin'.

6. Decide on your presentation. You can structure the oral history as a running narrative, like the excerpt from *Foxfire,* or as a series of questions and answers, as in the following example:

> *Back when you were making fifty-six dollars a month, what was Etta doing?*

> *Charlie:* She was at home looking after the family. She has never worked away from home.

Oral History   **105**

Guidelines for Evaluation

A good oral history . . .

- engages the interest of the reader with an introduction that supplies background information
- includes the speaker's exact words
- presents details that give a well-rounded portrait of the speaker
- uses ellipses to indicate omissions from direct quotes
- shows a logical organizational pattern

Reteaching

Assess the needs of students who were not successful in developing an effective oral history. Assign the appropriate Handbook Mini-Lessons, along with the support materials for each lesson. Concepts commonly requiring reteaching for this assignment are

Interviewing Skills: Handbook 27
Dialogue in Nonfiction: Handbook 22

The following suggestions and resources may also be useful.

1. Introductions To help students make their introductions more effective, suggest that they work with partners to answer these questions: Whom did I interview? What is the topic of the interview? Where did the interview take place? Is the setting important? Is there anything else my readers need to know in order to understand the words of the speaker? Have partners work together to revise their introductions based on the answers to the questions.

2. Organization You might work with students to create outlines from their index cards. Compare the outlines with the final oral histories and discuss changes that would make the histories more effective.

Extension and Enrichment

- Your class might plan a program for a presentation to parents or senior citizens. A small committee might be responsible for overall planning. Each student writer might choose either to be a narrator or to portray the person he or she interviewed.

Writing
—TIP—

Show where you have deleted material from a direct quotation by using ellipses.

1. Go back to the source. The best person to note inaccuracies and missing information in your history is the individual who was the subject. After you get some response from peer readers, show the person you interviewed your draft of the oral history. Ask such questions as:

> Did I represent your words accurately?
> Have I painted a realistic portrait of you?
> Would you like to add, change, or delete anything?

2. Revise your draft. Think about how the person you interviewed responded to the oral history and change it accordingly. Then proofread for spelling, grammar, and mechanical errors. Be sure to check your use of ellipses.

PUBLISHING AND PRESENTING

- **Read your oral history aloud to the class.** Also, play selected passages of the interview tape to let your classmates hear the person's own voice and words.
- **Display your written oral history and taped interview.** Ask if your local library or historical society would like to display your work or sponsor an oral presentation with the person you interviewed.
- **Make a collection of your oral histories.** Use *Foxfire* magazine as a model. If your school or local printer has desktop publishing capabilities, work together to produce and distribute your collection.

On the Lightside

FOLK ETYMOLOGY

The story is often told about a prince who was so pleased with the roast he was eating that he tapped it with his sword and dubbed it Sir Loin. If only it were true! The real story behind the word *sirloin* is much less dramatic. The *sir* comes from the French *sur*, meaning "above," so the sirloin is merely the piece of meat above the loin.

The tale of the prince is an example of folk etymology. Many times, the origin of a word is obscure or difficult to understand, so people come up with a simpler explanation. For example, it might seem obvious that a greyhound is a dog with grey coloring. Yet the *grey* in its name comes from an early Scandinavian word meaning "dog."

Sometimes, words themselves change over the centuries to reflect folk explanations. For instance, the *hang* in *hangnail* began as *ange*, an Old English word meaning "painful." Since the word refers to a piece of skin hanging from a fingernail, however, people gradually added the *h. Muskrat* comes from the Algonquian word *musquash;* it has nothing to do with either musk or rats.

Other times, folk explanations simply seem right. The popular salad made of shredded cabbage may get its name—*coleslaw*—from the Dutch words for *cabbage* and *salad,* but many people think that this cool, refreshing side dish tastes better as *cold slaw*.

Folk tales about the meaning of words often appear to be more logical—and certainly more romantic—than the real thing.

Starting from Literature

Objective

To use a professional model of a story-board as a springboard for writing

Teaching Strategies

Motivate

Ask students if they have ever used or seen their parents use an automated teller machine. Discuss with them the advantages and disadvantages of using such a machine.

Tap Prior Knowledge

Ask students how a cartoon strip tells a story (through frames that contain images and written dialogue). Then find out if any students are familiar with the term *story-board*. (Their knowledge may come from movies and television. Some students may have friends or family members who are employed in some aspect of advertising.) If none of your students are familiar with the term, ask them how they think television commercials or programs are planned.

Set a Purpose

Discuss the side-column notes before students read the sample storyboard. Remind students to read the material both above and below each image before proceeding to the next image. Suggest that as students read they pay attention to the kind of information the storyboard contains. Encourage them to try to imagine how the commercial would actually appear on television.

Related ASSIGNMENT

Storyboard

Although we usually think of narratives as stories that are written down or told orally, they can also be presented visually. Film, for example, is a familiar medium for visual narratives. Cartoons, dramatic scenes, and commercials are all narratives.

A storyboard serves as a drafting device for a visual narrative. The storyboard shown in the model is from a television advertisement for an automobile financing company. Notice that each sequence of the three-frame storyboard can be read like a separate paragraph; notes above the drawing establish the setting and dialogue below carries the action.

108

Sequence No.: 1
Camera Treatment: *Open long shot. Empty bank lobby with video monitors, no tellers.*
Time: *30 seconds*
Transition to next sequence: *Zoom in on customer.*

Video Teller: Hello, I'm Leona, your automatic teller. Can I help you with a student loan?
Customer: No, an auto loan, Leona. (Customer pushes fast forward button on remote control unit. Teller bounces around screen, then stops at:)
Teller: A home improvement loan?
Customer: Ugh!

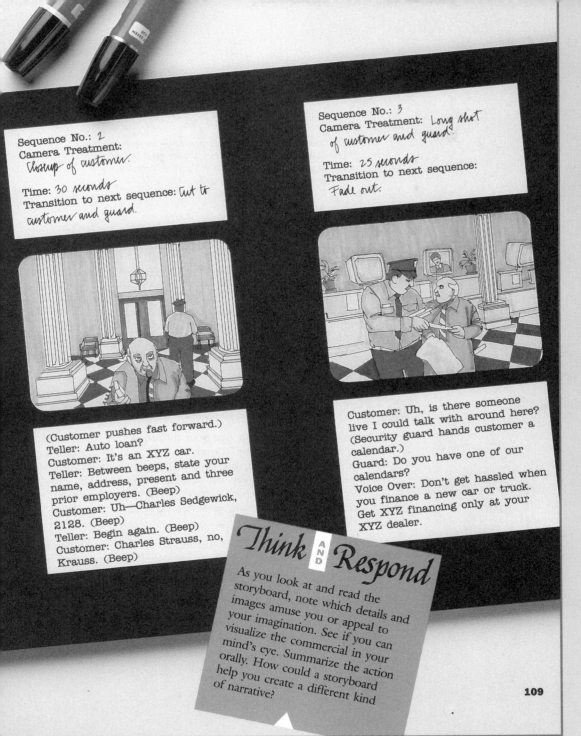

Sequence No.: 2
Camera Treatment:
Closeup of customer.

Time: 30 seconds
Transition to next sequence: Cut to
customer and guard.

(Customer pushes fast forward.)
Teller: Auto loan?
Customer: It's an XYZ car.
Teller: Between beeps, state your
name, address, present and three
prior employers. (Beep)
Customer: Uh—Charles Sedgewick,
2128. (Beep)
Teller: Begin again. (Beep)
Customer: Charles Strauss, no,
Krauss. (Beep)

Sequence No.: 3
Camera Treatment: Long shot
of customer and guard.

Time: 25 seconds
Transition to next sequence:
Fade out.

Customer: Uh, is there someone
live I could talk with around here?
(Security guard hands customer a
calendar.)
Guard: Do you have one of our
calendars?
Voice Over: Don't get hassled when
you finance a new car or truck.
Get XYZ financing only at your
XYZ dealer.

Think AND Respond

As you look at and read the storyboard, note which details and images amuse you or appeal to your imagination. See if you can visualize the commercial in your mind's eye. Summarize the action orally. How could a storyboard help you create a different kind of narrative?

109

Elicit Personal Responses

After students have examined the storyboard carefully, have them discuss their responses. Note how in this format the visual element dominates. The directions and dialogue support the images.

Explore the Author's Techniques

Review the storyboard as a class, discussing the writer's techniques and the elements he or she included. For example, point out that the material above the image includes identifying information, brief and precise directions for the camera operator (Page 108, frame 1: Open . . . shot. Empty . . . tellers.), the interval of time required, and a device for moving to the next scene. (Page 108, frame 1: Zoom . . . customer.)

In the panels below the image, the author includes dialogue and stage directions, using the traditional format for stage presentations. (Page 108, frame 1: Customer: . . . Leona. [Customer . . . unit.]) With very few words, the author succeeds in matching dialogue to images to create a humorous effect.

In addition, point out that the writer introduces the setting and the major characters in the first frame. The second and third frames develop the action.

Guiding Your Writers

Objectives

1. To identify a purpose and audience for a storyboard
2. To create a plan for a storyboard, including sketches of scenes, dialogue, sound effects, and directions to actors and camera operators
4. To prepare, evaluate, revise, and share a storyboard

Preteaching

Preview the assignment, noting any skills and concepts that students may need help with before they begin planning their storyboards. The Thinking Skills Transparencies as well as the mini-lessons listed below may help you in your selection and instruction. The cross references in the pupil text will give students access to the same lessons for independent study.

> **Handbook Mini-Lessons**
> - Writing Variables, pp. 311–315
> - Types of Organization, pp. 331–334
> - Appropriate Details, p. 355
> - Dialogue in Plays and Skits, p. 436

Teaching Strategies

Management Tip

Allow students to collaborate with partners or in small groups during the planning stage. Some students may want to brainstorm ideas for commercials or television show episodes. After students have identified a major focus, suggest that they discuss the characters, settings, and events that they will include in their storyboards. Just as people in advertising often work together as part of creative teams, you might allow pairs of students to develop a single storyboard.

INVITATION TO Write

The storyboard in the model was done for a humorous television advertisement. Now create your three-to-five-frame storyboard, either for a TV commercial or for a scene from a situation comedy.

Storyboards include elements used in all narratives. They have characters and a setting, follow a logical sequence, and use well-chosen details. In fact, storyboards are a kind of shorthand for the actual film or videotape. A storyboard consists of a series of rough sketches of important scenes, instructions to the camera operator, and details of the audio portion of the narrative. It can be used as a problem-solving technique in creating the actual pieces. The audio and visual descriptions and camera notes for each scene are arranged sequentially on small cards or panels called *frames*.

PLANNING YOUR STORYBOARD

1. Determine your purpose and your audience. A storyboard can be used to plan a television commercial, such as the model for an automobile financing company, or to develop an episode for a situation comedy series, or to plan any number of visual pieces. How will you use it? Is your purpose to entertain or to get people to buy a particular product? Will your audience be adults or children? How long will your episode be?

2. Sketch out a plan. Think through the entire commercial or episode. Plan the scenes you want to include in your storyboard. Choose the visual images and details, as well as the music and dialogue for each scene. To help organize your thoughts, make a simple outline or a chart with separate columns for audio and visual details.

3. Use technical terms. To give proper audio and camera directions, you will need to use technical audiovisual terms. Notice that some of the following terms are used in the model storyboard.

HANDBOOKS
FOR HELP & PRACTICE

Writing Variables, pp. 311–315

Types of Organization, pp. 331–335

Appropriate Details, pp. 355–356

Dialogue in Plays and Skits, p. 436

110   Workshop 3

Springboard

To provide students with more background knowledge, suggest that they watch a few television commercials closely. Students should try to observe the number of sequences, the kinds of camera shots and transition devices, the characters, dialogue, settings, and major events in each commercial. You might also suggest that students use a stopwatch or a watch with a second hand to time the commercials. As an alternative, you might record some commercials and view them in class. Have students identify and discuss the elements listed above.

- **closeup**   a camera shot that shows a small area of the scene
- **cut**   to move abruptly from one camera view to another
- **fade**   to gradually decrease or increase the strength of an audio or video signal
- **long shot**   a camera shot that shows a wide area of the scene
- **voice over**   the voice of an unseen narrator in a video production
- **zoom**   a camera technique that makes a scene seem suddenly closer or farther away

PREPARING YOUR STORYBOARD

1. Choose a format.   You may want to use a format like the one in the model or prepare each sequence on a separate sheet of poster board.

2. Include the necessary information.   No matter what format you choose, leave space for audiovisual information and additional notes to the camera operator. Notice how these are handled on the model storyboard. Use the following suggestions as guidelines:

- **Video**   Draw the placement of characters and objects in the scene. The drawing need not be a work of art. Pictures cut out of magazines or stick figures will do the job.
- **Audio**   Indicate all dialogue and music and include a verbal description of any action that takes place in the scene.

Storyboard   **111**

Writing
—**TIP**—

If your commercial or episode is a long one, consider presenting a few scenes from the beginning, the middle, or the end.

Guidelines for Evaluation

An effective storyboard . . .

- includes characters, a setting, and a series of events
- fully describes the action through images, camera directions, and dialogue arranged in frames
- presents the frames in a logical order
- includes realistic time allotments
- matches audio components to art
- contains realistic, convincing dialogue
- reflects an awareness of audience

Reteaching

Assess the needs of students who were not successful in developing an effective storyboard. Assign the appropriate Handbook Mini-Lessons, along with the support material listed for each lesson. Concepts commonly requiring reteaching for this assignment are

Types of Organization: Handbook 4
Dialogue in Plays and Skits:
    Handbook 22

The following suggestions and resources may also be useful.

1. Integrating Images and Dialogue Students who had difficulty coordinating images and dialogue might benefit from creating cartoon strips, focusing on the story elements without concern about time allotments, camera directions, and the like. After the cartoons are completed, have students work in small groups to provide the rest of the storyboard details.

2. Logical Order Students who had difficulty arranging their frames in a logical sequence might benefit from using Thinking Skills Worksheet: Chronological Order. Then have volunteers share their storyboards, and work as a group to identify problems and find solutions.

Extension and Enrichment

- Suggest that students review their journals for events or experiences that might be converted to a movie or television production. Interested students can select an event, consider how the event might be portrayed in film, and create a storyboard for one or two scenes.

- **Camera notes** Put yourself in the place of a camera operator and decide which camera treatment will produce the visual image you want. Consider the angles you want to use and the distance from which you will shoot each scene. Estimate how long each shot will take by timing the dialogue in the scene.

REVIEWING YOUR WRITING

1. Make sure your storyboard is complete. It should include enough words, pictures, and camera directions to give an accurate indication of what the finished video will be like.

2. Evaluate your storyboard. Ask yourself the following questions to help you judge the effectiveness of your work.

- Do the art, camera directions, and audio script fully describe the action that will take place?
- Is the sequence of frames logical?
- Are the suggested camera treatments effective?
- Would it be possible to complete the action and deliver the dialogue in the time allotted?
- Does the audio fit the action suggested by the art?
- Is the dialogue realistic and convincing?
- Are the information presented and the techniques used appropriate for the intended audience?

3. Ask for peer evaluation. Get your classmates' reactions to the questions listed above. If they see problems, ask them for suggestions on how to improve your storyboard.

PUBLISHING AND PRESENTING

- **Organize an exhibit.** Inquire about using a public area in your school, such as a corridor bulletin board or library showcase, to display the storyboards your class has produced.
- **Get an expert opinion.** Share your work with someone who is experienced with commercial advertising or video work. Ask this person to critique your storyboard. If you are interested in pursuing this kind of work, you might also prepare a list of questions to ask the person about his or her career.
- **Make a video.** Under your teacher's guidance, complete your commercial or TV sitcom scene as a video presentation.

Literature Connection

Discuss the fact that stories and novels are often adapted to film and television productions. Suggest that interested students consider stories that they are reading in literature and select a short scene from one of these works to develop for a visual medium. Students should then create a storyboard for the scene. Point out that, depending on the selection, students may have to create additional dialogue or use only a portion of the existing dialogue for their storyboard.

Sentence
COMPOSING

Delayed Modifiers

Experienced writers sometimes place adjectives after (rather than before) the person, place, or thing they describe to add interest, variety, and style to their sentences. Notice how the author, instead of writing "The <u>somber and dull</u> forests," adds power to the model sentence by delaying the adjectives that describe the forest.

MODEL

The forests, <u>somber and dull</u>, stood motionless and silent on each side of the broad stream.

Joseph Conrad, "The Lagoon"

A. Combining Sentences Combine the two sentences by placing the adjectives from the second sentence in the place indicated by a caret ($\wedge$).

Example	The forests,$_\wedge$, stood motionless and silent on each side of the broad stream. The forests were somber and dull.
Combined Sentence	The forests, <u>somber and dull</u>, stood motionless and silent on each side of the broad stream.

1. A bird somewhere, $_\wedge$, called for its friends. The bird was lonely and lost.
   Robert Lipsyte, *The Contender*

2. The red fearless eyes still looked at him, $_\wedge$. The eyes were impersonal and unafraid and detached. **John Steinbeck, *The Red Pony***

3. The old house was the same, $_\wedge$, but as we stared down the street, we thought we saw an inside shutter move. The house was droopy and sick.
   Harper Lee, *To Kill a Mockingbird*

4. The screen glowed silver, and soon life began to unfold, $_\wedge$. Life was beautiful and passionate and sad. **William Faulkner, "Dry September"**

5. The diggers gathered about the rim of the pit, $_\wedge$. The diggers were staring. **Edmund Ware, "An Underground Episode"**

6. A sigh, $_\wedge$, marked an almost imperceptible pause, and then his words flowed on, without a stir, without a gesture. The sigh was short and faint.
   Joseph Conrad, *Tales of Unrest*

Sentence Composing: Delayed Modifiers

Objectives

1. To combine sentences, placing adjectives in the postnominal position
2. To write original sentences that imitate professional models that have delayed adjectives
3. To expand sentences by adding delayed adjectives

Preteaching

These exercises focus on the use of delayed adjectives to achieve sentence variety and emphasis. You may want to review or refer students to Handbook 34, Using Modifiers: Adjectives, pages 620–625; Handbook 37, Using Verbals and Appositives: Participles, pages 683–684.

7. The swan, ∧ , looked at them remotely. The swan was sad-eyed.
   Pablo Neruda, "Three Poems and an Essay"

8. This is a snail shell, ∧ . The shell is round, full, and glossy as a horse chestnut.
   Anne Morrow Lindbergh, *Gift from the Sea*

9. The snow was still falling, ∧ , and it melted on the wooden cages and made the red lettering on the shutters glisten. The snow was soft and wet.
   Pierre Gascar, "The Animals"

10. In the dusk it appeared as a crouched and shadowy animal, ∧ . The animal was silent, gloomy, capable.
    Edmund Ware, "An Underground Episode"

B. Imitating Sentences Each sentence below contains an adjective series placed after the person, place, or thing it describes. Write a sentence that imitates the structure of each model.

Important: Imitate as many of the sentence parts as possible, not just the underlined adjective series.

Model Around the rocket in four directions spread the little town, green and motionless in the Martian spring.
Ray Bradbury, *The Martian Chronicles*

Student Sentence Near the center of the car showroom glistened the new model, sleek and stunning with its Plexiglas top.

1. I remembered that they were iris, blue and yellow and plum purple.
   Morris West, *The Salamander*

2. Then, as the reporters wander away, he sits slumped in a corner of the room, dejected, drained, and alone.
   Wayne Swanson, "How the Other League Lives"

3. Over his shoulder he carried a gunny sack, lumpy and full.
   John Steinbeck, *The Red Pony*

4. But I see its cinders red on the sky,/And hear its engine steaming.
   Edna St. Vincent Millay, "Travel"

5. Then they fled, houseless and floodless, down the valley, as their village, shredded and tossed and trampled, melted behind them.
   Rudyard Kipling, *The Jungle Book*

C. Expanding Sentences Become a partner with a professional writer. Copy each sentence and add a description containing an adjective series that blends with the rest of the sentence. Place your description after what is underlined. Use commas where needed. The author's original sentences are on page 306.

Sentence to Expand	The first thing Rainsford's eyes discerned was the largest man Rainsford had ever seen—<u>a gigantic creature</u>. **Richard Connell, "The Most Dangerous Game"**
Student Expansion	The first thing Rainsford's eyes discerned was the largest man Rainsford had ever seen—a gigantic creature, <u>fierce as a tiger, strong, but actually gentle as a baby</u>.
Author's Expansion	The first thing Rainsford's eye discerned was the largest man Rainsford had ever seen—a gigantic creature, <u>solidly made</u> <u>and black-bearded to the waist</u>.

Important: The goal is not to duplicate what the professional writer wrote but to add something that blends well with the original sentence.

1. <u>His guard</u> bowed and handed him the immense bow and quiver.
   James Clavell, *Shogun*

2. <u>A policeman</u> dragged his nightstick along the bars of an iron fence.
   Robert Lipsyte, *The Contender*

3. <u>Her voice</u> seemed to his ears to have lost some of its beauty.
   Honoré de Balzac, "La Grande Breteche"

4. It was a <u>heavy sound</u>.
   Theodore Taylor, "The Cay"

Application Write a descriptive paragraph. In one or more of the sentences, place the modifiers after, rather than before, the word they describe. Notice how delayed modifiers add interest and variety to your writing.

Grammar Refresher The model sentences in this workshop contain adjectives and participles that function as adjectives. To learn more about adjectives, see Handbook 34, pages 620–624. To learn more about participles, see Handbook 37, pages 683–685.

Sentence Composing **115**

4

Informative Exposition: Classification

Overview

Informative exposition, writing that explains or informs, can take several forms including classification—the examination of a subject in relation to its characteristics or to the larger group of which it is a part. By classifying a subject, students will apply and develop a critical thinking skill that will aid their comprehension of concepts and ideas in all subject areas. Workshop 4 includes the following Guided and Related Assignments:

1. **Guided: Definition** shows students how to identify the category to which a subject belongs and how to examine its characteristics; it also discusses how to explain a broad subject by breaking it down into its parts.

2. **Related: Extended Metaphor** builds on the skill of identifying characteristics introduced in the Guided Assignment by showing students how to develop a literary comparison based on these characteristics.

3. **Related: Comparison and Contrast** extends the classification skills introduced in the Guided Assignment by helping students use definition to compare two subjects effectively.

Teaching Preview

Preparation Guide

1. Use the Overview on this page and the Teacher's Choice descriptions on page 117 as a basis for deciding which assignment(s) to teach.

2. Preview the assignments and the teacher's notes and identify concerns that may require preteaching or extra support given your class's abilities. The handbook

mini-lessons suggested within the lesson may also provide guidance.

3. Preview the chart below for support materials in the Teacher's Resource File that may be used with this Workshop. Resources are for use with the Guided Assignment unless otherwise noted.

Support Materials

WRITER'S CRAFT RESOURCES

Prewrite and Explore
Thinking Skills Transparencies, pp. 3–4
Thinking Skills Worksheets, p. 2

Draft and Discover
Elaboration, Revision, and Proofreading Worksheets, p. 7

Revise Your Writing
Guidelines for Writing Assessment and Portfolio Use, pp. 11, 28–30
Peer Response Guides, pp. 15–16
Student Revision Model Transparencies, pp. 15–18
Elaboration, Revision, and Proofreading Worksheets, p. 8

Assessment
Tests and Writing Assessment Prompts, p. 4

Extension Activities
Writing Prompts for Fine Art Transparencies, pp. 8, 11, 12, 16, 18, 22
Writing from Literature, pp. 1–10, 13–18, 21–30, 33–36, 39–44
Standardized Test Practice

 Educational Technology
(available separately)
Writer's DataBank
Electronic English Handbook
Multimedia Workshop
Your Personal Trainer for the New SAT
In Perspective (videodisc)

• •

OTHER RESOURCES

Books and Journals
Moffett, James. *Active Voice.* Portsmouth: Boynton, 1992.

 Films and Videos
It's Like This. Agency for Instruc. Tech. (30 min.)
"Write On!" *ITV Series* (Pkg. 8). TV Ontario. (25 min.)

 Computer Software
Developing Writing Skills. Intellectual Software (Div. of Queue, Inc.). Apple family, 3 disks.
Success with Writing. Scholastic. Macintosh, 1MB.

Workshop Management Guidelines

The chart below indicates the number of days recommended for each phase of the Guided and Related Assignments. Stars indicate portions of the assignment that may be completed outside the classroom if time is limited or if teachers wish the activity to be completed by students independently.

DEFINITION

Starting from Literature ....1 day
Prewrite ....2–3 days*
Draft ....2–3 days*
Revise ....1 day
Publish ....1 day
Learning ....1 day*
Reteaching ....open
Extension/Enrichment..................... open
Sentence Composing......................1 day*

EXTENDED METAPHOR

Starting from Literature ....1 day
Understanding Extended
    Metaphors ....1 day
Writing ....1–2 days*
Reviewing...1 day
Publishing ....1 day

COMPARISON AND CONTRAST

Starting from Literature ....1 day
Preparing/Writing.............................1 day*
Reviewing...1 day
Publishing ....1 day

Linking Literature, Writing, and Grammar

The following options may be used to provide students with an integrated language experience. Begin by assigning and discussing any of the recommended pieces of literature. Use the suggested strategy to provide a link to the Guided Assignment.

LINKING LITERATURE AND WRITING

Option 1

Starting Point: "Los Angeles Notebook" by Joan Didion on pages 118–119 of *The Writer's Craft*

Strategy: Use the teaching suggestions on pages 118–119 to lead students into the Guided Assignment.

Option 2

Starting Point: "The Most Dangerous Game" by Richard Connell

Strategy: Before students read the story, ask them to define game. Then, after students have read the story, ask them to define game again, imagining how Rainsford or Zaroff might define it. Based on that discussion, suggest that students write the definition of another word that has more than one meaning.

Option 3

Starting Point: "Rhinoceros" by Adrien Stoutenberg

Strategy: As students respond to this poem, ask them to point out the details that give this description its impact. Also discuss the unexpected details and expressions that help the reader gain a fresh perspective on the animal. Explain that these same techniques can be used to describe or define any subject in a fresh and exciting way. As an example, have students read the Joan Didion piece on pages 118–119 and lead them into the Guided Assignment.

LINKING WRITING AND GRAMMAR

Before the drafting or revision stage of this assignment, tell students that clear definitions often require the use of comparisons. Ask students to find examples in their own papers as you write the following examples on the board.

The blue whale is similar to the sei whale but is up to forty-five feet *longer*.

The sperm whale is the *largest* of the toothed whales.

Porpoises are the *smallest* cetaceans, even smaller than dolphins.

Go over the rules of comparison on pages 631–637 of the Grammar and Usage Handbook. If problems of comparison still appear on student papers, assign the exercises on those pages for reteaching. Additional practice can be found in the *Grammar and Usage Practice Book* on pages 99–102.

Objective

To use a quote as a springboard to informal writing

Using the Prompt

The writing activities suggested on this page are designed to be informal, spontaneous, and ungraded. Encourage students to use their imaginations freely in the selection of subjects and in the form and wording of their explanations.

Model the activity by describing a game, sport, or hobby that you enjoy. Then ask students to discuss their favorite activities and elicit a brief oral explanation of each. Present the ideas in the Additional Sketches section as equally attractive springboards to writing.

Direct students to save their explanations in their writing portfolios for possible use in the workshop that follows.

Sketchbook

Basketball is one-on-one and burn-on-burn.
Basketball is ballet with defense.
Basketball is a blur of acrobatic giants, perilous abandon, and ram-slam-in-your-mother's-eyes dunk shots.
And for even the most casual fan, basketball can also be a dribbling, leaping, flowing salvation.

Charles Rosen
GOD, MAN AND BASKETBALL JONES

Describe or explain a game, sport, or hobby you enjoy. Write your description in prose or poetry. Start each paragraph or stanza with: "(Your subject) is. . . ."

Additional Sketches

Many words for common things began as proper names. For example, *leotard* comes from the man who invented it, Jules Leotard. What thing could be named after you? Explain why.

Define an emotion, such as love, hate, or anger.

Informative Exposition: Classification

Guided Assignment
DEFINITION

Related Assignment
EXTENDED METAPHOR

Related Assignment
COMPARISON AND CONTRAST

Y ou open your locker and out tumbles everything—books, long-forgotten notes, homework assignments, weeks-old food, a jacket you thought was lost, and a smelly sneaker. What do you do as you start to clean up? You may not think about it, but you begin to classify the contents, deciding what you should save and what you should throw into the trash can. Writers use classification too, grouping people, places, things, and ideas according to common characteristics. In the next three assignments, you will examine ways you can use classification to create clear definitions, comparisons, and metaphors.

117

Objectives

Guided Assignment:
DEFINITION
To recognize examples of extended definition and to plan, draft, revise, proofread, and share an extended definition

Related Assignment:
EXTENDED METAPHOR
To identify the characteristics of extended metaphor and to write, review, and share an extended metaphor

Related Assignment:
COMPARISON AND CONTRAST
To identify the characteristics of comparison and to write, review, and share a comparison of two people or things

Teacher's Choice

Guided Assignment
Definition This assignment is appropriate for most students because it can accommodate a wide range of topics and skill levels, and it draws on students' particular interests. The assignment also reinforces students' ability to classify and analyze information—prerequisites to the process of synthesis, which students will explore in Workshop 5. This assignment may be most useful after students have had experience with writing descriptions.

Related Assignments
Extended Metaphor This assignment is especially appropriate for advanced students and those keenly interested in literature. Visual learners may find photographs or other works of art useful springboards to writing.
Comparison and Contrast This assignment may be useful with students who are interested in the natural and social sciences. Ties to literature are also evident.

Assignment Rationale

Extended definitions are woven into the fabric of most expository writing. Productive thought depends on—and is stimulated by—clear definition of terms. An entire field of study—philosophy—has been largely devoted to defining ideas such as truth, beauty, existence, and justice. In daily life, juries decide cases based on whether the defendant's actions fit a precise definition of a crime. In writing a definition, students will need to find precise, vivid words to define their subjects. This skill is basic to all types of written and oral explanation.

Starting from Literature

Objective

To respond to a professional model of an extended definition as a springboard to writing

Teaching Strategies

Motivate

Ask students how they would explain an unusual environmental phenomenon to someone who had never experienced it. For example, how would they describe snow to someone from central Africa or a rainforest to a Greenlander? Elicit that clear definition requires knowledge of the subject, awareness of the audience, and precise wording.

Tap Prior Knowledge

Ask students how changes in weather affect them emotionally. Does snow make them feel happy and energetic or cozy and peaceful? Explain that in this excerpt Joan Didion describes an unusual wind found in southern California and relates its effects on people.

Guided ASSIGNMENT

Definition

If you look up a word such as *wind* in a dictionary, you will find a definition. But does that tell you all you want to know about the wind? To define a term, object, or idea, you need to examine it more closely, using a variety of strategies to discover its characteristics.

In her essay "Los Angeles Notebook," journalist and novelist Joan Didion defines a peculiar type of wind. As you read, look for the details she uses to describe the qualities of this wind and the ways it affects people.

From
"LOS ANGELES NOTEBOOK"
by Joan Didion

~ There is something uneasy in the Los Angeles air this afternoon, some unnatural stillness, some tension. What it means is that tonight a Santa Ana will begin to blow, a hot wind from the northeast whining down through the Cajon and San Gorgonio Passes, blowing up sandstorms out along Route 66, drying the hills and the nerves to the flash point. . . .

~ I recall being told, when I first moved to Los Angeles and was living on an isolated beach, that the Indians would throw themselves into the sea when the bad wind blew. I could see why. The Pacific turned ominously glossy during a Santa Ana period, and one woke in the night troubled not only by the peacocks screaming in the olive trees but by the eerie absence of surf. The heat was surreal. The sky had a yellow cast, the kind of light sometimes called "earthquake weather." . . .

~ The Santa Ana, which is named for one of the canyons it rushes through, is a foehn wind, like the foehn of Austria and Switzerland and the hamsin of Israel. There are a number of persistent malevolent winds, perhaps the best

118

known of which are the mistral of France and the Mediterranean sirocco, but a foehn wind has distinct characteristics: it occurs on the leeward slope of a mountain range and, although the air begins as a cold mass, it is warmed as it comes down the mountain and appears finally as a hot dry wind. Whenever and wherever a foehn blows, doctors hear about headaches and nausea and allergies, about "nervousness," about "depression." In Los Angeles some teachers do not attempt to conduct formal classes during a Santa Ana, because the children become unmanageable. In Switzerland the suicide rate goes up during the foehn, and in the courts of some Swiss cantons the wind is considered a mitigating circumstance for crime. Surgeons are said to watch the wind, because blood does not clot normally during a foehn. A few years ago an Israeli physicist discovered that not only during such winds, but for the ten or twelve hours which precede them, the air carries an unusually high ratio of positive to negative ions. No one seems to know exactly why that should be; some talk about friction and others suggest solar disturbances. In any case the positive ions are there, and what an excess of positive ions does, in the simplest terms, is make people unhappy.

The Scream, by Edvard Munch, 1893

Think AND Respond

Joan Didion used this essay to create a disturbing image of the Santa Ana wind. After reading her description, how do you think a Santa Ana wind would make you feel? What types of details does she use to create the mood? What ideas does her essay give you for a subject you could explore?

119

Set a Purpose

Before students read the excerpt, focus on the side-notes. Have a volunteer locate and read aloud the dictionary definition of *wind.* Discuss the information the definition provides and the limitations of such definitions. Suggest that students read the excerpt to learn more about a specific kind of wind.

Think and Respond

Elicit Personal Responses

Discuss students' responses to the excerpt, focusing on the questions listed in Think and Respond. Have students find examples of the specific details Didion uses to describe the *foehn* wind.

Explore the Author's Techniques

To help students use the excerpt as a model for writing, review the essay as a class, discussing some of Didion's techniques. For example, point out that Didion begins with a haunting, vivid description of a Santa Ana (Page 118, paragraph 1: . . . a hot wind . . . flash point.) and then moves into a first-person description of her experience with the wind. (Page 118, paragraph 2: I could . . . why. The Pacific . . . surf.) Didion then explains some of the characteristics of a *foehn* wind (Page 119, paragraph 1: . . . it occurs . . . wind.) and its effects on the people who experience it. (Page 119, paragraph 1: In Los Angeles . . . unmanageable. In Switzerland . . . crime.)

Link Literature to Writing

Point out that Didion's definition is effective because the author herself seems excited by her subject. It is something she learned a bit about, then investigated further. Suggest that as students begin to plan their own definitions in the following assignment, they search for subjects that interest them as much as the *foehn* wind intrigues Didion. As they write, encourage them to recall how Didion used specific details to help her readers understand the characteristics and effects of her subject.

Prewrite and Explore

Objectives

1. To use prewriting activities to generate ideas for an extended definition
2. To choose a topic, gather information, and identify purpose and audience for an extended definition

Preteaching

Preview the Prewrite and Explore section. If there are skills or concepts that your students may need help with, present them at this point. The Thinking Skills Transparencies and the mini-lessons listed below may help you in your selection and instruction. The cross references in the pupil text will give students access to the same lessons for independent study.

> **Handbook Mini-Lessons**
> * Personal Techniques, pp. 317–320
> * Asking Questions, p. 327
> * Brainstorming, pp. 323–324, 329
> * Creating Charts, pp. 358–359
> * Sources of Information, pp. 476–478

Teaching Strategies

Modeling

Model the second Exploratory Activity by making a quick list of things you are well acquainted with (''teaching'' and ''learning,'' for example) as well as things you'd like to know more about (''alpine hiking,'' for example).

Stumbling Block

Some students may be diffident about revealing areas of personal knowledge or interest. Point out this definition is not intended to be a highly technical description of a complex object; it can be about anything, tangible or intangible. Point out too that the subject does not have to be new to the audience. It can be as common as a boiled egg as long as it is explained in an interesting way.

INVITATION TO Write

Joan Didion defined the term *Santa Ana* through comparisons and examples. Now it is your turn to write an extended definition of a term, object, or idea.

We all agree on the definitions of the words *friend, freedom, values, order, safety, efficiency, kindness, relationship,* and *loyalty*—right? Wrong. Every day people discuss, debate, and argue about the meanings of these words. Why? Many words—like these—stand for complex ideas that cannot be adequately covered in a brief dictionary definition. Even simple words can mean different things to different people. That's why not only in conversations but also in all kinds of writing, you will find writers providing extended definitions.

PREWRITE AND EXPLORE

HANDBOOKS
FOR HELP & PRACTICE

Personal Techniques, pp. 317–320
Asking Questions, p. 327
Brainstorming, pp. 323–324, 329
Creating Charts, pp. 358–359
Sources of Information, pp. 476–478

1. Look for ideas. Good topics are ones that you have a special knowledge about or interest in. What topics do you know enough about to explain? What concepts would you like to know more about? What ideas have you encountered that puzzled or intrigued you? If you have trouble finding a topic, the following activities may help you come up with good writing ideas.

Exploratory Activities

* **Knowledge inventory** What special knowledge do you have as a result of your studies, hobbies, extracurricular activities, or personal experiences? Freewrite about terms, objects, or concepts you could define.
* **Listing** Make a list of topics that you have experience with or that you know a great deal about or things you have never really understood but would like to understand.

Springboard

Share with students the following quote from Mark Twain, in which he describes some of the characteristics of friendship: ''The holy passion of Friendship is of so sweet and steady and loyal and enduring a nature that it will last through a whole lifetime, if not asked to lend money.'' As a warm-up activity, have students brainstorm in small groups other characteristics that might be included in a definition of *friendship*. If you wish, you might allow interested students to work together to develop the definition for this assignment. Students might take a humorous, ''Twain'' approach.

- **Asking questions**   Imagine that you are writing for an encyclopedia in the year 2055. What might you write about? Let your imagination run wild. Ask yourself some "What if" questions to come up with possible topics for encyclopedia articles of the future. You might ask, "What if creatures were discovered that swim in deep space? What would they look like? (glowing jellyfish?) What would they be called? (astroplasm?) How would they survive? (by having built-in biological nuclear reactors?)"
- **Brainstorming**   Didion's choice to write about the wind seems a bit unusual. Working alone or with a small group, brainstorm other occurrences in nature that could have a significance worth exploring.
- **Reading literature**   Think of an abstract quality demonstrated by a character in a novel or short story. For example, Rainsford in "The Most Dangerous Game" demonstrates ingenuity. Choose such a trait and define it.

2. Select a writing topic.   Look over the ideas you have come up with by doing the Exploratory Activities. You might try freewriting about one or two of the most promising ideas to decide if you want to continue with any of them. If you are not satisfied with the topic, you also might consider the ideas you experimented with in the Sketchbook on page 116, or check the "Apply Your Skills" section on page 131 for possible topics.

One student writer, Marianne, recalled a favorite children's book that contained a picture of trolls. This got her thinking about imaginary creatures, so she brainstormed the following list.

ONE STUDENT'S PROCESS

Bigfoot	Jack Frost	ghost
Easter bunny	troll	Medusa
elf	Loch Ness monster	unicorn
giant	vampire	witch
gremlin	werewolf	genie

 Individualizing Instruction

Cultural Differences   Encourage students from diverse cultural backgrounds to consider definitions of objects, customs, or other aspects of their culture that may not be familiar to other students. For example, a Native American student might explain a custom such as *potlatch* (traditional gift-giving banquet of northwest coastal Indians), or a Japanese student might define *samurai*.

LEP Students   This assignment provides many opportunities for these students to expand their English vocabularies as they look for topics and explore ways to explain the various characteristics and attributes of a subject in detail. Frequent discussion will help students make the most of these language-building experiences. For this reason, you might allow these students to work with English-proficient partners to find a subject for, plan, and develop an extended definition.

Basic Students   You might direct these students away from abstract ideas as writing topics and toward concrete objects.

Teaching Tip: Topics

Refer students to the Ideas for Writing booklet or the Data Sheets for additional ideas for topics.

Teaching Tip: Dictionary Definition

Choose a word from Marianne's list on page 121 (*troll*, for example). Read aloud the dictionary definition of *troll*. Then model how to write a dictionary-type definition in which you classify a troll and point out some of its unique characteristics. Refer to the sample definition of *shuttle*, and structure your definition in the same way, using the headings *term, group,* and *difference*. Then invite a volunteer to follow the same procedure to define the word *genie*. Suggest that students try these strategies as they begin to gather information about their subjects.

 Individualizing Instruction

Learning Styles Visual learners will find diagrams and drawings particularly useful as they explore their subjects.

Basic Students Reinforce basic students' use of reference works such as encyclopedias and dictionaries as they research their definitions.

Teaching Tip: Examples of Definition

Read aloud examples of definitions found in literary works your students are reading. Consider any genre—nonfiction, fiction, poetry, or drama. Point out any comparisons or analyses in the examples. Also see the Literature Connection below.

Many of the creatures on Marianne's list seemed childish, but the term *gremlin* caught her eye. She looked in the dictionary, which defined *gremlin* as "a small imaginary creature humorously blamed for the faulty operation of airplanes or the disruption of any procedure." She knew she had found her topic.

3. Gather supporting information. A good extended definition will elaborate on its subject with specific details. You can use many different approaches to define a term. In fact, a combination of methods usually works well. If you need help finding support, try using several of the following techniques.

Strategies

What details can I use?

- **Use a dictionary.** In addition to giving you a brief definition of the topic, what other information, like the word's history, or *etymology,* does the dictionary supply? Sometimes the dictionary will use the word in an example sentence. What other ideas does the information in the dictionary entry trigger?
- **Write a dictionary-type definition.** Think of the group to which the subject that you want to define belongs. Then think about how the subject differs from other members of the group. For example, space *shuttle* belongs to the group, space *vehicles,* but it differs from many other space vehicles because it is reusable and lands like an airplane. Your dictionary-type definition of *space shuttle* might look something like this:

Term	Group	Difference
The *shuttle* is	a space vehicle	that is reusable and that lands like an airplane.

- **Make a drawing or diagram to show what you are defining.** For example, if you were explaining an *internal-combustion engine,* you might include a diagram of the engine with parts such as pistons and spark plugs labeled.
- **Make a sensory observation chart.** Use five columns labeled *Sight, Sound, Touch, Taste,* and *Smell.* In each column write appropriate details about your topic. Find as many different words to describe the senses as you can.

Literature Connection

Story to Read You might refer students to "A Mother in Mannville" by Marjorie Kinnan Rawlings, which offers examples in an effort to define *integrity*.

- **Make a list of examples.** In defining the Santa Ana, Didion compares it to the *foehn* of Austria and Switzerland and the *hamsin* of Israel. You can also give examples of what a thing is like.
- **Describe what makes up your subject.** A definition of *Senate* might be "a federal legislative body of the United States, made up of two elected officials from each state."
- **Analyze the subject.** Tell what the parts are, how the parts are connected, and what their functions are.
- **Make a cluster.** Write the topic in the center of a piece of paper and circle it. Then around your topic list some words, ideas, people, objects, or places that you associate with your topic. Draw lines from your topic to each of your associations. Then outside the associations make notes describing their qualities or meanings. What is each like? How is each related to the main topic?

4. Clarify your goals and audience. Ask yourself, "What interesting or unusual goals could my writing have?" For example, Joan Didion wanted to create an eerie image of the Santa Ana. Then consider the form that will help you accomplish your goals. Will you write an essay, as Didion did, a more straightforward encyclopedia-type entry, a magazine article, a humorous essay, or a satire? To help you decide, also think about who your readers will be and what form will be best for their needs.

 Writer's Choice Do you want your paper to be factual (objective) or emotional (subjective)? The choice is yours and will depend a great deal on your topic.

Writing
TIP

Try exploring your subject in several of these ways and you'll have a great deal of information to choose from as you draft.

The Definition **123**

Draft and Discover

Objectives

1. To draft an extended definition, using appropriate organization of specific details
2. To respond to one's own writing and the writing of peers

Preteaching

Preview the Draft and Discover section for skills or strategies with which students may need special help. The Elaboration Worksheets from the Revision, Proofreading, and Elaboration Worksheets booklet as well as the mini-lessons listed below may be useful in your selection and instruction.

> #### Handbook Mini-Lessons
> - Types of Organization, pp. 331–334
> - Types of Elaboration, pp. 351–354
> - Choosing Appropriate Details, p. 355

Teaching Strategies

Modeling

Supply a one-sentence definition of a topic you have chosen. For example, you might say, "Alpine hiking is a sport that combines the benefits of exercise with the opportunity for an unparalleled view of the world." Show how you used classification in your one-sentence opener by classifying alpine hiking as a sport and then went on to describe two of its effects.

 #### Individualizing Instruction

Advanced Students Encourage these students to experiment with form and style, creating definitions that depart from the standard expository essay. You might suggest that they write a definition as a poem or as an extended description of an item in a catalogue.

HANDBOOKS
FOR HELP & PRACTICE

Types of Organization, pp. 331–335

Types of Elaboration, pp. 351–354

Choosing Appropriate Details, pp. 355-356

PROBLEM
S O L V I N G

How do I develop my ideas?

DRAFT AND DISCOVER

1. Begin your draft. Look over the information you have gathered and consider how you want to begin. One way is to include a one-sentence definition early in the paper. Note how Didion did this by defining *Santa Ana* in her second sentence.

2. Think about the organization of your draft. After you have given a simple definition, the way you present the rest of your information depends on the types of details you have gathered. These are some common approaches:

- **General to specific** Begin with a broad definition and then proceed to more specific details. After Didion gave the general definition of a *Santa Ana,* she went on to give specific details by comparing it to other winds and by stating its effect on people.
- **Analysis** After the first paragraph, devote each of the rest of your paragraphs to the parts, aspects, or subgroups you have identified.

- **Narration** Explain how the subject came to be as it is. Tell its background, history, and development, using chronological order.
- **Classification** Place examples of your subject, for example, *wind,* into categories such as beneficial, neutral, and destructive. Examine each category in turn.

3. Elaborate on ideas. Joan Didion used examples and sensory details to develop her ideas. What will you use? Look over the information you generated when you did the activities for "Gather

---

Science Connection

Organizational Patterns Point out that definition is often used in the expository writing found in science textbooks or magazines. Suggest that students look for excerpts in which a term is defined. Ask students to note the organization of the material and to look especially for general-to-specific, analysis, and classification patterns.

Supporting Information" on page 122. The following strategies might help you develop some of your ideas further.

Strategies

- **Description** Use as many of the five senses as practical to show what your topic is like.
- **Comparison** Compare and contrast your object with similar ones. Note how Didion compared the Santa Ana to other types of winds.
- **Metaphors and similes** Use these figures of speech to capture the reader's interest by comparing your object to something unusual.

 Writer's Choice All of the above strategies can be used to develop definition compositions. It is up to you to choose the one that will work best with your subject, purpose, and intended audience.

Marianne began her draft with a paragraph defining her central term, *gremlins*. Then she developed the rest of her composition with examples. The following is the beginning of her unrevised first draft.

ONE STUDENT'S PROCESS

A gremlin is a tiny creature that lives for one purpose and one purpose only—to mess stuff up. There are many types of gremlins. Road Gremlins. These creatures have a range that extends over the entire civilized part of the globe. However, like rats, they congregate in large congested cities. They eat holes in asphalt and concrete —causing potholes. They also burrow just beneath the surface of roads, parking lots, driveways, and so on. Computer gremlins. These little guys eat the information stored on computer disks.

4. Take a break. Then go back to your draft with a fresh eye and use questions such as the following to recognize the strengths and weaknesses in what you have written.

If possible, hold brief, spontaneous conferences with students who request them during the drafting process. This will reduce the need for on-paper troubleshooting later.

Peer Response

Remind students that they can choose any means of peer response. Some students may ask peers to answer specific questions from this page or to complete the Peer Response Guide for this assignment. Others may want peers to provide free-form comments. Students may arrange for one peer reader or several.

Revise Your Writing

Objectives

1. To evaluate the responses to a draft of an extended definition
2. To use the responses and a set of standards to revise a draft
3. To proofread for errors in spelling, grammar, usage, and mechanics

Preteaching

Preview the Revise Your Writing section. Based on this preview and your knowledge of students' drafts, identify skills and strategies that you want to review. The Student Revision Model Transparency as well as the mini-lessons listed below may be useful in your selection and instruction.

> **Handbook Mini-Lessons**
> - Unity in Compositions, p. 363
> - Coherence in Compositions, pp. 368–369
> - Sharing During Writing, p. 401
> - Using Appositives, p. 693

Teaching Strategies

Critical Thinking

Evaluating As a class, discuss the Standards for Evaluation. You might then suggest that each student review his or her draft and peer reader comments and use a scale of 1 to 5 to rate the draft on each characteristic. The values students assign to each standard will help them prioritize their revision efforts.

REVIEW YOUR WRITING

Questions for Yourself

- Would someone who had never heard of my subject understand it on the basis of what I have written?
- Did I provide the most effective details and examples to define my topic?
- Did I choose the most appropriate method of organization?

Questions for Your Peer Readers

- Were you previously familiar with the topic that I've written about? Did you learn anything new?
- What parts of my writing should I make clearer?
- Did you find my composition interesting or amusing as well as informative? What should I do to improve reader interest?
- After reading my draft, how would you define my subject? Summarize my definition.

HANDBOOKS
FOR HELP & PRACTICE

Unity in Compositions, pp. 363–364
Coherence in Compositions, pp. 368–369
Sharing During Writing, pp. 401–402
Using Appositives, pp. 693–695

REVISE YOUR WRITING

1. Evaluate your response. Review your own thoughts and the responses of your peer readers. Also keep in mind the following characteristics, which are often used to evaluate a definition:

Standards for Evaluation

An effective definition . . .

- clearly states the subject to be defined and elaborates on the general definition with specific details.
- uses description, comparison, figurative language, and other appropriate means to elaborate on ideas.
- demonstrates a clear sense of audience through the use of appropriate language and choice of details.
- has a well-developed introduction, body, and conclusion.
- uses a logical and effective organizational pattern.
- uses transitional words and phrases to show relationships among ideas.

2. Problem solve. Decide which responses you want to use and then rework your draft. Marianne made these changes in response to suggestions by one peer reader.

ONE STUDENT'S PROCESS

They also burrow just beneath the surface of roads,
¶ There are also the
parking lots, driveways, and so on. Computer gremlins.

These little guys eat the information, or data, stored on
all
computer disks. When grades get mixed up in the cen-

tral office and the **A** students get **F**'s, this is due to

computer gremlins. When the bank makes an error in

someone's account, this is due to computer gremlins.
and   the   that   all   the blame
When bills come in the mail that are wrong, this is

belongs
also due to the computer gremlins.
Some gremlins are merely irritating, like the
Transmission gremlins that cause screens to blank

out or commercials to sound louder than programs.

Computer gremlins and road gremlins are different topics. Maybe they don't belong in the same paragraph?

Good examples and details.

You keep repeating "this is due to computer gremlins." Could you change it?

Isn't the shift to transmission gremlins kind of abrupt?

Grammar TIP

Capitalize the word you are defining only if it is a proper noun —for example, Santa Ana.

The Definition **127**

Social Studies Connection

Current Events   Point out that in order for us to understand current events, we must continually learn the definitions of new terms—those associated with technological advances, new diseases, geographical features, and current issues and trends. Have each student read a newspaper to find terms that would need to be defined for a reader twenty or thirty years ago.

Circulate among those students with whom you have not yet conferred to see that the word choice in their definitions is appropriate and clear. You might share with students the following general rule on word choice from William Strunk, Jr., and E. B. White's *The Elements of Style:* ''Prefer the specific to the general, the definite to the vague, the concrete to the abstract.''

Guidelines for Evaluation
The following guidelines may be used for a close evaluation of an extended definition. See the Guidelines for Evaluating Writing in the Teacher's Resource File for additional help with holistic or analytic scoring.

Ideas and Content
- clearly states the subject of the extended definition
- classifies the subject into a larger category, if appropriate, and differentiates the subject from other members of the category
- uses specific details to develop the definition
- elaborates on ideas, using description, comparison, and figurative language as appropriate
- reflects an awareness of audience in word choice and details

Structure and Form
- contains a thorough introduction, body, and conclusion
- is organized logically
- uses transitions to indicate relationships among ideas

Grammar, Usage, and Mechanics
- uses standard grammar and usage
- uses correct spelling, capitalization, and punctuation

You might have students evaluate their own definitions, using the Guidelines for Evaluating Writing form for this assignment. Review the form, adding your own assessment. You might concentrate on ideas, content, structure, and form, rather than on grammar and mechanics.

Publish and Present

Objective

To publish and present an extended definition

Teaching Strategies

Collaborative Opportunity

Students might enjoy working in pairs or small groups to create definition posters, with one student illustrating another student's definition.

Personal Touch

If you have written an extended definition, share it by reading it aloud. Ask a few volunteers to read their definitions to the class as well.

3. Proofread your work. Make a clean copy incorporating all your changes. Then look for errors in grammar, punctuation, and spelling.

LINKING
GRAMMAR **AND** WRITING
USING APPOSITIVES

An appositive is a word or phrase that renames something. Writers often use appositives in one-sentence definitions. An appositive is set off from the rest of the sentence with commas. Appositives are sometimes introduced with *or*.

The designer's spring collection includes pants and jacket ensembles with cravats, **or neckties.**

Jimson weed, **a poisonous plant related to the tomato,** was originally called *Jamestown weed*.

The dodo, **a large, flightless bird,** was driven to extinction.

See Grammar Handbook 37, pages 693–695 for additional help with this problem.

P UBLISH AND PRESENT

HANDBOOKS
FOR HELP & PRACTICE

Publishing Your Work,
pp. 402–403

- **Make a mini-encyclopedia.** With some of your classmates, gather the definitions written by the other students in your class. After deciding on an organizational pattern such as alphabetical or subject area, join the definitions together in a booklet. Duplicate the booklet for the whole class.
- **Read your work aloud in a small group.** Take turns responding to one another's work. Limit the responses of group members to positive comments only.
- **Create definition posters.** Display them in a corner of the classroom. Find examples of your subject in magazines and newspapers and place these examples, along with your composition, on the poster.
- **Save your work in your writing portfolio.** Compare this composition with another composition you wrote several months ago.

Off the Record

"Why do I get the feeling, Miss Branson, that you're not coming back on Monday?"

Gremlins

Marianne Morley

You jump onto your bicycle, ready to tear down the street, but no, during the night, somehow, a tire went flat. You screw a new light bulb into a socket. You flip the switch. The bulb fizzles and goes out. You lay out the supplies for a school project. You turn your back for a moment. An item you absolutely need disappears. You walk down the street. Your shoelace comes untied. You bend down to tie it. It snaps in two.

These kinds of things happen all the time, but we rarely stop to think what causes them. Who lets the air out of our bicycle tires? Who puts bad light bulbs into new bulb containers? Who steals supplies when your back is turned? Who unties shoelaces and frays them so they'll break?

Gremlins do.

"What's a gremlin?" you may ask. A gremlin is a tiny creature who lives for one purpose and one purpose only—to cause trouble. No one has ever actually seen a gremlin (for all we know, they may be invisible), but we do know they exist because we see their handiwork wherever we look.

Consider the road gremlins. These creatures have a range extending over the entire civilized part of the globe, but like rats, they love to congregate in large, congested cities. They eat holes in asphalt and concrete—a

Includes an interesting and well-developed introduction

Clearly states the subject

Demonstrates clear sense of audience through use of questions and everyday language

Uses a logical organizational pattern—three types of gremlins

The Definition **129**

Discuss the model with students. Refer to Marianne's draft, and point out how she has improved her essay by developing an engaging introduction. Ask students to point out passages in the model that they found especially interesting or effective. Encourage them to explain *why* the passages are successful.

Reteaching

Assess the needs of students who were not successful in developing an extended definition and identify two or three areas in which additional practice is needed. Assign the appropriate Handbook Mini-Lessons, along with the support materials listed for each lesson. Concepts commonly requiring reteaching for this assignment are

Types of Organization: Handbook 4
Types of Elaboration: Handbook 8
Choosing Appropriate Details: Handbook 8

The following suggestions and resources may also be useful.

1. Organization Review with students the organizational patterns on page 124. Have students who had difficulty with organization make after-the-fact diagrams or outlines of their definitions, labeling them according to type, such as general to specific, analysis, and so on. If possible, work with students in groups, discussing their diagrams and outlines and suggesting other organizational patterns.

2. Details Use Thinking Skills Worksheet: Questioning to review with students ways to generate details. Then have students circle the descriptive details that strengthen their definitions. Have them draw lines through the details that do not strengthen the definitions or are not relevant. This will help students determine if they need more, fewer, or different details.

3. Grammar and Usage: Appositives From students' drafts choose pairs of sentences that might have been combined by using appositives. Work with students to combine the sentences. You might use one of the exercises in Grammar Handbook 37, Using Verbals and Appositives: The Appositive Phrase, p. 693, to provide additional practice.

Extension and Enrichment

• Poets often have favorite words—words whose sound or "feel" they like. Urge students to identify some of their favorite words and to write expressive definitions of them.

• Invite students to imagine that they are hosting a group of visitors from outer space. Their guests have asked them to name and explain the single most important quality of the human species. Suggest that students identify the quality and write a definition for the visitors.

Uses description, comparison, and figurative language to elaborate on details

Uses transitional words and phrases to show relationships among ideas

Includes a well-developed body with specific details

Provides a strong conclusion

kind of pothole pot roast. They also burrow just beneath the surface of roads, parking lots, driveways, and so on, causing little raised bumps and cracks. Millions of dollars are spent annually to repair the damage these creatures do.

There are also the computer gremlins. These little guys eat the information, or data, stored on computer disks. When grades get mixed up in the central office and all the A students get F's, when the bank makes an error in someone's account, when the bills that come in the mail are all wrong—the blame belongs to the computer gremlins.

Some gremlins are simply irritating, like the television transmission gremlins that cause screens to blank out or commercials to sound louder than programs. Other gremlins are life threatening, like the ones that tamper with the brakes of cars or the landing gear of airplanes. No facet of life is free of them, and once you become aware of their existence, you'll see them everywhere.

So, the next time you don't have your homework done, don't fall back on one of those lame old excuses like "I forgot it at home," or "It must have fallen out of my notebook," or "I accidentally dropped it into the fish tank this morning and didn't have time to recopy it." Instead, blame it on the gremlins. They'll be happy to take the credit.

WRITER TO WRITER

It is a great mistake to regard a dictionary definition as "telling us all about" a word.

S. I. Hayakawa, U.S. Senator and author

1. Reflect on your writing. Now that you have completed your composition that defines and have read several others, think about the process you followed. Ask yourself the questions below and record your answers in your writing log or attach the page you record your answers on to your definition.

- What did you learn from writing this composition that you might use in the future? In particular, what ways of defining ideas can you use in other pieces of writing?
- Of all the definitions you've read (Didion's, the student's, any of your classmates', and your own), which ones did you like the most? Why did you like them? What made these good definitions? What do you think made them good pieces of writing?

2. Apply your skills. Try your hand at one or more of the following activities.

- **Cross curricular** Choose a key term from a math or science book. Write a brief definition of the term. Then do some thinking and reading about the subject in preparation for writing a longer, extended definition.
- **Literature** Read a poem that defines an abstract term, such as "Spring is like a perhaps hand" by e.e. cummings. Then try writing your own poem. Choose an abstract term like *beauty, justice, friendship,* or *love.* Write a series of vivid, concrete images—thing you can see, touch, taste, hear, or smell—that define the term for you.
- **Related assignments** Follow the suggestions on pages 134–142 to write an extended metaphor or a comparison and contrast composition.

◀ FOR YOUR **PORTFOLIO**

The Definition **131**

Learning from Your Writing Process

Objective

To analyze and reflect upon what has been learned about the writing process and about the writing of an extended definition

Teaching Strategies

Reflecting on the Process

After students have written their responses to the first group of questions, suggest that they meet in small groups to discuss the second group of questions. Have groups summarize their discussions for the class.

Writing Portfolio

Ask students to keep their responses to the questions with their final definitions in their writing portfolios. At this point students might want to look back in their portfolios and assess which of the skills and insights they have gained thus far may help them most in future writing.

Summary and Closure

Before proceeding to the next assignment, be sure students have internalized the following key ideas:

1. An effective extended definition uses specific details to classify and explain fully a term, object, or idea.

2. Description, comparison, metaphors, and similes are often used to define a term, object, or idea.

3. Because people can disagree on the connotations of even the most familiar words, extended definition is an important communicative tool for writer and reader alike.

Give students time to summarize what they have learned by describing the characteristics of an effective extended definition and by explaining why knowing how to write extended definitions will help them in other school subjects.

Starting from Literature

Objective

To respond to a model of an extended metaphor as a springboard to writing

Teaching Strategies

Motivate

Ask students to discuss the kinds of advice parents and other adults give children. Invite volunteers to tell about advice they have been given and their response to it. Point out that the mother in the poem shares some advice with her child.

Tap Prior Knowledge

Ask students to recall times when they used a comparison to describe something. ("That soccer game was the battle of the century!") Invite examples from the class. Explain that the mother in the poem gives advice about facing life by using a special kind of a comparison.

Set a Purpose

Before students read the poem, discuss the side-column notes and review the definition of a metaphor. Make sure students understand that the poem compares life to the process of climbing a staircase. Review the purpose-setting statement at the end of the side column, and suggest that students read the poem with that purpose in mind.

Related ASSIGNMENT

Extended Metaphor

In "Mother to Son," Langston Hughes uses a metaphor, a figure of speech that makes a direct, but often subtle, comparison between two unrelated things. The mother in the poem describes her life experiences in terms of climbing a staircase.

When literal wording alone isn't adequate, writers often use metaphors to express ideas, moods, or experiences. They speak of one thing as if it were another, different thing. As you read the poem, look for details and descriptions that help you understand what kind of life the mother had.

132

MOTHER TO SON
by Langston Hughes

Well, Son, I'll tell you
Life for me ain't been no crystal stair
It's had tacks in it,
And splinters,
And boards torn up,
And places with no carpets on the floor,

Bare.
But all the time
I'se been climbin' on
And reachin' landin's
And turning corners
And sometimes goin' on in the dark
Where there ain't been no light.
So, Boy, don't you turn back.
Don't you set down on the steps
'Cause you find it's kinder hard.
Don't you fall now—
For I'se still goin', Honey,
I'se still climbin'
And life for me ain't been no crystal stair.

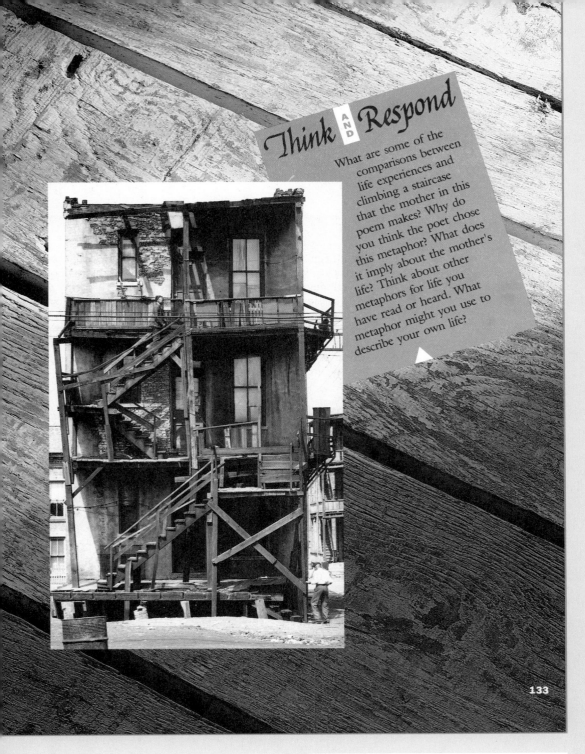

Think AND Respond

What are some of the comparisons between life experiences and climbing a staircase that the mother in this poem makes? Why do you think the poet chose this metaphor? What does it imply about the mother's life? Think about other metaphors for life you have read or heard. What metaphor might you use to describe your own life?

Think and Respond

Elicit Personal Responses

Point out the Think and Respond questions, and have students write in their journals their personal responses to the poem. At this time you might also suggest that students freewrite for several minutes in response to the last question. Then discuss the poem as a class, focusing on the specific comparisons the mother makes and how she reveals that her life has been difficult. Invite volunteers to share any metaphors for their own lives that their freewriting may have produced.

Explore the Author's Techniques

To help students identify techniques that might be helpful in their writing, direct a careful examination of the poem. For example, point out that Langston Hughes establishes the comparison in the first stanza (Page 132, stanza 1, line 2: Life . . . stair.) He continues the comparison throughout the poem, giving specific examples and painting vivid word pictures that reveal the mother's experiences. (Page 132, stanza 1, lines 3–6: It's had . . . floor . . . ; Stanza 2, lines 4–7: . . . And . . . light.) Point out too how Hughes establishes a sharp contrast through his word choice (*crystal* and *tacks, splinters, boards*). At the end of the poem, he repeats the metaphor, leaving his reader with a moving, dramatic image.

You might also point out that Hughes employs nonstandard usage, an element that adds realism and helps the reader better understand the speaker—a courageous and optimistic mother giving advice to her son.

Link Literature to Writing

Remind students that they use metaphors in their everyday speech. (''That test was a breeze.'' ''Our vacation was a disaster.'') With a little planning and imagination, students can turn those one-sentence comparisons into interesting extended metaphors. Suggest that as students develop their metaphors in the assignment that follows, they keep in mind how Langston Hughes continued the comparison throughout the poem and included specific, vivid examples.

Springboard

Share the following quotation: ''In literature, there are only oxen. The biggest ones are the geniuses—the ones who toil eighteen hours a day without tiring.'' (Jules Renard) Ask students to identify and discuss the metaphor. Suggest that students freewrite or brainstorm with partners to come up with a few metaphors that might describe them as writers.

Literature Connection

Author Note Born in Joplin, Missouri, in 1902, award-winning writer Langston Hughes was one of the greats among the many talented Harlem Renaissance artists. Hughes's works include poems, short stories, novels, nonfiction titles, and children's books. Hughes died in 1967.

Extended Metaphor **133**

Guiding Your Writers

Objectives

1. To recognize possible uses of extended metaphor
2. To choose a subject, a metaphor, and an appropriate form for an extended metaphor
3. To write, review, and share an extended metaphor

Preteaching

Preview the rest of the assignment. If there are skills or concepts with which students may need help, present them at this time. The Thinking Skills Transparencies and the mini-lessons listed below may be useful in your selection and instruction. The cross references in the pupil text will give students access to the same lessons for independent study.

> **Handbook Mini-Lessons**
> - Types of Organization, pp. 331–335
> - Denotative/Connotative Meaning, p. 411
> - Literal/Figurative Language, pp. 413–414
> - Using Correct Comparisons, pp. 634–635

Collaborative Opportunity

Provide opportunities for interested students to collaborate as they search for subjects and metaphors. Encourage students to ask themselves and one another, "Do I (you) know enough about this (the metaphor) to make several comparisons?"

INVITATION TO Write

In "Mother to Son," Langston Hughes uses an extended metaphor to compare life experiences to climbing a staircase. Now write an extended metaphor of your own in the form of a paragraph or a poem.

As with all figurative language, metaphors can help a writer achieve more exact descriptions and express more meaning than is possible with literal language. A **metaphor** links two unlike things by defining or discussing one thing in terms of the other. A metaphor does not use comparing words such as *like* or *as,* but links the two items directly. In an **extended metaphor,** two unlike things are compared throughout a piece of writing. For example, the comparison of getting through life to climbing a staircase is extended throughout Hughes's poem "Mother to Son."

UNDERSTANDING EXTENDED METAPHORS

HANDBOOKS
FOR HELP & PRACTICE

Types of Organization, pp. 331–335

Denotative/ Connotative Meaning, p. 411

Literal/Figurative Language, pp. 413–414

Using Correct Comparisons, pp. 634–635

1. Identify possible uses.   Look again at the extended metaphor in "Mother to Son." Try rewriting the poem in a few sentences of ordinary, literal language, describing the mother's life without using metaphors. Then consider how the mother's experience and advice are made more understandable and more moving by the use of the stair metaphor.

Now think about ways you can use metaphors. For example, could an extended metaphor help you clarify an explanation in a report? Describe a character in a story? Convey an image in a haiku or another kind of poem? Express your feelings about a personal experience in a poem or paragraph? Perhaps a metaphor could help you sway a reader in a persuasive piece or define an unfamiliar object or idea in an essay.

Literature Connection

Poem to Read   You may want to read aloud or suggest that students read "Dandelions" by Deborah Austin, "Training" by Demetrio Herrera, or "Fog" by Carl Sandburg, other examples of extended metaphor in poetry.

2. Choose a subject. Now consider specific subjects that might be made clearer by the use of a metaphor. You might choose a complex theory you need to explain, a personal belief you want to express, an object or idea you are trying to define, or an experience or feeling you want to share.

3. Pick a metaphor. Look for a specific metaphor to fit your subject. Brainstorm for familiar and recognizable objects, ideas, or activities that could be associated with your subject. For example, if you were trying to think of a metaphor to express the pain of separation, you might try thinking of images you associate with leave-taking, or a break or split, such as departing trains, a broken chain, or the setting sun. What connections or associations do you think led Langston Hughes to choose a staircase metaphor?

4. Choose a form. Consider whether you are more comfortable writing prose or poetry. In poetry, the sound and rhythm of the words are as important as the idea. If you choose to write prose, write a few sentences—a paragraph or two—rather than a whole essay or story.

5. Find the comparisons. Try to match the individual characteristics of the two things you are writing about. Hughes used the corners, turnings, and darkness to represent life's problems. What could you use? For example, suppose your subject is friendship and your metaphor is a garden. Parts of friendship might include the kinds or levels of friendship, traits that are important in friends, and experiences shared with friends. Your comparisons might be varieties of flowers (roses, daisies, marigolds, orchids), their traits (scent, beauty, hardiness), and types of soil and weather necessary for their growth.

WRITING AN EXTENDED METAPHOR

1. Test your metaphor. Make sure your metaphor is appropriate for your subject. Look at the ideas you've brainstormed. Is the metaphor you've chosen strong enough to sustain a poem or paragraph? If not, find another metaphor or a new theme.

2. Write your poem or narrative. Remember your purpose and the form you have chosen. For a poem, you may want to focus more on

Writing
——TIP——

In choosing a metaphor, think about things you are familiar with—football, shopping, love, or even TV, for example.

Teaching Tip: Comparisons

Students may find a comparison chart helpful as they are identifying the characteristics they will compare. To avoid stretching or forcing the metaphor, encourage students to limit their specific comparisons to three or four. You might find the Compare and Contrast Chart Thinking Skill Transparency useful.

Guidelines for Evaluation
An effective extended metaphor . . .
- describes or defines a person, object, or idea by comparing it to something else without using the words *like* or *as*
- makes a comparison that is appropriate and strong enough to support the piece of writing
- continues the comparison throughout the piece of writing
- does not include clichés or mixed metaphors
- includes expressive language that enhances the comparison

Social Studies Connection

Place Descriptions Interested students might develop a metaphor for their city or town or for places they have visited or read about. The metaphor should reflect their impressions of the place. For example, New York City may suggest a swarm of bees; Boston, a tangled web of streets, and so on.

Reteaching

Assess the needs of students who were not successful in developing an effective extended metaphor. Assign the appropriate Handbook Mini-Lessons, along with the support materials listed for each lesson. Concepts commonly requiring reteaching are

Denotative/Connotative Meaning:
Handbook 18
Literal/Figurative Language:
Handbook 18

The following suggestions and resources may also be useful.

1. Undeveloped Metaphor Students sometimes choose a suitable metaphor but have difficulty in developing descriptive details. Use the Category Questions Transparency from the Thinking Skills Transparencies to help these students develop their metaphor further. Have a volunteer offer a metaphor and discuss with students how to answer the questions. Then have students use the questions to generate details about their own metaphor before reworking their poem or paragraph.

2. Use of Clichés Remind students that an effective metaphor captures the reader's attention because it presents a new or unusual way of looking at an object or idea; it is not merely a trite comparison. For example, explain to students that to say something is ''easy as pie'' is not an example of a metaphor, but of a cliché. Have students record on index cards as many clichés as they can find. Suggest that they use the cards to create a ''Not Wanted'' bulletin board display. Have students check their poem or paragraph for these clichés and change any they find into a fresh image.

Extension and Enrichment

• Ask students to search for professional examples of extended metaphor in poems, prose, and song lyrics. You might provide class time for students to share their examples. Then have the class vote on their favorite metaphor. Before the vote is taken, you may want to allow students to campaign for their favorites by explaining why each metaphor is appealing.

a feeling or image, using poetic devices such as rhythm and, perhaps, rhyme. For prose, you will need to develop your metaphor in terms of specific comparisons.

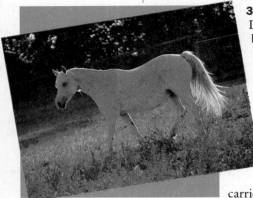

A horse of a different color.

3. Make sure your comparisons are consistent. Langston Hughes did not confuse his metaphor by mentioning unrelated details. For example, his speaker did not suddenly mention getting "stuck in the mud" in her "journey through life." Keep your metaphor on track as well.

4. Make the image fresh. Look for unusual subjects to compare or for unique ways of expressing similarities.

Although Langston Hughes's stair metaphor is not altogether new, his fresh way of expressing it and the consistency with which he carries it through his poem make it an effective and memorable comparison.

REVIEWING YOUR WRITING

1. Check the strength of your metaphor. Read your work aloud to see if the metaphor holds up throughout. Are there weak comparisons that don't seem consistent with the basic metaphor? Is there anything confusing in the way you have expressed your metaphor? Have you used the best words to convey your ideas?

2. Ask a classmate to read your poem or paragraph. Then discuss with your classmate how well your extended metaphor conveys your meaning.

PUBLISHING AND PRESENTING

• **Find a painting.** If your extended metaphor is in paragraph form, find a reproduction of fine art that represents the ideas you are trying to communicate.
• **Write a song.** Turn your poem into a song by composing music to go with the words. Perform your song on piano or guitar, or ask a friend to perform it.

On the Lightside

TEENAGER

It may come as something of a surprise, but until the 1940's teenagers did not exist. If you look in an old dictionary, the closest

you will find is *teenage*, a seldom-used term for the brushwood that is gathered to make fences and hedges. *Teen* is listed as an obsolete word for injury or misery.

There were no teenagers primarily because there was little need for the word. The group of young people between the ages of thirteen and nineteen did not have much in common. Many people in their mid- and late teens were already earning a living or raising a family, so they had little to do with their younger brothers and sisters just entering the teen years. All of that changed with the advent of universal public education in the twentieth century. When school became the common ground for young people throughout their teen years, teenagers emerged as a large and easily identifiable bloc. By the mid-1940's the word *teenager* had become a commonly used description.

Now, teenagers are perhaps the single most identifiable age group in society. Music, clothes, consumer goods, movies, television, and language all bear the stamp of teenagers and teen culture. Although the word *teenager* didn't even exist fifty years ago, today advertisers and merchants would be lost without it!

137

On the Lightside

When discussing this feature, ask students for examples of words and terms that have come into the language since they learned to speak. For example, *video cassette recorder* was not in use during their early childhood. Many of the words they mention will be as a result of technological advances.

Discuss the slang words currently in use by students. Compare them to words of the sixties, such as *groovy* and *far out*. You might suggest that students compile a dictionary of terms used by teenagers today.

Starting from Literature

Objective

To respond to a model of comparison and contrast as a springboard to writing

Teaching Strategies

Motivate

Ask students to recall two movies they have seen recently or two books they have read. Invite volunteers to describe the two items, identify the one they preferred, and explain their reasons.

Tap Prior Knowledge

Ask students to think about the last thing they purchased, such as a piece of clothing, a tape, or a magazine. How did they decide what to buy? Did they have to make a choice between two or more items? What factors did they consider in order to make the decision?

Set a Purpose

Point out that many decisions are based on comparison and contrast, or an analysis of how two things are alike and different. Voters, for example, compare candidates before going to the polls; employers compare the backgrounds and experience of prospective employees. Refer students to the side-column notes, and emphasize that comparison can also be used to deepen understanding of something. Point out the purpose-setting statement at the end of the side column. Have students read the excerpt with that purpose in mind.

Related **ASSIGNMENT**

Comparison and Contrast

FROM
FIFTH CHINESE DAUGHTER
JADE SNOW WONG

Is your favorite music different from the kind your parents like? Are the clothes you are wearing now the same as the ones you wore a year or two ago? Why wasn't the sequel to last year's blockbuster movie as good as the original? To analyze and describe similarities and differences, writers use comparison and contrast.

In *Fifth Chinese Daughter,* Jade Snow Wong compares her Chinese upbringing with that of a typical American classmate. As you read the excerpt, think about what the author learns about herself by making this comparison.

There was good to be gained from both [cultures] if she could find the right combination. She studied her neighbor in class, Stella Green, for clues.

Stella had grown up reading Robert Louis Stevenson, learning to swim and play tennis, developing a taste for roast beef, mashed potatoes, sweets, aspirin tablets, and soda pop, and she looked upon her mother and father as friends. But it was very unlikely that she knew where her great-grandfather was born, or whether or not she was related to another strange Green she might chance to meet.

Jade Snow had grown up reading Confucius, learning to embroider and cook rice, developing a taste for steamed fish and bean sprouts, tea, and herbs, and she thought of her parents as people to be obeyed. She not only knew where her ancestors were born but where they were buried, and how many chickens and

138

roast pigs should be brought annually to their graves to feast their spirits. She knew all of the branches of the Wong family, the relation of each to the other, and understood why Daddy must help support the distant cousins in China who bore the sole responsibility of carrying on the family heritage by periodic visits to the burial grounds in Fragrant Mountains. She knew that one could purchase in a Chinese stationery store the printed record of her family tree relating their Wong line and other Wong lines back to the original Wong ancestors.

Golden Pheasant

*Quilt, Star of Bethlehem.
Cotton, printed, pieced and
applique. 120 x 120 inches
The Metropolitan Museum of Art,
Sansbury-Mills Art Fund, 1973*

Think AND Respond

What points about her upbringing did Jade Snow Wong compare with Stella Green's? Why do you think she chose these particular aspects of her life to focus on? How could you use a comparison to understand something better or to help you make a choice?

139

Springboard

You may wish to share the following Chinese proverb during discussion of the excerpt from *Fifth Chinese Daughter:* "To forget one's ancestors is to be a brook without a source, a tree without a root." Ask students how the proverb relates to the traditions practiced by the Wong family.

Literature Connection

Author Note Jade Snow Wong was born in San Francisco in 1922. Her autobiography, *Fifth Chinese Daughter,* from which the excerpt was taken, was published in 1950. Wong's other publications include *No Chinese Stranger* and *The Immigrant Experience,* both works of nonfiction. In addition to being a writer, Jade Snow Wong is also a potter.

Think and Respond

Elicit Personal Responses

Suggest that students use the Think and Respond questions to help them formulate their reactions to the selection. After students have written their personal responses, discuss the characteristics of each culture that Jade Snow Wong chose to compare.

Explore the Author's Techniques

You can help your students improve their writing by encouraging them to experiment with the techniques of fine writers. To that end, discuss the techniques used by Jade Snow Wong in the selection from *Fifth Chinese Daughter.* For example, point out that she first describes, by providing specific examples, certain characteristics of her American classmate's culture. (Page 138, paragraph 2: Stella . . . friends. But . . . meet.) In this paragraph, Wong establishes the points of comparison—activities, tastes, attitudes toward parents, knowledge of family. She then contrasts, or shows the differences between, the two cultures by giving specific examples of those same characteristics or features in her culture. Wong describes each attribute in the same order, concluding with what she most likely perceives as the greatest difference between them—knowledge of ancestors. (Page 138, paragraph 3: Jade . . . obeyed. Page 139, paragraph 1: She . . . spirits. She . . . mountains. She . . . ancestors.)

Link Literature to Writing

Remind students that they frequently make comparisons. They may compare the qualities of various friends, the advantages of one method of study over that of another, or like Jade Snow Wong, compare aspects of their lives with that of others. Explain to students that the following assignment will help them develop their own comparisons. Suggest that as students write, they recall how Jade Snow Wong compared certain characteristics of two subjects by providing specific examples.

Guiding Your Writers

Objectives

1. To identify two items and a purpose for a comparison
2. To choose and organize points of comparison
3. To write, review, publish and share a comparison

Preteaching

After reviewing the rest of the assignment, determine whether you want to review specific skills and concepts before students begin to write. The Thinking Skills Transparencies and the mini-lessons listed below may help you plan that instruction. The cross references in the pupil text will give students access to the same lessons for independent study.

Handbook Mini-Lessons

- Elaboration, pp. 351–354
- Creating Charts, pp. 358–359
- Coherence in Compositions, pp. 368–369
- Using Specific Words, pp. 383–385

Teaching Strategies

Modeling

Consider illustrating comparison and contrast by drawing a Venn diagram on the board. You might use yourself and another teacher or Stella and Jade Snow Wong as subjects. Draw two overlapping circles, and write the name of the first subject in one circle and the second subject in the other. List shared characteristics or similarities in the intersecting part of the circles and distinguishing characteristics or differences in the outer part of each circle. Suggest that students might want to use such a device as they explore their potential subjects.

INVITATION TO Write

Jade Snow Wong learned a great deal about her own upbringing by comparing it with her classmate's. Now write a comparison of your own in which you explain how two people or things are alike and how they are different.

You make comparisons every day—choosing between two items on a menu or judging the competing claims of products, for example. When you compare and contrast items like these, you must first break each subject into its component parts, much as you did when writing a definition. You can then identify the specific ways each subject is similar to or different from the other. When you present the results of your comparison in a formal essay, you are both providing information and offering judgments to your reader.

HANDBOOKS
FOR HELP & PRACTICE

Elaboration, pp. 351–354

Creating Charts, pp. 358–359

Coherence in Compositions, pp. 368–369

Using Specific Words, pp. 383–385

PREPARING THE COMPARISON

1. Give yourself a purpose. There are many reasons for writing comparisons. You might want to learn about an unfamiliar object by comparing it to something familiar. You might compare two products or ideas in order to persuade your audience that one is better. You might want to write a review, comparing a book or movie to certain criteria or standards. Sometimes, you can even find a solution to a problem by comparing the advantages and disadvantages of two different courses of action.

2. Decide what you will compare. A comparison works best when the items share certain important characteristics or features. For example, you could compare playing a violin with playing an electric guitar, but since the two are so different, you are not likely to find any interesting parallels or understand either one any better as a result of comparing them. On the other hand, if you were to compare popular music of the 1990's with music of the 1950's, you are more likely to gain new insights into both.

Humanities Connection

Music and Art Interested students may want to compare two kinds of music, focusing on similarities in instruments, lyrics, and so on. Or students might compare two styles of painting, two works by a particular artist, or the techniques of two different artists.

3. Choose features that will help you accomplish your purpose.
Since Jade Snow Wong's purpose was to understand her own family background better, she chose to compare everyday features of her upbringing with those of her classmate's. Similarly, if your purpose is to discover how popular music reflects the concerns of listeners, you will choose to compare features like instruments used, content of songs, and concert styles.

4. Chart your points of comparison. Charting is a technique that lets you see relationships among features. Understanding these relationships can help you decide how to organize the ideas in your essay. To begin your chart, draw three columns. Label the first column "Points of Comparison," and under it, list the features you are comparing. On the top of the second and third columns, write the names of the items you are comparing—"1950's" and "1990's" for example. Then fill in the last two columns with notes summarizing the results of your comparison. How sharp are the distinctions between the two things? Have you discovered more similarities than differences or vice versa?

WRITING A COMPARISON

1. Choose an organizational pattern. There are two basic patterns for organizing the points of comparison. Using the **subject-by-subject** pattern, you would discuss all the features about one subject and then discuss all the features about the other. Ms. Wong uses this pattern in first describing Stella Green's upbringing and then her own. A second option is **feature-by-feature** comparison. Following this pattern, you would move back and forth between the two subjects, comparing and contrasting each feature.

2. Begin writing. Relax as you begin to put your ideas on paper. You can always make revisions later. Remember your purpose for comparing the items you are writing about. Support your purpose with persuasive language and good examples.

3. Give specific examples. Vivid examples help the reader visualize the things being compared. Jade Snow Wong, for example, notes Stella's "taste for roast beef, mashed potatoes, sweets, aspirin tablets, and soda pop" and her own "taste for steamed fish and bean sprouts, tea, and herbs." These specific examples reinforce the difference between the two girls' lives.

Comparison/Contrast **141**

Guidelines for Evaluation

Good comparisons . . .

- show how two objects, persons, or ideas are alike and different
- reflect a clear purpose
- contain specific, vivid examples
- use either a subject-by-subject or feature-by-feature organizational pattern
- include transitional words and phrases that signal similarities or differences
- display standard grammar and usage
- include correct capitalization, spelling, and punctuation

Reteaching

Assess the needs of students who were not successful in developing an effective comparison. Assign the appropriate Handbook Mini-Lessons, along with the support materials listed for each lesson. Concepts commonly requiring reteaching for this assignment are

Elaboration: Handbook 8
Coherence in Compositions: Handbook 10

The following suggestions and resources may also be useful.

1. Lack of Similarities and Differences Remind students that the purpose of a comparison is to point out similarities and differences. Work with those students who had difficulty coming up with and organizing these characteristics. Model on the board a list of similarities and differences between two concrete objects such as a typewriter and a computer. Work with students to identify points of comparison such as physical components, uses, and cost. Then have students make the same kind of list for their topic before they rework their comparison.

2. Lack of Coherence Review the transitional devices in Handbook 10, pages 364–366, with students whose comparisons are choppy. Suggest that students review their comparisons and locate each similarity and difference. Have students note whether they used a transitional word or phrase to signal the similarity or difference. If they have not, suggest that they add a transition so that their ideas will flow smoothly.

4. Include contrasting details. Contrasting, or pointing out differences, can be a good way to explore your subject. In a comparison of popular music eras, for example, you might write, "Popular music groups today give highly theatrical concert performances featuring flashing lights, dance movements, and various special effects. In the 1950's, however, concerts were simpler with emphasis on songs about the feelings and problems of youth." This use of a specific contrasting detail makes your point more effectively than simply writing, "Concerts today are more complex than concerts in the 1950's."

5. Use transitional words and phrases. *Likewise, both, similarly,* and *in the same way* help point out similarities. Differences can be indicated by words and phrases like *but, instead, on the other hand, however, in contrast to,* and *on the contrary.*

REVIEWING YOUR WRITING

1. Read and evaluate your comparison. Have you shown how the two persons or things are alike, while clearly making a distinction between them? Is your purpose for making the comparison clear? Are your examples vivid and specific?

2. Ask your classmates to read your comparison. Ask your readers to summarize the main points of your comparison. Do their summaries agree with what you intended to say? If not, what revisions would make your meaning clear?

3. Revise your comparison. Do you need to add one or more points of comparison? Do you need to trim or expand your writing in certain places? Will a different choice of words make a point clearer or more persuasive?

PUBLISHING AND PRESENTING

- **Prepare a chart that sums up your points of comparison.** Post this chart along with your first and final drafts as an illustration of the writing process.
- **Present your comparison orally.** This would be especially appropriate if your comparison reviews a book or movie or describes an interesting or unusual object. After reading, ask classmates for questions that explore the points you have compared.

142   Workshop 4

Social Studies Connection

Using Textbooks Suggest that students peruse their social studies textbooks for comparisons of groups of people, civilizations, major historical events, or historical figures. Encourage students to evaluate the comparisons by considering the following questions: What features of the subjects are compared? Does the comparison include vivid examples? How is the comparison organized? Interested students may find subjects that they want to investigate further and use as the basis for another comparison.

Sentence

Inverted Word Order

Experienced writers sometimes achieve variety in their sentences by changing the traditional order of words. Compare the two sentences below.

Little <u>ants</u> <u><u>ran</u></u> over the gray skin of the face.
Over the gray skin of the face <u><u>ran</u></u> little <u>ants</u>.

Stephen Crane, *The Red Badge of Courage*

In the first sentence, the subject (underlined once) comes before the verb; in the second, the verb (underlined twice) comes first. Inverting the usual subject-verb order draws attention to words and phrases other than the subject of the sentence. It also allows the writer to begin a sentence in an unusual way.

MODELS

1. Over the gray skin of the face <u>ran</u> little <u>ants</u>.
   Stephen Crane, *The Red Badge of Courage*

2. Sad <u>were</u> the <u>lights</u> in the houses opposite.
   Katherine Mansfield, "A Cup of Tea"

3. Here <u>lies</u> a <u>lady</u> of beauty and high degree.
   John Crowe Ransom, "Here Lies a Lady"

A. Rearranging Sentences The following original sentences have been changed so that the subject appears before the verb. Rearrange each sentence so that the verb comes before the subject. Use the words in parenthesis to begin and end the sentences.

1. The <u>feet</u> of three flying policemen <u>pounded</u> down the steps and upon the platform. (Down / policemen)   **Henry Sydnor Harrison, "Miss Hinch"**

2. This humble <u>kitchen</u> <u>was</u> a strange place for such occupants! (A / kitchen)
   Charlotte Brontë, *Jane Eyre*

3. The <u>chanter</u> <u>sat</u> reading the Psalter in a low steady tone in the far corners.
   (In / tone)   **Leo Tolstoy, "Childhood, Boyhood, Youth"**

4. A <u>girl</u> <u>was lying</u> face downwards quite still on the ground, with her arms clasping the trunk of a large tree. (Lying / girl)

Elizabeth Howard, "Three Miles Up"

Objectives

1. To rearrange sentences so that the verb precedes the subject
2. To write sentences that imitate professional models with inverted subject-verb order
3. To combine sentences to match professional models with inverted subject-verb order
4. To write a paragraph containing sentence imitations

Preteaching

These exercises focus on the use of inverted subject-verb order to achieve sentence variety. You may want to review or refer students to Grammar Handbook 29, The Sentence and Its Parts: Subjects in Unusual Positions, pp. 508–509; and Grammar Handbook 35, Using Prepositions, Conjunctions, and Interjections: What Is a Preposition? pp. 652–654.

ANSWER KEY

A. Rearranging Sentences

1. Down the steps and upon the platform pounded the feet of three flying policemen.
2. A strange place for such occupants was this humble kitchen!
3. In the far corners sat the chanter reading the Psalter in a low steady tone.
4. Lying face downwards quite still on the ground, with her arms clasping the trunk of a large tree, was a girl.

B. Imitating Sentences

Answers will vary.

B. Imitating Sentences In each model sentence the verb appears before the subject. Write a sentence that imitates the structure of each model sentence.

Important: Imitate as many of the sentence parts as possible, not just the part where the verb appears before the subject.

> ***Example***   Over the gray skin of the face <u>ran</u> little <u>ants</u>.
> **Stephen Crane, *The Red Badge of Courage***

> ***Imitation***   Through the canyons near the ravine <u>flew</u> majestic <u>eagles</u>.

1. On the table in the middle of the room <u>lay</u> the <u>coffin</u>.
   Leo Tolstoy, "Childhood, Boyhood, Youth"

2. There <u>sat</u> my <u>mother</u>
   With the harp against her shoulder,
   Looking nineteen,
   And not a day older.
   Edna St. Vincent Millay, "The Ballad of the Harp Weaver"

3. Deep down here by the dark water <u>lived</u> old <u>Gollum,</u> a small slimy creature.
   J.R. R. Tolkien, *The Hobbit*

4. There, lying to one side of an immense bed, <u>lay grandpa</u>.
   Katherine Mansfield, "The Voyage"

C. Combining Sentences The model sentences below, from a paragraph in John Steinbeck's *Of Mice and Men,* describe the interior of a bunkhouse. Use the skills you learned on page 53 to break down each sentence into its parts. Then combine the sentences listed below each model to create a sentence that matches the structure of each Steinbeck sentence. You will create a paragraph that describes a theater complex.

> ***Example***   In three walls there were small, square windows, and in the fourth, a solid door with a wooden latch.
> a. On two levels there were theaters.
> b. The theaters were small, intimate.
> c. On the third there was a grand auditorium for widescreen movies.

> ***Combined Sentence***   On two levels there were small, intimate theaters, and on the third, a grand auditorium for widescreen movies.

1. Against the walls were eight bunk beds, five of them made up with blankets, the other three unmade, exposing the burlap ticking on their mattresses.
   a. In the lobby were five concession counters.
   b. Four of them were jammed with customers.
   c. The other one was deserted.
   d. The deserted one was showing a "closed" sign on the countertop.

2. Over each bunk there was nailed a wooden apple crate containing two wooden shelves for the personal possessions of the occupant of the bunk.
   a. Over the concession counters was suspended a giant marquee.
   b. The marquee was listing show times.
   c. The show times were for all the movies playing at the theaters.

3. On these shelves were loaded little articles: soap, shaving cream, combs, brushes, razors, and medicines.
   a. On this marquee were featured many attractions.
   b. The attractions were dramas, adventures, mysteries, and comedies.

4. Near one wall there was a black cast-iron stove, its stovepipe going straight up through the ceiling.
   a. Across from the concession counters there was a staircase.
   b. The staircase was magnificent, red-carpeted.
   c. Its steps were leading up to the main auditorium.

5. In the middle of the room stood a big square table littered with playing cards, and around it were wooden apple boxes for the card players to sit on.
   a. On the stage of the auditorium hung a plush velvet curtain.
   b. The curtain was bordered with gold trim.
   c. Behind it was the silver screen.
   d. The screen was for the movie to project on.

Application Write a paragraph describing your room at home, one of your classrooms, or some other place. Include sentences that have the same structure as some of the model sentences from John Steinbeck's paragraph describing the bunkhouse. Underline your sentence imitations.

Grammar Refresher In the sentences in this workshop, the verb comes before the subject. To learn more about inverted subject-verb order, see Handbook 29, pages 508–509. Also, many of the sentences begin with prepositional phrases. See Handbook 35, pages 653–654 to learn more about introductory prepositional phrases.

Sentence Composing **145**

5

Informative Exposition: Analysis

Overview

Informative exposition, writing that explains or informs, can take several forms: classification, as in Workshop 4, and in this Workshop, analysis. Students will apply analysis by describing a process, which, in turn, will lead to better understanding of whole/part relationships and sequencing. These skills are essential for most kinds of writing and much everyday oral communication as well. Workshop 5 includes the following Guided and Related Assignments:

1. **Guided: Describing a Process** builds fundamental analytical skills by inviting students to describe a process based on personal experience or reading.

2. **Related: Cause-and-Effect Analysis** helps develop the skill of identifying patterns of cause and effect, within the context of process description.

3. **Related: Flowchart** further develops skills introduced in the Guided Assignment by asking students to analyze a process in visual form.

Teaching Preview

Preparation Guide

1. Use the Overview on this page and the Teacher's Choice descriptions on page 147 as a basis for deciding which assignment(s) to teach.

2. Preview the assignments and the teacher's notes and identify concerns that may require preteaching or extra support given your class's abilities. The handbook mini-lessons suggested within the lesson may also provide guidance.

3. Preview the chart below for support materials in the Teacher's Resource File that may be used with this Workshop. Resources are for use with the Guided Assignment unless otherwise noted.

Support Materials

WRITER'S CRAFT RESOURCES

Prewrite and Explore
Thinking Skills Transparencies, pp. 15–16
Thinking Skills Worksheets, p. 10

Draft and Discover
Elaboration, Revision, and Proofreading Worksheets, p. 9

Revise Your Writing
Guidelines for Writing Assessment and Portfolio Use, pp. 12, 31
Peer Response Guides, pp. 17–18
Student Revision Model Transparencies, pp. 19–22
Elaboration, Revision, and Proofreading Worksheets, p. 10

Assessment
Tests and Writing Assessment Prompts, p. 5

Extension Activities
Writing Prompts for Fine Art Transparencies, pp. 7, 9, 15, 19, 20, 21
Writing from Literature, pp. 1–2, 11–14, 21–22, 25–28, 31–32, 43–44
Standardized Test Practice

 Educational Technology (available separately)
Writer's DataBank
Electronic English Handbook
Multimedia Workshop
Your Personal Trainer for the New SAT
In Perspective (videodisc)

● ●

OTHER RESOURCES

Books and Journals
Claggett, Fran. *Drawing Your Own Conclusions: Mapping Metaphors in the English Classroom:* Portsmouth: Boynton, 1992.

 Films and Videos
Branches of Government Series. National Geographic Society. Color film or color video. (22–23 min each)
Luther's Choice. Films for the Humanities and Science. (56 min.)

Writing Skills—The Stages of Writing. Beacon Films. (15 min.)

 Computer Software
ClarisWorks. Vers.2.0. Claris. Macintosh.
Inspiration. Vers. 4. Inspiration Software. Macintosh.

Workshop Management Guidelines

The chart below indicates the number of days recommended for each phase of the Guided and Related Assignments. Stars indicate portions of the assignment that may be completed outside the classroom if time is limited or if teachers wish the activity to be completed by students independently.

DESCRIBING A PROCESS

Starting from Literature ....1 day
Prewrite ....1–2 days*
Draft ....1–2 days*
Revise ....1–2 days*
Publish ....1–2 days
Learning ....1 day*
Reteaching ....open
Extension/Enrichment.....................open*
Sentence Composing......................1 day*

CAUSE-AND-EFFECT ANALYSIS

Starting from Literature ....1 day
Preparing...1 day*
Drafting ....1–2 days*
Reviewing...1 day*
Publishing...................................1–2 days

FLOWCHART

Starting from Literature ....1 day
Planning ....1 day*
Drawing ....1 day*
Reviewing..1 day*
Publishing....................................1–2 days

Linking Literature, Writing, and Grammar

The following options may be used to provide students with an integrated language experience. Begin by assigning and discussing any of the recommended pieces of literature. Use the suggested strategy to provide a link to the Guided Assignment.

LINKING LITERATURE AND WRITING

Option 1

Starting Point: "Slice of Life" by Russell Baker on pages 148–149 of *The Writer's Craft*

Strategy: Use the teaching suggestions on pages 148–149 to lead students into the Guided Assignment.

Option 2

Starting Point: *The Miracle Worker* by William Gibson on pages 631–701 of McDougal, Littell's *Literature and Language,* Grade 9.

Strategy: As students read, respond to, and perhaps act out this play, have them consider Anne Sullivan's work with Helen Keller as a process. Sullivan undoubtedly arrived at the Keller home with certain ideas about how the process would work. As she launched into it, she had to adjust to difficult conditions. Encourage students to recognize that examining a process may lead to unexpected insights and then introduce the Guided Assignment.

Option 3

Starting Point: "How to Tell a Story" by Mark Twain

Strategy: As students read this essay, have them note the specific, pragmatic points Twain makes. Present the essay to students both as a description of the storytelling process and as an example of how entertaining and individualistic a process description can be. Have students share responses to particular passages that amuse, inform, or both. As a further example of humor used in the description of process, have students read Russell Baker's "Slice of Life" on pages 148–149 and lead them into the Guided Assignment.

LINKING WRITING AND GRAMMAR

Before the drafting or revision stage of this assignment, tell students that process descriptions often involve repeated use of pronouns. Point out that it is critical for readers to understand to whom or what a pronoun refers. Have students find pronouns with ambiguous referents as you write the following on the board.

Faulty: Ted and Janet were supposed to give us tickets to the concert, but we ended up going to the theater without them.

Correct: Ted and Janet were supposed to give us tickets to the concert, but we ended up going to the theater without the tickets.

Faulty: Richard saw the paper clips underneath the rubber bands, so he picked them up.

Correct: Richard saw the paper clips underneath the rubber bands, so he picked up the paper clips.

Go over the rules for pronoun usage on pages 568–569 of the Grammar and Usage Handbook. If problems having to do with pronouns still appear on student papers, assign the exercises on those pages for reteaching. Additional practice can be found in the *Grammar and Usage Practice Book* on pages 53–54.

Sketchbook

Objective

To use a literary excerpt as a springboard to informal writing

Using the Prompt

The writing activities suggested in the Sketchbook are designed to be informal and ungraded so that students feel free to experiment and to take risks.

The idea of a time machine has captured the imagination of people of all generations. Have students name movies and television programs that incorporate the idea of time travel. Some examples might be *Back to the Future* and *Star Trek*. As you discuss the excerpt and the questions that follow it, have volunteers tell about a time machine of their own creation and about where this machine might take them. Suggest that students think about their destination and about one thing they might teach or learn from the people they meet. Some students might want to work collaboratively, brainstorming ideas with a partner or in a small group before writing their responses. Students may also use the idea in the Additional Sketches section as an alternative to the time travel prompt.

Suggest that students save their writing activities for possible use in the workshop that follows.

Sketchbook

It was at ten o'clock to-day that the first of all Time Machines began its career. I gave it a last tap, tried all the screws again, put one more drop of oil on the quartz rod, and sat myself in the saddle. . . .

H. G. Wells
THE TIME MACHINE

What if a time machine took you to another era? What age would you like to have lived in? How would your life have been different then? How would it have been the same? What could you learn from the people living in that time period? What could you teach them?

Additional Sketches

How do they do that? How does it work?

Write a recipe. It could be directions for cooking something, but it doesn't have to be. It could be a recipe for success, for happiness, or for anything else you can think of.

146

WRITER'S **5** WORKSHOP

Informative Exposition: Analysis

Guided Assignment
DESCRIBING A PROCESS

Related Assignment
CAUSE-EFFECT ANALYSIS

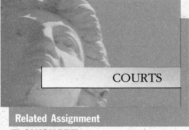

COURTS

Related Assignment
FLOWCHART

Y ou're in charge of lighting for the school play when suddenly all the lights go out. Fortunately the shop teacher has taught you how to analyze the problem—how to look at it closely to see what's happening—and what steps to take to deal with it. Quickly, you are able to locate the problem and fix it so the show can go on. When someone tells you how to do something, how something happens, or how something works, he or she is explaining a process. In this workshop you will explore a process you are curious about and share your knowledge with others. You will then apply your insights about describing a process to a cause-effect analysis and a flowchart.

147

Objectives

Guided Assignment:
DESCRIBING A PROCESS
To recognize the explanation of a process and to use prewriting activities to plan a process description and to draft, revise, proofread, and share a process description essay

Related Assignment:
CAUSE-AND-EFFECT ANALYSIS
To plan, write, review, and share a cause-and-effect analysis

Related Assignment:
FLOWCHART
To plan, make, revise, and share a flowchart of a process

Teacher's Choice

The following information may help you choose the assignments that best fit the needs and interests of your students.

Guided Assignment
Describing a Process Process descriptions help students become comfortable with accurate, detailed description and chronological order. This Guided Assignment may be most useful early in the year as preparation for cross-curricular writing.

Related Assignment
Cause-and-Effect Analysis This assignment helps students learn to analyze events or situations to determine cause-and-effect relationships, a skill that will prove useful in the study of literature, science, and social studies.

Flowchart Because this assignment teaches students how to present a detailed process in a visual format, it is especially appropriate for visual learners. The assignment also reinforces the ability to interpret information presented graphically, a skill students can apply in social studies, science, and mathematics.

Assignment Rationale

A process description explains how to do a particular thing or how something works or happens. In writing such a description, students learn to analyze the process, identify the necessary steps, describe the steps clearly and completely, and arrange them in logical order. This assignment fosters the ability to analyze and to think clearly and logically, skills that are essential in any kind of writing as well as in any practical field of endeavor.

Starting from Literature

Objective

To respond to a professional model of a process description as a springboard to writing

Teaching Strategies

Motivate

Ask students who carves the Thanksgiving turkey at their home and if that chore or any other chore has ever caused any problems. Elicit from students any humorous incidents that they may remember.

Tap Prior Knowledge

Have students speculate on the process of carving a turkey or completing some other task. Could they explain the process? Invite volunteers to describe briefly how to do a familiar household chore.

Guided ASSIGNMENT

Describing a Process

from "Slice of Life"
by Russell Baker

How to carve a turkey:

Have you ever heard of Murphy's Law, which states that "Everything that can go wrong will go wrong"? Russell Baker's explanation of how to carve a turkey presents a hilarious case of Murphy's Law in action. The essay itself, however, is an example of something well done. It explains a process so clearly, completely, and engagingly that you can "see" each step. As you read, notice how Baker helps you follow each step in a complicated, if slightly odd, process.

148

Assemble the following tools—carving knife, stone for sharpening carving knife, hot water, soap, wash cloth, two bath towels, barbells, meat cleaver. If the house lacks a meat cleaver, an ax may be substituted. If it is, add bandages, sutures and iodine to above list.

Begin by moving the turkey from roasting pan to a suitable carving area. This is done by inserting the carving knife into the posterior stuffed area of the turkey and the knife-sharpening stone into the stuffed area under the neck.

Thus skewered, the turkey may be lifted out of the hot grease with relative safety. Should the turkey drop to the floor, however, remove the knife and stone, roll the turkey gingerly in the two bath towels, wrap them several times around it and lift the encased fowl to the carving place.

You are now ready to begin carving. Sharpen the knife on the stone and insert it where the thigh joins the torso. If you do this correctly, which is improbable, the knife will almost immediately encounter a barrier of bone and gristle. This may very well be the joint. It could, however, be your thumb. If not, execute a vigorous sawing motion until satisfied that the knife has been defeated. Withdraw the knife and ask someone nearby, in as testy a manner as possible, why the knives at your house are not kept in better carving condition.

Exercise the biceps and forearms by lifting barbells until they are strong enough for you to tackle the leg joint with bare hands. Wrapping one hand firmly around the thigh, seize the turkey's torso in the other hand and scream. Run cold water over hands to relieve pain of burns.

Now, take a bath towel in each hand and repeat the above maneuver. The entire leg should snap away from the chassis with a distant crack, and the rest of the turkey, obedient to Newton's law about equal and opposite reactions, will probably come to rest in someone's lap.

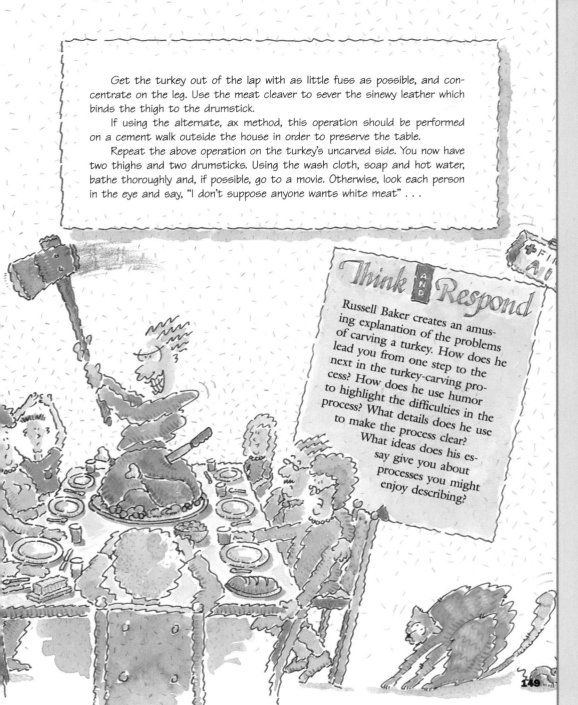

Get the turkey out of the lap with as little fuss as possible, and concentrate on the leg. Use the meat cleaver to sever the sinewy leather which binds the thigh to the drumstick.

If using the alternate, ax method, this operation should be performed on a cement walk outside the house in order to preserve the table.

Repeat the above operation on the turkey's uncarved side. You now have two thighs and two drumsticks. Using the wash cloth, soap and hot water, bathe thoroughly and, if possible, go to a movie. Otherwise, look each person in the eye and say, "I don't suppose anyone wants white meat" . . .

Think AND Respond

Russell Baker creates an amusing explanation of the problems of carving a turkey. How does he lead you from one step to the next in the turkey-carving process? How does he use humor to highlight the difficulties in the process? What details does he use to make the process clear? What ideas does his essay give you about processes you might enjoy describing?

149

Literature Connection

Author Note Russell Wayne Baker, a columnist for *The New York Times*, has won two Pulitzer Prizes. The first was awarded for distinguished commentary in 1979; the second in 1983 for *Growing Up*. Sometimes compared to Mark Twain and James Thurber, Baker has a fine, humorous style as seen in this excerpt from ''Slice of Life.''

Set a Purpose

Before students read the excerpt, discuss the side-column notes. Emphasize that, although Russell Baker's account is written tongue-in-cheek, it does provide a model of an effective description of a process. Have students read the excerpt, keeping in mind the purpose-setting statement given at the end of the side-column.

Think and Respond

Elicit Personal Responses

Before discussing the excerpt, have students write their personal responses in their journals or learning logs. After allowing sufficient time for them to formulate responses, encourage students to share their responses, focusing on the details Baker includes.

Explore the Author's Techniques

As you guide students through a close reading of the piece, have them note the order in which the process is described and the techniques the writer uses to draw the reader in. For example, in listing the tools for carving, Baker includes items such as a bar of soap and bath towels. The reader is instantly aware that something funny is in store. However, Baker uses clear transitional devices (Page 148, paragraph 6: Now, . . . maneuver.) and proceeds to follow strict chronological order. His use of precise, descriptive words (Page 148, paragraph 1: Assemble . . . cleaver. If it is . . . list. Paragraph 5: Wrapping . . . scream. Page 149, paragraph 1: Use . . . drumstick.) creates an interesting counterpoint to the ludicrous results of his efforts.

Link Literature to Writing

Point out that Baker wrote his description of a process to entertain rather than to inform. However, his word choice and logical ordering of details make his essay a model for the description of any process. Explain that in the following Guided Assignment students will have the opportunity to choose a topic and formulate their own process description. Suggest that as students write, they remember the use of precise words and logically ordered details that they saw in Baker's essay.

Prewrite and Explore

Objectives

1. To use prewriting activities to generate ideas for a description of a process
2. To select a topic and explore goals and audience for a process description
3. To gather and organize information for a process description

Preteaching

Preview the Prewrite and Explore section. If there are skills or concepts that your students may need help with, present them at this point. The following mini-lesson references may help you in your selection and instruction. The cross-references in the pupil text will give students access to the same lessons for independent study.

Handbook Mini-Lessons

- Sharing Techniques, pp. 323–325
- Appropriate Details, p. 355
- Solving Problems, pp. 456–458
- Sources of Information, pp. 476–478
- Interviewing Skills, pp. 481–482

Teaching Strategies

Modeling

Show a videotape of a professional football or basketball player in action. If possible, show the action in slow motion. Encourage students to identify the steps followed and list them on the board. If videotapes are unavailable, you might have a student athlete pantomime the steps used to complete an action and list them on the board.

Individualizing Instruction

LEP Students Encourage students to identify processes with which they are familiar and to dramatize or sketch the steps for a peer who can help supply English words.

Russell Baker provided comical instructions for carving a turkey. Now write your own description of a process—one that shows how to do something, tells how something works, or explains how an event takes place.

Does everyone know how to play Monopoly, or how Joe Montana scored a touchdown with just seconds to go? Of course not. That's why process explanations are so useful. They help people learn from each other about how to do something, how something works, or how an event happened. To help others learn about processes you understand, you need to analyze what goes into the process—what steps are involved and sometimes what skills and materials are needed. In the assignment that follows, you will analyze a process and share information by explaining the process to others.

PREWRITE AND EXPLORE

HANDBOOKS
FOR HELP & PRACTICE

Sharing Techniques, pp. 323–325
Appropriate Details, p. 355
Solving Problems, pp. 456–458
Sources of Information, pp. 476–478
Interviewing Skills, pp. 481–482

1. Look for ideas. You complete, observe, or are part of different processes every day. Think about which of these processes most interest you, or try one or more of the following activities to help you identify a process you would like to explain.

Exploratory Activities

- **Observing** Watch favorite performers or athletes in motion and make notes or sketches of the steps they use to complete an action. You may also want to study photos or videotapes.
- **Brainstorming about science and history** Complete the sentence "I wonder how . . ." in as many ways as possible. Perhaps you've always wondered how volcanoes erupt, how a microwave oven works, or how the Statue of Liberty was designed and installed. Let your mind roam free to think of ideas that intrigue you.

Springboard

Present as a warmup exercise a rapid association of ideas. Begin by mentioning a person, place, thing, or idea. Students should then supply as many "how-to" topics as they can that are related to that idea. For example, the first word mentioned might be *school*. The students may suggest topics, such as how to use the computers in the computer lab or how to study for a test. Continue supplying topics until all ideas have been exhausted.

- **Inventing** Think of games or machines you might like to invent and how they might work. You might enjoy brainstorming ideas with a partner and trying them out together.
- **Interviewing** Think of something you wish you knew how to do, such as the Heimlich maneuver, and interview someone in your community who is familiar with the process.
- **Reading literature** Think of fictional works you've read, such as Jack London's "To Build a Fire," in which an explanation of a process adds reality to a scene. Consider a process you might explain as part of a realistic narrative of your own.

One student, Danny, decided to observe his favorite athletes—professional baseball players. He videotaped a baseball game and observed the tape in slow motion, making sketches and notes about pitching and batting. His sketches and notes about pitching follow.

PROBLEM

S O L V I N G

How can I find a process that is interesting or important to me?

ONE STUDENT'S PROCESS

1. stands on mound, leaning toward home plate
2. watches catcher for a sign
3. shifts his weight to his back leg and goes into a windup
4. brings his front leg up waist high, rotates his body away from home plate
5. reaches pitching hand back toward second, swings his raised leg, and pushes off his back leg
6. brings pitching arm around, elbow first, and releases the ball about a foot in front of his head

Informative Writing **151**

Off the Record

"You can observe a lot just by watching."
Yogi Berra
Former catcher,
New York Yankees

Teaching Tip: Goals

Remind students that, although the general goal of many process descriptions is to inform, their goal might also be to amuse or to persuade. Emphasize that as students work through the assignment, they may modify their initial goal or change it altogether.

Teaching Tip: Audience

Discuss with students the important fact that most writing is intended for an audience and that the writer must keep the audience in mind if the writing is to be effective. Suggest that students try to put themselves in the place of their intended audience as they rehearse their explanations to themselves.

Teaching Tip: Gathering Information

Students who intend to gather information through interviews may benefit from the following reminders:

1. Make an appointment with the person to be interviewed.

2. Prepare for the interview by doing some background research and preparing key questions.

3. Follow up short answers with questions that elicit more detail.

4. Take notes during the interview.

5. If you do not understand an answer or explanation, ask for clarification.

 Individualizing Instruction

LD Students To assist these students with organization, suggest that they write each step in the process they are describing on a 3'' by 5'' card. They can then rearrange steps easily as they try to discover the best order for their descriptions.

To be sure that you understand your process, try demonstrating it. If it can't be demonstrated, try explaining it to a friend.

2. Select a writing topic you would like to work with. Choose a process you will enjoy writing about and one you think is useful for people to understand. Make sure you know enough about the process or can find the information you will need. If you are having trouble finding a topic, you may wish to refer to the "Apply Your Skills" section on page 161 or to the topics you explored in the Sketchbook on page 146.

3. List your goals. Once you choose a topic, think about what you want to accomplish in your writing. Russell Baker, for example, wanted his writing to amuse. Danny, who observed baseball players in motion, wanted to answer all those people who complain that baseball is a slow game. He wanted to help them understand how much speed and precision are involved in the pitching and batting processes. If your goals are not yet clear to you, don't worry. Your purpose may become clearer as you begin drafting.

4. Identify your audience. The information you provide and the way you present it will vary depending on who your audience is. Before preparing an explanation of how to set up a darkroom, for example, you need to know if your audience consists of experienced photographers or beginners. To analyze your readers and tailor your explanation to their needs, consider the following questions:

- How much do your readers already know about the topic you are writing about?
- What types of information will be most interesting and helpful to them?
- What are the most important pieces of information they should know about your topic?

5. Gather information. If necessary, continue observing or researching the process to answer your questions about it. After watching baseball players, for example, Danny still wondered exactly how fast a baseball travels and how long it takes pitchers and batters to complete their processes. He decided to do research to find out.

6. Organize your information. A process is usually described in chronological order; that is, the writer tells the steps in the order that they occur in time. Notice how Russell Baker first told readers to gather materials and move the turkey to a carving area, then explained how to sharpen the knife, and so on. Begin organizing your information by making a numbered list of all the steps in the process, arranging the steps in chronological order.

Also consider whether there is any background information your readers will need before you begin explaining the process. If you are explaining something that readers can do themselves, are there any materials they need to gather or skills they must have before they can do the process? Plan to give this information at the beginning of your explanation, as Russell Baker did.

DRAFT AND DISCOVER

1. Begin your draft. Begin your draft by explaining why the process is important, useful, or worth understanding. Then, with your writing goals in mind, try to describe the process in a lively way that will engage the reader's interest. One of the best ways to accomplish this is to concentrate on telling or showing why this process is important or interesting to you. If you have trouble making your writing lively, try one or more of the following techniques.

Strategies

- **Description** Provide enough details so that readers can understand the process exactly or, if appropriate, repeat the steps themselves. Use precise, vivid words to describe the process. In "Slice of Life," for example, Russell Baker used the words *torso, posterior, thigh, drumstick,* and *gristle* to identify parts of a turkey. He used the vivid words *skewered, sawing,* and *sever* to describe the carver's motions.
- **Definition** To keep your readers from becoming confused, define any special terms they might not understand.
- **Illustrations** Look for places where illustrations might help your readers understand the process you are explaining. Often a simple diagram can show an action that is difficult to explain in words. A flowchart can help readers understand at a glance how all the steps in a process are related. See the Related Assignment on page 168 for help in creating a flow chart.
- **Ways to begin** Use your introduction to establish clearly for your readers what you will be explaining. Think of ways to make your readers recognize why

HANDBOOKS

Writing Introductions, pp. 341–342
Using Diagrams, pp. 357–358

PROBLEM
S O L V I N G

How can I make my writing lively?

Informative Writing **153**

Springboard

Have small groups of students spend a few minutes brainstorming a list of transitions that might be useful in a process description. Invite groups to share their lists with the class.

Draft and Discover

Objectives

1. To draft a description of a process, using logical order and smooth transitions
2. To respond to one's own writing and the writing of peers

Preteaching

Preview the Draft and Discover section to identify concepts, skills, or strategies that students may need special help with. The mini-lessons listed below may help you in your selection and instruction.

Handbook Mini-Lessons
- Writing Introductions, pp. 341–342
- Using Diagrams, pp. 357–358

Teaching Strategies

Personal Touch

Share with students any notes you have made about a process description you plan to write. As you share your notes on your goal, describe the thinking processes you used. For example, you might choose to write about how to clean a teenager's room. Your purpose might be to provide useful tips to your teenaged son or daughter (or sister or brother) and to do it in a humorous way. Encourage students to comment on your goals.

Teaching Tip: Introductions

Call attention again to Russell Baker's essay, and discuss how he established his topic and the tone of his essay in the first paragraph. Point out that if Baker's only goal had been to inform, he probably would have chosen a more serious tone. But because he intended to amuse the reader, he wrote his description in a light-hearted fashion. Allow interested students to confer with one another about their introductions and the tone they might take in their descriptions.

Encourage students to use dictionaries and thesauruses to find vivid and precise words that will make for lively writing. Suggest that students consult with a writing partner to come up with descriptive words and phrases.

Managing the Paper Load

To help you discover major problems early on, ask students to place numbers in the margin of their papers to identify where each new step in the process begins. Then confer briefly with each student. Review the sequence of steps to be sure they are in a logical order and note whether the draft includes a clear introduction. Close reading of the description should be deferred until a later time.

they want to know about your process. You will also want to establish your tone—serious, casual, humorous—right from the start.

2. Make smooth transitions Use words such as *first, next, before, after, while,* and *finally* to help readers follow the sequence of steps in the process. Notice how effectively Baker made transitions in "Slice of Life."

Danny decided to begin his draft by explaining why he thought it was important for people to understand the processes of pitching and batting. His opening paragraph was directly related to his purpose for writing. Then he began explaining the steps in the pitching process in chronological order.

ONE STUDENT'S PROCESS

Some people complain that baseball is a slow-moving game. Yet each showdown between a pitcher and a batter is a battle of reflexes and timing played out at lightning speed.

The pitcher stands on the mound, leaning toward home plate. He watches the catcher give the sign for the pitch. Then he shifts his weight to his back leg and goes into his windup. He brings his front leg up waist high and rotates his body away from home plate. This builds up the momentum he needs to make a fast pitch. His pitching hand reaches back toward second base, he swings his raised leg toward home, and pushes off his back leg for added power. He brings his pitching arm around, elbow first, and releases the ball when it is about a foot in front of his head.

3. Review your writing. When you complete a rough first draft, put it aside for a few hours or a day. Then reread your draft yourself or ask a peer reader to respond to it. Questions such as the following may help you discover strengths and weaknesses in your explanation of a process.

R E V I E W   Y O U R   W R I T I N G

Questions for Yourself

- Have I made it clear why I think this process is important or interesting?
- Have I explained all the steps in the process?
- Are there places where I could make the steps in the process easier to follow or understand?
- Have I included all the information readers need to know?

Questions for Your Peer Reader

- Could you follow the order of the steps in the process? Have I put them in an order that makes sense to you?
- Is there any step in the process that you're unsure about or have a question about?
- Are there any places where I give more information than you need?
- Have I used any terms you don't know?
- What is the most interesting part of the process for you?
- How could I get you more interested or involved in this process?

Writer's Choice After your first revision, you might want to ask someone new to read the new version. Often a "fresh eye" can spot strengths and weaknesses that you and your first reader missed.

Writing
— TIP —

If you are writing directions for how to do something, ask a peer reader to try following the directions and completing the process.

The Simple Voting Machine, by Rube Goldberg

Informative Writing   **155**

Revise Your Writing

Objectives

1. To evaluate the responses to a draft of a process description
2. To use the responses and a set of standards to revise the draft
3. To proofread for errors in spelling, grammar, usage, and mechanics

Preteaching

Skim the Revise Your Writing section. Use the information in this section as well as your understanding of any problems students had during drafting to identify the skills, concepts, and strategies you want to review. The mini-lessons listed below may be helpful.

> #### Handbook Mini-Lessons
> - Coherence in Compositions, pp. 368–369
> - Peer Response, pp. 378–382
> - Using Specific Words, pp. 383–385
> - Varying Sentence Beginnings, pp. 416–418
> - Pronoun Agreement, pp. 565–566

Teaching Strategies

Critical Thinking

Judging As students evaluate the comments of peer readers, you might suggest that they ask themselves these questions: How can I do what the peer reader suggests? Will following this suggestion improve my description? Is there some other change I can make that will improve what I have written?

Coherence in Compositions, pp. 368–369
Peer Response, pp. 378–382
Using Specific Words, pp. 383–385
Varying Sentences, pp. 416–418
Pronoun Agreement, pp. 565–566

REVISE YOUR WRITING

1. Evaluate your responses. Review your own thoughts and the responses of your peer readers. Also keep in mind the following characteristics of an effective explanation of a process.

Standards for Evaluation

An effective explanation of a process . . .

- states the topic and purpose clearly in a strong introduction.
- includes all the necessary steps in the process in the correct sequence.
- defines all unfamiliar words.
- uses clear, specific language to describe the process completely so that another person could complete each step.
- demonstrates a clear sense of the audience through the use of appropriate language and details.
- uses transition words and phrases to make the sequence of steps clear.
- demonstrates an awareness of effective paragraphing.
- includes sentences with a variety of structures.

2. Problem-solve. Decide which responses you want to use and then rework your draft. Danny made the following changes in response to suggestions by one peer reader.

Science Connection

Students might bring to class examples of process descriptions from their science textbooks. Ask them to identify the characteristics of process description in the examples. Discuss the purpose of the explanations and the audience for which they are intended. Then determine what criteria these descriptions meet and how they might be improved.

ONE STUDENT'S PROCESS

Most major league pitchers can throw the ball about ninety miles an hour, so once the ball has been released, the batter has less than half a second to make up his mind whether to swing. In the first tenth of a second, he tries to figure out what kind of pitch *— a fast ball or a curve ball, for example —* has been thrown. If he decides to swing, he must start his motion. He has already taken his stance so that he'll be ready to begin the stride. *Once he completes the stride, by moving his front foot forward eight to twelve inches,* The rest of his body soon follows as he begins his swing. *First* His hips rotate toward the pitcher. *and then* His shoulders and his arms continue the forward motion. *of the swing* With a firm grip on the bat, he tries to make contact when the ball is about two feet in front of the plate. If he does all this effectively, he may soon be safe at first base, or better yet, circling the bases for a home run. If he miscalculates his moves the slightest bit, the count will be 0-1 against him, and he could be on his way to striking out. It's hard to believe that so much could happen so quickly—in less than one second after he *the pitcher* releases the ball. With so much going on every time the ball is pitched—nearly 200 times a game—baseball is hardly a slow-moving game. In fact, the opposite is true. The game moves so fast that it's hard for many people to appreciate what a contest of time and percision it really is.

Good use of facts—I never thought about how much is going on.

I think I missed something. When did he finish his stride and what exactly happens in the stride?

Are these actions all connected? Are they all part of the swing?

Excellent conclusion, but shouldn't you start a new paragraph?

Guidelines for Evaluation

The following guidelines may be used for a close evaluation of a process description. See the Guidelines for Evaluating Writing in the Teacher's Resource File for additional help with holistic or analytic scoring.

Ideas and Content
- makes clear the purpose of the description
- identifies the process
- includes all necessary steps
- clearly describes each step
- defines technical or unfamiliar terms
- uses vivid and precise words

Structure and Form
- focuses on a single process
- uses chronological order effectively
- uses transitions to make sequence clear
- groups related sentences into paragraphs
- demonstrates a clear sense of audience
- includes a variety of sentence structures

Grammar, Usage and Mechanics
- uses standard grammar and usage
- punctuates sentences correctly
- uses correct spelling

Modeling

After reviewing the Standards for Evaluation with students, discuss One Student's Process. Focus on the helpfulness of the peer reader's comments and on Danny's changes. Consider sharing your draft, discussing the changes you will make in it. Invite students to comment. If you wish to provide another example of revision, use the Student Revision Model Transparency for this assignment.

Linking Grammar and Writing

The description of a process may become confusing if verb tense is not consistent. Usually a process is described in the present tense and often in imperative sentences. Students should read their descriptions, focusing on consistency of tense. See pages 603–609 in Grammar Handbook 33 for a review of verb tense.

Individualizing Instruction

Basic Students You might have these students work in pairs with advanced students, who can help them locate and correct errors in their descriptions.

Managing the Paper Load

You need not grade all of the points listed in the Standards for Evaluation. You may wish to give two grades: one for content and structure, another for language and mechanics. Make sure students are aware of the criteria on which their descriptions will be evaluated.

Publish and Present

Objective

To publish and present the description of a process

Teaching Strategies

Speaking and Listening

Allow volunteers to read their process descriptions aloud. Coach students to read slowly and clearly enough to be understood. After a description has been read, have volunteers describe as many of the steps in the process as they can.

COMPUTER TIP

Experiment with formatting your description on the computer, adding headings, subtitles, and spacing. Try using boldfacing and underlining to highlight headings or important terms.

Grammar TIP

One quick way to define an unfamiliar term is to use an appositive, a noun or pronoun that follows another noun or pronoun and identifies or explains it.

HANDBOOKS

FOR HELP & PRACTICE

Discussion Skills, pp. 479–480

---

3. Proofread your work. Make a clean copy that incorporates all your changes. Then look for errors in grammar, punctuation, and spelling. Correct these mistakes so that readers will not be distracted by them. Before you publish your final draft, decide whether to add headings, illustrations, or flowcharts.

GRAMMAR AND WRITING

Pronoun Reference

In explaining a process, it is important that each pronoun you use refer clearly to the noun it is replacing. Otherwise, readers will be confused about what is happening in each step. If a pronoun reference is unclear, repeat the noun instead, as in the following example.

PROBLEM: Before you wrap the cloth around the stick, be sure to cut slashes in both ends of *it*.

CORRECTED: Before you wrap the cloth around the stick, be sure to cut slashes in both ends of *the stick*.

See Grammar Handbook 32, page 568 for additional help with this problem.

PUBLISH AND PRESENT

- **Prepare a videotape of the process, if possible.** In your video, demonstrate the process while explaining it orally. Perhaps you can donate your video to the school library.
- **Present an oral report.** If you have explained how something happens, present your explanation orally, using appropriate props, photographs, illustrations, or flowcharts for support.
- **Demonstrate the process to an audience of your choice.** For example, if you write about the process you use to study for a particular subject, demonstrate the skill in a tutoring session with someone who needs help in that subject.
- **Have a classroom skills exchange.** If many students explain practical skills, choose a skill you would like to learn and try following the directions in your classmate's explanations.

Baseball: A Game of Split-Second Timing

Danny Giambelli

Some people complain that baseball is a slow-moving game. Yet each showdown between a pitcher and a batter is in fact a battle of precise reflexes and split-second timing played out at lightning speed.

Consider, for example, what the batter sees in the second or two it takes for the pitcher to release the ball. The pitcher stands on the mound, leaning toward home plate. He watches the catcher give the sign for the pitch. Then he shifts his weight to his back leg and goes into his windup. He brings his front leg up waist high and rotates his body away from home plate. This builds up the momentum he needs to make a fast pitch. While his pitching hand reaches back toward second base, he swings his raised leg toward home and pushes off his back leg for added power. Finally, he brings his pitching arm around, elbow first, and releases the ball when it is about a foot in front of his head.

Most major league pitchers can throw the ball about ninety miles an hour, so once the ball has been released, the batter has less than half a second to make up his mind whether to swing. In the first tenth of a second, he tries to figure out what kind of pitch—a fast ball or a curve ball, for example—has been thrown. If he decides to swing, he must start his motion. He has

Introduction explains why the process is interesting

Presents all necessary steps in sequential order

Uses effective transitions to make the sequence of steps clear

Informative Writing **159**

Literature Connection

Poem to Read   Students might enjoy reading ''The Double-Play,'' a poem by Robert Wallace. Though not a strict process description, the poem describes how a double-play happens. After students have read the poem, you might have them list the steps involved in the process of making a double-play.

Using the Model

Have students compare the completed description on pages 159 and 160 with the earlier versions and discuss the following questions: In what way has Danny improved his earlier drafts? How has Danny made use of peer comments? Encourage students to use the annotations in the side column to discuss the elements of the final description.

Reteaching

Assess the needs of students who were not successful in developing an effective description of a process and identify two or three areas in which additional practice is needed. Assign the appropriate Handbook Mini-lessons, along with the support materials listed for each lesson. Concepts commonly requiring reteaching for this assignment are

Graphic Devices, Handbook 9
Transitional Devices, Handbook 10

The following suggestions and resources may also be useful.

1. **Vivid Language**   Remind students that vivid language is necessary for a successful description. To help students brainstorm appropriate word choices, use the Vocabulary Development booklet. Then have students review their descriptions, underlining all the verbs. Students should then try to find more precise substitutes for generic verbs. For example, *pull* might be replaced by *tug, wrench, yank,* and so on. Suggest that these students consult a thesaurus or dictionary to find appropriate substitutes.

2. **Audience**   Remind students that their choice of audience should dictate the type of vocabulary and amount of explanation needed in their essay. Have students explain who their target audience is and what they have done to make their writing appropriate for that audience. In a small group, discuss the kinds of accommodations that must be made for specific audiences.

Extension and Enrichment

• Have students bring to class several examples of process writing. They will find these in magazines, newspapers, and manuals that accompany various types of equipment. They will also find interesting examples of this type of writing in the novels of Hemingway, Melville, and Sinclair Lewis. Discuss the effectiveness of these examples. Have students speculate on why novelists include this type of writing in their work. *(It adds realism and interest and speaks to the innate curiosity of human nature.)*

• Compile a class scrapbook of various examples of process descriptions. You might divide the entries into several classifications: literary, historical, scientific, popular writing (newspapers and magazines), and product instructions.

• Encourage students to select the best examples of process descriptions they have found. These may be chosen from those presented or gathered by the class or they may represent their own private finds. Suggest that the students keep these as models in their writing portfolios.

Uses examples to explain steps in the process

Sums up the significance of the process in an effective conclusion

already taken his stance so that he'll be ready to begin his stride. Once he completes his stride, by moving his front foot forward eight to twelve inches, the rest of his body follows as he begins his swing. First his hips rotate toward the pitcher, and then his shoulders and his arms continue the forward motion of the swing. With a firm grip on the bat, he tries to make contact when the ball is about two feet in front of the plate. If he does all this effectively, he may soon be safe at first base, or better yet, circling the bases for a home run. If he miscalculates his moves the slightest bit, the count will be 0-1 against him, and he could be on his way to striking out.

It's hard to believe that so much could happen so quickly—in less than one second after the pitcher releases the ball. With so much going on every time the ball is pitched—nearly 200 times a game—baseball is hardly a slow-moving game. In fact, the opposite is true. The game moves so fast that it's hard for many people to appreciate what a contest of timing and precision it really is.

LEARNING FROM YOUR WRITING PROCESS

WRITER TO WRITER

There is only one trait that marks the writer. He is always watching. It's a kind of trick of mind and he is born with it.
Morley Callaghan, Canadian novelist and short-story writer

1. Reflect on your writing. Ask yourself the following questions, and record any useful thoughts or ideas in your own writing log:

- What techniques did I find helpful in writing my process explanation?
- What was most difficult about writing this piece?
- How successful was I in analyzing all the steps in the process?

2. Apply your skills. Try one or more writing activities in the following areas.

- **Cross curricular** Visit a science class and observe an experiment in progress. Ask questions about the experiment and take notes on it. Then submit an explanation of the process to the person you observed and ask how well you explained the process.
- **Literature** Read a biographical or autobiographical selection, such as "A Christmas Memory," "These Were the Sioux," or "I Know Why the Caged Bird Sings." Describe a process that was common in the time and place described in the selection but is unusual in your own time and place.
- **General** Call a representative of a local organization, such as a recycling group, the police department, the fire department, or your local Red Cross. Ask if there are any health- or safety-related processes you can help the organization to educate the public about. Prepare pamphlets or posters about the process and distribute or display them at your local shopping mall.
- **Related assignments** Follow the suggestions on pages 162–171 to write a cause-effect analysis or create a flowchart.

◄ FOR YOUR **PORTFOLIO**

Informative Writing **161**

Objective

To analyze and reflect upon what has been learned about the writing process and the writing of a description of a process

Teaching Strategies

Reflecting on the Process

Encourage students to share their thoughts as well as to suggest any other questions that might be useful in thinking about the writing experience. Suggest that students think about and try to recognize the things that went especially well, not just those that were not successful.

Writing Portfolio

Suggest that students save their evaluations with their final process descriptions in their writing portfolios. Encourage students to review their self-evaluations from the Guided Assignment in Workshop 4, in which they explored another kind of informative writing. How do their assessments differ? Do they see any common strengths or weaknesses?

Summary and Closure

Before proceeding to the next lesson, be sure students have internalized the following key ideas:

1. A process description explains how to do something, how something works, or how an event happened.

2. An effective process description includes a clear explanation of the steps, logical order, and appropriate transitions.

3. Many informational books are based entirely on descriptions of process. However, this type of writing is also found in short stories and novels.

Give students time to summarize what they have learned by describing the characteristics of an effective description of a process and by explaining how the skill of writing effective process descriptions can help them in other school subjects, particularly science and social studies.

Springboard

After students have discussed the Morley Callaghan quote on this page, suggest that they work in small groups to brainstorm other traits that writers may have in common. Emphasize that students can take a humorous or serious approach to the task. Invite groups to find creative ways to share their results with the class.

Starting from Literature

Objective

To respond to a professional model of a cause-and-effect analysis as a springboard to writing

Teaching Strategies

Motivate

Take an informal poll of the approximate number of hours students spend watching television and briefly discuss their viewing habits. Then ask students to imagine that suddenly a fascinating new form of entertainment (perhaps a medium in which the viewer becomes part of the program) is introduced. Ask students to speculate on the effects of such a phenomenon.

Tap Prior Knowledge

Ask students what media were popular before the advent of television. Elicit that people were entertained by radio programs and movies. If possible, play a tape of an old radio drama or variety show, and have students discuss what they know of old-time radio and its stars. You might also ask students what they know about the movie-going habits of older relatives or friends and neighbors who attended movies in the 1940's.

Set a Purpose

Before the students read the excerpt from *The Americans*, refer them to the side-column notes. Ask students to predict some of the effects of television on radio and movies. Then have students read the excerpt, remembering the purpose-setting statement given at the end of the side column. Suggest that students might also want to note as they read whether or not their predictions were accurate.

Related ASSIGNMENT

Cause-and-Effect Analysis

From
THE AMERICANS
by Jordan, Greenblatt, and Bowes

n ordinary or puzzling subject can take on new meaning if you explore its ties to the past or future. Often, a cause-and-effect analysis can help you discover these connections, revealing both the reasons for and consequences of an event, as well as its connection to many broader situations.

This excerpt examines the effects of the coming of television on the radio and movie industries. As you read the excerpt, look for examples of cause-and-effect relationships.

The media directly affected by the rise of television were radio and motion pictures. Radio was radically changed but not financially hurt. Expensive drama and variety shows disappeared. Instead, radio stations became local institutions, providing popular music, capsule news, and community services. The number of stations rose by 50 percent and advertising revenues went up by 35 percent in ten years.

The change in the film industry was more drastic. The studio system of Hollywood was a highly industrialized operation that turned out 600 or more feature films a year. The films were distributed through 18,500 theaters which, in 1946, drew an incredible 90 million paid admissions per week. From the very beginning, TV cut into this rich market. People stayed home to watch the little screen. By 1950, 5000 theaters had turned into bowling alleys and supermarkets or simply stood dark, while the number of paid admissions had fallen by half.

As the decade progressed, business became even worse. Studios terminated the contracts of their stars and rented their facilities to independent producers or sold the land to real-estate developers for office buildings, apartment houses, and hotels. In 1960 only fourteen feature films were made by the studios. The rest were turned out by independents or by filmmakers in Europe and elsewhere.

To compete with the little screen in the living room, movie makers

162

concentrated on color
and spectacle. Elaborate musical
numbers, panoramic battle sequences, and numbing
special effects were commonplace. Along with color and
stereophonic sound, several widescreen techniques were
used to make movies seem more realistic. There was even
a brief revival of three-dimensional films for which the
audience had to wear cardboard eyeglasses with polarized
lenses. Nothing helped. By 1960 only 27 percent of the
population over five years of age was going to the movies
each week, down from 70 percent in 1946. And the bottom
had not yet been reached.

One result was that motion pictures were no longer a
national unifying force. Once, they had appealed to all
ages and classes. Every war film made in the 1940s had
representatives of at least four or five different ethnic
groups as members of the army platoon or flying squadron that performed heroic deeds against the Axis. Now
the motion picture market fragmented. Films were made
to appeal to special markets such as young children, or
teenagers, or adults, or science fiction fans, or martial arts
fans, or, as in the 1970's, blacks. Their subject matter and
stars varied. So did the values they presented.

Think AND Respond

In what ways did the coming of
television affect the radio and
movie industries? What techniques
do the authors use to explain the
effects they have identified? What
types of details do they present to
support their analysis? What other
developments, besides television,
have had a major impact on our
daily lives? How might a cause-
and-effect analysis help you analyze one of these developments?

163

Think and Respond

Elicit Personal Responses

Using the Think and Respond questions
to stimulate reactions, students should
write their personal responses in their journals or reading logs. You might model the
process for them by sharing some of your
thoughts about a development that im-
pacts daily life. An example might be the
telephone, which has made the art of
friendly-letter writing almost obsolete.
Shopping by phone has become an important time-saving practice. On the other
hand, unnecessary or unwelcome calls
often waste time. After students have formulated their responses, elicit the effects
of television on radio and movies.

Explore the Authors' Techniques

To help students identify the techniques
of professional writers and to encourage
experimentation with such techniques,
point out some of the elements that make
this excerpt effective. For example, call attention to how the authors apply the principle of economy. The subject is introduced
in the first sentence and the rest of the first
paragraph explains the effects of television
on radio. (Page 162, paragraph 1: Radio
. . . hurt. Expensive . . . disappeared. Instead . . . services. The . . . years.) The authors then make a smooth transition to the
effect on films.

In the second paragraph, the authors
present statistics that substantiate the
dramatic drop in film audiences. (Page
162, paragraph 2: By 1950 . . . half.) They
further explore the effects of empty theaters on the large studios (Page 162, paragraph 3: Studios . . . hotels.) and the
changes in film techniques that were made
to regain audiences. (Page 163, paragraph
1: To . . . spectacle. Elaborate . . . commonplace. Along . . . realistic.)

Students should note that the authors
present a number of effects resulting from
one key event—the advent of television.

Link Literature to Writing

As students write their own analyses,
suggest that they recall how the authors of
the model provided a clear, logical explanation of several effects and supported their
explanation with solid facts.

Guiding Your Writers

Objectives

1. To identify a topic and a purpose for cause and effect analysis
2. To identify the cause and effect pattern(s) associated with the topic
3. To write, review, and share a cause and effect analysis

Preteaching

Skim the remainder of the assignment, noting any skills or concepts your students may need help with. The Thinking Skills Transparencies and the mini-lessons listed below may help you in your selection and instruction. The cross reference in the pupil text will give students access to the same lessons for independent study.

> **Handbook Mini-Lessons**
> - Types of Organization, pp. 331–335
> - Coherence in Compositions, pp. 368–369
> - Faulty Reasoning, pp. 453–455

Teaching Strategies

Modeling

Encourage students to use diagrams as they explore the causes and effects associated with their topics. You might draw on the board a diagram that illustrates some of the effects of television, using the information from the excerpt. Write the word *television* and draw a box or circle around it. From the box or circle draw a series of vertical lines; next to each jot down a few words that indicate the particular effect. You might also provide a generic diagram for a causal chain, drawing a series of boxes or circles connected by arrows or lines. You may also want to use the cause-and-effect Thinking Skills Transparencies from the Teacher's Resource File.

INVITATION TO Write

This excerpt presents the effects of television on the radio and movie industries. Now write a cause-and-effect analysis, explaining the relationship between an event and its cause or between an event and its effects.

When you explain why something happened or why certain conditions exist, or when you examine the result of an action, you are using cause-and-effect analysis. Like writing that explains a process, cause-and-effect analysis relies on sequence, one event or action leading to another. The sequence in cause-and-effect writing is unique, however, because one event is *responsible* for another one. Not only does one event come before the other, but it also *causes* the second event to happen.

PREPARING FOR A CAUSE-AND-EFFECT ANALYSIS

HANDBOOKS
FOR HELP & PRACTICE

Types of Organization, pp. 331–335
Coherence in Compositions, pp. 368–369
Faulty Reasoning, pp. 453–455

1. Identifying a cause-and-effect situation. First, identify your topic by exploring an intriguing or important event or action. Brainstorm to generate lists of events and their possible causes and effects. You might think about an occurrence that had a great impact on society. For instance, what caused the Great Depression? What were the results? Similarly you could explore a current situation and think about its possible effects. What might the results of continued environmental pollution be, for example? Or you might consider what motivated a person who has had an important impact on society. For example, what principles sustained Nelson Mandela through twenty-seven years in prison?

2. Explore the relationship of cause to effect. Examine the topic you have chosen to see which of several cause-and-effect patterns it matches. For example, is there a single cause and effect, or a single cause with multiple effects, or perhaps a causal chain where A

Social Studies Connection

History, Geography, and Economics All these subjects deal with causes and effects. You might discuss the following chain of causes and effects: the Industrial Revolution caused the rise of factories. The need for cheap labor resulted in the employment of children. The plight of the children eventually caused the enactment of child labor laws. Ask students to consider topics they are currently examining in social studies. Invite volunteers to share with the class cause and effect relationships associated with those topics. Students might draw on the board diagrams that illustrate the relationship (causal chain; single cause and effect; single cause, several effects).

causes B, B causes C, and so on? It is possible that a situation is a mix of these patterns. Notice that in the excerpt, a single event, the arrival of TV, had multiple effects. These effects can also be viewed as forming a causal chain: The rise of television caused a sharp decrease in movie audiences, which in turn led Hollywood to put more effort into elaborate spectacles and special effects.

3. Be sure your events are linked causally. Do not confuse events that simply follow one after another in time with a true cause-and-effect relationship. Be sure that one event *causes* another. For example, an article that examines the movements along the regional fault lines preceding an earthquake in Northern California explores a cause-and-effect relationship. In contrast, an article that reports the events during the 1906 San Francisco earthquake is not necessarily a cause-and-effect analysis.

4. Identify your purpose. Will the purpose of your analysis be to give your readers greater understanding of your subject, as was the case with the TV article, or do you want to persuade readers to share your views? For example, if you were trying to promote recycling, you might discuss the long-term negative effects on the environment of indiscriminate garbage disposal. You could then discuss the positive effects of recycling bottles, cans, and newspapers, and of using biodegradable containers and packaging.

DRAFTING A CAUSE-AND-EFFECT ANALYSIS

1. Invite your reader into your discussion. In your introduction, present the situation or event you are examining, and make the purpose of your analysis clear. Also, let your reader know whether you will explore causes, effects, or both. To add interest, you might begin with a provocative question or a startling prediction. Include any background information that the reader will need to understand the situation.

2. Organize the causes and effects into a coherent pattern. Cause-and-effect writing usually follows one of two organizational patterns. In the **cause-to-effect pattern,** you begin by stating the causes and then proceed to the effect or effects. In the **effect-to-cause pattern,** you begin by showing the effect or effects and then examine what caused them.

Writing
TIP

If your analysis contains a causal chain, you might use chronological order and present your information in narrative form.

Critical Thinking

Analyzing You might provide several sample sentences and work with students to identify those that contain true cause-and-effect relationships. (*Cause and effect:* "I forgot my keys, so I couldn't get in the house." *Not cause and effect:* "I went shopping, and then I stopped at the bank.") Emphasize the importance of analyzing events carefully to avoid inferring causal relationships where none exist.

Guidelines for Evaluation
A good cause-and-effect analysis . . .
- describes clearly the relationship of cause to effect
- includes an engaging introduction that states the topic and the parameters of the analysis
- displays coherent organization, using either a cause and effect pattern or an effect to cause pattern
- organizes details logically, using either chronological order, order of importance, or familiar to unfamiliar order
- uses appropriate transitional devices to indicate causes and effects
- contains an ending that states the significance of the findings, makes a prediction, or draws a conclusion
- demonstrates a knowledge of standard grammar and correct usage, capitalization, punctuation, and spelling

Literature Connection

Essay to Read Students will enjoy reading James Thurber's short essay, "The Night the Bed Fell," a humorous account of a chain of events in which each event causes the next.

Reteaching

Assess the needs of students who were not successful in developing an effective cause-and-effect analysis. Assign the appropriate Handbook Mini-Lessons, along with the support materials listed for each lesson. Concepts commonly requiring reteaching for this assignment are

Types of Organization: Handbook 4
Faulty Reasoning: Handbook 24

The following suggestions and resources may also be useful.

1. Lack of Causes and Effects Use Thinking Skills Worksheets: Cause and Effect 1 and 2 to help students understand the relationship between ideas. You might wish to use the diagrams to model the possible effects of commonplace events such as oversleeping on a school day or studying diligently for a test. Then have students work in pairs to diagram the relationships in their essay, adding or deleting ideas as necessary.

2. Weak Conclusions Remind students that a strong conclusion leaves the reader with something to think about. Refer to the example of a purpose (to promote recycling) on page 165. Discuss with students what a writer with such a purpose might want to include in his or her conclusion. Elicit suggestions (predict the success of recycling, and so on). Encourage students to review their purposes for clues that will help them revise their conclusions, leaving the reader with something to think about.

Extension and Enrichment

• Groups of students might work together to identify a problem in the school or classroom. Groups can explore the causes of the problem, discuss suggestions for correcting it, and predict some of the effects of each remedy. Students might express their ideas in a letter to their home room teacher or principal.

The 1929 stock market crash and closing of the banks was the result of irresponsible investing and lack of regulation.

With either pattern, there are three methods you can use to organize your details and examples. You can use **chronological order,** listing the causes and effects in the order in which they occurred. In **order of importance** organization, start with the most important or least important cause or effect and move through your list to the other end of the scale. With **familiar-to-unfamiliar order,** start with the best-known cause or effect and then proceed to less familiar causes and effects. Analyze your material to determine the best method of organization.

3. Write an ending. End your analysis in one of three ways: by drawing a conclusion, stating the significance of your findings, or making a prediction. If you used the order-of-importance method of organization, you may want to restate your most important point. With the chronological-order method, restate the initial cause and contrast it with the final effect. Be sure your ending paragraph is strong and compelling.

REVIEWING YOUR WRITING

1. Make sure connections are clear. Transition words such as *because, if . . . then, since, so, as a result,* and *therefore* can be effective in showing cause-and-effect relationships and connections.

2. Evaluate the relevance of your ideas. Examine the clarity of your ideas and also be sensitive to any information that, although interesting, is not pertinent to your analysis.

3. Have a classmate read your analysis. Ask him or her to comment on the strong points and to make suggestions for improvement.

PUBLISHING AND PRESENTING

• **Submit your analysis to the school or community newspaper.**
• **Convert your writing to a flowchart, graph, or table.**
• **Consider an oral presentation.** Use this idea if you are showing effects as part of a persuasive paper.

On the Lightside

THE ADMIRAL SPEAKS COBOL

One of the foremost language experts of the past fifty years has worked with languages that are never spoken and are not even intended for communication between people. Instead, these languages are the languages of computers.

The expert is Navy Admiral Grace M. Hopper, a pioneer in developing computer systems and computer languages. During her 43-year military career, which ended in 1986, she was in the forefront of the computer revolution. When she began, each computer had its own unique language, so communication between machines was difficult, and new programs had to be written for each machine. Hopper created the computer language COBOL (Common Business-Oriented Language), which was the first language that could be used

by computers made by different manufacturers. She also worked to bring computer users together by standardizing computer languages.

Along the way, Hopper had an impact on English as well. In 1945, she and her colleagues coined some terms that are familiar to all computer users. The computer they were using at the time stopped working one day, and when they took it apart they found that a moth had become caught in one of the circuits. *Debugging*, the now-popular term for checking a system or program for errors, had a very literal meaning when Hopper and her colleagues removed the dead moth from their computer. Ever since, computer glitches have been known as *bugs*.

167

Before students read the selection, encourage discussion of computer experiences and languages. Then have students read the selection to identify the problem Admiral Hopper solved by creating COBOL.

After students have read the selection, you might present the following statements for student reaction:

1. Learning a foreign language is easier than learning a computer language.

2. Learning a foreign language is more useful than learning a computer language.

3. All computers should "speak" the same languages.

4. All computer language is not really language.

Starting from Literature

Objective

To respond to a model as a springboard to creating a flowchart

Teaching Strategies

Motivate

Bring to class a clipping from a local newspaper that reports crimes committed in the area. Have students note if any suspects have been apprehended. Discuss where the suspects might be now, two weeks from now, or a month from now.

Tap Prior Knowledge

Ask students to think about ways that detailed information, such as population statistics or the functions of a system of the human body, is sometimes presented. Elicit from students that graphs, charts, tables, and other graphic devices are often used to present complex information. Point out that the model explains the criminal justice system by means of a flowchart, a kind of graphic device.

Set a Purpose

Discuss the side-column notes. Point out that the flow chart includes several possible courses or outcomes that may occur after a suspect has been apprehended. Encourage students to examine the flowchart carefully, keeping in mind the purpose-setting question given at the end of the side column.

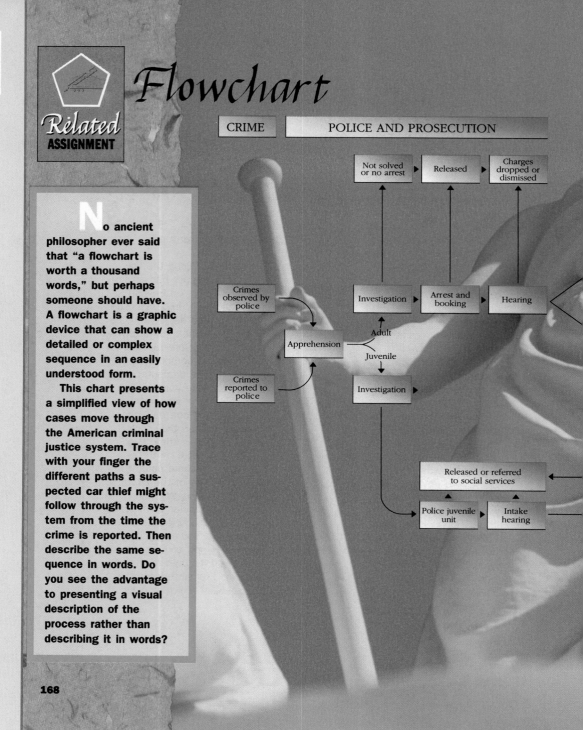

Related ASSIGNMENT

Flowchart

No ancient philosopher ever said that "a flowchart is worth a thousand words," but perhaps someone should have. A flowchart is a graphic device that can show a detailed or complex sequence in an easily understood form.

This chart presents a simplified view of how cases move through the American criminal justice system. Trace with your finger the different paths a suspected car thief might follow through the system from the time the crime is reported. Then describe the same sequence in words. Do you see the advantage to presenting a visual description of the process rather than describing it in words?

168

CRIME | POLICE AND PROSECUTION

Not solved or no arrest

Released

Charges dropped or dismissed

Crimes observed by police

Investigation

Arrest and booking

Hearing

Apprehension

Adult

Juvenile

Crimes reported to police

Investigation

Released or referred to social services

Police juvenile unit

Intake hearing

COURTS		
Arraignment ▶	Trial ▶	Sentencing
Dismissed ▶	Acquitted ▶	Appealed
Dismissed ▶	Acquitted ▶	Fined
Arraignment ▶	Trial ▶	Sentencing

Judicial hearing

CORRECTIONS	
Penitentiary ▶	Parole
Probation	
Jail	
Probation	
Juvenile home ▶	Parole
Probation	

Out of system

Think AND Respond

How did this flowchart make it easy to follow the various steps in the criminal justice system? How did the flowchart make clear that an accused person might take more than one route through the system? Can you think of other processes that could be made clearer by using a flowchart or similar diagram?

169

Think and Respond

Elicit Personal Responses

After students have had sufficient time to examine the flowchart, encourage them to respond to the questions on this page, writing their answers in their journals or learning logs. Then discuss their responses as a class, focusing on the advantages of presenting information by means of a flowchart.

Explore the Author's Techniques

Have students examine the chart carefully as a class. Call attention to the headings, and point out that they show the four main divisions of the process. Note how the author includes the major steps in the process in the order in which they occur. Each step is enclosed in a box, and arrows indicate flow and various alternate routes. Branches show the different courses followed by adults and juveniles. Finally, point out that the author condenses the explanation of the steps into single words and phrases.

Link Literature to Writing

Point out that the flowchart of the criminal justice system is just one example of a process that can be explained in this manner. In the assignment that follows, students will have the opportunity to explain a process by creating their own flowcharts. As they plan and make their flowcharts, students should try to apply the author's techniques of including major steps in order, using headings to indicate major divisions, showing alternate routes, and using concise words and phrases to explain the steps.

Social Studies Connection

Print Materials Suggest that students find examples of flowcharts in their social studies textbooks or in news magazines. Ask students to bring the examples to class and to discuss whether they think the graphic presentation of information is more understandable than a written explanation might have been.

Guiding Your Writers

Objectives

1. To recognize the advantages of presenting information in a flowchart
2. To choose and analyze a process for a flowchart
3. To make, revise, and share a flowchart of a process

Preteaching

Preview the rest of the assignment to identify skills or concepts with which your students may need help. The mini-lessons listed below may be useful in your selection and instruction. The cross references in the pupil text will give students access to the same lessons for independent study.

Handbook Mini-Lessons
- Writing Variables, pp. 311–316
- Peer Response, pp. 378–382
- Evaluating Ideas, pp. 452–453

Teaching Strategies

Teaching Tip: Topics

Brainstorm with the class a list of possible topics, and write them on the board. To get students started you might suggest a process yourself such as how to complete and file an income tax return. You might also refer students to the *Ideas for Writing* booklet.

Teaching Tip: Audience

Remind students to consider their intended audience as they plan their flowcharts. By its nature, a flow chart is brief, and the format does not allow for explanation of terms. The intended audience should also influence the complexity of organization in the flowchart.

Writing — TIP

Don't try to show everything. Include only the most important options and possible outcomes.

HANDBOOKS
FOR HELP & PRACTICE

Writing Variables, pp. 311–316
Peer Response, pp. 378–382
Evaluating Ideas, pp. 452–453

INVITATION TO Write

The flowchart on pages 168–169 gives an overview of how the American criminal justice system works. Now draw a flowchart for a similarly complex process.

A flowchart is especially helpful in presenting a complex process or a chain of events in which several different pathways or outcomes are possible. An effective flowchart clarifies the relationship among the steps in the process in a minimum of space and with the fewest number of words.

PLANNING A FLOWCHART

1. Choose a process to chart. Remember that flowcharts work best for processes that have a complex series of steps. Appropriate subjects might include the following: *How do green plants turn water and carbon dioxide into oxygen and carbohydrates? How does a bill become a law at the federal or state level? How are lithographs produced?*

2. Analyze the process. First list the basic steps in the process. Also list any alternative routes that might be taken, and any questions or options you need to consider. Next, organize the list. Group related thoughts or actions together, and arrange them in sequence. To show optional pathways, imitate the use of boxes and arrows in the flowchart on the criminal justice system.

DRAWING THE CHART

1. Decide on the starting and ending points. What part of the process will your chart follow? Consider the options you want to include and how many alternate pathways you will need.

For example, if you plan to describe how a play goes from script to first performance, you will omit steps showing how the play is reviewed and evaluated by critics and the public.

2. Think about how your chart will look. In which direction will it flow? Because we read from top to bottom and from left to right, these are the most common ways to design a flowchart. Also think about how to identify key points in the process. For example, the model uses boxes for key points in the criminal justice system.

 Writer's Choice Sometimes a different graphic pattern may be appropriate for a flowchart. For example, a process such as the cycle of precipitation may be best represented by a circle.

3. Sketch your chart. Use as few words as possible. You might find it easier to complete one main path from start to finish before you add any optional paths.

REVIEWING YOUR WRITING

1. Examine your first draft. Are the major steps and connections between them clear and complete? Are the important optional pathways indicated as alternative outcomes? Does the diagram make the process easy to follow?

2. Show your flowchart to someone else. Choose a person who is interested in the process but has limited knowledge about it. Ask that person if he or she can follow the process by studying your flowchart. If there are problems, ask the person to pinpoint steps that are not clear or to indicate if a necessary step has been left out.

3. Revise the chart based on your feedback. Incorporate any changes recommended by your reader which will make your chart easier to understand.

PUBLISHING AND PRESENTING

- **Put your chart to practical use.** Use your flowchart in a class assignment or share it with your study group in preparing for a test.
- **Give an oral presentation.** Describe the process, using your flowchart as a visual aid.

Writing
TIP

In tracing the process of a computer game, you might want to follow one path through to its conclusion, and then return to another path, rather than trying to deal with all the options at once.

Science Connection

Science Processes Many scientific processes can be represented in a flowchart. Suggest that students skim a chapter of their science textbook to find a verbal description of a scientific process. Encourage students to develop a flowchart for the process and to use the chart to help them understand and remember how the process works.

Guidelines for Evaluation

An effective flowchart . . .
- presents the major steps in a process in chronological order
- uses arrows and boxes or circles to indicate flow and alternate routes
- uses key words and phrases to explain steps
- includes headings to indicate any major divisions in the process

Reteaching

Assess the needs of students who were not successful in developing an effective flowchart. Assign the appropriate Handbook Mini-Lessons, along with the support materials listed for each lesson. Concepts commonly requiring reteaching are

Types of Organization: Handbook 4
Evaluating Ideas: Handbook 24

The following suggestions and resources may also be useful.

1. Weak Organization Remind students that for a flowchart to be successful events must be arranged chronologically. Suggest that students who had difficulty write each major step on an index card. Use one student's set of cards to model on the board how to arrange the cards to form a flowchart. Have students discuss and supply missing steps. Then have students work with partners to arrange their cards in logical order.

2. Lack of Key Words and Phrases Have students explain one or two steps in their process to you. Write their explanation on the board. Then work with them to condense the explanation by identifying a few key words or phrases from the material on the board.

Extension and Enrichment

- Interested students might work in groups to develop practical flowcharts for use in your school. For example, students might develop a flowchart that explains how to use the card catalogue and display the chart in the library.

After students have read and discussed the selection, ask them to name familiar places and to share any information they may have about the origin of those place names.

Because it is unlikely that students will know the origins of all the names they suggest, encourage them to select a place name to investigate further. You might then have students write a brief description of how the place got its name or give a short oral report. Some students may prefer to show the various renditions of the name in a chart, indicating the order in which changes occurred.

On the Lightside

PLACE NAMES

The explorers of the New World learned many place names from the Native Americans. However, the paths those names have followed in becoming a part of the language have sometimes been as twisted as the trails followed by the explorers.

The seventeenth-century French explorers Jacques Marquette and Louis Joliet traveled up and down the Mississippi River to places we now call *Wisconsin, Des Moines, Peoria, Missouri, Omaha, Wabash,* and *Kansas.* However, some of these names bear little resemblance to the names Marquette and Joliet first heard. *Wisconsin,* for example, comes from a Native-American word of uncertain meaning, *Mesconsing.* To the Frenchmen, it sounded like "Ouisconsing," and that is how they wrote it down. The English changed it to its present form, since the French word sounded like "Wisconsin" to them.

Des Moines followed an even more twisted path. Marquette and Joliet found a tribe called the Moingouena living on a river in what we now know as Iowa. The Frenchmen named the river after the tribe, Riviere des Moingouenas, and later shortened it to Riviere des Moings. *Moings,* however, is similar to the French word *moines,* which means "monks." Over time, their discovery came to be called *des Moines,* which means "of the monks." The names of the city and river Des Moines have nothing to do with monks. The name is simply the result of the jumbled influences of the past.

Sentence
COMPOSING

Introductory Prepositional Phrases

By beginning a sentence with one or more prepositional phrases, a writer sets the stage for the information that follows. Individual phrases answer such questions as *Which one? What kind? How? When? Where?* or *To what extent?*

MODELS

1. <u>On Monday</u> Laurie came home late, full of news.

    Shirley Jackson, "Charles"

Using a series of phrases can establish an entire scene or explain a set of circumstances.

2. <u>After years</u> <u>of home cooking</u> <u>on Earth</u> he had grown too fat for his old Adnaxian Air Force uniform.

    Henry Gregor Felsen, "The Spaceman from Adnaxas"

A. Beginning Sentences with Prepositional Phrases Reword each sentence in its original form by placing the underlined prepositional phrase or phrases at the beginning of the sentence. Use a comma after the opening prepositional phrase or series of phrases.

1. A green star rose <u>above the blue hills</u>.   **Ray Bradbury, *The Martian Chronicles***

2. Queenie shakes herself and trembles <u>on a farther shore</u>.

    Truman Capote, "A Christmas Memory"

3. Pompeii's 25,000 people awakened to another hot day in that hot summer <u>at dawn, on the twenty-fourth of August, in the year 79</u>.

    Robert Silverberg, "Pompeii"

4. Pies were baking in the oven <u>inside Mrs. O'Brien's kitchen</u>.

    Ray Bradbury, "I See You Never"

5. Miss Hinch had killed John Catherwood <u>in a tiny little room within ten steps of Broadway, at halfpast nine o'clock on a fine evening</u> with the light sword she used in her famous representation of "The Father of His Country."

    Henry Syndor Harrison, "Miss Hinch"

B. Unscrambling Sentences   Unscramble the sentence parts and write the resulting sentence. The sentence parts can be unscrambled in more than one acceptable way, but begin your sentence with a prepositional phrase or series of phrases.

1. a. I am a large, big-boned woman
   b. in real life
   c. with rough, man-working hands
   Alice Walker, "Everyday Use"

2. a. a Republic sniper lay watching
   b. on a roof-top
   c. near O'Connell Bridge
   Liam O'Flaherty, "The Sniper"

3. a. the man was still asleep
   b. his head back against the wall
   c. snoring slightly on the intaking breath
   d. in the far corner
   Ernest Hemingway, "The Undefeated"

4. a. Henry tried to explain
   b. watching the same shows
   c. during the commercials
   d. that there were millions of other Earth families
   Henry Gregor Felson, "The Spaceman from Adnaxas"

5. a. was a rock-like hump
   b. in front of them
   c. where no rock should be
   d. only three or four yards away
   William Golding, *Lord of the Flies*

C. Expanding Sentences   In each of the first five sentences that follow, the prepositional phrase is given, but not the rest of the sentence. In the next five sentences, the prepositional phrase is omitted. Finish each sentence by telling what happened. Use your imagination and fill your sentences with vivid details and varied sentence structures. Look on page 306 to see how the authors finished their sentences.

1. On stormy nights, . . .   **Joseph Conrad, "The Idiots"**

2. At the top of the bank, . . .   **J.R.R. Tolkien, *The Fellowship of the Ring***

3. With a head start, . . .   **Jean McCord, "The Cave"**

4. Up the rising slope, down through the drifts, along a creek bottom to the rising ground of the next ridge, . . .

      Adrienne Richard, "One Christmas in Montana"

5. In the front hall, under a large picture of fat, cheery monks fishing by the riverside, . . .   **Katherine Mansfield, "Sixpence"**

6. . . . Frodo for the first time fully realized his homelessness and danger.

      J.R.R. Tolkien, *The Fellowship of the Ring*

7. . . . , Trurl, the constructor, built an eight-story thinking machine.

      Stanislaw Lem, "Trurl's Machine"

8. . . . , my schooner lay moored to a rotting dock in St. Pierre harbor.

      Farley Mowat, "Whales for the Killing"

9. . . . , the fog had risen as high as the top of the ridges, and the whole house was swallowed up in it.   **Caroline Gordon, "The Captive"**

10. . . . , she saw herself, her hair hanging wild, her long bare legs scratched, her broadly smiling face dirt-streaked, her torn skirt dangling, her dog laughing up at her.   **Dorothy Canfield Fisher, "The Apprentice"**

Application This familiar sentence begins with several prepositional phrases: <u>Over the river</u> and <u>through the woods</u>, <u>to Grandmother's house</u> we go. To practice the pattern taught in this lesson, think of destinations that you have traveled to, or ones you would like to travel to. Then write several imitations of this sentence. Next, choose one of your sentences to use as the first sentence in a paragraph in which you describe your trip to this destination.

Grammar Refresher To learn more about prepositional phrases, see Handbook 35, pages 653–655.

6

Informative Exposition: Synthesis

Overview

Informative exposition, writing that explains or informs, can take several forms: classification and analysis, as in Workshops 4 and 5, and in this Workshop, Synthesis. Like classification and analysis, synthesis is a critical thinking skill with many applications to students' writing, oral communication, and school and job effectiveness. Synthesis requires students to gather information from numerous sources to make judgments, and then turn those judgments into recommendations. Workshop 6 includes the following Guided and Related Assignments:

1. **Guided: Essay of Advice** develops the ability to synthesize elements into a unified whole by asking students to give advice on a subject they know about.

2. **Related: Consumer Report** relates the concept of advice introduced in the Guided Assignment to consumer goods and services.

3. **Related: Problems and Solutions** builds on skills developed in the Guided Assignment by giving students a fictional problem on which to offer advice.

Teaching Preview

Preparation Guide

1. Use the Overview on this page and the Teacher's Choice descriptions on page 177 as a basis for deciding which assignment(s) to teach.

2. Preview the assignments and the teacher's notes and identify concerns that may require preteaching or extra support given your class's abilities. The handbook mini-lessons suggested within the lesson may also provide guidance.

3. Preview the chart below for support materials in the Teacher's Resource File that may be used with this Workshop. Resources are for use with the Guided Assignment unless otherwise noted.

Support Materials

WRITER'S CRAFT RESOURCES

Prewrite and Explore
Thinking Skills Transparencies, pp. 19–20
Thinking Skills Worksheets, p. 12

Draft and Discover
Elaboration, Revision, and Proofreading Worksheets, p. 11

Revise Your Writing
Guidelines for Writing Assessment and Portfolio Use, pp. 13, 32
Peer Response Guides, pp. 19–21
Student Revision Model Transparencies, pp. 23–26
Elaboration, Revision, and Proofreading Worksheets, p. 12

Assessment
Tests and Writing Assessment Prompts, p. 6

Extension Activities
Writing Prompts for Fine Art Transparencies, pp. 13, 14, 17, 18
Writing from Literature, pp. 1–6, 9–12, 17–20, 23–24, 29–42
Standardized Test Practice

 Educational Technology
(available separately)
Writer's DataBank
Electronic English Handbook
Multimedia Workshop
Your Personal Trainer for the New SAT
In Perspective (videodisc)

• •

OTHER RESOURCES

Books and Journals
Romano, Tom. *Clearing the Way: Working with Teenage Writers*. Portsmouth: Heinemann, 1992.

 Films and Videos
"Hard News." *Garage Gazette Series*. Access Network. (15 min.)

Computer Software
MindWriter. The Daedalus Group, Inc. PC/MS-DOS.
Step Write Up! Focus Media. Apple family. Macintosh, PC/MS-DOS.
Success with Writing. Scholastic. Apple family. Macintosh, PC/MS-DOS.

The following options may be used to provide students with an integrated language experience. Begin by assigning and discussing any of the recommended pieces of literature. Use the suggested strategy to provide a link to the Guided Assignment.

LINKING LITERATURE AND WRITING

Option 1

Starting Point: "How to Read Faster" by Bill Cosby on pages 178–179 of *The Writer's Craft*

Strategy: Use the teaching suggestions on pages 178–179 to lead students into the Guided Assignment.

Option 2

Starting Point: "The Lady, or the Tiger?" by Frank Stockton

Strategy: As part of your discussion of this short story, ask students to imagine that they are onlookers at the trial, perhaps friends of the youth. Prompt a wide-ranging conversation in which students share possible advice they would give to the youth on which door to pick, to the princess on how to intervene to save the youth's life, and to the king concerning changes in his system of justice. Conclude the discussion by leading into the Guided Assignment.

Option 3

Starting Point: "The Birds" by Daphne du Maurier

Strategy: As students read and discuss the story, have them focus on moments when the characters, under imminent attack by the birds, must decide what to do. Have students note whether the decisions the characters make are ones that help them or get them further into trouble. Then have students imagine that they are among the characters in the story. What advice would they give to help the other birds? Explain that we give and are given advice every day about major and minor issues. As an example, have them read Bill Cosby's "How to Read Faster" on pages 178–179 and lead them into the Guided Assignment.

LINKING WRITING AND GRAMMAR

Before the drafting or revision stage of this assignment, tell students that they can combine simple sentences into compound sentences with a conjunction such as *and* or *but,* or with a conjunctive adverb such as *therefore* or *consequently.* In the former case, the sentences are separated by a comma before the conjunction; in the latter case, by a semicolon before the conjunctive adverb and a comma after it. Write the following examples on the board as students look for examples of both types in their own writing. (You may wish to have students practice changing one type of compound sentence into the other.)

I warned him not to go out in the blizzard; **however,** he went anyway. (conjunctive adverb)

I warned him not to go out in the blizzard, **but** he went anyway. (conjunction)

Go over the rules for conjunctive adverb usage on page 666 and for compound sentence formation on page 737 of the Grammar and Usage Handbook. If problems still appear on student papers, assign the exercises on those pages for reteaching. Additional practice can be found in the *Grammar and Usage Practice Book* on pages 115–118.

Workshop Management Guidelines

The chart below indicates the number of days recommended for each phase of the Guided and Related Assignments. Stars indicate portions of the assignment that may be completed outside the classroom if time is limited or if teachers wish the activity to be completed by students independently.

ESSAY OF ADVICE

Starting from Literature ....1 day
Prewrite ....2–3 days*
Draft ....1–2 days*
Revise ....1–2 days*
Publish ....1–2 days
Learning...1 day*
Reteaching ....open
Extension/Enrichment.....................open*
Sentence Composing......................1 day*

CONSUMER REPORT

Starting from Literature ....1 day
Developing ....1–2 days*
Writing ....1–2 days*
Reviewing ....1–2 days*
Publishing...................................1–2 days

PROBLEMS AND SOLUTIONS

Starting from Literature ....1 day
Thinking Through ....1–2 days*
Writing ....1–2 days*
Reviewing ....1–2 days
Publishing...................................1–2 days

Sketchbook

Objective

To use a brief definition as a springboard to informal writing

Using the Prompt

Explain that the writing activities in the Sketchbook provide an opportunity for students to write informally without concern about grades. Encourage students to experiment as they write and to express themselves freely.

Before students write, invite volunteers to tell what the word *handicap* means to them. Since it is likely that students will mention physical handicaps such as blindness or deafness, emphasize that not all handicaps are of this type. Discuss handicaps that are not instantly recognizable such as shyness or a lack of self-confidence.

Allow students who wish to discuss their ideas with partners before writing to do so. Make sure students understand that they are free to write about one of the ideas in the Additional Sketches section if these prompts offer a better stimulus for writing.

Ask students to save their writing in their writing portfolio for possible use in the workshop that follows.

Sketchbook

A handicap is a disadvantage of some kind. What handicap do you have? Is it one that other people notice or one that only you are aware of? What would life be like if you didn't have that handicap? What would life be like if you had a different handicap?

Additional Sketches

When did you give someone advice? What was the result?

If you could save only one possession, what would it be? Why?

176

WRITER'S **6** WORKSHOP

Informative Exposition: Synthesis

Guided Assignment
ESSAY OF ADVICE

Related Assignment
CONSUMER REPORT

Related Assignment
PROBLEMS AND SOLUTIONS

In 1964, an American physicist named Robert A. Moog invented a musical instrument that electronically analyzes and combines sounds. It was the first commercially successful synthesizer. Just as Moog's invention synthesizes sounds to make music, writers synthesize information in order to write. They analyze and combine ideas to make judgments, reach conclusions, and give recommendations. In this workshop you will study ways you can synthesize information to give advice, make informed consumer decisions, and solve problems.

177

Objectives

Guided Assignment:
ESSAY OF ADVICE
  To recognize essays of advice and to use prewriting activities to draft, revise, proofread, and share an essay of advice

Related Assignment:
CONSUMER REPORT
  To choose a subject and develop evaluation standards for a consumer report and to write, review, and share a consumer report

Related Assignment:
PROBLEMS AND SOLUTIONS
  To identify a problem and possible solutions and to write, review, and share a solution to a problem

Teacher's Choice

Guided Assignment
  Essay of Advice Most students will profit from this assignment, which requires them to draw on personal experiences to offer advice. Because the assignment introduces students to the skill of synthesizing, it is most useful after students have had experience with analysis, such as that required in a process description.

Related Assignment
  Consumer Report More advanced students and students interested in the scientific process will welcome the challenge of developing standards for judging a product. Because the assignment offers the opportunity for "hands-on" research, it is especially appropriate for kinesthetic learners.

  Problems and Solutions This assignment helps students develop practical problem-solving skills that they can apply in many areas of life and in the study of other subjects, particularly science, literature, and social studies.

Starting from Literature

Objective

To respond to a professional model of an essay of advice as a springboard to writing

Teaching Strategies

Motivate

Ask students if they would like to be able to read faster and how they think someone like Bill Cosby could help them master this skill. Discuss with students what qualifications a person must have in order to give advice in an area.

Tap Prior Knowledge

Have students brainstorm a list of techniques for reading quickly. Ask students how they learned these techniques. Then discuss Bill Cosby's qualifications for giving advice on this matter. Some students may be aware that Mr. Cosby holds a doctorate in education. Explain that study for an advanced degree involves a great deal of reading.

"**I**f I were you . . ."

"My advice to you is . . ."

"What would you do if you were me?"

How many times do you think you've heard those words, or said them? Most people love to give advice. However, even the best advice is harder to take than to give. People who give advice successfully— newspaper columnists, members of the clergy, lawyers, doctors, financial experts, or friends and relatives—have the skill of writing or speaking in a way that makes people pay attention.

In the following passage, notice how Bill Cosby gives authoritative advice in a friendly way.

178

Essay of Advice

How to Read

by Bill Cosby

When I was a kid in Philadelphia, I must have read every comic book ever published. I zipped through all of them in a couple of days, then reread the good ones until the next issues were published. As I got older, though, my eyeballs must have slowed down. I mean, comic books started to pile up faster than my brother Russell and I could read them. It wasn't until much later, when I was getting my doctorate, that I realized it wasn't my eyeballs that were to blame. The problem is that there is too much to read these days, and too little time to read every word of it. That's when I started to look around for common-sense, practical ways to help me read faster. I found three that are especially good. And if I can learn them, so can you—and you can put them to use immediately.

The first way is previewing. It is especially useful for getting a general idea of heavy reading like long magazine or newspaper articles and nonfiction books. To preview, read the entire first two paragraphs of whatever you've chosen. Next read only the first sentence of each successive paragraph. Then read the entire last two paragraphs. This will give you a quick, overall view of the long, unfamiliar material. It will keep you from spending time on things you don't really want—or need—to read.

The second way to read faster is skimming. It is a good way to get a general idea of light reading like popular magazines or the sports and entertainment sections of the paper. It is also a good way to review material you've read before. To skim, think of your eyes as magnets. Force them to move fast. Sweep them across each and every line of type. Pick up only a few key words in each line. You will end up reading about half the words in *less* than half the time it would take to read every word.

The third way to increase your reading speed is clustering. Clustering trains you to look at groups of words rather than one at a time. . . . To practice clustering, begin with something easy to read. Read it as fast as you can. Concentrate on seeing three to four words at once rather than one word at a time. Then reread the piece at your normal speed to see what you missed the first time. Practice fifteen minutes every day until you can read clusters without missing much the first time.

So now you have three ways to help you read faster: previewing to cut down on unnecessary heavy reading; skimming to get a quick, general idea of light reading; and clustering to increase your speed and comprehension. With enough practice, you'll be able to handle more reading at school and at home in less time. You should even have enough time to read your favorite comic books!

Think AND Respond

What do you note about the tone of Cosby's essay? How did he organize his ideas to present them effectively? If you wanted to give advice to someone, what might Cosby's essay teach you about how to do it?

Literature Connection

Author Note William Henry Cosby, Jr., (1937–), better known as Bill, is an award-winning comedic and dramatic actor. He is also well known for his comedy albums and television commercials. Cosby holds a doctorate in education from the University of Massachusetts. His publications include *Fatherhood*, *Time Flies*, and *The Wit and Wisdom of Fat Albert*.

Set a Purpose

Discuss the side-column notes, allowing volunteers to describe briefly times when they have given or asked for advice. Refer students to the purpose-setting statement at the end of the side column on page 178, and have them read the selection.

Think and Respond

Elicit Personal Responses

Give students an opportunity to share their responses with the class, focusing on the ways in which Cosby makes his advice palatable and easy to understand.

Explore the Author's Techniques

You may want to use close reading to identify the techniques employed by the author. For example, point out how Cosby immediately engages the interest of the reader by sharing a childhood experience and by using an informal, conversational tone. (Page 178, paragraph 1: When . . . published. I zipped . . . published.) He then introduces his topic and establishes his credentials as a bona fide advice-giver on the subject. (Page 178, paragraph 1: I mean . . . them. It . . . blame. That's . . . faster. I . . . good.) Point out the one-two-three organization of the body of advice, and note how Cosby explains each method clearly and directly in a separate paragraph. Finally, call attention to the conclusion, in which Cosby summarizes the three methods and their purposes and points out the advantage of following his advice.

Link Literature to Writing

Point out that Cosby draws on his own experience as a child and as an adult student to formulate advice on reading. The advice he gives is not original. Students may recognize that the content of his advice is similar to what they have heard in the classroom. Yet Cosby makes an impact on the reader because his introduction is relevant to students' interests and because he gives his advice in a friendly, sympathetic way. Suggest that as students formulate their essays of advice in the Guided Assignment that follows, they explore ways in which they can affect an audience by referring to their personal experience and by their choice of tone.

Prewrite and Explore

Objectives

1. To use prewriting activities to generate ideas and determine a topic for an essay of advice
2. To explore audience, purpose, and format for an essay of advice
3. To gather information for an essay of advice

Preteaching

Preview the Prewrite and Explore section to identify skills and concepts that your students may need help with before prewriting. The Thinking Skills Transparencies and the mini-lessons listed below will aid you in your selection and instruction. The cross references in the pupil text will give students access to the same lessons for independent study.

> #### Handbook Mini-Lessons
> - Writing Variables, pp. 311–316
> - Personal Techniques, pp. 317–320
> - Sources of Information, pp. 476–478
> - Interviewing Skills, pp. 481–482

Teaching Strategies

Management Tip

You might set aside an area in the classroom and stock it with letters and essays of advice from magazines, newspapers, and books. Students might browse through these materials as they search for topics and plan their essays.

INVITATION TO Write

Bill Cosby gave good advice on a subject he knew about from personal experience. Now write your advice on a subject you know well.

Advice can be as specific and practical as how to interview for a job, or as broad and emotional as how to get over disappointment in love. Whatever the subject, advice is a blend of knowledge and experience. You wouldn't tell someone how to interview for a job—or how to get over a broken heart—unless you had done it yourself or at least read a great deal about it. The fact that it's a personal recommendation based on your own knowledge and experience makes advice different from an unsupported opinion or a set of step-by-step process directions.

PREWRITE AND EXPLORE

HANDBOOKS
FOR HELP & PRACTICE

Writing Variables, pp. 311–316
Personal Techniques, pp. 317–320
Sources of Information, pp. 476–478
Interviewing Skills, pp. 481–482

1. Find a topic. Think about the kinds of expertise you have that you could share with others. You might want to use one or more of the following activities to help you find, or remember, your areas of expertise. You may also want to check your writing for the Sketchbook on page 176 or the "Apply Your Skills" section on page 191 for ideas.

Exploratory Activities

- **Listing** Take a sheet of paper and write a list of topics you know a great deal about. Think about your hobbies, talents, or special skills, or about things for which you just seem to have a knack. For example, do you know how to avoid arguing with your parents, how to *win* arguments with your parents? Don't be modest—make the longest list you can.

- **Surveying** Ask friends and family members to tell you what kinds of advice they think you are qualified to give.
- **Recalling** Think about past situations in which you either gave or received good advice. What was useful about the advice? What wasn't useful about it?
- **Analyzing** What problems strongly concern you? For instance, have you thought a lot about how to resist peer pressure? Do you have tips for a friend who isn't doing well in school? The problems that concern you are often the ones you could help others solve.
- **Reading literature** Think about characters in stories or books you would have liked to be able to help. For instance, what would you tell Penelope in *The Odyssey* about how to deal with the suitors?

One student, Kathleen, made the following list of things she knew about or was good at doing. She circled the one she thought would make the most original and useful topic.

PROBLEM
S O L V I N G

How can I decide what type of advice to give?

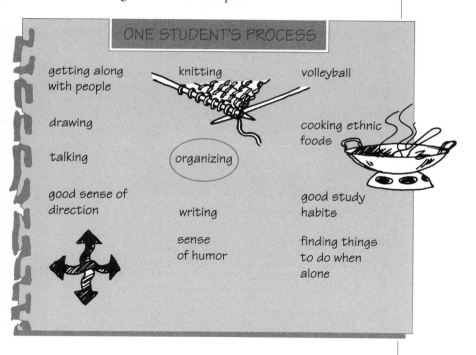

ONE STUDENT'S PROCESS

getting along with people

knitting

volleyball

drawing

cooking ethnic foods

talking

organizing

good sense of direction

writing

good study habits

sense of humor

finding things to do when alone

Personal Touch

You might plan to do the assignment yourself as students work through it. As students select activities from this page, share with them a list of topics on which you could give advice. Later, as students develop their plans, comment on your purpose, format, and anticipated audience. Invite students to ask questions or to make observations about your plans.

Individualizing Instruction

LEP Students Suggest that these students work with English-proficient partners. Encourage pairs to work through the exploratory activities together. The English-proficient student can supply precise English words for concepts with which the LEP student might struggle. The LEP student might help the partner to clarify ideas by asking questions.

Teaching Tip: Topics

If students have difficulty recalling events, suggest that they use categories such as birthday celebrations, holidays, sports, first day of school, new family members, weddings, or household emergencies to help them remember occasions when they have given or received advice. Students might also use the Data Sheet for this assignment as they search for topics.

Modeling

You might model the Literature Exploratory Activity by sharing advice you would like to give a character in one of your favorite novels or short stories. Invite volunteers to describe any appropriate situations from material they are reading in literature. You might also use the Literature Connection on page 182.

Springboard

Students may enjoy discussing the following piece of advice from Mark Twain: "Don't part with your illusions. When they are gone you may still exist but you have ceased to live." You might have students find the definition of *illusion,* and discuss what Twain might have meant (assumptions and beliefs about the way the world works, dreams, and so on). Students might then discuss in small groups or freewrite in their journals their particular "illusions." Which ones would they advise others to hold on to? Why?

Teaching Tip: Audience

Suggest that students think of two contrasting occasions on which they have received advice, one on which their response was positive and another when they resented the advice. Ask students to think about why they responded differently. Suggest that most audiences will be receptive to advice if it is given in a positive way and if the writer takes care to avoid both censure and condescension.

 Individualizing Instruction

Basic Students The students may be most successful in writing a personal letter of advice.

Gifted and Talented Students Students who are interested in dramatic arts might enjoying collaborating on the creation of a radio call-in show or "hot line." Students can work together to create questions and responses that give advice on several topics. You might allow students to present the show for the class at the end of this Guided Assignment.

Auditory Learners These students might also benefit from the above activity, which would allow them to work with others to prepare and present advice orally.

Writing
—TIP—

If your advice tells how to solve a problem, use a chart to brainstorm. Divide a sheet of paper into two columns labeled "Problem" and "Solution" and list ideas.

2. Share your ideas. Once you have identified a few promising ideas, share them with some classmates. Listen for their ideas about points you might make.

3. Select a topic. Freewrite for ten minutes on a topic that interests you. See how much advice you can come up with, and decide if this idea is the one you want to pursue. You don't have to know everything about your topic, but personal interest and experience will help. For example, Bill Cosby has a strong interest in education and literacy, so giving advice about reading was a logical choice.

 Writer's Choice Do you want to give advice about a serious issue or a lighthearted, funny one?

4. Think about your audience. This is especially important in the advice field. After all, your main goal is to get your audience to heed your words. In order to do that, you have to know who the audience is, what they already know about the subject, and what advice they may already have obtained. Once you know their needs and background, you can analyze how to meet those needs. Judging from his language, tone, and approach, what audience do you think Cosby was writing for?

5. Think about your purpose and format. Advice can be written in the form of an essay, a letter, a question-and-answer column, an advertisement, and more. Writing a general statement of purpose that includes your audience—like the one Kathleen wrote below—can help you focus your writing and determine your format.

ONE STUDENT'S PROCESS

My audience is other teens and my purpose is to motivate them to set goals and take action to reach them. The process can be tremendously rewarding.

Kathleen thought she could use her experience from organizing a hotline to help other teens work together to make their voices heard. She decided to write an essay to present her advice.

182 Workshop 6

Literature Connection

Story to Read "The Secret Life of Walter Mitty," by James Thurber, has a central character who could probably use some sound advice. You might want to have students read this short story and discuss the kind of advice they would give Walter Mitty.

6. Gather information. Think about the facts, details, and steps you need to discuss in order to explain your advice. Your advice may appear as a series of informal tips, as a more formal set of steps toward a goal, as a single long answer to a question, or perhaps as a chart. You might take a very detailed approach or concentrate on key points. Also consider whether you need to consult outside sources. Even if you know your subject well, you may still need to do library research or interview other experts. For instance, you may be an experienced runner, but may still want to consult a sports physician on how to avoid injuries and dehydration.

DRAFT AND DISCOVER

1. Begin your draft. The form of your draft will vary depending upon the type of advice you are giving. However, you generally should begin by clearly stating your subject and stating your qualifications to give the advice. Some of the following strategies may be helpful in developing your draft.

Strategies

HANDBOOKS
FOR HELP & PRACTICE

Thesis Statements,
pp. 343–344
Coherence in
Compositions,
pp. 368–369
Types of
Conclusions,
pp. 371–373
Solving Problems,
pp. 456–458
Synthesizing
Material,
pp. 468–469

- **Describing a process** If you are giving "how to" advice, try breaking it down into a stepwise process. Arrange the steps in chronological order; give details for each step; define unfamiliar terms and procedures; tell what supplies are needed, if any; and describe the desired results. Notice how Bill Cosby described *three* different processes in his essay.

- **Cause and effect** The action you are recommending will be a cause that may have certain effects on your readers and other people. Examine the causes and effects of your advice. Make the logical connections clear by using transitions and organization, such as chronological order, order of importance, or familiar-to-unfamiliar order.

Advice Essay **183**

Draft and Discover

Objectives

1. To draft an essay of advice, using such strategies as describing a process, analyzing cause and effect, or explaining a problem and a solution
2. To analyze one's own writing and the writing of peers

Preteaching

Read through the Draft and Discover section to identify those strategies or skills with which students may need help before drafting. You may find the mini-lessons listed below, as well as the Elaboration Worksheets from the Revision, Proofreading, and Elaboration booklet, useful in your selection and instruction.

> **Handbook Mini-Lessons**
> - Thesis Statements, pp. 343–344
> - Coherence in Compositions, pp. 368–369
> - Types of Conclusions, pp. 371–373
> - Solving Problems, pp. 456–458
> - Synthesizing Material, pp. 468–469

Teaching Strategies

Teaching Tip: Specific Details

To help students include sufficient detail in their drafts, you might suggest that they imagine an occasion on which a person would utilize their advice. Have they included everything the advisee would need to know?

 Individualizing Instruction

LD Students To help the students organize their drafts, you might provide them with a sheet that lists the major sections to be included. (For example, First paragraph: subject and qualifications; Middle paragraphs: advice; Last paragraph: summarize.)

Personal Touch

Allow students to see you working on the first draft of your essay of advice. You might read your draft to the class, encouraging students to critique your paper and to offer suggestions for improvement. Make notes of the students' suggestions for use in your revision. Remind students that even the most successful professional writers can profit from the feedback of their editors or peers.

Peer Response

As students arrange for peer response, remind them that they may want to use the Peer Response Sheets for this assignment. You might also suggest that students pay special attention to tone in the essays they are reading.

PROBLEM SOLVING

How can I present my ideas effectively?

Writing **TIP**

Do you want to use a friendly, personal tone, a serious, formal tone, or some combination? To help make sure the tone you use is the one you actually intended, read your draft aloud.

• **Problem and solution** Writing advice is often a form of problem solving. As when solving any problem, define it clearly and specifically first. Then analyze it in detail, list possible solutions, explore each possible solution, and decide on the one that seems most likely to solve the problem. Examine the range of possible results, as well as what to do if the solution doesn't work.

2. Take a break. Set your draft aside for a while; then evaluate it yourself and with peer readers you trust. The questions below may help focus your review process.

REVIEW YOUR WRITING

Questions for Yourself

• Have I said what I intended to say? Are the points I planned to make presented in logical order?

• Is my advice based on actual knowledge and research? Did I pretend to know more than I truly did?

• Is my advice realistic? Will my readers be able to follow it without difficulty?

• If I've used unfamiliar terms, have I explained them adequately?

Questions for Your Peer Readers

• Do you feel my tone is friendly and helpful?

• Do I sound like a reasonable and responsible advisor that you can take seriously?

• Do I sound like I know what I'm talking about? What details might make my advice more authoritative?

• Do I make my points clearly and illustrate them well?

• What do you wish I had said more about? At what points did you feel I said too much?

• Does my advice make sense? Are the tips I give specific and helpful?

• Would you be able to act on my advice?

Social Studies Connection

Current Events Suggest that students think about a community problem or controversy with which they have some knowledge or experience. Ask students to identify a person who might be in a position to effect a change and to formulate advice for that person. Students might share their ideas with the class or actually write a letter of advice to the person.

Writer's Choice You can write your advice from the first-person, second-person, or third-person point of view. Which would be best for your audience?

REVISE YOUR WRITING

1. Evaluate your responses. Go over the responses that you have received from your peer readers, and decide what changes you want to make. Bear in mind the following standards for effective advice essays:

Standards for Evaluation

An effective advice essay . . .

- states the subject clearly in an effective introduction.
- shows your qualifications to give advice on the topic.
- provides suggestions that are workable.
- provides specific details to illustrate and support each point.
- respects the needs and identity of the audience.
- uses appropriate language and tone for the audience.
- uses a clear and logical structure to organize your advice.

COMPUTER TIP

Make a second copy of your draft to experiment with as much as you like. Keep the original untouched so you won't lose material when revising.

HANDBOOKS
FOR HELP & PRACTICE

Peer Response, pp. 378–382

Sentence Length/ Structure, p. 416

Evaluating Ideas, pp. 452–453

Revise Your Writing

Objectives

1. To evaluate the responses to a draft
2. To revise a draft based on self-evaluation, the responses of others, and a set of standards
3. To proofread for errors in spelling, grammar, usage, and mechanics

Preteaching

Skim this portion of the lesson to identify the skills you want to review before students revise. Keep in mind the problems noted in students' first drafts. The mini-lessons listed below as well as the Student Revision Model Transparency and the Revision and Proofreading Worksheets from the Revision, Proofreading, and Elaboration booklet may help you in your selection and instruction.

> **Handbook Mini-Lessons**
> - Peer Response, pp. 378–382
> - Sentence Length/Structure, p. 416
> - Evaluating Ideas, pp. 452–453

Teaching Strategies

Critical Thinking

Evaluating In responding to peer comments, students should evaluate the responses in light of their writing goals and anticipated audience. You might suggest that students ask themselves the following questions: Will this suggestion help me clarify what I have to say? Does this response suggest that I need more information? If I decide to reject a suggestion, what is my reason for doing so?

Modeling

Follow up on your first draft and the student responses you received. Read your completed draft, showing how you incorporated comments and explaining why you rejected others. To further prepare students for revising, you might use the Student Revision Model Transparency for this assignment.

Guidelines for Evaluation

The following guidelines may be used for a close evaluation of an essay of advice. See the Guidelines for Evaluating Writing in the Teacher's Resource File for additional help with holistic or analytic scoring.

Ideas and Content
- contains an introduction that clearly states the subject and presents the writer's qualifications
- includes interesting, practical suggestions
- uses specific details to elaborate on each point
- demonstrates awareness of audience in content, word choice, and tone

Structure and Form
- demonstrates a clear, logical organizational structure
- includes transitional words and phrases as appropriate

Grammar, Usage, and Mechanics
- uses standard grammar and usage
- uses correct spelling, capitalization, and punctuation

Managing the Paper Load

You may want to focus on content and structure as you evaluate students' essays, using the Guidelines for Evaluation given above or the Guidelines for Evaluating Writing checklist and Sample Papers for this assignment. If you use the latter, return the checklist with the essay so students can note specific areas that were weak.

2. Problem-solve. Rework your draft, addressing the specific problems you and your peer readers have uncovered. Below, notice the changes that Kathleen made in response to her classmates' comments:

ONE STUDENT'S PROCESS

These are excellent suggestions. But what do you mean by "public relations"?

How do you get people on your side?

In order to make the project work, you have to move it out beyond the core group. That means public relations. The public will become your source of volunteers, money, and support. Another crucial step is to contact officials, businesspeople, and other citizens who may be able to help—or hinder—your project. Get as many important people on your side as possible.

Talk to people, make speeches, contact a newspaper reporter, hand out flyers.

In our case, we spoke personally to the mayor of our town, the public relations chiefs of the local telephone company and the local hospital, several legislators, members of the clergy, and owners of businesses.

3. Proofread your work. Make a clean copy of your draft and check it for errors in grammar, usage, and mechanics. Be sure you have used complete sentences and punctuated them correctly. Do any sentences sound confusing or unclear? Are all your verb tenses consisent? Have you made any typing mistakes? Try to imagine that you did not write your draft, and see if you can be as objective as possible about how it sounds. What do you notice now that you did not see before?

Springboard

You might have students submit anonymous written requests for advice. Then ask for volunteers for a panel of "experts" from the class, who will read the requests and prepare responses. The panel can then respond to the questions in a panel discussion. Other students may contribute additional advice extemporaneously. Students may also question the panelists on their qualifications for offering advice. Explain the entire activity beforehand to help avoid the submission of any questions that are too sensitive for class discussion.

LINKING
GRAMMAR **AND** WRITING

CONJUNCTIONS AND CONJUNCTIVE ADVERBS

Using conjunctive adverbs such as *therefore, however, consequently,* and *moreover* can be an effective way to state the results, consequences, or benefits of advice. When two clauses are linked by a conjunctive adverb, use a semicolon to separate the clauses and place a comma after the conjunctive adverb.

USING A CONJUNCTIVE ADVERB

We convinced the manager of the pizzeria that helping us would be good publicity; consequently, he became our first sponsor.

See Grammar Handbook 35, pages 663–665 for additional help.

PUBLISH AND PRESENT

- **Submit your essay for publication.** Send it to a special interest magazine or newspaper. Include a cover letter explaining who you are, where you are from, and what prompted you to write the essay.
- **Start an advice column.** Approach the editor of your school newspaper, or create a bulletin board for advice in your classroom. Encourage your friends to read each other's advice and write some of their own.
- **Share your advice in a speech.** Rehearse and then deliver your speech to classmates, friends, or family. Make a tape of it to listen to later. Make changes as needed to increase the speech's effectiveness.
- **Include your advice in a letter to someone who could use it.** Then discuss the recipient's reactions.
- **Keep your advice in your writing portfolio.** Read it to yourself in a month or two. At that time you may see your ideas and writing differently.
- **Share your advice.** Get together with a group of classmates and read your essays aloud.

Grammar TIP

Don't use the same form of compound sentence throughout. Vary your sentence structure to make your advice more engaging.

HANDBOOKS
FOR HELP & PRACTICE

Publishing Your Work, pp. 402–403

Publish and Present

Objective

To publish and to present an essay of advice

Teaching Strategies

Modeling

Review the essay of advice you have written. Then discuss with students what medium of publication might be used for it. Make a choice of an appropriate medium and explain your reasons for the choice. Encourage students to explain their choices of publication.

Speaking and Listening

You might arrange a whole-class or small-group reading session followed by a question-and-answer period. Volunteers can read their essays aloud, and listeners can ask questions, either about the content or about the writing process. (For example, Where did you get your ideas? Why did you choose to write a letter?) Such a session will help students benefit from the writing experiences of their peers.

Using the Model

After students have read the model, discuss the annotations in the side bar. Invite volunteers to identify any other elements of the essay that they found especially effective, helpful, or interesting.

Reteaching

Assess the needs of students who were not successful in developing an effective essay of advice and identify two or three areas in which additional practice is needed. Assign the appropriate Handbook Mini-Lessons, along with the support materials listed for each lesson. Concepts commonly requiring reteaching are

Writing an Introduction: Handbook 6
Coherence in Paragraphs: Handbook 10
Coherence in Compositions: Handbook 10

The following suggestions and resources may also be useful.

1. Lack of Specific Details In a small group, work with students who did not include sufficient specific details. Have each student read aloud one or two major points from his or her essay. Then ask questions to elicit more detail ("Can you give me an example?" "What would I do first?" "What would I need to do that?"), and have students make notes as they answer.

2. Weak Structure Hand out sheets on which you have written an outline with the following headings: Introduction, Major Points of Advice, and Conclusion. Leave space under each heading for student responses. Have each student who demonstrated difficulty with organization make a brief outline of the essay, identifying each of the three parts. Then work with students or suggest that they work with partners to correct any structural problems revealed by their outlines.

Uses appropriate language and tone for the audience

States the subject clearly in the introduction

Demonstrates the author's qualifications

Uses a clear organizational structure

Gives specific practical details

ONE STUDENT'S PROCESS

How to Make Your Voice Heard

Kathleen McAllister

Did you ever feel that no matter how many good ideas teenagers have, adults won't take us seriously? I used to feel that way too. Recently, however, I saw proof that if we work hard at making our voices heard, we can have an effect. I joined with a group of friends in persuading our community to establish a hotline for teenagers. The hotline is a phone number anyone can call, without giving his or her name, and talk to a teenage volunteer who will listen. The experience taught me that teenagers can make a difference. Here are steps you can take to make your voice heard.

The first step is to find a few friends, or even just one, who share your feelings. By seeking out early supporters, you do three things at once. First, you find out how strong or weak the appeal of the idea is. Second, by brainstorming the idea you strengthen it. Finally, if the idea convinces your listeners, you develop a pool of co-workers. In our case, the idea for the hotline started in a discussion a group of us were having over pizza, so we had a ready-made set of founders.

Once you have your core group, draw up a plan of action and divide the work among you. In particular, think about the following questions. What materials do you need to accomplish your goal? For instance, a hotline requires telephones, a small office, one or more desks, and volunteers. It also requires money for equipment, publicity, and rent. Try to have a good idea from the outset of what you'll need to buy and how much it will cost. Ask yourselves, too, what specific skills or knowledge you have that will help you achieve the goal.

Health Connection

Health Advice Most health textbooks and magazines include information on a variety of related subjects: how to maintain body weight, how to choose a balanced diet, how to pursue an exercise program, how to insure good mental health, how to avoid substance abuse, and so on. Suggest that small groups of students gather information of this type. Groups might then combine this information with their own knowledge and personal experience to develop advice on a health-related topic.

One of us was a good artist who drew a striking publicity poster; another was a persuasive talker who became our top fund-raiser; and one of us had a social-worker parent who became our advisor.

In order to make the project work, you have to move it out beyond the core group. That means public relations. Talk to people, make speeches, contact a newspaper reporter, hand out flyers—do whatever you can to spread your idea. The public will become your source of volunteers, money, and support. Another crucial step is to contact officials, businesspeople, and other citizens who may be able to help—or hinder—your project. Get as many important people on your side as possible. In our case, we spoke personally to the mayor of our town, the public relations chiefs of the local telephone company and the local hospital, several legislators, members of the clergy, and owners of businesses. All of them praised our idea. We soon learned, though, that praise isn't enough. We had to persuade them to act on their beliefs. For instance, we found an empty room in a social service agency and asked the director to let us use it. We convinced the manager of the pizzeria that helping us would be good publicity; consequently, he became our first sponsor.

Six months after our original inspiration, our words and enthusiasm had been transformed into a real hotline. I'll never forget how it felt to sit at the volunteer's desk that first evening. The early calls were from friends and relatives congratulating us. Later, serious calls flowed in. Today we're an established part of the community. Helping people is like physical exercise—you can feel yourself growing. Is there something you want to do that would make the world better, for teenagers or anyone else? Take my advice, and do it.

Considers the identity of the audience

Proposes workable solutions

• A group of students may want to take Kathleen's advice and create plans for an "advice center" at your school. Students might consider how student and teacher volunteers might staff such a center, when the center would operate, and so on. If students are interested, they might actually propose such a program.

• Some students might arrange for a representative of a health or safety organization or for another faculty member with expertise in some area to address the class. After the presentation, students might evaluate the advice both for content and method of presentation.

Off the Record

"I was your guidance counselor when you were a high school student here, Marvin, but now that you're on your own, you'll have to make your own business decisions."

Learning from Your Writing Process

Objective

To analyze and reflect upon what has been learned about the writing process and the writing of an essay of advice

Teaching Strategies

Critical Thinking

Inferring Students might ask themselves the following questions about the author comment on this page: What can I infer from the writer's statement about taking advice? How does this inference apply to the advice I have given in my essay? Why is the best advice often not heeded?

Reflecting on the Process

Briefly discuss the variety of advice formats students have read, heard, and worked on during the assignment, including your own. You might then model the process of reflecting on the writing experience by answering the first question on this page about your own essay. Remind students that they are free to make notes about any aspect of their writing experience; they are not limited to answering the questions on this page.

Writing Portfolio

After analyzing their responses to this assignment, students should place their evaluations, drafts, and final essays in their Writing Portfolios. You might suggest that students compare their final essays with their drafts, and note specific areas of improvement. Suggest that students make notes about any other changes they may want to make.

LEARNING FROM YOUR WRITING PROCESS

WRITER TO WRITER

"When giving advice—whether in writing or in person—first ask lots of questions about the situation. Remember there will be pluses and minuses to each solution you come up with. I give fabulous advice—if only I took it!"

Judith Stone, advice columnist for *Glamour* magazine

FOR YOUR PORTFOLIO

1. Reflect on your writing. Now that you have read advice essays by Bill Cosby and a student and have written one of your own, think about the writing process involved. Ask yourself questions such as those listed below. Record any useful responses you might have in your writing log or attach the answers to the final paper you submit.

- What did I enjoy most about giving advice? What did I enjoy least?
- How is writing advice different from the other kinds of writing I have done? What tips and suggestions might I give someone who is approaching this kind of writing for the first time?

Springboard

Ask students to reflect in their journals how the abstract picture *Twin Sisters* might be interpreted to illustrate some important points about writing advice (for example, two heads are better than one, looking at the world through a different point of view, or empathizing with the person(s) you are advising).

- When I look at my writing from earlier in the year, can I see my writing process changing? What parts of the writing process are easier for me now? What parts are still troublesome? What might I try next time to make them easier?
- What new problems arose in the advice assignment that weren't present in others? How did I deal with them?
- What new approaches did I learn from writing advice that I could use when writing other kinds of material?

2. Apply your skills. Try one or more writing activities in the following areas:

- **Cross-curricular** Think about something you have learned to do in science, music, art, shop, or another subject. For example, you might have learned how to measure the diameter of a star, to weld scrap metal, or to play a synthesizer. Write an article helping others learn the skill.

- **Literature** Write a letter of advice to a literary character who affected you. For example, you might tell the king in "The Lady or the Tiger?" how to be a better ruler.

- **History** Think of an historical figure you have studied who was facing a major decision—for example, Julius Caesar thinking about crossing the Rubicon River into Italy or Queen Elizabeth I deciding what to do about Mary, Queen of Scots. Write a letter giving him or her your advice.

- **General** With a small group of friends, write several letters that a group of confused parents of teenagers might send to a newspaper advice columnist. Then write the columnist's answers. Each of you might want to role-play a specific fictionalized parent. Use your knowledge, experience, and imagination to create parents who really need advice, as well as to suggest realistic solutions to their problems.

- **Related assignments** Follow the suggestions that you will find on pages 192–202 to write a consumer report and a problem/solution essay.

Advice Essay **191**

Reprinted by Permission of UFS, Inc.

Summary and Closure

Before proceeding to the next lesson, be sure students have internalized the following concepts.

1. An essay of advice makes a recommendation that is based on the personal experience and knowledge of the writer.

2. Advice can take a variety of forms—a letter, magazine article, newspaper column —depending on the writer's purpose and the intended audience.

3. An effective essay of advice includes the qualifications of the writer, an appropriate tone, practical suggestions, and clear organization.

Ask students to summarize what they have learned in this assignment by describing the key characteristics of an effective essay of advice. Students should also specify in what contexts they might be likely to use their skill in writing an essay of advice.

Springboard

Students may enjoy writing letters to a professional advice columnist. Suggest that students skim newspapers and magazines to identify a prospect. You might then brainstorm as a class a list of questions that students might like to ask the columnist. If any students receive a response, have them share it with the class.

Starting from Literature

Objective

To respond to a model of a consumer report as a springboard to writing

Teaching Strategies

Motivate

Ask students what kinds of sandwiches they eat for lunch and what motivates them to choose these kinds of sandwiches. Are they influenced by taste alone or do other factors affect their choices? Have students discuss the extent to which their choice of sandwiches might change were they to gain new information about calories, fat content, and other nutritional considerations.

Tap Prior Knowledge

Take a poll of what students know about the comparative merits of the sandwiches discussed in the consumer report—peanut butter, American cheese, bologna, and tuna. Have students rate the sandwiches by giving each a ranking of 1 to 4 on the following criteria: calories, total fat content, cholesterol content, and protein. Have students compile their results.

Set a Purpose

Discuss the side-column notes. Ask students to read to find out how well their own predictions match the findings of the report as well as to focus on the purpose stated at the end of the side column.

Related
ASSIGNMENT

Consumer Report

BETWEEN THE BREAD
FROM CONSUMER REPORTS

Have you ever started to buy or use a product only to realize that you know little or nothing about it? As a consumer you are constantly faced with choices. Would it be helpful to get some advice about the best product or service available? What you need is a consumer report.

In this report, the writer discusses the nutritional value of a favorite sandwich spread, peanut butter, and compares it with that of other popular sandwich fillings. As you read, look for the types of information the author includes in this evaluation.

Every day, about one out of six Americans eats peanut butter. By year's end, we've gobbled enough of the stuff to make 10 billion peanut butter and jelly sandwiches. . . .

Peanuts aren't really nuts but legumes, like peas and beans. Like those vegetables, peanuts (and their butter) are a good source of protein and dietary fiber. A three-tablespoon serving of peanut butter provides about a third of an adult's daily protein requirement and as much fiber as a bowl of raisin bran.

Although peanuts alone are a good source of protein, that protein is incomplete because some essential amino acids are present in proportions that don't match the ones people need for good nutrition. Add the spread to a slice of bread, however, and you improve the quality of the protein. Peanut butter also contains dietary fiber and B vitamins. It has a lot of fat, but most of the fat is unsaturated—that is, it tends not to raise blood cholesterol levels. (As plant seeds, peanuts themselves contain virtually no cholesterol.)

The Government requires all brands [of peanut butter] to be at least ninety percent peanuts, so any difference in the lesser ingredients doesn't add up to much. (Salt is an exception. Some brands . . . leave it out.) The stabilizer in regular peanut butter contributes saturated fat, but not enough to worry about. . . .

We compared a peanut butter sandwich with three other popular sandwiches—American cheese, beef bologna, and chunk light tuna packed in water.

The only one of the sandwich fillers with fiber, peanut butter is also the only one that contains virtually no cholesterol. It has the least sodium of the four, and less saturated fat than the cheese and bologna sandwiches. It's also likely to cost the least.

On the other hand, the peanut butter sandwich contains much more total fat and calories than the tuna sandwich. And it has less calcium than the cheese sandwich. The moral, as usual: Eat a varied diet.

192

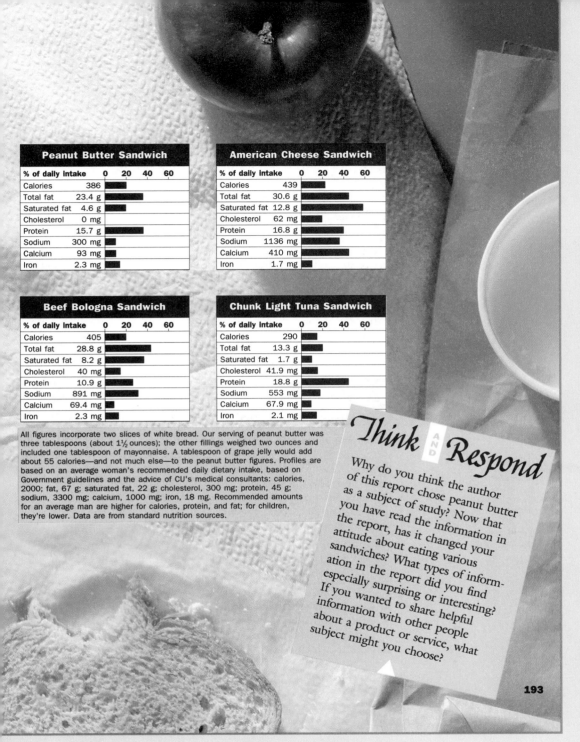

Peanut Butter Sandwich					
% of daily intake		0	20	40	60
Calories	386				
Total fat	23.4 g				
Saturated fat	4.6 g				
Cholesterol	0 mg				
Protein	15.7 g				
Sodium	300 mg				
Calcium	93 mg				
Iron	2.3 mg				

American Cheese Sandwich					
% of daily intake		0	20	40	60
Calories	439				
Total fat	30.6 g				
Saturated fat	12.8 g				
Cholesterol	62 mg				
Protein	16.8 g				
Sodium	1136 mg				
Calcium	410 mg				
Iron	1.7 mg				

Beef Bologna Sandwich					
% of daily intake		0	20	40	60
Calories	405				
Total fat	28.8 g				
Saturated fat	8.2 g				
Cholesterol	40 mg				
Protein	10.9 g				
Sodium	891 mg				
Calcium	69.4 mg				
Iron	2.3 mg				

Chunk Light Tuna Sandwich					
% of daily intake		0	20	40	60
Calories	290				
Total fat	13.3 g				
Saturated fat	1.7 g				
Cholesterol	41.9 mg				
Protein	18.8 g				
Sodium	553 mg				
Calcium	67.9 mg				
Iron	2.1 mg				

All figures incorporate two slices of white bread. Our serving of peanut butter was three tablespoons (about 1½ ounces); the other fillings weighed two ounces and included one tablespoon of mayonnaise. A tablespoon of grape jelly would add about 55 calories—and not much else—to the peanut butter figures. Profiles are based on an average woman's recommended daily dietary intake, based on Government guidelines and the advice of CU's medical consultants: calories, 2000; fat, 67 g; saturated fat, 22 g; cholesterol, 300 mg; protein, 45 g; sodium, 3300 mg; calcium, 1000 mg; iron, 18 mg. Recommended amounts for an average man are higher for calories, protein, and fat; for children, they're lower. Data are from standard nutrition sources.

Think AND Respond

Why do you think the author of this report chose peanut butter as a subject of study? Now that you have read the information in the report, has it changed your attitude about eating various sandwiches? What types of information in the report did you find especially surprising or interesting? If you wanted to share helpful information with other people about a product or service, what subject might you choose?

193

Elicit Personal Responses

Discuss the Think and Respond questions, encouraging students to express their honest reactions to the article and to comment specifically on how the author helped consumers through this report. Ask students to share some of their ideas for the subject of a consumer report.

Explore the Author's Techniques

As a class, discuss some of the techniques used by the author of the report. For example, the author makes sure readers know exactly what peanuts are and what the most important nutritional components of peanut butter and the peanut butter sandwich are (Page 192, paragraphs 2 and 3). The author also explains away any differences among peanut butter brands (Page 192, paragraph 4) before proceeding with any comparisons. The author then explains the methodology used in gathering information for the report (Page 192, paragraph 5) and summarizes the findings (Page 192, paragraphs 6 and 7). The author presents the data on which conclusions are based in easy-to-read charts (Page 193). The report concludes with a recommendation based on the findings (Page 192, paragraph 7: "The moral, as usual: Eat a varied diet.")

Link Literature to Writing

Point out that this report comparing peanut butter sandwiches with other sandwiches is just one example of a consumer report. Suggest that, as students develop their own consumer reports in the assignment that follows, they keep in mind how the author of the model carefully defined what he was evaluating before proceeding to explain his evaluation techniques and results. Also suggest that they keep in mind how clearly the author presented his data through charts and how succinctly he explained the conclusions he drew from his data.

Health Connection

Nutrition Encourage students to become familiar with nutritional labeling by having them compare breakfast cereals. Ask each student to list the following nutritional information per serving from the box of a favorite breakfast cereal: calories, protein (g), carbohydrate (g), fat (g), cholesterol (mg), sodium (mg), and potassium (mg). Have students compare their findings.

Guiding Your Writers

Objectives

1. To choose a subject and identify a purpose for a consumer report
2. To develop standards and objective tests for evaluation
3. To write, review, and share a consumer report

Preteaching

Scan the assignment to identify those skills and concepts with which students may need help. You may find the Evaluation Matrix in the Thinking Skills Worksheets as well as the mini-lessons listed below helpful. The cross references in the pupil text will give students access to the same lessons for independent study.

> **Handbook Mini-Lessons**
> - Brainstorming, pp. 323–324
> - Using Specific Words, pp. 383–385
> - Evaluating Ideas, pp. 452–453

Teaching Strategies

Cooperative Learning

Encourage students to work in small groups to develop a consumer report. After brainstorming to find a subject, students might divide the tasks of developing evaluation standards and carrying out tests, with each group member responsible for some aspect of the research. Students might then collaborate to organize, write, and revise the report.

INVITATION TO Write

This excerpt gave information about the nutritional value of peanut butter. Now write a consumer report that would help others choose a product or service that best fits their needs.

A consumer report is a form of advice that describes a product or service and offers an evaluation or opinion about its quality and reliability. People often use consumer reports to help them choose intelligently from among the different brands of the same product or some other popular item. Newspapers and TV shows often provide consumer reports in the form of book, movie, or restaurant reviews. Several consumer magazines, such as *Consumer Reports,* publish evaluations based on in-depth analyses and testing of products or services.

DEVELOPING A CONSUMER REPORT

HANDBOOKS

FOR HELP & PRACTICE

Brainstorming, pp. 323–324
Using Specific Words, pp. 383–385
Evaluating Ideas, pp. 452–453

1. Choose a product or service to evaluate. What product or service could you study in a way that might be helpful to other consumers? What products, such as shampoo or snack food, do you select and buy for yourself? What services do you purchase? What are you considering buying? Make a list of products and services you use and that you would enjoy evaluating for others. Choose the one you feel most qualified to discuss.

Writer's Choice Do you want to describe only one product or service, or would it be useful to compare two or more similar ones?

2. Consider whether the subject is appropriate for a report. Is it of interest to others? Will you be able to test it adequately or speak to others who have used it? Are there other similar products or services to which you could compare it?

Springboard

Bring to class two products that you have on hand, such as two "how-to" books on the same subject, two news magazines, or two brands of furniture polish. As a warm-up, brainstorm with students some of the standards against which the items might be evaluated. To help students get started, explain what you would expect from such a product.

3. Identify your purpose. Do you want to show whether your subject is a good buy? Do you want to compare it to other similar products (three brands of running shoes, for example) or services and show which one is best? Do you want to investigate possible dangers or threats to health associated with the item?

4. List your standards for evaluation. What should your subject do, be like, or provide? For example, running shoes should support your feet, feel good, and provide traction. Will you also judge your subject in terms of appearance or durability or price?

5. Use objective tests if possible. Read labels and other material from the manufacturer. Compare this information to the claims made for the product or service, or to information about similar products or services. You may also conduct your own tests. For example, pour milk on cereal, taste it at regular intervals, and record how long the cereal stays crisp.

6. Make subjective judgments when necessary. Try the product or service. After you've had some experience with it, ask yourself questions like these: How does it make you feel? How do you like its style? Is it good value for its price?

WRITING A CONSUMER REPORT

1. Introduce your subject. Describe the product or service that you studied and what you were trying to find out about it. Briefly list the standards you used in evaluating it. If you had expectations about the subject, tell what they were here.

2. Choose your tone. Decide on the tone you want your report to have. Will it be formal and objective, like the model or more informal and personal? The subject of your report will help establish the tone. So will the nature of your audience.

3. Describe your experience. Explain your tests and standards fully. Show how the subject did or did not meet each standard. Also, discuss how well your subject lives up to any claims made by the manufacturer of the product or the provider of the service. For example, if Korner Kritters claims to "stay crisper, longer" than other cereal brands, did you find that to be so? Give your personal reaction to using the product or service. Did you feel satisfied or disappointed after using it?

Writing
— TIP —

A good way to show a comparison of products or services is in a chart that lists how each one met your standards or tests.

Assess the needs of students who were not successful in developing an effective consumer report. Assign the appropriate Handbook Mini-Lessons, along with the support materials listed for each lesson. Concepts commonly requiring reteaching for this assignment are

Evaluating Ideas: Handbook 24
Synthesizing Material: Handbook 25

The following suggestions and resources may also be useful.

1. Inadequate Standards Provide students who had difficulty developing standards with several sample consumer reports, both professional and student models. In a small group identify the standards for evaluation in each example, and discuss why the particular features were chosen. Have students discuss possible standards for their product and then rework their report.

2. Lack of Recommendations Remind students that an important element of a consumer report is the recommendation of a product. Ask students who did not include a recommendation to orally summarize the information they gathered. Then ask leading questions such as, "Will you buy this product in the future?" "Why or why not?" or "Which item did you prefer?" "Which item would you tell your friends to buy?" "Why?" After students have answered the questions, suggest they incorporate recommendations into their reports.

Extension and Enrichment

• Students might use the results of their research to create a commercial or some other kind of advertisement for a product or service. If students choose to develop a commercial, remind them of the techniques they learned in the Related Assignment "Storyboard" (Workshop 3).

4. Summarize with a recommendation. This is the most important part of the report and should clearly reflect your opinion of whether consumers will be satisfied with the product or service you tested. If you have mixed reactions, they should be stated here. Your recommendation should be based on both your objective analysis and your subjective, or personal, reaction to it.

REVIEWING YOUR WRITING

1. Revise your report for usefulness. Read over your report to make sure a reader could use it to make a purchasing decision. Add any missing details. Check to see that you have clearly described the standards and tests you used to make your evaluation.

2. Proofread your report. Make sure it does not contain factual errors about the products or services. Check to see that you have correctly spelled proper names and accurately quoted information such as prices and product or service addresses.

PUBLISHING AND PRESENTING

- **Create a consumer handbook.** Compile the consumer reports written by classmates or reports you find in newspapers and magazines into a collection of consumer advice.
- **Send your report to the company that makes the product or offers the service.** Consumer opinions are valued by businesses, and your report should be useful to those who market the product or service.
- **Suggest the inclusion of a consumer column to your school newspaper.** Submit your report and a summary of its findings to the newspaper.

196 Workshop 6

On the Lightside

THE NEW PUNCTUATION

As section chief with the Department of Words and Letters, I have . . . develop[ed] a new punctuation more in keeping with today's usage.

The purpose of punctuation, as I understand it, is to make meanings of sentences unmistakably clear, something which I believe the new punctuation accomplishes.

The Halt—Stronger than a period. The halt signals an abrupt and serious stop.

1. . . . that's it, folks ⊙
2. The next one who speaks is middle class ⊙

The Crescendo—Used to show something is building, as anger.

1. If I have to tell you to sit down one more time, Sitzfleish, I'll explode ₀₀₀°
2. Here's Johnnny ₀₀₀°

The Delta-Sarc—indicates spoken sarcasm.

1. I'll just bet you do △
2. Brilliant, Harold, now what do we do △

The Sigh—Used to emphasize resignation.

1. Oh well, I guess so ⁊⟩
2. Isn't she magnificent ⁊⟩

The Diddledy Dot—The diddledy dot is used to indicate frivolity.

1. Oh ho, he makes $400,000 a year, does he ₀°₀

2. Sorry, didn't mean to walk in on you like that ₀°₀

A Word About Pausals

Pausals are used in place of knowledge to fill the gaps and ellipses in our speech. Because of their frequency . . . they require symbols.

This is the symbol for "you know," by far the most popular crop of pausals.

1. I'd like to go ⋇, but I can't. ⋇ how it is, ⋇, if I could, I would, ⋇.

This is the symbol for "uh," somewhat old-fashioned but still very much with us.

1. Ladies and gentlemen, I'd, ⸦, like to tell you, a, ⸦, few things about, ⸦, the company.

The symbol for "agh," the lesser of the pausal weeds but the choice of some.

The Segue—The segue is used to make elegant transitions, as from the middle of a sentence or paragraph . . . to the end. Usually it is made with subtle prose; however, when the writer has nothing to say, he may substitute the segue.

The Fin—The end. Finality. That's it baby.

Lewis Burke Frumkes

197

Allow students ample time to read about, enjoy, and perhaps experiment with Lewis Burke Frumkes' new punctuation. You might have students compose sentences using the new punctuation marks. Encourage students to share and discuss their sentences with the class.

Starting from Literature

Objective

To respond to a literary excerpt as a springboard to writing

Teaching Strategies

Motivate

Ask students to think about problems they may have had in the past or those that face them now. Suggest that all people have problems and that those who are successful in life work out solutions. Discuss with students people they know or have read about who have solved problems in their lives.

Tap Prior Knowledge

Have students recall their favorite characters from literature and discuss how they dealt with the problems that faced them. Did they solve their problems alone or did they seek help? Encourage students to suggest alternate courses of action that the characters might have followed.

Set a Purpose

Discuss the side-column notes, and ask students to restate Harry's problem. Then call attention to the purpose-setting statement at the end of the side column, and have students read the excerpt.

Related ASSIGNMENT

Problems and Solutions

from

THE TORN INVITATION

by Norman Katlov

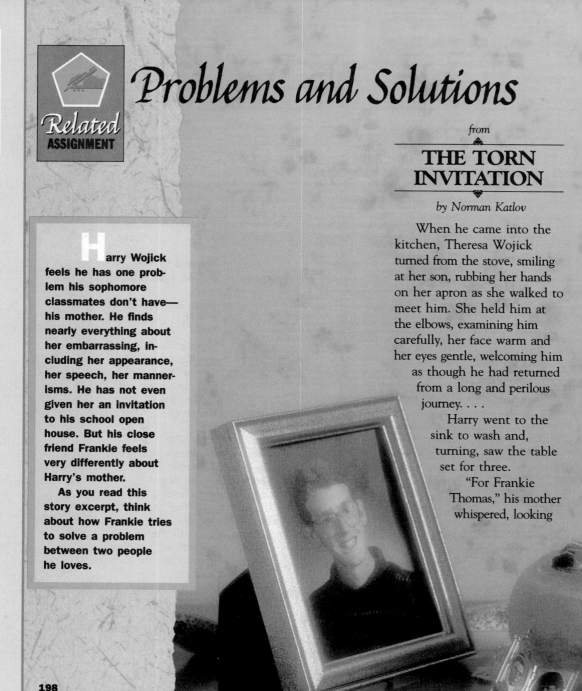

Harry Wojick feels he has one problem his sophomore classmates don't have—his mother. He finds nearly everything about her embarrassing, including her appearance, her speech, her mannerisms. He has not even given her an invitation to his school open house. But his close friend Frankie feels very differently about Harry's mother.

As you read this story excerpt, think about how Frankie tries to solve a problem between two people he loves.

When he came into the kitchen, Theresa Wojick turned from the stove, smiling at her son, rubbing her hands on her apron as she walked to meet him. She held him at the elbows, examining him carefully, her face warm and her eyes gentle, welcoming him as though he had returned from a long and perilous journey. . . .

Harry went to the sink to wash and, turning, saw the table set for three.

"For Frankie Thomas," his mother whispered, looking

198

at her son. "His mother is gone again till half the night, and leaves cold cuts. Boy like Frankie to eat cold cuts," she whispered. "You call him, Harry."

"Why can't she learn to speak English?" he asked himself savagely, turning away. "She's been here long enough!"

Harry walked through the short hall and stood under the arch which led into the living room. He saw the frail, black-haired boy with whom he had grown up, sitting in the chair under the lamp. "Hey, Frankie," Harry said. "Come on and eat." Harry whistled shrilly and came back into the kitchen.

He pulled the chair out and held it suspended off the clean, bare floor, his fingers tightening on the wood. There, next to his plate, was the white, square envelope, and atop it, covered by a transparent sheet of thin paper, was the embossed invitation.

Harry looked at his mother, who had her back to him, busy at the stove. He heard Frankie coming through the house and knew [that Frankie had put the invitation there], *knew* it. He moved the chair at last and sat down and, without touching it, his hands holding his knees, he read the invitation from the faculty of Hamilton High School to an open house in honor of all the students' mothers.

It was tomorrow.

Harry knew *that* all right. Had known it for ten days and had kept it a secret. . . .

Think AND Respond

Harry saw his mother as a problem. Do you think Harry had other problems that he didn't see? Was Frankie helpful in solving Harry's problems? Have you ever, like Harry, had a painful problem with another person? Or, like Frankie, have you seen a friend in a difficult situation and wanted to help? What solutions did you try? How successful were you?

199

Literature Connection

Author Note Norman Katlov was born in Russia in 1918. His knowledge of the experiences of immigrants may well be reflected in this excerpt. A versatile writer, Katlov has authored several books, scripts for television shows and a film, as well as a variety of material for newspapers and magazines.

Think and Respond

Elicit Personal Responses

Discuss responses to the excerpt, focusing on students' reactions to Frankie's solution. Ask students to suggest other solutions Frankie might have tried and to consider the possible effects of each.

Explore the Author's Techniques

You might call on volunteers to read the story aloud, paragraph by paragraph. Pause for discussion after each section, focusing on the elements Katlov introduces. For example, he introduces Theresa, presenting her as a caring and loving person. (Page 198, paragraph 1: She held . . . journey.) He then reveals one of the problems and Harry's feelings about it. (Page 198, paragraph 3: "For . . . son. "His . . . cuts. Boy . . . whispered. Page 199, paragraph 1: "Why . . . away.) Finally, Katlov reveals the major conflict and Frankie's attempt to solve it. (Page 199, paragraph 3: There . . . invitation. Paragraph 4: He heard . . . it. Paragraph 6: Had known . . . secret.) Ask students to speculate on the reasons Frankie might have had for his actions. What outcome did Frankie hope for or expect?

Link Literature to Writing

Point out that the excerpt provided an example of a personal problem and an attempt to resolve it. Suggest that as students approach the assignment that follows, they think about problems that they, other people, or fictional characters like Harry have experienced. How might those problems be solved?

Guiding Your Writers

Objectives

1. To identify and explore the causes and effects of a problem
2. To determine and evaluate several possible solutions
3. To write, review, and share an explanation of a solution to a problem

Preteaching

Preview the lesson, identifying those skills or concepts with which students may need help. The Problem-Solution Matrix in the Thinking Skills Worksheets as well as the mini-lessons listed below may help you in your selection and instruction. The cross references in the pupil text will give students access to the same lessons for independent study.

> **Handbook Mini-Lessons**
> - Thesis Statements, pp. 343–344
> - Faulty Reasoning, pp. 453–455
> - Solving Problems, pp. 456–458

Teaching Strategies

Modeling

Ask students to identify a typical school or classroom problem. Briefly explore the causes, and brainstorm with students several possible solutions. Discuss the ramifications of each solution, modeling the process that students will employ in this assignment.

Teaching Tip: Topics

Encourage students to review their journals for problems they have written about in the past or for their reactions to stories and the problems of particular characters.

INVITATION TO Write

In the excerpt, Frankie tried to help solve the problem between Harry and his mother. Now write how you would solve this or another problem by offering possible solutions or reasonable advice.

One of the most common experiences in life is facing problems and finding solutions. Trying to solve a problem often involves analyzing many different pieces of information. After combining the information into a whole picture, you can offer advice, either face to face or in writing. Fictional writing often has a powerful effect on us because it deals with problems or conflicts that we ourselves face. By studying these problems, offering advice, or exploring solutions, we can become better problem-solvers in our own lives.

THINKING THROUGH A PROBLEM AND SOLUTION

HANDBOOKS
FOR HELP & PRACTICE

Thesis Statements, pp. 343–344
Faulty Reasoning, pp. 453–455
Solving Problems, pp. 456–458

1. Choose a problem. Find a situation that has meaning to you or to others. You may analyze a problem or conflict in a work of fiction such as "The Torn Invitation" or another story. Consider choosing a work of fiction that has characters like people you know or problems that seem familiar to you. You may want to explore a real problem that you or someone you know has experienced. However, remember that dealing with a real-life problem may require that you give special consideration to the privacy and feelings of the people involved.

2. Study the problem. State the problem briefly in your own words. Try to figure out how the problem developed and whether it could have been avoided. For example, if you were analyzing Harry's problem, you might say: "Harry is ashamed of his mother because she is an immigrant. Why can't he see what a good, warm-hearted person she is? Is he ashamed of his own background in some way?"

200 Workshop 6

Literature Connection

Epic and Story to Read Remind students that an epic often involves a journey on which a hero solves many problems. *The Odyssey*, by Homer, provides many examples of problems and solutions. You might also suggest that students read "Thank You M'am" by Langston Hughes. The characters in this short story confront problems in an unusual way.

3. Think about the people involved. Identify what you know about their behavior and personalities. Try to see and understand the point of view of each person. If you are exploring "The Torn Invitation," you might consider Harry's need to be accepted by people at his school and his fear that his mother may embarrass him. Frankie, on the other hand, has reason to respond to Theresa Wojick's warmth and friendship. If you are analyzing an experience of your own, try to step back and view it as someone else would see it.

4. List three possible solutions. Be logical. Aim for reasonable, honest solutions. Take into account the personalities of the people involved, as well as how time and other circumstances affect their lives. Perhaps if Harry could see the difficulties his mother experiences in adjusting to both a strange culture and a new language, he might become more understanding.

5. Try out each solution in your mind. Consider the fact that people don't always act logically and that there are no instant or perfect solutions. If you were crafting an ending for Harry's story, for example, it would not be believable for Harry's mother to take one English lesson and "shine" the next day at the open house.

Writing
TIP

You might choose a movie that ends with an unresolved problem and try resolving the conflict.

Problems
and Solution **201**

Critical Thinking

Evaluating As students explore possible solutions, they may find a simple three-column chart (*Column 1:* Possible Solution or Alternative; *Column 2:* +; *Column 3:* −) helpful for identifying the positive and negative aspects of each solution and for choosing the most appropriate solution. You might also call attention to the Problem-Solution Matrix in the Thinking Skills Worksheets as another useful kind of graphic device.

Guidelines for Evaluation

An effective solution . . .

- provides a clear and concise statement of the problem
- explains the importance or significance of the problem, if appropriate
- gives a workable solution, reasons for the solution, and suggestions for implementing the solution
- includes examples and illustrations that clarify the problem and solution
- includes a conclusion that restates the significance of the problem or the importance of the solution, if appropriate
- uses correct grammar, usage, spelling, capitalization, and punctuation

Reteaching

Assess the needs of students who were not successful in developing an effective solution. Assign the appropriate Handbook Mini-Lessons, along with the support materials listed for each lesson. Concepts commonly requiring reteaching are

Solving Problems: Handbook 24
Adding Detail: Handbook 14

The following suggestions may also be useful.

1. Undeveloped Problems A story writer must clearly reveal a problem, not just state that one exists. In a small group work with students to revise one or two of the students' papers in which the problem is unfocused or undeveloped. Help students develop a clear understanding of the problem and strategies for revealing it to readers. You may want students to use the Problem-Solution Matrix in the Thinking Skills Worksheets.

2. Nonworkable Solution Have each student explain the solutions he or she considered to a partner. Students might consider the following questions to determine the best solution: Can this solution be implemented? Will both people accept this solution? How will this solution solve the problem? You may wish to model this process before asking students to do it.

Extension and Enrichment

• Groups of students might develop and role-play for the class scenes that illustrate the problems they described and their solutions. Each group should select one problem from group members' papers, taking care to choose a problem that is not too sensitive or private to be shared. A problem from a story would be most appropriate. After the role-play, invite the class to comment on the solution.

Writing
TIP

Consider the possibilities of compromise, one of the most effective problem-solving techniques.

WRITING ABOUT A PROBLEM AND SOLUTION

1. State the problem clearly and concisely. It is sometimes helpful to explain why the reader should care about solving the problem.

2. Offer your best solution. If you are exploring several solutions, be sure to include the merits and drawbacks of each.

3. Tell why you think your solution is workable. Explain why the solution is a reasonable one for the people involved. Then list the actions they need to take to implement the solution.

REVIEWING YOUR WRITING

1. Reread your writing for clarity. Have you summed up the problem accurately? Have you explained your solution clearly? As you reread, check to see that you have used examples and illustrations where necessary to clarify your points.

2. Ask a partner to evaluate your solution. If you are writing in response to a story, ask someone who has read the story to comment on your solution. You may wish to discuss how your solution compares with that of the author.

3. Review your conclusion. If you are addressing a personal or social problem, have your conclusion restate the significance of the problem or the importance of the solution.

PUBLISHING AND PRESENTING

• **Hold a round-table discussion.** If you have written about Harry's problem in "The Torn Invitation," talk with other students who wrote about the same subject. Read and evaluate your solutions. If possible, find and read the complete story, and compare the solution in the story with your proposed solutions.

• **Share your paper with others.** If you have written about a real problem, and if you are confident that your solution is sensitive to the needs and interests of all the people involved, consider offering it privately to those who requested it.

Sentence
COMPOSING

Infinitive Phrases

To express ideas efficiently, experienced writers often use infinitive phrases as subjects, direct objects, or modifiers.

> **MODELS**
>
> 1. <u>To keep silent about this amazing happening</u> deepened the shock for me. (Infinitive phrase used as a subject)
>   **John Knowles, _A Separate Peace_**
>
> 2. I want <u>to be an honest man and a good writer</u>. (Infinitive phrase used as a direct object)
>   **James Baldwin, _Notes of a Native Son_**
>
> 3. I was pronounced competent <u>to paddle my own bicycle without outside help</u>. (Infinitive phrase used as an adverb)
>   **Mark Twain, "Taming the Bicycle"**

A. Combining Sentences Combine the sentences by putting the infinitive phrase from the second sentence into the first sentence. Write the complete sentence.

1. He had forgotten to do something. He had forgotten <u>to build a fire and thaw out</u>.
   Jack London, "To Build a Fire"

2. He staggered with fatigue on his way to the Clydes', and paddled the length of their pool, stopping again and again with his hand on the curb. He kept stopping <u>to rest</u>.
   John Cheever, "The Swimmer"

3. The moon was higher, riding high and clear of the dust at last, and after a while the town began to do something. The town began <u>to glare beneath the dust</u>.
   William Faulkner, "Dry September"

4. Catherine looked at the books lying around his room, and asked if she might borrow the stories of Isaac Babel. She wanted the stories <u>to read on the train</u>.
   Doris Lessing, "Homage to Isaac Babel"

5. Although Bertha Young was thirty, she still had moments like this when she wanted to do many things. She wanted <u>to run instead of walk, to take dancing steps on and off the pavement, to bowl a hoop, to throw something up in the air and catch it again, or to stand still and laugh at—nothing—at nothing simply</u>.
   Katherine Mansfield, "Bliss"

Objectives

1. To combine sentences by adding infinitive phrases
2. To unscramble sentence parts, varying the placement of infinitive phrases
3. To write original sentences that imitate the structure of professional models with infinitive phrases

Preteaching

These exercises focus on the use of infinitive phrases. You may want to use or refer students to Grammar Handbook 37, Using Verbals and Appositives: Infinitives, pages 686–687.

ANSWER KEY

A. Combining Sentences
Answers will vary. Authors' original sentences are given below.
1. He had forgotten to build a fire and thaw out.
2. He staggered with fatigue on his way to the Clydes', and paddled the length of their pool, stopping again and again with his hands on the curb to rest.
3. The moon was higher, riding high and clear of the dust at last, and after a while the town began to glare beneath the dust.
4. Catherine looked at the books lying around his room, and asked if she might borrow the stories of Isaac Babel to read on the train.
5. Although Bertha Young was thirty, she still had moments like this when she wanted to run instead of walk, to take dancing steps on and off the pavement, to bowl a hoop, to throw something up in the air and catch it again, or to stand still and laugh at—nothing—at nothing simply.

B. Unscrambling Sentences

Answers will vary. Authors' original sentences are given below.

1. A man walked by, stepping into the gutter to skirt them.

2. Accompanied by a great number of selected people, the emperor went forth to visit the two wily swindlers.

3. Mrs. Botkin, an egg-shaped little woman with wispy hair that lay on her forehead like valentine lace, looked at her husband and started to say something.

4. Her hands shaking, she picked up the long sword, drew it out of the scabbard, and prepared to follow him through the wall.

5. To pay the doctor, she was forced to sell her last valuable possession, her husband's sewing machine.

C. Imitating Sentences

Answers will vary.

B. Unscrambling Sentences Unscramble and write each sentence, adding commas where needed. The sentence parts can be unscrambled in more than one acceptable way. Try placing the infinitive phrases in different positions.

1. a. stepping into the gutter
   b. a man walked by
   c. to skirt them   **James Agee, "Rufus"**

2. a. to visit the two wily swindlers
   b. accompanied by a great number of selected people
   c. the emperor went forth
                    Hans Christian Andersen, "The Emperor's New Clothes"

3. a. looked at her husband and started
   b. an egg-shaped little woman with wispy hair
   c. to say something
   d. that lay on her forehead like valentine lace
   e. Mrs. Botkin   **Evan Connell, Jr., "The Condor and the Guests"**

4. a. her hands shaking
   b. she picked up the long sword
   c. and prepared
   d. drew it out of the scabbard
   e. to follow him through the wall   **James Clavell, Shogun**

5. a. to sell her last valuable possession
   b. her husband's sewing machine
   c. she was forced
   d. to pay the doctor   **John Hersey, Hiroshima**

C. Imitating Sentences Each sentence below contains at least one infinitive phrase. Imitate the structure of the model, using your own content. *Important:* Imitate as many of the sentence parts as possible, not just the underlined infinitive phrase(s).

1. To say he was ugly would be unjust, and to say he was handsome would be gross exaggeration.   **John Henrik Clarke, "The Boy Who Painted Christ Black"**

2. To keep a sense of proportion, that was the main thing.
                                    James Hilton, Goodbye, Mr. Chips

3. He stared at his framed baby picture in the parlor, and turned away sick with fear and the effort to touch, to retain, to grasp himself for only a moment.   **Thomas Wolfe, Look Homeward, Angel**

4. They began <u>to ransack the floor</u>: pulled the beds away from the walls, tore clothes off hooks in the closets, pulled suitcases and boxes off shelves.

James Thurber, "The Night the Ghost Got In"

5. It became his habit <u>to creep out of bed even before his mother was awake,</u> <u>to slip into his clothes, and to go quietly down to the barn to see Gabilan.</u>

John Steinbeck, _The Red Pony_

Application In the musical, *Man of La Mancha,* Don Quixote sings about his quest—that is, his goal in life. In one sentence, using a long series of infinitive phrases, he describes that quest:

> To dream the impossible dream,
> to fight the unbeatable foe,
> to bear with unbearable sorrow,
> to run where the brave dare not go,
>
> To right the unrightable wrong,
> to love pure and chaste from afar,
> to try when your arms are too weary,
> to reach the unreachable star,
>
> This is my quest to follow that star,
> no matter how hopeless, no matter how far,
> to fight for the right without question or pause,
> to be willing to march into hell for a heavenly cause.
>
> And I know if I'll only be true to this glorious quest,
> that my heart will lie peaceful and calm when I'm laid
>   to my rest. . . .

Joe Darion, _Man of La Mancha_

Write a long sentence imitating the one above. Arrange your series of infinitive phrases as a list to resemble a poem, either rhymed like the model or unrhymed. You might want to use one of the following topics: your dream, your ambition, your hope, your desire, or your own quest.

Grammar Refresher All model sentences in this workshop contain infinitive phrases. To learn more about infinitive phrases, see Handbook 37, pages 686–687.

Sentence Composing **205**

7 Persuasion

Overview

Persuasion is writing that attempts to convince the reader to adopt the writer's position on an issue or to take action. Students will apply the skills of definition, classification, analysis, and synthesis that they developed in previous Workshops as they write to persuade a targeted audience. Workshop 7 includes the following Guided and Related Assignments:

1. **Guided: Supporting Opinions** builds on the skills of definition, analysis, classification, and synthesis developed in preceding Workshops by inviting students to identify issues they already care strongly about and to write persuasively in support of their positions.

2. **Related: Letter to the Editor** develops skills introduced in the Guided Assignment by asking students to express opinions in a familiar format.

3. **Related: Critical Review** builds on the skills of evaluating and expressing opinions introduced in the Guided Assignment by encouraging students to view real-world entertainment experiences in critical terms.

Teaching Preview

Preparation Guide

1. Use the Overview on this page and the Teacher's Choice descriptions on page 207 as a basis for deciding which assignment(s) to teach.

2. Preview the assignments and the teacher's notes and identify concerns that may require preteaching or extra support given your class's abilities. The handbook mini-lessons suggested within the lesson may also provide guidance.

3. Preview the chart below for support materials in the Teacher's Resource File that may be used with this Workshop. Resources are for use with the Guided Assignment unless otherwise noted.

Support Materials

WRITER'S CRAFT RESOURCES

Prewrite and Explore
Thinking Skills Transparencies, pp. 25–26
Thinking Skills Worksheets, p. 17

Draft and Discover
Elaboration, Revision, and Proofreading Worksheets, p. 13

Revise Your Writing
Guidelines for Writing Assessment and Portfolio Use, pp. 14, 33–35
Peer Response Guides, pp. 23–24
Student Revision Model Transparencies, pp. 27–30
Elaboration, Revision, and Proofreading Worksheets, p. 14

Assessment
Tests and Writing Assessment Prompts, p. 7

Extension Activities
Writing Prompts for Fine Art Transparencies, pp. 10, 12, 15, 16, 18, 20
Writing from Literature, pp. 1–44
Standardized Test Practice

 Educational Technology
(available separately)
Writer's DataBank
Electronic English Handbook
Multimedia Workshop
Your Personal Trainer for the New SAT
In Perspective (videodisc)

OTHER RESOURCES

Books and Journals
Fabiano, Theodore F. and F. Todd Goodson. "Political Rhetoric and the English Classroom." *English Journal.* 82.8 (1993): 50–52.
Jackson, Jeanne M. "There Ought to Be a Law: The Legislative Forum." *English Journal.* 80.7 (1991): 34–37.

Films and Videos
T.J.'s Rights. Film Ideas, 1992. (18 min.)

Computer Software
CAW: Computer Assisted Writing. Educational Activities, Inc. Apple family, PC/MS-DOS (double disk drive required).
Decisions, Decisions Series. (10 titles) Tom Snyder Productions. Apple family, Macintosh, PC/MS-DOS.
Persuasive Essay, Jr. Intellectual Software (Div. of Queue, Inc.). Apple family.

Workshop Management Guidelines

The chart below indicates the number of days recommended for each phase of the Guided and Related Assignments. Stars indicate portions of the assignment that may be completed outside the classroom if time is limited or if teachers wish the activity to be completed by students independently.

SUPPORTING OPINIONS

Starting from Literature .... 1 day
Prewrite .... 3–4 days*
Draft .... 2–3 days*
Revise .... 1–2 days*
Publish .... 1–2 days
Learning .... 1 day*
Reteaching .... open
Extension/Enrichment .... open*
Sentence Composing .... 1 day*

LETTER TO THE EDITOR

Starting from Literature .... 1 day
Examining the Issue .... 1–2 days*
Writing .... 1 day*
Reviewing .... 1 day*
Publishing .... 1–2 days

CRITICAL REVIEW

Starting from Literature .... 1 day
Thinking Through .... 1–2 days*
Writing .... 1 day*
Reviewing .... 1 day*
Publishing .... 1–2 days

Linking Literature, Writing, and Grammar

The following options may be used to provide students with an integrated language experience. Begin by assigning and discussing any of the recommended pieces of literature. Use the suggested strategy to provide a link to the Guided Assignment.

LINKING LITERATURE AND WRITING

Option 1

Starting Point: "Non-Jocks Deserve a Chance" by Susan Swartz on pages 208–209 of *The Writer's Craft*

Strategy: Use the teaching suggestions on pages 208–209 to lead students into the Guided Assignment.

Option 2

Starting Point: "The Secret Life of Walter Mitty" by James Thurber on pages 35–40 of McDougal, Littell's *Literature and Language,* Grade 9.

Strategy: As students read and discuss this short story, have them imagine that they are someone close to Mitty—perhaps his wife, doctor, friend, or co-worker. Invite them to speak persuasively to Mitty in an attempt to bring him out of his fantasy world. After students decide which attempt at persuasion was most effective, lead them into the Guided Assignment.

Option 3

Starting Point: "Fire and Ice" by Robert Frost

Strategy: As students read and discuss the poem, have them choose which kind of ending for the world they would prefer—in fire or in ice. Have them give persuasive reasons for their choice. Also discuss which approach Robert Frost favors and his reasons. Remind students that identifying and evaluating reasons or arguments that support a piece of persuasive writing are important for readers and writers. Then lead them into the Guided Assignment.

LINKING WRITING AND GRAMMAR

Before the drafting or revision stage of this assignment, tell students that effective persuasion demands writing that moves the reader. One of the most reliable methods of strengthening your position is to express the reasons for your thinking in appropriate phrases and clauses. Ask students to find examples of the effective use of phrases and clauses in their own writing as you write the following examples on the board:

Weak: I support the school building program. New construction is expensive. Teachers need space to teach effectively.

Strong: Although new construction is expensive, I support the school building program because teachers need space to teach effectively.

Go over pages 721–734 of the Grammar and Usage Handbook. If problems still appear on student papers, assign the exercises on those pages for reteaching. Additional practice can be found in the *Grammar and Usage Practice Book* on pages 145–154.

Sketchbook

Objective

To use a personal experience as a springboard to informal writing

Using the Prompt

Before students write, remind them that the activity is informal and that you will not grade their sketches.

Bring in samples of reviews to share with students, or you might record and play a videotape of a televised movie review, such as those given by Roger Ebert and Gene Siskel. Discuss the samples, and encourage students to respond to the writing prompt. Some students may wish to work alone; others, in pairs as if they were Siskel and Ebert, each writing a review of the same movie. If students prefer, they can respond to one of the ideas in the Additional Sketches section.

Suggest that students save their sketches in their Writing Portfolios for possible use in the following workshop.

Sketchbook

Newspapers and magazines often run short "capsule" reviews of movies, videos, plays, television programs, record albums, concerts, and even restaurants. Now it's your turn to become a critic. Write your thoughts about something you've seen or heard recently or a restaurant where you've eaten.

Additional Sketches

Write a letter of appreciation. Perhaps someone did you a big favor, or perhaps someone did something small that has had a lasting impact on you. Begin, "Dear _____ , there's something I've been wanting to tell you."

Write an advertisement for yourself. Be sure to mention your best qualities.

206

WRITER'S **7** WORKSHOP

Persuasion

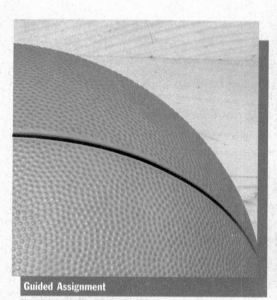
Guided Assignment
SUPPORTING OPINIONS

Related Assignment
LETTER TO THE EDITOR

Related Assignment
CRITICAL REVIEW

Every day you encounter persuasive messages. Television ads scream "Buy me!" Politicians seek your support. Critics give thumbs up or thumbs down to the latest books and movies. Even your friends try to convince you to go along with their wishes.

In all these cases, people use techniques of persuasion to achieve their goals. Persuasive writing attempts to influence the opinions of others or convince people to take a specific action. In this workshop you will learn how to use the elements of persuasive writing to support a position, express your opinion in a letter to the editor, and evaluate literary works in a critical review.

207

Objectives

Guided Assignment:
SUPPORTING OPINIONS
To take a position on an issue and to draft, revise, proofread, and share a piece of persuasive writing

Related Assignment:
LETTER TO THE EDITOR
To identify an issue and to write, review, and share a letter to the editor

Related Assignment:
CRITICAL REVIEW
To choose a work to evaluate and to write, review, and share a critical review

Teacher's Choice

Guided Assignment
Supporting Opinions This assignment helps students learn to identify, analyze, and develop logical arguments that support their opinions in issues—skills that are essential in everyday life. Arguing for their views and defending their positions vis-a-vis others, students learn how to appeal to their audience. Because writers of persuasion must distinguish fact from opinion, evaluate evidence, and draw conclusions, this assignment is probably most useful after students have had experience with exposition.

Related Assignment
Letter to the Editor This assignment helps students focus on an issue and develop rational support for their opinions. The assignment is not as extensive as the Guided Assignment; consequently, you may want to use it as a springboard into the Guided Assignment with basic and learning disabled students.
Critical Review In this assignment, students write a critical review of a movie or literary work. The assignment may be most useful when taught in conjunction with a unit on literature or the media.

Assignment Rationale

Persuasion is an integral part of the modern world. On a daily basis people are bombarded with a variety of messages that employ sophisticated persuasive techniques. Throughout their lives, students will be called upon to evaluate messages of this kind as well as to argue effectively their own positions. This assignment helps students develop skills that will make them astute evaluators of information and successful proponents of their positions.

Starting from Literature

Objective

To respond to a model of persuasive writing as a springboard to writing

Teaching Strategies

Motivate

Ask students if they would like to master the art of "winning" an argument or of convincing others to respond in a certain way. Invite discussion, and suggest that this assignment will help students learn some of the techniques of effective persuasion.

Tap Prior Knowledge

Ask students if there is some area in which they are not especially talented, such as music, art, or sports. Discuss how students feel when they are in classes with people talented in those areas. What would they like to change about the way they are treated? How would they convince others to make a change?

Guided ASSIGNMENT

Supporting Opinions

"NON-JOCKS DESERVE A CHANCE"
by Susan Swartz

A lawyer files a brief to try to convince the judge that her client is innocent. An employee writes a memo to try to "sell" a product idea to his boss. A group of citizens writes a joint letter to the newspaper about the problem of toxic waste. All of them will have a better chance of success if they know how to write a strong persuasive paper.

In her newspaper column, Susan Swartz tries to persuade gym teachers to be more generous to students who aren't good at sports. As you read, notice the way she uses reasoning, specific evidence, and personal style to get her point across.

◆ As we embark on another school year, could we have the attention of the teachers with the whistles around their necks and the clipboards in their hands?

◆ Some people from childhood on consider a ball a terrifying thing. If it's round and belongs to some sport they see it as the enemy, be it a big one that is supposed to soar over the net or a bitty sphere that fits into a hole in the ground.

◆ It is said that some 50 percent of Americans grow up shying away from sports. And they're not all female. Some of you are to blame.

◆ How do you treat the class klutz? Do you only add to her agony when she comes to you banged around by the scorn

208

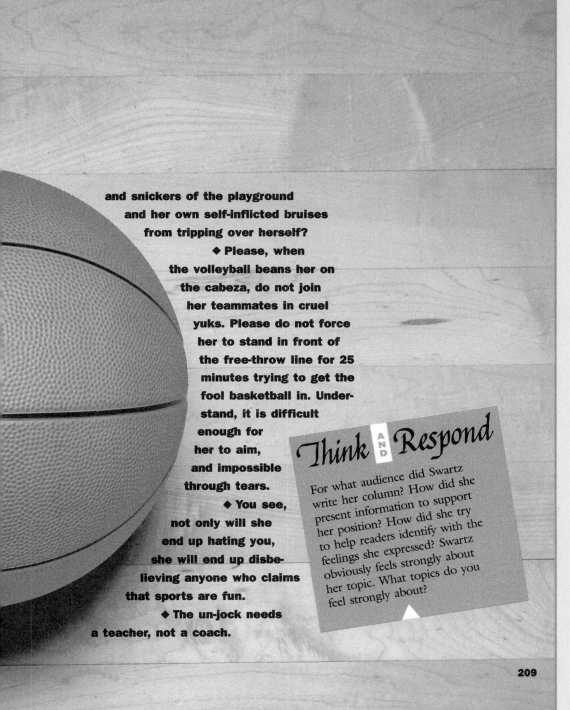

and snickers of the playground
and her own self-inflicted bruises
from tripping over herself?
◆ Please, when
the volleyball beans her on
the cabeza, do not join
her teammates in cruel
yuks. Please do not force
her to stand in front of
the free-throw line for 25
minutes trying to get the
fool basketball in. Understand, it is difficult
enough for
her to aim,
and impossible
through tears.
◆ You see,
not only will she
end up hating you,
she will end up disbe-
lieving anyone who claims
that sports are fun.
◆ The un-jock needs
a teacher, not a coach.

Think AND Respond

For what audience did Swartz write her column? How did she present information to support her position? How did she try to help readers identify with the feelings she expressed? Swartz obviously feels strongly about her topic. What topics do you feel strongly about?

209

Set a Purpose

Referring to the side-column notes, ask students to suggest other situations in which persuasion would be necessary. Then call attention to the purpose given at the end of the side column, and have students read the article.

Think and Respond

Elicit Personal Responses

Have students restate Swartz's position. Then focus discussion on the kinds of information she uses to convince gym teachers to change their attitudes.

Explore the Author's Techniques

Review the article, pointing out some of the author's techniques. For example, point out that Swartz begins by addressing her audience directly. (Page 208, paragraph 1: As we . . . hands?) She provides background information about the issue, offering specific facts, examples, (Page 208, paragraph 2: Some . . . thing. If it's . . . ground.) and statistics. (Page 208, paragraph 3: It is . . . sports.) Swartz then reveals her opinion (Page 208, paragraph 3: Some . . . blame.) and offers support for it by giving several examples. (Page 208, paragraph 4: How . . . klutz? Do . . . herself. Page 209, paragraph 2: Please . . . yuks. Please . . . in.) Lastly, Swartz offers specific reasons why gym teachers should change (Page 209, paragraph 2: You . . . fun.) and gives a final recommendation. (Page 209, paragraph 3: The un-jock . . . coach.) You might also point out that Swartz uses a light tone and some humor, but it is clear that she takes the issue seriously.

Link Literature to Writing

Point out that Susan Swartz wrote persuasively about an issue that concerned her. She stated her opinion, offered support for it, and made a recommendation for a change. Suggest that as students approach the assignment that follows, they think about issues that concern them and how, like Susan Swartz, they might persuade others to make a change.

Prewrite and Explore

Objectives

1. To use prewriting techniques to identify, define, and take a position on an issue for a piece of persuasive writing
2. To identify purpose, goals, audience, and form for persuasive writing
3. To develop and collect facts, examples, observations, and authoritative opinions to support a position

Preteaching

Preview the Prewrite and Explore section. If there are skills or concepts with which students may need help before prewriting, present them at this time. The Cluster Diagram and the Spider Map in the Thinking Skills Worksheets as well as the mini-lessons listed below may help you in your selection and instruction. The cross references in the pupil text will give students access to the same lessons for independent study.

> **Handbook Mini-Lessons**
> - Writing Techniques, pp. 320–323
> - Sharing Techniques, pp. 323–325
> - Creating Charts, pp. 358–359

Teaching Strategies

Modeling

Consider modeling the first Exploratory Activity on page 210 by offering and writing on the board one idea for each of the four categories. Invite students to add to the list.

INVITATION TO Write

Susan Swartz wrote persuasively about the plight of "un-jocks." The following activities will help you to write a persuasive essay on an issue you feel strongly about.

Whether you want to convince a friend to attend a party or you want to persuade the school board to increase funding for extra-curricular activities, you need to understand how to support your position. The starting point is to make clear for yourself what the issue is all about. Find where you stand, and give your reasons. Even when you're sure you are right, prepare yourself for questions and challenges. By responding to them, you can strengthen your argument.

PREWRITE AND EXPLORE

HANDBOOKS

FOR HELP & PRACTICE

Writing Techniques, pp. 320–323

Sharing Techniques, pp. 323–325

Creating charts, pp. 358–359

1. Identify an issue. Should police be allowed to search school lockers? Should baseball players be paid more than nurses? Every day, issues clamor for our attention and sometimes lead us to take action. The following activities may help you pin down issues you feel strongly about and find one to discuss in a paper. If you have trouble finding a topic, look at the suggestions under "Apply Your Skills" on page 221.

Exploratory Activities

- **Listing** Make a list of things you've noticed people disagreeing about. Use these categories to organize your list: world issues, national issues, local issues, personal issues.
- **Journal** Your writer's journal can be an excellent source of issues. Perhaps you've recorded an argument you had with one of your friends, or recorded your reaction to a news story.

Springboard

To help prepare students for the writing activity in this assignment, you might have them locate and bring in examples of persuasive writing about some current event. Students might look on the editorial page of a newspaper or in a magazine. Suggest that students make notes about the issue, the position the writer takes on the issue, and specific details that support the writer's position. Have students attach their notes to the example and display both pieces on the bulletin board.

- **Brainstorming** Write the heading "If I Ruled the World" at the top of a sheet of paper. With two or three classmates, make a list of issues that are important to you and what you would do about them.
- **Reading literature** Think about the conflicts in works you've read. For example, the barber in "Lather and Nothing Else" by Hernando Tellez had to decide whether or not to kill his enemy. If you had to choose sides in such a conflict, which side would you be on?

2. Share promising ideas. Look over the ideas you've generated, and narrow your choices down to the most promising issues. Then share them with classmates, listening for their responses to your ideas and also listening for issues mentioned by other students that you might like to pursue.

3. Select and define an issue. Select the issue that seems most promising to you and freewrite for ten minutes presenting your view of it. Don't hesitate to present arguments against your position; you will want to consider and perhaps deal with opposing positions as you write. If you have trouble defining your issue, try listing the basic ideas or positions involved. Here is the list one student, Helen, made of the positions on the issue of product-testing on animals.

Writing
—TIP—
Look for issues that have a personal meaning to you.

ONE STUDENT'S PROCESS

animals are subjected to testing for consumer products

some manufacturers conduct cruel experiments that ignore animal rights

some animal rights advocates want tests on animals stopped even when helpful to humans

some scientists feel other testing methods can be used

I Stand Here—I love animals, think unnecessary testing should be stopped

 Individualizing Instruction

Learning Styles Help visual learners choose an issue by bringing in current news magazines and allowing students to browse through the photographs. Visual and auditory learners might also watch or listen to a news analysis program on television or radio for ideas on current or controversial issues.

Spot Check

As students work through the exploratory activities to select a topic, make sure they are looking at controversial issues and not just matters of personal preference.

Stumbling Block

As students identify and explore their topics for persuasive writing, encourage them to analyze their feelings about the issue carefully. If after defining the issue they are still unsure about how they feel about it, encourage them to look for another topic. (You might refer students to the Data Sheets and the Ideas for Writing Booklet as other sources of ideas for topics.) Emphasize that it is very difficult to persuade someone else about something you are not sure of yourself.

Analyzing As students begin to explore their goals for writing, have them carefully analyze what goals are feasible. For example, it most probably would not be possible to persuade a school administration to excuse from gym class those students who are not good at sports. However, it might be possible to persuade gym teachers to be more understanding of those students.

Individualizing Instruction

Learning Styles As students consider forms for their writing, you might suggest that visual and auditory learners collaborate on a persuasive piece. Students might prepare a video or photographic essay accompanied by an original script.

Management Tip

Allow students a sufficient amount of time to research their issues before they begin drafting. Emphasize that successful persuasion results, at least in part, from a knowledgeable, authoritative presentation of information.

---

4. Determine your purpose and personal goals. Do you want to change the minds of your readers, make them take an action, or, like Susan Swartz, make them see a different point of view?

As you focus on your issue, ask yourself, "How is the issue personally important to me? If I'm successful, what effect will my writing about it have on readers?" The answers may not be totally clear until you have a chance to examine your issue more deeply.

5. Identify your audience. Thinking about your audience is especially important in persuasive writing because you are trying to have a real effect on people's views and actions. Are they students your own age, or adults? Are they a handful of people you know, or thousands of strangers? Do they hold similar, opposite, or undecided views? Also think about the background information your audience will need.

What is the best way to reach my audience?

6. Choose a form. Your view of who makes up your audience will help you choose the best way to appeal to your audience. For instance, to address your whole community you might write a letter to the editor of your newspaper. To organize a school food drive you might write a speech to deliver to your class and other classes. Susan Swartz wrote a newspaper column to present her position. Persuasive writing can take many other forms, such as editorials, books, leaflets, advertisements, sermons, and essays. You may choose to wait until you have a clear idea of what you want to say before deciding on a form.

7. Explore the issue. Now that you've defined your position, you need to gather facts, examples, observations, and authoritative opinions to support it. Here are three useful techniques. You can begin by writing down everything you know about the issue and see where the gaps are. Those gaps are where you'll want to concentrate your follow-up research. A second technique is to divide the page into two columns labeled "Pro" (for) and "Con" (against). Either write both columns yourself or ask another writer to fill in one of them while you take the other. Change roles so each of you has a chance to be both pro and con. A third way of exploring an issue is to invent two fictional characters and write a dialogue in which they argue about it.

 Writer's Choice You can decide how much personal emotion to include in your argument. You can rely on objective facts, or you can talk about your own feelings, depending on your particular topic and audience.

Social Studies Connection

History Persuasive writing has played a significant role in historical events. You might provide an example such as Thomas Paine's pamphlet "Common Sense," which influenced the American Revolution. (Consider reading portions of the pamphlet aloud in class.) Have students research other pieces of persuasive writing that influenced the course of events. You might suggest the speeches of historical figures, such as Martin Luther King, Jr., or Winston Churchill.

DRAFT AND DISCOVER

1. Begin your draft. Take the plunge and start drafting. Refer to your earlier plans as much as you like. Be sure you define the issue, state your position, and give sound reasons for others to agree with you. The following strategies may help.

Strategies

- **Definition** Make sure your readers understand the basic facts of the issue. Susan Swartz does this in the second and third paragraphs of her column.
- **Comparison and Contrast** Compare and contrast the pros and cons of the issue, the similarities and differences of the opposing sides, the advantages and disadvantages that might occur from adopting each view.
- **Cause and Effect** State what beneficial effects will result from adopting your view and what harmful effects will result from the opposing view. Swartz claims that negative coaching will lead to hatred of sports.

2. Organize your draft. There are two common ways of organizing persuasive papers. The *persuasive-descriptive* form develops from reason to reason, giving supporting details for each. The *persuasive-classificatory* form develops the pros and cons of one side first, then turns to the pros and cons of the other side.

HANDBOOKS
FOR HELP & PRACTICE

Types of Organization, pp. 331–335

Writing Introductions, pp. 341–342

Thesis Statements, pp. 343–344

Types of Conclusions, pp. 371–373

Critical Thinking/ Writing, pp. 452–458

In the movie *Inherit the Wind*, Spencer Tracy, as Clarence Darrow, uses his powers of persuasion to influence the jury.

Persuasion **213**

Draft and Discover

Objectives

1. To draft a piece of persuasive writing that defines an issue and supports the position taken, using appropriate organizational strategies
2. To respond to one's own writing and the writing of peers

Preteaching

Preview the Draft and Discover section to pinpoint skills or strategies with which students may need help before drafting. The Elaboration Worksheet from the Revision, Proofreading, and Elaboration booklet as well as the mini-lessons listed below may help you in your selection and instruction.

Handbook Mini-Lessons
- Types of Organization, pp. 331–335
- Writing Introductions, pp. 341–342
- Thesis Statements, pp. 343–344
- Types of Conclusions, pp. 371–373
- Critical Thinking/Writing, p. 452–458

Teaching Strategies

Teaching Tip: Organization

As students prepare to organize their drafts, point out that some issues naturally lend themselves to one type of organization. Issues that have two clear opposing sides (the development of nuclear weapons, for example) may be best developed using the persuasive-classificatory approach. If students intend to persuade their audience to take a particular course of action (protecting the environment, for example) for which there is no clear opposing side (no one would argue in favor of pollution), the persuasive-descriptive form is more appropriate.

LD Students Provide students with an outline form and work with them to add appropriate details.

PROBLEM

S O L V I N G

How should I present my argument?

PERSUASIVE-DESCRIPTIVE

INTRODUCTION
State the problem, your choice of side, and basic reasons for your choice.

REASON 1
(with evidence and details)

REASON 2
(with evidence and details)

REASON 3
(with evidence and details)

CONCLUSION
Restate the problem and your choice.

PERSUASIVE-CLASSIFICATORY

INTRODUCTION
State the problem, both sides, and your choice.

SIDE A
Pros—reasons for
Cons—reasons against

SIDE B
Pros—reasons for
Cons—reasons against

CONCLUSION
State your recommendation, with reasons.

As you write, think about what you need to say to help yourself and your readers understand the issue better. Don't ignore possible objections to your views; acknowledge them, and try to answer them. Maintain a reasonable tone throughout. In your conclusion, you may wish to simply summarize your position, or you could provide a call for action to address the issue you have discussed.

Notice how Helen began her draft with a summary of her position on using animals to test products. From her opening paragraph, you can see she chose the persuasive-descriptive form to organize her paper.

ONE STUDENT'S PROCESS

> More than 100 million animals die each year in the laboratories of the world. A large percentage are tested unnecessarily. This unnecessary and cruel testing must be stopped because (1) it is immoral, (2) it is threatening the environment, and (3) there are other testing methods that can be used.

214   Workshop 7

Springboard

Have students watch a news analysis program on television and keep notes about persuasive techniques used by the commentator. You might have students answer the following questions: What was the issue? What was the commentator's opinion about the issue? What specific details did the commentator use to support his or her opinion?

3. Examine your reasoning. As you write, take care to use words that say precisely what you mean. Avoid vague judgment words such as *good, bad, right,* or *wrong* unless you can defend your judgment with logical arguments. In addition, faulty reasoning can weaken your persuasive powers. Illogical arguments and unfair uses of language are the pitfalls of persuasion. Beware of:

- *loaded language*—taking unfair advantage of the emotional connotations of words
- *circular reasoning*—trying to prove a statement simply by repeating it in different words
- *the cause and effect fallacy*—assuming that one event caused a second event just because it came before it
- *the either/or fallacy*—assuming there are only two choices
- *over-generalization*—a generalization that is too broad to prove
- *bandwagon appeal*—trying to persuade people to follow the crowd
- *name-calling*—an argument that discusses who a person is, not what he or she thinks

For more information on avoiding logical fallacies, see Handbook 24, "Strategies for Critical Thinking and Writing," pages 453–454.

4. Test your arguments. Invite your fellow writers to challenge your position. This will help you strengthen your draft as you go on to revise. Try to survive the following knockdown attempts.

- **Believing and doubting** Have another writer make up two lists about your draft: a list of reasons to believe your position and a list of reasons to doubt it. Reading the lists will help you add reasons to your side and predict challenges to it.
- **Devil's advocate** Appoint another writer to devise every possible reason not to believe your position. This is called playing devil's advocate. In return, you get to be devil's advocate for the other person's paper.
- **Reluctant reader** Ask another writer to read your draft and consider taking some action on it. If your reader would be reluctant to act on what you've written, your draft may need to be more persuasive.
- **Free-for-all** Tape up your draft, along with everyone else's, around the room. For the next day or so, let everyone read everyone else's drafts and tape up responses to individual points.

Cartoon from *Wishful Thinking*, by David Sipress. Copyright ©1987 by David Sipress. Reprinted by permission of Harper Collins Publishers.

Persuasion **215**

Teaching Tip: Reasoning

Caution students against making a claim that something is "immoral" even though that argument is used successfully in One Student's Process. An argument of immorality is very difficult to support and often diverts attention from more productive arguments. For example, instead of claiming that drug abuse is immoral, it is probably better to point out that it is harmful to one's physical and mental health. That argument can easily be supported with specific evidence.

Individualizing Instruction

LEP Students The students may need special help with judgmental language, especially loaded language. Encourage them to use a thesaurus to help them determine precise connotations of words and to find appropriate synonyms. They might also work with English-proficient partners who can help them with word choice.

Management Tip

As students work together to test one another's arguments, you might be on the look-out for too much negative feedback that could be demoralizing to certain students. Remind students that the purpose of testing is to offer helpful suggestions for strengthening an argument, not to destroy an argument.

Peer Response

Have students exchange papers with a peer reader, preferably someone with whom they have not yet worked on this assignment. Make the Peer Response Worksheet for this assignment available to those students who wish to use it.

Revise Your Writing

Objectives

1. To evaluate peer responses to a draft of persuasive writing
2. To use the results of a self-evaluation, peer comments, and a set of standards to revise a draft
3. To proofread for errors in spelling, grammar, usage, and mechanics

Preteaching

Preview the Revise Your Writing section. Based on the section and on any problems you noted in student drafts, identify skills you want to review. The Student Revision Model Transparency and the Revision and Proofreading Worksheets from the Revision, Proofreading, and Elaboration booklet as well as the mini-lessons listed below may help you in your selection and instruction.

> **Handbook Mini-Lessons**
> - Peer Response, pp. 378–382
> - Grammatical Voice, pp. 417–418
> - Evaluating Ideas, pp. 452–453
> - Faulty Reasoning, pp. 453–455

COMPUTER TIP

Invite another writer to type in comments and questions in a different font. Answer them, and then erase the reader's comments.

HANDBOOKS
FOR HELP & PRACTICE

Peer Response,
pp. 378–382
Grammatical Voice,
pp. 417–418
Evaluating Ideas,
pp. 452–453
Faulty Reasoning,
pp. 453–455

 Writer's Choice Do you want to maintain your original position or reevaluate it in light of your responses?

5. Take a break. Give your draft a rest. Then return to it by asking yourself—and your peer readers—challenging questions such as the following.

REVIEW YOUR WRITING

Questions for Yourself

- Does my paper help me understand the issue more completely?
- Do I clearly state the nature of the issue and my position on it?
- Do I recognize possible objections to my views? Do I answer them?
- Have I included facts and details to support my position?
- Have I included a strong conclusion?

Questions for Your Peer Readers

- Is my paper interesting to read?
- Does the opening make the issue clear?
- Where do you think my position is strongest? Where do you think my position is weakest?
- Does my paper sound as if I respect you as a reader? Does my paper sound as if I respect those who disagree with me?
- Can you think of other points to support my view? To oppose it?

REVISE YOUR WRITING

1. Evaluate your responses. Think about your own and your readers' reactions to your paper. Which ones have hit on points that you ought to change? Also keep in mind these guidelines for evaluating persuasive writing.

Social Studies Connection

History One of the most famous debates over a controversial issue took place in a courtroom between two of the most persuasive speakers in American history—Clarence Darrow and William Jennings Bryan. You might have students research the Scopes Trial and write a brief report on the issue in question, the arguments of both sides, and the final outcome.

Standards for Evaluation

Effective persuasive writing . . .

- states the topic clearly in an effective introduction.
- supports a clearly stated opinion with facts or reasons, and elaborates on each reason.
- maintains a reasonable tone.
- takes opposing views into account and answers them.
- uses language effectively and avoids faulty logic.
- includes a conclusion that sums up reasons or provides a call to action.

2. Problem-solve. Rework your draft to fix the problems you have identified. Helen made the changes below after a peer reader wrote suggestions on her first draft.

Writing TIP

To give your writing a lively, personal tone, imagine that your reader is sitting across the table from you.

ONE STUDENT'S PROCESS

Most of us go through our entire lives without ever seeing an animal dying in a labratory cage. Its easy for us not to think about the suffering thats involved, because we don't see it.

More than 100 million animals die each year in the labatories of the world.

For a moment, however, try to imagine an island populated by 100 million sick, injured, and dying animals—mice lumpy with tumors, cats writhing in pain after surgery, rabbits blinded by irritating chemicals, pregnant baboons injured in staged automobile accidents, dogs with stomachs weighed down by lethal doses of shoe polish or floor wax.

According to veterinarian and animal-rights advocate Dr. Michael W. Fox,

I agree that it's a terrible situation. Perhaps more details could make it seem more real.

The figure 100 million is impressive. Where did you get it?

Teaching Strategies

Modeling

To prepare students for revising, discuss the Standards for Evaluation and One Student's Process. You might also use the Student Revision Model Transparency for this assignment, discussing the effects of changes on the content and structure of the paper.

Guidelines for Evaluation

The following guidelines may be used for a close evaluation of a persuasive paper. See the Guidelines for Evaluating Writing in the Teacher's Resource File for additional help with holistic or analytic scoring.

Ideas and Content
- clearly states the issue and an opinion in an interesting introduction
- includes facts and reasons that support the opinion
- uses statistics and/or specific details to elaborate on reasons
- anticipates and answers objections to the argument
- demonstrates an awareness of audience in word choice, details, and voice

Structure and Form
- develops arguments in a logical and coherent manner
- summarizes arguments or appeals for action in a concluding paragraph

Grammar, Usage, and Mechanics
- uses standard grammar and usage
- uses correct spelling, capitalization, and punctuation

Linking Grammar and Writing

You might point out that in persuasive writing, the writer often uses the editorial "we" and addresses the reader in the second person "you." (Refer to Swartz's article on pages 208–209.) Advise students that if they choose to do that, they should do it consistently throughout their papers. They should not switch back and forth, sometimes referring to the reader as "some gym teachers" and sometimes as "you." Suggest that students review their papers for this element.

Managing the Paper Load

You might use the Guidelines for Evaluating Writing and the Sample Papers for this assignment from the Teacher's Resource File to evaluate students' papers. Consider having students use the same checklist to evaluate their final papers.

Publish and Present

Objective

To publish and present a piece of persuasive writing

Teaching Strategies

Collaborative Opportunity

Students who have written on topics that would be of particular concern to other teenagers might work together to plan a presentation for another class. Students could read their papers, give speeches followed by a question and answer period, present a panel discussion, and so on. Encourage students to devise a creative means of presentation.

3. Proofread your work. Make a clean copy of your paper and then check it for errors in grammar, usage, and mechanics. If you've used statistics to support your argument, make sure they're accurate.

LINKING GRAMMAR AND WRITING

Active Versus Passive Voice

Good persuasive writing usually uses the active voice to make readers feel involved.

PROBLEM: The same reactions are not always shared by people and animals.

CORRECTED: People and other animals don't always share the same reactions.

See Grammar Handbook 33, pages 590–592, for additional help with this problem.

HANDBOOKS
FOR HELP & PRACTICE

Publishing Your
Work,
pp. 402–403
Discussion Skills,
pp. 479–480

PUBLISH AND PRESENT

- **Create a leaflet or brochure out of your persuasive paper.** Illustrate it and distribute copies.
- **Give an oral report based on your paper.** Instead of just reading your report aloud, adapt it for a more informal presentation. You might give a brief introduction to your report and then hold a question-and-answer session to involve your classmates.
- **Form a readers' circle.** Get together with peers who have written on the same topic or related topics. Use your discussion as a launching pad for exploration of related topics.
- **Keep your paper in your writing portfolio.** Refer to it whenever you write another persuasive piece.

Literature Connection

Essay to Read   You might have students read "An Editorial Lost in a News Item" by Louis Nizer and make a concise statement of Nizer's opinion.

Product Testing on Animals Is Wrong!

Helen Tanaka

Most of us go through our entire lives without ever seeing an animal dying in a laboratory cage. It's easy for us not to think about the suffering that's involved, because we don't see it. For a moment, however, try to imagine an island populated by 100 million sick, injured, and dying animals—mice lumpy with tumors, cats writhing in pain after surgery, rabbits blinded by irritating chemicals, pregnant baboons injured in staged automobile accidents, dogs with stomachs weighed down by lethal doses of shoe polish or floor wax. According to veterinarian and animal-rights advocate Dr. Michael W. Fox, more than 100 million animals die each year in the laboratories of the world. A large percentage are used for testing the latest brand of sunblock or other commercial products. This unnecessary and cruel testing must be stopped because it is immoral, it is threatening the environment, and there are other testing methods that can be used.

The most important reason to stop such testing is simply that it's wrong to make living creatures suffer, especially on so large a scale and for so little reason. Even though they can't talk or use tools, animals are conscious beings who have feelings. Some people even claim that animals are more sensitive to pain and fear than human beings, because they can't understand what's happening or see an end to the pain.

A second reason to stop testing is that the use of laboratory animals is already destroying environments throughout the world. A quarter of a million primates—

Appeals to audience in an appropriate voice

States the topic clearly in an effective introduction

Supports opinion with detailed reasons

Cites facts to support opinions

Using the Model

After students have read Helen's final essay, discuss it as a class, using the annotations to focus on the effectiveness of the introduction, the facts and details provided to support each reason, and the final recommendations.

Reteaching

Assess the needs of students who were not successful in developing an effective piece of persuasive writing and identify two or three areas in which additional practice is needed. Assign the appropriate Handbook Mini-Lessons, along with the support materials listed for each lesson. Concepts commonly requiring reteaching for this assignment are

Types of Organization: Handbook 4
Faulty Reasoning: Handbook 24

The following suggestions and resources may also be useful.

1. Lack of Position Statement in the Introduction Assemble a small group of students whose papers did not include a clear statement of the issue or position in their introductions. Duplicate the weak sample paper for this assignment from the Teacher's Resource File or ask a student to offer his or her paper for the group session. As a group, read the paper, formulate a statement of the issue and the position, and work together to revise the introduction. Then have students revise their own papers.

2. Lack of Specific Reasons Have students use the analysis frame from the Thinking Skills Worksheet to make a quick list of reasons that support their position. Suggest that pairs work together to flesh out weak areas, adding details from their prewriting notes or making notes about reasons that need to be further researched.

3. Grammar and Usage: Faulty Pronoun References Use Handbook 32 to review pronoun reference. Then have each student exchange his or her paper with a partner, who should identify the noun to which each pronoun refers. If a particular pronoun reference is unclear, have partners work together to correct the error.

Extension and Enrichment

- Have students choose a national or international issue to explore. Suggest that they use the techniques they have learned in this lesson to write a letter to their senator stating and supporting an opinion on the issue.
- Encourage a number of interested students to form an informal group to meet regularly to debate issues of concern. You might help students organize the group, prepare a list of issues to be discussed, and determine a meeting time and place.

Uses persuasive language

Conclusion provides a call to action

chimpanzees, monkeys, baboons—are killed for laboratory purposes every year. These species are in real danger of extinction. In addition, human expeditions threaten the forest environments where these animals live. Go into a rain forest with a troop of twenty or more people, trap most of its primates, and you'll also disrupt its food chain, its vegetation, and the populations of "bystander" animal species.

A third reason is that alternative techniques can be used instead of animal experiments. Experiments can be done on tissue cultures or through computer simulations instead of on whole animals. Often, new products can be tested on human tissue samples obtained from operating rooms or from volunteers. Tests done on human tissues are often more accurate in predicting harmful effects to human beings than tests done on animals. People and other animals don't always share the same reactions. It is not unusual for a substance to seem safe when tested on guinea pigs but to cause unexpected health problems on people. Therefore, manufacturers who test new products on animals may be tragically fooling themselves.

Animal-rights advocates suggest solving the problem by *replacing* animals with other experimental techniques, *reducing* the number of animals that have to be used, and *minimizing* their suffering during those experiments that are necessary. As individuals, we can all work toward those goals by joining groups such as the Humane Society or the ASPCA that lobby for animal rights. The place to begin is in your library. Read about the subject, find the organizations in your area—then do your part!

Off the Record

TEACHERS' LOUNGE

"The kids don't listen, so I have to repeat myself. I'm always repeating myself. You know, always saying the same thing more than once. I say it once, and they make me say it again. . . ."

W R I T E R   T O   W R I T E R

Writers write to influence their readers . . . but always, at bottom, to be more themselves.

Aldous Huxley, British author of Brave New World and other novels

1. Reflect on your writing. Think about the process you have engaged in while writing your essay. Then write an "afterword" for your paper in which you comment on your experience with persuasive writing. Here are some questions for you to consider:

- Where did you find an issue?
- What problems did you face in elaborating on the topic? in doing research? in organizing the paper?
- Which was harder, finding the facts or expressing them? Why?
- Look at Susan Swartz's column, Helen Tanaka's essay on animal testing, and your own work. What problems do you think the writers faced in turning their ideas into words? How did they—and you—solve them?

2. Apply your skills. Try one or more writing activities in the following areas:

- **Cross curricular** Choose an event you have learned about in history. Write a paper stating why you feel the event was either helpful or harmful to humanity.
- **Literature** Choose a realistic story or novel you have read this year such as "The Circuit" by Francisco Jiménez or "Initiation" by Sylvia Plath, and write a paper convincing the reader that the author did or did not accurately portray human life.
- **Art** Write a paper about any work of visual art in one of your textbooks. Persuade readers about the artist's effective or ineffective use of color, space, line, shading, or texture.
- **Related assignments** Follow the suggestions in pages 222–231 to write a letter to the editor and a critical review.

◄ FOR YOUR **PORTFOLIO**

Learning from Your Writing Process

Objective

To analyze and reflect upon what has been learned about the writing process and the writing of a persuasive essay

Teaching Strategies

Reflecting on the Process

You might have students work in small groups to discuss these questions. Suggest that students take notes during the discussion, and then invite a representative from each group to report on the major points raised in the discussion.

Writing Portfolio

Have students keep their notes and final essays in their Writing Portfolios.

Summary and Closure

Before proceeding to the next lesson, be sure students have internalized the following concepts:

1. Persuasive writing strives to convince others to follow a particular course of action or to agree with a certain point of view.

2. Effective persuasive writing clearly explains an issue and a position, supports the position with reasons, facts, and details, and makes a recommendation to the audience.

3. Effective persuasive writing uses sound, logical reasoning to present an argument.

Allow students time to summarize what they have learned by describing the characteristics of effective persuasive writing and by telling why knowing how to use persuasive writing might help them in other school subjects and in everyday life.

Starting from Literature

Objective

To respond to a model of a letter to the editor as a springboard to writing

Teaching Strategies

Motivate

Make a list of several issues on the board, such as academic grading systems, drunk driving, unemployment, and the federal budget deficit. Encourage students to express their feelings about each issue. During discussion help students realize that people usually feel most strongly about issues that directly affect their lives.

Tap Prior Knowledge

Ask students if they have read a book or seen a movie or television show that depicted a particular group of people in an unfair or distorted way. Have volunteers discuss such experiences, and ask how someone might respond to such a portrayal. Explain that the writer of the sample letter to the editor expresses her opinion about what she considers an unfair portrayal of single-parent families, an issue that directly affects her.

Set a Purpose

Discuss the side-column notes, encouraging students to mention any particular articles to which they had a definite response. Then call attention to the purpose-setting statement at the end of the side column, and have students read the letter.

Related
ASSIGNMENT

Letter to the Editor

* * * * * *

Have you ever read an article in a newspaper or magazine that caused you to react with anger, enthusiasm, skepticism, or some other strong emotion? Perhaps you wanted to express your feelings or urge other readers to take some action.

The following letter from a parent expresses her strong opinion about a book excerpt published in a newspaper.

As you read this letter to the editor, notice how the letter writer uses examples from her own life to support her opinion.

Dear Editor:

As a single female parent with two jobs, it is difficult for me to adequately express my displeasure with the excerpt from "Life without father: America's greatest social catastrophe" by Nicholas Davidson, which recently appeared in your paper.

As a parent and the product of a single female parent family, I find it continually frustrating and demoralizing that single-parent families, particularly those headed by black females, are always portrayed as failures.

Having obtained three degrees, I do not consider myself a failure. It enrages me when I read articles that appear to imply that single female parent families are to blame for all the ills of society, especially the decay of the traditional family structure.

Further, as a proud single parent of two daughters, one a soon-to-be graduate of the University of Michigan and the other a freshman honor student at Luther South High School, I believe that they have every possibility of becoming successful.

As young black women, my daughters should not become victims of yet another prejudice based upon the family structure from which they come.

No rational person would begin to suggest that single-parent families are preferable or desirable; however, they are a growing reality.

Yours truly,

Aurie A. Pennick
Chicago

Think AND Respond

As you read this letter to the editor, consider how strongly the writer must have felt about the issue of single-parent families to have written this letter to the newspaper. What have you read recently that made you stop and think or that caused you to comment to your friends about an issue? Could your comments become part of a letter to an editor?

Think and Respond

Elicit Personal Responses

Refer to the Think and Respond questions, and ask students to identify the implications about single-parent families to which the writer responds. (Paragraphs 2 and 3 in model). Focus further discussion on other issues that might provide the basis for a letter to the editor.

Explore the Author's Techniques

Help students use the sample letter as a model for their own letters by examining some of the author's techniques. Point out that the author begins her letter with a statement of the issue and her opinion, and includes a specific reference to the item to which she is responding. (Page 222, paragraph 1: As a . . . paper.) She identifies the points with which she takes exception. (Page 222, paragraph 2: As . . . failures. Paragraph 3: It enrages . . . structure.) and supports her opinion with personal examples. (Page 222, paragraph 1: As a . . . jobs . . . . Paragraph 2: As a . . . family . . . . Paragraph 3: Having obtained . . . failure. Paragraph 4: Further . . . successful.) Finally, she makes an implicit suggestion about a change in attitude toward those people raised in single-parent families led by black women. (Page 222, paragraph 5: As . . . come.)

Link Literature to Writing

Emphasize that Aurie Pennick wrote a letter to the editor because she felt strongly about the portrayal of single-parent families led by black women. She wanted to let people know that not all such families are failures, and she used specific examples to illustrate that fact. As students prepare to write a letter to the editor in the assignment that follows, have them consider issues they care about and think about how they might support their opinions with specific examples.

Guiding Your Writers

Objectives

1. To identify an issue and a purpose for writing a letter to the editor
2. To write, review, and share a letter to the editor

Preteaching

Preview the lesson for any skills or concepts with which students may need help. The mini-lessons listed below may help in your selection and instruction. The cross references in the pupil text will give students access to the same lessons for independent study.

> **Handbook Mini-Lessons**
> - Thesis Statements, pp. 343–344
> - Empty Sentences, pp. 391–393
> - Evaluating Ideas, pp. 452–453

Teaching Strategies

Modeling

Have students bring in examples of letters to the editor that they find especially persuasive or interesting. Discuss the issues presented in the letters, how the writers state and support their opinions, and why students find the letters interesting.

Individualizing Instruction

Basic Students Help students select topics that are limited in scope, such as issues revolving around the community or school. As students explore their opinions and collect information, provide opportunities for them to discuss their plans with you or with partners.

INVITATION TO Write

This letter to the editor expresses the writer's strong opinion about a book excerpt on families headed by single women. Now write your own letter to the editor expressing your opinion on an issue you feel strongly about.

A letter to the editor is a piece of persuasive writing in which you can present your views, evaluate events, and respond to others' opinions. The "Letters to the Editor" section in a newspaper or magazine also provides a forum for readers to respond to previously published articles. By writing a letter to the editor, you gain an opportunity to convince other readers of your point of view and to point out the flaws in others' arguments.

EXAMINING THE ISSUE

HANDBOOKS
FOR HELP & PRACTICE

Thesis Statements,
pp. 343–344

Empty Sentences,
pp. 391–393

Evaluating Ideas,
pp. 452–453

1. Choose an issue. Be aware of your own reactions as you read the paper, listen to the radio, watch the news, and talk with friends. What article, review, or event in the news caused you to react with strong emotion? If you feel strongly about several issues, you might want to choose a local, rather than a national, problem. For example, a letter about your school's sports program might have a more immediate impact than one about the scoring system for Olympic athletic competitions.

2. Examine your ideas. Ask yourself some questions: How do I feel about this issue? What are the facts as I know them? Are my conclusions supported by facts, examples, expert opinions, or observations? What personal experiences can I use? Try freewriting for several minutes, clustering, or charting to explore your knowledge of the issue.

3. Establish your purpose. Do you want only to argue your opinion forcefully in order to change other people's minds about the issue, or do you want also to persuade others to pursue a particular course of action?

224   Workshop 7

Springboard

Divide the class into two groups. Have one group read the newspaper for several days. (If your community has more than one newspaper, assign each newspaper to a separate group of students.) Have the other group watch the local and national newscasts on television. As students watch or read, have them make lists of issues that could serve as topics for letters to the editor. (If possible, students reading newspapers should bring in articles.) Have students share their lists and articles with the class.

WRITING THE LETTER

1. Include an introduction. Your introductory sentence or paragraph should identify what you are writing about and why you are qualified to comment. For example, if you were annoyed by a negative review of a recent rock concert, you might say that you've followed the band's career, are familiar with its music, and want to offer an audience member's point of view about the concert. The woman who wrote the model letter explained immediately that she had firsthand knowledge of the situation described in the book excerpt.

2. Support your opinions. Avoid merely venting your emotions. For example, it's better to explain *why* you believe the town needs a new football stadium than it is to complain that local politicians are incompetent or corrupt for not supporting the construction. Bolster your opinions with facts. If you believe the present stadium is crumbling, present evidence such as the cost of replacing bleachers damaged by weather conditions. A talk with a local architect or construction engineer may provide the supporting facts you need. Quote the opinion of others only if they are experts, are personally involved in the issue, or are public officials with responsibilities in this area.

3. Write a conclusion. End with a brief statement that leaves your readers with your most important thought or recommendation. The model letter, for example, ends with a clear statement in which the writer tells why she feels that the book excerpt was misleading and harmful.

4. Keep your letter simple. Your letter should be brief, well-constructed, and grammatically correct, as well as thoughtful and clear. Remember that the editor may need to shorten or excerpt your letter for publication. Keeping your letter short and organized will help the editor and may increase the chance that it will be picked for publication.

5. Use the correct format. Begin with "Dear Editor", and close with your full name and address. Usually, only your name and city are published, but editors may want to verify an address to be sure a letter is genuine. Newspapers and magazines automatically reject letters that are sent to them without names. However, they will often agree to an author's request to remain anonymous and not publish the name and address.

Writing TIP

You many find it easier to write the introduction *after* you have drafted the rest of the letter.

Letter to Editor **225**

Teaching Tip: Supporting Opinions

Emphasize the importance of including ample reasons, facts, and examples which make an argument convincing and credible. To help students focus on this essential element of persuasion, you might suggest that they make lists or charts that delineate each type of supporting information. As students draft their letters, they should refer to their lists, incorporating those pieces of information that are most persuasive and authoritative.

Teaching Tip: Proofreading

Stress the fact that a letter with errors is often disregarded (a letter of application for a job is a good example) even though the message may be worthwhile. Students should take extra care as they proofread, and they may want another person to proofread their letter a second time.

Guidelines for Evaluation

A good letter to the editor . . .
- includes an introduction that makes a clear statement of the issue and the opinion
- supports the opinion with facts and with examples
- contains a conclusion that makes a recommendation or emphasizes an important point
- uses correct format
- uses correct grammar, usage, spelling, capitalization, and punctuation

Assess the needs of students who were not successful in developing an effective letter to the editor. Assign the appropriate Handbook Mini-Lessons, along with the support material listed for each lesson. Concepts commonly requiring reteaching for this assignment are

Thesis Statements: Handbook 6
Types of Elaboration: Handbook 8
Evaluating Ideas: Handbook 24

The following suggestions and resources may also be useful.

1. Misstatement of the Issue or Opinion
Assemble a small group of students who had difficulty with this element. Have each student briefly explain his or her issue and opinion. Then work together to fashion a one-sentence declaration of each issue and opinion, and write the sentences on the board.

2. Inadequate Supporting Details
Help students develop support for their opinions by working with them in small groups to develop a list of resources. Ask questions such as the following: What experience have you had with the issue? What library resources such as newspapers, magazines, or books might offer background facts or statistical information? What people in the community might supply information about the issue? You might also have students use the Analysis Frame from the Thinking Skills Worksheets to record details to support their opinions. After students have adequate details, suggest they rework their letters.

Extension and Enrichment

• Students might exchange letters with partners, assume the role of editor, and write responses to the letters. Suggest that in their responses students might comment on the particular arguments of the writer, refute or agree with specific points, and state whether or not they agree with the proposed recommendation or suggestion. Allow interested pairs of students to share their letters and responses with the class.

REVIEWING YOUR WRITING

1. Reread and evaluate your letter. Did you state your opinion clearly? Did you support it with facts and examples? Did you provide complete, accurate, and convincing information?

2. Proofread your letter for grammar and spelling. Don't risk rejection of your important ideas because of careless mistakes.

3. Ask a classmate to read your letter. A good letter to the editor should be clear even to those who did not read the original article you may be responding to or who are not familiar with the issues you are addressing. Show your letter to one or two classmates whose opinions you trust. Ask them if your points are clear and adequately supported.

PUBLISHING AND PRESENTING

• **Send it off.** If you are responding to an article, send your letter to the publication that printed the article.
• **Attract local attention.** If you wrote about a local issue such as school discipline or the need for a local recreation center, send the letter to an appropriate periodical. A local community newspaper, for example, would be more likely to publish your letter about a neighborhood problem than a regional magazine.
• **Post your letter on the bulletin board.** If appropriate, attach a copy of the article to which you are responding. If you are curious about others' reactions, attach a "Comments" sheet and a pencil on a string.

M.R. Tingley, courtesy London Free Press

226   Workshop 7

On the Lightside

TREE-BENDER OR MUD-SENDER?

Who hasn't made a belly-flop? The answer is many people in Rhode Island, who commit belly-bumpers. There are also Ohioans who sometimes do belly-slappers. In Kansas, people have been known to make belly-landings.

What is another word for a heavy rain? It is a dam-buster in Alabama, a hay-rotter in Virginia, a tree-bender in Massachusetts, a mud-sender in California, and a stump-washer in South Carolina.

American English is rich in variations from one part of the country to another. The words that make up these colorful regional dialects are being collected in an ambitious new dictionary, *The Dictionary of American Regional English.* This five-volume work is the result of interviews with 2,777 people from every part of the country. More than 2.5 million responses were collected, and the words are being organized to show where they are used, who uses them, and the history behind the words. The entire dictionary will not be completed until the mid-1990's.

As time passes, regional differences in America are fading. Through this ambitious project, however, the distinctive qualities of America's many dialects are being recorded. "We're doing a job of historical preservation," said Frederic G. Cassidy, the dictionary's editor in chief. "We want to represent accurately the way people talk in the United States."

227

When discussing this feature, elicit other examples of regional word usage from students. Ask students for their opinions about why regional language differences are disappearing in America. Encourage them to consider the roles of contemporary media and public education.

Your students may be interested in compiling a dictionary of regional words, based upon their own experiences and interviews with friends and family members.

Starting from Literature

Objective

To respond to a professional model of a critical review as a springboard to writing

Teaching Strategies

Motivate

Have two volunteers who have seen the same movie present a "mock" Siskel and Ebert review. Then discuss as a class each reviewer's opinion of the movie, and encourage other students to offer their opinions as well.

Tap Prior Knowledge

Ask students to recall instances when they expressed their opinions about a book, a recording, or a movie, and influenced their friends' actions as a result. What opinion did they offer? What specific details about the work did they point out? How did their friends respond?

Set a Purpose

Refer to the side-column notes and briefly discuss any professional reviews students recall reading or hearing. Then point out the purpose-setting statement and question at the end of the side column. Have students read the review, noting the reviewer's opinion and how he supports it.

Critical Review

Related ASSIGNMENT

There is some truth to the saying, "Everybody is a critic." Certainly, everyone has opinions that are eagerly shared with others.

You are a critic, too. Your feeling of pleasure or dissatisfaction in response to a work of art or literature is an evaluation, a comment. When you put your opinions into words and share them with other people, you are writing a critical review.

As you read this newspaper review of a performance of *The Piano Lesson* by August Wilson, look for the places where the reviewer gives his responses to the performance. What reasons or examples does he give to support his views?

THE PIANO LESSON

by Richard Christiansen

The Piano Lesson, [August Wilson's] latest drama, which opened Monday night at Goodman Theatre, is set in the 1930's, when new aspirations of black people, still hobbled by old prejudices, were finding expression in changing times.

Boy Willie, who storms in from the South and settles into his sister Berniece's house in the North at the play's beginning, is a black man looking toward a future in which he at last can make his mark in the world.

After years of menial servitude, this proud, dirt-ignorant man has the chance to buy land of his own from a descendant of the white man who had owned his ancestors as slaves.

Boy Willie's plan is simple: To help buy the land, he will sell an old, beautifully carved piano that has been in his family since slave times to a dealer who is acquiring these now valuable examples of black folk art.

To Boy Willie, the piano is nothing but a piece of wood, to be traded off for good land he can call his own. But to Berniece, who bitterly opposes him, that old piano has a soul. It is a treasure bought with their family's blood, and she will never let it go. . . .

If *The Piano Lesson* is not a completely well-ordered play, it is a work of incredibly rich scenes and powerful moments.

Wilson's language, which makes uncommon beauty out of common talk, time and again soars with lyric beauty in whole stretches of action, or in a single succinct phrase.

Boy Willie's language is rough and unlearned, but it is filled with power, and when he shouts defiantly to the demons of his past and the terrors of his future, "Boy Willie was here!", his is a cry of unmistakable triumph. . . .

S. Epatha Merkerson makes the bitterness and repression of the unhappy Berniece audible in her strained voice and visible in her tightly wound body, while Charles S. Dutton, as Boy Willie, pushes the play forward with such tremendous physical momentum that he sometimes comes close to going over the top. . . .

When four . . . men, gathered around a kitchen table, join voices in an old work song that gradually, inexorably builds from a simple chant to a climatic chorale of great joy, this towering play's flaws seem irrelevant.

Here is theater of unquenchable and irresistible power.

Think AND Respond

What was this reviewer's response to *The Piano Lesson*? What details does the reviewer use to support his views and shape your opinion about the play? What play, book, or movie have you seen or read lately that you would like to tell others about? Would you recommend the work or tell them to avoid it? What reasons would you provide in your evaluation?

Springboard

Before students begin their critical reviews, have them think about and discuss what E. B. White means in the following verse:

The critic leaves at curtain fall
To find, in starting to review it,
He scarcely saw the play at all
For watching his reaction to it.

Literature Connection

Author Note Richard Christiansen (1931–) professional critic, writer, and editor, has held a variety of positions in journalism in Chicago. The review from which this excerpt was taken appeared in the *Chicago Tribune,* where Christiansen has served as critic and entertainment editor.

Think and Respond

Elicit Personal Responses

Discuss the Think and Respond questions, encouraging students to state Christiansen's opinion of the *The Piano Lesson* and to point out the supporting details he includes. You might also suggest that students imagine they have tickets to the play. Have them write in their journals responses to the following questions: How did the reviewer make you anticipate seeing the play? With which character in the play might you sympathize?

Explore the Author's Techniques

Help students use Christiansen's critical review as a model for their own writing by examining some of his techniques. Point out that the author explains the setting of the story (Page 228, paragraph 1: *The Piano . . . times.*) and reveals the play's central conflict without fully disclosing the plot or the ending (Page 228, paragraph 2: Boy . . . world. Paragraph 3: After . . . slaves. Paragraph 4: Boy . . . art. Paragraph 5: But . . . soul. It . . . go.) He lets the reader know what he considers the play's shortcomings, then concentrates on his opinion of the play's strengths. (Page 228, paragraph 6: If . . . moments.) Point out that Christiansen focuses on certain elements of the play—the language (Page 229, paragraph 1: Wilson's . . . phrase. Page 229, paragraph 2: Boy . . . triumph.) and the actors' effective portrayal of the two main characters (Page 229, paragraph 2: S. Epatha . . . top.). His use of a quote and a description of a particular scene help him make his point. (Page 229, paragraph 2: Boy . . . triumph. Page 229, paragraph 3: When . . . irrelevant.) Finally, Christiansen gives his opinion in one concise statement. (Page 229, paragraph 4: Here . . . power.)

Link Literature to Writing

Point out that while most students will not become professional critics like Richard Christiansen, they will often be called upon to give their critical opinions of books or movies. Suggest that as students learn to write a critical review, they think about how Christiansen describes certain aspects of the plot and then focuses on several key elements that support his opinion.

Guiding Your Writers

Objectives

1. To choose a movie, play, or literary work to review
2. To develop criteria and an approach for evaluation
3. To write, review, and share a critical review that states and supports an opinion

Preteaching

Preview the rest of the lesson to identify any skills or concepts with which students may need help. The Evaluation Matrix in the Thinking Skills Worksheets and the Thinking Skills Transparencies as well as the mini-lessons listed below may help you in your selection and instruction.

> ### Handbook Mini-Lessons
> - Appropriate Details, p. 355
> - Point of View, pp. 430–433
> - Evaluating Ideas, pp. 452–453

Teaching Strategies

 Individualizing Instruction

Advanced/Gifted and Talented Students Encourage advanced students and students who are gifted or especially interested in literary analysis to choose a challenging work to review. You might suggest *Great Expectations* by Charles Dickens in addition to other appropriate works.

Teaching Tip: Evaluation Criteria

Write on the board the names of one or two works your class has read recently. If possible, include a movie and play your students have watched. Brainstorm a set of criteria for each item, helping students understand the kinds of standards that might apply to each medium or genre. For example, the quality of a performance may be an important part of a movie or play, and plot is probably a key element in any work of fiction.

INVITATION TO Write

This review offered a professional critic's opinion of a play. Now write your own evaluation of a play, book, or movie, or of any other work that you know well.

A critical review always involves an opinion, or judgment, about the quality or effectiveness of something. It may also provide readers with a basis for making their own judgments or decisions. Like any statement of opinion, a critical review depends on sound reasons and clear examples to make its point convincing.

THINKING THROUGH YOUR RESPONSE

1. Choose a work to evaluate. Select a play, book, or movie that you have seen or read and about which you have strong positive or negative feelings. For example, the reviewer of *The Piano Lesson* clearly wanted to share the experience of seeing the play.

2. Clarify your standards. Be clear about the standards, or criteria, against which you are judging the work. You might create a list of questions such as these: *Was the purpose of the work fulfilled? Did it make me think? Was it believable? Was it performed or executed well? Would I read or see or hear it again? Would I recommend it to others?*

3. Make a list of your responses. On a chart, write down both good and bad aspects of the work you are evaluating. Use the questions you developed earlier as a guide. Give an example from the work to support your opinion of each aspect.

4. Identify your main point. After reviewing the good and bad aspects on your list, choose the overall point you want to make. Were you mainly delighted, bored, angry, or stimulated by the work?

HANDBOOKS
FOR HELP & PRACTICE

Appropriate Details, p. 355

Point of View, pp. 430–433

Evaluating Ideas, pp. 452–453

Springboard

Have students locate in newspapers and bring to class examples of critical reviews of books and movies. You might have students annotate the reviews, noting the reviewer's opinion and the information he or she provides to support the opinion. Display the examples and encourage students to use them as models as they plan and write their own reviews.

Literature Connection

Stories to Read Two short stories that might provoke interesting critical reviews by students are "Charles" by Shirley Jackson and "Antaeus" by Borden Deal.

WRITING THE RESPONSE

1. Create a statement of opinion. To guide you as you write, draft a statement that sums up your overall evaluation of the work. This statement can be placed early in the review or used as a summary. Notice how the reviewer of *The Piano Lesson* sums up his main point in the last sentence of the review.

2. Begin your draft with a summary of the work. The summary may be short or more extensive, as in the review of *The Piano Lesson*.

3. Present supporting evidence. Give specific material from the play that supports your opinion. You may begin with supporting evidence and end with a statement of opinion. Or you may start with your opinion and follow it up with reasons, facts, and examples.

REVIEWING YOUR WRITING

1. Examine the extent of your coverage. Does your review tell enough about the work so that a reader can understand what it is about? Does it tell too much? Is your review an interesting piece of writing in itself? Is your opinion stated clearly, argued fairly, and supported by reasons, facts, and examples?

2. Share your writing. Ask someone who is unfamiliar with the work you reviewed to respond to your writing. Your reader can tell you if you have been clear and complete.

3. Look at the ideas of others. If the work was evaluated by a professional critic or reviewer, compare your review with that of the professional. On what points did you agree or disagree?

PUBLISHING AND PRESENTING

- **Display your reviews.** If other students reviewed the same work, display all of the evaluations, together with any professional reviews, on the bulletin board.
- **Hold a discussion.** Get together with several classmates who reviewed the same work. After each of you has given your evaluation, engage in a debate about the merits of the work.
- **Create a review column.** With your class, try to establish a regular review column in the school newspaper.

Writing
TIP

Don't reveal the whole plot of a movie or book. Give your readers a chance to find out for themselves.

Guidelines for Evaluation

A good critical review . . .
- gives a summary that is sufficient for a reader to understand the general focus of the work but that does not disclose the entire plot
- contains a clear statement of the writer's opinion
- supports the opinion with examples, facts, and reasons
- uses standard grammar and usage and correct spelling, capitalization, and punctuation

Reteaching

Assess the needs of students who were not successful in developing an effective critical review. Assign the appropriate Handbook Mini-Lessons, along with the support materials listed for each lesson. Concepts commonly requiring reteaching are

Point of View: Handbook 21
Evaluating Ideas: Handbook 24

The following suggestions may also be useful.

1. Lack of Statement of Opinion If students' reviews lacked a clear statement of opinion, work with them to review their reactions from their prewriting notes. Using the notes of a volunteer, write on the board a list of one set of reactions. Use the list to develop a one-sentence statement of overall opinion. Then have students review their notes and write an opinion statement, using your example as a model.

2. Lack of Specific Responses and Supporting Information If students' writing contained too many general statements such as "I liked the movie because it was interesting," work with them to describe specific responses by modeling sentences such as "I liked the plot because it kept me on the edge of my seat, waiting to see what would happen next." "I liked the main character because I have had some of the problems she faced, and I understood what she was going through." As students formulate specific responses, elicit from them one or two details that relate to each response.

On the Lightside

You might read the class one of the stories of the furies, Vulcan, or Hercules. Point out that flowers such as the hyacinth and narcissus, planets such as Pluto and Uranus, and constellations such as Orion are named after figures from Greek mythology. Ask students to research one of these figures or any other Greek figure whose name or some derivative of the name has become a word commonly used in English. Have students write a brief synopsis of the story and share it with the class.

On the Lightside

FOR YOUR AMUSEMENT

When you listen to music or visit a museum, nine Greek goddesses are looking after you. These nine goddesses, the Muses, cared for artists in Greek mythology. They dwelt in the springs and fountains at the base of sacred Mount Parnassas, and each Muse was a source of inspiration for a form of music, poetry, art, or the sciences.

Their inspiration continues in the words that have been made from their name. *Music* can be traced to the Greek word *mousikos,* meaning "belonging to the Muses." *Museum* is from *mouseion,* the "temple of the Muses." *Muse* itself means a spirit or power watching over artists, poets, and musicians; in a more general sense, it simply means the power of inspiration. *Amuse* and *bemuse* are also closely associated with the Muses.

Greek mythology has been a rich source of words

that have unusual stories behind them. *Siren,* for example, can be traced to the mythic creatures of the same name who were half woman and half bird. They sat on the rocks by the shore and used their sweet singing to lure ships to destruction. *Echo* comes from the Greek nymph Echo, who talked too much. As punishment, she was allowed only to repeat what others said. She wasted away in sadness until nothing was left of her but her voice. *Titan, fury, Herculean,* and many other words commonly used today can also be traced to the stories of the supernatural heroes of ancient civilization.

232

Sentence
COMPOSING

Adverb Clauses That Tell Time

When composing sentences, effective writers often begin by telling what happened *when, while, before, as,* or *after* another event happened. They use adverb clauses, often at the beginning of their sentences, to make these time relationships clear.

MODELS

1. <u>When</u> he reached the dining room, he sat down at a table near the window.　**Willa Cather, "Paul's Case"**

2. <u>While</u> we were waiting for the coffee, the head-waiter, with an ingratiating smile on his false face, came up to us bearing a large basket full of huge peaches.
Somerset Maugham, "The Luncheon"

3. <u>Before</u> the girls got to the porch, I heard their laughter crackling and popping like pine logs in a cooking stove.
Maya Angelou, *I Know Why the Caged Bird Sings*

4. <u>As</u> Gregor Samsa awoke one morning from uneasy dreams, he found himself transformed in his bed into a gigantic insect.　**Franz Kafka, "The Metamorphosis"**

5. <u>After</u> they had dived and come up, they swam around, hauled themselves up, and waited their turn to dive again.　**Doris Lessing, "Through the Tunnel"**

A. Expanding Sentences　Only the introductory adverb clauses are given for sentences 1–5. Finish these sentences by telling what happened. Then look on page 307 to see what the authors added to the adverb clauses to finish their sentences.

1. When Mama and I came home from work a little after eight, . . .
Gerda Weissman Klein, "All But My Life"

2. While Nick walked through the little stretch of meadow alongside the stream, . . .　**Ernest Hemingway, "Big Two-Hearted River"**

3. As she headed down the hall to her next class, . . .
Toni Cade Bambara, "Geraldine Moore the Poet"

Sentence Composing: Adverb Clauses That Tell Time

Objectives

1. To expand sentences beginning with adverb clauses
2. To complete sentences by adding adverb clauses
3. To write original sentences that imitate professional models with introductory adverb clauses

Preteaching

These exercises focus on the use of adverb clauses. You may want to review or direct students to Grammar Handbook 39, Clauses and Sentence Structure: Adverb Clauses, pp. 729–730.

ANSWER KEY

A. Expanding Sentences
Answers will vary.

B. Adding Adverb Clauses
Answers will vary.

C. Imitating Sentences
Answers will vary.

4. Before she could put a stop to it, . . .

Ambrose Stack, "The Strangers That Came to Town"

5. After he had disappeared down the road with his suitcase strapped on his shoulders, . . . **Katherine Anne Porter, "The Cracked Looking-Glass"**

B. Adding Adverb Clauses The adverb clause has been removed from each of the following sentences. All that remains is the introductory adverb itself. Add an adverb clause that blends with the rest of the sentence. Write the complete sentence. Then look on page 307 to see how the authors began their sentences.

1. Before. . . , the farmers were self-sufficient in a way they never were to be again. **Harry Crews, *A Childhood***

2. As. . . , she was greeted by a rush of warm air, in sharp contrast to the cool wind on her back. **Yong Ik Kim, "The Sea Girl"**

3. While. . . , I stood there, throwing the ball at the apartment building that faced the street. **Steve Allen, "The Sidewalk"**

4. After. . . , she turned and gave a full, severe look behind her where she had come. **Eudora Welty, "A Worn Path"**

5. When. . . , you get very sleepy at times, and the hours seem to pass like lazy cattle moving across a landscape. **James Hilton, *Goodbye, Mr. Chips***

C. Imitating Sentences Imitate the following sentences, using your own content. Write about anything you want, but use sentence structures that resemble the models.
Important: Imitate as many of the sentence parts as possible, not just the adverb clauses.

1. Before he went up into the blue hills, Tomas Gomez stopped for gasoline at the lonely station. **Ray Bradbury, *The Martian Chronicles***

2. As he walked along, drawing his lungs full of cold air, his happiness increased, and the idea of a baby party appealed to him more and more.
F. Scott Fitzgerald, "The Baby Party"

3. While other families built small fortunes, bought Fords and radios, put in electricity and went twice a week to the moving pictures in Monterey or Salinas, Junius degenerated and became a ragged savage.
John Steinbeck, *The Red Pony*

4. After it hovered uncertainly in the air, the plane settled clumsily on the ground, stumbled to a stop, and then waddled into the brightly lighted area around the terminal building, wheezing and gasping.

Robert Bingham, "The Unpopular Passenger"

5. When he was done, when he had gathered eggs that had remained hidden for weeks, Jody walked down again past the cypress tree, and past the bunkhouse toward the pasture.   **John Steinbeck, *The Red Pony***

Application   Below is just one sentence—a long sentence that begins with a series of adverb clauses. It is an adaptation of a sentence from "Letter from Birmingham Jail" by Reverend Martin Luther King, Jr. Notice how the repetition of the adverb clauses creates emphasis.

> When you have seen vicious mobs lynch your mothers and fathers and drown your sisters and brothers, when you have seen hate-filled policemen curse and kick your black brothers and sisters, when you see the vast majority of your twenty million Negro brothers smothering in an airtight cage of poverty in the midst of a wealthy society, when you suddenly find your tongue twisted and your speech stammering as you seek to explain to your six-year-old daughter why she can't go to the public amusement park that has just been advertised on television and see her cry when she is told that Funtown is closed to colored children, when you take a long trip and find it necessary to sleep night after night in the uncomfortable corners of your automobile because no motel will accept you, you will then understand the horror of prejudice.

Write a similar but shorter sentence. Choose one of the ideas below—or one of your own. Use at least three *when* clauses in a series.

a. When. . . , when. . . , when. . . , you will then understand the demands in a teen-ager's life.

b. When. . . , when. . . , when. . . , you will then grasp what it takes to be an athlete.

c. When. . . , when. . . , when. . . , you will then experience real happiness.

d. When. . . , when. . . , when. . . , you will then be a true friend.

Grammar Refresher   All model sentences in this workshop contain adverb clauses. To learn more about adverb clauses, see Handbook 39, pages 729–732.

Sentence Composing   **235**

Writing About Literature

Overview

Writing about literature is frequently required of students in school. The process of responding to a piece of literature involves the thinking skills of analyzing, evaluating, making inferences, and drawing conclusions. Writing about literature also provides students with the opportunity to express their opinions on a wide range of topics. Workshop 8 includes the following Guided and Related Assignments:

1. **Guided: Personal Response to Literature** develops the skills of analyzing, evaluating, making inferences, and drawing conclusions by asking students to choose a piece of literature and respond to it in-depth.

2. **Related: Point of View** builds on skills introduced in the Guided Assignment by having students analyze a character from fiction or history.

3. **Related: Responding to Media** encourages students to apply critical thinking developed in the Guided Assignment to pieces from the mass media.

Teaching Preview

Preparation Guide

1. Use the Overview on this page and the Teacher's Choice descriptions on page 237 as a basis for deciding which assignment(s) to teach.

2. Preview the assignments and the teacher's notes and identify concerns that may require preteaching or extra support given your class's abilities. The handbook mini-lessons suggested within the lesson may also provide guidance.

3. Preview the chart below for support materials in the Teacher's Resource File that may be used with this Workshop. Resources are for use with the Guided Assignment unless otherwise noted.

Support Materials

WRITER'S CRAFT RESOURCES

Prewrite and Explore
Thinking Skills Transparencies, pp. 11–12
Thinking Skills Worksheets, p. 7
Writing from Literature, pp. 1–44

Draft and Discover
Elaboration, Revision, and Proofreading Worksheets, p. 15

Revise Your Writing
Guidelines for Writing Assessment and Portfolio Use, pp. 15, 36–38
Peer Response Guides, pp. 25–26
Student Revision Model Transparencies, pp. 31–34
Elaboration, Revision, and Proofreading Worksheets, p. 16

Extension Activities
Writing Prompts for Fine Art Transparencies, pp. 13, 19, 20, 22
Standardized Test Practice

 Educational Technology
(available separately)
Writer's DataBank
Electronic English Handbook
Multimedia Workshop
Your Personal Trainer for the New SAT
In Perspective (videodisc)

OTHER RESOURCES

Books and Journals
Fehlman, Richard H. "Making Meanings Visible: Critically Reading TV." *English Journal*. 81.7 (1992): 19–23.
Sheridan, Daniel. "Writing in Response to Literature: The Paper of Many Parts." *English Journal*. 82.6 (1993): 58–63.

Computer Software
"Romeo and Juliet, a Play Study" (and other titles). *Write On: Secondary Classics Series I & II*. Humanities Software. Apple family, Macintosh, PC/MS-DOS.
"To Kill a Mockingbird." *Write On: Multimedia Study Bundles*. Humanities Software. Apple family, Macintosh, MPC; Videocassette or Laserdisc.

Linking Literature, Writing, and Grammar

The following options may be used to provide students with an integrated language experience. Begin by assigning and discussing any of the recommended pieces of literature. Use the suggested strategy to provide a link to the Guided Assignment.

LINKING LITERATURE AND WRITING

Option 1

Starting Point: "Traveling Through the Dark" by William Stafford on page 238 of *The Writer's Craft* and on pages 133–135 of McDougal, Littell's *Literature and Language,* Grade 9.

Strategy: Use the teaching suggestions on pages 238–239 to lead students into the Guided Assignment.

Option 2

Starting Point: *The Tragedy of Romeo and Juliet* by William Shakespeare on pages 716–842 of McDougal, Littell's *Literature and Language,* Grade 9.

Strategy: As you read and discuss all or part of the play, encourage students to keep a reading response log. This will help generate ideas for personal response essays. List the major elements of literature that they might focus on: plot, characters, theme, and language. Point out that these are elements that may be part of the focus of their work as they complete the Guided Assignment.

Option 3

Starting Point: Haiku by Basho, Buson, Wallace Stevens, and Jack Kerouac

Strategy: As you read and discuss these very brief poems, have students freewrite their immediate responses. Students may wish to build on their freewriting to create essays. In discussion, emphasize the roles of sensory imagery, figurative language, and understatement in haiku.

LINKING WRITING AND GRAMMAR

Before the drafting or revision stage of this assignment, tell students that in discussing works of literature they will often use pronouns instead of the names of characters and will need to choose correctly between the nominative and objective cases of the pronoun. Ask students to find examples of both in their own writing as you write the following examples on the board:

Incorrect: Romeo hoped the future would be bright for Juliet and he.

Correct: Romeo hoped the future would be bright for Juliet and him. *(objective)*

Incorrect: Him and Tybalt had a sword fight.

Correct: He and Tybalt had a sword fight. *(nominative)*

Go over the rules of pronoun usage on pages 547–555 of the Grammar and Usage Handbook. If problems of pronoun case still appear on student papers, assign the exercises on those pages for reteaching. Additional practice can be found in the *Grammar and Usage Practice Book* on pages 37–38.

Workshop Management Guidelines

The chart below indicates the number of days recommended for each phase of the Guided and Related Assignments. Stars indicate portions of the assignment that may be completed outside the classroom if time is limited or if teachers wish the activity to be completed by students independently.

PERSONAL RESPONSE TO LITERATURE

Starting from Literature ....1 day
Prewrite ....1–2 days*
Draft ....1–2 days*
Revise ....1–2 days*
Publish ....1–2 days
Learning ....1 day*
Reteaching ....open

POINT OF VIEW

Starting from Literature ....1 day
Choosing ....1–2 days*
Writing ....1 day*
Reviewing ....1 day*
Publishing...................................1–2 days

RESPONDING TO MEDIA

Starting from Literature ....1 day
Evaluating...................................1–2 days*
Drafting ....1 day*
Reviewing ....1 day*
Publishing...................................1–2 days

Sketchbook

Objective

To use a work of art as a springboard to informal writing

Using the Prompt

Make sure students understand that their sketches will not be graded. Encourage students to be as imaginative as they can, and point out that they need not share their sketches with anyone.

Before students begin writing, you might discuss the piece of art as a class. Have students examine the way the characters are dressed, the expressions on their faces, and any other details that seem significant. Students might then brainstorm additional questions about the art. What is the significance of the title *Nighthawks*? What are the characters' relationships to one another? Where have they been?

Point out the Additional Sketches and remind students that they are free to use those ideas as alternatives. Ask students to save their writing in their Writing Portfolios for possible use in the workshop that follows.

Sketchbook

Nighthawks, Edward Hopper

The time is late at night; the place a lonely diner. Who are these people? Why are they here? What are they saying?

Additional Sketches

Write a dialogue between you and a literary character.

What stories and poems that you have read stick in your mind? Why?

236

Humanities Connection

Art Note Edward Hopper (1882–1967) painted familiar urban American scenes in a realistic style that revealed their strangeness and created a sense of loneliness. He used light masterfully to isolate people and objects in space, such as the eerie glow that bathes the all-night diner in *Nighthawks*, shown above.

WRITER'S **8** WORKSHOP

Writing About Literature

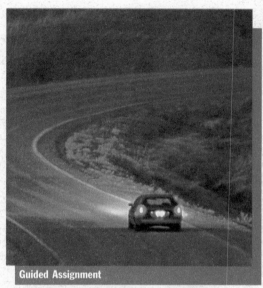

Guided Assignment
PERSONAL RESPONSE TO LITERATURE

Related Assignment
POINT OF VIEW

Related Assignment
RESPONDING TO MEDIA

It's the year 50,000 B.C. You and the other members of your clan are sitting in a cave where a storyteller chants the legend of how people learned to make weapons. At the close of the story, clan members murmur, shiver, and nod approval.

As long as stories and poems have existed, their audiences have been responding to them. In this workshop, you will get a chance to develop your own skills at writing personal responses to literature. You can apply your skills as you respond to an event from a character's point of view as well as an event reported by the media.

237

Writer's Workshop 8:
Writing About Literature

Objectives

Guided Assignment:
PERSONAL RESPONSE TO LITERATURE
To write a personal response to a piece of literature

Related Assignment:
POINT OF VIEW
To write, review, and share a piece of writing from the point of view of a character from literature

Related Assignment:
RESPONDING TO MEDIA
To write, review, and share a response to a media piece

Teacher's Choice

The following information may help you choose the assignments that best fit the needs and interests of your students.

Guided Assignment

Personal Response to Literature This Guided Assignment is intentionally based on reader-response theory as opposed to the more critical, analytic approach to literature. Students explore their own feelings about a piece of literature rather than try to dissect the mechanics of the work. The approach taken in this assignment is considered an effective way to teach literature and is particularly helpful to less experienced readers. You will probably want to coordinate the use of this assignment with your literature curriculum, perhaps using it after students have had several experiences with literature but early enough in the year to help them develop the habit of keeping a reading response log.

Related Assignments

Point of View You may want to use this assignment in conjunction with the study of characterization or point of view in literature.

Responding to Media This assignment teaches students to be critical listeners and readers. It can be particularly useful in the study of current events.

Guided
ASSIGNMENT

Personal Response to Literature

Assignment Rationale

In this assignment students are encouraged to focus on the feelings and ideas that a literary work stimulates, thus developing an awareness of the interactive nature of reader and text. As students examine their responses, their appreciation of literature is enhanced, and they develop the ability to analyze, make inferences, and draw conclusions.

Starting from Literature

Objective

To respond to a poem as a springboard to writing

Teaching Strategies

Motivate

Ask several students to share their responses to a particular book or movie. As a class, discuss the different responses, focusing on the various interpretations people have of the same work. Discuss the fact that personal experiences influence our interaction with works of literature.

Tap Prior Knowledge

Ask students if they have ever seen an injured or sick animal that they have been powerless to help—perhaps in a movie, on the news, or in real life. Ask students how they felt. What thoughts did they have? Tell students that in the poem they will be reading, a motorist encounters a deer along the road and has to make a difficult decision.

Whether it's a storyteller's tale, or a poem, short story, novel, or play, literature invites you into a particular world and encourages you to experience someone else's feelings, thoughts, and actions. It asks you to call up your own memories and experiences, too, and to examine them in light of what you've read.

In the following poem, the speaker tells about finding a dead deer by the side of a road. As you read, notice how the speaker only hints at his own thoughts and feelings, allowing you to summon up your own reactions.

238

Traveling Through the Dark
by William Stafford

Traveling through the dark I found a deer
dead on the edge of the Wilson River road.
It is usually best to roll them into the canyon:
that road is narrow; to swerve might make more dead.

By glow of the tail-light I stumbled back of the car
and stood by the heap, a doe, a recent killing;
she had stiffened already, almost cold.
I dragged her off; she was large in the belly.

My fingers touching her side brought me the reason—
her side was warm; her fawn lay there waiting,
alive, still, never to be born.
Beside that mountain road I hesitated.

The car aimed ahead its lowering parking lights;
under the hood purred the steady engine.
I stood in the glare of the warm exhaust turning red;
around our group I could hear the wilderness listen.

I thought hard for us all—my only swerving—
then pushed her over the edge into the river.

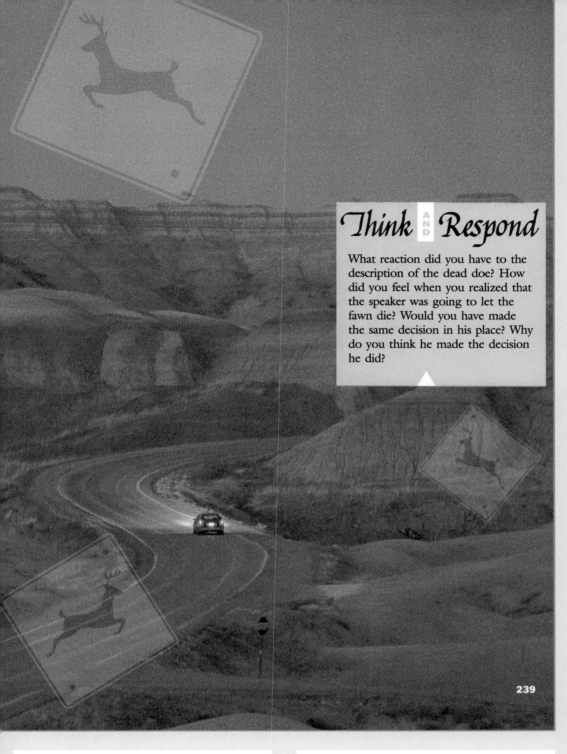

Think AND Respond

What reaction did you have to the description of the dead doe? How did you feel when you realized that the speaker was going to let the fawn die? Would you have made the same decision in his place? Why do you think he made the decision he did?

239

Springboard

Share this quote from Emily Dickinson: "If I read a book and it makes my whole body so cold no fire can warm me, I know that it is poetry. If I feel physically as if the top of my head were taken off, I know that is poetry." Have students freewrite a response, considering the possibility of a physical reaction to a literary work.

Set a Purpose

Read and discuss the side-column notes. Call attention to the purpose-setting statement at the end of the column, and encourage students to pay close attention to their thoughts and feelings as they read the poem.

Think and Respond

Elicit Personal Responses

Because this poem is especially moving, you may want to have students write personal responses before discussion. Ask students to share their first and strongest impression about the poem.

Explore the Author's Techniques

To help students understand their responses to the poem, work through it carefully with students. In "Traveling Through the Dark," Stafford uses suspense—revealing the plot and setting (Stanza 1: Traveling . . . road. It . . . dead. Stanza 2: By . . . cold. I . . . belly.), the speaker's predicament (Stanza 3: My . . . born.), and conflict (Stanza 3: Beside . . . hesitated.), and finally, at the end of the poem, the speaker's decision (Stanza 5: I thought . . . river.). By building slowly toward this climax, Stafford heightens the reader's interest and emphasizes the seriousness of the speaker's situation.

You might also call attention to and discuss the poet's use of "swerve" in the poem. (Stanza 1: . . . to swerve . . . dead. Stanza 5: I . . . river.) Point out that both uses of the word refer to a kind of departure from a set course. Ask students what else the poet might mean by "swerving" in the last stanza of the poem.

Link Literature to Writing

Explain that in the assignment that follows, students will formulate a personal response to another piece of literature. Suggest that as they approach the assignment, they recall the feelings and thoughts that "Traveling Through the Dark" aroused in them.

Prewrite and Explore

Objectives

1. To begin a reading response log and to identify a work of literature to explore
2. To use prewriting activities to explore and respond to a work of literature
3. To identify a topic and audience for a personal response essay

Preteaching

Preview the Prewrite and Explore section. If there are skills or concepts with which students may need help before prewriting, present them at this time. The Writing About Literature Booklets as well as the mini-lessons listed below may help you in your selection and instruction. The cross references in the pupil text will give students access to the same lessons for independent study.

> **Handbook Mini-Lessons**
> - Personal Techniques, pp. 317–320
> - Writing Techniques, pp. 320–323
> - Analysis Frame, p. 360
> - Reading Skills, pp. 462–463

Teaching Strategies

Modeling

Read aloud one of your favorite poems or short stories for the class. Model on the board some of your initial responses to the piece. Invite students to share their reactions as well.

Individualizing Instruction

Basic and LD Students Help basic students and learning disabled students with low reading levels select works that are manageable and at a comfortable independent reading level. If students express a strong interest in a work that is a bit difficult, you might arrange for an initial oral reading by an advanced student.

INVITATION TO Write

Literary works like William Stafford's poem stir personal responses in readers. Now record your responses to one or more literary works. Then reread, reconsider, and revise one response as an essay to share with your classmates.

When people talk with each other about the books they've read or the films and TV shows they've seen, they often end up with a better understanding of their own experience, of other people, and of the works themselves. Writing a literary response—a reaction to a piece of writing—is also a way to explore the experience. A good place to start is a **reading response log,** a journal in which you record your thoughts about a work of literature while it's still fresh in your mind. A reading log can become your conversational partner, giving you a chance through your writing to discover what you think and feel. It lets you explore a piece in some detail, and can be used as a launching pad for a more formal paper or discussion.

▶ PREWRITE AND EXPLORE

HANDBOOKS
FOR HELP & PRACTICE

Personal Techniques, pp. 317–320

Writing Techniques, pp. 320–323

Analysis Frame, p. 360

Reading Skills, pp. 462–464

1. Begin keeping a reading response log. Yours can be included in your writing journal or kept in a separate notebook. Make entries as you read or whenever you finish each work you study.

2. Choose a piece of literature to explore. You may choose a poem or story you are studying, or a favorite piece of your own. For example, you might consider the short story "Thank You, M'am" by Langston Hughes or the poems "Birches" by Robert Frost or "Women" by Alice Walker.

3. Write your reactions. The experience of reading literature is sometimes called "the making of meaning." In other words, whenever you read, you are interpreting and reacting to the ideas and images of the writer. The most appropriate response is *any* response you happen to have. It might be a prediction, a question, a comment,

240 Workshop 8

Springboard

To help students become aware of the skills they already use in responding to movies, television shows, and recordings, and to realize that they can apply those same skills when responding to literature, you might suggest the following warm-up activity. Have students record their responses to movies, television shows, and songs for several days. Then have them share their responses in small groups, discussing their particular reactions and noting how they expressed them.

or a feeling. Only you know what your strongest responses are. Pay attention to what you are thinking, feeling, and wondering as you read a literary work.

Your shortest responses may be no longer than a single word ("Wow!") or a question mark (?) after a passage you don't understand. Some may be a sentence or phrase; others may require a paragraph or more to explore your feelings fully. You are likely to write such extended responses at moments when you experience some break-through in your understanding of a difficult idea or realize something important about a text that you hadn't realized before. If you have trouble knowing what to write, try some of the following activities:

Exploratory Activities

- **Pointing** As you read, keep track of passages that catch your attention—anything from a single word to a whole scene. They may be passages that puzzle you or excite you, that you enjoy or you *don't* like.
- **Focused freewriting** When you finish your first reading of a work, complete a five-minute rewrite. Respond by focusing partic-ularly on any problems you experienced in understanding what you read. As an alterna-tive, use one of these prompts to help you start writing:

  Reading this work, I noticed . . .
  In this work, I liked . . .
  After reading this work, I wonder . . .
  For me the most important word in this work is _____ because . . .
  For me the most important line in this work is _____ because . . .
  Reading this work makes me think of . . .

- **Sharing** In a group of three or four stu-dents or with the whole class, read aloud the passages you noted in your journal and listen to the passages selected by other students. Talk with classmates about why you—and they—chose these passages.

The Sonnet by William Mulready, 1839

Personal Response to Literature **241**

Teaching Tip: Recording Reactions

Suggest that students record any reactions that they think are worthwhile. Point out that if students are uncertain about the value of a particular reaction, they should still make note of it. They cannot "overwrite" personal responses at this stage.

Spot Check

As students finalize their choices, check to make sure that the piece selected is ap-propriate for the ability level of that stu-dent. If it is inappropriate, you may wish to offer several alternatives.

Humanities Connection

Art Note *The Sonnet*, an oil painting by Wil-liam Mulready (1786–1863), portrays a scene of young love. Mulready employed a favorite technique—painting a thin layer of bright color over a white background—that makes the scene appear to glow. Ask: How does this tech-nique heighten the painting's theme?

Critical Thinking

Analyzing Work through One Student's Process with the class. Point out how Blair indicates the stanza to which he is responding. He also uses direct quotes in his reading log, asks questions, and reports his feelings. Finally, he summarizes his overall feelings about the poem. Suggest that students try some of these techniques as they continue to respond to their chosen works.

 Writer's Choice Read the responses in your journal. Do you see one you could expand into an essay? If not, will you reread some of the literature or find a new piece?

Reading for his own enjoyment, Blair found William Stafford's "Traveling Through the Dark" in a poetry anthology in his town library. After he took the book home and read the poem, he wrote the following entry in his log.

ONE STUDENT'S PROCESS

I read this poem three times without stopping to respond. I know I should have stopped to respond, but I just kept reading it again and again. It's about a man who finds a dead deer on the side of the road at night. Here's my response after my third reading.

<u>stanza 1:</u> He says "it is usually best to roll them into the canyon." But why does he make it *his* business to roll the deer off the side of the road? I wouldn't want to touch a dead animal.

<u>stanza 3:</u> He's surprised that the cold deer has a warm belly and then he realizes there's a baby deer inside waiting to be born. The dead deer is pregnant! How awful, the phrase "never to be born." I was shocked when I got to this part.

<u>stanza 4:</u> He says "around our group I could hear the wilderness listen." What group? He and the dead deer and the baby inside its mother? Yes, because he is alone. The poem says "I found a deer," not "we."

<u>stanza 5:</u> He pushes the deer over the cliff or bank into the river. Why? Couldn't he get somebody to operate and save the baby? What does he mean when he says "I thought hard for us all"?

This is a sad poem and not hard to understand, except I don't agree with the way the man acted. Couldn't he try to save the unborn deer?

4. Read and rewrite. If you are working with a short poem, reread it several times, making new response entries with each reading. If you are working with a short story or long poem, reread it one more time, responding as you read and especially as you complete your second reading.

 Writer's Choice Do you want to zero in on one specific reaction to the piece you are reading, or continue exploring several reactions?

5. Find a topic for your response essay. Look over your journal entries for the work you are going to write about. Pay special attention to the entries that seem to have the most to say about the literary work, about the difficulties of reading it, or about you as the reader. Select one entry or several related ones as the basis for your response paper. You might ask yourself what your thoughts, feelings, or questions are about any one of these elements of the work:

- the plot or events that take place
- the characters in the work
- the setting—time, place, atmosphere—where the events occur
- the theme or main idea the work conveys to you
- the voice or character of the speaker or narrator

6. Identify your audience. In literary response essays, it's important to have a feel for how familiar or unfamiliar your audience is with the work you are discussing. Think about what your classmates will need to know in order to understand your response.

DRAFT AND DISCOVER

1. Consider the form. Your response essay will probably consist of at least three parts.

- The **introduction** should familiarize your reader with the story or poem. It need not be a complete plot summary or retelling, but it must give your reader enough information for a rough understanding of the work.
- The **body** of your paper will then tell about your response to the work. It should explain what your response was and why you felt as you did.
- Your **conclusion** should present an overall reaction to the work.

PROBLEM SOLVING

How do I decide which aspect or aspects of the work I want to respond to?

HANDBOOKS
FOR HELP & PRACTICE

Types of
Conclusions,
pp. 371–373
Paraphrases and
Summaries,
pp. 464–465

Personal Response
to Literature   **243**

Suggest that students reread their stories or poems on different days if possible, or at least at different times during the day. Point out that their thoughts and feelings will vary slightly from day to day, depending upon their circumstances and mood.

Critical Thinking

Analyzing As students select a topic and clarify a focus for their essay, you might have them look ahead to Blair's draft on page 244. Point out that Blair focused on his responses and attempts to understand the main character's decision and motivation, key elements in the poem.

Draft and Discover

Objectives

1. To draft an essay that expresses a personal response to a piece of literature and that includes specific reactions and supporting details
2. To respond to one's own writing and that of a peer

Preteaching

Preview the Draft and Discover section for skills or strategies with which students may need special help. The Elaboration Worksheet from the Revision, Proofreading, and Elaboration booklet as well as the mini-lessons listed below may be useful in your selection and instruction.

> **Handbook Mini-Lessons**
> - Types of Conclusions, pp. 371–373
> - Writing Paraphrases and Summaries, pp. 464–465

Modeling

Refer to the favorite piece of literature that you shared earlier with the class. Model a topic for the piece and discuss the elements you might include in a summary and in the body of a draft. Emphasize that it is important to include specific details but only those that help develop the topic.

 Individualizing Instruction

Learning Styles Some students might benefit from the structure that an informal outline or chart would provide. Suggest that these students list the details they want to include in the introduction, body, and conclusion.

COMPUTER ──TIP──

If you are having difficulty getting started, type out on your computer the response entry that will be the basis for your paper.

2. Write the draft. Some of your journal entries may already be early drafts of a response essay. Expand on them by explaining more fully what you were thinking and feeling and why. Quoting directly from the literary work at key points in your paper will support your opinions and can help readers better understand your response. Using quotations can also give your readers a feel for the work. However, be careful not to overuse quotations. What is important is *your* response. Paraphrasing—summing up passages from the work in your own words—is another good strategy for supporting your opinions and for bringing the work closer to the reader.

Look at the first draft of Blair's response essay. Can you see how it is a revision of responses in his log?

ONE STUDENT'S PROCESS

This poem, "Traveling Through the Dark," is about a man who sees a dead deer on the side of the road and starts to push it off the road. But he notices that the deer is a pregnant mother with a baby deer alive inside it. But he still pushed the deer off the road into a river.

My response to the poem was at first to feel angry at the man. Why didn't he try to save the baby by calling a vet to operate? That's what I would do. But after many readings I realized that the man did what he thought was right for the mother and baby deer and that it was hard for him to do it. He says "I thought hard for us all, then pushed her over the edge into the river." I think he probably thought about what a hard life the fawn would have if it was born prematurely without a mother. By saving its life, he might have just been giving it a slower death. The speaker probably also thought about how guilty he would feel for killing the fawn. And about the fact that all living things have to die someday. That's what I would be thinking about in his situation. He was trying to do what he thought was best. I'm just not sure that I agree with him.

3. Review your paper. After you complete your draft, put it aside for a while to get a new perspective on it. Then reread it. Look and listen for places where you aren't making clear sense or where you're saying something that isn't exactly true. Consider rewriting those sentences or rethinking the ideas behind them. Ask yourself—and a peer reader or readers—questions such as the following.

R E V I E W   Y O U R   W R I T I N G

Questions for Yourself
- Did I find or get at the issue that really matters to me?
- Do I give the title of the work and tell something about the work in my introduction?
- Does the way I explain my response to the work still make sense to me?
- Have I changed my mind about all or part of my response?
- Do my feelings about the work come through?

Questions for Your Peer Readers
- Do you understand what the story or poem is about from my paper?
- Can you see why I responded to the work in the way that I did?
- Can you tell me in your own words what you think my response is?
- Are there parts of the story or poem I should have responded to, but didn't?
- What feeling or feelings came through strongest in my writing?
- What would you like to know more about?

Ask for any additional help you would like as well, including editorial suggestions for fixing awkward sentences in your paper.

 Writer's Choice Do you want to continue with this draft, or might you want to change your response entirely?

Writing
═TIP═

Don't be afraid to change your mind about your response to the literary work.

Revise Your Writing

Objectives

1. To evaluate responses to a draft of a personal response to literature
2. To use the responses, the results of a self-evaluation, and a set of standards to revise a draft of a personal response essay
3. To proofread for errors in grammar, spelling, usage, and mechanics

Preteaching

Preview the Revise Your Writing section. Use the material in the section and your knowledge of any problems in students' drafts to identify the skills or strategies you wish to review. The Student Revision Model Transparency, the Revision and Proofreading Worksheets, and the mini-lessons listed below may be helpful in your selection and instruction.

Handbook Mini-Lessons

- Coherence in Compositions, pp. 368–369
- Revising for Ideas, pp. 375–376
- Adding Detail, pp. 386–388
- Quotation Marks, pp. 795–796

Teaching Strategies

Critical Thinking

Evaluation Prepare students for evaluation of their peer responses and for revision by discussing in detail One Student's Process, the Student Revision Model Transparency for this assignment, and the Standards for Evaluation. To help students organize their revision efforts, you might suggest that they transfer their responses to the "Questions for Yourself," their peer reader's suggestions, and any notes they may make about their drafts in light of the Standards for Evaluation to one sheet of paper. They can then review all comments, and circle those that seem most significant to them.

HANDBOOKS

FOR HELP & PRACTICE

Coherence in Compositions, pp. 368–369

Revising for Ideas, pp. 375–376

Adding Detail, pp. 386–388

Quotation Marks, pp. 795–796

REVISE YOUR WRITING

1. Evaluate your responses. Review your own thoughts and the reactions you got from your peers. Also keep in mind the following characteristics of strong personal responses to literature.

Standards for Evaluation

An effective response . . .

- includes an introduction that identifies the literary work and clearly states your overall response to it.
- tells enough about the literary work so that readers can understand your response.
- contains clearly described, specific reactions and responses to the literary work, well supported by quotations and details.
- uses language and details that are appropriate for your audience.

2. Problem-solve. Use the suggestions above, and your own and your peer's responses, to help strengthen your draft. Here is how Blair revised a paragraph of his essay.

ONE STUDENT'S PROCESS

This is an excellent point. I'd try to emphasize it.

How do you feel about that?

He probably thought about what it would feel like to be a newborn—maybe premature—fawn brought into this world without a mother? If he had saved the fawn, he might have just been giving it a slower death. ~~Another thing I thought~~ The poem also made me think about ~~was~~ the fact that all things die.

It's strange to realize it can happen in an instant. The deer was full of life one moment and a dilemma for a passerby the next.

246 Workshop 8

---

3. Proofread your work. Make a clean copy that incorporates all your changes. Then find and correct any errors in spelling, grammar, and punctuation. Make sure all quotes from the text are exact.

LINKING
GRAMMAR **AND** WRITING
Quoting from a Poem or Story

Be sure to enclose exact quotes from a poem or story in quotation marks. Use an ellipsis (. . .) to show where you have omitted words. Put a slash-mark (/) wherever your quotation from a poem includes a line break.

PROBLEM: He says "I thought hard for us all, then pushed her over the edge into the river."

CORRECTED: He says "I thought hard for us all . . . /then pushed her over the edge into the river."

See Grammar Handbook 41 for additional information on using quotation marks.

HANDBOOKS
FOR HELP & PRACTICE

Discussion Skills, pp. 479–481

PUBLISH AND PRESENT

- **Form a readers' circle.** With several other writers who wrote about the same piece of literature, read your essays aloud and discuss how similarly or differently you approached the work.
- **Compile a book of literary essays.** Present a copy to the school library as a guide for other students who might be looking for interesting pieces of literature to read and discuss.
- **Read your response to literature aloud to your class.** You may wish to begin by reading an excerpt of the literary selection you chose. Invite questions and comments.

Personal Response to Literature **247**

The following guidelines may be used for a close evaluation of a personal response essay. See the Guidelines for Evaluating Writing in the Teacher's Resource File for additional help with holistic or analytic scoring.

Ideas and Content
- clearly identifies and summarizes the literary work in an introduction
- describes specific responses to the work
- uses quotations and details to support responses
- clearly states an overall reaction to the work either in the introduction or in the conclusion
- demonstrates an awareness of audience in word choice and detail

Structure and Form
- focuses on a topic
- is organized logically with a distinct and focused introduction, body, and conclusion

Grammar, Usage, and Mechanics
- includes standard grammar and usage
- uses correct spelling, capitalization, and punctuation

Publish and Present

Objective

To publish and present a personal response essay

Teaching Strategies

Teaching Tip: Sharing

In addition to the publishing options students select from this page, you might also have them display their essays in the classroom. After students have had a chance to read them, discuss which of the works students would like to read and why.

Using the Model

Ask students how their initial response to "Traveling Through the Dark" compares with Blair's responses. Review the annotations and suggest that students evaluate their final essay or the essay of a partner in the same way.

Reteaching

Assess the needs of students who were not successful in developing an effective personal response essay and identify two or three areas in which additional practice is needed. Assign the appropriate Handbook Mini-Lessons, along with the support materials listed for each lesson. Concepts commonly requiring reteaching for this assignment are

Paraphrases and Summaries: Handbook 25.
Adding Detail: Handbook 14.

The following suggestions may also be useful.

1. Inappropriate Summaries Gather a small group of students who had difficulty summarizing a literary work. Read aloud a short story or a poem ("The Sniper" by Liam O'Flaherty or "Lucy Gray" by William Wordsworth, for example). Work with students to list the main events in the work and to describe the events in a three- or four-sentence summary.

2. Lack of Specific Responses If some students did not include specific, well-supported responses, provide and discuss these examples of an empty response ("I don't like the characters.") and a specific response ("The characters seem wooden and unreal."). Work with students to review and evaluate their responses against these statements to identify those that are not specific. Then have students work with partners to reread their literature selections, revise empty responses, and find specific details to support the revised responses.

Introduction identifies and briefly summarizes the work

Provides a clear, specific reaction to the work

Supports reaction with quotation from the work

Sums up reaction in an effective conclusion

248 Workshop 8

ONE STUDENT'S PROCESS

Response to William Stafford's "Traveling Through the Dark"

Blair Tremaine

"Traveling Through the Dark" is a poem about a man who drives along a country road at night and sees a dead deer by the side of the road. He gets out of his car to push the deer into the canyon off the narrow road. He is concerned that other drivers might swerve to avoid the dead deer and then have accidents, possibly killing themselves or their passengers or people in oncoming cars. When he starts to move the deer, he feels that its belly is warm. Then he realizes that the dead deer is a mother with an unborn fawn alive inside her. The man thinks for a while and then pushes the deer off the road into the river.

When I first read this poem I thought the speaker was cruel to dump the dead deer in the river with its unborn baby inside. I wondered why he didn't operate on the mother or call a vet. But after many readings I realized that he did what he thought the mother and baby would want him to do, and that it was hard for him. He says he "thought hard for us all . . . /then pushed her over the edge into the river." I think "for us all" means for the two deer and for himself and for all living things. What would it feel like to be a newborn—maybe premature—fawn brought into this world without a mother? If he had saved the fawn, he might have just been giving it a slower death. The poem also made me think about the fact that all things die. It's strange to realize it can happen in an instant. The deer was full of life one moment and a dilemma for a passerby the next.

I don't know if I could do what the man in the poem did and I'm not sure he did the right thing. But he was trying to do what he thought was best. In this particular situation nothing he did could have been kind, but he tried to do what was least cruel.

WRITER TO WRITER

Originality does not consist in saying what no one has ever said before, but in saying exactly what you think yourself.

Sir James F. Stephen, British journalist and judge

1. Reflecting on your writing. Now that you have read William Stafford's poem and Blair Tremaine's response and have created a literary response essay of your own, think about the process you used. Ask yourself the following questions, and jot down your responses in your writer's log.

- If I had it to do over again, would I choose to write about the same literary text or a different one? Why?
- How did writing about the literary work affect my understanding or appreciation of the work?
- How was my style in this literary essay different from my style in other kinds of writing? How was it similar? Was my style appropriate?
- Did I learn anything new about literature by writing this essay? If so, what?

2. Apply your skills. Try one or more writing activities in the following areas.

- **Cross curricular** Find a historical document discussed in a history or social studies textbook, such as the *Declaration of Independence*. Write your response to the document.
- **The arts** Find a painting, sculpture, or piece of music that especially affects you either positively or negatively. Write your response to it.
- **Current events** Read or listen to a speech by an official or candidate. Write your response to it.
- **Drama** Think about a movie, play, or television show you have seen recently. Write your response to it.
- **Related assignments** Follow the suggestions on pages 250–260 for responding to a character and to media.

▶ FOR YOUR
PORTFOLIO

Personal Response
to Literature **249**

Learning from Your Writing Process

Objective

To analyze and reflect upon what has been learned about the writing process and about writing a personal response to literature

Teaching Strategies

Reflecting on the Process

Remind students to note any other responses they have to their writing experience in addition to those stimulated by the questions. A quick review of their self-evaluations and peer reader's comments might help students formulate complete responses.

Writing Portfolio

Have students keep their responses to the writing experience with their final essays in their Writing Portfolio.

Application

You might provide students who choose the second activity in the "Apply Your Skills" section with one or more of the Fine Art Transparencies from the Teacher's Resource File.

Summary and Closure

Before students proceed to the next assignment, make sure they have internalized the following concepts:

1. Writing a personal response to literature requires careful reading and awareness of one's own thoughts and feelings.

2. An effective personal response essay includes a brief summary of the work, specific responses, and details that support each response.

Allow students time to summarize what they have learned by describing the characteristics of a personal response to literature. Ask students to consider how the skills they have learned in this assignment might help them in the study of literature and other school subjects.

Starting from Literature

Objective

To respond to a literary excerpt as a springboard to writing

Teaching Strategies

Motivate

Ask students if they have ever wished to be inside somebody's "skin" and to experience life as that person experiences it. Whom would they choose? Why?

Tap Prior Knowledge

Ask students if they have ever been responsible for a younger brother, sister, or neighbor. How did they feel toward that person? Resentful? Protective? Explain that the excerpt is about a girl who, among other things, takes care of her brother.

Set a Purpose

Before students read the excerpt, discuss the side-column notes. Encourage students to imagine as they read that they are the main character in the story. Have them think about how she feels and the kind of person she is.

Related ASSIGNMENT

Point of View
from RAYMOND'S RUN

by Toni Cade Bambara

Have you ever encountered a character in a story whom you felt you really understood? Why do you think you felt so sympathetic to that character? A short story often invites you to share the experiences of a character by seeing and responding to events from that character's point of view.

In this story, Squeaky has a special relationship with her brother Raymond, who has physical and mental handicaps. As you read the story, put yourself in Squeaky's place. Can you understand what is going on in her mind? Can you see her point of view?

250

I don't have much work to do around the house like some girls. My mother does that. And I don't have to earn my pocket money by hustling; George runs errands for the big boys and sells Christmas cards. And anything else that's got to get done, my father does. All I have to do in life is mind my brother Raymond, which is enough.

Sometimes I slip, and say my little brother Raymond. But as any fool can see he's much bigger, and he's older too. But a lot of people call him my little brother cause he needs looking after cause he's not quite right. And a lot of smart mouths got lots to say about that too, especially when George was minding him. But now, if anybody has anything to say to Raymond, anything to say about his big head, they have to come by me. And I don't play the dozens or believe in standing around with somebody in my face doing a lot of talking. I much rather just knock you down and take my chances, even if I am a little girl with skinny arms and a squeaky voice, which is how I got the name Squeaky. And if things get too rough, I run. And as anybody can tell you, I'm the fastest thing on two feet.

There is no track meet that I don't win the first place medal. I used to win the twenty-yard dash when I was a little kid in kindergarten. Nowadays, it's the fifty-yard dash. . . .

I take my time getting to the park on May Day because the track meet is the last thing on the program. The biggest thing on the program is the May Pole dancing, which I can do without, thank you, even if my mother thinks it's a shame I don't take part and act like a girl for a change. You'd think my mother'd be grateful not to have to make me a white organdy dress with a big satin sash, and buy me new white baby-doll shoes that can't be taken out of the box till the big day. You'd think she'd be glad her daughter ain't out there

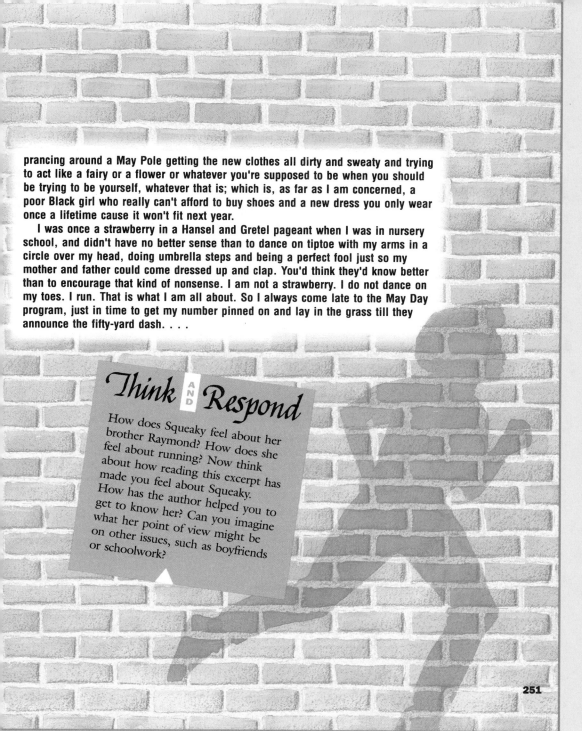

prancing around a May Pole getting the new clothes all dirty and sweaty and trying to act like a fairy or a flower or whatever you're supposed to be when you should be trying to be yourself, whatever that is; which is, as far as I am concerned, a poor Black girl who really can't afford to buy shoes and a new dress you only wear once a lifetime cause it won't fit next year.

I was once a strawberry in a Hansel and Gretel pageant when I was in nursery school, and didn't have no better sense than to dance on tiptoe with my arms in a circle over my head, doing umbrella steps and being a perfect fool just so my mother and father could come dressed up and clap. You'd think they'd know better than to encourage that kind of nonsense. I am not a strawberry. I do not dance on my toes. I run. That is what I am all about. So I always come late to the May Day program, just in time to get my number pinned on and lay in the grass till they announce the fifty-yard dash. . . .

Think AND Respond

How does Squeaky feel about her brother Raymond? How does she feel about running? Now think about how reading this excerpt has made you feel about Squeaky. How has the author helped you to get to know her? Can you imagine what her point of view might be on other issues, such as boyfriends or schoolwork?

251

Literature Connection

Author Note   Toni Cade Bambara, African-American writer and editor, was born in New York in 1939. Bambara's works include *The Sea Birds Are Still Alive: Collected Stories, Gorilla, My Love,* and *The Salt Eaters.*

Think and Respond

Elicit Personal Responses

To help students better understand Squeaky, you may want to read the excerpt aloud or have a volunteer read it. Then discuss the Think and Respond questions, focusing on what students have learned about Squeaky.

Explore the Author's Techniques

To help students understand how Toni Cade Bambara reveals the makeup of her main character, discuss the excerpt carefully. Call attention to the use of the pronoun "I," and explain that the story is written in the first person, from the main character's point of view. By using the first-person point of view, Bambara allows Squeaky to share her thoughts and feelings directly. Point out the informal tone (Page 250, paragraph 2: But as any . . . too.), vocabulary and expressions (Page 250, paragraph 2: And I don't . . . talking.), and sentence structure (Page 250, paragraph 4: You'd think . . . year.), and emphasize that Bambara writes as her character would speak, thus helping the reader understand and relate to her. Discuss how Bambara reveals Squeaky's attitudes toward her brother (Page 250, paragraph 2: But now . . . me.), toward running (Page 250, paragraph 2: And if . . . run. And as . . . feet. Page 251, paragraph 2: That . . . about.), and toward "girlish" things. (Page 250, paragraph 4: The biggest . . . change.)

Link Literature to Writing

Point out that by reading the excerpt carefully, students have learned a great deal about how Squeaky thinks and feels. Explain that in the following assignment, students will have the opportunity to "take on" a character and write from that character's perspective. Suggest that as they write, students think about how their character thinks and feels and might express himself or herself.

Guiding Your Writers

Objectives

1. To identify and analyze a character from a literary work
2. To create an original situation for the character
3. To write, review, and share a piece of writing from the point of view of that character

Preteaching

Preview the rest of the assignment for any skills or concepts with which students may need help. The Category Chart in the Thinking Skills Transparencies and the Thinking Skills Worksheets and the mini-lessons listed below may help you in your selection and instruction. The cross references in the pupil text will give students access to the same lessons for independent study.

Handbook Mini-Lessons
- Varieties of Language, pp. 409–411
- Point of View, pp. 430–433
- Dialogue in Fiction, pp. 434–435

Teaching Strategies

Teaching Tip: Finding a Character

Work closely with students as they choose a character to analyze. You might brainstorm in class a list of characters appropriate for this assignment. Also see the Literature Connection below.

INVITATION TO Write

In "Raymond's Run", Toni Cade Bambara presents Squeaky's experiences from Squeaky's point of view. From the point of view of a character from a literary work, write about an event or situation not presented in that work.

The term "point of view" refers to the perspective from which a story is told. When a story is written from a character's point of view, the reader learns very directly how that character responds to the events and situations of his or her life. When you respond to a piece of literature by writing from a character's point of view, you can broaden your understanding of the story by discovering aspects of the character you might not have seen otherwise. By putting yourself in a character's place and trying to imagine how he or she would react in a new situation, you can also enrich your appreciation of the original story.

HANDBOOKS
FOR HELP & PRACTICE

Varieties of Language, pp. 409—411

Point of View, pp. 430—433

Dialogue in Fiction, pp. 434—435

CHOOSING A CHARACTER

1. Choose a character. You may choose Squeaky or any character from a work of literature—a novel, a short story, an essay, or a play. You don't have to choose the main character, but you do need enough information about how the character thinks, speaks, or behaves so that you can analyze how he or she might respond in a particular situation.

Writer's Choice For a history class report, ask if you may write from the point of view of a famous historical character, rather than writing the usual third-person narrative report.

2. Analyze the character. Get to know him or her from the dialogue, from the plot events, and from other clues in the story, such as how different people react to the character. In your mind, picture the character's physical appearance and style. Think about his or her personality.

Literature Connection

Stories to Read Students might enjoy reading the following stories written from the first-person point of view: "Everyday Use" by Alice Walker, "The Cave" by Jean McCord, "A Mother in Mannville" by Majorie Kinnan Rawlings, and "Antaeus" by Borden Deal.

For example, what is Squeaky like as a person? She describes herself as "a little girl with skinny arms and a squeaky voice." What else do you learn about her approach to life and other people?

3. Relate the character to yourself. List ways in which the character is like you and ways in which he or she is different. Underline the traits that are most unlike your own. This kind of comparison gives you a more personal connection with the character.

4. Invent a situation. You may choose to write about a natural extension of the story, such as Squeaky's training Raymond for his first race, or you may write about something not hinted at in the story, such as Squeaky's getting an after-school job or becoming interested in a boy. Whatever situation you choose to explore from the character's point of view, it must be something that seems to arise naturally out of the character's life.

WRITING THE RESPONSE

1. Choose a form. If your character kept a *diary,* what would he or she write in it? What events and feelings would be described? A diary entry could reveal the character's innermost thoughts and might provide an opportunity to explore his or her secret hopes and fears. Writing a *personal letter* would require you to imagine the person to whom your character is writing. An *essay* or *letter to the editor* would provide a chance for the character to express his or her thoughts about a subject in a more formal way. If the first form you try doesn't fit your character, try another until one feels right.

2. Use language that is appropriate for your character. Ask yourself questions like these: How formally or informally would my character speak? For example, would he or she use slang or highly figurative language? Would the character express strong emotion or look at events coolly from a distance?

Grammar
─TIP─

Decide whether your character is going to speak in the present or past tense, and maintain that tense throughout.

Point of View **253**

Teaching Tip: Analyzing a Character

You might suggest that students use a category chart to help them analyze their characters. (See Writing Handbook 9, Using Graphic Devices, pp. 357–360, for an example. You may also want to use or refer students to the Category Chart in the Thinking Skills Transparencies and in the Thinking Skills Worksheets.) Possible categories include *Physical Characteristics, Personal Qualities,* and *Goals or Aspirations.* You might model such a chart using Squeaky as the subject. Suggest that students refer to the charts as they write, making sure that what they write is in keeping with the information listed in their charts.

Guidelines for Evaluation
Effective writing from a character's point of view . . .
- reflects an understanding of the character's thoughts, feelings, and actions
- contains original situations or events consistent with the character's life
- uses a voice and language in keeping with the character
- contains only those grammar and usage errors that are consistent with those the character might have made

Science Connection

Students who want to experiment further with writing from a character's point of view might imagine they are an astronaut such as Buzz Aldrin or Neil Armstrong, the first men on the moon, or Sally Ride, the first American woman in space. Have students research the person and write about an experience in space from that person's point of view.

Reteaching

Assess the needs of students who were not successful in developing an effective piece written from a character's point of view. Assign the appropriate Handbook Mini-lessons, along with the support materials listed for each lesson. Concepts commonly requiring reteaching for this assignment are

Point of View: Handbook 21
Varieties of Language: Handbook 18

The following suggestions and resources may also be useful.

1. Lack of an Original Situation Help students who had difficulty creating an original, believable situation by reviewing the things one character did in a particular story. Elicit from a volunteer the things his or her character did, and make a list on the board. Have the volunteer suggest one or two other things the character might do in another story. Write the suggestions on the board, comparing each to the other items on the list. Help students evaluate whether the original events seem believable and in keeping with the actual story events listed. Suggest that students use this process to develop and evaluate a new situation for their papers.

2. Inconsistent Voice and Language Have students tape-record a passage from the story in which their character is speaking and a passage from their own writing. Suggest that students listen to both passages several times, and underline sentences in their paper that sound stilted or out of character. Students can then work with you or a partner to revise those sections of their papers.

Extension and Enrichment

• Have students present a talk show in which they portray their characters, other literary characters, or historical figures. Divide the class into small groups, and appoint one member of each group talk show host. Have students work together to research their characters and prepare interview questions. Allow groups to present their shows for the class.

REVIEWING YOUR WRITING

1. Go back to the source. Reread the work you chose or the excerpts from "Raymond's Run." Do they reveal a character that is consistent with the character who "wrote" your piece? If not, work on your writing until it reflects the character created in the original work.

2. Read your writing aloud. Do you hear the character's voice in your words? Does your writing sound as if it could have come from him or her? Is the style of your writing similar to the character's style?

3. Proofread your character's writing. Remember that you reveal the personality of your character through his or her voice and style. One way to do this is to have the character make certain "mistakes" in grammar, usage, and mechanics. For example, Squeaky might leave out a *would* or an *am* from time to time or use a run-on sentence, but her writing rings true for her character. Make sure any such mistakes your character makes are consistent and appropriate.

PUBLISHING AND PRESENTING

• **Make a booklet.** If several of you have written from Squeaky's point of view, form a group and collect the writings into a booklet that explores Squeaky's character beyond "Raymond's Run." See if the Squeaky that is revealed in the book is a consistent character or if the personality traits revealed in some narratives contradict those revealed in others.
• **Tape character sketches.** With others, create a tape or video of "living character sketches."
• **Present your character.** Read your writing aloud to the class. If others are familiar with the same character, discuss whether he or she is believably reflected in your writing.

254   Workshop 8

On the Lightside

THE SCOTS-IRISH

The roots of American country music are generally traced to the hills of Appalachia, but they actually go one step farther into the past. Listen to a country song, and you may actually be hearing music passed down from the ballads of the Scottish lowlands in the sixteenth and seventeenth centuries.

The Scots-Irish settlers came to America in great numbers in the 1700's. They moved through the Cumberland Gap and settled in the frontier land of the Appalachian Mountains. They brought with them a rich oral culture that survives today in the speech and music of Appalachia. Phrases such as *bonnyclabber* for curdled sour milk and *flannelcake* for wheat cake come from the Scots-Irish. So do pronunciations such as "tharr" for *there* and "barr" for *bear*.

The settlers also brought with them the Scots-Irish storytelling tradition. Their stories and ballads, told with attention to the colorful turn of phrase, have had a strong influence on American country music. As Robert McCrum, William Cran, and Robert MacNeil note in *The Story of English,* "Today, the ballads of the Scots-Irish that traveled here during the eighteenth century are imitated and reproduced from Arkansas to Alberta, by singers like Dolly Parton and Kenny Rogers who have internationalized a style that was once confined to the hills."

255

When discussing this selection, you may want to obtain a recording of early American folk songs from your local library, as well as recordings of American country and bluegrass music. Play the recordings and point out the similarities between the early songs and the modern music, particularly the narrative element—often a tale of tragic love. You may also wish to read aloud one or more of the many versions of the Scottish ballad "Barbara Allen's Cruelty" or the ballads "Sir Patrick Spens" and "Lord Randall." Point out how these old Scottish ballads contain many of the same elements as the modern music—the use of narrative, repetition, and vernacular.

Objective

To respond to a newspaper article as a springboard to writing

Teaching Strategies

Motivate

Ask students if they think the media always present information objectively and accurately, and invite discussion. Encourage students to give examples of biased as well as objective messages.

Tap Prior Knowledge

Ask students to discuss what they know about energy sources and consumption in the United States. Call attention to the headline of the newspaper article, and encourage discussion of the impact of oil drilling on the environment.

Set a Purpose

Discuss the side-column notes, and call attention to the purpose-setting question at the end of the column. Point out the Oil vs. Environment head on page 257, and suggest that as students read or immediately after reading the selection, they jot down some of the details offered on each side of the issue.

Related
ASSIGNMENT

Responding to Media

Oil potential spawns fears in Alaska tribe

Every day you are bombarded with information from radio, television, magazines, newspapers, movies, billboards, and books. To make sense of all these messages, which sometimes are confusing and contradictory, you must learn to respond to them personally and critically. As you read the newspaper article on this page, think carefully about the information you are being given. Are both sides of the issue being presented fairly?

From USA TODAY

Trimble Gilbert's people have lived in Arctic Village, Alaska, in the barren prairie of the Arctic Circle, for 1,000 years. From the world beyond, they want only privacy.

But Gilbert, and about 300 Gwich'in Indians holding a tribal meeting in Arctic Village this week, now find themselves caught up in an environmental drama that stretches to the Persian Gulf 6,000 miles away.

Arctic Village lies in the shadow of the ghostly, frozen Arctic National Wildlife Refuge, home to a 1.5-million-acre coastal plain some think could be a mother lode of oil.

"North America's Saudi Arabia," is what some have called the ANWR; others report the smell of oil in the snow.

Congressional interest in exploring the ANWR—opposed by the Gwich'in who fear it would disrupt the caribou they depend on for subsistence and culture—was put on hold after [recent] . . . oil spills.

But [tension in the Middle East] has scrambled the picture. Some Congress members are now eyeing the ANWR, as well as offshore sites in Florida, California and the Northwest.

"We're proud to be in the United States, to be American Indians. But we can see the future," says Gilbert, the chief, spokesman and pastor for the Gwich'in—pronounced *GWI-chin*—of Arctic Village. "If we lose the caribou, we don't know how we're going to live here."

To environmentalists, renewed interest in ANWR—as well as calls to lift [the] . . . ban on drilling in coastal areas in the Lower 48—is both an overreaction and a symptom of a nonexistent national energy policy. . . .

256

OIL VS. ENVIRONMENT

CARIBOU COMMUTE: Critics say oil operations could alter migration routes for 180,000 caribou on the refuge. Herds such as this one—pictured outside refuge land—roam hundreds of miles.

Photos by H. Darr Beiser, USA TODAY

CONCERNED FOR CARIBOU: Peter Tritt, Arctic Village Postmaster, says the Gwich'in Indians, through oil drilling, could 'make a lot of money. But money doesn't last long. Caribou last forever.'

"Before Congress acts," [says former Wisconsin senator Gaylord Nelson], it "ought to hold the administration's seat to the fire on an energy and conservation policy with some teeth in it.". . .

Oil analysts . . . agree that a new policy is needed. But what they want is renewed exploration for domestic oil. . . .

As domestic options go, the ANWR is a potential bonanza.

Set up in 1960 to preserve wildlife like caribou, polar bears and musk oxen—only Congress can open it to exploration—ANWR has a 19% chance of being able to produce as much as 9.6 billion barrels of oil in its lifetime.

The USA uses about 8 million barrels of oil a day, half of it imported. . . .

In order to keep up domestic supply, "we need to have the ANWR option pay off," says [Stephen] Chamberlain, [head of exploration for the American Petroleum Institute.] "We obviously think it's one of the best prospects in the United States for a large, world-class oil field."

There's also great support for opening the A N W R in Alaska, where oil pays for 85% of the state budget and bonus checks of roughly $900 each to all state residents. . . .

In Arctic Village, population 100, the Gwich'in will meet all week to plot strategy on the ANWR.

Politics and oil revenues mean little here. . . .

"We can make a lot of money (from drilling)," says Peter Tritt, Arctic Village's postmaster, a wry man who holds court over cups of coffee at the village store. "But money doesn't last long. Caribou last forever."

Think AND *Respond*

Which side of the ANWR issue did the writer of this article seem to be on? Which phrases or passages lead you to this conclusion? Did the writing, or the images that accompanied the article, affect your opinion?

Copyright 1990, USA TODAY, Reprinted with permission.

257

Guiding Your Writers

Objectives

1. To identify, analyze, and evaluate a media piece
2. To write, review, and share a response to a media piece

Preteaching

Preview the remainder of the assignment. Present any skills or concepts with which students may need help. The mini-lessons listed below may help in your selection and instruction. The cross references in the pupil text will give students access to the same lessons for independent study.

Handbook Mini-Lessons

- Writing Variables, pp. 311–315
- Thesis Statements, pp. 343–344
- Coherence in Compositions, pp. 368–369
- Faulty Reasoning, pp. 453–455

Teaching Strategies

Management Tip

Allow students several days to review and make notes about media pieces. Suggest that students record their thoughts and reactions in their journals or logs. In addition, encourage students to keep print pieces so that they can refer to them later as they make their final choices and begin their analyses. If possible, students might make videotapes or recordings of pieces from television or radio.

Critical Thinking

Analyzing Review the difference between fact and opinion. Remind students that a fact is a statement that can be proved or shown to be true, while an opinion offers a personal view or preference. Ask students for examples of statements of fact and opinion, and write them on the board. Discuss and analyze the statements as a class, noting strategies for distinguishing between the two such as asking the question "Can this be proved?"

INVITATION TO Write

Articles such as the ANWR story appear in newspapers and magazines every day. As a critical reader, you should respond to these articles thoughtfully. Practice this skill by writing a critical response to a media piece.

It is through the media that we receive most of our information about the world. Therefore, the media are often responsible for shaping our views or opinions of current events and issues. However, because reporters, editors, broadcasters, and other writers often manipulate information to match their own opinions about an issue, it is important to evaluate everything you hear and read rather than accept it as true simply because it is reported in the media.

EVALUATING A MEDIA PIECE

1. Choose a media piece. As you read newspapers, magazines and advertisements, listen to the radio, and watch television, pay attention to how you react to the information you receive. Focus your attention on a piece to which you respond strongly.

2. Determine the purpose of the media piece. Is the intent to inform, entertain, persuade, or a combination of these? The main purpose of the newspaper article excerpted here, for example, was to inform. Note, however, that it also served the secondary purpose of trying to persuade readers to support the environmental point of view.

3. Identify the assumptions of the producers of the piece. Ask yourself what ideas, beliefs, and values are being assumed or communicated. For example, is the most important aspect of the ANWR problem truly the preservation of the reserve, or do you think the oil crisis creates a more important issue?

4. Evaluate the claims of the piece. Is the information accompanied by convincing evidence and support, or is the presentation

HANDBOOKS

FOR HELP & PRACTICE

Writing Variables, pp. 311–316

Thesis Statements, pp. 343–344

Coherence in Compositions, pp. 368–369

Faulty Reasoning, pp. 453–455

258   Workshop 8

Springboard

As a warm-up activity, show videotapes of television commercials. Discuss each commercial, focusing particularly on the goals, assumptions, and claims of the advertisers. For example, if the commercial advertises toothpaste, are the advertisers assuming that people want to be beautiful, popular, attractive to the opposite sex, or have healthy teeth?

biased or designed to appeal to the emotions alone? Does any of the information seem inaccurate or incomplete? For example, in the ANWR article, do the photographs and the references to the people of Arctic village help create an emotional response in the reader? Note specific examples from the media piece that support your conclusions.

5. Record your personal reactions. If you found yourself getting angry as you read, listened, or watched, write that down, but also try to figure out what aspect of the piece triggered your response.

DRAFTING YOUR RESPONSE PAPER

1. Review your notes. Evaluate your specific responses to be sure they are supported with examples. Eliminate general, unsubstantiated statements: "I don't agree" is not a sufficient response unless you specify with what and why you don't agree.

2. Write an introductory paragraph. Begin with a summary of the main points of the media piece and your overall reaction to these points. Do you agree or disagree, and what is the basis for your reaction? An overview is all that is necessary here. You will offer support for your views in the body of your paper.

3. Organize your material. Look for overall patterns in the piece and group your responses into categories, such as positive/negative or agree/disagree. There are several ways to organize your response paper: you can follow the structure of the media piece, responding to each point or argument as the author presents it, or you can group your responses into patterns, perhaps first discussing the points with which you agree, followed by those with which you disagree.

4. Draft the body and conclusion of your paper. Develop your ideas fully in the body, giving reasons, facts, and examples to support your views. End with a conclusion that sums up or restates your views, perhaps with a recommendation for further action.

 Writer's Choice You might want to include a copy or a transcription of the media piece to which readers can refer when they read your response.

Writing
—TIP—
Direct quotations from the media piece can provide excellent support for your statements.

 Individualizing Instruction

Learning Styles Auditory learners may benefit most from an analysis of a radio or television piece; visual learners, from magazine advertisements or televised pieces.

Advanced Students Encourage these students to choose a more challenging media piece, such as a documentary or "docudrama" that may contain a subtle slant.

Teaching Tip: Faulty Reasoning

As students analyze their media pieces and begin to draft, you might want to review some of the elements of faulty reasoning, especially with students whose media pieces are persuasive in nature. See Writing Handbook 24, pages 452–458, or the Guided Assignment for Workshop 7, page 208.

Modeling

You may want to model on the board an introduction for a response to a media piece. (You might use one of the commercials discussed earlier. See Springboard, page 258.) Emphasize the importance of including information that will give the reader a general sense of the piece.

Guidelines for Evaluation
A good response to the media . . .
- contains a summary of the piece in an introduction
- makes a clear statement of the writer's general reaction to the piece
- includes facts, reasons, and examples that support the reactions
- contains a conclusion that restates or summarizes reactions or makes a recommendation
- is organized in a logical and coherent manner
- uses standard grammar and usage and correct capitalization, spelling, and punctuation

Assess the need of students who were not successful in developing an effective response to a media piece. Assign the appropriate Handbook Mini-lessons, along with the support material listed for each lesson. Concepts commonly requiring reteaching are

Thesis Statements: Handbook 6
Types of Elaboration: Handbook 8

The following suggestions and resources may also be useful.

1. Weak Organization On the board make a simple outline or chart that reviews each organizational strategy mentioned in the text (page 259: following point-by-point the organization of the media piece itself and arranging and discussing responses in categories), and discuss each method with students who demonstrated weak organization. Help students review their papers to determine a more effective organizational strategy. Suggest that students make an outline before revising their papers.

2. Lack of Supporting Information If students' writing lacked adequate supporting information for their responses, help them identify specific parts of the piece that spurred their reactions by asking leading questions such as, ''At what point did you feel that you were being manipulated?'' or ''When were you certain you agreed?'' As students review their media pieces to find examples and details in response to your questions, have them make notes about specific references that they might add to their papers.

REVIEWING YOUR WRITING

1. Reread your response paper. Make sure that all of your statements are supported by examples from the media piece and that your point of view is developed clearly and logically.

2. Have several peer readers respond to your work. First ask them to read the media piece and respond to it personally. Then ask them to read your response paper. Was their response to the piece similar to yours or different? Did your paper change their minds?

3. Revise and write a final draft. Make any changes that clarify or strengthen your response. Proofread your work, checking for errors in punctuation and capitalization. Be especially careful in the spelling of proper names and places.

PUBLISHING AND PRESENTING

- **Read your written response to the class.** Then lead a class discussion, inviting each individual to give a personal response to the media piece.
- **Submit your response paper in the form of a letter to the editor.** You may especially wish to do this if you responded to a newspaper or magazine article.
- **Present your response in an alternative medium.** For example, if you responded to a radio announcement, present your response in the form of a magazine article. If you read a newspaper article, present your response as a radio commentary.

Sentence
COMPOSING

Adjective Clauses

Effective writers sometimes expand sentences by adding relative clauses that function as adjectives. Using clauses that modify nouns or pronouns allows writers to clarify relationships and avoid needless repetition. In this lesson, you will learn how to use clauses that begin with *who, which,* and *that.*

MODELS

1. My mother is descended from the younger of two English brothers named Lambton, <u>who settled in this country a few generations ago</u>.
   Mark Twain, "Mental Telepathy"

2. His black hair, <u>which had been combed wet earlier in the day</u>, was dry now and blowing.
   J. D. Salinger, "The Laughing Man"

3. He looked at me the way people look at a dog <u>that can't learn even the simplest trick</u>.
   Steve Allen, "The Sidewalk"

A. Combining with *Who* Expand the first sentence by inserting at the caret ∧ information from the second sentence. Begin your insertion with *who.* Commas are indicated where needed.

Example	My mother is descended from the younger of two English brothers named Lambton, ∧ . The Lambtons settled in this country a few generations ago.
Combined Sentence	My mother is descended from the younger of two English brothers named Lambton, <u>who settled in this country a few generations ago</u>. **Mark Twain, "Mental Telepathy"**

1. His gaze returned unsteadily to Montag, ∧ . Montag was now seated with a book in his lap.   **Ray Bradbury, *Fahrenheit 451***

Sentence Composing: Adjective Clauses

Objectives

1. To combine sentences by adding adjective clauses that begin with *who, which,* and *that*
2. To write original sentences that imitate professional models with adjective clauses

Preteaching

These exercises focus on the use of adjective clauses. You may want to review or direct students to Grammar Handbook 39, Clauses and Sentence Structure: Adjective Clauses, pp. 725–726; Grammar Handbook 41, Punctuation: Commas with Non-essential Clauses, p. 781.

ANSWER KEY

A. Combining with *Who*

1. His gaze returned unsteadily to Montag, who was now seated with a book in his lap.

2. She got very excited whenever she passed a desk and could pick up the homework from a student who had remembered to do the assignment.

3. Because my work was in a field that brought me into contact with the people who produced television shows, I was asked one day to appear on one.

4. The carpenter, who had been a soldier in the Civil War, came into the writer's room and sat down to talk of building a platform for the purpose of raising the bed.

5. My aunt was a warm-hearted, misty-eyed woman, who had no children of her own, who fussed over me from the moment I arrived until the moment I left, and who was continually giving me nickels from the cash register and pretending that we mustn't let my uncle know.

B. Combining with *Which*

1. His numerous legs, which were pitifully thin compared to the rest of his bulk, waved helplessly before his eyes.

2. Along with my classmates, I shoveled all day, digging up rubbery red clay, to a depth of four feet, barely clearing a ten-by-twenty-foot sector, which was our class's quota for the day.

3. Smog, which was once the big attraction of Los Angeles, can now be found all over the country, from Butte, Montana, to New York City.

4. Lily was still wearing her wedding sandals, which had begun to blister her.

5. There, in his room on the ground floor, to the right of the front door, Father Kleinsorge changed into a military uniform, which he had acquired when he was teaching at the Rokko Middle School in Kobe, and which he wore during air-raids.

---

2. She got very excited whenever she passed a desk and could pick up the homework from a student ∧ . The student had remembered to do the assignment.   **Toni Cade Bambara, "Geraldine Moore the Poet"**

3. Because my work was in a field that brought me into contact with the people ∧ , I was asked one day to appear on one. The people produced television shows.   **Lynn Caine, *Lifelines***

4. The carpenter, ∧ , came into the writer's room and sat down to talk of building a platform for the purpose of raising the bed. The carpenter had been a soldier in the Civil War.   **Sherwood Anderson, *Winesburg, Ohio***

5. My aunt was a warm-hearted, misty-eyed woman, ∧ , ∧ , and ∧ . This woman had no children of her own. This woman fussed over me from the moment I arrived until the moment I left. This woman was continually giving me nickels from the cash register and pretending that we mustn't let my uncle know. (Hint: Use *who* three times in a row.)   **Richard T. Gill, "The Ten-Dollar Bill"**

B. Combining with *Which* Expand the first sentence by inserting information from the second sentence. Begin the inserted information with *which*, and place the information directly after the word or phrase it modifies. Remember to use commas to set off the new information.

1. His numerous legs waved helplessly before his eyes. His legs were pitifully thin compared to the rest of his bulk.   **Franz Kafka, "The Metamorphosis"**

2. Along with my classmates, I shoveled all day, digging up rubbery red clay, to a depth of four feet, barely clearing a ten-by-twenty-foot sector. The sector was our class's quota for the day.   **John Knowles, *A Separate Peace***

3. Smog can now be found all over the country, from Butte, Montana, to New York City. Smog was once the big attraction of Los Angeles.   **Art Buchwald, "Fresh Air Will Kill You"**

4. Lily was still wearing her wedding sandals. The sandals had begun to blister her.   **Joan Aiken, "Searching for Summer"**

5. There, in his room on the ground floor, to the right of the front door, Father Kleinsorge changed into a military uniform. The uniform he had acquired when he was teaching at the Rokko Middle School in Kobe, and the uniform he wore during air-raids. (Hint: Use *which* twice.)   **John Hersey, *Hiroshima***

C. Combining with _That_ Expand the first sentence by inserting information from the next sentence(s). Begin the inserted information with _that_. When you combine the sentences, no commas are needed because the added information is essential to the meaning of the sentence.

1. My father loved all instruments. The instruments would instruct and fascinate.   **Eudora Welty, _One Writer's Beginnings_**

2. On Sunday mornings Momma served a breakfast. The breakfast was geared to hold us quiet.   **Maya Angelou, _I Know Why the Caged Bird Sings_**

3. At once Fujiko got up and motioned him to wait as she rushed noiselessly for the swords. The swords lay in front of the _takonama_, the little alcove of honor.   **James Clavell, _Shogun_**

4. She was a large woman with a large purse. The purse had everything in it but a hammer and nails.   **Langston Hughes, "Thank You, M'am"**

5. The trick, according to Chiang, was for Jonathan to stop seeing himself as trapped inside a limited body. The limited body had a forty-two-inch wingspan and performance. The performance could be plotted on a chart. (Hint: Use _that_ two times.)   **Richard Bach, _Jonathan Livingston Seagull_**

Application Write sentences that imitate the structure of each of the model sentences below. Imitate as many of the sentence parts as possible, not just the underlined parts. Then write a paragraph that includes one of the sentences you wrote. Notice how the structure of your sentence adds variety to the paragraph.

1. There are many people around nowadays <u>who seem to appreciate the fact that a family can go on an outing without being out</u>.   **Patrick F. McManus, "A Fine and Pleasant Misery"**

2. There is no way <u>that you could talk any language of peace</u> to vicious men <u>who treated defenseless women and children in that manner</u>.   **Winnie Mandela, "Solitary Confinement"**

Grammar Refresher All of the model sentences in this workshop contain adjective clauses, which often begin with _who, which,_ or _that_. To learn more about adjective clauses and how to punctuate them, see Handbook 39, pages 725–729.

C. Combining with _That_
1. My father loved all instruments that would instruct and fascinate.
2. On Sunday mornings Momma served a breakfast that was geared to hold us quiet.
3. At once Fujiko got up and motioned him to wait as she rushed noiselessly for the swords that lay in front of the takonama, the little alcove of honor.
4. She was a large woman with a large purse that had everything in it but a hammer and nails.
5. The trick according to Chiang, was for Jonathan to stop seeing himself as trapped inside a limited body that had a forty-two-inch wingspan and performance that could be plotted on a chart.

Application
Answers will vary.

9

Reports

Overview

Report writing is a common denominator of most areas of academic study—including social studies, English, and science. Students will call on the thinking and writing skills introduced in the preceding Workshops as they learn to gather, assimilate, and present information. The research skills they develop will serve them well in many careers. Workshop 9 includes the following Guided and Related Assignments:

1. **Guided: The Short Research Paper** builds on subject matter that students are already interested in as a foundation for developing skills of information- gathering, documentation, and organization.

2. **Related: The I-Search Paper** further extends the skills treated in the Guided Assignment by asking students to write a research report with a personal focus; it encourages students to explore their own discovery process as part of a research narrative.

Teaching Preview

Preparation Guide

1. Use the Overview on this page and the Teacher's Choice descriptions on page 265 as a basis for deciding which assignment(s) to teach.

2. Preview the assignments and the teacher's notes and identify concerns that may require preteaching or extra support given your class's abilities. The handbook mini-lessons suggested within the lesson may also provide guidance.

3. Preview the chart below for support materials in the Teacher's Resource File that may be used with this Workshop. Resources are for use with the Guided Assignment unless otherwise noted.

Support Materials

WRITER'S CRAFT RESOURCES

Prewrite and Explore
Thinking Skills Transparencies, pp. 3–4, 15–16
Thinking Skills Worksheets, pp. 2, 10

Draft and Discover
Elaboration, Revision, and Proofreading Worksheets, p. 17

Revise Your Writing
Guidelines for Writing Assessment and Portfolio Use, p. 16
Peer Response Guides, pp. 27–28
Student Revision Model Transparencies, pp. 35–42
Elaboration, Revision, and Proofreading Worksheets, p. 18

Extension Activities
Writing Prompts for Fine Art Transparencies, pp. 8, 10, 11, 19
Standardized Test Practice

Educational Technology
(available separately)
Writer's DataBank
Electronic English Handbook
Multimedia Workshop
Your Personal Trainer for the New SAT
In Perspective (videodisc)

OTHER RESOURCES

Books and Journals
Macrorie, Ken. *The I-Search Paper.* Portsmouth: Boynton, 1988.

 Films and Videos
The Academic Edge: Learning to Use Your Library. Journal Films, Inc., 1989. (18 min.)
"The Research Paper." *Write Course Series.* Dallas Comm. Coll. Dist. (30 min.)

Computer Software
MasterWrite. Mindscape. Apple family.
Owens, Peter. *Research Paper Writer.* Tom Snyder Productions. Macintosh, Mac Network, CD-ROM.
Thomas, Owen and Irene Thomas. *The Writing Workshop.* Milliken. Apple family.

Workshop Management Guidelines

The chart below indicates the number of days recommended for each phase of the Guided and Related Assignments. Stars indicate portions of the assignment that may be completed outside the classroom if time is limited or if teachers wish the activity to be completed by students independently.

SHORT RESEARCH PAPER

Starting from Literature .... 1 day
Prewrite .... 1–3 days*
Research .... 1–2 weeks*
Draft .... 1 week*
Revise .... 3–5 days*
Publish .... 1–1.5 weeks
Learning .... open*
Reteaching .... open
Extension/Enrichment .... open*
Sentence Composing .... 1 day*

I-SEARCH PAPER

Writing .... 1–2 weeks*

Linking Literature, Writing, and Grammar

The following options may be used to provide students with an integrated language experience. Begin by assigning and discussing any of the recommended pieces of literature. Use the suggested strategy to provide a link to the Guided Assignment.

LINKING LITERATURE AND WRITING

Option 1

Starting Point: from *The Broken Spears,* by Miguel Leon-Portilla, on pages 266–267 of *The Writer's Craft*.

Strategy: Use the teaching suggestions on pages 266–267 to lead students into the Guided Assignment.

Option 2

Starting Point: poems about the *Odyssey* such as "Penelope" by Dorothy Parker, "An Ancient Gesture" by Edna St. Vincent Millay, and "Siren Song" by Margaret Atwood

Strategy: While reading these poems and comparing them to the way Homer presents the identical events in the lives of Odysseus and Penelope, help students understand that the writers are using and responding to primary source materials as students themselves will be using and responding to research materials as they complete the Guided Assignment.

Option 3

Starting Point: "I Hear America Singing" by Walt Whitman

Strategy: Have students read Whitman's "I Hear America Singing." As a class, brainstorm a number of possible research topics that the poem inspires.

LINKING WRITING AND GRAMMAR

Before the drafting or revision stage of this assignment, review with students the rules for punctuating the titles of research sources. Ask students to find examples in class readings. Meanwhile, write the following examples on the board:

The poem "I Hear America Singing" appears in Walt Whitman's book of poetry called *Leaves of Grass*.

Go over the rules for punctuating titles on page 800 of the Grammar and Usage Handbook. If problems of source punctuation still appear in student papers, assign the exercises on those pages for reteaching. Additional practice can be found in the *Grammar and Usage Practice Book* on pages 199–200.

Sketchbook

Objective

To use a list of statements as a springboard to informal writing

Using the Prompt

These writing activities are informal and should not be graded so that students feel free to explore and to take risks.

As students choose a topic and begin to list what they know, encourage them to write their ideas as they occur, without concern about organization. When students finish, invite volunteers to share their lists and to mention any questions about their topics that came to mind as they wrote.

If they prefer, students can use the ideas in the Additional Sketches section. Suggest that students keep their lists in their writing portfolios for possible use in the workshop that follows.

Sketchbook

What would you like to know more about? What perplexes you? Choose a topic, and then write all the things you do know about it. Write as long a list of statements as you can. Some of them might be very simple, but that's fine, because they will lead you to more things you know. Here's one example:

Apartheid

It is a single word.
It's an unusual looking and sounding word.
It means racial segregation.
From news reports I can tell it's a serious problem in
*   South Africa.*
Here are some of my feelings about apartheid: . . .

Additional Sketches

Keep writing things you know—even when what you know is that you are uncertain about something.

What recent discovery fascinates you? Describe it for a friend.

What famous person do you especially admire? Who is this person? Tell everything you know about him or her.

264

WRITER'S 9 WORKSHOP

Reports

Guided Assignment
THE SHORT RESEARCH PAPER

Related Assignment
THE I-SEARCH PAPER

In art class, your teacher asks you to write a short biography of Vincent van Gogh. Your biology teacher asks for a report on the migration patterns of monarch butterflies. In economics class, your assignment is to report on the major products of a country. What do these assignments have in common? For all of them, you will need to do research, gathering information from outside sources rather than just relying on your own knowledge and experience. In this workshop you will develop your skills in researching and writing reports for your academic classes. You also will learn how to use research skills for papers with a more personal focus.

265

Objectives

Guided Assignment:
THE SHORT RESEARCH PAPER
To research and document information for a short report and to draft, revise, proofread, and share a short report

Related Assignment:
I-SEARCH PAPER
To identify the characteristics of a research report with a personal focus and to write a report with a personal focus

Teacher's Choice

The following information may help you choose the assignments that best fit the needs and interests of your students.

Guided Assignment
The Short Research Paper Most students will benefit from this Guided Assignment, which provides a model report as well as a step-by-step approach to selecting and researching a topic and writing a report about it. Students will use the skills they develop in the assignment in many curricular areas. The assignment is most useful after students have had experience with expository writing (Workshops 4, 5, and 6).

Related Assignment
I-Search Paper This assignment is particularly useful with students who lack the self-discipline to complete a formal report, but who respond well to instruction based on personal experience. It should help clarify the connection between writing and thinking, as well as lead to an appreciation of the discovery-through-research process.

Starting from Literature

Objective

To respond to a professional model of a research report as a springboard to writing

Teaching Strategies

Motivate

Inform students that even before Columbus came to America, the Aztec, Native American Indians of what is now Mexico, had one of the most advanced civilizations in the world. Their capital city, so magnificent that those who saw it could hardly believe their eyes, was built on a piece of land thought to be worthless. What was that city like, and how had the Aztec made so much of so little?

Tap Prior Knowledge

Encourage students to share any information they have about ancient cities they have studied or read about. Explain that in this excerpt Miguel Leon-Portilla describes what he has learned about Tenochtitlan, the capital city of the ancient Aztecs.

Guided ASSIGNMENT

The Short Research Paper

Almost every time you read a nonfiction book or a newspaper or magazine article, you are reading a type of research report. The authors have gathered together information from a variety of sources, analyzed it, and presented their findings.

The following excerpt is taken from a book about the Spanish conquest of the Aztec civilization in Mexico. As you read, notice the wealth of detail the author uncovered during his research. See how he uses that material to make the Aztec capital, which was destroyed nearly 500 years ago, come alive again.

266

The beginnings of the Aztec capital were very humble. It was founded on a low-lying island so undesirable that other tribes had not bothered to occupy it. The [native] chronicles describe the difficulties with which the Aztecs managed to build a few miserable huts and a small altar to their supreme deity, the war-god Huitzilopochtli. But their fierce will overcame every obstacle. Less than two

TENOCHTITLAN, THE AZTEC METROPOLIS

from *The Broken Spears*, by Miguel Leon-Portilla

centuries later, the Spanish conquistador Bernal Diaz del Castillo thought that the wonders he beheld must be a dream. . . .

Tenochtitlan was divided into four great sections. To the northwest stood Cuepopan, "the place where flowers bloom," which now forms the *barrio* or sector known as Santa Maria la Redonda; to the southwest, Moyotlan, "the place of the gnats," later dedicated by the Spanish missionaries to the honor of St. John the Baptist; to the southeast, Teopan, "the place of the gods," which included the precinct of the main temple and which was known in colonial times by the name of San Pablo; and to the northeast, Atzacoalco, "in the house of the herons," which became the site where the missionaries built the church of San Sebastian.

The two most important places in the capital were the sacred precinct of the main temple, with its related temples, schools and other structures (in all, it contained seventy-eight buildings), and the huge plaza in Tlatelolco that served as the principal market place, offering an astonishing variety of products from far and near. The walled precinct of the main temple formed a great square measuring approximately five hundred yards on each side. Today nothing is left of the temple except a few remains . . . .

The population of Tenochtitlan at the time of the Conquest has been the subject of considerable controversy, but beyond question it must have amounted at least to a quarter of a million. The activities were many and colorful. Fiestas, sacrifices and other rituals were celebrated in honor of the gods. Teachers and students met in the various *calmecac* and *telpuchalli,* the pre-Hispanic centers of education. The coming and going of merchant canoes and the constant bustle in the Tlatelolco market impressed the Spaniards so much that they compared the city to an enormous anthill. The military exercises and the arrival and departure of the warriors were other colorful spectacles. In brief, the life of Tenochtitlan was that of a true metropolis. The city was visited by governors and ambassadors from distant regions. Gold, silver, rich feathers, cocoa, bark paper and other types of tribute, along with slaves

and victims for the human sacrifices, streamed in along the streets and canals. The Spaniards were right: Tenochtitlan was indeed an anthill, in which each individual worked unceasingly to honor the gods and augment the grandeur of the city.

Think AND Respond

What types of details about the Aztec capital did Miguel Leon-Portilla present? What types of sources do you think he used? If you had to prepare a report on the ancient Aztecs, how would *you* go about it? Where would you look? What sources would you go to?

Literature Connection

Author Note Born in Mexico City in 1926, Miguel Leon-Portilla studied in Los Angeles before returning home to earn his Ph.D. and to teach ancient Mexican history. Fluent in six languages, Leon-Portilla has written a variety of material in both English and Spanish.

Set a Purpose

Before students read the excerpt, discuss the side-column notes. Be sure students realize that authors cannot rely on their own knowledge to write articles but must collect information from various sources. Point out the purpose-setting statement at the end of the side column and have students read the excerpt.

Think and Respond

Elicit Personal Responses

Refer to the Think and Respond questions and have students share their responses with the class. Encourage students to take notes about sources and procedures for report writing that are suggested during discussion.

Explore the Author's Techniques

Discuss the excerpt with students, focusing on the kinds of information Leon-Portilla includes and the techniques he uses to communicate that information. For example, point out that the author first provides a historical perspective. He then describes the sections of the city as it was then, as well as information about what certain areas later became. (Page 266, paragraph 2: To the northwest . . . the Baptist. Page 267, paragraph 1: The walled . . . side. Today . . . remains.) To this description of the physical elements of the city, Leon-Portilla adds information about the population and the activities taking place. He uses precise words and phrases that help the reader imagine the place. (Page 267, paragraph 2: The coming . . . anthill. Gold . . . canals.) Emphasize that the author has collected much information and has woven the details together to provide a clear report about Tenochtitlan.

Link Literature to Writing

Inform students that much research was probably needed before Leon-Portilla could write about this ancient Aztec city. To accomplish that research and continue with the project long enough to produce a finished piece of writing, he must have been very interested in his topic. Suggest that in the assignment that follows, students select topics that fascinate them enough to sustain them through the project.

Prewrite and Explore

Objectives

1. To use prewriting techniques to choose and limit a topic for a short report
2. To identify a purpose and to write a statement of controlling purpose for a report

Preteaching

Preview the Prewrite and Explore section. If there are skills or concepts your students need help with before prewriting, present them now. The Thinking Skills Transparencies and the mini-lessons listed below may help your selection and instruction. The cross-references in the pupil text give students access to the same lessons for independent study.

> **Handbook Mini-Lessons**
> * Beginning the Writing Activity, pp. 311–316
> * Finding Ideas, pp. 317–325
> * How to Limit a Topic, pp. 327–329

Teaching Strategies

Modeling

Briefly discuss the meanings of *subject* and *topic*. Then model the process of generating ideas by making a list of a few subjects. Focus on your own particular interests or on current events. Then break down each of those subjects into two or three specific writing topics for a short report.

Management Tip

You might confer with ninth-grade teachers of other subjects to find out what students are studying. Discuss ways to coordinate this Guided Assignment with the research projects students are working on in other classes.

INVITATION TO Write

Miguel Leon-Portilla used his research skills to explore a historical topic. Pick a subject that interests you, then research and write a short report that will teach you and your audience more about it.

Writing a report is an opportunity not only to expand your knowledge but also to integrate new information with what you already know. In the process, you may discover new ways of thinking about a subject. As you proceed through what at first may seem like a complex process, remember that when you write a research report, you gather information about your topic from a variety of sources and then present that information clearly and accurately.

PREWRITE AND EXPLORE

HANDBOOKS
FOR HELP & PRACTICE

Beginning the Writing Activity, pp. 311–316
Finding Ideas, pp. 317–325
How to Limit a Topic, pp. 327–329

1. Look for subjects that interest you. What are you curious about? What have you always wanted to know? Even if your teacher has assigned a general subject for your report, let your own personal interests and skills help you find a **topic,** a specific aspect of that subject to explore. For example, imagine that your science teacher has assigned a research report on the atmosphere. If you've always been interested in rainbows, writing about the topic of rainbows would satisfy the requirements of the assignment and hold your attention as well. Other students might be more interested in floods or tornadoes. Try one or more of the following activities to help you generate ideas for the topic of your report.

Exploratory Activities

* **Listing** If your broad subject was *not* assigned, make a list of interesting subjects, such as your hobbies, ideas you are studying in your classes, current events, and special interests you want to know more about.

Social Studies Connection

Students who enjoyed reading about Tenochtitlan may want to write about other ancient cities, such as Athens, Babylon, Memphis, Thebes, Rome, or Jerusalem. Some students may prefer to research and write about a Native American culture or about the Aztec, Incan, or Mayan civilization.

- **Clustering** Write your assigned subject or a broad area of interest in the center of a piece of paper and circle it. Outside the circle, write any related ideas that occur to you. Circle these and draw lines connecting them to the central subject. Branch out from each of the related ideas in the same way.
- **Knowledge inventory** Write down everything you already know about your assigned subject or area of interest. Include information you have learned in school, information from your own experience and reading, and information obtained from other people. At the bottom of the page, write down some questions about the subject to which you would like to find answers.
- **Freewriting** Write for at least ten minutes about a subject you find interesting, and see where your words take you. Then review your writing to see if you've generated any possible report topics.
- **Reading literature** Think about the authors whose work you have been reading, such as James Thurber, Robert Frost, and Alice Walker. What would you like to know about them, about the types of writing they do, or about the subjects they explore in their writing?

2. Choose a topic. If you're not satisfied with any of the topic ideas you've come up with, look over the writing you did for the Sketchbook on page 264 or check the "Apply Your Skills" section on page 286 for other options. Now choose your favorite idea and do some preliminary reading about it to make sure that the topic will hold your interest over time. You can get a general overview of a topic by reading relevant articles in encyclopedias or in specialized dictionaries.

3. Narrow your focus. You may need to narrow your topic to a size that's manageable in a short report. If your topic is too broad, you'll have trouble choosing from among the many sources of information on the topic, and your writing will be unfocused. To see how your topic can be divided into smaller parts, try scanning the tables of contents or the indexes of books on the subject. You may continue to refine your topic as you conduct research and write your report.

One student, Lisa Kaplan, listed her report ideas and evaluated them in the journal entry shown on the next page. Throughout this workshop, you will follow the process Lisa used in researching and writing her report.

Writing
TIP

Your daily newspaper can be a source of ideas for topics.

PROBLEM
SOLVING

How can I choose a topic?

Research Paper **269**

Research Paper **269**

Critical Thinking

Analyzing To help students get a feel for material appropriate for a report, ask them to analyze and to discuss Lisa's selection of a topic. Why were *robots* and *the Vietnam War* too broad? What would writers have to include in reports on such topics? What makes Lisa's third topic too subjective? How could she have revised this topic idea so that it would have been suitable for a research report?

Collaborative Opportunity

Allow students to work with partners to try out their report topics. Ask students to share what they already know about their topics and to discuss what information they hope to find. Partners should tell what they would like to know about the topic. Encourage each student to decide whether his or her topic is appropriate as planned or should be expanded, limited further, or otherwise adjusted.

Stumbling Block

Students may have trouble understanding how identifying their purposes and goals can help them limit their topics or find their own unique angles on the topics. Review these concepts by discussing how purposes and goals have influenced other kinds of writing students have done. Then discuss the purpose chart on this page. Have each student create such a chart for his or her own topic, identifying an appropriate aspect of the topic for each of the purposes given. Students can work in pairs or in groups of three to review their charts and discuss alternative ways of using purposes and goals to refine and limit their topic ideas.

ONE STUDENT'S PROCESS

POSSIBLE TOPICS	COMMENTS
robots	too broad
the Vietnam War	too broad
"How I Learned to Improve My Memory"	too subjective

Maybe I could narrow the topic of robots to a more manageable size. The history of robots? The future of robots? How robots work? I'll have to do some preliminary research to find the right boundaries.

Lisa Kaplan had seen robots in action during a school field trip to an automobile manufacturing plant, and she wanted to learn more about them. She read the entries on robots in *The World Book Encyclopedia* and the *Encyclopaedia Britannica*, and she read a magazine article about them too. As a result, Lisa discovered that she was interested both in the history of robotic technology and in prospects for future uses of robots. Lisa therefore decided to pursue this topic, since she knew she would be able to find the information she needed in a variety of sources.

4. Determine your purpose. Your purpose is your reason for writing. Considering why you want to write about your topic can help you find your own unique angle, or approach to the topic. Also think about your personal goals, or what you want to accomplish in your report. The chart below shows how a writer's purpose might determine what aspect of a topic he or she pursues.

Purpose	Topic
To inform the audience	How robots have changed our world
To compare and contrast	Robots vs. human beings
To examine cause and effect	The impact of robotics on assembly-line manufacturing jobs
To analyze the topic	Robots: masters or slaves?

 Writer's Choice Do you want to sketch out your purpose now or wait until you have done more research? If you are already familiar with your topic, try to determine your purpose and goals early in your writing process.

5. Write a statement of controlling purpose. Once you have narrowed your report topic to a manageable size and decided what you want your writing to accomplish, you're ready to write a statement of controlling purpose. This statement briefly tells what your report will be about. A statement of controlling purpose can help you stay focused on your topic as you look for sources of information and take notes from those sources. After you've completed your research, you will use your statement of controlling purpose as the basis of your thesis statement.

Once Lisa had decided to write about the history and the future promise of robotics, she knew what direction her research would take. Here is her statement of controlling purpose.

> I will examine the history of robotics and see how engineers think robots might be used in the future.

RESEARCH YOUR TOPIC

1. Prepare research questions. First spend some time thinking about what you want to learn. Then make a list of questions your research can answer. Use these questions to focus your search for sources and to guide you in gathering material to use in your writing.

2. Look for the best sources. For a listing of books on your topic, check your library's card or computer catalog. In addition, you may find lists of relevant, timely articles on your topic in a magazine index, such as the *Readers' Guide to Periodical Literature,* or a newspaper index, such as the *New York Times Index.*

3. Use your library's reference materials. If you read an encyclopedia entry as part of your preliminary research, check to see if any related entries are cross-referenced at the end. Those entries might give you important background material or help you to further refine, or narrow, your report topic. Also ask your librarian for names of references that you might find useful in researching your topic. The chart on the next page lists reference materials commonly found in libraries.

 Writer's Choice The library is not the only place where you can learn about your topic. Try interviewing people who know about your subject. Also check to see if any documentaries on your subject are available on videotape.

As this poster shows, robots took center stage in science-fiction films of the 1950's.

HANDBOOKS
FOR HELP & PRACTICE

Taking Notes,
pp. 459–461
Paraphrases and
Summaries,
pp. 464–465
The Library and
Other Information
Sources,
pp. 470–478
Outline Form,
pp. 816–817

Research Paper   **271**

Teaching Tip: Statement of Controlling Purpose

A student who has done enough preliminary research to narrow his or her topic to a manageable scope should be able to write a statement of controlling purpose that defines the central problem his or her research will solve. Students who have trouble with this task may be unclear about what they want to accomplish in their reports. Remind students that a statement of controlling purpose is flexible and may be changed or refined at any time during the research or drafting process.

Spot Check

At this point you may want to confer briefly with students, checking appropriateness of topics and providing assistance with statements of controlling purpose as needed.

Research Your Topic

Objective

To gather, record, document, and organize information for a report.

Preteaching

Preview the Research Your Topic section for skills or concepts with which students may need help before they begin researching. The mini-lessons listed below will help you in your selection and instruction.

> **Handbook Mini-Lessons**
> - Taking Notes, pp. 459–461
> - Paraphrases and Summaries, pp. 464–465
> - The Library and Other Information Sources, pp. 470–478
> - Outline Form, pp. 816–817

 Individualizing Instruction

Auditory Learners Encourage auditory learners to gather information by interviewing others. Help them to identify experts who are accessible and may be willing to be interviewed. Suggest that students study Writing Handbook 27, pages 481–492, to help them prepare.

Management Tip

A library can be intimidating to infrequent users, and many students may be unsure of the location of reference books and other aids. If possible, arrange a tour of your school or local library; a reference librarian can explain how to find source listings in the card or computer catalog and how to use magazine and newspaper indexes.

Critical Thinking

Analyzing   Discuss the kinds of references included in the chart. Ask students to analyze each kind (dictionaries, encyclopedias, and so on) and determine its appropriateness for their topics and purposes.

 ## Individualizing Instruction

Basic Students   Some students may feel overwhelmed by the prospect of finding a variety of sources and gathering information from them—even before they go to the library for the first time. These students may benefit from making a step-by-step plan—and a schedule for their research process. They will feel successful as they accomplish each small goal, cross tasks off their lists, and meet their own deadlines.

Visual and Auditory Learners   These students might look for filmstrips, audiotapes, and videotapes on their topics.

Advanced Students   Encourage these students to broaden the scope of their search for information. Suggest that they conduct at least one interview, or, if their topics are suitable, look for information in primary sources.

COMPUTER TIP

Ask a librarian whether your library subscribes to an information service. If so, you may be able to use it to access databanks containing the most current information on a wide variety of topics.

Library Reference Materials

Reference	Contents	Examples
Dictionaries	Spellings, pronunciations, and meanings of words	*Webster's New World Dictionary*
Encyclopedias	Detailed articles on many subjects	*Encyclopaedia Britannica, The World Book Encyclopedia, Encyclopedia of Computer Science, Dictionary of American History, Harper Encyclopedia of Science*
Almanacs and yearbooks	Up-to-date facts, statistics, and unusual information	*Facts on File, Information Please Almanac*
Atlases	Detailed maps and geographical information	*National Geographic Atlas, Times Atlas of the World*
Biographical references	Detailed information about the lives of well-known people	*Dictionary of American Biography, Webster's New Biographical Dictionary, Dictionary of American Authors*
Vertical file	Pamphlets, booklets, catalogs, handbooks, and clippings filed by subject	
Indexes	Listings of articles that have appeared in periodicals	*Readers' Guide to Periodical Literature, Social Science Index, General Science Index, Art Index*

4. Make source cards. For each source you think you might use, record complete publication information on a three-by-five-inch index card. You will need this information when you credit the source for ideas in your report and when you create a Works Cited list. Be sure to number each source in the upper right-hand corner of the card for reference during note taking. That way, you can jot down the source-card number in your notes, instead of rewriting the title and the author's name, each time you use the source. Also include on each card a library call number and a note about where you found the source, in case you ever need to find it again. These guidelines and models show what to include on source cards.

Guidelines for Source Cards

- **Books** Write the author or editor's complete name, the title, the name and location of the publisher, and the copyright date.
- **Magazines and newspapers** Write the author's complete name, the article's title, the name and date of the magazine or newspaper, and the page number(s) of the article.
- **Encyclopedias** Write the author's complete name (if given), the entry title, and the name and copyright date of the encyclopedia.

Research —TIP—

Notice that the order and the punctuation of the information on these source cards matches the format of the same information in the Works Cited entry models on page 281.

Source Card for Encyclopedia Entry

⑤
Entry title
Liao, Thomas T. "Robot." The World Book

Encyclopedia. 1993 ed.
Encyclopedia title/Copyright date

School Library

Source Card for Magazine or Newspaper Article

②
Article title
Colligan, Douglas. "Robotic Soul."

Omni June 1985: 66+.
Name and date of publication/Page number(s)

Source Card for Book

Source number ③
Author   Book title
Higgins, Mike. A Robot in Every Home.

Oakland: Kensington, 1985.
City of publication/Publisher/Copyright date

Location of source   TJ211
Public Library   H5
          Library call number 1985

Emphasize to students the importance of recording complete, accurate publication information for all usable sources. A student who overlooks this step or does the work carelessly will be unable to provide accurate documentation of his or her sources or to create a Works Cited list—two very important elements in the final draft of a research report. Give students time to practice making source cards in class; ask them to record publication information from several sources you provide, using the examples on this page as models. Provide an answer key so that students can check their own answers once they've completed the assignment.

Linking Grammar and Writing

Have students examine the three model source cards. Ask what generalizations they can make about the treatment of book and article titles. Review the rules for using underlining and quotation marks with titles (see Grammar Handbook 41, page 800), and have students complete the exercises on pages 800–802 if necessary.

Social Studies Connection

Professional Journals Invite interested students to locate a professional history or geography journal. Ask students to look at several articles to determine if the authors have provided bibliograhies. Students might also note how the authors have cited sources within the articles. Have students share what they find with the class.

Teaching Tip: Taking Notes

As they take notes, many students will overuse quotations, preferring to copy directly from their sources instead of writing paraphrases and summaries of the material. As a result, these students will be less likely to develop a real understanding of their topics, and their lack of understanding will be apparent in their final reports. Tell students that the best way for them to check their understanding of the material they read is to write paraphrases or summaries in their own words. Encourage them to reserve quotations for only those occasions when the author's point is particularly persuasive or well said. Also remind students that even when they rewrite material in their own words, they still need to document the source of their ideas; note cards should include source references and page numbers.

Modeling

Using an overhead projector, model the process of writing a paraphrase and a summary of a passage from a book or magazine article on the topic of your choice. First share the original text with students, then take them through the process of rewriting each sentence of supporting detail in your own words. When you're ready to write the summary, ask students to identify the passage's main idea for you before you begin to write. As an alternative, keep your paraphrase on the projector and have students work independently to write their own summaries of the passage. Ask several students to read their summaries aloud before you use the overhead projector to display your own summary.

 Individualizing Instruction

LEP Students Because LEP students may not have an extensive English vocabulary, you might suggest that they work with English-proficient partners who can help them restate information from their sources.

---

5. Take notes from your sources. As you review your sources, look for information that suits your purpose and that answers your research questions. When you find material you may want to include in your report, take notes, using one or more of the following techniques.

- **Quotation** Copy from the original text word for word, including all punctuation. Put quotation marks at the beginning and the end of the quotation. Use this note-taking method when you think the author's own words would best support a point you want to make in your report.
- **Paraphrase** Rewrite material from the source in your own words. You might simplify the language, use synonyms, and restructure the sentences. A paraphrase captures both the main idea of a passage and the supporting details, so use this method when your notes need to be very detailed.
- **Summary** In your own words, record only the main idea of a passage. Write a summary when you need to remember the author's general idea.

To take notes efficiently, follow these guidelines.

> ### Guidelines for Note Taking
>
> - Use a separate four-by-six-inch index card for each piece of information. At the top of each card, write a brief heading that summarizes the main idea of the note. This heading will help you sort your cards into groups when you're ready to organize your material and write an outline.
> - In the upper right-hand corner of each note card, write the number of the corresponding source card.
> - At the bottom of each note card, indicate whether the material is a quotation, a paraphrase, a summary, or an idea of your own. This will help you to remember whether the idea needs to be credited to a source.
> - At the end of each note, write the number of the page on which you found the material in your source. You'll need the page number to give credit to the source if you use the information in your report; you may also need it to verify a fact or a quotation or to gather more information from the source.

274   Workshop 9

Off the Record

"When you steal from one author, it's plagiarism; if you steal from many, it's research."
Wilson Mizner (1876–1933), American writer

Here is a note card Lisa wrote as she read one of her sources.

Source number ④

Computers and Robotics   Main idea

Developments in computer technology have meant that robots can perform a wide range of movements and do complex kinds of work. To program a single-armed robot, you move it through the motions a human arm would make. The movements are then recorded in the computer's memory. Robots on assembly lines have changed the way cars are made. 116   Page number

(Paraphrase)   Type of note

6. Write a thesis statement. A thesis statement can help you focus your draft and can keep you on the right track as you write. After you've completed your research, try to identify the main idea that you want to develop in your report. Then write a sentence or two—a **thesis statement**—clearly stating that main idea. A thesis statement may also indicate the organizational pattern you will follow and reflect your tone and point of view. Look again at your statement of controlling purpose; you may be able to use it as a basis for your thesis statement.

Remember Lisa's statement of controlling purpose.

> I will examine the history of robotics and see how engineers think robots might be used in the future.

This statement helped Lisa focus her research and find information that supported her purpose. However, Lisa found some material about how robots are used today that she wanted to include in her report. She wrote the following thesis statement and incorporated it in her introduction.

> The past and present uses of robotic technology give us clues to what robots will be able to do in the future.

7. Begin organizing your information. Read over your note cards and sort them into groups. The information on the cards in each group should be related in some way; the main-idea headings on the cards may help you find connections among the notes. Set aside any cards containing information that does not fit in with the other material you have gathered. You may not need them when you draft your report.

Research TIP

Stick to your topic as you take notes. If your source is a book, the index and the table of contents can help you find useful sections. Headings in bold type signal key passages in articles. See Handbook 25, pages 459–469, for more information on taking notes and incorporating source material in your writing.

Writing TIP

A thesis statement tells the main idea of a piece of writing in the same way that a topic sentence tells the main idea of a paragraph.

Learning Styles   Although some students will have difficulty putting the information they have gathered into standard outline form, **visual learners** as well as other students may find it easier to use charts, diagrams, or other graphic devices. (Direct students to Writing Handbook 9, pages 357–360, for explanations and examples of such devices.)

Teaching Tip: Outlines

Use Lisa's topic outline to review standard outline form. Tell students whether you will be evaluating their outlines, and indicate whether you prefer them to write topic outlines or sentence outlines. Direct them to the Appendix, pages 816–817, for a model of each outline type.

Managing the Paper Load

Confer briefly with each student during outlining to determine if students have sufficient information and a workable plan of organization. Alert students to any problems you notice. You might also identify students who have mastered the required organizational skills. Have those students work collaboratively with students who are having trouble organizing their material.

8. Make a working outline.   If you make an outline, or plan, of the order in which you will present your information, drafting your report will be easier. In addition, making an outline helps to ensure that you won't leave out any of the material you want to include. To begin, arrange your groups of related note cards so that the ideas flow logically from one group to the next. Then use the main ideas and supporting details in your note cards for the headings and subheadings of your outline. Guidelines for standard outline form, as well as models of both sentence and topic outlines, can be found in the Appendix, pages 816–817.

9. Stay flexible.   Remember that your working outline is only a plan for you to follow as you write. In doing other kinds of writing, you have learned that you may start off in one direction and then decide you'd rather go in another. This may also be your experience in writing a research report, so feel free to change your mind—and your plan—as you draft your report.

Lisa's working topic outline is shown below. Notice that she organized much of her information in chronological order.

Writing —TIP—

Before you make a standard outline, try using a graphic organizer—such as a cluster, a time line, or a tree diagram—to help you see how your information and your ideas are related.

ONE STUDENT'S PROCESS

Robots: They've Come a Long Way,
but Where Are They Headed?

Introduction—playwright Karel Čapek's futuristic vision of robotics versus reality: the past, present, and future of robots
 I. What a robot is
 II. Comparison of 1950's robots with robots of the 1990's
   A. Development of George Devol's first model robot
   B. Industrial uses for these "first-generation" robots
 III. "Second-generation" robots with sensory abilities
 IV. "Third-generation" robots—looking to the future
   A. Personal robots
   B. Robots in medicine, industry, outer space

276   Workshop 9

DRAFT AND DISCOVER

1. Begin writing. Gather together your note cards and your outline and begin writing wherever you feel comfortable. Some writers like to begin with the introduction; others prefer to start somewhere in the middle. Just make sure that you write one or more paragraphs for each of the headings in your outline and that you put the paragraphs in order before you review your writing and revise your draft. Remember that your outline is like the picture on the cover of a jigsaw puzzle—it serves as a reference so that you'll always know how your pieces should fit together in the end.

2. Find the best way to present your information. Depending on your topic, you may find one or more of these strategies useful.

Strategies

- **Description and definition** Present the basic characteristics of your subject by means of details and examples. This is the strategy Leon-Portilla used in his description of Tenochtitlan.
- **Classification** Analyze your subject in terms of a category to which it belongs, or compare and contrast your subject with others.
- **Cause and effect** Examine changes over time by showing what happens when one event leads to another.

Writer's Choice You may find that your note cards don't contain all the information you need. In that case, stop drafting and do more research or go on to another section of your outline and do more research later.

3. Share your own ideas and interpretations. Writing a report involves more than just stringing together the information you found in your sources; it involves analyzing the ideas of others and then sharing your conclusions. You should, however, use the facts, examples, and other evidence you've gathered to back up your own ideas and to show why you believe the ideas are valid.

HANDBOOKS
FOR HELP & PRACTICE

Beginning a Draft,
pp. 340–344
Drafting Paragraphs,
pp. 345–350
Elaboration,
pp. 351–356
Unity, Coherence, and
Transitional Devices,
pp. 361–370

Writing
TIP

Spatial order, order of importance, and chronological order are other organizing strategies. Pages 330–335 have more information on these and other strategies.

Research Paper **277**

Objectives

1. To draft a short report using parenthetical notes for documentation
2. To respond to one's own writing and to the writing of one's peers

Preteaching

Preview the Draft and Discover section. Present any skills or concepts students may need help with before drafting. The Elaboration Worksheet from the Revision, Proofreading, and Elaboration booklet, as well as the mini-lessons listed below, may help you in your selection and instruction.

> **Handbook Mini-Lessons**
> - Beginning a Draft, pp. 340–344
> - Drafting Paragraphs, pp. 345–350
> - Elaboration, pp. 351–356
> - Unity, Coherence, and Transitional Devices, pp. 361–370

Teaching Strategies

Linking Grammar and Writing

Briefly review sentence fragments. Ask volunteers to offer fragments from their note cards, then have them show on the board how they might change the fragments into sentences. Students might also refer to page 524–525 in Grammar Handbook 30 for a review of sentence fragments.

Modeling

When students write research reports for the first time, they often string together the material they've recorded in their notes instead of presenting their own analysis and using the material they've gathered as evidence to support it. Emphasize the importance of using the drafting process to explain to others what one has learned. If you've been working on a report along with your students, share one or two paragraphs from the body of your draft, showing them how you've explained a concept in your own words and how you've included documented material from sources to elaborate your explanation.

Teaching Tip: Introductions

Emphasize the importance of creating an introduction that immediately engages the reader. You might briefly review the following strategies, which are discussed on pages 341–342 of Writing Handbook 6: startling or interesting facts; vivid, detailed description; questions; incidents or anecdotes; and quotations.

Teaching Tip: Plagiarism

Review the definition of *plagiarism* with students and make sure they understand what the penalty will be if they plagiarize in their reports. Remind them that it is not enough simply to put another person's ideas in different words; there must always be a parenthetical note indicating the source and the page number, and complete publication information for the source must appear in the Works Cited list.

Critical Thinking

Judging   Encourage students to review their drafts for possible plagiarism. They should check that each direct quotation has been written and punctuated exactly as it was in the original source. In addition, each quotation, paraphrase, and summary must be documented properly. Remind students to refer to the Guidelines for Parenthetical Documentation on this page as they credit their sources.

Writing TIP

You may credit your sources with footnotes or endnotes instead of parenthetical documentation. Check with your teacher to see which method you should use.

---

4. Avoid plagiarism.   You must tell your readers where you got the facts and examples you're including in your report. If you do not credit, or document, your sources, you will commit **plagiarism—** the dishonest presentation of someone else's ideas as your own. You must credit the sources of all direct quotations, paraphrases, and summaries, but you do not need to credit a source for common information that many people have. In addition, you do not need to document your own thoughts and ideas.

5. Document your sources.   Parenthetical documentation is the most common way of crediting sources in the body of a paper. When you use this form of documentation, you include in parentheses after each quotation, paraphrase, or summary enough information about the source to enable a reader to find the full source entry on the Works Cited page. Usually, a parenthetical reference consists of a title or author's name followed by a page number. Remember to underline book titles and use quotation marks around magazine or encyclopedia article titles. Follow these guidelines for parenthetical documentation; see Lisa's final draft on pages 283–285 for examples.

Guidelines for Parenthetical Documentation

- **Work by one author**   Put the author's last name and the page reference in parentheses: (Connolly 41). If you mention the author's name in the sentence, put only the page reference in parentheses: (41).

- **Work by more than one author**   Put the authors' last names and the page reference in parentheses: (Wilk and McColley 253). If a source has more than three authors, give the first author's last name followed by *et al.* and the page reference: (Kelsey et al. 150).

- **Work with no author given**   Give the title (or a shortened version of it) and the page reference: ("Robots and You" 31).

- **One of two or more works by the same author**   Give the author's last name, the title or a shortened version, and the page reference: (Awrey, "Robot Control" 26).

- **Two or more works cited at the same place**   Use a semicolon to separate the entries: (Dietz 88; Golanski 143).

Springboard

   From your own reading material, select and bring in a few articles with particularly engaging introductions. Share the articles with students, and explain why each introduction "hooked" you. Encourage students to comment on the introductions as well.

6. Examine your draft. Set your completed draft aside overnight, or, if possible, for a few days to get a fresh perspective on it. Then reread your draft and let a peer read and respond to it. The following questions can guide your review.

R E V I E W   Y O U R   W R I T I N G

Questions for Yourself
- Have I met the requirements of this assignment?
- Have I written a thesis statement and developed it in the body of my report?
- Are my facts and quotations accurate? Have I documented my sources correctly?
- Are my ideas developed clearly and logically? How might my material be organized more effectively?
- Have I included all the material I want to present? Have I achieved my purpose and goals? What changes, additions, or deletions should I make?

Questions for Your Peer Readers
- What did you like most about my report?
- Which parts—if any—did you have trouble following?
- What do you need more information about?
- What parts could I leave out?
- Did the introduction capture your interest?
- Did the conclusion successfully sum up the report?

 Writer's Choice Consider the beginning and the ending of your report. Can you begin with a fascinating fact or a short narrative? In your conclusion, can you summarize your research or restate your thesis in different words?

R EVISE   YOUR   WRITING

1. Evaluate your responses. Consider the responses you have received and decide what changes you want to make. Keep in mind the following characteristics of good research reports.

HANDBOOKS
FOR HELP & PRACTICE

Types of Revision,
pp. 375–376

Proofreading,
pp. 376–377

**Self-Assessment
and Peer Response,**
pp. 378–382

Achieving Clarity,
pp. 383–390

Punctuating Titles,
pp. 800–801

Auditory Learners These students may benefit form hearing their reports read aloud by peers.

Revise Your Writing

Objectives

1. To evaluate responses to a draft of a short report
2. To use the responses and a set of standards to revise the draft
3. To prepare a Works Cited List
4. To proofread for errors in spelling, grammar, usage, and mechanics, and to follow MLA guidelines for manuscript preparation

Preteaching

Preview the Revise Your Writing section. On the basis of that preview and any problems you have spotted in student drafts, identify the skills and strategies you want to review. The Student Revision Model Transparencies and the Revision and Proofreading Worksheets from the Revision, Proofreading, and Elaboration booklet, as well as the following list of mini-lessons, may be helpful.

Handbook Mini-Lessons
- Types of Revision, pp. 375– 376
- Proofreading, pp. 376– 377
- Self-Assessment and Peer Response, pp. 378–382
- Achieving Clarity, pp. 383–390
- Punctuating Titles, pp. 800–801

Teaching Strategies

Teaching Tip: Standards for Evaluation

Discuss with students the Standard for Evaluation list. Ask which of these standards they feel are most important and which elements they struggle with most. Some students may wish to focus on a few specific standards as they revise their work; they should submit lists of those standards when they turn in their final drafts for assessment.

Critical Thinking

Analyzing   Discuss the changes Lisa make in this paragraph from her first draft. Point out that Lisa turned a quotation into a paraphrase, added documentation in two places, and deleted an unnecessary sentence. Tell students that these are precisely the kinds of revisions they should be making in the second and third drafts of their reports. (Some students will need to make more substantive content and organizational changes in their second drafts.) You may also wish to use the Student Model Transparency for this assignment to help students see other kinds of revisions they may want to make in their drafts.

Writing TIP

Read your draft aloud to yourself in private to hear whether it flows smoothly.

Standards for Evaluation

An effective research report . . .

- begins with an interesting introduction, including a thesis statement that reveals the topic and purpose of the report.
- develops the topic completely with appropriate details.
- contains accurate, relevant facts.
- documents sources correctly.
- presents ideas in a logical sequence.
- uses transitions to show the relationships among ideas.
- uses exact quotations from sources effectively but sparingly to support ideas.
- has a satisfying conclusion that summarizes the research or restates the thesis in different words.
- includes a correctly formatted Works Cited list.

2. Problem-solve.   Rework your draft, incorporating the revisions you have decided to make. Notice the changes Lisa made in response to comments from a classmate.

ONE STUDENT'S PROCESS

I think you could make the definition clearer in your own words.

Is the second sentence really necessary?

This is an interesting way to look at robots. What source are you quoting from?

Draft:

A robot is "a mechanical device or apparatus that is ~~made operational by the application of programmic instructions.~~" ~~The term is also used for people who work mechanically or without original thought.~~ The instructions for ~~robots~~ are stored in a computer. By changing the program, a person can alter the robot's behavior. Thus, according to one expert, a robot is "a computer to which limbs, organs, tools, and other equipment have been attached." (Barrett 37).

that operates by following a program, or set of instructions, that specifies its tasks (Liao 369).

se

280   Workshop 9

Off the Record

CALVIN AND HOBBES / By Bill Watterson

3. Prepare a Works Cited list. First gather all the source cards for sources you actually used and documented in your report. Then alphabetize them by author's last name or, where no author is given, by first word of the title. Then use the publication information on the cards to create a Works Cited list to attach to the end of your report.

The following samples show what information to include and what spacing and punctuation to use. You can also use Lisa's Works Cited list on page 285 as a model.

Models for Works Cited Entries

Book: One author	Ackerman, Diane. A Natural History of the Senses. New York: Random, 1990.
Book: Two or more authors	Commager, Henry Steele, and Raymond H. Muessig. The Study and Teaching of History. Columbus: Merrill, 1980.
Book: Editor but no single author	Carpenter, Humphrey, ed. The Letters of J.R.R. Tolkien. Boston: Houghton, 1981.
Magazine article	Batten, Mary. "Life Spans." Science Digest Feb. 1984: 46–51.
Newspaper article	James, Noah. "The Comedian Everyone Loves to Hate." New York Times 22 Jan. 1984, sec. 2: 23.
Unsigned encyclopedia entry	"Robot." Encyclopaedia Britannica: Micropaedia. 1993 ed.
Signed encyclopedia entry	Berkowitz, Gerald M. "Čapek, Karel." The World Book Encyclopedia. 1993 ed.
Personal interview	Barber, Theodore. Personal interview. 29 Nov. 1993.

Review the forms of Works Cited entries that students are most likely to use. Point out that most entries can be broken down into three distinct parts, each of which ends with a period: author's name, title, and publication information. Remind students that they don't need to memorize the forms given on this page; rather, they should use them—and Lisa's Works Cited entries on page 285—as models when they are ready to alphabetize their source cards and create their own Works Cited lists. Be sure to have a copy of the *MLA Handbook for Writers of Research Papers* available as a reference in your classroom. Students using resources for which entries are not modeled here (e.g., film, audiotape, or videotape) will need to look up the correct documentation formats in the *MLA Handbook.*

Guidelines for Evaluation

The following guidelines may be used for a close evaluation of a research report. See the Guidelines for Evaluating Writing in the Teacher's Resource File for additional help with holistic or analytic scoring.

Ideas and Content
- includes an introduction with a thesis statement that clearly conveys the topic and purpose of the report
- contains appropriate details that develop the topic
- includes pertinent, accurate facts gathered from appropriate sources
- uses quotations appropriately
- demonstrates effective paraphrasing and summarizing techniques

Structure and Form
- contains an introduction, body, and conclusion
- demonstrates a logical ordering of ideas
- includes appropriate transitions
- contains proper documentation, including parenthetical notes and a Works Cited list

Grammar, Usage, and Mechanics
- uses standard grammar
- uses correct punctuation
- uses correct spelling

Managing the Paper Load

Because students will be asked to write reports throughout high school, you will probably want to read their final reports closely. Consider assigning two grades, one for content, focusing on the development of the topic, and another for structure and form, paying special attention to organization and the proper use and documentation of sources. Make sure students are aware of your criteria as they revise.

Teaching Tip: Publishing and Presenting

Students can work in teams to create visual aids to enhance their oral reports. Students who do not wish to make oral presentations might display their reports in the classroom for others to read.

Writing
—TIP—

Make sure all quotations are exact and enclosed in quotation marks.

4. Proofread your report. Correct any errors you might have made in grammar, spelling, and mechanics. Then make a clean final copy of your report, following the Modern Language Association's guidelines for manuscript preparation, listed below.

MLA Manuscript Guidelines

- **Typing or printing** Type your final draft on a typewriter, or if you are using a word processor, print out a letter-quality copy. Do not justify the lines. If you have to write your final copy by hand, use dark blue or black ink and make sure your handwriting is neat and legible. Use only one side of the paper.

- **Paper** Use 8½-by-11-inch, white, nonerasable paper.

- **Margins** Except for page numbers, leave one-inch margins on all sides of the paper. Indent the first line of each paragraph five spaces from the left margin. Indent set-off quotations (those of more than four lines) ten spaces from the left margin. Do not indent long quotations from the right.

- **Spacing** The entire paper—including the heading and title on the first page, the body of the paper, quotations, and the Works Cited list—should be double-spaced.

- **Heading and title** One inch from the top of the first page and flush with the left margin, type your name, your teacher's name, the course name, and the date on separate lines. Below this heading, center the title on the page. Do not underline the title or put it in quotation marks, and do not use all capital letters.

- **Page numbers** Number all pages consecutively in the upper right-hand corner, one-half inch from the top. You may type your last name before the page number to identify your work in case a page is misplaced.

5. Share your report with others, then save it in your portfolio. Get together with a small group of classmates who share similar interests, and read your report aloud. Alternatively, give an oral presentation of your report to your entire class, adding graphs, drawings, models, or photographs.

Lisa Kaplan
Mr. Swidler
English I
15 May 1994

Robots: They've Come a Long Way
but Where Are They Headed?

"A new world has risen," announces a robot leader, "the rule of the robot." The year is 1920, and in his play R.U.R., the Czech writer Karel Čapek is taking an eerie look into the future. In this new world, people have created humanlike machines that are more precise and reliable than people are. Society becomes dependent on mechanical workers, and this new race goes on to dominate human beings and threaten them with extinction.

Čapek couldn't have been more right—or more wrong. A new world <u>has</u> risen since 1920, and society <u>is</u> now dependent on mechanical workers. Today's robots, however, can't think and feel the way those in Čapek's futuristic play do. Not yet, anyway. What predictions can we make about the future? The past and present uses of robotic technology give us clues to what robots will be able to do.

A robot is a mechanical device that operates by following a program, or set of instructions, that specifies its task (Liao 369). These instructions are stored in a computer. By changing the program, a person can alter the robot's behavior. Thus, according to one expert, a robot is "a computer to which limbs, organs, tools, and other equipment have been attached" (Barrett 37).

Rapid advances in electronics during and after World War II and the development of the computer microchip in the late 1950's provided the technology necessary for the inventor George J. Devol, Jr., to create the first practical robot. It was a computerized arm that

Begins with an engaging introduction to capture readers' interest

Includes a thesis statement

Uses exact quotations effectively

Research Paper **283**

Using the Model

Discuss Lisa Kaplan's final draft with students. Ask them to comment on Lisa's introduction, explaining why it is effective. Call attention to the documentation in the report and emphasize the importance of crediting certain pieces of information. After the discussion you might have students exchange their reports with partners and annotate the papers in the same way the model is annotated.

Reteaching

Assess the needs of students who were not successful in developing an effective research report and identify two or three areas in which additional practice is needed. Assign the appropriate handbook mini-lessons, along with the support materials listed for each lesson. Concepts commonly requiring reteaching for this assignment are

Thesis Statements: Handbook 6
Paragraphs and Summaries: Avoiding Plagiarism: Handbook 25
Types of Conclusions: Handbook 11

The following suggestions and resources may also be useful.

1. Paraphrasing and Summarizing Review the definitions of these terms and make sure students understand the differences between them. Select a short passage from a textbook, an encyclopedia, or a magazine and share a copy with students. On the board model how to write a paraphrase and a summary of the passage.

2. Structure Have students find several feature articles in periodicals. Work with students to identify the introduction and the paragraphs that form the body and the conclusion of each article. Students might label the parts of the articles and keep them for future reference. Students can label the sections of their own drafts and work on reorganizing their body paragraphs so that ideas flow from one to the next.

Extension and Enrichment

• Students might interview several friends, relatives, and acquaintances to discover whom each considers his or her hero. Students can then write short reports identifying and profiling these heroes.

• Some students might enjoy researching and writing short reports about the origin and development of their favorite sports. Recommend that they research when and where the sports originated, who invented the sports, how popular the sports are with spectators and players, and how the sports have changed over the years.

Links ideas with transitions

Presents ideas in a logical sequence

Documents sources correctly

Conclusion sums up report and makes reference to introduction

could perform routine tasks precisely (Asimov 865).

Like Devol's early models, the robot of today is usually a stationary structure with a single arm. The arm can lift objects and use simple tools (Asimov 35), making it ideal for repetitive tasks on factory assembly lines. Most industrial robots are found in the automobile industry, welding, spray painting, cutting, drilling, and polishing (Asimov and Frenkel 46–68).

Already, however, engineers have progressed beyond these "first-generation" robots, which simply perform repetitive tasks (Barrett 39). "Second-generation" robots, although still stationary, have basic sensing abilities. Some can "see" with a television camera or "feel" with sensors attached to their "hands" (Marsh 20–21). They can even interact with their surroundings. One of these intelligent robots harvests oranges in Florida, choosing only the ripe ones to pick (Barrett 38–39).

Engineers are now developing "third-generation" robots, such as the "personal robot," which can be programmed to serve food, clean house, or act as a watchdog (Asimov and Frenkel 95–107). They are working on robots that can diagnose illness, mine for precious metals, and even rescue fire victims (Barrett 39; Colligan 67–69). In addition, the factories of the future may be filled with computer-controlled robots. Some of these factories may be in outer space or on the moon, and some may contain robots producing other robots (Marsh 24–25, 30–31).

As the future of robotics unfolds, we need to keep Karel Čapek's vision from becoming reality. As one writer put it, "No one knows how the real-life super-robot story will end. But it seems likely that, one day in the distant future, we will find out" (Higgins 894).

Works Cited

Asimov, Isaac. *Asimov's New Guide to Science.* New York: Basic, 1984.

Asimov, Isaac, and Karen A. Frenkel. *Robots.* New York: Harmony, 1985.

Barrett, F. D. "The Robot Revolution." *Futurist* Oct. 1985: 37–40.

Colligan, Douglas. "Robotic Soul." *Omni* June 1985: 66+.

Higgins, Mike. *A Robot in Every Home.* Oakland: Kensington, 1985.

Liao, Thomas T. "Robot." *The World Book Encyclopedia.* 1993 ed.

Marsh, Peter. *Robots.* New York: Warwick, 1983.

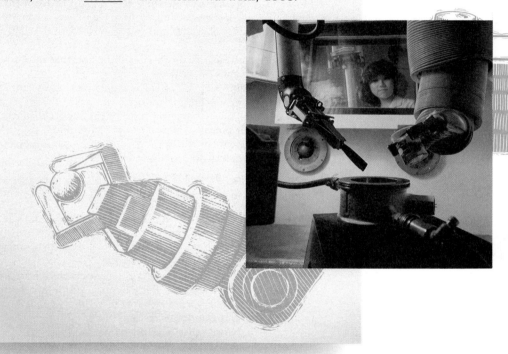

Literature Connection

Essay to Read Students may enjoy reading "Pompeii" by Robert Silverberg. Invite students to discuss the details Silverberg includes and to speculate on his sources of information.

Learning from Your Writing Process

Objective

To analyze and reflect upon what has been learned about the writing process and the writing of a short report

Teaching Strategies

Reflecting on the Process

Each student need not answer every question in the *Reflect on your writing* section. You may prefer to have each student preview the questions and choose one or two that suggest insights he or she would like to share. Discuss answers with the entire class.

Writing Portfolio

Students should attach their responses to their final reports and save their work in their writing portfolios. Answers can be written in the form of resolutions that, if followed, will help improve their future writing. However, remind students that they should also think about and record any strategies or ideas that worked well and they they want to remember to use again.

Summary and Closure

Before proceeding to the next lesson, make sure that students understand and can apply the following key concepts:
1. Short reports are often required in different curriculum areas.
2. Short reports are also found in various periodicals and reference books.
3. Information gained from others should be quoted exactly, paraphrased, or summarized—and then correctly documented—in a short report.

Provide time for students to summarize what they have learned by describing the characteristics of short reports and by explaining why knowing how to write a research report might help them in other school subjects.

LEARNING FROM YOUR WRITING PROCESS

WRITER TO WRITER

I have rewritten—often several times—every word I have ever published. My pencils outlast their erasers.

Vladimir Nabokov, novelist, critic, translator

FOR YOUR **PORTFOLIO**

1. Reflect on your writing.   Now that you've written a research report and read two others, think about your writing process. Ask yourself questions such as the following and record your thoughts in your journal or in an afterword you can attach to your report.

* How did my process for writing a report differ from the process I used in other types of writing?
* How did careful planning and outlining before drafting affect the final product?
* What specific research techniques did I use that might help me in other types of writing?
* What techniques that I learned in other writing assignments were helpful in writing my report?
* How did the voice, tone, and style of my report differ from those of other pieces of writing in my portfolio?
* Which aspects of the writing process are becoming easier for me? Which aspects do I still need to work on?

2. Apply your skills.   Use your research skills as you try one or more of these writing activities.

* **Science**   Pick a scientific question such as "How did the universe begin?" or "What happened to the dinosaurs?" or "What is gravity?" Research and write about how scientists' answers to the question have changed over time.
* **Literature**   Research and write a brief biography of an author you admire or have studied. For example, you might write about William Shakespeare or Homer, telling what is known about his life and examining various theories about who actually wrote the works that bear his name.

Off the Record

"At first I thought Professor Finton's seating chart was wrong, but it wasn't."

INVITATION TO Write

Write an I-Search paper, a research report with a personal focus.

Related ASSIGNMENT

Just recently, I experienced the pain and trauma of almost losing a loved pet. Mandy was only a four-and-one-half-month-old puppy when, on a Friday night in October, she was suddenly struck with a severe illness.

With a heavy heart and a guilty feeling, I took Mandy to the vet on Monday . . . . I had assumed that Mandy wouldn't get parvo since all our neighbors' dogs had been vaccinated against the illness. Where else could she get it? Little did I know that Mandy could contract the disease just from walking on the grass outside our door. This was the beginning of my education on parvovirus.

Caren Rice, student, Saddleback Community College

This excerpt is from the introduction to an I-Search paper, a research report with a personal focus. You can write an I-Search paper with only a few modifications to the strategies and techniques presented in the guided assignment.

WRITING AN I-SEARCH PAPER

1. Choose a topic. The topic of an I-Search paper should be something you *need* to find out for some reason of your own, no matter how unimportant it may seem to others.

Woman With Dog, by
Pierre Bonnard, 1922
© The Phillips Collection,
Washington, D.C.

I-Search   **287**

Guiding Your Writers

Objectives

1. To identify a topic and a purpose for an I-Search paper
2. To gather information about the topic
3. To write an I-Search paper that includes information about the topic, the process itself, and the significance of the experience

Preteaching

Preview the assignment for skills and concepts with which your students may need help. The mini-lessons listed below may help you in your selection and instruction. You may also want to refer students to these mini-lessons for their own independent study.

Handbook Mini-Lessons
- Personal Techniques,
  pp. 317–320
- Writing the Introduction,
  pp. 341–342
- Coherence in Compositions,
  pp. 368–369

Teaching Strategies

Modeling

Discuss the excerpt and the introductory paragraph, making sure students understand the definition of an I-Search paper. Ask students why Caren Rice investigated parvovirus.

As students research their topics, encourage them to use index cards to record information and sources. Review how to paraphrase information, and emphasize the importance of restating in one's own words information from another source. You might also suggest that students note on the backs of the cards their thoughts about the information and about how they found it.

Teaching Tip: Organization

Review the basic parts of a report. Emphasize that the introduction should make a clear statement of the topic and that the body should contain an explanation of the information students found. Point out that because the report should also include a description of the process, students will probably want to arrange their details in chronological order. Finally, remind students to write a conclusion that both summarizes what they have learned and describes the significance of the research experience.

Peer Response

Encourage students to exchange their drafts with partners. You might brainstorm with students a list of pertinent questions for their readers, such as the following: Do you understand why this topic is important to me? Is there any information in my draft that seems incomplete or that you are still wondering about? Can you explain how I went about gathering information?

Managing the Paper Load

You will probably want to focus your evaluation of the I-Search reports on two or three important elements. You might rate the papers in terms of the following key points: significance of the subject to the writer, variety of relevant information, and awareness of the discovery process.

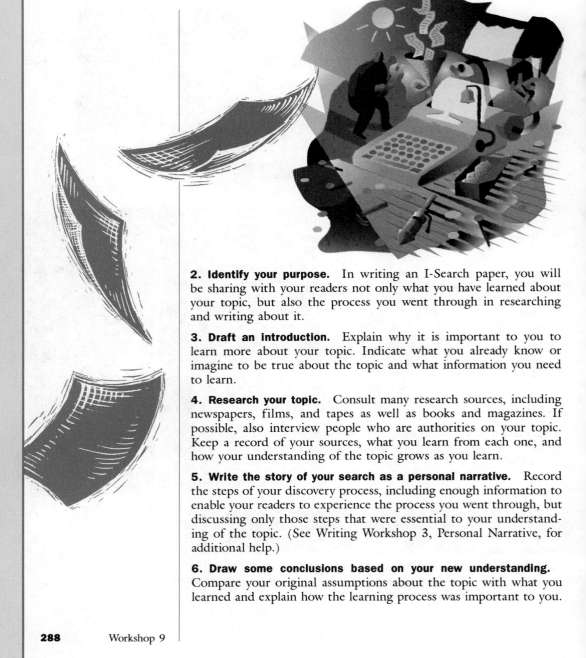

2. Identify your purpose. In writing an I-Search paper, you will be sharing with your readers not only what you have learned about your topic, but also the process you went through in researching and writing about it.

3. Draft an introduction. Explain why it is important to you to learn more about your topic. Indicate what you already know or imagine to be true about the topic and what information you need to learn.

4. Research your topic. Consult many research sources, including newspapers, films, and tapes as well as books and magazines. If possible, also interview people who are authorities on your topic. Keep a record of your sources, what you learn from each one, and how your understanding of the topic grows as you learn.

5. Write the story of your search as a personal narrative. Record the steps of your discovery process, including enough information to enable your readers to experience the process you went through, but discussing only those steps that were essential to your understanding of the topic. (See Writing Workshop 3, Personal Narrative, for additional help.)

6. Draw some conclusions based on your new understanding. Compare your original assumptions about the topic with what you learned and explain how the learning process was important to you.

288   Workshop 9

Humanities Connection

Art Note   *Woman with a Dog* (1922), pictured on the previous page, is a painting by Pierre Bonnard (b. 1867, France, d. 1967). The young Bonnard was influenced by the Nabis, artists known for their intimate, domestic scenes. During his mature, Intimist period, he experimented with the use of warm, subdued colors to suggest the affection and comfort of quiet lives.

PREPOSITION AT END

A friend of mine—let's call him Buster—who is a high school English teacher tells me that a colleague of his encountered him on the way to lunch one day and said, "Here's something you will appreciate. The kids in my history course had to write a short piece on the Civil War and, believe it or not, I spent a quarter of an hour lecturing them on not ending a sentence with a preposition. That's not my subject, but I felt I had to do it because the offenses in their writing were so flagrant." Then, according to Buster, the conversation went something like this:

"I don't know what you're getting at," said Buster, as solemnly as he could.

"I was telling them," said the colleague, "that it wasn't good English to end a sentence with a preposition."

"I still don't know what you are talking about," said Buster.

"Are you kidding?" said the colleague. "You're an English teacher, aren't you? I talked to them about the rule that you shouldn't end a sentence with a preposition. You understand that, don't you?"

"Maybe you don't know what rules are for," said Buster, still with a straight face.

The colleague looked at him for a moment, puzzled and annoyed, then said, "I don't know what you're up to, but . . ."

"You mean you don't know to what I am up," said Buster, "or perhaps up to what I am. Right?"

I am not sure they are on speaking terms any more . . .

So many authorities on usage have tried to correct the impression that it is wrong to end a sentence with a preposition that I almost feel as if I were flogging a dying horse. But the horse doesn't die . . .

The origin of the misguided rule [that it is wrong to end a sentence with a preposition] . . . derives from Latin, and in . . . Latin . . . prepositions do usually stand before the words they govern. But . . . in English, prepositions have been used as terminal words in a sentence since the days of Chaucer, and in that position they are completely idiomatic. [For example,] in such idiomatic sentences as "I don't know what you're talking about," or "you don't know what rules are for" . . . the stress falls toward the end [of the sentence] and the words are sufficiently strong to sustain that stress.

Theodore M. Bernstein

289

On the Lightside

This feature deals with the mistaken idea that a sentence should not end with a preposition. Point out that a preposition *usually* precedes its object, but does not have to. Have students identify the sentences in Buster's speech that end with a preposition and reword them so that the preposition precedes its object, noting that the revised sentences sound awkward and unnatural.

Sentence Composing: Review

Objectives

1. To write original sentences that imitate professional models containing introductory modifiers, delayed modifiers, inverted subject-verb order, introductory prepositional phrases, infinitive phrases, adverb clauses that tell time, and adjective clauses
2. To identify those particular elements in the model sentences

Preteaching

These exercises review the skills that students have learned in the previous sentence composing exercises. You may want to review or direct students to Grammar Handbook 34, Using Modifiers: Adjectives, pp. 620–621; Grammar Handbook 37, Using Verbals and Appositives: Participles, pp. 683–685; Infinitives, pp. 686–687; Grammar Handbook 29, The Sentence and Its Parts: Subjects in Unusual Positions, pp. 508–509; Grammar Handbook 35, Using Prepositions, Conjunctions, and Interjections: What Is a Preposition? pp. 652–654; Prepositional Phrases as Modifiers, pp. 657–659; Grammar Handbook 39, Clauses and Sentence Structure: Adverb Clauses, pp. 729–730; Adjective Clauses, pp. 725–726.

Sentence
COMPOSING

Reviewing Sentence Composing Skills

In the preceding sentence composing exercises, you studied how professional writers use unusual word order, phrases, and subordinate clauses to add interest and variety to their sentences.

Skill 1: Introductory Modifiers (pages 81–83)

Curious, they gathered at the cab window.
> **Glendon Swarthous, *Bless the Beasts and the Children***

Skill 2: Delayed Modifiers (pages 113–115)

The forests, somber and dull, stood motionless and silent on each side of the broad stream. > **Joseph Conrad, "The Lagoon"**

Skill 3: Inverted Word Order (pages 143–145)

Over the gray skin of the face ran little ants.
> **Stephen Crane, *The Red Badge of Courage***

Skill 4: Introductory Prepositional Phrases (pages 173–175)

After years of home cooking on Earth he had grown too fat for his old Adnaxian Air Force uniform.
> **Henry Gregor Felsen, "The Spaceman from Adnaxas"**

Skill 5: Infinitive Phrases (pages 203–205)

I was pronounced competent to paddle my own bicycle without outside help. > **Mark Twain, "Taming the Bicycle"**

Skill 6: Adverb Clauses That Tell Time (pages 233–235)

When he reached the dining room, he sat down at a table near the window. > **Willa Cather, "Paul's Case"**

Before the girls got to the porch, I heard their laughter crackling and popping like pine logs in a cooking stove.
> **Maya Angelou, *I Know Why the Caged Bird Sings***

Skill 7: Relative Clauses (pages 261–263)

My mother is descended from the younger of two English brothers named Lambton, who settled in this country a few generations ago.
> **Mark Twain, "Mental Telepathy"**

A. Imitating Sentences Write a sentence that imitates the structure of each model sentence.

Important: Imitate as many of the sentence parts as possible, not just the underlined part(s).

1. <u>At daylight</u> I was half wakened by the sound of chopping.
   Marjorie Kinnan Rawlings, "A Mother in Mannville"

2. <u>When he was over eighty</u>, Chips used to recount that incident with many chuckles. **James Hilton, *Goodbye, Mr. Chips***

3. Some older guys with their caps on backward are leaning against the fence, swirling basketballs on the tips of their fingers, waiting for all these crazy people <u>to clear out</u> so they can play.
   Toni Cade Bambara, "Raymond's Run"

4. <u>Rigid</u>, I began climbing the rungs, slightly reassured by having Finny right behind me. **John Knowles, *A Separate Peace***

5. I mean <u>to live a simple life, to choose a simple shell I can carry easily</u>—like a hermit crab. **Anne Morrow Lindbergh, *Gift from the Sea***

6. <u>When I was a small child</u>, there was no library for Negroes in our city, and not until a Negro minister invaded the main library did we get one.
   Ralph Ellison, *Shadow and Act*

7. His gaze returned unsteadily to Montag, <u>who was now seated with a book in his lap</u>. **Ray Bradbury, *Fahrenheit 451***

8. <u>In front of the house</u>, sloping down to the river, <u>is</u> a <u>garden</u> where the box-trees bordering the footpaths, all neatly trimmed in former days, now grow in wild freedom. **Honoré de Balzac, "La Grande Breteche"**

9. <u>As the boy grew</u> he ran with his village kind, as young antelope run together. **Mari Sandoz, *These Were the Sioux***

10. <u>Surprised</u>, I found myself a good distance ahead of Andries.
    Peter Abrahams, *Tell Freedom*

11. Suddenly, my own face, <u>reflected</u>, startles me witless.
    Annie Dillard, *Pilgrim at Tinker Creek*

12. <u>Comfortable and compact</u>, it sits curled up like a cat in the hollow of my hand. **Anne Morrow Lindbergh, *Gift from the Sea***

13. <u>While he was slipping them on</u>, the car veered toward a young couple crossing the street. **Robert Lipsyte, *The Contender***

Sentence Composing **291**

14. He bequeaths me his fragile eighteenth-century cologne bottle, <u>crystal with encrusted specks of gold</u>. **Anaïs Nin, *The Diary of Anaïs Nin***

15. <u>When Daru turned out the light</u>, the darkness seemed <u>to coagulate all of a sudden</u>. **Albert Camus, "The Guest"**

16. Packs of little kids, <u>raggedy and skinny</u>, raced past him along the gutter's edge, kicking empty beer cans ahead of them.
Robert Lipsyte, *The Contender*

17. Let us not seek <u>to satisfy our thirst for freedom</u> by drinking from the cup of bitterness and hatred. **Martin Luther King, Jr., "I Have a Dream"**

18. There <u>is</u> <u>something</u> uneasy in the Los Angeles air this afternoon, some unnatural stillness, some tension. **Joan Didion, "Los Angeles Notebook"**

19. Never, never <u>may</u> the <u>fruit</u> <u>be plucked</u> from the bough and gathered into barrels. **Edna St. Vincent Millay, "Never May the Fruit Be Plucked"**

20. <u>Nearby grew the "tree of true knowledge,"</u> as Samutchoso called it.
Laurens van der Post, *The Lost World of the Kalahari*

21. <u>In relief, in humiliation, in terror</u>, he understood that he, too, was an appearance, that someone else was dreaming him.
Jorge Luis Borges, "The Circular Ruins"

22. <u>When the whistle woke him</u>, he clutched quickly at his breast pocket, glancing about him with an uncertain smile. **Willa Cather, "Paul's Case"**

23. <u>Through the torn window</u> <u>appeared</u> the <u>timelessness</u> of an impermeably clouded late summer afternoon.
Elizabeth Bowen, "The Happy Autumn Fields"

24. <u>In the shallows</u>, face downward, <u>lay</u> the <u>oiler</u>.
Stephen Crane, "The Open Boat"

25. Father Kleinsorge went <u>to fetch water for the wounded in a bottle and a teapot he had borrowed</u>. **John Hersey, *Hiroshima***

26. <u>After our few chores around the tumble-down shanty</u>, Joey and I were free <u>to run wild in the sun with other children similarly situated</u>.
Eugenia Collier, "Marigolds"

27. <u>Raw, gentle, and easy</u>, it mizzled out of the high air, a special elixir, tasting of spells and stars and air, carrying a peppery dust in it, and moving like a rare light on his tongue.
Ray Bradbury, *The Martian Chronicles*

28. On the wall hung a clock that had long since stopped.

   Aharon Megged, "The Name"

29. When Atticus switched on the overhead light in the livingroom, he found Jem at the window, pale except for the vivid mark of the screen on his nose.

   Harper Lee, _To Kill a Mockingbird_

30. The horses stopped to breathe again, and the guard got down to skid the wheel for the descent, and open the coach-door to let the passengers in.

   Charles Dickens, _A Tale of Two Cities_

31. At the end of the straight avenue of forests, the sun appeared unclouded and dazzling, poised low over the water that shone smoothly like a bank of metal.

   Joseph Conrad, "The Lagoon"

32. To escape the wolf pack which all the other players became, he created reverses and deceptions and acts of sheer mass hypnotism which were so extraordinary that they surprised even him; after some of these plays I noticed him chuckling to himself, in a kind of happy disbelief.

   John Knowles, _A Separate Peace_

33. The light began to fade, and Dorothy called them in for more cake and lemonade, and then it was time to calm down the girls who were cranky, say good-bye, and start back to Harlem.

   Robert Lipsyte, _The Contender_

34. Whenever the memory of those marigolds flashes across my mind, a strange nostalgia comes with it and remains long after the picture has faded.

   Eugenia Collier, "Marigolds"

35. He tended to eat the same meals over and over and to wear the same clothes, to drop off his cleaning on a certain day and to pay all his bills on another.

   Ann Tyler, _The Accidental Tourist_

B. Identifying Sentence Composing Skills For each sentence in Exercise A, identify the skill or skills illustrated by the underlined parts: introductory modifier, delayed modifier, inverted word order, introductory prepositional phrase, infinitive phrase, adverb clause that tells time, or relative clause.

Application From a recent piece of writing select seven sentences at random. Experiment with each sentence, adding phrases or clauses or changing the word order, using the skills you have studied in these exercises.

Writing for Assessment

Overview

Writing for assessment requires of students all the writing and critical thinking skills covered in previous Workshops and also demands that students develop strategies and techniques for applying these skills under the pressure of a testing situation. Students learn how to analyze essay test prompts, approach test questions in the proper frame of mind, organize information, and write within time constraints. The test-taking skills they develop will have application throughout their academic and business careers. Workshop 10 includes the following Guided and Related Assignments:

1. **Guided: Responding to Essay Questions** develops skills of writing for assessment through a set of procedures and strategies for dealing with essay questions on tests.

2. **Related: Responding to a Writing Prompt** asks students to apply skills covered in the Guided Assignment in briefer form and with a non-academic prompt.

Teaching Preview

Preparation Guide

1. Use the Overview on this page and the Teacher's Choice descriptions on page 295 as a basis for deciding which assignment(s) to teach.

2. Preview the assignments and the teacher's notes and identify concerns that may require preteaching or extra support given your class's abilities. The handbook mini-lessons suggested within the lesson may also provide guidance.

3. Preview the chart below for support materials in the Teacher's Resource File that may be used with this Workshop. Resources are for use with the Guided Assignment unless otherwise noted.

Support Materials

WRITER'S CRAFT RESOURCES

Prewrite and Explore
Thinking Skills Transparencies, pp. 3–4, 23–24
Thinking Skills Worksheets, pp. 2, 14

Draft and Discover
Elaboration, Revision, and Proofreading Worksheets, p. 19

Revise Your Writing
Guidelines for Writing Assessment and Portfolio Use, p. 17
Elaboration, Revision, and Proofreading Worksheets, p. 20

Assessment
Tests and Writing Assessment Prompts, p. 8

Extension Activities
Writing Prompts for Fine Art Transparencies, pp. 9, 13, 16, 17
Standardized Test Practice

 Educational Technology
(available separately)
Writer's DataBank
Electronic English Handbook
Multimedia Workshop
Your Personal Trainer for the New SAT
In Perspective (videodisc)

· ·

OTHER RESOURCES

Books and Journals
Benson, Barbara P. "Effective Tests: Let Them Write!" *English Journal.* 80.2 (1991): 74–79.
Pratt, John Clark. "Writing Under Pressure: Examinations and Other Timed Indignities." *Writing from Scratch.* Lanham, Md.: Hamilton Press, 1987: 85–94.

Computer Software
"Answering Essay Questions," *Write On: Life Skills Series.* Humanities Software. Apple family, Macintosh, PC/MS-DOS.
Essay Ease. Mindplay. Apple family.
"Writing," *Homework Helper.* Spinnaker. Apple family, PC/MS-DOS.

Workshop Management Guidelines

The chart below indicates the number of days recommended for each phase of the Guided and Related Assignments. Stars indicate portions of the assignment that may be completed outside the classroom if time is limited or if teachers wish the activity to be completed by students independently.

RESPONDING TO ESSAY QUESTIONS

Starting from Literature .... 1 day
Prewrite .... 1 days*
Draft .... 1 day*
Revise .... 1 day
Apply Your Skills .... 1–2 days*
Reteaching .... open
Sentence Composing .... 1 day*

RESPONDING TO A WRITING PROMPT

Completing Writing Assessments .. 1 day*
Apply Your Skills .... 1–2 days*

Linking Literature, Writing, and Grammar

The following options may be used to provide students with an integrated language experience. Begin by assigning and discussing any of the recommended pieces of literature. Use the suggested strategy to provide a link to the Guided Assignment.

LINKING LITERATURE AND WRITING

Option 1

Starting Point: from *The Tragedy of Romeo and Juliet* by William Shakespeare, on pages 296–297 of *The Writer's Craft* and on pages 716–845 of McDougal, Littell's *Literature and Language,* Grade 9.

Strategy: Use the prompt on page 298 of *The Writer's Craft.*

Option 2

Starting Point: *Great Expectations* by Charles Dickens

Strategy: You may wish to discuss with the class how they might go about responding to the following prompts: "Compare and contrast the two endings of *Great Expectations* and state your reasons for preferring one of them" or "Explain the changes that come over one of the following characters during the course of the novel: Pip, Estella, Miss Havisham." Alternatively, you might work as a class to compose a prompt on an aspect of *Great Expectations* to help reveal what test-writers look for and how they proceed.

Option 3

Starting Point: "A Poison Tree" by William Blake

Strategy: You may wish to discuss with the class how they might go about responding to the following prompt: "Using quotations from the poem, show how Blake uses metaphor to express his feelings about love and hate, friendship and enmity."

LINKING WRITING AND GRAMMAR

Before the drafting or revision stage of this assignment, point out that in writing under time pressure, people often make errors of agreement, especially in difficult areas such as the agreement of subject and verb in compound sentences. Have students look for correct and incorrect agreement in their own writing as you write the following on the board:

Love and marriage *go* together like a horse and carriage. (subjects joined by *and* take plural verb)

Is Jason or Jennifer here today? (singular subjects joined by *or* or *nor* take singular verb)

Neither the star quarterback nor his teammates expect to lose the big game tomorrow.

The star quarterback *doesn't* expect to lose the big game tomorrow, and neither do his teammates. (singular subject and plural subject joined by *or* or *nor* take verb or verbs agreeing with the nearest subject)

Go over the rules for verb agreement on pages 700–703 of the Grammar and Usage Handbook. If problems on verb agreement still appear in student papers, assign the exercises on pages 705–706 for reteaching. Additional practice can be found in the *Grammar and Usage Practice Book* on pages 133–140.

Sketchbook

Objective

To use questions about a popular subject as a springboard to informal writing

Using the Prompt

The activities on this page are meant to stimulate students and generate spontaneity. They should not be graded.

Since music is a topic most young people feel strongly about, the questions on this page should provoke a lively discussion. You might also want to have students discuss why each generation of teenagers seems to "invent" its own style of music. After students become interested in the topic, have them write their responses to the questions. Allow students to select and write about a topic from the Additional Sketches section if they prefer.

Encourage students to keep their writing in their Writing Portfolios for possible future use.

Sketchbook

Is music important to you and the people around you? Why do you like the music you do?

Additional Sketches

What have you done that made you proud?

What was a turning point in your life?

294

WRITER'S 10 WORKSHOP

Writing for Assessment

Guided Assignment
RESPONDING TO ESSAY QUESTIONS

Related Assignment
RESPONDING TO A WRITING PROMPT

W hen taking essay tests, have you ever felt like you were running a losing race against the clock? You can win these races, but to do so you need to be wise as well as swift. Responding to essay questions involves many of the same writing and thinking strategies you have studied in the preceding workshops. In this workshop you will learn strategies you can use to beat the clock and write essay answers that are clear, logical, and to the point. You will also study strategies for writing answers to other types of tests, such as writing assessments.

295

Objectives

Guided Assignment:
RESPONDING TO ESSAY QUESTIONS
   To learn strategies for writing responses to essay questions

Related Assignment:
RESPONDING TO A WRITING PROMPT
   To learn strategies for analyzing writing assessment prompts and writing appropriate responses

Teacher's Choice

   The following information may help you choose the assignments that best fit the needs and interests of your students.

Guided Assignment
   Responding to Essay Questions For most students, the need to acquire the skills covered in this assignment—analyzing, planning answers for, and responding to essay questions—is pressing. Mastery of these skills will increase student confidence with and ability to answer essay questions in various disciplines. You will probably want to use this assignment early in the school year and then perhaps repeat it later, when students' writing skills have progressed.

Related Assignment
   Responding to a Writing Prompt This assignment allows students to transfer many of the skills acquired in the Guided Assignment. You will probably want to use the assignment after students have had experience with each of the writing modes.

Students will be asked to demonstrate their knowledge throughout their academic lives. For this reason, they must be taught how to respond to test questions in order to communicate their knowledge effectively. This is best accomplished not by the force-feeding of facts, but by teaching students strategies that will help them achieve maximum results from their efforts.

Starting from Literature

Objective

To respond to an excerpt and questions as a springboard to writing a response to an essay question

Teaching Strategies

Motivate

Ask students if they would like to learn how to approach tests with confidence, and invite discussion. Ask students what strategies they presently use to do well on tests.

Tap Prior Knowledge

Ask students if they have ever "frozen" after reading an essay question. Were they unsure about how to begin? Discuss their experiences.

Set a Purpose

Discuss the side column notes. Suggest that as students read the excerpt and questions, they think about what the questions are asking and how they might go about planning answers.

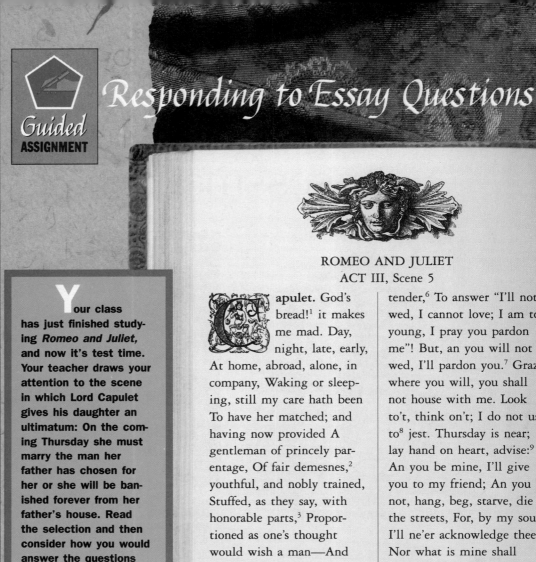

Guided ASSIGNMENT

Responding to Essay Questions

Your class has just finished studying *Romeo and Juliet,* and now it's test time. Your teacher draws your attention to the scene in which Lord Capulet gives his daughter an ultimatum: On the coming Thursday she must marry the man her father has chosen for her or she will be banished forever from her father's house. Read the selection and then consider how you would answer the questions that follow it.

ROMEO AND JULIET
ACT III, Scene 5

Capulet. God's bread![1] it makes me mad. Day, night, late, early, At home, abroad, alone, in company, Waking or sleeping, still my care hath been To have her matched; and having now provided A gentleman of princely parentage, Of fair demesnes,[2] youthful, and nobly trained, Stuffed, as they say, with honorable parts,[3] Proportioned as one's thought would wish a man—And then to have a wretch puling[4] fool, A whining mammet,[5] in her fortunes tender,[6] To answer "I'll not wed, I cannot love; I am too young, I pray you pardon me"! But, an you will not wed, I'll pardon you.[7] Graze where you will, you shall not house with me. Look to't, think on't; I do not use to[8] jest. Thursday is near; lay hand on heart, advise:[9] An you be mine, I'll give you to my friend; An you be not, hang, beg, starve, die in the streets, For, by my soul, I'll ne'er acknowledge thee, Nor what is mine shall never do thee good. Trust to't.[10] Bethink you. I'll not be forsworn."[11]

1. *God's bread:* an oath on the sacred communion bread 2. *demesnes:* wealth 3. *parts:* qualities 4. *puling:* whining 5. *mammet:* doll 6. *in her fortunes tender:* when good fortune is offered her

7. *pardon you:* be glad to see you gone 8. *I do not use to:* I do not usually 9. *advise:* be advised 10. *Trust to't:* be assured to it 11. *be forsworn:* break my vow

Think and Respond

Elicit Personal Responses

Discuss the Think and Respond questions, focusing on the strategies students
would use to analyze the questions. You
might list their ideas on the board, and
then return to the list for discussion after
students have completed the assignment.

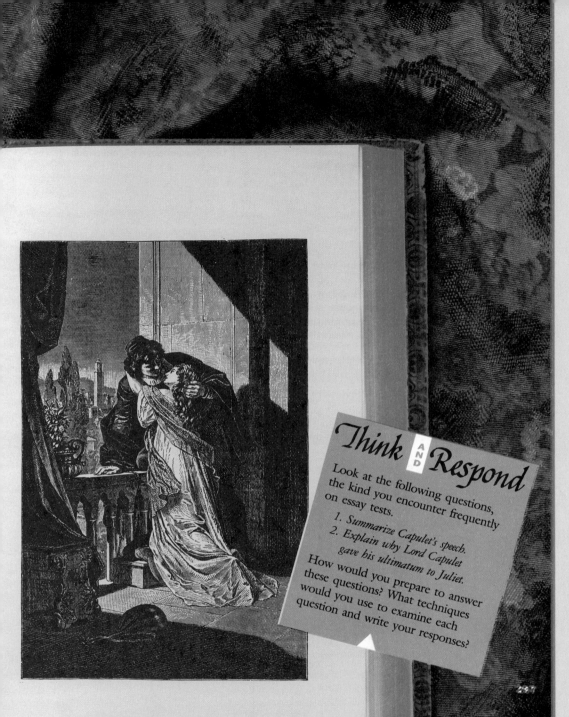

Think AND Respond

Look at the following questions,
the kind you encounter frequently
on essay tests.

1. Summarize Capulet's speech.
2. Explain why Lord Capulet
   gave his ultimatum to Juliet.

How would you prepare to answer
these questions? What techniques
would you use to examine each
question and write your responses?

Literature Connection

Author Note   William Shakespeare is the
author of some of the most enduring plays in
English literature. It is believed that *Romeo and
Juliet*, the tragedy from which the excerpt was
taken, was written in or around 1596. Although
Shakespeare died more than 300 years ago, his
plays are still performed and read today.

Springboard

Groups of students might enjoy dramatizing or
planning a Reader's Theater presentation of
one or more scenes from *Romeo and Juliet*.
(The excerpt is from Act III, Scene 5.) Students
might create other essay questions based on
the scenes that the groups dramatize.

Prewrite and Explore

Objective

To learn strategies for preparing to respond to an essay test, including budgeting time, analyzing test questions, planning an answer, and formulating a thesis statement

Preteaching

Preview the Prewrite and Explore section and identify any skills or concepts with which students may need help. The Cluster Diagram in the Thinking Skills Transparencies and the mini-lessons listed below may be helpful in your selection and instruction. The cross references in the pupil text will give students access to the same lessons for independent study.

> ### Handbook Mini-Lessons
> - Using Graphic Devices, pp. 357–360
> - Reading Skills, pp. 462–463
> - Synthesizing Material, pp. 468–469
> - Essay Tests, pp. 486–487

Teaching Strategies

Teaching Tip: Guiding the Reading

Because students will be asked at the end of this assignment to summarize the speech given in the excerpt, work with students as a class to read and "translate" the excerpt.

Critical Thinking

Drawing Conclusions Ask students why it would be wise to budget most of their time for the 75-point essay question. *(If they receive the highest score on that question, they will already have passed the test; if they answer every multiple choice question correctly but have no time left for the essay question, their score will be 25.)* Consider other combinations of objective and essay question point values and ask students how they would budget their time.

INVITATION TO Write

Here is a question such as you might encounter on an essay test: Explain why Lord Capulet gave his ultimatum to Juliet.

You probably know that success on essay tests is largely a matter of studying hard and knowing the material. However, even if you know the material well, you can still improve your test performance by knowing how to plan your responses. Just as athletes examine their opponents in order to develop a game plan to help them win, you can examine tests in order to develop strategies that will help you answer questions more effectively.

HANDBOOKS
FOR HELP & PRACTICE

Graphic Devices, pp. 357–360

Reading Skills, pp. 462–463

Synthesizing Material, pp. 468–469

Essay Tests, pp. 486–487

PREWRITE AND EXPLORE

1. Preview the test. First, carefully read all the questions and directions to get an overview of what you are expected to do. Then budget your time. For example, if a test contains twenty-five multiple choice questions worth a total of 25 points and one essay question worth 75 points, you should budget most of your time for the essay question.

2. Analyze the questions. The key to answering essay questions is understanding what you are expected to do. Read each question carefully and determine exactly what the question is asking. Look for the key words that tell you what to do.

When you answer an essay question, you are asked to respond to a prompt. A **prompt** is a word or direction that tells you to perform a specific thinking or writing task. The chart that follows shows key words commonly used in prompts along with strategies for responding to questions with those prompts.

298   Workshop 10

Responding to a Prompt

Analyze Break something down to its component parts; explain the function of each part and show how each part relates to the whole.

Compare Show how two or more things are alike and how they are different; support and emphasize the similarities and differences you point out with details and examples.

Contrast Show how two or more things are different; support and emphasize differences you point out with details and examples.

Describe Provide word pictures; use precise details that show you clearly understand the main or the distinctive characteristics of the process, term, or concept you are describing.

Discuss Provide general statements supported with facts and details that show how well you understand key points or relationships.

Explain Make a problem, a relationship, or a process clear and understandable; include examples, reasons, or facts to show how a process or reaction happens, why a specific thing occurs, or what has caused a particular problem.

Identify/Define Provide specific facts or details to establish or explain the unique identity of a significant process, character, or event.

Interpret Explain in your own words the meaning or importance of something; supply examples, facts, or reasons to support your main ideas.

Summarize Give a condensed version of a process, event, or sequence, briefly covering the most important points and omitting the less important acts and details.

PROBLEM

S O L V I N G

What strategies should I use to answer the question?

The prompt in the essay question about *Romeo and Juliet* asks you to "explain" why Lord Capulet gave his ultimatum to Juliet. To answer this question, you need to include reasons, facts, and other details to support your explanation of what has caused Lord Capulet's behavior.

3. Respond to the prompt. Begin planning your answer. Remember that you will have little or no time to revise, so plan carefully. As you plan, jot down notes, use clustering, or make an outline to help you refresh your memory about the main points of the subject and to help you organize your ideas. Clustering can be particularly useful for questions that ask you to give examples or to compare and contrast.

To answer the question about *Romeo and Juliet,* one student, Theresa, reread the passage from Lord Capulet's speech. Then, drawing on the speech and her knowledge of the play as a whole, she made these notes as she refreshed her memory and organized her ideas.

ONE STUDENT'S PROCESS

—Juliet threatens her father's authority.
—Capulet's authority represents the authority of the social system, makes the conflict more than just personal.
—Capulet feels good of family is at stake.
—Capulet thinks he knows best what's good and right for Juliet.
—Capulet doesn't want to be embarrassed. Made a promise to his friend about Juliet's marriage, so his honor is at stake.

Natalie Wood and Richard Beymer in the movie version of Leonard Bernstein's *West Side Story*, a musical version of Shakespeare's *Romeo and Juliet*.

4. Develop a thesis statement. The thesis statement should contain your main idea and show that you understand the question. A good thesis statement can set a goal for your answer and keep you on track as you write. Here is the thesis statement Theresa wrote to begin her answer.

ONE STUDENT'S PROCESS

Lord Capulet gave his ultimatum to Juliet because her refusal to marry the husband he had chosen for her challenged his authority.

DRAFT AND DISCOVER

1. Begin with your thesis statement. Meet the question head on by stating your main idea and then supporting it with facts, examples, and other details.

2. Move smoothly from one idea to the next. Use your prewriting notes or outline to guide your writing, and use transitions to move from one point to another. Don't be afraid to include any new ideas that occur to you. In fact, you may find that you change your mind about all or part of your answer as you write. Since you won't have time to reorganize your essay, simply acknowledge the change. Teachers will respect your thinking as you write.

3. End with a strong conclusion. Your conclusion should restate your thesis in light of the evidence you have presented in the main part of your essay.

4. Reread your essay. Ask yourself questions like those listed below to guide you in recognizing the strengths and weaknesses of your answer.

REVIEW YOUR WRITING

Questions for Yourself
- Does my response directly answer the question?
- Have I covered all the points I intended to?
- Do I need to include more facts or details?
- Does my summary restate my main point?

HANDBOOKS
FOR HELP & PRACTICE

Thesis Statements, pp. 343–344
Appropriate Details, pp. 355–356
Types of Conclusions, pp. 371–373

Writing
——**TIP**——
Leave space as you write so you can make changes and corrections neatly later.

Assessment **301**

Draft and Discover

Objective

To learn strategies for writing answers to essay questions, including supporting the main idea, using transitions, and developing a conclusion

Preteaching

Preview the Draft and Discover section for skills and strategies with which your students may need help. The Elaboration Worksheet and the mini-lessons listed below may be helpful in your selection and instruction.

> *Handbook Mini-Lessons*
> - Thesis Statements, pp. 343–344
> - Appropriate Details, p. 355
> - Types of Conclusions, pp. 371–373

Teaching Strategies

Stumbling Block

Some students tend to mistake quantity for quality and assume that long answers indicate a great amount of knowledge. As a result, they may produce long, rambling answers rather than lean, well-focused replies. Discuss this fact with students, and emphasize the importance of including only material that supports the thesis.

Off the Record

"Here's my test, Mr. Sauer. I've left a few intentional mistakes. I wonder if you'll be able to find them."

Revise Your Writing

Objective

To learn strategies for revising answers, including reviewing questions and preliminary notes and rereading for problems and errors

Preteaching

Preview the Revise Your Writing section and identify skills or strategies with which students may need help. The Revision and Proofreading Worksheets, the Student Revision Model Transparency, and the mini-lessons listed below may be helpful in your selection and instruction.

Handbook Mini-Lessons
- Unity in Compositions,
  pp. 363–364
- Coherence in Compositions,
  pp. 368–369
- Types of Revision, pp. 375–376
- Self-Editing, p. 378

Guidelines for Evaluation
A good essay answer . . .
- gives the main idea in a clear thesis statement
- uses facts, examples, and reasons to support and elaborate on the main idea
- is organized logically
- uses transitions effectively
- is comprehensive, responding to all parts of the question
- summarizes main ideas in a conclusion
- reflects an understanding of the test situation in word choice

HANDBOOKS

FOR HELP & PRACTICE

Unity in
Compositions,
pp. 363–364
Coherence in
Compositions,
pp. 368–369
Types of Revision
pp. 375–377
Self-Editing,
p. 378

R EVISE YOUR WRITING

1. Reread each question. You will have to work quickly to revise your essay, and you will not have time to make major revisions. However, you should take time to reread each question to make sure you have understood and responded to the prompt.

2. Recheck your prewriting notes. See if there is anything from your prewriting notes that you would like to add.

Keep in mind the following guidelines for a good test essay.

Standards for Evaluation

An effective essay answer . . .

- includes a clear statement of thesis.
- supports the main idea with facts, examples, and other details.
- moves smoothly from one idea to another.
- responds to key words in the question.
- covers all the points in the question.
- uses language that is appropriate for the test situation.
- includes a strong conclusion that summarizes the ideas.
- uses transitional words and phrases to show the relationships among ideas.

Portrait of Erasmus
by Hans Holbein
the Younger.

Humanities Connection

Art Note *Portrait of Erasmus* is an oil painting by Hans Holbein the Younger (b. 1497?, Germany, d. 1543). Desiderius Erasmus (b. 1469, Holland, d. 1536)—the subject of Holbein's painting—is generally considered to be the greatest scholar of the northern Renaissance. As writer and editor, he established universally accepted standards for evaluating the authenticity and meaning of historical documents. Ask: For what kinds of writing projects might you need to analyze historical documents?

3. Check for problems and errors. Correct any problems you find. First deal with problems in content and organization. Then go back and correct any errors in grammar or mechanics. Use proofreading symbols to mark your changes. Insert missing details with carats. Lengthy inserts can be written on a separate page.

Consider how Theresa responded to the prompt, developed her response, structured her essay, and revised it.

ONE STUDENT'S PROCESS

Lord Capulet gave his ultimatum to Juliet because her refusal to marry the husband he had chosen for her challenged his authority.

Capulet believed the good of his family was at stake. By choosing a good match for Juliet, he was making sure that she would be well taken care of. He felt he knew what was best for his daughter and what was right for her.

However, this was more than a personal issue between Capulet and his daughter. In the society of the 1300's, a father's authority over his family was absolute. It was common practice for fathers to arrange the marriages of their daughters. Capulet's authority represented the authority of the entire social system.

Lord Capulet also did not want to be embarrassed. He had promised his daughter's hand in marriage. If he broke his promise, he felt he would be dishonored.

Thus, in giving Juliet his ultimatum, Capulet reflected his belief that he needed to defend his duty to his family, his right as a father, and his honor in the community.

Clearly states thesis. Responds to key words in the question.

Supports main idea with details.

Uses transitional words to show relationships among ideas.

Moves smoothly from one idea to another.

Includes a strong conclusion.

APPLY YOUR SKILLS

Now try responding to a prompt. Write a short summary of Capulet's speech on page 296. Refer to the suggestions in this workshop.

Assessment   **303**

Discuss the annotations, and point out the revisions the student made in her answer. Emphasize that students will probably not have time to rewrite the entire draft and will have to make changes directly on the original. Emphasize the importance of making changes that improve an answer, and remind students that legible handwriting is a must.

Apply Your Skills

Objective

To plan, write, and revise an essay answer to a question

Teaching Strategies

Teaching Tip: Analyzing a Prompt

You may want to review briefly the kind of answer called for by the key word *summarize*. (See page 299.) Remind students that their summaries must be written in their own words, although they may want to include quotations from the speech that illustrate and support key points.

Reteaching

Assess the needs of students who were not successful in developing an effective essay answer and identify two or three areas in which additional practice is needed. Assign the appropriate Handbook Mini-Lessons, along with the support material listed for each lesson. Concepts commonly requiring reteaching for this lesson are

Synthesizing Material: Handbook 25
Thesis Statements: Handbook 6
Essay Tests: Handbook 28

Guiding Your Writers

Objectives

1. To learn strategies for analyzing a writing assessment prompt
2. To learn strategies for planning and writing a response to a writing assessment prompt
3. To write a response to a writing assessment prompt

Preteaching

Preview the assignment and identify skills or strategies with which your students may need help. The Cluster Diagram in the Thinking Skills Transparencies and the Thinking Skills Worksheets as well as the mini-lessons listed below may be helpful in your selection and instruction. The cross references in the pupil text will give students access to the same lessons for independent study.

> #### Handbook Mini-Lessons
> - Writing Variables, pp. 311–315
> - Thesis Statements, pp. 343–344
> - Unity in Compositions, pp. 363–364
> - Coherence in Compositions, pp. 368–369
> - Types of Conclusions, pp. 371–373

Teaching Strategies

Teaching Tip: Analyzing Prompts

Select some of the prompts from the Writing Prompts for Assessment booklet in the Teacher's Resource File. Work with students to help them identify the purpose, mode, audience, and format that each prompt requires.

Related ASSIGNMENT

INVITATION TO *Write*

Write a letter describing your community to a teenaged student living in a foreign country. In your letter, include descriptions of the people, the physical setting, and other features of your community.

In addition to the essay tests you take in your classes, you may also be asked to complete writing assessments that check your overall writing skills. Like essay questions, writing assessments call on you to respond to specific prompts. These prompts often require you to consider your purpose, your mode of writing, your audience, and your writing format. Above is an example of the kind of question you might find on a writing assessment.

You can use these steps to help you improve your performance on writing assessments.

HANDBOOKS
FOR HELP & PRACTICE

Writing Variables, pp. 311–316
Thesis Statements, pp. 343–344
Unity in Compositions, pp. 363–364
Coherence in Compositions, pp. 368–369
Types of Conclusions, pp. 371–373

COMPLETING WRITING ASSESSMENTS

1. Consider your purpose. Look for key words in the question that will help you determine the purpose of your writing. Check to see whether you are expected to inform your audience, persuade them, express your feelings or opinions, or do something else.

2. Choose your mode. The mode is the strategy you use to accomplish your purpose. Examples of modes include description, narration, definition and classification, and comparison and contrast.

3. Identify your audience. The assessment question may specify an audience. The audience might be one person, such as a friend, teacher, or elected official, or it might be a group, such as your classmates or the members of your community. If no audience is specified, imagine your audience as a teacher or other adult who is interested in your skills as a writer.

4. Identify the format. The assessment question may ask you to write within a specific format. Examples of formats include essays, letters, and newspaper articles.

Here is how one student examined the sample prompt, identified the key words, and decided what was expected of him.

ONE STUDENT'S PROCESS

Write a <u>letter</u> <u>describing</u> your community to a <u>teen-aged student</u> living in a <u>foreign country</u>. In your letter, include descriptions of the people, the physical setting, and other features of your community.

Purpose: inform
Mode: description
Audience: foreign student
Format: letter

5. Respond to the assessment question. After you have examined the question and determined what is expected of you, follow the steps you would use in responding to an essay question.

- Begin planning your response by making notes, using clustering, or writing an informal outline.
- Develop a thesis statement to get a goal for your writing and keep you on track.
- As you write, use transitions to move smoothly from one idea to the next.
- End with a strong conclusion.
- Review your writing, looking first for problems in content and organization and then for errors in grammar and mechanics.

▲PPLY YOUR SKILLS

Now see how well you can respond to an assessment test question. Write your answer to the sample question on page 304. If you need help, refer to the suggestions on these two pages.

Completing
Writing Assessment **305**

COMPOSING

Author Expansions

You have used your sentence composing skills to complete sentences begun by professional writers. Now look at the sentences they wrote. What qualities do your sentences share? What differences do you see?

Delayed Modifiers, Exercise C, page 115

1. His guard, ever present, bowed and handed him the immense bow and quiver.

2. A policeman, bored and tired, dragged his nightstick along the bars of an iron fence.

3. Her voice, usually so pure and musical, seemed to his ears to have lost some of its beauty.

4. It was a heavy sound, hard and sharp, not rolling.

Introductory Prepositional Phrases, Exercise C, pages 174–175

1. On stormy nights, when the tide was out, the bay of Fougere, fifty feet below the house, resembled an immense black pit, from which arose mutterings and sighs as if the sands down there had been alive and complaining.

2. At the top of the bank, the horse halted and turned about neighing fiercely.

3. With a head start, none of them could catch me, and I raced along as fast as I'd ever run in my life before.

4. Up the rising slope, down through the drifts, along a creek bottom to the rising ground of the next ridge, we plodded.

5. In the front hall, under a large picture of fat, cheery monks fishing by the riverside, there was a thick, dark horsewhip that had belonged to Mr. Spears's father.

6. In that lonely place, Frodo for the first time fully realized his homelessness and danger.

7. Once upon a time, Trurl, the constructor, built an eight-story thinking machine.

8. On a moonless night in August 1961, my schooner lay moored to a rotting dock in St. Pierre harbor.

9. By that time the fog had risen as high as the top of the ridges, and the whole house was swallowed up in it.

10. In the long mirror across the room, she saw herself, her hair hanging wild, her long bare legs scratched, her broadly smiling face dirt-streaked, her torn skirt dangling, her dog laughing up at her.

Adverb Clauses That Tell Time, Exercise A, page 233

1. When Mama and I came home from work a little after eight, Papa was usually going to bed.

2. While Nick walked through the little stretch of meadow alongside the stream, trout had jumped high out of the water.

3. As she headed down the hall to her next class, Geraldine remembered that she hadn't done the homework for English.

4. Before she could put a stop to it, some of their classmates scoffed at the leaf-lard-and-black-bread sandwiches they ate for lunch, huddled in one corner of the recreation room, dressed in their boiled-out ragpickers' clothes.

5. After he had disappeared down the road with his suitcase strapped on his shoulders, Roseleen had gone back in the house and had looked at herself in the square looking glass beside the kitchen window.

Adverb Clauses That Tell Time, Exercise B, page 234

1. Before tobacco came to Bacon County, the farmers were self-sufficient in a way they never were to be again.

2. As she thrust her head into the small room, she was greeted by a rush of warm air, in sharp contrast to the cool wind on her back.

3. While he scrubbed the sidewalk, I stood there, throwing the ball at the apartment building that faced the street.

4. After she got to the top, she turned and gave a full, severe look behind her where she had come.

5. When you are getting on in years (but not ill, of course), you get very sleepy at times, and the hours seem to pass like lazy cattle moving across a landscape.

Dynamism of Forms, by Gino Severini, 1912

Writing Handbook

The mini-lessons in this Handbook may be used for a variety of purposes.

Preteaching—to introduce specific writing concepts and skills before beginning a Guided or Related Assignment

Reference—to provide extra help and practice as students problem-solve their way through a piece of writing

Reteaching—to remedy specific problems noted in student writing

To match mini-lessons to an assignment, see teaching notes in the Writer's Workshop, and Handbook cross-references on the pupil page.

Sketchbook

Objective

To use a cartoon as a springboard to informal writing

Using the Prompt

Remind students that Sketchbook activities are meant to encourage risk-taking and experimentation and are not graded.

Encourage students to think of topics with which they are very familiar. Many students will probably be familiar with pets or pet owners, but encourage students to think of other familiar topics as well. Hobbies, fashion, or particular sports, for example, are likely to be very familiar to different students.

Be sure students recognize that the activity is completely open-ended and that their writing may take any form—an anecdote, a poem, a cartoon, a comic strip, a story, an opinion essay, etc. Be sure, too, that students recognize that they may write about their responses to or opinions of the cartoon itself.

Use the ideas from the Additional Sketches section as an alternative for students who prefer a different starting point. Have students keep their writing in their Writing Portfolios for possible use in later writing.

Sketchbook

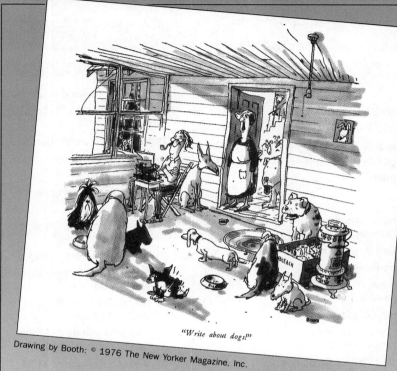

"*Write about dogs!*"

Drawing by Booth: © 1976 The New Yorker Magazine, Inc.

. . . Or about cats, or other pets, or about pet owners, or about this cartoon, or . . . .

Additional Sketches

What's in your closet?
What makes you angry, glad, or sad?

310

Beginning the Writing Activity

Almost every activity in life involves writing. As a student, you are asked to do expository and imaginative writing as well as reports and test answers. To find a job, you may need to write résumés, cover letters, and employment applications. Businesspeople write proposals, memos, and speeches. Almost everyone writes notes and letters, and many people write just for themselves. Each writing activity is different, and analyzing its **variables,** or parts, can help you get started. These variables include: **topic, purpose, personal goals, audience, form,** and **voice.**

THE WRITING VARIABLES

You may make decisions about some of these variables before you begin writing and about others later on, after you have gathered ideas or tried them out in an experimental draft. Consider each of the variables separately and think about how changing it would affect your writing as a whole.

Sometimes one or more of the writing variables are determined by the writing activity itself. When you are given a writing assignment, analyze it to determine which variables are specified and which you must decide on.

Topic

Topic is the key writing variable. It is important to choose one that you are interested in and can develop adequately. Suppose that you are assigned to write a speech on any topic of your choice. Should you choose a topic that you already know a great deal about or one that you aren't so familiar with but are curious about?

Each choice has advantages and disadvantages. If you choose a topic that you already know about, you will not have to spend much time gathering ideas. Instead, you can draw heavily on your own knowledge. However, such a topic might not prove as interesting to explore as one that involves learning new things. If you choose an unfamiliar topic, you will have to spend time learning about it, but this learning can be part of the excitement of the writing process.

Beginning the
Writing Activity **311**

Objectives

1. To identify and analyze writing variables
2. To explore approaches to determining variables

Handbook Mini-Lessons

For information on topics related to analyzing the writing activity, see the following mini-lessons.

- Finding Ideas, pp. 317–325
- Limiting a Topic, pp. 327–329
- Personal Voice and Style, pp. 405–408

Teaching Strategies

Motivating

Have students name public figures whom they admire—singers, actors, politicians, and so on. Ask volunteers to think of ways each of these figures might need to use writing in his or her daily life.

Critical Thinking

Making Comparisons Ask students which of the two types of topics they would prefer to write about: a familiar topic or an unfamiliar one. Have students explain the reasons for their choices.

Modeling

To help students see unusual angles or approaches to a topic, suggest this topic to the class: Animals That Help People. Then model for students some original approaches you might take to the topic and write your ideas on the chalkboard. Some possibilities might include looking at the topic from an animal's point of view; interviewing people whom animals have helped; and researching the most unusual incidence of animal aid.

Teaching Tip: Purpose

Have students look through newspapers or magazines to find examples of articles or advertisements that fill one or more of the purposes stated: self-expression, information, entertainment, analysis, or persuasion. Encourage students to discuss how the writer fulfilled the purpose.

Writing
—**TIP**—

Remember that whatever topic you choose, it should be one that you find interesting. If you find it interesting, chances are your readers will too.

For example, one student, who had been a latchkey child, decided to write about safety tips for children who spend time alone at home after school. This topic provided a nice balance between what she already knew and needed to find out: she had some ideas based on her own experience as a child and a baby-sitter, and would research others.

WRITER TO WRITER

To decide on a topic, I have to think about why I am writing and who will be reading my writing.

**Lisa Korpan, student
Northfield, Illinois**

When choosing a topic, keep in mind that specific topics are easier to research than general ones, concrete subjects are easier than abstract ones, and older events are easier to research than recent ones. For example, the topic "The United States Space Program" is too general to cover in a short report. Your research and writing will be more focused if you choose a more specific topic, such as "The *Apollo 11* Moon Landing." Because this mission occurred several decades ago, finding books and articles about it will be easy. However, don't rule out writing about current events that really excite you.

Sometimes your teacher will give you a subject to write about. Even then, though, you should search for new angles or unexpected approaches to make the topic your own. For example, if your teacher assigned you to write about the *Apollo 11* moon landing, you might decide to write about the memories of people who were children at the time of the landing. You could start your research by interviewing people in your own family. For more help with finding a topic, see Writing Handbook 2, pages 317–325.

Purpose

Sometimes the purpose of a writing activity is given. For example, you may be asked to write a letter persuading your principal to approve a class trip. Analyze any writing assignment to determine if the purpose is stated. If you must decide on your purpose, remember that you don't have to choose it before you begin writing. It may evolve later. Some of the most common purposes for writing

Art Connection

Point out to students that visual artists create their works with a purpose in mind, just as writers do. Have students think about works of art they admire, or provide a book with art reproductions for them to look at. Use the following questions to generate student discussion about artists' purposes for creating: Why do you think the artist chose the medium he or she worked in? What was the artist trying to communicate? How effectively did the artist accomplish his or her purpose?

are **to express yourself, to inform, to entertain, to analyze,** and **to persuade.** However, a piece of writing seldom has only one purpose. For example, you might persuade readers of the dangers of riding a bicycle without a helmet by informing them of the number of injuries to riders who don't wear helmets.

Statement of Controlling Purpose   One way to clarify your purpose for writing is to compose a **statement of controlling purpose** explaining what you want your writing to accomplish. This statement is a tool for planning and focusing your writing but does not actually appear in the piece of writing itself. Some statements of controlling purpose for various types of writing are shown below. Notice that each statement contains a key word that tells the purpose of a particular composition, such as to *explain, entertain, define,* and *narrate.*

> **Writing that explains a process**   The purpose of this speech is to explain to new speech club members how to prepare a dramatic interpretation.
>
> **Writing that entertains**   The purpose of this skit is to entertain, by parodying, or poking gentle fun at, the process of running for a student council office.
>
> **Writing that defines**   The purpose of this essay is to define the word *energy* and to give examples of the kinds of energy that are used in modern industrialized nations.
>
> **Writing that narrates**   The purpose of this newspaper article is to tell the story of our volleyball team's trip to play in a tournament in California.

Personal Goals   Your statement of controlling purpose will help you establish your general reason for writing. In addition, you may want to consider your own **personal goals**—what you hope your writing will accomplish for you. For example, a personal goal for writing a personal narrative may be to feel closer to someone with whom you shared an important experience. A personal goal for writing a newspaper story about a school club you belong to may be to inform others about the activity. A personal goal for writing a report on careers in health care may be to help you decide whether you would enjoy working in that field.

The student who wanted to write safety tips for children left alone at home wanted to inform people of the dangers children might face and persuade them to avoid those dangers. Her personal goal was to help other people benefit from the experiences of her own family and other families she knew.

Beginning the
Writing Activity   **313**

Audience

Sometimes your audience is chosen for you, and you know who your reader or readers will be. For example, suppose your teacher asks you to write an article for your school newspaper. In that case your audience is the students in your school. At other times you can choose your audience. For example, if you are writing a short story, you might write for a general audience, for young children, or for people your own age. You can get a feel for your audience by asking questions such as these:

- What information do my readers need? What do they already know?
- What part of my subject will my readers find most interesting?
- What will they agree or disagree with?
- What kind of language will be most appropriate to this audience?

Answering these questions can help you tailor your writing to the people who will be reading or hearing it. In turn, understanding your audience will often help you determine the details to include and the form, language, and tone of your writing. For example, if you were writing a skit for young children, you would use simpler language than if you were writing for adults. If you were writing about American high schools for your classmates, you could assume that they already knew a great deal about the subject; for an audience of foreign exchange students, you would have to provide more background information.

The student who wanted to write safety tips for children couldn't decide whether to address parents or the children themselves, so she decided to divide her writing into two parts—one to the parents and the other to the children.

Form

The **form** is the type of writing in which you express your ideas. The form you choose will help to determine the length, organization, and shape of your writing. It will also help to determine what kinds of details and what kind of language you will use. The following list includes some of the many forms that a piece of writing can take.

Boxing by Alexander Archipenko, 1914. Collection, Museum of Modern Art, New York

314 Writing Handbook

Forms of Writing

advertisement	history	paraphrase
anecdote	instructions	play
announcement	joke	poem
autobiography	journal entry	poster
book review	lab report	proposal
cartoon	legend	questionnaire
catalog	letter	recipe
classified ad	limerick	résumé
dialogue	magazine article	report
essay	meeting minutes	short story
family history	movie review	speech
freewriting	news report	summary

The student who wanted to write safety tips for children decided to draft a letter to parents and attach it to a safety poster that would get the children's attention.

Voice

You have probably noticed that you do not use the same kind of speech all the time. You speak one way when you are with your friends, another way when participating in a class discussion, and still another way when giving a formal report. These different ways of speaking are your various **voices.**

Different kinds of writing require different voices. When writing a formal report, for example, you may use a voice that is authoritative, unbiased, and factual. When telling a ghost story, you may take on a voice that is imaginative and emotional. Choosing an appropriate voice for a piece of writing is a little like taking on the role of a character in a play. When writing a report, you might imagine that you are a teacher, giving a lecture about a subject that fascinates you. When writing a ghost story, you can pretend that you have been frightened by mysterious events, and then imagine how you would tell your own story.

The student writing safety tips for children knew she wanted to write in a serious but conversational tone in her letter to the parents and to use simple language and a reassuring tone in her poster for the children.

Collaborative Opportunity

Have students work in small groups to determine possible audiences for the forms listed in the chart. Each group can choose four or five forms and work together to find two possible audiences for each form.

Managing the Paper Load

Students can work in small groups to evaluate each others' variables charts for Exercises A and B. Encourage students to discuss the decisions they have made and their appropriateness to the assignment. If students disagree with others' choices, they should give reasons for their criticisms.

Additional Resources
- Writing Resource Book, pp. 1–2

ANSWERS TO PRACTICE YOUR SKILLS

A. Answers will vary. Be sure that students address all the variables noted in the chart, as shown in the example below.
Topic: Recycling in my town
Purpose: To gather support
Audience: Junior high school students
Form: Speech
Voice: Serious, committed
B. Answers will vary.

Keep in mind that you do not have to make all your decisions about writing variables at the beginning of the writing process. Instead, relax and try out different approaches. For example, you might start freewriting on a topic and then discover that you really want to write about only some part of it or about another topic altogether. You may begin writing an essay but decide as you write that a better approach would be to present the same information as a dialogue between two characters. You might write a journal entry you don't intend to share with anyone and later decide you'd like to revise your writing and present it to an audience.

These early stages of writing can be fun: think of the different stages as a chance to try out ideas, experiment with the writing variables, and discover what you want to say and the best way to say it.

Practice Your Skills

A. Imagine that your teacher has asked you to write a speech on some issue related to conservation. Decide on a specific topic you might like to write about, what your purpose for writing might be, what audience you might like to speak to, and what kind of voice you might use. Copy the writing variables chart below and fill in your ideas. If there are any variables you'd like to make a decision about later in the writing process, explain why you prefer to defer this decision and what factors might influence the choice you ultimately make.

TOPIC _____

PURPOSE _____

AUDIENCE _____

FORM _____ *Speech* _____

VOICE _____

B. Now imagine that your teacher asked you to present the same topic in a letter. To whom would you write? How might the other writing variables change? Fill in a new writing variables chart showing some of the changes you might decide to make.

History Connection

Have students use what they have learned about writing variables to analyze an assignment from history class. Have them make a variables chart such as the one in Exercise A for a recent assignment and fill it in appropriately. This will encourage students to think about writing variables in other educational settings.

How Do I Find Ideas?

The Polish-American writer Sholem Asch once wrote, "It has been said that writing comes more easily if you have something to say." That is, if you can find great ideas that really excite *you* and seem important to *you,* you're more likely to create a piece of writing that will interest your readers as well.

Sometimes you may know right away what you want to write about, but other times, your ideas may not come as easily as you would like. The following exploratory techniques can both help you find good ideas and elaborate, or develop, them.

PERSONAL TECHNIQUES

Often your best source of ideas is *you.* You can start simply by looking inside yourself to discover what you know and remember, what you've seen and done, what you like and dislike, what you wonder about, and what you dream about.

Recalling Your own mind is a gold mine of ideas waiting to be uncovered through recalling, or thinking back on, your experiences. The following list describes some specific techniques you can use to jog your memory about past events in your life:

- Look through an album of family photographs, a scrapbook, an old yearbook, a family history, or your diary or journal for material that will jog your memory.
- Choose an important time, place, person, or thing from your life and write down all the information and feelings you can recall about it.
- Talk to a friend or family member about experiences you have shared. Even if other people remember an incident differently, their memories are likely to activate your own and give you new insights.

Writing
─TIP─

Never sell yourself short. Your own ideas, experiences, and observations can be important and interesting to others.

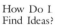

How Do I
Find Ideas? **317**

How Do I Find Ideas?

Objectives

- To learn and apply personal, writing, and sharing techniques for stimulating writing

Handbook Mini-Lessons
For information on topics related to finding ideas, see the following mini-lessons.
- Developing Ideas, pp. 351–354
- Graphic Aids, pp. 357–360
- Oral Skills, pp. 479–482

Teaching Strategies

Motivating

Read the quotation from Sholem Asch aloud. Ask volunteers to interpret the quotation, paying special attention to the phrase "something to say." (Possible response: *an exciting or important idea to communicate.*) Have students give examples of works they have read in which they feel the writer had "something to say."

Listening and Speaking

Encourage students to prepare a list of questions they can use when interviewing a friend or family member. Stress that the questions should serve to clarify and broaden the students' own memories of the shared event. *Who, what, when, why,* and *where* questions will be helpful, as will questions such as "How did the event make you feel?"

The ideas for my stories usually come from my personal experiences or I get an idea from something someone says.

**Wayne Jarmon, student
Birmingham, Alabama**

Conducting an Interest Inventory Have you designed a computer program or your own clothes? Do you read articles on the history of baseball or the history of cartoons just for fun? Chances are, there are certain types of events, information, or activities that tend to grab your attention and hold your interest. You may even be an expert on something. Conducting an interest inventory can help remind you of those areas of life about which you are most curious and might have the most to say.

Questions for Conducting an Interest Inventory

- Which magazines do I read regularly? Which articles do I particularly remember? Did I save any of them?
- What is the last book I read for my own pleasure?
- What TV documentaries have I enjoyed?
- What sports and hobbies do I enjoy? What kind of lessons would I most like to take if I could?
- What careers interest me?
- Who is the person I most admire? Why?

Using Trigger Words The great nineteenth-century British statesman Benjamin Disraeli used to thumb through the dictionary for

Sports Connection

Have students tailor the Interest Inventory questions in the student book to *one* particular sport—gymnastics, soccer, football, diving, and so on. Students can use the questions to determine which sport most interests them and to find out how much they actually know about the sport. They may wish to produce a piece of writing using their inventory.

words that would jolt, or trigger, his imagination. You can use Disraeli's technique by thinking about trigger words such as these:

discovery	heart	outer space
freedom	money	school
friendship	nature	secret
happiness	nightmare	work

Notice how one student used the word *discovery* to trigger ideas.

Trigger Word: Discovery

Buried treasure?
Explorers looking for lost continent?
Doctors seeking cures for diseases?
Something unexpected about a person who seemed ordinary?
Finding out something new about myself? After a challenge?
Finding something that was lost—many years later?
Solving a mystery?

Creative Questioning   A good way to stir up ideas in your mind and see things in a fresh light is to ask **creative questions.** Use your imagination to think of unusual, even silly, "what if" questions. Just by forming these questions you will begin thinking creatively, and the answers may lead you to some original results. Here are some sample "what if" questions:

- **What if I combined two objects that are normally separate?** (Someone thought to put an alarm clock and a radio together, creating the clock radio.)
- **What if I put two opposing ideas together?** (Can you create a dessert that is both hot and cold?)
- **What if I used an object in a new or unusual way?** (Fashion designers always find new ways to use scarves.)
- **What if a person, place, object, event, or idea had never happened?** (Imagine the world without cars.)
- **What if I changed just one part of a thing or situation?** (Someone thought of putting wheels on skis so that skiers could stay in shape year-round.)
- **What if I changed an object's composition or shape in some way?** (The invention of plastic revolutionized the manufacture of thousands of things.)

How Do I
Find Ideas?   **319**

Cooperative Learning

Have students work in teams to practice creative questioning on each other. Each team can choose two of the questions listed and come up with a new, imaginative idea. Students can then compare their ideas with those of their classmates to gain a better understanding of the limitlessness of imagination.

Springboard

Read this quotation by Walter Kaufman aloud to students: "The world of reason is poor compared to the world of the senses—until *or, but, because, when, if,* and *unless* populate it with endless possibilities." Have students discuss the quotation as it pertains to the idea of creative questioning. Then have students brainstorm other words that help "populate the world of reason with possibility."

Allow students to share and discuss their lists with the class as a whole.

- **What if relationships were different?** (What if a brother or sister changed places with one of your parents?)
- **What if I changed the location of something?** (What would happen if a skyscraper were built in a jungle?)
- **What if people changed their actions in some way?** (What if people slept all day and stayed awake all night?)

Gleaning The word *glean* means "to gather bit by bit." When you glean, you gather interesting sights, sounds, words, and ideas the way an insect collector gathers interesting specimens. However, gleaning is not just gathering; it also involves thinking about the ideas you gather and determining how they might be used in a piece of writing.

Keep an open mind as you go through your day. Ideas for writing may occur to you, even at the most unexpected times. Later, when you add these ideas to your journal, story ideas or other writing topics may emerge. Notice how one student gleaned an idea for a piece of writing while observing a construction site.

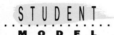

There's a woman wearing a suit and a hard hat, talking to the supervisor. She's pointing to something on the blueprint. I never realized that architects visit the building site; that would be fun! Wonder what else they do.

Now she's pointing at the cement mixer. The glop coming down the chute is lumpy, and steam is rising from it. I never saw steam come from concrete! And shouldn't it be smooth? Now the supervisor picks up a bullhorn and shouts, "Stop the pouring!"

What's going on? Something must be wrong. This would make a funny story: A truck carrying oats is highjacked, and the missing cargo is found in a cement mixer!

WRITING TECHNIQUES

Writing itself can be a good source of writing ideas. Try to jot down your ideas freely without worrying about organization or style. There are several techniques for doing this.

Freewriting The key to freewriting is the word *free*. Freewriting is private; you don't have to share ideas with anyone, so you can relax

---

 Individualizing Instruction

Learning Styles Students should be aware that gleaning can take many forms. For those students who learn best visually, taking photographs of places, people, or events can be helpful. For those who learn auditorily, having a tape recorder handy will aid them in noting ideas as they occur. Other students may prefer to have their journals close at hand as they go about their daily activities. Stress that gleaning is often a spur-of-the-moment activity; opportunities to glean should not be lost.

Teaching Tip: Gleaning

Point out that the notes in the model offer the writer an opportunity to develop several ideas. Ask students to consider what other writing ideas the gleaning notes might inspire. (Possible responses include: *a description of an architect's job; an essay on the formation of concrete; a love story about the female architect and the supervisor.*)

Teaching Tip: Freewriting

Some students might find the concept of freewriting confusing and may feel that this exercise obfuscates writing ideas rather than clarifying them. Point out that freewriting helps to loosen ideas from the mind, just as shaking a fruit tree loosens fruit, leaving it free to fall.

and let your thoughts flow. These steps will help you get started.

1. Start with any idea you want to explore. You might begin by asking youself, "What's on my mind today?" You can use a picture, an experience, or even just a word to get your thoughts going.
2. Write whatever comes into your mind.
3. Keep your pen moving. Try to let it "think" for you. Let yourself follow ideas where they take you. Don't worry about spelling, grammar, or punctuation; just keep going.
4. Time yourself. Write nonstop for three to five minutes.

Here is an example of freewriting from one student's journal:

It's snowing again. Snow seems terrific at first, but by February I'm sick of it just dirty and slushy. Boots, sweaters, coats, scarves, gloves—always losing them. Wish I lived someplace warmer.

Florida, Arizona. Aunt Fay in Arizona. Visited her once sure is different there. So hot. Not much green. Huge cactuses—weird looking—needles, odd shapes, no leaves. Wonder why they're so different from other plants. Report topic?

Invisible Writing   One way to make sure that you don't try to control or critique your writing while you're generating ideas is to do some invisible writing. Get two pieces of blank paper, some carbon paper, and either a pen that has run out of ink or a thin metal object with a tip shaped like that of a pen. When you write with the inkless implement on a blank sheet of paper on top of carbon, the writing will show only on the page underneath. This way you can record your thoughts without analyzing them.

Stumbling Block

The concept of invisible writing might confuse those students who feel that not seeing what they are writing is unacceptable. Ask these students to consider how unanalyzed writing could be useful to them. (Possible response: *It allows freer thought and flow of ideas.*) Point out that going back and seeing what they have written can reveal surprising new ideas and show them the wide scope of their imaginations.

Math Connection

Point out to students that while the study of mathematics might not seem to be conducive to the germination of ideas for writing, freewriting about math can generate ideas that might surprise them. Encourage them to study the freewriting model and then freewrite for a couple of minutes on mathematics. Students can then discuss the ideas they have generated.

You can sharpen your powers of observation and gather writing ideas at the same time by listing all of the details of something you've observed. Here is an example of a list you might make after taking a walk on the beach:

endless white sand	cry of sea gulls
baby blue sky	deserted
clear, cool water	sparkle of sun on sand
curve of larger waves	wet sand khaki colored
hiss of foam on sand	disappearing footprints
cloudless	bleached driftwood
salt on skin	tiny silver fish darting
crash of waves	dazzling brightness
slight breeze	shells washed up on shore
smell of seaweed	sky reflected in pools

Using a Journal A **journal** is your own place for writing what you want, when you want, without worrying about crossing every *t* and dotting every *i*. You can keep a journal for enjoyment, for clearing your mind, and for freeing your imagination.

A journal can be a place where you practice and experiment with different writing styles. Many writers, including professionals, keep journals so that they can record their observations, reactions, and feelings for later use in their writing. (See Writer's Workshop 1 to learn more about how to make best use of your journal as a source of writing ideas.)

There are no rules for journal keeping; it is a highly individualized process. However, the tips that follow will help you to get started:

- **Find a format that works for you.** Whether you write in a spiral-bound notebook, a composition book with a drawing on the cover, or a file folder of loose-leaf paper, your journal should feel comfortable and inviting.
- **Carry your journal with you, or keep it in a handy place.** Write in it whenever and wherever inspiration strikes.
- **Date your journal entries.** Dates provide a simple way of organizing your material. They also serve as useful landmarks when you later read and think about entries.

Journal writing gives you a chance to do some mental "housecleaning." It can also provide good ideas for assigned writing. Most important, perhaps, is what happens when you read your entries in the future. They remind you how it felt to be you at another time

COMPUTER TIP

If you have a word processor, you can do invisible writing by working with the terminal screen light turned down so that you cannot see the writing on the screen.

Personal Touch

If you kept a journal in the past, tell students how you used the journal and the ways in which it helped you in your writing. Students might enjoy an anecdote about the way you feel now reading what you wrote in the past. How do those entries document your changing thoughts and feelings?

Springboard

Show students a fine art reproduction of a landscape. Then have students imagine that they inhabit the landscape and make a list of sensory details from the world of the painting in which they are projecting themselves. Remind them to include details of smell, sound, touch, and taste, as well as sight, using their imaginations.

in your life. To see how journalist Bob Greene used his high school journal years later to evoke vivid memories of growing up, see Writer's Workshop 1, page 28.

Keeping a Sourcebook or Clip File You may want to set aside part of your journal as a **sourcebook,** a place to collect interesting quotes, observations, magazine or newspaper articles, song lyrics, and photos to use as a source of writing ideas. Instead, you may keep your collection in a file folder, called a **clip file.** Many professional writers keep files of clippings from the magazines and newspapers they read. These can be a valuable source of ideas. When you need something to write about, you can simply go to your clip file and rummage around.

Collect anything that catches your interest. You can quote a passage from a book, a lyric from a song, or a line from a movie. You can cut a cartoon out of a newspaper, an advertisement out of a brochure, or an amusing or interesting picture out of a magazine. (Of course, you can do this only to your own property. When collecting from library materials, copy, trace, or photocopy the material you want to save.) You might even include in your sourcebook or clip file a four-leaf clover or a ticket stub from a concert you really enjoyed.

SHARING TECHNIQUES

Most writers agree that writing is primarily a solitary activity. There comes a time when every writer must sit down alone and put thoughts onto paper. However, throughout the writing process, you can benefit from sharing ideas with other people. Two (or three or ten) heads are often better than one, and this is especially true when it comes to generating ideas. If you need some help coming up with ideas for writing, you might try getting together with your classmates and friends to share ideas by brainstorming or discussing.

Brainstorming When people brainstorm, they let their thoughts run free to come up with as many ideas as possible. One of the rules of brainstorming is that no idea should be considered too ridiculous, inappropriate, or irrelevant to mention. Simply begin talking about the chosen topic and come up with as many ideas as you can as fast as you can. Have one person in your group act as recorder and write down the ideas.

How Do I
Find Ideas?   **323**

Although you can brainstorm alone, you can often get a more interesting variety of ideas by brainstorming in a group. Here, for example, is a list generated by a group of students new to the United States. They brainstormed about situations and things that were new and strange to them.

supermarkets	English	American sports
cold weather	department stores	dirt bikes
snow	electric stove	MTV
heavy clothing	new friends	language
shopping	new foods	American schools

Keep the following guidelines in mind when brainstorming:

Guidelines for Brainstorming

• By yourself or in a group, list every thought that comes into your mind about a subject.

• Do not organize or order the ideas.

• Do not "censor" any idea as too inappropriate, impossible, or unrelated to be useful. In a group brainstorming session, no one is allowed to criticize anyone else's ideas, and everyone is encouraged to build on other people's ideas.

Discussion A discussion can be a good way to explore ideas in depth with other people. For example, the group of students who brainstormed the ideas above might also hold a discussion in which they all described in detail the most difficult situations they had

Speaking and Listening

Allow students to practice the art of controlled discussion by dividing the class into small groups and inviting them to discuss their own experiences as the "new kid" in a situation. Encourage students to think out loud to develop ideas about the problems of adjusting to a new environment.

faced in adjusting to American life, as well as the funniest things that had happened to them since they arrived. They might then decide to come up with a list of suggestions for easing the transitions of future new students. In a discussion, each participant is free to speak at length on a particular topic, and everyone is invited to react to what is being said. "Thinking out loud" about your ideas and hearing other people's ideas can help you figure out what you really think, what ideas you really care about, and how much you have to say on a particular topic.

Other Techniques Many graphic devices, which are used primarily as aids in developing a topic, can also help you when you are searching for writing ideas or need to break a large subject down into a smaller, more manageable topic. You'll find many examples of graphic aids and suggestions for using them in Writing Handbook 9, pages 357–360.

Practice Your Skills

A. Choosing a subject from the list below, or one of your own, use recalling, listing, gleaning, or freewriting in your journal to generate writing ideas.

photographs	hunger	red
marathons	winter	success
plastic	steam	stars

B. Form a small group with some classmates and brainstorm ideas about the topics listed in Exercise A. Afterward, have a class discussion in which you compare the results of your individual freewriting and group brainstorming. Which resulted in more creative, usable ideas for writing?

C. Using any number of the subjects on the following list, combined in any way you like, write five "what if" questions and the answers in your journal. See how creative you can be. Can you come up with an invention? A story idea? An idea for a party? A new solution to an old problem?

lamp	zebra	mail carrier
Alaska	mask	ancient Rome
rock musician	eclipse	tangerine
eraser	tree	saxophone
February	green	paper
highway	onion	truckdriver

Collaborative Opportunity

You might have students complete Exercise C cooperatively. Working in pairs, students can write five "what if" questions each, then have their partners propose answers to the questions. This will help expand the imaginative possibilities of the exercise.

Additional Resources
- Writing Resource Book, pp. 3–4
- Thinking Skills Transparencies: Cluster Diagram
- Fine Art Transparencies

Social Studies Connection

CNN Television's "Crossfire," PBS's "Frontline," and ABC's "Nightline" are often conducted in a discussion format. Encourage students to watch these shows to see how articulate discussion can effectively raise and clarify ideas. Provide students with an opportunity to report on the most effective speakers and their standpoints.

Math Connection

Point out to students that information in graph or table form is often interesting enough to spark a writing idea. Have students look at tables or graphs in newspapers or almanacs you have provided or in their math textbooks. They can then suggest ideas for writing based on the graphic information.

Discuss the difference between ideograms and phonetic spellings. Ideograms for two similar sounding words would probably not look at all alike. Unlike early Chinese, written English came into being as a phonetic system for recording oral language. However, even our own language is no longer truly phonetic.

Students may have wondered why common spellings, such as *ough,* have several pronunciations, as in *rough, bough, thought, though,* and *through.* Discuss this with students, eliciting other examples, and explain that English spelling is only about 60% phonetic. Show students samples of Chaucer's Middle English and Shakespearean English to illustrate how much the language changed within two hundred years. Explain that although our spoken language has continued to change, many word spellings were standardized by the advent of the printing press in the mid-1400's.

Tell students that the International Phonetic Alphabet contains symbols for every sound used in human speech and is used by scientists and linguists to record speech exactly as it is spoken. You may wish to invite a linguist to further address this interesting topic with your class.

On the Lightside

PEKING OR BEIJING

In the past decade Peking, the capital of China, has disappeared. So have Canton, Tibet, and Inner Mongolia. In their places are Beijing, Guangzhou, Xizang, and Nei Mongol.

China has not changed, but the system for translating the Chinese language has. Since Chinese does

not use the same alphabet as English, translation is a complex process. Unlike English, which is written using the 26-character Roman alphabet, Chinese is written in pictorial symbols called ideograms. The Chinese people must learn about 6,000 ideograms to be able to communicate effectively, and there are a total of about 45,000. Translating Chinese involves spelling words so that they sound like their Chinese pronunciation.

For more than a century a process called the Wade-Giles system was the most widely used means of transcribing Chinese. *Peking, Mao Tse-Tung,* and *Chou En-Lai* are the products of the Wade-Giles system. In 1979, however, the Chinese government adopted a new system. It is called Pinyin, which is Chinese for "phonetic spelling," and it uses Roman letters in a different manner. So Peking has become Beijing, Mao Tse-Tung is Mao Zedong, and Chou En-Lai is Zhou Enlai.

The Pinyin system is simpler than Wade-Giles, but its adoption has caused many adjustments in the West. Mapmakers in particular have been confronted with a country in which all the familiar places have been wiped off the face of the map.

326

How to Limit a Topic

An important decision to make when you are prewriting is whether to limit your topic, and if so, how much. One factor to consider in making your decision is any length requirements you've been given. For example, if you are writing a three-page paper, you can't cover a topic as broad as the history of music. You need to limit your topic to something you can cover well in three pages, such as musical notation. Another factor to consider is how much detail you need or want to include. For example, if you want to persuade your readers that popular music today is better than when your parents were in school, you need to include details to prove your point. One way would be to limit your topic to a comparison of the two types of lyrics.

Some techniques that can help you limit a topic are asking questions, using graphic devices, and brainstorming.

ASKING QUESTIONS

You can limit a broad topic by asking questions beginning with *who, what, where, when, why,* and *how.* Suppose your assignment is to write a report on the solar system. Here are some questions you might ask yourself to limit that topic:

1. Who discovered the planets?
2. What is the solar system made up of?
3. Where do astronomers do their work?
4. When did people first explore the solar system?
5. Why do some planets have moons?
6. How has our view of the solar system changed over the years?

Using the fifth question as a starting point, you might decide to write a paper describing the moons of Neptune.

Writing
TIP

Don't stop after writing a few questions. List as many questions as you can to discover the best way to approach a topic.

16th Century Astrologer looking through his telescope at the sky. 19th century woodcut

How to Limit a Topic **327**

Writing Handbook 3:
How to Limit a Topic

Objectives

1. To learn how to limit a topic to accommodate length restrictions
2. To apply strategies such as questioning, brainstorming, and graphic devices to limit a topic.

Handbook Mini-Lessons
For information on topics related to limiting a topic, see the following mini-lesson.
• Finding Ideas, pp. 317–325

Teaching Strategies

Individualizing Instruction

Learning Styles Students will be drawn to particular techniques for limiting a topic depending on their primary learning styles. During any practice exercises you may plan, consider grouping auditory learners in brainstorming cells while providing visual learners with opportunities to work on graphic devices.

WRITING HANDBOOK 3

Just as you can use graphic devices to find ideas, you can also use them to limit your topic. Two of the graphic devices discussed in Writing Handbook 9—clustering and idea trees—are particularly useful in limiting your topic. (See pages 357–358.) Both clusters and tree diagrams help you see what you already know and generate related ideas that can serve as a topic.

In clustering you begin by writing the name of a general topic—the "nucleus" word—on a piece of paper and circling it. Then, outside the circle, write any word or idea that you associate with the nucleus word. Put each new idea in its own circle, and connect it with a line to the nucleus word or to any other word you have written. Branch out spontaneously from the new ideas in the same way, using lines to show relationships between words.

For example, a student needed to write a five-page report about music. He thought his writing would mean more to a reader if he included details such as the names of singers and musicians, song titles, and lyrics. Study the word cluster he made to limit his topic.

Notice that the student eventually identified three major ideas associated with music: "classical," "singers," and "changes since 1960's." After completing the cluster, the student examined the ideas branching off from each of those main ideas to determine which offered the kind of details he wanted to include. He finally decided to write his paper on changes in music since the 1960's.

Tree diagrams work very much like clustering. Begin by writing a central idea, such as "medicine." Then write related ideas branching from it, connected by lines. These might be: "hospital," "pharmacy," and "doctor's office." Next narrow your main ideas further, until you find an appropriate, and interesting, report topic. For example, the main idea "doctor's office" might lead to the more limited topic "the waiting room."

BRAINSTORMING

Another way to narrow a topic is by brainstorming. When you brainstorm to limit a topic, work with a small group of your peers to think about ideas related to the topic and share any ideas you think of without stopping to judge their quality.

Suppose you and a friend were brainstorming on the topic "sports." You might come up with the following ideas: record-holders, Babe Ruth, amateur sports, unusual sports, women in sports, early American games. From these ideas you might decide to write about women in sports. To narrow your focus, you could visit the library and look for information on this topic. There you might learn about Althea Gibson, a tennis champion who paved the way for black women in tennis. You could then write a paper about Althea Gibson and her greatest accomplishments.

WRITER TO WRITER

Brainstorming among a number of people has been the root of any success I've had in writing.

**Jason Boettcher, student
Seattle, Washington**

Practice Your Skills

Choose one of the topics below or one of your own. Use questioning, clustering, a tree diagram, or brainstorming to limit your topic and narrow the focus.

teenagers	art	government
festivals or holidays	India	music
outdoor adventures	insects	humor

How Do I Plan and Organize My Writing?

Objectives

1. To identify types of organization: main ideas and supporting details; chronological order; spatial order; order of importance, degree, or quality; cause and effect order; classification; comparison/contrast; part-to-part organization
2. To rewrite a paragraph to improve its organization

Handbook Mini-Lessons

For information on topics related to planning and organizing writing, see the following mini-lessons.
- Writing Thesis Statements and Topic Sentences, pp. 343–344
- Revising for Form, p. 376

Teaching Strategies

Motivating

Discuss the sometimes humorous but often frustrating replies students have received when asking directions to an unfamiliar destination. Have students list the shortcomings of those instructions: important details omitted, irrelevant details included, directions given out of order, and so forth. Explain that writing, like oral directions, is only as effective as its organizational strategy—the subject of this lesson.

WRITING
HANDBOOK
4

How Do I Plan and Organize My Writing?

After you have chosen a topic and gathered some ideas, you need to organize your thinking and plan your writing. This will help both you and your reader understand what you want to say. Planning your approach and organizing ideas is like packing for a trip. To do it well, you must know something about where you are going. First you lay out everything you think you will take. After more thought, you might decide to leave some things out or add others.

The way you plan and organize your writing will be determined by the material you're writing about, just as the way you pack for a trip is determined by your destination. For example, if you are writing a report on a subject you know only a little about, you must do a good deal of planning and research before you begin to write. On the other hand, if you are suddenly inspired to write a story, you might begin writing immediately and carefully revise your first draft later.

W R I T E R   T O   W R I T E R

Human life itself may be almost pure chaos, but the work of the artist . . . is to take these handfuls of confusion . . . and put them together in a frame to give them some kind of shape and meaning.

Katherine Anne Porter, short story writer and novelist

Organizing your writing is like asking, "Where do I want to go, and how do I get there from here?" Writers, like travelers, can ask themselves this question at any stage in their process, but they usually have some idea of their goal at the beginning. Some writers like to organize their ideas before they begin writing. They often use outlines to plan their work. Other writers like to get their ideas down on paper first, and work out the organization as their writing develops. Many writers use a combination of these techniques. (For more information on outlines, see the Appendix, pages 816–817, and Guided Assignment 9, "The Short Research Paper," pages 265–286.)

Springboard

You might introduce the concept of order in writing by encouraging students to discuss the following quote: "Good order is the foundation of all things." (Edmund Burke, *Reflections on the Revolution in France*, 1790) Have students then discuss what order has to do with good writing. What happens when writing seems random?

TYPES OF ORGANIZATION

Main Idea/Supporting Details   One way of organizing your ideas is to sort them according to whether they are the big ideas—the principal messages you want to convey—or smaller details that support and illustrate those ideas.

Suppose you have brainstormed ideas for a short piece about soccer, your favorite sport. You noticed that many of your ideas are about improving your skills, so this becomes the main idea. In your notes, you cross out phrases about equipment, rules, and other ideas not related to skills and circle the notes that do apply.

Chronological Order   Writers often present events in chronological order, or the order in which they occur. This organization is especially useful in telling a story or explaining a process.

One way of organizing ideas chronologically is to make a time line—a list of events arranged in the order in which they happened. For example, you could use the time line below to develop a paragraph about the invention of the bicycle.

Comte Mede de Sivrac (France) 2-wheeled scooterlike vehicle	Baron Karl von Drais (Germany) steering bar	Kirkpatrick Macmillan (Scotland) foot pedals	Pierre and Ernest Michaux (France) front wheel, two cranks	Pierre Lallement and James Carroll (U.S.) first U.S. patent	Archibald Sharp (Britain) spoke tension wheel	J.K. Starley (Britain) chain transmission, equal wheels	John Dunlop (Scotland) pnuematic tire
1790	1816	1839	1861	1866	1876	1885	1888

When using chronological order, remember to signal changes in time by using transitional words and phrases. Notice how the writer of the following passage uses transitions.

LITERARY MODEL

Soon the biggest of the boys poised himself, shot down into the water, and did not come up. . . . **After a long time,** the boy came up on the other side of a big dark rock, letting the air out of his lungs in a sputtering gasp and a shout of triumph. **Immediately** the rest of them dived in. **One moment,** the morning seemed full of chattering boys; **the next,** the air and surface of the water were empty.

Doris Lessing, "The Tunnel"

Writing TIP

Try using graphic devices to organize a main idea and its supporting details.

Teaching Tip: Main Idea/ Supporting Details

Copy each sentence of a paragraph in random order on the chalkboard. Add irrelevant sentences. Ask volunteers to cross out sentences that do not belong and number those remaining in the order in which they should appear, beginning with the main idea. Discuss with students how they distinguished relevant from irrelevant information, main idea from supporting details.

Teaching Tip: Chronological Order

On individual index cards, type or print each sentence of the instructions for making or assembling an object. Have students examine the transitional words and phrases that signal time in order to reconstruct the directions in their chronological order.

Visual Learners The terms for the various kinds of organizational order may be more meaningful and more easily remembered if students are encouraged to design a symbol representing each name. For example, a horizontal arrow might represent spatial order; a vertical arrow, order of importance. Two-headed arrows might remind students that their order may be from right to left or left to right, least to most or most to least important. These symbols, placed beside their notes during prewriting, can be a constant reminder to follow that order and direction during writing.

Teaching Tip: Order of Importance

Demonstrate the humor of sentences violating the principle of order of importance, such as "He was an excellent writer who wrote twenty outstanding novels, used a ballpoint pen, won a Nobel Prize for Literature, and used correct punctuation."

Writing —TIP—

Familiar forms of spatial organization include top to bottom, left to right, near to far, back to front, and inside to outside.

Spatial Order Visual details are often easiest to understand when they are described in spatial order, or according to their position in space. Suppose you want to explain how video cassettes are organized at a local store. The most natural way would be to proceed from section to section, starting at one end of the store and ending at the far end.

The simplest spatial-order descriptions are written from a single physical point of view, or **vantage point.** If you are describing a street, for instance, pretend you are standing at a particular spot on that street and describe what you can see from there. If you decide to move down the street at some point—perhaps in order to describe what's around the corner—make sure to alert your reader to the change by using transitions.

In the following passage, Jack London uses spatial order to organize his description of a complex landscape. He uses the transitions *on one side, beyond the pool,* and *below* as if giving directions to a hiker.

> **On one side,** beginning at the very lip of the pool, was a tiny meadow, a cool, resilient surface of green that extended to the base of the frowning wall. **Beyond the pool** a gentle slope of earth ran up and up to meet the opposing wall. Fine grass covered the slope—grass that was spangled with flowers, with here and there patches of color, orange and purple, and golden. **Below,** the canyon was shut in. . . . The walls leaned together abruptly and the canyon ended in a chaos of rocks, moss-covered and hidden by a green screen of vines.
>
> **Jack London, "All Gold Canyon"**

Order of Importance, Degree, or Quality Sometimes, especially in persuasive or informative writing, you may want to order details based on their importance, usefulness, familiarity, or some other quality. This order can be from most to least or from least to most of the quality. For example, to present information quickly for hurried readers, most news stories are written with the most important facts in the first paragraph and the least important facts at the end. On the other hand, if you were writing a letter to the newspaper editor urging people to fight pollution, you might build your argument from the least to the most important points to arouse emotions.

332 Writing Handbook

Springboard

Have fun reviewing the material by supplying a phrase, sentence, title, lyric, or line of poetry as a clue to an organizational pattern. Ask volunteers to solve the riddle. ("Like a Rolling Stone"—comparison/contrast; "Time After Time"—chronological order; "laughing on the inside, crying on the outside"—spatial order)

Notice how, in the next paragraph, the writer begins with a little-known detail about the brain and ends with a fact almost everyone has experienced—that thinking can be hard work.

▼

> The more than 100,000 chemical reactions that occur in the brain each second require huge amounts of the body's stored energy. In fact, the brain can burn as many calories in intense concentration as the muscles do during exercise. That's why thinking can feel as exhausting as a physical workout.
>
> **Mark McCutcheon, _The Compass in Your Nose_**

Cause-and-Effect Order When you hear a good joke, you laugh. This is a familiar cause-and-effect relationship. One event (the cause) brings about another (the effect). At times, you may want to describe a chain of causes and effects in order to show clearly how they are connected. In the following paragraph, a writer explains the chain of events that produced much of the art we see today in public buildings.

▼

> **cause**
> **effect**
>
> **cause**
>
> **effect**
>
> In the 1930's disaster struck the United States. A great depression swept across the country, bringing massive unemployment in its wake. . . . The black art movement might have floundered completely but for the Federal Works Project. The government provided financial aid to both black and white artists. Commissions to paint murals—pictures which are painted directly on a wall or ceiling—were given to black artists. Colorful murals began appearing on the walls of government buildings, schools, hospitals, and libraries all over America.
>
> **Marcella Thum, _Exploring Black America_**

Causal organization can help you explain things like how machines work or why the continents move. You can also use it in fiction. For example, you might explain why a character fears enclosed places by describing how she got lost in a cave as a child. Transitions such as _therefore, as a result,_ and _consequently_ can help you signal the causes and effects you are describing.

Teaching Tip: Cause and Effect

To demonstrate the relationship between cause and effect, state a cause beginning with the word _because_ ("Because inflation has eroded the value of the dollar . . . ") and have volunteers supply an effect ("its purchasing power declines each year"). Reverse the procedure, stating an effect ending with _because_ and having volunteers supply one or more causes: ("Baseball is our national pastime because . . . many people like to watch it; it is a simple game to understand; it has been played in the United States for a century and a half").

Social Studies Connection

Historical Papers Ask students to analyze a short but powerful historical speech or document such as "The Gettysburg Address." Is it organized by one or more than one type of order? Have students quote portions that illustrate their reasoning.

Challenge students to list other comparison words that signal classification (Possibilities include: *both, all, a majority, a percentage.*)

Classification   A common way to organize ideas is to classify, or group them, on the basis of size, color, value, or some other characteristic. The following writer classified music according to styles.

S T U D E N T
M O D E L

> Recently I've been listening to jazz, which, according to my father, is America's outstanding contribution to the art of music. I enjoy ragtime, a piano style with an almost mechanical sound; the blues, especially the funky voices of Bessie Smith and Blind Lemon Jefferson; and the high-intensity sound of hard-bop groups like those led by Sonny Rollins and Horace Silver.

Some useful comparisons to signal classification are *some, one kind, another, a third group,* and *others.*

Comparison/Contrast   When you want to discuss the characteristics of two or more subjects, you may want to organize the details in a comparison/contrast framework. There are two basic ways to do this—by subject or by quality. You can treat each subject separately, discussing all of its qualities, or treat each quality individually, discussing how it compares in each subject. See how Maya Angelou uses a subject organization to compare graduating girls and boys.

L I T E R A R Y
M O D E L

> The girls often held hands and no longer bothered to speak to the lower students. There was a sadness about them, as if this old world was not their home and they were bound for higher ground. The boys, on the other hand, had become more friendly, more outgoing. A decided change from the closed attitude they projected while studying for finals. Now they seemed not ready to give up the old school, the familiar paths and classrooms.
>
> **Maya Angelou, *I Know Why the Caged Bird Sings***

Transitions such as *one, the other, on one hand, on the other hand, however, in contrast, similarly,* and *likewise* will alert your reader to a comparison/contrast organization.

Part-to-Part Organization   For some pieces of writing you will not want to use a general organizing principle. Instead, you can connect each idea logically to the one that follows it. Notice how part-to-part organization works in the following paragraph.

Springboard

Inform students that from now on there will be "order in the school." Divide the class into eight groups and assign one type of organization to each group. Students are to find and copy examples of their order from text and reference books used in connection with their various classes. Have each group share their findings with the class.

For centuries, the Chinese had taught that it was uncouth and barbaric to serve a large carcass that in any way resembled the original animal. In addition, it was considered impolite to expect a dinner guest to struggle through a dissection that could have been done before-hand, in the kitchen, out of sight. . . . That belief dictated food size, which in turn suggested a kind of eating utensil. Chopsticks—of wood, bone, and ivory— were perfectly suited to conveying the precut morsels to the mouth, and the Chinese word for the implements, *kwai-tse,* means "quick ones." Our term "chopsticks" is the English phonetic version of *kwai-tse.*

Charles Panati, *Extraordinary Origins of Everyday Things*

Practice Your Skills

A. Read each group of details and identify the method that should be used to organize them in paragraph form.

1. Dogs need: food, shelter, companionship, exercise, and training
   Cats need: food, shelter, less companionship, can live outdoors, need no training
2. write paragraph   gather ideas to develop topic
   write topic sentence   choose and limit topic
3. students are often too tired to do their homework
   high school kids want spending money
   their grades often drop
   they get jobs after school
4. dimly lit lobby   busy downtown street
   crowded dance floor   brightly painted entrance

B. Rewrite the paragraph below so that it is well organized. Choose any method of organization you feel is appropriate and indicate the method you used.

> In today's fast-moving economy, people often change jobs a dozen or more times in their lives. Years ago communities were closer-knit and more stable than they are today. Freedom to move makes people's lives exciting and interesting. Only a generation or two ago, people usually remained in the same community throughout their lives. Families today move from place to place more readily than they once did. The stable communities of the past offered people security and a closeness with neighbors that are rare in today's society.

Managing the Paper Load

You need not attempt to collect, correct, and record each Practice Your Skills paper. Instead, circulate around the room as students are working, spot checking and helping with problem areas as needed. Volunteers can give the answers to Exercise A while students correct their own papers. Exercise B should provoke a lively discussion as students read and discuss their responses. Be sure students understand that more than one method of organization is acceptable.

ANSWERS TO PRACTICE YOUR SKILLS

A. 1. Comparison/Contrast Order
   2. Chronological Order
   3. Cause and Effect Order
   4. Spatial Order
B. Methods of organization may vary. The following rewritten paragraph combines comparison/contrast and cause and effect orders.

Years ago communities were closer-knit and more stable than they are today. Only a generation or two ago, people usually remained in the same community throughout their lives. Today, because of our fast-moving economy, people often change jobs a dozen or more times during their lives. As a result, families move from place to place more readily than they once did. Although freedom to move makes people's lives exciting and interesting, it is not without its price. The stable communities of the past offered people security and a closeness with neighbors that are rare in today's society.

Additional Resources
• Writing Resource Book, pp. 7–8

Art Connection

Art Styles Ask students to research and describe two styles of art. Allow them to choose the type of organization or organizations they consider most appropriate for the information they want to include in their writing.

Drafting as Experimentation and Discovery

Objectives

1. To recognize drafting as a process of exploration that can lead to new questions, ideas, and personal insights
2. To understand the benefits and uses of adventuresome drafting and careful drafting
3. To relate drafting to revision

Handbook Mini-Lessons

For information on topics related to drafting as experimentation and discovery, see the following mini-lessons.

- How Do I Begin a Draft? pp. 340–344
- Drafting Paragraphs, pp. 345–350
- Using Graphic Devices, pp. 357–360
- Point of View, pp. 430–433

Teaching Strategies

Motivating

Ask your class to think of other activities besides writing which make use of some kind of drafting process to experiment before a final product is completed (for example, *drawing, painting, architecture, computer programming, choreography, composing*). Encourage students who may have talent in artistic or musical areas to see that drafting is a process with which they are already familiar.

Drafting as Experimentation and Discovery

Ray Bradbury, the author of hundreds of science fiction and fantasy stories, once said, "Creativity is continual surprise." Because intuition and discovery in writing are important to Bradbury, he does not work from an outline or plan. Instead he writes spontaneously, experimenting with ideas and watching his stories take shape as he types draft after draft.

You are probably asking yourself, "But who wants to write a draft and then revise it? That means writing at least twice, which is at least twice as much work." Writing a draft and revising it later, however, can be both easier and more satisfying than trying to get everything right the first time. Drafting makes the act of writing a part of the learning process, not just a way of expressing what you already know.

Drafting has other advantages as well. When you write a draft, you don't have to worry about proper punctuation, capitalization, and spelling. You don't have to worry about all the rules of writing that appear in textbooks. Instead you can just play with an idea to see where it leads. Once you learn to approach drafting as play—as experimenting with ideas to see where they take you—you'll understand why many writers enjoy this phase of the writing process.

DRAFTING AS DISCOVERY

If you start drafting by just thinking aloud on paper, coming up with ideas and seeing where they lead, you may be surprised at what happens. To write means to experiment with and discover your own thoughts and feelings.

> ### WRITER TO WRITER
>
> I don't really know what I'm going to say. In the end it's a process of discovery, rather than of putting something in that I know beforehand.
>
> **Saul Bellow, novelist**

Eve,
by B.M. Jackson, 1967
The Vietnam War
touched many
people's lives.

For example, suppose that you have an idea for a short story. As part of the prewriting process, you imagine a couple of characters. Maybe one of the characters is a man who used to be a pilot in the Vietnam War. Today he earns his living as a crop-duster for farms in the Midwest. Perhaps the other character is the man's teen-age son, who is scared to death of flying. You want to tell the story of their relationship. To see whether this idea works, you decide to write a draft.

Start by imagining your characters in a specific situation—maybe having breakfast together.

Clay looked at his father sitting across from him at the kitchen table. He seemed to have aged ten years in the past few months. Clay's mom silently fixed breakfast as his father suddenly began talking.

"Did I ever tell you the story of that last mission?" Clay shook his head, knowing that nothing would stop his dad from repeating the story for the hundredth time.

"Those were the days of real challenge and real courage," Clay's father continued. "Not like today."

STUDENT
M O D E L

Drafting as
Experimentation   **337**

Drafting as Experimentation   **337**

Teaching Tip: Setting

Have a student read the draft passage aloud. Ask, "How does the author let you know Clay and his father are now in the plane?" *(Clay's father gazes out the window of the cockpit).* Make sure students understand that at this stage of drafting, an abrupt change in setting is acceptable. In a final draft the author will have to clarify such transitions.

Critical Thinking

Interpreting Have students provide possible answers to the rhetorical questions about the characters. Explain that the purpose of drafting is to explore possible ideas as answers and that there are no right or wrong answers.

Speaking and Listening

You might want to develop the plot of the story by having your students try round-robin storytelling. In this technique, a group of five to ten students comes up to the front of the class. Each student takes a brief turn telling a part of the story until it comes to a natural conclusion.

While you are writing these first few sentences, you begin to realize that your story is going to be about Clay and his father's different definitions of courage and Clay's coming of age. You begin to sense that the setting—breakfast time in the family's kitchen—is not the best setting for a story about courage. You decide not to interrupt your writing "flow" to rewrite the opening sentences. Instead you continue drafting with the characters in a new setting—a private plane in flight.

> "This is the only place where things seem real to me," Clay's father told him, gazing out the cockpit window at the miniature world below.
> "Dad, I want to turn around. We were supposed to have been back an hour ago. Mom's going to be worried."
> "Sure it's your mother who's worried?" he asked, with an insinuating smile.
> Clay didn't answer, didn't say a word. In the silence, the father and son heard something that they knew meant trouble . . . .

By putting your characters in a more dangerous setting, you have provided an opportunity for the two men to *show*—not just *tell*—how they are or are not courageous. Will the plane develop engine trouble? Will the father, the son, or both show courage or fear? How? Will the father and son come to understand and appreciate each other? These and many other intriguing questions will be answered as you follow your ideas wherever they lead you. Later, as you revise, you can remove the references to the kitchen in the opening sentences and add references to the plane to establish the setting.

One of the most exciting moments in writing is when you discover what you really think and understand for the first time how your ideas fit together. This kind of discovery is one of the rewards of drafting.

Kinds of Drafting

There are two basic kinds of drafting—adventuresome drafting and careful drafting. We've already seen an example of the adventuresome draft, in which you write without an elaborate plan, trying out ideas and exploring them to see where they lead.

338   Writing Handbook

Literature Connection

Bring in photocopies of first drafts by writers with whom your students are familiar, such as Steinbeck or Dickens. Examples of first drafts can often be found as illustrations in biographies of authors. Have students examine the changes the authors made and discuss the reasons for the changes.

Social Studies Connection

Ask students what kinds of missions a pilot like Clay's father might have flown during the Vietnam War. Encourage them to speculate why he might need to repeat his story so many times.

You might, however, use a more careful kind of drafting. For example, suppose you are writing a report about the growth of industry in the United States between 1860 and 1900. You probably would begin by doing research and then develop a detailed writing plan or outline that might include the following four main points: the beginning of the factory system; the inventions that made the Industrial Revolution possible; the movement of working people from farms to cities; and the way all of these things changed life in America.

As you work out the writing plan for a careful draft and actually begin writing, you try to establish the connections among your four main points. You see at once how some of them fit together, but you must consciously build connections among others. To do this, ask yourself questions like these: What is the relationship between these ideas? What details will help me move from this idea to that one? How can I shape the writing so that I will be able to connect one point to another?

For example, you might want to show that the movement of people from farms to cities changed life in America by reducing the number of family farms. This process of linking ideas is sometimes called **bridge building.** It is an especially important part of writing a careful draft.

Drafting and Revision

Because drafting is a process of discovering and exploring ideas on paper, it usually involves a certain amount of rethinking. For this reason, drafting and revision often occur simultaneously. In fact, some people revise and reshape their writing extensively during the drafting process. Nevertheless, it is important to keep the purpose of drafting in mind and not get bogged down fixing details. Remember, the goal of drafting is to get your ideas down on paper by letting your words flow freely. You can revise your writing in a second draft. In fact, revision can be seen as the process of writing a series of drafts, each more complete, careful, and refined than the one before.

Although drafts are usually imperfect, they often contain interesting and useful ideas expressed in a fresh, lively way. Like many professional writers, you may want to save your earlier drafts to review during the final stages of revising a piece of writing. You may find that some of your best phrases or passages emerged when you were writing freely, and you may want to use them in the final version of your work.

Writing
—**TIP**—

To help you determine connections among ideas, you may want to draw a diagram or other graphic representation.

Drafting as
Experimentation   **339**

Learning Styles Auditory learners may prefer drafting by dictating their ideas into a tape recorder. Visual learners will probably appreciate using particular graphic devices to organize their ideas.

Linking Grammar and Writing

Make clear that writers can choose whether or not to correct errors in grammar, spelling, and mechanics during the drafting stage. While some writers feel compelled to correct any mistake they see, others prefer to let their thoughts flow freely by deferring correction until the proofreading stage.

Computer Tip

Point out that some writers keep separate "discard" files of passages they have cut from their work, but which they consider worth saving for possible use elsewhere. Another way of saving deleted passages on a computer disk is to put them in a different font or within brackets.

Additional Resources
- Writing Resource Book, pp. 9–10

Springboard

Create an Idea Chart like this on the board:

Characters   *Setting*   *Problem*
Clay, father   Plane   engine trouble

Call on students to suggest as many story ideas as they can think of from these three elements. Next ask students to choose their own characters, setting, and problem and to freewrite as a springboard

to drafting. Finally, ask students to use their freewriting ideas to write a paragraph of a possible story. Encourage interested students to complete their stories.

How Do I Begin a Draft?

Objectives

1. To recognize and apply various techniques for beginning a draft
2. To identify thesis statements and topic sentences as helpful ways to present main ideas in expository writing

Handbook Mini-Lessons

For information on topics related to beginning a draft, see the following mini-lessons.

- How Do I Find Ideas?
  pp. 317–325
- How Do I Plan and Organize My Writing? pp. 330–335
- Drafting Paragraphs, pp. 345–350

Teaching Strategies

Motivating

Choose several topics of current concern to your students, including social, school, or community issues, or current events. Write the topics on the board. Ask students to freewrite for five minutes on the topic of their choice. Tell them not to worry about starting at the beginning. After five minutes, ask students to look over their writing to see if anything they have written might make an effective beginning for a paper. Have students share their ideas with the class.

WRITING
HANDBOOK
6

How Do I Begin a Draft?

Some writers find that the most difficult part of the drafting process is getting started. Many end up staring at a blank sheet of paper, frustrated by the difficulty of getting those first few ideas down. That doesn't have to be the case, though, because you can begin anywhere in your draft and in any way that's comfortable. Once you are ready to draft the beginning of your piece, you can write either your introduction or a thesis statement or topic sentences.

GETTING STARTED

The introductory paragraph of a paper can be a very difficult place to start writing. You might find it easier to begin with another part of your composition. Here are some guidelines for starting at a point other than the introduction.

Guidelines for Starting in the Middle

- Develop the best ideas you have gathered from your prewriting and sharing techniques.
- Look at what you've written and start to play with the ideas. Reorganize, move ideas around, delete unnecessary ideas, and strengthen weak sections by adding details.
- Think about where the ideas you have written might lead. Also think about how you might lead into, or introduce, what you have already written.

The "starting-in-the-middle" technique can work for any kind of writing—expressive and imaginative, as well as expository. For example, imagine that you want to write a mystery story. You have a key scene in mind, and you know who your characters will be. The trouble is, you don't know how you want to begin your story, and you're not sure how to conclude it. You can begin writing with your key scene. Once you have that on paper, you can more easily go back and write an introduction telling who your characters are and how the plot begins. You may even think of new angles and plot twists after beginning in the middle.

Writing the Introduction

At some point, however, you will have to draft the actual beginning of your piece—the introduction. An introduction usually serves two purposes:

- to catch the reader's attention
- to suggest or state the main idea

If the piece of writing is a single paragraph, the introduction may be only one or two sentences long. If the piece is a longer composition or report, the introduction may be a paragraph or more in length.

A strong opening is crucial if you are to catch your readers' attention. The first several sentences are especially important. You can experiment with the following techniques.

Startling or Interesting Facts An unusual fact can disturb, surprise, or inform your readers or make them curious. Notice how the writer uses the words *alarming evidence* to introduce the fact that more than half the adults in the survey do not exercise enough.

> Alarming evidence about the state of fitness—or lack of it—in the United States continues to mount. A Centers for Disease Control survey of more than 25,000 adults revealed that 55 percent *do not* exercise three times a week for 20 minutes at a time, the minimum amount needed to provide health benefits.
>
> ***Runner's World***

Vivid, Detailed Description A graphic, mysterious, or sensory description of a person or place can capture the reader's imagination. Here, the author presents a vivid description of events and only at the end tells the reader when they took place.

> Everywhere, over the entire earth, volcanoes spewed gases into the sky. As heat and gas rose into the atmosphere, massive clouds formed, blotting out the stars. From one end of the globe to the other, lightning storms cracked and flashed. This is what the earth was like four and a half billion years ago.

Writing
—TIP—

Use your opening paragraph to engage your readers' attention. It can also introduce your topic or story idea.

PROFESSIONAL
M O D E L

STUDENT
M O D E L

Teaching Tip: Setting a Purpose

Reassure students that they do not have to memorize the labeled techniques. The point is for students to learn how to get started at writing, and the labeled techniques are helpful tools. The key thing for them to remember is to "play with the ideas," counteracting their inhibitions and loosening up the flow of writing.

Music Connection

You might bring in records or tapes with famous musical introductions, such as the opening movement of Beethoven's Fifth Symphony or a currently popular song with an identifiable introduction. Discuss how any good introduction grabs your attention and makes the listener or reader want to continue.

Individualizing Instruction

Advanced Students The Bulwer-Lytton Contest, an annual competition sponsored by San Jose State University, challenges entrants to compose the "worst" possible opening sentence to a novel. (The contest pokes fun at Edward Bulwer-Lytton who opened his 1830 novel *Paul Clifford* with the cliche, "It was a dark and stormy night.") The results of this contest are published in Penguin Paperbacks, *It Was a Dark and Stormy Night* and *Son of It Was a Dark and Stormy Night*, edited by Scott Rice. You may want to pick out some examples of "winning" sentences and encourage advanced students to enter the contest.

Teaching Tip: Resources

Discuss with students where they might find materials for their introductions. For example, they might look for quotations in *Bartlett's Quotations;* they can find statistics in reference books such as *Statistical Abstracts,* as well as many newspaper and magazine articles; and they can get anecdotes, descriptions and facts from books, magazines, and newspapers.

PROFESSIONAL
M O D E L

PROFESSIONAL
M O D E L

PROFESSIONAL
M O D E L

Questions A question can get your reader thinking and wanting to read on to find the answer. Notice how this question gets the reader interested in discovering more about the earth's *"cousin"*.

▼

Does earth have a giant cousin in space? A team from the Smithsonian Astrophysical Observatory has reported . . . a planet ten times more massive than Jupiter . . . about 90 light-years from earth. **National Geographic**

Incidents or Anecdotes A bit of retelling—of a story or one interesting event—adds human interest that can draw a reader into a piece. The conflict between neighbors told here would cause most readers to want more of the story.

▼

A man in Cambridge, Massachusetts, took his neighbor to court because the neighbor hadn't cut his grass in fourteen years. **Andrew A. Rooney**

Quotations A quotation can personalize and add interest to a piece of writing. The quotation chosen by this writer brings something inanimate to life.

▼

"A flute," wrote an early nineteenth-century British critic, "is a musical weed which springs up everywhere." **Nancy Toff**

Springboard

Ask students to compose a thesis statement for this lesson. (A possible thesis statement might be something like this one: *You can begin anywhere in your draft and you can introduce your subject in many different, effective ways*).

Writing Thesis Statements and Topic Sentences

Any of the techniques for introductions described on the preceding two pages can be effectively used to open a piece of nonfiction writing. Remember, however, that in much of the nonfiction writing you do, your introduction should not only capture your readers' attention but also reveal the main idea of the rest of the composition. You can express this main idea in a thesis statement that you include in your introductory paragraph or paragraphs. The main point of each of the paragraphs following your introduction may be expressed in a topic sentence.

> In writing, I always make an outline where I put the topic sentences for each paragraph and then I put ideas under them. It seems to work very well.
>
> **Tom Adams, student**
> **San Marcos, California**

Thesis Statement A **thesis statement** is one or two sentences that clearly express the main point or idea that will be developed in a composition. An effective thesis statement does more than tell what your paper is about, however. It may convey your point of view or perspective on your topic, and it may signal your paper's overall organization.

Imagine, for example, that you are writing an informative essay explaining the United States government's system of checks and balances. You might write the following thesis statement and include it in your introduction:

> How does the United States Constitution prevent any of the branches of government—executive, legislative, or judicial—from becoming too powerful? It provides for a system of checks and balances, allowing each branch to have some control over the other.

Topic Sentence In the same way that a thesis statement expresses the main idea of a composition, a **topic sentence** states the main idea of a single paragraph. All the other sentences in the paragraph support or elaborate this idea.

How Do I
Begin a Draft?   **343**

Collaborative Opportunity

Exercise B provides an excellent collaborative opportunity. Pairs or small groups of students may work together to choose topics and techniques. Each group may choose either to write an introduction collaboratively or to have each member write an introduction for a different topic. In the latter case, the members can exchange papers and respond to one another's work.

Managing the Paper Load

None of the exercises in this lesson need to be graded. Exercise A may remain completely private as a journal entry. Exercise B is suited for reading aloud and peer response. Exercise C requires discussion rather than writing.

Additional Resources
• Writing Resource Book, pp. 11–12

A topic sentence is often most effective at the beginning of a paragraph. Keep in mind, however, that it may appear later in the paragraph—even at the end, to summarize or reinforce the paragraph's main idea.

Imagine that on a home economics test you are asked to write a paragraph explaining why people should try cooking in a wok—a frying pan with a convex bottom, commonly used in China. You might begin your paragraph with a topic sentence such as the following:

> One of the quickest and most healthful ways to prepare food is to cook it in a wok.

All the other sentences in your paragraph could support this idea with specific facts, examples, and details about cooking food in a Chinese wok.

Practice Your Skills

A. Choose one of the topics listed below and gather some ideas about it. Then, starting anywhere, write one or two paragraphs for a piece on that topic.

• hurricanes	• television
• a musical instrument	• a famous athlete
• diets	• Africa
• pollution	• movie making
• maturity	• money

B. Choose a topic from those listed below and write one or two introductory paragraphs for a nonfiction essay on the topic. Use one of the techniques described in this handbook, and be sure to include a thesis statement.

• similarities and differences between two products
• your house—from a pet's perspective
• why recycling is everyone's responsibility
• how to pack for a long trip
• advantages and disadvantages of automatic teller machines

C. Look through a variety of magazines for articles with introductions that capture your attention. Bring a few of these articles to class and share them with a small group of your classmates. Identify the technique each writer uses to introduce his or her article and discuss whether it makes for an effective beginning. Also look for a thesis statement and any topic sentences the writer may have used.

Drafting Paragraphs

WHAT IS A PARAGRAPH?

A **paragraph** is a group of sentences that are related to one another and to a main idea. A paragraph may stand alone, as in a one-paragraph answer to a test question, or it may be part of a longer piece of writing.

All good paragraphs share three characteristics: **unity, coherence,** and **elaboration.** A paragraph is unified when all its sentences support the main idea. A paragraph is coherent when all its sentences are related to one another and flow logically from one to the next. A paragraph is well elaborated when its main idea is supported with details and information.

Read the following paragraph and find the sentence that doesn't relate to its main idea:

Paragraph Without Unity

In ancient Greek mythology, gods and goddesses sometimes used their powers to punish humans who exhibited qualities they found offensive. For example, the goddess Athena turned Arachne, a weaver, into a spider after Arachne boasted about her skill. Hercules himself could boast that he had the greatest powers of all the gods. Likewise, the gods punished Narcissus for being too vain; he became the flower that bears his name.

The sentence about Hercules disrupts the paragraph's unity. It does not relate to the main idea—which is expressed in the first sentence—so it should be deleted. Try reading the paragraph again, skipping the sentence about Hercules. The paragraph will seem more unified because both example sentences support the main idea.

The following paragraph contains a great deal of information about space exploration, but is it clear how it all fits together?

Paragraph Without Coherence

During the 1960's, America achieved great successes with its space program. In 1969, the *Apollo 11* mission landed the first Americans on the moon. The first American in space was Alan B. Shepard, who made a solo flight in May 1961. Shepard's achievement was followed by a round-the-world space flight by John Glenn. After *Sputnik*, the National Aeronautics and Space Administration, or NASA, was formed.

Drafting Paragraphs **345**

Drafting Paragraphs

Objectives

1. To recognize the importance of unity, coherence, and elaboration to a good paragraph
2. To identify the topic sentence as the one that states the main idea of the paragraph
3. To understand that paragraphs without topic sentences must still contain related ideas

Handbook Mini-Lessons

For information on topics related to drafting paragraphs, see the following mini-lessons.
- Elaboration: How Do I Develop Ideas? pp. 351–356
- Unity, Coherence, and Transitional Devices, pp. 361– 370

Critical Thinking

Analyzing The examples on the first two pages of this lesson explain problems with paragraphs and give students the tools to analyze their own writing. Ask students to analyze problems with unity, coherence, and elaboration in paragraphs from papers they have written.

Writing
TIP

Don't be too concerned about when to start a new paragraph in your first draft. Focus on paragraphing as you revise.

The paragraph lacks coherence because the information is not presented in an organized way, and the relationships among the ideas are not clear. Compare the following version, which has been revised to make it more coherent:

Revised, Coherent Paragraph

During the 1960's, America achieved great successes with its space program. When the Soviet Union launched its first satellite, *Sputnik*, in 1957, the United States met the challenge by forming the National Aeronautics and Space Administration, or NASA. NASA then embarked on a series of highly successful missions. In May 1961, NASA put the first American in space— Alan B. Shepard. Shepard's achievement was followed by a round-the-world space flight by John Glenn. Finally, in 1969 came the high point of America's space program: the *Apollo 11* mission landed the first Americans on the moon.

In the revised paragraph the relationship between *Sputnik* and NASA is made clear. So is the relationship between NASA and the U.S. space missions. In addition, the details about space missions appear in a logical order, the order in which they occurred. The reader can easily understand the chronology of the events.

Read the following paragraph, which discusses the connection between weather and human behavior. Even though the paragraph is unified and coherent, it lacks elaboration.

Poorly Elaborated Paragraph

Weather often affects the way people think and act. If we think about why we feel good or bad on a given day we can often trace the cause to the weather. Many people find this to be true in their own lives.

This paragraph presents a main idea but does not provide specific facts, examples, or sensory details to support it. The second and third sentences merely restate the main idea in different words. Such repetition offers nothing to hold the reader's attention. Compare the following, more strongly elaborated version.

Revised, Strongly Elaborated Paragraph

Weather often affects the way people think and act. Most people feel more cheerful when the sun is shining and the sky is blue than when it is cloudy or raining. When it is gray and humid out, they may feel weighed down, even depressed. As for snow, people's emotions may vary, depending on whether it means "No school today" or "I have to shovel the walk."

USING TOPIC SENTENCES

A paragraph is often built on a **topic sentence,** a sentence that states the main idea, or topic, of the paragraph. Sometimes the topic sentence establishes what will be said in the paragraph. Other times the topic sentence summarizes what has been said. A topic sentence can be found anywhere in a paragraph—at the beginning, at the end, or in the middle.

Beginning with the Topic Sentence As you read the following paragraph, notice how the main idea is stated in its first sentence. All the other sentences illustrate or "prove" the main idea with specific details. This is one of the most common ways to develop a paragraph.

LITERARY
MODEL

The town was dead. Its beds were empty and cold. The only sound was the power hum of electric lines and dynamos, still alive, all by themselves. Water ran in forgotten bathtubs, poured out into living rooms, onto porches, and down through little garden plots to feed neglected flowers. In dark theaters, gum under the many seats began to harden with tooth impressions still in it.

Ray Bradbury, *The Martian Chronicles*

Moon Rise, Hernandez, New Mexico, 1941. Photograph by Ansel Adams

Drafting Paragraphs **347**

Cooperative Learning

Divide the class into small groups. Give each group a topic sentence. For example: Parents should (not) restrict their children's television watching. Summer is (not) the best season of the year. Tobacco advertising should (not) be outlawed. Students should (not) take part in developing their high school's dress code. Each group should try to come up with a paragraph that is unified and coherent and that elaborates the main idea. Have the groups share their paragraphs with the class.

Individualizing Instruction

LEP and ESL Students These students may find it most effective to put a topic sentence at the start of each paragraph. Explain that this approach provides the most obvious and clearest approach to paragraphing.

Teaching Tip: Topic Sentence Placement

Have students read the Bradbury paragraph. Ask students why the topic sentence could not have been placed at the end of the paragraph as it is written (*"Its beds were empty and cold"* would have an unclear antecedent). Ask students how Bradbury might have recast his paragraph to put the topic sentence at the end (*He might have written, "Every bed in town was empty and cold"*). Ask how this recasting might have changed the paragraph (*putting the topic sentence at the end might have heightened suspense about what had happened*).

Humanities Connection

Art Note Shown is the photograph, *Moon Rise, Hernandez, New Mexico,* 1941, by the internationally acclaimed photographer Ansel Adams (b. 1902, San Francisco, d. 1984). In his work, Adams combined an artist's eye with a naturalist's appreciation of the environment. He is especially known for his technical innovations in photography and his masterly portrayals of nature's beauty and force. Each of his pictures made a strong statement supported by the sensory details within the frame.

Critical Thinking

Making Inferences Ask students why they think the writer of this paragraph put the topic sentence at the end instead of at the beginning. *(This placement of the topic sentence creates suspense. Since most readers would not be able to identify the name Ehrich Weiss, they would wonder who the character was. Because most people have heard of Harry Houdini, their curiosity would be satisfied by the topic sentence at the end.)*

Teaching Tip: Topic Sentences

Point out that few professional writers construct paragraphs by consciously thinking, "Where shall I put my topic sentence?" Most professional writers work more intuitively. After all, they became writers because they possessed special facility at writing good paragraphs and sentences. Remind students that even though they may never become professional writers, they will certainly be writers of school papers, and they may eventually write business memos, briefs, letters, and reports. Since most people cannot write intuitively, they must think consciously about paragraph construction.

Ending with the Topic Sentence Now look at a paragraph in which the topic sentence appears at or near the end. In this position, it makes a point or sums up what precedes it.

> He was born Ehrich Weiss in 1874. As a young child, he taught himself to make small items appear and disappear. Because Ehrich's family was quite poor, he went to work for a locksmith at the early age of 12. Before long, he knew how to pick almost any lock in existence. *Thus began the career of Harry Houdini—one of the most remarkable magicians of all time.*

Using Topic Sentences in Other Positions Topic sentences can also appear anywhere in the paragraph. In the following paragraph, Bruce Catton describes how Charleston, the site of the Democratic convention in 1860, was strangely unlike all other American cities. He puts his topic sentence in the middle for descriptive purposes.

> At first glance, it looked familiar enough, a quiet American city of 40,000 people spread out on a flat peninsula between two rivers to face the sea . . . . *Yet, there was a strangeness here, as if Charleston were a stage set designed to remind outlanders that along this coast which had been stained by so much history, life had found a pattern unlike that which the rest of America knew.* The shops seemed unexpectedly quaint, almost foreign . . . . There were palmettos in the streets, unfamiliar blossoms topped the garden walls and gleamed in the half-hidden lawns, and in the park along the Battery the twisted live oaks were dripping with Spanish moss . . . . The coaches and omnibuses that clattered down to the docks moved with a negligent, leisurely haste.
>
> **Bruce Catton, *The Coming Fury***

Drafting Paragraphs Without Topic Sentences Not every paragraph has a topic sentence. Sometimes the topic has been stated in an earlier paragraph or will be stated in a paragraph that follows. In that case, the topic sentence is merely implied, rather than stated directly in the paragraph itself. Other times there is no topic sentence at all. This happens most frequently in a **narrative,** or story.

Mathematics Connection

Encourage students to see a paragraph as a mathematical set. Draw a Venn diagram of a paragraph, such as the Bradbury paragraph, on the board. The topic sentence, "The town was dead," is a large circle, a set. Every other sentence is a subset of that sentence—a smaller circle within the larger one. In this particular paragraph, few or none of the secondary circles interlock—beds and bathtubs do not intersect. These subsets may, however, have smaller subsets within them—for instance, water in bathtubs and water on porches.

Paragraphs that are used simply to advance the action or provide description have no real topic by themselves—they just move the plot forward or clarify the setting.

Using Implied Topic Sentences The following narrative paragraph does develop a single idea. However, no individual sentence in the paragraph states this topic. In other words, this paragraph has an **implied topic sentence.**

> The man in the black suit threw the last items into the leather suitcase and yanked at the zipper. He glanced at the clock on the mantel and saw that it was 2:17. Forty-three minutes, he calculated quickly. Was it enough time to get to the airport? Perspiration beaded his upper lip as he snatched his tickets off the dresser. Grabbing his suitcase, he raced out of the room. What if he couldn't catch a cab? He would have to, he thought.

Even when there is no topic sentence, each paragraph should contain related ideas or present a single incident or description. Notice how in the paragraph above every sentence supports the implied topic sentence: *The man was trying to get to the airport on time*.

WRITER TO WRITER

I believe a story can be wrecked by a faulty rhythm in a sentence . . . or a mistake in paragraphing, even punctuation. Henry James is the maestro of the semicolon. Hemingway is a first-rate paragrapher . . . . I don't mean to imply that I successfully practice what I preach. I try, that's all.

Truman Capote, novelist

Practice Your Skills

A. Revise the following paragraphs to make them unified and coherent. Rearrange sentences and add transitions as needed.

1.   In 1848, gold was discovered at Sutter's Mill in California. California is heavily populated. People staked out claims and

Teaching Tip: Implied Topic Sentences

Point out that paragraphs with implied topic sentences are common in literature, especially in descriptive passages. Ask students to find examples in a story they have read recently.

Individualizing Instruction

Learning Styles For visual learners, emphasize the typographical aspect of paragraphing. The length of a paragraph and the way indentations look on the page affect the reader's emotions and pace. Ask auditory learners how they might note paragraph breaks while reading aloud *(pausing or changing tone at the beginning of the new paragraph).*

---

panned for gold. A few of them became rich. News of the discovery spread throughout the world. The first organized group of American settlers came to California in 1841. Most of the prospectors found little or no gold.

2.   Birds and reptiles share similarities but display just as many differences. Both birds and reptiles, having a backbone, are called vertebrates. Birds are warmblooded; their body temperature remains about the same regardless of the temperature of their surroundings. Humans are warmblooded also. The body of a bird is covered with feathers. The body of a reptile is covered with dry, scaly skin. Reptiles are coldblooded, that is, their body temperature changes with that of their surroundings.

B. Choose two of the topic sentences below. For each one, list at least four specific facts or details that elaborate the main idea.

• People are often afraid of new situations and experiences.
• Walking through the forest, we could tell that winter was on the way.
• Creativity often strikes when you least expect it.

C. In each of the following paragraphs, identify the topic sentence and tell whether it appears at the beginning, at the end, or in the middle of the paragraph.

1.   All forests go through stages of development. First a cleared area is created either by humans or by a natural event. Then pines or other softwoods begin to spring up. Next hardwoods begin to grow, and the forest is mixed. As the forest matures, it becomes composed increasingly of hardwoods.

2.   When an amateur musician looks for a teacher, what characteristics should the teacher have? How can musicians find time to practice? How can beginners overcome their frustrations and fears of failure? These are just a few of the questions answered in Stephanie Judy's new book, *Making Your Own Music (And Making Music Your Own).*

3.   Ants live in colonies with thousands, even millions, of other ants—female workers, males, and one queen. Each type of ant has specific jobs to perform. The queen's most important job is to lay eggs. The female worker ants build the nest, find food, carry the food back to the colony, take care of the young, and fight enemies. The main purpose of male ants is to fertilize the eggs that the queen lays.

Elaboration: How Do I Develop Ideas?

Once you've gathered together a few main ideas, you've come a long way toward producing a piece of writing. However, to breathe life into those ideas, you need to develop, or elaborate, them. Your main ideas must be supported, explained, described, and even, sometimes, questioned. Elaborating your ideas is one of the most important tasks that you have as a writer.

TYPES OF ELABORATION

There are many types of details you can use to elaborate, or support, a main idea. You can choose among such possibilities as facts and statistics, sensory details, incidents, specific examples, and research. Sometimes an anecdote or a quotation can provide just the right support for an idea. You will need to select the types of elaboration that best fit your purpose, audience, and topic.

Facts and Statistics   Facts are statements that can be proven through observation, experience, consulting a reference work, or speaking with an authority. For example, the statement "Piranhas rarely attack people" is a fact. If you doubt the statement, you can easily check it in an encyclopedia. **Statistics** are facts about people, the weather, business, and so on, that involve numbers, such as, "In the United States, about 90 percent of high-school students attend public schools." In the following paragraph find the facts and statistics the writer used to develop her main idea.

> Fibrillations of the heart, a rapid quivering of muscle fibers rather than the contractions needed to pump blood, is one of the leading causes of sudden death by heart attack. A study . . . compared cardiac arrest victims treated by emergency medical technicians [EMTs] to those treated by paramedics. The eventual survival rate among those patients treated by EMTs was only six percent. This rate rose dramatically, to twenty-seven percent, for patients treated by paramedics.
> **Sharon Balter, "State of the Art of Emergency Care"**

WRITING HANDBOOK 8

PROFESSIONAL
M O D E L

Elaboration   **351**

Writing Handbook 8:
Elaboration: How Do I Develop Ideas?

Objectives

1. To understand and apply the techniques of elaboration
2. To respond to models of elaboration

> **Handbook Mini-Lessons**
>
> For information on topics related to topic of elaboration, see the following mini-lessons.
> - Using Graphic Devices, pp. 357–360
> - Developing Study and Research Skills, pp. 459–468
> - Using the Library and Other Sources of Information, pp. 470–477
> - Interviewing Skills, pp. 481–482

Teaching Strategies

Motivating

Ask students what comes to mind when someone tells them, "You're going to love this!" when talking about a movie, book, or television show. Point out that most people want to know more. They want to know why they will love it, or what is special about it. Without additional information, the first statement has little impact. When speakers provide additional information, they are elaborating on their first ideas. Tell students that they will learn many new ways to elaborate ideas.

Critical Thinking

Generalizing   Discuss with students what makes someone an authority on a topic, and why their families or best friends might not be authorities. Help them come up with general guidelines that help them identify authorities.

Sensory Details Words that appeal to the five senses provide sensory detail. They help develop an idea by telling how things look, sound, smell, taste, or feel. If you use exact, vivid sensory words, you can help readers experience the scene or event you are writing about. In the following paragraph, look for sensory details that help bring the scene to life.

> Early morning is a time of magic in Cannery Row. In the gray time after the light has come and before the sun has risen, the row seems to hang suspended out of time in a silvery light. The streetlights go out, and the weeds are a brilliant green. The corrugated iron of the canneries glows with the pearly lucence of platinum or old pewter. No automobiles are running then. The street is silent of progress and business. And the rush and drag of the waves can be heard as they splash in among the piles of the canneries. It is a time of great peace, a deserted time, a little era of rest.
>
> **John Steinbeck, *Cannery Row***

WRITER TO WRITER

My writing often starts with an attention getter, such as painting a vivid word picture.

Ryan Bevington, student
Seattle, Washington

The most vivid descriptions *show* rather than *tell* what the writer means. They are concrete and specific rather than abstract and general. Precise details let your readers figure out what an object, person, or scene is like. You can paint a picture of something without telling your readers how to understand it. In the following examples, notice how showing and telling create very different experiences for a reader.

Telling   Riley's Place is a busy restaurant at lunchtime.

Showing   Waiters banged dishes onto bare metal tables; knives and forks clattered together; customers shouted above the din. It was lunchtime at Riley's Place, and there wasn't a seat in the house.

Incidents Narrating or telling about an event can help you convey your idea or enlarge its significance. You probably use this technique in speaking, by making a statement and then telling a story to elaborate. The following paragraph begins with a topic sentence. The author then supports this idea with examples, including a story.

> Unfortunately, nature is very much a now-you-see-it, now-you-don't affair. A fish flashes, then dissolves in the water before my eyes like so much salt. Deer apparently ascend bodily into heaven . . . . For a week last September migrating redwing blackbirds were feeding heavily down by the creek at the back of the house. One day I went out to investigate the racket; I walked up to a tree, an Osage orange, and a hundred birds flew away. They simply materialized out of the tree. I saw a tree, then a whisk of color, then a tree again. I walked closer and another hundred blackbirds took flight. Not a branch, not a twig budged. Or, it was as if the leaves of the Osage orange had been freed from a spell in the form of red-winged blackbirds; they flew from the tree, caught my eye in the sky, and vanished. When I looked again at the tree the leaves had reassembled as if nothing had happened.
>
> **Annie Dillard, *Pilgrim at Tinker Creek***

Examples Sometimes a main idea can be supported with one or more specific examples. The main idea of the following paragraph is that toy designers search ceaselessly for the blockbuster toy that will become the rage, outselling all others. Notice how the writer has provided examples of such toys in the following excerpt.

Writing
── **TIP** ──
Use of the first-person narrative in relating an incident can add a powerful, personal quality to a piece of writing.

> The life of the modern toy designer is an unending search for the next Hula Hoop, the next Rubik's Cube, the next Teenage Mutant Ninja Turtle. Unfortunately, no one has yet devised a foolproof formula for predicting just what makes a new toy "fun." . . . A single hot toy can bring in $100 million in retail sales in a single season; a hot toy that unexpectedly goes cold (remember the Cabbage Patch Kids? Teddy Ruxpin?) can help push a company into bankruptcy.
>
> **Doug Steward, "In the Cutthroat World of Toy Sales, Child's Play Is Serious Business"**

Elaboration   **353**

Individualizing Instruction

LEP Students To give students an immediate sense of success with elaborating, invite them to give brief oral descriptions that elaborate on the idea, "Most school mornings start off the same way." After they have told what their mornings entail, point out that they have just used incidents to elaborate.

Teaching Tip: Incidents

Some students may correctly point out that Dillard's description includes many sensory details. Reinforce the insight that various techniques support one another in writing. Elaboration is not an either-or choice.

Teaching Tip: Examples

Invite students to elaborate further on Steward's main idea by coming up with additional examples of toys and game fads. The activity will be fun for most students and will give them quick and concrete practice in providing examples.

Auditory Learners   Auditory learners often excel at remembering quotations that they hear. Encourage them to keep notebooks of interesting remarks, and to include the date they heard them, the speakers' names, and the circumstances.

Teaching Tip: Quotations

Work with students to brainstorm sources of quotations. Point out, if necessary, that the quotation in the excerpt came from a printed source. Then develop a list of other sources, including spoken arts recordings, broadcasts, and books of quotations.

PROFESSIONAL
M O D E L

Quotations   Sometimes another person has said something so perfectly and eloquently that you'll want to use it to add force and depth to your own words. Other times, a quotation can be used as an example, to illustrate a point you want to make. In the following paragraph, notice how the writer has used quotations.

> We are used to running until we run down, but the lesson of the mountains is that the race is to the steady, not to the swift. "In time you'll learn that, generally speaking, the way to hurry is not to hurry but to keep going," walker Colin Fletcher advises in his manual on the subject. "To this end I have two walking speeds: slow and slower." With experience, the right pace for mountains becomes second nature. Take one step and all the others fall naturally into place. The greatest pride in walking in mountains, the badge of maturity, is not in reaching the summit but in reaching it in stride.
>
> **Paul Bruchow, *The Necessity of Empty Places***

SOURCES OF ELABORATION

Once you have decided on the type of elaboration appropriate for your topic, there are several sources and techniques you can use to gather the information.

Questioning   Questioning is one of the best ways both to find and elaborate on ideas. When you question, you think about what you don't know but would like to learn more about. Begin by simply writing the words *who, what, when, why,* and *how* at the top of a sheet of paper. Then come up with a list of questions of anything you wonder about your topic. As in brainstorming and freewriting, try to let your mind roam freely as you write questions, and don't evaluate any of your ideas in advance. Some questions may serve as guides for research; others will direct you to information you already have.

Exploratory Techniques   The exploratory techniques for finding ideas discussed in Writing Handbook 2 (pages 317–325) are also helpful in elaborating on those ideas. These techniques include recalling, using trigger words, freewriting, invisible writing, listing, using a journal, brainstorming, and discussion.

354   Writing Handbook

Research You may find you need factual information to elaborate on your topic. Two good ways of acquiring facts are using the library and interviewing. In the library, research your topic in the card catalog or computerized library catalog system. Discuss any special questions you have with a librarian. If your topic is current, you may know or know about people who might be able to answer questions. Set up an interview, and make a list of questions to ask. Take notes or tape-record your interview. The information you gain can be quoted or paraphrased in your writing. (See Writing Handbook 25, pages 464–465.)

Graphic Devices Graphic devices can also be an excellent way to elaborate on your topic. Several of the devices discussed in Writing Handbook 9 on pages 357–360, such as clustering, charting, and using an analysis frame or idea tree, can provide helpful information.

CHOOSING APPROPRIATE DETAILS

How will you know what type of details to use in developing a piece of writing? The answer depends on the purpose and personal goals of your writing. If your main purpose is to persuade someone about a particular course of action, facts and statistics that support your viewpoint will be very useful. On the other hand, if your goal is to describe accurately and precisely a particular person, place, or thing, then sensory details generally will be more appropriate.

In the following paragraph, notice how the writer chose appropriate details to elaborate on what her father loved.

LITERARY
M O D E L

My father loved all instruments that would instruct and fascinate. His place to keep things was the drawer in the "library table" where lying on top of his folded maps was a telescope with brass extensions . . . . In the back of the drawer you could find a magnifying glass, a kaleidoscope, and a gyroscope kept in a black buckram box, which he would set dancing for us on a string pulled tight. He had also supplied himself with an assortment of puzzles composed of metal rings and intersecting links and keys chained together, impossible for the rest of us, however patiently shown, to take apart; he had an almost childlike love of the ingenious.

Eudora Welty, *One Writer's Beginnings*

Elaboration   **355**

Individualizing Instruction

Basic Students You may wish to review good general sources of information with students, including almanacs, encyclopedias, atlases, and *Facts on File*. In addition, review ways to access information through the card catalog or computer. Remind them that books are listed by topic, title, and author.

Cooperative Learning

Divide the class into small teams of three or four students and assign each a topic to research. However, have each student concentrate on using only one section of the library: the reference section, the periodical section, and the nonfiction section, for instance. Students can present the information orally, but should name each source.

Individualizing Instruction

Visual Learners Visual learners should be encouraged to use graphic devices as sources of information, as well as methods of elaboration. Encourage them to find as many examples of different graphic devices as possible, including maps, charts, graphs, and diagrams.

Modeling

You may wish to model Exercise B by having volunteers give informal oral descriptions of the way good pizza tastes. Help students elaborate on vague words such as "delicious," suggesting specific details about the sauce, the cheese, the crust, and the toppings.

Additional Resources
- Writing Resource Book, pp. 16–17
- Elaboration, Revision, and Proofreading Worksheets

Practice Your Skills

A. Choose two of the following main ideas. Follow the suggestions in parentheses to come up with other ideas that support or develop the main idea.

1. Weather often affects the way people think and act.
   (*Suggestion:* Brainstorm with others to recall specific examples of human behavior you have observed during storms or times of intense heat or cold.)
2. The engine of the car coughed and sputtered, fouling the air with smoke.
   (*Suggestion:* Observe cars in a parking lot or on the highway to gather sensory details.)
3. It was one of the largest and busiest airports in the country.
   (*Suggestion:* Develop questions and use them to research in reference books for facts and statistics about an airport, its employees, passengers, and planes.)
4. The California Gold Rush began in 1848.
   (*Suggestion:* Use gleaning and research techniques to gather facts and statistics about the topic and develop a time line of events.)
5. People often lavish affection on their pets.
   (*Suggestion:* Interview a veterinarian or a pet-store owner to gather facts or specific examples about the attention and care some owners give their pets.)
6. Baseball is a thinking person's game.
   (*Suggestion:* Talk to your friends who watch or play baseball to collect anecdotes that illustrate this statement.)
7. The ancient Greeks made revolutionary contributions to humanity.
   (*Suggestion:* Develop an appropriate definition of *revolutionary* and select examples from reference books that fit your definition.)

B. Choose one of the following sentences and turn it into a paragraph that shows rather than tells your reader.

- The pizza tasted good.
- My room was a mess.
- The roller-coaster ride was scary.
- _____ was acting strangely.
- The street was crowded.
- The ballpark was deserted.
- My parents seemed angry.
- The party was fun.
- The band was really rocking.
- The trip was a long one.
- Moving day was tiring.

Music Connection

Have students find reviews of musical performances to see how reviewers elaborate on their main ideas, and to see the kinds of details they focus on. Encourage students to look for reviews of the kinds of music that they enjoy hearing.

Using Graphic Devices

At various points during the writing process you may find it difficult to sort out your ideas because you cannot clearly "see" what you are thinking. Using graphic devices—making pictures of what's on your mind—is a good way to help organize your ideas and generate new ones. Some of the graphic devices shown in this lesson can help you find ideas. Others will be more helpful in later stages of the writing process, when you begin elaborating and organizing your ideas, or when you are drafting and revising.

USING DIAGRAMS

Clustering is a way of showing the relationships among ideas. It is a particularly good way to generate ideas because it allows related ideas to "grow" freely from one another. In a **cluster,** a number of related ideas are grouped together using circles and lines. Two similar ways to show related ideas are **idea trees** and **spider maps.** In an idea tree, the main ideas are shown as "branches" and related ideas as "twigs" on the branches. In a spider map, related ideas are connected like the legs on a spider. Study the examples below.

Cluster—Threatened and Endangered Species

Writing
TIP

Graphic devices can be helpful in both generating and developing ideas.

Writing Handbook 9:
Using Graphic Devices

Objectives

1. To recognize and use clusters, idea trees, and spider maps to find ideas for writing
2. To recognize and use observation charts, category charts, comparison-contrast charts, and analysis frames to help organize and elaborate details during writing

Handbook Mini-Lessons
For information on topics related to using graphic devices, see the following mini-lessons.
- How Do I Find Ideas?
  pp. 317–325
- Elaboration: How Do I Develop Ideas? pp. 351–355

Teaching Strategies

Motivating

Ask students to recall times when they either gave or received complicated directions to a place. Elicit that, at some point, people usually want to draw a map because a graphic representation is, for many people, the most efficient method for visualizing and following a route. Explain that graphic devices available to writers serve a similar purpose.

Teaching Tip: Graphics

Remind students that they need not worry about the aesthetics of the graphic devices they create because the purpose of such devices is to assist them in seeing the relationships and connections among ideas.

Show students any graphic device that you may have generated in the past to guide your own writing. Explain why you used that particular device.

 Individualizing Instruction

LEP Students These students will usually interpret information that is presented graphically with less difficulty than textual material. Determine that they understand the vocabulary used in the graphic aids.

Modeling

Consider modeling an observation chart, using the classroom as the subject. Enlist the aid of students in completing the chart.

Idea Tree— Canned-Food Collection

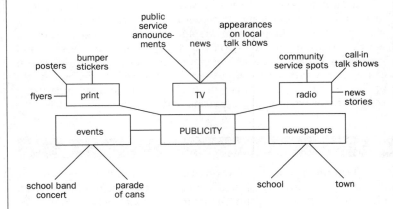

Spider Map—Publicity Options

CREATING CHARTS

Charting is a good way to generate details in an orderly fashion. For example, if you were collecting details for a description and wanted to make sure you had sensory details for as many of the five senses as possible, you could use an **observation chart** like the one below.

Subject Observed—Car Chase	
Visual Details	car speeding red light police car chasing
Sounds	siren blaring
Smells	exhaust fumes
Tastes	exhaust fumes
Feel/Textures	rush of air as I stood on curb

Science Connection

You might want to point out that scientists use versions of observation charts to record experiments and to make precise records of visual investigations. Ask students to identify situations where such charts would be most useful to scientists. Invite students who have created observation charts in science courses to share them with the class.

Another good device to use when generating details is a **category chart.** This kind of chart is more flexible than an observation chart because instead of listing details according to the five senses, you can list them in categories you create to suit your subject. Here is a category chart you might make if you were collecting details for a description of a person.

Subject Observed—Man on a Bus

Mannerisms	Physical Features	Clothing
twitch of left eye	tall	battered gray hat
rapid movement of hands while speaking	medium build	gray trench coat
	red hair	black boots
	freckles	red scarf

If you need to compare and contrast two or more things, you can collect details in a **comparison-and-contrast chart.** Write the subject in your chart's title. List the items you would like to compare across the top and the categories or characteristics you are comparing down the side. Then fill in details for each item, as in the following chart.

Items Being Compared— Professional and Amateur Athletes

	Pros	Amateurs
Payment	living wage	none
Skill	high level	high level
Specific sport	any	any
Appear in ads for pay	many do	some do

Critical Thinking

Analyzing Ask students to identify types of writing for which a comparison-contrast chart would be extremely useful. (writings that examine and analyze alternative choices) Remind students that such writing often uses the similarities and differences between two options to recommend a course of action.

Social Studies Connection

If national, local, or school election time is at hand, you might ask students to make an analysis frame that sets forth the qualities needed in a candidate for a particular office. Students could later generate a comparison-contrast chart in which they compare the qualities of the two leading candidates.

As you circulate around the room while students are working, watch for signs of halted progress. You may wish to work with a group of students having difficulty as other students work independently.

ANSWERS TO PRACTICE YOUR SKILLS

A. Answers will vary. No matter which of the three devices students choose, a good diagram will be richly detailed, with at least two branches stemming from the core topic and a variety of second- and third-level associations. A well-constructed diagram need not look elegant but should at least be legible and should be well enough organized to allow a reader to follow each train of associations.

B. Answers will vary. Successful charts will be complete and well organized. If students make an observation chart, they should record information relevant to all the senses. If they make a category chart, they should record information about a complete range of distinct (nonoverlapping) categories relevant to the subject. In either case, you should be able to see the categories at a glance and be able to tell in which category each detail belongs.

C. Answers will vary. Students' charts should cover both similarities and differences in a broad range of significant categories and should reflect a careful study of the two magazines.

D. Answers will vary. A well-constructed analysis frame will identify the field being analyzed in the large box. Each subsequent level of boxes should represent a complete analysis of the box to which they are related—that is, they should be comprised of all the components that make up the larger category. The chart should be neat and easy to follow, and the analysis should be carried out to at least two levels below the overall topic.

Managing the Paper Load

Have students react to each others' graphic devices. Make yourself available for guidance and advice.

Additional Resources
- Writing Resource Book, pp. 18–20
- Thinking Skills Transparencies: Analysis Frame

USING AN ANALYSIS FRAME

A simple way of showing details that are related to one main idea is by using an analysis frame. Write the overall idea you want to analyze in a large box at the top of your paper. Then list the components that contribute to that idea in smaller, connected boxes underneath. Here is an analysis frame a student made to examine the features to be considered in choosing a car.

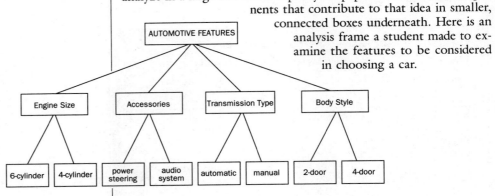

Practice Your Skills

A. Choose three of the following subjects. Following the examples shown in this handbook, construct either a cluster, an idea tree, or a spider map for each subject.

how humans use animals	things I fear
life in the city	life in the country
planning a party	information in a newspaper
the truth about sharks	popularity
jewelry	flying
frozen food	insects
water	reunions

B. Using an observation chart or a category chart, collect details about a person, place, or event you can observe in your school or neighborhood.

C. Make a comparison/contrast chart in which you compare and contrast characteristics of two magazines you have read or two games you have played.

D. Make an analysis frame in which you analyze the qualities needed to make a good athlete or performer in a field of your choice.

Unity, Coherence, and Transitional Devices

Good writing is a pleasure to read because it expresses ideas clearly and flows smoothly. It is unified and coherent. In a piece of writing that is **unified,** all the sentences or paragraphs support one main idea. In a piece of writing that is **coherent,** all the sentences or paragraphs follow one another in a logical manner. The connection between ideas is strengthened by the use of **transitional devices.**

UNITY IN PARAGRAPHS

You can achieve unity in your paragraphs in several ways. In most paragraphs, a good topic sentence plays a key role in establishing unity. If you relate all of the details to your topic sentence, your paragraph will be unified. (See "Topic Sentences," pages 343–344.) If there is no topic sentence, unity is achieved when all of the sentences support the implied main idea or when they follow a logical progression, as in a narrative.

Related Details In a unified paragraph, every detail supports the topic sentence or implied main idea; that is, all of the sentences in the paragraph explain the writer's most important point.

In the following paragraph about the famous composer Richard Wagner, the first sentence establishes the main idea that the composer's behavior is like that of a six year old. Notice that the details in the rest of the paragraph support that idea.

> He had the emotional stability of a six-year-old child. When he felt out of sorts, he would rave and stamp, or sink into suicidal gloom and talk darkly of going to the East to end his days as a Buddhist monk. Ten minutes later, when something pleased him, he would rush out of doors and run around the garden or jump up and down on the sofa, or stand on his head. He could be grief-stricken over the death of a pet dog, and he could be callous and heartless to a degree that would have made a Roman emperor shudder.
>
> **Deems Taylor, "The Monster"**

PROFESSIONAL
MODEL

Unity and
Coherence   **361**

Writing Handbook 10:

Unity, Coherence, and Transitional Devices

Objectives

1. To recognize and achieve unity and coherence in paragraphs and compositions
2. To use transitional devices to achieve coherence

Handbook Mini-Lessons

For information on topics related to unity, coherence, and transitional devices, see the following mini-lessons.
- Types of Organization, pp. 331–335
- Drafting Paragraphs, pp. 345–350
- What Are the Types of Revision? pp. 375–377
- Correcting Problem Sentences, pp. 391–399

Teaching Strategies

Critical Thinking

Analyzing Ask students how well the sentences which follow the topic sentence, "He had the emotional stability of a six-year-old child," support the main idea. Do students agree that six-year-olds are erratic in their behavior, callous, and heartless? If not, ask them what comparison they might substitute for the one in the topic sentence.

Visual Learners Convey the concept of unity by examining what makes a piece of art, such as a painting by Rembrandt, unified. Note how all the elements—color, composition, subject matter—work together to provide a single feeling or impression. Have students consider what would happen if the artist had made a different choice in one of these elements; if he had painted the background of a portrait in primary colors, for example, or had used a broad brush. As students evaluate their writing for unity—particularly if their writing includes description—have them create a painting in their minds of the images they've written. They can revise or delete those details that disrupt the overall unity of impression.

Teaching Tip: Implied Main Idea

Point out to students that descriptive paragraphs frequently have no stated main idea. A writer who supplies a wealth of details to describe a spectacular view would not say, "The view from the terrace was breathtaking," but would *show* the view to the reader.

Unity is particularly important in writing descriptions. When you describe a person or an object, you want to create a single, unified impression. To do this, carefully choose details that contribute to that impression.

In describing a classic car, for example, you might brainstorm a list of details about the car. Then you would eliminate those details that don't fit the impression.

Compare the two sentences below. Which one creates a unified impression?

1. The classic car had a glistening red hood, worn upholstery, and precise pin-striping along its side.
2. The reflective chrome, precise pin-striping, and glistening, red hood caught nearly everyone's eye.

As you probably agree, the second sentence gives a unified impression because all the details point to the attractiveness of the car, whereas the first one introduces an unattractive element—the worn upholstery.

Implied Main Idea The second sentence about the classic car gives an impression that is not directly stated. Sometimes the main idea of a paragraph also is not directly stated, but the paragraph is unified because all the sentences point to one idea.

Logical Progression Often, in narrative writing, the main idea is neither stated nor implied. In the following paragraph, unity is achieved because each detail in the paragraph follows logically from those that precede it.

362 Writing Handbook

> The nursery was silent. It was empty as a jungle glade at hot high noon. The walls were blank and two dimensional. Now, as George and Lydia Hadley stood in the center of the room, the walls began to part and recede into crystalline distance, it seemed, and presently, an African veldt appeared, in three dimensions; on all sides, in colors reproduced to the final pebble and bit of straw. The ceiling above them became a deep sky with a hot yellow sun.
>
> **Ray Bradbury, "The Veldt"**

Points to remember in writing unified paragraphs are summarized in the following chart. These guidelines will be useful for any type of writing that you do.

Guidelines for Achieving Unity in Paragraphs

- If the paragraph has a topic sentence, check to make sure that the other sentences support it.
- If your paragraph's main idea is implied rather than directly stated, check to see that each sentence advances that idea.
- If you are writing a description, make sure that the words you choose and the details you include create a unified impression.
- If you are writing a narrative paragraph in which the main idea is neither stated nor implied, make sure that each sentence connects logically to the one before it and the one after it.

UNITY IN COMPOSITIONS

Unity is important not only in individual paragraphs but also in whole compositions. To achieve unity in a composition, you should be sure that each body paragraph relates directly to the main idea of your composition. For example, suppose that you have written a three-paragraph piece about swimming as a form of exercise and have asked a peer reader to respond.

Unity and
Coherence   **363**

Critical Thinking: Inferring Sequence

Using the paragraph provided, discuss how each detail leads logically to the next. Choose another paragraph from a Bradbury or other story to write on the board, but write the sentences out of order. Ask students to recreate the original sequence. (This might be a good cooperative learning activity. Divide the class into groups and give each group a different narrative paragraph to put into correct sequence.)

Stumbling Block

Students who have difficulty understanding the concept of unity in writing might be helped if you compare it with unity in other fields they are more familiar with. Ask students with expertise in music, art, or drama to discuss unity as it applies to their specialty. In classical drama, for example, the principle of unity required a play to have a single action represented as occurring in one place on one day.

Literature Connection

For unity in composition, Lincoln's Gettysburg Address makes a great model. It is brief, to the point, and perfectly clear. Most important, it is unified around the idea of a nation dedicated to the idea that "all men are created equal."

- Paragraph one describes how swimming shapes up the body.
- Paragraph two describes how swimming improves lung capacity and blood pressure.
- Paragraph three describes swimming accidents.

Your peer reader would probably tell you that your composition is not unified because the third paragraph is unrelated to swimming as a form of exercise.

COHERENCE IN PARAGRAPHS

A paragraph may be unified, but if the ideas do not flow clearly, it will not be coherent. In a coherent paragraph, the sentences all follow logically from one to another and the connection between ideas is obvious. Sentences can be organized in many logical patterns, including chronologically or spatially, by cause and effect or comparison and contrast, or by order of importance, degree, or familiarity. (See "Types of Organization," pages 331–335.) To connect sentences, you can use transitional devices.

WRITER TO WRITER

Word-carpentry is like any other kind of carpentry; you must join your sentences smoothly.

Anatole France, French novelist and critic

Transitional Devices

Transitional devices are words and phrases that connect ideas and can help you achieve coherence in your writing. There are transitions showing time, space, sequence, degree, comparison and contrast, cause and effect, and other relationships.

Time When you are narrating or explaining a process that involves time, consider using some of the following transitions.

Transitions That Show Time

after	before	finally
next	then	again
during	the next day	while
every time	always	meanwhile

Note the transitions showing time in the following paragraph. Without the transitions, the reader has no way of knowing how the events are related to one another and the paragraph loses coherence.

> During 1989, several Eastern European governments fell. *First,* the communist government of Hungary fell. *Shortly after,* Romania's government fell. *Then* the people of Lithuania began to clamor for freedom.

Space When you are writing descriptions, you should use transitions that help the reader picture the relationships among the objects you are describing. The following are just a few of the many spatial transitions that you might find useful.

Transitions That Show Space

behind	in front of	on the left of
below	over	around
here	in the center	on top of

Think about how the transitions showing space in the following paragraph help you form a mental picture by telling you where each item is located.

> *In the center of* the ad is a woman drinking milk. *Beside* her is a man watching as if admiring her good sense. *Above* the photo, the word *natural* is written in capital letters. A small box *below* the photo contains nutritional information on milk.

Degree When you are explaining the relative importance of items or ideas, you can use transitions such as the following.

Transitions That Show Degree

first	second	mainly
more important	less important	least important

In the following paragraph, note that *first* and *second* are used to show importance, not time or sequence.

> There are many reasons to begin an aerobic exercise program. *First,* you will look better. *Second,* you will feel better. Perhaps even *more important,* you will tone your muscles. However, *most important* of all, you will derive enormous cardiovascular benefits.

Comparison and Contrast When you are comparing and contrasting people, places, things, or ideas, you can use some of the following transitions to show the relationship between your choice of subjects.

THE FAR SIDE By GARY LARSON

People who don't know which end is up.

Unity and Coherence **365**

Individualizing Instruction

LD Students Explain to students that they may find it helpful to plan descriptive writing by making a drawing to sketch out the subject's location and show component parts. They may find it even easier to work from a photograph or reproduction of the place or object they intend to describe.

Teaching Tip: Degree

Remind students that, as writers, they will make decisions about the relative importance of items or ideas. The words they use should make it clear to their readers just which item or idea they consider to be the most or least important.

Transitions That Show Comparison

as	than	similarly
in the same way	likewise	also
either . . . or	neither . . . nor	

Transitions That Show Contrast

yet	but	however
unlike	in contrast	instead
on the contrary	on the other hand	

Note how the use of transitions in the following paragraph clarifies one difference between Generals Grant and Lee.

> Ulysses S. Grant was described as having an abrupt manner. *Likewise,* he was not always described as a gentleman. *On the other hand,* Robert E. Lee was a figure of refinement, a model of decorum.

Cause and Effect When you are describing a cause-and-effect relationship, you can use transitions to alert your reader to either the cause or the effect. Following are just a few of the many transitions that signal a cause-and-effect relationship.

Transitions That Show Cause and Effect

because	therefore	since
consequently	as a result	so that
although	for this reason	if, then

Pay attention to the transitions in the following paragraph. Note that if the word *consequently* were missing, the sentence would not make sense and the paragraph would not have coherence.

> The first mechanical clocks were invented in Europe when the majority of the population could not read. *Therefore,* many people could not read even the simple numbers on a clock. *Consequently,* the clocks tolled or chimed the hour.

Other Relationships If you are introducing examples, emphasizing a point, or adding more information, consider using the following words and phrases to make the relationship between the ideas clear and your writing coherent.

Transitions That Introduce Examples

as	for example	for instance
like	such as	to illustrate
that is	namely	in particular

Transitions That Signal Emphasis
indeed   in fact   in other words

Transitions That Signal More Information
in addition   besides   furthermore
moreover   also   as well as
similarly

Transitions That Signal Explanation
for example   that is   in other words

Words and Phrases That Refer and Connect

The relationship of ideas in some paragraphs is made clear by chains of words. These paragraphs do not rely on typical transitions such as *first* or *consequently*. Instead, coherence is achieved through the use of pronouns or synonyms.

Pronouns Using pronouns to refer to a previously named noun in a paragraph is a good way to achieve coherence in your writing. Notice how forms of the pronoun *it* have been used to replace the word *kitten* in the following paragraph.

> A kitten is playing with *its* classical plaything, a ball of wool. Unfailingly, *it* begins to paw at the object, first gently and enquiringly with outstretched forearm and inwardly flexed paw. Now with extended claws, *it* draws the ball toward *itself*.
>
> **Konrad Lorenz, "On Feline Play"**

Cat and Kittens; AMERICAN; National Gallery of Art, Washington; Gift of Edgar William and Bernice Chrysler Garbish.

Writing TIP

In choosing transitions as you write, think of what you would say if you were speaking.

PROFESSIONAL MODEL

Unity and Coherence   **367**

Teaching Tip: Pronouns and Coherence

You can effectively demonstrate the role that pronouns play in linking sentences to each other by reading aloud one or two paragraphs, substituting nouns for the pronouns that refer to the nouns. In addition to establishing coherence, pronouns make it possible to avoid what would otherwise be deadly repetition of nouns.

Humanities Connection

Art Note The nineteenth-century American artist of the primitive painting *Cat and Kittens*, (c. 1872/73) is unknown. An artwork is considered "primitive" if the artist has little or no formal training. The primitive artist relies on natural talent and instincts rather than learned techniques to achieve coherence in the work. The power of primitive art usually derives from its simplicity and directness. Ask:

When might you choose a simple, direct style or tone in your writing?

Stumbling Block

While synonyms allow students to link words or ideas without repetition, they must take care to be precise in their word usage. You might want to solicit a list of synonyms for common words, such as "pretty" or "famous," and then discuss the connotations these words carry. "Notorious," for example, does not mean exactly the same thing as famous.

Teaching Tip: Repetition

Point out to students that repetition within a paragraph may serve several purposes. For example, repetition in the following example from Mark Twain's *Autobiography* serves to establish coherence and to create an emphatic tone: "*Of all* the *creatures* that were made he [man] is the *most* detestable. *Of* the entire brood, he is the *only one*—the *solitary one*—that possesses malice. That is the basest of *all* instincts, passions, vices—the *most* hateful. He is the *only creature* that inflicts *pain* for sport, knowing it to be *pain*. . . . Also— in *all* the list, he is the *only creature* that has a nasty mind."

Synonyms You can also achieve coherence by using a series of closely related words or ideas. Note how the related terms *blight, evil, spell, maladies, sickened, shadow of death,* and *illness* link the sentences in the following paragraph.

▼

> Then a strange *blight* crept over the area and everything began to change. Some *evil spell* had settled on the community: mysterious *maladies* swept the flocks of chickens; the cattle and sheep *sickened* and died. Everywhere was a *shadow of death.* The farmers spoke of much *illness* among their families.
>
> **Rachel Carson, "A Fable for Tomorrow"**

COHERENCE IN COMPOSITIONS

Transitional words and other devices are important for achieving coherence not only in paragraphs but also in compositions. You can link your paragraphs by using transitional words or by repeating, rephrasing, or using closely related words.

Transitional Words In the following example, note the transitional word that strengthens the link between paragraphs.

▼

> In Outward Bound, learning about yourself is the main objective. By being faced with the physical challenge, for example, of hiking across the desert for a stretch of eighteen hours, you can discover new strengths and abilities. You might learn that you can navigate well or simply that you can hike for an extended period of time.
>
> *Besides* learning about yourself, you also learn how to work within a group. In Outward Bound, you might be roped to a group trying to scale the face of a steep mountain, everyone working together to accomplish the climb. Working within a team is a vital skill you will have to master in Outward Bound.

Repeated Words Repeating an important word from an earlier sentence or paragraph can help your reader see the connection among your ideas. In the next selection, notice the repetition of *flower.*

Suggest that students work in groups to examine multi-paragraph pieces of writing to find evidence of transitional words that link paragraphs. Students may also investigate for synonyms of closely related words in the writing that they examine. Ask them to bring good examples to the attention of the entire class.

PROFESSIONAL
M O D E L

Carol Duke has built her life around *flowers*. Even when she is not in the garden at . . . her hilltop home in Williamsburg, Massachusetts, she is immersed in flowers—teaching, lecturing, designing, and arranging. She has created arrangements for clients as diverse as the New York City Ballet, the Chase Manhattan Bank . . . .

For Carol, a visual artist by training, *arranging flowers* is an ideal blend of her interests in art and gardening.

Polly Bannister, "The Next-to-Last Word in Flower Arranging"

Rephrasing Another way to link your paragraphs is by rephrasing a word or term that was mentioned earlier in the selection. Notice how the expression *exercise just for sheer pleasure* has been rephrased to link the paragraphs in the following model.

PROFESSIONAL
M O D E L

"A runner's biggest bugaboo is the stopwatch," says Jim Couts, a sports psychology consultant in Long Beach, California. "Many runners feel compelled to keep track of how long it takes to go from here to there, and as Type A personalities, they're uptight and under too much stress. They definitely need to learn to *exercise just for sheer pleasure*."

The perfect place to experience *such a refreshing change* is the swimming pool. A cool, clear pool becomes the perfect think tank— a refuge where you can improve your mental training without overworking your body. The water insulates and protects you from outside stimuli, allowing you to think without interruption.

Lynne Cox, "Into the Think Tank"

Unity and
Coherence   **369**

Practice Your Skills

A. Rewrite the following paragraphs, improving the unity and coherence. Delete details that do not support the main idea of each paragraph. Arrange the remaining details in the most appropriate logical order and add transitions where they are needed.

1.   Surfing was invented in Hawaii. Modern surfers use boards of fiberglass. When early European explorers first came to Hawaii, they were surprised to find the natives riding waves. They stood on wooden planks and rode to the shore with great daring and skill. The Europeans soon learned this peculiar sport, which came to be known as "surfing." The sport was slow to catch on in Europe and America. In the 1960's the sport became popular due to movies about teen beach parties and surfing songs by groups like the Beach Boys. Even now, California is still sometimes called "The Surfing Capital of the World." In the old days, members of the Hawaiian royalty would surf to show their courage. The Hawaiians were also known to be great boat builders.

2.   A show horse must exhibit the best qualities of its breed to excel in competition. Arabian horses, for example, are known for their widely set eyes and flared nostrils. Their legs are slender, ending in delicate fetlocks and tapering hooves. Their necks are arched, rising elegantly and proudly from sculptured withers, or shoulders. Their chests are deep and wide, and they generally have full, sloping backs and arched tails. As their name implies, these elegant show horses were first bred by nomadic Arabs. Their horses were the most prized possessions of these tribes.

B. Read the two paragraphs that follow. Then rewrite them using transitional devices to make a stronger link between the paragraphs. Also add transitions within each of the paragraphs where they are needed.

    It is a hot day for the annual boat race at Montauk Bay. Spectators line the shore, eagerly awaiting the beginning of the race. Brightly colored sailboats jam the harbor. The captains and crews board their boats. They carefully survey their equipment. Sails are tightened, ropes are retied, knots are checked, and navigation equipment is logged in.

    Boating accidents are often the result of not checking things on board or of ignoring foul weather. It is important that rules are followed to ensure a safe race. The captain and crew should survey the equipment on board in order to uncover any problems.

How Do I Write a Conclusion?

WRITER TO WRITER

If I didn't know the ending of a story, I wouldn't begin. I always write my last line, my last paragraphs, my last page first.

Katherine Anne Porter, novelist

Like songs, films, ballets, and basketball games, the writing you do needs an ending, or **conclusion.** There are many types of conclusions you can choose from; however, they all generally should do the following:

- wrap up the ideas in the work
- follow logically from the introduction and body of the work
- not introduce new, unrelated material
- provide the writing with a feeling of finality
- leave the reader with something to think about

TYPES OF CONCLUSIONS

A conclusion, like an introduction, should support your writing purpose and personal goals. Typical methods for concluding your writing are presented below and on the following pages.

Restating the Main Idea You can sometimes conclude a composition by simply restating the main idea.

> Dinosaurs ruled the earth for 150 million years, but 65 million years ago their reign ended. Although there are still questions about what caused their death, it seems clear that changes in climate played a role. The failure of the dinosaurs to adapt to a new climate brought about their downfall.

A similar way to conclude a composition is to summarize or restate the main ideas or topic sentences of the body paragraphs. Each sentence in such a conclusion summarizes the ideas from a different body paragraph of the composition.

Writing
TIP

A conclusion that summarizes generally works best in a long work that covers much material.

STUDENT MODEL

How Do I Write
a Conclusion?   **371**

Generalizing About the Information Given You may want to conclude a composition by making a general statement, or **generalization,** about the information you have dealt with. The following generalization ties together information about three separate artists.

> Robert Frost didn't publish his first book of poems until his late thirties. Vladimir Horowitz, in his eighties, was still one of the greatest pianists on earth. Grandma Moses didn't start painting until her seventies, and she was still going strong in her nineties. Obviously, age is no barrier to accomplishment in the arts.

Making a Prediction In the following example, the writer concludes by speculating on the possibility of travel between stars some time in the distant future. Notice his unusual, but effective, technique of adding a one-sentence "clincher" at the end.

> It is difficult to go to the stars. But it is not impossible. There are not one, but many, many future-magic technologies, all under intensive development for other purposes, that, if suitably modified and redirected, can give the human race a magic starship that will take us to the stars.
>
> And go we will.
>
> **Robert L. Forward, *Future Magic***

Asking a Question Writers sometimes conclude by asking a question that sums up their opinions:

> Of all the causes that attract the attention of these young people, the plight of nature is one which may truly be a last call. Things wild and free are being destroyed by the impersonality of our attitude toward the land. What better way to fight the destruction of nature than to place in the hands of the young this powerful plea for a land ethic?
>
> **Carolyn and Luna Leopold,**
> **Introduction to *A Sand Country Almanac***

Teaching Tip: Asking Questions

Explain to students that the question asked in the model is a *rhetorical* question —that is, a question that is meant to emphasize a point rather than to elicit an answer.

372 Writing Handbook

Off the Record

"Which, of all defects, has been the one most fatal to a good style? The not knowing when to come to an end."
—Sir Arthur Helps
Companions of My Solitude

Making a Recommendation Writers often conclude persuasive pieces with a recommendation for action.

> It is a terrible, an inexorable law that one cannot deny the humanity of another without diminishing one's own: in the face of one's victim, one sees oneself. Walk through the streets of Harlem and see what we, this nation, have become.
> **James Baldwin, "Fifth Avenue Uptown: A Letter from Harlem"**

Ending with the Last Event Some narratives—pieces of writing that tell stories—simply end with the last incident.

> Oh, horror upon horror!—the ice opens suddenly to the right, and the left, and we are whirling dizzily, in immense concentric circles, round and round . . . . The circles grow rapidly small—we are plunging madly within the grasp of the whirlpool—and amid a roaring, and bellowing, and thundering of ocean tempest, the ship is quivering—oh God!—and—going down!
> **Edgar Allan Poe, "MS Found in a Bottle"**

Practice Your Skills

The following paragraphs are the conclusions of short persuasive papers. Decide which conclusion is weak and which is strong. Explain your answer and rewrite the weak conclusion.

1. For the school, a student newspaper provides a popular extracurricular activity to keep students constructively occupied. For the students, it provides valuable instruction in a variety of fields, including writing, photography, and typesetting. Perhaps most important, it gives students the satisfaction of seeing an excellent final product that they themselves created. It is clear, then, that since the newspaper provides major benefits for both school and students, discontinuing it would be a serious mistake.

2. In conclusion, then, golfers should use caddies rather than electric carts. My father was a caddie when he was a boy, and he still enjoys playing golf today. I've never played golf, myself—I like tennis. But at least if you walk instead of ride in a cart, you get some exercise. Of course, if you carry your own bag you get still more exercise.

Writing TIP

Restating and summarizing are good ways of concluding expository pieces. Predictions, questions, and recommendations are effective conclusions for persuasive writing.

How Do I Write a Conclusion? **373**

You might tell students that the French settlers of Acadia in Nova Scotia were expelled from Canada in 1755 because they refused to accept British rule. By 1790 more than 4,000 Acadians had settled in Southern Louisiana.

Encourage students to research the origin and meaning of some of the terms from Cajun culture such as *jambalaya, gumbo, creole, lagntappe,* and *mirliton.* Challenge students to find additional Cajun terms.

On the Lightside

SPEAKING CAJUN

Perhaps you have tasted gumbo, or jambalaya, or creole, or other Cajun dishes. These complex recipes are reflections of the culture of the Cajuns, who have lived for more than two hundred years in the bayous of southern Louisiana. During this time, however, the Cajuns have contributed more than food; they have also created a rich and hearty language called the Cajun dialect. Like their food, the Cajun language is a spicy mixture. It is basically a form of French, but it also includes seasonings from English, Native-American languages, African languages, and the French spoken in Canada.

The story of the Cajun language begins in 1604, when French settlers founded the colony of Acadia in Canada. When the British captured the colony, they forced out everyone who would not swear allegiance to the British. Many of the Acadians moved to Louisiana. There they established their own communities and maintained a separate culture. Their French language did not have the words to describe some of the things they encountered in this frontier land, so they borrowed words from the English settlers, Native Americans, and slaves they encountered in this new homeland. Over time, they even changed their own name to Cadian, and finally to Cajun.

Today Cajuns still live in southern Louisiana. Their language, like their food, remains a zesty part of American culture.

374

374

What Are the Types of Revision?

Revision is like taking a rough diamond and cutting and polishing it into a finished gem. You begin with raw material—a rough draft. You then revise this material to create the finished product, your final draft. However, revising is not limited to the final stages of writing; it can occur at any time during the process. For more information about the stages of the writing process and for detailed revision checklists, see "Thinking Through Your Writing Process," page 22.

WRITER TO WRITER

I review my writing every time I write something new to see what mistakes I've made.

Adalberto Pina, student
Boston, Massachusetts

There are three basic types of revision—**revising for ideas,** or what you say, **revising for form,** or the way you say it, and **proofreading,** or correcting mistakes in usage, grammar, and mechanics. You generally will need to do at least one, and possibly all of these types of revision to improve your draft. Consider the possibility of inviting an outside response. Often it is worthwhile to get ideas for revision from other people—your classmates, your peers, and perhaps from your teacher.

Revising for Ideas

Most writers begin revising by looking at the content of their rough draft. They read over their work to make sure it has a clear focus that accomplishes their goals and that all necessary ideas have been included. They also look for ideas that are unnecessary or distracting from their main focus. Here is the rough draft of a paragraph from a student's composition.

> Konrad Lorenz showed that when a bird is born, the bird looks around for its mother. it follows its mother around, imitating her actions. When it sees its mother and hears it's mother's voice, it forms an imediate bond. By imitating its mother, the young bird learns how to swim to find food and to communicate with other birds.

Writing Handbook 12:
What Are the Types of Revision?

Objectives

1. To identity three types of revisions: revising for ideas, revising for form, and proofreading
2. To understand and apply techniques of revising for ideas and form
3. To understand and apply proofreading techniques

Handbook Mini-Lessons

For information on topics related to the types of revisions, see the following mini-lessons.

- Self-Editing and Peer Response, pp. 378–382
- How Can I Achieve Clarity? pp. 383–389
- Point of View, pp. 430–433
- Drafting Paragraphs, pp. 345–349
- Unity, Coherence, and Transitional Devices, pp. 361–369

Teaching Strategies

Teaching Tip: Revision

Emphasize to students that a check must always be made to see if the three types of revision mentioned here are necessary. While a paper may not need to undergo each type of revision, every paper must be carefully assessed to determine what kinds of revision will be necessary.

Critical Thinking

Analyzing Have students study the model paragraph for other ideas that may need revision or clarification. *(Possible example: the author points out that the young bird learns from its mother how to swim. Since only some birds swim, Lorenz must have focused on particular kinds of birds. Should they be specified?)*

Reading this draft, one of the writer's classmates pointed out that he didn't know who Konrad Lorenz was. Was he a scientist? The writer decided to insert this information in the first sentence when revising the draft.

Revising for Form

When you revise for form, you make sure that your composition has unity and coherence, that your ideas are elaborated fully, that each paragraph deals with a separate idea, and that you used transitions to make the order of the ideas clear. You also look for places where sentences can be combined to eliminate unnecessary repetition.

In the student's rough draft, the sentence "When it sees its mother and hears it's mother's voice, it forms an immediate bond" describes an event that occurs *before* the bird begins to follow its mother around. Therefore, the student decided to move the sentence to make the order of the events clear.

Proofreading

Proofreading is often the final step in the revising process. When you proofread, you look for and correct errors you may have missed or possibly introduced in earlier revisions. Focus on punctuation, capitalization, spelling, grammar, and usage. Notice how the student corrected such errors in the draft below. The student also typed and penciled in the revisions.

> In the 1960's austrian psychologist Konrad Lorenz showed that when a bird is born, it looks around for its mother. it follows its mother around, imitating her actions. When it sees its mother and hears it's mother's voice, it forms an imediate bond. By imitating its mother, the young bird learns how to swim to find food and to communicate with other birds. This process of bonding with the mother and learning from her actions is called imprinting.

Teaching Tip: Proofreading

Whenever students are engaged in proofreading, urge them to break up the task into at least three stages: grammar and usage, punctuation, and capitalization and spelling. When it comes to spelling, a useful resource to have available is one or more of those small spelling guides that are designed for use by secretarial workers. These books spell and divide into syllables virtually every word students will be called upon to use. They are convenient and easy to handle.

Practice Your Skills

Revise the passage below, using the proofreading symbols and handwritten editorial comments as your guide. Feel free to make other changes as well.

I wonder what Helen Keller's life would have been like if she hadn't had all those disadvantages. Probably she would have been a great person. I mean greater, or great in a different way. Maybe she would have become an actress, a musician, or a painter. Or scientist. There are two selections in our Literature textbook about her. There's the play, The Miracle Worker and the other is an essay by Helen Keller. She must have been extremely smart. She wrote very well. But she needed Anne Sullivan's help to "talk" to other people. She couldn't look into a microscope or telescope, or see a painting or hear music. Anne Sullivan was really great for sticking with her and teaching her so much. Helen's parents loved her even though they didn't know how to help her until Anne Sullivan came along. Yes, Helen Keller was one of those rare people who would have been great no matter what they did. But her gifts might have been lost to the world if Anne Sullivan hadn't discovered them. Until then, people thought she was an uncontrollable child who didn't have any intelligence at all and would never learn. Anne Sullivan was strict but that was because she loved Helen and wanted her to learn.

What disadvantages?

I don't know who Anne Sullivan is.

This sentence seems out of place.

Does her refer to Anne or Helen?

This seems to belong earlier in the composition.

What Are Types of Revision? **377**

Self-Assessment and Peer Response

Objectives

1. To understand and apply strategies for self-assessment
2. To understand the role of the peer reader and to elicit and benefit from peer response
3. To respond effectively to another person's writing

Handbook Mini-Lessons

For information on topics related to self-assessment and peer response, see the following mini-lessons.

- What Are the Types of Revision? pp. 375–377
- Sharing and Publishing, pp. 401–403

Teaching Strategies

Critical Thinking

Drawing Conclusions Ask students why it is *not* a good idea for self-assessment to take place immediately after a first draft is completed. *(Writers must detach themselves from their work to gain objectivity. If self-editing begins immediately after drafting, the writer may overlook problems that some time away from the paper will reveal.)*

Teaching Tip: Self-Assessment

Students may need to examine a paper several times in order to revise it completely. A piece of writing can rarely be examined and revised once for all deficiencies. Students may wish to make an outline of a draft to check for organizational problems first; after revising it and adding missing information, they can review it again for usage and spelling mistakes.

WRITING
HANDBOOK
13

Self-Assessment and Peer Response

Like other parts of the writing process, revision offers you many choices. When you revise, you can choose the revision method that best suits you and your writing situation. Two possible approaches to revision are self-assessment and peer response. These two methods can provide you with a wide range and variety of responses.

SELF-ASSESSMENT

When you assess your own work, you revise with little or no assistance from other people. This can be difficult, because you must try to look at your writing objectively, as though you were seeing it for the first time. Here are general guidelines for revising your own work:

- **Read your work aloud.** Hearing your words spoken sometimes reveals hidden problems.
- **Outline your work.** Although many writers use outlining as a tool for planning and organizing their writing, you may also make an outline to check the structure of your work after you have written a rough draft.
- **Read your work from the point of view of your audience.** Ask yourself, "If I were this person, would everything in this piece be clear? Would I need more background information? What would I find confusing or uninteresting?"
- **Use revision checklists.** Check for specific problems with content, form, sentence structure, grammar, usage, and mechanics. The Revision Checklists in "Thinking Through Your Writing Process," page 22, may help.

Visage et Main, by Fernand Leger, 1953

PEER RESPONSE

Writers often don't see problems in their own work because of their emotional attachment to it, or they may be too harsh on themselves and make unnecessary changes. In both situations, the solution is simple: have someone else review your writing and make suggestions for improving it. A classmate who reads and comments on your work is called a **peer reader.** The suggestions and comments made by a classmate are called **peer response.**

You can use responses to your writing at various points in the writing process and for various reasons. These responses can help you determine what you want to say; find new ideas; gain perspective; see what works; organize and clarify material; and improve an argument.

W R I T E R   T O   W R I T E R

When I finish writing a story, I read it over and try to picture it happening in my mind. If there is a part that seems out of place, I'll try to fix it. Also, I'll read it out loud to someone. I'll find the point where they lose interest and change it.

Leslie Gewin, student
Birmingham, Alabama

What to Ask Your Peer Reader

The most valuable feedback that a peer reader can give you is an honest account of his or her own experience with your writing. To gain insights into the reader's experience with your work, ask him or her questions such as the following:

- "Say back to me in your own words what you hear me stating in my writing."
- "Which words or phrases stick in your mind? Which passages or features did you like best?"
- "What do you hear as my main point or idea (or event or feeling)? What supporting ideas do you think are most effective? least effective?"
- "What ideas, feelings, beliefs, and opinions are suggested in my writing but not actually stated directly? What would you like to hear more about?"
- "Does my writing arouse any emotion in you? If so, what emotion do you feel?"
- "Who do you think my audience is? Does my writing seem appropriate for that audience?"
- "What, specifically, could I do to improve my organization? the development of my main ideas?"
- "What, specifically, could I do to make the relationships between my ideas clearer?"

Self-Assessment and
Peer Response   **379**

Critical Thinking: Analyzing

Ask students which of the questions to the peer reader might be most appropriate for a personal narrative, for an editorial, for an expository theme, or for any other kinds of writing with which your students are familiar. Ask students to come up with other possible questions for the types of writing you discuss.

Humanities Connection

Art Note The picture on the previous page, *Visage et Main* (1953), which in French means "face and hand," is a painting in the cubist form by Fernand Leger, (b. 1881, France, d. 1955). Cubism is a technique in which the painter portrays the human figure as combinations of geometric, mechanical shapes. Leger was the only French master who devoted his life's work to the cubist movement.

Ask: What effect does this painting have on you? How does the painter create the effect?

Teaching Tip: Reader as Helper

Point out to students that in a very real sense the peer reader is the writer's helper and assistant. As readers, students can make clear to their peers what worked and what didn't in a piece of writing. In turn, they can get similar guidance. Being constructive means peer readers should never begin by saying to themselves, "What can I find wrong with this?" Readers must always be aware of what they have been asked to listen for and respond to. For example, not every writer will ask a reader for specific suggestions for revision.

TIP

Before you begin work with a peer reader, make a list of questions you want to ask. Tailor your questions to the type of writing you are revising.

The questions that you ask your peer reader will change according to the type of writing you are revising. You will probably think of questions you want to ask in addition to the ones listed above. Remember that your peer response can be only as good as the questions you ask: if you ask for little guidance, you will receive little. If you ask for a lot of help, that's what you will get.

How to Help Your Peer Reader

The best way to help your reader show you his or her reaction to your writing is to *listen* to what is said. Sometimes it's difficult to hold back when you want to defend or explain yourself. Remember, though, that after you have heard your reader through, *you* will make the final decision about how you change your writing.

Here are tips on getting the most benefit from peer response.

- Don't try to explain or apologize for your writing.
- Don't respond until your readers have fully reacted to your work.
- Ask questions that require more than a yes or no answer so your readers can come up with their own judgments.
- Above all, don't tell your readers how you want them to respond to your writing. Allow them to respond freely; then make your own choices about revising your work.

How to Respond to the Writing of Others

Just as you might ask for peer response from a classmate, you must be prepared to give your own response to someone else's work. There is one important rule to keep in mind when responding to another's writing: *Be constructive, not destructive.* Your role is not to judge the writing, but simply to share politely and positively what happened to you when you read it.

Generally, when you are responding to someone else's writing, make sure that you have enough time to think about and absorb the material. Don't hurry your response.

When you give your response, try to relate your points to specific parts of the writing. Don't omit any kind of response, even if you're not sure that your response is "sensible." Try not to evaluate or advise the writer in abstract terms. Just tell him or her what you experienced; in other words, what you enjoyed, what you were confused by, or what you felt was particularly effective. The most valuable thing you can do is to tell the writer what you really saw and how you really reacted to the writing.

Springboard

You might want to share this sentence by Ralph Waldo Emerson with the class: "Tis the good reader that makes the good book." Discuss how this thought illuminates the relationship between a writer and a peer reader.

Ways of Responding

Some of the ways you can respond to another student's writing include **pointing, summarizing, telling,** and **finding holes.** One student, who had just read a novel set in the late nineteenth century, decided to write a short story set in that historical period. Here are two paragraphs of her story. Several responses given by her peer reader follow.

▼

She was the only child at the convent, but she blended in perfectly with the black-robed nuns. She had dark hair and eyes, a silent walk, and a way of watching and saying nothing that belonged in the quiet corridors and peaceful gardens.

Every day, that unnatural peace was shattered by Mr. Shote. Mother Superior had arranged for him to come and tutor the girl, because she never left the convent grounds. Mr. Shote was a large man with a red face and a beard. He joked as often as he scolded. The nuns liked him, but the first day the girl saw him she turned pale as a ghost and ran away, screaming.

Pointing   You might point out the words and phrases that had the strongest impact on you.

> "I liked the phrases 'black-robed' and 'unnatural peace.' They establish an ominous mood. The simile 'pale as a ghost' seemed like a cliché, though."

Summarizing   Quickly summarize your main impressions of the work. Ask the writer if this was the main idea or impression he or she was trying to convey.

Off the Record

"You can't fake it. Bad writing is a gift."
Richard Le Gallienne
quoted in *Pieces of Hate*
by Heywood Broun

Teaching Tip: The Reader/Writer Relationship

The best author-editor relationships are marked by mutual admiration and respect. This also holds true for the peer reader-writer relationship. You might want to share with students the following passage from a letter that editor Maxwell Perkins wrote to author F. Scott Fitzgerald, having them note Perkins' positive, respectful tone. The book Perkins is talking about is *The Great Gatsby*, which he had just received in first-draft form. His tone is one that every peer reader should adopt. "I think you have every right to be proud of this book. It is an extraordinary book, suggestive of all sorts of thoughts and moods. . . . I could go on praising the book and speculating on its various elements and meanings, but points of criticism are more important now. I think you are right in feeling a certain slight sagging in chapters six and seven, and I don't know how to suggest a remedy." In the peer reader-writer relationship, sometimes the peer reader will be able to suggest a remedy or help the writer come up with his own remedy.

Gifted and Talented Students Have these students prepare a model peer-editing conference with oral questions and responses. You might videotape the conference and allow the entire class to view the tape.

ANSWERS TO PRACTICE YOUR SKILLS

A. The process for self-editing and the final versions will vary. An edited version of the paragraph is shown in the example below.
In 1987, an Indian burial ground was discovered in a field in Kentucky. The men who found the field leased digging rights from the current owner and uncovered relics, which they later sold. Native Americans protested their actions and called what had been done looting and grave robbing. Thus began a serious inquiry into the question of who should own such cultural relics: those who located them or the descendants of those who buried them.
B. The process for self-editing as well as the openings to the stories, the questions, and the revisions will vary.

Additional Resources
- Writing Resource Book, pp. 28–29
- Peer Response Guides

"A mysterious little girl lives in a convent and, for some reason, fears the man who has come to tutor her. Is this the main idea of your story?"

Telling Try to tell the writer what your experience was as you read the work and how you reacted to the characters or descriptions in the piece.

"I like the little girl living in the convent, maybe because it reminds me of some movies I used to like. Also, she's mysterious; I don't know why she's there. And then I got really interested in the teacher, Mr. Shote. I thought, though, that if he was to be a scary character, he shouldn't seem so jolly."

Finding Holes When you find holes, or missing information, in a piece of writing, try to point out to the writer what you believe is missing.

"I was confused about what the girl was doing at the convent. If it is a mystery, you might want to imply that readers will find out about it later."

Practice Your Skills

A. Read the following piece and imagine that you wrote it yourself. Assess the piece, using one of the methods described in this handbook.

In 1987, an Indian burial ground was discovered in a field in Kentucky. The men who found the field took the relics they uncovered and sold them after leasing the digging rights from the owner. Native Americans protested the looting, calling it grave robbing, thus opening a serious inquiry into who should own such cultural relics: the public or private individuals.

B. Write the opening to a story based on one of the ideas below. Then give your story opening to a classmate for peer response. Choose questions to ask your peer reader from those listed on page 379. Use your reader's responses to revise your opening.

- a tornado in a small Indiana town
- a rock concert in a huge stadium
- opening night at a state fair
- a lost pet
- moving to another neighborhood
- a tie-breaking eleventh inning
- a roller coaster ride

How Can I Achieve Clarity?

Divers dislike going into unclear, murky water because of the danger of becoming lost or confused. Readers dislike wading through unclear writing for the same reasons. Getting lost trying to follow a writer's ideas or becoming confused by the presentation of the ideas can be a frustrating experience. Therefore, when revising a piece of writing, try to make your ideas as clear as possible. Asking yourself the following questions may be helpful: Will my reader understand this? Is there any way that I can make my ideas clearer?

One way to make your writing clear is to organize it carefully. Other techniques you can use to ensure the clarity of your writing are to use specific words, add details, and create paragraphs that highlight groups of related ideas.

USING SPECIFIC WORDS

The English language offers you a great many choices as a writer. The effectiveness of your writing depends, to a great extent, on your word choice, or diction. One very important quality to look for in the words you choose is precision. Words should be specific enough to convey exactly what you mean.

Specific Nouns   Nouns are specific when they refer to individual or particular things. If you refer to a *mountain,* you are being general. If you refer to *Mount Kilimanjaro,* you are being specific. Specific nouns help your reader identify the who, what, and where of your message.

Specific Verbs   Verbs are the most powerful words in sentences. They convey the action, the movement, and sometimes the drama of thoughts and observations. Suppose you read over a draft and find a sentence such as this one.

> The child ran down the narrow street.

How can you add interest to the sentence and satisfy your reader's desire to know more? The first thing you could do is replace the general noun *child* with a specific name. You might ask yourself, Is the verb *ran* descriptive enough to capture the reader's attention? Are there other words that are more specific? Our rich and varied language has many words to describe specific types of

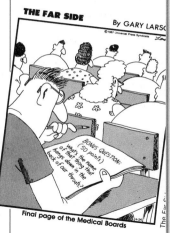

THE FAR SIDE   By GARY LARSON

Final page of the Medical Boards

Clarity   **383**

Writing Handbook 14:
How Can I Achieve Clarity?

Objectives

1. To recognize and use specific words
2. To identify and use effective techniques for adding details
3. To identify and use effective techniques for paragraphing

Handbook Mini-Lessons

For information on topics related to clarity, see the following mini-lessons.

- Unity, Coherence, and Transitional Devices, pp. 361–369
- How Can I Make My Language Richer? pp. 409–415
- Building Your Vocabulary, pp. 438–451

Teaching Strategies

Motivating

Ask students to listen carefully and follow your instructions. Then read the following: "Take out your books and before you do that write your name, but anyway, examine the verso page of any randomly selected spread and if you can identify an idea like any you have expressed in a recent paper pass it to your left and then read your partner's idea."

Use the ensuing confusion and predictable questions ("Which book?" Write our name on what? "What is a verso page?") to emphasize the importance of clarity in language and to begin a discussion of how more clarity can be achieved.

Collaborative Opportunity

Have students work together to find as many synonyms as possible for general nouns and verbs. They can begin with this list: NOUNS: *ruler* (king), *tool, worker, result, art;* VERBS: *make, get, confuse, neglect, revise.* After students have exhausted their own word inventories for synonyms of the general words, they may consult a thesaurus or dictionary of synonyms for additional possibilities.

Teaching Tip: Specific Modifiers

Point out that while many synonyms exist for most adjectives and adverbs, each specific modifier usually has a slightly different connotation, which underscores the importance of choosing these modifiers carefully. As an example, list the following synonyms for the adjective *beautiful* on the board, and discuss with students the connotation of each: *lovely, handsome, pretty, bonny, comely, fair, good-looking, glorious, splendid, resplendent, sublime, superb, exquisite, elegant,* and *choice.*

Writing
—TIP—

Keep an ongoing list of powerful sensory modifiers and refer to it frequently when writing.

running, such as *bolt, race, careen, scamper, dart, scramble, fly, scurry, gallop, zoom, dash,* or *flee.* Choosing one of these can make your writing clearer and more lively.

Specific Modifiers As you select modifiers, there are three general rules to remember:

- **Don't overuse modifiers.** If you choose your nouns and verbs well, you will not need as many modifiers. For example, the verb *trudge* is more effective than the phrase *walk slowly.*
- **Avoid empty modifiers.** These include words such as *nice, good, really, interesting, wonderful, great, excellent, awful, terrible, awesome.* All these modifiers do is express approval or disapproval. They do not tell why the writer approves or disapproves.
- **Use your senses.** There are many modifiers that enliven language by appealing to the senses of sight, hearing, touch, taste, and smell. Sight words can describe colors, such as *azure* or *jet;* shapes, such as *portly;* textures, such as *glossy;* or appearances, such as *ramshackle.* Sound words describe what you hear, such as *raucous* or *gurgling.* Touch words describe how things feel, such as *spongy* or *gritty.* Taste words, such as *tangy* or *burnt,* describe a taste; and smell words tell about odors, such as *spicy* or *acrid.* When you use these words, your writing usually becomes more descriptive, more interesting, and more effective.

WRITER TO WRITER

I try to use all the senses when I write. I like to compare things to something else. I open a jar of vanilla or smell a magnolia and think, what does this scent remind me of? I'm always transforming anything that's happening in my life into language.

Sandra Cisneros, writer and teacher

Using the Thesaurus and the Dictionary Two tools that can help you to choose specific, interesting words are the thesaurus and the dictionary. Suppose that you have written the following sentence:

The injured player walked off the football field.

Springboard

Write this sentence on the board: "The *thin* man *fell* to the ground." Challenge students to replace the underlined words with as many specific synonyms as possible. Set a time limit and explain that the winner will be the student with the longest list of synonyms that make sense.

The verb *walked* is not very clear because it doesn't tell the reader how the player walked. To find a replacement for the word, you might look in a thesaurus, which lists synonyms, or words that are similar in meaning. Your thesaurus may be a book, or it may be a part of the word-processing program you are using. Under the entry for *walk,* you might find some of the following synonyms: *amble, hike, hobble, journey, march, meander, pace, parade, perambulate, plod, promenade, ramble, rove, saunter, stray, stroll, traipse, traverse, wander.*

Based on the list from the thesaurus, you might choose to replace *walk* with *hobble.* Your next step would be to check the word *hobble* in a dictionary to make sure that it has the precise meaning you want to convey. In the dictionary you would find an entry such as the following:

Notice that this dictionary entry not only confirms that *hobble* is the right word to use, but it also tells you the proper past-tense form—*hobbled.* Therefore, you can revise your sentence as follows:

The injured player hobbled off the football field.

Nearly everyone has had the experience of trying to assemble an item that is described as "easy to assemble," only to find that the enclosed instructions are difficult or impossible to follow. Ask students to recount some of their experiences. What details were missing from the directions? What assumptions did the writer of the directions make about the necessity of certain details that turned out not to be valid?

ADDING DETAIL

Often your writing is unclear and readers get lost because you have provided too little information. Showing your work to a peer reader can help you identify such problems. If you think that your ideas need to be made clearer with additional information, there are three methods of elaborating to consider: **adding description, adding explanation,** and **showing rather than telling.**

Adding Description   Some statements in your writing can be clarified by adding description. Suppose that you are writing a paragraph about how to make a perfect omelet. One sentence of your paragraph reads as follows:

Whip the eggs and milk until it looks just right.

This sentence is unclear because the reader won't necessarily know what "just right" means. You can make the statement clearer by adding descriptive details.

Whip the eggs and milk until the milk, egg whites, and yolks are completely blended and the entire mixture is a uniform, frothy yellow.

Adding Explanation   Sometimes, when you show work to a peer reader, he or she will fail to understand what you are saying. Often the reason for this may be that the reader needs more explanation. The types and sources of elaboration, or further explaining, are discussed in Writing Handbook 8, pages 351–356.

Suppose that you are writing a report about the rain forests of South America. One part of your report reads as follows:

Over half of the known species of animals and plants inhabit the rain forests of South America. Legislation is urgently needed to protect the forests.

A reader who doesn't know anything about the rain forests would find this part of the report confusing. The relationship between the two sentences isn't clear, so the reader won't understand why the forests need protection. The problems with the paragraph can be solved by adding additional information, or explanation.

Over half of the known species of animals and plants inhabit the rain forests of South America. The rain forests are thus the most important of all habitats for life on earth. Unfortunately, these forests are disappearing at an alarming rate. It has been estimated that as many as 3,000 acres of rain forest are being cleared each hour for building, farming, and cattle grazing. When the land is cleared, the plants and animals on it die. Many live nowhere else on the earth. Therefore, if we are to avoid mass extinction of rain-forest life, the governments of South America must pass laws to protect the forests.

Destruction of a Brazilian rain forest.

Combining Detail and Specific Words It is not always enough just to be specific. Sometimes your writing requires more details. A piece of writing that has precise words, adequate detail, and appropriate explanation is clear and satisfying to the reader, even if, like the following paragraph, it only describes how a can opener works.

▼

A can opener has a sharp-edged cutting blade or wheel that slices into the lid. A toothed wheel fits beneath the lip of the can, and rotates the can so that the cutting wheel is forced into the lid. Two further toothed wheels—one above the other —form a pair of spur gears to transmit the turning force from the handle.

David Macaulay, *The Way Things Work*

Rain Forest Column XV, by Louise Nevelson, 1967.

PROFESSIONAL
M O D E L

Clarity   **387**

Teaching Tip: Adding Exposition

Remind students that the amount and kind of detail needed to make a piece of exposition clear depends partly on the audience. Readers who know a great deal about rain forests and the roles they play may be able to get along with less information than the model paragraph provides. Readers unfamiliar with rain forests, however, absolutely need the additional details.

Humanities Connection

Art Note *Rain Forest Column XV*, 1967, is a relief by sculptor Louise Nevelson (b. 1899/1900, United States, d. 1988). In sculpture, a relief is a work in which figures and forms stand out against a surrounding flat surface. The success of a relief depends upon the detail and precision of the sculpted shapes. Because the original column was made of wood (which decays over time), Nevelson sought to preserve the clarity of the relief by casting it in bronze, a wear-resistant metal. She disassembled the work and cast each form separately. She then applied black paint to restore the wood effect. Though dissatisfied with the result in this work, Nevelson never abandoned her efforts to achieve permanence in art through preservation of detail.

Marcel Marceau, famous French mime (pantomimist), in character as Bip.

Notice the specific verbs such as *slices* and *rotates*. Would *cuts* and *turns* convey the meaning as well? Notice, too, the specific nouns and modifiers, such as *toothed wheels* and *spur gears*. Each word is exact. Yet it is more than exactness and specificity that make the writing effective. The author has included just enough details to explain how a can opener works.

Showing Rather Than Telling   Which of the two sentences that follow interests you more?

I was angry when I saw Angelo riding the black and gold BMX racing bike I had been saving up to buy.

When I saw Angelo riding the black and gold BMX racing bike I had been saving up to buy, my heart began to pound, I could feel my cheeks get hot, and I felt as if I could actually spit fire.

If you find you are more interested in the second sentence, you are like most readers, who prefer showing to telling. The second sentence makes it possible for us to imagine the speaker's face reddening, hear his or her heart pounding, and feel the intensity of the anger expressed in the simile "as if I could actually spit fire." The reader has been shown the anger rather than simply told about it.

Adding description and explanation to your work will help you show your readers what is happening. They will become involved and be inspired to read on.

P ARAGRAPHING

Paragraphing is the process of separating a group of ideas into smaller groups of related ideas. A piece of writing that is properly divided into paragraphs is easy for the reader to follow and understand.

Some writers begin their work by gathering ideas and then dividing these ideas into groups. Each group of ideas is then used to develop a separate paragraph. Other writers try to get all their ideas down quickly in a draft. They then go back and revise their work to create paragraphs. Often this revision involves moving ideas around. You might find, for example, that an idea that you placed in one paragraph should be moved into a different paragraph, with other ideas that are related to it. Keep the following guidelines in mind when you consider the paragraphing in a rough draft.

Guidelines for Paragraphing

Nonfiction

- **Look for changes in content.** When a new idea is introduced or the topic changes, begin a new paragraph.

- **Make sure that each paragraph presents a set of related ideas and has a specific purpose.**

- **Think about the order of your paragraphs.** Do they follow reasonably from one another, or should they be rearranged in an order that would be clearer to your reader?

- **Look for paragraphs that present too many ideas.** Decide how it would be possible for you to break those ideas into more manageable units.

- **Watch for unnecessary or unrelated ideas in a paragraph.** Consider deleting them or moving them to another paragraph.

- **Look for places where your ideas seem to shift in direction or focus.** Consider creating new paragraphs in these places or, if necessary, deleting unrelated material.

- **Add transitions, if necessary, to make the order of your ideas clearer.**

Fiction

- **Look for any major change in the setting or place where the action is occurring.** Create a new paragraph whenever those changes occur.

- **Look for changes in time.** Create new paragraphs to signal these shifts.

- **Look for major changes in the action.** These may occur with changes of scene, or they may occur within the same scene. Create a new paragraph to make it clear that a change has occurred.

- **Examine your dialogue and create a new paragraph whenever the speaker changes.**

- **Look for shifts in person and point of view.** Decide whether these are appropriate. If they are, create paragraphs there. If they are not, eliminate the shifts or provide enough information to make the situation clear.

Clarity **389**

Individualizing Instruction

LD Students The guidelines for paragraphing may seem overwhelming to these students. To help them gain understanding, choose some simple paragraphs from textbooks or other reading materials and discuss the reasons for the paragraph breaks.

Answers will vary in some instances. Good answers should approximate the examples shown.

1. More specific replacements for *smart* might be *intelligent, rational,* and *clever.* Replacements for *afraid* might be *fearful, alarmed,* and *apprehensive.*

2. More specific replacements for *touching* might be *examining, inspecting, scrutinizing,* and *investigating.* Replacements for *moving* might be *shifting, manipulating,* and *transporting.*

3. Exposition may resemble the following example: "The computer asks questions to clarify the symptoms, and the doctor supplies the needed information. The computer then responds by suggesting the types of treatment that would be most beneficial."

4. An appropriate replacement would resemble the following example: "Perhaps one day we will have to deal with computers that pout, whine, shout, and hurl software at us—and not only make mistakes but invent excuses for their mistakes."

5. Paragraphs should begin on lines 1, 6, 10, 17, and 20.

Additional Resources

- Writing Resource Book,
  pp. 30–32

Practice Your Skills

Study the sample composition that follows. Then rewrite the composition to improve its clarity. Follow the directions given at the end.

Artificial Intelligence

1 Can you imagine a computer developing a mental illness? Arthur C.
2 Clarke did. In his novel *2001: A Space Odyssey,* Clarke created a
3 smart computer named Hal that becomes afraid and turns on its
4 creators. Like a human being, Hal feels emotions, such as love
5 and distrust, and when these emotions get out of hand, trouble
6 follows. Will it ever be possible for computers to become that
7 much like humans? No one knows for sure. However, many
8 scientists throughout the world are currently working on ways to
9 make computers more like people. The science of modeling human
10 behaviors on computers is called *artificial intelligence.* One
11 successful area of research into artificial intelligence has
12 to do with what are known as expert systems. An expert
13 system is a computer program that has been taught much of
14 what an expert in a given field would know. Today there are many
15 expert systems available for medical diagnosis. The user—
16 probably a doctor—types in a patient's symptoms.
17 Another successful research area is robotic movement.
18 The computer is attached to mechanical "arms" and "legs." It uses
19 information from the environment to control the limbs for
20 touching objects or moving across a floor. Will computers ever
21 learn to do all of these things as well as human beings can?
22 Probably not, at least not for many, many years. Nevertheless,
23 the new science of artificial intelligence has yielded interesting
24 results. Perhaps one day we will have to deal with
25 computers that pout or become paranoid the way Hal did
26 in Clarke's novel. Only time will tell.

1. Look at the sentence on lines 2–4. Replace the words *smart* and *afraid* with more specific modifiers. Use a thesaurus and dictionary to help you.
2. Replace the words *touching* and *moving* on line 20 with more specific verbs. Use a thesaurus and dictionary to help you.
3. On line 16, add exposition to tell readers how a doctor might find computer diagnosis valuable.
4. Replace the sentence on lines 24–26 with one that shows rather than tells what a near-human computer might be like.
5. Decide where the composition should be broken into paragraphs. Rewrite it in paragraphed form.

Correcting Problem Sentences

Good sentences communicate ideas clearly and hold your reader's attention. When revising a draft, always check to see if you can improve your sentences. Look particularly for sentences that are empty, stringy, overloaded, or padded.

CORRECTING EMPTY SENTENCES

Empty sentences are ones that do not really say anything. Some empty sentences simply repeat an idea that has already been stated. Others make a statement but fail to support it with a fact, a reason, or an example.

Eliminating Repeated Ideas

Your writing will be easier to read and much more interesting if you eliminate unnecessary repetition. Notice the strategies used to eliminate repetition in the following examples:

Repetitive   The unemployment rate in the city was high, and many people were out of work.

Strategy   The clause "many people were out of work" repeats the idea that "the unemployment rate in the city was high." Omit the second clause.

Revised   The unemployment rate in the city was high.

Correcting Problem
Sentences   **391**

Writing Handbook 15:
Correcting Problem Sentences

Objective

To identify and correct empty sentences, stringy sentences, overloaded sentences, and padded sentences

Handbook Mini-Lessons
For information on topics related to correcting problem sentences, see the following mini-lessons.
- Transitional Devices, pp. 364–367
- How Can I Vary My Sentences? pp. 416–418
- Sentence Combining, pp. 419–429
- Clauses and Sentence Structure, pp. 721–748

Writing
— TIP —
Repetition is often hard to spot in your own writing. It's a good idea to ask a peer reader for help.

Teaching Strategies

Collaborative Opportunity

As students address each type of problem sentence, have them work in groups of three to identify examples of each type in their own writing, perhaps from materials in their Writing Portfolios. Students should read each other's writing, identify problem sentences, and discuss possible corrections. Each writer should then decide if and how revisions will be made. Consider transferring specific problem sentences and revisions to overhead transparencies. Examples could then be examined and discussed by the entire class.

Repetitive	On Tuesday our class is going on a field trip. Our class is going to the art museum. We can go only if the bus is running. Fifteen students are in our class.
Strategy	Many sentences are used to convey few ideas. Combine sentences to eliminate repetition and choppiness.
Revised	If the bus is running on Tuesday, our class of fifteen students is going on a field trip to the art museum.

Adding Supporting Details   Many sentences are empty because they make general statements that are not supported by reasons, facts, or examples. Notice how the following sentences were improved:

Unsupported	I like Aim cameras because they are the best.
Strategy	Add facts to support your point of view.
Revised	I like Aim cameras because they are easier to use and take sharper pictures than other cameras.

Unsupported	Animals are fun.
Strategy	This sentence is so general that it doesn't say much. Use examples to help your readers understand what you mean.
Revised	Pet dogs and cats can be fun to watch when they get into frustrating situations because their facial expressions seem almost human.

Guidelines for Correcting Unsupported Sentences

- Look for statements in your writing that will make the reader ask *why?*
- Provide facts, reasons, and examples to support each claim. If you cannot, eliminate the claim.
- Be sure to add any transitional words and phrases that are needed for clarity and coherence.

W R I T E R T O W R I T E R

Using examples or details gives your topic support that is necessary to back up your opinion.

Diane Ceisel, student
Northfield, Illinois

Practice Your Skills

Revise these empty sentences, following the directions given. There is no single "correct" answer.

In items 1–6, delete repeated ideas or combine sentences to eliminate repetition.

1. Many bicyclists are interested in the Tour de France because it is an interesting bicycle race.
2. The pit bull knew I was afraid of him. He could sense my fear.
3. Diane was unjustifiably rude to her friends. She was rude for no good reason. She thought she was superior.
4. If you have ever been to Yellowstone Park, you know what a wonderful time you can have there. This park is a place to visit often. At Yellowstone Park, there is always something enjoyable to do, no matter how many times you have been there.
5. Have you ever been to a crowded concert? If you have not been to a crowded concert, you do not know what it is like to see a concert with 10,000 people.
6. On Saturday, we are going hiking. I am sure it will be a good hike if the park is not crowded. There are five of us going hiking, and everyone wants a good climb.

In items 7–12, correct the empty sentences by adding the reasons, facts, or examples described in parentheses.

7. Newspapers inform the public on current national and local events. Newspapers have advantages over television newscasts. (more in-depth coverage, readers can take their time and absorb more information)
8. The ocean is a great body of water that covers 70 percent of the earth's surface. The ocean can be dangerous. (storms common and unpredictable, no fresh water)
9. According to federal law, you must be eighteen years old before you can vote. This law is (fair/unfair) and (should not/should) be changed. (Support your opinion with your own reasons.)
10. The Renaissance was a time of great human achievement. The arts, especially, flowered at that time. (some of greatest painters and sculptors ever known, their works still survive)
11. The Red Cross is an organization that works to relieve human suffering. Its services are widespread. (disaster relief—fires, floods, earthquakes—throughout world)
12. I want to buy a car this year. It would cost as much money as I have in my savings account. My parents do not approve of the idea. (Tell how much the car costs and why your parents object.)

Springboard

Tell students that writers sometimes provide many details to make a humorous point. Read Mark Twain's description of a river pilot of whom he was not particularly fond: "He was a middle-aged, long, slim, bony, smooth-shaven, horse-faced, ignorant, stingy, malicious, snarling, fault-finding, mote-magnifying tyrant." Challenge students to write a similar detail-heavy description.

CORRECTING STRINGY SENTENCES

As you create a draft, or when you revise, look for stringy sentences. A stringy sentence contains too many ideas connected loosely by the word *and*. These sentences are difficult to follow because the reader must first sort out the ideas and then figure out how they are related. Here is an example:

Stringy The plane ran out of fuel, and it was forced to make an emergency landing, and no one was hurt, and one wing grazed the ground and broke off.

Notice that the relationships among the ideas in this sentence are not clear. Instead, the ideas are simply strung together with *and*'s. When you find such a sentence in your own writing, take it apart and think about the ideas it expresses.

Broken down The plane ran out of fuel.
It was forced to make an emergency landing.
No one was hurt.
One wing grazed the ground and broke off.

Ask yourself how the ideas are related. For example, in what order did events occur? Are any events related by cause and effect? Do you want to compare or contrast events?

Once you understand how the ideas are related, combine them again. Avoid overusing the word *and*. Instead, choose words that show the relationships between your ideas. Good connecting words include *if, then, because, when, therefore, while, although, which, as,* and *that.*

Revised   Because the plane had run out of fuel, it was forced to make an emergency landing. Though one wing grazed the ground and broke off, no one was hurt.

Practice Your Skills

Revise these stringy sentences by breaking them down into their parts and then recombining them. Add words to clarify the relationships among ideas.

1. The tourists went to the Louvre Museum, and they saw the *Mona Lisa,* and later they saw the Eiffel Tower, and they took several photographs of the structure.
2. I went to the annual art fair, and I purchased some paintings, and the paintings were oils, and then I bought some sculptures.
3. Ana auditioned for the play, and she read a monologue from *Romeo and Juliet,* then she sang a song from *West Side Story.*
4. Juan walked up the steps of the deserted house, and then he turned the knob on the front door, and he heard voices, and the voices were loud.
5. I saw a lightning bolt in the sky, and the sky was gray, and then I heard a clap of thunder and it frightened me.
6. Andy got a part-time job, and he works at the stadium, and he's saving for a new ten-speed bicycle.
7. Pedro learned how to windsurf, and he felt he needed a wet suit, and then he could surf in cold water, and he could continue to surf for hours.
8. The karate instructor demonstrated the basic maneuvers, and the maneuvers were very precise and difficult, and then she showed her students how to block their opponents' moves.
9. Mom lost her car keys, and we searched the entire house for them, and they finally showed up in her coat pocket, and she was very grateful we had found them.
10. The house looked very old, and it needed a paint job, and the shutters needed to be replaced, and my parents wondered whether the house was worth buying.

Correcting Problem
Sentences   **395**

CORRECTING OVERLOADED AND PADDED SENTENCES

Writing requires effort, and you might be reluctant to cut a single word. However, your writing will be much clearer and more streamlined if you learn to spot unnecessary wordiness.

Overloaded Sentences Sometimes the relationships between the ideas in a sentence are clear, but the sentence is still overloaded with too many ideas. Readers are exhausted by the time they reach the end of such a sentence because they haven't had time to pause and absorb the individual ideas in it. Try reading the following overloaded sentence and then study the strategy for revising it.

Overloaded	The California condor, which has the largest wingspan of any bird in North America, once ruled the air over the western portion of the continent, but now this magnificent bird is nearing extinction, for only about twenty survive, all of these in zoos, which makes it especially important for zookeepers to breed them in captivity.
Strategy	The writer has tried to communicate too many ideas in one sentence. Break the sentence into separate sentences, each expressing one or two ideas. One possibility is suggested below.
Revised	The California condor has the largest wingspan of any bird in North America. Once this magnificent bird ruled the air over the western portion of the continent, but now it is nearing extinction. Only about twenty survive, all of these in zoos. Consequently, zookeepers must breed condors in captivity if the species is to survive.

Padded Sentences Unlike an overloaded sentence, a padded sentence does not contain too many ideas. Instead, it uses more words than are necessary to communicate an idea. Although padded sentences may be grammatically correct, their wordiness makes them difficult to follow. As you revise your writing, remove the padding and shorten wordy expressions.

- **Taking out Extra Words** The following expressions contain extra words that merely repeat ideas. For every expression listed in the box, you will find a simpler way of saying the same thing.

Springboard

Provide students with these and other examples of padded expressions. Challenge students to reduce each expression to a single word: "in the event that" *(if);* "a large number of" *(many);* "because of the fact that" *(because);* "during the time that" *(while);* "in the very near future" *(soon);* "in close proximity" *(near).* Encourage students to add to the list.

Notice how removing the padding in the following sentences makes the meaning clearer:

Padded Pat hasn't been to school due to the fact that she is ill.
Revised Pat hasn't been to school because she is ill.

Padded What I want to say is that fad diets can harm your body and increase your likelihood of binge eating and weight gain.
Revised Fad diets can harm your body and increase your likelihood of binge eating and weight gain.

• **Reducing Clauses to Phrases** Frequently you can eliminate padding by reducing clauses beginning with *who is, that is,* or *which is* to simple phrases. Look at these examples:

Padded Skydiving, which is often considered a dangerous sport, requires specific training and equipment.
Revised Skydiving, often considered a dangerous sport, requires specific training and equipment.

Padded The statue that is in the plaza towers over the capital.
Revised The statue in the plaza towers over the capital.

Padded Kate Bush, who is now a solo performer, was formerly a backup vocalist for Peter Gabriel.
Revised Kate Bush, now a solo performer, was formerly a backup vocalist for Peter Gabriel.

Correcting Problem Sentences **397**

Teaching Tip: Padded Sentences

Point out to students that some padding comes from the use of inflated expressions that have become familiar because they are used by government officials and members of the legal profession. While these expressions sound impressive, their essential message can often be communicated in a single word. Some examples: "at this moment in time" (*now*); "due to the fact that" (*because*); "at your earliest convenience" (*soon*).

 Individualizing Instruction

ESL Students Stress to these students the difference between oral and written language. Point out that although many of the expressions listed in the box are used in conversation, they are usually eliminated in writing.

A. Answers will vary. Good revisions will eliminate overloaded sentences, as shown in the examples below.

1. Like detectives searching for clues, archaeologists search to discover the secrets of ancient civilizations. They investigate, for example, the culture of the ancient Egyptians who built splendid temples, tombs, and statues. Many of the Egyptian structures are covered with hieroglyphics, a type of writing that combined pictures with symbols that denote sounds.

2. Archaeologists rely on scientific aids, including aerial photography and electric current. Aerial photography may show traces of buried structures. When passed through the ground, electric current can measure the ground's moisture, indicating any ancient buildings that remain.

3. Among the most important spices, salt comes from the ocean or from deposits on land that was once covered by oceans. Incidentally, the mining of salt gave the city of Salzburg in Austria its name. *Saltzberg* means "salt city" in German. The city was so named because famous salt mines were located near it during the Middle Ages.

4. Boston, located on the eastern coast of Massachusetts, is a city of firsts. These firsts include the first public park in America, which was established in 1634. Boston Latin School, the first public school in America, still exists. Boston also established the first public library, the first lighthouse, and the first railroad. Finally, Boston University became the first college to admit women to all of its departments.

5. The grandparents of Lawrence Douglas Wilder, who was named after the poet Paul Laurence Dunbar and the abolitionist Frederick Douglass, were slaves. The legacy of slavery did not keep Wilder from realizing his dream of a successful political career. He fulfilled his dream in 1990 when he became the governor of Virginia, the first elected black governor in American history.

6. William Shakespeare, considered to be the greatest dramatist in history, wrote many plays. He earned his reputation by creating unforgettable characters who possess universal qualities and by displaying rare skill in the brilliant use of poetic language.

B. Answers will vary slightly. Good revisions will promote clarity, as shown in the examples below.

1. Tonight's football game at Central High has been postponed until tomorrow.

Practice Your Skills

A. Break down these overloaded sentences into separate sentences that express one or two ideas.

1. Like detectives, archaeologists, who study ancient objects and buildings, search for clues to the secrets of ancient civilizations such as that of the ancient Egyptians, who built splendid temples, tombs, and statues, many covered with hieroglyphics, which were a type of writing that combined pictures with symbols for sounds.

2. Archaeologists rely on scientific aids, which include aerial photography and electric current, because aerial photography may show traces of buried structures and electric current passed through the ground can measure the ground's moisture and, thus, show if any ancient buildings remain.

3. Salt, among the most important spices, comes from the ocean or from mining the salt deposits on land that was once covered by oceans, which explains the significance of the name of the city of Salzburg, in Austria, which means "salt city" in German, so named because during the Middle Ages there were famous salt mines located near the city.

4. Boston, located on the eastern coast of Massachusetts, is a city of firsts, including the first public park in America, established in 1634, and the first public school, the Boston Latin School (which is still in existence), as well as the first public library, lighthouse, and railroad in America, in addition to which Boston University was the first college to allow women into all its departments.

5. The grandparents of Lawrence Douglas Wilder, who was named after the poet Paul Laurence Dunbar and the abolitionist Frederick Douglass, were slaves, but this did not keep Wilder from realizing his dream, which was to have a successful political career, a success he realized in 1990 when he became governor of Virginia—the first elected black governor in American history.

6. William Shakespeare, who wrote many plays, is considered to be the greatest dramatist in history because he created unforgettable characters who had universal qualities and because he used language that was both brilliantly poetic and dramatic, and such skillful use of language is rare.

B. Revise each sentence by taking out extra words that do not add to the meaning of the sentence. Simplify *who, that,* and *which* clauses into phrases.

1. It just so happens that the football game between George Washington High School and Central High has been canceled for tonight and rescheduled for tomorrow.

2. What I want to do is finish this article and submit it to *Life* magazine for the September issue.
3. Congresswoman Connor, who is a member of the Committee on Armed Forces, submitted a report on defense spending.
4. Dion left the reception early on account of the fact that he had to attend another party, which was a retirement celebration for his boss.
5. Being that the trial was held in Washington, D.C., the press coverage was especially heavy.
6. The state track meet, which was the year's most important sporting event, attracted talent scouts from many universities.
7. What I think is that if you don't believe in your own abilities, no one else will, and the reason is that people are attracted to others with high self-esteem.
8. The point is that the Guggenheim Museum, which is located in New York City, attracts many tourists, partly due to the fact of the building's unusual design.

C. This short essay contains many problem sentences. Revise the essay, correcting empty, stringy, overloaded, and padded sentences.

The Statue of Liberty, which was given to the United States by France in 1884 is one of the best-known symbols of freedom in the world. It is a symbol that is familiar to millions of people around the world. A Frenchman, who was named Alexandre Gustave Eiffel (who was the same man who designed the Eiffel Tower) built the supporting framework, and the statue was finished in pieces in France, and then it was sent to the United States, and then it was assembled.

The statue depicts a strong, proud woman in a loose robe. Pride and strength emanate from her gaze and from her stance. Her right arm holds a torch, and her left arm a tablet, and the point is that this tablet bears an inscription and the date of the Declaration of Independence.

The statue stands on an island, which is called Liberty Island, which is in the middle of New York Harbor, where it has welcomed a great many thousands and thousands of immigrants with its inscription, on the tablet, which reads, in part, "Give me your tired, your poor, your huddled masses yearning to breathe free, the wretched refuse of your teeming shore. Send these, the homeless, tempest-tost to me. I lift my lamp beside the golden door!" which is a stirring comment on the fact that the United States is a nation of immigrants. Visitors from around the United States and the world come to see the statue.

2. I want to finish this article and submit it for the September issue of *Life*.
3. Congresswoman Conner, a member of the National Security Committee, submitted a report on defense spending.
4. Dion left the reception early to attend his boss's retirement party.
5. The press coverage was especially heavy because the trial was held in Washington, D.C.
6. The state track meet, the year's most important sporting event, attracted scouts from many universities.
7. If you don't believe in your own abilities, no one else will, because people are attracted to others who have high self-esteem.
8. The Guggenheim Museum in New York City attracts many tourists, partly because of the building's unusual design.
C. Answers will vary. A good revision will address all of the sentence problems identified, as shown in the example below.
The Statue of Liberty, given to the United States by France in 1884, is a symbol of freedom to millions of people throughout the world. Alexandre Gustave Eiffel, the Frenchman who designed the Eiffel Tower, built the statue's supporting framework. The statue itself was finished in pieces in France and sent to the United States, where it was assembled.
The Statue of Liberty depicts a woman in a loose robe whose gaze and stance communicate pride and strength. Her right arm holds a torch. In her left arm is a tablet bearing an inscription and the date of the Declaration of Independence.
Americans and visitors from other countries come to see the statue, which stands on Liberty Island in the middle of New York Harbor. The inscription on the tablet has welcomed many thousands of immigrants: "Give me your tired, your poor, your huddled masses yearning to breathe free, the wretched refuse of your teeming shore. Send these, the homeless, tempest-tost to me. I lift my lamp beside the golden door!" The words provide a stirring comment about the United States as a nation of immigrants.

Additional Resources
• Writing Resource Book, pp. 33–35
• Elaboration, Revision, and Proof-reading Worksheets

After students have read the feature, pose the question ''Can an illiterate person function in society?'' Discuss the difficulties of being unable to read or write. Encourage students to compare and contrast the difficulties experienced by an illiterate person today and in Sequoyah's time.

You might also prompt discussion of Sequoyah's undertaking, encouraging students to speculate about the process of developing an alphabet. Suggest that students research the Cherokee alphabet or the development of the English, Chinese, or Russian alphabets. Have students share their research with the class.

On the Lightside

THE CHEROKEE LANGUAGE

For centuries Native-American lore was passed down through the

generations mainly by word-of-mouth. At the beginning of the nineteenth century, however, a Cherokee named Sequoyah gave his people the ability to keep a written record of their culture.

As a child, Sequoyah had been fascinated by the "talking leaf" used by white settlers. He had seen these people write messages on paper and then read them; he wondered why his own people did not know the secret of the talking leaf. The question continued to haunt Sequoyah as he grew up. Although he became an accomplished silversmith, painter, and warrior, he—like the rest of his people—was illiterate. Then, a hunting accident left him partially crippled. With time on his hands, he began to investigate the mystery of the talking leaf. For twelve years he studied the way the Cherokee people spoke, and he developed a way to break down Cherokee words into individual sounds. Adapting letters from English, Greek, and Hebrew, he developed an alphabet of eighty-six symbols, each corresponding to a syllable of spoken Cherokee language. At last, the Cherokee people had a system for reading and writing their own language.

The alphabet Sequoyah invented earned him the respect of his own people and of the nation. Developing an entirely new alphabet had been a giant undertaking. For Sequoyah's efforts, the giant California redwood trees—the sequoias—were named after him.

Sharing and Publishing

Sometimes what you write is so private that you want to keep it to yourself. In most cases, though, the purpose of writing is to communicate with an audience, to share your thoughts and ideas with others.

WRITER TO WRITER

What I like best about writing is having someone understand and enjoy my work.

Rita Colafella, student
Watertown, Massachusetts

SHARING DURING THE WRITING PROCESS

Sometimes writers get stuck in the middle of a draft and don't know what to do next. Sometimes they get so caught up in their writing that they can't tell whether an idea is working well or not. If you find yourself worrying about the quality of what you've written or wondering what to do next, you might consider asking for help. Often another person's reactions can help you decide exactly what you need to do to improve your work or move ahead with confidence. Different people can provide a wide range of responses to your work. You can share your work in progress with relatives and friends. You can share it with a teacher in a writer's conference. You can also share it with your classmates, perhaps in a small-group discussion session.

There are many ways to share your work during the writing process. The following are some possibilities. See "Self-Assessment and Peer Response," pages 378–382, for specific suggestions on using peer response.

- Discuss your ideas with someone without showing that person what you've written. This is a good way to gather fresh ideas.
- Read all or part of your notes, outline, or draft to the other person.

Writing Handbook 16:
Sharing and Publishing

Objectives

1. To understand the benefits of sharing writing with others during the writing process
2. To recognize the various methods of publishing that are available

Handbook Mini-Lessons

For information on topics related to sharing and publishing, see the following mini-lessons.
- Self-Assessment and Peer Response, pp. 378–382
- Oral Communication Skills, pp. 479–482

Teaching Strategies

Teaching Tip: Sharing

Impress upon students that writing is often an all-consuming activity that demands a great deal of intense effort. It can be so tiring that the writer can reach a point where he or she can no longer judge whether or not the work is moving in the originally anticipated direction. It is at that point that the writer needs a fresh and objective look. Student peers can serve this function for each other.

Sharing and Publishing **401**

When students are working on a piece of writing, set aside a period of time each day when help and guidance can be secured. During this block of time, encourage students to use any of the suggested ways of sharing work. Students will benefit from knowing that a sharing period is a normal and natural part of the writer's work day.

COMPUTER TIP

Ask someone to sit at your terminal to read what you've written. You could even ask the other person to type in ideas or suggestions.

• Give all or part of your material to the other person to read and comment on.
• Arrange for a writer's conference with your teacher. Bring all of the work that you have done on the piece of writing. Also bring your writing portfolio.
• Hold a group discussion with other writers from your class who are working on similar projects. Share your work in progress and discuss ways to improve it.

Before you share your writing, compile a list of questions about aspects of your work that you would like your peer reader to respond to. That way, your reader will know what to look for as he or she reads your work and can focus on the problems that most concern you. For example, you might ask, "Do these ideas seem to work well together?" or "Are the steps in this process clear to you?" or "Can you tell why the main character is acting the way she does?" When your reader reacts to your work, he or she may also offer advice for improving your writing. Of course, thank your reader for the suggestions, but decide for yourself whether incorporating them will actually improve your writing.

PUBLISHING YOUR WORK

Once you have completed a piece of writing you are proud of, it is especially satisfying to share the finished product with an appropriate audience. The following list describes some of the ways you can publish your completed work.

Methods of Publishing

- Send your work in a letter to a friend or relative.

- Submit your work to your school newspaper or literary magazine. If your school doesn't have a literary magazine, consider starting one with some other students and a faculty sponsor.

- Submit your work to your community newspaper.

- Offer your work to the editor of a group, club, or organization newsletter such as ones produced by YMCAs, Boys' and Girls' Clubs, churches, synagogues, and school clubs.

- Photocopy your work onto a transparency to be used with an overhead projector.

- Form or join a writing exchange group. Simply get together with friends or classmates, in or out of school, and share your writing with one another.

- Store your work in a folder or writing portfolio that you can share with others. You can use a folder with several pockets to separate your writing into different categories.

- Present your work orally in a report, a speech, a reading, an oral interpretation, or a dramatic performance.

- Make a cassette recording of your work and create a listening center with other students.

- Make arrangements to have your work read at a school assembly or over the school's public address system.

- Save your work on a computer disk and exchange disks with another writer who has access to a computer. Add your "reviews" of each other's work and exchange disks again.

- Make your writing part of a poster, a collage, or a bulletin board display.

- Enter your work in a contest sponsored by a community organization or a magazine.

- Get a copy of *Writer's Market* or *Market Guide for Young Writers* at a local library. Look in these books for information about publishers that accept work by young people.

- Make your own book, magazine, newspaper, pamphlet, or flier and distribute it yourself.

Writing TIP

Be flexible about the final form your writing will take. Try to stay open to creative ideas for presenting your work.

Collaborative Opportunity

Consider forming a group of students who would be interested in writing related papers on the various aspects of a topic or an issue. The general topic might relate to a social studies class or to a science class, or it might deal with a current issue of interest to students. Together, the students could identify subtopics of the general topic and make assignments to members of the group. The members of the group could function as peer readers as the work progresses.

Individualizing Instruction

Learning Styles To involve students of varying ability levels and learning styles to the maximum degree possible, consider establishing a bi-monthly class magazine. The availability of desktop publishing makes it possible to utilize all kinds of talents in such an enterprise. Some students could handle article-selection tasks, others could undertake editorial matters, and still others could participate in design, art, and production. Such a magazine could provide a ready outlet for student abilities. It could also be distributed to parents and serve a public relations function for your writing program.

Additional Resources
- Writing Resource Book, p. 36

Springboard

Encourage students to create a class booklet called "Publishing Opportunities for High School Students." Help them research unusual and creative ways to get published and to record what they learn in the booklet. At the end of the year, provide a copy for each student.

Sketchbook

Objective

To use a comic strip as a springboard to informal writing

Using the Prompt

Before beginning the activity, point out that Sketchbook activities are ungraded and are meant as opportunities to experiment with writing.

Discuss with students the way in which writers sometimes adopt the persona of someone else and use that person's point of view and voice to describe events. Ask students what benefits a writer might reap from writing as if he or she were someone else. Students should recognize that the writer might be able to create humor or create a tone very different from what he or she would ordinarily use.

Ask students to identify popular fictional private detectives, either from books or from television or film, and characteristics they associate with them. If necessary, suggest such fictional detectives as Sherlock Holmes, Thomas Magnum, and "Dirty" Harry Callaghan. Ask students to adopt the persona of one of these detectives or of the character Calvin imagines himself as in the comic strip as they write about an everyday scene.

Use the ideas in Additional Sketches with those students who find these to be better starting points for writing. Encourage students to keep their writing in their Writing Portfolios. Point out that there may be ideas in their Sketchbook writing that they will want to develop at a later time.

Sketchbook

Calvin and Hobbes

You, a hard-bitten private eye, are on a case. Choose an everyday scene and write about it in the style of a detective mystery.

Additional Sketches

What is your personal style? What's unique about the way you dress, act, or think?

If you were a building, what would you be like?

404

Finding a Personal Voice and Style

WHAT IS VOICE?

When you answer the telephone, you can often tell immediately who is on the other end just by the sound of the person's voice. Just as every person has a distinct speaking voice, every writer has a distinct "writing voice." You can often identify an author by the "sound" of his or her writing. As you write, you will develop your own distinct writing voice and learn to adapt that voice to different writing situations.

What makes one voice different from another? The answer can be put in one word—style. Style is all the characteristics that make something unique. Imagine, for example, that you are going to a party. The clothes you choose to wear will depend to some degree on the type of party it is. To a large extent, however, your choices will reflect elements of your personality and your feelings about yourself.

Like the style expressed by your choice of clothes, the style expressed in your writing is determined by choices you make, often unconsciously, of these important elements:

- sentence structure
- diction
- tone

WRITER TO WRITER

Be yourself. No one but Tom Clancy writes like Tom Clancy.

Sean Ellars, student
Cedar Rapids, Iowa

Sentence Structure

One important element of a writer's style is the type of sentences the writer tends to use—long or short, complicated or simple, meandering or direct. Usually, one type of sentence comes more naturally to a writer because it is part of his or her true voice. However, writers may use a variety of sentence types in different situations to make their writing interesting and appropriate for their audience.

Writing
TIP

When you feel uncomfortable writing in a particular voice, try writing your first draft in a more natural voice for you. You can then revise the voice once you have your ideas on paper.

Finding a Personal
Voice and Style   **405**

Writing Handbook 17:
Finding a Personal Voice and Style

Objectives

1. To identify three elements that help determine personal voice and style: sentence structure, diction, and tone
2. To identify and contrast four kinds of diction: concrete, abstract, formal, and informal
3. To apply strategies to develop a personal voice and style through imagination and experimentation
4. To write a paragraph that compares and contrasts three examples of voice and style

Handbook Mini-Lessons

For information on topics related to voice and style, see the following mini-lessons.

- The Writing Variables, pp. 311–316
- Using Specific Words, pp. 383–385
- Varieties of Language, pp. 409–411
- Using Grammatical Voice, pp. 417–418

Teaching Strategies

Peer Response

If students have built up sufficient trust, you might suggest they identify the characteristic sentence structure, diction, and tone of each others' everyday speech.

Linking Grammar and Writing

As students consider sentence structure, they may need to review the characteristics of a complete sentence. Refer them to Grammar Handbook 29. Then have students look at the sentence fragments used by O. Henry: ''Her Jim.'' Ask them to consider what the author's intentions might have been in using this sentence fragment. *(Point out that writers usually have a specific reason for ''breaking'' a standard grammatical principle. Here O. Henry is using a fragment to emphasize the character's attachment to her husband.)*

 Individualizing Instruction

Kinesthetic Learners Refer to the quote that describes poetry using concrete diction. To dramatically define the concept of concrete words, consider allowing students to be mobile for a minute or two, with the goal of finding objects in the room to touch, smell, hear, look at. When they return to their seats, ask them to jot down some concrete descriptive words about their experience. To define the concept of abstract words, have students make a list of concrete objects paired with abstract concepts. For example: clock=time, window=vision, floor=stability, wall=support.

Sometimes short, simple sentences can be dramatic. In the following passage, for example, the character's bleak financial situation is emphasized by the author's use of short sentences stripped down to the bare essentials.

> Twenty dollars a week doesn't go far. Expenses had been greater than she had calculated. They always are. Only one dollar and eighty-seven cents to buy a present for Jim. Her Jim.
>
> **O. Henry, "The Gift of the Magi"**

Some writers make good use of long, complicated sentences. Notice how one writer captured the speed and force of a flooding stream by using a long, streaming sentence:

> It smashes under the bridge like a fist, but there is no end to its force; it hurtles down as far as I can see till it lurches round the bend, filling the valley, flattening, mashing, pushed, wider and faster, till it fills my brain.
>
> **Annie Dillard, *Pilgrim at Tinker Creek***

Diction

Another important element of a writer's style is diction, or the type of words the writer tends to use. A writer's diction may be concrete or abstract, formal or informal.

Concrete vs. Abstract Diction Concrete words are ones that name or describe things you can see, hear, smell, touch, or taste. The words *onion, buttery, pink,* and *squirm* are all concrete words. Abstract words name things that cannot be perceived through the senses. The words *truth, justice,* and *independence* are abstract. Notice how the following passage discusses an abstract subject—poetry—using concrete diction:

> A poem should move you. It should burn like fire, should wring you like a dishrag; it should toss you on your back and go soaring off into the clouds.

Formal vs. Informal Diction Formal English is a serious, dignified way of speaking or writing that is appropriate for serious occasions. Informal English is the more conversational language we use in everyday situations. Some words, such as *perspiration,* are formal. Other words, such as *sweat,* are informal. If you were writing a story about a long-distance runner, you might use the informal word *sweat.* If you were writing a formal essay on how the human body functions during exercise, you might use the formal word *perspiration.* Sometimes, however, writers deliberately mix levels of diction to make a statement about a character or situation.

Tone

Another important stylistic choice you make is the choice of a particular tone. The tone of a piece of writing is its emotional effect and is determined by the writer's attitude toward the subject. If you are writing directions, for example, you would probably use a matter-of-fact tone. If you were writing a persuasive letter warning about the dangers of pollution, you might use an alarmed tone. Decide what tone of voice you want to create in a piece of writing and choose words that will help convey that emotional effect.

DEVELOPING YOUR WRITING VOICE

You do not use the same speaking voice to tell a joke to a friend, to read a story to a child, and to speak to a friend's mother on the telephone. Yet the voice you use in each situation is recognizably yours and not someone else's. One of the secrets of good writing is to learn to vary your writing voice in different situations and yet always be yourself.

In some writing situations, you can use the same voice you use in everyday conversation. For example, when writing a personal letter to a friend, you want to write as if you were speaking directly to your friend. In other writing situations, however, you need to modify your voice and may even need to imagine yourself playing a part in order to create an appropriate voice.

Finding a Personal Voice and Style **407**

When writing a formal research report, for example, you might imagine yourself an expert, which you really are. When you write dialogue for fictional characters, you need to imagine how those particular people would speak and use the voices your characters would use.

If you have trouble finding your voice in certain writing situations, try to loosen up. Don't worry about getting your writing voice exactly right in your first draft. Experiment with different voices, using freewriting and journal writing to find a natural, comfortable rhythm.

Practice Your Skills

Read each of the following passages from well-known short stories. Consider the sentence structure, diction, and tone of each. Write a paragraph comparing and contrasting the three writers' voices and styles.

Paris Street, by Edward Hopper, 1906. Oil on wood.

But even here the exuberant and barbaric fancy asserted itself. This vast amphitheater, with its encircling galleries, its mysterious vault, and its unseen passages, was an agent of poetic justice, in which crime was punished, or virtue rewarded, by the decrees of an impartial and incorruptible chance.

Frank R. Stockton, "The Lady, or the Tiger?"

Rainsford held his breath. The general's eyes had left the ground and were traveling inch by inch up the tree. Rainsford froze there, every muscle tensed for a spring. But the sharp eyes of the hunter stopped before they reached the limb where Rainsford lay; a smile spread over his brown face . . . . The general was playing with him! The general was saving him for another day's sport! The Cossack was the cat; he was the mouse. Then it was that Rainsford knew the full meaning of terror.

Richard Connell, "The Most Dangerous Game"

She was one of those pretty and charming girls, born, as if by an accident of fate, into a family of clerks. . . . She dressed plainly because she could not afford fine clothes. . . . She grieved incessantly, feeling that she had been born for all the little niceties and luxuries of living. She grieved over the shabbiness of her apartment, the dinginess of the walls, the worn-out appearance of the chairs, the ugliness of the draperies. All these things, which another woman of her class would not even have noticed, gnawed at her and made her furious.

Guy de Maupassant, "The Necklace"

408 Writing Handbook

Humanities Connection

Art Note *Paris Street,* 1906, is an oil painting on wood by American artist Edward Hopper (b. 1882, New York, d. 1967). Hopper primarily painted American scenes; however, early in his career, he traveled to Europe and recorded his impressions in works like this one. Although Hopper sometimes worked in watercolors, his primary medium was oils. Ask: How is a painter's experimentation with different media like a writer's use of different voices, styles, and tones?

How Can I Make My Language Richer?

Careful attention to the underlying meanings of the words you use, the way the words sound, and how you put them together to describe things can make your writing come alive. You can enrich your writing by being aware of the varieties of language you can draw on, stating exactly what you mean, using words that appeal to the ear, and creating unusual comparisons.

VARIETIES OF LANGUAGE

When you write, you communicate not only through what you say but also through the way you say it. The way you use language can help you establish such important elements as character and mood in stories or tone and purpose in letters or news stories. You can use language differently in various situations as you tailor your message to your audience and purpose. A knowledge of the varieties of language available to you can help you vary and enrich your writing.

WRITER TO WRITER

Language grows out of life, out of its needs and experiences.

Anne Sullivan, Teacher of Helen Keller

Standard English

Standard English follows widely accepted guidelines for correct usage. It is the language of most professional writing in magazines, books, and newspapers, and of most national radio and television commentators. This textbook presents many of the rules and guidelines for using standard American English.

Formal and Informal English Standard English can be divided into two varieties, formal and informal. These are not separate categories, but two ends of a spectrum. **Formal English** is appropriate in any situation that is serious, dignified, or ceremonial. **Informal English,**

Writing Handbook 18:
How Can I Make My Language Richer?

Objectives

1. To identify the varieties of standard English and recognize the characteristics of formal and informal usage, idioms, slang, and dialects
2. To learn the difference between denotation and connotation
3. To identify three sound devices: onomatopoeia, alliteration, and assonance
4. To understand the difference between literal and figurative language and to identify three types of figurative language: simile, metaphor, and personification
5. To rewrite and revise paragraphs to include richer language

Handbook Mini-Lessons

For information on topics related to enriching language, see the following mini-lessons.

- Personal Techniques, pp. 317–320
- Personal Voice and Style, pp. 405–408
- Using Dialogue Effectively, pp. 434–436
- Using Reference Works, pp. 473–475

Teaching Strategies

Motivating

Have students think about what "richness" in music means to them. Ask them what aspects of their favorite music makes it "come alive" for them. Point out that "rich" music has depth, a pleasing interplay of a variety of elements: melody, harmony, tempo, dynamics, words, orchestration. In writing, too, variety leads to richer language.

Individualizing Instruction

Basic Students Provide individual guidance to students to help them locate examples of rich language from their own work in their writing portfolio or from books, essays, and poems that they identify as personal favorites.

Collaborative Opportunity

Students might enjoy creating slang mini-dictionaries in groups of two or three. First they could spend some time in conversation, then create a written dialogue using slang words. After the dialogue is complete, group members could be assigned specific words to define formally. Groups could then compare their definitions, looking for any disagreements about perceived meanings.

Personal Touch

Consider sharing your own place of origin, and/or some aspects of your background related to dialect. Give students some examples of words or phrases unique to a geographical region with which you are familiar.

The Three Stooges:
Moe, Larry, and Curly

also known as conversational or colloquial English, is appropriate in everyday situations.

Both formal and informal English use correct grammar; however, they differ in tone, vocabulary, and structure.

	Formal English	Informal English
Tone	Serious, reserved, academic, ceremonial	Personal, friendly, conversational
Vocabulary	May use long or less common words; avoids clipped words and contractions	Uses simple words; often uses clipped words and contractions
Structure	Long, carefully constructed sentences	Sentences of varied lengths, similar to conversation

Idioms and Slang One characteristic of informal English is the presence of colloquial expressions such as **idioms** and **slang.** Idioms are words and phrases that have a meaning different from the literal meaning of the words. Some examples are, "Hold your tongue" and "You're pulling my leg." Slang consists of expressions coined by members of a group. Slang is appropriate only in very informal situations.

Many dictionaries indicate whether a word or phrase is considered informal English, an idiom, or slang. Such labels help you to match the appropriate type of language to your writing purpose.

Dialects The varieties of English used in different places and by different groups of people are called **dialects.** Everyone speaks a particular dialect; none is more "correct" than another. Dialects can differ from one another in pronunciation, grammar, vocabulary, spelling, and punctuation. For example, a New Yorker may say "stand on line," when someone from California would say "stand in line." A person in southern Illinois may pronounce *greasy* as *greezy,* while someone from northern Illinois may pronounce it *greecy*. For the past tense of the verb *dive*, a person from Wisconsin may say *dove*, while someone from Kentucky says *dived*. A Canadian writes *colour* where an American writes *color*.

410 Writing Handbook

Literature Connection

Mark Twain's short story "Buck Fanshaw's Funeral" provides excellent examples of the differences in formal and informal language, dialects, and idioms. Students could read and report on the story. They will likely enjoy the humorous confusion that results from a clash of dialects.

Using Varieties of Language in Writing

Just as the different levels of language add variety to oral communication, they can be used to enhance written pieces as well. Here are some ways you can use different varieties of language to enrich your writing.

- When creating characters, as in a short story, use different types of language to distinguish one character from another. The language characters use in dialogue can help reveal their personalities.
- When writing lighthearted stories, essays, letters, or poems, use informal English to establish the tone.
- When writing serious essays, newspaper articles, or letters of application, especially for people you don't know, use somewhat more formal English to make the seriousness of your purpose clear.
- Most published writing falls between the extremes of formality and informality.

DENOTATIVE AND
CONNOTATIVE MEANING

Choosing words that reflect your exact meaning also can make your writing richer. Words have two kinds of meanings—**denotative meanings,** which are their dictionary definitions, and **connotative meanings,** which involve the emotions and other associations that come to people's minds when they hear or read a word. Both types of meanings are at work in every piece of writing.

Consider the word *home,* for example. The denotative meaning of *home* is "a place where a person lives." For many people, however, *home* means much more than just a place to eat and sleep. A person might associate *home* with comfort, security, family, personal belongings, and friends, for example. Connotative meaning is very important in writing because your readers' personal feelings and associations influence their response to your words.

Persuasive writing is especially dependent on connotative meaning. A writer of an advertisement, for example, might describe a particular soap as *economical.* However, the writer would not call the soap *cheap*—even though *economical* and *cheap* both have the denotative meaning "low-priced"—because its connotations include "poorly made," and "not worth buying."

How Can I Make My
Language Richer?   **411**

Stumbling Block

Some students may not easily pick up on the difference between denotative and connotative meaning. You may wish to try this exercise with them: As you write word-pairs on the chalkboard, have students free-associate and jot "feeling" words on their papers in response. Ask: "How does the first word in this pair make you feel? What feelings arise when you read the second word in the pair?" After they have a list of their responses, ask them to go to a dictionary and look up the formal definitions of the words on the chalkboard. (Use word-pairs like: *young/immature, kill/murder, educated/highbrow, accident/blunder, disappointment/dud, uninformed/stupid, casualty/victim.*) What observations can they make about how the word-pairs are similar in *definition* but different in *feeling?*

Critical Thinking

Judging   Help students increase their abilities to work with subtle differences in word connotation by first referring them to the second example that advertises "cheap" soap. Have students try to come up with a few similar sentences—denotatively correct, but connotatively confusing, misleading, or humorous. They may choose to start with popular advertising slogans, changing key words to give new, probably undesirable, connotations. Alternatively, you might have basic students work together in groups to analyze the use of connotations in current advertising copy.

Refer to the Thurber excerpt and ask students to name some sounds they hear in a typical day. Invite them to come up with words (real or made-up) that could describe those sounds with onomatopoeia.

Refer to the Noyes excerpt and ask students to substitute words that don't begin with the same letter for *cobbles, clattered,* and *clashed.* Ask them to read their new sentence aloud. Then have them describe the mood or impact that alliteration conveyed.

Refer to the Frost excerpt and ask: Suppose Frost had chosen "flame and cold" instead of "fire and ice"? Have students listen to your reading of the excerpt with the substituted words. Ask for their feelings about how the word changes affected the mood of the piece of writing.

SOUND DEVICES

Not only the meanings, but also the actual sounds of words can enrich both prose and poetry. Three kinds of devices that writers often use to create pleasing patterns of sound are **onomatopoeia, alliteration,** and **assonance.**

Onomatopoeia Onomatopoeia is the use of words that suggest or imitate sounds. Words such as *hum, murmur, squish, crackle,* and *buzz* are examples of onomatopoeia. Use of such words can create clear sound images in your writing as the following example illustrates.

> The pounding of the cylinders increased: ta-pocketa-pocketa-pocketa-*pocketa-pocketa*.
>
> **James Thurber, "The Secret Life of Walter Mitty"**

Alliteration Alliteration is the repetition of a consonant sound at the beginnings of words. Alliteration draws attention to words a writer wants to emphasize and can create special moods, such as the noisy urgency of the following repeated *c* sounds.

> Over the cobbles he clattered and clashed in the dark innyard.
>
> **Alfred Noyes, "The Highwayman"**

Assonance Assonance is the repetition of a vowel sound within words. Like alliteration, assonance emphasizes certain words and can help create a mood. It can also help establish connections between words. Notice how the repetition of the long-*i* sound helps connect the words *fire, ice, I,* and *desire* in this excerpt.

> Some say the world will end in fire,
> Some say in ice.
> From what I've tasted of desire
> I hold with those who favor fire. . . .
>
> **Robert Frost, "Fire and Ice"**

412 Writing Handbook

Literature Connection

You may wish to read or have a student read Edgar Allan Poe's poem "The Bells." It makes abundant use of all three kinds of sound devices: onomatopoeia, alliteration, and assonance.

LITERAL AND FIGURATIVE LANGUAGE

Understanding the effects of literal and figurative language and how to use them can also enrich your writing. **Literal language** is straightforward and matter-of-fact. The words mean just what they say.

Literal   The Broncos won the game 44–9.

In contrast, **figurative language** makes statements that are poetic and imaginative. When you use figurative language, you enrich your writing by expressing your ideas vividly. However, you don't expect people to take your statements literally.

Figurative   In a game that seemed to last a week, the Broncos destroyed the Patriots.

This sentence is not a simple statement of facts. The Broncos did not actually destroy the Patriots, and the game did not actually go on for a week. The writer uses nonliteral, figurative language to communicate vividly the idea that the game was one-sided and took a long time to play.

Types of Figurative Language

Among the most common types of figurative language are **simile, metaphor,** and **personification.** Using figurative language involves seeing connections between things that are basically dissimilar and using specific techniques to make a comparison.

Simile   A simile compares two unlike things using words such as *like* or *as*. "His hands are like leather" and "Her voice was as irritating as fingernails on a chalkboard" are examples of similes.

To create a simile, choose something you want to describe, such as a woman. Decide on a characteristic you would like to focus on, the woman's beauty, for example. Next think of something else that has this same characteristic, for example, a flower. Finally relate the second thing to the first using a word such as *like* or *as*.

> My love is like a red, red rose.
>
> **Robert Burns**

Writing
—**TIP**—

Use figurative language sparingly. Two metaphors are not usually better than one.

LITERARY
M O D E L

Teaching Tip: Figurative Language

Before students look at the Broncos-Patriots sentence as an example of figurative language, have them think of some recent pep rally slogans for their school sports teams. Ask them why the use of figurative language is more effective in these kinds of slogans. Point out that it gives the slogans more power and emotional impact. You may wish to have students try to change the slogans into literal language, and discuss the difference in impact.

Critical Thinking

Making Comparisons Help students quickly get a feel for the nature of simile and metaphor by using a quick question and answer activity. Use a series of "What is a _____ like?" questions. Students should respond with first-impression comparisons.

Metaphor A metaphor makes a comparison without using the words *like* or *as*. Sometimes metaphors imply comparisons without stating them directly. "The moon was a ghostly galleon" and "Alex weaseled out of the job" are both metaphors. A galleon, a large, three-masted sailing ship, carries associations of slow, majestic, mysterious movement over the ocean, shaping a vivid picture of how the moon sails through the sky. Weasels are long, quick, and often thought of as sneaky creatures, an effective description of a person smoothly and slyly avoiding work.

In making a metaphor, like a simile, you decide what to describe, pick a characteristic to focus on, and think of something else with the same characteristic. You then describe the first thing as though it were the second. For example, one writer decided to describe a pheasant, to focus on its startling color and thought of the similar brightness of a jewel.

LITERARY
M O D E L

A pheasant cock sprang into view,
A living jewel, up he flew.

Robert P. Tristram Coffin

Personification Personification is a simile or metaphor that attributes human qualities to nonhuman objects.

> The tree stood straight and strong and tall, like an old warrior.

> The engine gasped and groaned, protesting against the cold night air.

Avoiding Clichés

Some phrases that contain figurative language are used so often that they hold little interest for most readers. These worn-out comparisons are called **clichés.** "He eats like a bird" and "She's as busy as a bee" are clichés.

Compare the following similes.

Cliché	Shira was quiet as a mouse.
Fresh Comparison	Shira was quiet as a snowflake.

You have probably heard the first comparison so many times that it doesn't even make you stop to think about how quiet a mouse can be. The second comparison, however, should make you imagine the perfectly soundless fall of a snowflake.

414 Writing Handbook

Teaching Tip: Personification

The concept of personification could become more real to students through the following identification exercise. Say: "Imagine you are a (car, tree, skyscraper, etc.)." After students have thought about it for a while, ask them how they feel. Then have them jot down some phrases to describe the "experience" of a car, tree, skyscraper, etc. Point out that they now have some material to work with in developing sentences that contain personification.

Peer Response

To practice identifying clichés, students could freewrite a paragraph starting with: "It was a dark and stormy night . . . ." They should try to load the rest of the paragraph with as many clichés as possible. Have students exchange papers, circle any clichés they find, and replace them with fresh uses of figurative language.

Springboard

Photocopy a local sports column for distribution in class. Have students find examples of figurative language, and circle and label them.

Practice Your Skills

A. The following paragraph is part of a formal report. It contains several varieties of language. Rewrite the paragraph to eliminate all informal language and slang.

> Pet gerbils should be fed commercial gerbil pellets or a mixture of fruits, small seeds, and raw vegetables. Watching them eat is a real blast, because they stuff a lot of food in the pouches of their cheeks. Water should be made available in their cages, though they sure don't drink much. Gerbils get water mostly through moisture in the food they eat. If cared for properly, a pet gerbil should live up to four years, or round about that.

B. Write the word from each group below that is commonly used in your community. Then locate someone in your community who is from a different region of the United States. List the words he or she used in that region. Make a list of the regional differences in dialects.

1. **carbonated drink:** pop, soda, soda pop, tonic, soft drink
2. **sink fixture:** faucet, spigot, tap
3. **green vegetable:** snap bean, green bean
4. **insect that glows at night:** firefly, glowworm, lightning bug, candle bug
5. **large sandwich meant to be a meal in itself:** hero, submarine, hoagie, hoagy, grinder, poor-boy
6. **vehicle for small baby:** baby buggy, baby cab, baby carriage, baby coach
7. **amusement park ride (on tracks):** coaster, roller coaster, rolly-coaster, shoot-the-chutes

C. Revise the following paragraph using sound devices and figurative language to make it more vivid and interesting. Follow these suggestions: (1) use a simile; (2) replace clichés; (3) use a metaphor; (4) use a sound device; (5) use personification.

> (1) Reading mysteries is fun. (2) They can keep you on the edge of your seat. (3) A good mystery keeps you wondering who did it. (4) Sometimes the tension is almost unbearable, however. (5) When you solve the mystery, you might even feel as if you've won a battle of wits.

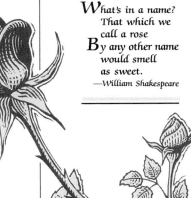

What's in a name? That which we call a rose B*y any other name would smell as sweet.*
—William Shakespeare

How Can I Make My Language Richer? **415**

Managing the Paper Load

As an alternative to having students rewrite the entire paragraph on gerbils, you may wish to have them make a list of the informal phrases and slang words. Students could then pair each item with a self-developed formal phrase or word.

Additional Resources
- Writing Resource Book, pp. 39–40

How Can I Vary My Sentences?

Objectives

1. To identify four ways of varying sentences: using different kinds of sentences, varying sentence length and structure, varying sentence beginnings, and varying grammatical voice
2. To revise passages to vary the sentences

Handbook Mini-Lessons

For information on topics related to sentence variety, see the following mini-lessons.

- Eliminating Repeated Ideas, pp. 391–392
- The Sentence and Its Parts, pp. 497–523
- Active and Passive Voice, pp. 590–592
- Clauses and Sentence Structure, pp. 721–748

Teaching Strategies

Motivating

Ask students to think about what they mean when they say: "Let's do something different." How would they describe what is good about *routine* in life compared with what is pleasing about surprises or *variety*? Ask them to describe what would make for monotony in life—and in writing. Point out that one way writers try to avoid monotony for their readers is by varying sentences.

WRITING
HANDBOOK
19

How Can I Vary My Sentences?

Sentences are one of the basic building blocks in writing. You can vary them in numerous ways to add impact and interest to your writing.

Using Different Kinds of Sentences

There are four different kinds of sentences you can use to give your writing variety: **simple, compound, complex,** and **compound-complex.**

A **simple sentence** has one independent clause.

Typhoons are similar to hurricanes.

A **compound sentence** has two or more independent clauses.

Typhoons are similar to hurricanes, but they tend to be stronger and larger.

A **complex sentence** has one independent clause and one or more subordinate clauses.

Typhoons are violent tropical storms that occur in the western Pacific.

A **compound-complex sentence** has two or more independent clauses and one or more subordinate clauses.

As typhoons gather intensity, they move slowly westward, but their circular winds are very strong.

You can avoid monotony in your writing by using these different sentence types to draw attention to single ideas or to group related ideas.

Varying Sentence Length and Structure

Short, simple sentences can be direct and graceful. However, occasional use of longer, more elaborate sentences will add richness to your writing. Often you can combine short sentences to form longer ones that are more interesting.

Simple	Willa Cather wrote about the American frontier. She wrote about pioneers and farmers. She celebrated the virtues of hard work and compassion.
More Complex	Writing about the pioneers and farmers of the American frontier, Willa Cather celebrated the virtues of hard work and compassion.

Varying Sentence Beginnings

Series of sentences that all begin the same way can be monotonous. For example, a series of sentences beginning with *she* makes the following paragraph choppy and dull.

Paragraph Without Variety

She heard about Galveston's devastating hurricane. She went to Texas, bringing a small staff with her. She participated in the last disaster relief work of her career. She was seventy-eight years old. She was a remarkable woman. She was Clara Barton. She was the founder of the American Red Cross.

Note how much richer the paragraph sounds when the writer varies sentence beginnings by using different adverbs and a gerund phrase and varies the types and structures of the sentences as well.

Paragraph with Variety

Almost as soon as the devastating hurricane hit Galveston, she heard about it. Immediately, she went to Texas, bringing a small staff with her. There she participated in the last disaster relief work of her career. Being seventy-eight years old did not stop her. Who was this remarkable woman? She was Clara Barton, founder of the American Red Cross.

To vary the beginnings of your sentences, examine your writing for sentences beginning with *the* and pronouns such as *he, she,* and *it.* Most writers overuse these words. Also, consider beginning your sentence with other parts of speech. Especially effective beginnings include verb forms, adverbs, and prepositions.

Using Grammatical Voice

Another way to vary your writing is through grammatical voice. There are two grammatical voices to choose from: active and passive. The active voice places the emphasis on the doer of the action.

Active   Nelson Mandela led the South African people in protest.

The doer of the action, Nelson Mandela, is the focus here.

In the passive voice, on the other hand, the action itself is emphasized, not the doer. The doer is either not named or is named in a phrase that follows the verb.

Passive   Mandela was freed after twenty-seven years. (Doer of the action not named.)
Passive   After twenty-seven years, Mandela was freed by President F. W. de Klerk. (Doer named after the verb.)

Speaking and Listening

Ask a volunteer to read aloud the paragraph without sentence variety and the paragraph with variety. Lead students to recognize that varying sentences in everyday speech greatly increases the impact and interest of our oral communication with others.

Teaching Tip: Active and Passive Voice

Some students may fall into the habit of using the passive voice almost exclusively because they feel it sounds more "professional" or "educated." Help them see how using the active voice can deliver clarity and power. Ask students to compare the following sentence with that of the police report which follows it: "Johnson threw open the door, fired five blasts, and lunged into the room." "The door was opened by Johnson, five rounds were discharged from his weapon, and he became situated in the room." Point out that the police report uses the passive tense in an attempt to promote objectivity. The other sentence, however, has more impact on the reader.

Humanities Connection

Point out that visual artists, like writers, add interest to their works by varying factors such as light, background, subject, point of view. Suggest that students check out oversized books on painting or photography from the library. Have them report on the techniques artists use to add variety to their work.

Managing the Paper Load

Rather than having students rewrite the paragraph in Exercise B, you may wish to have them jot down the passive verbal phrases they find. Students should then pair those phrases with their own suggestions for active voice alternatives.

Additional Resources
• Writing Resource Book, pp. 41–42

Caesar Augustus, Roman Emperor. Marble statue portraying Caesar as a god.

A sentence in the active voice is stronger, more lively, and more direct than one using the passive voice. Although you may want to use the passive voice when you don't know the doer of the action or to vary your writing, you should strive to use the active voice as much as possible.

Practice Your Skills

A. Rewrite the following paragraph, using different kinds of sentences, combining some to produce longer, more elaborate sentences, and varying the way the sentences begin. Suggested changes for individual sentences are: (2)–(3) make a simple sentence by turning *September* into an appositive; (4)–(6) make a compound sentence containing three independent clauses; (7) begin with a transitional word; (8)–(9) make a compound sentence.

(1) The names of the months come from Latin names for numbers. (2) The word for the seventh month in the Roman calendar is September. (3) It comes from the Latin word meaning "seven." (4) The eighth month, October, comes from the word meaning "eight." (5) The ninth month, November, comes from the word meaning "nine." (6) The tenth month, December, comes from the word meaning "ten." (7) The months of July and August are different. (8) July is named after Julius Caesar. (9) August is named after Augustus Caesar.

B. Rewrite one of the following paragraphs, changing the passive voice to the active voice in each case where the emphasis should be placed on the doer of the action.

1. Why are some movies called *blockbusters?* Are blocks busted by movies? Actually, it is likely that *blockbuster* was first used by pilots during World War II. What was meant by *blockbuster* was a large aerial bomb. It was thought of as any bomb big enough to destroy a whole city block. The word was later picked up by people in show business. It was used by show business people to mean "a huge success."

2. The earliest steam engine was described—and perhaps invented—by Hero, an ancient Greek scientist. It was built by the Greeks from a small hollow sphere mounted on a pipe. Steam was forced through the pipe into the sphere. The sphere was made to whirl by steam coming from two L-shaped jets in its sides. No useful work, however, was performed by steam engines for hundreds of years. The Greek steam engine could be said to be an invention whose time had not yet come.

Sentence Combining

When you draft or revise, one way to add interest and variety to your writing is to combine some related sentences and sentence parts to form single sentences that carry more meaning and are more economical. You can use several strategies.

COMBINING SENTENCES AND SENTENCE PARTS

In reviewing your own writing, you may find sentences or sentence parts that express similar ideas, contrasting ideas, or a choice between ideas. These sentences or sentence parts may be combined by using **conjunctions,** such as *and, but,* or *or,* which connect words or groups of words. When combining sentences with a conjunction, you use a comma; when combining sentence parts, you do not.

To join similar ideas, use the conjunction *and.* To join contrasting ideas, use the conjunction *but.* To show a choice between ideas, use a comma and the conjunction *or.* Complete sentences with similar ideas can also be joined by a semicolon.

Separate Sentences (similar ideas)	Jupiter has sixteen known moons. *Saturn has eighteen known* moons.
Combined Sentence	Jupiter has sixteen known moons, and *Saturn has eighteen.*
Separate Sentences (similar ideas)	The low-pressure system and storm will probably pass today. *Tonight will most likely be calm.*
Combined Sentence	The low-pressure system and storm will probably pass today; *tonight will most likely be calm.*
Separate Sentences (contrasting ideas)	High-heeled shoes are considered to be stylish. Most high-heeled shoes are *uncomfortable to walk in.*
Combined Sentence	High-heeled shoes are considered to be stylish, but most are *uncomfortable to walk in.*

Sentence Combining **419**

Objective

To recognize sentences that should be combined and apply techniques for combining sentences

Handbook Mini-Lessons
For information on topics related to sentence combining, see the following mini-lessons.
- Correcting Problem Sentences, pp. 391–399
- How Can I Vary My Sentences? pp. 416–418
- The Sentence and Its Parts, pp. 497–518

Teaching Strategies

Motivating

Have students consider how a painter mixes colors on a palette to produce a work of visual art. Ask them how combining colors can make visual art more interesting. How would a painting be different if artists could only use primary colors? Elicit the response that working with primary colors alone would severely limit artistic interest and variety. Point out that, in the same way, when writers use only short, simple sentences they run the risk of producing choppy, repetitive pieces of writing.

Linking Grammar and Writing

In order to determine when to use a comma in the combining exercises, students may need to review the difference between a compound sentence (two or more independent clauses) and a sentence with a compound predicate (in which the verbs refer to the same subject). The first case requires a comma; the latter does not. Refer students to Grammar Handbooks 29: Compound Sentence Parts, pp. 517–520 and 41: The Comma, pp. 772–785.

ANSWERS TO PRACTICE YOUR SKILLS

A.

Answers to sentences 4–6 may vary slightly.
1. Daniel Boone explored the Kentucky wilderness and searched for Indian trails.
2. Reptiles are numerous in the tropics, but many live in colder climates.
3. The weather will be good for the marathon in the spring or in the fall.
4. Tonight's concert has been canceled, but refunds will be available tomorrow.
5. Mammals may lay eggs or bear live young. OR: Mammals may lay eggs, but some bear live young.
6. Texas had been claimed for Spain in the early 1500's but remained unoccupied by Spaniards for almost two centuries.

B.

Answers will vary slightly. However, good answers will use the conjunctions and commas properly, as in the examples shown below.

Hot-air balloons and gas balloons are both used for sport ballooning. Balloonists compete in races and rallies. Sport balloons are considered easy to operate, but balloonists must pay attention to weather conditions. Balloonists should ascend in the early morning or late afternoon.

Writing
—TIP—

Look for repetitions of nouns and pronouns in your writing. Combine sentences to avoid such repetition.

Separate Sentences (choice between ideas)	We could take the train to the park. *My mom could drive.*
Combined Sentence	We could take the train to the park, or *my mom could drive.*

When you combine sentence parts, no comma is necessary. Notice in the following sentences the differences between combining sentences and combining sentence parts.

Combined Sentences	They could rent a good movie, or they could sunbathe at the beach.
Combined Sentence Parts	They could *rent a good movie or sunbathe at the beach.*

Practice Your Skills

A. Combine each pair of sentences. In sentences 1–3, use the word in parentheses to join the sentences. Omit the words that are underlined.

In sentences 4–6, decide on your own how you will join the sentences.

1. Daniel Boone explored the Kentucky wilderness. <u>Daniel Boone</u> searched for Indian trails. (Use *and.*)
2. Reptiles are numerous in the tropics. Many <u>reptiles</u> live in colder climates. (Use *but.*)
3. The weather will be good for the marathon in the spring. <u>It will also be good</u> in the fall. (Use *or.*)
4. Tonight's concert has been canceled. Refunds will be available tomorrow.
5. Mammals may lay eggs. Some mammals bear live young.
6. Texas had been claimed for Spain in the early 1500's. It remained unoccupied by Spaniards for almost two centuries.

B. Read the following passage and then rewrite it, combining the sentences in parentheses. Omit the words that are underlined. You may need to add *and, but, or,* and commas.

(1) (Hot-air balloons are used for sport ballooning. Gas balloons <u>are also used for sport ballooning</u>.) (2) (Balloonists compete in races. They <u>participate in</u> rallies.) (3) (Sport balloons are considered easy to operate. Balloonists must pay attention to weather conditions.) (4) (Balloonists should ascend in the early morning. <u>It is also good to balloon in the</u> late afternoon.)

ADDING WORDS TO SENTENCES

Sometimes you can combine sentences by transferring a key word from one sentence to another. You often will be able to combine the sentences without changing the form of the word. However, occasionally you will need to add an ending such as *-y, -ed, -ing,* or *-ly.*

Separate Sentences	He was in an *exuberant* mood. His mood was contagious.
Combined Sentence	His *exuberant* mood was contagious.
Separate Sentences	Butter the pan. Pour the cake batter into the pan.
Combined Sentence	Pour the cake batter into the *buttered* pan.
Separate Sentences	She painted the storm windows with a narrow brush. She was *careful.*
Combined Sentences	She *carefully* painted the storm windows with a narrow brush.

Often you can combine sentences in a number of ways. For example, you could have combined the sentences above in this way: "She painted the storm windows *carefully* with a narrow brush."

In the following examples, although there may be a number of ways to combine the sentences, usually only one combined sentence will be given.

You may be able to combine more than two sentences when one sentence carries the main idea and each of the other sentences adds only one detail. You may need to use a comma or the word *and.*

Separate Sentences	The skis were strapped to the top of the car. They were *long* and *shiny.* The car was *compact.*
Combined Sentence	The *long, shiny* skis were strapped to the top of the *compact* car.
Separate Sentences	Write the following sentence. The sentence is *simple.* Write it *carefully.*
Combined Sentence	*Carefully* write the following *simple* sentence.

Some students may assume that long, combined sentences are always better than short sentences. Remind them that short and long sentences work together in good writing. Thus, writers avoid both excessive choppiness and potential confusion on the part of readers. Good writing should vary sentence length and structure to provide an unobtrusive "rhythm" for the flow of ideas.

Critical Thinking

Generalizing After students have studied the examples of combined sentences, remind them that in many cases, they could have been combined differently. Point out specific examples from the text and ask students if they can think of other ways the sentences could have been combined. For example: "Strapped to the top of the compact car were long, shiny skis."

Managing the Paper Load

Consider using sentences 1–5 of Exercise A as a verbal exercise rather than a written one. Call on volunteers to respond with their answers before requiring the written work in sentences 6–10.

Modeling

Notice that in Exercise A sentences 6–10 call for more personal judgment from the students. Model the method you would use to combine sentences in sentence 6. Point out that the second and third sentences in this example refer to the clay and the sculptor, respectively. Thus, *soft* and *old* could be used as adjectives in the first sentence to produce: "The old sculptor molds the soft clay."

Performance art combines the visual with other art forms.

Practice Your Skills

A. Combine each pair or group of sentences. In sentences 1–5, use the directions in parentheses and eliminate the underlined words. In sentences 6–10, decide on your own how to join the sentences. Remember, you may need to change the form of a word.

1. The ruby sparkled in the light. The ruby glistened. (Use *-ing*.)
2. "Thank you," Margaret said, smiling. Margaret's smile was bright. (Use *-ly*.)
3. Al walked across the porch. The porch creaked. (Use *-y*.)
4. The ancient map was etched in stone. The ancient map had many details. (Use *-ed* and a comma.)
5. The animal looked hungry. The animal was large. She was in a playful mood. (Use a comma.)
6. The sculptor molds the clay. The clay is soft. The sculptor is old.
7. A police officer caught the thief running from the scene of the crime. The officer wore a uniform.
8. The musicians practiced in the recording studio. They were famous. They practiced all day.
9. I can run on any track. I can run swiftly. I can run easily.
10. The shopkeeper surveyed her store. Her expression was proud.

B. Rewrite the following passage. Eliminate the underlined words and combine the pairs or groups of sentences in parentheses. Decide on your own how to combine the sentences in the last paragraph by connecting words or changing the form of a word.

(1) (Music takes many forms. It also reflects various ways of life.) (2) (At first, music existed only as voice sounds. These sounds were simple and natural.) (3) (Eventually, people made music with objects. There were many different objects.) (4) (The ancient Egyptians clapped sticks together. They clapped in a rhythmical pattern. They also jingled metal rods.) (5) (The early Chinese played an instrument called the zither. This instrument was interesting.) (6) (It had forty strings stretched across a board. The strings were stretched tightly.)

The ancient Greeks used the alphabet for musical tones. They were creative. The Romans copied Greek music. They also invented an instrument called the tuba. The musicians in India used formulas called ragas. The formulas were complex.

INSERTING WORD GROUPS

Sometimes a group of words from one sentence can be added to another sentence, eliminating unnecessary repetition. You may be able to add a group of words to another sentence without changing their form. Occasionally, however, you may need to change the form of one of the words by adding *-ing* or *-ed*.

Separate Sentences	The clowns were amusing. They were *in the miniature car.*
Combined Sentence	The clowns *in the miniature car* were amusing.
Separate Sentences	The meet is at our track. The meet is *next on the schedule.*
Combined Sentence	The *next scheduled* meet is at our track.

One way of adding a group of words from one sentence to another sentence that refers to the same thing is by using an **appositive phrase.** An appositive phrase is a group of words, set off by commas, that refers to the same thing as another group of words. You can think of an appositive phrase as a way of renaming or explaining something. It usually closely follows the word or phrase it identifies.

Separate Sentences	The Rocky Mountains are *the largest mountain system in North America.* The Rocky Mountains form the Continental Divide.
Combined Sentence with Appositive Phrase	The Rocky Mountains, *the largest mountain system in North America,* form the Continental Divide.

Practice Your Skills

A. Combine each of the following pairs or groups of sentences. In sentences 1–5 eliminate the underlined words. Additional clues are provided in parentheses. In sentences 6–10, decide on your own how to combine the sentences.

1. The detour signs are posted every twenty-five miles. <u>The signs are posted</u> along Route 91.
2. The construction crew worked steadily. <u>They</u> stopped only for a quick break. (Use *-ing.*)

Linking Grammar and Writing

Students may be better able to catch the essence of the appositive phrase if you use the words, *namely,* or *which is/are* to explain its use in a sentence. Students needing further help or background can be directed to Grammar Handbook 37: Using Verbals and Appositives.

 Individualizing Instruction

Basic Students Provide more practice for these students by listing words on the chalkboard. Have students call out two simple descriptive sentences about the word that you list. Then work together, verbally, combining the two sentences. For example: If you list *car*, students may call out, "John drives a car" and "The car is red." The combined sentence would be: "John drives a red car."

A. Answers will vary in sentences 1–10. However, good answers will use conjunctions and commas properly, as shown in the examples below.

1. The detour signs are posted every twenty-five miles along Route 91.
2. The construction crew worked steadily, stopping only for a quick break.
3. The artifacts, kept in glass displays, were carefully guarded.
4. Alexander the Great, one of the greatest generals in history, was king of Macedonia.
5. At the end of the hall is a metal door leading to a secret chamber.
6. An architect designed the new capitol building on Jefferson Avenue in memory of Senator Deaver.
7. The author, often called the literary genius of her decade, has written several historical novels.
8. The telegram was from defense attorney Anita Lownsberry Sanchez.
9. The store contains antique furniture and glass dating to the nineteenth century.
10. Rescue workers combed through the piles of debris, looking for survivors.

B. Answers will vary. However, good revisions will address the problems identified on the pupil page, as shown in the examples below.

1. Baseball, one of the most popular sports in the United States, has an interesting history.
2. Some people claim that baseball evolved from another game, rounders.
3. The British played rounders as early as the 1600's.
4. American colonists in New England played it in the 1700's.

Although rounders was a game that involved hitting a ball with a bat and advancing around the bases, it was different from baseball. Soaking, the technique of throwing the ball at the runner, was changed by the Americans, who preferred tagging the runner.

The playing field for rounders was in the shape of an irregular pentagon, measuring over thirty-nine feet on three sides and twenty-eight feet on the other two. Instead of three bases, there were four posts, not including the batting square, the place where the batsman would stand.

Managing the Paper Load

For Exercise B, rather than having students rewrite the first paragraph, you may wish to call on students to suggest how they would combine the sentences. Jot their responses on the chalkboard and evaluate/revise together.

---

3. The artifacts were kept in glass displays. <u>The displays were</u> carefully guarded. (Use a comma.)
4. Alexander the Great was king of Macedonia. <u>He was</u> one of the greatest generals in history. (Use commas.)
5. At the end of the hall is a metal door. <u>It</u> leads to a secret chamber. (Use -*ing*.)
6. An architect designed the new capitol building. The building is on Jefferson Avenue near Rhodes Boulevard. He designed it in memory of Senator Deaver.
7. The author has written several historical novels. The author is often called the literary genius of her decade.
8. The telegram was from Anita Lownsberry Sanchez. She is a defense attorney.
9. The store contains antique furniture and glass. The furniture and glass date back to the nineteenth century.
10. Rescue workers combed through the piles of debris. They looked for survivors.

B. Rewrite the following passage. Eliminate the underlined words and combine the pairs or groups of sentences in parentheses. Decide on your own how to combine the sentences in the last two paragraphs. In your new sentences you will have to separate some groups of words with commas, and you may have to add -*ing* or -*ed* to a word in the group.

(1) (Baseball has an interesting history. <u>Baseball</u> is one of the most popular sports in the United States.) (2) (Some people claim that baseball evolved from another game. <u>This game was called</u> rounders.)

(3) (The British played rounders. <u>They played it</u> as early as the 1600's.) (4) (American colonists played it. <u>They played</u> in New England. <u>They played</u> in the 1700's.)

Rounders was different from baseball. Rounders was a game that involved hitting a ball with a bat and advancing around the bases. Soaking took the place of tagging the runner. Soaking was the technique of throwing the ball at the runner. Americans changed this practice. They changed this into tagging the runner.

The playing field for rounders was in the shape of an irregular pentagon. The field measured over thirty-nine feet on three sides. It measured twenty-eight feet on the other two sides. Instead of three bases, there were four posts. They did not include the batting square. The batting square was the place where the batsman would stand.

COMBINING WITH *WHO, WHICH, AND THAT*

If you have mentioned a person, place, or thing in one sentence and then provided details about it in another, you can often combine the two sentences using *who, which,* or *that.*

Separate Sentences	The student received a grant. She *wanted to study genetics.*
Combined Sentence	The student **who** *wanted to study genetics* received a grant.
Separate Sentences	Marie Curie won the Nobel Prize for chemistry. She *founded the Radium Institute in Paris.*
Combined Sentence	Marie Curie, **who** *founded the Radium Institute in Paris,* won the Nobel Prize for chemistry.

Use **who** to combine sentences if the subject is a person. If the details you add are essential to understand that subject, as in the first example, no comma is needed. If the details are not essential to understanding the subject, as in the second example, they are set off with commas.

Separate Sentences	Here is a machine called a respirator. The machine *helps patients breathe.*
Combined Sentence	Here is a machine called a respirator **that** helps patients breathe.
Separate Sentences	Political campaigns need committed and hardworking volunteers. Political campaigns *are very exciting.*
Combined Sentence	Political campaigns, **which** *are very exciting,* need committed and hardworking volunteers.

Use **that** or **which** to combine sentences if the subject is a place or thing. If the added details are essential to understand the subject, as in the first example, use *that* without commas. If the details are not essential, use *which* and add commas.

Sentence Combining **425**

Double Wedding Ring Quilt, by Emily Hasbrouck, 1930-1940.
From the permanent collection of the Museum of American Folk Art.

ANSWERS TO PRACTICE YOUR SKILLS

A. Answers will vary in sentences 6–10. However, good answers will use *who, which,* and *that* properly, as shown in the examples below.

1. This is the puppy that I told you about.
2. This computer, which is used for word processing, uses floppy disks.
3. Nancy, who was the president of the student council, suggested the theme for the homecoming float.
4. The awards program, which aired in over 2 million households, originated in Los Angeles.
5. The comedian, who was on several television specials, made the audience laugh hysterically.
6. I need the safe key that is in my purse.
7. The jewels that were Mrs. Lee's were sold at the auction.
8. The senators who represented my state supported the bill.
9. The plane, which had encountered turbulence, landed safely.
10. The manager, who had coached the team for twenty years, retired the pitcher in the seventh inning.

Practice Your Skills

A. Combine each pair of sentences. In sentences 1–5, eliminate the underlined words and follow the clues in parentheses. In sentences 6–10, use *who, which,* or *that.*

1. This is the puppy. I told you about <u>him.</u> (Use *that*.)
2. This computer uses floppy disks. <u>This computer</u> is used for word processing. (Use *which* and commas.)
3. Nancy suggested the theme for the homecoming float. <u>Nancy</u> was the president of the student council. (Use *who* and commas.)
4. The awards program originated in Los Angeles. <u>The program</u> aired in over 2 million households. (Use *which* and commas.)
5. The comedian made the audience laugh hysterically. <u>She</u> was on several television specials. (Use *who* and commas.)
6. I need the key to the safe. The key is in my purse.
7. The jewels were sold at the auction. They were Mrs. Lee's.
8. Senators supported the bill. The senators represented my state.
9. The plane landed safely. The plane had encountered turbulence.
10. The manager retired the pitcher in the seventh inning. The manager had coached the team for twenty years.

B. Rewrite the following passage. Eliminate the underlined words and combine the pairs of sentences in parentheses. Decide on your own how to combine the sentences in the last paragraph. Use *who,* *that,* or *which* with or without commas, as appropriate.

(1) (Film uses an immense vocabulary of images. <u>It</u> is a form of communication.) (2) (Film communication starts with the shot. <u>The shot</u> is film's basic unit.)

(3) (Directors talk to their audiences through the use of shots. <u>The directors</u> are in charge of all aspects of production.) (4) (I. Pudovkin wanted directors to observe things, then show them. <u>He</u> was an early Russian film director.)

(5) (Directors can spend hours preparing for a shot. <u>This shot</u> may be seen for only a few seconds.)

A director must select an angle. This angle has a particular perspective. The long shot is one perspective. A long shot includes the entire area of action. The long shot can present an overview to the viewer. The long shot was the only shot in the early days of film. The medium shot is another alternative. The director often chooses this alternative. The usual distance for a shot is the medium shot. It is an intermediate shot between the long shot and the close-up. The close-up shot is an effective tool. Directors often use this tool to display emotion.

COMBINING SENTENCES
WITH CONJUNCTIONS

Often you can combine sentences in ways that make the relationships between your ideas clearer. To combine sentences in this way, you need to use a word that shows relationships, such as a **subordinating conjunction.** Subordinating conjunctions such as those shown below can express relationships of time, cause, or condition.

Subordinating Conjunctions for Sentence Combining

Time	Cause	Condition
when	as	although
until	for	unless
while	because	whether (or not)

 Individualizing Instruction

Gifted and Talented Students For Exercise B, you may wish to ask gifted students to freewrite a third paragraph beginning with: "If I were a film director, I would . . ." Instruct them to vary short and long sentences for a smooth flow of ideas.

Critical Thinking

Judging Ask students to consider what kinds of writing topics would call for numerous expressions of time relationships (training manuals or cookbooks) or cause relationships (history or economics textbooks).

Notice how subordinating conjunctions are used to combine sentences and show relationships between them.

Separate Sentences   The soldiers stood respectfully at attention. *The flag was raised high above the army base.*

Combined Sentence   The soldiers stood respectfully at attention **while** *the flag was raised high above the army base.*

Separate Sentences   Jerry enjoyed the New York Philharmonic's performance. *He usually attends rock concerts.*

Combined Sentence   Jerry enjoyed the New York Philharmonic's performance **although** *he usually attends rock concerts.*

The subordinate idea also can be placed at the beginning of the sentence, followed by a comma.

Although *Jerry usually attends rock concerts,* he enjoyed the New York Philharmonic's performance.

Practice Your Skills

A. Combine the following pairs of sentences. In sentences 1–5, follow the directions enclosed in parentheses. In sentences 6–10, decide which subordinating conjunction to use.

1. Barbara walked home. Her brother offered to drive her. (Use *although*.)
2. The play was postponed. The star broke his leg. (Use *because*.)
3. Alonzo ignored Tanya's comments. She teased him. (Use *when*.)
4. The students listened quietly. Juan told the class about his three-week trip to Europe. (Use *when*.)
5. Children are receptive to computers. They learn about them at an early age. (Use *because*.)
6. Jim is a good athlete. He isn't as good as a professional.
7. The crowd at the stadium was enormous. The football game was the first of the season.
8. I enjoyed tutoring foreign students in chemistry. It took a great deal of time.
9. The police officer called for back-up help. She heard a gunshot.
10. Everyone wants tickets. The ice extravaganza comes to town only once a year.

B. Rewrite the following passage, combining the sentences in parentheses. Use an appropriate subordinating conjunction.

(1) (Photography offers a wide variety of career opportunities. Many events and people need to be visually documented.) (2) (Commercial photography is one of the most popular fields for the prospective photographer. Many other fields present career opportunities.) (3) (Commercial photographers take pictures for advertisements. They work with varied subject matter.) (4) (Commercial photographers must be skilled and imaginative. They are creating memorable images.) (5) (Portrait photographers pose their subjects. People often feel awkward about posing.) (6) (Photojournalists may work for only one newspaper or magazine. Some work for and sell their photographs to various publications.) (7) (Scientific photographers must be specialists in their particular fields. They work with highly complex subject matter.)

C. Revise the following passage, using any of the sentence-combining techniques.

The Mayas developed an extraordinary civilization in Central America. The Mayas were a Native American people. The Mayan civilization reached its peak about A.D. 300. It continued to flourish for almost six hundred years. The Mayas made advances in astronomy. The advances were outstanding. They also developed an accurate calendar. The Mayas did not have schools. The children learned by observing and helping adults.

Entire Mayan families lived together in one domicile. This included parents, children, and grandparents. They constructed their houses from poles. The poles were lashed together. They used leaves and grass to weave roofs for their homes. The leaves were of palm. The grass was dried.

Mayan farmers raised beans, corn, and squash. Mayan farmers lived in rural homes or small villages. The farmers cleared their fields during the harvest. They used stone axes to do this.

Mayan figure

Sentence Combining **429**

B. Answers will vary slightly.
1. Photography offers a wide variety of career opportunities because many events and people need to be visually documented.
2. Although many other fields present career opportunities, commercial photography is one of the most popular fields for the prospective photographer.
3. When commercial photographers take pictures for advertisements, they work with varied subject matter.
4. Commercial photographers must be skilled and imaginative because they are creating memorable images.
5. Portrait photographers pose their subjects, although people often feel awkward about posing.
6. Although photojournalists may work for only one newspaper or magazine, some work for and sell their photographs to various publications.
7. Scientific photographers must be specialists in their particular fields because they work with highly complex subject matter.
C. Answers will vary. However, a good revision will use a number of the sentence-combining techniques identifed on the pupil pages, as shown in the example below.
The Mayas, who were a Native American people, developed an extraordinary civilization that reached its peak about A.D. 300 and continued to flourish for almost six hundred years. The Mayas made outstanding advances in astronomy and also developed an accurate calendar.
Entire Mayan families, including parents, children, and grandparents, lived together in one domicile. Although the Mayas did not have schools, Mayan children learned by observing and helping adults.
Living in rural homes or small villages, Mayan farmers raised beans, corn, and squash. The farmers used stone axes to clear their fields during the harvest.

Spot Check

As you circulate among students, check for proper punctuation of their combined sentences. When you find fragments or run-ons, suggest procedures for revising to make them effective complete sentences.

Additional Resources
- Writing Resource Book, pp. 43–47
- Elaboration, Revision, and Proofreading Worksheets

Point of View

Objectives

1. To identify the first-, second-, and third-person points of view in writing
2. To identify appropriate uses of various points of view in fiction and nonfiction
3. To use an appropriate point of view in writing

Handbook Mini-Lessons

For information on topics related to point of view, see the following mini-lessons.

- Personal Voice and Style, pp. 405–408
- Varieties of Language, pp. 409–411

Teaching Strategies

Motivating

Have students consider how a major league baseball game differs for a player, an umpire, or a coach. Point out that each of these figures *experiences* the game from a different perspective. Ask students how people with different points of view might write about the game. For example, how would a player's diary entry differ from a coaching or scouting report?

Critical Thinking

Analyzing Ask students where they might encounter the type of third-person account given here of the fire *(in a newspaper)*. Ask if a first-person point of view might appear in such an article *(yes, but only in a direct quotation)*.

Point of View

One important choice you need to make when you write is what **point of view** to use. Point of view is the vantage point from which you write, your "angle" on your topic. The point of view you choose depends on whose story you want to tell, how formal you want your writing to be, and how much closeness you want to set up between you and your readers.

THREE POINTS OF VIEW

There are three basic points of view: first-, third-, and second-person. To understand these points of view, consider an apartment building that burned to the ground. Spectators cheered as a fire-fighter led a child to safety. If you asked the child what happened, you would learn about it from his personal point of view as a participant in the action.

> I don't know what happened. Smoke was everywhere and I kept coughing and screaming "Help!" out the window. Then this woman got there and told me to follow her. We kind of crawled down the halls. That's how we got out.

A story narrated by a participant using pronouns such as *I, me, my, we,* and *our* is told from the **first-person point of view.**

On the other hand, spectators might tell the story of what they saw but not include their own experience. As you read, what differences do you notice in the information you receive from this narrative compared with what you learned from the child's version?

> After the firefighters thought that they had everyone out of the building, they heard a child crying for help. One firefighter rushed into the flaming building, found the child, and led him to safety.

A story of other people's experiences narrated by an observer is told from the **third-person point of view.** The use of pronouns such as *they, it, her, him,* and *she* signals this point of view.

The first-person and third-person points of view are used in many types of writing. The **second-person point of view** is usually used for specific purposes, such as giving directions and instructions. The pronoun *you* is often used as the subject, though it may be implied rather than stated, as in this passage.

To protect your family from fires, follow these rules:

1. Install smoke detectors in your home, and check them regularly to make sure that they are working.
2. Always have a fire extinguisher on hand. Explain to young children that it is not a toy.
3. Make sure that there are two exits from every part of your house.
4. Hold regular fire drills using these exits.
5. Choose a place for your family to meet after exiting your house. Make sure the spot is at a safe distance from the building.

W R I T E R   T O   W R I T E R

The first piece I wrote this year I did in the first-person. It was fun. For my next piece I used first-person, but the subject matter didn't fit, so I changed to third. It was great!

Brad A. Mullin, student
Cedar Rapids, Iowa

USING VARIOUS POINTS OF VIEW

Sometimes the choice of point of view for a piece of writing is obvious. For example, personal letters and journal entries are normally written from a first-person point of view; instructions, directions, and commands, from a second-person point of view.

In many types of writing, however, the decision about point of view is not so obvious. Both first-person and third-person points of view can be used effectively in fiction and nonfiction. Here are some guidelines to help you decide which point of view to use.

Point of View in Fiction

In writing fiction, such as a short story, if you want your narrator to participate in the story, choose the first-person point of view. Your reader will be drawn into the story, seeing into the character's mind and feeling what the character feels. Note that a first-person narrator does not have to be the writer, but can be any character you choose.

Point of View   **431**

Speaking and Listening

Have a volunteer read the excerpt from "Autumntime." Then elicit responses to the excerpt. Lead students to conclude that because this piece is written in the first person, the language conveys the melancholy feeling of the character in a direct way. Challenge a student to transpose the excerpt orally from first to third person. Ask students to describe the difference in effect. *(Normal conversation is usually in the first person. The character's feelings are less direct because they are filtered through the perceptions of a third-person narrator.)*

Teaching Tip: Point of View

Some students may feel that the excerpt from White's book could have been written in either first or third person and thus conclude that point of view is an arbitrary choice in fiction. Have these students re-read the excerpt from *The Once and Future King* and then a later passage from the same book that delves into Merlyn's thoughts as this passage does the Wart's. Point out that the author would have lost this option if he had chosen to write in the first-person.

Dad used to tell me stories about the trees that still existed when he was a boy. There weren't very many even then, with the urbanization program in full swing, but most people had seen at least one tree by the time they started school. It wasn't like nowadays, at any rate. Oh, I've seen the plastic trees; practically every street has a few of them. But you can tell the plastic ones are artificial just from looking at pictures in the microdot library.

A. Lentini, "Autumntime"

Use the third-person point of view in fiction if you do not want your narrator to participate in the action but only to describe it.

The Wart did not know what Merlyn was talking about, but he liked him to talk. He did not like the grown-ups who talked down to him, but the ones who went on talking in their usual way, leaving him to leap along in their wake, jumping at meanings, guessing, clutching at known words, and chuckling at complicated jokes as they suddenly dawned. He had the glee of the porpoise then, pouring and leaping through strange seas.

T. H. White, *The Once and Future King*

Point of View in Nonfiction

When writing personal and informal nonfiction, such as autobiographies and personal narratives, consider using the first-person point of view. First-person makes the writing direct and personal.

When spring came to St. Louis, I took out my first library card, and . . . spent most of my Saturdays at the library (no interruptions) breathing in the world of penniless shoeshine boys who, with goodness and perseverance, became rich, rich men, and gave baskets of goodies to the poor on holidays. The little princesses who were mistaken for maids, and the long-lost children mistaken for waifs, became more real to me than our house, our mother, our school, or Mr. Freeman.

Maya Angelou, *I Know Why the Caged Bird Sings*

Springboard

Read the opening sentence or sentences of a variety of pieces of writing and challenge students to identify which point of view is used in each. Then ask them to evaluate the effectiveness of the openings. From their ratings, can they conclude that they prefer a particular point of view? If so, which one do they prefer?

Nonfiction writing such as essays, biographies, and news articles—whether formal or informal, personal or impersonal—often uses the third-person point of view.

It's the job of the dictionary editors to keep tabs on new words and new uses of old ones. At G. & C. Merriam Company, the country's biggest dictionary-makers, twenty full-time lexicographers [dictionary-makers] keep a constant lookout for verbal novelties.

Many words are gathered but few are chosen. Here are some (courtesy of *Compton's Yearbook*) that are now being watched as possible candidates for the dictionary.

automobilitis: the problems caused by the increasing use of automobiles

carboholic: a compulsive eater   **Stephen Rosen, *Future Facts***

These sculptures are one artist's solution to automobilitis.

Practice Your Skills

A. Study the following writing ideas. Decide which point of view would be most effective for each one. Write the first sentence of an opening paragraph in the point of view you have chosen.

1. a persuasive argument that students should be able to spend their free time any way they choose
2. an informative article on handwriting analysis
3. a comparison of yourself at age six and now
4. a humorous definition of baseball
5. a story in which the main character is orbiting the earth

B. Rewrite the first-person narrative by Maya Angelou on page 432. Tell the story from the point of view of the librarian who observed the little girl absorbed in her reading every Saturday.

Point of View   **433**

Social Studies Connection

To better understand the importance of point of view in writing, you might have students read and compare two written sources of information about a particular issue or period in American (or world) history: a primary source such as an autobiography of someone who lived through the time and a secondary source such as a textbook account of the event, issue, or period.

Using Dialogue Effectively

Objective

To identify the ways dialogue enhances fiction and nonfiction writing and conveys information in plays and skits

Handbook Mini-Lessons

For information on topics related to using dialogue effectively, see the following mini-lessons.

- Finding a Personal Voice and Style, pp. 405–408
- Point of View, pp. 430–433

Teaching Strategies

Motivating

Invite students to think about times they have overheard a conversation. Ask them what we can learn about someone just from hearing that person speak. (For example, we may be able to tell: what part of the country he or she is from; the person's level of education; the person's mood; the person's needs or desires.) Ask in what ways listening to someone speaking might reveal aspects of his or her character. Elicit the response that speech is a major expression of personality and, thus, can reveal character.

WRITING
HANDBOOK
22

Using Dialogue Effectively

Dialogue is conversation between two or more people. Writers use dialogue in works of all kinds—fiction, nonfiction, plays, and poems—to add life and interest to their work.

USING DIALOGUE IN FICTION

Fiction includes short stories, novels, tall tales, and other kinds of imaginative prose writing. Most fiction contains two types of writing: **narration,** in which the narrator describes events, and **dialogue,** in which characters speak. Dialogue can add many different kinds of information to fiction writing.

Dialogue to Reveal Character   Notice how the author uses dialogue in this passage to reveal what the characters are like. Notice, too, how speaker's tags—*He said, I said*—identify who is speaking.

LITERARY
MODEL

He said, "I can chop some wood today."
I said, "But I have a boy coming from the orphanage."
"I'm the boy."
"You? But you're small."
"Size don't matter, chopping wood," he said. "Some of the big boys don't chop good. I've been chopping wood at the orphanage a long time."

Marjorie Kinnan Rawlings, "A Mother in Mannville"

Dialogue to Reveal Information   Sometimes dialogue provides background. In this example, the dialogue helps identify the setting.

LITERARY
MODEL

"Off there to the right—somewhere—is a large island," said Whitney. "It's rather a mystery."
"What island is it?" Rainsford asked.
"The old charts call it 'Ship Trap Island,' " Whitney replied. "A suggestive name, isn't it? Sailors have a curious dread of the place. I don't know why. Some superstition."

Richard Connell, "The Most Dangerous Game"

Dialogue to Present Events Dialogue can also present the events of a story. Note how the author uses dialogue in this example to show how the frightened girl woke her brother.

> "Come on, wake up."
> "What for? Go 'way."
> I was lost for a reasonable reply. I could not say, "I'm scared, and I don't want to be alone," so I merely said, "I'm going out. If you want to come, come on."
>
> **Eugenia Collier, "Marigolds"**

W R I T E R   T O   W R I T E R

> Sometimes I needed to make dialogue do three or four or five things at once—reveal what the character said but also what he thought he said, what he hid, what others were going to think he meant, and what they misunderstood, and so forth—all in a single speech.
>
> **Eudora Welty, novelist**

U SING DIALOGUE IN
NONFICTION

Nonfiction includes all writing that deals with real, not imaginary, people and events. Dialogue is often used in autobiographies, biographies, and newspaper and magazine articles. Note how this biographer used dialogue to show Abraham Lincoln's quick wit.

> A foreign diplomat demurred at Lincoln's condemning a certain Greek history as tedious: "The author of that history, Mr. President, is one of the profoundest scholars of the age. Indeed, it may be doubted whether any man of our generation has plunged more deeply in the sacred fount of learning."
> "Yes," said Lincoln, "or come up drier."
>
> **Carl Sandburg, <u>Abraham Lincoln: The War Years</u>**

Using Dialogue
Effectively   **435**

Speaking and Listening

To practice using dialogue to *show* what's happening rather than just to *tell* it, consider using this activity: Ask students to try to convey a specific action scene by writing just four lines of dialogue between two speakers. Call on students to read their dialogues aloud while classmates try to guess the specific action and setting the writer had in mind. Also, have peers comment on the naturalness of speech (or lack of it) in the dialogue.

Individualizing Instruction

ESL Students These students may need extra help in understanding the conventions of written dialogue because these conventions vary among languages. Refer students to Grammar Handbook 41, pages 795–801.

Literature Connection

Hemingway's short story "A Clean Well-Lighted Place" uses dialogue almost exclusively to reveal character and feelings. You may wish to have students read the story and report on whether they think his dialogue is "natural sounding" or somewhat contrived (as some critics suggest) and what effect they feel Hemingway was attempting to create.

Literature Connection

Students may enjoy reading Shirley Jackson's short story "The Lottery" as an example of dialogue that powerfully portrays events (in the second half of the story). Students could be asked to comment on the eerie effect seemingly normal dialogue can have when set in a threatening situation.

Stumbling Block

Some students may have trouble writing dialogue that sounds like spoken language. To help them get the feel for how spoken language looks in writing, suggest they read various forms of transcripts (for example, *The White House Transcripts*, which should be available in the local library). Another option would be to have students tape-record ten minutes of a TV sitcom, and transcribe it. Have them use their transcriptions to find differences in spoken and written language.

ANSWERS TO PRACTICE YOUR SKILLS

Answers will vary. A good revision will use dialogue in ways identified in the pupil pages, as shown in the example short story below.

"Chin, come to the main deck," shouted Sarah, the starship commander, over the intercom. When the science adviser arrived, Sarah directed him to the window. "That asteroid; it's headed right for us. Activate the laser and blast it."

Chin thought this was a bad idea. "Commander, we should take evasive action. Chunks of debris from a blast like that could destroy us."

While Sarah and Chin argued, the asteroid glanced off the side of the ship and spun off into space.

"Are you okay?" asked Chin.

"Yeah. I'm okay. But don't even *think* about questioning an order again, mister."

Peer Response

Have students exchange rewritten paragraphs. Peer readers should look for natural speech in the dialogue. Have them circle portions that need revision and work with each other to rewrite.

> ### Additional Resources
> - Writing Resource Book, pp. 50–51

PROFESSIONAL MODEL

Writing **TIP**

When repeating the words of a real person, as in a biography, nonfiction essay, or interview, make sure to quote the person exactly.

USING DIALOGUE IN PLAYS AND SKITS

Because plays and skits consist almost entirely of dialogue, the dialogue must convey a great deal of information. It must not only tell about events that occur offstage, but also must convey what characters are thinking and feeling.

The following example shows how a single portion of dialogue can provide information, offer insights about character, and give stage directions.

▼

> **James:** What is it, a game?
> **Annie [curtly]:** An alphabet.
> **James:** Alphabet?
> **Annie:** For the deaf. (**Helen** *now repeats the finger movements in air, exactly, her head cocked to her own hand, and* Annie's *eyes suddenly gleam.*) Ho. How *bright* she is!
>
> William Gibson, *The Miracle Worker*

Guidelines for Writing Dialogue The most important thing to remember is that dialogue should sound like natural speech. Use the kinds of sentence fragments and contractions that speakers commonly use, and try to make the dialogue fit the situations.

Practice Your Skills

Rewrite this piece of narration as you would for either a short story or a play. Use narration and dialogue for a story and dialogue and stage directions for a play.

> Sarah, the starship commander, shouted over the intercom for her science adviser, Chin, to come to the main deck. When Chin arrived, she asked him to look through the window at the asteroid headed directly for the ship. Sarah ordered Chin to activate the ship's laser to blow the asteroid apart. Chin thought this was a bad idea because large pieces of the asteroid might collide with the ship. He suggested taking evasive action. While Sarah and Chin argued, the asteroid glanced off the side of the ship and spun off into space. Chin asked Sarah if she was all right. Sarah said she was but that Chin had better not disobey an order again.

Off the Record

Paula Danziger, author of young-adult books, says, "The teacher I remember most is a guy named Paul Abramson, who said to me one day, 'Danziger, get rid of the gum.' I said, 'But I just put it in my mouth and the flavor's not gone.'" They compromised. She could chew if she stood in the garbage can. "He allowed for lunacy, which I think is absolutely necessary."

Sketchbook

In 1956, a newspaper drew this portrait of life "in a time not very far away." What do you see in the future, not very far away?

This is your future

3D Color TV Wall Panel · Slide-back Roof · Personal Helicopter and Roof Landing Area · Moving Stairway · House-control Panel

Glass Walls · Dust-free Floors · Menu Selector and Microwave Stove · Giant-size Fruit · Ultrasonic Laundry · Electrical Heat Unit · Phono-vision Room

Additional Sketches

How might life be different if we started out as old people and gradually grew younger until we were just babies?

What have you accomplished in the last month? Summarize your achievements.

437

Objective

To use a portrait of life in the near future as a springboard to informal writing

Using the Prompt

Be sure students understand that the writing activities suggested in the Sketchbooks are designed to be informal in order to allow risk-taking and experimentation and will not be graded.

Ask students to discuss the kinds of changes that have altered people's lives in the past forty years. Students may suggest such things as computerization, increased television viewing, increases in pollution and population, new musical styles, mobile telephones and fax machines, or the increased speed of telecommunications.

Encourage students to brainstorm changes that might take place in the next forty years. How will people communicate? How will they get to school or work? What labor-saving devices may make life even easier? What kinds of music will be popular? What will people wear? What will hair styles be like?

Some students may benefit from drawing their own portraits of life "in a time not very far away" before they begin writing. These students might then write short or lengthy captions to accompany their drawings.

Use the ideas in the Additional Sketches section with students who prefer a different starting point. Encourage students to keep their writing in their Writing Portfolios for possible use in future writing projects.

Building Your Vocabulary

Objectives

1. To identify and use various strategies of inferring word meaning from context
2. To infer word meaning by analyzing word parts

Handbook Mini-Lessons

For information on topics related to building vocabulary, see the following mini-lessons.
- How Can I Achieve Clarity? pp. 383–390
- How Can I Make My Language Richer? pp. 409–415

Teaching Strategies

Motivating

Point out that having a good vocabulary is not just an academic requirement; it has very practical value. Have students read the first paragraph and try to report specific ways good vocabulary could help in the life situations mentioned there. Encourage students to respond with personal examples from their own past experience.

WRITING
HANDBOOK
23

Writing
— TIP —

In your writing, be sure to give your readers context clues for words that may be un-familiar to them.

Building Your Vocabulary

A good vocabulary is a valuable asset in many life situations— meeting people, explaining your ideas and feelings, looking for a summer job, reading a newspaper, listening to an interview, or even writing a paper for history class. A personal vocabulary plan can help you develop your word power.

Using a vocabulary notebook is a good way to build your vocabulary. When you come across an unfamiliar word, jot it down in a notebook or in a special section of your journal. You might like to jot down the entire sentence as an example of how the word is used. Once a week, sit down with your list of words, a dictionary, and a thesaurus. Look up the words and create a sentence using each. Try to use these words in your conversation and writing to make them part of your active vocabulary.

INFERRING WORD MEANINGS FROM CONTEXT

Before using a dictionary to look up a word in your vocabulary notebook, try figuring out what it might mean. Like a detective searching for clues at the scene of a crime, you can often learn the meaning of an unfamiliar word by examining the "scene," or **context,** in which the word is used. The sentence or group of sentences in which the word appears may contain clues to its meaning. Based on these clues, you can **infer,** or make an educated guess about, the meaning. Some types of context clues are **definition and restatement, example, comparison and contrast,** and **cause and effect.**

Definition and Restatement In a definition or restatement clue, a writer reveals the meaning of a word by defining it or by restating it in different words. Definition and restatement clues are often signaled by certain key words or phrases.

Key Words Indicating Definition and Restatement

in other words	this means	that is
to put it another way	which is to say	or

The clues can also be signaled by punctuation, such as a dash. According to the dictionary, *grueling* means "extremely trying; exhausting." In the example below, notice how the phrase following the dash provides this dictionary definition.

> The long climb up the steep cliff was a *grueling* experience— **one that left us utterly exhausted.**

A common type of restatement is the **appositive.** It is often set off by commas, as shown in the following example.

> The directors of the zoo announced the purchase of a pair of *quetzals,* **crested birds native to Central America.**

Using Examples   Examples can also help you determine the meaning of an unfamiliar word. You will find that certain key words often introduce examples.

Key Words Indicating Examples

like	for instance	this
such as	especially	these
for example	other	to illustrate

The examples and key words in the following sentence help you determine the meaning of *memorabilia*—mementos.

> A small Georgia museum contains some excellent Civil War *memorabilia,* **such as** flags, maps, guns, and uniforms.

Sometimes the unfamiliar word is itself one of the examples of a familiar word.

> A few small mammals, **such as** the Australian *wombat,* are in danger of becoming extinct.

Comparison   In a comparison clue, the writer compares the unfamiliar word with other, more familiar words. You can use these comparisons to unlock the meaning of an unknown word.

Key Words Indicating Comparison

like	in the same way	as	similar to

Linking Grammar and Writing

You may wish to help students distinguish a fine point of grammar here: appositives that are set off by commas compared to appositives that have a restrictive function (not set off by commas). Use this sentence as an example: *My son Bob is the quietest of the three boys.* Notice that the sentence would have commas before and after "Bob" if he were the only son in the family: *My son, Bob, is an only child.* Point out that this distinction frequently comes into play when referring to authors and their works. For example, no comma is used in *Smith's play* The Grammarian *was better than the others.* See Grammar Handbook 37: Appositives, p. 693.

In the following example, notice how the key word *like* and the comparison help you understand the word *ocotillo*.

> The *ocotillo,* **like** many other desert plants, has stiff, thorny stems and branches that protect it against grazing animals.

A **simile** is a special kind of comparison between two unlike things using the word *like* or *as*. Similes are often used in poetry. The following simile gives you a clue to the meaning of *salutary*.

> The letter from home was a *salutary* influence on Ginger: **like** a swim on a hot day, it helped her to regain her energy.

Contrast In a contrast clue, the writer contrasts an unfamiliar word with something familiar. Specific words signal a contrast clue.

Key Words Indicating Contrast		
on the contrary	on the other hand	but
although	in contrast to	unlike

In the following example, the key word and the contrast clue help you determine the meaning of *mollify*.

> His intention was to *mollify* her, **but instead** his words seemed to make her even more angry.

Cause and Effect Finding context clues helps you understand the relationships between ideas. One very common relationship between ideas is cause and effect. Key words that may signal cause and effect are listed below.

Key Words Indicating Cause and Effect			
as a result	consequently	because	when
as a consequence	therefore	since	then

Notice how the use of the key word and the cause-and-effect relationship in the following sentence help you determine the meaning of *noxious*.

> We knew the fumes were *noxious* **when** everyone became ill.

440   Writing Handbook

Stumbling Block

When looking for key words in the context as word meaning clues, some students may take a very mechanical approach. They may pay little attention to the content of the passage while just scanning for the key words. Stress the value of letting the *ideas* come through the context.

Critical Thinking

Inferring Sequence   Emphasize the skill it takes to distinguish true cause and effect from mere coincidence in the thinking process. Have students practice distinguishing the proper and improper use of cause and effect key words. Call out paired events (with a key word indicating cause and effect) and have students respond with: "proper" or "improper." For example: *The rooster crowed; consequently, the sun rose.* (improper)

Literature Connection

The poets of the Romantic era are a key source for examples of simile and metaphor. Suggest, for example, that students read Percy Bysshe Shelley's "To a Skylark" to find the many different ways a bird can be compared to abstract concepts.

Inference from General Context   Context clues sometimes do not appear in the same sentence as the unfamiliar word. In the following paragraph, a sentence containing the term *obsolescence* is followed by a sentence containing an explanation and examples.

> Much of the American economy is based on the principle of planned *obsolescence*. Consumer groups have criticized manufacturers for turning out products that are designed to wear out in a short time, although the technology exists to make longer-lasting products.

From the general context in which *obsolescence* appears, you probably inferred that it means "the state of being no longer useful."

Sometimes context clues are included in several sentences. Try to determine the meaning of *impromptu* from the following series of descriptive details.

> It was a hot summer Sunday. Suddenly, there was a power failure. Soon most houses had lost their air-conditioned coolness, and people began to drift outdoors in search of a breeze. Soon, food began to appear, and an *impromptu* block party developed. All around me, people were getting acquainted.

Based on the information in the paragraph, you should have been able to guess the meaning of *impromptu*—"unplanned."

W R I T E R   T O   W R I T E R

I discovered that when I write I have a larger vocabulary than when I speak.

**Beth Hill, student
Tuscaloosa, Alabama**

Edgar Bergen,
ventriloquist,
used his dummy
Charlie McCarthy
to entertain people.

Building Your
Vocabulary   **441**

ESL Students   Being able to infer word meanings from general context is crucial for anyone trying to learn another language. Help these students see the benefit of reading blocks of text (in the examples) without stopping for every unknown word. Point out the connection between this approach to reading and the way they listen to conversations to pick up the "gist" or main flow of ideas.

Personal Touch

You may wish to share some examples from your own experience of learning new vocabulary upon entering a new area of study or vocation (especially new technical terms). Explain to students how you had to use inferring/investigating skills to master new procedures or become familiar with a new environment.

Science Connection

The process of inference has its counterpart in science in the methods of induction and experimentation. Ask students to describe how the scientific method makes use of "clues." Clarify the difference between deductive and inductive reasoning in science and logic.

Practice Your Skills

A. The sentences below contain words that may be unfamiliar. Using context clues, write the letter of the best meaning for each italicized word.

1. Several *lustrous* objects brightened the room: a chrome sculpture, a crystal chandelier, and sparkling silver doorknobs.
   - a. stolen
   - b. expensive
   - c. shining
   - d. handmade

2. I like a *succinct* sports announcement, not one that rambles.
   - a. brief; clear
   - b. witty; joking
   - c. wise; well informed
   - d. wordy; repetitious

3. Some nations have unwisely *exploited* their colonies, taking as much wealth out of them as they could.
   - a. taken advantage of
   - b. enslaved
   - c. destroyed
   - d. bought and sold

4. Sonia's personality is an *amalgam* of the most desirable traits of the other members of her family—her mother's sense of humor, her father's cheerfulness, and her grandfather's calm.
   - a. cause
   - b. contrast
   - c. mixture
   - d. abundance

5. Because Shannon complained of difficulty reading the chalkboard at school, her parents suspected she was *myopic*.
   - a. fatigued
   - b. lazy
   - c. malnourished
   - d. nearsighted

6. A rainbow is an *evanescent* thing; it gradually disappears, leaving only a memory.
   - a. temporary
   - b. shaped like an arch
   - c. balanced
   - d. beautiful

7. Like any other beginner, a *novice* in the kitchen is likely to make mistakes.
   - a. cook
   - b. young person
   - c. helper
   - d. someone new to an activity

8. Of course this narrative is *fictitious;* the story has no basis in fact.
   - a. colorful
   - b. changeable
   - c. important
   - d. imaginary

9. The child was *precocious*. She could read before she started nursery school.
   - a. hard to manage
   - b. ahead in development
   - c. likely to brag
   - d. very young

10. A guinea pig is *vulnerable*. It can't fight well, it can't run fast, and it has no tough hide or bad scent to protect it.
    - a. hopeless
    - b. lovable
    - c. popular as a pet
    - d. easily hurt

ANSWERS TO PRACTICE YOUR SKILLS

A. Context Clues in Sentences

1. c; 2. a; 3. a; 4. c; 5. d; 6. a; 7. d; 8. d; 9. b; 10. d; 11. d; 12. b; 13. b

11. Tell me the *gist* of the movie. I don't have time for a long description right now.
   a. rating
   b. characters
   c. complete explanation
   d. <u>main idea</u>
12. The story is too *somber*. I prefer something with a more cheerful ending.
   a. sleepy
   b. <u>sad</u>
   c. lengthy
   d. noisy
13. A distinct feeling of *anxiety* about the future replaced her peace of mind.
   a. quiet
   b. <u>uneasiness</u>
   c. understanding
   d. interest

B. Read each of these passages. Then write the letter that represents the best definition of the italicized word.

Richard M. Nixon, former President of the United States, was a master at circumlocution.

1. Many politicians are masters at the art of *circumlocution*. This fact is often illustrated in press conferences. In response to a controversial question posed by a reporter, some politicians can talk for several minutes without ever really answering the question.
   a. <u>talking around a subject</u>
   b. moving from place to place
   c. pleasing people
   d. lying
2. Most Americans would find it difficult to adapt to the *ascetic* lifestyle of a monk. Garage door openers, dishwashers, garbage disposals, stereos, and color televisions—the luxuries that many Americans consider necessities—are missing from a monk's life.
   a. religious
   b. extravagant
   c. vigorous
   d. <u>self-denying</u>
3. One young scientist used a laser to create a *hologram* of an apple for her exhibit. Viewers could see all sides of the apple.
   a. <u>three-dimensional image of a scene or object</u>
   b. moving picture
   c. scene painted on a large wall
   d. life-sized scene

Building Your Vocabulary   **443**

Individualizing Instruction

Advanced Students If advanced students finish Exercise B well ahead of others, have them make lists of as many synonyms and antonyms they can give for the italicized words in the exercise.

Managing the Paper Load

For Exercise B, you may wish to have students exchange papers for grading. Students should correct the wrong responses by writing definitions (from a dictionary) of misunderstood words.

4. Since her injury, Eileen Gardner was able to do little more than watch television and carry out light chores around the house. Though she had been a capable athlete, her muscles were beginning to *atrophy*. Then she decided to rebuild them.
   a. waste away   c. strengthen
   b. develop   d. elongate

5. A true *gastronome* like Julia Child is probably unimpressed by the billions of hamburgers sold by fast-food restaurants. Known as "The French Chef," Ms. Child is the author of a number of books on French cooking. For her, the measure of cooking rests more in the quality than in the quantity of the final product.
   a. a world traveler   c. a fast-food lover
   b. an expert on fine foods   d. a busy person

6. The Battle of Antietam was the bloodiest twelve hours of the Civil War: 22,719 soldiers were killed or wounded. Yet Clara Barton did not turn back in horror from the *carnage* of the battlefield. She had taken upon herself the duty of nursing the injured. She did not flinch from stepping across corpses to the mangled survivors to fulfill that duty.
   a. combat   c. filth
   b. enemy   d. mass killing

7. When news broke out that a tanker had spilled tons of oil off shore, students from the local high school rushed to the beach. There they cleaned oil from the feathers of helpless sea birds. The students had *mitigated* at least some of the damage caused by the spill.
   a. made worse   c. caused
   b. made milder or less serious   d. ignored

8. The negative effects of the new insecticide have angered local residents. In an attempt to *pacify* its outraged neighbors, the Kental Corporation has offered to pay for any damage. The offer is not enough. Residents say that money cannot make up for their fear, worry, and loss of crops.
   a. make fun of   c. accuse
   b. soothe   d. mislead

9. Friday was the *antithesis* of the rest of that whole, miserable week. The sun shone for the first time, the air was warm, and the pools of water began slowly to evaporate.
   a. cause   c. last day
   b. opposite   d. best

10. In his old age, Frank led a *sedentary* life. Most days he read his books and tended to his carrier pigeons.
    a. settled   c. sad
    b. vigorous   d. angry

ANALYZING WORD PARTS

Most English words are composed of smaller units, called **word parts.** Each word part—base word, prefix, or suffix—carries its own meaning. If you know the meanings of the parts, you may be able to infer the meaning of the entire word.

Base Words   Words that lie at the heart of longer words are called **base words.** New words are often created by adding other word parts to base words. For example, here are four words formed by adding word parts to the base word *trust:*

> distrust   trustful   mistrust   untrustworthy

Notice how each word was formed. If you know the meaning of the base word, you can begin to understand the longer words.

Prefixes   A **prefix** is one or more syllables placed at the beginning of a base word to change or extend its meaning. When you know the meaning of a prefix, you can often figure out the meaning of a word.

Prefix	+	Base Word	=	New Word
in-	+	correct	=	incorrect
extra-	+	ordinary	=	extraordinary
mis-	+	manage	=	mismanage

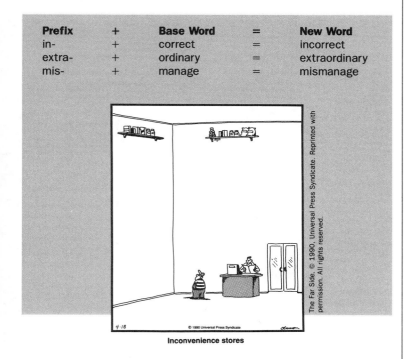

4-18   © 1990 Universal Press Syndicate

Inconvenience stores

Building Your
Vocabulary   **445**

Critical Thinking

Generalizing   Students can work on developing their own examples of words that have prefixes and/or suffixes to supplement the ones given in the text. After students study a particular kind of prefix or suffix example, write a prefix or suffix on the board and have students call out base words that could be attached to it.

The prefixes in the following chart mean "not" or "the opposite of." For example, whereas *appropriate* means "suitable," *inappropriate* means "not suitable."

Prefixes That Reverse Meaning

Prefix	Meaning	Example
dis-	the opposite of	displace
in-	not	inconsiderate
		intolerable
ir-	not	irregular
		irresponsible
im-	not	immobile
		immaterial
il-	not	illegible
		illiterate
non-	not	nonessential
		nonpoisonous
un-	the opposite of	untie
		unstable

The following prefixes show relationships in time or space. For example, *submerge* means "place under water."

Prefixes That Show Relationships

Prefix	Meaning	Example
sub-	beneath, lower	subcommittee
		substructure
pre-	before	prepaid
ante-	before	antecedent
post-	after	postdated
super-	over, above, beyond	superstructure
		superhuman
circum-	around	circumscribe
re-	back, again	return
		reappear
extra-	outside, beyond	extralegal
		extraordinary

The following prefixes show judgment. For example, *malprac-tice* means "improper practice."

Prefixes That Show Judgment

Prefix	Meaning	Example
pro-	in favor of	probusiness
contra-	opposed to	contradict
anti-	against	antislavery
mis-	wrong	misplace
mal-	bad, badly	malnourished

Suffixes A **suffix** is one or more syllables placed at the end of a base word to form a new word. In the following chart, note how suffixes have been added to base words to form new words.

Base Word	+	Suffix	=	New Word
compose	+	*-er*	=	composer
fury	+	*-ous*	=	furious
percent	+	*-age*	=	percentage

The spelling of a base word may change when a suffix is added. For example, the *y* in *fury* is changed to *i* when *-ous* is added. For information about spelling rules for adding suffixes, see the Appendix, page 828.

Noun Suffixes Syllables that form a noun when added to the end of a base word are called **noun suffixes.** The noun suffixes in the chart below mean "one who does something" or "that which does something."

Noun Suffixes That Refer to Action

Suffix	Example	Suffix	Example
-arian	humanitarian	*-ist*	botanist
-eer	puppeteer	*-ian*	electrician
-er	computer	*-or*	actor

Building Your Vocabulary   **447**

Noun suffixes are sometimes used to create abstract words, words that describe a state of being or a quality. For example, by adding the suffix *-dom* to the base word *bore,* you get the abstract noun *boredom,* which means "the state of being bored."

Noun Suffixes That Form Abstract Words

Suffix	Examples
-ance, -ence	relevance, dependence
-ation, -ition	admiration, recognition
-dom	wisdom, boredom
-hood	statehood, womanhood
-ism	realism, patriotism
-ment	amazement, encouragement
-ness	cleverness, kindness
-ship	leadership, friendship
-tude	attitude, gratitude
-ity	sanity, rapidity

Number Three,
by Jackson Pollock, 1949

Adjective Suffixes Suffixes that change base words to adjectives—words that modify nouns and pronouns—are called **adjective suffixes.** For example, the suffix *-able* changes the word *believe* into the adjective *believable.*

Adjective Suffixes

Suffix	Meaning	Examples
-ous	full of	glorious, wondrous
-ose	full of	verbose
-ful	full of	graceful, bountiful
-al	relating to	regional, fanatical
-ic	pertaining to	scientific, symbolic
-ical	pertaining to	historical, economical
-ish	relating to	stylish, smallish
-ive	pertaining to	active, manipulative
-able	capable of being	imaginable, workable
-less	without	blameless, doubtless
-like	like	childlike, catlike

Verb Suffixes Syllables that change base words to verbs are called **verb suffixes.** For example, the suffix *-en* changes the base word *short,* an adjective, into the verb *shorten.*

Verb Suffixes

Suffix	Meaning	Example
-ate	become, make	illuminate
-en	become, make	strengthen
-fy	become, make	liquefy
-ize	become, make	finalize

Practice Your Skills

A. Draw lines to separate each word into its parts—prefix, base, and suffix. Determine the meanings of the prefix and suffix. Then, determine the meaning of the entire word.

    Example   un/avoid/able = not able to be avoided

1. inexcusable
2. immortality
3. nonconformism
4. mismanagement
5. prearrangement
6. irregularity
7. disadvantageous
8. precolonial
9. malodorous
10. inhumanity

For Exercise A, rather than having each student do all ten words, consider assigning one word to groups of two or three students. After they have worked together to separate the word and define the base word, they could report their results to the larger group.

ANSWERS TO PRACTICE YOUR SKILLS

A. 1. in/excus/able = not able to be excused

  2. im/mortal/ity = the state of not being mortal; never dying

  3. non/conform/ism = a state or position of not conforming

  4. mis/manage/ment = wrong or improper managing

  5. pre/arrange/ment = the state or practice of arranging beforehand

  6. ir/regular/ity = the quality of not being regular or predictable

  7. dis/advantage/ous = the state of not having advantage

  8. pre/coloni/al = relating to the time before colonization

  9. mal/odor/ous = the quality of having a bad odor

  10. in/human/ity = the state of not being humane, or kind

Spot Check

As you circulate among students during Exercise B, watch for spelling errors that can creep in even when students have chosen the proper suffixes.

B. 1. agreement
   2. catlike
   3. auctioneer
   4. brighten
   5. tactful
   6. knighthood
   7. violinist
   8. global
   9. criticize
   10. courageous
   11. freedom
   12. secretive
   13. alienate
   14. merciless
   15. fluidity

C. 1. c; 2. d; 3. b; 4. d; 5. d; 6. b; 7. d;
8. d; 9. a; 10. c; 11. c; 12. b; 13. d; 14. a;
15. d.

B. In each of the following sentences, there is a blank followed by a base word in parentheses. Add a suffix to the base to form the correct part of speech to fit the sentence.

> **Example**   At the village water station, engineers added chemicals to _____ (pure) the water. *purify*

1. The leaders of the two neighboring nations decided to meet annually for friendly talks, and this _____ (agree) lasted for thirty peaceful years.
2. With _____ (cat) movements the burglar circled the house quickly and silently.
3. The _____ (auction) was well known throughout the country for her sense of humor.
4. Those blinking neon signs will _____ (bright) the street, turning it colorful and exciting.
5. Nina tried to think of a _____ (tact) way of telling her boyfriend that he had egg on his shirt.
6. Sir Gawain, taking his _____ (knight) very seriously, spent most of his adult life defending King Arthur.
7. May Shin shouted with joy after hearing she was now a _____ (violin) with the Springfield Symphony Orchestra.
8. Unlike traditional warfare, a nuclear war could easily result in _____ (globe) devastation.
9. When the team started to lose, the fans started to _____ (critic) the coach.
10. Alonso dove into the icy waters of Lake Michigan to save a drowning person and for this _____ (courage) act was given the Citizen's Award.
11. The immigrants had little money and few possessions, but they took great joy in their _____ (free).
12. Although she had nothing to hide, Allison was very _____ (secret) about her activities.
13. He may find that his behavior will _____ (alien) even his best friends.
14. The queen dealt harshly with her subjects' disobedience by imposing _____ (mercy) punishments.
15. The performers moved with great _____ (fluid) through the complicated steps of the dance.

C. Write the letter that represents the best definition for each italicized word.

1. *antislavery*
   a. after slavery
   b. before slavery
   c. opposed to, or against slavery
   d. in favor of, or for slavery

450   Writing Handbook

450   Writing Handbook

2. *postmeridian*
   a. come back again
   b. before noon
   c. around evening
   d. after noon

3. *disquiet*
   a. a quiet mood
   b. the lack of mental peace
   c. anger; disgust
   d. suddenness

4. *illimitable*
   a. not legal
   b. one who places limits
   c. able to be confined
   d. without limit; infinite

5. *impractical*
   a. difficult to practice
   b. perfectly possible
   c. involved in preparation
   d. not practical

6. *inglorious*
   a. full of glory
   b. dishonorable
   c. beautiful; magnificent
   d. victorious

7. *mischance*
   a. luck, fortune
   b. misconduct
   c. another chance; second try
   d. bad luck; unlucky incident

8. *pro-American*
   a. not an American
   b. a professional athlete
   c. opposed to America
   d. in favor of America

9. *nonmetallic*
   a. not made of metal
   b. like metal
   c. an unknown metal
   d. a metalworker

10. *supernatural*
    a. frightening
    b. fiction
    c. beyond the natural world
    d. less than natural

11. *statistician*
    a. one who studies oceans
    b. a photographic machine
    c. one who works with numbers
    d. full of static

12. *untactful*
    a. nonviolent
    b. lacking skill in dealing
       with people
    c. polite; diplomatic
    d. adhesive

13. *imprecise*
    a. not fast
    b. proper
    c. well proportioned
    d. not exact

14. *incurable*
    a. unable to be remedied
    b. long-lasting
    c. not caring
    d. able to be corrected

15. *antifreeze*
    a. favoring cold
    b. a children's game
    c. against heat
    d. a substance that prevents
       water from freezing

Building Your
Vocabulary **451**

To extend Exercise C for more practice, tell students to pick one of the "wrong" lettered options and try to make another new word with the base word using *that* definition. (Use the following numbers: 1d, proslavery; 2b, antemeridian; 3a, quietude or quietness; 4c, limitable; 5b, practicable or practical; 8a, un-American)

Additional Resources
- Writing Resource Book, pp. 52–53
- Vocabulary Development

Writing Handbook 24:
Strategies for Critical Thinking and Writing

Objectives

1. To use critical thinking skills to evaluate ideas
2. To recognize and correct examples of faulty reasoning
3. To use problem-solving techniques

Handbook Mini-Lessons

For information on topics related to strategies for critical thinking and writing, see the following mini-lessons.

- Beginning the Writing Activity, pp. 311–316
- Unity, Coherence, and Transitional Devices, pp. 361–370
- What Are the Types of Revision? pp. 375–377
- Correcting Problem Sentences, pp. 391–399
- Developing Study and Research Skills, pp. 459–469

Teaching Strategies

Motivating

Have students draw on their own experiences in evaluating ideas. You might want to mention that school elections, sports events, movies, and musical groups all require evaluation. Discuss methods that they have used to evaluate ideas. Then relate these methods to evaluating ideas during the writing process.

Strategies For Critical Thinking and Writing

To a large extent, writing is about thinking and making choices. Three areas in which you need to apply your thinking skills when writing are evaluating ideas, recognizing faulty reasoning, and solving problems.

EVALUATING IDEAS

When to Evaluate No matter who you are and what your age, you are always exposed to new ideas that you must evaluate, or judge. For example, when you watch an interview on television or read an editorial in the newspaper, you should not assume that the ideas are valid merely because these ideas were broadcast or printed.

You also will need to evaluate your own ideas, thinking carefully about what you say or write, how well your ideas are presented, and the effect they may have on others. Based on this evaluation, you must be prepared to rethink your ideas, and perhaps throw them out and start over.

For example, you need to evaluate ideas at many points throughout your writing process. In prewriting, you evaluate possible topics and supporting ideas. As you draft you monitor how well your ideas are working and evaluate new ideas and approaches as they emerge. During revising you look at your writing as a whole and evaluate your peers' responses to it in deciding how to make it stronger. Finally, you evaluate publishing options and choose the one that will best present your piece of writing.

How to Evaluate When you evaluate ideas, whether your own or someone else's, you must consider not only their content, but also their purpose, presentation, and effect on an audience. Ask yourself questions such as these: Are the ideas accurate? Are they well supported and presented? Do they accomplish their purpose?

For example, suppose you wrote the following paragraph in a persuasive piece about saving endangered animals.

> Many of you probably have never seen a whooping crane or a rhinoceros or a whale in its natural habitat. You probably never will either unless something is done soon to protect these

endangered species. People must be made aware of the problem and work to find a solution because it is important to help threatened wildlife survive.

Assuming you did research on endangered species before beginning to write, you know that your facts are accurate. You have not supported those facts well, however, because you have not told your readers why saving the animals is important. Without strong arguments supporting your statements, your writing will not accomplish its purpose—convincing people to protect endangered wildlife.

RECOGNIZING FAULTY REASONING

One standard for judging ideas is the quality of thinking used to arrive at them. Faulty, or illogical, reasoning can produce misleading or even false ideas. This type of thinking is sometimes purposely used in advertising, political slogans and statements, and persuasive writing. Two kinds of faulty reasoning—**logical fallacies** and **improper appeals to emotion**—are discussed below. Learning to recognize them will help you to evaluate information you read and hear, and to avoid this type of faulty reasoning in your own writing.

Types of Logical Fallacies

The common types of logical fallacies include overgeneralization, circular reasoning, and the either/or and cause-and-effect fallacies.

Overgeneralization A **generalization** is a statement that applies to many persons, places, or things. When a generalization becomes so broad that it can be easily disproved, it is an **overgeneralization.** Overgeneralizations are signaled by words such as *everyone, no one, always, never, best,* and *worst.* A writer who states, "No one travels by railroad anymore," is guilty of overgeneralization because as long as one person travels by train, the statement is false.

Circular Reasoning The attempt to prove a statement simply by repeating it in different words is called **circular reasoning.** For example, a writer who states, "We should protect endangered animals because it is important to help threatened wildlife survive" is using circular reasoning and has not told the reader why it is important to help endangered species.

Critical Thinking
and Writing   **453**

Individualizing Instruction

Basic Students Create and distribute checklists like the following for basic students to use to evaluate a piece of writing.
1. What is the main idea? _____
2. What is the author's purpose? _____
3. Are the facts accurate? O Yes O No
Examples of inaccurate facts: _____
4. Are opinions supported with clear reasons or details? O Yes O No
Examples of unsupported opinions: _____
5. Does the author succeed in his or her purpose? O Yes O No
Explain your answer: _____
Guide students to use their checklists to evaluate the model paragraph on pages 452–453. Discuss their findings, and urge them to use similar questions to evaluate samples of their own writing in their Writing Portfolios. You may wish to create similar checklists for students to use later in this lesson when they examine faulty reasoning and strategies for problem solving.

Individualizing Instruction

LEP Students Ask these students to watch commercials on television with the sound off. Without the distraction of language, LEP students may be more able to identify the use of visual fallacies or misrepresentations (for example, objects are made to appear larger; certain images are focused on).

Teaching Tip: Demonstrating Logical Fallacies

Use diagrams on the board to emphasize the components of each fallacy. For example, for circular reasoning, write, *1 = 1.* Show students that the model sentence for circular reasoning contains two equal parts (two clauses that mean essentially the same thing). For the either/or fallacy on the next page, draw a circle in which you write: *We need more city revenue.* Then draw several "solution" lines radiating from the problem. Write the two that are given in the fallacy, and have students suggest further solutions.

Either/Or Fallacy A writer who states that there are only two alternatives, when actually there are many, is using the **either/or fallacy.** The statement "Either we raise taxes or we close the parks" is an example of this fallacy because it leaves no room for other solutions. For example, one way to keep the parks open without raising taxes might be to charge an entry fee.

Cause-and-Effect Fallacy When one event follows another, you might assume, falsely, that the first event caused the second. For example, if you found that it rained every time you washed the family car, you might stop washing the car. Yet the two events are not related.

Improper Appeals to Emotion

Besides being able to recognize and avoid logical fallacies, you should also be able to identify improper appeals to emotion. Although emotional appeals can be used properly and effectively, sometimes people in advertising and politics use these appeals improperly. The following are some examples of improper appeals to emotions.

Bandwagon The argument that you should believe or do something because everyone else does, is called a **bandwagon** appeal. For example, the statement "Everyone's eating more fiber these days" doesn't give you any proof that eating fiber is good for you. It simply suggests that you should eat it because other people do.

Snob Appeal One common form of bandwagon is **snob appeal,** which implies that a belief or action will make you part of an elite group. "Own a Golden Arrow—a special car for special people" is an example of snob appeal.

Loaded Language Many words have two kinds of meanings, **denotative** and **connotative.** The denotative meaning of a word is its dictionary meaning. The connotative meaning is the emotional associations that people have with the word. **Loaded language** is a type of emotional appeal that takes advantage of connotative meanings or emotional associations. The denotative meaning of the word *mutt,* for example, is "a mixed-breed dog." However, the connotative meaning of "an inferior dog of little value" is negative and would offend many dog lovers.

During the '50's phone booth "stuffing" was a fad that had great bandwagon appeal.

Teaching Tip: Connotative Meanings

Use a thesaurus entry to dramatize the differences among the connotative meanings of "synonyms," pointing out that although the words technically mean the same thing, they contain many subtle shades of meaning. For example, use the entry for *silent,* pointing out the differences among *noiseless, peaceful, inaudible, wordless, speechless, reserved, uncommunicative, tongue-tied,* and *bashful.*

Name-Calling By using **name-calling,** or pointing out something negative about a person, the writer can distract the reader from the real issues. The statement "Smyth can't possibly understand what poverty is all about because he is a mindless twit" is an example of name-calling. The writer expresses a low opinion of Smyth's intelligence, rather than contradicting Smyth's opinions about poverty with facts and logical reasoning.

Practice Your Skills

A. Determine what type of faulty reasoning or improper appeals to emotions appear in each statement below. Then work with a partner discussing ways in which each statement might be revised to make it logical or fair.

1. Nowadays if you are not a straight-A student, you won't get into college.
2. Mr. Gomez is a sour man with a silly attachment to the past; of course, his lectures about the history of South America will be boring.
3. Friday's game ended in embarrassing defeat for the team and the entire student body. We propose, therefore, that games never again be scheduled for Friday the 13th.
4. You basically have two choices in life—a career as a Scrooge in business or a career of poverty in the arts.
5. Team sports are more fun than individual sports because working with a team is more fun than working alone.
6. Regular teen-agers go out for sports. Only saps work on the school newspaper.
7. All of us want to be rich and famous someday, whether or not we admit it.
8. Why would you endorse a lowlife like that when everyone who is anyone supports the mayor?
9. This school deserves praise for social awareness. One of our students is on the local conservation task force.
10. The present committee has always planned picnics for days that turn out to be rainy; we need a new committee.

B. Working with a group of students, put together a bulletin-board display on logical fallacies and improper appeals to emotion in advertising. Clip advertisements from newspapers and magazines that contain examples of each. Be especially alert for ads directed toward teen-agers. Attach each ad to a sheet of paper. Label the fallacies and improper appeals to emotions, and then explain why each ad is illogical or unfair.

Critical Thinking
and Writing　　**455**

Literature Connection

Poem to Read Point out that poets rely on the connotative meanings of words to convey their messages. Students may enjoy reading the poem "Casey at the Bat" by Ernest Lawrence Thayer and discussing (1) the poet's use of words with strong connotative meanings; and (2) how the fans of both teams might use loaded language to describe the game.

C. Answers will vary. A good revision will replace such fallacies as overgeneralization and circular reasoning with more realistic statements based on facts and reasons, as shown in the example below.

I think we should not run the story about the humane society. I took a poll of our readers and found that 75% of them have "little or no interest" in animal issues. I think our readers might find a story about the new volleyball coach more interesting, since many readers have written to ask for profiles of new faculty members.

Management Tip

To introduce the section on solving problems, have students discuss such school-related problems as finishing a report on time or managing the commitments of homework and after-school sports. Then decide on one common problem. Use this problem as a model and apply the Guidelines for Problem Solving that follow. Discuss each step of the process, and make appropriate notations on the board.

C. In the following piece of persuasive writing, the editor of a school newspaper argues to one of her staff members that a story about the local humane society should not be run in the school paper. Read the memo and identify examples of logical fallacies and improper appeals to emotion. Then revise the memo to make it a better piece of persuasive writing.

> I think we should kill the story about the humane society. Everyone thinks that animal issues are boring. Besides, only wimps are interested in stories like this. The story about the new volleyball coach would be more interesting because this is the kind of story our readers will find interesting.

SOLVING PROBLEMS

Evaluating ideas and identifying faulty reasoning are important skills in themselves, but they are especially useful in solving problems. Problem solving is a vital skill for daily living, involving everything from putting together an appropriate outfit to deciding how to reduce litter and pollution in your community. The basic steps in problem solving are shown in the following chart.

Guidelines for Problem Solving

- **Define the problem.** State the problem clearly. The more specific you are, the more likely you are to find a solution.

- **Explore the problem and list possible solutions.** Describe the problem, analyze it, and ask questions. To help you find solutions, see the list of strategies on page 457.

- **Decide on one solution.** Explore and consider the effects of each solution. Then choose the one that seems to solve the problem in the best way.

- **Try out the solution.** Use it to solve the problem.

- **Examine the results.** If the solution does not work well, try another approach.

Often, you will have no trouble identifying a problem, but may not be able to think of possible solutions. The following strategies may be helpful.

Strategies for Finding Solutions

- **The trial-and-error method**   Use brainstorming to come up with a list of solutions. They try each solution, one at a time, and choose the one that works best.

- **The goal-oriented method**   Compare and contrast the present situation with your goal. Ask yourself, "What are the differences between the current situation and my goal?" List these differences. Then work on each difference, one at a time, until you achieve your goal.

- **The divide-and-conquer method**   If the problem is complex, don't try to solve it all at once. Instead, divide the problem into parts and solve each part separately.

- **The past-experience method**   Think about similar problems you've solved. Will the same solution work now?

- **The simplification method**   Go straight to the heart of the problem. Ignore the details. Solve the heart of the problem first. Then concentrate on the details.

- **The "what if?" method**   Ask yourself *what if* questions, in which you imagine things to be different from the way they are. Doing so will often lead you to a creative solution.

Critical Thinking and Writing   **457**

Science Connection

Discuss how the scientific method relates to the use of a carefully planned problem-solving strategy. Ask students to supply examples from their science classes. They may cite such examples as Alexander Fleming's discovery of penicillin, Louis Pasteur's discovery of the germ theory, or another similar discovery.

Teaching Tip: Strategies for Finding Solutions

Using the common problem that the students have selected, discuss specific ways to implement each type of strategy.

Cooperative Learning

Select a common school or community problem that was not previously used as an example in class and that will provide ample opportunity for a wide range of possible solutions. Divide the class into groups and assign each member of the group a specific role in solving the problem. For example, assign one student the role of group moderator, another the role of note-taker, and the others the roles of "strategy planners," giving each a specific type of strategy method to apply to the problem. Have the members report their findings to the class.

Relate Singer's quotation to the questions writers must ask themselves as they begin to revise a piece of writing. Point out that one way to overcome doubts about where and how to start a rewrite is to use such problem-solving strategies as "divide and conquer" to make a seemingly large task much easier to accomplish. Ask students how they might use the other strategies in the revision process.

Peer Response

Discuss the various strategies that students suggest for responding to a peer reader's remarks. Then have them select pieces of their own writing from their Writing Portfolios to give to peer readers. Have them apply the critical thinking and problem-solving skills they have learned to plan effective strategies for creating revisions based on their peer readers' remarks.

Additional Resources
- Writing Resource Book, pp. 54–55
- Thinking Skills Transparencies: Problem-Solution Matrix

ANSWERS TO PRACTICE YOUR SKILLS

A.–B. Answers will vary but should reflect students' understanding of the problem-solving guidelines and strategies discussed in this handbook.

WRITER TO WRITER

Experience has shown me that there are no miracles in writing. The only thing that produces good writing is hard work. It's impossible to write a good story by carrying a rabbit's foot in your pocket.

Isaac Bashevis Singer, fiction writer

Problem solving is also an important skill for writers; in fact, you can look at a writing activity as just a problem to be solved. For example, suppose that you have done a mathematics project in which you generated some tessellations, or repeating patterns, and wrote a report on how to create them. You gave your report to a peer reader for response and received the following comments: "I really like your tessellations, but don't think I could make any of my own just from reading your report. I'm confused about what materials I need, and I'm not sure in what order I should do things."

From these comments, you can see two problems with your writing: the materials are not clearly specified and the steps of the process are confusing. You can solve the first problem easily by listing the materials needed before describing the steps of the process.

You may not be sure, however, how to make the process of creating a tessellation clear to your readers. To solve this problem, you can use the goal-oriented approach. First write down the steps you used in creating your tessellations. Then compare those steps with the instructions in your report. Finally, make any necessary changes and add transitions to clarify the order.

Practice Your Skills

A. Imagine that you have written a short story. Your peer readers agree that the main character does not seem real. One tells you that the dialogue and the character's actions do not seem believable. Using the guidelines for problem solving and the strategies for finding solutions, list ways you could revise your story to bring your character to life.

B. Suppose that you are assigned to write an editorial for the school newspaper. Your editors say that your reasoning is weak. Use the guidelines for problem solving to come up with ways to persuade your readers.

Developing Study and Research Skills

As you continue through school, you will begin to realize that despite the differences among your classes, they almost all require the same basic study skills. Again and again, you will be asked to evaluate assignments, read for specific purposes, take notes, and synthesize material. By mastering these study skills, you can learn with less effort and more enjoyment.

Evaluating Assignments

In most classes you will be given assignments on a regular basis. These assignments will usually be either **short-term,** taking a day or less to do, or **long-term,** requiring more than a day. Almost all writing assignments are long-term, so you will need to plan time to gather and organize ideas, write drafts, and revise.

The following guidelines will help you carry out any assignment successfully.

1. **Keep an assignment log.** Reserve a special place in a notebook or folder for writing down all your assignments.

2. **Write down all the necessary information.** Make sure that you understand the assignment, including clarifying anything that is unclear. Write down what needs to be done, what materials you will need, what form your final product should take, and when it is due.

3. **Make a plan for carrying out the assignment.** On a sheet of paper, list all the steps needed to carry out the assignment.

4. **Keep a weekly schedule.** Use a small, portable calendar to make a schedule for yourself every week. Update the schedule each time you get an assignment.

TAKING NOTES

When you read, it's always a good idea to take notes on what you are reading. Even if you never look back at these notes, the action of taking them will help you register the material and increase the likelihood that you will remember it.

Writing Handbook 25:
Developing Study and Research Skills

Objectives

1. To identify and apply techniques for managing time effectively
2. To use note-taking as a study aid
3. To understand and apply strategies for effective and efficient reading
4. To incorporate source materials in writing through paraphrases and summaries
5. To interpret graphic aids.

Handbook Mini-Lessons
For information on topics related to study and research skills, see the following mini-lessons.
- How to Limit a Topic, pp. 327–329
- How Do I Plan and Organize My Writing? pp. 330–335
- Using Graphic Devices, pp. 357–360
- Using the Library and Other Sources of Information, pp. 470–478

Teaching Strategies

Modeling

Many students may have trouble listing the steps needed to carry out an assignment. They know the goal, but are unable to identify individual steps needed to reach it. Model the process by showing them the daily steps they could take on a simple project, such as finishing a book report in a week.

Teaching Tip: Notetaking

Remind students to note why the dates, names, or places that they write down are important. A date with no other information is not helpful. Some students may wonder why notetaking helps them remember material. Explain that people remember what they have organized better than they remember unorganized material. As proof, ask students to remember these numbers: 4 3 1 3 2 4 3 4 2 4. Few will be able to. Now ask them to remember these numbers: one number 1, two 2's, three 3's, and four 4's. Most will remember the organized numbers better.

 Individualizing Instruction

Learning Styles Although some students will be able to use the modified outline form for notetaking, others will do better if they first take their notes, then go back and organize them. They can organize them in one of two ways, either by recopying them, or by numbering related ideas with the same numbers.

LD Students Most learning disabled students will have prior experience using an assignment log. Contact their Special Education Teacher to discuss which type of log they are using. Learning disabled students will benefit from using a "highlighter" marker when reviewing their notes. They can highlight the key words, group related ideas, identify the main idea, and so on by colors.

Guidelines for Taking Notes

- **Take notes on all important information.** This information can come from your teacher, other students, labwork, reading, or yourself.

- **Look and listen for key words.** These include *most important, for these reasons, first, for example,* and *to review.* Such key words often signal facts and ideas that should be remembered.

- **Do not try to write down every word.** Write down important facts only, such as names, dates, definitions, people, places, events, and ideas.

- **Keep your notes in one place.** Use a separate tablet, notebook, or section of a notebook for each subject. Write the date on each page of notes.

- **Go back over your notes as soon as you can.** Group related ideas together; add words and phrases to make your notes understandable later. Recopy your notes if necessary.

Two techniques that can significantly improve your ability to take notes efficiently are using a modified outline form and using abbreviations.

Modified Outline Form A formal outline (see Appendix, pages 816–817) is probably too structured to use in most note-taking situations. A modified outline form, however, can help you organize main ideas and related details efficiently when taking notes. In the following example, notice that main ideas are placed to the left. Related details are introduced by dashes and indented beneath the main ideas to which they refer. As with all the notes, writing in phrases instead of complete sentences allows you to follow the lecture or reading more closely.

Notice that an informal outline differs from a formal outline in several specific ways.

- Main ideas and details are not set off by numerals and letters.
- It is not necessary to have two or more points under each heading.
- Headings do not have to be written in parallel grammatical form.

April 23

The Middle Ages

Time period—about 1,000 years
 —Beginning: mid 400's, end of Roman Empire
 —Ending: mid 1400's
Social Divisions
 —Clergy
  —priests
  —monks
  —nuns
 —Nobility
  —kings
  —princes
  —dukes
  —knights

Abbreviations If your notes are to be complete, you must be able to record information quickly. Using abbreviations and symbols can help you take notes more effectively. Omitting the period after an abbreviation will also save time. The following chart suggests abbreviations to use, but develop ones that work for you.

Some Abbreviations and Symbols for Note-Taking

w/o	without	def	definition
&,+	and	*	important
#	number	re	regarding
>	more than	<	less than
~	approximately	=	equals
y	why	∴	therefore

Teaching Tip Abbreviations

Suggest that students who use many abbreviations go through their notes soon after taking them to be sure the abbreviations are legible and understandable. If they are not, students who discover this soon after notetaking will be better able to recreate the original ideas.

Science Connection

Assign students to preview one chapter in a science book. Encourage them to spend no more than five or ten minutes looking over the material. Then have them note at least three things they now know about the chapter that they did not know before.

Some writing is easy to read; other writing is much more difficult to understand. A few simple strategies can help you improve your reading skills no matter what you have to read.

Previewing Previewing means looking over the material to see what it's about. This strategy is especially important for reading informative material. To preview, follow these steps.

1. Read the first two paragraphs of a chapter.
2. Read the first sentence of each paragraph that follows.
3. Read the last two paragraphs.
4. Scan all information presented in graphics or in special type.

Questioning After previewing reading material, note questions that you expect the material will answer. Then, as you read, look for answers to your questions and write them down. Sometimes your reading will raise questions that are not answered. Write these questions down so that you can ask them during a class discussion or in a conference with your teacher.

Predicting As you read, make guesses, or predictions, about what might happen next. Jot these down. This strategy is especially important when you read fiction.

Identifying Main Ideas As you read, look for main ideas. They often appear as the topic sentences of paragraphs. They also can appear in introductory and concluding paragraphs. Jot down definitions of key terms and important statistics, names, and dates.

Identifying Relationships As you read, try to figure out how each part of the reading relates to other parts. Look for these elements.

- **Relationships between main ideas and supporting details.** You need to know which ideas the author is emphasizing. Once you identify a main idea, look for how this idea is supported and developed.
- **Sequence relationships.** Pay close attention to the order of events in your reading.
- **Cause-and-effect relationships.** Look for instances in which one occurrence or group of occurrences causes another.

Making Inferences An **inference** is a conclusion that you make based on what you know. For example, suppose you read the following sentences in a book on world geography.

Modeling

Model for students the kinds of questions readers ask themselves. For instance, if you were reading a section called State Nicknames, questions might include: Do all states have them? What's the nickname of my state? How do states get nicknames?

Critical Thinking

Analyzing Discuss with students what word cues help them identify relationships between ideas. Help them realize that transition words, such as *for example, first,* or *because,* which they are encouraged to use in writing, also help readers because they show how ideas are related.

Springboard

To encourage students to think about the accuracy of what they read, have them learn about so-called facts that have turned out not to be true. You may wish to have them look in such books as *The Dictionary of Misinformation,* or else research famous hoaxes like the Cardiff giant.

At the very top of Mount Everest, the highest mountain on earth, explorers have found limestone. Limestone is formed when the shells of animals break down and pile up at the bottom of the sea. As these shells continue to pile up over millions of years, they are squeezed together to form limestone deposits.

Based on this passage, you can infer that the highest point on earth was once covered by an ocean. As you read, record your inferences, or conclusions about the reading, in your notes.

Responding With Your Own Ideas and Opinions Remember that your own ideas and opinions are important and that no book, not even a textbook, is right all of the time. As you read, jot down your thoughts about the material. If you disagree with the author, make a note telling why. If the reading material gives you an idea that you'd like to use later on for a piece of writing, jot that down, too.

Reviewing Your Reading Once you have finished reading the material carefully, review your notes. You may wish to organize them by making separate lists containing questions and answers about the reading, main ideas, key terms, definitions, and ideas and opinions you want to develop later.

Reading Rates

Not all written material can or should be read the same way. Sometimes you only need a general idea of what the material is about or a specific piece of information. Other times, you want to read slowly and carefully. It is important that you learn how to adjust your reading rate to suit the material.

Skimming When **skimming,** you move your eyes quickly over a page or an entire selection. You skim to get a general idea of your reading material, to study for a test, and to review material you have already read. As you skim, you glance at titles, topic sentences, chapter headings, and highlighted words or phrases. You also look at graphic aids and at the table of contents, index, or glossary.

Scanning **Scanning** involves moving your eyes quickly across a line or down a page to locate particular information. You scan material to look for a specific fact or for specific information, such as a date, a definition, or a name and number in a telephone book.

Slow and Careful Reading If you want to absorb all the information in a book, you must read it slowly and carefully, as described in this handbook.

Writing
—**TIP**—
You may want to keep an ongoing list of ideas and opinions that you can use as a springboard when you are given an open-ended writing assignment.

Basic, LD, and LEP Students Many of these students may not at first understand how a reader can infer that the highest point on earth was once covered by an ocean. Walk such students through the paragraph, showing them that limestone, found at the very top of Mount Everest, was formed at the bottom of the sea. How then did it get to the top? The sea must have been there.

When doing research for a report, you may collect information from many different sources. You can incorporate material written by someone else into your writing in two ways. You can quote the source directly, or you can paraphrase the information or summarize it. You will also find the skills of paraphrasing and summarizing useful when you are reading for your own information or studying for a test.

Paraphrasing When you **paraphrase** something, you rewrite it in your own words. A paraphrase is about as long as the original source and includes almost all the ideas. One way to paraphrase is simply to rewrite each sentence of the original in your own words. Another way is to make a list of all the ideas in the source and then write original sentences containing those ideas.

For example, in doing research for a history report on the foods eaten by early Native Americans, a student read the following paragraph.

> The art involved in popping corn is at least five thousand years old, perfected by the American Indians. They clearly appreciated the difference between sweet corn (for immediate eating), field corn (as cattle feed), and so-called Indian corn, which has sufficient water content for popping.
> **Charles Panati, "Extraordinary Origins of Everyday Things"**

The student decided to use this material in her report, and paraphrased it as follows. Note that she was careful to mention the source of the information.

> According to Charles Panati, Native Americans have popped corn for five thousand years or more. They knew and used sweet corn—eaten without cooking, field corn—for livestock, and what is known as Indian corn—used for popping because it contains water.

Critical Thinking

Making Comparisons Have students compare and analyze Panati's paragraph with the student's paraphrase. From the original they can infer, for instance, that since water is required for corn to pop, field corn and sweet corn are too dry. They should notice that the paraphrase includes all the ideas of the original without repeating words or phrases.

Social Studies Connection

Assign students to look in current newspapers and news magazines for examples of graphic aids. Have them photocopy or summarize the material to help others appreciate the variety of information that can be presented this way.

Summarizing A **summary,** also known as a **précis,** is similar to a paraphrase. In both cases you rewrite material from your source, putting it in your own words. The difference is that when writing a summary, you rewrite the material in fewer words. To write a summary, list the main ideas in your source, leaving out ideas that are not important. Whenever possible, combine ideas using a shorter, more general phrase. When you finish listing the main ideas, write a few short sentences explaining the ideas.

For example, the student writing the history report could have decided to summarize rather than paraphrase the information about popcorn, as follows.

▼

> Native Americans have eaten corn raw, popped it, and fed it to cattle for five thousand years or more.

Whether you are writing a paraphrase or a summary, make sure that you are true to your source material. Try to preserve the original writer's ideas without oversimplifying or changing them.

Avoiding Plagiarism

Plagiarism is the uncredited use of another person's words or ideas. Treating someone else's words or ideas as your own is dishonest. You don't need to credit your source if the ideas you pick up are general knowledge and are stated in your own words. However, when you paraphrase or summarize someone else's original ideas or research, or quote someone's exact words, you must credit your source by mentioning where the information came from.

Often the best way to document your sources is to insert brief **parenthetical notes** (references in parentheses) whenever you use someone else's words, facts, or ideas. (See Writer's Workshop 9, "The Short Research Paper," page 278, for documentation guidelines.)

W R I T E R   T O   W R I T E R

Adam was the only man who, when he said a good thing, knew that nobody had said it before him.

Mark Twain, American novelist and humorist

Critical Thinking

Evaluation Help students develop criteria to determine what ideas are "general knowledge." Facts that are readily available in any almanac, dictionary, or common reference book, for instance, fall into that category, but so do ideas that students have read and heard repeatedly. Unusual facts that readers might question should be credited, however, as should another person's conclusions.

Developing Study
and Research Skills   **465**

Individualizing Instruction

LEP Students Graphic aids are usually quite useful to LEP students, because they contain only limited numbers of words that must be translated or understood. However, they also provide very little context that students can use to decipher unfamiliar words. Often, you can help by quickly reading the material aloud once. This often provides enough information so that they can later go back on their own and read the material more carefully.

Modeling

Model for students the process of reading a table. Use the example in the book, helping students understand, for instance, that the parenthetical note tells them that the numbers shown are not decimals, and that some information, such as the year, may not be labeled.

INTERPRETING GRAPHIC AIDS

Information often can be presented clearly and economically in visual form, and much reading material includes graphic aids such as charts, tables, diagrams, maps, and graphs. Here are some general guidelines for studying these graphic aids and specific suggestions for reading tables and graphs.

Common Graphic Aids

Type	Purpose	Study Tips
Pictures, Sketches, Diagrams	To illustrate text; to show the parts or functions of the subject	Read caption or title; relate image to text; note labels of parts
Maps	To display geographical areas of distribution	Read caption or title; find legend or key
Tables, Charts, Graphs	To list information; to compare information	Read caption or title; check key to determine organization

Reading Tables Tables present large amounts of information—either numerical or verbal—simply and clearly. Imagine how many words you would need to present the information listed in the following table.

Average Hours of TV Usage per Day in America
(6.28 means six hours and twenty-eight minutes of viewing.)

	1971	1976	1984	1985	1986	1987
February	6.53	6.49	7.38	7.49	7.48	7.35
July	5.08	5.33	6.26	6.34	6.37	6.32
Year's Average	6.01	6.11	7.08	7.07	7.10	7.10

Every table presents information about one or more subjects that are called **variables** because the numbers associated with them vary. In this table, variables in vertical columns include the number of hours and minutes of watching television in a single year. Variables in horizontal rows indicate the amounts of watching in six different years.

Reading Graphs   Graphs are used to show relationships among sets of variables. To understand a graph, read the title and the key to symbols and abbreviations. Then determine what variables are presented by the graph and how they are related.

In a **circle graph**, or **pie graph**, the circle represents 100 percent, or the whole, of something. The sections within the circle graph represent parts of the whole.

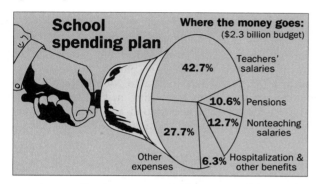

School spending plan

Where the money goes:
($2.3 billion budget)

- 42.7% Teachers' salaries
- 10.6% Pensions
- 12.7% Nonteaching salaries
- 6.3% Hospitalization & other benefits
- 27.7% Other expenses

Bar graphs usually show one variable expressed in numbers and the other variable expressed in words. Each bar is labeled with the names of both variables. The "name variable" in the bar graph below is the name of a continent, and the "number variable" is the population density per square mile in the country.

Population Density of the Continents*

- Asia: 176 per sq. mi.
- Europe: 168 per sq. mi.
- Africa: 48 per sq. mi.
- North America: 43 per sq. mi.
- South America: 39 per sq. mi.
- Australia: 5 per sq. mi.

1986 estimates based on the latest figures from official government and United Nations sources.
*Antarctica has no permanent population.

Teaching Tip: Graphic Aids

Encourage students who photocopy graphic aids to note the author, title, publisher, date, and page of the source, so that facts taken from the charts or graphs can be documented.

Computer Tip

Students who enjoy working with computers may enjoy using them to make pie charts, line, or bar graphs. These can be created using graphics programs, financial programs, and many integrated programs.

Critical Thinking

Evaluation Help students evaluate the usefulness of different kinds of graphic aids. Help them recognize that bar graphs, for instance, make it easy to compare information, while pie charts and circle graphs make it easy to spot a major trend.

Math Connection

Have students look in math books to find information about creating different kinds of graphs. Have them work together in groups to create sets of instructions for making line, bar, and pie graphs.

Learning Styles   Visual learners may learn information quickly from charts and graphs. On the other hand, kinesthetic learners should be encouraged to create their own charts and graphs.

Modeling

Synthesizing may be a difficult concept for students to understand, so model how it might work. You might suggest, for example, that students imagine they have gathered population data from one source, rainfall and climate data from others. From this, they might synthesize the information that most of the world's people live within 60° of the equator. They might use their data to support the reasons why people live there rather than at the poles.

Guidelines for Reading Graphs

- Read the title or caption of the graph to see what relationship is being illustrated.

- Determine what graphic element expresses the relationship, for example, bars in a bar graph or wedges in a pie graph.

- Read any explanation given of the graph numbers.

- Relate the number variables with the name variables in the graphs and explain their message in words.

SYNTHESIZING MATERIAL

After you have read the material for your assignment and taken notes on it, you need to be able to put the information you have together in a way that makes it clear to you. **Synthesis** is the act of recombining ideas to form something new. When you synthesize material, you consider the information and ideas in a source or in several sources and integrate them with what you already know about the topic.

Guidelines for Synthesizing

- Take notes on your reading, paying special attention to information, ideas, and graphic aids that you can use in your writing.

- Look over your notes and organize them. Link related ideas and themes.

- Decide what elements from your notes are important to your synthesis. How does this new material fit in with what you already know?

- Write a topic sentence combining ideas from your notes in a new way.

- Find information in your notes that will support the main idea of your writing.

Practice Your Skills

Follow these numbered directions one at a time. Do not read through all of the directions first.

1. Skim the encyclopedia article below. Note the topic sentence and boldfaced words. Make a list of questions to answer after doing an in-depth reading.
2. Scan the article to identify examples of carnivorous animals that have canine teeth. Write your answer.
3. Read the article carefully and take notes. Then use the notes to write a paraphrase and a summary of the article.
4. Add an explanation of the table's information to your notes. Use the notes to synthesize ideas from the selection and the table. Write a topic sentence based on your synthesis.

Carnivorous mammals. Some mammals are carnivorous. They eat animal flesh. Many of them are speedy animals that catch, hold, and stab their prey with long, pointed canine teeth. Such mammals, which include leopards, lions, and wolves, do not thoroughly chew their food. They swallow chunks of it whole. Dolphins, seals, and other fish-eating mammals also use their teeth to grasp prey, which they swallow whole. Some carnivorous mammals commonly feed on the remains of dead animals, instead of hunting and killing fresh prey.

The World Book Encyclopedia

Table of Average and Maximum Longevity of Certain Carnivores

Carnivore	Average Lifespan	Maximum Lifespan
Black bear	18 years	36 years
Red fox	7 years	14 years
Leopard	12 years	19 years
Tiger	16 years	26 years
Lion	15 years	25 years

Have students work individually, jotting down their answers. But instead of evaluating answers individually, have a group discussion, in which answers are compared and explained.

ANSWERS TO PRACTICE YOUR SKILLS

Although answers will vary, they should be similar to the examples shown below.

1. What are some carnivorous mammals? What is special about them? How long do they live?
2. leopards, lions, wolves
3. Notes on the table will vary, but should include the disparity between carnivores' average lifespan and their maximum lifespan. Paraphrases and summaries will vary, but summaries should be shorter than paraphrases.
4. Possible topic sentence: Carnivorous mammals have different lifespans as well as different eating habits.

Additional Resources
- Writing Resource Book, pp. 56–59

Using the Library and Other Sources of Information

Objectives

1. To learn how library materials are classified and arranged
2. To learn the features and functions of specific types of reference works
3. To explore other sources of information

Handbook Mini-Lessons

For information on topics related to the library and other sources of information, see the following mini-lessons.
- Developing Study and Research Skills, pp. 459–469
- Interviewing Skills, pp. 481–482

Teaching Strategies

Collaborative Opportunity

Have students work in groups to find out how to operate any mechanized research tools available at your school library, such as microfilm or microfiche readers and on-line computer catalogs. Have group members talk with a library staff member for instruction, use the machine, and write a group report to share the information with other students.

Using the Library and Other Sources of Information

Today's libraries are media centers, not merely book rooms. In a typical modern library, you can find not only books, but also magazines, newspapers, videotapes, audiotapes, computer files, pamphlets, brochures, and other materials that provide information and stimulate your imagination.

ORGANIZATION OF THE LIBRARY

To locate resources in a library, you need to be familar with the way libraries are organized. Most libraries organize their materials into the following sections.

- **Stacks**   shelves containing both fiction and nonfiction books
- **Search Tools: Catalogs and Indexes**   card catalog and on-line computer catalog containing information about library materials and their locations
- **Reference**   dictionaries, encyclopedias, almanacs, and atlases
- **Periodicals**   newspapers and magazines
- **Audiovisual**   films, tapes, and records
- **Young Adult and Children's Section**   books for younger readers

In the library, books are separated into four main types: **fiction, nonfiction, biography,** and **reference.** Each type of book is usually stored in a different part of the library, on shelves that are marked with numbers or letters that help you to find specific works.

Fiction   Novels and short-story collections are usually arranged on the shelves in alphabetical order by author. For example, to find *The Pearl* by John Steinbeck, you would look in the fiction section for authors whose last names begin with *S.*

Nonfiction   Nonfiction books are numbered and arranged according to broad subject categories. For example, science books are shelved together, as are books on sports. Each subject category is further divided into subsections. Under science, for example, you will find subsections covering fields such as astronomy, biology, chemistry, earth science, and physics.

Most libraries classify their collection of nonfiction books according to the **Dewey Decimal System.** This system, which is named for librarian Melvil Dewey, classifies all books by number in ten major subject categories.

000–099	General Works	encyclopedias, handbooks
100–199	Philosophy	psychology, ethics
200–299	Religion	the Bible, theology, mythology
300–399	Social Science	government, education, law
400–499	Language	languages, grammars, dictionaries
500–599	Science	mathematics, chemistry, biology
600–699	Technology	medicine, cooking, inventions
700–799	Fine Arts	music, painting, theater, sports
800–899	Literature	poetry, plays, essays
900–999	History	biography, travel, geography

In the Dewey Decimal System, each major group is also subdivided. The 800's section, for instance, is further divided into 810 for American Literature, 820 for English Literature, and so on. A subcategory such as American Literature is further broken down into 811 for Poetry and 812 for Drama, continuing up to 819.

Instead of the Dewey Decimal System, some libraries use the **Library of Congress Classification,** or **LC.** The LC system uses twenty-one broad categories designated by letters of the alphabet. A second letter is added for a subdivision within a category. For example, *Q* identifies science, and *QB* designates astronomy. The LC system is most often used in large public libraries and university libraries.

Biography and Autobiography Libraries often shelve biographies and autobiographies in a separate section. Books in this area are usually labeled with a *B* and are arranged in alphabetical order by the last name of the person the book is about. A book containing the biographies of two or more persons is called a **collective biography.** The Dewey Decimal number of collective biographies is 920.

Reference Books Reference books are also shelved together, often with the letter *R* above the classification number. These books cannot be checked out; they are only to be used in the library building.

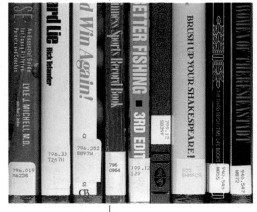

Modeling

Use these questions to model the process of locating books by using card and computer catalogs.

    1. Does the library have any books written by _____?

    2. Does the library have any books on the subject of _____?

    3. Does the library have the book entitled _____?

Show the students that once they consult the catalog, their knowledge of the Dewey Decimal System and the library floor plan will help them to locate a book. Follow the modeling activity with a specific book-locating assignment for each student. You might also have them write "process" papers or numbered lists that summarize the steps of using the catalog system and the Dewey Decimal System to locate books. Have them keep these papers in their Writing Portfolios for future reference.

 Individualizing Instruction

LD Students Students who have *limited long-term memory* would benefit from a one-to-one tour of the library. This can be done by having an advanced student accompany the learning disabled student, if a teacher is not available. The learning disabled student should be responsible for making a map, outline, or cue cards of the library. It is important for the student to know what books are in the reference section. Reference material is often easier for these students to use when doing research because it is summarized. A separate map, outline, or cue cards can be made of the books in the reference section.

THE CARD CATALOG

You can easily locate a book you need by using the card catalog, a cabinet of small drawers or file trays containing alphabetically arranged cards. Some libraries keep their card catalogs in book form. Each card lists information about a book that the library has on its shelves. For nonfiction books the card also carries the classification number, often referred to as the **call number,** in the upper left-hand corner. The call number is a location code that directs you to the shelf in the library where a particular book is located. The same call number you found on the catalog card will be on the spine of the book.

Subject, Author, and Title Cards The card catalog contains three different types of cards. **Subject cards** help you locate a book on a topic of interest when you do not know a specific author or book title. Subject headings are printed at the top with the author's name and the book's title listed below. Many different kinds of books may be listed under one subject heading. **Author cards** help you locate a book if you do not know the title. The author's name appears on the top line of an author card, last name first. **Title cards** help you if you know the title of a book but not the author. The title of a book is written at the top of the title card, with the author's name directly underneath.

Cross-Reference and Guide Cards Cards that read *See* and *See also* are called **cross-reference cards.** They refer you to another subject heading in the catalog that will give you the information you want. **Guide cards** are blank cards with a guide word printed on a tab that projects above the other cards. Guide cards aid you in finding other catalog cards quickly.

Computerized Catalogs Many public libraries offer a computerized catalog system that is more compact and often easier and quicker to use than the card catalog. If you know the author, title, or subject of a book, the computer will tell you if the library has it. If you need a listing of the books the library has on a certain subject, type in the subject, and the computer will provide a list of titles and call numbers of books available. Computerized catalog systems vary from library to library so it is important for you to familiarize yourself with the particular system that your library offers.

REFERENCE WORKS

The reference works in the library are like an army of experts working for you. Some of the most useful reference works are discussed below.

Encyclopedias These are collections of articles on many subjects. They can be general, such as *The World Book,* or specialized, such as *The Baseball Encyclopedia.* The articles are usually arranged alphabetically in separate volumes. Guide letters on the spine of each volume and guide words at the top of the pages aid you in finding your subject. Most encyclopedias also include a separate index in which you can look up topics.

Almanacs and Yearbooks Published annually, almanacs and yearbooks are useful sources for facts and statistics on current events, government, economics, population, sports, and other fields. The *Guinness Book of World Records* and the *World Almanac and Book of Facts* are frequently used almanacs.

Biographical References Biographical dictionaries contain brief biographical notes about contemporary and historical figures from all over the world. Longer biographical articles can be found in encyclopedias. *The Biography Index* lists the reference books in which information on specific people can be found.

Literary Reference Books References that are especially helpful for literary research include *Bartlett's Familiar Quotations*—well-known quotations and proverbs arranged by author, topic, and key word—and *Granger's Index to Poetry*—a collection of poems indexed by subject, author, title, and first line.

Vertical File Current information in the form of pamphlets, handbooks, booklets, and clippings is kept in a set of file cabinets called the **vertical file.**

Atlases Besides maps, an **atlas** also contains interesting data on a number of subjects. You can often find sections on population, temperatures, oceans, and place names. Another source for information on places is a **geographic dictionary.**

Periodicals These important resources for current topics include magazines, journals, and newspapers. Recent issues are usually kept on open racks. Back issues are stored in bound volumes or on microforms.

Writing ── TIP ──

Before you begin researching a project, make a list of possible reference works to consult. You can add to your reference list as you proceed.

Cooperative Learning

Divide the class into cooperative learning teams. Give each team a broad topic, such as "The 1988 Olympic Games in Seoul, Korea" or "Facts About Denmark." Assign the members within each group a specific role. You may wish to assign each a specific type of reference work to consult. Have each member first write a "process plan" about what information he or she hopes to gather from the source. Then have them proceed to a research session, report their findings at a group meeting, and use all of their information to create a group report.

Microforms To save space, magazine and newspaper articles are often stored on **microforms,** very small photographs of printed pages. The microforms are stored on filmstrips, called **microfilm,** and on film cards, called **microfiche.** Microforms are viewed on a special machine that your librarian can help you use.

The Readers' Guide to Periodical Literature The *Readers' Guide to Periodical Literature* is an invaluable aid for finding magazine articles, stories, and poems published in over two hundred magazines. Articles are listed alphabetically by author and subject.

Dictionaries A **dictionary** is much more than just a tool for checking definitions and spellings. The entry word is usually divided into syllables and includes information such as the following.

- **pronunciation,** explained in the pronunciation key
- **part of speech**
- **inflectional endings,** changes in the form of a word
- **synonyms and antonyms**
- **derived words,** words from a common root word
- **usage and field labels,** which tell whether a word is colloquial, slang, or dialectical and may tell the field of knowledge in which the word is used

Dictionary Entry for irregular

irregular (ir reg′ yōō lər, i reg′–; –yə–) *adj.* [ME. ¢ OFr. *irregulier,* \ ML. *irregularis:* **see** IN-² & REGULAR] **1.** not conforming to established rule, method, usage, standard, etc; out of the ordinary; anomalous. **2.** not conforming to legal or moral requirements; lawless; disorderly. **3.** not straight or even; not symmetrical; not uniform in shape, design, or proportion. **4.** uneven in occurrence or succession; variable or erratic ☆**5.** having minor flaws or imperfections: said of merchandise. **6.** *Bot.* not uniform in shape, size, etc., as the petals of flowers **7.** *Gram.* not inflected in the usual way *[go is an irregular verb]* **8.** *Mil.* not belonging to the regularly established army —*n.* **1.** a person or thing that is irregular **2.** a soldier who belongs to an irregular military force ☆**3.** [*usually in pl.*] irregular merchandise —**ir·reg′u·lar′i·ty** *n., pl.* **-ties** — **ir·reg′u·lar·ly** *adv.*

SYN.—**irregular** implies deviation from the customary or established rule, procedure, etc. [an *irregular* conduct]; **abnormal** and **anomalous** imply deviation from the normal condition or from the ordinary type, **abnormal** stressing a typical form or character [a man of *abnormal* height], and **anomalous,** an exceptional condition or circumstance [in the *anomalous* postion of a leader without followers]; **unnatural** applies to that which is contrary to the order of nature or to natural laws [an *unnatural* appetite for chalk] *ANT.* **regular, normal, natural**

Webster's New World Dictionary

A dictionary is the writer's most valuable key to unlocking the wonderful world of words and their meanings. In the dictionary will be found, not only the proper spelling of words, but the various meanings and connotations. Every profession and field has its own definitions, and most can be found in a comprehensive dictionary.

Thesauruses A **thesaurus** is a storehouse of synonyms and antonyms. If you need a synonym for a word, a thesaurus offers a quick way to see all the possibilities. Precision in writing depends on accurate word choice, and a thesaurus can help you find the words you need. Keep in mind, however, that synonyms have similar meanings, not identical ones. If you use an unfamiliar synonym from a thesaurus, check its precise meaning in a dictionary to be sure it fits the use you intend.

Thesaurus Entry for *danger*

DANGER—1. *Nouns.* **danger,** chance, hazard, insecurity, jeopardy, peril, unsafety, risk, pitfall, endangerment; storm brewing, clouds gathering, clouds on the horizon; crisis. **dangerousness,** riskiness, touch and go, unsafety, treachery; venturousness, etc. (see *Adjectives*). [*dangerous person*] **menace,** threat, serpent, viper; dangerous woman, *femme fatale* (F.).
2. *Verbs.* **endanger,** expose to danger, hazard, jeopardize, peril, imperil, risk, speculate with, venture, compromise. [*accept danger*] **risk,** hazard, venture, adventure. dare, stake, set at hazard, speculate.
3. *Adjectives.* **dangerous,** chancy, risky, ticklish, touch-and-go, venturous, venturesome, adventurous, adventuresome, speculative; hazardous, perilous, parlous, precarious, insecure, jeopardous, critical, queasy, unsafe, ugly, treacherous, serpentine, viperous. See also CHANCE, FEAR, THREAT, WARNING.
Antonyms—See PROTECTION.

Roget's Thesaurus

Most thesauruses arrange the entry words in alphabetical order, but not all. *Roget's Thesaurus,* for example, arranges words into categories according to ideas. If the thesaurus you are using does not arrange the entries alphabetically, consult the index to learn how to locate words.

Using the Library   **475**

Teaching Tip: Using the Thesaurus

From samples of their own writing, have students search for sentences containing such vague words as *nice, good, bad, big,* or *happy.* Have them use thesauruses to find synonyms with more precise meanings, and to rewrite the sentence two or three times, each time with a different synonym. Discuss how the meaning of the sentence changes. Using the model thesaurus entry, provide this example: *He was a dangerous man; He was an adventurous man; He was a treacherous man.*

Brainstorm ideas with students as to what types of experts are available at school, in the community, and at home. For example, a relative from another culture could be consulted as an expert on everyday life in that culture; a teacher who collects antiques might be consulted as an expert on early American furniture; and so on. You might make an interviewing assignment in order to have students seek out experts in fields that interest them.

OTHER SOURCES OF INFORMATION

In addition to reference works in libraries, writers can consult several other sources of information. These include experts, government agencies, computer services, and the media.

Experts When you're looking for information or viewpoints on a particular topic, you should consider interviewing an expert, someone who knows a lot about a particular subject. You can find experts in your own circle of relatives and friends, as well as at schools and universities, in businesses, and in local arts centers and museums.

Government Agencies One of the primary roles of the government is to provide information to the public. You can contact local government agencies through your town hall or mayor's office for information on local issues. You can also contact state and federal government agencies for information on their programs. A federal agency —the General Services Administration Consumer Information Center—offers a catalog listing over one hundred free or inexpensive government pamphlets on various subjects. To receive this catalog, write to: Consumer Information Catalog, P.O. Box 100, Pueblo, CO 81002.

Computer Services If you have access to a computer and a modem, you can use a computer information service. A modem allows you to hook up a computer to a telephone line. You can then dial an information service and use on-line encyclopedias or learn about topics such as current events, sports, and weather. Check to see if your school or library subscribes to one of the computer information services now available.

Literature Connection

Newspaper columnists are experts with an identifiable point of view. They can be excellent sources of information from their individual perspectives. Introduce students to the work of such acclaimed newspaper columnists as Art Buchwald, Ellen Goodman, Mike Royko, and H. L. Mencken. Collections of their works have been published in book form.

The Media A **medium** is a method of communication that is used to reach large numbers of people. The following chart shows the various kinds of media.

Audiovisual Media

Broadcast Media	Narrowcast Media	Other Audiovisual Media
radio	computer	videocassette tapes
noncable	networks	and discs
television	cable/pay	audiotapes, records, CDs
	television	films and filmstrips
	facsimile	photographic prints
	machines	and slides
		transparencies
		computer discs and
		software

Print Media

books	magazines	fliers
newspapers	letters	posters/billboards

The major purposes of the media, like the purposes of writing, are to inform, entertain, and persuade. To understand which of these purposes a particular medium is stressing and to be sure you use the media responsibly, keep these guidelines in mind.

- **Vary the media that you use.** Reading newspapers and magazines will help you get a broader perspective than just watching television news programs.
- **Respond actively to what you see and hear.** Develop a critical attitude, asking questions such as the following: Is this program meant to be informative, entertaining, persuasive, or some combination of these? What am I learning about myself and the world? Is what I am seeing accurate? objective? biased?
- **Share observations about the media.** Discussing the media with others will help you interpret the messages critically.
- **Keep a media journal.** In a section of your writing journal, collect clippings or retell interesting stories from the media. Comment critically on radio and television programs and news events. List ideas you might use in your writing.

Critical Thinking

Making Comparisons Go through newspapers and news magazines with students, pointing out the differences between news stories containing unbiased reporting of facts and feature stories or columns in which opinions are expressed. Discuss critical thinking skills (see Handbook 24) that readers can use to evaluate content, tone, and purpose of a piece of writing.

Practice Your Skills

A. Use the card catalog or computer catalog in your library to find a listing for each of the following books. Write the title, author, call number, and publication date for each.

1. a book about John F. Kennedy; a book by John F. Kennedy
2. a book on Renaissance art
3. a book with statistics on immigration to the United States
4. a book with plays by Eugene O'Neill and Tennessee Williams
5. a book about cross-country skiing

B. List the subject cards that will direct you to books on the following topics.

1. "Peanuts" cartoons
2. repairing minibikes
3. developing photographs
4. stamp collecting
5. popular music
6. the origin of the Olympics
7. the first astronauts
8. how films are made
9. fashions of today's youth
10. the first television program

C. Choose one of the topics listed below, and imagine you are going to write a research report on it.

early television comedians
drug education
immigration into your state
mental health clinics
how your town was founded
methods of voting
history of income tax
why the census is important

1. Make a research plan that includes all of the appropriate library reference works you could use. Describe the order in which you would use them, how you would use each of them, and what kind of information you would gather from each.
2. Make a list of other research tools you would use to find information on your topic. Use a telephone book to find local, state, or federal agencies that might know about your topic.
3. Include a list of media, such as magazines of educational television programs that might provide information on your topic.

Oral Communication Skills

Long before you learned to write, you were speaking and listening—sharing ideas orally. Speaking and listening skills remain important throughout your life, and they extend and reflect your writing skills. Good oral communication skills will be particularly helpful to you in taking part in discussions and interviews, both in and out of school.

DISCUSSION SKILLS

Like a writing activity, a discussion must have a purpose that all participants agree to. Common purposes for discussions include sharing information on topics of mutual interest, solving problems, and planning for group activities.

During discussions, people may express a variety of viewpoints. This makes discussions lively, but it can also make reaching agreement difficult. When groups share ideas about controversial topics, members may conclude by "agreeing to disagree." However, when groups have to solve problems or agree on a course of action, participants may need to try approaches such as those below.

- **Compromise.** Sometimes group members may need to give up some of their demands to gain support for their most important concerns.
- **Redefine the issue.** Group members may misunderstand one another's positions. Restating the issue in a different way may allow everyone to come to agreement.
- **Find a new alternative.** If the group finds none of the proposed courses of action acceptable, the group should come up with new ones, possibly by brainstorming.
- **Postpone the discussion.** Sometimes a group may find that more information is needed or that group members have become too emotional. In these cases, the group may need to reschedule the discussion.

Formal Group Discussions

Many discussions take place within formal groups. For example, your class may discuss political issues or develop ideas for sets for a school play. Outside of school, you may be involved in formal group discussion of a club trip or a neighborhood clean-up project.

Discussion at the highest level: Ronald Reagan and Mikhail Gorbachev

Oral Communication Skills **479**

Objectives

1. To identify the elements of formal and informal group discussions
2. To identify and practice good interviewing skills

Handbook Mini-Lessons

For information on topics related to oral communication skills, see the following mini-lessons.

- How to Limit a Topic, pp. 327–329
- Strategies for Critical Thinking and Writing, pp. 452–458

Teaching Strategies

Motivating

Point out that most people spend more time speaking than they do writing. In fact, effective oral communication benefits everyone, not just those involved in negotiations or interviewing. Tell students that in this lesson they will learn skills they can use outside of school as well as within.

Teaching Tip: Discussion Skills

If necessary, give examples of each of the skills listed. One example of compromise might be having both parties agree to drop their least important demand; an example of redefining an issue might be focusing on the hours someone works and not the hourly wage; finding new alternatives means not being bound to only those solutions already suggested; and postponing is usually most effective when a new date is scheduled.

Critical Thinking

Evaluating Have students discuss what qualities would make each of the people listed either effective or ineffective: a chairperson, for instance, should not be partial to one person; a recorder should be accurate; and a participant should participate.

Teaching Tip: Goals

Have students identify the goals of each stage of a formal group discussion. You may find it helpful to imagine what might happen without a particular stage.

 Individualizing Instruction

LEP Students Some students may find it difficult to participate fully in large group discussions because speakers may change quickly or two may try to talk at once. As a result, a student may be trying to listen to one speaker, while processing what another has said. Encourage students to speak up and ask for explanations when necessary. If this happens so frequently that it becomes disruptive, schedule frequent breaks in the discussion so that students can summarize the material.

Formal discussion groups usually include a **chairperson,** a **recorder,** and **participants.**

The **chairperson** begins the discussion by introducing the topic, stating discussion aims, and mentioning key points to be considered. This person also ensures that only one person speaks at a time and is responsible for bringing the discussion to an orderly conclusion.

The **recorder** takes notes about what is said. Later he or she organizes the notes and shares them with group members by distributing copies or reading them at a future meeting.

The **participant** takes part in the discussion, speaking only when recognized by the chairperson. Participants should support their statements with facts, examples, or authoritative opinions. They should listen attentively and try to see each other's points of view.

Formal group discussions usually develop in five stages.

1. Planning and preparation Participants often meet before the discussion to define its purpose and narrow the topic. They may also outline points to be discussed. All participants should prepare for the discussion by gathering information about the topic and organizing their ideas.

2. Statement of subject and purpose The chairperson opens the discussion by explaining its purpose.

3. Definition of key terms Group members agree on the definitions of terms that will be central to the discussion.

4. Analysis The group discusses the topic in detail. During the analysis, the chairperson may need to encourage the group to stick to the topic and keep its purpose in mind.

5. Summary The chairperson summarizes the major points and decisions made during the discussion and notes any further actions that need to be taken.

Less Formal Group Discussions

Most approaches used in formal discussions can be applied in less formal discussions. When you discuss your writing in a peer response group, for example, you may want to appoint a chairperson to ensure that discussion is orderly. You may even want someone to act as recorder and take notes. You will certainly want to establish what the discussion is about and why it is being held. By following the procedures of formal discussions, informal groups can develop ideas efficiently in a cooperative, friendly atmosphere.

Broadcast Media Connection

Encourage students to watch a television announcer without turning up the sound or to listen to a radio announcer who is speaking in a foreign language. Have students see how much they can learn from nonverbal cues, such as tone of voice or gesture.

Practice Your Skills

As your teacher directs, get together with classmates in small groups. Decide among yourselves who will be the discussion chairperson, recorder, and participants. Then, have a discussion about a topic of mutual interest. Follow the guidelines on page 480 for conducting a formal discussion.

INTERVIEWING SKILLS

Interviewing people is an important way to gather information that you can use in writing, such as reports, articles, or stories. Sometimes you will be the subject of an interview. For example, you may be asked for information about yourself when applying for a job, college admission, or a scholarship.

Whether you are the interviewer or the person being interviewed, the following steps can help you be more effective. For more information, see "Oral History," pages 102–106.

1. Agree on a time and place. Whether the interview is by telephone or in person, agree on a time and place that is convenient for you and the other person.

2. Arrive on time and be prepared. If you cannot keep an interview appointment, call in advance and reschedule the interview. If you are conducting the interview, learn ahead of time about the topics to be discussed. Then write questions on index cards or a notepad, leaving space for answers. If you are being interviewed, list the questions you might be asked, and practice answering them. Here are some typical questions:

> What are your strong and weak points?
> What are some of your interests?
> Do you get along well with others?
> What are your plans for the future?

3. Dress carefully and appropriately. Proper clothing and grooming tell others you are serious about this meeting.

4. During the interview, listen carefully and be polite. Make eye contact, smile, and show interest. Observe common courtesies such as saying "please," and don't interrupt your subject. Be aware of your body language, too. Crossing your arms, for example, can convey either aggression or fear. Be sure to ask follow-up questions for clarification or to get more information.

Writing
TIP

In an interview, avoid asking questions that can be answered yes or no so that your subject will respond fully, giving as much information as possible.

Modeling

Help students recognize the difference between asking a yes/no question and asking an open-ended one. For instance, "Do you like this school?" may elicit less information than "What do you like most and least about this school?"

Teaching Tip: Interview Preparation

Tell students that in the reference section of the library they will find books that contain information about some companies they might interview with. These books—such as *The Occupational Outlook Handbook*—may give the histories of companies, provide the names and titles of people in charge, and discuss benefits.

Critical Thinking

Judging Have students develop criteria for what constitutes "appropriate" dress and behavior. Point out that gum chewing, for instance, is too informal for an interview and might also prejudice a subject. Have students discuss reasons for other strictures.

Oral Communication Skills **481**

Stumbling Block

Many notetaking interviewers find that their subjects' spoken words outstrip their ability to write. Point out that most subjects are flattered when an interviewer says, "That's interesting. Could you wait while I get that down?"

 Individualizing Instruction

Basic Students These students may find that transcribing an entire interview is tedious and partly wasted time. Instead, suggest that they first listen to a tape from start to finish. Then have them go back and listen for specific information or quotations that they want to transcribe.

Collaborative Opportunity

After all the interviews have been finished, have the students work together to create a list of interviewing tips to be kept as a class resource.

Additional Resources
• Writing Resource Book,
  pp. 62–63

5. Tape record the interview or take careful notes. To ensure an accurate record, consider tape recording the interview, but only after getting permission from the person you are interviewing. If you plan to quote the person in your writing, ask permission to do this, too. If you take notes instead of making a tape recording, jot down main ideas. However, try to capture some important ideas in the exact words of your subject. Beneath each main idea, list words and phrases about the thoughts the person expresses relating to that main idea. Take down word-for-word only statements that you plan to quote.

6. Express your appreciation. As you leave, let the person know that you are grateful for his or her time. As soon as possible after the interview, write a short, formal thank-you note.

7. If you were the interviewer, organize your notes. Rewrite your notes while the interview is fresh in your mind. If you taped the interview, make a written copy of the interview, possibly by writing each question and answer on an index card. Once you have a clean copy of your interview or notes, organize the material. Also record the following information about the interview: the person's name and position; the interview date; whether the interview was by phone, person, or letter; and how the interview was recorded (on tape or in notes).

8. If you were the interviewer, share your final product with the person you interviewed. Give the person you interviewed a chance to correct mistakes in your report of the interview by sending him or her a copy for review.

Practice Your Skills

With a partner, play the part of the interviewer and then the person who is being interviewed in one of the situations below. List five questions the interviewer would ask and use these questions during the interviews. If possible, videotape the interview so that you can study your body language.

1. You are writing a history paper about the Battle of the Bulge during World War II. You will be interviewing a veteran of that war.

2. You are writing an article for the school newspaper about the basketball team and its prospects for the coming season. You will be interviewing the coach.

482 Writing Handbook

Taking Tests

Winning a chess game requires strategy and concentration. Good chess players often plan their moves far in advance. Test taking, too, requires planning and strategy, and your scores reflect your knowledge not only of the subject, but of test-taking strategies as well.

In school, you are assessed on the basis of two kinds of tests—classroom tests, which measure your knowledge of the specific topics covered in your courses and textbooks, and standardized tests, which measure your general knowledge. Helpful strategies for preparing for classroom tests are listed below.

Midway through the exam, Allen pulls out a bigger brain.

- Confirm what kind of test it will be and precisely what material it will cover.
- Allow sufficient study time; study on a regular basis.
- Review your notes. Highlight or underscore key points.
- Skim any reading to be covered by the test. Carefully reread any material you aren't sure of; quiz yourself by answering any questions written in your textbook.
- Answer any study questions provided by your teacher; develop a list of your own study questions and answer them in writing.
- Make separate lists of important facts and formulas.
- Use memorization techniques.

OBJECTIVE TESTS

An objective test question has a single correct answer. When taking an objective test, work quickly through the questions that are easy for you. Mark difficult questions and return to them later. If you cannot determine the answer, guess.

There are basically four kinds of objective items on classroom tests. Strategies for answering each type of question and sample questions are shown in the chart on the next pages.

Taking Tests **483**

Writing Handbook 28:
Taking Tests

Objectives

1. To learn and practice strategies for taking various kinds of classroom tests
2. To learn and practice strategies for answering questions on standardized tests such as the college board exams

Handbook Mini-Lessons
For information on topics related to taking tests, see the following mini-lessons.
- Building your Vocabulary, pp. 438–451
- Solving Problems, pp. 456–458
- Reading Skills, pp. 462–463

Teaching Strategies

Teaching Tip: How to Study

Encourage students to relate their own experiences in preparing for tests. What difficulties have they encountered? How might the guidelines help them? How much study time do they feel is "sufficient"? Have students apply the guidelines to draft a study plan and schedule for an upcoming test.

 Individualizing Instruction

LD Students Have these students brainstorm some of the distractions that occur when they take a test (for example, noises and time limits). When students become aware of how they are distracted, they can develop coping techniques (for example, move away from peers, practice taking timed tests). Identify the testing situations in which such changes can be made to accommodate for distractions (appropriate for informal classroom tests—not formal standardized test situations).

Modeling

Distribute copies of a test that students have recently taken that contains various types of objective questions. Model the process of marking difficult questions, moving on to answer less difficult ones, and then returning to those that remain unanswered. Ask students why this strategy may be effective.

Objective Test Strategies

True/False

You are asked to tell whether a statement is true or false.

1. If any part of a statement is false, the whole statement will be false.
2. Words such as *all, always, only,* and *never* often appear in false statements.
3. Words such as *generally, probably, some, usually, often,* and *most* often appear in true statements.

Matching

You are asked to match items in one column with corresponding items in a second column.

1. Check the directions to see whether each item is used only once and whether some are not used at all.
2. Read all items in both columns.
3. Match those items you know first.
4. Cross out items as you match them, unless items are used more than once.

Multiple Choice

You are asked to choose the best answer from a group of answers provided.

1. Read all choices before answering.
2. Eliminate incorrect answers.
3. Choose the answer that is most complete or accurate.
4. Note choices including "none of the above" or "all of the above."

Completion

You are asked to fill in a blank in a statement.

1. Make sure your answer fits grammatically.
2. If several words are needed, write in all of them.
3. Write legibly, using proper spelling, grammar, punctuation, and capitalization.
4. Give only information that directly responds to the question and completes the sentence.

Springboard

To practice strategies for answering objective questions, have students create questions for a classroom version of a television game show. To make the game doubly useful, have them base their questions on a unit of study for which they need review for an upcoming test. Have students take turns being contestants and emcees.

Sample Test Questions

True/False

_____ Amphibians are cold-blooded animals that live only in water.

_____ Newts are amphibians.

_____ If a newt loses a leg, often the leg will grow back.

_____ Amphibians never develop lungs.

Matching

_____ 1. simile

_____ 2. personification

_____ 3. metaphor

_____ 4. paradox

_____ 5. hyperbole

A. I'm so happy about my promotion I could cry.

B. The room was as gloomy as a November day.

C. The sun smiled on all of us that day.

D. I told you a million times I'm not going to the game.

E. The road was a ribbon of moonlight.

Multiple Choice

Mark Twain was born in

A. St. Louis, Missouri

C. Hannibal, Missouri

B. Florida, Missouri

D. none of the above

Mark Twain wrote

A. *Roughing It*

C. *The Guilded Age*

B. *Life on the Mississippi*

D. all of the above

Completion

Feudalism was the political and military system of western Europe during the _____ .

In the feudal system a piece of land given in return for services was called _____ .

In feudal times a person bound to the lord's land and transferred with the land to a new owner was called _____ .

A _____ held land and did homage to a lord.

Teaching Tip: Test Taking

Discuss the sample test, having students identify which clues or strategies the test-taker should use to answer the questions.

Managing the Paper Load

Have students exchange papers to correct each other's tests. Then discuss the answers and provide review for any students who require it.

Practice Your Skills

On a separate paper, write answers to the following questions.

1. Answer the statements below by writing *True* or *False*.
   A. Standardized tests cover material you are currently studying.
   B. You should complete difficult questions first, and save easier ones for when you may be rushed for time.
   C. In matching questions, the same answer item may be used more than once, and some items may not be used at all.
   D. Completion questions always require one-word answers.

2. Match the objective tests with their strategies.
   1. True/False   A. Make sure your answer fits grammatically into the space provided.
   2. Multiple Choice   B. Read all items in both columns before starting.
   3. Completion   C. Remember that if any part of a statement is not true, the entire statement is not true.
   4. Matching   D. Choose the most complete or accurate answer provided.

3. Choose the best answer of the four choices given. Which one of the following types of objective test questions does not present a choice of answers?
   A. matching   B. multiple choice
   C. true/false   D. completion

4. Supply the words or phrases that best complete the sentence. In a true/false question, words such as _____ , _____ , _____ , and _____ often appear in false statements.

SHORT-ANSWER
AND ESSAY TESTS

Short-Answer Questions Always respond to short-answer questions in complete sentences. Answer completely, but be brief and to the point. Concentrate on the content of your answer first, and then go back and rework your sentences to correct errors in mechanics, if necessary. In the following example, note how the answer is given in a complete sentence and how it provides the three facts requested.

When, where, and by whom was paper invented?

Paper was invented in China by Ts'ai Lun in A.D. 105.

Essay Questions Essay questions that appear on classroom tests require lengthier, more detailed explanations than short-answer questions. On a social studies test, for example, you might be asked to describe three of the earliest river-valley civilizations. Such a question would require at least three paragraphs, one for each civilization.

When answering an essay question, you will go through a shortened version of the writing process. Make a short outline before you begin to write to help you organize your ideas. First write down your thesis in a topic sentence. Then quickly list the most important points you want to include to support, or prove, that thesis. Each point will be a separate paragraph. Referring to the outline as you write will help you remain focused on your main points. End your essay with a strong conclusion. Most likely, you will have little time to revise your writing.

Panel from a wooden box found in Ur, one of the earliest cities in southwest Asia.

Practice Your Skills

Allow yourself no more than fifteen minutes to answer the following essay test question. Is it necessary to provide wheelchair ramps for the physically disabled on all street corners and in all municipal and government buildings? Why or why not?

STANDARDIZED TESTS

The amount of study that you can do for standardized tests is limited. However, you can prepare for standardized tests by understanding the kinds of questions they include.

Reading Comprehension Questions

A reading comprehension item requires you to read a passage and then answer several questions about it. Preview the questions before reading the passage. Then read the passage quickly but carefully, looking for answers to these questions. Note also the main

Taking Tests   **487**

Humanities Connection

Art Note *Panel from Wooden Box* found in Ur. Ur was a city in ancient Sumer (now southeastern Iraq). Sumer is believed to be the birthplace of the world's first civilization. The Sumerians invented cuneiform, the first writing system. In cuneiform, symbolic wedge-shaped marks replaced images such as those on the panel.

Distribute copies of pages from standardized test booklets, using them as models as students read about and discuss the various types of questions. Point out that standardized tests usually provide multiple-choice answer selections, and that students indicate their answers by filling in spaces on an answer sheet.

 Individualizing Instruction

Basic Students Use several simple examples of analogies to model the process of figuring out the relationships between components. For example, use:

1. stove:kitchen :: bed:bedroom
2. big:small :: night:day
3. skin:person :: rind:melon
4. foot:leg :: hand:arm

idea and pay attention to words that show relationships. Read all the answer choices first, and then choose the one that best answers the question. Watch for answers that are only partially correct.

Vocabulary Questions

These questions measure vocabulary skills and are of four types—synonym, antonym, sentence completion, and analogy. Each kind requires you to apply critical thinking skills as well as your knowledge of language.

Synonyms You identify the word or phrase closest in meaning to the given word. Study the following sample.

> INTERROGATE   (A) imprison   (B) punish   (C) question
>   (D) torture   (E) curse

Read all the options before choosing. People who are interrogated may be imprisoned, tortured, or punished; but *interrogate* actually means "question."

Antonyms You choose the word or phrase that is most nearly opposite the given word.

> DEPRESS   (A) force   (B) clarify   (C) loosen
>   (D) allow   (E) elate

Depress means both "to push down" and "to sadden." No antonym of "to push down" (such as *raise*) is given. However, *elate* is the opposite of *sadden* and is, therefore, the best choice.

Sentence Completion You select the word or words that best fit the meaning of the sentence. Your completed sentence must make sense and be grammatically correct.

> Marcia was _____ by the team's refusal to accept her, yet she _____ her training program.
> (A) encouraged . . . joined   (B) frustrated . . . continued
> (C) annoyed . . . quit   (D) discouraged . . . discontinued

Try all the options before you choose. Although this question might appear difficult at first, only choice *B* is logical.

Analogies You are given a related pair of words and asked to select a second pair of words that expresses a similar relationship.

> COLT:HORSE   ::   (A) dachshund:dog   (B) robin:bird
>   (C) herd:buffalo   (D) fawn:deer

488   Writing Handbook

Mathematics Connection

Relate analogies to mathematical ratios, using these examples. Have students gifted in math suggest additional ones.

1/2 is to 1 as 2 is to 4
10 is to 5 as 8 is to 4

The colon between the words means "is to." Think of analogy questions as a type of sentence completion problem. Translate the analogy into a statement such as this:

A colt is to a horse as a _____ is to a _____ .

First, establish the relationship between colt and horse by devising a sentence that relates the pair.

A colt is a young horse.

Then try each of the paired answers in your sentence by asking yourself these questions.

A dachshund is a young dog?   A robin is a young bird?
A herd is a young buffalo?   A fawn is a young deer?

Only the last sentence expresses the correct relationship, so *D* would be the correct answer.

Grammar, Usage, and Mechanics This type of test question measures language skills. You are given a sentence with certain parts underlined and are asked to tell whether there is an error in grammar, usage, punctuation, or capitalization—or no error at all. If you see an error, mark the corresponding letter on your answer sheet. If there is no error, mark "No error." Read the directions carefully, however. Some tests contain more than one error per item.

Here is an example of a grammar/usage question that you might find on a standardized test.

<u>Although</u> both Jennifer and Heather <u>are</u> talented, each <u>have</u>
   A   **B**   **C**
very distinct kinds of ability. <u>No error</u>
                            D

In the test sentence above, *each* is singular and requires the singular verb *has*. Therefore, *C* is the error in the sentence. You would mark *C* on your answer sheet.

Here is an example of a question that tests punctuation or capitalization:

Mark <u>T</u>win wrote <u>"T</u>he Celebrated Jumping Frog of Calaveras
    A   **B**
County" before he wrote *The <u>a</u>dventures of Huckleberry*
                                C
Finn. <u>No error</u>
      D

All major words in the titles of books are capitalized; therefore, *C* marks the error in this sentence.

Management Tip

Use the guidelines to summarize effective strategies for both classroom and standardized tests, highlighting any areas that you feel may need further review or practice. You might also copy and distribute the guidelines for students to use as they prepare for upcoming tests.

Additional Resources

- Writing Resource Book, pp. 64–66
- Standardized Test Practice
- Vocabulary Development

Taking the Test

Your performance on tests can be further improved by the application of good test-taking strategies. You can use the following helpful techniques when you take both classroom and standardized tests.

1. Survey the test.
2. Plan your time. Read all the directions, decide in which order to answer the questions, and allow time for review.
3. Read each test item carefully.
4. Begin by answering the questions that you know.
5. Be careful when using answer sheets. Fill in each answer circle darkly and completely and make thorough erasures. Be sure that the number of the test item corresponds with the number on the answer sheet.
6. For essay tests, read all directions and questions before beginning so that you do not repeat yourself.

Practice Your Skills

1. Choose the word that is closest in meaning to the given word.

   ENIGMATIC   (A) instant   (B) automatic
          (C) ridiculous   (D) mysterious

2. Choose the word that is most nearly opposite the given word.

   MALEVOLENT: (A) sickly   (B) malicious
          (C) kind   (D) fast

3. Select the words that best fit the meaning of the sentence.

   Since last year's total population of our town was 9,020, this year's _____ of 9,010 showed a _____ of ten people.
   (A) dispersion . . . relocation   (B) tally . . . decrease
   (C) decrease . . . recount   (D) calculation . . . remainder

4. Select the pair of words that expresses a similar relationship to the given pair.

   BIRD : FLOCK   ::   (A) caterpiller : butterfly   (B) colt : horse
          (C) robin : sparrow   (D) wolf : pack

5. Write the letter that corresponds to any error.

   On the first day of her vacation, Jill <u>laid</u> in the sun at Clearwater
                                                      A

   <u>Beach</u> for over <u>two</u> hours. <u>No error.</u>
   B   **C**   **D**

Sketchbook

*H*ome is the place where, when you have to go there,
They have to take you in.

Robert Frost
"THE DEATH OF THE
HIRED MAN"

How would you define *home*? Or how would you define *family* or *friends* or some other term related to your daily life? In a sentence or paragraph, write what you think is a suitable definition. Then compose one or two paragraphs that recreate a scene from your daily life. The scene, which could be humorous or serious, should illustrate your definition. Use a variety of sentence types, and, if you include dialogue, pay attention to your punctuation.

Additional Sketches

Imagine that you are a reporter at a memorable, though fictitious, event, such as the discovery of the lost continent of Atlantis by deep-sea divers. Write a dramatic account of the event, using vivid adjectives and verbs, which conveys its importance and excitement.

You are on a lonely stretch of road. Why are you there? Where did you come from and where are you going? How long have you been on this road? What do you see on either side of the road? What time of day is it? Describe in narrative form what you notice and feel.

491

Objective

To use a quotation and a cartoon as a springboard to informal writing

Using the Prompt

Before beginning the activity, be sure students understand that Sketchbook writing is ungraded. It is designed to be informal and to offer opportunities for experimenting with writing techniques.

Ask students how Robert Frost's definition of *home* differs from a dictionary definition. Students should see that it is very subjective and represents the emotion-laden point of view of one individual. Then ask in what ways the cartoon is like Frost's definition of *home*. Help students recognize that the cartoon underscores how varied and individual the idea of home can be.

Have students brainstorm a list of general words associated with everyday life. The list should include the words *home*, *family*, and *friends* from the student text but might also include such words as *love*, *health*, *security*, *well-being*, and *peace*. Then have students choose words for their definitions and paragraphs. Encourage students to take a completely individual approach and to be completely subjective in their definitions. Students may find it useful to generate ideas about their words by using cluster diagrams or spider maps before they begin writing.

Ideas in the Additional Sketches section can be used as alternatives if some students find these ideas a better starting point. Encourage students to keep their writing in their Writing Portfolios. They may wish to use some of the ideas they have developed in later writing.

Swinging, by Vasily Kandinsky, 1925

Grammar and Usage Handbook

The mini-lessons in this Handbook may be used for a variety of purposes.

Direct Teaching—to cover a specific language skill in depth

Preteaching—to introduce a specific language skill before the revision stage of an assignment (see Teaching Preview pages in this Teacher's Edition for suggestions).

Reteaching—to remedy specific problems noted in student papers

These exercises enable you to discover the areas of strengths and weaknesses in your students' backgrounds. The items are constructed similarly to some standardized tests that students will encounter as they move through high school. The range of errors tested include those of grammar, usage, spelling, punctuation, and capitalization. Use this assessment as a formal diagnostic tool or as an informal means of deciding what grammar handbooks you will emphasize.

Additional Resources
- Standardized Test Practice

Skills Assessment Pretest
1. C—his *or* her
2. A—whom
   C—really beloved
3. B—from the Phoenicians
4. B—attendant
   C—taught
5. A—ever
   B—communicate
6. E
7. A—The Book of Lists
   C—any other names

Directions One or more of the underlined sections in the following sentences may contain errors of grammar, usage, punctuation, spelling, or capitalization. Write the letter of each incorrect item; then rewrite the item correctly. If there is no error in an item, write E.

> **Example** Most <u>historians think</u> that John Quincy Adams was
>   A
> America's greatest <u>Secretary of State</u>, and <u>all agree</u> that William
>   B   C
> Seward <u>and him</u> were the top two. <u>No error</u>
>   D   E
>
> **Answer** D—and he

1. Every <u>jazz</u> musician <u>has</u> <u>their</u> own style <u>of playing</u>. <u>No error</u>
          A   B   C   D   E

2. Joan of Arc, <u>who</u> many writers have featured in <u>their</u> stories and plays, was a <u>real beloved</u>
             A   B   C
   heroine of <u>France</u>. <u>No error</u>
             D   E

3. The Greeks <u>got</u> their alphabet <u>off the Phoenicians</u>, <u>whose empire</u> covered modern-day
              A   B   C
   Lebanon and <u>parts of</u> Syria and Israel. <u>No error</u>
                D   E

4. Clint Eastwood <u>has said</u> that his job <u>as a gas station attendent</u> <u>learned</u> him <u>more than</u> his
                    A   B   C   D
   college courses in business did. <u>No error</u>
                                E

5. People today hardly <u>never</u> <u>comunicate</u> <u>with smoke signals</u>, though the ancient Chinese and
                        A   B   C
   Greeks <u>did</u>. <u>No error</u>
          D   E

6. The first <u>television</u> broadcasts <u>began</u> in the United States <u>in 1928</u>, but it was difficult to
               A   B   C
   see the images very <u>well</u>. <u>No error</u>
                    D   E

7. The reference work <u>"The Book of Lists"</u> <u>reports</u> that Tiger and Samantha are more
                        A   B
   popular than <u>any</u> names for cats, <u>including</u> Morris and Puff. <u>No error</u>
             C   D   E

8. Although both Beatrix Potter and <u>himself</u> wrote stories about <u>Peter Rabbit</u>, Thornton
   A   **B**
   W. Burgess is <u>incorrectly</u> <u>reguarded</u> as the creator of the character. <u>No error</u>
           C   **D**   **E**

9. Scientists wonder <u>wheather</u> the big-bang theory <u>explains</u> the existence <u>of matter</u> in
                  A   **B**   **C**
   the <u>universe?</u> <u>No error</u>
       D   **E**

10. <u>The Betty Ford Clinic</u> became famous as a center for <u>Drug and Alcohol</u> rehabilitation
    A   **B**
    <u>largely because</u> of the <u>clinics'</u> treatment of public figures. <u>No error</u>
        C   **D**   **E**

11. The right to <u>freedom of expression</u> is often <u>endangered</u> even though <u>we Americans</u> enjoy
                A   **B**   **C**
    the protection of the <u>Bill of Rights</u>. <u>No error</u>
                D   **E**

12. Students who <u>set</u> down to read <u>James Joyce's</u> *Dubliners* might be surprised <u>to learn that</u>
              A   **B**   **C**
    the book was rejected twenty-two times before <u>it was published</u>. <u>No error</u>
                                     D   **E**

13. When Robert Redford <u>turned down</u> the leading role in *The Graduate,* the part <u>went to</u>
                   A   **B**   **C**
    Dustin Hoffman, who was <u>more better</u> suited to it. <u>No error</u>
                   D   **E**

14. Each of <u>the Brontë sisters</u>—Charlotte, Emily, and Anne—had <u>their</u> <u>own</u> particular style of
           A   **B**   **C**
    writing and view <u>of the world</u>. <u>No error</u>
                    D   **E**

15. There have <u>supposedly</u> been hundreds of sightings of the Loch Ness monster, but <u>them</u>
               A   **B**
    reports are latecomers <u>compared</u> with reports of the Abominable Snowman, <u>which began</u>
                        C   **D**
    in the fifteenth century. <u>No error</u>
                           E

16. <u>Pluto's orbit</u> is so eccentric that <u>it's</u> currently closer to the <u>sun</u> than <u>neptune</u>, temporarily
    A   **B**   **C**   **D**
    making that planet number eight. <u>No error</u>
                                E

17. <u>Yiddish, usually</u> considered a variant of <u>German,</u> has its own grammar, dictionaries, and
    A   **B**
    <u>literature, and</u> is written in the <u>hebrew</u> alphabet. <u>No error</u>
        C   **D**   **E**

18. Jane <u>Addams founder</u> of <u>Hull House, was</u> the first <u>American</u> woman to win the
    A B C
    <u>Nobel Peace Prize.</u> <u>No error</u>
    D E

19. <u>Among</u> the <u>most popular</u> verse forms in the <u>world are</u> <u>haiku, and the limerick.</u>
    A B C D
    <u>No error</u>
    E

20. <u>Language</u> sets humans apart from other living <u>creatures it</u> allows people to express ideas
    A B
    by saying things in a way that may have never been <u>spoke</u> <u>before.</u> <u>No error</u>
    C D E

21. <u>*Snow White and the seven dwarfs*</u> <u>are</u> one of <u>Walt Disney's</u> most famous <u>full-length</u>
    A B C D
    animated films. <u>No error</u>
    E

22. Written history <u>began</u> in the <u>rich, fertile</u> Tigris-Euphrates river <u>valley, in</u> the country
    A B C
    called <u>Mesopotamia.</u> <u>No error</u>
    D E

23. <u>The myth that</u> Abraham Lincoln <u>wrote</u> the Gettysburg Address <u>onto the back</u> of an
    A B C
    envelope <u>has been disproved</u> by recorded facts. <u>No error</u>
    D E

24. <u>Reviewer Brooks Atkinson</u> wrote of Farley Granger in a theatrical production of <u>*pride*</u>
    A B
    <u>*and predjudice,*</u> "Farley Granger <u>played Mr. Darcy</u> with all the flexibility of a <u>telegraph</u>
    C D
    <u>pole.</u> <u>No error</u>
    E

25. Kris Kristofferson <u>taught</u> English to <u>West Point</u> cadets before he <u>became</u> a <u>songwriter,</u>
    A B C D
    <u>singer, and actor.</u> <u>No error</u>
    E

The Sentence and Its Parts

THE COMPLETE SENTENCE

Sometimes in conversation we use only parts of sentences.

Not now.　　That one.　　Yes.　　Over the hill.

In standard written English, however, complete sentences are important. With them, we can express our ideas more clearly.

A sentence is a group of words that expresses a complete thought.

The following groups of words are sentences:

Alicia agreed to the plan.
That red car is blocking the alley.
The alarm at the bank sounded late last night.

When part of an idea is missing from a sentence, the group of words is a sentence fragment.

A sentence fragment is a group of words that does not express a complete thought.

Agreed to the plan. (Who agreed?)
That red car. (What about the red car?)
Late last night. (What happened?)

You can learn more about sentence fragments in Handbook 30.

Practice Your Skills

A. CONCEPT CHECK

Fragments　Write *S* for each group of words that is a sentence. For each sentence fragment, write *F*.

1. Professional baseball player William Ellsworth Hoy.
2. This remarkable man was born in 1862.
3. Threw out the first ball of the 1961 World Series.
4. At the age of 17, Hoy opened a cobbler's shop.
5. An outstanding player on Houckton, Ohio, sandlots.
6. Won a position on a professional team in Oshkosh, Wisconsin.
7. At 24 Hoy was small—five feet four and 148 pounds.
8. Also profoundly deaf.
9. At first Hoy had trouble with his hitting.
10. Because he could not hear the umpire call strikes and balls.

Writing Theme
Baseball Heroes

The Sentence
and Its Parts　　**497**

Grammar Handbook 29:

The Sentence and Its Parts

The Complete Sentence

Objectives

- To distinguish between complete sentences and sentence fragments
- To employ revision skills to rewrite sentence fragments as complete sentences
- **Writing** To demonstrate an understanding of complete sentences by eliminating sentence fragments from writing

Teaching Strategies

Speaking and Listening

Have students select a topic and allow them to freewrite for a limited time. After students finish, ask volunteers to read parts of their writing. Point out that in this prewriting stage, incomplete thoughts are often expressed. Then discuss how the continuous use of fragments in writing would affect the communication of ideas. Point out how writing differs from conversation, in which fragments are also used. Emphasize that although the intended thought in a fragment may be clear to the writer, the reader may not have been provided with enough information to understand the idea.

Note: For related instructional material, see "What Is a Sentence Fragment?" on pages 524–525 and "Using Clauses Correctly" on pages 742–743.

Answers to Practice Your Skills appear on next page.

B. DRAFTING SKILL

Writing from Fragments Writers frequently use sentence fragments when making notes. Later they rewrite those fragments as sentences. Use the fragments below to draft at least five sentences about William Ellsworth Hoy. Add words or combine fragments.

1. Invented the umpire's visual signals
2. For strike, ball, safe, and out
3. Not his only remarkable achievement
4. Seventeen-year career in professional baseball
5. Many records and awards
6. At age 38, led the league in putouts, assists, and fielding
7. Only winner of the triple crown of fielding in the history of the game
8. Put out three runners at home plate with a throw from center field
9. All in one game
10. Amazing, small, gentlemanly cobbler from Ohio

C. APPLICATION IN WRITING

Letter to the Editor Use the information in the two exercises you have just read to write a letter to a newspaper editor. Take a position for or against inducting William Ellsworth Hoy into the Baseball Hall of Fame at Cooperstown, New York. Mention some of Hoy's accomplishments and explain why you think they were—or were not—important enough to qualify him. When you have written your letter, check to see that it does not contain sentence fragments.

KINDS OF SENTENCES

Sentences can be grouped into four basic categories, depending on the purpose of the writer or speaker.

1. A declarative sentence makes a statement. It always ends with a period (.).

A beautiful opera house overlooks the harbor of Sydney, Australia.

2. An interrogative sentence asks a question. It ends with a question mark (?).

When did the United States buy Alaska?

3. An imperative sentence gives a command. It usually ends with a period (.). An imperative sentence may sometimes end with an exclamation point (!) when the writer wants to make a strong command.

Do ten more push-ups. Hurry up!

4. An exclamatory sentence expresses strong emotion. It ends with an exclamation point (!).

I passed the test! What a day this has been!

Practice Your Skills

A. CONCEPT CHECK

Kinds of Sentences Write *Declarative, Interrogative, Imperative,* or *Exclamatory* to identify each of the following sentences.
1. Do you remember facts easily?
2. Has your mind ever gone blank during a history test?
3. What a frightening feeling that can be!
4. Fortunately, you can improve your memory and your ability to recall facts.
5. For example, how can you learn a list of words for a class?
6. Scientists have a suggestion for you.
7. First, write the beginning letters of the words.
8. Then create a sentence with the initial letters of the words in your lists.
9. For example, the sentence "My very eager monkey just slid under Nan's poinsettia" is a clue to the names of the planets—Mercury, Venus, Earth, Mars, Jupiter, Saturn, Uranus, Neptune, Pluto.
10. Say! What a way to study!

> **Writing Theme**
> Powers of the
> Mind

The Sentence
and Its Parts   **499**

B. Revision Skill

Punctuating Sentences
Punctuation is added on page.

1. Interrogative
2. Declarative
3. Interrogative
4. Declarative
5. Declarative
6. Imperative
7. Interrogative
8. Imperative
9. Exclamatory
10. Declarative
11. Imperative *or* Exclamatory
12. Exclamatory
13. Imperative
14. Imperative
15. Imperative

Additional Resources

• Grammar and Usage Practice
  Book, pp. 3–4

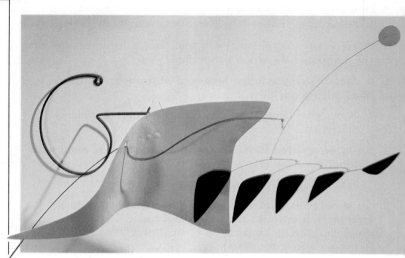

Yellow Whale, by
Alexander Calder, 1958
Painted sheet metal
and wire, 45″ wide.
Collection of Howard
and Jean Lipman

B. REVISION SKILL

Punctuating Sentences   Writers improve the clarity of their sentences by punctuating them properly. Write *Declarative, Interrogative, Imperative,* or *Exclamatory* to identify each of the following sentences. Then add the appropriate end punctuation.

1. Do you know anything about daydreams?
2. Daydreams are a form of imagination that allow you to temporarily escape the reality and facts of everyday life.
3. Are daydreams sometimes useful?
4. You can put bits and pieces of experiences into new forms that lead to invention and creativity.
5. In daydreams you can explore possibilities for your future.
6. Put yourself in a different frame of mind.
7. What would you like to do or be?
8. Imagine yourself as an astronaut visiting another planet, a rock star on stage, or a corporate executive at a meeting.
9. What powerful motivation daydreams provide!
10. Daydreams are a means for planning and problem solving.
11. Imagine the inventions that may have started this way. or !
12. What wonderful plots were woven from imaginings!
13. Choose some leisure time each day for daydreaming.
14. Try daydreaming before attempting any creative activity.
15. Just remember, daydreams know no bounds.

Humanities Connection

Art Note   The sculptor Alexander Calder is considered the inventor of the mobile, which is a work of art that is constructed of various materials and that moves, usually by air currents. Calder's dynamic mobiles are crafted of shapes cut from riveted sheet metal and wire. The shapes, balance, and movement of his mobiles contribute to their beauty and powerful effect on viewers. The young Calder earned a B.S. in Mechanical Engineering. (Mechanical engineers study the effects that energy and forces have on objects.) Ask: How do you think Calder's engineering background influenced his artistic development?

C. APPLICATION IN LITERATURE

Identifying and Punctuating Sentences The following sentences are spoken by Alice and a queen in Lewis Carroll's *Through the Looking Glass.* Write the end mark that is appropriate for each. Then identify each sentence as *Declarative, Interrogative, Imperative,* or *Exclamatory.*

(1) Alice: Can you keep from crying by considering things?
(2) Queen: That's the way it's done.
(3) Let's consider your age to begin with.
(4) Alice: I'm seven and a half, exactly.
(5) Queen: I'm just one hundred and one, five months, and a day.
(6) Alice: I can't believe that. or !
(7) Queen: Can't you?
(8) Try again: draw a long breath and shut your eyes.
(9) Alice: One can't believe impossible things. or !
(10) Queen: Why, sometimes I've believed as many as six impossible things before breakfast.

CHECK POINT
PAGES 497–501

Tell whether each item is a sentence or fragment. Then add words to develop each fragment into a sentence. Add the correct end punctuation to each sentence, including the revised ones. Then identify each sentence as *Declarative, Interrogative, Imperative,* or *Exclamatory.*

1. Have you ever heard of extrasensory perception?
2. The usual abbreviation ESP
3. An awareness of something without the use of any of our sense organs
4. How extraordinary reading someone else's thoughts would be!
5. Telepathy is one kind of ESP.
6. Considerable debate within the scientific community about the validity of ESP
7. Can you foretell future events?
8. Another kind of ESP, precognition
9. Has much research been done on the many kinds of ESP?
10. Try some experiments in card guessing.
11. Tested clairvoyance at a university
12. Don't overestimate psychokinesis, or mind over matter.
13. Can anyone influence the outcome of a roll of the dice?
14. What I'd give to have ESP!
15. How exciting the discoveries of the future will be!

Writing Theme
Extrasensory Perception

C. Application in Literature
Identifying and Punctuating Sentences
Punctuation is added on page.
  1. Interrogative
  2. Declarative
  3. Imperative
  4. Declarative
  5. Declarative
  6. Declarative *or* Exclamatory
  7. Interrogative
  8. Imperative
  9. Declarative *or* Exclamatory
  10. Declarative

CHECK POINT
PAGES 497–501

You may wish to use the following checkpoint exercises as an informal evaluation of student mastery of the concepts covered in this handbook.

WRITING THEME   Extrasensory Perception

You might encourage students to do additional research on this theme and use it as the subject of a research report.
Sentences from fragments will vary. See typical sentences below. Punctuation is added on page.
  1. S Interrogative
  2. F The usual abbreviation for the term is ESP. Declarative
  3. F ESP is an awareness of something without the use of any of our sense organs. Declarative
  4. S Exclamatory
  5. S Declarative
  6. F There is considerable debate within the scientific community about the validity of ESP. Declarative
  7. S Interrogative
  8. F Some people seem to possess another kind of ESP, precognition. Declarative
  9. S Interrogative
  10. S Imperative
  11. F Scientists tested clairvoyance at a university. Declarative
  12. S Imperative
  13. S Interrogative
  14. S Exclamatory
  15. S Exclamatory

Complete Subjects and Predicates

Objectives

Teaching Strategies

Teaching Tip: Subjects and Predicates

Students may need additional guidance in identifying complete subjects and predicates. Help them verbalize the identification process by asking "Who or what is this sentence about?" to identify the subject and "What statement is made about the subject?" to identify the predicate.

Collaborative Opportunity

Group students for a creative writing activity. Have a student begin a story by writing a complete subject and then pass the paper to the next student to write a predicate that completes the sentence and begins to develop a story line. Have students continue around the group, alternating subjects and predicates until the story is complete. Have students share their stories with the class.

> **Additional Resources**
> - Grammar and Usage Practice Book, pp. 5–6

WRITING THEME   The Brontë Sisters

Suggest that interested students consider using this theme as a writing topic for an assignment in Writer's Workshop 8: Writing About Literature.

A. Concept Check

Complete Subjects
Answers are underlined on page.

COMPLETE SUBJECTS AND PREDICATES

A sentence has two parts: the subject and the predicate. The subject tells whom or what the sentence is about. The predicate tells what the subject is, what the subject does or did, or what happened to the subject.

Subject	Predicate
The volcano	erupted again.
A reporter from the paper	relayed the news.
Helen Keller	became a writer.

The complete subject includes all the words that identify the person, place, thing, or idea that the sentence is about. The complete predicate includes all the words that make a statement about the subject.

A complete subject or predicate may consist of one word or a number of words.

Complete Subject	Complete Predicate
Continents	drift.
The plants in the classroom	need more sunlight.
Basketball and astronomy	are two of my interests.

Practice Your Skills

A. CONCEPT CHECK

Complete Subjects   Write the complete subject of each of these sentences.

1. The remarkably talented Brontë sisters lived in England during the early and middle 1800's.
2. Charlotte, Emily, and Anne all became writers.
3. They grew up on the lonely moors of Yorkshire.
4. The Brontës were a family who believed in educating themselves at home.
5. The society of other children was not a part of their lives.
6. Their isolation allowed the sisters and their brother time for pretending.
7. The four Brontë children invented strange and fascinating imaginary lands.
8. Fantastic characters and complicated stories were spun out of their active imaginations.

Writing Theme
The Brontë Sisters

9. Each of the three sisters remembered these childhood stories as an adult.

10. Some of the events and characters even appeared in the Brontës' books.

B. CONCEPT CHECK

Complete Predicates   Write the complete predicate of each of these sentences.

(1) Charlotte Brontë's novel *Jane Eyre* tells the story of a courageous and independent young woman. (2) Jane's cruel aunt treats the orphan girl badly. (3) She sends Jane to Lowood, a boarding school for homeless girls. (4) The young girl learns many hard lessons about life. (5) Jane leaves the school after eight years. (6) She takes a job as a governess at Thornfield. (7) The story of Jane's romance begins there. (8) She meets the fascinating and mysterious Mr. Rochester. (9) Secrets from his past complicate the story. (10) The plot of *Jane Eyre* has become the model for many Gothic romance novels of the present day.

Emily, Charlotte, Bramwell, and Anne Brontë. Drawing by Bramwell Brontë

SIMPLE SUBJECTS AND PREDICATES

The simple subject is the key word or words in the complete subject.

The simple subject names the person, place, thing, or idea the sentence is about. Modifying words are not part of the simple subject. A simple subject may include more than one proper noun. In the following sentences the simple subjects are printed in boldface type.

Complete Subject	Complete Predicate
John Lennon	wrote many songs.
One of my friends	plays the trumpet.
Star Wars	is a good movie.

The Sentence and Its Parts   **503**

Simple Subjects and Predicates

Objectives

- To identify the simple subject of a sentence
- To identify the simple predicate of a sentence
- To identify verb phrases in sentences
- **Writing**   To expand sentences by adding words to the subject or predicate

Teaching Strategies

Linking Grammar and Writing

Point out to students that although short, direct sentences can be very effective, sentence expansion is a way to add variety and improve the interest level of their writing. Ask students to review one of their rough drafts to see whether any sentences can be improved by adding words or phrases to the subject or predicate. As part of their revision process, have students rewrite these sentences.

 Individualizing Instruction

ESL Students   In Korean, Japanese, Hindi, and related languages, the verb always occurs at the end of the sentence. Some ESL students may have difficulty locating the verb in English sentences, particularly when the verb is an unfamiliar one.

> **Additional Resources**
> - Grammar and Usage Practice Book, pp. 7–8

Writing Theme
Thunderstorms

The simple predicate, also called the verb, is the main word or words in the complete predicate.

The simple predicate, or **verb,** tells what the subject is or does. Other words that add to the meaning of the predicate are not part of the verb. In the following sentences the verbs are boldfaced.

Complete Subject	Complete Predicate
All the lines in this picture	**converge.**
I	**returned** home.
The radio	**was** once a novelty.

Finding the Verb and the Subject

In any sentence, the verb and the simple subject, referred to in this textbook as the **subject,** are the most important words.

To find the key words in a sentence, first find the verb. It will express some kind of action or state of being. Then place the words *who* or *what* in front of the verb. The answer will tell you the subject.

> An attendant at the station checked the oil.
> *Verb:* checked
> *Who checked?* attendant
> *Subject of verb:* attendant

Sentence Diagraming   For information on diagraming the subject and verb of a sentence, see page 830.

Practice Your Skills

CONCEPT CHECK

Simple Subject and Predicate   Make two columns and label them *Subject* and *Verb.* For each sentence, write the simple subject and the simple predicate in the proper column.

1. Thunderstorms fascinate people all over the world.
2. Lightning fills the sky with electric brightness.
3. The air echoes with the crackly, rumbly sound of thunder.
4. These dramatic natural events are beautiful but sometimes scary.
5. In fact, one recorded thunderstorm went far beyond scary.
6. For one thing, this storm stretched for 40,000 miles.
7. The circumference of the earth is only about 25,000 miles.
8. Still, this "impossibly" large storm existed.
9. Two *Voyager* spacecraft recorded it in 1980 and 1981.
10. This spectacular storm raged on the planet Saturn.

The Verb Phrase

A verb may consist of one or more words. It may consist of a **main verb** and one or more **helping verbs,** also called **auxiliary verbs.**

A verb phrase consists of a main verb and one or more helping verbs.

Helping Verb	+	Main Verb	=	Phrase
was		sinking		was sinking
must have		caused		must have caused

Venice *is sinking* one-fifth of an inch each year.
The storm *must have caused* the damage to the house.

Common Helping Verbs

be (*and its forms:* am, are, is, was, were, being, been)
have (*and its forms:* has, had)
do (*and its forms:* does, did)

can	may	must	shall	will
could	might	ought	should	would

Some of these words can also be used as main verbs.

The ostrich *has* a life span of fifty years. (Main verb)
It *has disappeared* from much of Africa. (Helping verb)

Practice Your Skills

A. CONCEPT CHECK

Simple and Complete Subject and Predicate Write each of the following sentences. Draw a vertical line between the complete subject and the complete predicate. Then draw one line under the simple subject and two lines under the verb or verb phrase.

1. A famous place in London | is Madame Tussaud's Exhibition.
2. This museum | contains lifelike wax figures of famous people.
3. Nearly three million people | visit the museum yearly.
4. The realism of the exhibits | has astounded visitors.
5. Marie Tussaud | exhibited wax figures for the first time in 1802.
6. Marie's uncle | had taught her the art of wax sculpting at his museum in Paris.

WRITING THEME   London, England

Encourage interested students to consider this writing theme as they brainstorm possible topics for a Writer's Workshop.

A. Concept Check
Simple and Complete Subject and Predicate
Answers are underlined on page.

Additional Resources
• Grammar and Usage Practice Book, pp. 9–10

B. Drafting Skill

Sentence Expansion

Answers will vary. See typical answers below.

1. Visitors to London love to walk along the mall from Trafalgar Square to Buckingham Palace.   Predicate

2. They gaze at the beautiful paintings in the National Gallery at Trafalgar Square.   Predicate

7. Sympathy for the king |earned Marie a prison term during the French Revolution.
8. She |modeled the heads of revolutionary leaders and victims of the guillotine as part of her punishment.
9. London |became her home after her term in prison.
10. Many of the famous people of her time |served as her subjects.
11. Figures of wax |almost came to life under Marie's skilled fingers.
12. Descendants of Marie Tussaud |maintain the museum even today.
13. Celebrities |have occasionally donated their clothes for the figures of themselves.
14. The exhibits in the museum |change every year.
15. Visitors to the museum |can see figures ranging from Henry VIII's wives to Princess Diana.

B. DRAFTING SKILL

Sentence Expansion   Use sentence expansion to improve the interest and variety of the sentences below. Expand each sentence by adding words or phrases to the subject or predicate. Tell whether the material was added to the subject or to the predicate. (Information in parentheses suggests content to add.)

1. Visitors to London love to walk along the mall. (They walk from Trafalgar Square to Buckingham Palace.)
2. At Trafalgar Square, they gaze at paintings. (The paintings are beautiful. The paintings are in the National Gallery.)

St. Paul's from Bankside, Southwark by William Richardson, 1883

Humanities Connection

Art Note   *St. Paul's from Bankside,* painted by artist William Richardson (b. 1842, England, d. 1877), captures the masterwork of architect Sir Christopher Wren (b. 1632, England, d. 1723). Following the Great Fire of 1666, Wren was commissioned to redesign and rebuild London. St. Paul's Cathedral (1672) was the centerpiece in his vision of the revitalized city. Wren is generally considered to be England's greatest architect. His innovative designs for domes and steeples have inspired architects for centuries.

3. The Nelson column at the end of the square is massive. (It is 125 feet tall. It is made of granite.)
4. Colorful troops change the guard at the Horse Guard Palace. (The troops are the queen's Household Cavalry.)
5. Nearby, a bobby guards the door at number 10 Downing Street. (This is the Prime Minister's house.)
6. The famous Clock Tower is visible from Trafalgar Square. (This is the tower from which Big Ben booms out the hour.)
7. In the square itself, visitors can see hundreds of pigeons. (They can feed them, too.)
8. Now they pass the lake in St. James's Park. (The lake is peaceful and glistening.)
9. Snow-white geese swim by. (The geese seem proud of their gracious home.)
10. The visitors often stop to look at the gardens in the park. (The gardens are beautifully kept.)
11. The Queen Victoria Memorial stands at the end of the mall. (It is impressive.)
12. Buckingham Palace, however, is the real attraction of the walk. (It is huge and stately.)
13. Buckingham Palace does not look much like a castle. (It differs from the kind of castle you find in a fairy tale)
14. Inside, however, a real queen and her family live. (They work and play there, too.)
15. With luck, a visitor may get a glimpse of the queen on this route. (It is the mall which serves as the chief route for royal parades.)

C. APPLICATION IN WRITING

Writing for a Diary Entry   A writer often keeps a diary, or journal, when traveling, to record experiences, describe unusual sights, or note events that hold personal meaning. Later the writer may use a diary entry as the basis of a description in a travel article or even in a novel or short story. Rewrite the diary entry below to create a short description of a visit to the National Gallery in London. Add a subject or a predicate whenever one is needed.

> Went to the National Gallery today. A remarkable collection of paintings. The Rembrandt self-portraits. I loved seeing how he changed over his lifetime. A face full of intelligence and ambition, later wisdom and compassion. Lights and darks of his other paintings. Walked for a long time among the English landscape paintings by Turner and Constable. What gentle beauty! Maybe my favorite—people's faces in the cafeteria where I had lunch.

The Sentence
and Its Parts   **507**

3. The 125-foot granite Nelson column at the end of the square is massive.   Subject
4. Colorful troops of the queen's Household Cavalry change the guard at the Horse Guard Palace.   Subject
5. Nearby, a Bobbie guards the door at the Prime Minister's house at number 10 Downing Street.   Predicate
6. The famous Clock Tower, from which Big Ben booms out the hour, is visible from Trafalgar Square.   Subject
7. In the square itself, visitors can see and feed hundreds of pigeons.   Predicate
8. Now they pass the peaceful, glistening lake in St. James's Park.   Predicate
9. Snow-white geese, seeming proud of their gracious home, swim by.   Subject
10. The visitors often stop to look at the beautifully kept gardens in the park.   Predicate
11. The impressive Queen Victoria Memorial stands at the end of the mall.   Subject
12. The huge and stately Buckingham Palace, however, is the real attraction of the walk.   Subject
13. Buckingham Palace does not look much like the kind of castle you find in a fairy tale.   Predicate
14. Inside, however, a real queen and her family live, work, and play.   Predicate
15. With luck, a visitor may glimpse the queen on this route, which serves as the chief route for royal parades.   Predicate

C. Application in Writing
Writing for a Diary Entry
Answers will vary. See typical answer below.
I went to the National Gallery today, where I saw a remarkable collection of paintings. The Rembrandt self-portraits were fascinating. I loved seeing how the artist changed over his lifetime. In his early years, his face was full of intelligence and ambition. Later, it showed wisdom and compassion. I walked for a long time among the English landscape paintings by Turner and Constable. What gentle beauty they exhibited! Maybe my favorite sights, however, were people's faces in the cafeteria where I had lunch.

Subjects in Unusual Positions

Objectives

- To identify the subject and verb in sentences in which the order is inverted, in sentences beginning with *Here* and *There,* in interrogative sentences, and in imperative sentences
- **Writing** To demonstrate revision skills by inverting subjects and verbs for sentence variety

Teaching Strategies

Linking Grammar and Literature

Point out that poetry often contains sentences in which the order of the words is inverted, as in the following line from Walt Whitman's "I Hear America Singing":

I hear America singing, the varied carols I hear. . .

Ask students to find the inverted word order in the quotation. Then ask them to bring in other poems or literary excerpts in which the word order is inverted and identify the subjects and predicates in each example. Point out to students that occasional use of inverted word order can add variety to their writing.

Stumbling Block

For students who have difficulty locating the subject in sentences in which the word order is inverted, emphasize asking *who* or *what* the sentence is about or *who* or *what* is the "doer" in the sentence.

Additional Resources
- Grammar and Usage Practice Book, pp. 11–12

SUBJECTS IN UNUSUAL POSITIONS

In most sentences the subject comes before the verb or verb phrase. Sometimes, however, this order is changed to give sentences some variety.

Sentences with Inverted Order

A sentence is in inverted order when the verb or any part of the verb phrase comes before the subject.

In the following examples, each subject is underlined once and each verb is underlined twice.

Along the drive to the house <u>were</u> tall <u>trees</u>.
Next to the ocean liner <u>chugged</u> the <u>tugboat</u>.
<u>Hidden</u> from view <u>were</u> three <u>pedestrians</u>.
<u>Parked</u> in the driveway <u>was</u> a shiny red <u>convertible</u>.

To find the subject, first locate the verb or verb phrase. Then place the words *who* or *what* before the verb or verb phrase. The word that answers the question is the subject.

Out of the magician's hat squirmed ten white rabbits.
Verb: squirmed
Who or what squirmed? rabbits
Subject: rabbits

Sentences Beginning with *Here* or *There*

In some sentences beginning with *Here* or *There,* the subject follows the verb.

Here <u>is</u> the <u>photo</u> for my identification card.
There <u>are</u> ten <u>questions</u> on the form.

Interrogative Sentences

In interrogative sentences the subject typically comes either after the verb or between parts of the verb.

<u>Is</u> the new <u>gym</u> ready for use?
<u>Are</u> all your <u>sweaters</u> the same color?
<u>Did</u> <u>you</u> <u>see</u> Allan's new ten-speed bicycle?
<u>Have</u> the <u>students</u> <u>written</u> in their journals today?

To find the subject of an interrogative sentence, change the sentence to a declarative one. Then find the verb and ask *who?* or *what?*

> Is Appomattox in Virginia?
> *Declarative:* Appomattox is in Virginia.
> *Verb:* is
> *What is?* Appomattox
> *Subject:* Appomattox

In interrogative sentences beginning with *Who, What, Where, When, Why,* and *How,* the subject often comes between parts of the verb.

> Who will the winner be?
> What did you say?
> Where was the treasure hidden?
> When will the World Series end?
> Why doesn't he listen?
> How can you finish this job?

Sometimes a word such as *who* or *what* is the subject. Then the subject comes before the verb.

> What was the verdict in the trial?
> Who is directing the film?

Subjects in Imperative Sentences

Imperative sentences give commands or state requests. In an imperative sentence the subject is usually not stated. Since a command or a request is always given to the person spoken to, the subject of such a sentence is *you.* When the subject *you* is not stated, it is said to be understood.

Although the first word in an imperative sentence is often a verb, a word like *Please* or a phrase like *For heaven's sake* sometimes precedes the verb.

> Leave the package here.
> (*You* is the understood subject of *Leave.*)
> Please revise this draft.
> (*You* is the understood subject of *revise.*)

What are the imperative sentences in the cartoon at the right? Are the subjects stated or understood?

Sentence Diagraming For information on diagraming interrogative and imperative sentences, see page 830.

THE FAR SIDE   By GARY LARSON

© 1985 Universal Press Syndicate

The Far Side, ©1985 Un...

"Hold still, Omar. ... Now look up. Yep. You've got something in your eye, all right—could be sand."

The Sentence
and Its Parts   **509**

WRITING THEME   Words

Suggest that interested students use this theme as the alternative topic when completing a writing application activity in this handbook.

A. Concept Check

Subjects in Unusual Positions
Subjects and verbs or verb phrases are underlined, and imperative sentences are indicated by (You), on page.

B. Revision Skill

Sentence Variety
1. From Latin come a great many English words.
2. There is one from a Latin joke or pun, in fact.
3. Have you heard the word *tandem?*
4. Picture a carriage with two horses harnessed one behind the other.
5. There are two seats, one behind the other, on a tandem bicycle.
6. From the real meaning of the word *tandem* comes the humor.
7. Doesn't the Latin word *tandem* mean either "one behind the other" or "two"?
8. Look up the origin of *tandem.*
9. Here is the pun.
10. From a Latin word meaning "at length" or "at long last" comes the word *tandem.*

Writing Theme
Words

Writing
—TIP—

Variety is important in good writing.

Practice Your Skills

A. CONCEPT CHECK

Subjects in Unusual Positions   Write the simple subject and the verb or verb phrase in each of the following sentences. For imperative sentences write (*You*) to indicate the subject.

1. Have you ever traced a word back to its origin?
2. There are thousands of interesting word histories.
3. Take, for instance, the word *disaster.* (You)
4. Here is an example of a word with a Latin root—*astrum,* or "star."
5. Add the negative prefix *dis-* to *-astrum.* (You)
6. From the negative influence of stars supposedly come "disasters."
7. Into your mind probably leap visions of earthquakes, floods, shipwrecks, and volcanic eruptions.
8. But do the stars really play a part in such events?
9. There is no scientific reason for such a belief.
10. Out of the superstitions of ancient cultures grow some interesting word meanings.

B. REVISION SKILL

Sentence Variety   Too many sentences that sound alike may make your writing uninteresting. To gain experience with some less common sentence structures, rewrite most of the sentences below so that the verbs come before the subjects. Follow the directions given in parentheses.

1. A great many English words come from Latin. (Begin the sentence with *From Latin.*)
2. One is from a Latin joke or pun, in fact. (Begin the sentence with *There is.*)
3. You have heard the word *tandem.* (Change to a question.)
4. You can picture a carriage with two horses harnessed one behind the other. (Change to an imperative sentence.)
5. Two seats, one behind the other, are on a tandem bicycle. (Begin the sentence with *There are.*)
6. The humor comes from the real meaning of the word *tandem.* (Begin the sentence with *From the real meaning.*)
7. The Latin word *tandem* does not mean either "one behind the other" or "two." (Change to a question.)
8. You can look up the origin of *tandem.* (Change to an *imperative sentence.*)
9. The pun is here. (Begin the sentence with *Here.*)
10. The word *tandem* comes from a Latin word meaning "at length" or "at long last." (Begin the sentence with *From a Latin word.*)

A. Complete Subjects and Predicates Draw a vertical line between each complete subject and complete predicate. Underline the simple subject once and the verb twice.

1. The ancient Cambodian <u>city</u> of Angkor | <u>was</u> the capital of the Khmer kingdom from 800 until 1431.
2. This amazing <u>metropolis</u> | <u>covered</u> forty square miles.
3. This <u>wonder</u> of the ancient world | <u>contained</u> elaborate temples, roads, irrigation canals, reservoirs, and hospitals.
4. <u>Angkor</u> | <u>was captured</u> by Thai troops in 1431.
5. Apparently, the Khmer <u>people</u> | <u>abandoned</u> their capital in great haste.
6. The nearby <u>jungle</u> | <u>covered</u> Angkor very quickly with a thick green blanket.
7. The sleeping <u>city</u> | <u>was</u> not <u>rediscovered</u> until the nineteenth century.
8. A French <u>naturalist</u> | <u>stumbled</u> accidentally into the overgrown ruins of the once-majestic Angkor.
9. Henri <u>Mouhat</u> | <u>was</u> only <u>looking</u> for rare butterflies.
10. <u>He</u> | <u>found</u> one of the world's most remarkable and civilized "lost" cities instead.

B. Verbs and Verb Phrases Write the <u>verb or verb phrase</u> in each sentence below. Then write the <u>subject</u>. Watch for unusual kinds of sentences.

1. Down through the centuries <u>have come</u> <u>tales</u> of another "lost" place.
2. <u>Have</u> <u>you</u> ever <u>heard</u> of Atlantis?
3. A famous Greek <u>philosopher</u> <u>describes</u> the mysterious continent and its legendary city.
4. Here <u>is</u> the <u>story</u>.
5. Beyond the Pillars of Hercules <u>lay</u> a vast <u>island</u> larger than Asia Minor.
6. For 9,000 years <u>it</u> <u>had been</u> a powerful kingdom.
7. Indeed, the <u>armies</u> of Atlantis <u>had overrun</u> all the lands of the Mediterranean.
8. There <u>was</u> almost no <u>resistance</u> to their power.
9. Then, suddenly, over this great continent <u>flowed</u> the <u>waters</u> of the sea.
10. Into the world of fantastic and mythical legend <u>went</u> the underwater <u>city</u>.

Writing Theme
Lost Cities

The Sentence
and Its Parts   **511**

CHECK POINT
PAGES 502–510

You may wish to use the following check-point exercises as an informal evaluation of student mastery of the concepts covered in this handbook.

WRITING THEME   Lost Cities

Invite students to consider how they might use this writing theme to generate topics for Writer's Workshop 9.

A. Complete Subjects and Predicates
Answers are underlined on page.

B. Verbs and Verb Phrases
Answers are underlined on page.

- To identify direct objects and indirect objects in sentences

Teaching Strategies

Critical Thinking

Synthesizing Label three columns on the chalkboard: "action verb," "indirect object," and "direct object." Allow students to fill in words in the columns. Have them create sentences using the key words on the board in the correct functions.

OBJECTS OF VERBS

The two main kinds of verbs are **action verbs** and **linking verbs.**

An action verb describes an action. It tells that something is happening, has happened, or will happen.

Samantha *collects* seashells.   Mr. Klein *delivers* newspapers.
We *skated* on Duck Lake.   I *slept* well afterward.

A linking verb, sometimes called a state-of-being verb, links the subject with another word or words in the predicate.

Ramon *is* an expert swimmer.   The frog *became* a prince.
The captain *was* a good leader.   My aunts *are* teachers.

Complements

Some action verbs do not need other words to complete their meaning in a sentence. The action they describe is complete.

The players *rested*.   The rain finally *stopped*.
Nathan *was worrying*.   The T-shirt *will fade*.

However, other action verbs—and all linking verbs—are incomplete by themselves. They need additional words to complete their meaning. These other words are called **complements.**

A complement is a word that completes the meaning of a predicate.

The italicized verbs below are followed by complements.

Action Verbs
Kazuo *reserved* a space.
Lila *remembered* the formula.

Linking Verbs
Pat *is* a student.
The music *sounded* familiar.

The two kinds of complements that complete the meaning of action verbs are **direct objects** and **indirect objects.** The complements that complete the meaning of linking verbs are **predicate nominatives** and **predicate adjectives.**

Direct Objects

A direct object receives the action of an action verb. It answers the question *what?* or *whom?*

Our pharmacy sells stamps. (Sells what? Sells *stamps*. *Stamps* is the direct object.)

To find the direct object, first find the verb. Then form a question by placing *whom?* or *what?* after the verb. The direct object answers this question.

A verb that takes a direct object is called a **transitive verb.** You will learn about transitive and intransitive verbs on pages 588–589.

Indirect Objects

If a sentence has a direct object, it may also have another kind of complement called an **indirect object.**

An indirect object tells *to whom?* or *for whom?* or *to what?* or *for what?* about an action verb. The words *to* and *for* are not used in the actual sentences, however.

A sentence can have an indirect object only if it has a direct object. The indirect object always comes before the direct object. To find the indirect object in a sentence, first find the direct object. Then ask *to whom?* or *to what?* or *for whom?* or *for what?* The indirect object answers these questions.

> Andrea handed the teller her deposit. (Handed what? *Deposit* is the direct object. Handed it to whom? *Teller* is the indirect object.)

Individualizing Instruction

Visual Learners Help visual learners to understand the concept of indirect objects by using a diagram like the following:

Mom baked a cake for ⟨John⟩.

Mom baked ⟨John⟩ a cake.

Basic Students Help basic students to make a list of verbs that commonly support an indirect object, for example: *give, make, take, bring, show.* You may wish to suggest that they refer to this list as they complete the exercise.

Additional Resources
• Grammar and Usage Practice Book, pp. 13–14

WRITING THEME Fossils

You may want to encourage interested students to do further research on this topic and use it as the subject for an expository writing assignment.

Concept Check
Indirect Objects and Direct Objects
Student answers should be in columns.
1. have left (V), us (IO), messages (DO)
2. can examine (V), None, skeletons (DO)
3. offer (V), world (IO), evidence (DO)
4. provide (V), None, specimens (DO)
5. unearth (V), None, fossils (DO)
6. gave (V), museum (IO), mammoth (DO)
7. produce (V), None, fossils (DO)
8. promote (V), None, formation (DO)
9. give (V), us (IO), information (DO)
10. found (V), None, footprints (DO)
11. had seen (V), None, footprints (DO)
12. have given (V), scientists (IO), deal (DO)
13. have identified (V), None, hundreds (DO)
14. can tell (V), observer (IO), size (DO)
15. reveals (V), None, length (DO)

Writing Theme
Fossils

Fossil remains of a trilobite, extinct for millions of years.

When the word *to* or *for* appears in the sentence, the word that follows it is not an indirect object, even though it tells *to whom* or *for whom* about the action of the verb.

Mrs. Wong sent us a beautiful painting.
Mrs. Wong sent a beautiful painting to us.

In the first sentence, *us* is the indirect object of *sent*. It comes before the direct object, *painting*.

In the second sentence, *us* follows the word *to*. It comes after the direct object. Therefore, *us* is not an indirect object. It is the object of the preposition "to." (For more about prepositional phrases, see pages 653–658.) Verbs that often take indirect objects include *bring, give, hand, lend, make, offer, send, show, teach,* and *write*.

Sentence Diagraming For information on diagraming sentences with direct and indirect objects, see page 831.

Practice Your Skills

CONCEPT CHECK

Indirect Objects and Direct Objects Make three columns on your paper. Label them *Verb, Indirect Object,* and *Direct Object*. For each sentence, write those parts in the proper columns. If a sentence has no indirect object, write *None*.

1. Prehistoric animals have left us messages about ancient times.
2. At museums, visitors can examine huge skeletons of dinosaurs.
3. Skeletons offer the world evidence of ancient life.
4. Fossils provide even better specimens for study.
5. Scientists unearth fossils in many forms.
6. Natives of the North gave the museum a frozen mammoth.
7. Swampy or damp places produce more fossils than dry areas.
8. Minerals in water promote the formation of fossils.
9. Fossils give us information about ancient changes in climate.
10. In 1802 a farm boy found fossil footprints of a small dinosaur.
11. No one had ever seen fossil footprints before.
12. Since then, fossil footprints have given scientists a great deal of information.
13. Scientists have identified hundreds of extinct animals from fossil footprints.
14. Study of some footprints can tell an observer the size of a dinosaur.
15. The distance between footprints reveals to a scientist the length of the dinosaur's legs.

SUBJECT COMPLEMENTS

You learned earlier that a linking verb does not describe an action. It links the subject with another word in the sentence. This word, which identifies or describes the subject, is a **subject complement.**

A linking verb always needs a subject complement to complete its meaning in a sentence; otherwise, the meaning of the predicate is incomplete.

> The whooping crane is _____. (Is what? a rare *bird*)
> The math problem seemed _____. (Seemed what? *hard*)
> Chen was _____. (Was what? *late*)

In the sentences above, *bird, hard,* and *late* are subject complements.

The verb *be* is the most common linking verb. It has various forms, such as *am, is, are, was, were, will be, has been.*

Other Common Linking Verbs				
appear	feel	look	smell	taste
become	grow	seem	sound	

Two kinds of subject complements complete the meaning of linking verbs. These subject complements are called **predicate nominatives** and **predicate adjectives.**

A predicate nominative is a noun or pronoun that follows a linking verb and that identifies, renames, or explains the subject.

In each of the following sentences a noun or a pronoun follows a linking verb and names or identifies the subject.

> Squirrels are rodents.   The winner is he.

A predicate adjective is an adjective that follows a linking verb and that modifies or describes the subject.

In each of the following sentences the word that follows the linking verb describes or modifies the subject.

> Tomas must be weary.   The lake looks choppy.

The Sentence
and Its Parts   **515**

Objectives

- To identify predicate nominatives and predicate adjectives in sentences
- To distinguish among direct objects, indirect objects, predicate nominatives, and predicate adjectives in sentences
- **Writing** To use subject complements in writing

Teaching Strategies

Teaching Tip: Subject Complements

Emphasize the *completing* nature of subject complements; that is, they *complete* the meaning of linking verbs as well as add information about the subject of the sentence. To illustrate this concept, have volunteers generate unfinished sentences that have linking verbs and ask other students to provide an adjective or a noun to complete each sentence.

Collaborative Opportunity

Have pairs or small groups of students create sentences using each verb listed in the chart of other common linking verbs, except *seem,* as both a linking verb and an action verb. Challenge students to think of another verb that can be used in both ways, for example, *turn, remain, stay,* or *act.*

> **Additional Resources**
> - Grammar and Usage Practice Book, pp. 15–16

Suggest to students that they consider this writing theme as they develop a list of possible research report topics in Writer's Workshop 9.

A. Concept Check
Predicate Nominatives and Predicate Adjectives
1. important, Predicate Adjective
2. rituals, Predicate Nominative
3. joyous, Predicate Adjective
4. None
5. alike, Predicate Adjective
6. celebrations, Predicate Nominative
7. introductions, Predicate Nominative
8. None
9. None
10. glue, Predicate Nominative

B. Application in Literature
Complements
1. man, Predicate Nominative
2. funeral, Predicate Nominative
3. skirts, Direct Object
4. titles, Direct Object
5. achievement, Predicate Nominative
6. lords, Predicate Nominative
7. alone, Predicate Adjective
8. him, Indirect Object
9. steps, Direct Object
10. salute, Direct Object

Writing Theme
Rituals

Some verbs can be completed either by direct objects or subject complements. To determine what kind of complement follows the verb, ask: Is the complement receiving the action of the verb? Is the complement identifying the subject? Is the complement describing the subject?

> Luisa tasted the *strawberries*. (Direct object)
> The strawberries tasted *tart*. (Predicate adjective)
> Strawberries are a delicious *treat*. (Predicate nominative)

Sentence Diagraming   For information on diagraming sentences with subject complements, see page 832.

Practice Your Skills

A. CONCEPT CHECK

Predicate Nominatives and Predicate Adjectives   For each sentence write the subject complement, if there is one, and identify it as *Predicate Nominative* or *Predicate Adjective*. If there is no subject complement, write *None*.

1. Rituals are important in every society.
2. Weddings and funerals are two significant rituals.
3. Weddings are usually joyous.
4. A funeral, on the other hand, provides a time for mourning.
5. Rituals for the dead are not alike everywhere.
6. In some cultures funerals become celebrations for the newly freed soul.
7. Coming-of-age rituals can be serious introductions to the responsibilities of adulthood.
8. They may also contain pranks and jokes.
9. The importance of rituals appears frequently as a theme in literature.
10. In many ways rituals are the glue that holds a society together.

B. APPLICATION IN LITERATURE

Complements   Write the complements that are italicized in the following selection. Identify each by writing *Direct Object*, *Indirect Object*, *Predicate Nominative*, or *Predicate Adjective*.

> (1) Ezeudu was a great *man*, and so all the clan was at his funeral . . . . (2) It was a warrior's *funeral*, and from morning till night warriors came and went in their age groups. (3) They all wore smoked raffia *skirts*, and their bodies were painted with chalk and charcoal.

(4) Ezeudu had taken three *titles* in his life. (5) It was a rare *achievement*. There were only four titles in the clan, and only one or two men in any generation ever achieved the fourth and highest. (6) When they did, they became the *lords* of the land. Because he had taken titles, Ezeudu was to be buried after dark with only a glowing brand to light the sacred ceremony . . . .

It was then that the one-handed spirit came, carrying a basketful of water . . . . But the most dreaded of all was yet to come. (7) He was always *alone* and shaped like a coffin.

"Ezeudu!" he called in his guttural voice . . . . "If your death was the death of nature, go in peace. (8) But if a man caused it, do not allow *him* a moment's rest." (9) He danced a few more *steps* and went away.

The drums and the dancing began again and reached fever-heat. Darkness was around the corner, and the burial was near. (10) Guns fired the last *salute* and the cannon rent the sky.

Chinua Achebe, *Things Fall Apart*

C. APPLICATION IN WRITING

Writing a Letter Write a letter that you could send to a pen pal in another country. Choose a holiday or celebration with which you are familiar. Help your pen pal become familiar with this holiday or celebration by describing it in detail. Use several subject complements in your description.

Kwele Initiation Mask

Coming of Age Mask, Biombo People of Zaire

COMPOUND SENTENCE PARTS

The word *compound* means "having two or more parts." Each of the sentence parts described so far in this section—subjects, verbs, and complements—can be compound.

The parts of a compound construction are usually joined by one of these conjunctions: *and, or,* or *but.* Here are some examples of compound constructions.

Subjects	*Bats* and *sloths* like to hang upside down from tree branches.
Verbs	The archaeologist carefully *scraped* and *sorted* the shards of pottery.
Direct Objects	The children will play *charades* or *darts* after supper.
Indirect Objects	Carlos made *Roz* and *me* a Mexican dinner.

The Sentence
and Its Parts   **517**

C. Application in Writing
Writing a Letter
Answers will vary.

Compound Sentence Parts

Objectives

- To identify compound sentence parts
- To combine sentences to form compound sentence parts
- **Writing** To use compound sentence parts in writing

Teaching Strategies

Teaching Tip: Conjunctions

Point out to students that in addition to the single conjunctions listed in the lesson, compound sentence parts can be joined by pairs of conjunctions such as *both . . . and, either . . . or, neither . . . nor, not only . . . but also,* and *whether . . . or.* (See Grammar Handbook 35, pages 663–667.)

Linking Grammar and Writing

Point out that using compound sentence parts is a way of relating connected ideas in writing. In addition, using compound sentence parts can help students streamline their writing. Suggest that students review one of their rough drafts to see how using compound sentence parts might improve their writing.

Humanities Connection

Art Note Shown are a *Kwele Initiation Mask* from the Congo and a *Coming-of-Age Mask* of the Biombo people of Zaire (artists unknown). A rite of passage, or initiation, is a ritual associated with a change of status for an individual and reinforces the bonds between the individual and society. The rites of passage is a universal theme in art and literature; and many cultures use stylized masks to represent the social rank—for example, adulthood—attained through initiation. Ask: What rites of passage are celebrated publicly in our society?

WRITING THEME   Comedy

You may want to encourage interested students to consider this theme as the basis for an independent or collaborative writing project.

A. Concept Check

Compound Sentence Parts
The compound parts are underlined on page.
1. radio, vaudeville, Direct Object
2. huge, ornate, Predicate Adjective
3. varied, exciting, Predicate Adjective
4. singers, comedians, Subject
5. audiences, hosts, Indirect Object
6. sang, danced, Verb
7. Movie stars, athletes, Subject
8. players, cowhands, Indirect Object; love, applause, Direct Object
9. booed, hissed, Verb
10. home, forerunner, Predicate Nominative

B. Drafting Skill

Eliminating Unnecessary Words
Answers will vary. See suggested answers below.
1. Lily Tomlin and Bill Cosby are fine comedians. (Subject)
2. Both created and portrayed unusual characters. (Verb)
3. Tomlin's characters are lively and realistic. (Predicate Adjective)
4. Tomlin's Ernestine, a telephone operator, is outrageous and endearing. (Predicate Adjective)
5. Comedy clubs and records gave Cosby his first successes. (Subject)
6. Cosby has written books and stories. (Direct Object)

| Predicate Nominatives | Carl Sandburg was a *poet, historian,* and *biographer.* |
| Predicate Adjectives | Often the weather was *clear* but *cold.* |

Sentence Diagraming   For information on diagraming sentences with compound parts, see pages 832–833.

Practice Your Skills

A. CONCEPT CHECK

Compound Sentence Parts   Write the compound parts in the following sentences. Identify the compound part by writing *Subject, Verb, Direct Object, Indirect Object, Predicate Nominative,* or *Predicate Adjective.* If there is no compound part, write *None.*

1. In the days before television, people enjoyed radio and vaudeville.
2. The old vaudeville theaters were huge and sometimes ornate.
3. The acts in a show were deliberately varied and exciting.
4. Many famous singers and comedians started their show business careers in vaudeville.
5. George Burns frequently tells audiences and talk-show hosts stories about his days "on the boards."
6. Fred Astaire sang and danced his way into movies from vaudeville.
7. Movie stars and athletes often appeared on the vaudeville stage.
8. The audiences gave singing baseball players and dancing cowhands their love and applause.
9. However, they often booed and hissed poorer acts off the stage.
10. The vaudeville theater was the home of American comedy and the forerunner of the television variety shows.

B. DRAFTING SKILL

Eliminating Unnecessary Words   Skillful writers eliminate unnecessary words. One way to do this is to use compound sentence parts. Combine the sentences below by using compound sentence parts. Tell which part of the sentence was made compound. Remember that compound subjects require a plural verb.

1. Lily Tomlin is a fine comedian. So is Bill Cosby.
2. Both created unusual characters. They portrayed them too.
3. Tomlin's characters are lively. They are realistic too.
4. Tomlin's Ernestine, a telephone operator, is outrageous. She is endearing too.
5. Comedy clubs gave Cosby his first successes. So did records.
6. Cosby has written books. He has written stories as well.

Writing Theme
Comedy

7. Cosby told audiences tales about Fat Albert. He told readers too.
8. Cosby treats childhood with great humor. Tomlin does also.
9. Tomlin's child character Edith Anne is frank. She is also funny.
10. Today Cosby and Tomlin are successful comedians. They are successful actors too.

C. APPLICATION IN WRITING

Writing a Critical Comparison   All people in show business have to deal with critics and criticism. Comedians are no exception, even though it is very difficult to explain humor. Choose two comedians or comic actors from television or movies. In a paragraph or two, explain ways in which they are similar and ways in which they are different. You may want to say what you like about each of them. Use compound sentence parts in several of your sentences.

CHECK POINT
PAGES 512–519

A. Subject Complements   Identify each italicized word as *Direct Object, Indirect Object, Predicate Nominative,* or *Predicate Adjective.*

1. Michelangelo was a great *artist.*
2. He has given the *world* grand and powerful works of art.
3. Several popes hired *him* as a painter, architect, and sculptor.
4. One of Michelangelo's works was a *tomb* ordered by Pope Julius II.
5. From 1508 to 1512 he painted the *ceiling* of the Sistine Chapel in Rome.
6. The paintings are astonishingly *beautiful.*
7. These frescoes show nine *scenes* from the Old Testament.
8. The ceiling became his most famous *achievement.*
9. In 1524 he designed a *library* for Pope Clement.
10. The Medici rulers gave *Michelangelo* many commissions.
11. He designed the *Medici Chapel* for them.
12. This project is more *complete* than any of his other large scuptural or architectural works.
13. He became chief *architect* for St. Peter's in Rome.
14. Michelangelo designed its monumental *dome.*
15. He remained *productive* as an artist well into his seventies.
16. His writings include some three hundred *sonnets.*
17. Michelangelo's reputation was *immense* in his own time.
18. His influence on Western art remains *unequalled.*
19. One other artist gave *Michelangelo* competition.
20. Leonardo da Vinci was his greatest *rival.*

Writing Theme
Great Artists

The Sentence and Its Parts   **519**

7. Cosby told audiences and readers tales about Fat Albert. (Indirect Object)
8. Cosby and Tomlin treat childhood with great humor. (Subject)
9. Tomlin's child character Elizabeth Anne is frank and funny. (Predicate Adjective)
10. Today Cosby and Tomlin are successful comedians and actors. (Predicate Nominative)

C. Application in Writing
Writing a Critical Comparison
Answers will vary.

CHECK POINT
PAGES 512–519

You may wish to use the following check-point exercises as an informal evaluation of student mastery of the concepts covered in this handbook.

WRITING THEME   Great Artists

You may wish to suggest that interested students consider using this theme as a subject for an assignment in a Writer's Workshop.

A. Subject Complements
1. Predicate Nominative
2. Indirect Object
3. Direct Object
4. Predicate Nominative
5. Direct Object
6. Predicate Adjective
7. Direct Object
8. Predicate Adjective
9. Direct Object
10. Indirect Object
11. Direct Object
12. Predicate Adjective
13. Predicate Nominative
14. Direct Object
15. Predicate Adjective
16. Direct Object
17. Predicate Adjective
18. Predicate Adjective
19. Indirect Object
20. Predicate Nominative

B. Compound Sentence Parts Write the compound sentence parts in the following sentences. Then tell whether each one is a *Compound Subject, Verb, Direct Object, Indirect Object, Predicate Nominative,* or *Predicate Adjective.*

1. Leonardo da Vinci was a great painter and scientist.
2. His brilliant mind and deep curiosity inspired his interest in a wide variety of subjects.
3. The young Leonardo studied art, engineering, and architecture.
4. Later he became a writer, inventor, botanist, biologist, and musician.
5. Two of his well-known masterworks were the *Mona Lisa* and the *Last Supper.*
6. Leonardo gave his landscapes and portraits a fresh approach.
7. His observations and sketches filled many notebooks.
8. Leonardo visualized and sketched ideas for many new machines.
9. His inventions were ingenious and amazingly precise.
10. Far ahead of his time, he invented a helicopter, bicycle, airplane, and parachute.
11. In fact, he made the first accurate drawings and paintings ever done of the human body.
12. Accuracy and precision were enormously important to Leonardo da Vinci.

Sketches of the human figure and a flying machine, by Leonardo da Vinci

Humanities Connection

Art Note *Proportions of the Human Figure* by Leonardo da Vinci (b. 1452, Italy, d. 1519) is one of the first accurate drawings of the human anatomy ever done. *Flying Machine* is only one example of his many ingenious inventions. Leonardo was the definitive Renaissance man. He excelled in virtually every intellectual pursuit. His genius ranged from classical painting and sculpture to engineering and science. When you consider Leonardo's genius and creativity, you can truly imagine that for him "there were not enough hours in the day." Ask: If you could interview Leonardo, what three questions would you ask him?

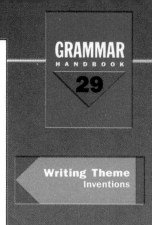

GRAMMAR
HANDBOOK
29

Writing Theme
Inventions

A. Sentence Fragments and Sentence Types   Some of the following groups of words are sentence fragments. On your paper, write *fragment* if the item is a fragment and rewrite it as a sentence. If the item is a sentence, identify it as *Declarative, Interrogative, Imperative,* or *Exclamatory* and add the correct end marks.

1. Scissors were invented during the Bronze Age.
2. In early forms, two blades were linked by a *C*-shaped spring.
3. Pivoted type of iron and stainless steel
4. Aren't scissors somehow associated with mortality in Greek mythology?
5. Wielded by Atropos, one of the three Fates
6. Sheared the thread of each mortal's life
7. Imagine needing two hands for scissors. or !
8. Did the Romans invent one-handed sheep shears?
9. Virtually identical to the type in use today
10. Scissors for domestic use became common in England during Elizabethan times.
11. What a long time ago that was!
12. Would you ever expect to import a pair of scissors?
13. Shears and scissors of high quality are produced in Sheffield, England.
14. Archaeological findings confirm the popularity of scissors all over the world.
15. Pairs of scissors roughly 3,500 year old

B. Simple Subjects and Verbs   Write each of the following sentences. Underline the simple subject once and the verb or verb phrase twice. Watch for unusual kinds of sentences. If the subject is not directly stated, write (*You*) in parentheses.

1. Simplicity is the key to a great invention.
2. Think of the changes in daily life during the last few decades. (You)
3. High technology has caused some of them.
4. Simple inventions, however, have been responsible for many other changes.
5. In just about any office, for example, there exist hundreds of simple, useful inventions.
6. Take the paperclip or the rubber band, for example. (You)
7. There are staplers, felt tip pens, thumbtacks.
8. In the time before word processors, consider how liquid correction fluid for typewriters changed office life. (You)
9. These simple devices seem to have been around forever.
10. Someone, however, invented each of them.

The Sentence
and Its Parts   **521**

Application and Review

These activities have been designed to allow your students to apply concepts presented in this handbook. Exercise A requires students to recognize sentence fragments and to identify types of sentences. Exercises B and C require students to identify simple and complete subjects and verbs, respectively. Exercise D requires students to identify direct objects, indirect objects, predicate nominatives, and predicate adjectives.

Additional Resources

- Tests and Assessment, Mastery Tests, pp. 35–42
- Elaboration, Revision, and Proofreading Worksheets, p. 21

WRITING THEME   Inventions

Encourage interested students to consider this writing theme as they develop topics for Writer's Workshop 5: Informative Exposition: Analysis.

A. Sentence Fragments and Sentence Types

Sentences from fragments will vary. See typical answers below. End marks are added to sentences on page.

1. Declarative
2. Declarative
3. F Later a pivoted type of scissors was constructed of iron and stainless steel.
4. Interrogative
5. F Scissors were wielded by Atropos, one of the three Fates.
6. F Atropos sheared the thread of each mortal's life.
7. Imperative
8. Interrogative
9. F Roman sheep shears were virtually identical to the type in use today.
10. Declarative
11. Exclamatory
12. Interrogative
13. Declarative
14. Declarative
15. F Archaeologists have found pairs of scissors roughly 3,500 years old.

B. Simple Subjects and Verbs

Answers are underlined on page.

C. Complete Subjects and Predicates

Answers are underlined on page.

D. Sentence Parts

Subjects and verbs are underlined on page.

1. inventor, PN
2. world, IO; invention, DO
3. childhood, DO
4. famous, PA
5. envy, PN
6. simple, PA
7. improvement, PN
8. bags, DO
9. intense, PA
10. machines, DO
11. her, IO; tasks, DO
12. machines, DO
13. dignified, PA; friendly, PA
14. member, PN
15. Knight, IO; patent, DO

C. Complete Subjects and Verbs   On your paper, write each of the following sentences. Underline the complete subject once and the complete predicate twice. Watch for unusual kinds of sentences. If the subject is not directly stated, write (*You*).

1. The Chinese invented paper over 2,000 years ago.
2. Have you heard of Cai Lun?
3. Some people credit him with the invention of paper in A.D. 105.
4. There is no truth to this story, however.
5. From Shensi province have come samples of much older paper.
6. Did the Chinese invent printing too?
7. First there was printing from large stone blocks.
8. Think of the importance of this invention! (You)
9. Even more important was the invention of movable type.
10. About 1045, Bi Sheng made characters in clay.
11. He set them in wax.
12. From the inked characters came the printed words.
13. Imagine the impact of this invention! (You)
14. How did printing reach the West from China?
15. It might have come over the Silk Road to Arabia.

D. Sentence Parts   Write the following sentences. Underline the subject once and the verb twice. Above each Direct Object (*DO*), Indirect Object (*IO*), Predicate Nominative (*PN*), or Predicate Adjective (*PA*) write the appropriate abbreviation. Some parts may be compound.

1. Margaret E. Knight was a very productive inventor.
2. She gave the world her first invention at the age of twelve.
3. Later in life, she recalled her childhood.
4. "I was famous for my kites."
5. "My sleds were the envy of all the boys in town."
6. Knight's first patented invention was simple.
7. It was an improvement on a paper-feeding machine.
8. With her invention, the machine could fold square-bottomed paper bags.
9. Knight's interest in heavy machinery was intense.
10. She improved and created machines for the textile, paper, shoe, and building-construction industries.
11. Sometimes factories gave her specific tasks.
12. At other times, Knight perfected her machines independently.
13. According to reports, Margaret Knight was dignified but friendly.
14. She was a respected member of the manufacturing community.
15. The U.S. Patent Office gave Knight her last patent after her death at seventy-six.

On the Lightside

WRITER'S RULES

Readers of this column often send in original material they hope to see us publish. Here are *my* guidelines for good writing for those potential *Omni* contributors.

"Hang him, you idiots! Hang him! . . . 'String-him-up' is a figure of speech!"

The FAR SIDE Cartoon by Gary Larsen reprinted by permission of Chronicle Features. San Francisco, California

- Avoid colloquial stuff.
- Do not use a foreign term when there is an adequate English *quid pro quo.*
- It behooves the writer to avoid archaic expressions.
- Do not use hyperbole; not one writer in a million can use it effectively.
- Avoid cliches like the plague.
- Mixed metaphors are a pain in the neck and should be thrown out the window.
- Placing a comma between subject and predicate, is not correct.
- Parenthetical words however must be enclosed in commas.
- Consult a dictionary frequently to avoid mispelling.
- Don't be redundant.
- Don't repeat yourself or say what you have said before.
- Remember to never split an infinitive.
- The passive voice should not be used.
- Use the apostrophe in it's proper place and omit it when its not needed.
- Don't use no double negatives.
- Proofread carefully to see if you have any words out.
- Hopefully, you will use words correctly, irregardless of how others use them.
- Never use a long word when a diminutive one will do.
- Subject and verb always has to agree.
- No sentence fragments.
- Remember to finish what

Scot Morris

This feature humorously parodies a grammatical list of "do's and don't's" that professional writers often encounter. You might have individual students explain the error or stylistic faux pas in each rule. Then encourage the class to make up its own list of writer's rules, using other familiar grammatical maxims, as in "Avoid overuse of excessive, extraneous, distracting, and redundant modifiers."

Writing Complete Sentences

What Is a Sentence Fragment?

Objectives

- To identify complete sentences and sentence fragments
- **Writing** To demonstrate revision skills by rewriting sentence fragments as complete sentences
- **Writing** To use sentence fragments for effect in writing

Teaching Strategies

Teaching Tip: Context

Remind students that very few of us use complete sentences all the time, especially in speaking. When we talk, however, the immediate context of our conversation, as well as our gestures and intonations, makes our meaning clear. But in writing, the writer and the reader are usually at a distance—in both time and space—and so fragments are more difficult to interpret.

 Individualizing Instruction

ESL Students In some languages, it is grammatically correct for the subject to drop out. (Spanish, Vietnamese, and Korean are three examples.) Explain to these students that in English the subject cannot be inferred from the inflected verb and therefore must be stated.

GRAMMAR
HANDBOOK
30

Writing Complete Sentences

WHAT IS A SENTENCE FRAGMENT?

A group of words that is only part of a sentence is called a sentence fragment.

A sentence fragment is often confusing because it does not express a complete thought. Sometimes the subject is left out, and the reader wonders *whom* or *what* the sentence is about. At other times the verb is omitted. Then the reader wonders *what happened?* or *what about it?*

Fragment   Shifted into lower gear. (Who shifted? The subject is missing.)

Sentence   The trucker shifted into a lower gear.

Fragment   The quarterback near the ten-yard line. (What happened? The verb is missing.)

Sentence   The quarterback fumbled near the ten-yard line.

Sometimes both the subject and verb are missing.

Fragment   In the middle of the lake. (Who or what is in the middle of the lake? What is happening there?)

Sentence   A canoe tipped over in the middle of the lake.

Fragments Due to Incomplete Thoughts

When you are in a hurry, you sometimes jot down only bits of ideas. As a writer, you understand these fragments of ideas. However, they will probably seem unclear to your reader because at least part of the subject or predicate is missing.

Look at this note left by a student. What does this series of fragments mean?

> Up late listening to birthday albums. Forgot alarm. Borrowed money from jar. Working late—more tonight.

These complete sentences show what the writer meant:

> I was up late listening to the albums you gave me for my birthday. I forgot to set the alarm and was late this morning. I borrowed lunch money from the emergency jar. I'm working late today—I'll explain more when I get home tonight.

524 Grammar Handbook

Fragments Due to Incorrect Punctuation

All sentences end with one of three punctuation marks: a period, a question mark, or an exclamation point. Sometimes a writer uses one of these punctuation marks too soon. The result is an incomplete idea, or sentence fragment.

Fragment	The storm struck. Without warning.
Sentence	The storm struck without warning.
Fragment	We canceled the picnic. And went home.
Sentence	We canceled the picnic and went home.
Fragment	Everyone's efforts had been wasted. Because no one checked the weather forecast.
Sentence	Everyone's efforts had been wasted because no one checked the weather forecast.
Fragment	What lesson did we learn? About planning ahead?
Sentence	What lesson did we learn about planning ahead?

Fragments Used for Effect

Professional writers know how and when to use fragments for special purposes.

> "It's because," she hiccups, "I *am* too old. Old and funny."
> "Not funny. Fun. More fun than anybody."
> **Truman Capote, "A Christmas Memory"**

> And, indeed, it is a kind of ocean. Scented acres of holiday trees, prickly-leafed holly.
> **Truman Capote, "A Christmas Memory"**

> Despair? Did someone say despair was a question in the world?
> **Lorraine Hansberry, *To Be Young, Gifted, and Black***

The first example above conveys a character's feelings through natural-sounding dialogue; the second sets a scene in a succinct, or brief, way; the third uses a single word to emphasize an idea.

To use sentence fragments effectively, a professional writer must create surrounding sentences that supply needed information and offer the reader a complete idea. If you intentionally use a fragment in your own writing, check to see if you are communicating clearly. (Have you written an intentional fragment that really works, or is it a confusing fragment that needs revision?) Remember that complete sentences usually are the best means for expressing ideas well.

Writing
—**TIP**—
To avoid sentence errors, remind yourself to use a complete sentence to express a complete thought.

Speaking and Listening

Some students may recognize sentence fragments more easily when they are read aloud. Ask a volunteer to read the student note in the text and then read the revised version. Help students to hear the choppy "sound" of the fragments as compared with the flowing "sound" of the complete sentences.

Because sentence fragments often cause confusion for readers, encourage students to avoid them in their public writing. Ask students to review one of their rough drafts to find sentence fragments caused by the incorrect insertion of end punctuation. Have students rewrite these fragments as complete sentences.

Teaching Tip: Purpose of Fragments

Point out that many slogans such as "No Smoking" are made up of fragments. These fragments, in conjunction with colorful graphics and symbols such as Smokey the Bear, convey a memorable message. Ask students to brainstorm a list of slogans based on fragments and discuss the differing effects they evoke.

 Individualizing Instruction

ESL Students Remind these students that although oral English often includes sentence fragments, sentence fragments are not acceptable in writing, unless used for effect.

> **Additional Resources**
> • Tests and Assessment, Pretests, pp. 11–12
> • Grammar and Usage Practice Book, pp. 19–20

Literature Connection

Linking Grammar and Literature Point out that the following famous lines from Shakespeare's *Romeo and Juliet* are fragments:

A plague o' both your houses! (111, 1, 86)
Unseemly woman in a seeming man! (111, 3, 116)

Ask students to reread these lines and the surrounding passages to identify the context clues Shakespeare uses to make the fragments clear to his reader.

Writing Theme

You may want to suggest that interested students note this theme in their journals to consider as a topic for a short story or a personal narrative.

Managing the Paper Load

Prepare and make answer key material for Exercise A available to students for self-check. Then have students do Exercises B and C for a grade.

WRITING THEME   Families in Literature

A. Concept Check
Fragments
   1. S
   2. F
   3. S
   4. F
   5. S
   6. S
   7. F
   8. F
   9. F
  10. S
  11. S
  12. F
  13. F
  14. S
  15. S

B. Revision Skill
Correcting Unclear Fragments
Answers wil vary. See typical answers below. As an alternative strategy, allow students to combine fragments correctly with other complete sentences to form new sentences.

   Louisa May Alcott made an important contribution to American literature. Her honest, human portraits of family life had immediate and wide appeal. The most famous of her books, *Little Women,* was an immediate bestseller. The publisher could not keep up with the orders from bookstores. Thousands of them poured in from all over the country. Young women strongly identified with the sisters in the book. The independent, tomboyish Jo especially appealed to them. Millions of tears were shed over the terrible illness of little Beth. She had always been the gentlest of the sisters. Alcott's faithful readers had no idea that she was also the author of dozens of stories of a very different kind. Her lively fiction included adventure stories and popular thrillers.

Writing
—— **TIP** ——

A fragment is not an effective device if it causes a reader to pause in confusion.

Practice Your Skills

A. CONCEPT CHECK

Fragments   Write *S* for each group of words that is a sentence. Write *F* for each fragment.

1. Stories about families have always been popular.
2. Often, the stories of Greek mythology.
3. Brothers are likely to be quarreling with their sisters for reasons of jealousy or greed.
4. For example, Poseidon, the god of the sea, with Demeter, the goddess of the harvest.
5. During the Middle Ages, family stories in literature often included conflict.
6. One son often battles with another son for possession of the throne.
7. Destroyed each other in order to take control of the kingdom.
8. Bickering and jealousy even in the legends of King Arthur and his knights.
9. Arthur's half-sister, Morgan Le Fay, his sworn enemy.
10. The second wife of King Melodeus tried to poison the king's son Tristam because she was jealous.
11. In Elizabethan times, the outcomes of family conflicts in Shakespeare's plays and could be either tragic or comic.
12. King Lear and his three daughters or Petruchio and his wife Katherina, for instance.
13. In the nineteenth century, novels more with everyday life.
14. Russian novelist Leo Tolstoy suggested that readers preferred stories about families in conflict.
15. "All happy families are alike," he wrote, "but an unhappy family is unhappy after its own fashion."

B. REVISION SKILL

Correcting Unclear Fragments   Improve the following paragraph by rewriting the five fragments as complete sentences.

> Louisa May Alcott made an important contribution to American literature. Her honest, human portraits of family life. The most famous of her books, *Little Women,* was an immediate bestseller. The publisher could not keep up with the orders from bookstores. Poured in from all over the country. Young women strongly identified with the sisters in the book. Especially the independent, tomboyish Jo. Millions of tears were shed over the terrible illness of little Beth. The gentlest of the

sisters. Alcott's faithful readers had no idea that she was also the author of dozens of stories of a very different kind. Including adventure stories and popular thrillers.

C. APPLICATION IN LITERATURE

Using Fragments Effectively As you have learned, professional writers sometimes use fragments for special purposes. Find the fragments in the following passage. Write them on your paper and then add words to make them complete sentences. Compare the two versions and suggest why Saroyan used the fragments in his writing.

(1) [Homer McCauley] got out of bed and brought out his body-building course from New York and began reading the instructions for the day. (2) His brother Ulysses watched, as he always did . . . . (3) After some ordinary preliminary exercises, including deep breathing, Homer lay flat on his back and lifted his legs stiffly from the floor.

(4) "What's that?" Ulysses said.

(5) "Exercises."

(6) "What for?"

(7) "Muscle."

(8) "Going to be the strongest man in the world?"

(9) "Naah."

(10) "What then?"

(11) "You go back to sleep," Homer said.

(12) Ulysses got back in bed but sat up, watching.

(13) At last Homer began to get dressed.

(14) "Where you going?"

(15) "School."

William Saroyan, _The Human Comedy_

C. Application in Literature
Using Fragments Effectively

Answers will vary. See typical answers below. Fragments are underlined on page.

5. "These are exercises."
6. "What are they for?"
7. "I'm building muscle."
8. "Are you going to be the strongest man in the world?"
9. "Naah, I'm not."
10. "What are you going to be then?"
14. "Where are you going?"
15. "I'm going to school."

Saroyan used fragments to represent conversation. In conversations, people often use fragments.

What Is a Run-on Sentence?

Objectives

- To identify run-on sentences
- **Writing** To demonstrate revision skills by correcting run-on sentences

Teaching Strategies

Critical Thinking

Analyzing In order to identify run-on sentences, students need to be able to recognize the two sets of subjects and verbs that make them up. You might name these sentence parts for the first sentence (contestant hesitated; buzzer sounded), and then ask volunteers to identify the subjects and verbs in the remaining run-ons.

 Individualizing Instruction

Basic Students Remind students that they will need to decide which commas lead to run-on sentences in the exercises. One useful strategy for these students is to check to see which exercise items contain more than one complete thought.

Teaching Tip: Linking Ideas

Help students see that in the process of correcting run-on sentences they can more clearly show the relationship of ideas. For example, using the connecting word *but* shows contrast; the word *consequently* shows a cause-and-effect relationship. Have students discuss and evaluate the relationships between ideas suggested by other connecting words used to correct run-on sentences in the examples and exercises in the text.

WHAT IS A RUN-ON SENTENCE?

A run-on sentence is two or more sentences written incorrectly as one.

A run-on sentence is confusing because it does not show where one idea ends and another one begins. A run-on often occurs because a writer fails to use an end mark to signal the end of a sentence.

Run-on	The contestant hesitated too long the buzzer sounded.
Correct	The contestant hesitated too long. The buzzer sounded.

Another type of run-on error is called a **comma splice** or **comma fault.** In this case, the writer mistakenly uses a comma instead of a period.

Comma Splice	Ray began as a backup singer, now he sings lead.
Correct	Ray began as a backup singer. Now he sings lead.

Correcting Run-on Sentences

The run-on sentences above were rewritten as two sentences. There are several other ways to correct run-ons. If the ideas expressed are closely related, you may wish to join them in a single sentence.

Run-on	Susan already excels in art, now she wants to study music.
Correct	Susan already excels in art, and now she wants to study music.

Run-on	Mary Alice was shy at first, she quickly felt more at ease.
Correct	Mary Alice was shy at first, but she quickly felt more at ease.

You can join sentences with a semicolon.

Run-on	The judge entered the courtroom, everyone rose.
Correct	The judge entered the courtroom; everyone rose.

You can join sentences with a semicolon and a conjunctive adverb followed by a comma. See page 666 for a list of conjunctive adverbs.

Run-on	The evidence was overwhelming the jury returned a verdict of guilty.
Correct	The evidence was overwhelming; consequently, the jury returned a verdict of guilty.

Practice Your Skills

A. CONCEPT CHECK

Run-on Sentences Write *R* for each run-on sentence. Write *S* for each correctly written sentence. Rewrite the run-on sentences correctly.

1. Lawyers have not always gone to law schools, they learned their profession in law offices.
2. In both England and America, before the American Revolution, the clerks in law offices included many students.
3. Young men were apprentices to older lawyers, at that time, only men could practice law.
4. The young law student served a lengthy apprenticeship after that the student took an examination.
5. Some young men passed the examination, they became attorneys.
6. In the late 1770's, some universities began to offer lectures on law by famous lawyers.
7. Later, in 1817, Harvard Law School was founded, it is the oldest law school in the United States.
8. Today, most major universities in the United States have law schools.
9. The classes in these schools are made up of men and women of every background.
10. Many of the graduates never practice law instead they become social workers, politicians, or diplomats.

B. REVISION SKILL

Avoiding Run-on Sentences Run-on sentences make writing difficult to read and understand. An important part of revising your work is being sure to eliminate these errors. Find the run-on sentences in these paragraphs and rewrite the paragraphs correctly.

The first female lawyer in the United States was Arabella Babb Mansfield, she graduated from Iowa Wesleyan College in 1866. For the next three years, she worked as an apprentice in a law office. Her husband also studied law both of them took the Iowa bar examination.

Mrs. Mansfield passed the examination with high scores. Her husband passed, too, he was automatically permitted to practice law. In fact, all successful male examinees were automatically admitted to the Iowa Bar Association, Mrs. Mansfield was not.

Arabella Mansfield took her case to court. In June of 1869, a judge ruled in her favor, she was admitted to the bar.

Complete Sentences **529**

Additional Resources
• Grammar and Usage Practice Book, pp. 21–22

WRITING THEME Lawyers

Encourage interested students to think about how they might narrow this topic to use as a possible subject for a Writer's Workshop assignment.

A. Concept Check
Run-on Sentences
Students' sentences will vary. See typical answers below.
1. R Lawyers have not always gone to law schools. Formerly, they learned their profession in law offices.
2. S
3. R Young men were apprentices to older lawyers. At that time, only men could practice law.
4. R The young law student served a lengthy apprenticeship. After that, the student took an examination.
5. R Some young men passed the examination; then they became attorneys.
6. S
7. R Later, in 1817, Harvard Law School was founded. It is the oldest law school in the United States.
8. S
9. S
10. R Many of the graduates never practice law; instead, they become social workers, politicians, or diplomats.

B. Revision Skill
Avoiding Run-on Sentences
Answers will vary. See suggested answers below.
The first female lawyer in the United States was Arabella Babb Mansfield. She graduated from Iowa Wesleyan College in 1866. For the next three years, she worked as an apprentice in a law office. Her husband also studied law. Both of them took the Iowa bar examination.
Mrs. Mansfield passed the examination with high scores. Her husband passed, too. He was automatically permitted to practice law. In fact, all successful male examinees were automatically admitted to the Iowa Bar Association. Mrs. Mansfield was not.
Arabella Mansfield took her case to court. In June of 1869, a judge ruled in her favor. She was admitted to the bar.

Writing Theme
Orson Welles

Orson Welles, starring in the role of *Citizen Kane*, 1941

530 Grammar Handbook

C. APPLICATION IN WRITING

Transcripts   Imagine yourself learning to be a court reporter. Since an important part of your job will be to record accurately and quickly everything that happens and everything that is said in the courtroom, you are practicing writing with time limits.

Choose any scene, event, or conversation, preferably one that is fast paced. Give yourself a time limit of three minutes and write, as rapidly as you can, everything you see and hear. Then read through your account and write a paragraph from it, changing fragments and run-ons into correct sentences.

CHECK POINT
PAGES 524–530

A. Write *S* for each group of words that is a complete sentence. For each sentence fragment, write *F*. Then add words or combine ideas to change the fragments into sentences.

1. The remarkable movie *Citizen Kane*.
2. About a colorful newspaper publisher.
3. The character of Kane was based on William Randolph Hearst.
4. Portraying a publishing tycoon's ambition, ruthlessness, and love.
5. The brilliant young director, Orson Welles, also played the lead.
6. Appeared in movie theaters in 1941.
7. New and intriguing filmmaking techniques were used.
8. Revolutionized the use of the soundtrack.
9. Hearst tried to stop its release.
10. Considered one of the greatest American films of all time.

B. Write *S* for each group of words that is a correctly written sentence. For each run-on sentence, write *R*. Then rewrite each run-on sentence correctly.

1. Orson Welles even arrived in Hollywood as a celebrity he was already considered a "boy genius."
2. At twenty-two Welles founded the Mercury Theater in New York.
3. He also created the Mercury Theater of the Air, it was a radio program.
4. He broadcast *The War of the Worlds* and caused a national panic.
5. People truly thought the earth had been invaded by Martians.
6. Welles produced, directed, wrote, and starred in *Citizen Kane*.
7. He made many movies, most were important in film history.
8. He was known for experimentation and unusual film techniques.

A. Complete Sentences, Fragments, and Run-ons Write *S* for each correctly written sentence, *F* for each fragment, and *R* for each run-on. Then rewrite all fragments and run-ons as complete sentences.

1. Many mystery writers with pseudonyms, or pen names.
2. Writers famous for other types of writing.
3. For example, C. Day Lewis wrote poetry under his own name, he wrote mysteries as Nicholas Blake.
4. A writer's pen name may even be an aristocratic title.
5. One such writer of detective stories, Edward John Moreton Drax Plunkett, became famous under his short pen name, Lord Dunsany.
6. Usually, a pseudonym masks one writer sometimes it masks two of them.
7. Two cousins, Frederic Dannay and Manfred B. Lee, wrote their detective fiction as Ellery Queen.
8. Frequently the pen names chosen by writers are men's names.
9. Often, however, a woman behind a pseudonym.
10. Anthony Gilbert is really Lucy Malleson, Gordon Daviot is Elizabeth MacKintosh.
11. One of the most famous names in mystery writing, Agatha Christie, not a pseudonym.
12. Born Agatha Mary Clarissa Miller in 1890.
13. Married first to Colonel Archibald Christie but later to Max Mallowan.
14. Dozens of her detective novels bear the Christie name, she published romantic fiction as Mary Westmacott.
15. Sometimes the mystery is who, exactly, wrote the mystery!

B. Correcting Fragments and Run-on Sentences The following paragraphs contain fragments and run-ons. Rewrite the paragraphs and correct these errors. Check your capitalization and punctuation carefully.

You may be familiar with Scotland Yard. From watching British mystery movies. However, it isn't in Scotland and it isn't a yard, it is a nickname. For the metropolitan Police Force of London.

Scotland Yard got its name from a short street in London. This street was the site of a palace. Where visiting Scottish kings stayed. In 1829 the palace became London's police center. In 1890 the police moved into offices on the Thames Embankment, these offices were named New Scotland Yard.

Writing Theme
Names and
Pen Names

Application and Review

These activities have been designed to allow your students to apply concepts presented in this handbook. Exercises A, B, and C require students to recognize and correct sentence fragments and run-ons. Exercise D challenges students to construct a paragraph based on fragments and run-ons.

> ### Additional Resources
> - Grammar and Usage Practice Book, Mastery Tests, pp. 43–46
> - Elaboration, Revision, and Proofreading Worksheets, p. 22

WRITING THEME   Names and Pen
                Names

Invite interested students to explore how they might develop this theme into a possible topic for a Writer's Workshop assignment.

A. Complete Sentences, Fragments, and Run-ons
Students' sentences will vary. See typical answers below.
  1. F There are many mystery writers with pseudonyms, or pen names.
  2. F Some are writers famous for other types of writing.
  3. R For example, C. Day Lewis wrote poetry under his own name; he wrote mysteries as Nicholas Blake.
  4. S
  5. S
  6. R Usually, a pseudonym masks one writer. Sometimes it masks two of them.
  7. S
  8. S
  9. F Often, however, there is a woman behind a pseudonym.
  10. R Anthony Gilbert is really Lucy Malleson. Gordon Daviot is Elizabeth MacKintosh.
  11. F One of the most famous names in mystery writing, Agatha Christie, is not a pseudonym.
  12. F She was born Agatha Mary Clarissa Miller in 1890.
  13. F She was married first to Colonel Archibald Christie but later to Max Mallowan.
  14. R Dozens of her detective novels bear the Christie name. She published romantic fiction as Mary Westmacott.
  15. S

B. Correcting Fragments and Run-on Sentences
You may be familiar with Scotland Yard from watching British mystery movies. However, it isn't in Scotland, and it isn't a yard. It is a nickname for the Metropolitan Police Force of London.

Scotland Yard got its name from a short street in London. This street was the site of a palace where visiting Scottish kings stayed. In 1829 the palace became London's police center. In 1890 the police moved into offices on the Thames Embankment. These offices were named New Scotland Yard.

C. Proofreading
Errors are underlined on page.

Names of some flowers come from Greek history and mythology. The gentian is an example. It was named after King Gentius of ancient Illyria. The iris was named after Iris, goddess of the rainbow. There is a reason for its name. Like a rainbow, irises come in a variety of colors. The narcissus bears the name of a handsome youth. He so loved gazing at his own reflection in a pool of water that he finally pined away and was turned into a flower. These yellow trumpetlike flowers beside a pond suggest the nodding head of Narcissus. The hyacinth's name also has a story. One day Apollo was throwing the discus with a young man named Hyacinthus. The god of the west wind, Zephyrus, was angry with Hyacinthus. He caused the discus to strike the young man and kill him. From his blood sprang the flower that now bears his name.

D. Writing Complete Sentences
Answers will vary.

A good paragraph will contain no fragments or run-on sentences. It should, however, contain complete sentences, as shown in the examples below.

Criminals in real life and in fiction eventually discover that there is no perfect crime. Although they use false names, false beards, and false clues to disguise their identities, criminals always leave a trail of some type.

The lives of detectives in real life and in fiction are filled with danger and adventure. They discover evidence, decipher clues such as fingerprints, and solve mysteries. As members of local law enforcement agencies, detectives capture and bring criminals to justice.

C. Proofreading The following first draft of a paragraph contains sentence fragments and run-ons, as well as errors in punctuation, spelling, and usage. Rewrite the paragraph, correcting the errors. Then proofread your work carefully. (You may use a dictionary for help.)

Names of some flowers come from Greek history and mythology. The gentian is an example, it was named after King Gentius of aincient Illyria. The iris named after iris, goddess of the rainbow. There is a reason for its name, like a rainbow, irises come in a variety of colors. The narcissus bares the name of a handsome youth. So loved gazing at his own reflecshun in a pool of water that he finally pined away and was turned into a flower. These yellow trumpetlike flowers besides a pond suggest the nodding head of Narcissus. The hyacinths name also has a story, one day Apollo was throwing the discus. With a young man named Hyacinthus. The god of the west wind, Zephyrus was angry with Hyacinthus. Caused the discus to strike the young man and kill him. From his blood sprang the flower that now bears his name.

D. Writing Complete Sentences A first step in writing is to make notes of ideas to develop. These notes usually are in the form of phrases, rather than complete sentences. Use some of the following phrases to write a paragraph. Be sure that your paragraph contains no fragments or run-on sentences.

1. Detectives and criminals in real life and fiction.
2. False names, false beards, false clues
3. Disguise their identities
4. Leave a trail of some type
5. Discover evidence and solve mysteries
6. Filled with danger and adventure
7. Clues such as fingerprints
8. Caught and brought to justice
9. Local law enforcement agencies
10. No perfect crime

Using Nouns

WHAT IS A NOUN?

A noun is a word that names a person, place, thing, or idea.

Persons	aunt, doctor, Gregory, Anita Cruz
Places	kitchen, hotel, Savannah, West Virginia
Things	blanket, mirror, lightning, Statue of Liberty
Ideas	freedom, intelligence, sincerity, democracy

Practice Your Skills

CONCEPT CHECK

Understanding Nouns Make four columns labeled *Persons, Places, Things,* and *Ideas.* Find at least fifteen nouns in the following paragraphs and list each in the proper column.

(1) At that time, Shozo Shimada was Seattle's most successful Japanese businessman. (2) He owned a chain of stores which extended not only from Vancouver to Portland, but to cities in Japan as well. (3) He had come to America in 1880, penniless but enterprising, and sought work as a laborer. (4) It wasn't long, however, before he saw the futility of trying to compete with American laborers whose bodies were twice his in muscle and bulk. (5) He knew he would never go far as a laborer, but he did possess another skill that could give him a start toward better things. (6) He knew how to sew. (7) He set aside his shovel, bought a second-hand sewing machine, and hung a dressmaker's sign in his window. (8) He was in business.

(9) In those days there were some Japanese women in Seattle who had neither homes nor families nor sewing machines and [who] were delighted to find a friendly Japanese person to do some sewing for them. (10) They flocked to Mr. Shimada with bolts of cloth, elated to discover a dressmaker who could speak their native tongue and sew western-styled dresses for them. (11) My father came to America in 1906 when he was not yet twenty-one. . . . (12) He landed in Seattle on a bleak January day . . . (13) and then allowed himself one day of rest to restore his sagging spirits . . . (14) He went to see Mr. Shozo Shimada to whom he carried a letter of introduction.

Yoshiko Uchida, "Of Dry Goods and Black Bow Ties"

GRAMMAR HANDBOOK 31

Writing Theme
Success Factors

Grammar Handbook 31:
Using Nouns

What Is a Noun?

Objective

- To identify nouns

Teaching Strategies

Teaching Tip: Nouns

Students may need additional help in identifying ideas that nouns can name. Ask students to generate nouns that refer to qualities (such as sincerity and intelligence), doctrines (such as democracy and equality), and feelings (such as enthusiasm and suspicion).

> ### Additional Resources
> - Tests and Assessment, Pretests, pp. 13–14
> - Grammar and Usage Practice Book, pp. 23–24

WRITING THEME   Success Factors

Concept Check
Understanding Nouns   Student answers should be in columns that contain at least fifteen of the following nouns.

Persons:	Shozo Shimada, businessman, laborer, laborers, women, families, person, Mr. Shimada, dressmaker, father, Mr. Shozo Shimada
Places:	Vancouver, Portland, cities, Japan, America, Seattle
Things:	time, chain, stores, 1880, work, bodies, muscle, bulk, things, shovel, sewing machine, sign, window, business, days, homes, sewing machines, sewing, bolts, cloth, tongue, dresses, 1906, day, letter
Ideas:	futility, skill, start, rest, spirits, introduction

Kinds of Nouns

Objectives

- To identify common, proper, concrete, abstract, collective, and compound nouns
- **Writing** To employ the revision technique of replacing vague words with precise nouns
- **Writing** To use specific nouns in description

Teaching Strategies

Linking Grammar and Literature

Give students copies of the poem "Jabberwocky" by Lewis Carroll. Ask them to list the recognizable nouns in the poem and to substitute an English noun for each fictitious one. Urge students to include common, proper, abstract, concrete, collective, and compound nouns in their substitutions. Ask them to discuss the clues they used to identify each Jabberwocky noun; for example, the letter s signaling a plural or its position after "the."

 Individualizing Instruction

ESL Students These students will also need to distinguish between countable and uncountable nouns. All abstract nouns are uncountable. Some concrete nouns, such as *water* and *gold*, are also uncountable. Remind them that uncountable nouns do not have plural forms. Some uncountable nouns, however, end in s (news, politics).

Remind ESL students also that a collective noun as the subject of a sentence usually takes the singular form of the verb. ("The group is ready to go.")

Writing
—**TIP**—
Choose the noun that names exactly what you mean. Don't write *bird* if you mean *canary*.

KINDS OF NOUNS

Nouns may be classified in several ways.

Common and Proper Nouns

A common noun is a general name for a person, place, thing, or idea. A proper noun is the name of a particular person, place, thing, or idea.

Look at the following examples. As you can see, proper nouns begin with capital letters, and they may consist of more than one word.

Common Nouns	Proper Nouns
city	Burlington
mayor	Mayor Ortiz
game	Super Bowl
street	Storrow Drive
river	Rio Grande

Concrete and Abstract Nouns

A concrete noun names an object that can be seen, heard, smelled, touched, or tasted. An abstract noun names something that cannot be perceived through the senses.

Concrete Nouns	Abstract Nouns
Marcia	kindness
thunder	skill
perfume	truth
water	generosity
banana	courage
rocket	sorrow

Collective and Compound Nouns

A collective noun names a group of people or things.

committee	club	team	herd
crowd	class	flock	family

A compound noun contains two or more words. It may be written as one word, as two words, or with a hyphen.

sunlamp	ice hockey	one-half
earthworm	light bulb	great-aunt
bookcase	Main Street	runner-up

Practice Your Skills

A. CONCEPT CHECK

Kinds of Nouns   Write the underlined nouns in each sentence. Identify each noun as *Common, Proper, Collective,* or *Compound.* All nouns will fit at least one category, and some will fit more than one.

> **Example**   The <u>stagehands</u> are a helpful <u>group</u>.
> stagehands—Common, Compound
> group—Common, Collective

When you have finished, write three of the underlined nouns that are *Concrete* and two that are *Abstract.*

1. The <u>process</u> of producing a play can take many <u>weeks</u> or even months.
2. It begins with careful research by the <u>director</u> and a <u>team</u> of designers.
3. They try to imagine how the play—for example, Shakespeare's tragedy <u>*Hamlet*</u>—should be presented on their particular type of <u>stage</u>.
4. The shape of the <u>theater</u> will affect how the <u>audience</u> experiences the action of the play.
5. The director and the costume and set designers act as a <u>committee</u> in producing the play.
6. <u>*Hamlet,*</u> like many <u>cliffhangers</u>, is full of both surprises and <u>suspense</u>, especially the scenes with the ghost of Hamlet's father.
7. In this drama about a <u>crown prince</u> of Denmark, <u>Shakespeare</u> explores <u>emotions</u> beneath the surfaces of complicated family <u>relationships</u>.
8. The <u>set</u> and costumes for this drama should express the <u>darkness</u> of the emotions and events that lie at the heart of a tragedy.
9. For this reason, the <u>costume designer</u> avoids creating clothing based on cheerful <u>colors</u>, seeking instead to clothe the actors in shades of grey and black.
10. As a comment on some troublesome situation, <u>people</u> often quote this line from <u>*Hamlet:*</u> "Something is rotten in the state of <u>Denmark.</u>"

Using Nouns   **535**

Additional Resources
• Grammar and Usage Practice Book, pp. 25–26

WRITING THEME   Theater

Recommend that interested students note this theme in their journals as a possible topic for a current or future Writer's Workshop assignment.

A. Concept Check
Kinds of Nouns
　1. process—Common, Abstract; weeks—Common, Abstract
　2. director—Common, Concrete; team—Common, Collective, Concrete
　3. *Hamlet*—Proper, Concrete; stage—Common, Concrete
　4. theater—Common, Concrete; audience—Common, Collective, Concrete
　5. committee—Common, Collective, Concrete
　6. *Hamlet*—Proper, Concrete; cliffhangers—Common, Compound, Abstract; suspense—Common, Abstract
　7. crown prince—Common, Compound, Concrete; Shakespeare—Proper, Concrete; emotions—Common, Abstract; relationships—Common, Abstract
　8. set—Common, Concrete; darkness—Common, Abstract
　9. costume designer—Common, Compound, Concrete; colors—Common, Concrete
　10. people—Common, Collective, Concrete; *Hamlet,* Proper, Concrete; Denmark—Proper, Concrete

The Uses of Nouns

Objective

- To identify nouns used as subjects, direct objects, indirect objects, and predicate nominatives

Teaching Strategies

Critical Thinking

Classifying Have students generate sentences that use nouns as subjects, direct objects, indirect objects, and predicate nominatives. Ask volunteers to identify the functions of these nouns in the sentences according to the four categories.

Teaching Tip: Uses of Nouns

Remind students that the subject of a sentence tells what the sentence is about. The direct object receives the action of the verb. The indirect object tells to whom, for whom, to what, or for what an action is performed. A predicate nominative follows a linking verb and renames the subject of the sentence.

Linking Grammar and Writing

Point out that precise word choice is an important part of effective writing. For example, in a description, the use of specific nouns helps the reader form a clear picture of the subject. Encourage students to review one of their rough drafts to see how they might use specific nouns to improve their writing.

> **Additional Resources**
> - Grammar and Usage Practice Book, pp. 27–28

B. REVISION SKILL

Precise Word Choice Good writers think carefully about word choices. For example, using *canoe* instead of *boat* paints a concrete and specific picture for the reader. Improve the following paragraphs by replacing the vague underlined words with precise nouns. You may use a dictionary or thesaurus for help.

(1) A play director tries to match his or her <u>thought</u> of the characters to flesh-and-blood actors. (2) During tryouts, the theater lobby echoes with the <u>talk</u> of actors hoping for parts in the play. (3) Once a cast has been chosen, the director becomes the actors' <u>helper</u>.

(4) Between rehearsals, actors memorize their lines and quickly grab some <u>food</u>. (5) They may rush to the wardrobe room for their <u>clothes</u>. (6) One actor may be insisting that he must wear a <u>hat</u> in the first scene. (7) Another is demanding a pair of <u>shoes</u> for the second act.

(8) In the meantime, the set builders work steadily, creating <u>things</u> for the stage. (9) An <u>expert</u> will make a lighting chart of the play, scene by scene. (10) The entire <u>group</u> cooperates to prepare for opening night.

C. APPLICATION IN WRITING

Set Description Choose a scene from a novel or story you have read. Write a brief description of the stage setting that would be needed in presenting the scene as a play. Include information about various characters, costumes, stage sets, scenery, lighting, music, and sound effects. Use specific nouns to identify the people and objects.

THE USES OF NOUNS

A noun may act as a subject, a direct object, an indirect object, or a predicate nominative. Study the following examples.

Subject	*Meteorologists* study the weather. (*Meteorologists* is the subject of the verb *study.*)
Direct Object	The magician amazed the *audience*. (*Audience* receives the action of the verb *amazed.*)
Indirect Object	The coach showed the *quarterback* a new play. (*Quarterback* tells to *whom* the play was shown.)
Predicate Nominative	Lyn Walker is a carpenter's *assistant*. (*Assistant* follows the linking verb *is.*)

Practice Your Skills

CONCEPT CHECK

Uses of Nouns Write each italicized noun and tell how each is being used.

1. Nearly a thousand years ago, a *civilization* flourished in an area of New Mexico called Chaco Canyon.
2. The Navajo have given the *people* the name of Anasazi.
3. "Anasazi" is their *term* for "ancient ones."
4. The Anasazi built impressive *villages* about A.D. 1000.
5. They developed a sophisticated *culture*.
6. Then this *culture* vanished, mysteriously, about A.D. 1300.
7. Today the *land* of the Anasazi is the Chaco Culture National Historic Park.
8. Archaeologists search the *ruins* for clues about the Anasazi.
9. Research gives *archaeologists* insights into Anasazi culture.
10. According to experts, the sudden disappearance of the Anasazi is still a *mystery*.

C H E C K P O I N T
PAGES 534–536

A. Label four columns *Common, Proper, Collective,* and *Compound.* Write each noun from the sentences in the correct columns. Some nouns will belong in two categories. Then list eight *Concrete* nouns from the sentences and three *Abstract* nouns.

1. Eons ago, a powerful species of animal ruled the earth.
2. Through vast swamplands stalked these huge reptiles known now as dinosaurs.
3. Western America was tropical then, like the lands around the Amazon.
4. The big animals inhabited an area from the Pacific Ocean toward the Mississippi River.
5. One type, the brontosaurus, weighed more than thirty tons.
6. With its tapering tail, it measured up to sixty feet.
7. Despite its threatening size, this creature grazed peacefully on marshland plants.
8. The tyrannosaurus, member of another dinosaur group, was smaller than the brontosaurus but possessed much greater strength and ferocity.
9. This species had small forelegs but powerful hindquarters.
10. Over one-half of the motion pictures made about dinosaurs have used the tyrannosaurus as a model.

Writing Theme
Early Civilizations

Writing Theme
Dinosaurs

Using Nouns   **537**

"Must you always eat as if there's no tomorrow?"

B. Write the italicized noun in each sentence. Tell whether the noun is functioning as a *Subject, Direct Object, Indirect Object,* or *Predicate Nominative.*

1. One of the greatest mysteries of science is the sudden *extinction* of the dinosaurs.
2. After being dominant for 130 million years, these monstrous *lords* of the earth vanished.
3. With them disappeared about *half* of the species of life on this planet.
4. The *greenhouse effect* might explain the disappearance.
5. Rising temperatures could have destroyed the *balance* of life.
6. However, rock samples from Gubbio, Italy, gave *scientists* a more convincing explanation.
7. A large *quantity* of iridium was found in rocks dating from the end of the dinosaur era.
8. Iridium is a rare *metal* that is more common in space than on earth.
9. Walter Alvarez was a *geologist* who studied the ore samples from Italy.
10. They gave *Alvarez* the idea that a meteorite might have struck the earth.

11. The meteorite's gigantic impact created a *crater* 200 kilometers (124 miles) wide.
12. Its *force* threw a huge amount of dust into the air.
13. The dust dispersed into the atmosphere, completely blocking out the *sunlight* for several years.
14. The results were icy *temperatures* and extinction of many life forms.
15. This theory gives *humanity* more reasons to look to the skies.

THE PLURALS OF NOUNS

Nouns that name one person, place, thing, or idea are called **singular nouns.** Nouns that name more than one are called **plural nouns.** The following rules tell how to form the plurals of nouns.

1. **To form the plural of most nouns, just add *-s.***

    prizes   dreams   circles   stations

2. **For most singular nouns ending in *o*, add *-s.***

    solos   halos   studios   photos   pianos

    For a few nouns ending in *o*, add *-es.*

    heroes   tomatoes   potatoes   echoes

3. **When the singular noun ends in *s, sh, ch, x,* or *z,* add *-es.***

    waitresses   brushes   ditches   axes   buzzes

4. **When a singular noun ends in *y* with a consonant before it, change the *y* to *i* and add *-es.***

    army—armies   candy—candies   baby—babies
    dairy—dairies   ferry—ferries   conspiracy—conspiracies

    When a vowel (*a, e, i, o, u*) comes before the *y*, just add *-s.*

    boy—boys   way—ways   array—arrays
    alloy—alloys   weekday—weekdays   jockey—jockeys

5. **For most nouns ending in *f* or *fe*, change the *f* to *v* and add *-es* or *-s.* Since there is no rule, you must memorize such words.**

    life—lives   calf—calves   knife—knives
    thief—thieves   shelf—shelves   loaf—loaves

    For some nouns ending in *f*, add *-s* to make the plural.

    roofs   chiefs   reefs   beliefs

Using Nouns   **539**

The Plurals of Nouns

Objectives

- To form the plurals of nouns
- To correct errors in the use of plural nouns
- **Writing**   To use the plurals of nouns correctly

Teaching Strategies

Personal Touch

You might wish to share with the class your personal methods for remembering the spellings of plural nouns. For example, you might point out that the plurals of nouns that end in *o* and refer to music are formed by adding only -s: *pianos, solos, concertos, cellos.*

Individualizing Instruction

ESL Students   In Japanese and Korean, nouns have no plural forms. Therefore, native speakers of these languages must pay particular attention to the use of plural endings in English.

Linking Grammar and Writing

Emphasize to students that checking for the correct spellings of plural nouns and other words is an important part of proofreading during the writing process. Ask students to review one of their rough drafts to see whether they need to correct the spellings of any plural nouns. Encourage them to make these corrections as a regular step in their proofreading process.

WRITING THEME   Natural Disasters

You may want to encourage students to do research on this theme and use it as the subject for an assignment in a Writer's Workshop.

A.   Concept Check

Plurals of Nouns
1. travelers, deer, sheep
2. passes, Rockies
3. men, missionaries
4. cliffs, deposits
5. pickaxes, echoes
6. cars, teeth
7. leaves, trees
8. tons, roofs
9. stories, heroes
10. children, boulders

Writing TIP

Check the dictionary if the plural of a word is formed in an unusual way.

Writing Theme
Natural Disasters

6. **Some nouns have the same form for both singular and plural.**

   deer   sheep   moose   salmon   trout

7. **For some nouns, the plural is formed in a special way.**

   man—men   goose—geese   ox—oxen
   woman—women   mouse—mice   child—children

8. **For a compound noun written as one word, form the plural by changing the last word in the compound to its plural form.**

   stepchild—stepchildren   firefly—fireflies

   If the compound noun is written as a hyphenated word or as two separate words, change the most important word to the plural form.

   brother-in-law—brothers-in-law
   life jacket—life jackets

Practice Your Skills

A. CONCEPT CHECK

Plurals of Nouns   Rewrite the nouns in parentheses by changing each to its plural form.

1. Before 1845, most (traveler) through British Columbia's Crowsnest Pass were Indians, along with some (deer) and mountain (sheep).
2. The Crowsnest is the most southerly of the three (pass) through the Canadian (Rocky).
3. The first European (man) to explore the pass were prospectors and (missionary).
4. Rising above the pass, the (cliff) of Turtle Mountain were found to be rich in (deposit) of coal.
5. In 1896, the sounds of railway workers' hammers and (pickax) raised (echo) through the pass.
6. Railroad (car) carried their loads of coal through the (tooth) of the mountains.
7. On April 29, 1903, the (leaf) on Turtle Mountain's (tree) began to tremble.
8. The side of the mountain broke away, sending 70 million (ton) of rock plunging onto the (roof) of the town below.
9. The survivors of the avalanche later told many (story) of (hero) who helped save others.
10. Three (child) survived because a cascade of (boulder) carried their bedroom along like a surfboard.

B. PROOFREADING SKILL

Correct Plural Forms   Rewrite this paragraph, correcting all errors. Pay special attention to plural nouns. There are fifteen errors.

> The <u>streakes</u> of fire across the summer <u>skys</u> are caused by chunks of rock called meteors. When a <u>meteor</u> enters the atmosphere and survives <u>it's</u> plunge to earth, it is called a meteorite. While most meteors are burned in the atmosphere. Huge <u>craters</u> throughout the world exist to <u>testify</u> that <u>other's</u> have fallen to earth. A large meteorite can strike the ground with the force of several <u>ton</u> of <u>dynamite?</u> Near <u>Winslow Arizona</u> is a major meteor crater <u>600</u> <u>foots</u> deep and three-quarters of a mile across. When a <u>majer</u> meteorite fell in Siberia in 1908, <u>tree's</u> were blown over for thirty <u>mile</u>, and earth <u>tremores</u> were felt all over the world.

C. APPLICATION IN WRITING

Eyewitness Report   You are in your living room. Suddenly there is a mild earthquake, strong enough to knock things off shelves. In one or two paragraphs, describe the scene. Then check the spelling of each plural noun.

THE POSSESSIVES OF NOUNS

Possessive nouns show ownership or belonging.

> the *child's* coat (The child owns the coat.)
> the *cat's* paw (The paw belongs to, or is part of, the cat.)
> the *girl's* health (The health is part of the girl.)

Possessive nouns are formed by adding an apostrophe (') and an *-s* or only an apostrophe to the noun. Possessive nouns may also be singular or plural. Look at these three examples of possessive nouns.

> My *mother's* car is in the garage.
> My *parents'* car is in the garage.
> The *children's* bicycles are in the garage.

There are three rules for forming the possessives of singular and plural nouns.

1. **If a noun is singular, add 's.**

> mother—my *mother's* car
> Ross—*Ross's* desk

B. Proofreading Skill
Correct Plural Forms
   The streaks of fire across the summer skies are caused by chunks of rock called meteors. When a meteor enters the atmosphere and survives its plunge to earth, it is called a meteorite. While most meteors are burned in the atmosphere, huge craters throughout the world exist to testify that others have fallen to earth. A large meteorite can strike the ground with the force of several tons of dynamite. Near Winslow, Arizona, is a major meteor crater 600 feet deep and three-quarters of a mile across. When a major meteorite fell in Siberia in 1908, trees were blown over for thirty miles, and earth tremors were felt all over the world.

C. Application in Writing
Eyewitness Report
Answers will vary.

The Possessives of Nouns

Objectives

- To form possessive nouns correctly
- To correct errors in possessive forms

Teaching Strategies

Critical Thinking

Synthesizing   Have small groups or teams of students challenge other teams to form the possessives of nouns they have selected. Encourage students to use both singular and plural nouns and to refer to the rules for forming possessives.

Stumbling Block

Students sometimes confuse the plural forms of nouns with possessives. Help them recognize that apostrophes are used to show possession, not plurality.
singular noun: student
plural noun: students
singular possessive: student's
plural possessive: students'
For more help with apostrophes, see pages 793–794.

 Individualizing Instruction

ESL Students   Point out to these students that the only time we are likely to use the preposition *of* to show possession is when the noun is a thing, not a person; for example, "the color of the house."

Managing the Paper Load

Prepare and make an answer key available for students to use with Exercise A. Have them complete the remaining exercises for a grade.

WRITING THEME   Touring Bands

Suggest that interested students add this theme to a list of possible topics for writing assignments.

A. Concept Check

Possessive Nouns
Student answers should be complete sentences.

1. sun's
2. Women's
3. Cars'
4. David's
5. amplifiers'
6. César Rosa's
7. bass's
8. drums'
9. crowd's
10. nation's

Writing Theme
Touring Bands

Exception: The *s* after the apostrophe is dropped after *Jesus'*, *Moses'*, and certain names in classical mythology (*Zeus'*). These possessive forms, therefore, can be pronounced easily.

2. **If a noun is plural and ends with s, just add an apostrophe.**

> parents—my *parents'* car
> the Santinis—the *Santinis'* home

3. **If a noun is plural but does not end in s, add 's.**

> women—the *women's* coats
> people—the *people's* choice

Practice Your Skills

A. CONCEPT CHECK

Possessive Nouns   Each sentence below contains one singular noun or one plural noun that must be made possessive. Rewrite the sentences, inserting the correct possessive nouns.

1. The sun heat bakes the streets of East Los Angeles.
2. Women and men's eyes narrow against the glare.
3. Cars chrome bumpers, newly buffed, are glinting in the light.
4. David arms ache as he unloads his equipment from the van.
5. The heat even seems to increase both amplifiers weight.
6. Guitarist César Rosa garage is to be the rehearsal studio.
7. Neighbors gather as the bass unmistakable booming notes signal the band to begin.
8. The drums heavy thumping rhythms fill the afternoon air.
9. The music grows louder, prompted by the crowd cheers.
10. One of the nation best rock-and-roll bands, Los Lobos, has never lost touch with the neighborhood that nourished it.

Los Lobos,
Hispanic rock music
group

B. PROOFREADING SKILL

Focus on Possessives   Rewrite the following paragraph, correcting all errors. Pay special attention to the use of possessive nouns. There are ten errors.

A touring <u>musicians</u> life is less romantic than it may seem. Too often it <u>consist's</u> of late nights, fast-food meals, and fitful rest on the tour <u>buses</u> uncomfortable seats. Dressing-room <u>facilitys</u> are primitive and not always clean. The sharpness of a <u>bands</u> sound and the clarity of <u>it's</u> lyrics are at the mercy of the sound system in each hall. From one night to the next, the audience's response can swing from indifference to ecstasy. The music of the other acts on the bill may often be totally at <u>odd's</u> with your own. However, <u>their</u> is an energy in the music that can stir your blood and set your spine shaking. Give yourself over to the rhythm, let your <u>finger's</u> fly across the instrument you play, and, before you know it, <u>lifes'</u> sorrows will take a back seat to the beat.

Paul McCartney, composer and musician

CHECK POINT
PAGES 539–542

A. On your paper, write the plural form of each of these singular nouns.

1. avenue
2. tax
3. laborer
4. child
5. cry
6. stereo
7. hero
8. woman
9. wharf
10. lunch
11. foot
12. boy
13. story
14. doorway
15. thief
16. path
17. roof
18. echo
19. alley
20. potato

B. Write the possessive form of each italicized noun in the following sentences.

1. The first tokens of change in a neighborhood that is sliding into urban decay are the *owners* signs in the windows of various stores.
2. Each *sign* bold letters announce the depressing news, "Everything Must Go."
3. One by one the many *shops* lighted windows go dark.
4. *People* glances slide past the boarded storefronts.
5. Soon the rattling thunder of construction *workers* equipment splits the air.
6. The brick fronts of these structures come down, exposing a *building* interior.

Writing Theme
Urban Renewal

B. Proofreading Skill
Focus on Possessives
A touring musician's life is less romantic than it may seem. Too often it consists of late nights, fast-food meals, and fitful rest on the tour buses' uncomfortable seats. Dressing-room facilities are primitive and not always clean. The sharpness of a band's sound and the clarity of its lyrics are at the mercy of the sound system in each hall. From one night to the next, the audience's response can swing from indifference to ecstasy. The music of the other acts on the bill may often be totally at odds with your own. However, there is an energy in the music that can stir your blood and set your spine shaking. Give yourself over to the rhythm, let your fingers fly across the instrument you play, and, before you know it, life's sorrows will take a back seat to the beat.

CHECK POINT
PAGES 539–542

You may wish to use the following checkpoint exercises as an informal evaluation of student mastery of the concepts covered in this handbook.

WRITING THEME   Urban Renewal

A.

1. avenues
2. taxes
3. laborers
4. children
5. cries
6. stereos
7. heroes
8. women
9. wharves
10. lunches
11. feet
12. boys
13. stories
14. doorways
15. thieves
16. paths
17. roofs
18. echoes
19. alleys
20. potatoes

B.

1. owners'
2. sign's
3. shops'
4. People's
5. workers'
6. building's

7. Gradually, the *laborers* efforts turn a three-story building into a hole in the ground.
8. The surrounding fence is quickly covered with graffiti, amateur *artists* images, and *everybody* posters.
9. Many *spectators* eyes are drawn to the holes in the fence.
10. Passers-by watch as the new *structure* concrete foundation is poured.
11. *Cranes* cables lift steel girders high in the sky.
12. The architect compares his new tower to *Olympus* peak.
13. The windows, mirrors of black glass, reflect *children* antics from the sidewalk.
14. The building *owner* worried manner relaxes as offices are rented.
15. The building stands, still and tall, awaiting its new *tenants* first steps.

Les Constructeurs,
by Fernand Léger, 1950

C. Complete each sentence by writing a noun of the type called for in parentheses.

1. In response to urban crowding and _____ demand for more office space, architects developed the skyscraper. (plural possessive)
2. Once Elisha Otis had perfected the passenger elevator, a _____ taller than five stories became practical. (singular)
3. The use of iron for reinforcement made the _____ job of raising a skyscraper easier and safer. (singular possessive)
4. Since 1930, one of New York's most famous _____ has been the Empire State Building. (plural)
5. While other buildings may be taller, none has sparked its _____ imagination and sense of romance like the Empire State. (plural possessive)

544 Grammar Handbook

Humanities Connection

Art Note   The work of Fernand Léger (1881–1955) sprang from an interest in cubism. With his use of tubular shapes, Léger's style is considered an expression of his fascination with machines. Ask: How does the use of shapes in *Les Constructeurs* offer a fresh view of its subject? Could Léger have achieved the same effect with a realistic painting? Why or why not?

Writing Theme
Famous Tricksters

A. Identifying Types of Nouns Write each noun in the following sentences. Identify the noun according to its kind: *Common, Proper, Collective, Compound.* Remember, some nouns will fit more than one category. Afterward, write three *Concrete Nouns* and two *Abstract Nouns* that appear in the sentences.

1. A famous trick was played at ancient Troy, in Asia Minor.
2. Homer tells about it in his epic poem *The Iliad.*
3. The poem describes the final battles before the fall of the city of Troy.
4. An army from Greece had been attacking the city for ten years.
5. King Priam was then ruling the Trojan people.
6. His army was inspired by the valor of his son Hector.
7. Hector seemed without an equal in strength and courage.
8. On the battlefield, Hector killed the best friend of the Greek hero Achilles.
9. In a rage, the Greek warrior defeated Hector and killed him.
10. Afterward, the spirit of the Trojan community faltered.
11. Then the clever Greek leader Odysseus hatched a scheme against Troy.
12. The Greek invaders retreated, leaving behind a huge wooden horse as a gift.
13. Relieved, the unsuspecting Trojans brought the horse into the city and held a victory celebration.
14. That night, a team of Greek soldiers emerged from their hideaway inside the horse.
15. They opened the city gates to the Greeks, and Troy was conquered.

B. Identifying the Uses of Nouns Write each italicized noun and tell whether the noun is used as a *Subject, Direct Object, Indirect Object,* or *Predicate Nominative.*

1. Time has only increased the *reputation* of Harry Houdini, the American magician noted for his sensational stunts.
2. Houdini won international *acclaim* for his puzzling and complicated escapes.
3. Difficult challenges gave this world-famous *artist* little trouble.
4. Hanging upside down from America's tallest buildings, this *wizard* wriggled out of straitjackets with ease.
5. In London, he offered the citizens a unique *opportunity* to imprison him by any possible means.
6. Newspaper *editors* therefore located a British blacksmith who had spent five years perfecting unbreakable handcuffs.

Using Nouns   **545**

Application and Review

These activities have been designed to allow your students to apply concepts presented in this handbook. Exercise A requires students to identify types of nouns. Exercise B requires students to identify the use of nouns. Exercises C and D require students to form the plurals and possessives of nouns.

> *Additional Resources*
> - Tests and Assessment, Mastery Tests, pp. 47–52
> - Elaboration, Revision, and Proofreading Worksheets, p. 23

WRITING THEME   Famous Tricksters

A. Identifying Types of Nouns
1. trick—Common; Troy—Proper; Asia Minor—Proper, Compound
2. Homer—Proper; poem—Common *or* epic poem—Common, Compound; *The Iliad*—Proper
3. poem—Common; battles—Common; fall—Common; city—Common; Troy—Proper
4. army—Common, Collective; Greece—Proper; city—Common; years—Common
5. King Priam—Proper, Compound; people—Common, Collective
6. army—Common, Collective; valor—Common; son—Common; Hector—Proper
7. Hector—Proper; equal—Common; strength—Common; courage—Common
8. battlefield—Common; Hector—Proper; friend—Common; hero—Common; Achilles—Proper
9. rage—Common; warrior—Common; Hector—Proper
10. spirit—Common; community—Common, Collective
11. leader—Common; Odysseus—Proper; scheme—Common; Troy—Proper
12. invaders—Common; horse—Common; gift—Common
13. Trojans—Proper; horse—Common; city—Common; celebration—Common
14. night—Common; team—Common, Collective; soldiers—Common; hideaway—Common; horse—Common
15. gates—Common; Greeks—Proper; Troy—Proper

Answers to second part of Activity A will vary. See typical answers below.
Concrete: Troy, Homer, poem, battles, army, Greece, people, friend, horse, gates, Greeks . . .
Abstract: fall, years, valor, strength, courage, scheme . . .

B. Identifying the Uses of Nouns
1. reputation, Direct Object
2. acclaim, Direct Object
3. artist, Indirect Object
4. wizard, Subject
5. opportunity, Direct Object
6. editors, Subject

7. handcuffs, Direct Object
8. end, Predicate Nominative
9. artist, Subject
10. message, Direct Object

C. Forming the Plurals and Possessives of Nouns

Student answers should be in columns.

1. impostor, impostor's, IMPOSTORS, impostors'
2. thief, THIEF'S, thieves, thieves'
3. SISTER-IN-LAW, sister-in-law's, sisters-in-law, sisters-in-law's
4. discovery, discovery's, discoveries, DISCOVERIES'
5. sorceress, sorceress's, SORCERESSES, sorceresses'
6. riddle, RIDDLE'S, riddles, riddles'
7. STRATEGY, strategy's, strategies, strategies'
8. wish, wish's, WISHES, wishes'
9. OCTOPUS, octopus's, octopuses/octopi, octopuses', octopi's
10. fantasy, FANTASY'S, fantasies, fantasies'
11. sash, sash's, SASHES, sashes'
12. ASSEMBLY LINE, assembly line's, assembly lines, assembly lines'
13. HOAX, hoax's, hoaxes, hoaxes'
14. FOLLY, folly's, follies, follies'
15. NOOSE, noose's, nooses, nooses'

D. Correct Plural and Possessive Forms

Student answers should be complete sentences.

1. travels, Troy's
2. Greeks', gods'
3. storms, invaders'
4. Odysseus', Polyphemus'
5. Greeks', monster's
6. lives, troops
7. wits', giant's
8. Cyclops', knives
9. trickster's, bellies
10. men-at-arms, adventures

7. Before a spellbound crowd, Houdini tested and fought the *handcuffs* for over an hour before he freed himself.
8. In California, a daring trick was nearly the *end* of Houdini as he clawed his way out from under six feet of earth.
9. The skillful escape *artist* escaped from New York's East River after being chained and nailed in a packing case.
10. Even today, Houdini's legend suggests a powerful *message:* the human spirit cannot be kept in chains.

C. Forming the Plurals and Possessives of Nouns Make four columns and label them *Singular, Singular Possessive, Plural,* and *Plural Possessive.* Write each of the following fifteen nouns in the correct column. Then write the three other forms of each noun, each in its proper column.

1. impostors	6. riddle's	11. sashes
2. thief's	7. strategy	12. assembly line
3. sister-in-law	8. wishes	13. hoax
4. discoveries'	9. octopus	14. folly
5. sorceresses	10. fantasy's	15. noose

D. Correct Plural and Possessive Forms Rewrite the sentences below, changing each italicized singular noun to either its plural or possessive form. Some nouns need to be both plural and possessive.

1. Homer's tales recount the *travel* of Odysseus after *Troy* fall.
2. The *Greek* savage destruction of Troy aroused many of the *god* wrath.
3. They caused violent *storm* to lash all the *invader* ships.
4. *Odysseus* ships were blown off course to *Polyphemus* island in the land of the Cyclops.
5. The *Greek* hunger made them kill some of this *monster* sheep.
6. In revenge, Polyphemus took the *life* of most of the *troop.*
7. At his *wit* end, Odysseus finally devised a plan to free the survivors from the depths of the *giant* cavern.
8. Odysseus destroyed the *Cyclops* one eye with a wooden spear carved by the *knife* of his soldiers.
9. The *trickster* crew clung to the wool on the *belly* of several sheep.
10. The Greek *man-at-arms* escaped and sailed away to many further *adventure*—and tricks.

546 Grammar Handbook

Using Pronouns

WHAT IS A PRONOUN?

A pronoun is a word that is used in place of a noun or another pronoun.

Pronouns help present ideas clearly and efficiently. First of all, they help prevent unnecessary repetition. They are also used as transitional devices to tie sentences or paragraphs together.

The noun or pronoun that a pronoun stands for is called its **antecedent.** Find the antecedent of the italicized pronouns below.

> Lin was late because *she* missed the bus. (*She* refers to the noun *Lin. Lin* is the antecedent of the pronoun *she*.)
> Raúl read the book and returned *it* to the shelf. (*It* refers to the noun *book. Book* is the antecedent of the pronoun *it*.)

The antecedent may be made up of two or more nouns.

> The coaches, players, and fans appeared happy as *they* arrived. (The antecedent of *they* is *coaches, players,* and *fans*.)

Pronouns may also be the antecedents of other pronouns.

> You missed *your* bus.   They knew *their* way.

The antecedent and the pronoun may appear in the same sentence, or the antecedent may appear in the preceding sentence.

> The tractor pushed the stones and bricks. *It* cleared a path. (*It* refers to the antecedent *tractor.*)

Occasionally the antecedent appears after the pronoun.

> After *he* studied, Bill rested. (*Bill* is the antecedent of *he*.)

Practice Your Skills

A. CONCEPT CHECK

Pronoun Antecedents   Write the antecedent of each italicized pronoun in the following sentences. Remember that the antecedent may appear in another sentence.

1. Maggie Lena Walker, the first black woman bank president, did not begin *her* remarkable business career in the usual way.

Writing
TIP

Pronouns can serve as devices to connect ideas and make your writing flow more smoothly.

Writing Theme
Business Leaders

Using Pronouns   **547**

Grammar Handbook 32:
Using Pronouns

Objectives

- To identify the antecedents of pronouns
- **Writing**   To use pronouns to provide transitions

Teaching Strategies

Teaching Tip: Antecedents

To illustrate how the use of pronouns prevents repetition of words, have students read the example sentences aloud, substituting the antecedent for the pronoun in each sentence. In addition, you may wish to have other students try giving directions for some simple task without using pronouns. The repetitive results will provide another illustration of the function of pronouns.

Additional Resources

- Tests and Assessment, Pretests, pp. 15–16
- Grammar and Usage Practice Book, pp. 33–34

WRITING THEME   Business Leaders

A. Concept Check
Pronoun Antecedents
   1. her, Maggie Lena Walker

2. its, college
3. her, Maggie Lena Walker
4. her, mother
5. their, teachers
6. it, potential
7. she, Maggie
8. its, cooperative
9. them, Promotions
10. she, Maggie
11. his, Armstead Walker, Jr.
12. He, Armstead Walker, Jr.
13. They, Armstead, Maggie
14. herself, Walker; its, organization
15. her, Maggie Walker

B. Drafting Skill

Providing Transitions

(1) An innovative and resourceful American businesswoman was Sarah Walker. (2) She was a widow with a young daughter. (3) To help support her, Sarah worked as a washerwoman for eighteen years. (4) They were long, hard years. (5) However, Walker then invented a hair preparation especially useful for black women. (6) It was an immediate success. (7) To demonstrate her preparation door-to-door, she used "Walker Agents." (8) They were organized into clubs with prizes for sales. (9) Her sales methods helped make Walker wealthy, and they also made her a leader in American business. (10) Walker's initiative was remarkable, and she turned it into a triumphant success.

2. She was never able to attend a college famous for *its* business program.
3. In fact, a college education was unlikely for *her.*
4. Maggie's mother had spent *her* early life as a slave and later earned her living doing laundry.
5. Maggie was lucky enough, however, to attend a school where the teachers took an active interest in *their* students.
6. These teachers were aware of Maggie's potential and encouraged *it.*
7. Maggie graduated from Armstrong Normal School when *she* was sixteen and became a teacher.
8. At the same time, she began working for an insurance cooperative that had *its* headquarters in Richmond, Virginia.
9. Promotions came quickly to Maggie at the company, and she accepted *them* eagerly.
10. Eventually *she* gave up her job as a teacher.
11. Armstead Walker, Jr., proposed to Maggie, and she became *his* wife.
12. *He* was a building contractor in Richmond.
13. *They* were married in 1886.
14. Walker distinguished *herself* by vastly increasing her organization's membership as well as *its* assets.
15. In 1902 Maggie Walker earned *her* place in banking history by founding the St. Luke's Penny Savings Bank.

B. DRAFTING SKILL

Providing Transitions   Sometimes a pronoun refers to a noun in a preceding sentence.

> Many important black businesspeople flourished in the early part of this century. Several of *them* were women.

Them helps tie the two sentences together by referring back to *businesspeople.* Such words are called **transitional devices.** Write the sentences below in paragraph form. Substitute pronouns for any italicized words or groups of words to provide transitions.

1. An innovative and resourceful American businesswoman was Sarah Walker.
2. *Sarah Walker* was a widow with a young daughter.
3. To help support *the daughter,* Sarah worked as a washerwoman for eighteen years.
4. *The eighteen years* were long, hard years.
5. However, Walker then invented a hair preparation especially useful for black women.
6. *The hair preparation* was an immediate success.

7. To demonstrate her preparation door-to-door, *Walker* used "Walker Agents."
8. *Walker Agents* were organized into clubs, with prizes for sales.
9. Her sales methods helped make Walker wealthy, and *her sales methods* also made her a leader in American business.
10. Walker's initiative was remarkable, and she turned *Walker's initiative* into a triumphant success.

PERSONAL PRONOUNS

Personal pronouns change form to refer to (1) the person speaking, (2) the person spoken to, or (3) the person or thing spoken about.

1. First-person pronouns refer to the person speaking.

   I pole vault.   *We* collect old magazines.

2. Second-person pronouns refer to the person spoken to.

   Did *you* bring *your* calculator?   *You* should go too.

3. Third-person pronouns refer to the person or thing spoken about.

   She asked *him* a question.   *They* opened *it* immediately.

The chart below shows the forms of the personal pronouns.

	Singular	**Plural**
First Person	I, me (my, mine)	we, us (our, ours)
Second Person	you (your, yours)	you (your, yours)
Third Person	he, she, it him, her, it (his, her, hers, its)	they, them (their, theirs)

First- and third-person pronouns change form to show singular and plural. Third-person singular pronouns also change to show gender.

Masculine	he, him, his (refer to males)
Feminine	she, her, hers (refer to females)
Neuter	it, its (refer to things and often to animals)

Objectives

- To identify personal pronouns by person, number, and case
- To identify the correct pronouns to complete sentences
- **Writing** To use pronouns to reflect point of view
- **Writing** To demonstrate revision skills by replacing nouns with pronouns to avoid repetition

Teaching Strategies

 Individualizing Instruction

LEP Students You may wish to review each of the cases of pronouns individually. Have students copy the following chart or devise their own.

CASE	PART OF SENTENCE
Nominative	subject, predicate nominative
Objective	direct object, indirect object, object of preposition
Possessive	subject, predicate nominative, direct object, object of preposition, adjective

ESL Students Because there are no personal pronouns in Japanese, Japanese students will have difficulty using personal pronouns in English. They are accustomed to using honorific words and expressions to convey similar meaning. Be aware, also, that in some other languages, including Spanish and French, nouns are classified grammatically as either masculine or feminine, and pronouns agree with them. Native speakers of these languages may have trouble with the concept of neuter gender. In addition, note that the pronoun *you* has various forms (familiar, formal, masculine, feminine) in other languages. In English the pronoun *you* has only one form, the plural, for both singular and plural.

Linking Grammar and Writing

Point out that pronouns are used to establish point of view in writing. Have students examine examples of professional writing in which personal pronouns reflect first-person, second-person, and third-person points of view. Discuss the different effect that each point of view creates.

Additional Resources
• Grammar and Usage Practice Book, pp. 35–36

WRITING THEME   Fathers

Suggest that interested students brainstorm to make a list of topics related to the theme of fathers to use for future writing assignments.

A. Concept Check
Personal Pronouns
Pronouns are underlined on page.
1. My, first-person; his, third-person
2. he, third-person
3. They, third-person; their, third-person
4. My, first-person; theirs, third-person
5. their, third-person
6. you, second-person; it, third-person; you, second-person
7. his, third-person; my, first-person
8. he, third-person; me, first-person; Your, second-person; she, third-person; her, third-person
9. my, first-person; We, first-person; your, second-person
10. My, first-person; it, third-person; he, third-person; him, third-person

B. Application in Literature
Personal Pronouns
1. He, third-person, singular; my, first-person, singular; I, first-person, singular; him, third-person, singular
2. We, first-person, plural; our, first-person, plural
3. us, first-person, plural
4. She, third-person, singular
5. I, first-person, singular
6. she, third-person, singular
7. me, first-person, singular; it, third-person, singular

Possessive Pronouns

Personal pronouns that show ownership are **possessive pronouns.** In the preceding chart, possessive pronouns are in parentheses. For further discussion of possessive pronouns, see page 553.

Practice Your Skills
A. CONCEPT CHECK

Personal Pronouns   Write the personal pronouns in each of the following sentences. Tell whether each pronoun is a first-person, second-person, or third-person pronoun.

1. My father was born in Alma, Wisconsin, where his father was a teacher.
2. The children at the school where he taught lived on farms.
3. They all helped their parents, who were dairy farmers.
4. My grandfather's family had a farm also; theirs was small but productive.
5. Alma, Wisconsin, started out as a port city where barges took on cargo for their trips south.
6. If you visit it today, you can still see the old docks.
7. When his son was six, my grandfather left Alma and became a school principal in a larger town.
8. Much later he told me, "Your grandmother hated to move because she had a rose garden that was the joy of her life."
9. However, my grandmother said, "We decided that moving was worthwhile for your grandfather's career."
10. My father says Alma, as it looked when he was growing up, was for him the most beautiful place on earth.

B. APPLICATION IN LITERATURE

Personal Pronouns   Write the italicized pronouns in the following paragraphs. Identify each as a first-person or third-person pronoun. Then tell whether the pronoun is singular or plural. Notice how the pronouns add a feeling of warmth and closeness to the passage.

(1) *He* had become blood of *my* blood; he the strong swimmer and *I* the boy clinging to *him* in the darkness. (2) *We* swam in silence, and in silence we dressed in *our* wet clothes, and went home. (3) There was a lamp lighted in the kitchen, and when we came in, the water dripping from *us,* there was my mother. (4) *She* smiled at us. (5) *I* remember that she called us "boys." (6) "What have you boys been up to?" *she* asked, but my father did not answer. (7) As he had begun the evening's

experience with *me* in silence, so he ended *it*. (8) *He* turned and looked at me. (9) Then he went, *I* thought, with a new and strange dignity, out of the room.

Sherwood Anderson, *Discovery of a Father*

C. APPLICATION IN WRITING

Point of View   Rewrite the passage below, using third-person pronouns. Continue the narrative by adding a conclusion of your own.

> I remember very clearly my father and the sidewalk. I could not have been more than nine. I was walking beside my father in the bright sunshine when he stopped.
>
> "Look at the sidewalk," he said. "Tell me what color it is."
>
> "It's gray," I said, a little puzzled.
>
> "You didn't look. Really look at it."
>
> So I looked again. Then, in the bright sun, I could see colors. When I looked more closely, I saw flashes of yellow, red, and blue. My shadow was a vibrant purple.
>
> "That's the way the whole world is," my father said, gazing down at me. "It shares its secrets slowly." Then we walked on.

The Cases of Personal Pronouns

A personal pronoun, like a noun, can function as a subject, an object, a predicate nominative, or a possessive. Unlike a noun, however, a personal pronoun changes its form, or case, depending on its use in a sentence. The three cases of a pronoun are the **nominative case,** sometimes called the subject form; the **objective case,** sometimes called the object form; and the **possessive case.**

Nominative Case   *He* pitched. (*He* is the subject.)
Objective Case   Riley tagged *him.* (*Him* is the direct object.)
Possessive Case   *His* pitch was wild. (*His* shows possession.)

The Nominative Case   Use the nominative case when a pronoun is a subject or a predicate nominative.

Nominative Case	
Singular	I, you, he, she, it
Plural	we, you, they

Subject   *I* drew a map.
                    You need to leave for school now.
                    She plotted our route.

Predicate   That student must be *he.* (*He* follows the linking verb
Nominative   *must be.*)
                    The early-morning caller was *he.* (*He* follows the linking verb *was.*)

The subject forms of pronouns are also used for predicate pronouns. If the subject form does not sound natural to you, try reversing the subject and the predicate pronoun. The sentence should still sound correct.

The singer was *she.*   *She* was the singer.

For a more complete discussion of predicate nominatives, see pages 515–516.

Usage Note   The expression *It's me* is frequently heard in informal conversation even though it is not grammatically correct. The linking verb *is* calls for a complement in the nominative case: *It is I, This is she.* Most people consider *It's me* acceptable. However, avoid this phrase in formal writing or speaking.

The Objective Case Use the objective case when a pronoun is a direct object, an indirect object, or the object of a preposition.

Objective Case	
Singular	me, you, him, her, it
Plural	us, you, them

Direct Object	The answer surprised *her*.
	Are you following *us?*
	Dennis introduced *them* to his neighbor.
Indirect Object	Carole sent *them* a souvenir of her trip.
	The principal gave *him* some good advice.
	Please lend *me* a pen.

The third use of the objective case is the object of a preposition. Prepositions are connecting words like *to, for, into,* and *with.* A pronoun that follows such a word is the object of the preposition.

Object of	They gave a surprise party for *me*.
Preposition	Give this book to *her*.

For further discussion of prepositions, see pages 652–662.

The Possessive Case Use the possessive case to show ownership.

Possessive Case	
Singular	my, mine, your, yours, his, her, hers, its
Plural	our, ours, your, yours, their, theirs

Possessive pronouns are often used by themselves. The possessive pronouns *mine, yours, his, hers, its, ours,* and *theirs* replace nouns that function as subjects, predicate nominatives, and objects.

Subject	*Yours* are the best lines in the play.
Predicate Nominative	The leading role is *hers*.
Direct Object	I've heard your lines, but I haven't heard *his*.
Object of Preposition	Your part sounds interesting; now I'll tell you about *mine*.

Using Pronouns   **553**

Writing Theme
The Nobel Prize

Greek coin

At other times, possessive pronouns are used with the nouns they refer to. In this case the possessive pronouns *my, your, his, her, its, our,* and *their* function as adjectives.

Read *your* lines slowly and clearly. (*Your* functions as an adjective modifying the noun *lines.*)

In this textbook, however, a possessive pronoun that functions as an adjective is considered a pronoun, not an adjective.

Practice Your Skills

A. CONCEPT CHECK

Pronoun Case Write each italicized pronoun in the paragraph below, and identify that pronoun's case as *Nominative, Objective,* or *Possessive.*

(1) Throughout history people have awarded prizes for achievements *they* have valued. (2) In ancient Greece, athletes received laurel wreaths for *their* skills. (3) The martial arts were valued in the Roman Empire; gladiators most skilled in *them* were given money, and a man could make *his* fortune fighting. (4) Kings and queens award high honors for individuals' service to *their* monarch. (5) For distinction in motion pictures, *we* have the Academy Awards. (6) If *you* were to write a great book, *your* achievement might win *you* a Pulitzer Prize. (7) Among the most famous prizes in the world today are the Nobel Prizes, named for Alfred Nobel, who established *them* in 1896.

B. DRAFTING SKILL

Pronoun Case Write the correct pronouns for the sentences below. Choose from those given in parentheses.

1. Alfred Nobel, the son of an inventor, was born in Stockholm, Sweden, but as a teenager (he, him) spent a year in the United States studying engineering.
2. (Him, He) returned to Sweden and studied explosives, developing a method of combining nitroglycerin with an absorbent substance to form dynamite.
3. Nobel's invention changed the methods of warfare, making (it, its) more violent.
4. Eight years before (he, him) died, Nobel read (his, him) own obituary, mistakenly printed in a French newspaper.
5. (He, Him) realized the negative image that many people had of (he, him).

Humanities Connection

Art Note Pictured on *Moneta con spiga di grano* or *Coin with the Top Part of a Grain Stalk* is an imagined likeness of the head of Arethusa, a nymph in Greek mythology. According to myth, to protect her from a hunter, the gods changed Arethusa into a stream of water on the mythical island of Ortygia. Arethusa is also the name given to a famous fountain that flows from an underground stream. This fountain is located near the city of Syracuse on the Mediterranean island of Sicily. The coin, now associated with a castle in Milan, Italy, may be Sicilian in origin. Stalks of grain from the spring harvest—also depicted on the coin—were symbols of rebirth and renewal to the ancient Greeks and Romans. Ask: Why do you think the artist associated the grain stalk with the likeness on the coin?

6. Assessing his achievements, Alfred Nobel decided to add to (they, <u>them</u>).

7. Before he died in 1896, (<u>he</u>, his) left (he, <u>his</u>) fortune to establish international prizes in different fields.

8. The first Nobel Prize for physics went to Wilhelm Roentgen for (him, <u>his</u>) discovery of what (us, <u>we</u>) know as X-rays.

9. In 1903 the Curies received the physics prize for work (<u>they</u>, them) did on radioactivity.

10. Admirers of William Butler Yeats's poetry were not surprised when the prize for literature went to (he, <u>him</u>) in 1923.

11. The 1938 winner for literature was Pearl Buck, in part for (she, <u>her</u>) most famous novel, *The Good Earth.*

12. Although the Nobel Prize for peace is usually given to an individual, (its, <u>it</u>) has sometimes been given to an organization.

13. In 1965 (it, <u>its</u>) recipient was UNICEF, the United Nations Children's Fund.

14. Nobel Prize winners' diplomas include descriptions of (them, <u>their</u>) work.

15. (Their, <u>They</u>) also receive cash awards that Alfred Nobel set aside in (him, <u>his</u>) will.

C. REVISION SKILL

Avoiding Repetition   Repetition of nouns often produces tiresome writing. In the following passage, decide which italicized nouns should be replaced with personal pronouns to avoid repetition.

Yasunari Kawabata, first Asian to win the Nobel Prize in literature, 1968

The Curies were a family famous for winning Nobel Prizes. (1) *Pierre Curie* was born in Paris in 1859 and educated at the Sorbonne, where *Pierre Curie* later became a professor. (2) *Pierre Curie's* wife, *Marie,* was born in Warsaw in 1867 and was educated at first by *Marie's* father. (3) Later *Marie* also attended the Sorbonne, where *Marie* received a doctorate. (4) *Pierre and Marie* then worked as a team in *Pierre and Marie's* research on radioactivity. (5) In the process of *Pierre and Marie's* work, *Pierre and Marie* discovered polonium and radium. (6) For this work *Marie* received a Nobel Prize in 1903 jointly with *Marie's* husband and Henri Becquerel. (7) Then, in 1906, *Pierre Curie* died after *Pierre Curie* was run over by a cart. (8) After *Pierre's* death, Marie succeeded *Pierre* at the Sorbonne. (9) In 1911 *Marie* received another Nobel Prize for *Marie's* work in chemistry. (10) The family tradition continued when the Curies' daughter Irène and *Irène's* husband Frédéric received the prize in 1935 for *Irène and Frédéric's* research in radioactivity.

Gabriela Mistral, Chilean poet and Nobel Prize winner

Reflexive Pronouns and Intensive Pronouns

Objectives

- To identify and use correctly reflexive and intensive pronouns
- **Writing** To use intensive pronouns to create emphasis

Teaching Strategies

Teaching Tip: Intensive Pronouns

Intensive pronouns are usually stressed when used in oral situations. Help students hear this emphasis by reviewing orally with them sentences that contain intensive pronouns. Then discuss the subtle differences in sentence connotation made by the addition of an intensive pronoun.

 Individualizing Instruction

ESL Students Explain that idiomatically, a reflexive pronoun preceded by the preposition "by" means alone. Compare the following sentences:

I bought myself a new car.
I myself bought a new car.
I bought a new car by myself.

Additional Resources

- Grammar and Usage Practice Book, pp. 39–40

REFLEXIVE PRONOUNS AND INTENSIVE PRONOUNS

Reflexive pronouns and intensive pronouns are formed by adding *-self* or *-selves* to certain personal pronouns.

Singular myself, yourself, himself, herself, itself
Plural ourselves, yourselves, themselves

Reflexive pronouns reflect an action back on the subject and add necessary information to the sentence.

Kim bought *herself* a digital watch.
Doug and Steve made *themselves* a snack.

Intensive pronouns are used to emphasize a noun or pronoun.

They do not add information to a sentence. If intensive pronouns are removed, the meaning of the sentence does not change.

Maggie *herself* opened the vault.
The neighbors *themselves* cleaned the alley.

A reflexive or an intensive pronoun must have an antecedent.

Incorrect *Myself* knitted this sweater.
Correct *I* knitted this sweater *myself*.

Incorrect You can come with Ann and *myself*.
Correct You can come with Ann and *me*.

Practice Your Skills

A. CONCEPT CHECK

Reflexive and Intensive Pronouns Identify each pronoun in the sentences below as *Reflexive* or *Intensive*.

1. The word *hieroglyphics* <u>itself</u> originally meant "sacred writing."
2. The ancient Egyptians thought of <u>themselves</u> as having received writing from their gods.
3. Several ancient peoples used hieroglyphics to express <u>themselves</u>.
4. Each culture developed for <u>itself</u> a form of picture writing.
5. I <u>myself</u> find this combination of art and language fascinating.
6. A picture of a man feeding <u>himself</u> is believed to mean "eat."
7. Some hieroglyphics were written so hastily that the pictures <u>themselves</u> remain mysterious.
8. Today we do not trouble <u>ourselves</u> with using images for words.
9. However, our alphabet <u>itself</u> developed from pictures.
10. If you want to challenge <u>yourself</u>, take a course in hieroglyphics!

B. DRAFTING SKILL

Creating Emphasis Writers can use intensive pronouns to create emphasis and clarity.

> The scholar spoke to the reporter.
> The scholar herself spoke to the reporter.
>   (Emphasis on *scholar*)
> The scholar spoke to the reporter himself.
>   (Emphasis on *reporter*)

Add intensive pronouns to emphasize elements in the sentences below.

1. I slowly entered the pyramid. Near the door, I saw the marble tablet.
   a. Emphasize that it was the speaker who entered the pyramid.
   b. Emphasize that it was the pyramid that the speaker entered.
   c. Emphasize the tablet's location near the entrance.
   d. Emphasize the particular tablet that the speaker saw.

2. June collected some of the scattered fragments.
   a. Emphasize that it was June who acted.
   b. Emphasize the importance of the fragments.

3. "It seems to me, June," said Dr. Dias, raising his eyebrows, "that you have discovered some hieroglyphics in the tomb."
   a. Emphasize the importance of Dr. Dias.
   b. Emphasize the importance of the discoverer.
   c. Emphasize where the discovery occurred.

Using Pronouns   **557**

CHECK ✓ POINT
PAGES 547–557

You may wish to use the following checkpoint exercises as an informal evaluation of student mastery of the concepts covered in this handbook.

WRITING THEME Political Holidays

A.

Personal pronouns are underlined on page.

1. him, Diego, Objective
2. their, People, Possessive
3. He, Diego, Nominative; his, Diego, Possessive
4. him, Diego, Objective; he, Diego, Nominative; its, Fourth of July, Possessive; it, Fourth of July, Nominative
5. His, Diego, Possessive; him, Diego, Objective
6. He, Diego, Nominative; she, Juana, Nominative
7. She, Juana, Nominative; their, Diego, Juana, Possessive; them, towns, Objective
8. it, Fifth of May, Objective
9. they, Diego and his family, Nominative; his, Diego, Possessive
10. his, Diego, Possessive; he, Diego, Nominative; his, Diego, Possessive

B.

1. themselves, Reflexive, Catholics
2. They, Personal, Catholics
3. himself, Intensive, Catesby
4. his, Personal, king
5. he, Personal, Catesby
6. him, Personal, Fawkes; himself, Reflexive, Catesby; his, Personal, Catesby
7. himself, Reflexive, Fawkes

CHECK ✓ POINT
PAGES 547–557

A. Write each personal pronoun and its antecedent. Identify the case of each pronoun as *Nominative, Objective,* or *Possessive.*

1. Diego watched the fireworks explode above <u>him</u>.
2. People were raising <u>their</u> voices to celebrate the holiday.
3. <u>He</u> was spending <u>his</u> first summer in the United States.
4. To <u>him</u> the Fourth of July was fun, and <u>he</u> understood <u>its</u> importance, but <u>it</u> wasn't *Cinco de Mayo*.
5. <u>His</u> sister Juana told <u>him</u> that many cities and towns in the United States celebrated the Mexican defeat of the French.
6. <u>He</u> was sure <u>she</u> was right.
7. <u>She</u> added, however, that <u>their</u> small town wasn't one of <u>them</u>.
8. The Fifth of May had passed, and no one had noticed <u>it</u>.
9. When <u>they</u> were still following the harvest, Diego and <u>his</u> family had celebrated with the other migrant workers.
10. Diego was glad <u>his</u> father had a permanent job here on the farm, but <u>he</u> couldn't help missing <u>his</u> own country.

B. Write each italicized pronoun and identify it as *Personal, Intensive,* or *Reflexive.* Then write its antecedent.

1. In 1605 certain Catholics in England were organizing *themselves* to overthrow the Protestant government.
2. *They* were led by Robert Catesby, whose father had been imprisoned for refusing to leave the Catholic Church.
3. Catesby *himself* had once been imprisoned for taking part in a plot against Queen Elizabeth I.
4. Catesby planned to blow up the building in which Parliament met, at a time when the king and *his* advisers would be there.
5. Catesby was known to the government, so *he* needed to find someone unknown, someone like Guy Fawkes.
6. Rather than endanger Fawkes by meeting with *him himself,* Catesby sent *his* cousin to explain the plot.
7. Having agreed to participate, Fawkes called *himself* John Johnson.

Fourth of July on the River, by Susan Slyman, New York, 1985

558 Grammar Handbook

Humanities Connection

Art Note Shown is *Fourth of July on the River* (1985), an acrylic painting by Susan Slyman. Acrylics (synthetic imitations of oils) are a recent innovation in painting made possible by technology. Ask: If you were *writing* a description of a Fourth of July celebration, which elements would you choose to focus on? Why?

8. The plotters rented a house next to the Parliament building, and *they* tried to tunnel to a spot under the meeting room.

9. When *they* found that the work would take too long, they abandoned *it* and rented a cellar under the meeting room.

10. There Fawkes hid twenty barrels of gunpowder, concealing *them* under piles of wood and coal.

11. Had members of the Gunpowder Plot found *themselves* a solution?

12. The scheme took a different turn because one plotter had a relative in Parliament whom *he* wished to save.

13. The letter *he* sent warning *his* relative of danger led to the discovery of the plot.

14. Soon all the plotters, including Fawkes *himself*, were arrested.

15. Today, on Guy Fawkes Day, the English set bonfires on which *they* burn stuffed figures called "guys."

DEMONSTRATIVE PRONOUNS

The **demonstrative pronouns** are *this, that, these,* and *those*. *This* and *these* point out people or things that are near in space or time. *That* and *those* point out people or things that are farther away.

This is my laboratory manual.

That is yours on the table.

These are rubber boots with a fur lining.

Those near the door are leather.

Usage Note The words *this, that, these,* or *those* may be used as adjectives.

That is an antique clock. (Pronoun)
That clock is an antique. (Adjective)

These are retouched photographs. (Pronoun)
These photographs are retouched. (Adjective)

Those are Sam's skates. (Pronoun)
Those skates are Sam's. (Adjective)

Using Pronouns **559**

Demonstrative Pronouns

Objectives

- To identify and correctly use demonstrative pronouns
- **Writing** To use demonstratives correctly in giving directions

Teaching Strategies

Critical Thinking

Inferring Have pairs of students create sentences with missing demonstrative pronouns. Explain that the sentences will have to include clues to number and location. Then ask students to challenge other pairs to supply the correct demonstrative pronouns. Encourage students to explain what words in each sentence provided the clues.

Additional Resources

- Grammar and Usage Practice Book, pp. 41–42

You may want to suggest that students brainstorm a list of topics for description and refer to it when they write a description in Writer's Workshop 2.

A. Concept Check
Demonstrative Pronouns

Those are climbing roses along the far wall;
  These at my right shoulder don't climb at all.
And those in the distance are handsome and tall,
  In contrast with these, which are lovely but small.

The trowel in my pocket, yes, this, is brand new;
  The trowel at my aunt's house is older, and blue.
I need to plant bulbs where the ground is so flat.
  Which trowel should I use, do you think, this or that?

My dad told me some seeds, like these in my hand,
  Grow best in a spot where the soil's mixed with sand.
But those you are holding do well, so they say,
  When planted in earth that is ninety parts clay.

All gardens are freshest and coolest at dawn
  When thin morning sunbeams creep over the lawn.
But this will be truly its loveliest soon,
  When bathed in the rays of the hot sun of noon.

B. Application in Writing
Stage Directions
Answers will vary.

Practice Your Skills

A. CONCEPT CHECK

Demonstrative Pronouns   Complete the following four stanzas. As you write the poem, fill in each blank with the correct demonstrative pronoun.

    _____ are climbing roses along the far wall;
      _____ at my right shoulder don't climb at all.
  And _____ in the distance are handsome and tall,
    In contrast with _____ , which are lovely but small.

The trowel in my pocket, yes, _____ , is brand new;
  The trowel at my aunt's house is older, and blue.
I need to plant bulbs where the ground is so flat.
  Which trowel should I use, do you think, _____ or _____ ?

My dad told me some seeds, like _____ in my hand,
  Grow best in a spot where the soil's mixed with sand.
But _____ you are holding do well, so they say,
  When planted in earth that is ninety parts clay.

All gardens are freshest and coolest at dawn
  When thin morning sunbeams creep over the lawn.
But _____ will be truly its loveliest soon,
  When bathed in the rays of the
  hot sun of noon.

B. APPLICATION IN WRITING

Stage Directions   Write stage directions for a scene from a play. Base your directions on a play you have read or make up a scene of your own. Describe the stage setting for your scene, including scenery, lighting, and audio effects. Direct the actors where to stand and when and where to walk. Tell them what gestures and tones of voice to use. Use a variety of pronouns.

INDEFINITE PRONOUNS

Indefinite pronouns do not refer to a definite person or thing. An indefinite pronoun usually does not have an antecedent.

> *Several* of the cars were over ten years old.

Occasionally an indefinite pronoun has an antecedent.

> The chess players began the game. *Both* were concentrating.

Some indefinite pronouns are singular, and some are plural. Others can be singular or plural, depending on the context.

Indefinite Pronouns			
Singular	another	each	everything	one
	anybody	either	neither	somebody
	anyone	everybody	nobody	someone
	anything	everyone	no one	something
Plural	both	few	many	others
	several			
Singular or Plural	all	any	most	none
	some			

Practice Your Skills

A. CONCEPT CHECK

Indefinite Pronouns Write the indefinite pronouns in each sentence. Identify each pronoun as *Singular* or *Plural*.

1. No one knows exactly how many people live in the United States, but the Bureau of the Census does its best to find out.
2. The census begins with a list of all of the households in the country.
3. Many people are hired, and some go from door-to-door.
4. Each of the apartments in a building is a separate entry.
5. Then the Bureau sends a form to everyone on the list.
6. Most of the households receive a short form to fill out.
7. Others receive a form with very detailed questions.
8. A difficulty arises when someone does not have a permanent home.
9. Special personnel try to contact anyone without a home.
10. If the census is to succeed, everybody must cooperate.

B. Drafting Skill

Achieving Clarity and Precision

Answers will vary. See typical answers below.

(1) In the Elm Street area, five of the families had been missed by the first census workers. (2) Five of the buildings on the west side of the street appeared to be factories. (3) However, Mr. Lee advised me that four of these had been converted to condominiums. Investigation proved this true. (4) A dozen of the residents who had not been interviewed were eager to provide information. (5) Without these data, the bureau could have called the statistics for the neighborhood invalid.

Interrogative Pronouns

Objective

- To identify and use interrogative pronouns correctly

Teaching Strategies

Speaking and Listening

If possible, play a recording or read aloud Abbott and Costello's famous routine, "Who's on First?" (See page 578.) The comedians rely on misunderstandings about pronouns to produce humor in this routine. In a discussion, elicit from students that puns are plays on words. Discuss how pronouns and puns are used to produce humor in this selection.

> ### Additional Resources
> - Grammar and Usage Practice Book, pp. 45–46

WRITING THEME Persephone

Application in Writing

Writing Study Questions

Answers will vary. See typical answers below.

1. Who was the most powerful of the gods?
2. Whose is the title of god of the underworld?
3. Whom did Hades kidnap?
4. Which seasons are explained by the myth?
5. What does Demeter's grief cause?

B. DRAFTING SKILL

Achieving Clarity and Precision Overuse of indefinite pronouns can produce unclear writing. Rewrite the report below, replacing the italicized pronouns with specific words to make the information more precise. You may need to invent details.

(1) In the Elm Street area, *several* of the families had been missed by the first census workers. (2) *Most* of the buildings on the west side of the street appeared to be factories. (3) However, *someone* advised me that *many* of these had been converted to condominiums. Investigation proved this true. (4) *Some* of the residents who had not been interviewed were eager to provide information. (5) Without these data, *anyone* could have called the statistics for the neighborhood invalid.

INTERROGATIVE PRONOUNS

Interrogative pronouns are used to ask questions.

The interrogative pronouns are *who, whom, whose, which,* and *what.* An interrogative pronoun does not have an antecedent.

Who won an Emmy Award?   *Which* is your favorite?
Whom did Gloria call?   *What* was that noise?
Whose is this parka?

Usage Note Three interrogative pronouns, *what, whose,* and *which,* can also be used as adjectives.

Which bike is yours?   *What* grade did you get?

Practice Your Skills

APPLICATION IN WRITING

Writing Study Questions Using a variety of interrogative pronouns, write five questions about the Greek myth of Persephone.

Father: Zeus, most powerful of the gods
Mother: Demeter, goddess of growing things
Kidnapped by Hades, god of the underworld
Lived as Hades' wife in the underworld
The myth explains the seasons of summer and winter.
The six months Persephone spends on earth are warm and lovely.
During the time Persephone spends with Hades, Demeter grieves.
Demeter's grief causes the earth to be cold and barren.

Writing Theme
Persephone

RELATIVE PRONOUNS

A **relative pronoun** is used to relate, or connect, an adjective clause to the word or words it modifies. An adjective clause is a group of words that modifies a noun or pronoun. The clause has a subject and verb, but it cannot stand alone as a complete sentence. The noun or pronoun that the adjective clause modifies is the antecedent of the relative pronoun. The relative pronouns are *who, whom, whose, which,* and *that.*

The author, *whose book we discussed,* is not well known. (*Whose* is a relative pronoun. Its antecedent is *author.*)

The play *that we saw* is a musical about cats. (*That* is a relative pronoun. The antecedent of *that* is *play.*)

Depending on their use in a sentence, *who, whom, whose,* and *which* may be either relative pronouns or interrogative pronouns.

Interrogative Pronoun   *Who* is your favorite player?
Relative Pronoun   Keith Hernandez, *who* used to play for the Mets, is my favorite player.

Sometimes inexperienced writers rely too heavily on dependent clauses that begin with relative pronouns. Overuse of such constructions as *which is . . . , that is . . . ,* and *who will be* can be corrected by omitting the clause or rewording the sentence.

Unneeded Clause   The *Titanic,* which was thought to be unsinkable, sank on its first voyage.
Improved   The *Titanic,* thought to be unsinkable, sank on its first voyage.

Practice Your Skills

CONCEPT CHECK

Relative Pronouns and Their Antecedents Write each relative pronoun and its antecedent.

1. Checkers, which in England is called *draughts,* is an ancient game.
2. The two people who play need foresight and concentration.
3. The checkerboard, which is marked with sixty-four light and dark squares, may be any size for informal play.
4. There are twenty-four playing pieces that are divided between the players.

Writing
―TIP―
Use *who* to refer to people. *Which* refers to animals or things. *That* refers to people, animals, or things.

Writing Theme
Board Games

Using Pronouns   **563**

Relative Pronouns

Objective

- To identify relative pronouns

Teaching Strategies

Linking Grammar and Literature

Have students identify the relative pronouns in the following passage from "Raymond's Run" by Toni Cade Bambara:

"So I keep Raymond on the inside of me, and he plays like he's driving a stage coach; which is OK by me so long as he doesn't run me over or interrupt my breathing exercises, which I have to do. . . ."

Suggest that students read through other parts of this story to find additional examples of the use of relative pronouns.

Individualizing Instruction

ESL Students There is no true relative pronoun in Chinese. Chinese students will have difficulty using this grammatical form.

> **Additional Resources**
> - Grammar and Usage Practice Book, pp. 47–48

WRITING THEME   Board Games

Concept Check
Relative Pronouns and Their Antecedents
Relative pronouns are underlined on page.
  1. which, Checkers
  2. who, people
  3. which, checkerboard
  4. that, pieces

5. The official diameter of each piece, which is round and flat, varies from 1¼ to 1½ inches.
6. The player whose checkers are darker is said to have black pieces, and the other player has the colored pieces.
7. The players draw lots, which decides the playing order.
8. The player who makes the first move uses the black pieces.
9. A player's checkers, which are all of the same color, are arranged on the dark squares of the three closest rows.
10. During a tournament game, players are forbidden to do anything that might distract an opponent.

CHECK POINT
PAGES 559–564

Identify the italicized word or group of words in each sentence as an *Adjective* or a *Pronoun*. Then identify each pronoun as *Demonstrative, Indefinite, Interrogative,* or *Relative*.

1. *What* was the greatest volcanic eruption in history?
2. The answer depends on how *one* defines greatness.
3. If you define it in terms of fame, perhaps the greatest was the eruption of Mount Vesuvius, *which* destroyed Pompeii in A.D. 79.
4. If you define it by forcefulness, *everyone* would agree that the greatest eruption occurred in 1883.
5. Krakatoa is the name of *that* volcano.
6. *This* was also the name of an island in what is now Indonesia.
7. The eruption destroyed the island, but later eruptions, *some* as late as 1928, have formed a new island.
8. *This* island is called Anak Krakatoa, or Child of Krakatoa.
9. The eruptions *that* destroyed Krakatoa caused a great catastrophe.
10. During the night of August 26, houses on another island, *which* was one hundred miles away, were shaken to pieces by these tremors.
11. The next morning, *no one* failed to see the thick smoke.
12. *That* cloud of ash rose 50 miles into the air.
13. The explosions *that* occurred were heard two thousand miles away.
14. *All* life on the islands closest to Krakatoa was destroyed.
15. *These* islands were covered with a thick layer of ash.
16. It took five years for *anything* to grow again.
17. *Which* of the effects of the eruption were the worst?
18. Sailors *who* could not navigate their ships through the masses of floating ash might say *those* were the worst.
19. Relatives of the people *who* were drowned when a 120-foot-high tidal wave swept inland might say *that* was the worst.
20. *Who* can really decide on the worst aspect of a disaster?

AGREEMENT WITH ANTECEDENTS

Pronouns must agree with their antecedents in number, gender, and person.

Use a singular pronoun to refer to a singular antecedent. Use a plural pronoun to refer to a plural antecedent.

> The artist set up *her* easel by the river. (The singular pronoun *her* refers to the singular antecedent *artist*.)

> The artists displayed *their* paintings in the park. (The plural pronoun *their* refers to the plural antecedent *artists*.)

Pronouns in the third-person singular must also agree with their antecedents in gender.

> Shelly took *her* last exam this morning, but Jason will take *his* tomorrow. (*Her* refers to the feminine antecedent *Shelly; his* refers to the masculine antecedent *Jason*.)

Notice in the preceding examples that the pronouns and antecedents also have another form of agreement. They are all in the third person.

Fallingwater, Bear Run, Pennsylvania, 1936. House designed by world famous architect, Frank Lloyd Wright, illustrates nature and architecture in harmony.

Practice Your Skills

CONCEPT CHECK

Agreement with Antecedents Write the pronoun which correctly completes each sentence. Identify the antecedent of each pronoun.

Writing Theme
Martin Luther King, Jr.

1. By October 1964, Martin Luther King, Jr., had already spent many years of _____ life working for civil rights.
2. The struggle for voter registration was at _____ peak.
3. Black citizens were insisting on _____ right to use all public facilities.
4. When the telephone rang at the King home, _____ often signaled an incident of hatred and abuse.
5. One morning, when Mrs. King picked up the receiver, _____ received a different kind of shock.
6. A man from the Associated Press was calling, and _____ said, "We have just received a message from Norway."
7. The Nobel Prize committee had announced that _____ was awarding Dr. King the Nobel Prize for peace.

Humanities Connection

Art Note Built in 1936, the Kaufmann house, *Falling Water*, at Bear Run, Pennsylvania, is one of the masterpieces of the internationally acclaimed architect, Frank Lloyd Wright (b. 1867, United States, d. 1959). Wright believed that a building should ''flow'' into its surroundings and achieved this effect in the Kaufman house by building it over a waterfall, and extending the terraces above the water to frame the scene. Wright's structures also incorporated the natural materials and colors of the setting. This house was built from the rough stone found in the region.

8. her, Mrs. King; he, husband
9. he, Dr. King; him, Dr. King
10. we, Martin and I

Additional Resources

• Grammar and Usage Practice
Book, pp. 49–50

8. Mrs. King at once called _____ husband at the hospital, where
_____ was having an examination.
9. Dr. King had been sleeping, and when _____ received the news,
it occurred to _____ that he might be dreaming.
10. Mrs. King wrote later, "Though _____ were very happy, both
Martin and I realized the tremendous responsibility that this
placed on him."

Martin Luther King, Jr.,
receiving the Nobel
Peace Prize in 1964.

Indefinite Pronouns as Antecedents

When the antecedent is an indefinite pronoun, determine
whether it is singular or plural. A pronoun must agree in number
with its antecedent. Therefore, use the singular possessive pronouns
his, her, and *its* and the singular reflexive pronouns *himself, herself,* and *itself* with the singular indefinite pronouns.

Each of the stores set *its* own hours.
Each of the women introduced *herself.*
Neither of the men gave *himself* enough time for the trip.
Someone forgot *his* hockey skates in the boys' locker room.
Someone forgot *her* handbag.
Someone forgot *his or her* backpack.

The phrase *his or her* is sometimes used to show that the indefinite pronoun may refer to a male or a female.

The plural pronouns *their* and *themselves* are used with the
plural indefinite pronouns.

Both of the swimmers timed *their* sprints.
All of the tourists found *themselves* lost without guidebooks.

For indefinite pronouns that may be either singular or plural, determine the number from the meaning of the sentence.

Singular All of the water has chemicals in *it*.
Plural All of the streams have chemicals in *them*.

Do not be confused by a phrase that appears between an indefinite pronoun and a possessive pronoun.

Incorrect One of the girls left *their* umbrella. (The possessive pronoun should agree with *one*, not with *girls*.)
Correct One of the girls left *her* umbrella.

Practice Your Skills

A. CONCEPT CHECK

Indefinite Pronouns Write the indefinite pronoun in each sentence.

1. When artists create original art, each reveals his or her own way of looking at the world.
2. Most, such as Rembrandt, depict a recognizable world.
3. In contrast, some, such as Picasso, urgently impress their own personalities on us in disorienting ways.
4. However, neither of those two artists ever fails to intrigue us.
5. All of the truly great artists give us glimpses of new worlds.

B. DRAFTING SKILL

Connecting Ideas The correct use of pronouns and antecedents can clarify relationships between ideas. Supply each missing pronoun below and identify its antecedent.

(1) Many of our early photographers found _____ work treated merely as a fad. (2) One, however, named Alfred Stieglitz, eventually saw _____ work accepted as art. (3) Each of his photographs is remarkable for _____ technical innovations. (4) Several of his most famous photographs used as _____ subject Georgia O'Keeffe, the artist who became his wife. (5) Much of her work had the Southwest as _____ theme. (6) Most of O'Keeffe's paintings have an abstract, yet sensuous, quality about _____ . (7) Both of these artists, Stieglitz and O'Keeffe, did _____ best to redefine art. (8) Everyone, according to Stieglitz, should continually reconsider _____ definition of art. (9) Few of the first modern artists had _____ work exhibited in the United States until Stieglitz opened a gallery in 1905. (10) Anyone who studies modern art should devote some of _____ time to these artists.

Writing Theme
Artists

 Individualizing Instruction

ESL Students Remind these students that uncountable nouns such as "water" are singular. Therefore, indefinite pronouns occurring with uncountable nouns will be singular.

Additional Resources
• Grammar and Usage Practice Book, pp. 51–52

WRITING THEME   Artists

A. Concept Check
Indefinite Pronouns
Answers are underlined on page.

B. Drafting Skill
Connecting Ideas
1. their, Many
2. his, One
3. its, Each
4. their, Several
5. its, Much
6. them, Most
7. their, Both
8. his or her, Everyone
9. their, Few
10. his or her, Anyone

C. Proofreading Skill

Correcting Antecedent Agreement

Errors are underlined on page.

Everybody who looks at Dorothea Lange's photographs will find his or her own meaning for her work. However, no one can experience her pictures without being deeply affected. Though all of the pictures are of the Depression era, they are not a cold record of fact. Lange's compassion projects through the lens to the lines on every face.

Lange began her career as a portrait photographer in San Francisco. She tried to make each of her photographs a timeless record of its subject. One day she saw a young unemployed worker through the window of her studio. Someone else might have turned his or her back on a sight so common. Lange, however, decided to capture the time in which she lived. No one captured it better.

Teaching Strategies

Stumbling Block

Often students do not initially recognize what is ambiguous in cases of vague pronoun use. It may be helpful to supply additional examples and have students verbalize the confusing elements as well as possible solutions.

C. PROOFREADING SKILL

Antecedent Agreement Rewrite the paragraphs below, correcting all errors. Pay particular attention to pronoun agreement as you rewrite each sentence.

Everybody who looks at Dorothea Lange's photographs will find <u>their</u> own meaning for her work. However, no one can experience her pictures <u>with out</u> being deeply <u>effected</u>. Though all of the pictures are of the Depression era, <u>it</u> is not a cold record of fact. <u>Langes</u> compassion projects <u>threw</u> the lens to the lines on every face.

Lange began her career as a portrait photographer in <u>san francisco</u>. She tried to make each of her photographs a timeless record of <u>their</u> subject. One day she saw a young <u>unemploied</u> worker through the window of her studio. Someone else <u>might</u> have turned <u>their</u> back on a sight so common. Lange, however, decided to capture the <u>Time</u> in which she lived. No one captured it <u>more</u> better.

VAGUE PRONOUN REFERENCE

When you write or speak, be sure that each pronoun refers clearly to its antecedent. If a pronoun appears to have more than one antecedent or if there is no apparent antecedent, the pronoun reference is vague. Study the examples of vague pronoun reference in the following sentences. Can you think of other ways to correct the sentences?

Incorrect	We saw the cat's shadow, and then it ran away. (*It* obviously refers to the cat, although the actual antecedent in the sentence is *shadow*.)
Correct	We saw the shadow, and then the cat ran away.
Incorrect	Jean called Harriet when she arrived in town. (Does *she* refer to Jean or to Harriet?)
Correct	When Harriet arrived in town, Jean called her.
Incorrect	In this article *it* tells about the new subway tunnel.
Correct	This article tells about the new subway tunnel.
Incorrect	Outside the concert hall, *they* put up barricades.
Correct	Outside the concert hall, the police put up barricades.
Incorrect	On most airlines, *you* need a carrier for *your* dog.
Correct	Most airlines require carriers for dogs.

Practice Your Skills

A. REVISION SKILL

Clarifying Vague Pronoun Reference Rewrite each sentence below to correct vague pronoun reference. You may need to invent details.

1. In 55 B.C. Julius Caesar was the Roman governor of Gaul, which they call France today.
2. The Romans had conquered many lands, but they were not always as submissive as they thought.
3. Because the conquered peoples tended to rebel against their rulers, they always needed to be alert.
4. Caesar's soldiers had a hard task, for the Gauls were about to rebel, and Caesar believed that the Britons were plotting with them.
5. In Caesar's *Commentaries,* it tells the story of how he took five thousand soldiers and sailed to Britain.
6. The Romans fought with the Britons, and after they won a few battles, they set up a camp.
7. However, winter was coming on, when you find it difficult to live off the land; so Caesar withdrew until the next summer.
8. Although Caesar managed to conquer the local British chieftain, he was not the ruler of the entire country.
9. As the army marched inland, he met with surprise attacks.
10. They never fail to point out in history texts that Caesar's army left its mark on each culture it touched.

B. PROOFREADING SKILL

Correcting Vague Pronoun Reference Rewrite the paragraphs, correcting vague pronoun reference and other errors.

> After occupying britain for three months, Caesar returned to Gaul. The Romans realized it would have been difficult to defeat the Britons because they had no central government. Instead, each of the British tribes controlled their own territory. You would have had to fight each tribe separately.
>
> In Caesar's account of his invasion of Britain, it gives one of the earliest descriptions of its people. Spirits were said to live in rocks and trees, and they believed that the oak tree was especially sacred. The Britons new how to make pottery and to weave wool into cloth. Their culture, however, proved warlike, fighting among themselves with swords and spears.
>
> Although Caesar did not succede, Roman soliders conquered the Britons one hundred years later. After they prevailed, they remained as part of a Roman province for more than three hundred years.

Additional Resources
- Grammar and Usage Practice Book, pp. 53–54

WRITING THEME Julius Caesar

A. Revision Skill

Clarifying Vague Pronoun Reference
Answers will vary. See typical answers below.

1. In 55 B.C. Julius Caesar was the Roman governor of Gaul, which is called France today.
2. The Romans had conquered many lands, but the vanquished were not always as submissive as the Romans thought.
3. Because the conquered peoples tended to rebel against their rulers, the Romans always needed to be alert.
4. Caesar's soldiers had a hard task, for the Gauls were about to rebel, and Caesar believed that the Britons were plotting with the Gauls.
5. Caesar's *Commentaries* tells the story of how Caesar took five thousand soldiers and sailed to Britain.
6. The Romans fought with the Britons, and after the Romans won a few battles, they set up a camp.
7. However, winter was coming on, when it was difficult to live off the land; so Caesar withdrew until the next summer.
8. Although Caesar managed to conquer the local British chieftain, that chieftain was not the ruler of the entire country.
9. As Caesar's army marched inland, it met with surprise attacks.
10. History texts never fail to point out that Caesar's army left its mark on each culture it touched.

B. Proofreading Skill

Correcting Vague Pronoun Reference
Answers will vary. See typical answers below. Errors are underlined on page.

After occupying Britain for three months, Caesar returned to Gaul. The Romans realized it would have been difficult to defeat the Britons because the Britons had no central government. Instead, each of the British tribes controlled its own territory. The Romans would have had to fight each tribe separately.

Caesar's account of his invasion of Britain gives one of the earliest descriptions of its people. Spirits were said to live in rocks and trees, and the oak tree was believed to be especially sacred. The Britons knew how to make pottery and to weave wool into cloth. Their culture, however, proved warlike. They were constantly fighting among themselves with swords and spears.

Although Caesar did not succeed, Roman soldiers conquered the Britons one hundred years later. After the Romans prevailed, Britain remained as part of a Roman province for more than three hundred years.

Objectives

- To use pronouns correctly in compound constructions
- To use correctly pronouns that have compound antecedents joined by *or* or *nor*
- To use pronouns correctly in comparisons
- To distinguish between possessive pronouns and contractions
- To use *who* and *whom* correctly
- To use *we* and *us* correctly with nouns
- To use *them* and *those* correctly
- **Writing** To demonstrate revision skills by correcting pronoun errors

Writing Theme
Man's First Flight

PROBLEMS WITH PRONOUNS

Many of the most common errors in both writing and speaking result from the improper use of pronouns. When you use pronouns, watch for these problems.

Pronouns in Compound Construction

Pronouns in compound constructions often cause difficulty. In the sentences below, which form in parentheses is correct?

> *Laura* and (I, me) learned judo. (*Laura and I* is the compound subject. The nominative form, *I,* is correct.)
> Sheila practices with him and (I, me). (*Him and me* is the compound object of the preposition *with.* The objective form, *me,* is correct.)

In a compound construction, you can tell which pronoun form is correct by saying the sentence twice, trying out each pronoun separately. For instance, in the second example above, say: *Sheila practices with him. Sheila practices with me.*

Practice Your Skills

CONCEPT CHECK

Compound Constructions Write the correct pronoun for each sentence.

1. My family and (me, I) stood watching Orville and Wilbur Wright on a desolate beach at Kitty Hawk.
2. We did not know that this would be a historic day for Orville and (he, him).
3. Both Wilbur and (him, he) had come here before to test gliders.
4. Now (us, we) and four others watched them test *Flyer.*
5. The December weather punished (they, them) and (we, us).
6. Strong winds ripped Mom's hat off, and my sister and (her, she) chased it.
7. Wilbur yelled at Mom and (she, her) to step out of the way.
8. Orville reclined along the lower wing, and Wilbur ran alongside the plane and (he, him).
9. *Flyer* rose into the air, moved unsteadily, and came down 120 feet from the others and (I, me).
10. Although the Wright Brothers were initially ignored by the press, history finally credited (they, them) and their machine with achieving the first successful powered flight.

Orville and Wilbur Wright making the first flight at Kitty Hawk, North Carolina, 1903.

Compound Antecedents Using *Or* or *Nor*

When two or more singular antecedents are joined by *or* or *nor,* use a singular pronoun.

Neither *Jeff* nor *Alonso* received *his* test results.

When two or more plural antecedents are joined by *or* or *nor,* use a plural pronoun to refer to them.

Neither the *dancers* nor the *actors* brought *their* costumes.

When one singular antecedent and one plural antecedent are joined by *or* or *nor,* use the noun nearer the verb to determine whether the pronoun is singular or plural.

Neither *Alice* nor the other *guests* brought *their* swimsuits.

Pronouns in Comparisons

When a pronoun is part of a comparison using *than* or *as,* use the nominative form. If words are omitted from the comparison, supply the missing words. Then you will be able to choose the correct form.

Gina is two years older than *I.* (Think: older than *I* am.)

Using Pronouns   **571**

WRITING THEME   Mystery Writers

Drafting Skill
Antecedent Agreement
1. she
2. her
3. their
4. his
5. her
6. her
7. he
8. their
9. I
10. its

Writing Theme
Mystery Writers

Practice Your Skills

DRAFTING SKILL

Antecedent Agreement Write the correct pronoun in each sentence.

1. JAN: Agatha Christie is good, but another novelist—Phyllis Dorothy James—is better than _____ .
2. CHRIS: I disagree. It's true that neither Christie nor P. D. James lets _____ readers down, but Christie's plots are great puzzles.
3. JAN: Puzzles or mazes have _____ appeal, but it's the detective that really makes the difference.
4. CHRIS: Right! Either Hercule Poirot or Sherlock Holmes finds _____ way to the top of most readers' list of favorites, and Poirot is Christie's creation.
5. JAN: Neither Jane Marple nor Agatha Christie can really think _____ way logically through a mystery.
6. CHRIS: Nonsense. Christie or her heroine can use _____ reasoning powers better than James's Cordelia Gray.
7. JAN: Poirot is always trusting his "little grey cells" instead of scientific evidence. James's Adam Dalgleish is much more systematic than _____ .
8. CHRIS: Neither the average reader nor the critics can deny _____ frustration when Poirot proves the least likely suspect guilty in *The Murder of Roger Ackroyd*.
9. JAN: Give up. You're just not going to sway as loyal a James fan as _____ .
10. CHRIS: In the end, either sales figures or literary history will stamp _____ decision on this question.

Possessive Pronouns and Contractions

Do not confuse the possessive pronouns *its, your, their,* and *whose* with the contractions *it's, you're, they're,* and *who's*. In a contraction, the apostrophe shows where letters have been left out.

Contractions   *It's* time to leave. (*It's = It is*)
You're ready, aren't you? (*You're = You are*)
They're leaving tomorrow. (*They're = They are*)
Who's coming to the lecture? (*Who's = Who is*)

The possessive form of a personal pronoun has no apostrophe.

Possessive Pronouns   Put the kitten in *its* basket.
Here are *your* report covers.
We gave them *their* tickets.
Whose book is this?

To decide which word is correct in a sentence, substitute the words the contraction stands for. If the sentence sounds right, then the contraction is correct. If it doesn't, a possessive pronoun is required.

Who and Whom

Many people have trouble deciding when to use *who* and *whom*. *Who* is in the nominative case. It is used as a subject.

> *Who* tuned our music teacher's piano?
> *Who* is there?
> *Who* will call for tickets?

Whom is in the objective case. Although it may not always sound natural to you, it must be used when the sentence requires an object.

> *Whom* did the Steiners see? (*Whom* is the direct object of the verb *did see*. The Steiners did see *whom*.)
> About *whom* will you write your biography? (*Whom* is the object of the preposition *about*. You will write about *whom*.)

Be especially alert to sentences that begin with an interrogative pronoun and end with a preposition. Such sentences also use *whom*.

> *Whom* was the message directed to? (*Whom* is the object of the preposition *to*. The message was directed to *whom*.)

We and Us with Nouns

The pronouns *we* and *us* are often used with nouns: *we students, us students*. Use *we*—in the nominative case—if the noun is the subject of the sentence.

> *We* hikers hacked our way through brush. (*Hikers* is the subject.)

Use *us*—in the objective case—if the noun is an object.

> Nothing can stop *us* hikers. (*Hikers* is the direct object.)

To decide whether to use *we* or *us,* think of the sentence without the noun. For instance, in the first example above, think: *We hacked our way.* In the second example, think: *Nothing can stop us.*

Using Pronouns   **573**

Off the Record

"George Moore wrote brilliant English until he discovered grammar."

—Oscar Wilde

Them and *Those*

Them is a pronoun and is used only as an object. It is not used as a subject or as any other part of speech. *Those,* on the other hand, is a demonstrative pronoun that can also be used as an adjective. Do not use *them* in place of *those*.

Incorrect	*Them* are my favorite snacks. (*Them* is used incorrectly as the subject of the sentence.)
Correct	*Those* are my favorite snacks.
Incorrect	A search party found *them* explorers. (*Them* is used incorrectly as an adjective.)
Correct	A search party found *those* explorers.

Practice Your Skills

A. CONCEPT CHECK

Pronoun Usage   Write the word that completes each sentence.

(1) (Who, Whom) decided that all astronaut candidates should be test pilots? President Eisenhower settled this issue. (2) He realized that astronauts were people for (who, whom) life-risking situations were an everyday occurrence. (3) (Them, Those) first candidates had to be less than six feet tall. (4) (You're, Your) probably wondering why. (5) Candidates had to fit into the *Mercury* capsule (whose, who's) size was governed by the number of booster rockets it carried. (6) Such considerations seem strange to (we, us) earthbound spectators. (7) Later in the space program, only (those, them) candidates with a Ph.D. in science could qualify. (8) In the shuttle era, NASA changed many of (its, it's) requirements. (9) Candidates' ages no longer applied, nor did (they're, their) height. (10) In addition, many Americans were glad that six of (those, them) 1978 candidates were women.

B. PROOFREADING SKILL

Correcting Pronoun Errors   Rewrite the following passage, correcting all errors in grammar, usage, and mechanics. Pay special attention to errors in pronoun usage.

A young man whom loved flying stood before his st. Louis backers.

One said, "Perhaps its because us bankers are not fliers, but we wonder if a multiengine craft would be more certain to get across the atlantic?"

"No," replied Lindbergh. "<u>Them</u> are harder to handle in rough weather; and if I lose an engine over the <u>Ocean</u>, I won't make it."

Later the plane's <u>designer's</u> tried to make Lindbergh accept <u>they're</u> recommendation that he not place a large gas tank where the windshield should be. They thought there couldn't be any flier to <u>who</u> fuel was that important.

In spite of many other hardships such as <u>them</u>, Lindbergh made his historic <u>flite</u> successfully

CHECK POINT
PAGES 565–575

A. Correct all errors in pronoun usage.

1. Truly great athletes add <u>his or her</u> own chapter to sports history.
2. Each has <u>their</u> own style of excellence.
3. <u>Whom</u> was the "Greatest Female Athlete of the Century"?
4. <u>It says</u> in the record book that it was Mildred (Babe) Didrikson.
5. In 1932, at a national track meet, she scored thirty points by herself, defeating the second-place team <u>who's</u> score was twenty-two points.
6. Neither the public nor the writers could get <u>its</u> fill of her.
7. All of the excitement over her Olympic medals made <u>their</u> way into newspapers around the world.
8. However, <u>them</u> achievements did not bring financial security.
9. <u>Its</u> an odd combination, but eventually she earned her living performing in vaudeville and in exhibition games.
10. Finally Didrikson became a professional golfer, and <u>it</u> made her a millionaire.

B. Rewrite each sentence that has a pronoun error, correcting the error. If a sentence has no error, write *Correct.*

1. <u>Whom</u> was named "Greatest Male Athlete of the Century" in 1950?
2. It was Jim Thorpe, <u>who's</u> heritage was Native American.
3. In high school his skills earned his football team and <u>he</u> honors.
4. <u>Us</u> sports fans know of his performance at the 1912 Olympics.
5. He won two gold medals but was forced to return <u>it</u>.
6. <u>They</u> discovered he had played baseball for money.
7. According to Olympic rules, this made him a professional.
8. He was disqualified by the people <u>whom</u> had honored him.
9. Everyone had <u>their</u> own opinion about what should be done about Thorpe's situation.
10. In 1982 the Olympic Committee restored his medals.

You may wish to use the following checkpoint exercises as an informal evaluation of student mastery of the concepts covered in this handbook.

WRITING THEME   Great Athletes

A.
Errors are underlined on page.
1. Truly great athletes add their own chapter to sports history.
2. Each has his or her own style of excellence.
3. Who was the "Greatest Female Athlete of the Century"?
4. The record book says that it was Mildred (Babe) Didrikson.
5. In 1932, at a national track meet, she scored thirty points by herself, defeating the second-place team whose score was twenty-two points.
6. Neither the public nor the writers could get their fill of her.
7. All of the excitement over her Olympic medals made its way into newspapers around the world.
8. However, those achievements did not bring financial security.
9. It's an odd combination, but eventually she earned her living performing in vaudeville and in exhibition games.
10. Finally Didrikson became a professional golfer, and golf made her a millionaire.

B.
Errors are underlined on page.
1. Who was named "Greatest Male Athlete of the Century" in 1950?
2. It was Jim Thorpe, whose heritage was Native American.
3. In high school his skills earned his football team and him honors.
4. We sports fans know of his performance at the 1912 Olympics.
5. He won two gold medals but was forced to return them.
6. Officials discovered he had played baseball for money.
7. Correct
8. He was disqualified by the people who had honored him.
9. Everyone had his or her own opinion about what should be done about Thorpe's situation.
10. Correct

Application and Review

These activities are designed to allow your students to apply concepts presented in this handbook. Exercises A and B require students to identify kinds of pronouns and the cases of pronouns. Exercise C challenges students to correct errors in pronoun usage. Exercises D and E require students to solve pronoun problems by choosing the correct pronouns.

> ### Additional Resources
> • Tests and Assessment, Mastery Tests, pp. 53–60
> • Elaboration, Revision, and Proofreading Worksheets, p. 24

WRITING THEME   Historic Figures and Periods

Suggest that interested students brainstorm topics related to this theme to use for writing assignments in their history class.

A. Identifying Pronouns
Pronouns are underlined on page.
1. Who, Interrogative
2. He, Personal; one, Indefinite; who, Relative
3. who, Relative; himself, Intensive
4. He, Personal; something, Indefinite; that, Relative; itself, Reflexive
5. that, Relative
6. This, Demonstrative
7. Nobody, Indefinite; anything, Indefinite; that, Demonstrative
8. His, Personal
9. Anyone, Indefinite; who, Relative
10. It, Personal; which, Relative

B. Identifying Pronoun Case
1. she, Nominative
2. her, Objective
3. him, Objective
4. he, Nominative
5. her, Possessive; their, Possessive
6. them, Objective
7. We, Nominative; her, Possessive
8. They, Nominative
9. It, Nominative; her, Possessive
10. she, Nominative; they, Nominative; her, Possessive

C. Correcting Pronoun Errors
Errors are underlined on page.
1. Everyone should read the Greek and Roman myths for himself or herself.
2. Of the twelve male and female Olympians, each had his or her own powers and duties.
3. However, all of the gods and goddesses owed their allegiance to Zeus, the most mighty.
4. The myths tell of how the gods helped heroes.
5. One of the gods lent his winged sandals

GRAMMAR
HANDBOOK
32

Writing Theme
Historic Figures and Periods

A. Identifying Pronouns   Write each pronoun and identify it as *Personal, Intensive, Reflexive, Demonstrative, Indefinite, Interrogative, or Relative.*

1. Who was Nicholas Cugnot?
2. He was one of the pioneers who developed the automobile.
3. Cugnot, who was himself a captain in the French Artillery and an engineer, wanted to build a machine to haul a cannon.
4. He wanted to create something that could propel itself.
5. Cugnot designed a three-wheeled vehicle that was steam-powered.
6. This is generally considered to have been the first automobile.
7. Nobody had ever seen anything like that before.
8. His carriage had a huge boiler ahead of the driving wheel.
9. Anyone who laughed at this monstrosity was proved wrong.
10. It could go three miles an hour, which was remarkable for the day.

B. Identifying Pronoun Case   Write the italicized pronouns in the sentences below. Then identify the case of each pronoun as *Nominative, Objective,* or *Possessive.*

1. In Germany *she* was known as Sophie Friederike Auguste, but she was known to history as Catherine the Great.
2. The title of Grand Duchess Catherine Alekseyevna came to *her* at age fourteen when she was promised in marriage to Grand Duke Peter of Russia.
3. Peter took the throne, but she replaced *him* and took power.
4. Soon afterward, *he* died, possibly murdered in a brawl.
5. During *her* reign, Russia's poor peasants showed *their* dissatisfaction by revolting frequently.
6. Catherine tried unsuccessfully to establish a system of education for *them*.
7. *We* know much about Catherine from *her* letters.
8. *They* reveal a witty, energetic woman.
9. *It* was common for *her* workday to be fifteen hours long.
10. In addition to letters, *she* wrote many comedies, proverbs, and stories, and *they* have added to *her* colorful reputation.

C. Correcting Pronoun Errors   Rewrite the following sentences, correcting all errors in pronoun usage.

1. Everyone should read the Greek and Roman myths for themselves.
2. Of the twelve male and female Olympians, each had their own powers and duties.
3. However, all of the gods and goddesses owed his or her allegiance to Zeus, the most mighty.
4. In the myths they tell of how the gods helped heroes.
5. One of the gods lent their winged sandals to Perseus.

6. Sometimes the gods grew angry, and it caused problems.
7. Some took his anger out on humans.
8. When Arachne angered the goddess Minerva, she turned her into a spider.
9. In our modern culture, it shows how myths are still relevant.
10. Several of the months take its names from gods and goddesses.

D. Using Pronouns Correctly Write the correct pronoun for each sentence.

1. Uncle Abe is going to build his family and (we, us) houses.
2. In 1952 Dad and (him, he) designed our first homes.
3. Neither they nor (I, me) can wait for the house-raising party.
4. John says that either you or (he, him) will win the footrace.
5. You are a better racer than (him, he).
6. Either the twins or Ann will bring (their, her) songbook.
7. Between you and (I, me), I hope Aunt Lydia doesn't cook.
8. It is (her, she) who adds so much salt to everything.
9. She is always asking John and (I, me) to pluck the hen.
10. The next village and (we, us) have fifty families now.
11. Soon the men will build a school for them and (we, us).
12. The teacher will live with either my cousins or (we, us).
13. Ann and (me, I) heard the pastor talk of a possible college.
14. (Him, He) and the village council have discussed the plan.
15. Expect a letter from my family and (I, me) next month.

E. Solving Pronoun Problems Write the correct pronoun for each sentence.

1. (We, Us) typists know that *qwerty* is not a foreign word.
2. (They're, Their) the first letters on the top row of a typewriter.
3. Perhaps (your, you're) question is "Why this arrangement?"
4. Charles Sholes, (who, whom) developed the first typewriter, had a very good reason.
5. In order to avoid type bars clashing, (them, those) letters most often used in English were not placed near one another.
6. Sholes, for (who, whom) inventing was a sideline, was a senator from Wisconsin.
7. His first typewriter made (it's, its) appearance in 1874.
8. (Who, Whom) was interested in (those, them) strange-looking new machines?
9. Mark Twain, (who's, whose) book *Life on the Mississippi* is a classic, bought one.
10. In fact, records about his work suggest that (it's, its) the first literary manuscript to have been typed.

6. Sometimes the gods grew angry, and their anger caused problems.
7. Some took their anger out on humans.
8. When Arachne angered the goddess Minerva, Minerva turned her into a spider.
9. Our modern culture shows how myths are still relevant.
10. Several of the months take their names from gods and goddesses.

D. Using Pronouns Correctly
Answers are underlined on page.

E. Solving Pronoun Problems
Answers are underlined on page.

If possible, play a recording of this selection. Abbott and Costello rely on comic characters as well as misunderstandings about pronouns to produce humor in this routine.

On the Lightside

WHO'S ON FIRST?

The antics of Abbott and Costello kept audiences laughing for almost thirty years. From 1929 until 1957 the team performed on the vaudeville stage, for radio and TV, and in a series of successful movies. The following sketch is their most famous routine. Every time they did it, they changed it slightly.

Bud: You know, strange as it may seem, they give ballplayers peculiar names nowadays. On the St. Louis team Who's on first, What's on second, I Don't Know is on third.

Lou: That's what I want to find out, the names of the fellows on the St. Louis team.

Bud: I'm telling you. Who's on first, What's on second, I Don't Know is on third.

Lou: You know the fellows' names?

Bud: Yes.

Lou: Well, then, who's playing first?

Bud: Yes.

Lou: I mean, the fellow's name on first base.

Bud: Who.

Lou: I'm askin' you, who is on first.

Bud: That's the man's name.

Lou: That's whose name?

Bud: Yes.

Lou: Well, go ahead, tell me.

Bud: Who is on first base.

Lou: That's what I'm tryin to find out. Wait a minute. Tell me the pitcher's name.

Bud: Tomorrow.

Lou: You don't want to tell me today?

Bud: I'm telling you, man.

Lou: Then go ahead.

Bud: Tomorrow.

Lou: You gotta catcher?

Bud: Yes.

Lou: The catcher's name?

Bud: Today.

Lou: Today. And Tomorrow's pitching.

Bud: Now you've got it.

Lou: Now, I throw the ball to first base.

Bud: Then who gets it?

Lou: He'd better get it! (frenzied) Now I throw the ball to first base.

Bud: Uh-huh.

Lou: Who picks up the ball and throws it to What. What throws it to I Don't Know. I Don't Know throws it back to Tomorrow. A triple play!

Bud: Yeah, it could be.

Lou: Another guy gets up and it's a long fly ball to center. Why? I don't know. And I don't care.

Bud: What was that?

Lou: I said, I don't care.

Bud: Oh, that's our shortstop.

Bud Abbott and Lou Costello

Sketchbook

"Urban-belief tales" are a popular form of modern folklore. One well-known urban tale concerns alligators that supposedly lurk in city sewers. Another tells of a hitchhiker who eerily appears on the road every twenty miles. Write a complete version of one of these tales, or invent a similar story. Use a variety of descriptive verbs, adjectives, and adverbs.

To show how your mind freely flows from one idea to the next, try some freewriting. Jot down what you are thinking as your thoughts flow through your mind, or write what you imagine someone else, such as your friend or teacher, is thinking at a particular moment. Don't worry about writing complete sentences. Feel free to use sentence fragments.

Additional Sketches

You are a millionaire writing your will. Tell what you intend to leave to your friends, relatives, or your favorite pet. Explain why each is receiving a particular gift or legacy. Use a variety of pronouns.

579

Objective

To use the idea of an "urban-belief tale" as a springboard to informal writing

Using the Prompt

Be sure students understand before they begin writing that Sketchbook activities are meant to tap students' spontaneous creativity and are designed to encourage experimentation and risk taking; they are not graded.

Give students additional background on urban-belief tales: They are a common form of contemporary American folklore. Storytellers generally relate them as if they were real-life experiences, and many such tales even appear as genuine news stories in newspapers or on television. However, when an effort is made to prove them, they turn out to have no basis in fact.

To give students additional ideas, you might suggest the following sketches of well-known urban-belief tales.

- A man discovers that the fast-food chicken he has bought at a take-out shop is really batter-fried rat.
- When bouffant hair was popular, a girl styled her hair and then did not comb it again for weeks. A bee fell into her hair and, unable to escape, stung her badly.

The Additional Sketches section can be used to provide an alternative if some students prefer a different starting point. Ask students to keep their writing in their Writing Portfolios, for reference during future writing projects.

These exercises allow your students to practice skills acquired in Handbooks 29–32. You may wish to use the exercises to provide a thorough review of the material in these chapters or to evaluate student mastery of the concepts.

Additional Resources
- Grammar and Usage Practice Book, pp. 61–63
- Standardized Test Practice

Skills Assessment Test 1
1. B—the universe
   C—their
2. B—skies
   D—geese
3. A—chocolate syrup
   D—that was!
4. B—Spielberg
5. A—they *or* these
6. A—It's
   D—discoveries

Directions   One or more of the underlined sections in the following sentences may contain errors of grammar, usage, punctuation, spelling, or capitalization. Write the letter of each incorrect item, then rewrite the item correctly. If there is no error in an item, write E.

Example   Edith Hamiltons' book *Mythology* makes it clear. That
                            A   **B**
Zeus' power was not unlimited. No error
C   **D**   **E**

Answer   A—Edith Hamilton's; B—clear that

---

1. Although it is commonly accepted by astronomers and other scientists that the Universe
   A   **B**
   has many "black holes," the proof of they're existence is based entirely on theoretical
                                        C   **D**
   mathematics. No error
   E

2. Yearly, each spring and fall, the skys over the Mississippi Valley are filled with songbirds,
                A   **B**   **C**
   cranes, gooses, and other migratory fowl signaling the change of seasons. No error
           D   **E**

3. When 250 gallons of sweet, sticky choclate syrup spilled on a Los Angeles freeway in
                                       A   **B**
   the spring of 1977, cars were backed up for hours. What a colossal traffic jam that was.
                 C   **D**
   No error
   E

4. Stephen Spielberg worked with Harrison Ford when he directed the action film
                      A   **B**   **C**
   Raiders of the Lost Ark. No error.
   D   **E**

5. Cab Calloway, Duke Ellington, and Louis Armstrong—them were some of the greatest
                                                       A **B**   **C**
   entertainers of all time. No error
                 D   **E**

6. Its important to recognize that Cuban doctor Carlos Juan Finlay's research into the
   A   **B**
   transmission of yellow fever formed the basis of Walter Reed's discoverys about the
                                    C   **D**
   disease. No error
           E

7. E
8. D—"Sun's Day." *Monday*
9. B—Robert's
   C—Robert and her
10. E
11. A—Whom
    B—Pulitzer Prize
12. A—The *Dictionary of Misinformation*
    corrects
    D—misquotations
13. A—independently
    D—himself
14. C—than she
15. C—and they
16. C—musician
    D—he

7. When American frontiersman Davy Crockett <u>left home</u> <u>at the age of thirteen</u>, he <u>found</u>
                                           A   **B**   **C**
<u>himself</u> on a cattle drive <u>headed for Virginia</u>. <u>No error</u>
  D   **E**

8. The word *Sunday* <u>comes from</u> the <u>Anglo-Saxon</u> words *Sunna Daeg,* which mean
           A   **B**   **C**
"Sun's Day," *Monday* is from *Monan Daeg,* or "Moon's Day." <u>No error</u>
     D   **E**

9. Although Elizabeth Barrett Browning's poetry is <u>as widely known as</u> her husband
                                       A
<u>Roberts'</u>, most scholars who compare <u>Robert and she</u> consider him to be the
 B   **C**
<u>more important</u> poet. <u>No error</u>
   D   **E**

10. Neither Stevie Wonder <u>nor</u> Ray Charles <u>was</u> blind at birth, but both <u>have lived</u> with
                      A   **B**   **C**
blindness most of <u>their</u> lives. <u>No error</u>
             D   **E**

11. "<u>Who</u> did the <u>pulitzer prize</u> in journalism honor this year?" I <u>asked, leafing</u> through the
   A   **B**   **C**
Raleigh News and Observer. <u>No error</u>
       D   **E**

12. <u>In the *Dictionary of Misinformation* it corrects</u> some <u>commonly</u> held <u>beliefs</u> and
                      A   **B**   **C**
<u>missquotations</u>. <u>No error</u>
  D   **E**

13. Michael Faraday and Joseph Henry <u>independantly</u> but simultaneously <u>made a</u> discovery
                             A   **B**
<u>that led to the development of electricity</u>, and each claimed credit for <u>themself</u>. <u>No error</u>
               C   **D**   **E**

14. Mary Wollstonecraft Shelley <u>never doubted</u> that her husband would be <u>more famous</u>
                            A   **B**
<u>than her</u>, even after she <u>wrote</u> *Frankenstein*. <u>No error</u>
  C   **D**   **E**

15. <u>There are</u> giant twelve-foot lizards on the volcanic <u>island</u> of <u>Komodo, and them</u> are
  A   **B**   **C**
known as <u>Komodo</u> dragons. <u>No error</u>
        D   **E**

16. <u>Director</u> Mike Nichols might not seem <u>to have</u> much in common with <u>musican</u> Andre
  A   **B**   **C**
Previn, but Previn and <u>him</u> were both born in Berlin, Germany. <u>No error</u>
                 D   **E**

17. E
18. B—we farmers
19. E
20. B—his
    C—Germany
21. E
22. D—the spacecraft
23. A—children in
24. D—later, it was not
25. A—Those
    C—gorilla

17. <u>Dr. Mary McCleod Bethune</u> <u>was</u> a presidential <u>advisor; moreover</u>, she founded Bethune-
                         A   **B**   **C**

    Cookman <u>College</u>. <u>No error</u>
             D   **E**

18. It is commonly believed that pigs are dirty <u>animals, but</u> <u>us farmers</u> know that since they
                                            A   **B**

    don't sweat, <u>they</u> must wallow in mud to cool off. <u>No error</u>
      C   **D**   **E**

19. <u>In 1917</u>, militant <u>American</u> women <u>fought</u> for the passage of a <u>constitutional</u>
      A   **B**   **C**   **D**

    amendment giving women the right to vote. <u>No error</u>
                                         E

20. Each of the pioneers of the gasoline engine automobile, Karl Benz and Gottlieb <u>Daimler</u>,
                                                                A

    built <u>their</u> first cars in <u>germany</u> in the <u>1880's</u>. <u>No error</u>
        B   **C**   **D**   **E**

21. <u>Although its</u> final title was *Of Mice and Men*, John <u>Steinbeck's</u> classic was originally
      A   **B**   **C**

    titled *Something That Happened*. <u>No error</u>
          D   **E**

22. In 1976 the Americans sent two *Viking* <u>spacecraft</u> to <u>Mars</u>, and <u>they</u> provided us with
                               A   **B**   **C**   **D**

    the best photographs of Mars to date. <u>No error</u>
                             E

23. The practice of adopting <u>children. In</u> ancient Sumeria <u>came about</u> so that a childless
                       A   **B**

    couple <u>could pass</u> <u>its</u> worldly belongings to an heir. <u>No error</u>
         C   **D**   **E**

24. The sport <u>of bowling</u> had <u>its</u> origins in ancient <u>Egypt. In Germany</u> thousands of years
           A   **B**   **C**

    later. <u>It was not</u> a sport but part of a religious ceremony. <u>No error</u>
        D   **E**

25. <u>Them</u> people <u>who</u> believe the <u>Gorilla</u> is a fierce animal are <u>wrong; it</u> is quiet, slow, and
      A   **B**   **C**   **D**

    primarily vegetarian. <u>No error</u>
                    E

Using Verbs

WHAT IS A VERB?

A verb is a word that expresses action, condition, or state of being.

The two main kinds of verbs are action verbs and linking verbs. Helping, or auxiliary, verbs are sometimes used with them.

Action Verbs

An action verb tells that something is happening, has happened, or will happen. It may describe physical or mental action.

> I *am thinking* about the answer. (mental action)
> Juan *considered* all his options. (mental action)
> The storm *raged* for several hours. (physical action)
> I *will write* the answer on the board. (physical action)

Linking Verbs

A linking verb, sometimes called a state-of-being verb, links the subject with words in the predicate.

> Claude Monet *was* a painter. (The linking verb *was* links the subject *Claude Monet* to *painter.*)
> The contestants *appeared* nervous. (The linking verb *appeared* links the subject *contestants* to *nervous.*)

Common Linking Verbs

be (am, are, is, was, were, been, being)	look	smell	seem
	appear	taste	sound
become	feel	grow	remain

Some verbs can be used as either linking verbs or action verbs.

Linking Verb	Action Verb
The stew *smelled* delicious.	The chef *smelled* the stew.
That bread *tasted* fresh.	Hannah *tasted* the fresh bread.
The hikers *grew* weary.	This farmer *grows* soybeans.
Jamie *felt* tired.	Rudy *felt* the soft velvet.

Writing
—TIP—

Overuse of state-of-being verbs can produce weak writing. Watch for opportunities to replace "be" verbs with strong action verbs.

What Is a Verb?

Objectives

- To identify action verbs and linking verbs
- To identify verb phrases, helping verbs, and main verbs
- **Writing** To use precise action verbs in writing

Teaching Strategies

Stumbling Block

Action verbs such as *think* and *consider* are sometimes difficult for students to perceive as actions, since no physical movement is required. Have students generate a list of other action verbs that refer to mental or emotional activity.

 Individualizing Instruction

ESL Students Remind these students that adjectives, not adverbs of manner, follow linking verbs: *He looked handsome,* not *He looked handsomely.*

Linking Grammar and Writing

Have students review a piece of writing in progress, or a passage in their journal or portfolio, to see where they might substitute specific action verbs for less precise linking verbs.

Writing Theme
Memories

To decide whether a word is an action verb or a linking verb, see how it is used in the sentence. Does it express or describe an action, or does it link the subject with a word in the predicate?

Practice Your Skills

A. CONCEPT CHECK

Types of Verbs　On your paper, write the italicized verbs from the excerpt below. Tell whether each verb is an action verb or a linking verb. Notice the variety of verbs the author used.

(1) Our house was gray, square, and *had* a very high peaked roof. (2) Under the roof was an attic, and it *was* big and filled with dust and dusty boxes and empty jars. (3) The attic had no floor, only the ceiling below, and I used to *sneak* up to its peacefulness and sit just as quietly as the dust and *feel* alone. (4) It had one small dusty window where I could sit and *watch* the road that ran in front of our house. (5) It was old and gravel and *went* nowhere. . . .

(6) We *were* very poor, and I wore striped overalls and homemade shirts of flannel. (7) In the winter I *wore* a mackinaw coat and high-top brown leather work shoes that had funny round hard toes. (8) But in the summer I *ran* around in

my dusty, and as Mom would say, "rusty" feet. (9) We also *ate* the same things for dinner as for supper. (10) We *had* pinto beans and fried potatoes with gravy and flat bread. (11) Breakfast was dried milk and bread which *tasted* much better with sugar.

(12) I didn't have toys, so whenever Edmund *bought* Linda Beth some new ones, I usually *played* with the old ones when he was not at home. (13) When he was at home, I often just *went* away by myself and *was* quiet. (14) But if he was asleep I sat at the kitchen table and *talked* with Mom while she *cooked* or sewed. (15) I *liked* to do that more than most other things.

Durango Mendoza, "A Short Return"

B. REVISION SKILL

Using Vivid Action Verbs By replacing dull verbs with more specific action verbs, a writer can make a description more effective. Keep in mind that action verbs, as well as linking verbs, can sometimes be dull. Revise the following paragraph by replacing the italicized verbs or phrases with livelier action verbs.

(1) Few memories *stay* in my mind more than the time I *saw* the space shuttle *go* into orbit. (2) At sunrise the giant rocket *was bright* on the distant launch pad. (3) Thousands of spectators *were* by their cars and *looked* expectantly in the same direction. (4) At T minus ten seconds, the crowd *said* the seemingly magic words: ". . . ten, nine, eight. . . ." (5) At zero, great billows *came* from the engines, and the air seemed to *fill* with thunder as the shuttle *moved* into the sky. (6) As the image of the shuttle *went away*, ideas of space travel *were* in my head, *taking* me to new worlds of the imagination.

C. APPLICATION IN WRITING

Character Description Recall someone from your past who made a lasting impression on you. Write a brief description that captures the essence of that person's appearance, personality, and distinguishing gestures. Use precise action verbs to bring your portrait into sharp focus for your readers. See the examples below. Check to see that any linking verbs you use are essential and are as effective as your action verbs.

Imprecise	Precise
said	shouted, whispered
ran	dashed, loped, rocketed
turned	spun, whipped around

Using Verbs **585**

9. ate, Action Verb
10. had, Action Verb
11. tasted, Linking Verb
12. bought, Action Verb; played, Action Verb
13. went, Action Verb; was, Linking Verb
14. talked, Action Verb; cooked, Action Verb
15. liked, Action Verb

B. Revision Skill
Using Vivid Action Verbs
Answers will vary. See typical answers below.
(1) Few memories linger in my mind more than the time I watched the space shuttle blast into orbit. (2) At sunrise the giant rocket glistened on the distant launch pad. (3) Thousands of spectators waited by their cars and peered expectantly in the same direction. (4) At T minus ten seconds, the crowd uttered the seemingly magical words: ". . . ten, nine, eight. . . ." (5) At zero, great billows spewed from the engines, and the air seemed to explode with thunder as the shuttle shot into the sky. (6) As the image of the shuttle receded, ideas of space travel swam in my head, shuttling me to new worlds of the imagination.

C. Application in Writing
Character Description
Answers will vary.

Helping Verbs

A main verb—either action or linking—sometimes has one or more helping verbs, also called **auxiliary verbs.** In these examples, the helping verbs are in italic type. The main verbs are in boldface.

That tree *will* **grow** fuller every year.
Their dog *has been* **barking** all night.

The most common helping verbs are forms of *be, have,* and *do.* Several other verbs can also be used as helping verbs.

Common Helping Verbs				
Be	is, am, are, was, were, be, been, being			
Have	has, have, had			
Do	does, do, did			
can	will	shall	may	must
could	would	should	might	

The main verb and one or more helping verbs make up a **verb phrase.**

Helping Verb(s)	+	Main Verb	=	Verb Phrase
am		laughing		am laughing
had		thought		had thought
did		consider		did consider
will be		applauding		will be applauding

Sometimes the helping verb and the main verb are separated. The words that come between them are not part of the verb phrase. In the following examples, the verb phrase is italicized. Remember that the contraction *n't* is not part of the verb.

He *should*n't *have been swimming* in that area.
Did the press secretary *speak?*

The forms of *be, have,* and *do* can also be used as main verbs.

Main Verb	Helping Verb
Samantha *was* busy.	Samantha *was preparing* lunch.
Jill *has* a project.	Jill *has finished* her sculpture.
We *did* the puzzle.	*Did* you *complete* the puzzle?

Practice Your Skills

A. CONCEPT CHECK

Verb Phrases   On your paper, make two columns, labeled *Helping Verb* and *Main Verb*. Find the verb phrase in each of the following sentences and write each part in the proper column.

1. The Austrian composer Wolfgang Amadeus Mozart (1756–1791) has often been cited as the perfect example of a child prodigy.
2. By age five, the remarkably gifted child had composed his first music for piano.
3. The young Mozart could create entire musical scores in his head.
4. Then he would write the notes on paper without hesitation.
5. The people around him, however, must have found him remarkably difficult at times!
6. Outspoken and self-possessed, he was constantly insulting them.
7. Even as an adult, Mozart did not behave according to other people's expectations.
8. He simply would not please his wealthy patrons with their favorite kinds of music.
9. Did he, perhaps, sense the applause of future generations?
10. Could this have been a reason for such unbounded confidence?

B. DRAFTING SKILL

Using Helping Verbs   Helping verbs "help" by making the meaning of main verbs clear and precise. On your paper, complete each of the following sentences by adding one or more helping verbs that fit the meaning. Then underline the complete verb phrase. (For some sentences, suggestions are given in parentheses.)

> **Example**   This composer _____ _____ taken the title of her symphony from a poem by Walt Whitman. (Express possibility.)
> This composer <u>may have taken</u> the title of her symphony from a poem by Walt Whitman.

(1) Music _____ changed significantly since the beginning of the twentieth century. (2) Changes in other art forms _____ _____ influenced the form and feeling of modern music. (Express possibility.) (3) For example, composers _____ _____ studied the works of the new French painters at the turn of the century. (Express certainty.) (4) In addition, the literature of their time _____ _____ inspired such composers as Claude Debussy and Benjamin Britten. (Express possibility.)

Additional Resources
• Grammar and Usage Practice Book, pp. 67–68

WRITING THEME   Music

A. Concept Check
Verb Phrases
Answers are underlined on page.

Helping Verb	Main Verb
1. has been	cited
2. had	composed
3. could	create
4. would	write
5. must have	found
6. was	insulting
7. did	behave
8. would	please
9. Did	sense
10. could have	been

B. Drafting Skill
Using Helping Verbs
Answers will vary. See typical answers below.

(1) Music has changed significantly since the beginning of the twentieth century. (2) Changes in other art forms could have influenced the form and feeling of modern music. (3) For example, composers must have studied the works of the new French painters at the turn of the century. (4) In addition, the literature of their time could have inspired such composers as Claude Debussy and Benjamin Britten.

Using Verbs   **587**

(5) Could new technology have served as a source for some of the recent changes in music? (6) Certainly, modern composers have taken common city sounds as musical themes. (7) Conversely, in modern American music, listeners can often find themes from the nation's musical past. (8) Charles Ives and Aaron Copland, for example, have incorporated the melodies of old hymns into their works. (9) Finally, new electronic instruments have significantly affected the range of an orchestra's sounds. (10) Current American composers such as Joelle Wallach, David Del Tredici, and John Adams did not hesitate to use such untraditional instruments as vibraphones, bullhorns, and synthesizers.

C. Application in Writing
The Review
Answers will vary.

Transitive and Intransitive Verbs

Objective

- To identify transitive and intransitive verbs

Teaching Strategies

Teaching Tip: Transitive and Intransitive Verbs

Encourage students to look for a receiver of the action of the verb to determine whether the verb is transitive or intransitive. Students may find this memory device helpful: the first two letters of transitive (*tr*) can stand for "takes receiver." Then have students expand on the exercises by using the given verbs in new sentences, changing them from transitive to intransitive and vice versa where possible.

---

(5) _____ new technology _____ served as a source for some of the recent changes in music? (Suggest possibility.) (6) Certainly, modern composers _____ taken common city sounds as musical themes. (7) Conversely, in modern American music, listeners _____ often find themes from the nation's musical past. (8) Charles Ives and Aaron Copland, for example, _____ incorporated the melodies of old hymns into their works. (9) Finally, new electronic instruments _____ significantly affected the range of an orchestra's sounds. (10) Current American composers such as Joelle Wallach, David Del Tredici, and John Adams _____ not hesitate to use such untraditional instruments as vibraphones, bullhorns, and synthesizers.

C. APPLICATION IN WRITING

The Review   Listen to a concert broadcast on a public radio or television station. Take notes as you listen. Use your notes to write a short review of the performance. Describe what was good about the performance and suggest what could have been improved. As you draft and revise your review, pay special attention to appropriate helping verbs such as *could, should, would,* and *might.*

TRANSITIVE AND INTRANSITIVE VERBS

In many sentences, an action verb expresses an idea by itself. In other sentences, a direct object is needed to complete the action of the verb. The **direct object,** as you have learned, tells who or what receives the action of the verb.

Verbs that have direct objects are called transitive verbs.

They *extended* the ladder to the second floor.
(The direct object *ladder* completes the action of the verb *extended.*)
He carefully *stored* the rope. (The direct object *rope* completes the action of the verb *stored.*)

Verbs that do not have direct objects are called intransitive verbs.

We *met* in the park.
Everyone *rested* for a while.
Hal *slept* in the chair.

In the preceding examples, the words after the verb do not complete the action of the verb.

Some action verbs are always transitive; others, always intransitive. Many verbs, however, may be transitive in one sentence and intransitive in another. Compare the sentences below. The direct objects are in boldface type.

Transitive Verb	**Intransitive Verb**
We *played* the **tape** over and over.	We *played* all afternoon.
The winners *celebrated* their **victory.**	Their fans *celebrated* too.
Irma *practiced* her **speech.**	Yvonne also *practiced* this morning.

Linking verbs are always intransitive because they never take direct objects.

Those flowers *are* lilies. (*Lilies* is a predicate nominative that renames the subject. It is not a direct object and does not complete the action of the verb.)

They *seem* healthy. (*Healthy* is a predicate adjective that describes the subject. It is not a direct object.)

Practice Your Skills

CONCEPT CHECK

Transitive and Intransitive Verbs Write the verb in each of the following sentences and identify it as *Transitive* or *Intransitive*. If the verb is transitive, write its direct object.

1. The Spanish artist Salvador Dali (1904–1989) is probably the most surrealistic of all painters.
2. Throughout the history of art, most painters have portrayed the real world.
3. Today's abstract painters, on the other hand, emphasize pure shapes and color.
4. Surrealist painters—creative innovators in artistic perception and technique—do neither.
5. In surrealist art, painting and sculpture portray images of the mind.
6. Most of Dali's colorful paintings resemble wild dreams or strange fantasies.
7. A viewer would certainly not find the scenes in Dali's paintings anywhere in the real world.

Writing Theme
Salvador Dali

Photo by Philippe Halsman ©Yvonne Halsman

Using Verbs **589**

Active and Passive Voice

Objectives

- To identify verbs in the active voice and passive voice
- **Writing** To demonstrate revision skills by using passive voice verbs to avoid the use of "you"

Teaching Strategies

Linking Grammar and Writing

Remind students that the use of the active voice can make their writing stronger and more direct. Ask students to review one of their rough drafts and see if any sentences can be improved by changing passive voice verbs to the active voice. Also, encourage students to check to see where they might use passive voice verbs to avoid awkward "you" constructions. Have students rewrite these sentences as part of their revision process.

Critical Thinking

Have students find examples of the use of passive voice verbs in newspaper articles. Ask students to discuss why they think the writers decided to use the passive voice in these sentences.

---

8. Still, like painters centuries before, Dali painted with great attention to highly realistic detail.
9. His paintings, therefore, often appear almost photographic, like snapshots of dreams.

10. In Dali's world, real-looking pocket watches melt over real-looking stones next to real-looking skeletons.
11. The remarkable result, of course, is a very unreal, surrealistic landscape.
12. Dali's paintings are, in one sense, blueprints of his extraordinary imagination.
13. His exceedingly strange but technically polished work disturbs some people.
14. Others have sensed an underlying humor in his bizarre images and landscapes.
15. Like many other modern artists, Dali left interpretation of his paintings up to the individual viewer.

ACTIVE AND PASSIVE VOICE

The **voice** of a verb tells whether the subject performs the action of the verb or receives the action. There are two verb voices in English: the active voice and the passive voice. Only action verbs have voice. Linking verbs do not.

A verb is in the active voice when the subject of a sentence performs the action.

Shakespeare *wrote* that play in the sixteenth century.

In the sentence above, the subject *Shakespeare* performs the action of the verb *wrote*. Therefore, *wrote* is said to be in the active voice.

A verb is in the passive voice when the subject of a sentence receives the action.

That play *was written* by Shakespeare in the sixteenth century.

590 Grammar Handbook

Humanities Connection

Art Note Salvadore Dali (1904–1989) was a surrealist painter who described his work as "hand-painted dream photographs." His paintings often contain juxtapositions of incongruous and puzzling objects and symbols that create a nightmarish mood. Ask: What mood is created in *The Persistence of Memory*? How did Dali create the mood?

In the sentence on the preceding page, the subject *play* receives the action of the verb *was written*. When the subject is the receiver or the result of the action, the verb is said to be in the passive voice.

The passive voice is made by using some form of the helping verb *be* with the past participle of an action verb. The receiver of the action comes before the verb; it is the subject of the sentence.

Active Voice	**Passive Voice**
Maria *tutors* the boys.	The boys *are tutored* by Maria.
Lee *finished* the job.	The job *was finished* by Lee.
Ann *hammered* the nail.	The nail *was hammered* by Ann.

To change a particular sentence from active to passive voice, the verb in the original sentence must be transitive; that is, it must have a direct object. Only verbs that have direct objects can be changed from active to passive. In the sentences above, notice that the direct objects become the subjects and the subjects become the objects of prepositions.

With a verb in the passive voice, it is not always necessary that the performer of the action be named in the sentence. In the following example, the person who wrote the play is not mentioned.

> That play was written in the sixteenth century.

Be careful not to confuse the term *action* with the term *active*. They do not have the same meaning. Most action verbs can be in either the active or passive voice.

Using Voice in Writing

In general, use the active voice when you write. It is stronger, more lively, and more direct. The active voice uses fewer words than the passive and highlights the person who is performing the action. Compare these two sentences.

Active   Carla fixed the lamp.
Passive   The lamp was fixed by Carla.

Occasionally, however, the passive voice is appropriate. Use the passive when you want to stress the receiver of an action or when the performer of the action is unknown or unimportant.

> The entire city block was demolished by the sudden, ferocious tornado.
> According to the records, our town hall was built at the turn of the century.
> The municipal election results were announced.

Additional Resources
- Grammar and Usage Practice Book, pp. 71–72

WRITING THEME   Puppets

Have interested students brainstorm to create a list of possible writing subjects based on this theme.

A. Concept Check

Active and Passive Voice
Verbs are underlined on page.
1. Active
2. Passive
3. Passive
4. Active
5. Passive
6. Passive
7. Passive
8. Passive
9. Active
10. Passive

B. Revision Skill

Avoiding the Use of "You"

Answers will vary. See suggested answers below.

  Marionettes and rod puppets differ from hand puppets in several ways. (1) A marionette can be controlled by strings or wires that are attached to its body. (2) Usually, strings are attached to the head, shoulders, hands, and knees. (3) The audience cannot see the puppeteers, who are hidden behind curtains above the stage. (4) In contrast, a puppeteer operates a rod puppet by sticks or rods. (5) Rod puppets can be used to represent figures other than people. (6) For example, clouds, flowers, or just simple shapes can be portrayed by rod puppets. Rod puppets are featured in a form of Japanese theater called *bunraku* (doll theater). (7) In *bunraku*, a puppeteer dressed in black operates the rod behind each doll.

Writing Theme
Puppets

Practice Your Skills

A. CONCEPT CHECK

Active and Passive Voice   Write the <u>verbs</u> in the following sentences. Then tell whether each verb is in the *Active Voice* or the *Passive Voice*.

1. Puppets <u>have</u> always <u>enjoyed</u> widespread popularity in Europe.
2. In Germany and Austria, puppet theater <u>is known</u> as *Kasperltheater*.
3. The most prominent puppet character in Germany <u>was called</u> Kasperle.
4. The character <u>developed</u> in the 1600's.
5. Kasperle <u>was brought</u> to Germany by traveling puppeteers.
6. A universally popular character, he <u>was featured</u> in marionette productions of *Faust*.
7. Later, he <u>was adapted</u> as a hand puppet.
8. In England, Kasperle <u>was</u> commonly <u>known</u> as Punch.
9. In America, Punch and Judy shows <u>have entertained</u> audiences since colonial times.
10. Today, both adults and children <u>are charmed</u> by a more sophisticated form of puppets, the Muppets.

B. REVISION SKILL

Avoiding the Use of "You"   In formal writing the pronoun *you* should be used only to mean "you the reader." In some cases changing a verb from the active to the passive voice will eliminate awkward *you* constructions. In other cases a noun should be substituted for *you*. In the paragraph below, eliminate the use of *you* in sentences 1, 2, 5, and 6 by changing the verbs to the passive voice. In sentences 3, 4, and 7, supply a new subject.

  Marionettes and rod puppets differ from hand puppets in several ways. (1) You control a marionette by strings or wires that are attached to the body of the puppet. (2) Usually, you attach strings to the head, shoulders, hands, and knees. (3) You cannot see the puppeteers, who are hidden behind curtains above the stage. (4) In contrast, you operate a rod puppet by sticks or rods. (5) You can use rod puppets to represent figures other than people. (6) For example, you can portray clouds, flowers, or just simple shapes. Rod puppets are featured in a form of Japanese theater called *bunraku* (doll theater). (7) In *bunraku* you can see the puppeteer dressed in black operating the rod behind each doll.

A. Write the verb in each of the following sentences. Then tell whether it is an *Action Verb* or a *Linking Verb*.

1. Louis Armstrong <u>was</u> one of the greatest trumpeters in history.
2. This jazz revolutionary <u>changed</u> forever America's most original musical form.
3. A native of New Orleans, Armstrong <u>played</u> the bugle as a boy.
4. Later, in Chicago, he <u>performed</u> as a soloist with jazz orchestras.
5. Armstrong soon <u>grew</u> famous for his dazzling techniques.
6. Naturally, other jazz musicians <u>imitated</u> his innovations.
7. The Louis Armstrong style, however, always <u>remained</u> distinctive.
8. His playing certainly never <u>seemed</u> effortless.
9. A handkerchief across his sweaty brow <u>became</u> his trademark.
10. Extraordinary talent and a bright, warm personality <u>earned</u> Armstrong worldwide acclaim and respect.

B. APPLICATION IN LITERATURE

Active and Passive Voice Identify each italicized verb or verb phrase as the *Active* or *Passive* voice. Then, for each verb in the active voice, write whether it is *Transitive* or *Intransitive*.

> After breakfast there was a ceremony that (1) *was observed* every week without fail. First (2) *came* the hoisting of the flag. Snowball (3) *had found* in the harness-room an old green tablecloth of Mrs. Jones's and (4) *had painted* on it a hoof and a horn in white. This (5) *was run* up the flagstaff in the farmhouse garden every Sunday morning. . . . After the hoisting of the flag all the animals (6) *trooped* into the big barn for a general assembly which was known as the Meeting. Here the work of the coming week (7) *was planned* out and resolutions (8) *were put* forward and debated. . . . The Meeting always (9) *ended* with the singing of *Beasts of England,* and the afternoon (10) *was given* up to recreation.
>
> **George Orwell,** *Animal Farm*

C. Rewrite the following paragraph, correcting any errors in spelling, capitalization, and mechanics. Also correct weak writing by changing passive voice verbs to active voice.

> Born in england in 1612, the poet Anne Bradstreet's life began while <u>William</u> Shakespere was still alive. At the age of sixteen she was married to <u>Simon</u> Bradstreet, and two <u>year's</u>

Writing Theme
Revolutionary Figures

You may wish to use the following Checkpoint exercises as an informal evaluation of student mastery of the concepts covered in this handbook.

WRITING THEME   Revolutionary Figures

A.
Verbs are underlined on page.
1. Linking Verb
2. Action Verb
3. Action Verb
4. Action Verb
5. Linking Verb
6. Action Verb
7. Linking Verb
8. Linking Verb
9. Linking Verb
10. Action Verb

B. Application in Literature
Active and Passive Voice
1. Passive
2. Active, Intransitive
3. Active, Transitive
4. Active, Transitive
5. Passive
6. Active, Intransitive
7. Passive
8. Passive
9. Active, Intransitive
10. Passive

C.
Errors are underlined on page. Answers will vary. See suggested answers below.

The poet Anne Bradstreet was born in England in 1612, while William Shakespeare was still alive. At the age of sixteen she married Simon Bradstreet, and two years later they sailed for America. The couple lived in Massachusetts, where Mr. Bradstreet served as governor. However many hardships an unfamiliar world imposed on her, Anne took the time to create some memorable poems. Her work treated the details of daily life with simplicity and honesty—in spite of the fact that other colonists may have felt it inappropriate for a woman to write poetry. The verse of one of America's first significant writers also beautifully represents early New England Puritanism.

Objective

- To write the principal parts of regular verbs

Teaching Strategies

Collaborative Opportunity

Challenge small groups of students to create a quiz game that requires answers involving the identification of the four principal parts of regular verbs. Set aside time in class for students to play the game.

> **Additional Resources**
> - Grammar and Usage Practice Book, pp. 73–74

later they sailed for America. The couple lived in Massachusets, where Mr. Bradstreet served as governor. However, Many hardships were imposed on her by an unfamiliar world, Anne took the time to create some memorable Poems in spite of the fact that other colonists may have felt it inapropriate for a woman to write poetry. The details of dailey life were treated with simplicity and honesty in her work. Early New england Puritanism is also beautifully represented in verse by one of Americas first significant writer's.

PRINCIPAL PARTS OF REGULAR VERBS

Every verb has four basic forms, called principal parts. The principal parts are the present, the present participle, the past, and the past participle.

Present	Present Participle	Past	Past Participle
learn	(is) learning	learned	(have) learned
open	(is) opening	opened	(have) opened
walk	(is) walking	walked	(have) walked

For all verbs, the present participle is formed by adding *-ing* to the present form. The present participle is used as a main verb with a form of the helping verb *be*.

No one *is listening* to my explanation.

The past participle of **regular verbs** is formed by adding *-ed* or *-d* to the present form. The past participle is used with a form of the helping verb *have* to form the perfect tenses.

No one *had listened* before now.

Verbs whose past participles are formed in other ways are called **irregular verbs.**

The spelling of some regular verbs changes when *-ing* or *-ed* is added to the present form.

Present	Present Participle	Past	Past Participle
try	(is) trying	tried	(have) tried
slip	(is) slipping	slipped	(have) slipped
notice	(is) noticing	noticed	(have) noticed
knit	(is) knitting	knitted	(have) knitted

594 Grammar Handbook

Practice Your Skills

CONCEPT CHECK

Principal Parts of Regular Verbs Make four columns labeled *Present*, *Present Participle*, *Past*, and *Past Participle*. Write each italicized verb below in the appropriate column and then complete the chart.

1. It might be said that the English scientist Sir Isaac Newton (1642–1727) *succeeded* in shrinking the world.
2. His study of the laws of motion has *influenced* space scientists.
3. Application of Newton's theories has *resulted* in space travel and orbiting communication satellites.
4. Two of Newton's basic principles *apply* to astrophysics.
5. First, all physical actions *involve* equal and opposite reactions.
6. Rockets at the moment of liftoff are *demonstrating* this principle.
7. Second, objects in motion *tend* to remain in motion.
8. Accordingly, space probes, once free of the earth's and sun's gravity, *continue* endlessly onward.
9. They *travel* without engines or fuel.
10. Information provided by communication satellites is *closing* gaps in world understanding.

"Nothing yet.... How about you, Newton?"

The Far Side, cartoon by Gary Larson, reprinted by permission of Chronicle Features

PRINCIPAL PARTS OF IRREGULAR VERBS

Verbs whose past and past participle are not formed by adding *-ed* or *-d* to the present are **irregular verbs.**

Present	Present Participle	Past	Past Participle
cost	(is) costing	cost	(have) cost
lose	(is) losing	lost	(have) lost
wear	(is) wearing	wore	(have) worn
sing	(is) singing	sang	(have) sung
take	(is) taking	took	(have) taken

Because the principal parts of irregular verbs are formed in a variety of ways, you must either memorize these parts or refer to a dictionary. The principle parts for regular verbs are given only if they involve a spelling change. For irregular verbs, the dictionary will give two forms if both the past and past participle are the same, as in *catch, caught.* It will give three forms if all principal parts are different, as in *ring, rang, rung.*

Using Verbs   **595**

Individualizing Instruction

LEP Students/Basic Students Oral practice is important in learning the principal parts of irregular verbs. Have students make flashcards for some of the more commonly used verbs from the groups in the lesson. Tell them to write the present form of the verb on the front and the other forms on the back. Let students quiz each other aloud to memorize the parts of these verbs.

Linking Grammar and Writing

Point out that checking for the correct usage of the past and the past participle forms of irregular verbs is a part of proofreading during the writing process.

Additional Resources
- Grammar and Usage Practice Book, pp. 75–76

WRITING THEME Impulse Buying

Concept Check
Principal Parts of Irregular Verbs
  1. burst
  2. set
  3. cut
  4. burst
  5. brought
  6. cost
  7. told
  8. cut
  9. sat

Writing Theme
Impulse Buying

Irregular verbs can be broken down into the five main groups that follow.

Group 1 The irregular verbs in this group have the same form for the present, the past, and the past participle. *Hit, let, put,* and *set* are also in this group.

Present	Present Participle	Past	Past Participle
burst	(is) bursting	burst	(have) burst
cost	(is) costing	cost	(have) cost
cut	(is) cutting	cut	(have) cut

Group 2 The irregular verbs in this group have the same form for the past and the past participle.

Present	Present Participle	Past	Past Participle
bring	(is) bringing	brought	(have) brought
lead	(is) leading	led	(have) led
lose	(is) losing	lost	(have) lost
sit	(is) sitting	sat	(have) sat
teach	(is) teaching	taught	(have) taught

Here are some sentences with verbs from Group 2.

> I always *lose* my best tapes. (present)
> The path *led* into the field. (past)
> I have *sat* here for almost an hour. (past participle)

Practice Your Skills

CONCEPT CHECK

Principal Parts of Irregular Verbs Write the past or past participle of each verb in parentheses.

1. Wayne (burst) angrily into the living room.
2. He (set) a pile of packages on the table.
3. He (cut) the string from one package and pulled something out.
4. Looking at his purchase, he tried to recapture the joy it had given him, but the bubble had (burst).
5. He had (bring) home a leather jacket and should have been happy.
6. The jacket had (cost) over a hundred dollars.
7. However, a friend he met on the way home (tell) him the jacket would go on sale the very next day.
8. Wayne could have (cut) the expense in half if he had waited for a sale.
9. For a while, he just (sit) sulking on the sofa.

10. lost
11. brought
12. lost
13. led
14. taught
15. told

Additional Resources
• Grammar and Usage Practice
  Book, p. 77

10. He had (lose) more than fifty dollars!
11. His part-time job (bring) in only about that much weekly.
12. "I have (lose) an entire week's pay," he said disconsolately to himself.
13. His annoyance (lead) him to question his eagerness to buy the jacket.
14. The disappointment had (teach) him a lesson about impulse buying.
15. Wayne had (tell) himself that many times before he felt any better.

Group 3 The past participle of the irregular verbs in this group is formed by adding *-n* or *-en* to the past form.

Present	Present Participle	Past	Past Participle
break	(is) breaking	broke	(have) broken
choose	(is) choosing	chose	(have) chosen
freeze	(is) freezing	froze	(have) frozen
speak	(is) speaking	spoke	(have) spoken
steal	(is) stealing	stole	(have) stolen
tear	(is) tearing	tore	(have) torn
wear	(is) wearing	wore	(have) worn

Here are some sentences with the verbs from Group 3.

I *wear* those heavy socks with these boots. (present)
He *chose* a red bicycle this time. (past)
She *has spoken* at assembly before. (past participle)

Practice Your Skills

A. CONCEPT CHECK

More Irregular Verbs Write the past or past participle of each verb in parentheses.

1. For centuries people have (choose) bowling or similar sports as forms of recreation.
2. Ancient Egyptians (steal) away from work in the middle of the day to play such games.
3. Early sources have (speak) of games called *kegles* or *ninepins*.
4. In the early nineteenth century Washington Irving (speak) of ninepins in his stories.
5. Many Americans (choose) bowling as their favorite sport as its popularity began to grow in the post-World War II years.

Writing Theme
Sports

WRITING THEME   Sports

A. Concept Check
More Irregular Verbs
  1. chosen
  2. stole
  3. spoken
  4. spoke
  5. chose

6. chosen
7. wore
8. broken
9. worn
10. stolen

B. Revision Skill

Checking Verb Forms

(1) In almost every sport, it is important that people check whether they <u>have chosen</u> the right clothes. (2) Anyone whose hands or feet have <u>almost frozen</u> on a ski slope knows this fact. (3) Many weekend football players have <u>broken</u> bones because they played without padding. (4) Hikers who have mistakenly worn flimsy clothes probably <u>tore</u> them on the first thorny bush they encountered. (5) Active tennis players and even leisurely golfers <u>have often spoken</u> about the need for wearing the proper shoes for a particular sport.

> **Additional Resources**
> • Grammar and Usage Practice Book, p. 78

6. Modern bowlers often have (choose) to compete in amateur or professional leagues.
7. League bowlers used their own shoes and (wear) special shirts that identified them as team members.
8. No one has (break) Earl Anthony's record of 1981 to 1983.
9. Aleta Sill had (wear) the women's international crown after the championship tournament in 1985.
10. Mark Roth has (steal) honors for lifetime earnings, a distinction formerly held by Earl Anthony.

B. REVISION SKILL

Checking Verb Forms Checking to see if you have used the correct verb forms is an important part of the revision process. The sentences in the following paragraph have errors in verb forms. Rewrite the paragraph below correctly, correcting all errors in the use of verb forms.

> (1) In almost every sport, it is important that people check whether they have chose the right clothes. (2) Anyone whose hands or feet have almost froze on a ski slope knows this fact. (3) Many weekend football players have broke bones because they played without padding. (4) Hikers who have mistakenly wore flimsy clothes probably teared them on the first thorny bush they encountered. (5) Active tennis players and even leisurely golfers have often spoke about the need for wearing the proper shoes for a particular sport.

Group 4 In the irregular verbs in this group, the vowel changes in the past and the past participle. The vowel changes from *i* in the present form to *a* in the past form and to *u* in the past participle.

Present	Present Participle	Past	Past Participle
begin	(is) beginning	began	(have) begun
drink	(is) drinking	drank	(have) drunk
ring	(is) ringing	rang	(have) rung
shrink	(is) shrinking	shrank	(have) shrunk
sing	(is) singing	sang	(have) sung
sink	(is) sinking	sank	(have) sunk
swim	(is) swimming	swam	(have) swum

Here are some sentences with verbs from Group 4.

We *sing* in that choir. (present)
Someone *drank* the last of the juice. (past)
The boats in the harbor *have sunk*. (past participle)

Practice Your Skills

A. CONCEPT CHECK

More Irregular Verbs Write the appropriate past or past participle form of each verb given in parentheses.

1. Many champion swimmers (begin) their swimming careers at a very early age.
2. In some cases they (swim) before they were able to walk.
3. Some of their parents probably (shrink) with concern at taking such young children into swimming pools.
4. Then, to their surprise, they found that their infants (swim) almost naturally.
5. One reason is that infants have not (begin) to fear the water.
6. Another reason is that baby fat makes most infants naturally buoyant; few have (sink) quickly when released in water.
7. One father said that he (sing) to his child to keep her happy in the water.
8. He also observed that although she (drink) a lot of water before she learned to swim, it didn't seem to bother her.
9. For years, swimming teachers have (sing) the praises of early lessons.
10. In fact, by age ten, most future champions have (swim) hundreds of miles.

B. PROOFREADING SKILL

Correcting Verb Forms Proofread the following paragraph. Then rewrite it correctly. Pay attention to the use of irregular verbs.

Many athletes have swimmed the English channel. Once a feat that even the hardy had shrank from, people eventualy begun to think of it as somewhat comonplace. However, on September 3 1964 Lenore Modell made the accomplishment seem important again. Lenore was one of those miraculous califonia water-babies who had began to swim at an early age.

Thirty eight years had passed. Since the Channel had first been swam by a woman. A large crowd gathered on the cliffs of dover and their voices sung out with chants of encouragement. At South foreland Point on the opposite shore, a crowd waited and drunk steaming beverages to ward off the chill. Over fifteen hours passed, and hopes of her arrival had almost sank. She had nearly swam up Dover Harbor by mistake, but a tide carried her to her goal. Lusty cheers rung out for this young woman who had just passed her fourteenth birthday—the youngest swimmer to conquer the Channell.

WRITING THEME **Infant Swimmers**

A. Concept Check
More Irregular Verbs
1. began
2. swam
3. shrank
4. swam
5. begun
6. sunk
7. sang
8. drank
9. sung
10. swum

B. Proofreading Skill
Correcting Verb Forms
Errors are underlined on page.

Many athletes have swum the English Channel. Once a feat that even the hardy had shrunk from, people eventually began to think of it as somewhat commonplace. However, on September 3, 1964, Lenore Modell made the accomplishment seem important again. Lenore was one of those miraculous California water-babies who had begun to swim at an early age.

Thirty-eight years had passed since the channel had first been swum by a woman. A large crowd gathered on the cliffs of Dover, and their voices sang out with chants of encouragement. At South Foreland Point on the opposite shore, a crowd waited and drank steaming beverages to ward off the chill. Over fifteen hours passed and hopes of her arrival had almost sunk. She had nearly swum up Dover Harbor by mistake, but a tide carried her to her goal. Lusty cheers rang out for this young woman who had just passed her fourteenth birthday—the youngest swimmer to conquer the channel.

Group 5 In this group of irregular verbs, the past participle is often formed by adding *-n* or *-en* to the present form. In the following list, notice the similarity between the present form and past participle form.

Present	Present Participle	Past	Past Participle
come	(is) coming	came	(have) come
do	(is) doing	did	(have) done
drive	(is) driving	drove	(have) driven
eat	(is) eating	ate	(have) eaten
fall	(is) falling	fell	(have) fallen
give	(is) giving	gave	(have) given
go	(is) going	went	(have) gone
grow	(is) growing	grew	(have) grown
know	(is) knowing	knew	(have) known
ride	(is) riding	rode	(have) ridden
rise	(is) rising	rose	(have) risen
run	(is) running	ran	(have) run
see	(is) seeing	saw	(have) seen
take	(is) taking	took	(have) taken
throw	(is) throwing	threw	(have) thrown
write	(is) writing	wrote	(have) written

Here are some sentences with verbs from Group 5.

Every summer they *grow* corn in their garden. (present)
Yesterday they *went* to a museum and to a play. (past)
I *have ridden* my last horse. (past participle)

Practice Your Skills

A. CONCEPT CHECK

More Irregular Verbs Write the appropriate past or past participle form of each verb given in parentheses.

1. As the country (grow), cattle drives became an important step in feeding the nation, but that is not why cowboys are remembered.
2. Many colorful stories have been (write) about the way of life of the cowhands who (drive) the cattle to market.
3. Imagine a typical cattle drive a century ago: the sun has not (rise), but the cowhands' day has already begun.
4. By dawn they have (eat) their breakfast at the chuck wagon and are on their horses.
5. Although they have (see) many hardships, they like the freedom of the rugged trail.

Additional Resources
• Grammar and Usage Practice Book, pp. 79–80

WRITING THEME   Food

A. Concept Check
More Irregular Verbs
  1. grew
  2. written, drove
  3. risen
  4. eaten
  5. seen

Box T. Ranch, Arizona, by Erwin E. Smith, 1909–1910. The Box T. Ranch cook working in the noonday sun.

6. When they started this drive, they (take) only a few personal belongings, only what would fit in their saddlebags.
7. They (know), even then, that any extra weight would tax their horses' strength—and they were right.
8. Before sunset on that first day, they had already (ride) dozens of miles through heat and dust.
9. Even a hundred years ago, though, city dwellers may have (take) for granted the beef on their tables.
10. Today, we should remember and admire the oldtime cowhands for what they (do) to keep a growing nation fed

B. DRAFTING SKILL

Using Correct Verb Forms   Some of the verbs have been omitted in the following paragraph. Refer to the list of Group 5 verbs on the preceding page. Choose verbs from this list to fill in the blanks. Be sure to choose the correct form of each verb.

(1) Until recently people _____ little thought to the relationship between nutrition and health. (2) For years people simply _____ whatever food was easily obtained. (3) The science of nutrition _____ into existence only in the twentieth century. (4) In the past, most of our clues about nutrition were _____ from the symptoms and illnesses doctors _____ in patients who were malnourished. (5) Today, technology can measure almost instantly the effect of food that has been _____ . (6) As a result, as much has been _____ about

Using Verbs   **601**

preventive care as has been published about treatment. (7) Many articles note that the incidence of certain ailments such as high blood pressure and heart disease has _____ drastically in recent years. (8) In many cases specialists have _____ patients extensive guidance on improving diet as a way of avoiding such medical problems. (9) In fact, some patients have _____ their pills away as their knowledge has _____ about cooking and eating properly. (10) Gradually, we are all _____ to realize that our eating habits _____ much more than satisfy hunger.

C. PROOFREADING SKILL

Checking Verb Forms   Proofread the following paragraph. Then rewrite it correctly. Pay special attention to the correct use of irregular verbs.

Have you ever <u>heared</u> about the <u>Grate</u> Molasses Flood of <u>1919 It</u> happened on a <u>brite january</u> day in <u>Boston most</u> people had just <u>ate</u> lunch when a giant molasses tank <u>bursted</u>. Fourteen thousand tons of thick, sticky syrup <u>come</u> pouring out in a brown fifteen-foot wave. The wave was not "as slow as molasses in January." It moved at thirty-five miles per hour and destroyed everything in <u>it's</u> path. <u>Twenty one</u> people <u>losed</u> <u>there</u> lives; one hundred and fifty were injured.

C H E C K ✔ P O I N T
PAGES 594–602

Write the appropriate past or past participle form of each verb given in parentheses.

1. The world has (see) some clever hoaxes over the centuries.
2. One of the best (grow) from the ingenious imagination of one Horace Cole.
3. Mr. Cole (choose) the British Navy as the target of his best practical joke.
4. As his allies in the hoax, he (take) four young English gentlemen and the young writer Virginia Woolf.
5. If the Admiral at Weymouth had (know) Cole, he might not have welcomed four Abyssinian princes aboard the *Dreadnought*.
6. On the other hand, he might not have recognized the young man behind a bushy mustache he had (grow) overnight.

7. The princes themselves, three of the men and Virginia Woolf, (wear) flowing robes and heavy makeup.
8. Their interpreter, Virginia's brother, (run) the most serious risk of discovery.
9. He had (throw) on only a little stage makeup and was pretending to be from Germany.
10. One more friend (fall) in with the scheme, sending a telegram signed by a high government official to the Admiral.
11. When Horace Cole—calling himself Herbert Cholmondeley of the British Foreign Office—(bring) the Abyssinian princes onto the ship, they were received with great ceremony.
12. In fact, the Admiral himself (lead) the visitors around the ship.
13. Since none of the hoaxers (speak) the Abyssinian language, they simply (throw) up their hands in wonder at each new sight.
14. If the navy had (catch) on, the "princes" might have (swim) back to shore.
15. As it was, they had only one punishment: by the end of the day, the princes had not (eat) for fear of smearing their makeup.

VERB TENSE

By changing the form of a verb, you can indicate whether something is happening now, has happened in the past, or will happen in the future. These changes in form are called **tenses.**

English verbs have three simple tenses (present, past, and future) and three perfect tenses (present perfect, past perfect, and future perfect). The tenses are formed by using the principal parts and the helping verbs *have, has, had, will,* and *shall.*

Three Spheres II, by M.C.Escher, 1946.

Using Verbs **603**

Humanities Connection

Art Note   In the lithograph *Three Spheres II* (1946) by M. C. Escher (b. 1898, the Netherlands, d. 1971), a picture of the artist at work on this composition appears in the center sphere. Note that the drawing table reflects each sphere, and the spheres reflect on one another. Escher believed that space and time were continuous and interrelated; and his belief in an orderly world are clearly represented in this print. Ask: What do you think the spheres represent in life?

Verb Tense

Objectives

- To identify the six main verb tenses and use them correctly
- **Writing** To demonstrate revision skills by correcting errors in verb tenses

Teaching Strategies

Teaching Tip: Verb Tense

You might want to clarify the six main tenses with the use of a time line. Position a short sentence in the present tense in the middle of the line. Write the sentence in the past tense at the extreme left. Give within each sentence a time indicator such as *yesterday.* Then fill in a separate time line with sentences written in perfect tenses. This will help illustrate the relative aspect of the perfect tenses. Ask students to generate other sentences in each tense.

Stumbling Block

Students may have difficulty distinguishing the difference between the ideas of tense and principal parts. Clarify that the principal parts of verbs are used to form the six verb tenses reviewed in the lesson.

Linking Grammar and Writing

Have students keep a scrapbook of newspaper and magazine articles that illustrate the six main tenses covered in the lesson. Encourage students to label the verb tenses they find in the articles.

Simple Tenses

Use the **present tense** to show an action that occurs in the present. To form the present tense, use the first principal part of the verb (the present form) or add *-s* or *-es* to the present form.

> I *know* the answer.
> Cathy *knows* the answer.

Use the **past tense** to show an action that was completed in the past. To form the past tense of regular verbs, add *-ed* or *-d* to the present form. To form the past tense of irregular verbs, use the past form listed as one of the principal parts.

> I *asked* for information.
> They *knew* the solution.

Use the **future tense** to show an action that will occur in the future. To form the future tense, use the helping verb *will* or *shall* with the present form.

> Cristo *will help* us.
> I *shall* not *go*.

Perfect Tenses

Use the **present perfect tense** to show an action that was completed in the recent past or at an indefinite time in the past or one that began in the past and continues to the present. To form the present perfect tense, use the helping verb *has* or *have* with the past participle.

> She *has gone* home.   They *have* finally *arrived*.

Use the **past perfect tense** to show an action that preceded another past action. To form the past perfect tense, use the helping verb *had* with the past participle.

> They *had left* before we came.
> The plane *had* just *taken* off when we arrived at the terminal.

Use the **future perfect tense** to show an action that will occur before another future action or time. You can form the future perfect tense by using the helping verbs *will have* or *shall have* with the past participle.

> By Sunday, the team *will have played* twelve schools.
> By noon tomorrow, I *shall have completed* my four final exams.

Writing
— **TIP** —

Effective use of verb tenses aids a writer in showing the order of events.

Verb Conjugation

A **verb conjugation** is a list of all the forms of a verb. The conjugation below shows the six tenses of the regular verb *watch*.

Simple Tenses

	Singular	Plural
Present Tense		
First Person	I watch	we watch
Second Person	you watch	you watch
Third Person	he, she, it watches	they watch
Past Tense		
First Person	I watched	we watched
Second Person	you watched	you watched
Third Person	he, she, it watched	they watched
Future Tense		
First Person	I will (shall) watch	we will (shall) watch
Second Person	you will watch	you will watch
Third Person	he, she, it will watch	they will watch

Perfect Tenses

	Singular	Plural
Present Perfect Tense		
First Person	I have watched	we have watched
Second Person	you have watched	you have watched
Third Person	he, she, it has watched	they have watched
Past Perfect Tense		
First Person	I had watched	we had watched
Second Person	you had watched	you had watched
Third Person	he, she, it had watched	they had watched
Future Perfect Tense		
First Person	I will (shall) have watched	we will (shall) have watched
Second Person	you will have watched	you will have watched
Third Person	he, she, it will have watched	they will have watched

Managing the Paper Load

Pair students for Exercise A. Discuss answers orally, and then assign Exercises B and C for independent work.

WRITING THEME Flight

You may want to suggest that interested students do further research on this theme and use it for the subject of a writing assignment for a history or science class.

A. Concept Check

Simple and Perfect Verb Tenses
1. had designed, Past Perfect
2. have found, Present Perfect
3. seems, Present
4. resists, Present
5. allows, Present
6. had fallen, Past Perfect
7. drifted, Past
8. landed, Past
9. will have improved, Future Perfect
10. will descend, Future

Writing Theme
Flight

Eric Bigler, a quadriplegic for 15 years, is an applications programmer and sky dives in tandem.

Practice Your Skills

A. CONCEPT CHECK

Simple and Perfect Verb Tenses Write the verb in each of the following sentences. Then identify its tense.

1. Leonardo da Vinci had designed a parachute about four hundred years before the invention of the airplane.
2. Historians have also found a description of a parachute in a sixteenth-century novel.
3. The principle behind a parachute's design seems fairly simple.

4. Air inside the canopy resists the pull of gravity on the parachutist.
5. A hole at the top of the parachute allows a little air through.
6. Earlier parachutes—without the air hole—had fallen too slowly.
7. During this slow fall, the parachute often drifted long distances sideways.
8. The parachutist, therefore, often landed in a dangerous or at least undesirable location.
9. In the future, however, parachute technology will no doubt have improved.
10. A jumper will descend more confidently and with greater accuracy toward a target.

B. REVISION SKILL

Achieving Clarity Using the wrong tenses in your writing will result in confusion. Use the directions in parentheses after each sentence to revise the italicized verbs.

(1) Few people *traveled* in an airship. (present perfect)
(2) Airships *were* large balloonlike aircraft filled with a lighter-than-air gas. (simple present) (3) Flammable hydrogen *has filled* the early airships. (simple past) (4) Traveling at about 78 mph, they *have made* transatlantic trips before commercial propeller planes. (past perfect) (5) People who *traveled* by airship say it is the nicest way to fly. (present perfect) (6) The flight *will feel* smooth and quiet. (simple present) (7) However, since the fiery *Hindenburg* disaster in 1937, people *fear* flying in airships. (present perfect) (8) Today engineers *have filled* airships with nonflammable helium. (simple present) (9) *Have* airships *made* a commercial comeback? (simple future) (10) Perhaps someday people *have forgotten* the past. (future perfect)

C. APPLICATION IN WRITING

A Poem Write a poem about flying. Decide whether you want to set the action in the past, the present, or the future. When you revise, check to make sure your verb tenses are appropriate and logical. Just to get started you might want to borrow one of these lines:

"Oh I have slipped the surly bonds of earth,
 And danced the skies . . ."

John Gillespie Magee, Jr., "High Flight"

"You cannot fly like an eagle with the wings of a wren."

William Henry Hudson

"Oh that I had wings like a dove!"

Psalms 55:6

PROGRESSIVE VERB FORMS

Each of the simple and perfect tenses has a **progressive form** that shows continuing action. The progressive form is made by using a tense of the helping verb *be* with the present participle.

Present Progressive	We are reading.
Past Progressive	We were reading.
Future Progressive	We will be reading.
Present Perfect Progressive	We have been reading.
Past Perfect Progressive	We had been reading.
Future Perfect Progressive	We will have been reading.

Encourage interested students to note this theme in their journals to use as a topic for a science writing project.

Concept Check

Progressive Verb Forms
1. was traveling, Past Progressive
2. was submitting, Past Progressive
3. had been using, Past Perfect Progressive
4. had been making, Past Perfect Progressive
5. had been waiting, Past Perfect Progressive
6. have been improving, Present Perfect Progressive
7. are telephoning, Present Progressive
8. are using, Present Progressive
9. will be employing, Future Progressive
10. will have been working, Future Perfect Progressive

Avoiding Shifts in Tense

Objectives

- To learn how to avoid improper shifts in verb tense
- **Writing** To demonstrate revision skills by correcting improper shifts in verb tense

Teaching Strategies

Collaborative Opportunity

Challenge students to create their own tests that cover shifts in verb tense. Have students take each other's tests as a collaborative learning opportunity.

Linking Grammar and Writing

You might wish to have students look through one of their rough drafts to make sure they have avoided improper shifts in verb tenses. Have students make necessary corrections as part of the proofreading process.

Practice Your Skills

CONCEPT CHECK

Progressive Verb Forms   Write each progressive verb form used in the following sentences. Then identify its tense.

1. On February 14, 1876, Alexander Graham Bell's design for a telephone was traveling on its way to the patent office.
2. On that very same day, just a few hours behind Bell, a man named Elisha Gray was submitting his own designs.
3. By 1876 people had been using the word *telephone* for about fifty years.
4. Scientists had been making correct assumptions about the mechanics of sound vibrations since the early 1800's.
5. In the meantime, the telephone had simply been waiting to be invented.
6. Since Bell's work in 1876, scientists have been constantly improving upon Bell's original design.
7. Today, people are telephoning with the aid of computers and fiberoptic technology.
8. Nevertheless, telephones today are still using the same method for the conversion of sound into electrical signals that Bell used in the nineteenth century.
9. What technology telephones will be employing in the year 2100 is anyone's guess.
10. It is certain, however, that scientists will have been working diligently on that very technology for decades.

AVOIDING SHIFTS IN TENSE

When two actions occur at the same time, use the same tense for both actions.

> Galileo *was* a professor at Pisa University, and there he *conducted* his experiments. (Both actions occurred in the past.)
> Tara *is mowing* the lawn while we *are weeding* the flower beds. (Both actions occur in the continuing present.)

Avoid unnecessary shifts in tense between sentences or within paragraphs.

Incorrect   The early pioneer settlers *built* homes as soon as they arrive on the prairie.

Correct   The early pioneer settlers *built* homes as soon as they *arrived* on the prairie.

Practice Your Skills

A. CONCEPT CHECK

Shifts in Tense From the verbs given in parentheses, write the verb needed to avoid a shift in tense.

1. The year was A.D. 900, and salt (is, <u>was</u>) literally worth its weight in gold.
2. Then as now, it was hot in West Africa, where the sun (bakes, <u>baked</u>) the land.
3. So, in those days, people (value, <u>valued</u>) salt because it was needed to replace sodium lost through perspiration.
4. Of course they also preserved and (flavor, <u>flavored</u>) their food with salt.
5. In southern Ghana at that time, gold was plentiful in the gold fields of Wangara, but salt (is, <u>was</u>) scarce and therefore treasured.
6. Today, we think of gold as very valuable and probably (<u>find</u>, found) it hard to imagine having too much of it.
7. However, because they had gold in abundance, the people of Wangara (trade, <u>traded</u>) it for scarce items.
8. They willingly offered a pound of gold and (take, <u>took</u>) in return a pound of the vital crystal, salt.
9. The people of the northern Sahara gladly (fill, <u>filled</u>) their bags with gold and rode off on their camels.
10. When you (<u>season</u>, seasoned) your scrambled eggs the next time, consider the value of salt.

B. REVISION SKILL

Avoiding Shifts in Tense Unnecessary shifts in tense can confuse your reader by making the sequence of events unclear. Revise the following paragraph, correcting any unnecessary or confusing shifts in tense.

> (1) One hundred years ago, the ghost towns of the West flourished and thrived. (2) In Nevada alone, almost 1,300 towns <u>prosper</u> and then <u>die</u>. (3) Most <u>are founded</u> when gold, silver, and copper were discovered. (4) Thousands of people came hoping to strike it rich. (5) Many <u>are</u> young, earnest, and honest. (6) Others, however, were outlaws who <u>prey</u> on the innocent miners. (7) The towns lasted as long as the mines continued to be productive. (8) When the mines closed, the towns <u>become</u> deserted. (9) Today, some ghost towns are reviving and <u>had</u> been attracting tourists. (10) If there is a stream near the ghost town, many tourists <u>had tried</u> their luck at panning for gold; sometimes they even find a bit of gold dust or a tiny nugget.

Using Verbs **609**

Writing Theme
Valuable Resources

Additional Resources
- Grammar and Usage Practice Book, pp. 85–86

WRITING THEME   Valuable Resources

You may want to suggest that students brainstorm a list of topics related to this theme for use in the Writer's Workshops on expository writing.

A. Concept Check
Shifts in Tense
Answers are underlined on page.

B. Revision Skill
Avoiding Shifts in Tense
Errors are underlined on page.

(1) One hundred years ago, the ghost towns of the West flourished and thrived. (2) In Nevada alone, almost 1,300 towns prospered and then died. (3) Most were founded when gold, silver, and copper were discovered. (4) Thousands of people came, hoping to strike it rich. (5) Many were young, earnest, and honest. (6) Others, however, were outlaws who preyed on the innocent miners. (7) The towns lasted as long as the mines continued to be productive. (8) When the mines closed, the towns became deserted. (9) Today, some ghost towns are reviving and have been attracting tourists. (10) If there is a stream near the ghost town, many tourists try their luck at panning for gold; sometimes they even find a bit of gold dust or a tiny nugget.

You may wish to use the following Checkpoint exercises as an informal evaluation of student mastery of the concepts covered in this handbook.

WRITING THEME   Agnes De Mille

A.

1. Past
2. Present
3. Past Perfect
4. Past
5. Past Progressive
6. Future
7. Past
8. Present Progressive
9. Present Perfect
10. Present Perfect

B.

Verbs are underlined on page.

1. wrote—Past
2. will read—Future
3. played—Past
4. danced—Past
5. writes—Present
6. realize—Present
7. was—Past

Writing Theme
Agnes De Mille

Agnes De Mille, world famous dancer and choreographer

A. Write the tense of the italicized verb or verb phrase in each of the following sentences.

1. Agnes De Mille *changed* the world of dance forever.
2. Awkward as a child, she *is* now a legend.
3. Her training for a career as a dancer *had begun* late, at the age of thirteen.
4. Although she was a diligent student, her early professional work *met* with little success.
5. She trained as a classical dancer but *was* always *dreaming* of a career in theater and movies, perhaps influenced by her father, a playwright, and uncle, a movie director.
6. Dance historians *will* probably *say* the turning point in her career came with her choreography for the musical *Oklahoma!*
7. Before *Oklahoma!,* dancing in a musical *had* nothing to do with the story line of the play.
8. De Mille's choreography, however, *is* always *moving* the story along.
9. The story it tells in *Oklahoma!* is powerful, emotional, and funny and *has become* just as popular as the music itself.
10. Musical choreography *has* never *returned* to the essentially meaningless kicks and taps of the era before De Mille.

B. For each of the following sentences, write the verb or verb phrase that avoids an unnecessary shift in tense. After each verb, identify its tense.

1. When Agnes De Mille was in her forties, she (writes, wrote) a book about her life as a dancer.
2. This lively story of struggle and triumph will remain a favorite with readers, and artists of all kinds (read, will read) it with interest and enjoyment for years to come.
3. Of her early days in New York, she writes, "I continued to give auditions although it (plays, played) havoc with my practice schedule.
4. In the course of time . . . I (dance, danced) before every known manager and agent in New York. . . ."
5. De Mille goes on to tell about her many rejections and disappointments, and she (writes, wrote) with self-effacing good humor about her embarrassments.
6. "As I write this," she comments, "I (realize, realized) none of it seems seriously distressing.
7. I certainly had enough to eat, and there (was, will have been) money to carry on for several recitals.

8. But if I could not get into the commercial theater, I (can, <u>could</u>) not function.
9. A dancer has only ten good years of performing life, and I (will have begun, <u>had begun</u>) late."
10. De Mille sh<u>ows how</u> difficult and rewarding life as an artist (<u>is</u>, will be).

U SING THE RIGHT VERB

The following pairs of verbs are sometimes confused.

Bring and *Take*

Present	Present Participle	Past	Past Participle
bring	(is) bringing	brought	(have) brought
take	(is) taking	took	(have) taken

Bring refers to movement toward the speaker. *Take* refers to movement away from the speaker.

> *Bring* that hammer to me, please.
> When you go home, *take* your tools with you.

Learn and *Teach*

Present	Present Participle	Past	Past Participle
learn	(is) learning	learned	(have) learned
teach	(is) teaching	taught	(have) taught

Learn means "to gain knowledge or skill." *Teach* means "to help someone learn."

> We *are learning* the metric system.
> Ms. Rivera *taught* us the metric system.

Let and *Leave*

Present	Present Participle	Past	Past Participle
let	(is) letting	let	(have) let
leave	(is) leaving	left	(have) left

Let means "to allow or to permit." *Leave* means "to go away from."

> The landlord *will let* us stay until the end of the month.
> They *have left* without their books.

Using Verbs **611**

Using the Right Verb

Objectives

- To correctly use verbs often confused
- **Writing** To demonstrate revision skills by correcting errors in the use of verbs often confused

Teaching Strategies

Critical Thinking

Synthesizing Have students write usage rules for other troublesome verb pairs, such as *lend* and *borrow*, *affect* and *effect*, *can* and *may*, and *imply* and *infer*, and share the rules with the class. Encourage students to write original sentences to illustrate the verb pairs.

Additional Resources
- Grammar and Usage Practice Book, pp. 87–88

WRITING THEME *Pygmalion*

You might want to suggest that interested students use *Pygmalion* as the subject of a personal response to literature in Writer's Workshop 8.

A. Revision Skill

The Right Verb

1. The actress stepped onto the stage and faced Ms. Brown's class. "Here on the set of the show, I will teach you about George Bernard Shaw's *Pygmalion.*

2. The play tells of Henry Higgins, a language expert, who takes a poor flower girl named Eliza—played by me—into 'is 'ome right 'ere," the actress said, letting her voice slip into Eliza's cockney accent and dropping all the *h*'s.

3. "He has only one interest in her: to teach her proper English.

4. He plans to take her out in high society and pass her off as a lady in order to win a bet with a friend.

5. Correct

6. Correct

7. "At an ambassador's grand reception," the actress continued, "Higgins lets Eliza mingle with the guests and watches their reactions carefully.

8. Correct

9. Shaw lets the audience draw their own conclusions regarding the ethics of Higgins's experiment.

10. Correct

11. As the actress concluded, the students thanked her for all she had taught them.

12. "If you bring your programs to me after tonight's performance," she said, "I will be happy to autograph them."

B. Application in Writing

Dialogue

Answers will vary.

Practice Your Skills

A. REVISION SKILL

The Right Verb Many of the following sentences contain errors in the use of *bring, take, learn, teach, let,* and *leave.* Rewrite those sentences, correcting the errors. If a sentence has no error, write *Correct.*

1. The actress stepped onto the stage and faced Ms. Brown's class. "Here on the set of the show, I will learn you about George Bernard Shaw's *Pygmalion.*

2. The play tells of Henry Higgins, a language expert, who takes a poor flower girl named Eliza—played by me—into 'is 'ome right 'ere," the actress said, leaving her voice slip into Eliza's cockney accent and dropping all the *h*'s.

3. "He has only one interest in her: to learn her proper English.

4. He plans to bring her out in high society and pass her off as a lady in order to win a bet with a friend.

5. Several scenes bring the audience into Eliza's intense elocution lessons."

6. Behind the actress, the set moved, and the revolving stage brought an elegant English drawing room into view.

7. "At an ambassador's grand reception," the actress continued, "Higgins leaves Eliza mingle with the guests and watches their reactions carefully.

8. He has taught her so well that all the guests believe her to be a princess.

9. Shaw leaves the audience draw their own conclusions regarding the ethics of Higgins's experiment.

10. As the play ends, Eliza leaves the unlovable Henry Higgins behind and plans to marry a charming but worthless-seeming gentleman named Freddy."

11. As the actress concluded, the students thanked her for all she had learned them.

12. "If you take your programs to me after tonight's performance," she said, "I will be happy to autograph them."

B. APPLICATION IN WRITING

Dialogue Create a brief dialogue that might continue the story of the characters in *Pygmalion,* or write a scene for an original play in which one character attempts to prove a point by teaching something to another character. In your dialogue, use several of the verb forms you have studied in this lesson.

Lie and Lay

Present	Present Participle	Past	Past Participle
lie	(is) lying	lay	(have) lain
lay	(is) laying	laid	(have) laid

Lie is an intransitive verb that means "to rest in a flat position" or "to be in a certain place." It does not take a direct object. *Lay* is a transitive verb that means "to place." It takes a direct object.

Lie on the sofa until you feel better.

The papers *lay* in a heap on the floor.

Lay your jackets there. (*Jackets* is the direct object.)

He *laid* a wreath on the grave. (*Wreath* is the direct object.)

Amish community barn raising

Rise and Raise

Present	Present Participle	Past	Past Participle
rise	(is) rising	rose	(have) risen
raise	(is) raising	raised	(have) raised

Rise is an intransitive verb that means "to go upward." It does not take a direct object. *Raise* is a transitive verb that means "to lift" or "to make something go up." It takes a direct object.

Steam *rises* and disappears.

The tax *has risen* to 8 percent.

Raise the curtain slowly. (*Curtain* is the direct object.)

The workers *raised* the barn. (*Barn* is the direct object.)

Using Verbs **613**

WRITING THEME Birds

Encourage students to add this theme to a
list of possible topics for a science paper.

A. Concept Check

The Right Verb
Answers are underlined on page.

Sit and Set

Present	Past Participle	Past	Past Participle
sit	(is) sitting	sat	(have) sat
set	(is) setting	set	(have) set

Sit is an intransitive verb that means "to occupy a seat." It does
not take a direct object. *Set* is a transitive verb that means "to
place." It usually takes a direct object.

> She usually *sits* next to me in class.
> Finally, all the passengers *had sat* down.
> *Set* those boxes on the table. (*Boxes* is the direct object.)
> Someone *has set* one cup on top of the other. (*Cup* is the
> direct object.)

Practice Your Skills

A. CONCEPT CHECK

The Right Verb Write the verb form in parentheses that correctly
completes each of the following sentences.

1. It is 1820, and the sun has barely (risen, raised).
2. Crossing the dim room, an artist (sits, sets) a pouch on the table.
3. His paper and pencils are (lying, laying) neatly in place.
4. He takes a small bundle from the pouch and (lays, lies) it on the table.
5. Carefully unwrapping it, he (sits, sets) the delicate object in a wooden frame.
6. As he is (sitting, setting) down, he hears a mournful warbling from outside.
7. He crosses to the window and (rises, raises) the curtain.

8. Bright sunlight falls across the table where his subject and instruments (lie, lay).
9. The artist listens to the lonely bird outside and then (sits, sets) down.
10. John James Audubon studies the delicate body of the warbler before him and (rises, raises) his pencil to begin a sketch.

B. REVISION SKILL

Choosing the Correct Word When you revise, make sure that your words express the meaning you intend. The following sentences contain errors in the choice of verbs. Rewrite the sentences, correcting the errors.

1. "The sun had not yet raised, and all,
    Save the warblers of the woods, was still."
2. As this couplet demonstrates, songbirds have often risen writers to poetic inspiration.
3. The warblers that set in treetops in countless poems and stories actually include 120 species of small songbirds.
4. The significance of the New World warbler's name lays in its similarity to European, Asian, and African cousins.
5. Its dwelling places lay mainly in the forests, brush, and grassy swamps of North America and Central America.
6. Warblers' nests are usually found in trees or bushes but may also set in a hole on the forest floor.
7. As soon as eggs hatch in the nest, both parents share the duties of rising the two to five young birds.
8. Since warblers are active insect-eaters, they can often be seen setting watchfully among leaves and grass, waiting for food to appear.
9. Some species also raise up to catch insects on the wing, from small flies to grasshoppers.
10. Most warblers have weak, raspy songs, but a few species rise their voices clearly and beautifully.

C. PROOFREADING SKILL

Checking Verb Forms Proofread the following paragraph. Then rewrite it correctly. Pay special attention to the use of correct verb forms.

When one sets in the woods at sunrise, he or she can clearly hear the melodic dawn chorus of birds. Experiments have learned naturalists that birds early morning activity is the result of several "triggers," or stimuli that evoke responses in behavior. One trigger occurs when the light intensity changes; another trigger occurs when the temprature raises and insects begun to stir. Singing leaves other birds know that a territory is taken. Woodland birds have adapted there behavior to correspond to their environment. And the activities of both their prey and their competitors. The key to understanding the importance of triggers and the resulting behavior lays in carful, patient observation in the field.

One of director Alfred Hitchcock's most famous films was *The Birds*.

Photo by Philippe Halsman © Yvonne Halsman

Using Verbs   **615**

B. Revision Skill
Using Correct Word Choice
1. "The sun had not yet risen, and all,
    Save the warblers of the woods, was still."
2. As this couplet demonstrates, songbirds have often raised writers to poetic inspiration.
3. The warblers that sit in treetops in countless poems and stories actually include 120 species of small songbirds.
4. The significance of the New World warbler's name lies in its similarity to European, Asian, and African cousins.
5. Its dwelling places lie mainly in the forests, brush, and grassy swamps of North America and Central America.
6. Warblers' nests are usually found in trees or bushes but may also sit in a hole on the forest floor.
7. As soon as eggs hatch in the nest, both parents share the duties of raising the two to five young birds.
8. Since warblers are active insect-eaters, they can often be seen sitting watchfully among leaves and grass, waiting for food to appear.
9. Some species also rise up to catch insects on the wing, from small flies to grasshoppers.
10. Most warblers have weak, raspy songs, but a few species raise their voices clearly and beautifully.

C. Proofreading Skill
Checking Verb Forms
Errors are underlined on page.

When one sits in the woods at sunrise, he or she can clearly hear the melodic dawn chorus of birds.* Experiments have taught naturalists that birds' early morning activity is the result of several "triggers," or stimuli that evoke responses in behavior. One trigger is the change in light intensity; another trigger occurs when the temperature rises and insects begin to stir. Singing lets other birds know that a territory is taken. Woodland birds have adapted their behavior to correspond to their environment and the activities of both their prey and their competitors. The key to understanding the importance of triggers and the resulting behavior lies in careful, patient observation in the field.

*For the first sentence also accept revisions such as the following: "When sitting in the woods at sunrise, one can clearly hear the melodic dawn chorus of birds."

You may wish to use the following Checkpoint exercises as an informal evaluation of student mastery of the concepts covered in this handbook.

WRITING THEME   Self-Assertion

A.
Answers are underlined on page.

B.
Errors are underlined on page.

William Garwood of Evanston, Illinois, invented one of America's favorite treats—the ice-cream sundae. In the 1880's an Evanston law was passed that prohibited the sale of soda-water drinks on Sunday. Garwood's temper rose at this news. He was certain to lose some of his Sunday ice-cream soda business. "I'll teach them!" he shouted. He quickly set a soda glass on the counter and filled it with ice cream and syrup with the soda left out. Garwood called his creation a "Sunday." Later the spelling was changed to "sundae." However he spelled it, the news of his creation certainly brought him happy customers, sitting at the counter.

Writing Theme
Self-Assertion

A. Write the verb form in parentheses that correctly completes each of the following sentences.

1. Dust (raised, <u>rose</u>) in the air like hot gold clouds, and the battle raged on as if it would never end.
2. Running toward the exhausted soldiers, Molly Pitcher (<u>brought</u>, took) them water from the nearby spring.
3. A winter at Valley Forge with her husband had (<u>taught</u>, learned) Molly how strong Washington's troops were—and how brave.
4. But even among strong soldiers, the dust and heat of battle can (<u>raise</u>, rise) a fierce thirst.
5. Suddenly, Molly saw her husband, John, fall; he (laid, <u>lay</u>) in a heap beside his cannon.
6. With a feeling of dread, she ran to him and (sat, <u>set</u>) her pitcher on the ground beside him.
7. When she saw he had been overcome by heat, Molly pulled him into the shade and (<u>let</u>, left) him rest there.
8. Then she snatched up the ramrod that was (<u>lying</u>, laying) beside John's cannon.
9. Watching John had (learned, <u>taught</u>) Molly what to do: "Load!" she shouted, then pushed the ramrod down the barrel of the cannon.
10. She did not know it then, but her courage had just (brought, <u>taken</u>) Molly beyond the annals of history and into the world of legend.

B. The following paragraph contains errors in spelling, capitalization, usage, and punctuation. Rewrite the paragraph, correcting all of these errors. Pay particular attention to errors arising from incorrect verb usage.

William Garwood of Evanston, Illinois, invented one of <u>america's</u> favorite <u>treets</u>—the ice-cream sundae. In the 1880's an Evanston law was passed that prohibited the <u>sail</u> of soda-water drinks on Sunday. <u>Garwoods</u> temper <u>rised</u> at this news. He was certain to <u>loose</u> some of his Sunday ice-cream-soda business. <u>I'll learn them</u>! he shouted. He <u>quickley</u> <u>sat</u> a soda glass on the counter and filled it with ice cream and syrup, with the soda <u>leaved</u> out. Garwood called his creation a "Sunday" <u>later</u> the spelling was changed to <u>"sundae"</u>. However he spelled it, the news of his creation certainly <u>bringed</u> him happy customers, <u>setting</u> at the counter.

Writing Theme
Stories

A. Identifying Types of Verbs Write the verb in each sentence and tell whether it is *Action* or *Linking*. Then tell whether each action verb is *Transitive* or *Intransitive*.

1. Stories, or narratives, <u>take</u> many forms.
2. The modern short story, with its emphasis on character, mood, and theme, <u>is</u> familiar to readers of today.
3. Most of us naturally <u>remember</u> the dramatic, plot-heavy fairy tales from our childhood days.
4. Tall tales about trickster rabbits, coyotes, or ravens <u>have</u> always <u>been</u> popular among America's native cultures.
5. Among pioneers, lumbermen, and railroad workers, tall tales about larger-than-life human heroes—Pecos Bill, Paul Bunyan, and John Henry—<u>became</u> standard entertainment after a long day's work.
6. A tall tale <u>involves</u> a special literary technique: exaggeration, or hyperbole.
7. A narrative's purpose often <u>determines</u> its form.
8. For example, a fable usually <u>ends</u> with a moral.
9. A story's form <u>may</u> also <u>develop</u> out of a particular cultural tradition or custom.
10. In ancient cultures, for instance, stories usually <u>took</u> the form of poetry rather than of prose.

B. Using Principal Parts and Tenses of Verbs Draw four columns and label them *Present, Present Participle, Past,* and *Past Participle.* In the columns, write the principal parts of the following verbs. Then choose three of the verbs and write them in each of the six main tenses.

1. tell	5. write	9. explain	13. report	17. refer
2. describe	6. relate	10. speak	14. narrate	18. compose
3. conclude	7. sing	11. recite	15. say	19. persuade
4. cut	8. catch	12. taste	16. fall	20. lead

C. Choosing the Correct Verb Write the correct verb in each of the following sentences.

1. Anecdotes have often (stole, <u>stolen</u>) the show from longer stories because of their short, friendly character.
2. These short, true accounts (<u>bring</u>, take) the past closer to their eager listeners.
3. Sometimes they (learn, <u>teach</u>) us lessons about life.
4. More often, they (lie, <u>lay</u>) a picture of foolishness or some other human quality before us.
5. A favorite kind of anecdote (<u>lets</u>, leaves) us learn surprising facts about some ordinary thing.

Application and Review

These activities are designed to allow your students to apply concepts presented in this handbook. Exercise A requires students to identify types of verbs. Exercise B requires students to form the principal parts of verbs. Exercise C requires students to choose verbs correctly. Exercises D and E require students to use verb tense and voice correctly.

> ### Additional Resources
> - Tests and Assessment, Mastery Tests, pp. 61–68
> - Elaboration, Revision, and Proof-reading Worksheets, p. 25

WRITING THEME   Stories

A. Identifying Types of Verbs
Verbs are underlined on page.

1. Action, Transitive	6. Action, Transitive
2. Linking	7. Action, Transitive
3. Action, Transitive	8. Action, Intransitive
4. Linking	9. Action, Intransitive
5. Linking	10. Action, Transitive

B. Using Principal Parts and Tenses of Verbs
Student answers should be in columns. Answers are listed in the following order: Present; Present Participle; Past; Past Participle. Answers for the three verbs will vary.

1. tell; (is) telling; told; (have) told
2. describe; (is) describing; described; (have) described
3. conclude; (is) concluding; concluded; (have) concluded
4. cut; (is) cutting; cut; (have) cut
5. write; (is) writing; wrote; (have) written
6. relate; (is) relating; related; (have) related
7. sing; (is) singing; sang; (have) sung
8. catch; (is) catching; caught; (have) caught
9. explain; (is) explaining; explained; (have) explained
10. speak; (is) speaking; spoke; (have) spoken
11. recite; (is) reciting; recited; (have) recited
12. taste; (is) tasting; tasted; (have) tasted
13. report; (is) reporting; reported; (have) reported
14. narrate; (is) narrating; narrated; (have) narrated
15. say; (is) saying; said; (has) said
16. fall; (is) falling; fell; (has) fallen
17. refer; (is) referring; referred; (have) referred
18. compose; (is) composing; composed; (have) composed
19. persuade; (is) persuading; persuaded; (have) persuaded
20. lead; (is) leading; led; (have) led

C. Choosing the Correct Verb
Answers are underlined on page.

D. Using Verb Tense and Voice For each sentence, supply the correct form of the verb that appears in italics. Rewrite the sentence, using the verb tense and voice indicated in parentheses. In at least one sentence, use a progressive form.

1. *The Valkyrie,* one of Richard Wagner's operas, *tell* the story of a disobedient daughter and the punishment her father must impose. (Present Tense, Active Voice)
2. Always popular with audiences, the opera *perform* for the first time in 1870. (Past Tense, Passive Voice)
3. Years earlier, Wagner *inspire* by Norse mythology. (Past Perfect Tense, Passive Voice)
4. Accordingly, his characters are no mere mortals; they are Wotan, father of the gods, and his warrior daughter Brünnhilde, who *doom* to stay within a magic ring of fire. (Present Tense, Passive Voice)
5. As part of a scheduled recital, one of America's most famous sopranos *sing* several excerpts from this opera. (Future Tense, Active Voice)

E. Using Verbs Correctly The following paragraph is weak because some verbs are in the passive voice and some sentences contain improper shifts in tense. Replace the italicized passive verbs with active ones, and make any other necessary corrections, such as corrections in spelling.

> (1) During the Middle Ages (A.D. 400–1500), many folk tales *were composed* by European peasants. (2) Some stories told about real people and events, and others <u>are</u> fantasies and legends. (3) No one wrote down these stories; instead, traveling <u>mistrels</u> and common people <u>tell</u> them to one another, sometimes in the form of songs. (4) In the mid–1800's, many of these folk tales *were* still *being told*. (5) To the delight of children everywhere, most of the stories, including "Cinderella" and the legends of Robin Hood and Friar Tuck, *have been collected* and *published*.

WORD TORTURE

Irregular verbs often cause problems. In this column, Nathaniel Benchley considers one of these problems. Could you come up with a satisfactory answer to Mr. McIntyre's question?

In his column a short time ago Mr. O. O. McIntyre asked who could tell, without looking it up, the present tense of the verb of which "wrought" is the past participle. That was, let us say, of a Thursday. Today my last fingernail went.

At first, I thought that it was so easy that I passed it by. But, somewhere in the back of that shaggy-maned head of mine, a mischievous little voice said, "All right—what is it?"

"What is what?" I asked, stalling.

"You know very well what the question was. What is the present tense of the verb from which the word 'wrought' comes?"

I started out with a rush. "I *wright*," I fairly screamed. Then, a little lower, "I wrught." Then, very low, "I wrouft." Then silence.

From that day until now I have been muttering to myself, "I wright—I wraft—I wronjst. You wruft—he wragst—we wrinjsen."

I'll be darned if I'll look it up, and it looks now as if I'll be incarcerated before I get it.

People hear me murmuring and ask me what I am saying.

"I wrujhst," is all that I can say in reply.

"I know," they say, "but what were you *saying* just now?"

"I wringst."

This gets me nowhere. While I am working on it, however, and just before the boys come to get me to take me to the laughing academy, I will ask Mr. McIntyre if he can help me out on something that has almost the same possibilities for brain seepage. And no fair looking *this* up, either.

What is a man who lives in Flanders and speaks Flemish? A Flem? A Flan? A Floom? (This is a lot easier than "wrought," but it may take attention away from me while I am writhing on the floor.) And, when you think you have got it the easy way, remember there is another name for him, too, one that rhymes with "balloon." I finally looked that one up.

At present I'm working on "wrought."

Nathaniel Benchley

"Word Torture" by Nathaniel Benchley provides a humorous follow-up to "Principal Parts of Irregular Verbs" in Handbook 33, Using Verbs. When discussing the feature, draw the parallel to sports trivia or other trivia questions that delight and torture people. Pose the same question to the students that Benchley ponders, "What is the present tense of the verb of which *wrought* is the past participle?" (*Worken*, a Middle English word meaning "to work," is the present tense verb.) Have students find the answer to the other question Benchley poses.

Encourage students to begin lists of grammar trivia questions in their journals. Such an activity might spark a serious interest in the study of grammar.

Using Modifiers

Adjectives

Objectives

- To identify adjectives and the words they modify
- **Writing** To use precise adjectives in writing

Teaching Strategies

Speaking and Listening

Ask students to bring to class detailed pictures from magazines and newspapers. As part of a class discussion, have students create descriptions of the pictures, using vivid and colorful adjectives. Discuss how modifiers can be used to bring a description to life by making details seem real to the reader.

 Individualizing Instruction

ESL Students In Spanish, the adjective usually follows the noun (without a comma). Spanish-speaking students will therefore need to pay close attention to this punctuation note.

Vietnamese and Russian are examples of languages that contain no articles. Some ESL students will have particular difficulty using "a," "an," "the," and no article (the zero article) correctly. These students will need concentrated practice in the use of articles.

GRAMMAR HANDBOOK 34

Using Modifiers

ADJECTIVES

Modifiers are words that change or limit the meaning of other words. One kind of modifier is an adjective.

An adjective is a word that modifies a noun or a pronoun.

An adjective can change or limit the meaning of a noun or a pronoun by answering one of these questions:

What Kind?	*shiny* floor, *hilarious* story, *windy* day
Which One or Ones?	*that* girl, *next* time, *those* cars, *last* exit
How Many? or	*three* months, *several* boxes, *less* pain,
How Much?	*more* snow

More than one adjective may modify the same noun or pronoun.

Four festive musicians wore masks. (*How many* musicians? *Four* musicians. *What kind* of musicians? *Festive* musicians.)

Adjectives are usually placed immediately before the noun or pronoun they modify. Occasionally, however, a writer may decide to add variety to a sentence by putting adjectives in other positions. Notice the pleasing rhythm created by the unusual adjective placement in the following sentences.

The runners, *confident* and *eager,* started the race.

Confident and *eager,* the runners started the race.

Punctuation Note Adjectives that appear in these positions are set off from the rest of the sentence by commas or a comma.

Articles

The most common adjectives are the **articles** *a, an,* and *the. The* is the **definite article.** It points out a specific person, place, thing, or idea.

Keep *the* ball in play. (a particular ball)

A and *an* are **indefinite articles.** They do not point out a specific person, place, thing, or idea.

Did you bring *a* ball? (not a specific ball)
He made *an* error on the play. (not a specific error)

Fastnacht carnival in Basil, Switzerland. What words would you choose to describe this event?

620 Grammar Handbook

Use the indefinite article *a* before a word beginning with a consonant sound: *a* ball, *a* game. Use the indefinite article *an* before a word beginning with a vowel sound: *an* error, *an* honor.

Proper Adjectives

One special kind of adjective is the **proper adjective.**

A proper adjective is formed from a proper noun. Proper adjectives are always capitalized.

Proper Noun	Proper Adjective
Japan	*Japanese* car
Mexico	*Mexican* culture
Shakespeare	*Shakespearean* sonnet
Bach	*Bach* aria
Hindu	*Hindu* philosophy

Predicate Adjectives

Another kind of adjective is the **predicate adjective.** Unlike most adjectives, predicate adjectives follow the words they modify.

A predicate adjective comes after a linking verb and modifies the subject of the sentence.

Nothing seemed *clear* anymore.
   (*Clear* modifies the subject, *nothing.*)
Her hair is *auburn.*
   (*Auburn* modifies the subject, *hair.*)

Clear and *auburn* are predicate adjectives. They follow the linking verbs *seemed* and *is,* and each modifies the subject of the sentence.

A predicate adjective can be compound, like other modifiers. In the following examples, two predicate adjectives follow each linking verb.

The car was *rusty* and *dilapidated.*
Angelo looked *tired* but *happy.*

For a review of linking verbs, see Grammar Handbook 33, pages 583–584.

Sentence Diagraming   For information on diagraming sentences with adjectives, see page 831.

Linking Grammar and Writing

Have students create a list of overused adjectives and challenge them to supply more precise synonyms. Then suggest that students review a rough draft or a piece in their Writing Portfolio to see where revising adjective choice would improve their writing.

WRITING THEME   Winterscapes

Encourage interested students to add this theme to an ongoing list of possible writing topics for a sensory description.

A. Concept Check

Adjectives
1. this, time; gray, night; Sunday, night
2. little, wind; white, curls; thin, curls; lonesome, curls; old, drifts
3. two, ruts; yellow, bus; choppy, hills; sand, hills
4. powdery, white; every, hill
5. some, bug; bewildered, bug; shifting, wind
6. storm-lost, valley; ranch, house

Gray, thin, lonesome, powdery, bewildered, and storm-lost help create the lonely mood.

B. Drafting Skill

Adding Details

Answers will vary. See suggested answers below.
1. ghostly
2. gloomy
3. Victorian
4. Bare
5. massive
6. leafless
7. ancient
8. Three
9. threatening
10. desolate

C. Application in Writing

A Description

Answers will vary.

Writing Theme
Winterscapes

Writing
TIP

Use only as many adjectives as needed to strengthen an effect.

Practice Your Skills

A. CONCEPT CHECK

Adjectives Write the italicized adjectives in the following paragraph from *Winter Thunder*. After each adjective, write the word that it modifies. Which adjectives help create the lonely mood?

(1) The snow began quietly *this* time, like an afterthought to the *gray Sunday* night. (2) The moon almost broke through once, but toward daylight, a *little* wind came up and started *white* curls, *thin* and *lonesome,* running over the *old* drifts left from the New Year storm. (3) Gradually the snow thickened, until around eight-thirty the *two* ruts of winding trails were covered and undisturbed except down in the Lone Tree district where an old *yellow* bus crawled heavily along, feeling out the ruts between the *choppy sand* hills. (4) The storm increased until all the air was a *powdery* white and *every* hill, every trace of road, was obliterated. (5) The bus wavered and swayed in its direction, . . . and then finally grasped at any footing, until it looked like *some* great snowy, *bewildered* bug seen momentarily through the *shifting* wind. (6) . . . Once the bus had to back down from a steep little patch that might have led into a *storm-lost* valley with a *ranch* house and warmth and shelter.

Mari Sandoz, *Winter Thunder*

B. DRAFTING SKILL

Adding Details Improve the passage below by replacing the vague, italicized adjectives and by filling the blanks with specific adjectives. Choose adjectives that maintain an eerie mood.

The winter moon cast a(n) (1) *unusual* glow along the (2) _____ path to the (3) _____ house. (4) _____ branches of a (5) *big* oak formed shadows across the face of the building. In fact, each (6) _____ limb seemed to reach out and encircle the (7) _____ structure. (8) *Some* paneless windows looked (9) _____ , like eyes staring at the (10) _____ landscape.

C. APPLICATION IN WRITING

A Description Imagine that you are visiting a land of ice and snow. In your journal describe what you experience. Convey a variety of sensations in what at first looks like a lifeless, empty scene. Check your description for precise adjectives.

NOUNS AND PRONOUNS AS ADJECTIVES

Both nouns and pronouns can sometimes function as adjectives in sentences.

Nouns as Adjectives

Possessive nouns function as adjectives in sentences. The possessive form of a noun ends in -'s or -s': *girl's, girls'.*

My *sister's* goal is to become an auto mechanic.
The coach collected the *players'* uniforms.

Other nouns function as adjectives without a change in form.

Fruit trees flourish in the *California* sun.

Pronouns as Adjectives

The following kinds of pronouns can function as adjectives.

Possessive	my, your, his, her, its, our, their
Indefinite	some, any, many, few, several, one
Demonstrative	this, that, these, those
Interrogative	what, which, whose

The candidates filed *their* petitions.
I received *several* packages.
That evidence should be disregarded.
Which book belongs to you?

Practice Your Skills

CONCEPT CHECK

Nouns and Pronouns as Adjectives   Identify each noun or pronoun used as an adjective. Write the word that each adjective modifies.

1. The use of flags, simple or elaborate, goes far back in world history.
2. In 3000 B.C. China's finest craftspeople made silk flags for their civic and religious occasions.
3. Which country first used a flag as a national symbol?
4. Rome's flag, created in 1219, was the first national flag.
5. A ship's flag has long been a tradition in sailing.
6. Bright pennants fly over school buildings and office complexes.

Writing Theme
Flags

Using Modifiers   **623**

Nouns and Pronouns as Adjectives

Objective

- To identify nouns and pronouns used as adjectives

Teaching Strategies

Teaching Tip: Adjectives

Stress that nouns and pronouns are used as adjectives when they answer one of the following questions: *What kind? Which one or ones?* or *How many or how much?*

 Individualizing Instruction

LEP Students/Visual Learners   Help students visually model the process of identifying nouns and pronouns used as adjectives by drawing arrows from the adjectives to the words they modify.

Additional Resources
- Grammar and Usage Practice Book, pp. 93–94

WRITING THEME   Flags

You may want to suggest that interested students do research on this theme and use it as the subject for a Writer's Workshop assignment in expository writing.

Concept Check
Nouns and Pronouns as Adjectives
1. world, history
2. China's, craftspeople; silk, flags; their, occasions
3. Which, country
4. Rome's, flag
5. ship's, flag
6. school, buildings; office, complexes

7. Car, dealers; their, prices
8. hospital, ships; many, facilities
9. Tokyo, stadium; Innsbruck, slope
10. this, flag

7. Car dealers use scraps of color to announce their low prices.
8. The flag of the American Red Cross has marked hospital ships and many special medical facilities in wartime.
9. Over a Tokyo stadium or an Innsbruck slope, the flag of the Olympics has become familiar to the whole world.
10. The joined circles of this flag represent five continents.

Immigrants inside Ellis Island checkpoint.

C H E C K ✔ P O I N T
PAGES 620–624

You may wish to use the following Checkpoint exercises as an informal evaluation of student mastery of the concepts covered in this handbook.

WRITING THEME   America's People

Encourage interested students to think about how they might narrow this theme to use as a topic for a social studies report.

1. life, story; our, country; its, people
2. Native, Americans; earliest, inhabitants
3. Other, citizens; American, citizens; many, nations; different, nations; African, nations
4. distant, countries; Asiatic, countries
5. nineteenth, century; European, immigrants
6. Their, reasons; various, reasons
7. Many, people; food, shortages
8. political, freedom
9. familiar, climates

Writing Theme
America's People

C H E C K ✔ P O I N T
PAGES 620–624

On your paper, write the adjectives in the following sentences. Tell which word each adjective modifies. Include nouns and pronouns used as adjectives, but do not include the articles.

1. The life story of our country is told in the faces of its people.
2. Native Americans were the earliest inhabitants of the land.
3. Other American citizens originally came from many different African nations.
4. Some came from distant Asiatic countries.
5. In the nineteenth century, European immigrants flocked here.
6. Their reasons for coming were various.
7. Many people migrated because of food shortages at home.
8. Some came in search of political freedom.
9. They settled in areas with familiar climates.

10. Numerous Scandinavian immigrants settled in the Midwest.
11. People from southern Italy chose sunny California.
12. Chinese and Japanese people found homes on the West Coast.
13. Some newcomers were serious and thrifty.
14. Others were jovial and energetic.
15. In recent years, newcomers have arrived from our neighbor countries.
16. America is like a colorful tile mosaic.
17. Each different cultural group contributes a new beauty.
18. New peoples introduce exotic and delicious foods.
19. They share lively music and expressive dances.
20. This variety gives our country its unique character.

ADVERBS

An adverb is another type of modifier.

An adverb is a word that modifies a verb, an adjective, or another adverb.

An adverb answers one of the following questions about the word it modifies:

How?	works *accurately,* studies *hard,* plays *well,* *quietly* walked
When?	opens *soon,* visited *yesterday,* exercises *daily,* was paved *recently*
Where?	stood *there,* sat *here,* sleeps *upstairs,* ran *everywhere*
To What Extent?	*almost* missed, *never* stops, *completely* finished

The adverbs *not* and *never* tell to what extent and when.

> We did *not* plant tulips this year. (*Not* modifies *did plant* and tells to what extent.)
> Those trees will *never* bloom. (*Never* modifies *will bloom* and tells when.)

Forming Adverbs

Many adverbs are formed by adding *-ly* to an adjective. Notice that the addition of *-ly* may cause a change in spelling.

weak + -ly = weakly	formal + -ly = formally
possible + -ly = possibly	happy + -ly = happily

Adverbs

Objectives

- To identify adverbs and the words they modify
- **Writing** To use adverbs effectively in writing

Teaching Strategies

Teaching Tip: Adverbs

Emphasize that not all words ending in *-ly* are adverbs. Words such as *friendly, costly,* and *lovely* are adjectives.

Linking Grammar and Writing

Point out that students can sometimes strengthen their writing by substituting strong verbs for combinations of intensifiers and adverbs. For example, "He spoke very softly" becomes "He whispered." Emphasize that overuse of intensifiers weakens writing.

Speaking and Listening

Have a volunteer give a demonstration of a simple process for a group of students or the class. Ask each observer to write a detailed description of the process. Have students read their descriptions aloud. Discuss the use of adverbs to create an accurate description.

Writing
TIP

Place limiting mod-
ifiers to reflect
your meaning. *He
nodded just to
me. He just nod-
ded to me.*

Commonly Used Adverbs				
afterward	fast	low	often	there
almost	forth	more	seldom	today
already	hard	near	slow	tomorrow
also	here	never	soon	too
back	instead	next	still	well
even	late	not	straight	yesterday
far	long	now	then	yet

Adverbs and the Words They Modify

Adverbs frequently modify verbs. An adverb may appear before or after the verb it modifies.

> We *proudly* displayed our posters.
> The line moved *quickly.*
> *Where* are you going? (*Where* modifies the verb *are going.*)

Adverbs sometimes modify adjectives and adverbs. Such adverbs usually tell to what extent something is true.

> My cousin is *partially* blind. (*Partially* tells to what extent. It is an adverb modifying the predicate adjective *blind.*)
> I did *very* well on the test. (*Very* tells to what extent. It is an adverb modifying the adverb *well.*)

Here is a list of adverbs that often modify adjectives or adverbs. These words are sometimes called **Intensifiers.**

> too   quite   rather   most   more   extremely
> just   nearly   so   really   truly   somewhat

Some words can either be adverbs or adjectives. *Late* is one of these words. Some others are *still, north, straight, hard, long,* and *high.*

> The doctor arrived too *late.* (adverb)

> Marta took that *late* train. (adjective)

Sentence Diagraming For information on diagraming sentences with adverbs, see page 831.

Practice Your Skills

A. CONCEPT CHECK

Adverbs   Write the adverbs in this paragraph and the word each modifies. Also tell that word's part of speech.

(1) At dawn the wind fell away, and the ship cruised slowly in the deceptively calm sea. (2) The crew had just finished its morning chores. (3) Suddenly the rain came down in torrents. (4) It soon filled the empty water drums. (5) Then the clouds lifted and the sun broke through. (6) Steam rose from the soaked decks and gradually drifted away. (7) By dark, however, the boat was pitching wildly. (8) Finally, the captain headed the ship south, and it eventually sailed beyond the squall.

B. DRAFTING SKILL

Choosing Adverbs   The novelist Henry James once wrote to a friend, "I'm glad you like adverbs—I adore them; they are the only qualifications I really much respect." Write the following passage twice, each time using different adverbs to fill each blank.

(1) Cheryl walked _____ down the block. (2) In the east, the sun had _____ risen. (3) She looked around _____ . (4) As she reached the end of the dock, a board creaked _____ under her foot. (5) The sound was _____ audible. (6) Cheryl breathed _____ . (7) Then she leaned _____ against a piling. (8) Above her, a bird called out _____ , exactly mirroring her own feelings. (9) The sound of voices talking _____ came to her from one of the boats. (10) She turned and walked _____ toward the source of the sounds.

C. APPLICATION IN WRITING

Describing a scene.   Adverbs help a writer describe action precisely. Imagine that you want to describe the scene below in a story. Use adverbs to recreate the image for your reader.

Additional Resources
- Grammar and Usage Practice Book, pp. 95–96

WRITING THEME   Sailing

A. Concept Check
Adverbs
1. away, fell, Verb; slowly, cruised, Verb; deceptively, calm, Adjective
2. just, had finished, Verb
3. Suddenly, came, Verb; down, came, Verb
4. soon, filled, Verb
5. Then, lifted, Verb; through, broke, Verb
6. gradually, drifted, Verb; away, drifted, Verb
7. wildly, was pitching, Verb
8. Finally, headed, Verb; south, headed, Verb; eventually, sailed, Verb

B. Drafting Skill
Choosing Adverbs
Answers will vary. See suggested answers below. Students should write the passage twice, with different adverbs.
1. quickly; slowly
2. already; barely
3. happily; cautiously
4. slightly; loudly
5. barely; very
6. hard; faster
7. briefly; momentarily
8. cheerily; mournfully
9. excitedly; secretively
10. rapidly; hesitantly

C. Application in Writing
Describing a Scene
Answers will vary.

Using the Correct Modifier

Objective

- To learn strategies for using adjectives and adverbs correctly

Teaching Strategies

Stumbling Block

Have students write several pairs of sentences with linking verbs that can also function as action verbs. The first sentence should use the verb as a linking verb followed by a predicate adjective. The second sentence should use the verb as an action verb modified by an adverb or adverb phrase.

 Individualizing Instruction

LED Students Suggest that students create a brief chart to help them distinguish adjectives and adverbs. Have students include on the charts the kinds of questions that adjectives and adverbs answer; for example, adverbs answer *how, where, when,* etc.

It is sometimes difficult to decide whether to use an adjective or an adverb. The following explanations and examples will help you choose the correct kind of modifier.

Adjective or Adverb?

In the following sentence, which modifier correctly completes the sentence—the adjective *sudden* or the adverb *suddenly*?

> The blast happened _____ .

To decide, ask yourself the following questions:

1. **What kind of word does the modifier describe?**

   If the modified word is an action verb, an adjective, or an adverb, use the adverb *suddenly*. If the modified word is a noun or a pronoun, use the adjective *sudden*.

2. **What does the modifier tell about the word it describes?**

   If the modifier tells *how, when, where,* or *to what extent,* use the adverb *suddenly*. If the modifier tells *which one, what kind,* or *how many,* use the adjective *sudden*.

   If you apply both tests to the sentence "The blast happened _____ ," you will be able to determine that the adverb *suddenly* is the correct choice to modify the verb *happened*.

Adverb or Predicate Adjective?

You have learned that a predicate adjective follows a linking verb and that the predicate adjective modifies the subject. Besides forms of *be*, other linking verbs are *become, seem, appear, look, sound, feel, taste, smell,* and *grow*.

> This melon smells sweet. (*Sweet* modifies *melon*.)
> The parking lot looks full. (*Full* modifies *lot*.)
> The thunder grew louder. (*Louder* modifies *thunder*.)

In the sentences above, the words *smells, looks,* and *grew* are linking verbs. Therefore, the words that follow them are adjectives. However, these same verbs can also be action verbs, as can *sound, appear, feel,* and *taste*. When these verbs are action verbs, they are followed by adverbs.

Here are sentences using the same words as linking verbs and as action verbs.

Linking Verbs with Adjectives	Action Verbs with Adverbs
The water *looked* clear.	Dave *looked* quickly.
The team *appeared* eager.	Clouds *appeared* suddenly.
This music *sounds* peaceful.	The alarm *sounds* often.
Tanya *felt* bad.	Al carefully *felt* the fabric.

If you have trouble deciding whether a sentence needs an adverb or a predicate adjective, ask yourself the following questions:

1. **Can you substitute *is* or *was* for the verb?** If you can, use an adjective.

2. **Does the modifier tell *how, when, where,* or *to what extent?*** If it does, use an adverb.

Practice Your Skills

CONCEPT CHECK

Correct Use of Modifiers Write the correct modifier for each sentence. Tell whether the modifier is an *Adjective* or an *Adverb*.

> **Example**   French photographers (frequent, frequently) use the Eiffel Tower as a subject for their work.
> (frequently, Adverb)

1. As a place to live, Paris fits an artist's needs (perfect, perfectly).
2. Many artists have used its scenic beauty (regular, regularly) as a backdrop for their work.
3. Although the idea of Paris as an ideal place for artists may seem (mythical, mythically), it is not a new notion.
4. Artists did not flock to Paris (sudden, suddenly).
5. Since the mid-1800's, the Parisian lifestyle has suited artists (ideal, ideally).
6. Artists from all over the world are attracted almost (instinctively, instinctive) to the picturesque corners of the city.
7. The narrow streets of the Left Bank have been (inspirationally, inspirational) to painters.
8. Many artists not (original, originally) from France were called "Bohemians," suggesting that they were gypsies.
9. If that idea was taken (literal, literally), it was incorrect.
10. However, the artistic lifestyle was (real, really) similar to that of wanderers.

Additional Resources
- Grammar and Usage Practice Book, pp. 97–98

WRITING THEME   Paris
Concept Check
Correct Use of Modifiers
Modifiers are underlined on page.
1. perfectly, Adverb
2. regularly, Adverb
3. mythical, Adjective
4. suddenly, Adverb
5. ideally, Adverb
6. instinctively, Adverb
7. inspirational, Adjective
8. originally, Adverb
9. literally, Adverb
10. really, Adverb

Writing Theme
Paris

11. Artists formed a community to help one another (brave, <u>bravely</u>) survive poverty and rejection.
12. Painters and poets gathered (regular, <u>regularly</u>) in cafés.
13. Some writers were (eager, eagerly) to describe Parisian life.
14. These descriptions can make one feel (<u>romantic</u>, romantically) about Paris and the artist's life.
15. Despite its beauty, however, many artists and writers can (<u>scarcely</u>, scarce) make a living in this capital of dreams.

CHECK ✔ POINT
PAGES 625–630

A. Write the adverbs in the following sentences. Tell which word or words each adverb modifies.

1. The most influential style of theater Italy has offered the world is probably the *commedia dell'arte*.
2. This very popular form of theater flourished around 1600.
3. *Commedia* actors never used complete scripts.
4. Much of the dialogue was cleverly improvised.
5. Many of the most famous *commedia* companies were composed almost entirely of family members.
6. Thus improvization was much easier and went smoothly.
7. Actors had to be prepared for anything their partners suddenly said.
8. Each member of the company usually specialized in the portrayal of a single character.
9. A mask clearly identified each character.
10. Audiences enthusiastically cheered their favorites and loudly booed villains.

Writing Theme
Theater

della Commedia Italiana (artist unknown) Milan, Italy

630 Grammar Handbook

Humanities Connection

Art Note   *della Commedia Italiana* (artist unknown), in English, means "from Italian Comedy." The actors in the Italian Comedy, or commedia dell'arte—which was popular in Italy during the Renaissance—played stock characters or stereotypes, such as the old man, the trickster, and the young lovers. Working from general outlines only, the actors improvised much of their dialogue—not unlike improvisational comedy groups do today. Performed outdoors in public places, the commedia dell'arte plays were filled with slapstick comedy, bright costumes, and interaction with the audience.

B. Write the correct modifier for each sentence. Tell whether the modifier is an *Adjective* or an *Adverb*.

1. The theatrical traditions in Europe and in the Far East have developed (independent, independently).
2. East Asian plays (original, originally) were written in Sanskrit.
3. Their plots (ordinary, ordinarily) centered on one main story.
4. Since there were no playhouses that were (permanent, permanently), temporary ones had to be constructed.
5. There was no scenery, so the shift of place and time suggested by dialogue and action could be (rapid, rapidly).
6. Costumes for the performances were (traditionally, traditional).
7. Makeup indicated a character's place of birth, social position, and historical period (perfect, perfectly).
8. The drum was (real, really) important, since it followed the speakers' voices closely and heightened tension.
9. Roles and emotions were divided into a number of (clear, clearly) different categories.
10. Sanskrit drama was (sure, surely) responsible for creating European interest in the theater of East Asia.

USING MODIFIERS IN COMPARISONS

Adjectives and adverbs can be used to compare two or more things. You might describe air mail as being faster or better than the pony express. Special forms of modifiers are used to make comparisons.

Degrees of Comparison

There are three degrees of comparison: the positive degree, the comparative degree, and the superlative degree.

A modifier in the **positive degree** describes one person, place, thing, idea, or action. The positive degree is the basic form of the modifier—the one you will find in the dictionary.

A modifier in the **comparative degree** compares two persons, places, things, ideas, or actions.

A modifier in the **superlative degree** compares three or more persons, places, things, ideas or actions.

Positive	Seikan is a *long* railroad tunnel in Japan.
Comparative	Seikan is *longer* than Burlington's Cascade Tunnel.
Superlative	Seikan is the *longest* railroad tunnel in the world.

Using Modifiers in Comparisons

Objectives

- To identify the three degrees of comparison and to form the comparative and superlative degrees of adverbs and adjectives correctly
- **Writing** To use the forms of comparison correctly in writing

Teaching Strategies

Cooperative Learning

Have small groups of students write consumer reports comparing products. As a prewriting activity, have students examine advertisements for similar products. After students have completed this prewriting activity, have them draft their reports. Encourage students to exchange drafts, focusing their comments on the effectiveness of the reports and the correct use of comparisons.

LEP Students Point out the following mnemonic device to students: in regular comparisons, *-er* (two letters) is added when comparing two things; *-est* (three letters) is added when comparing three things.

Linking Grammar and Literature

Have students identify the irregular comparison in the following line from the poem "Birches" by Robert Frost:

"One could do worse than be a swinger of birches."

Ask students to read through other poems and stories to find examples of comparative and superlative forms.

Regular Comparisons

Most modifiers change in regular ways to show comparison.

1. A one-syllable modifier forms the comparative and superlative by adding *-er* and *-est*.

Positive	Comparative	Superlative
big	bigger	biggest
wide	wider	widest
kind	kinder	kindest

2. Most two-syllable modifiers form the comparative and superlative by adding *-er* and *-est*: *clumsy, clumsier, clumsiest*. Sometimes, a two-syllable modifier sounds awkward when *-er* and *-est* are added. If so, use *more* and *most* to form the comparative and superlative degrees.

Positive	Comparative	Superlative
hopeful	more hopeful	most hopeful
cautious	more cautious	most cautious

Two-syllable adverbs that end in *-ly* form comparison by using *more* and *most*: *quickly, more quickly, most quickly*.

3. Modifiers of three or more syllables use *more* and *most* to form the comparative and the superlative.

Positive	Comparative	Superlative
beautiful	more beautiful	most beautiful
anxiously	more anxiously	most anxiously

Irregular Comparisons

Some modifiers have irregular comparative and superlative forms. These modifiers and their comparative and superlative forms are shown in the following list.

Positive	Comparative	Superlative
good	better	best
well	better	best
bad	worse	worst
much	more	most
many	more	most
far	farther	farthest
little	less or lesser	least

To make a negative comparison, use *less* and *least* before the positive form of the modifier: *helpful, less helpful, least helpful*.

Practice Your Skills

A. CONCEPT CHECK

Errors in Comparison Find the errors in comparison in the following sentences and write the sentences correctly. If a sentence has no error, write *Correct*.

> **Example** Of the two pharaohs, who was most powerful?
> Of the two pharaohs, who was the more powerful?

1. Tutankhamen is probably the more famous of all the pharaohs of Egypt.
2. His fame is not due to his having been the most great ruler.
3. In fact, compared to the previous pharaoh, Ikhnaton, Tutankhamen was least creative.
4. An artist and religious reformer, Ikhnaton wrote some of the most beautiful poetry of his time.
5. Inheriting the throne at age ten made King Tut one of the younger monarchs in Egyptian history.
6. No other pharaoh was given an elaborater tomb.
7. Many kings' tombs containing less treasure were robbed.
8. Tutankhamen's tomb was fortunater, however, lying undisturbed for 3,000 years.
9. Archaeologist Henry Carter made his more remarkable discovery when he found the tomb in 1922.
10. Now Tutankhamen lies in the National Museum in Cairo, most impressive in death than in life.

B. DRAFTING SKILL

Using Modifiers Correctly Complete each sentence by using the form of the modifier given in parentheses.

> **Example** The construction of the ancient pyramids required (much—comparative) workers than such a project would today. more

1. Egypt's pyramids are considered one of the (great—superlative) wonders of the world.
2. The (early—superlative) pyramids were built about 2700 B.C.
3. The three (famous—superlative) pyramids are in Giza.
4. The first pyramid at Giza was built by King Khufu and is (massive—comparative) than the other two.
5. It is (large—comparative) than any other ancient structure except the Great Wall of China.
6. Some people say that this pyramid is the (impressive—superlative) structure ever built.

Additional Resources
• Grammar and Usage Practice Book, pp. 99–100

Scarab beetles were considered sacred in early Egypt, and stylized versions were created in many materials.
The Metropolitan Museum of Art, Rogers Fund, 1935

WRITING THEME Ancient Egypt

Suggest that interested students note this theme in their journals as a possible writing topic in world history.

A. Concept Check
Errors in Comparison
Errors in comparison are underlined on page.
1. Tutankhamen is probably the most famous of all the pharaohs of Egypt.
2. His fame is not due to his having been the greatest ruler.
3. In fact, compared to the previous pharaoh, Ikhnaton, Tutankhamen was less creative.
4. Correct
5. Inheriting the throne at age ten made King Tut one of the youngest monarchs in Egyptian history.
6. No other pharaoh was given a more elaborate tomb.
7. Correct
8. Tutankhamen's tomb was more fortunate, however, lying undisturbed for 3,000 years.
9. Archaeologist Henry Carter made his most remarkable discovery when he found the tomb in 1922.
10. Now Tutankhamen lies in the National Museum in Cairo, more impressive in death than in life.

B. Drafting Skill
Using Modifiers Correctly
1. greatest
2. earliest
3. most famous
4. more massive
5. larger
6. most impressive

Using Modifiers **633**

7. smaller
8. better
9. least
10. worse
11. more interesting
12. higher
13. most freely
14. later
15. more quickly

C. Application in Writing
Writing an Ad
Answers will vary.

Using Correct Comparisons

Objectives

- To use comparisons correctly, avoiding double and illogical comparisons
- **Writing** To demonstrate revision skills by correcting errors in comparisons

7. The second pyramid was built by Khufu's son Khafre and is much (small—comparative) than the first.
8. Today, however, Khafre's pyramid is in (good—comparative) condition than his father's.
9. The third pyramid, which is the (less—superlative) well known of the three, was built for Menkaure.
10. The remains of the walls are in (bad—comparative) condition than the others.
11. However, some statues found in the pyramid complex are (interesting—comparative) because of their small size.
12. Generally, royal statues were of a (high—comparative) standard than private statues.
13. The statue of Menkaure and his wife, known for its dignity, was imitated (freely—superlative) by private sculptors for other statues in the pyramid complex.
14. Structures similar to the pyramids were built much (late—comparative) than those in Egypt.
15. These later pyramids were built (quickly—comparative) than those at Giza.

C. APPLICATION IN WRITING

Writing an Ad Advertising copywriters often use the comparative and superlative forms of modifiers. For example, a copywriter might describe an airline as the *friendliest* in the sky. Write an advertisement for a new museum exhibit. Use comparative and superlative forms to make the exhibit sound as fascinating as possible.

USING CORRECT COMPARISONS

The explanations that follow will help you use comparisons correctly.

Avoiding Double Comparisons

A double comparison occurs when *-er* or *-est* is used with *more* or *most*.

Incorrect	She can type more faster than I.
Correct	She can type faster than I.
Incorrect	Tokyo is the most largest of the three cities.
Correct	Tokyo is the largest of the three cities.

Avoiding Illogical Comparisons

An illogical comparison is one that does not make sense because of missing words or an illogical construction.

Unclear   A queen termite lives longer than any insect.

Clear   A queen termite lives longer than any *other* insect. (Since a queen termite is itself an insect, it can only live longer than *other* insects. Always use the word *other* when you compare one thing with all other things of the same kind.)

Unclear   Adrienne likes that movie better than Hernando.

Clear   Adrienne likes that movie better than Hernando *does*. (Adrienne does not like the movie better than she likes Hernando. Hernando does not like the movie as much as Adrienne does.)

Unclear   Mark's bicycle is newer than Fred.

Clear   Mark's bicycle is newer than Fred's. (The comparison is between Mark's bicycle and Fred's bicycle, not between Mark's bicycle and Fred.)

Practice Your Skills

A. CONCEPT CHECK

Correct Comparisons   Rewrite each sentence, correcting the error in comparison. If a sentence has no error, write *Correct.*

1. One of the most commonest weapons in history is the sword.
2. Some historians consider the sword more fascinating than any weapon.
3. Swords were developed from the more primitive flint weapons of Neolithic times.
4. Unlike later iron and steel swords, more earlier swords were made of softer metals such as bronze or copper.
5. The Vikings introduced a blade of carbonized iron that was much stronger than the Romans.
6. Western cultures favored a straighter blade more than Eastern cultures.
7. Of the weapons makers in Europe, the swordsmiths of Toledo, Spain, may have been the most finest.
8. For centuries, Spanish blades were more stylish than any weapons in Europe.
9. During the Renaissance, the European nobles developed a more intense interest in the art of dueling.
10. The Japanese revered swordsmanship even more than Europeans.

Writing Theme
Weapons and Armor

Using Modifiers   **635**

B. Proofreading Skill

Correcting Errors of Comparison

Answers will vary. See suggested answers below. Errors are underlined on page.

Throughout history soldiers have used special coverings for protection. These special coverings, or armor, made soldiers safer by guarding them against enemy weapons.

In the Stone Age, warriors used several layers of skin to protect themselves from club and ax attacks. Many years later, people made themselves shields and body armor from metal, a stronger material.

The metal suits from the Middle Ages were heavier than any other armor. These suits of armor, made from thin sheets of metal or metal links, covered knights from head to foot. Each knight hoped his armor would be stronger than anyone else's. Unfortunately, the weight of the metal suits often caused additional problems. If a knight fell, sometimes he couldn't get up again!

C H E C K P O I N T
PAGES 631–636

You may wish to use the following Checkpoint exercises as an informal evaluation of student mastery of the concepts covered in this handbook.

WRITING THEME   American Poets

Encourage interested students to consider using the theme as the subject for a Writer's Workshop assignment.

A.

Answers are underlined on page.

Japanese suit of armor from the Muromachi Period, c. 1550

Metropolitan Museum of Art, Rogers Fund, 1904

Writing Theme
American Poets

B. PROOFREADING SKILL

Correcting Errors of Comparison   Rewrite the following paragraphs, correcting all <u>errors</u> in the use of comparisons. Also, correct all errors in spelling and punctuation.

Throughout history soldiers have used special coverings for protection. These special coverings, or armor, made soldiers <u>more safer</u> by guarding them against enemy <u>weapons'</u>.

In the Stone Age, warriors used several layers of skins to protect themselves from club and ax <u>attacks?</u> Many years later, people made themselves <u>sheilds</u> and body armor from metal, a <u>more stronger</u> material.

The metal suits from the Middle Ages were heavier than <u>any armor</u>. These suits of armor, made from thin sheets of metal or metal links, covered knights from <u>hed</u> to foot. Each knight hoped his metal suit would be stronger than <u>any armor</u>. Unfortunately, the <u>wait</u> of the suits often caused additional problems. If a knight fell, <u>some times</u> he couldn't get up again!

C H E C K P O I N T
PAGES 631–636

A. Choose the correct modifier.

1. One of the (importantest, <u>most important</u>) poets in American literature is Emily Dickinson.
2. Although many of her poems sound simple, some are (more hard, <u>harder</u>) to understand than they seem at first.
3. Her (<u>earliest</u>, most early) poems were valentines.
4. Others were written for the (trivialest, <u>most trivial</u>) events.
5. Her (more late, <u>later</u>) verse, however, is often filled with profound philosophical questions about immortality.
6. Dickinson's imagination sometimes took her into (mysteriouser, <u>more mysterious</u>) realms than most of us inhabit.
7. Nevertheless, her unique poems were (best, <u>better</u>) than those of most other poets of her time.
8. In fact, many critics consider Dickinson one of the (most great, <u>greatest</u>) poets.
9. One of her (<u>most frequent</u>, frequentest) themes is the transformation of poverty into riches.
10. Although Emily Dickinson lived in the nineteenth century, many of her poems have a (most contemporary, <u>more contemporary</u>) feeling than some of the poetry of this century.

636 Grammar Handbook

Humanities Connection

Art Note   Shown is a suit of armor designed by the Japanese artisan, Yoshihisa Matahachiro (b. 1523, d. 1554). Japan in the 15th and 16th centuries was torn asunder by ruinous feudal wars that were fought by armor-clad warriors called *samurai*. The samurai followed a strict code of conduct known as *bushido* or "way of the warrior." Ironically, a calm realism dominates Japanese art of the time, the Muromachi period. Painters depicted contemplative monks, orderly gardens, and tea ceremonies. The artists seem to have been inspired by quiet and harmony, attributes missing from the social chaos surrounding them.

B. For each sentence, write the form of the modifier given in parentheses.

1. (Often—comparative) than not, Robert Frost is selected as America's premier poet.
2. For many decades, Frost has been the (popular—superlative) poet for the general reading public.
3. The (great—superlative) number of his poems are about nature.
4. His poem "Stopping by Woods on a Snowy Evening" is perhaps (familiar—comparative) to many readers than any other of his poems.
5. This lovely poem is (short—comparative) than most of his other works.
6. Nevertheless, its few lines deliver a message and feeling that are (meaningful—comparative) than many longer poems.
7. His (long—comparative) poems, such as "Birches," often depict New England landscapes.
8. In that poem, Frost looks back to days when he was (young—comparative).
9. The poem ends with the speaker's declaring that earth is the (good—superlative) place for love.
10. Frost's reverence for nature helped establish him as one of the (eminent—superlative) writers of his time.

C. Find the errors in comparison in these sentences and rewrite the sentences correctly. If a sentence has no error, write *Correct.*

1. Langston Hughes's poetry was in some ways creativer than other African-American poetry of his day.
2. Perhaps more than any poet of his time, Hughes wanted to incorporate the spirit of jazz into his poetry.
3. Hughes sought recognition as a black man more than the poet Countee Cullen.
4. Hughes's attraction to spirituals and blues was more stronger than to traditional English poetry.
5. His work had a greater oral quality than did most other poetry being written.
6. Hughes's use of dialect is one of his work's effectivest features.
7. However, sound in his poetry is not meaningfuller than imagery.
8. Hughes's images in "The Negro Speaks of Rivers" may be more memorable than those in any of his poems.
9. In that poem, the speaker describes how rivers have helped his spirit grow more profound.
10. Few poets of this century have written powerfuller about the African-American experience.

Langston Hughes, noted African-American poet

Using Modifiers **637**

B.
1. More often
2. most popular
3. greatest
4. more familiar
5. shorter
6. more meaningful
7. longer
8. younger
9. best
10. most eminent

C.
1. Langston Hughes's poetry was in some ways more creative than other African-American poetry of his day.
2. Perhaps more than any other poet of his time, Hughes wanted to incorporate the spirit of jazz into his poetry.
3. Hughes sought recognition as a black man more than did the poet Countee Cullen.
4. Hughes's attraction to spirituals and blues was stronger than to traditional English poetry.
5. Correct
6. Hughes's use of dialect is one of his work's most effective features.
7. However, sound in his poetry is not more meaningful than imagery.
8. Hughes's images in "The Negro Speaks of Rivers" may be more memorable than those in any of his other poems.
9. Correct
10. Few poets of this century have written more powerfully about the African-American experience.

- To recognize and avoid common problems with modifiers
- **Writing** To demonstrate revision skills by correcting errors in the use of modifiers

Teaching Strategies

 Individualizing Instruction

ESL Students In Spanish, double negatives are grammatically correct. In English, they are not. It will be helpful to make this comparison for Spanish-speaking students.

> *Additional Resources*
> - Grammar and Usage Practice Book, pp. 103–106

permission of Johnny Hart and Creators Syndicate

IF THERE'S ONE THING I HATE
ITS HAVING TO CHOOSE BETWEEN
TWO THINGS I DESPISE !

WOULD THAT BE A
TRIPLE NEGATIVE ?

638 Grammar Handbook

PROBLEMS WITH MODIFIERS

Certain modifiers are responsible for many of the errors found in writing. By studying the following pages and referring to them occasionally as you revise, you can avoid these modifier problems.

The Double Negative

A **double negative** is an error that occurs when two negative words are used and only one is necessary. Avoid using double negatives.

Incorrect	We didn't take no time-outs.
Correct	We didn't take *any* time-outs.
Incorrect	My sister never eats no dessert.
Correct	My sister never eats *any* dessert.
Incorrect	John couldn't eat nothing all day.
Correct	John couldn't eat *anything* all day.

Contractions like *couldn't* contain a shortened form of the negative *not*. Do not use other negative words after them.

Some common negative words are *no, none, not, nothing,* and *never*. Instead of these words, use *any, anything,* or *ever* after negative contractions.

Incorrect	Amy hasn't never seen the Tigers play.
Correct	Amy hasn't *ever* seen the Tigers play.
Incorrect	Michelle couldn't find no leeks at the market.
Correct	Michelle couldn't find *any* leeks at the market.
Incorrect	The new council didn't change nothing.
Correct	The new council didn't change *anything*.

Other negative words are *hardly, scarcely,* and *barely*. Do not use these words with negative contractions such as *hasn't, didn't,* and *couldn't*.

Incorrect	Rick couldn't barely control the machine.
Correct	Rick could *barely* control the machine.
Incorrect	The movers hadn't scarcely begun.
Correct	The movers had *scarcely* begun.
Incorrect	Lightning hardly never strikes houses.
Correct	Lightning *hardly* ever strikes houses.

Practice Your Skills

CONCEPT CHECK

Double Negatives Correct each sentence that contains a double negative. If a sentence has no error, write *Correct*.

1. Last night's basketball game wasn't hardly a contest at all.
2. The home team didn't play no defense the entire game.
3. The center wouldn't scarcely bother to run up the court.
4. He never put out no decent effort to rebound or to block the other team's shots.
5. The opposing center wasn't no faster or stronger than the home team's player.
6. In fact, he was shorter, but he gave no ground.
7. The home team couldn't shoot nothing but air balls in the third quarter.
8. The visitors didn't allow them no easy baskets.
9. Of course, the referees didn't give the locals no breaks.
10. Hardly any penalties were called on the visiting team.
11. It seemed as if the home team couldn't scarcely move without receiving a penalty.
12. We never have seen nothing like this disastrous game.
13. The visitors didn't barely disguise their glee.
14. We could hardly stand to watch all the high fives.
15. The home team couldn't have hung their heads no lower than they did after that game.

Those and *Them*

Those can be used as an adjective or a pronoun.

Where are the controls for *those* power saws? (Adjective)
Those are the Jackson twins. (Pronoun)

Them is never an adjective and cannot be used in place of *those*.

Incorrect   We framed *them* photos.
Correct   We framed *those* photos.

Unnecessary *Here* and *There*

"This here" and "that there" are repetitious phrases. The word *this* includes the idea of *here*. The word *that* includes the idea of *there*. Avoid "this here" and "that there."

Incorrect   *This* here sandwich is stale.
Correct   *This* sandwich is stale.

Using Modifiers   **639**

WRITING THEME   Basketball

Students might like to consider the theme of basketball for a personal narrative or a short story.

Concept Check
Double Negatives
Answers will vary. See suggested answers below. Errors are underlined on page.

1. Last night's basketball game was hardly a contest at all.
2. The home team didn't play any defense the entire game.
3. The center would scarcely bother to run up the court.
4. He never put out any decent effort to rebound or to block the other team's shots.
5. The opposing center wasn't any faster or stronger than the home team's player.
6. Correct
7. The home team couldn't shoot anything but air balls in the third quarter.
8. The visitors didn't allow them any easy baskets.
9. Of course, the referees didn't give the locals any breaks.
10. Correct
11. It seemed as if the home team could scarcely move without receiving a penalty.
12. We never have seen anything like this disastrous game.
13. The visitors barely disguised their glee.
14. Correct
15. The home team couldn't have hung their heads any lower than they did after that game.

Teaching Tip: Cultural Differences

Errors with double negatives and the use of *them*, *those*, *this*, and *that* are common in some nonstandard dialects. Stress the importance of knowing and using standard English in written communication and for school and business. Oral practice may also be helpful.

Grammar and Writing

Point out that problems with modifiers can interfere with clear communication in writing. Ask students to review one of their rough drafts and see if any errors in the use of modifiers must be corrected. Have students make these corrections as part of their proofreading process.

Using Modifiers   **639**

This Kind and These Kinds

This and *that* modify the singular nouns *kind* and *sort*. *These* and *those* modify the plural nouns *kinds* and *sorts*. *Kind* and *sort* are usually singular when the noun in the prepositional phrase following these words is singular.

> *This kind* of project is exciting. (*This kind* and *project* are singular.)
> *That sort* of movie disturbs me.

Kind and *sort* are usually plural when the noun in the prepositional phrase is plural.

> *These sorts* of rides are fun. (*These sorts* and *rides* are plural.)
> *Those kinds* of plans always fail.

Good and Well

Although *good* and *well* have similar meanings, you cannot always substitute one word for the other. Look at the following sentences. What would happen if you switched *good* and *well?*

> That is a *good* photo of you. (The adjective *good* modifies the noun *photo.*)
> You sing *well.* (The adverb *well* modifies the verb *sing.*)

Good is always an adjective, modifying a noun or a pronoun. *Good* is never used to modify a verb; the adverb *well* is used instead.

Incorrect Jeff planned the party good.
Correct Jeff planned the party well.

Well generally functions as an adverb. In the sentence above, for example, *well* is used as an adverb modifying an action verb. *Well* can also be used as a predicate adjective after a linking verb. When *well* is used as an adjective, it always means "in good health."

Incorrect Nina doesn't feel good: she has the flu.
Correct Nina doesn't feel *well:* she has the flu. (The adjective *well* modifies *Nina.*)

Usage Note Since *good* and *well* can both be adjectives, they can both be used as predicate adjectives following the linking verb *feel. Feel good* refers to happiness, comfort, or pleasure.

> I felt good when I saw that A on my paper.

Practice Your Skills

A. CONCEPT CHECK

Other Problems with Modifiers Write the <u>correct word or phrase</u> for each sentence.

1. (<u>This</u>, This here) kind of plane is often chartered to bring fishing parties to Canada.
2. (Them, <u>Those</u>) vacationers flew from Toronto to Moose Lake.
3. Summer brings (<u>this kind</u>, these kinds) of tourist to the Northwest Territories of Canada.
4. The fishing is supposed to be (well, <u>good</u>) this season.
5. Trout, bass, and other kinds of fish swim in abundance in (<u>these</u>, these here) chilly waters.
6. (Those kind, <u>Those kinds</u>) of lures attract trout.
7. Fly-casters line up along (them, <u>these</u>) shores to fish.
8. Deep-water enthusiasts succeed fairly (good, <u>well</u>) in trolling from a boat.
9. Visiting anglers are very (well, <u>good</u>) for the economy, but visitors can cause problems.
10. (That there, <u>That</u>) guide goes along partly to remind them not to litter the landscape.

B. REVISION SKILL

Avoiding Problems with Modifiers Rewrite each incorrect sentence, correcting <u>errors</u> in the use of modifiers. If a sentence has no error, write *Correct*.

1. We would all do <u>good</u> to become better acquainted with the habits of sharks.
2. That <u>there</u> aquarium has one of the largest collections of sharks in captivity.
3. Not all of <u>them</u> sharks are carnivorous, or flesh eating.
4. This kind of shark, the whale shark, isn't a meat eater.
5. <u>Them</u> huge whale sharks are over fifty feet long, but they manage to live on plankton.
6. Without a doubt, the most dangerous species is this <u>here</u> great white shark.
7. You have to do more than swim <u>good</u> to escape one of them.
8. It's good to remember that most shark attacks occur in warmer water.
9. <u>These</u> kind of attack sometimes occurs in just three feet of water or less.
10. <u>Them</u> beaches that are subject to shark activity usually have lookout towers and sirens.

C. Proofreading Skill

Correcting Errors with Modifiers

Scientists divide whales into two main groups according to their method of feeding. The larger group is called toothed whales. This kind of whale does not feed on anything smaller than fish. Among toothed whales are dolphins, porpoises, and killer whales.

Whales in the second group, called baleen whales, are larger than toothed whales. Baleen whales feed on tiny shrimplike animals known as plankton. The blue whale, part of this second group, is larger than any other animal. Oddly, the group of larger whales eats the smaller-sized food.

PAGES 638–642

You may wish to use the following Checkpoint exercises as an informal evaluation of students' mastery of the concepts convered in this handbook.

WRITING THEME   Weather

You may want to suggest that interested students do research on this theme and use it as the subject for an assignment in science.

A.

Answers will vary. See suggested answers below.

1. This magnificent cloud is called a cumulonimbus.
2. Cumulus, cumulonimbus, and others of these types of heavy clouds drift lower than 6,500 feet.
3. Those names for clouds are derived from Greek words.
4. Cumulonimbus weather is hardly what one could term tranquil.

C. PROOFREADING SKILL

Correcting Errors with Modifiers   Proofread the following paragraphs. Then rewrite them, correcting all of the errors, including errors in spelling, punctuation, and grammar. Pay special attention to the use of adjectives and adverbs.

Scientists divide whales into two main groups according to there method of feeding. The largest group is call toothed whales. These kind of whales do not feed on nothing smaller than fish. Among toothed whales are dolphins porpoises, and killer whales.

The second group, called baleen whales, is more larger in size than toothed whales, baleen whales feed on tiny shrimplike animales known as plankton. The blue whale, part of this second group, is larger than any animal. Oddly, the group of larger whales' eat the more smaller-sized food.

Scrimshaw on a whale tooth shows whalers towing a dead whale to their ship.

PAGES 638–642

A. The following sentences contain errors in the use of modifiers. Rewrite each sentence, correcting the error.

1. This here magnificent cloud is called a cumulonimbus.
2. Cumulus, cumulonimbus, and others of these type of heavy clouds drift lower than 6,500 feet.
3. Them names for clouds are derived from Greek words.
4. The weather they bring isn't hardly what one could term tranquil.

5. Rain, snow, thunder, and sometimes tornadoes accompany <u>them</u> clouds.
6. That <u>there</u> evil-looking cloud means that it will probably rain today.
7. <u>These</u> sort of cloud is common at this time of year.
8. In fact, those formations scarcely <u>never</u> pass over without bringing rain.
9. Of course, the rain is <u>well</u> for farmers and their crops.
10. However, some torrential downpours don't <u>never</u> seem to stop.
11. Those <u>there</u> clouds in the west are cirrus clouds.
12. Precipitation hardly <u>never</u> falls from these light, feathery clouds.
13. They nevertheless serve <u>good</u> as an indicator of storms to come.
14. Those <u>there</u> cirrus clouds, the cirrostratus, can thicken and descend to lower altitudes.
15. In the tropics, that <u>there</u> development can mean that a hurricane is forming.
16. Cirrostratus clouds also produce <u>them</u> lovely red sunrises.
17. However, remember this <u>here</u> saying, "Red sky at morning, sailors take warning."
18. It is <u>well</u> to realize that old sayings often have a basis in fact.
19. Thanks to weather satellites, we don't <u>never</u> have to guess at cloud movements again.
20. On the other hand, no matter how <u>well</u> our technology becomes, people will still complain about the weather.

B. Write the word or phrase that correctly completes each sentence.

1. On (<u>this kind</u>, these kinds) of summer day the sun seems to broil the earth.
2. It is difficult to believe (them, <u>those</u>) rays came from 93 million miles away.
3. (<u>This</u>, This here) spectroscope is an instrument used to study solar radiation.
4. It does a (<u>good</u>, well) job of measuring the wavelengths of sunlight, even when the sky is cloudy.
5. The instrument can measure (<u>those types</u>, those type) of rays that are invisible to the naked eye.
6. Scientists are determining that some of (them, <u>those</u>) rays can be harmful to human beings.
7. Prolonged exposure to the sun doesn't do your skin (no, <u>any</u>) good at all.
8. Of course, it always feels (well, <u>good</u>) to bask idly in the sun's warmth.
9. However, the fun isn't worth (<u>any</u>, no) serious health risks.
10. Even on an overcast day, (<u>that</u>, that there) shining star is a dangerous and even lethal force.

5. Rain, snow, thunder, and sometimes tornadoes accompany these clouds.
6. That evil-looking cloud means that it will probably rain today.
7. This sort of cloud is common at this time of year.
8. In fact, those formations scarcely ever pass over without bringing rain.
9. Of course, the rain is good for farmers and their crops.
10. However, some torrential downpours don't ever seem to stop.
11. Those clouds in the west are cirrus clouds.
12. Precipitation hardly ever falls from these light, feathery clouds.
13. They nevertheless serve well as an indicator of storms to come.
14. Those cirrus clouds, the cirrostratus, can thicken and descend to lower altitudes.
15. In the tropics, that development can mean that a hurricane is forming.
16. Cirrostratus clouds also produce those lovely red sunrises.
17. However, remember this saying, "Red sky at morning, sailors take warning."
18. It is good to realize that old sayings often have a basis in fact.
19. Thanks to weather satellites, we don't ever have to guess at cloud movements again.
20. On the other hand, no matter how good our technology becomes, people will still complain about the weather.

B.
Answers are underlined on page.

GRAMMAR HANDBOOK 34

Writing Theme
Modes of Travel

A. Identifying Modifiers Write the modifiers in the following sentences. Identify each modifier as an *Adjective* or an *Adverb* and tell which word it modifies. Include nouns and pronouns used as adjectives. Do not include articles or compound words such as *Mercury Theater* or *New Jersey*.

1. Who would imagine that a simple radio broadcast could cause a nationwide panic?
2. It was Halloween of 1938, and people crouched intently around their radios.
3. The Mercury Theater of the Air usually dramatized a famous novel every week.
4. Americans heard a nervous reporter breathlessly announce a truly fantastic event.
5. The reporter announced that a mysterious spaceship had landed in a small town in New Jersey.
6. Gruesome, tentacled creatures, he said, peered curiously from the ship's interior.
7. The clearly terrified reporter shakily continued his description of the eerie proceedings.
8. Suddenly, with brutal swiftness, a searing ray flashed from the spacecraft.
9. The radio was temporarily silent.
10. Listeners held one another tightly and looked nervously into the dark night.
11. Residents of New Jersey were probably the most frightened, but listeners across America reacted immediately and intensely.
12. Some people pleaded with local authorities to halt electrical power to reduce the dangers of alien attack.
13. This broadcast of "The War of the Worlds" fooled much of its radio audience completely.
14. Orson Welles, the writer and director, later apologized to the upset Americans for the clever Halloween prank.
15. The young director had unintentionally caused a panic.
16. He thought that he had plainly indicated that the upcoming broadcast was a dramatization of a popular novel.
17. Unfortunately, many people were not listening carefully or joined the program late.
18. Thoughtful listeners easily identified the spellbinding plot of *War of the Worlds* in spite of the fact that English settings had been imaginatively replaced with American ones.
19. This incident truly proved the remarkable power of radio.
20. Today, experts consider his spaceship saga to have been the peak of Welles's radio career and a highlight of early broadcasting.

Additional Resources
- Tests and Assessment, Mastery Tests, pp. 69–74
- Elaboration, Revision, and Proofreading Worksheets, p. 26

WRITING THEME Modes of Travel

Suggest that interested students note this theme in their journals for use as a possible writing topic.

A. Identifying Modifiers

1. simple, Adjective, broadcast; radio, Adjective, broadcast; nationwide, Adjective, panic
2. intently, Adverb, crouched; their, Adjective, radios
3. usually, Adverb, dramatized; famous, Adjective, novel; every, Adjective, week
4. nervous, Adjective, reporter; breathlessly, Adverb, announce; truly, Adverb, fantastic; fantastic, Adjective, event
5. mysterious, Adjective, spaceship; small, Adjective, town
6. Gruesome, Adjective, creatures; tentacled, Adjective, creatures; curiously, Adverb, peered; ship's, Adjective, interior
7. clearly, Adverb, terrified; terrified, Adjective, reporter; shakily, Adverb, continued; his, Adjective, description; eerie, Adjective, proceedings
8. Suddenly, Adverb, flashed; brutal, Adjective, swiftness; searing, Adjective, ray
9. temporarily, Adverb, silent; silent, Adjective, radio
10. tightly, Adverb, held; nervously, Adverb, looked; dark, Adjective, night
11. probably, Adverb, were; most, Adverb, frightened; frightened, Adjective, Residents; immediately, Adverb, reacted; intensely, Adverb, reacted
12. Some, Adjective, people; local, Adjective, authorities; electrical, Adjective, power; alien, Adjective, attack
13. This, Adjective, broadcast; its, Adjective, audience; radio, Adjective, audience; completely, Adverb, fooled
14. later, Adverb, apologized; upset, Adjective, Americans; clever, Adjective, prank; Halloween, Adjective, prank
15. young, Adjective, director; unintentionally, Adverb, caused
16. plainly, Adverb, indicated; upcoming, Adjective, broadcast; popular, Adjective, novel
17. Unfortunately, Adverb, were listening; not, Adverb, were listening; carefully, Adverb, were listening; late, Adverb, joined
18. Thoughtful, Adjective, listeners; easily, Adverb, identified; spellbinding, Adjective, plot; English, Adjective, settings; imaginatively, Adverb, had been replaced; American, Adjective, ones
19. This, Adjective, incident; truly, Adverb, proved; remarkable, Adjective, power
20. Today, Adverb, consider; his, Adjective, saga; spaceship, Adjective, saga; Welles's, Adjective, career; radio, Adjective, career; early, Adjective, broadcasting

B. Making Correct Comparisons Rewrite each incorrect sentence, correcting each error in the use of comparisons. If a sentence has no error, write *Correct*.

1. Although scientists can learn much about space from earthbound observations, artificial satellites make their studies more richer.
2. As early as the fifteenth century, people's ambitions reached more far than the planet's surface.
3. Experimentation with rockets was the significantest work done to make these dreams come true.
4. The USSR opened the space age when it launched *Sputnik I* on October 4, 1957, four months ahead of the launching of the first American satellite.
5. The Soviets were less fortunater with *Sputnik II,* which carried Laika, the first animal to orbit the globe.
6. *Sputnik II* orbited for 162 days, but Laika died on the sixth day, making the experiment least productive than the Soviets had hoped.
7. America's space program was different from Russia.
8. On January 31, 1958, America sent the sensitivist instruments then available into orbit to help study energy bands in space.
9. Since the 1950's, each country has produced exciting results from different but equally astounding feats in space.
10. Most progress in space exploration was made in the past few decades than in all previous centuries combined.
11. However, some people say that reality will never be amazinger than our vivid imaginations.
12. Space travel is one of the most commonest themes in science fiction today.
13. *Star Trek* has played more longer than most other television series.
14. Box-office earnings for *Star Wars* were higher than for any space film.
15. In the future, travel to other planets may be no difficulter than going to the movies.

C. Using Modifiers Correctly Many of the following sentences contain errors in the use of modifiers. Write each incorrect sentence, correcting the error. If a sentence contains no error, write *Correct*.

1. Few Americans now living will visit space, but many enjoy those there other stars from movies and television.
2. These kinds of star are recognized more often than the stars in the sky, such as Alpha Centauri.
3. A star's vehicle is frequent as familiar as his or her name.

B. Making Correct Comparisons
Errors are underlined on page.
1. Although scientists can learn much about space from earthbound observations, artificial satellites make their studies richer.
2. As early as the fifteenth century, people's ambitions reached farther than the planet's surface.
3. Experimentation with rockets was the most significant work done to make these dreams come true.
4. Correct
5. The Soviets were less fortunate with *Sputnik II,* which carried Laika, the first animal to orbit the globe.
6. *Sputnik II* orbited for 162 days, but Laika died on the sixth day, making the experiment less productive than the Soviets had hoped.
7. America's space program was different from Russia's.
8. On January 31, 1958, America sent the most sensitive instruments then available into orbit to help study energy bands in space.
9. Correct
10. More progress in space exploration was made in the past few decades than in all previous centuries combined.
11. However, some people say that reality will never be more amazing than our vivid imaginations.
12. Space travel is one of the most common themes in science fiction today.
13. *Star Trek* has played longer than most other television series.
14. Box-office earnings for *Star Wars* were higher than for any other space film.
15. In the future, travel to other planets may be no more difficult than going to the movies.

C. Using Modifiers Correctly
Errors are underlined on page.
1. Few Americans now living will visit space, but many enjoy those other stars from movies and television.
2. These kinds of stars are recognized more often than the stars in the sky, such as Alpha Centauri.
3. A star's vehicle is frequently as familiar as his or her name.

4. Correct

5. A more earthbound means of travel suits many popular stars quite adequately.

6. Roy Rogers didn't ever walk if he could ride his trusty horse, Trigger.

7. James Dean and Peter Fonda felt powerful as they rode down the highway on motorcycles.

8. Judy Garland's ride to Oz in a farmhouse was surely one of the most fantastic journeys ever taken.

9. Of course, everyone knows that many stars own those beautiful stretch limousines.

10. However, when people in Hollywood speak of star vehicles, they don't mean spaceships or anything like that.

11. In show business, a vehicle is a project that shows off an actor's talents well.

12. Harrison Ford's part in *Star Wars* was probably more important to his career than any other role he had played.

13. The movie *Alien* made Sigourney Weaver more famous than her stage work did.

14. Correct

15. That movie is itself a vehicle for terror.

D. Using Modifiers Correctly

(1) The yacht *Stars and Stripes* won the America's Cup in 1987, when it sailed the fastest of all the yachts. (2) The yacht's skipper, Dennis Conner, felt jubilant, for he had lost the cup four years earlier to an Australian boat. (3) For the 1983 competition, the Australians developed a boat that was quicker than Conner's. (4) Conner couldn't do anything to overcome the disadvantage in speed. (5) In preparing for the 1987 competition, Conner decided to employ high-technology boat designers to develop a sailboat that would be the most highly advanced of all the competitors. (6) His designers did well. (7) The boat they developed didn't lose any races in the final round. (8) In the first three races, Conner's sailboat beat its Australian competitor badly. (9) In the final race, the Australian boat was beaten worst of all. (10) Conner had regained the America's Cup easily.

4. The starship *Enterprise,* for example, is instantly associated with William Shatner, the star of *Star Trek*.

5. A more earthbound means of travel suits many popular stars quite adequate.

6. Roy Rogers didn't never walk if he could ride his trusty horse, Trigger.

7. James Dean and Peter Fonda felt powerfully as they rode down the highway on motorcycles.

8. Judy Garland's ride to Oz in a farmhouse was sure one of the most fantastic journeys ever taken.

9. Of course, everyone knows that many stars own them beautiful stretch limousines.

10. However, when people in Hollywood speak of star vehicles, they don't mean spaceships or nothing like that.

11. In show business, a vehicle is a project that shows off an actor's talents good.

12. Harrison Ford's part in *Star Wars* was probably more important to his career than any role he had played.

13. The movie *Alien* made Sigourney Weaver more famous than her stage work.

14. The creature in this movie uses a human as a vehicle.

15. That there movie is itself a vehicle for terror.

D. Using Modifiers Correctly Rewrite the following paragraph, correcting the errors in the use of modifiers.

(1) The yacht *Stars and Stripes* won the America's Cup in 1987, when it sailed faster of all the yachts. (2) The yacht's skipper, Dennis Conner, felt jubilantly, for he had lost the cup four years earlier to an Australian boat. (3) For the 1983 competition, the Australians developed a boat that was more quicker than Conner's. (4) Conner couldn't do nothing to overcome the disadvantage in speed. (5) In preparing for the 1987 competition, Conner decided to employ high-technology boat designers to develop a sailboat that would be the more highly advanced of all the competitors. (6) His designers did good. (7) The boat they developed didn't lose no races in the final round. (8) In the first three races, Conner's sailboat beat its Australian competitor bad. (9) In the final race, the Australian boat was beaten worse of all. (10) Conner had regained the America's Cup easy.

BIOGRAPHY OF A WORD

Time has a way of changing words. Some words undergo a change in reputation by moving up or down the social ladder. For example, *marshal,* which now refers to an esteemed occupation, once meant "one who held horses." On the other hand, *villain* meant "farmer."

Sometimes, little remains of the first spelling and meaning of the word. Take, for example, the adjective *tawdry,* which now means "cheap and gaudy, or showy." This word owes its existence to Ethelreda, the pious daughter of a seventh-century Saxon king.

Ethelreda was known and honored for her religious devotion and good works. However, she always regretted her youthful love of beautiful necklaces. She died of a throat disease, and she blamed the sickness on her early fondness for rich jewelry.

Ethelreda was named the patron saint of the island village where she had established a monastery, but already the forces of change were at work. She was remembered not as Saint Ethelreda, but as Saint Audrey, a shortening of Ethelreda. The townspeople honored her memory by selling necklaces of fine silk—Saint Audrey's laces—on her feast day. As time passed, these beautiful laces gave way to gaudy, poorly made scarves. By the 1700's, even the name had been cheapened. In common speech, "Saint Audrey" was pronounced "t Audrey." Soon the laces became Tawdry laces. Today *tawdry* is used to refer to anything cheap and showy. None of Ethelreda's spirit has survived in the word, and all that remains of her sainthood is the *t.*

647

After discussing the feature, tell students that *The Oxford English Dictionary* is a rich source for understanding the evolution of words. As examples, you might have students look up the changing definitions of *solicit, self,* or *sandwich.* Ask students to find the relationship between the term *politics* and the Greek word *polis.*

These exercises allow your students to practice skills acquired in Handbooks 33–34. You may wish to use the exercises to provide a thorough review of the material in these chapters or to evaluate student mastery of the concepts.

Additional Resources
- Grammar and Usage Practice Book, pp. 107–109
- Standardized Test Practice

Skills Assessment Test 2
1. A—worst
2. A—had stolen
3. A—Lazarus's
   C—than anyone else
4. D—their
5. B—Mayflower
   C—brought
6. B—had already been laid

Skills
A S S E S S M E N T

Directions One or more of the underlined sections in the following sentences may contain errors of grammar, usage, punctuation, spelling, or capitalization. Write the letter or letters of each incorrect item, and then rewrite the item correctly. If there is no error in an item, write E.

> **Example**   In the cathedral of Notre Dame, the windows make
> A   B
>
> beautiful patterns as light passes through them creations of colored
>   C   D
>
> glass. No error
>   E
>
> **Answer**   D—those creations

1. Of all age groups, the worse drivers, statistically, are between the ages of twenty and
   A   B   C
   twenty-four. No error
   D   E

2. When it was claimed that George Harrison had stole the tune for "My Sweet Lord"
   A
   from the song "He's So Fine," the jury agreed that the tunes were quite similar and
   B   C
   awarded damages. No error
   D   E

3. Emma Lazarus' poem on the Statue of Liberty has made her more famous than anyone
   A   B   C
   in her family in spite of the fact that her cousin became a Supreme Court justice.
                                                               D
   No error
   E

4. In *Romeo and Juliet,* Romeo tells Mercutio and Tybalt to lay down there swords and
                    A   B   C   D
   stop fighting. No error
                  E

5. In the fall of 1620, the "Mayflower" took a small group of families here from England.
            A   B   C   D
   No error
   E

6. By the end of the Civil War, a telegraph line had already been lain from New York to
                      A   B   C
   San Francisco. No error
   D   E

7. Possibly <u>no one</u> <u>will ever explain</u> the sightings of the Loch Ness monster and the
   _A   _B
   Abominable Snowman, but <u>these kind</u> of mystery will <u>always</u> fascinate people. <u>No error</u>
        _C   _D   _E

8. Diana Ross <u>has sung</u> <u>not only</u> in the <u>United States</u> but also in other countries <u>all over</u>
        _A   _B   _C   _D
   the world. <u>No error</u>
        _E

9. When Theodore C. Sorensen <u>read</u> <u>John F. Kennedy's</u> preface to *Profiles in Courage,* it
        _A   _B
   made him <u>feel good</u> to realize how much Kennedy <u>apreciated</u> his contribution to the
        _C   _D
   book. <u>No error</u>
        _E

10. Did <u>Miss Havisham</u> in *Great Expectations* really think she looked <u>nicely</u> in the <u>ancient</u>,
         _A   _B   _C
    decaying wedding dress she <u>weared?</u> <u>No error</u>
         _D   _E

11. At the <u>1980 Winter Olympics</u>, speed skater Eric Heiden <u>skates</u> the 500-meter race <u>so</u>
         _A   _B   _C
    <u>quick</u> that he <u>set</u> a world record. <u>No error</u>
         _D   _E

12. <u>No one</u> <u>hadn't never</u> topped <u>Babe Ruth's</u> home-run record until Roger Maris <u>did so</u>
         _A   _B   _C   _D
    in 1961. <u>No error</u>
         _E

13. Recent studies of the <u>enviroment</u> show that <u>toxic waste</u> is a <u>more larger</u> problem
         _A   _B   _C
    <u>than scientists once thought</u>. <u>No error</u>
         _D   _E

14. Winston and <u>lady Churchill</u> <u>so hated</u> Graham Sutherland's portrait of the <u>British Prime</u>
         _A   _B   _C
    <u>Minister</u> that they refused to <u>leave it be</u> displayed. <u>No error</u>
         _D   _E

15. The <u>English</u> critic Walter Pater <u>wrote</u> more <u>emotionally</u> about art <u>than John Ruskin</u>,
         _A   _B   _C   _D
    who was equally famous. <u>No error</u>
         _E

16. Bricks were invented by the <u>Egyptains</u>, who <u>sat</u> <u>them</u> in the <u>sun to</u> bake and harden.
         _A   _B   _C   _D
    <u>No error</u>
         _E

17. In 1987 there <u>were</u> 2,810 accidents in U.S. nuclear power plants, about 25 <u>less</u> than
    A
    <u>them</u> <u>reported in</u> 1986. <u>No error</u>
    C   D   E

18. When theater <u>critic Ivor Brown</u> saw John Gielgud in tights as Romeo in <u>May of 1924</u>, he
    stated in his <u>review,</u> "Mr. Gielgud has the most meaningless legs <u>imagineable</u>." <u>No error</u>
    C   D   E

19. <u>Homing pigeons</u> usually navigate by the position of the sun; however, <u>these kind</u> of birds
    rely on the <u>earth's</u> <u>magnetic field</u> at night or on cloudy days. <u>No error</u>

20. This <u>week our</u> science teacher <u>learned us</u> that <u>banana</u> "trees" are actually giant <u>herbs</u>
    and not trees at all. <u>No error</u>

21. <u>Petrified</u> wood is not wood that <u>has turned</u> to stone but rather wood that <u>has acted</u> as a
    kind of <u>mold for</u> mineral deposits. <u>No error</u>

22. Most people in their lives will contract a <u>rhinovirus</u>, but since <u>it's</u> a trigger of the
    common cold, they <u>won't</u> grow <u>no</u> horns on their foreheads. <u>No error</u>

23. <u>In recorded history</u> no snow had ever <u>fell</u> on <u>West Palm Beach</u>, Florida, until <u>January 19,</u>
    <u>1977</u>. <u>No error</u>

24. One of French painter <u>Jacques Louis David's</u> most famous works, *Death of Marat,*
    depicts Jean Paul Marat, a martyr of the <u>French Revolution</u>, who was stabbed in <u>1793</u>
    <u>while in his bath.</u> <u>No error</u>

25. During <u>world war II</u>, the Nazis <u>stoled</u> the crown of <u>Charlemagne;</u> however, <u>American</u>
    soldiers eventually recovered it. <u>No error</u>

Sketchbook

You are this man. How did you get into this situation? What are you feeling now? How will you get down safely? Write a humorous, melodramatic narrative about your predicament. Try to select verbs, adverbs, and adjectives that convey the danger and absurdity of the moment.

Additional Sketches

Imagine you are visiting an exotic setting, either real or imaginary. Write a postcard home from this remote or romantic place. Describe in vivid detail where you are and what you have been doing.

You have just witnessed a theft, and the police need you to help them catch the thief. Describe as precisely as you can exactly what you saw at the scene of the crime, using concrete modifiers.

651

Objective

To use the image of a man in a bizarre and dangerous situation as a springboard to informal writing

Using the Prompt

Remind students that the writing activities suggested in the Sketchbook are designed to be informal in order to allow risk taking and discovery. They are not graded.

Many students may not recognize that the photograph shows silent film star Harold Lloyd in a famous scene from the 1923 movie *Safety Last*. The character he plays is a salesclerk who has climbed the side of a building, playing the role of a "human fly," in order to increase business at his store so that he can get a promotion, a raise, and the girl he loves.

Encourage students to brainstorm melodramatic details and humorous problems that might arise before and after they, as the character in the photograph, reach the clock. In addition to the questions in the student text, encourage them to think about such questions as: How high is the clock? How might the movements of the clock affect them? How might others try to assist them? In what ways might efforts at assistance either succeed or backfire?

Use the ideas in the Additional Sketches section with students who find that these ideas offer a better starting point. Encourage students to put their writing in their Writing Portfolios. They may wish to refer to them during future writing projects.

What Is a Preposition?

Objectives

- To identify prepositions
- To identify components of a prepositional phrase
- To distinguish between prepositions and adverbs
- **Writing** To use prepositional phrases to show relationships in writing

Teaching Strategies

Cooperative Learning

Ask each student to find a partner. Tell one student from each pair to draw a geometric pattern and then to orally instruct the partner to duplicate the design without looking at the other student's picture, relying only on oral instructions. Have students share results with the class and discuss the probable reasons for their success or difficulty. Elicit that careful use of spatial words is a key factor, including prepositional phrases that show relationships and make connections.

 Individualizing Instruction

ESL Students Certain Asian languages do not contain prepositions, or they contain very few. Native speakers of these languages will have difficulty distinguishing "He is in the game" and "He is at the game."

GRAMMAR
HANDBOOK
35

Writing TIP

When *as* is a preposition, it means "like" or "in the capacity of." When *but* is a preposition, it means "except."

Using Prepositions, Conjunctions, and Interjections

WHAT IS A PREPOSITION?

A preposition is a word used to show the relationship between a noun or pronoun and some other word in the sentence.

In the following examples, notice how changing the preposition can affect the meaning of the sentence as a whole.

> Sara skated *off* the ice.
> Sara skated *onto* the ice.
> Sara skated *over* the ice.

The prepositions *off, onto,* and *over* show the relationship between the noun *ice* and the verb *skated*. In each sentence, *ice* is the **object of the preposition.**

The following list presents words often used as prepositions. Some prepositions consist of two or three words. These are called **compound prepositions.**

Commonly Used Prepositions

about	at	down	near	to
above	before	during	of	toward
across	behind	except	off	under
after	below	for	on	underneath
against	beneath	from	onto	until
along	beside	in	out	up
among	between	inside	over	upon
around	but (except)	into	since	with
as	by	like	through	without

Commonly Used Compound Prepositions

according to	because of	in place of	on account of
ahead of	due to	in spite of	on top of
along with	in addition to	instead of	out of
as of	in front of	next to	prior to

The Object of the Preposition

The object of a preposition is always a noun, a pronoun, or a group of words used as a noun.

> **With poise,** Meryl Streep walked to the stage and accepted her Academy Award. (The noun *poise* is the object of the preposition *with*.)
>
> The city welcomed the British prime minister and scheduled a sightseeing tour *for him*. (The pronoun *him* is the object of the preposition *for*.)
>
> Give the Springsteen concert tickets *to whoever asks for them first*. (*Whoever asks for them first* is a group of words functioning as a noun. It is the object of the preposition *to*.)

Like the other sentence parts, the object of a preposition may be compound.

> *Between January* and *July,* Franklin gained twenty pounds. (*January* and *July* are the compound objects of the preposition *between*.)

The Prepositional Phrase

A prepositional phrase consists of a preposition, its object, and any modifiers of the object.

A preposition does not show relationships by itself. It always begins a phrase, a group of words without a subject or verb. The prepositional phrases in the following sentences are italicized.

> Martha indicated her approval *with a nod*.
> The figures *on a totem pole* have special significance.

There are three situations in which a prepositional phrase that comes at the beginning of a sentence should be followed by a comma.

1. If the phrase is followed by a natural pause when read:
   According to our town's fire marshal, working smoke detectors can save many lives.
2. After a series of prepositional phrases:
   After three weeks of heavy rain in April, the farmer's fields were wet and muddy.
3. To avoid confusion:
   Next to the new elementary school, houses were being built for employees of the city.

Using Prepositions,
Conjunctions, and
Interjections **653**

Speaking and Listening

Students may be interested to learn how often they use prepositions in their own speech. Ask student volunteers to address the class, each giving a description of a favorite film, book, or meal. Direct listeners to record the prepositions used. Discuss the results.

 Individualizing Instruction

ESL Students Hindi and other Indian languages contain postpositions, not prepositions. (Postpositions follow their objects.) Indian students will have trouble with the correct use of prepositions.

Linking Grammar and Writing

Point out that since prepositional phrases show relationships, they are especially useful in adding details to descriptions and connecting ideas in explaining a process or giving directions.

Additional Resources
- Tests and Assessment, Pretests, pp. 21–22
- Grammar and Usage Practice Book, pp. 111–112

WRITING THEME   Adaptable Animals

Suggest that interested students add this theme to an ongoing list of possible writing topics for expository writing or science papers.

A. Concept Check

Prepositional Phrases
Answers are underlined on page.

Writing Theme
Adaptable Animals

Preposition or Adverb?

Many words used as prepositions may also be used as adverbs. How can you tell if a word is a preposition or an adverb?

A preposition is never used alone. It is always followed by a noun or pronoun used as the object of the preposition. If the word does not have an object, it is probably an adverb.

The visitors walked *around the courtyard*. (Preposition)
The visitors walked *around*. (Adverb)

The giant sequoias towered *above the trail*. (Preposition)
The giant sequoias towered *above*. (Adverb)

Can you jump *over that hurdle?* (Preposition)
Can you come *over* later? (Adverb)

Practice Your Skills

A. CONCEPT CHECK

Prepositional Phrases   Write the prepositional phrases in the following sentences. Underline the preposition once and its object twice. Be aware that some sentences may have more than one prepositional phrase.

Example   The sun shines on the desert.

1. Can any creature live without water?
2. Many animals in the desert survive on water-rich food, but the kangaroo rat is a different sort of creature.
3. This distinctive little animal can be found in deserts all around the world.
4. The creature's long kangaroo-like back legs suggest the reason for its name.
5. A kangaroo rat can live for an indefinite period of time without any water.
6. Inside its body, this amazing creature produces its own water supply.
7. When the body of any creature oxidizes or "burns" food, it produces a small amount of water.
8. In contrast, the body of a kangaroo rat is so remarkably efficient that the little animal can live on the tiny quantity of water produced through this process.
9. Perhaps one can't squeeze water out of a stone, but the kangaroo rat can obtain it from a dry barley seed.
10. Few animals but the kangaroo rat seem so perfectly adapted to life in the desert.

B. APPLICATION IN LITERATURE

Prepositional Phrases Write ten of the prepositional phrases you find in the following passage. For each phrase, underline the preposition once and the object of the preposition twice. Notice how the author uses prepositional phrases to add detail to this description of nature in winter.

(1) Other interesting things are going on wherever there is shelter. (2) Slugs, of all creatures, hibernate inside a waterproof sac. (3) All the bumblebees and paper wasps are dead except the queens, who sleep a fat, numbed sleep, unless a mouse finds one and eats her alive. (4) Honeybees have their own honey for fuel, so they can overwinter as adults, according to Edwin Way Teale, by buzzing together in a tightly packed, living sphere. (5) Their shimmying activity heats the hive; they switch positions from time to time so that each bee gets its chance in the cozy middle and its turn on the cold outside. . . . (6) Ladybugs hibernate under shelter in huge orange clusters sometimes the size of basketballs.

Annie Dillard, *Pilgrim at Tinker Creek*

C. APPLICATION IN WRITING

Writing a Scientific Description Prepositions express relationships. Scientific descriptions of animals often include discussion of a creature's relationship to its environment. A snake, for example, exists quite nicely *without legs* and, *in a desert,* can often be found *under a rock,* hiding *from the hot sun.* Write a brief scientific description, using prepositions to show the relationship of a creature to its surroundings.

Using Prepositions,
Conjunctions, and
Interjections   **655**

B. Application in Literature
Prepositional Phrases
Answers are underlined on page.

C. Application in Writing
Writing a Scientific Description
Answers will vary.

You may wish to use the following Checkpoint exercises as an informal evaluation of student mastery of the concepts covered in this handbook.

WRITING THEME Cities of Italy

A.

1. through, Preposition
2. around, Adverb
3. by, Preposition
4. around, Preposition
5. to, Preposition
6. on, Preposition
7. next to, Preposition, Compound
8. above, Adverb
9. along with, Preposition, Compound
10. in front of, Preposition, Compound
11. inside, Adverb
12. through, Adverb
13. overhead, Adverb
14. below, Adverb
15. out of, Preposition, Compound

B.

Answers are on page.

Writing Theme
Cities of Italy

A. Write whether the italicized word in each sentence is a preposition or an adverb. Identify each compound preposition by writing *Compound.*

1. A trip to Rome is a journey *through* time.
2. Tourists can simply glance *around* to see layers of history.
3. Soaring modern skyscrapers and crumbling ancient ruins stand side *by* side.
4. Cars and buses speed *around* the ancient Colosseum.
5. Italian businesspeople rush *to* their workplaces.
6. Their stylish shoes pound *on* Roman roads constructed two thousand years earlier.
7. Commuters wait *next to* a temple honoring the Roman gods.
8. Looking up, you see the Pantheon rising *above.*
9. It is a reminder that modern Rome exists *along with* parts of the city Emperor Hadrian knew in A.D. 120.
10. Souvenir shops line the street *in front of* the Pantheon.
11. When you go *inside,* however, time seems to reverse.
12. Here is a vast room that the Renaissance artist Michelangelo probably walked *through.*
13. The twentieth century seems to vanish when you gaze in wonder at the Pantheon's expansive rotunda *overhead.*
14. You stop to marvel at the patterns in the floor *below.*
15. When you finally go *out of* the cool darkness and into the sunlight, an echo of ancient times goes with you.

B. Write the prepositional phrase or phrases in each sentence. Then underline the object of each preposition.

1. Venice is a favorite among tourists who travel to Italy.
2. In the city you can see an array of architectural styles.
3. Venice offers visitors the extravagance of the Gothic style and the restraint of the Renaissance style.
4. Take a gondola ride up the Grand Canal to St. Mark's Square.
5. When you step out of the boat, you will see the magnificent Doges' Palace with its pointed arches.
6. Over a narrow waterway is a bridge to a prison.
7. Just off the square is the Basilica of St. Mark.
8. Byzantine mosaics decorate the walls inside the building.
9. According to experts, however, the mosaics may be in danger because of flooding that occurs during the winter.
10. Some of the experts believe that Venice is sinking into the sea.

PREPOSITIONAL PHRASES AS MODIFIERS

Modifiers are often single words. However, groups of words may also function as modifiers. Prepositional phrases, for example, may work in the same way that adjectives or adverbs do to modify various parts of a sentence.

An adjective phrase is a prepositional phrase that modifies a noun or pronoun.

Like adjectives, adjective phrases tell *which one* or *what kind.* Here are three examples.

> The last room *on the right* is haunted.
> (*On the right* is an adjective phrase modifying the noun *room.* The phrase tells *which one.*)
> All *of the restaurant workers* wear weird purple hats.
> (*Of the restaurant workers* is an adjective phrase that modifies the pronoun *all.* The phrase tells *what kind.*)
> No one could explain the reason *for his sudden departure.*
> (*For his sudden departure* is an adjective phrase modifying the noun *reason.* The phrase tells *which one.*)
> The signs *with blue letters at the mall* list the stores.
> (*With blue letters* and *at the mall* are adjective phrases modifying the noun *signs.* The phrases tell *which ones.*)

An adverb phrase is a prepositional phrase that modifies a verb, an adjective, or an adverb.

Like adverbs, an adverb phrase tells *how, when, where,* or *to what extent* something occurred.

> The bottles are sealed *by a huge machine.*
> (*By a huge machine* is an adverb phrase telling *how.* It modifies the verb *are sealed.*)
> Hendricks sulked *on the beach.*
> (*On the beach* is an adverb phrase. It tells *where* about the verb *sulked.*)
> She was courageous *during the crisis.*
> (*During the crisis* is an adverb phrase. It tells *when* about the adjective *courageous.*)
> The sun shone hot *as fire.*
> (*As fire* is an adverb phrase. It tells *to what extent* about the adverb *hot.*)

Using Prepositions, Conjunctions, and Interjections

657

Writing
—TIP—

Prepositional phrases provide an effective way to add detail to writing.

Prepositional Phrases as Modifiers

Objectives

- To identify the functions of prepositional phrases
- **Writing** To use prepositional phrases as adjectival and adverbial modifiers

Teaching Strategies

Critical Thinking

Classifying Ask volunteers to generate sentences with prepositional phrases. Have other students classify each phrase as either adjective or adverb. Then ask still other students to classify each adverb phrase as modifying a verb, an adjective, or an adverb.

Linking Grammar and Literature

Have students identify the prepositional phrases used as modifiers in the following passage from "A Christmas Memory" by Truman Capote:

"The black stove, stoked *with coal and firewood,* glows *like a lighted pumpkin.* Eggbeaters whirl, spoons spin round *in bowls of butter and sugar,* vanilla sweetens the air, ginger spices it; melting, nose-tingling odors saturate the kitchen, suffuse the house, drift out *to the world on puffs of chimney smoke.*"

Have students identify the function of each prepositional phrase and then discuss how the phrases help the author bring his description to life by adding sensory details. Encourage students to read through the rest of this selection, or other stories, to see how authors use prepositional phrases in their writing.

Individualizing Instruction

WRITING THEME   Suspense

Encourage interested students to note this theme in their journals for use as a possible topic for imaginative writing.

A. Concept Check

Prepositional Phrases as Modifiers
1. of the hounds, baying, Adjective
2. On a ridge, climbed, Adverb
3. Down a watercourse, could see, Adverb; of a mile, quarter, Adjective
4. of General Zaroff, figure, Adjective
5. ahead of him, made out, Adverb; through the tall jungle weeds, surged, Adverb
6. by some unseen force, pulled, Adverb
7. in leash, must be holding, Adverb
8. on him, would be, Adverb

B. Drafting Skill

Adding Details
Answers will vary. See suggested answers below.
1. Clearly the victim had been murdered *in an unusual manner*.
2. When the body was discovered *in the office*, there was evidence *of the crime*.
3. Papers had been scattered *around the room*, and a letter opener was found *under the desk*.

Sometimes one prepositional phrase follows another. Sometimes both phrases modify the same word.

> We fished *with minnows during the evening*.
> (The adverb phrase *with minnows* tells *how* about the verb *fished*. The adverb phrase *during the evening* tells *when* about the verb *fished*.)

Frequently, however, the second phrase is an adjective phrase that modifies the object in the first phrase.

> Okawa topped the salad *with bits of cheese*.
> (The adverb phrase *with bits* tells *how* about the verb *topped*. *Of cheese* is an adjective phrase describing the noun *bits*.)

Sentence Diagraming   For information on diagraming prepositional phrases, see page 833.

Practice Your Skills

A. CONCEPT CHECK

Prepositional Phrases as Modifiers   Write the italicized prepositional phrases in the following passage. After each phrase tell what word the phrase modifies and whether the phrase functions as an adjective or adverb.

> (1) The baying *of the hounds* grew nearer, then still nearer, ever nearer. (2) *On a ridge* Rainsford climbed a tree. (3) *Down a watercourse,* not a quarter *of a mile* away, he could see the bush moving. (4) Straining his eyes, he saw the lean figure *of General Zaroff.* (5) Just *ahead of him* Rainsford made out another figure whose wide shoulders surged *through the tall jungle weeds*. (6) It was the giant Ivan, and he seemed pulled forward *by some unseen force*. (7) Rainsford knew that Ivan must be holding the pack *in leash*. (8) They would be *on him* any minute now.
> **Richard Connell, "The Most Dangerous Game"**

B. DRAFTING SKILL

Adding Details   Complete the following story, using prepositional phrases.

> (1) Clearly the victim has been murdered (*how*). (2) When the body was discovered (*where*), there was evidence (*what*). (3) Papers had been scattered (*where*), and a letter opener was

Painting by Gottfried Helnwein

658 Grammar Handbook

found (*where*). (4) (*When*), several police officers arrived on the scene to investigate the incident. (5) A detective dressed (*how*) followed them (*where*) and asked everyone to wait (*where*). (6) He had seen a shadowy figure climbing (*where*) and said he had an idea who it was.

C. APPLICATION IN WRITING

Writing an Opening Scene The opening scene of a story often sets the mood or captures the interest of the reader. Imagine an old deserted house with shutters that creak in the wind. Write the beginning of a story about that house. Describe a suspenseful moment in a mystery that takes place there. Use prepositional phrases to give readers a clear picture of the event.

USING PREPOSITIONS CORRECTLY

Often, prepositions are used incorrectly or unnecessarily. The following list describes some of the most common problems. Refer to it occasionally as you revise your writing.

Prepositions Often Misused

among, between *Between* refers to two people or things. *Among* refers to three or more.

There is a peace treaty *between* the two countries.
We divided the work *among* the four of us.

beside, besides *Beside* means "at the side of." *Besides* means "in addition to."

Secret Service agents stand *beside* the President.
There are other motives *besides* greed.

in, into *In* means "inside something." *Into* suggests motion from the outside to the inside.

Sis stayed *in* the car.
I went *into* the house.

off, from Do not use the word *off* when you mean *from*.

Incorrect   Tony borrowed a coat *off* me today.
Correct   Tony borrowed a coat *from* me today.

Using Prepositions Correctly

Objectives

- To identify correct usage of prepositions
- To correct errors in the use of prepositions and prepositional phrases

Teaching Strategies

 Individualizing Instruction

ESL Students The prepositions of time, *in*, *on*, and *at*, pose particular problems for these students, as in the following phrases:

in June
on Monday
at twelve o'clock
on June 1, 1991

The prepositions of location, *in*, *on*, and *at*, also pose problems, as in the following phrases:

on the train
in the car
at the airport

Visual representations, such as diagrams or cartoons, may help students to remember these concepts.

Linking Grammar and Writing

Point out to students that the errors in preposition usage discussed in this lesson can appear in writing. Ask students to read through one of their rough drafts to see if they have made any of these kinds of errors. Then have students revise these sentences as part of their proofreading process.

WRITING THEME   Electrical Inventions

Encourage interested students to brainstorm a topic related to this theme for use as the subject for a current or future expository writing or science assignment.

A. Concept Check

Using Prepositions
1. besides
2. among
3. into
4. from
5. on
6. among

Writing Theme
Electrical
Inventions

---

on, onto *On* means "upon something." *Onto* suggests motion to the top of something.

> The tag teams were *on* the beach.
> The beach ball sailed out *onto* the water.

Prepositions Used Unnecessarily

Prepositions like *at, of,* and *to* may be used unnecessarily. Often these prepositions come at the end of a sentence.

Incorrect   Where are my gym clothes *at?*
Correct   Where are my gym clothes?

Incorrect   Nicole could not feel her toes inside *of* her ski boots.
Correct   Nicole could not feel her toes inside her ski boots.

Incorrect   Where did the Brooklyn Dodgers move *to?*
Correct   Where did the Brooklyn Dodgers move?

Misplaced Prepositional Phrases

A prepositional phrase should be placed near the word it modifies. Otherwise the meaning of your sentence may not be clear.

Incorrect   Pablo told many stories of his fascinating childhood *in our class*. (Did Pablo spend his childhood in our class?)
Correct   *In our class*, Pablo told many stories of his fascinating childhood.

A. CONCEPT CHECK

Using Prepositions   Write the correct word or phrase from the pair in parentheses.

1. Many uses for electrical power were developed (beside, besides) the ones found by Thomas Edison.
2. There was much competition (among, between) the many inventors experimenting with electricity for musical instruments.
3. T. Cahill put his efforts (in, into) developing a massive generator.
4. The Hammond Corporation took the generator idea (off, from) Cahill to develop its first electronic organ.
5. The organ was polyphonic, which means that someone could play full chords (on, onto) it as well as just one note at a time.
6. The music synthesizer is (between, among) the electronic instruments that came into popular use during the 1960's.

7. It operates (off of, from) a coded tape with all the essential elements of a musical sound.
8. Pitch, duration, reverberation, and vibrato are all factors that can be punched (on, onto) the tape.
9. One difference (between, among) a synthesizer and an acoustic instrument is the synthesizer's ability to produce a wider variety of sounds.
10. However, most of our ideas about how music should sound come (off, from) acoustic instruments.

7. from
8. onto
9. between
10. from

B. REVISION SKILL

Avoiding Incorrect Usage The following sentences contain unnecessary prepositions and misplaced prepositional phrases. Revise the sentences to correct these errors.

1. Inside of a small attic in London's Soho district, John Logie Baird transmitted the first television image.
2. On October 2, 1925, Baird sent a picture of a ventriloquist's dummy to another room with very crude equipment.
3. Later he gave the first public demonstration in 1926 of television in England.
4. The Alexandra Palace in London is where the first television programs were broadcast at.
5. At the time, Baird had no idea where his invention would take entertainment to.

B. Revision Skill

Avoiding Incorrect Usage

Answers will vary. See suggested answers below.

1. *Inside* a small attic in London's Soho district, John Logie Baird transmitted the first television image.
2. On October 2, 1925, *with very crude equipment,* Baird sent a picture of a ventriloquist's dummy to another room.
3. Later, *in 1926 in England,* he gave the first public demonstration of television.
4. The Alexandra Palace in London is where the first television programs were broadcast.
5. At the time Baird had no idea where his invention would take entertainment.

Using Prepositions,
Conjunctions, and
Interjections **661**

C. Proofreading Skill

Correcting Errors with Prepositions
Errors are underlined on page.

Answers will vary. See suggested answers below.

At the age of thirty-two, Thomas Edison completed his most famous invention, the electric light. With great determination, he had spent two years searching for the right filament. Finally he tried carbonized thread inside his bulb, and the bulb glowed brightly for a day and a half. Today, it's hard to imagine the world without these lights.

Besides the electric light, Edison also invented the storage battery, the mimeograph, and the dictaphone. In addition, he improved many other inventions, such as the telephone and the typewriter. Where did he get all his ideas? Among his many inventions and improvements, the phonograph was Edison's personal favorite. By the time he died, he held patents for more than a thousand inventions.

CHECK POINT
PAGES 657–662

You may wish to use the following Checkpoint exercises as an informal evaluation of student mastery of the concepts covered in this handbook.

WRITING THEME   Sailing Mishaps

A.

1. in maritime history, Adjective
2. Near midnight, Adverb
3. off the Grand Banks, Adverb
4. of the supposedly unsinkable ship, Adjective
5. in the Atlantic Ocean's icy waters, Adverb
6. for the 2,224 people, Adjective
7. with help, Adverb
8. from his post, Adverb
9. for maritime safety, Adjective
10. in the shipping lanes, Adjective

C. PROOFREADING SKILL

Correcting Errors with Prepositions   Rewrite the following passage, correcting all of the errors. Pay particular attention to the use of prepositions and prepositional phrases.

At the age of 32, Thomas Edison completed his most famous invention, the electric light. He had spent two years searching for the right filament with great determination. Finally he tryed carbonized thread inside of his bulb, the bulb glowed brightly for a day and a half. Today, its hard to imajine the world without these lights.

Beside the electric light, edison also invented the storage battary, the mimeograph, and the dictaphone in addition, he improved many other inventions, such as the telephone and the typewriter. Where did he get all his ideas at. Between his many inventions and improvements, the phonograf was Edison's personal favorite. By the time he died, he hold patents for more than a thousand inventions.

CHECK POINT
657–662

A. Write the italicized prepositional phrase in each sentence. Then identify each phrase as *Adjective* or *Adverb*.

1. One of the greatest disasters *in maritime history* took place on April 14, 1912.
2. *Near midnight,* the luxurious passenger liner *Titanic* struck a mammoth iceberg.
3. The collision occurred *off the Grand Banks* of Newfoundland.
4. The iceberg ripped a three-hundred-foot gash in the side *of the supposedly unsinkable ship.*
5. Over fifteen hundred people—primarily the male passengers and crew—perished *in the Atlantic Ocean's icy waters.*
6. There were only 1,178 lifeboat spaces *for the 2,224 people* on board the ocean liner.
7. Perhaps the nearby liner *Carpathia* could have answered the ship's distress call *with help.*
8. However, at the time of the mishap, the *Carpathia's* radio operator was gone *from his post.*
9. As a result of this tragedy, an international commission drew up new rules *for maritime safety.*
10. The International Ice Patrol was established to watch for ice *in the shipping lanes.*

662 Grammar Handbook

B. Some of the following sentences contain <u>misused prepositions</u> or <u>misplaced prepositional phrases</u>. If a sentence has such an error, rewrite the sentence to correct the error. If there is no error in a sentence, write *Correct*.

1. The Bermuda Triangle has drawn many ships into its mysterious clutches.
2. This unexplained phenomenon exists in the North Atlantic off <u>of</u> the shores of the Bermuda Islands.
3. Many ships sailing there have disappeared from the face of the earth.
4. For example, the liner *Marie Celeste* was found <u>into</u> the triangle without its crew!
5. Besides the *Marie Celeste,* a number of other "ghost ships" have been discovered.
6. Scientists have come to examine the source of these disappearances from all over the world.
7. There is little agreement about the causes of the disappearances <u>between</u> these many investigators.
8. Some theories sound as if they have been borrowed <u>off</u> science-fiction writers.
9. Reports tell about evil aliens kidnapping sailors <u>in magazine articles</u>.
10. However, a less mysterious theory holds that these unexplained disappearances actually were caused by sudden storms or downward air currents.
11. Swift sea currents <u>out of the area</u> may have swept the wreckage away.
12. For all our scientific progress, we still cannot explain where the lost ships and sailors are <u>at</u>.

CONJUNCTIONS

A conjunction connects words or groups of words.

> Lee wrote *and* narrated the skits.
> You may go out tonight, *but* don't be late.
> Dr. No smiled *as* he entered the laboratory.
> My typing is fast; *however,* I usually make a few errors.
> George was tired *because* he ran two miles in the heat.

There are three kinds of conjunctions: coordinating, correlative, and subordinating conjunctions. Conjunctive adverbs also function as conjunctions.

Using Prepositions, Conjunctions, and Interjections **663**

Conjunctions

Objectives

- To identify coordinating and correlative conjunctions
- **Writing** To demonstrate revision skills by combining sentences using coordinating and correlative conjunctions

Linking Grammar and Writing

Discuss how writers can express different kinds of relationships between ideas through the use of different conjunctions. *And* joins ideas. *But* and *yet* express contrast. *For* and *so* indicate cause and effect. *Nor* expresses negation. *Or* communicates a choice.

Writing
TIP

Use a comma before a coordinating conjunction joining the clauses in a compound sentence.

Coordinating Conjunctions

Coordinating conjunctions connect ideas of equal importance. These ideas can be words, phrases, or complete sentences. A coordinating conjunction, however, is always one word.

Coordinating Conjunctions						
and	but	for	nor	or	so	yet

Words or groups of words connected by coordinating conjunctions include compound subjects, compound objects, compound verbs, and compound sentences.

Compound Subject	Did the Italians *or* the Chinese invent pasta?
Compound Object	We will visit New York *or* Miami sometime in June.
Compound Verb	Simon overslept *and* missed soccer practice.
Compound Sentence	The deadline is next week, *so* you still have time.

Correlative Conjunctions

Like coordinating conjunctions, **correlative conjunctions** join similar words or groups of words. However, these conjunctions are always used in pairs.

Correlative Conjunctions		
both . . . and	neither . . . nor	whether . . . or
either . . . or	not only . . . but also	

Notice the pairs of conjunctions in each of the following sentences.

> *Both* oak *and* walnut are used to make furniture.
> *Not only* did Rosa win, *but* she *also* broke her record.
> The coach debated *whether* to kick *or* to run.
> Allison *neither* studied *nor* slept that night.
> *Either* the video *or* the album won an award.

Practice Your Skills

A. CONCEPT CHECK

Conjunctions Write the conjunctions in the following paragraph. Then identify them as *Coordinating* or *Correlative* conjunctions.

Writing Theme
The Great Depression

(1) The careers of Dorothea Lange <u>and</u> Margaret Bourke-White, two famous American photographers, show some interesting similarities. (2) Both of them grew up in the East in the early 1900's, <u>and</u> both attended Columbia University, where they studied under the renowned photographer Clarence H. White. (3) By 1934 <u>both</u> Lange <u>and</u> Bourke-White were focusing on the Great Depression <u>and</u> the toll it was taking in rural America. (4) Their stark photos revealed with simple honesty how people lived, forcing the viewer to understand the reality of hardship. (5) <u>Not only</u> did the photos set the standards for the photo documentary, <u>but</u> they <u>also</u> called attention to the desperate needs of rural America.

B. DRAFTING SKILL

Sentence Combining Combine each pair of sentences by using the conjunction or conjunctions in parentheses. Adjust wording where necessary. Remember that a comma comes before a coordinating conjunction that joins clauses in a compound sentence.

1. The year 1929 brought America the stock market crash. It brought the Great Depression, too. (and)
2. As America seemed to grow more prosperous, wealthy people gambled their money in the stock market. Working-class people also gambled their money. (both . . . and)
3. Risking money on the stock market became a national pastime. Many people were affected by the crash. (so)
4. The value of stocks dropped faster and faster. Many people wanted to sell their stocks before they became useless. (not only . . . but also)
5. Obviously many Americans did not understand the significance of the crash. They tried to protect themselves by drawing all of their money out of their bank accounts. (for)
6. The banks did not have enough money to return to all the panicked savers at once. The government did not have enough money. (neither . . . nor)
7. Many people lost their life's savings. Banks were forced to close their doors. (and)
8. President Hoover wondered if he should take steps to change the situation. He wondered if he should rely on time to end the Depression. (whether . . . or)

Using Prepositions, Conjunctions, and Interjections **665**

Additional Resources
- Grammar and Usage Practice Book, pp. 115–116

WRITING THEME   The Great Depression

Encourage interested students to do research on this theme and use it for a possible social studies report.

A. Concept Check

Conjunctions
1. and, Coordinating
2. and, Coordinating
3. both . . . and, Correlative; and, Coordinating
4. None
5. Not only . . . but also, Correlative

B. Drafting Skill

Sentence Combining
1. The year 1929 brought America the stock market crash and the Great Depression.
2. As America seemed to grow more prosperous, both wealthy people and working-class people gambled their money in the stock market.
3. Risking money on the stock market became a national pastime, so many people were affected by the crash.
4. Not only did the value of stocks drop faster and faster, but also many people wanted to sell their stocks before they became useless.
5. Obviously many Americans did not understand the significance of the crash, for they tried to protect themselves by drawing all of their money out of their bank accounts.
6. Neither the banks nor the government had enough money to return to all the panicked savers at once.
7. Many people lost their life's savings, and banks were forced to close their doors.
8. President Hoover wondered whether he should take steps to change the situation or rely on time to end the Depression.

9. By 1932, millions of Americans had neither employment nor hope for change.
10. Hoover's conventional methods failed,
but Franklin Roosevelt helped pull the country to
its feet again by making bold changes.

Subordinating Conjunctions

Objectives

- To identify subordinating conjunctions and conjunctive adverbs
- **Writing** To combine sentences by using subordinating conjunctions and conjunctive adverbs

Teaching Strategies

Stumbling Block

Students may point out that they have often seen the words listed as conjunctive adverbs used at the beginning of sentences, rather than preceded by a semicolon as stated in the lesson. Explain that the words listed in the lesson are called conjunctive adverbs only if they join two sentences. These words may also be used as adverbs in simple sentences.

Collaborative Opportunity

Have students form teams and give each team a newspaper and markers. Allow fifteen minutes for students to circle as many subordinating conjunctions and conjunctive adverbs as they can find.

Writing
—**TIP**—

A comma is placed after a subordinate clause that begins a sentence.

9. By 1932, millions of Americans had no employment. They had no hope for change. (neither . . . nor)
10. Hoover's conventional methods failed. Franklin Roosevelt helped pull the country to its feet again by making bold changes. (but)

SUBORDINATING CONJUNCTIONS

A **subordinating conjunction** begins a clause that cannot stand alone and joins it to a clause that can stand alone. A **clause** is a group of words with a subject and verb. For a discussion of clauses, see Grammar Handbook 39, pages 721–734.

Commonly Used Subordinating Conjunctions

after	as though	if	so that	when
although	because	in order that	than	where
as	before	provided	unless	whereas
as if	even though	since	until	while

Each of the following two sentences contains a subordinating conjunction.

> The fans were quiet *while* the golfer putted.
> *Although* I prefer peaches, I also like strawberries.

Conjunctive Adverbs

Certain adverbs, called **conjunctive adverbs,** can join sentences.

Commonly Used Conjunctive Adverbs

accordingly	finally	instead	still
also	furthermore	nevertheless	therefore
besides	hence	otherwise	thus
consequently	however	similarly	

A conjunctive adverb is usually preceded by a semicolon and followed by a comma. In the three following examples, notice how conjunctive adverbs clarify the relationship between the two parts of the sentences.

> The chemical leak polluted the town's water; *consequently,* the town needed a new water supply.
> The evidence sounded convincing; *still,* the jury believed the defendant's story.
> The students took shelter in the basement; *otherwise,* they would not have survived the tornado.

Practice Your Skills

A. CONCEPT CHECK

Subordinating Conjunctions Write the subordinating conjunction or conjunctive adverb that is found in each of the following sentences and tell which it is.

1. Although Paul Robeson was the son of a former slave, he became a Phi Beta Kappa graduate of Rutgers University.
2. At Rutgers, he was twice named an All-American end in football; similarly, he starred in three other sports.
3. Robeson earned a degree from Columbia Law School in 1923; however, it was almost impossible for African Americans to practice law at that time.
4. Since he could not work as a lawyer, he pursued the career for which he became best known—that of singer and actor.
5. As if those accomplishments were not remarkable enough, in the 1930's he became an activist for international peace, racial justice, and fair labor practices.
6. He also became involved in some controversial international matters; consequently, he was criticized by some extremely conservative politicians in the United States.
7. Robeson's passport was canceled by the American government; furthermore, his acting and singing career suffered because of the criticism he received.
8. He had been hurt both professionally and personally; still, he continued to work for the humanist causes in which he believed.
9. He moved to London in 1958, where he was able to resume working in the theater.
10. Robeson did not become bitter about the treatment he had received; instead, he wrote a book, *Here I Stand,* reaffirming his political beliefs.

Using Prepositions, Conjunctions, and Interjections **667**

 Individualizing Instruction

LEP Students/Basic Students Place more emphasis on the function of conjunctive words and the use of punctuation than on the grammatical terms themselves.

Linking Grammar and Writing

Discuss the meaning of *subordinate* as "having lesser importance or a lower rank." As a way to establish which idea is the lesser of the two, model how each of the structures joined to a sentence by a subordinating conjunction becomes dependent on the main part of the sentence. Provide examples from professional writers to show the relationships between ideas in sentences with subordinating conjunctions.

> *Additional Resources*
> • Grammar and Usage Practice Book, pp. 117–118

WRITING THEME Paul Robeson
Encourage interested students to add this theme to their journals for use as the subject for a writing assignment.

A. Concept Check
Subordinating Conjunctions
Subordinating conjunctions and conjunctive adverbs are underlined on the page.
1. Although, Subordinating conjunction
2. similarly, Conjunctive adverb
3. however, Conjunctive adverb
4. Since, Subordinating conjunction
5. As if, Subordinating conjunction
6. consequently, Conjunctive adverb
7. furthermore, Conjunctive adverb
8. still, Conjunctive adverb
9. where, Subordinating conjunction
10. instead, Conjunctive adverb

Paul Robeson in *The Emperor Jones*, by Eugene O'Neill

B. DRAFTING SKILL

Establishing Relationships A subordinating conjunction establishes the relationship between the ideas in a sentence. Write each pair of sentences as one sentence, using the more appropriate conjunction in parentheses. The conjunction may be placed at the beginning of some sentences.

Paul Robeson had to struggle for dignified movie roles. He was a star. (unless, even though)

Paul Robeson had to struggle for dignified movie roles, *even though* he was a star.

1. Paul Robeson's first film was called *Borderline*. It is his stunning achievement as the lead in *The Emperor Jones* that is remembered as his debut. (after, although)

2. *Borderline* broke a major movie stereotype. It presented an African American as an intelligent, sympathetic person. (because, while)

3. Paul Robeson traveled to England. He appeared in *The Song of Freedom*. (as, where)

4. *The Song of Freedom* was another important step for Robeson and all African Americans in film. Race was not the primary issue of the story. (since, whereas)

5. Robeson became involved in the project. The character he was to play would be portrayed as a dignified human being. (in order that, still)

6. Robeson portrayed an African-American dockworker. Race did not play a part in the character's relationships with his fellow workers. (when, although)

7. Robeson wrote an article about uniting Eastern and Western cultures. He made the movie. (before, whenever)

8. The film's main character, Zinga, expressed similar ideas. Many people thought that the movie was based on Robeson's life. (because, while)

9. Some people still believe that this was true. The facts show that it was not the case. (so that, although)

10. People value the struggle for human dignity. Paul Robeson will be remembered. (because, although)

INTERJECTIONS

An interjection is a word or phrase used to express strong feeling or emotion.

Interjections express feelings such as joy, anger, terror, pain, fear, surprise, disgust, or sadness. Because interjections are not part of the main structure of the sentence, they are set off by an exclamation mark or a comma.

Unbelievable! Look at those giant submarine sandwiches.
Oh, I thought you were meeting me in the cafeteria.
We went to the shore, and, *oh,* it was fun.
Never! I couldn't think of going without my sister.

Practice Your Skills

A. CONCEPT CHECK

Prepositions, Conjunctions, and Interjections Write each italicized word and its part of speech.

1. *Wow!* Some news stories are stranger than fiction.
2. A New York cabdriver was held up *by* a passenger.
3. The passenger demanded $50, *and* the cabbie handed it over.
4. *Well,* after the thief had escaped, three other men jumped into the taxi.
5. *When* the cabbie told them about the robbery, they demanded the rest of her money.
6. Upset, the cabbie drove *until* she spotted a police officer.
7. The officer nodded sympathetically as he listened to the driver's amazing story, and then he asked for a ride *to* the police station.
8. *"Really!"* snapped the driver. "Those fellows took all my cash, and now you want me to drive you to the station."
9. The police officer said, "Those same three fellows just drove away *in* my squad car."
10. The cabbie rolled her eyes and sighed, *"Oh,* climb in."

B. APPLICATION IN WRITING

Writing a Narrative When people tell others about incidents in their lives, they often use interjections to convey their feelings about the events. Think of a visit to a museum or zoo, a show, a concert, or some other event that impressed you. Write a short descriptive narrative about the event, using interjections to show your reactions. Try to choose an event that allows you to express a variety of feelings.

> **Writing Theme**
> Life in the City

Using Prepositions, Conjunctions, and Interjections **669**

CHECK ✓ POINT
PAGES 663–669

You may wish to use the following Checkpoint exercises as an informal evaluation of student mastery of the concepts covered in this handbook.

WRITING THEME Overcoming Difficulties

A.

Conjunctions and interjections are underlined on student's page.

1. but, Coordinating conjunction; and, Coordinating conjunction
2. Oh, Interjection; and, Coordinating conjunction
3. if, Subordinating conjunction
4. neither, nor, Correlative conjunctions
5. and, Coordinating conjunction; instead, Conjunctive adverb
6. Although, Subordinating conjunction
7. not only, but also, Correlative conjunctions; and, Coordinating conjunction; and, Coordinating conjunction
8. When, Subordinating conjunction
9. and, Coordinating conjunction
10. Imagine, Interjection

B.

Answers are underlined on page.

Writing Theme
Overcoming
Difficulties

CHECK ✓ POINT
PAGES 663–669

A. Write the <u>conjunctions</u> and <u>interjections</u> in the following sentences. Identify each as a *Coordinating Conjunction, Correlative Conjunction, Subordinating Conjunction, Conjunctive Adverb,* or *Interjection.*

1. Elvis Presley was born on January 8, 1935, in a shack in Tupelo, Mississippi, but he rose to wealth and fame unrivaled in the history of rock music.
2. <u>Oh</u>, how his father, Vernon, worked to provide for his wife and son.
3. At about ten years of age, Elvis asked his parents if he could have a bicycle.
4. They had neither the money nor any way of obtaining it.
5. Gladys and Vernon Presley couldn't afford a bicycle; instead, they gave their son a guitar.
6. <u>Although</u> a guitar was not what he really wanted, the gift changed the boy's life.
7. He drew from <u>not only</u> gospel music but also country and rhythm and blues to develop his own unique style.
8. <u>When</u> "Heartbreak Hotel" hit the charts in 1956, it marked his first major success.
9. By the end of 1956, Elvis was a national celebrity and had made his debut in motion pictures.
10. <u>Imagine</u>! This stellar career started with a recording made as a birthday gift for his mother.

Top: Elvis Presley as a child in Tupelo
Bottom: Elvis Presley's first record album

B. Choose the subordinating conjunction or conjunctive adverb that most clearly expresses the relationship between the ideas in the following sentences.

1. (<u>Although</u>, When) noted American author Pearl Buck was born in Hillsboro, West Virginia, she grew up in China, where her parents worked as missionaries.
2. In fact, she learned to speak Chinese (because, <u>before</u>) she learned to speak English.
3. On several occasions, internal strife between rival political factions in China put her in danger; (<u>consequently</u>, however), she had to flee to safety.

4. Buck faced further hardship (until, when) her daughter was born severely handicapped.
5. (If, Provided) the astronomical medical costs were to be paid, Buck would have to sell a great many books.
6. Her first novel, *East Wind, West Wind,* sold well; (however, furthermore), it received unfavorable critical reviews.
7. *The Good Earth,* her best-known work, was a financial success; (otherwise, nevertheless), it was controversial.
8. Critics felt that farmers, like the novel's peasant hero Wang Lung, were unworthy to be cast as central characters; (still, therefore), Buck made farmers the heroes of her next two works.
9. Even the joy of winning a Nobel Prize for literature was marred (because, in order that) some writers criticized her for being too young to receive such an honor.
10. Buck produced an astounding number of fiction and nonfiction works—the total came to 65—(until, since) she died in 1973.

C. Write the following sentences, filling in the type of conjunction called for in parentheses. Some sentences may have more than one right answer.

1. In the 1400's, tales of churning waters inhabited by _____ monsters _____ the spirits of dead mariners chilled the souls of European sailors. (correlative)
2. Fear of the Sea of Darkness restricted exploration of the west coast of Africa _____ Gil Eannes changed the situation. (subordinating)
3. He had Prince Henry the Navigator on his side, _____ he had powerful superstitions to overcome. (coordinating)
4. This Portuguese explorer reassured his crew _____ they would remain calm. (subordinating)
5. _____ they finally rounded Cape Bojador, they were greeted by an unexpected sight. (subordinating)
6. In addition to a peaceful coastline, they found _____ calm seas _____ shoals of silvery sardines in the water. (correlative)
7. They had expected treacherous reefs; _____, they encountered the familiar plant rosemary growing on sandy shores. (conjunctive adverb)
8. It had taken fifteen years _____ as many attempts for sailors to sail beyond the legendary edge of the world. (coordinating)
9. The surge of discovery moved rapidly; _____, within only seventy years the remaining west coast of Africa had been mapped. (conjunctive adverb)
10. _____ Eannes opened a door, later explorers could go anywhere in Africa. (subordinating)

Pearl S. Buck, Nobel Prize for literature winner and noted author

Application and Review

These activities are designed to allow your students to apply concepts presented in this handbook. Exercise A requires students to identify prepositional phrases. Exercise B challenges students to identify other parts of speech in sentences.

Additional Resources

- Tests and Assessment, Mastery Tests, pp. 75–80
- Elaboration, Revision, and Proof-reading Worksheets, p. 27

WRITING THEME   California

A. Identifying Prepositional Phrases

1. to California, Adjective, expedition; at an Indian village, Adverb, stopped
2. of the village, Adjective, name
3. by a group, Adverb, had been settled; of Shoshones, Adjective, group
4. of the expedition, Adjective, leaders
5. of the Angels, Adjective, Queen
6. in California, Adjective, city; by the Spanish, Adverb, founded
7. Since that time, Adverb, has become; in the United States, Adjective, city
8. From the time, Adverb, held; of its origins, Adjective, time; for many people, Adjective, charm
9. of many Spanish-speaking people, Adjective, home
10. in its architecture, Adverb, reflects; in the breadth, Adverb, reflects; of its cultural diversity, Adjective, breadth

B. Recognizing Parts of Speech

1. either . . . or, Conjunctions, Correlative
2. If, Conjunction, Subordinating
3. when, Conjunction, Subordinating; from, Preposition
4. against, Preposition
5. because, Conjunction, Subordinating; on, Preposition
6. Gold, Interjection; at, Preposition
7. As, Conjunction, Subordinating; however, Conjunction, Conjunctive Adverb
8. and, Conjunction, Coordinating; of, Preposition
9. and, Conjunction, Coordinating
10. as, Preposition

GRAMMAR HANDBOOK
35

Writing Theme
California

A. Identifying Prepositional Phrases Write the prepositional phrase or phrases in each sentence. Label each phrase *Adjective* or *Adverb* and tell what word it modifies.

1. The year was 1769 when a Spanish expedition to California stopped at an Indian village.
2. The name of the village was Yang-Na.
3. It had been settled many years earlier by a group of Shoshones.
4. The leaders of the expedition renamed the place *Nuestra Señora la Reina de Los Angeles*.
5. That Spanish phrase means Our Lady Queen of the Angels.
6. Los Angeles was the second city in California founded by the Spanish.
7. Since that time, it has become the second largest city in the United States.
8. From the time of its origins, this city held a romantic charm for many people.
9. Los Angeles is still the home of many Spanish-speaking people.
10. Even now the city reflects its founders in its architecture and in the breadth of its cultural diversity.

B. Recognizing Parts of Speech Write the italicized words in the passage below. Then label each word *Preposition, Conjunction,* or *Interjection*. Identify conjunctions as *Coordinating, Correlative, Subordinating,* or *Conjunctive Adverbs*.

(1) The history of California has never been free of *either* conflict *or* drama. (2) *If* the story of this state could be summarized in a word, it might be "drama."

(3) California became a Mexican territory in 1821, *when* Mexico won independence *from* Spain. (4) Twenty-five years later, English-speaking Californians rebelled *against* Mexican rule. (5) This revolt was called the Bear Flag Rebellion *because* the Californians' flag had a grizzly bear *on* it.

(6) *Gold!* In 1848, *at* Sutter's Mill in the foothills of the Sierras, gold was discovered. (7) *As* the gold rush began in 1849, San Francisco had 800 inhabitants; *however,* two years later it had 25,000.

(8) In 1906, a tremendous earthquake *and* the resulting fire destroyed most *of* the city. (9) Seven hundred people died, *and* 300,000 were left homeless. (10) The people of San Francisco quickly rebuilt their city, and it has emerged *as* a key center of culture and industry.

On the Lightside

"STOP THE PRESSES!"

Occasionally, under the pressure of constant deadlines, an editor will goof, and the results can be hilarious, ludicrous, or macabre. Look at some irrepressible gaffes from actual newspaper and magazine articles:

- The accident occurred at Hillcrest Drive and Santa Barbara Avenue as the dead man was crossing the intersection.
- Mr. Benjamin Porter visited the school yesterday and lectured on "Destructive Pests." A large number were present.
- Columbia, Tennessee, which calls itself the largest outdoor mule market in the world, held a mule parade yesterday headed by the Governor.
- Zimbabwe Rhodesian guerrilla leaders demanded Monday that a Commonwealth peacekeeping force of several thousand men—one with teeth—be sent to enforce a cease-fire in the war against their forces.
- The assembly passed and sent to the senate a bill requiring dog owners in New York City to clean up after their pets, in penalty of $100 fine. The bill also applies to Buffalo.
- Recent tests conducted by a zoologist prove that grasshoppers hear with their legs. In all cases the insects hopped when a tuning fork was sounded nearby.

There was no reaction to this stimulus, however, when the insects' legs had been removed.

- Knicks Notes. Knicks open regular season on the road against Cleveland on October 28, then are at home the following night against Washington, during which time Senator Bill Bradley's uniform number 24 will be retired. Bradley will join former teammates Willis Reed, Dave DeBusschere and Walt Frazier in hanging from the Madison Square Garden rafters.
- *Moby Dick,* the great American classic by Herman Melville, will be seen again next week with veteran actor Victor Jory in the title role.
- Citizens of Santa Barbara County are faced with a tax rise. Most of the money raised would be used for five foot policemen.
- Gretzky won his sixth consecutive Hart Trophy as the NHL's Most Valuable Player, an unprecedented feat that tied him with Gordie Howe as a six-time winner.
- Gene Autry is better after being kicked by a horse.
- The ball struck him on the right temple and knocked him cold. He was taken to Sacred Heart Hospital where X-rays of his head showed nothing.

Richard Lederer

On the Lightside

This feature is a collection of editorial mistakes culled from newspapers and magazines. You might read your favorite aloud to the class and explain the source of the error. Then call on individual class members to do the same. Encourage the group to create their own collection of editorial gaffes as a class project. In addition to perusing local newspapers, students should consult national magazines, such as *The New Yorker,* that publish humorous editorial slip-ups on a regular basis.

673

Reviewing Parts of Speech

The Parts of Speech

Objectives

- To review the eight parts of speech
- To identify the part of speech of words in sentences

Teaching Strategies

Teaching Tip: Word Order

In many languages, a word's part of speech or function in a sentence is signaled by its ending. A noun, for example, has different endings when it is used as a subject or as an object. In English, word order is the most important factor in determining a word's part of speech and function. Word order alone can change the whole meaning of a sentence. For example:

The batter hit the ball.
The ball hit the batter.

◆ Individualizing Instruction

ESL Students As a review of the parts of speech, suggest that these students do a comparative analysis of English and their native languages. Do the same parts of speech also exist in their languages? If so, do they function the same way? If not, how are these ideas expressed in their languages? (For example, true adverbs do not exist in Arabic. Adverbial expressions are usually formed by a preposition and a noun.)

Additional Resources

- Tests and Assessment, Pretests, pp. 23–24
- Grammar and Usage Practice Book, p. 121

GRAMMAR HANDBOOK 36

Reviewing Parts of Speech

THE PARTS OF SPEECH

The following chart will help you review the eight parts of speech.

Part of Speech	Definition	Examples
Noun	names a person, place, thing, or idea	child, Montana, song, happiness
Pronoun	used in place of a noun or other pronoun	I, you, my, these, herself, who, all
Verb	expresses action or state of being	is, does, have, catch, tastes
Adjective	modifies a noun or a pronoun	purple, ten, tiny, old, lovely, Tom's
Adverb	modifies a verb, an adjective, or another adverb	very, too, well, here, not, yesterday, quickly
Preposition	shows a relationship between a noun or pronoun and another word	after, of, in, on, with, from, under, below, according to
Conjunction	connects words or word groups	and, but, or, if, neither . . . nor
Interjection	expresses emotion	Ouch! Terrific! Oh!

Luminous Zag: Night, by Louise Nevelson, 1971. Collection, the Solomon R. Guggenheim Museum, New York. Photo by Robert E. Mates

Practice Your Skills

CONCEPT CHECK

Parts of Speech   Identify the part of speech of each italicized word.

(1) Once upon a time, *Trurl,* the constructor, built an eight-story thinking machine. (2) *When* it was finished, *he* gave it a coat of *white* paint, trimmed the edges in lavender, stepped back, *squinted,* then added a little curlicue *on* the front and, where one might imagine the *forehead* to be, a few *pale* orange *polkadots.* (3) *Extremely* pleased *with himself,* he whistled an air *and,* as is always done on such occasions, *asked* it the ritual question of how much *is* two plus two. . . . (4) At last, when Trurl had grown extremely impatient, the machine ground to a halt and said in a voice like thunder, *SEVEN!*

Stanislaw Lem, "Trurl's Machine"

Writing Theme
Science Fiction

Using Words as Different Parts of Speech

The same word can be used as different parts of speech. A word might be used as a noun in one sentence and as a verb in another. The method for identifying a part of speech is to determine how a word functions in a sentence.

Noun or Verb?	The one-hundred-dollar *bill* has a picture of Benjamin Franklin. (*Bill* is a noun used as a subject.)
	The plumbers will *bill* us for their work. (*Bill* is used as the main verb.)
Noun or Adjective?	The artist folded *paper* into unusual shapes. (*Paper* is used as a noun, the direct object of *folded.*)
	At the picnic, we ate on paper plates. (*Paper* is used as an adjective, modifying *plates.*)
Pronoun or Adjective?	*What* is your favorite rock song? (*What* is used as a pronoun, the subject of the sentence.)
	What new shows are on TV now? (*What* is used as an adjective, modifying the noun *shows.*)
Adjective or Adverb?	A *low* wall surrounded the giant estate. (*Low* is used as an adjective, modifying the noun *wall.*)
	A seaplane cruised *low* over Myrtle Beach. (*Low* is used as an adverb, modifying the verb *cruised.*)
Adverb or Preposition?	After her persuasive speech, Inez sat *down.* (*Down* is used as an adverb, modifying the verb *sat.*)
	We sailed our raft *down* the Mississippi. (*Down* is used as a preposition.)

Parts of Speech   **675**

WRITING THEME   Science Fiction

You might want to encourage students to jot down ideas for their own science fiction stories and use them in creative writing activities.

Concept Check
Parts of Speech
   1. Trurl, Noun
   2. When, Conjunction, he, Pronoun; white, Adjective; squinted, Verb; on, Preposition; forehead, Noun; pale, Adjective; polkadots, Noun
   3. Extremely, Adverb; with, Preposition; himself, Pronoun; and, Conjunction; asked, Verb; is, Verb
   4. Seven, Interjection

◆ Individualizing Instruction

Basic Students   To illustrate the concept that one word may function in several ways, draw an analogy to a table, which can be used in several different capacities. You can write on a table, sit on it, stand on it, or even use it as a barricade (on its side) or as the foundation of a tent (upside down). It is the same piece of furniture functioning differently. So too, the word *table* can be a noun, a verb, or an adjective. You may want to provide the following examples:

Our Thanksgiving *table* was laden with food. (noun)
The committee will *table* the motion to raise taxes. (verb)
Near the sofa is a large *table* lamp. (adjective)

Teaching Tip: Word Endings

The addition of certain suffixes can change a word's part of speech. The most familiar may be the *-ly* ending that changes adjectives to adverbs, but students should be aware of others, such as *-ion* and *-ment,* which form nouns, *-able, -y,* and *-al,* which form adjectives, and *-ize,* which forms verbs.

Teaching Tip: Pronunciation

Point out that some words that can be used as more than one part of speech change pronunciation when they change part of speech; for example, *address, separate,* and *object.* Challenge students to find five more such words and write sentences that illustrate their parts of speech.

Linking Grammar and Writing

Lively dialogue often contains an interjection, the part of speech used more often in speech than in writing. Encourage students to compose a few lines of dialogue for their Writing Portfolios. Before they begin, discuss the interjections they might use.

WRITING THEME   The Performing Arts

Encourage students to consider writing a critical review or a personal narrative about a current play, film, or other artistic production.

A. Concept Check
Parts of Speech
1. play, Noun
2. play, Verb
3. That, Pronoun
4. that, Adjective
5. name, Verb
6. name, Noun
7. Never, Interjection
8. never, Adverb
9. after, Conjunction
10. After, Preposition

B. Drafting Skill
Experimenting with Parts of Speech
Answers will vary. See typical answers below.
1. Good *comedy* roles are quite rare. (Adjective)
2. *Those* whom we saw last night were delightful actors. (Pronoun)
3. Some comic performances are *fantastic* indeed. (Adjective)

Additional Resources
• Grammar and Usage Practice Book, p. 122

Writing Theme
The Performing Arts

Itzhak Perlman,
reknowned classical
violinist

676 Grammar Handbook

Preposition or Conjunction?	*After* the season, the debate team had an awards banquet. (*After* is used as a preposition.)
	After the moon came up, Tom and Huck sneaked out. (*After* is used as a subordinating conjunction beginning a group of words that contains a subject and a verb.)
Interjection or Adverb?	*Never!* I won't try sky diving again. (*Never* is used as an interjection.)
	Ms. Saito *never* raises her voice in class. (*Never* is used as an adverb, modifying the verb *raises*.)

Practice Your Skills

A. CONCEPT CHECK

Parts of Speech   Identify the part of speech of each italicized word in the following sentences.

1. To a child, outdoor *play* is usually more attractive than practicing music.
2. A musician, of course, must *play* for years to master an instrument.
3. *That* is why some budding musicians give up before learning to play well.
4. They simply lack *that* special motivation to persevere.
5. Can you *name* several respected musicians who overcame handicaps?
6. One *name* that comes to mind is Itzhak Perlman.
7. This victim of childhood polio said *"Never!"* to the idea of giving up.
8. Perlman *never* abandoned his study of the violin.
9. He continued to practice *after* he was stricken with the disease.
10. *After* years of study, he became a world-class virtuoso.

B. DRAFTING SKILL

Experimenting with Parts of Speech   The ability to use words as different parts of speech can be a useful skill in writing. Write each of the following sentences. Then, after each, write a sentence using the italicized word as a different part of speech.

1. *Comedy,* with its light tone and subtle wordplay, can be difficult to perform.
2. Only *those* actors with a knack for timing can handle comedy well.
3. *"Fantastic!"* an audience may say about a great comedian's performance.

4. Comedy looks easy to play but is achieved only through hard *work*.

5. For example, physical comedy, such as slapstick, calls for the agility and *control* of an athlete.

C. APPLICATION IN WRITING

The Synopsis   Some local newspapers give a brief synopsis, or summary, of the plot of each current film. Choose a current film and write your own synopsis of its plot. In the synopsis include five of the following words and use each of them as more than one part of speech: *act, film, open, wonderful, picture, that, one, some, praise, this.*

CHECK POINT
PAGES 674–677

A. Write each italicized word in these sentences and tell its part of speech.

1. Pablo Picasso was a *sort* of hero in the *art* world.
2. The respect and admiration he had did not depend *on* his *financial* success.
3. *Picasso's work* sold for millions of dollars only after the artist had been painting for decades.

Writing Theme
Heroes

The Three Musicians,
by Pablo Picasso

Parts of Speech   **677**

4. Comic actors often *work* on TV. (Verb)

5. Some comic actors must *control* their voices to achieve humorous sound effects. (Verb)

C. Application in Writing
The Synopsis
Answers will vary.

CHECK POINT
PAGES 674–677

These exercises allow your students to practice the skills acquired in this handbook. You may wish to use the exercises as an informal evaluation of student mastery of the concepts.
WRITING THEME   Heroes

A.

1. sort, Noun; art, Adjective
2. on, Preposition; financial, Adjective
3. Picasso's, Adjective; work, Noun

Humanities Connection

Art Note   Pablo Picasso (1881–1973) is considered one of the greatest artists of the twentieth century. In *The Three Musicians*, which is typical of Picasso's cubist works, the artist breaks his subject down into geometric shapes and then reassembles the shapes to offer the viewer a fresh and unusual perspective. Ask: What effect does this painting have on you?

4. Picasso had always been *greatly* respected for his courage *and* for his belief in his own art.
5. *Some* artists try to paint what the critics will *praise.*
6. *Others* attempt to paint what the galleries *can* sell.
7. Picasso would *paint* only *those* pictures he truly wanted to create.
8. *Bravo!* He demonstrated great personal *integrity.*
9. *This* stubborn independence of Picasso's earned him a *number* of enemies.
10. However, it eventually *cemented* his position *as* a hero of artists everywhere.
11. Many people feel that a *picture* by Picasso is more than an *extraordinary* work of art.
12. *For* them, his paintings are symbols of the triumphant freedom of *human* creativity.

B. APPLICATION IN LITERATURE

Parts of Speech   List the italicized words in the following selection and tell what part of speech each word is.

(1) [Theseus] had not gone *far* when he met a huge man in a bearskin carrying an *enormous* brass club. (2) *This* was *Corynetes,* the cudgeler, terror of travelers. (3) He reached out a hairy hand, seized Theseus by the throat, and lifted his club, which glittered *in* the hot *sunlight.*

(4) "Pardon me," said Theseus. (5) *"What* are you planning to do?"

(6) "Bash in *your* head."

(7) "Why?"

(8) "That's what *I* do."

(9) "A beautiful club you have *there,* sir," said Theseus.

(10) "So bright *and* shiny. (11) You know, it's a *positive* honor to have my head bashed in *with* a weapon like this."

(12) "Pure brass," growled the bandit.

(13) "Mmm . . . but is it *really* brass? . . . (14) A brass club *would be* too heavy to lift."

(15) "Not too heavy for me," said the bandit, "and it's pure brass. (16) Look. . . ."

(17) He held out his club, which Theseus accepted, smiling. (18) Swinging it in a *mighty* arc, he *cracked* the bandit's head as if it were an egg.

(19) "Nice *balance* to this," said Theseus. (20) "I think I'll keep it."

Bernard Evslin, *Heroes & Monsters of Greek Myths*

A. Recognizing the Parts of Speech List the italicized words in this passage and tell what part of speech each is.

(1) *At* 2 A.M. on October 12, 1492, Christopher Columbus landed on a *small* island in the New World. (2) *Many* of the facts of this historic voyage are known, *but* one simple question continues to bedevil historians and geographers—*where* did *Columbus* first land?

(3) Experts have argued their cases *for* many different islands in the Bahamas. (4) Indeed, over the years no fewer than *nine* landfall islands have been suggested, defended, and opposed. (5) Until recently, the choice of many scholars *had been* Watling Island, *which* was renamed San Salvador. (6) In 1986, a team led by Joseph Judge of The National Geographic Society *produced* what appears to be *conclusive* evidence that Columbus's first landing was at an island sixty miles southeast of Watling. (7) Using a sophisticated computer, Judge's team *electronically* re-created all the possible routes the fleet might have taken *across* the Atlantic. (8) *They* matched their data with detailed *descriptions* found in Columbus's log. (9) Line by line, information was *translated* and entered *into* the computer's complex program. (10) Computer analysis *indicated* that on October 12, Columbus's fleet would almost certainly have arrived at the tiny island of Samana Cay.

B. Understanding the Parts of Speech Write two sentences for each word below. Use the word as a different part of speech in each sentence.

sail   after   ship   what   sign   rose   around

C. Using Parts of Speech Complete this short story, using the parts of speech called for in the parentheses.

(1) It (verb) a dark (conjunction) (adjective) night. (2) The (adjective) sailors, (proper noun) and (proper noun), looked out at the (noun) shining (prepositional phrase).

(3) "There is no (noun) like this," said (proper noun). "I'd rather sail the (adjective) (noun) than live (prepositional phrase)."

(4) "Yes," said (proper noun) (adverb), "(pronoun) is the only life. (5) If only (pronoun) hadn't (verb) the ship."

GRAMMAR
HANDBOOK
36

Writing Theme
Ships and Sailing

Parts of Speech   **679**

Application and Review

These activities are designed to allow your students to apply concepts presented in this handbook. Exercise A requires students to recognize parts of speech. For Exercise B, students use given words as different parts of speech. Exercise C challenges students to complete a short story, using different parts of speech.

> **Additional Resources**
> • Tests and Assessment, Mastery Tests, pp. 81–84

WRITING THEME   Ships and Sailing

A. Recognizing the Parts of Speech
1. At, Preposition
   small, Adjective
2. Many, Pronoun
   but, Conjunction
   where, Adverb
   Columbus, Noun
3. for, Preposition
4. nine, Adjective
5. had been, Verb
   which, Pronoun
6. produced, Verb
   conclusive, Adjective
7. electronically, Adverb
   across, Preposition
8. they, Pronoun
   descriptions, Noun
9. translated, Verb
   into, Preposition
10. indicated, Verb

B. Understanding the Parts of Speech
Answers will vary.

C. Using Parts of Speech
Answers will vary. See typical answers below.
(1) It was a dark but peaceful night. (2) The weary sailors, Joe and Bob, looked out at the ocean shining in the moonlight.
(3) "There is no life like this," said Joe. "I'd rather sail the seven seas than live in any city."
(4) "Yes," said Bob contentedly, "this is the only life. (5) If only they hadn't sunk the ship."

Ella Flagg Young (1845–1918) was the first woman to serve as superintendent of schools in any large city. She did so in Chicago from 1909 to 1915. As we might gather from this On The Lightside feature, her chief contributions were of a practical nature: the introduction of such studies as home economics and manual training.

You may wish to challenge students to experiment and arrive at their own solutions to the nonsexist language problem, and then actually employ them for one week. Encourage students to record problems, successes, and frustrations in their journals.

You may also wish to point out that this is a timely problem. In many states, sex-neutral writing (as it is sometimes termed) has become part of the job of drafting legislation. For the drafters, the question is not whether to be nonsexist, but how to do so.

Revising laws is a huge undertaking (6,586 sections of statutes were affected in Minnesota alone) and raises many questions about people's ability to understand statutory language that is already difficult.

You may wish to have students research the current status of the statutory language in your state's legislation.

On the Lightside

HE'ER AND THON

In 1912 Ella Flagg Young, the superintendent of schools in Chicago, made this surprising statement to a group of principals:

"A principal should conduct his'er school so that each pupil is engaged in something that is profitable to him'er and where the pupil is required to use knowledge in school in accomplishing his'er task. . . ."

Young was bothered by a common problem with English—no single pronouns exist that can be used to refer to a nonspecific person of either sex. When a pronoun is needed to refer to a person of either sex, writers must either use "his or her," or randomly choose either the male or female pronoun. ("A principal should conduct his school . . .").

"The problem has bothered me frequently and the solution of it occurred to me on my way to this meeting," Young said. "Most pronouns of the feminine gender end in 'er, so all you have to do to make the common pronoun is to take the masculine form and add 'er."

Young created the following words: his'er, which joins his and her; him'er, for him and her; and he'er, for he and she. The principals enthusiastically agreed to implement Young's suggestion, but she had little success when she tried to gain national support.

Other people have also tried to fill the gap. In 1884 Charles Crozat Converse, a lawyer and hymn writer, made up thon.

"By cutting off the last two letters of the English word that and the last letter of the word one, and uniting their remaining letters in their original sequence in these two words, I produced that word now proposed for the needed pronoun," Converse said. He gave the following example: "If a Mr. or Mrs. A. comes to the courthouse on Monday, I will meet thon."

Over the years many other blends have been proposed, including hizer, shis, hom, shim, heesh, sheehy, and shey. Author June Arnold replaced all third-person pronouns with na and nan in her 1973 novel The Cook and the Carpenter, and other writers have penned their own personal solutions.

Although Converse's and Young's coinages have been included in some dictionaries, they have not become widely accepted. A writer still has no easy solution to his'er problem with pronouns.

Using Verbals and Appositives

GERUNDS

A **verbal** is a word formed from a verb that does not function as a verb. There are three types of verbals: **gerunds, participles,** and **infinitives.** Verbals and the phrases made from them can make your writing more fluid and efficient. The first verbals you will study are gerunds.

A gerund is a verb form that functions as a noun.

A gerund ends in *-ing*. It may be used like a noun is used—as a subject, a direct object, an object of a preposition, or a predicate nominative.

Subject	*Drawing* is Alissa's hobby.
Direct Object	Carmela tried *surfing*.
Object of a Preposition	The best place for *jogging* is the cinder trail around the Harvest Reservoir.
Predicate Nominative	One of the major industries of northern Minnesota is *mining*.

The Gerund Phrase

A gerund phrase consists of a gerund plus its modifiers and complements. The entire phrase functions as a noun.

Because a gerund is formed from a verb, it can have an object.

> We won by *scoring* a *touchdown* in the last minute. (*Touchdown* is the object of *scoring*.)

Like a verb, a gerund can be modified by adverbs.

> Lin started *laughing again*. (The adverb *again* modifies *laughing*.)

Since a gerund functions as a noun, it can also be modified by adjectives.

> *Quick thinking* saved us much embarrassment. (The adjective *quick* modifies *thinking*.)

Gerunds can also be modified by prepositional phrases.

> *Sitting on these benches* is uncomfortable. (*On these benches* modifies *sitting*.)

Using Verbals
and Appositives **681**

Gerunds

Objectives

- To identify and use gerunds and gerund phrases
- **Writing** To use gerunds and gerund phrases to improve awkward and unclear sentences

Teaching Strategies

Stumbling Block

Students may have difficulty distinguishing between "ing" verb phrases and gerunds. Point out that auxiliary verbs are present if an "ing" word is a verb form. (Volunteers *are* contributing their time. The charity *is* doing well.)

 Individualizing Instruction

LD Students Help students generate sentences modeled after those on the top half of page 681. First, provide gerunds for students to use as subjects, direct objects, objects of prepositions, and predicate nominatives. Then have volunteers provide gerunds for their classmates to use.

ESL Students Certain gerunds follow the verb "go" in idiomatic usage: go skating, go skiing, go bowling, go jogging, go shopping, etc. These expressions are problematic for ESL students. Explain that these are gerunds used as direct objects, answering the question "what?"

Linking Grammar and Literature

Ask students to find passages from literature that contain gerunds and gerund phrases.

WRITING THEME   Jazz

Students may want to write about the history of jazz or about the life of a jazz artist as the subject of a Writer's Workshop assignment.

A. CONCEPT CHECK
Using Gerunds and Gerund Phrases
Answers are underlined on page.

Writing Theme
Jazz

The entire gerund phrase, like a single-word gerund, functions as a noun.

Subject	*Eating pizza* was Joe's favorite pastime.
Direct Object	We enjoyed *seeing the movie a second time*.
Object of a Preposition	Kari got the concert tickets by *waiting in line overnight*.
Predicate Nominative	Nancy's favorite summer job was *working at the zoo*.

Usage Note   When a gerund is preceded by a noun or pronoun, the possessive form of that noun or pronoun must be used.

> *Aretha's coming late to music class* distracted the students who were practicing for the concert. (The possessive form, *Aretha's,* precedes a gerund.)
>
> My good math grade was due to *my completing the extra-credit assignment*. (The possessive form, *my,* precedes a gerund.)

Sentence Diagraming   For information on diagraming gerunds and gerund phrases, see page 834.

Practice Your Skills

A. CONCEPT CHECK

Using Gerunds and Gerund Phrases   Identify the gerund or gerund phrase in each sentence and write it on your paper.

1. Defining jazz correctly is difficult.
2. However, a key element in all jazz forms is improvising.
3. Early jazz musicians often developed their styles by listening to other musicians' works.
4. Writing down the notes of a composition was unusual in the early days of jazz.
5. Because ragtime musicians did make a practice of writing down their music, some critics did not accept ragtime as a legitimate form of jazz.
6. Imagine telling that to someone like Scott Joplin!
7. Composing ragtime piano pieces was Joplin's special talent.
8. One of his major achievements was popularizing ragtime with such compositions as "Maple Leaf Rag" and "The Entertainer."
9. He made listening to ragtime acceptable to jazz artists who played other styles of jazz.
10. By introducing ragtime abroad, musicians made it the first type of jazz known in Europe.

682 Grammar Handbook

B. REVISION SKILL

Using Gerunds and Gerund Phrases You can sometimes improve awkward or unclear sentences by using gerunds or gerund phrases. Rewrite each sentence below by replacing the underlined words with a gerund or gerund phrase.

1. Jazz developed from <u>the merger of</u> West African and southern American musical traditions.
2. <u>To play</u> jazz became popular at the end of the Civil War.
3. By 1910, music companies had begun <u>the production of</u> jazz records.
4. Southern riverboats carried jazz to the North by <u>the employment of</u> small bands.
5. Then, during the 1920's, a new way of <u>expression through dance</u> developed.
6. <u>The performance of</u> the Charleston soon became the "rage."
7. Many couples' greatest fun was <u>to dance</u> the night away.
8. Americans also greatly enjoyed <u>competition with each other</u> in dance contests.
9. Soon, musicians started <u>the organization of</u> big jazz bands.
10. What these players enjoyed most about jazz was <u>to make</u> a new kind of music together.

A 1926 *Life magazine* cover illustrates the dance craze of the 20's.

PARTICIPLES

A participle is a verb form that functions as an adjective.

You have learned that the **past participle** is one of the principal parts of a verb. The past participle of a regular verb is formed by adding *-d* or *-ed* to the present tense, as in *walk—walked, dance—danced*. The past participles of irregular verbs are formed differently and must be learned separately: *tear—torn, sing—sung*. For a review of irregular verbs and principal parts, see Grammar Handbook 33.

You have also learned that there is another kind of participle, called the **present participle.** The present participle is always formed by adding *-ing* to the present tense of the verb: *dance—dancing, sing—singing*.

Verb	Past Participle	Present Participle
look	looked	looking
bring	brought	bringing
cry	cried	crying

B. REVISION SKILL

Using Gerunds and Gerund Phrases
Answers will vary. See typical answers below.
   1. Jazz developed from merging West African and southern American musical traditions.
   2. Playing jazz became popular at the end of the Civil War.
   3. By 1910, music companies had begun producing jazz records.
   4. Southern riverboats carried jazz to the North by employing small bands.
   5. Then, during the 1920's, a new way of dancing developed.
   6. Performing the Charleston soon became the "rage."
   7. Many couples' greatest fun was dancing the night away.
   8. Americans also greatly enjoyed competing in dance contests.
   9. Soon, musicians started organizing big jazz bands.
   10. What these players enjoyed most about jazz was making a new kind of music together.

Participles

Objectives

- To identify participles and participial phrases
- **Writing** To use gerunds and participles correctly in sentences

Have two teams of students generate example sentences like the ones at the top of page 684. One team writes sentences with present participles; the other with past participles. Working against a time limit, team members compose as many sentences as possible, checking to ensure that each sentence contains the correct tense. At a given time, team members display their sentences on the board and help check each other's work.

Writing
—**TIP**—

Use a comma after a participial phrase that comes at the beginning of a sentence.

Participles are often used as parts of verb phrases: *had danced, am going.* When they are used as verbals, however, participles always function as adjectives. A participle modifies a noun or a pronoun.

> *Exhausted,* Lauren sat down with a sigh. (*Exhausted* is a past participle modifying the noun *Lauren.*)
> *Whistling,* he made his way home through the dark night. (*Whistling* is a present participle modifying the pronoun *he.*)
> A *fallen* tree blocked my driveway. (*Fallen* is a past participle modifying the noun *tree.*)
> The articles were new and neatly *arranged.* (*Arranged* is a past participle, used as a predicate adjective, modifying the noun *articles.*)

The Participial Phrase

A participial phrase consists of a participle plus its modifiers and complements. The entire participial phrase functions as an adjective.

Because a participle is formed from a verb, it can have an object.

> The goat *chewing the shoe* belongs to Carla. (*Shoe* is the object of the participle *chewing.*)

Also, the participle can be modified by adverbs or adverb phrases.

> We heard the foghorn *moaning in the distance.* (*In the distance* is a prepositional phrase modifying the participle *moaning.*)

The participial phrase, like the single-word participle, always functions as an adjective.

> *Sprinting wildly,* Carlos beat the throw to home plate. (*Sprinting wildly* modifies *Carlos.*)

Sentence Diagraming For information on diagraming participles and participial phrases, see page 834.

Participle, Gerund, or Verb?

All present participles, all gerunds, and some verbs in verb phrases end in *-ing.* To distinguish among them, ask the questions listed on the following page:

1. Is the word or phrase used as an adjective? If so, it is a participle or part of a participial phrase.

 Tuning the piano, Hank listened carefully to each note. (*Tuning the piano* is an adjective modifying *Hank.*)

2. Is the word or phrase used as a noun? If so, it is a gerund or part of a gerund phrase.

 Tuning the piano will improve its sound. (*Tuning the piano* is a noun and the subject of the sentence.)

3. Is the word conveying what the subject is doing and preceded by an auxiliary verb? If so, it is a verb in a verb phrase.

 Hank *had been tuning* the piano for two hours. (*Had been tuning* is a verb phrase.)

Practice Your Skills

A. CONCEPT CHECK

Participles Write the participle or participial phrase in each of the following sentences. After each participle or phrase, write the word it modifies.

1. Stars have varying degrees of brightness, or magnitude.
2. One measuring device for brightness is a photoelectric cell.
3. This cell, attached to a telescope in place of an eyepiece, can determine the brightness of a distant star.
4. Early astronomers, classifying stars on the basis of brightness, developed an odd numerical system.

Writing Theme
The Stars

Starry Night, by
Vincent van Gogh

Using Verbals
and Appositives   **685**

  Individualizing Instruction

LEP Students To reinforce students' understanding of adjectives, you might want to review the questions that adjectives answer: What kind? Which one or ones? How many? How much? (See Grammar Handbook 34, page 620.)

 Allow students to work in small groups to complete Exercise A and to develop sentences orally before completing Exercise B.

Additional Resources
• Grammar and Usage Practice Book, pp. 125–126

WRITING THEME   The Stars

Encourage students to research stars as a possible topic for a science assignment.

A. CONCEPT CHECK
Participles
Answers are underlined on page.

Sentence Variety

Answers will vary. See typical answers below.

1. Going to the planetarium was both fun and educational. (Gerund)
Going to the planetarium, I saw a falling star. (Participle)

2. Looking through telescopes is a major activity of astronomers. (Gerund)
Those girls looking through telescopes work after school at the planetarium. (Participle)

3. Developing our technology further means that we must encourage more students to develop an interest in math and science. (Gerund)
Developing our technology further, scientists work hard to build on their successes. (Participle)

4. Studying our solar system gave me a chance to study the rings of Saturn. (Gerund)
The Aztecs, studying our solar system, developed a highly accurate calendar. (Participle)

5. Is sparkling brightly a characteristic of all stars? (Gerund)
Sparkling brightly, stars appear closer than they actually are. (Participle)

Infinitives

Objectives

- To identify infinitives and infinitive phrases
- To determine the function of infinitives and infinitive phrases in sentences
- **Writing** To use infinitive structures in writing.

Teaching Strategies

Teaching Tip: Infinitives

You might wish to explain that the *to* of an infinitive is sometimes omitted after certain verbs, such as *let, make,* and *have.* To illustrate, provide students with the following sentence pairs:

- I *made* him *do* his homework.
  I *wanted* him *to do* his homework.
- She *let* her brother *go* first.
  She *asked* her brother *to go* first.
- He *had* them *sing* the song.
  He *told* them *to sing* the song.

The first sentence in each pair contains an infinitive, even though the *to* has been omitted. Point out that students may wish to use similar forms when they write their personal agendas for Exercise B on page 688.

---

5. A dim star has a larger assigned number than does a much brighter star.
6. Color is another attribute of stars studied by astronomers.
7. To the casual observer on earth, most sparkling stars seem bright white.
8. Trained astronomers, on the other hand, filter starlight through various colors.
9. The filtered light can be identified as red, yellow, white, or blue.
10. The color, observed with sophisticated instruments, indicates a star's temperature.

B. DRAFTING SKILL

Sentence Variety Compose two sentences for each of the phrases below. In one sentence, use the phrase as a gerund. In the other, use it as a participle. Label your sentences *Gerund* and *Participle.*

> **Example** peering into a telescope
> a. Peering into a telescope was a nightly ritual for Willie. (Gerund)
> b. Peering into a telescope one evening, Willie saw a luminous disk approaching. (Participle)

1. going to the planetarium
2. looking through telescopes
3. developing our technology further
4. studying our solar system
5. sparkling brightly

INFINITIVES

An infinitive is a verb form that usually begins with the word *to* and functions as a noun, adjective, or adverb.

You have learned that the word *to* is a preposition when it is followed by a noun or a pronoun as its object. However, when *to* is followed by a verb, it forms an infinitive. The *to* is called the *sign of the infinitive.* Compare these examples:

Prepositional Phrases	Infinitives
We went *to the juice bar.*	We went *to swim.*
Ms. Lin came home *to an empty house.*	Ms. Lin came home *to study.*
I shouted *to him.*	I shouted *to warn him.*

The Infinitive Phrase

An infinitive phrase consists of the infinitive plus its modifiers and complements. The entire phrase functions as a noun, an adjective, or an adverb.

Because an infinitive is formed from a verb, it can have an object.

> Megan planned *to have* a party. (*Party* is the object of the infinitive *to have*.)

An infinitive may be modified by adverbs or adverb phrases.

> The choir tried *to sing together*. (*Together* is an adverb modifying the infinitive *to sing*.)
>
> One customer demanded *to talk to my manager*. (*To my manager* is an adverb phrase modifying the infinitive *to talk*.)

Unlike gerunds and participles, infinitives can be used as more than one part of speech. An infinitive or infinitive phrase can be used as a noun, an adjective, or an adverb. Infinitives and infinitive phrases can function in many of the ways in which a noun functions. They are often used as subjects or direct objects.

Subject	*To learn a new language* takes time. (*To learn a new language* is the subject.)
Direct Object	Diane forgot *to send the entry fee*. (*To send the entry fee* is the direct object.)

The infinitive or infinitive phrase is used as an adjective if it modifies a noun or a pronoun. It is used as an adverb if it modifies a verb, adjective, or adverb.

Adjective	Shelly needs someone *to advise her*. (*To advise her* modifies the pronoun *someone*.)
Adverb	Miguel is afraid *to talk to Teresa*. (*To talk to Teresa* modifies the predicate adjective *afraid*.)

Usage Note A modifier placed between the word *to* and the verb of an infinitive is said to "split" the infinitive. Usually, a split infinitive sounds awkward and should be avoided.

Awkward	Marita tried to *patiently* wait.
Better	Marita tried to wait *patiently*.

Sentence Diagraming For information on diagraming infinitives and infinitive phrases, see page 835.

Using Verbals
and Appositives   **687**

Teaching Tip: Infinitives

Adjectival and adverbial uses of infinitives may be more difficult to identify than noun uses. Point out that an infinitive used as an adverb usually follows an adjective, as in "hard to do" or "too angry to speak." An infinitive used as an adjective usually follows a noun, as in "the candidate to beat" or "the place to visit," or a pronoun, as in "someone to do the work," and adds information about the word it modifies.

 ### Individualizing Instruction

ESL Students/LEP Students As a writing tip, suggest that these students copy the following list of words as examples of verbs that must be followed by a gerund, not an infinitive:

avoid	enjoy	practice
consider	finish	suggest
dislike	miss	

Linking Grammar and Writing

As students write longer sentences, they may have more than one infinitive structure in their work. Explain that in most cases, they should retain the *to* of each infinitive to preserve parallel structure. For example, *It is more fun to cook than to wash dishes* is clearer and less awkward than *It is more fun to cook than wash dishes*. Have students identify examples of infinitive structures in their writing and share them with the class.

 ### Individualizing Instruction

Basic Students Some students may confuse the preposition *to* with the infinitive *to*. Give them more example sentences such as those found on the bottom of page 686 to help them see the difference. (For example: Martha wanted to learn sign language. Ted rushed to the store.) Point out that *to* before a verb is an infinitive, while *to* before a noun is part of a prepositional construction. Then have students demonstrate understanding by giving sentences of their own orally using *to* as a preposition and as an infinitive. (See Grammar Handbook 35, page 652, for more on prepositions.)

**WRITING THEME   Dreams and
                   Fulfillment**

Suggest that students use the theme of
dreams and fulfillment as a possible topic
for writing a personal narrative.

A. CONCEPT CHECK

Infinitives and Infinitive Phrases
Answers are underlined on page.

B. APPLICATION IN WRITING

A Personal Agenda
Answers will vary.

Practice Your Skills

A. CONCEPT CHECK

Infinitives and Infinitive Phrases   Write the infinitive or infinitive phrase in each of the following sentences.

1. The dream of pilots Dick Rutan and Jeana Yeager was to fly around the world without refueling.
2. Scientific advances enabled them to make a very fuel-efficient and lightweight plane.
3. The *Voyager* was designed to be a flying fuel tank.
4. The weight of the fuel made it difficult for the plane to leave the ground.
5. In their tiny cockpit, Rutan and Yeager had to endure the constant buffeting of the plane.
6. When storms bashed the plane, the goal was just to survive.
7. Mechanical problems, such as a faulty fuel gauge and a stalled engine, continued to cause worry.
8. With fuel to spare, the *Voyager* returned home after 25,000 miles.
9. Thousands of people at Edwards Air Force Base cheered the pilots' courageous refusal to settle for anything less than victory.
10. The success of the *Voyager* may make it possible for planes to fly farther and more economically.

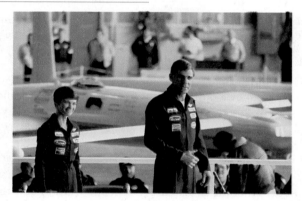

Voyager pilots,
Dick Rutan and
Jeana Yeager

B. APPLICATION IN WRITING

A Personal Agenda   Write a paragraph that briefly outlines your personal agenda, or list of things to do. Begin with the words *Now is the time in my life*. . . . Use an infinitive such as *to do research* or *to relax* to finish that sentence. Use at least three more infinitive structures in your personal agenda.

CHECK POINT
PAGES 681–688

A. Make two columns. In the first column, write the gerunds, gerund phrases, participles, and participial phrases from each of the following sentences. In the second column, tell whether a gerund is used as a *Subject, Direct Object, Object of a Preposition,* or *Predicate Nominative* and which word a participle modifies.

1. In the early nineteenth century, increased mechanization caused rapid growth in the production of goods.
2. Population increases further accelerated the development of manufacturing.
3. Thanks to the Industrial Revolution, the world had become a changed place.
4. The industrial age resulted in a dehumanizing way of life for the working classes.
5. For the first time in history, untiring machines dominated human lives.
6. In rural areas, a new farming machine might replace dozens of workers.
7. These rural workers protested their loss of jobs and income by rioting.
8. For many of these agrarian people, working in urban factories replaced farming.
9. Unfortunately for these former farmers, factory work was backbreaking and unrewarding.
10. Meeting the demand for more goods resulted in greatly overcrowded factories.
11. Manufacturing created densely populated and unhealthy city areas as well.
12. The dubious rewards of working in cities during the Industrial Revolution were drudging in sweatshops, living in slums, and being easily replaceable in a job.
13. Depending upon an employer for job security at this time became impossible.
14. In 1824, workers started forming trade unions.
15. Fearing loss of control over their employees, employers reacted with enormous hostility.
16. For the next century, labor and management could not avoid struggling against each other.
17. Breaking laws as well as centuries of tradition, labor demanded better working conditions.
18. Nevertheless, using pressure and often violence, mill owners resisted change.

> **Writing Theme**
> The Industrial
> Revolution

Using Verbals
and Appositives   **689**

CHECK POINT
PAGES 681–688

You may wish to use the following checkpoint exercises as an informal evaluation of student mastery of the concepts covered up to this point.

WRITING THEME   The Industrial Revolution

You may want to suggest that students consider using the Industrial Revolution as the subject of a research paper.

A.

1. increased, participle, mechanization
2. manufacturing, gerund. Object of Preposition
3. changed, participle, place
4. dehumanizing, participle, way; working, participle, classes
5. untiring, participle, machines
6. farming, participle, machine
7. rioting, gerund, Object of Preposition
8. working in urban factories, gerund phrase, Subject; farming, gerund, Direct Object
9. backbreaking, unrewarding, participles, work
10. Meeting the demand for more goods, gerund phrase, Subject; overcrowded, participle, factories
11. Manufacturing, gerund, Subject; populated, participle, areas
12. working in cities during the Industrial Revolution, gerund phrase, Object of Preposition; drudging in sweatshops, living in slums, being easily replaceable in a job, gerund phrases, Predicate nominatives
13. Depending upon an employer for job security at this time, gerund phrase, Subject
14. forming trade unions, gerund phrase, Direct Object
15. Fearing loss of control over their employees, participial phrase, employers
16. struggling against each other, gerund phrase, Direct Object
17. Breaking laws as well as centuries of tradition, participial phrase, labor; working, participle, conditions
18. using pressure and often violence, participial phrase, owners

B. Write the verbals or verbal phrases in each of the following sentences. Tell whether the verbal is a *Gerund,* a *Participle,* or an *Infinitive.* Tell whether each infinitive is used as a *Subject, Direct Object, Adjective,* or *Adverb.*

1. To define progress may seem difficult.
2. Advanced technology by itself may not improve the quality of human life.
3. Today, many thinking people would agree with that statement.
4. Leading scholars once believed that each advance in science and technology inevitably brought humanity farther along the road of progress.
5. The burden of warning the world about the dangers of technology often fell upon writers, artists, and craftspeople.
6. Charles Dickens, for example, wrote partly to entertain his readers and partly to inform society about the many evils of the Industrial Revolution.
7. At twelve, he had gone to work in a factory.
8. Disgusted by what he saw, Dickens wanted to protect children from those dangers.
9. Working twelve and fourteen hours a day resulted in a seriously deprived childhood, he thought.
10. With his novel *Oliver Twist,* Dickens tried to show the anguished life of England's industrial poor.
11. Starving children were forced into lives of crime and often met death at the hands of scoundrels and thieves.
12. Less dramatically, the artist William Morris led a battle to restore quality in furnishings and the arts.
13. Producing quality work was important to the workers, Morris declared.
14. A major element in happiness is the quality of taking pride in one's work.
15. To leave a factory with the thought "I made something really good today" builds a worker's sense of self-worth.
16. Morris believed that workers who made shoddy goods would not be pleased to use such goods.
17. Wearing shoddy clothes, sitting on cheap, ugly chairs, and looking at inferior pictures on the wall is hardly enjoyable.
18. It is degrading to live one's life surrounded by inferior objects, Morris believed.
19. Dickens and Morris believed that for progress to occur, it is sometimes necessary to pause.
20. Perhaps the right place to look for solutions to society's problems is in the past.

MISPLACED AND DANGLING MODIFIERS

Place a verbal or verbal phrase as close as possible to the word it modifies.

> I saw an alligator at the other side of that pond looking through my binoculars.

Did you find the sentence above unclear or perhaps humorous? If a verbal or verbal phrase is misplaced, it may appear to modify the wrong word and can confuse the reader. In addition, poorly placed modifiers distract the reader from what is actually being said. A word that modifies the wrong word or group of words is called a **misplaced modifier**.

Unclear   The three Simpson children attempted to wash the family dog, *giggling wildly.* (Is the dog *giggling wildly?*)

You can easily correct this sentence by bringing the participial phrase and the word it modifies closer together.

Clear   *Giggling wildly,* the three Simpson children attempted to wash the family dog. (The participial phrase *Giggling wildly* now clearly modifies *children.*)

Another kind of error is the **dangling modifier**. This error occurs when the word that the verbal phrase should logically relate to is not in the sentence.

Unclear   *To mow the lawn,* the grass must be dry. (Who will mow the lawn? The grass?)

One way to correct a dangling modifier is to add the word that the phrase logically relates to. Sometimes additional rewording is necessary to make the sentence clear.

Clear   *To mow the lawn,* you should make sure the grass is dry. (Notice how the wording of this sentence has been changed. The phrase *To mow the lawn* now modifies *you.*)

Using Verbals
and Appositives   **691**

Misplaced and Dangling Modifiers

Objectives

- To identify misplaced and dangling modifiers in sentences
- **Writing** To use revision skills to correct misplaced or dangling modifiers

Teaching Strategies

Linking Grammar and Writing

Two common errors in student writing are the use of dangling and misplaced modifiers. Have students select a piece of writing from their portfolios and scan it for the correct use of modifiers.

Writing Theme
Fireworks

Practice Your Skills

A. DRAFTING SKILL

Eliminating Misplaced and Dangling Modifiers Each of the following sentences contains either a misplaced modifier or a dangling modifier. Rewrite each sentence, finding and eliminating the misplaced or dangling modifier to make the intended meaning of the sentence clear.

1. Bursting colorfully in the sky, people love to watch Fourth of July fireworks.
2. By sending up luminous rockets of red and orange, the night sky is brightened by the exhibitors.
3. Whistling as they fall, some observers grow frightened by the loud displays.
4. To be comfortable, blankets were spread on the ground throughout the park.
5. Running from blanket to blanket, the park is full of laughing children.
6. Tired from strenuous activities, the celebration relaxes everyone, including the children.
7. Having come from all over the world, the Fourth of July is a special day for new citizens.
8. Tonight, before going home, fireworks will fade into the background.
9. To appreciate the meaning of the day, thoughts must turn to history and the values of the country.
10. With such thoughts in mind, people see all around them reasons for celebration walking home.

B. PROOFREADING SKILL

Using Modifiers Correctly Rewrite the following paragraph, correcting all errors. Be sure to revise any sentences that contain a misplaced modifier or a dangling modifier.

> Having been invented in China, people throughout the world still love fireworks today. Fireworks, safe only in the hands of an expert, is also called pyrotechnics. Combining gunpowder and other ingredients, most states prohibit the use of fireworks by individuals. In addition, the federal government limits the explosive power of fireworks. That can be used by individuals. Hollow tubes of paper are packed with gunpowder to create fireworks, coarse gunpowder propels rockets through the air. By adding special chemicals, beautiful colors are created in fireworks.

Off the Record

"A Freshman class, working on the improvement of sentence construction, were considering the sentence, 'Hurrying to school, his shoes came off at the corner.'

'What's wrong with it?' the teacher asked.

The students suggested several things, all of them wide of the mark. They seemed completely baffled. A minute of silence was suddenly ended by a loud chuckle and a voice that said, 'I know what's wrong with it. "Hurrying to school!" ' "

Ethel H. Gerstein
High Points

APPOSITIVES

An appositive is a noun or pronoun that usually follows another noun or pronoun and identifies or explains it.

The appositive adds detail to your writing. Unlike gerunds, participles, and infinitives, appositives are not based on verbs.

> Tim O'Brien, the novelist, is a Vietnam War veteran. (The appositive *the novelist* identifies *Tim O'Brien*.)
>
> Old Faithful, a geyser, erupts nearly every sixty-seven minutes. (*A geyser* identifies *Old Faithful*.)

The Appositive Phrase

An appositive phrase consists of the appositive and its modifiers.

> Jean Nicolet, the French explorer, landed on the shore of Green Bay in 1634. (The adjective *French* modifies the appositive *explorer*. The entire phrase identifies *Jean Nicolet*.)
>
> The giant panda, *a black and white bearlike animal of China and Tibet,* seldom eats anything but bamboo. (The adjectives *black, white,* and *bearlike* and the prepositional phrase *of China and Tibet* all modify the appositive *animal*. The entire phrase identifies *panda*.)

Sometimes the appositive phrase precedes—comes before—the word it modifies.

> *An epic tale of adventure and heroism,* the story of King Arthur is loved by people of all ages.

There are two kinds of appositives—nonessential and essential. A **nonessential** appositive adds extra meaning to a sentence that is already clear and complete. In other words, the sentence could be read without the appositive, and the main idea would still be clear. Set off nonessential appositives from the rest of the sentence with commas.

> Grover Cleveland, *a bachelor,* was married in the White House.

Essential appositives make the main idea of a sentence complete. If the sentence were read without the essential appositive, meaning would be lost. Commas are not used with essential appositives.

> The cartoon cat *Garfield* is overweight, out of shape, and grumpy.

Writing
—TIP—

Use appositives to work added information into a sentence.

Writing Theme
Bloomsbury

Practice Your Skills

A. CONCEPT CHECK

Appositives Write the appositive or appositive phrase in each sentence.

1. The London district Bloomsbury lent its name to a remarkable group of writers and artists.
2. The members of the Bloomsbury Group, all believers in the importance of art and social issues, began meeting in 1905.
3. Virginia Woolf, a writer of great stature, was the group's leader.
4. She was married to Leonard Woolf, author and social reformer.
5. Together, Virginia and Leonard ran the Hogarth Press, a publishing company for new and experimental work.
6. Their home in Bloomsbury, 46 Gordon Square, became a meeting place for young writers in rebellion against Victorian society.
7. John Maynard Keynes, a world-famous economist, was a frequent visitor there.
8. The author of *A Passage to India* and *A Room with a View,* E. M. Forster, also was a member of the group.
9. Virginia's sister Vanessa Bell was a painter and drew many artists into the group.
10. A collection of rebels and mavericks, the Bloomsbury Group now has a firm and highly respected place in the history of English literature.

LONDON
THE HOGARTH PRESS
1960

The Hogarth Press was a private project of Virginia Woolf and her friends. Portrait of Virginia Woolf at Asheham, by Vanessa Bell, 1912

B. DRAFTING SKILL

Eliminating Wordiness Using appositive constructions is one way to eliminate wordiness. Combine each pair of sentences by using an appositive phrase. Eliminate the italicized words and use commas where necessary.

1. In the heart of Bloomsbury is the British Museum. *The museum is* a treasure house of art objects and antiquities.
2. I spent Thursday touring the museum's marvelous galleries. *Thursday was* my second day in England.
3. One of the first things I saw was the Rosetta stone. *The Rosetta stone is* a flat stone inscribed in three languages.
4. The inscriptions were helpful in deciphering hieroglyphics. *Hieroglyphics are* the ancient Egyptians' system of writing.
5. The Elgin marbles are housed in a special room. *The Elgin marbles are* carvings from the Parthenon in Athens, Greece.
6. The Magna Carta is on display in the reading room. *The Magna Carta is* a document assuring all Britons of their basic rights and liberties.
7. It was signed in 1215 by King John at Runnymede. *Runnymede is* a field in Surrey on the Thames River.
8. The Upper Egyptian Galleries were the best of all. *The Galleries are* the home of the museum's mummies.
9. A special treat is hidden away on the upper floor of the museum. *That treat is* a collection of drawings by Michelangelo, Rubens, and Rembrandt.
10. After my visit, I relaxed at an English tea. *An English tea is* a light meal of dainty sandwiches, scones, and all the tea one can drink.

C H E C K   P O I N T
PAGES 691–695

A. Revise the following sentences to eliminate dangling and misplaced modifiers. You may need to add, rearrange, or change some words.

1. Traveling to Ireland, a medieval banquet in an Irish castle is a favorite activity for tourists.
2. Guarded by a giant wolfhound, our tourist group walked over the drawbridge.
3. Ladies in medieval costumes greeted the guests singing merrily by the fireplace.

Writing Theme
Ireland

Using Verbals
and Appositives **695**

B. DRAFTING SKILL
Eliminating Wordiness

Answers will vary. See suggested answers below.

1. In the heart of Bloomsbury is the British Museum, a treasure house of art objects and antiquities.
2. I spent Thursday, my second day in England, touring the museum's marvelous galleries.
3. One of the first things I saw was the Rosetta stone, a flat stone inscribed in three languages.
4. The inscriptions were helpful in deciphering hieroglyphics, the ancient Egyptians' system of writing.
5. The Elgin marbles, carvings from the Parthenon in Athens, Greece, are housed in a special room.
6. The Magna Carta, a document assuring all Britons of their basic rights and liberties, is on display in the reading room.
7. It was signed in 1215 by King John at Runnymede, a field in Surrey on the Thames River.
8. The Upper Egyptian Galleries, the home of the museum's mummies, were the best of all.
9. A special treat, a collection of drawings by Michelangelo, Rubens, and Rembrandt, is hidden away on the upper floor of the museum.
10. After my visit, I relaxed at an English tea, a light meal of dainty sandwiches, scones, and all the tea one can drink.

C H E C K   P O I N T
PAGES 691–695

You may wish to use the following checkpoint exercises as an informal evaluation of student mastery of the concepts covered in this handbook.

WRITING THEME Ireland

A.

Answers will vary. See typical answers below.

1. A medieval banquet in an Irish castle is a favorite activity for tourists traveling to Ireland.
2. Our tourist group walked over the drawbridge guarded by a giant wolfhound.
3. Singing merrily by the fireplace, ladies in medieval costumes greeted the guests.

4. Each guest in turn drew straws to select a king and queen for the evening.
5. Passing a beverage called mead, the servants bowed to the king and queen.
6. Using my imagination, I can still see the platters piled with food.
7. After we ate our dinner, entertainers in medieval dress were brought out.
8. We were regaled by the performers' juggling bright objects and singing madrigals.
9. Having been a professional comedian for years, the master of ceremonies had a lively comic routine.
10. After thoroughly enjoying the dinner and entertainment, we found a tour through the castle delightful.

B.
1. Ireland
2. Scotland
3. ''The land of saints and scholars''
4. the Celts
5. lovers of learning and of myth and saga
6. scholarly scribes and artists
7. handwritten and intricately decorated books
8. a national heritage
9. a period of the late 1800's and early 1900's
10. tall green mountains, rocky cliffs, and lush green plains
11. storytellers all
12. Gaelic and English

---

4. <u>Selecting a king and queen for the evening,</u> straws were drawn by each guest in turn.
5. The servants bowed to the king and queen <u>passing a beverage called mead.</u>
6. I can still see the platters piled with food <u>using my imagination.</u>
7. <u>After eating our dinner,</u> entertainers in medieval dress were brought out.
8. <u>Juggling bright objects and singing madrigals,</u> we were regaled by the performers.
9. The master of ceremony's comic routine was lively, <u>having been a professional comedian for years.</u>
10. <u>After thoroughly enjoying the dinner and entertainment,</u> a tour through the castle was delightful.

B. Write the appositive or appositive phrase in each of the following sentences.

1. The enchanted country <u>Ireland</u> has captured people's imaginations for centuries.
2. At one place, the Emerald Isle is less than fourteen miles from its nearest neighbor, <u>Scotland.</u>
3. <u>"The land of saints and scholars,"</u> Ireland is marked by many ruined castles and abbeys.
4. Its early inhabitants, <u>the Celts,</u> had once peopled vast tracts of Europe.
5. These early people, <u>lovers of learning and of myth and saga,</u> created a unique and powerful body of literature.
6. In the Dark Ages, Irish monks—<u>scholarly scribes and artists</u>—kept the Irish love of words alive.
7. Their output, <u>handwritten and intricately decorated books,</u> has been preserved in museums.
8. The Irish love of words, <u>a national heritage,</u> has contributed a wealth of great literature to the world.
9. The Irish Literary Revival, <u>the period of the late 1800's and early 1900's,</u> included such literary giants as James Joyce, William Butler Yeats, and George Russell.
10. The landscapes of Ireland, <u>tall green mountains, rocky cliffs, and lush green plains,</u> also are preserved in the literature of Irish writers.
11. Modern Irish people, <u>storytellers all,</u> still beguile their listeners by telling stories and anecdotes and relating the myths and history of their nation.
12. The official languages of Ireland, <u>Gaelic and English,</u> are spoken throughout the island nation, although few people today use Gaelic as their everyday language.

A. Application in Literature Write the italicized words or phrases in the following passage. Tell whether each verbal is a *Gerund, Participle,* or *Infinitive.*

 (1) The dragon Smaug approached the village. . . . *Roaring,* he swept back over the town. (2) A hail of dark arrows leaped up and snapped and rattled on his scales and jewels; and their shafts fell back, *kindled by his breath* burning and hissing into the lake. No fireworks you ever imagined equalled the sights that night. (3) At the *twanging of the bows* and the *shrilling of the trumpets,* the dragon's wrath blazed to its height, till he was blind and mad with it. (4) No one had dared *to give battle to him* for many an age; nor would they have dared now, if it had not been for the grim-voiced man (Bard was his name), who ran to and fro *cheering on the archers* and urging the Master *to order them* to fight to the last arrow.
 (5) Fire leaped from the dragon's jaws. He circled for a while high in the air above them, *lighting all the lake;* the trees by the shores shone like copper and like blood, with *leaping* shadows of dense black at their feet. (6) Then down he swooped, straight through the arrow-storm, reckless in his rage, taking no heed *to turn his scaly sides towards his foes,* seeking only to set their town ablaze.

J.R.R. Tolkien, *The Hobbit*

B. Sentence Combining Combine each pair of sentences by following the instruction in parentheses. Eliminate the italicized words and make any other necessary changes.

1. The dragon appears in mythology and folklore all over the world. *It is* a mythical beast resembling a large, fire-breathing lizard. (Use an appositive.)
2. In the Orient, dragons are considered benevolent. *They* represent supernatural wisdom and strength and ensure wealth and good luck. (Use two participles.)
3. In the West, they seem to have had only one purpose and were considered ferocious adversaries. *They* threatened heroes. (Use an appositive infinitive.)
4. •Dragons were thought of as forces of evil in the world. *They* guarded treasures and seized young damsels. (Use two participles.)
5. In ancient England, *something* became a major part of a knight's job. *Knights* fought dragons. (Use a gerund.)
6. The Welsh painted colorful and highly stylized dragons on royal banners. *The dragon* stands for sovereignty. (Use an infinitive.)

Application and Review

These activities are designed to allow your students to apply concepts presented in this handbook. Exercise A requires students to identify gerunds, participles, and infinitives. In Exercise B, students combine sentences using verbals and appositives. In Exercise C, students revise sentences by correcting misplaced and dangling modifiers. Exercise D challenges students to use verbal phrases to create their own myth or legend.

> ### Additional Resources
> - Tests and Assessment
>   Mastery Tests, pp. 85–90
> - Elaboration, Revision, and Proofreading Worksheets, p. 28

WRITING THEME **Myth and Legend**

You might suggest that students consider using the conventions of myth and legend in a creative writing assignment.

A. APPLICATION IN LITERATURE
 1. Roaring, Participle
 2. kindled by his breath, Participle
 3. twanging of the bows, shrilling of the trumpets, Gerunds
 4. to give battle to him, Infinitive; cheering on the archers, Participle; to order them, Infinitive
 5. lighting all the lake, Participle; leaping, Participle
 6. to turn his scaly sides towards his foes, Infinitive

B. Sentence Combining
Answers will vary. See suggested answers below.
 1. The dragon, a mythical beast resembling a large, fire-breathing lizard, appears in mythology and folklore all over the world.
 2. In the Orient, dragons are considered benevolent, representing supernatural wisdom and strength and ensuring wealth and good luck.
 3. In the West, they seem to have had only one purpose, to threaten heroes, and were considered ferocious adversaries.
 4. Dragons were thought of as forces of evil in the world, guarding treasures and seizing young damsels.
 5. In ancient England, fighting dragons became a major part of a knight's job.
 6. The Welsh painted colorful and highly stylized dragons on royal banners to stand for sovereignty.

7. The dragon is sometimes portrayed in various myths and legends as a two-sided being, preventing rain or sending it.

8. Oriental dragons, good and powerful spirits, are respected and friendly caretakers whose images scare away evil.

9. Guarding the air, sea, and earth was their sacred duty.

10. The Chinese use the dragon's power to control the rain needed to ensure a plentiful harvest.

C. Using Phrases Correctly

Answers will vary. See suggested answers below.

1. Writers have found King Arthur a fascinating figure—partly mythical, partly historical.

2. Historians believe that there was a real Arthur living in Wales in the sixth century.

3. However, it is the legendary Arthur, leading his knights of the Round Table at Camelot, who fascinates readers.

4. The table was said to hold places for 150 knights devoted to purity and honor.

5. Sitting at the table, Arthur's knights pledged themselves to follow the code of chivalry.

6. The knights organized guests to pursue this ideal.

7. Searching for the Holy Grail, Sir Galahad, one of Arthur's knights, met many dangers.

8. By falling in love, Sir Lancelot and Arthur's wife, Guinevere, brought disaster to King Arthur's court.

9. Following the code of chivalry, Arthur should have punished his wife and Lancelot.

10. Reluctant to denounce them, he violated the code, and Camelot was doomed.

D. Using Verbals

Answers will vary.

---

7. The dragon is sometimes portrayed in various myths and legends as a two-sided being. *It may* prevent rain or send it. (Use two participles.)

8. Oriental dragons are respected and friendly caretakers whose images scare away evil. *The dragons* are good and powerful spirits. (Use an appositive.)

9. *Something* was their sacred duty. *They* guarded the air, sea, and earth. (Use a gerund.)

10. The Chinese use the dragon's power. *The power* controls the rain needed to ensure a plentiful harvest. (Use an infinitive.)

C. Using Phrases Correctly Each of the following sentences contains a misplaced modifier or a dangling modifier. Revise the sentences to make the meaning clearer.

1. Partly mythical, partly historical, writers have found King Arthur a fascinating figure.
2. Living in Wales in the sixth century, historians believe that there was a real Arthur.
3. However, it is the legendary Arthur who fascinates readers leading his knights of the Round Table at Camelot.
4. Devoted to purity and honor, the table was said to hold places for 150 knights.
5. Arthur's knights pledged themselves to follow the code of chivalry sitting at the table.
6. Pursuing this ideal, quests were organized.
7. One of Arthur's knights, Sir Galahad, met many dangers searching for the Holy Grail.
8. Sir Lancelot and Arthur's wife Guinevere brought disaster to King Arthur's court falling in love.
9. Arthur should have punished his wife and Lancelot following the code of chivalry.
10. Reluctant to denounce them, the code was violated, and Camelot was doomed.

D. Using Verbals Use the following verbal phrases to create your own myth or legend.

1. brandishing her enchanted sword
2. menacing the villagers
3. to slay the beast
4. breathing green fire
5. exhausted from the epic struggle
6. to ensure their safety and tranquility

On the Lightside

THE WORD WIZARD

Comedians Bob and Ray performed comic radio interviews for almost fifty years, beginning in 1946.

Bob: And now it's time for another informative session with Doctor Elmer Stapley, the Word Wizard. Doctor Stapley is one of the nation's leading authorities on the meaning and derivation of English words. And he's here to answer the questions that you listeners send in about our language and its correct use. Doctor, our first letter to the Word Wizard comes from a woman in Ohio. She writes: "I am very upset about the grammar my nine-year-old son uses. Everyday, he comes home and says, 'I ain't gotten no money.' How can I explain this complicated mistake so he'll stop saying it?"

Stapley: Well, I don't see what's complicated. Just tell him to get a job and earn some money. Then he'll stop saying he doesn't have any.

Bob: Well, I don't think that quite answers the woman's question, doctor. Her son is only nine, so he can't very well get a job. I think she just wants to explain to him why it's wrong to say, "I ain't gotten no money."

Stapley: Well, problematically, the thing that's bothering her is that word "gotten." You see, her son is using the past icicle instead of the present tension. But that's hard to explain to a child. So I'd suggest having the kid use a completely different verbal and say, "I ain't in possession of no money."

Bob: And that's the only grammatical change . . . you'd recommend?

Stapley: Of course. And please don't try to change my mind— because once I've solved a problem, I remain abominable.

Bob: This last letter comes from a lady in North Carolina. And she writes: "I work on the switchboard for a firm called Fleckny, Ignass, Wateford and Swope. Frequently, I get calls from people who want to talk to Mr. Fleckny, Mr. Ignass, Mr. Wateford, or Mr. Swope. If they're all out to lunch, should I say, "None of them is here" or "None of them are here'?"

Stapley: The correct thing to say is: "All of them are not around."

Bob: Yes. I'm sure that would get the message across. Thank you for being with us today.

Stapley: Not at all. I was petrified to come.

Bob: Well, we always get a little nervous about having you here, too, but we seem to keep inviting you back anyway.

Bob Elliot and Ray Goulding

Allow time for students to read and enjoy this humorous excerpt from a radio show interview. Interested students may wish to take the parts of Bob and Doctor Stapley and read the script aloud to the class.

Define *malapropism*, the incorrect but humorous use of a word sounding somewhat like the one intended. Have students find examples of malapropism in the dialogue (*problematically* for *probably*, *icicle* for *participle*, *tension* instead of *tense*). Elicit from students the incorrect use of *abominable* and *petrified* and ask what words they would suggest as appropriate replacements. Have them also note Bob's responses to these words.

Discuss Doctor Stapley's proposed solution to the problem of the ungrammatical sentence. Have students identify and correct the errors in the sentence.

Your students might enjoy experimenting with malapropism or creating humorous responses to other questions about grammatical errors.

Making Subjects and Verbs Agree

Objectives

- To identify the correct form of a verb in relation to its subject
- To recognize errors in subject-verb agreement
- **Writing** To use correct subject-verb agreement in writing

Teaching Strategies

Individualizing Instruction

Basic Students Emphasize that the third-person singular form of a verb, unlike the singular form of most nouns, ends in -s and that the plural form of a verb, unlike the plural form of most nouns, does not usually end in -s. Remind students that the singular form of the verb ends in -s only in the third person and not with *I* or *you*.

ESL Students The singular verb form ending in -s is particularly difficult for ESL students. It is hard for many students to pronounce -s in spoken English, and therefore they often forget it. Reinforce the patterns of agreement in standard English through oral drill.

Linking Grammar and Writing

As students gain writing fluency and as their sentences become more complex, they learn to enrich sentences by adding descriptive phrases between subject and verb. These added phrases may often cause confusion in subject-verb agreement. Suggest that as students complete the Application in Writing assignments in this handbook, they double-check their sentences for agreement.

GRAMMAR HANDBOOK 38

Writing ─TIP─

If you suspect an agreement problem, carefully identify the subject.

Making Subjects and Verbs Agree

AGREEMENT IN NUMBER

The **number** of a word indicates whether the word is singular or plural. A word is **singular** when it refers to one thing and **plural** when it refers to more than one thing. If a subject and verb are the same in number, they agree.

A verb must agree in number with its subject.

If a subject is singular, its verb must be singular. If a subject is plural, then its verb must be plural. The singular form of a verb ends in -s. A plural verb does not usually end in -s.

Singular The <u>gymnast</u> <u>dismounts</u> gracefully.
     The <u>cat</u> <u>stalks</u> its prey.
     The <u>reporter</u> <u>rushes</u> to the scene.
Plural The <u>gymnasts</u> <u>dismount</u> gracefully.
     The <u>cats</u> <u>stalk</u> their prey.
     The <u>reporters</u> <u>rush</u> to the scene.

In a sentence with a verb phrase, the first helping verb must agree with the subject.

The corn <u>crop</u> <u>has</u> withered in the blazing August heat.
The <u>peaches</u> <u>have</u> been ripening for a month.

Agreement of subjects and verbs usually occurs naturally. However, problems may arise when the subject of the sentence is not clear.

The subject of the verb is never found in a prepositional phrase.

When you make subjects and verbs agree, disregard any prepositional phrase that separates the subject from the verb.

The <u>tapes</u> on this shelf <u>are</u> mine.
The <u>sound</u> of Bow Bells <u>is</u> familiar to Londoners.
Many <u>constellations</u> in the sky <u>have</u> names from Greek myths.

Phrases beginning with words such as *with, together with, including, as well as*, and *in addition to* are not part of the subject.

<u>Honesty</u>, as well as courage, <u>is</u> a virtue.
<u>Broccoli soup</u>, in addition to veal, <u>was prepared</u> by the chef.

Practice Your Skills

A. CONCEPT CHECK

Subject-Verb Agreement   Write the form of the verb that agrees with the subject of each of the following sentences.

1. The most famous example of Europe's museums (are, <u>is</u>) the Louvre, built as a fortress in 1200.
2. The original art galleries in the Louvre (<u>were</u>, was) commissioned by Catherine de' Medici.
3. The exhibit area of the museum, in addition to the offices, (<u>is</u>, are) now housed in four wings of a square courtyard.
4. Two kings of France (<u>were</u>, was) responsible for building the other two wings.
5. The Oriental Antiquities Department, including several divisions, (present, <u>presents</u>) a panorama of ancient Middle Eastern civilizations.
6. A very popular collection among these divisions (are, <u>is</u>) that of Egyptian Antiquities.
7. The well-known Department of Greek and Roman Antiquities (<u>traces</u>, trace) its origins all the way back to 1800.
8. Many works in the Louvre (<u>belong</u>, belongs) to the French schools of painting.
9. Drawings, together with furniture and sculpture, (is, <u>are</u>) also exhibited.
10. Curators at the museum (enriches, <u>enrich</u>) the collection through purchases and through the use of donations.

Mona Lisa,
by Leonardo da Vinci

B. DRAFTING SKILL

Making Subjects and Verbs Agree   Errors in subject-verb agreement are easy to make while drafting. Write each of the following sentences, using the correct present-tense form of the verb in parentheses.

1. Artists around the world often (try) watercolors at some point.
2. A box of six or eight cakes of watercolor pigment (cost) little.

Making Subjects
and Verbs Agree   **701**

Humanities Connection

Art Note   Leonardo da Vinci (b. 1452, Italy, d. 1519) was a multi-dimensional artist whose genius extended to many fields. The *Mona Lisa* illustrates da Vinci's power and innovation as an artist. It has a naturalness unusual for portraits of its time. This is due, in part, to da Vinci's rendering of the model's folded hands. Encourage students to formulate an idea for a painting and describe it accu-rately, using correct subject-verb agreement.

3. covers
4. varies
5. are
6. dry
7. is
8. involves
9. prevents
10. helps
11. shows
12. are
13. produces
14. is
15. apply

C. Proofreading Skill

Correcting Agreement Errors
Errors are underlined on page.

Among the most popular of American illustrators is Norman Rockwell (1894–1978). His paintings of familiar situations and common people tell accurate stories about American life. Best known are his cover illustrations for the *Saturday Evening Post* and other magazines. These covers are fine examples of Rockwell's detailed, realistic style.

Scenes from the circus appear frequently in Rockwell's work. He has also used the theater, parks, and homes as settings for his famous illustrations. A boxing ring, a blacksmith shop, and the White House are some of his more unusual settings. However, Rockwell is essentially an artist of the people. His most memorable paintings are simple, sentimental scenes of middle-class American life.

3. A large camel's-hair brush, together with three sable-hair brushes, (cover) the beginner's basic need.
4. The right position for holding these brushes (vary) with each artist.
5. The two different kinds of watercolor paints (be) transparent and opaque.
6. Watercolors on textured paper (dry) quickly.
7. The paint (be) applied directly to the dry surface in the dry-paper method.
8. An alternative technique to the dry method (involve) wetting the paper first and then applying pigment.
9. Heavier weight, along with certain textures, (prevent) the paper from shrinking.
10. The whiteness of the paper in watercolor paintings (help) provide light tones and highlights.
11. An underdrawing in very light pencil lines (show) only slightly through the transparent color.
12. Special colored pencils, in addition to paint, (be) used to create watercolors.
13. Water brushed over the pencil strokes (produce) the effect of a watercolor painting.
14. Practice, as well as careful technique, (be) needed for success in this art form.
15. Few hard-and-fast rules about technique (apply) to this very appealing form of painting.

C. PROOFREADING SKILL

Correcting Agreement Errors Proofread the following paragraphs. Rewrite them on your paper, correcting all errors. Pay particular attention to subject-verb agreement.

Among the most popular of American illustraters are Norman Rockwell (1894–1978). His paintings of familiar situations and common people tells accurate storys about american life. Best known is his cover illustrations for the *Saturday Evening Post* and other magazines. These covers are fine examples of Rockwells detailed, realistic stile.

Scenes from the cirkus appears frequentley in Rockwell's work. He has also used the theater, parks, and homes as settings for his famous illustrations a boxing ring, a blacksmith shop, and the White House is some of his more unusual settings. However, Rockwell is essentially an artist of the poeple. His most memerable paintings is simple, sentamental scenes of middle-class American life.

COMPOUND SUBJECTS

A compound subject whose parts are joined by *and* is plural. Therefore, it requires a plural verb.

> Jute and other natural <u>fibers</u> <u>are woven</u> together in the wall hanging.
> <u>Steve</u> and <u>Marcella</u> <u>write</u> for the student newspaper.
> The <u>players</u> and their <u>manager</u> <u>ride</u> the bus.

When the parts of a compound subject are joined by *or* or *nor*, the verb should always agree with the subject that is nearer to the verb.

> Neither Jan nor his <u>friends</u> <u>eat</u> sushi.
> Either the jugglers or the tightrope <u>walker</u> <u>performs</u> next in the big top.

Usage Note   Sometimes a subject appears to be compound when it is actually a single unit. In this case the subject takes a singular verb.

> <u>Peas and carrots</u> <u>is</u> a popular Danish dish.
> <u>Rock-and-roll</u> <u>was influenced</u> by American jazz.

Practice Your Skills

A. CONCEPT CHECK

Compound Subjects   Write the form of the <u>verb</u> that agrees with the subject of each sentence.

1. Not only humans but also some computers (is, are) able to reason and solve problems.
2. The concept and the technology of artificial intelligence (has, have) existed for barely thirty-five years.
3. In fact, the first researchers and inventors of "thinking" computers (is, are), in some cases, still active in the field.
4. Neither the uses nor the ultimate goal of artificial intelligence (has, have) been fully agreed on by scientists.
5. Today, "thinking" computers and industrial robots (has, have) the ability to diagnose diseases and locate minerals.
6. Such accomplishments are possible because a television camera or other optical devices (helps, help) a robot "see" the world.
7. Computer engineers or even the average perceptive trend watcher (predicts, predict) that "thinking" robots will soon help humankind in essential ways.

Writing Theme
Science

Making Subjects
and Verbs Agree   **703**

8. The nuts and bolts of a "thinking" computer (is, are) a sophisticated program loaded with information.
9. In these computers, a memory chip or an arithmetic chip (is, are) used in the circuit boards, depending on the specific task.
10. Ordinary computer wear and tear (is, are) a problem that is lessened by the use of magnetic tapes.

B. REVISION SKILL

Recognizing Compound Subjects   Some of the following sentences contain errors in subject-verb agreement. Rewrite the sentences correctly. If a sentence contains no error, write *Correct*.

1. Science and medicine has benefited greatly from the contributions of women throughout history.
2. Surgery and basic medical care for women was specialties of Aspasia, a female doctor who lived during the time of the Roman Empire.
3. Under the reign of Henry VIII in sixteenth-century England, either a woman or a man were allowed to practice medicine.
4. However, it was three centuries before an American woman or women from other countries was able to become licensed physicians.
5. Lucy Hobbs Taylor and Margaret Maltby was two of the first American women to earn graduate degrees in science and medicine.
6. By 1857, the doctors and nurses at the New York Infirmary for Women was all female, making that infirmary the first medical department solely for women.
7. Nevertheless, neither a female doctor nor a female scientist was fully acknowledged in the United States until World War I.
8. Since that time, many awards and honors has been given to Dr. Sylvia Earl Meads, a marine biologist.
9. Cancer chemotherapy research and many published studies has earned Dr. Jane C. Write an international reputation.
10. Scientific technology and applications has also been advanced by women's inventions, such as the submarine telescope and the snowplow.

C. APPLICATION IN WRITING

A Comparison   Think of two inventions that can be compared and write a paragraph about their similarities and differences. For example, you might choose to compare and contrast typewriters and word processors. Include sentences with compound subjects. Begin at least one sentence with *Both* and at least one with *Either*. Check for subject-verb agreement.

B. Revision Skill
Recognizing Compound Subjects
Errors are underlined on page.
  1. Science and medicine have benefited greatly from the contributions of women throughout history.
  2. Surgery and basic medical care for women were specialties of Aspasia, a female doctor who lived during the time of the Roman Empire.
  3. Under the reign of Henry VIII in sixteenth-century England, either a woman or a man was allowed to practice medicine.
  4. However, it was three centuries before an American woman or women from other countries were able to become a licensed physician.
  5. Lucy Hobbs Taylor and Margaret Maltby were two of the first American women to earn graduate degrees in science and medicine.
  6. By 1857, the doctors and nurses at the New York Infirmary for Women were all female, making that infirmary the first medical department solely for women.
  7. Correct
  8. Since that time, many awards and honors were given to Dr. Sylvia Earl Meads, a marine biologist.
  9. Cancer chemotherapy research and many published studies have earned Dr. Jane C. Write an international reputation.
  10. Scientific technology and applications have also been advanced by women's inventions, such as the submarine telescope and the snowplow.

C. Application in Writing
A Comparison
Answers will vary.

A. Write the form of the verb that agrees with the subject of each sentence.

1. Techniques of mass communication (is, are) a powerful force in many essential areas of our lives.
2. At home, newspapers and radios (allows, allow) us to receive important news from around the world.
3. A magazine article or a television program (provide, provides) entertainment or useful information.
4. At school, teachers and students (uses, use) a wide variety of textbooks on subjects ranging from astronomy to zoology.
5. An animated film about germs (show, shows) students processes they could not otherwise see.
6. Business, as well as industry, sometimes (make, makes) use of teletypewriters, which send and receive written messages over wires, often across great distances.
7. In addition, computers linked by a telephone wire (help, helps) many businesses exchange vast quantities of data at high speed.
8. In many industries, a training film or videotape recordings (provides, provide) valuable education for employees.
9. On a global level, the development of communication satellites (has, have) made worldwide television broadcasting possible.
10. Mass communication, in both our personal and public lives, (has, have) certainly made the world grow smaller.

B. Some of the following sentences contain errors in subject-verb agreement. On your paper, rewrite these sentences correctly. If a sentence has no error, write *Correct*.

1. Animals, including humans, uses their senses to communicate with other members of their species.
2. For example, the calls of a male robin warns other males that it is defending its territory.
3. The female of the species, however, are encouraged to approach for mating.

Writing Theme
Communication

In the early 1800's, each phone wire in New York City carried ONE phone call.

Making Subjects and Verbs Agree   **705**

You may wish to use the following Checkpoint exercises as an informal evaluation of student mastery of the rules for subject-verb agreement covered in this handbook.

Individualizing Instruction

LD Students   You might wish to use exercise A as an ungraded diagnostic exercise for LD students. Be sure that these students understand items 1, 5, 6, 7, 9, and 10, which deal with subject-verb agreement involving intervening phrases. Once you are sure students understand this concept, ask them to complete the remaining items that probe subject-verb agreement with compound subjects.

WRITING THEME   Communication

A.
Answers on page

B.
Errors are underlined on page.
1. Animals, together with humans, use their senses to communicate with other members of their species.
2. For example, the calls of a male robin warn other males that it is defending its territory.
3. The female of the species, however, is encouraged to approach for mating.

4. The albatross, as well as many other kinds of birds, performs a complicated courtship ritual to attract a mate.
5. Correct
6. Correct
7. Each kind of fiddler crab has its own claw-waving language.
8. The language of honeybees is more complex than that of spiders or fiddler crabs.
9. Correct
10. Distance, direction, and quality of the food source are revealed by the dance of the bees.
11. A ''kiss'' between prairie dogs helps each animal tell whether the other belongs to the same family group.
12. Neither a male antelope nor a female gypsy moth is able to communicate effectively without the use of scents.
13. The body or facial gestures are often used as communication tools by monkeys.
14. Hunched shoulders and bared teeth on a male baboon signal a threat to other baboons.
15. Correct

Indefinite Pronouns

Objectives

- To identify indefinite pronouns and to classify them as either singular or plural
- To identify and use verbs that agree with indefinite pronoun subjects
- **Writing** To use verbs that agree with indefinite pronouns in personal and assigned writing

Teaching Strategies

Stumbling Block

Students may have difficulty with the singular indefinite pronouns *each* and *neither*, which are often mistaken for plural pronouns because they are often followed by prepositional phrases that suggest a group of people or things. Provide additional examples of sentences in which these pronouns are used as subjects. You might write the following sentences on the board:

Each of my friends wants to go.
Neither of the workers has the time.

Erase the prepositional phrase in each sentence, and then have students read the shortened sentences aloud. Continue with additional examples of this type.

4. The albatross, as well as many other kinds of birds, <u>perform</u> a complicated courtship ritual to attract a mate.
5. Preening and dancing are performed as part of the ritual.
6. The male spider goes through elaborate gestures to tell his "lady love" that he is not a bit of dirt or a tasty fly.
7. Each kind of fiddler crab <u>have</u> its own claw-waving language.
8. The language of honeybees <u>are</u> more complex than that of spiders or fiddler crabs.
9. A forager bee that finds food does a dance to communicate information about the food to other members of the hive.
10. Distance, direction, and quality of the food source <u>is</u> revealed by the dance of the bees.
11. A "kiss" between prairie dogs <u>help</u> each animal tell whether the other belongs to the same family group.
12. Neither a male antelope nor a female gypsy moth <u>are</u> able to communicate effectively without the use of scents.
13. Body movement or facial gestures <u>is</u> often used as communication tools by monkeys.
14. Hunched shoulders and bared teeth on a male baboon <u>signals</u> a threat to other baboons.
15. However, no nonhuman animal, including the very intelligent chimpanzee, has ever been seen writing a message for other animals to read.

■ N D E F I N I T E   P R O N O U N S

To make a verb agree with an indefinite pronoun that is used as the subject, you must determine whether the pronoun is singular or plural.

Singular Indefinite Pronouns			
another	each	everything	one
anybody	either	neither	somebody
anyone	everybody	nobody	someone
anything	everyone	no one	

Singular indefinite pronouns take singular verbs.

<u>Nobody</u> here <u>knows</u> the answer.
<u>Everyone</u> who signed up to go <u>is</u> here.

706 Grammar Handbook

Plural Indefinite Pronouns

both	few	many	several

Plural indefinite pronouns take plural verbs.

<u>Several</u> of the candidates <u>agree</u> on the issues.

Singular or Plural Indefinite Pronouns

all	any	most	none	some

The pronouns in the box above take singular verbs when they refer to one thing. They take plural verbs when they refer to several things.

<u>All</u> of the casserole <u>is burned</u>.
<u>All</u> of the representatives <u>were</u> present.

<u>Most</u> of the lake <u>has</u> a mud base.
<u>Most</u> of the beaches <u>have</u> lifeguards.

<u>Some</u> of the treasure <u>has</u> never <u>been recovered</u>.
<u>Some</u> of the coal barges <u>are docked</u> at a pier in Duluth.

Practice Your Skills

A. CONCEPT CHECK

Verb Agreement with Pronouns   In each of the following sentences, write the present-tense form of the verb in parentheses.

1. Most of the world's zoos (resemble) miniature cities, with something to please nearly every animal lover.
2. Everything in a zoo (be) carefully selected for public appeal.
3. To allow better viewing, several of the best zoos now (minimize) the barriers between spectators and animals.
4. In these animal parks, many of the strangest animals on earth (be) on display and viewed from elevated trains.
5. Some of the zoo animals (come) directly from the wild.
6. Others, which require special attention, (be) bred at the zoo.

Writing Theme
Animals

Making Subjects
and Verbs Agree   **707**

B. Revision Skill

Making Verbs Agree with Pronouns
Errors are underlined on page.

1. Everyone always loves watching the antics of the bears at zoos and circuses.
2. Few of the spectators, however, realize that the bear is a relative of the dog, raccoon, and weasel.
3. Correct
4. Most of our familiarity with bears is based on the bear of North America.
5. Interestingly, black bears are not always black; some are brown or cinnamon in color.
6. Correct
7. Two behaviors, teasing or threatening an adult or cub, are unwise; either provokes an angry attack.
8. Nearly anything—fish, meat, nuts, or berries—makes a good meal for this animal.
9. All of these creatures are troublesome around campsites if food is left within their reach.
10. Correct

C. Application in Writing

A Plot Synopsis
Answers will vary.

> **Additional Resources**
> • Grammar and Usage Practice Book, pp. 137–138

---

7. At certain zoos, much of the bird population (consist) of very rare and marvelous species.
8. Few of the creatures at a zoo, however, (create) as fascinating or as popular a sight as a family of gorillas.
9. In addition to displaying such intriguing animals, many of the world's zoos (provide) valuable educational services such as lectures and classes.
10. Certainly one of the best sources of entertainment and instruction concerning nature's wonders (be) your local zoo.

B. REVISION SKILL

Making Verbs Agree with Pronouns Some of the following sentences contain errors in subject-verb agreement. Rewrite these sentences correctly, changing the form of the verb. If a sentence contains no error, write *Correct*.

1. Everyone always love watching the antics of the bears at zoos and circuses.
2. Few of the spectators, however, realizes that the bear is a relative of the dog, raccoon, and weasel.
3. In fact, many of the world's animal experts put the giant panda in the raccoon family.
4. Most of our familiarity with bears are based on the bear of North America.
5. Interestingly, black bears are not always black; some is brown or cinnamon in color.
6. One of this species, the Kermode's bear, has creamy white fur.
7. Two behaviors, teasing or threatening an adult or cub, are unwise; either provoke an angry attack.
8. Nearly anything—fish, meat, nuts, or berries—make a good meal for this animal.
9. All of these creatures is troublesome around campsites if food is left within their reach.
10. No one wants to argue with a five-hundred-pound beggar that can run twenty-five miles an hour.

C. APPLICATION IN WRITING

A Plot Synopsis Write a brief plot summary for a science-fiction story in which animals play a different role from that in our present culture. For example, your plot might involve animals that serve as assistants to humans. Your description should include several indefinite pronouns as subjects of sentences. Check for subject-verb agreement in your work.

OTHER AGREEMENT PROBLEMS

Several other situations can cause problems in subject-verb agreement.

Doesn't and Don't with Pronouns

Doesn't is singular. Use *doesn't* with singular indefinite pronouns and with the subjects *she, he*, and *it*. *Don't* is plural. Use *don't* with plural subjects, with plural indefinite pronouns, and with the personal pronouns *I, we, you,* and *they*.

It doesn't matter to me.	I don't like jogging.
He doesn't live near Seattle.	We don't watch much TV.
Everyone doesn't agree.	You don't come to the games.

Inverted Sentences

Sometimes the verb comes before the subject rather than after it. Such a sentence is called an **inverted sentence.** Inverted sentences occur as questions, as sentences beginning with *there, here,* or *where,* or as sentences beginning with phrases. To find the subject in an inverted sentence, turn the sentence around to its natural order, placing the subject first. Then make sure subject and verb agree.

Making Subjects
and Verbs Agree   **709**

Other Agreement Problems

Objectives

- To recognize and correct special subject-verb agreement problems
- To understand verb agreement with *doesn't* and *don't*

Teaching Strategies

 Individualizing Instruction

LEP Students Work with these students to help them determine the natural order of inverted sentences. Write several short, simple inverted sentences on the board: *Where is your book?; Here is my book; "Pop" goes the weasel; Were we shocked!* Demonstrate how to change word order by placing the subject before the verb. For each sentence, give students the first word or two as an oral prompt until they have mastered the process.

Does the <u>train</u> often <u>arrive</u> late? (The train does often arrive late.)
Here <u>is</u> your beach <u>towel</u>. (Your beach towel is here.)
Toward the clouds <u>floats</u> the <u>balloonist</u>. (The balloonist floats toward the clouds.)

Nouns Plural in Form

Some words appear to be plural. That is, they end in -s as mos plural nouns do. However, these words are singular in meaning *mumps, news, molasses*. Use a singular verb with such subject

Dark <u>molasses</u> <u>is</u> especially thick and gooey.
<u>Mumps</u> sometimes <u>causes</u> eye or ear problems.
The <u>news</u> today <u>is</u> better than yesterday's news.

Many words ending in *-ics* refer to a science or branch of stud and are considered singular: *physics, mathematics, genetics*. Occa sionally such a word is used with a plural verb, usually when th word refers to qualities.

<u>Physics</u> <u>is</u> taught at this school.
<u>Acoustics</u> <u>is</u> a useful science.
The <u>acoustics</u> here <u>are</u> good.
His <u>politics</u> <u>are</u> strange.

Collective Nouns

A **collective noun** names an entire group of people or thing *class, team, flock, crowd*. A collective noun may be either singula or plural. When the noun refers to the group as a single unit, it singular. Use a singular verb. When the collective noun refers to th individual members of the group, it is plural. Use a plural verb.

The <u>majority</u> of the recruits <u>complete</u> basic training in six weeks. (Individual recruits complete training.)
The <u>majority</u> <u>rules</u> in this club. (*Majority* is a single unit.)

Words of Amount and Time

Words and phrases that identify periods of time, weights, mea sures, and numbers, including fractions, are usually considered sing units. Use singular verbs with these words and phrases.

<u>Two hours</u> <u>is</u> a very long time to stand at attention.
Just <u>four teaspoons</u> of hot sauce <u>seasons</u> this chili to my taste.
About <u>two-thirds</u> of the fruit salad <u>has</u> disappeared already.

The livestock would gather every morning, hoping for one of Farmer Dan's popular "airplane" rides.

710 Grammar Handbook

Stumbling Block

Point out to students that when words of amount are used with nouns that don't function collectively (such as *fruit salad*) but individually (such as *people, words,* or *snowflakes*), they take plural verbs.

Four-fifths of these words were borrowed from other languages.

Those three snowflakes look very similar.

Titles

A title of any work of art, literature, or music is considered singular even though it may contain plural words.

> _Dubliners_, by James Joyce, <u>is</u> a book of short stories published in 1914.
>
> Vincent van Gogh's _The Potato Eaters_ <u>was</u> on display at the gallery.
>
> _Babes in Toyland_, with Stan Laurel and Oliver Hardy, <u>was</u> <u>filmed</u> in 1934.

Practice Your Skills

A. CONCEPT CHECK

Other Agreement Problems Write the correct form of the <u>verb</u> for each sentence.

1. (<u>Doesn't</u>, Don't) everyone enjoy a thrilling, well-executed performance?
2. A crowd of anxious fans (<u>sits</u>, sit) on the grass near the main runway.
3. With necks craned and eyes squinting, the crowd (<u>doesn't</u>, don't) seem aware of anything but the bright summer sky.
4. News of the Oshkosh Air Show (<u>has</u>, have) drawn thousands of spectators to Whittman Airfield.
5. There (is, <u>are</u>) some of the world's best precision fliers performing here.
6. Unlike audiences at many other air shows, this audience (<u>understands</u>, understand) the difficulties involved in aerobatic flight.
7. This (<u>does</u>, do) add to the challenge, performers say.
8. In fact, over three-quarters of the crowd (has, <u>have</u>) attended previous shows.
9. For a time, physics with its limitations (<u>seems</u>, seem) nonexistant.
10. Three hours (<u>seems</u>, seem) to vanish as aircraft of every age and type defy the <u>laws</u> of gravity.
11. A team of World War I fighter planes (<u>stages</u>, stage) a dogfight.
12. The Red Baron Squadron (flies, <u>fly</u>) upside down doing loops and tailspins in their open-cockpit Stearmans.
13. _Aerobatics_ by Don Berfiner (<u>includes</u>, include) a section on this famous group.
14. Above the crowded bleachers (buzz, <u>buzzes</u>) a swift German Messerschmitt.
15. Finally, out of the clouds (zooms, <u>zoom</u>) the Navy's Blue Angels for the finale.

Additional Resources
- Grammar and Usage Practice Book, pp. 139–140

WRITING THEME Daredevils

Writing Theme
Daredevils

A. Concept Check
Other Agreement Problems
Answers on page

B. Drafting Skill

Making Subjects and Verbs Agree

Answers will vary.

C. Proofreading Skill

Correcting Agreement Errors

Errors are underlined on page.

Into town come the circus performers, daredevils of a special kind. A trapeze troupe risk their lives high above the crowd. Perhaps genetics provides the talent, but practice develops experts. Another risk taker is the lion tamer. However, he doesn't show any fear, so the big cats will stay calm and manageable. Even the clowns encounter danger when they help string the rigging. With eager anticipation the crowd watches and loves every minute.

B. DRAFTING SKILL

Making Subjects and Verbs Agree   Complete each sentence, using a verb in the present-tense form. Make sure that your subjects and verbs agree.

1. Toward the apex _____ the seasoned mountaineers.
2. The team _____ down at high altitudes.
3. There _____ less oxygen and every movement counts.
4. Four hours _____ a long time as they inch their way upward over rocks and ice.
5. Often the expedition •_____ supplies to last for days.

C. PROOFREADING SKILL

Correcting Agreement Errors   Rewrite the following paragraph, correcting all errors. Pay special attention to subject-verb agreement.

> Into town comes the circus performers, daredevils of a special kind. A trapeze troupe risks their lives. High above the crowd. Perhaps genetics provide the talent, but practice developes experts. Another risk taker is the Lion tamer. However he don't show any fear, so the big cats will stay calm and managable. Even the clowns incounter danger when they help string the rigging. With eager anticipation the crowd watch and love every minute.

The Dare Devils skydiving in free-fall formation

In the following sentences, write the form of the verb that agrees with the subject.

1. Probably everyone in the United States (dreams, dream) of traveling to another country.
2. There (is, are) hundreds of places to go and things to do and see.
3. It (doesn't, don't) take much effort to find inexpensive ways to visit Europe, Asia, or Africa.
4. A couple of these methods (is, are) practiced by students around the world—backpacking and staying at youth hostels.
5. Either of these methods (helps, help) tourists on a budget.
6. In addition, *Europe on $25 a Day*, a popular travel book, (offer, offers) further advice.
7. For example, there (is, are) special discounts and bargains to watch for.
8. Most of the free events in Europe (is, are) as enjoyable as expensive forms of entertainment.
9. Few of the major tourist attractions (cost, costs) more than several dollars.
10. Besides the selection of specific points of interest, many of the most important decisions for travelers (involves, involve) lodging.
11. Neither a hotel's outside appearance nor its lack of a fancy lobby necessarily (indicate, indicates) its quality.
12. Some of the hotels (has, have) peeling paint on the outside and elegant rooms on the inside.
13. All of the hours spent finding the right hotel, however, (is, are) worthwhile.
14. Of course, everything, from selecting lodgings to deciding what clothes to pack, (depends, depend) on your destination.
15. A group of islands called Baleares, off the coast of Spain, (is, are) home to artists' colonies and spectacular beaches.
16. Anyone who believes in the Loch Ness monster (doesn't, don't) want to miss the lake region of Scotland.
17. From London's Heathrow Airport, forty-five minutes on the subway (delivers, deliver) the drama enthusiast to the West End theater district.
18. No one who loves grand opera, wonderful art, and delicious pasta (want, wants) to bypass Rome.
19. Politics (is, are) a lively process to observe in action at Bonn's parliament.
20. None of the entertainment spots at Monte Carlo (turns, turn) away patrons eager to celebrate.

Writing Theme
Travel

Making Subjects and Verbs Agree **713**

You may wish to use the following exercise as an informal evaluation of student mastery of the rules for subject-verb agreement covered in this handbook.

Managing the Paper Load

To limit the number of items to correct, you may wish to model the first five items orally in class.

WRITING THEME Travel

You may wish to encourage students to jot down this theme in their journals for use in a creative writing assignment such as a travel brochure, an advertisement, or a promotional poster.

Answers on page

Application and Review

These activities have been designed to allow students to apply concepts presented in this handbook. Exercise A requires students to write the correct present-tense form of verbs. Exercises B and C require students to recognize and correct errors in subject-verb agreement. Exercise D challenges students to complete sentences whose subjects require correct present-tense verb forms.

> **Additional Resources**
> • Tests and Assessment
>   Mastery Tests, pp. 91–94
> • Elaboration, Revision, and Proof-reading Worksheets, p. 29

WRITING THEME   Sports

A. Understanding Subject-Verb Agreement

1. is, Singular
2. depict, Plural
3. has, Singular
4. Do, Plural
5. consists, Singular
6. have, Plural
7. appears, Singular
8. exhausts, Singular
9. behave, Plural
10. is, Singular
11. strikes, Singular
12. strike, Plural
13. cross, Plural
14. shift, Plural
15. is, Singular

B. Correcting Agreement Errors

Errors are underlined on page.

1. *The Oxford Companion to Sports and Games* indicates that skiing is one of the oldest outdoor sporting activities in history.
2. A team of archaeologists in Sweden and Finland has discovered skis believed to be 4,500 years old.
3. In those days, a pair of skis was a necessity.
4. Hunting and traveling were much easier to do by gliding across deep snow.
5. Eventually, new boot bindings and ski designs were important in popularizing skiing as a sport.

GRAMMAR
HANDBOOK
38

Writing Theme
Sports

A. Understanding Subject-Verb Agreement   For each of the following sentences, write the correct present-tense form of the verb in parentheses. Then identify each subject and verb as *Singular* or *Plural*.

1. Neither the time nor the place of field hockey's origins (be) certain.
2. Early Greek artifacts and Egyptian drawings (depict) people holding what appear to be hockey sticks.
3. The size of teams in ancient times (have) not been established by archaeologists and art historians.
4. (Do) eleven players make up today's field hockey team?
5. The offense (consist) of five players and the defense of six.
6. The team all (have) the opportunity to score except for the full-backs and the goalie.
7. The give-and-take between the opposing teams (appear) strenuous.
8. Two hours of playing sometimes (exhaust) the best-conditioned athlete.
9. On the other hand, certain players in nearly every sport sometimes (behave) like bullies.
10. The bully, with its distinctive moves, (be) a play found only in field hockey.
11. Each of the players (strike) the ground on his or her side of the ball with the heel of the stick.
12. Players at this point (strike) the opponent's stick over the top of the ball.
13. Both forward lines (cross) the center line as soon as the bully is completed.
14. The halfbacks and fullbacks of the team losing the bully (shift) to their defensive positions.
15. Without doubt, the recipe for continual victories in hockey (be) skill, concentration, and a generous amount of risk taking.

B. Correcting Agreement Errors   Some of the following sentences contain errors in subject-verb agreement. Rewrite the sentences correctly. If there is no error in a sentence, write *Correct*.

1. *The Oxford Companion to Sports and Games* indicate that skiing is one of the oldest outdoor sporting activities in history.
2. A team of archaeologists in Sweden and Finland have discovered skis believed to be 4,500 years old.
3. In those days, a pair of skis were a necessity.
4. Hunting and traveling was much easier to do by gliding across deep snow.
5. Eventually, new boot bindings and ski designs was important in popularizing skiing as a sport.

6. Downhill racing and related events has become a worldwide sporting pastime since the 1924 Winter Olympics.
7. Every year now, an army of skiers carries their equipment and enthusiasm to resorts all across the United States.
8. There are many thrills for skiers who attempt such challenges as the slalom, transverse, and ruade.
9. Skiers on a leisurely cross-country excursion enjoys the quieter delights of the winter scenery.
10. The number of people who pursue the varied pleasures of this ancient sport don't seem to be diminishing.

C. Recognizing Agreement Errors Rewrite the following sentences, correcting errors in subject-verb agreement. If a sentence has no error, write *Correct*.

1. About 15 million Americans runs more than a mile several times a week.
2. The popularity of the sport has led to a wealth of scientific research.
3. Many advantages of running has been well documented.
4. This vigorous exercise strengthen the heart muscle.
5. It also releases a stress-reducing hormone in the brain.
6. There is, however, some disadvantages to running.
7. Shin splints, runner's knee, Achilles' tendonitis, and heel spurs is short-term runners' ailments.
8. More long-term damage result from running with minor injuries and overracing.
9. Most runners does not need to worry about serious injury.
10. A reasonable training program of up to thirty miles a week are considered safe.

D. Making Subjects and Verbs Agree Complete each sentence, using a verb in the present-tense form. Make sure that your subjects and verbs agree.
1. *The Wide World of Sports*
2. Anyone with an interest in sports
3. The host, together with guest experts
4. Everything from Ping-Pong to polo
5. One of the events
6. Excellent camera work and colorful commentary
7. Computer graphics
8. Both the athletes and their coach
9. Neither amateurs nor professionals
10. Two hours of playing

6. Downhill racing and related events have become a worldwide sporting pastime since the 1924 Winter Olympics.
7. Every year now, an army of skiers carry their equipment and enthusiasm to resorts all across the United States.
8. Correct
9. Skiers on a leisurely cross-country excursion enjoy the quieter delights of the winter scenery.
10. The number of people who pursue the varied pleasures of this ancient sport doesn't seem to be diminishing.

C. Recognizing Agreement Errors
Errors are underlined on page.
1. About 15 million Americans run more than a mile several times a week.
2. Correct
3. Many advantages of running have been well documented.
4. This vigorous exercise strengthens the heart muscle.
5. Correct
6. There are, however, some disadvantages to running.
7. Shin splints, runner's knee, Achilles' tendonitis, and heel spurs are short-term runners' ailments.
8. More long-term damage results from running with minor injuries and overracing.
9. Most runners do not need to worry about serious injury.
10. A reasonable training program of up to thirty miles a week is considered safe.

D. Making Subjects and Verbs Agree
Answers will vary. See typical answers below.
1. "The Wide World of Sports" is one of my favorite television programs.
2. Anyone with an interest in sports is likely to follow the Olympics.
3. The host, together with guest experts, is discussing stocks and bonds.
4. Everything from Ping-Pong to polo is available at one great vacation spot.
5. One of the events is being postponed.
6. Excellent camera work and colorful commentary make the film entertaining.
7. Computer graphics interests both my sister and me.
8. Both the athletes and their coach want a larger locker room.
9. Neither amateurs nor professionals ignore the advice of today's dietitians.
10. Two hours of playing seems sufficient.

As you discuss this feature, encourage discussion of the humor in Mr. Language Person's responses. Point out, however, that many writers do confuse *who* and *whom* and *affect* and *effect*. Discuss the correct use of these words.

Students might enjoy developing humorous questions and answers about other problems in grammar. Allow them to work in pairs.

On the Lightside

ASK MR. LANGUAGE PERSON

Once again it is time for "Ask Mr. Language Person," the popular feature wherein we discuss the kinds of common grammatical concerns with which common people tend to encounter problems with.

We'll begin with the first question:

Q: What is the purpose of the apostrophe?

A: The apostrophe is used mainly in hand-lettered small-business signs to alert the reader that an "S" is coming up at the end of a word, as in: WE DO NOT EXCEPT PERSONAL CHECK'S, or: NOT RESPONSIBLE FOR ANY ITEM'S.

Another important grammar concept to bear in mind when creating hand-lettered small business signs is that you should put quotation marks around random words for decoration, as in "TRY" OUR HOT DOG'S, or even TRY "OUR" HOT DOG'S.

Q: When do you say "Who," and when do you say "Whom"?

A: You say "who" when you want to find out something like, for example, if a friend of yours comes up and says, "You will never guess which of your immediate family members just lost a key limb in a freak Skee-Ball accident." You would then reply: "Who?" You say "whom" when you are in Great Britain or you are angry, as in: "And just WHOM do you think is going to clean up after these otters?"

Q: Like many writers, I often get confused about when to use the word "affect," and when to use "infect." Can you help me out?

A: Here is a simple pneumatic device for telling these two similar-sounding words (or gramophones) apart: Just remember that "infect" begins with "in," which is also how "insect" begins, while "affect" begins with "af," which is an abbreviation for "Air Force."

Q: Some business associates and I are trying to compose a very important business letter, and we disagree about the wording of a key sentence. My associates argue that it should be, "Youse better be there alone with the ransom money, on account of we don't want to have to whack nobody's limbs off." I say this is incorrect. Can you settle this argument?

A: Tell your associates they'd better bone up on their grammar! The sentence they're suggesting ends with the preposition "off," and should be corrected as follows: ". . . don't want to have to whack nobody's limbs off with a big knife."

Dave Barry

716

Sketchbook

You are the restaurant critic for your high-school newspaper. Your assignment is to visit the two best-known pizza parlors in the area to compare the pizzas they serve. As you list differences and similarities (in quality, price, service, and atmosphere), you will need to use a variety of prepositions, conjunctions, and interjections. Be sure to answer questions that readers of your column might have.

Additional Sketches

You are an advertising copywriter assigned to write a magazine ad for a new means of transportation. The manufacturers claim that the new vehicle will "make cars obsolete." Visualize a vehicle that could do that. How would it be better than a car? How would it move? What fuel would it use? How much would it cost to buy and run? You have a hundred words with which to persuade customers to buy the vehicle. Choose the most exciting and descriptive nouns, verbs, adjectives, and adverbs. Your boss says, "Make every word count!"

As the host of a talk show called "Off the Wall," you have invited several offbeat guests to appear on tonight's segment. To prepare for the interviews, you must make notes about each person. List some facts about three of the guests, using gerunds, participles, and appositives.

717

To play the role of restaurant critic as a springboard to informal writing

Using the Prompt

Before beginning the activity, underscore that Sketchbook activities are designed to be informal in order to encourage risk taking and experimentation; they are not graded.

Ask students to discuss any restaurant reviews they have read. What information did they find particularly useful? What additional information would they have liked to have?

If possible, have available the menus from the two best-known pizza restaurants in the area. Help students develop and complete a compare-and-contrast chart. Write the names of the two restaurants at the heads of two columns across the top of the chart of the things being compared. Ask students to brainstorm characteristics they will compare; list these down the left side of the chart. In addition to the items suggested in the student text, the list might include such characteristics as variety in pizza toppings; flavor of the sauces; size of the pizzas; appearance of the pizzas; and hours of operation.

Encourage students to use the information in the chart as the basis for a complete restaurant review. Remind them that additional ideas frequently come to people as they write, and stress that students should not feel limited to the ideas in the chart.

Present the Additional Sketches as alternative topics for students who prefer a different starting point. Encourage students to keep their writing in their Writing Portfolios. They may wish to refer to it during future writing projects.

These exercises allow your students to practice skills acquired in Handbooks 35–38. You may wish to use the exercises to provide a thorough review of the material in these chapters or to evaluate student mastery of the concepts.

Additional Resources
- Grammar and Usage Practice Book, pp. 141–143
- Standardized Test Practice

Skills Assessment Test 3
1. D—from each other
2. E
3. B—, all former Chicago Cubs,
4. B—lives
   C—are
5. C—is
6. B—doesn't
   D—Sir Joseph William Swan
7. A—In the family tree of American music,
   B—is
8. E

Skills

A S S E S S M E N T

Directions   One or more of the underlined sections in the following sentences may contain errors of grammar, usage, punctuation, spelling, or capitalization. Write the letter of each incorrect item, then rewrite the item correctly. If there is no error in an item, write E.

> **Example**   In a presidential <u>ellection</u>, voters <u>usually choose</u> <u>among</u>
>   A   B   C
> two <u>major</u> candidates. <u>No error</u>
>   D   E
> **Answer**   A—election; C—between

1. It is traditional <u>among blues musicians</u> to <u>borrow</u> guitar riffs <u>off each other</u>. <u>No error</u>
      A   B   C   D   E

2. Few contemporary writers <u>besides</u> Alice Walker are <u>equally admired</u> for the <u>literary value</u>
                              A   B   C
   and the popular appeal <u>of their work</u>. <u>No error</u>
                     D   E

3. Ernie Banks, <u>Billy Williams</u> and Fergie Jenkins <u>all former Chicago Cubs</u> are three Hall
                    A   B
   of Famers who <u>never</u> played in a <u>World Series</u>. <u>No error</u>
                  C   D   E

4. Some of the eerie coincidences <u>between</u> the <u>lifes</u> of Abraham Lincoln and John F.
                                    A   B
   Kennedy <u>is</u> almost too <u>astounding to believe</u>. <u>No error</u>
           C   D   E

5. <u>No playwright</u> of the past four hundred years <u>has rivaled</u> William Shakespeare, and four
      A   B
   centuries <u>are</u> a long time <u>to go unchallenged</u>. <u>No error</u>
           C   D   E

6. Thomas Edison was a great <u>scientist</u>, but he <u>don't</u> deserve credit for the light <u>bulb. It</u>
                             A   B   C
   was invented by <u>sir Joseph William Swan</u>. <u>No error</u>
                       D   E

7. <u>In the family tree of American music</u> rock-and-roll <u>are</u> descended from <u>jazz</u>, which is a
                     A   B   C
   <u>uniquely</u> American form. <u>No error</u>
     D   E

8. One of the shortest airline <u>flights</u> in the world <u>is</u> between <u>Papa Westray Island</u> and
                            A   B   C
   Westray Island in <u>Scotland; it</u> takes two minutes. <u>No error</u>
                  D   E

9. The authors Maj Sjowal and Per Wahloo, writing together, has become renowned for a
                    A   **B**   **C**
   series of detective novels. No error
           D   **E**

10. The history of newspapers starts in 59 B.C., when news were gathered for a
         A   **B**
    Roman gazette called *Acta Diurna (Action Journal)*. No error
       C   **D**   **E**

11. The candidate with her capable aides have complete control of the situation; we can
                  A   **B**   **C**
    expect a smoothly run campaign. No error
           D   **E**

12. Of the two sisters which one looks more like her Aunt? No error
              A   **B**   **C**   **D**   **E**

13. Is garlic the herb a member of the lilly family? No error
     A   **B**   **C**   **D**   **E**

14. The meeting's purpose is to rise public consciousness about environmental problems. No
        A   **B** **C**   **D**
    error
    E

15. Does anyone object to our tabeling this issue until the next meeting? No error
            A   **B** **C**   **D**   **E**

Directions Each of the following sentences contains a grammatical problem. On your paper write the letter of the sentence that best corrects the problem.

16. Chief Crazy Horse defeated General George Armstrong Custer leading a fierce and dedicated army of Native-American braves.
    A. General George Armstrong Custer leading a fierce and dedicated army of Native-American braves was defeated by Chief Crazy Horse.
    B. Leading a fierce and dedicated army of Native-American braves, Chief Crazy Horse defeated General George Armstrong Custer.
    C. Chief Crazy Horse defeated General George Armstrong Custer to lead a fierce and dedicated army of Native-American braves.

17. A
18. C
19. A
20. B

17. To understand many poems, they should be read out loud, just as songs must be sung and not merely looked at on a piece of paper.
    A. To understand many poems, one should read them out loud, just as one must sing songs and not merely look at them on a piece of paper.
    B. They should be read out loud, just as songs must be sung and not merely looked at on a piece of paper to understand many poems.
    C. Just as songs must be sung, to understand many poems, they should be read out loud, and not merely looked at on a piece of paper.

18. Marguerite de Pioche de la Vergne, a seventeenth-century Frenchwoman, is named as one of the first people to write a novel in *A Handbook to Literature*.
    A. A seventeenth-century Frenchwoman, Marguerite de Pioche de la Vergne, is named as one of the first people to write a novel in *A Handbook to Literature*.
    B. Marguerite de Pioche de la Vergne, a seventeenth-century Frenchwoman, is named as one of the first people to have written a novel in *A Handbook to Literature*.
    C. In *A Handbook to Literature*, Marguerite de Pioche de la Vergne, a seventeenth-century Frenchwoman, is named as one of the first people to write a novel.

19. People can be married at the age of eighteen in all states of the Union having parental consent, but not in Puerto Rico, which has an age limit of twenty-one.
    A. People having parental consent can be married at the age of eighteen in all states of the Union, but not in Puerto Rico, which has an age limit of twenty-one.
    B. Except in Puerto Rico, people can be married at the age of eighteen in all states of the Union having parental consent.
    C. Having an age limit of twenty-one, people can be married at the age of eighteen in all states of the Union having parental consent, but not in Puerto Rico.

20. Kurt Vonnegut began to write a novel about his visit to the Galápagos Islands plugging in the word processor.
    A. Kurt Vonnegut began writing a novel about his visit to the Galápagos Islands plugging in the word processor.
    B. Plugging in the word processor, Kurt Vonnegut began to write a novel about his visit to the Galápagos Islands.
    C. A novel about his visit to the Galápagos Islands plugging in the word processor was written by Kurt Vonnegut.

Clauses and Sentence Structure

WHAT IS A CLAUSE?

A clause is a group of words that contains both a subject and a predicate. There are two kinds of clauses: independent clauses and subordinate clauses.

Independent Clauses

A clause that can stand alone as a sentence is an independent, or main, clause.

Each sentence below has two independent clauses.

The <u>World Series</u> <u>ended</u>, and the football <u>season</u> <u>began</u>.
The <u>instructions</u> <u>were</u> vague, but the <u>nurse</u> <u>nodded</u>.

In both sentences, the subject of each clause has been underlined once. The verb has been underlined twice. The clauses in both examples can stand alone as sentences.

The World Series ended. The football season began.
The instructions were vague. The nurse nodded.

In the sentence below, which clause can stand alone as a sentence?

If the peace <u>treaty</u> <u>is signed</u>, the <u>President</u> <u>will return</u> to the
    United States tomorrow.

Both clauses have a subject and a verb. However, only the independent clause can stand alone as a sentence.

Not a Sentence   If the peace treaty is signed.
Sentence   The President will return to the United
                        States tomorrow.

Subordinate Clauses

A clause that cannot stand alone as a sentence is a subordinate clause. A subordinate clause is sometimes called a dependent clause.

Here are examples of subordinate clauses. In each clause the subject is underlined once and the verb twice.

when the <u>fog</u> <u>lifted</u>   that <u>I</u> <u>like</u> best
after <u>you</u> <u>leave</u>   where <u>she</u> <u>lived</u>

Clauses and
Sentence Structure   **721**

Grammar Handbook 39:

Clauses and Sentence Structure

What Is a Clause?

Objectives

- To distinguish independent clauses from subordinate clauses
- **Writing** To use a variety of subordinate clauses in writing

Teaching Strategies

Speaking and Listening

To help students understand subordinate clauses, have them read aloud the subordinate clauses in the text. Then have them decide whether the clause makes sense by itself. Ask how they would respond if a friend said to them, "When the fog lifted." Elicit that they would need more information to understand the message. Have students practice evaluating a number of independent and subordinate clauses in this way.

Basic Students You might want to explain to these students what the word *subordinate* means (lower in rank or less important). Also, explain that *dependent* means "something that depends on or relies on another thing." Emphasize that even though a subordinate clause contains a subject and a verb, it cannot be a sentence by itself.

WRITING THEME   Journeys

A. Concept Check
Independent and Subordinate Clauses
Answers are underlined on page. There is no subordinate clause in sentence 7.

Writing Theme
Journeys

To form a sentence with a subordinate clause, add an independent clause.

Subordinate ⌐ Independent ⌐
When the fog lifted, we could see the mountains.

Independent ⌐ Subordinate ⌐
This is the view that I like best.

If a clause can stand alone as a sentence, it is independent. If it cannot stand alone as a sentence, it is subordinate.

> The holiday was over before we knew it.
> The holiday was over. (The clause can stand alone as a sentence. It is an independent clause.)
> Before we knew it. (The clause cannot stand alone as a sentence. It is a subordinate clause.)

Certain words are frequently used to introduce subordinate clauses. You will learn more about introductory words on pages 725, 730, and 733. Some of them are listed below.

after	if	when	which
because	that	where	who

Do not confuse a clause with a phrase. A phrase does not have a subject and a verb. For discussion of phrases, see Handbooks 35 and 37.

Clause   The character *who wore a sly grin* seemed the most likely suspect. (The clause *who wore a sly grin* has a subject, *who,* and a verb, *wore*.)

Phrase   The character *wearing a sly grin* seemed the most likely suspect. (The participial phrase *wearing a sly grin* does not have a subject and a verb.)

Practice Your Skills

A. CONCEPT CHECK

Independent and Subordinate Clauses Write the following sentences. Draw one line under each subordinate clause and two lines under each independent clause. One sentence does not have a subordinate clause.

1. It was a cold, windy day at Kitty Hawk when two young men took their flying machine down to the beach.
2. The date, which became part of aviation history, was December 17, 1903.

3. A few spectators, who showed a mild interest in the proceedings, had gathered on the beach.
4. If the experiment were a success, it would open a whole world of possibilities.
5. The rickety contraption on the sand was the first airplane that was complete with engine and pilot seat.
6. The plane, which the two young men called the *Flyer,* was the first powered, controlled aircraft capable of sustained flight.
7. However, it was not the first flying invention; it had been preceded by numerous gliders.
8. After they had made attempts to improve the limited glider, the inventors saw the need for powered flight.
9. The two men, as you have probably already guessed, were Orville and Wilbur Wright.
10. Although there were several initial mishaps that day, the Wright brothers' airplane flew for 59 seconds, covering 852 feet.

B. APPLICATION IN LITERATURE

Clauses and Phrases Write the italicized words from each sentence in the literary excerpt below. Then tell whether the words make up a *Clause* or a *Phrase*.

(1) *Day had broken cold and gray,* exceedingly cold and gray, when the man turned aside (2) *from the main Yukon trail* and climbed the high earth-bank, (3) *where a dim and little-travelled trail led eastward* through the fat spruce timberland. (4) *It was a steep bank,* and he paused for breath at the top, (5) *excusing the act to himself* by looking at his watch. It was nine o'clock. There was no sun nor hint of sun, (6) *though there was not a cloud in the sky.* It was a clear day, and yet there seemed an intangible pall (7) *over the face of things,* a subtle gloom that made the day dark, and (8) *that was due to the absence of sun.* This fact did not worry the man. He was used to the lack of sun. It had been days (9) *since he had seen the sun,* and he knew (10) *that a few more days must pass* before that cheerful orb, due south, would just peep (11) *above the skyline* and dip immediately from view.

The man flung a look back (12) *along the way* he had come. The Yukon lay a mile wide and hidden (13) *under three feet of ice.* (14) *On top of this ice* were as many feet of snow. It was all pure white, rolling in gentle undulations (15) *where the ice-jams of the freeze-up had formed.*

Jack London, "To Build a Fire"

Iditarod Race,
Anchorage to Nome,
Alaska: The starting
line, 1988

Clauses and
Sentence Structure **723**

Individualizing Instruction

ESL Students Suggest that these students write about their journeys to this country. It may be easier for them to concentrate on clauses if they are writing about something real.

C. Application in Writing
The Plot Synopsis
Answers will vary.

C H E C K   P O I N T
PAGES 721–724

You may wish to use the following Checkpoint exercises as an informal evaluation of student mastery of types of clauses.

Managing the Paper Load

To limit the number of exercises to correct, you may wish to pair students for Exercise A and then have them discuss their answers orally. Then assign Exercise B for independent work.

WRITING THEME   Learning

A.
Subordinate clauses are underlined once and independent clauses are underlined twice on page.
1. Independent + Independent
2. Subordinate + Independent
3. Subordinate + Independent
4. Independent + Independent
5. Independent + Subordinate
6. Independent + Independent
7. Subordinate + Independent
8. Subordinate + Independent
9. Independent + Subordinate
10. Independent + Independent

C. APPLICATION IN WRITING

The Plot Synopsis Science-fiction stories often center around unusual journeys. Write a synopsis, or summary, of a science-fiction journey you have read about or seen in a movie or on television—or describe an imaginary journey of your own. Use a variety of subordinate clauses in your synopsis.

C H E C K   P O I N T
PAGES 721–724

A. Write the two clauses in each sentence and identify them as: *Independent + Independent, Subordinate + Independent,* or *Independent + Subordinate.*

1. Elizabeth Cady Stanton grew up in the early nineteenth century, and she had a beloved older brother.
2. Although Elizabeth's father loved her, he favored his son.
3. While she was still quite young, her brother died.
4. She wanted to comfort her father, and she also wanted his love.
5. She decided to learn how to do everything that boys her age did.
6. She wanted to learn to ride horses and climb trees, but she also wanted to learn Greek.
7. When she consulted her minister, he agreed to help.
8. Before much time had passed, he observed Elizabeth's intelligence and decided to let her father know.
9. Her father then enrolled her at the Johnstown Academy, New York, which made Elizabeth extremely happy.
10. She studied hard all year, and she won an award for Greek studies.

B. APPLICATION IN LITERATURE

Clauses Write each italicized group of words. Tell whether the word group is a *Phrase* or *Clause* and identify clauses as *Subordinate* or *Independent.*

(1) She was a large woman *with a large purse* that had everything in it but a hammer and nails. (2) *It had a long strap,* and she carried it slung across her shoulder. (3) It was about eleven o'clock at night, dark, and she was walking alone, *when a boy ran up behind her and tried to snatch her purse.* (4) The strap broke *with the sudden single tug* the boy gave it from behind. (5) But the boy's weight and *the weight of the purse combined* caused him to lose his balance. (6) Instead of taking off full blast *as he had hoped,* the boy fell on his back on the sidewalk and *his legs flew up.* (7) *The large woman simply turned around and kicked him right square in his blue-jeaned sitter.* (8) Then she reached down, picked the boy up by his shirt front, and shook him *until his teeth rattled.* (9) *After that* the woman said, "Pick up my pocketbook, boy, and give it here."

Langston Hughes, "Thank You, M'am"

Writing
—TIP—

Skillful use of clauses adds detail to a paragraph and variety to its sentences.

Adjective Clauses

An adjective clause is a subordinate clause that is used as an adjective to modify a noun or a pronoun.

Like adjectives, adjective clauses tell *what kind* or *which one* about a noun or a pronoun. However, an adjective clause usually follows the word it modifies.

Adjective   *Part-time* students are excused early.

Adjective Clause   Students *who work* part time are excused early.

Words That Introduce Adjective Clauses

Most adjective clauses are introduced by a relative pronoun:

Relative Pronouns   who   whom   whose   that   which

A relative pronoun links or relates the clause to the word it modifies. The relative pronoun also functions within the clause as a subject, an object, or a modifier.

Subject   There is the artist *who painted the mural.* (The relative pronoun *who* is the subject of the verb *painted* in the adjective clause.)

Clauses and
Sentence Structure   **725**

Adjective Clauses

Objectives

- To identify adjective clauses and the words that introduce them
- To distinguish between essential and nonessential adjective clauses
- **Writing** To use adjective clauses to expand and combine sentences

Teaching Strategies

 Individualizing Instruction

Basic Students You might wish to review the function of adjectives (see Grammar Handbook 34, page 620). Explain that adjective clauses answer the same questions and modify the same parts of speech as adjectives. Point out that the whole clause functions as a modifier.

When discussing relative adverbs, make sure students understand that these words introduce clauses that function as adjectives, not adverbs. An adjective clause introduced by a relative adverb modifies a noun or a pronoun; for example, the adjective clause introduced by *where* in the sample sentence modifies the noun *studio*.

 Individualizing Instruction

Advanced Students As the class completes the exercise on page 726, encourage these students to state the function of the relative pronoun within each adjective clause.

WRITING THEME Native American Culture

You might want to encourage students to do additional research on this theme and use it as the subject of a Writer's Workshop assignment.

Concept Check

Adjective Clauses
Clauses are underlined on page.
1. whose; artist
2. who; member
3. None (*that* omitted); exhibit
4. why; reason
5. that; arrowheads
6. None (*that* omitted); weapons
7. where; world
8. whose; culture

Direct Object	The person *whom we asked* was helpful. (The relative pronoun *whom* is the object of the verb *asked* in the adjective clause.)
Object of Preposition	The girl *with whom I spoke* is a cousin. (The relative pronoun *whom* is the object of the preposition *with* in the adjective clause.)
Modifier	Children *whose parents work here* go to the day-care center. (The relative pronoun *whose* modifies the subject of the adjective clause.)

Where, when, why, before, and *since* may also introduce adjective clauses. Such words are sometimes called **relative adverbs** or **coordinating conjuntions.**

We visited a studio *where recordings are made*.

The introductory word in an adjective clause can be omitted and the clause will still function as an adjective.

Lincoln is the President *most historians admire*. (The relative pronoun *whom* has been omitted.)

Sentence Diagraming For information on diagraming sentences with adjective clauses, see page 835.

Practice Your Skills

CONCEPT CHECK

Adjective Clauses Write the adjective clause in each sentence. Then underline the relative pronoun or relative adverb that introduces the clause. If the introductory word has been omitted, write *None*. After each clause, write the word that it modifies.

1. Edgar Heap of Birds is a contemporary artist whose work has been displayed all over the world.
2. He is a Cheyenne tribal member who expresses the Native American experience in his art.
3. This artist created a multimedia exhibit he called "Sharp Rocks."
4. He explained the reason why he gave the exhibit this name.
5. It refers to arrowheads that the Cheyenne used for defense.
6. Sharp rocks were also weapons the tribesmen used in hunting animals for food.
7. Today, Native Americans live in a world where destructive forces are at work against their culture.
8. The danger comes not from weapons but from a larger culture, whose "weapons" are television, radio, and other media.

Writing Theme
Native American Culture

9. This is not an enemy that can be fought with arrowheads.
10. Edgar Heap of Birds's exhibit "Sharp Rocks" appeared at a time when many artistic works actively promoted cross-cultural understanding.

Essential and Nonessential Adjective Clauses

An essential adjective clause is a clause that is essential to the meaning of the sentence.

If an essential clause is omitted, the meaning of the sentence changes or is incomplete. Because essential clauses are necessary to complete the meaning of the sentence, they are not set off with commas. Essential clauses are sometimes called restrictive clauses.

In the city, I need a bike *that can bounce out of potholes*. (Without the clause, the reader would not know what kind of bike is needed in the city.)

A nonessential adjective clause merely adds extra information to the sentence.

The meaning of the sentence would be complete and clear without the clause. Nonessential clauses, sometimes called nonrestrictive clauses, are set off with commas.

This touring bike, *which I borrowed from my aunt,* is perfect for the open road. (The clause simply adds more information to the sentence.)

In Handbook 41 you will learn more about identifying and punctuating essential and nonessential clauses.

Sentence Diagraming For more information on diagraming sentences with adjective clauses, see page 835.

Practice Your Skills

A. CONCEPT CHECK

Essential and Nonessential Adjective Clauses Write the adjective clause in each of the following sentences. Underline the subject in the clause once and the verb twice. After the clause, write the word that it modifies.

1. Sparta was the ancient Greek city-state where physical strength and skill were most highly admired.
2. In Athens, which was Sparta's greatest rival, intellectual achievement was greatly valued.

Writing Theme
Spartan Training

Clauses and
Sentence Structure   **727**

9. that; enemy
10. when; time

Teaching Strategies

Speaking and Listening

Make sure students understand the distinction between essential and nonessential clauses. Remind them that an essential clause is one that is necessary to the meaning of a sentence. To help students distinguish between these two types of clauses, suggest that they read the example sentences aloud, omitting the adjective clauses. Then have them determine whether the sentences make sense. In this way, they can determine whether clauses are essential or nonessential.

> *Additional Resources*
> - Grammar and Usage Practice Book, pp. 147–150

WRITING THEME   Spartan Training

A. Concept Check
Essential and Nonessential Adjective Clauses
Clauses are underlined on page.
  1. where physical strength and skill were most highly admired; city-state
  2. which was Sparta's greatest rival; Athens

3. who were the sons of citizens; youths

4. when they were born; time

5. who probably would not become strong healthy citizens; children

6. where they began their education; barracks

7. which included track, boxing, and wrestling; training

8. who were obedient; children

9. which was required for citizenship; training

10. who had wives; men

B. Drafting Skill

Sentence Combining

Answers will vary. See suggested answers below.

1. The pentathlon, which is still part of modern Olympic games, is one of the oldest Olympic events.

2. A pentathlete, who was the most admired athlete in the ancient Greek games, had to run, jump, and throw well.

3. All children who lived in Athens or Sparta learned these skills.

4. Because he believed in balance, Aristotle praised pentathletes, who were the most well-rounded athletes.

5. The pentathlon consisted of five events that required the athlete to have both upper- and lower-body strength.

6. One event required throwing the discus, which is a heavy, rounded stone, as far as possible.

7. In another, the pentathlete faced the stade (track) races, which demand sprinting speed.

---

3. All Spartan youths <u>who were the sons of citizens</u> were raised to be soldiers.

4. Spartans lived under government supervision from the time <u>when they were born</u>.

5. Weak children, <u>who probably would not become strong healthy citizens,</u> were left on a mountain to die.

6. At age seven, all Spartan boys went to live in government barracks, <u>where they began their education</u>.

7. This education was mostly physical training, <u>which included track, boxing, and wrestling</u>.

8. Even children <u>who were obedient</u> were whipped occasionally to make them better soldiers.

9. A man did not complete his military training, <u>which was required for citizenship</u>, until the age of thirty.

10. Even men <u>who had wives</u> continued to eat in the mess hall with the other soldiers.

B. DRAFTING SKILL

Sentence Combining Below are pairs of sentences. Combine them into one sentence with an adjective clause. Use commas where needed.

> **Example** The pentathlon was part of Spartan military training.
> The pentathlon is now classified as track and field.
> The pentathlon, which is now classified as track and field, was part of Spartan military training.

1. The pentathlon is one of the oldest Olympic events.
   It is still part of modern Olympic games.

2. A pentathlete had to run, jump, and throw well.
   He was the most admired athlete in the ancient Greek games.

3. All children learned these skills.
   The children lived in Athens or Sparta.

4. Because he believed in balance, Aristotle praised pentathletes.
   Pentathletes were the most well-rounded athletes.

5. The pentathlon consisted of five events.
   These events required the athlete to have both upper- and lower-body strength.

6. One event required throwing the discus as far as possible.
   The discus is a heavy, rounded stone.

7. In another, the pentathlete faced the stade (track) races.
   Stade races demand sprinting speed.

8. The competitor might eventually become a fine soldier.
   The Spartans rewarded the competitor.
9. The pentathlon reflected the culture of the Spartans.
   The Spartans highly valued war and preparation for it.
10. The modern Olympic pentathlon includes riding a horse, fencing, shooting, swimming, and running.
   The modern Olympic pentathlon is also based on military skills.

C. APPLICATION IN WRITING

A Comparison Adjective clauses are often used in comparisons. Write a paragraph comparing ancient Spartans and modern Americans. You could begin, "The ancient Spartans, who . . ." Use at least two other adjective clauses in your paragraph.

Adverb Clauses

An adverb clause is a subordinate clause that is used as an adverb to modify a verb, an adjective, or another adverb.

Adverb	We arrived *late*.
Adverb Clause	We arrived *after the bus had left*. (The adverb clause modifies the verb *arrived*.)
	We were sorry *that we had missed the bus*. (The adverb clause modifies the adjective *sorry*.)
	The bus left earlier *than we had expected*. (The adverb clause modifies the adverb *earlier*.)

Like adverbs, adverb clauses tell *how, when, where,* or *to what extent*. They can also tell *why, how much,* and *under what condition*.

How	They spoke *as though they had solved the crime*.
When	*Before it rained*, we planted the seeds.
Where	Many plants thrive *where the winter is cold*.
To What Extent	He does not play the flute *as well as Dermot does*.
Why	*Because a storm was coming*, school closed early.

In the following examples, the subject or the verb or both are omitted from an adverb clause. Clauses from which words have been left out are called **elliptical clauses**.

They are more experienced *than I*. (The verb has been omitted: *than I am*.)

Complete the test *as soon as possible*. (The subject and the verb have been omitted: *as soon as it is possible*.)

8. The competitor, whom the Spartans rewarded, might eventually become a fine soldier.
9. The pentathlon reflected the culture of the Spartans, who highly valued war and preparation for it.
10. The modern Olympic pentathlon, which is also based on military skills, includes riding a horse, fencing, shooting, swimming, and running.

C. Application in Writing
A Comparison
Answers will vary.

Adverb Clauses

Objectives

- To identify adverb clauses and words that introduce them
- **Writing** To use adverb clauses to combine and expand sentences

Teaching Strategies

Teaching Tip: Adverb Clauses

Remind students of the questions that adverb clauses answer and allow them to practice adding clauses to simple sentences. Point out the list of subordinating conjunctions on page 730. Tell students to look for these words as markers of adverb clauses.

Teaching Tip: Elliptical Clauses

Be sure that students understand the concept of omitted words and "understood" meaning. Point out that the omitted words can affect the meaning of the sentence. For example, *He likes her better than I* means "He likes her better than I do." *He likes her better than me* means "He likes her better than he likes me."

Individualizing Instruction

LD Students Provide each of these students with a list that includes the questions that adverb clauses answer, subordinating conjunctions, and sample sentences.

LEP Students Provide these students with additional practice in adverb clauses. Make a set of cards listing subordinating conjunctions. Give students an independent clause as an oral prompt. Then show them a card that contains an appropriate subordinating conjunction. Have individuals use the subordinating conjunction in an adverb clause that can be joined with the independent clause.

ESL Students These students often have difficulty using *although, even though,* and *though.* Point out that these three have the same meaning and are used to introduce adverbial clauses of concession. *Although* is the most formal of the three. *Even though* denotes the strongest sense of concession of the three.

Additional Resources
• Grammar and Usage Practice Book, pp. 151–152

WRITING THEME Maurice Prendergast

Concept Check
Adverb Clauses
Clauses are underlined on page.
1. (when) he was still a child; enjoyed
2. (Although) he was born in Canada and grew up in Boston; studied

Afternoon, Pincian Hill,
by Maurice
Prendergast, 1898
© The Phillips
Collection,
Washington, D.C.

Words Used to Introduce Adverb Clauses

Most adverb clauses start with a subordinating conjunction. A **subordinating conjunction** relates the subordinate clause to the independent clause. Look at the following list.

Commonly Used Subordinating Conjunctions

after	as though	provided that	until
although	because	since	when
as	before	so that	whenever
as if	even though	than	where
as long as	if	though	wherever
as soon as	in order that	unless	while

Practice Your Skills

CONCEPT CHECK

Adverb Clauses Write the <u>adverb clause</u> in each sentence. Put parentheses around the subordinating conjunction. Underline the subject once and the verb twice. Then write the word or words that the clause modifies.

1. Maurice Prendergast enjoyed drawing <u>when he was still a child.</u>
2. <u>Although he was born in Canada and grew up in Boston,</u> he studied art in Paris.

Humanities Connection

Art Note Maurice Prendergast (1859–1924) is considered one of the finest American watercolorists. He is noted for brightly colored geometric areas which seem to float within a scene. As in *Afternoon, Pincian Hill,* Prendergast often used broad splashes of color to create light, airy scenes full of vitality. Ask students to describe their feelings about the painting.

3. <u>When he was in France</u>, Prendergast admired the work of James Whistler.
4. <u>Since he carved picture frames for a living</u>, his interest in painting grew.
5. Prendergast is considered a postimpressionist <u>because he used broad areas of color.</u>
6. Watercolor was his preferred medium <u>when he was young.</u>
7. *Afternoon, Pincian Hill* is a watercolor he painted at age thirty-nine <u>while he was in Europe.</u>
8. <u>Although Prendergast used oils for his later works</u>, these had the same mosaic-like effect as his watercolors.
9. <u>While this talented painter's early works were lively and luminous</u>, his later paintings had a wistful look.
10. <u>Because the artist exhibited in unpopular shows</u>, his following was never great during his lifetime.

Punctuating Adverb Clauses

An adverb clause at the beginning or in the middle of a sentence is set off by commas. None is needed if the clause comes at the end.

> Although she was tired, Hannah did her exercises.
> Hannah, although she was tired, did her exercises.
> Hannah did her exercises although she was tired.

Sentence Diagraming For information on diagraming sentences with adverb clauses, see page 836.

Practice Your Skills

A. CONCEPT CHECK

Adverb Clauses Write the adverb clause in each sentence. Put parentheses around the subordinating conjunction, and underline the subject once and the verb twice. After the clause, write the word or words it modifies.

1. Many people build their own house, <u>even though the task can be time-consuming and exasperating.</u>
2. They usually opt for energy-saving features such as fuel-efficient furnaces and heat pumps, <u>although the initial cost can be high.</u>
3. They also incorporate solar panels into the roof design <u>whenever they can.</u>
4. <u>After the construction crews excavate the building site and put in the footing</u>, they pour concrete for the foundation.

Writing Theme
Homes

5. (As soon as) the concrete sets; arrive and start

6. (until) the roofline is completed; working

7. (so that) the interior is protected from wintry blasts of wind and summer heat; install

8. (before) they finish the outside shell with siding and shingles; install

9. (While) the carpenters are busy outside; arrive

10. (as) they get the house ready for occupancy; painting, installing

B. Drafting Skill
Combining Sentences

Answers will vary. See typical answers below.

1. Although the feudal lords of the Middle Ages had armies to protect them, the lords also built fortresses.

2. Since Europe was in a constant state of war, castles became crucial to defense.

3. Because there were no banks, grocery stores, or prisons, the castle had to fulfill all these functions.

4. When a castle was built atop a high, craggy hill, it was difficult to storm.

5. Since castles built on flat terrain were open to attack, moats became important.

6. Because high walls surrounding a castle were topped with battlements or fortifications, residents could hurl weapons at attackers.

7. Whenever attacks took place, women and children stayed in the keep, an inner tower.

8. Although modern movie sets show castles that have grandeur, medieval castles were usually cold, dark places.

9. Although in the last century people still occupied many castles, in our century most castles have become museums.

10. Where remnants of castles exist, they serve to illustrate earlier concepts of home.

5. As soon as the concrete sets, the carpenters arrive and start laying the joists for the ground floor.
6. Then they frame the walls with 2 by 4's, working steadily until the roofline is completed.
7. The insulators install thick batts of fiberglass in all of the outside walls so that the interior is protected from wintry blasts of wind and summer heat.
8. They install all windows and doors before they finish the outside shell with siding and shingles.
9. While the carpenters are busy outside, the electricians and plumbers arrive to install wiring and circuit breakers, water pipes and drains inside.
10. Many owners elect to complete the interior themselves, painting walls and installing floor tile and carpeting as they get the house ready for occupancy.

B. DRAFTING SKILL

Combining Sentences Combine each of the following pairs of sentences into one sentence with an adverb clause. The subordinating conjunction should reflect the relationship suggested in parentheses. Punctuate your sentence correctly.

1. The feudal lords of the Middle Ages had large armies to protect them.
   The lords also built fortresses. (contrast)
2. Europe was in a constant state of war.
   Castles became crucial to defense. (cause/effect)
3. There were no banks, grocery stores, or prisons.
   The castle had to fulfill all these functions. (cause/effect)
4. A castle was built atop a high, craggy hill.
   A castle was difficult to storm. (time)
5. Castles built on flat terrain were open to attack.
   Moats became important. (cause/effect)
6. High walls surrounding a castle were topped with battlements or fortifications.
   Residents could hurl weapons at attackers. (cause/effect)
7. Attacks took place.
   Women and children stayed in the keep, an inner tower. (time)
8. Modern movie sets show castles that have grandeur.
   Medieval castles were usually cold, dark places. (contrast)
9. In the last century people still occupied many castles.
   In our century most castles have become museums. (contrast)
10. Remnants of castles exist.
    They serve to illustrate earlier concepts of home. (place)

C. APPLICATION IN WRITING

A Letter You have been transported in time to a medieval castle. Write a letter about accomplishing simple, everyday tasks without modern conveniences. Your letter can be informative or humorous. Use a variety of adverb clauses. For example, you may wish to begin with "When I first saw the castle, I . . ."

Noun Clauses

A noun clause is a subordinate clause that is used in a sentence as a noun.

Noun clauses may be used in any way a noun is used. However, they most frequently function as subjects, direct objects, indirect objects, predicate nominatives, and objects of prepositions. Study the examples below. The sentences show the various ways noun clauses may be used.

Subject	Our greatest *concern* is creeping inflation. (Noun)
	<u>What</u> <u>concerns</u> us most is creeping inflation. (Noun Clause)
Direct Object	Can scientists predict *earthquakes*? (Noun)
	Can scientists predict <u>when</u> <u>earthquakes</u> <u>will</u> <u>occur</u>? (Noun Clause)
Indirect Object	We will give the first *caller* a free trip. (Noun)
	We will give <u>whoever</u> <u>calls</u> first a free trip. (Noun Clause)
Predicate Nominative	His problem was *survival*. (Noun)
	His problem was <u>how</u> <u>he</u> <u>might</u> best <u>survive</u> the shipwreck. (Noun Clause)
Object of Preposition	She was worried about the *results*. (Noun)
	She was worried about <u>whether</u> <u>she</u> <u>had placed</u> first in the meet. (Noun Clause)

Words Used to Introduce Noun Clauses

Noun clauses are introduced by relative pronouns and by subordinating conjunctions.

Pronouns	who, whom, whose, which, what, that, whoever, whomever, whatever
Subordinating Conjunctions	how, that, when, where, whether, why, if, since (For a complete list of subordinating conjunctions, see page 730.)

Sentence Diagraming For information on diagraming sentences with noun clauses, see page 836.

Clauses and Sentence Structure **733**

Noun Clauses

Objectives

- To identify noun clauses and words that introduce them
- **Writing** To use noun clauses in writing

Teaching Strategies

Linking Grammar and Literature

On the chalkboard write the following sentence from N. Scott Momaday's *The Way to Rainy Mountain*:

"They were an old council of warlords, come to remind and be reminded of *who they were*."

Have students find the noun clause (italicized) and then tell which word introduces the clause (*who*) and how the clause functions (object of preposition).

Stumbling Block

When discussing the words used to introduce noun clauses, elicit from students that these are the same words used to introduce adjective and adverb clauses. Emphasize that how a clause is used determines whether it is a noun clause, an adjective clause, or an adverb clause.

Writing Theme
Meteors and Comets

Writing
—— **TIP** ——

Skillful use of noun clauses makes expository writing clearer and more precise.

Practice Your Skills

A. CONCEPT CHECK

Noun Clauses and Their Functions Write the noun clauses in each of the following sentences. Tell whether the clause is used as a *Subject*, a *Direct Object*, an *Indirect Object*, a *Predicate Nominative*, or an *Object of a Preposition*.

1. What concerns many scientists is the chance of a collision between the earth and a large meteor.
2. When such a global collision might take place is, of course, unpredictable.
3. The scientists' main question, though, is whether any form of life could survive such a disaster.
4. They know that many small meteors have already hurtled through our atmosphere and crashed into the earth's surface.
5. From what observers deduce from past occurrences, a major collision could occur in the next 50,000 years.

6. Archaeologists have, in fact, suggested that this type of catastrophe resulted in the extinction of the dinosaurs.
7. Existing evidence gives whoever studies it an idea of problems following a massive collision, such as dangerous fires, intense heat, and heavy vapor.
8. The next issue is how any vegetation can grow under vapor clouds blocking the sun.
9. Whether such prehistoric collisions may have affected the planet is a fascinating question.
10. There is some irony in the question of whether such collisions may destroy our planet.

B. APPLICATION IN WRITING

The Explanation Much scientific writing involves explaining—describing how something works, why it happens, or how it began. Write a question about astronomy or about some other aspect of nature. Then write a paragraph that answers the question. In the first sentence of your explanation, reword your question as a noun clause. Use at least three other noun clauses in your paragraph.

CHECK POINT
PAGES 725–735

A. Write the subordinate clause in each of the following sentences. Tell whether the clause is an *Adjective Clause,* an *Adverb Clause,* or a *Noun Clause.* If it is an adjective or an adverb clause, write the word or words it modifies. If it is a noun clause, tell how it is used in the sentence.

1. Everyone should be aware that the food industry routinely adds vitamin supplements to products such as milk and bread, artificial coloring to butter and hot dogs, and chemical preservatives to all manner of products.
2. Some people make it a point to avoid eating foods with any type of additive, even though the Food and Drug Administration vouches for their safety.
3. They buy organically produced foods that are completely free of chemical additives of any kind.
4. You will have to decide for yourself where you stand on the issue.
5. If you are pursuing good nutrition, you must learn how to read food labels.
6. The government requires label information that specifies ingredients and nutritional value for most food products.
7. All the ingredients, which are listed in the order of amount used, must be clearly printed.
8. If food shoppers read labels carefully, they can go home with bags full of chemical-free foods.
9. The Food and Drug Administration determines what constitutes the "minimum daily requirement" of a nutritional element such as vitamin C or protein.
10. The manufacturer must tell what amount of each of these elements is in the product and then list the proportion of the daily requirement.
11. This information, which is called "percent of minimum daily requirements," is on the labels of all domestic foods.
12. You can make good food choices if you take the time to become familiar with food-label information.

> **Writing Theme**
> Food and
> Nutrition

Clauses and
Sentence Structure **735**

Sentence Structure

Objectives

- To recognize and classify simple sentences, compound sentences, complex sentences, and compound-complex sentences
- **Writing** To use sentence-combining skills to create compound, complex, and compound-complex sentences
- **Writing** To use revision skills to eliminate choppy sentences

B. Write the subordinate clauses in the following paragraphs. Tell whether each clause is an *Adjective Clause,* an *Adverb Clause,* or a *Noun Clause.*

(1) <u>If you ask Americans to name their favorite dish,</u> they might say hamburger or apple pie. (2) There are some people, however, <u>who consider pizza the most popular American food.</u> (3) The year 1984 marked the first time <u>when pizzerias outnumbered hamburger restaurants in the United States.</u> (4) Pizza is inexpensive. (5) This is no doubt one reason <u>why it is so popular.</u> (6) Also, it contains most of the basic nutrients that <u>are usually listed on food labels.</u>

(7) Pizza was invented in 1889, <u>when a baker from Naples prepared a special pie for the queen of Italy.</u> (8) Using tomato, basil, and mozzarella cheese, he produced a pie <u>that incorporated the red, green, and white of the Italian flag.</u> (9) If the baker saw some modern pizzas, he would discover <u>that they are stuffed or topped with everything from artichokes to zucchini, and in the Pacific Northwest, even pineapple.</u>

SENTENCE STRUCTURE

Sentences may be grouped into four categories according to purpose.

Declarative	We are raking leaves. (makes a statement)
Interrogative	Will you help? (asks a question)
Imperative	Join the group. (gives a command)
Exclamatory	How fast we'll finish! (expresses strong emotion)

Sentences may also be grouped into categories according to the number of independent and subordinate clauses they contain. There are four sentence structures: simple, compound, complex, and compound-complex.

Simple Sentences

A simple sentence contains one independent clause only.

The parts of a simple sentence may be compound. Each of the following sentences is a simple sentence with compound parts.

Compound Subject	*Freshmen* and *sophomores* faced one another on Field Day in a tug of war.
Compound Verb	They *struggled* and *strained* in the mud.

Compound Direct Object	The winners received *medals* and a *trophy*.
Compound Predicate Adjective	The losing team was *muddy* and *unhappy*.

Compound Sentences

A compound sentence contains two or more independent clauses that are joined together.

The clauses in a compound sentence may be joined with a comma and a coordinating conjunction: *and, but, nor, or, for,* or *yet.*

> The subway <u>car</u> <u>was crowded</u>, *but* <u>we</u> <u>piled</u> in anyway.
> Either <u>we</u> <u>are</u> late *or* <u>you</u> <u>are</u> early. (Note that a comma is not necessary in a short compound sentence.)

The clauses in a compound sentence may be joined by a semicolon.

> <u>Sharon</u> <u>writes</u> the newsletter; <u>we</u> <u>distribute</u> it.

The clauses in a compound sentence may also be joined by a semicolon and a conjunctive adverb: *therefore, however, moreover, nevertheless, consequently.* (For other conjunctive adverbs, see page 666.)

> <u>Alligators</u> <u>appear</u> slow; *nevertheless,* <u>they</u> <u>can move</u> quickly.
> (A conjunctive adverb is usually followed by a comma.)

Sentence Diagraming For information on diagraming compound sentences, see page 837.

Practice Your Skills

CONCEPT CHECK

Simple and Compound Sentences Write each sentence and label it *Simple* or *Compound.* Underline the <u>subject</u> of each independent clause once and the <u>verb</u> twice.

1. <u>Environmentalists</u> <u>are concerned</u> about many endangered species and <u>are striving</u> to increase public awareness of the problem.
2. The <u>United States</u> <u>has</u> already <u>lost</u> many native species; the <u>Carolina parakeet</u> and the <u>passenger pigeon</u> <u>are</u> now extinct.
3. The <u>whooping crane</u> and the <u>California condor</u> <u>have</u> long <u>been</u> on the endangered-species list; now the <u>bald eagle</u> and the <u>prairie dog</u> <u>are being threatened.</u>

Writing Theme
Endangered Species

Clauses and
Sentence Structure **737**

Teaching Strategies

Linking Grammar and Writing

Point out that the close relationship between the meanings of two sentences, not the shortness of the sentences, makes compounding possible. For example, the sentences *The bus was crowded* and *We piled on anyway* can be compounded but not *The bus was crowded* and *We bought a dog.*

Teaching Tip: Compound Sentences

As the class examines the sample compound sentences, ask students to pay particular attention to the use of coordinating conjunctions, conjunctive adverbs, and punctuation.

WRITING THEME Endangered Species

You might want to encourage students to do additional research on this theme and use it as the basis for an oral report or future writing assignment.

Concept Check

Simple and Compound Sentences
Subjects and verbs are underlined on page.
1. Simple
2. Compound
3. Compound

4. Simple
5. Compound
6. Simple
7. Simple
8. Compound
9. Simple
10. Compound
11. Compound
12. Compound

Teaching Strategies

Linking Grammar and Writing

Point out to students that complex sentences are extremely helpful tools for writers who wish to show the relationship of ideas. Such relationships include time sequence, cause and effect, concession, and specification. You may wish to add, however, that writers who value clarity avoid piling up too many subordinate clauses in one sentence.

WRITING THEME   Jet Propulsion

You might wish to encourage students to do additional research on this theme, make notes in their journals, and use their notes as the basis for a research report.

Concept Check
Compound and Complex Sentences
Subjects and verbs are underlined on page.
1. Compound
2. Complex

Writing Theme
Jet Propulsion

4. The <u>reasons</u> for the loss of so many species <u>are</u> complex.
5. Some animal <u>habitats</u> <u>have changed</u> or <u>vanished</u>, but in other cases, <u>animals</u> <u>have been killed</u> for sport or profit.
6. <u>Changes</u> in animal habitats <u>have occurred</u> because of the growth of population and industry.
7. <u>Forests</u> and <u>grasslands</u> <u>have been cleared</u> for housing.
8. <u>Pollution</u> from industrial waste <u>destroys</u> entire ecosystems, and one factory's <u>waste</u> <u>may eliminate</u> a hundred species.
9. A <u>campaign</u> for saving an endangered species <u>may appear</u> in the headlines and <u>alert</u> people temporarily.
10. The <u>buffalo</u> <u>was</u> once on the verge of extinction; so <u>was</u> the peregrine falcon; <u>they</u> <u>were</u> both <u>saved</u> through the concerted actions of dedicated environmentalists.
11. Unfortunately, <u>headlines</u> <u>change</u>, and public <u>concern</u> <u>may</u> not <u>last</u> long enough for the prevention of further damage.
12. <u>People</u> <u>grow</u> tired of hearing about the problem, yet <u>it</u> <u>will</u> never <u>disappear</u> by itself.

Complex Sentences

A complex sentence is one that contains an independent clause and one or more subordinate clauses.

↦——Independent Clause——↴ ↓↦——Subordinate Clause——↴
<u>Clara</u> <u>purchased</u> a typewriter although <u>she</u> <u>wanted</u> a computer.
  (complex sentence with an adverb clause)

↦——Subordinate Clause——↴ ↓↦——Independent Clause——↴
After <u>she</u> <u>cashed</u> her paycheck, my <u>mother</u> <u>bought</u> a VCR
↦——————Subordinate Clause——————↴
on which <u>she</u> <u>had left</u> a small deposit. (complex sentence with an adverb clause and an adjective clause)

Sentence Diagraming   For information on diagraming complex sentences, see page 837.

Practice Your Skills

CONCEPT CHECK

Compound and Complex Sentences   Write each sentence, and underline the <u>subject</u> of each clause once. Underline each <u>verb</u> twice. Label the sentence *Simple, Compound,* or *Complex.*

1. Most <u>people</u> <u>think</u> of jet propulsion as a twentieth-century phenomenon, but <u>they</u> <u>could</u> not <u>be</u> more wrong.
2. Long before there <u>were</u> airplanes, a Greek <u>mathematician</u> and <u>physicist</u> named Hero <u>built</u> the first jet engine.

3. The engine, or "aeolipile," was powered by steam, but it was not designed for any practical use.

4. Hero's engine consisted of a large kettle of boiling water that was connected to a metal ball by two bent pipes.

5. Steam rushed through holes on each side, and its force caused a rapid turning motion in the ball.

6. Later, the Chinese developed rocket power and were using it in military combat by the thirteenth century.

7. In 1678, Ferdinand Verbiest built a model carriage using a jet of steam for power.

8. Before the beginning of the twentieth century, John Barber had patented a gas turbine that was the ancestor of the turbojet.

9. It was a German company that built the first jet plane.

10. However, the basic idea has surely been around a long time.

Compound-Complex Sentences

A compound-complex sentence is a sentence that contains two or more independent clauses and one or more subordinate clauses.

    ┌─Independent Clause──┐ ┌─Subordinate Clause─┐
The instructor explained how a splint is made, and
┌──────────Independent Clause──────────┐
we practiced the technique on one another.

It may help you to think of a compound-complex sentence as a compound sentence with a subordinate clause.

Sentence Diagraming For information on diagraming compound-complex sentences, see page 837.

Practice Your Skills

A. CONCEPT CHECK

Compound, Complex, and Compound-Complex Sentences Write the following sentences. Underline the subject of each independent and subordinate clause once, the verb twice. Label each sentence *Compound, Complex,* or *Compound-Complex.*

1. If you visited the Tower of London, you might see a living, flying, burglar alarm.

2. It is a flock of ravens that lives in the tower, and these birds are fed by British tax money.

3. The Tower of London is actually made up of eight fortresses that have been built over the centuries.

Writing Theme
Inhabitants of
the Air

Clauses and
Sentence Structure **739**

3. Compound
4. Complex
5. Compound
6. Simple
7. Simple
8. Complex
9. Complex
10. Simple

Teaching Strategies

Linking Grammar and Literature

Point out that skillful writers make conscious decisions about crafting longer compound or complex sentences or shorter, more direct ones. Note that short sentences can evoke certain images and feelings. The following passage, for example, was spoken in 1890 by Crowfoot, a Blackfoot orator:

"What is life? It is the flash of a firefly in the night. It is the breath of a buffalo in the wintertime. It is the little shadow which runs across the grass and loses itself in the sunset."

Have students discuss why the shorter sentences work well in this passage.

> **Additional Resources**
> • Grammar and Usage Practice Book, pp. 155–160

WRITING THEME   Inhabitants of the Air

You might want to encourage students to do additional research on this theme and use it as the basis for an oral presentation to a class of younger students.

A. Concept Check
Compound, Complex, and Compound-Complex Sentences
Subjects and verbs are underlined on page.
1. Complex
2. Compound-Complex
3. Complex

4. Compound-Complex
5. Compound
6. Compound
7. Complex
8. Compound
9. Complex
10. Compound-Complex

4. Shortly after the first <u>fortress</u> <u>was built</u>, <u>flocks</u> of ravens <u>discovered</u> this new source of garbage, and <u>they</u> <u>came</u> from the nearby woods in search of food.

5. The <u>ravens</u> <u>became</u> regular visitors, but <u>they</u> <u>didn't become</u> guests of the nation until the seventeenth century.

6. Then, one night, <u>Tower Hill</u> <u>was attacked</u> by the enemies of the king, and the <u>ravens</u> <u>awoke</u>.

7. <u>They</u> <u>began</u> such a raucous battle that the king's <u>guardsmen</u> also <u>awoke</u>.

8. The <u>guardsmen</u> <u>fought</u> off the attack, and the <u>tower</u> <u>was saved</u>.

9. Since <u>he</u> <u>was grateful</u> to the ravens—and also a bit of a joker—<u>King Charles II</u> <u>ordered</u> protection for them.

10. Though three <u>centuries</u> <u>have passed</u>, there <u>are</u> still some <u>ravens</u> in the Tower of London, and <u>tourists</u> <u>love</u> to take pictures of England's flying burglar alarm.

Scarabs,
by M.C.Escher, 1935.

©1990 M.C. Escher Heirs/Cordon Art — Baarn — Holland

B. DRAFTING SKILL

Sentence Combining   Combine and rewrite the sentence sets below to make interesting compound, complex, or compound-complex sentences. Follow the directions given in parentheses. Use correct punctuation.

1. Insects are small. They are mighty. (Compound)
2. You consider their weight. They are in a sense the strongest creatures in nature. (Complex)

B. Drafting Skill

Sentence Combining

Answers will vary. See typical answers below.
1. Insects are small, but they are mighty.
2. If you consider their weight, they are in a sense the strongest creatures in nature.

Humanities Connection

Art Note   In his drawing *Scarabs,* M.C. Escher (1898–1971) plays on the symbolism of circular forms. Ask students how precise black lines and rounded shapes affect them. Remind them that the scarab was a talisman of eternal life in ancient Egypt. Does the drawing make them think of life? Encourage students to use as many different types of sentences as possible.

3. An adult human can pull nine-tenths of his or her own weight. A fully grown horse can pull about eight-tenths of its own weight. An insect can pull about twenty times its own weight. (Compound-Complex)

4. Grasshoppers are good jumpers. Frogs jump impressive distances, too. Their muscles are strong and quick. (Compound-Complex)

5. There is one kind of flea. It is often trained and used in flea circuses. (Complex)

6. This flea can make a standing jump of thirteen inches. It can reach a height of eight inches. (Compound)

7. A human athlete wanted to measure up to that flea. He or she would have to make a standing jump of 450 feet. The jump would reach a height of 275 feet. (Complex)

8. People once believed. Insects could fly as fast as planes. (Complex)

9. A dragonfly was supposed to be able to reach speeds of sixty miles an hour. A deer-botfly was supposed to reach speeds of 820 miles an hour. (Compound)

10. The truth is far from these exaggerations. It is still impressive. (Compound)

11. No insect can go faster than twenty-five miles an hour for long. Some can "sprint" at thirty-five miles an hour for a short distance. (Compound)

12. Most birds can't fly this fast. Few animals can outrace a mosquito. There are exceptions. (Compound-Complex)

13. One considers all these qualities. It remains true. The insect world's greatest strength lies in its adaptability. (Complex)

14. Insects are small and fragile. They exist in more life zones than do all other animals combined. (Compound-Complex)

15. Almost a million kinds of insects have been discovered by scientists. The number is growing every day. (Compound)

C. REVISION SKILL

Eliminating Choppy Sentences Revise the following paragraph by breaking up the strings of short sentences. Change some of the simple sentences into compound, complex, or compound-complex sentences. You may add or delete words as necessary. Also proofread and correct any errors in spelling or mechanics that you find. Make a clean copy of your revised paragraph.

> One of the worlds greatest delicacies is bird's-nest soup. This Oreintal soup is made with the white nests of a tiny bird. The birds are called swiftlets. The swiftlets build there nests on the high walls of sea caves. The caves are located along the coasts of Southeast Asia. The nests are very hard to find. They

3. Though an insect can pull about twenty times its own weight, an adult human can pull nine-tenths of his or her own weight, and a fully grown horse can pull about eight-tenths of its own weight.

4. Grasshoppers are good jumpers, and frogs jump impressive distances, too, because their muscles are strong and quick.

5. There is one kind of flea that is often trained and used in flea circuses.

6. This flea can make a standing jump of thirteen inches, and it can reach a height of eight inches.

7. If a human athlete wanted to measure up to that flea, he or she would have to make a standing jump of 450 feet that would reach a height of 275 feet.

8. People once believed that insects could fly as fast as planes.

9. A dragonfly was supposed to be able to reach speeds of sixty miles an hour, and a deer-botfly was supposed to reach speeds of 820 miles an hour.

10. The truth is far from these exaggerations, but it is still impressive.

11. No insect can go faster than twenty-five miles an hour for long, but some can "sprint" at thirty-five miles an hour for a short distance.

12. Although there are exceptions, most birds can't fly this fast, and few animals can outrace a mosquito.

13. When one considers all these qualities, it remains true that the insect world's greatest strength lies in its adaptability.

14. Insects are small and fragile, but they exist in more life zones than do all other animals combined.

15. Almost a million kinds of insects have been discovered by scientists, and the number is growing every day.

C. Revision Skill
Eliminating Choppy Sentences
Errors are underlined on page. Answers will vary. See typical answers below.

One of the world's greatest delicacies is bird's-nest soup. This Oriental soup is made with the white nests of tiny birds called swiftlets. On the high walls of sea caves that are located along the coasts of Southeast Asia, the swiftlets build their nests. These nests are very hard to find, but they are even harder to collect because they are very fragile. Nest collectors, who carry candles for light, use bamboo ladders to climb up the walls of the caves. Some of these ladders are 200 to 300 feet tall, and it can take as long as an hour to climb back down. The nests, however, are extremely valuable; in fact, they are actually worth their weight in gold. Because of the nests' value, the caves are guarded night and day to prevent outsiders from stealing them.

Using Clauses Correctly

Objectives

- To identify sentence fragments consisting of unattached subordinate clauses
- To use *who* and *whom* correctly
- **Writing**   To use revision skills to eliminate misplaced clauses

Teaching Strategies

Linking Grammar and Literature

Ask students why professional writers might sometimes use sentence fragments (to imitate speech patterns, to show a character's thoughts, to show interrupted actions). Elicit from students that sentence fragments are common in oral language and in written dialogue. Emphasize that nonfiction writers use complete sentences to express ideas and describe events.

WRITING THEME   The Leaning Tower of Pisa

Revision Skill

Eliminating Sentence Fragments

Answers will vary. See typical answers below.
1. Sentence
2. The tower looks as if it might fall over at any moment.
3. Sentence
4. Tourists, who visit the tower by the thousands every year, often wonder what makes it lean.
5. They always ask how the tipping happened.
6. The cause lies in the construction of the tower, which was begun in 1174.
7. Sentence

---

are even harder to collect. The nests are very fragile. Nest collectors use bamboo ladders to <u>clime</u> up the walls of the caves. Some ladders are 200 to 300 feet tall. Collectors carry candles for light. It can take as long as an hour to climb back down. The nests are extremely valuable. In fact, they are actually worth their <u>wieght</u> in gold. <u>Becauze</u> of the nests' value, the caves are guarded night and day to prevent theft.

U SING CLAUSES CORRECTLY

As you begin to add clauses to your sentences, watch for the problems of sentence fragments and misplaced clauses.

Avoiding Sentence Fragments

Although a subordinate clause has a subject and a verb, it cannot stand alone as a sentence because it does not express a complete thought.

The TV is on.   While the TV is on.

The first word group is a sentence. It expresses a complete thought. The subordinate clause *While the TV is on* leaves the reader wondering what happens while the TV is on. Treating a subordinate clause as a sentence is a common cause of fragments. You can correct this kind of sentence fragment by making the clause part of a sentence.

While the TV is on, we can't hear the doorbell.

Practice Your Skills

REVISION SKILL

Eliminating Sentence Fragments Decide whether each group of words below is a complete sentence or a sentence fragment. If the word group is a sentence, write *Sentence* on your paper. If the word group is a fragment, make it a complete sentence.

(1) Why is the Leaning Tower of Pisa one of the seven wonders of the modern world? (2) As if it might fall over at any moment. (3) It has, however, stood for hundreds of years. (4) Who visit it by the thousands every year. (5) How it happened. (6) The construction of the tower, which was begun in 1174. (7) It took nearly two hundred years to build the tower.

Writing Theme
The Leaning Tower of Pisa

(8) When the ground beneath the tower started to sink after the first three stories were built. (9) Until it was leaning more than sixteen feet out of line. (10) However, it has tipped only one more foot in the last one hundred years.

Avoiding Misplaced Clauses

Place adjective clauses and adverb clauses as close as possible to the words they modify. Otherwise the sentence may be absurd, inaccurate, or unintentionally humorous.

Unclear   They carelessly set the plant on a table that was dripping wet. (Since the clause seems to modify *table,* the sentence is not accurate.)

Clear   They carelessly set the plant that was dripping wet on a table.

Sometimes a misplaced clause makes the meaning of a sentence unclear. In the two revisions of the unclear sentence below, notice how the meaning changes.

Unclear   Mother told me as soon as I got home to start dinner. (The meaning is unclear.)

Clear   As soon as I got home, Mother told me to start dinner. (I was told as soon as I got home.)

Clear   Mother told me to start dinner as soon as I got home. (I was to start dinner as soon as I got home.)

Remember to place clauses correctly so that the intended meaning of a sentence is clear.

Practice Your Skills

REVISION SKILL

Eliminating Misplaced Clauses Rewrite the following paragraph, correcting each misplaced clause. Some sentences are correct.

(1) There are remnants of great stone cities in areas of Central America that were built by the Mayas. (2) Now the cities are overgrown by jungle plants which are joined by a network of magnificent paved roads. (3) Elaborate causeways, which had been accurately surveyed, were the work of skilled mathematicians. (4) At the height of its fame, one city possessed architecture as complex as ours today when splendid temples and halls were built. (5) A huge temple covered an acre that rose to a height of seventy-five feet. (6) Nearby were halls, which were supported by seventy decorated columns, as well as

> **Writing Theme**
> Mayan
> Civilization

Clauses and
Sentence Structure   **743**

7. The Well of Sacrifice, <u>which was a deep pit</u>, was also located in this city.

8. <u>While they were still alive</u>, men, women, and children were thrown into the pit to appease the gods.

9. The city thrived for a period that lasted for two hundred years and then, in the fifteenth century, came to a sudden and mysterious end.

10. The inhabitants, <u>whose fates remain unknown</u>, suddenly vanished from the city.

Teaching Strategies

Stumbling Block

Many students have difficulty using *who* and *whom* correctly. Be sure that students understand that the choice of *who* or *whom* depends on the pronoun's function in the clause. Thus "Give this to *whoever* answers the door" is correct because *whoever* is the subject in the clause, and "Give this to *whomever* you choose" is correct because *whomever* is the object in the clause.

Additional Resources
- Grammar and Usage Practice Book, pp. 161–166

WRITING THEME   Stonehenge

Concept Check
Who and *Whom*
Answers are underlined on page.

---

courtyards and sunken gardens. (7) The Well of Sacrifice was also located in this city <u>which was a deep pit</u>. (8) Men, women, and children were thrown <u>into the pit to appease the gods</u> while they were still alive. (9) The city thrived for a period <u>that lasted for two hundred years</u> and then, in the fifteenth century, came to a sudden and mysterious end. (10) The inhabitants suddenly vanished from the city <u>whose fates remain unknown</u>.

Using *Who* and *Whom*

Who is a subject form. *Whom* is an object form. The use of *who* or *whom* in a subordinate clause depends on whether the pronoun is used in the clause as a subject, a predicate nominative, or an object.

Subject	The outfielder *who **made** that catch* is a rookie.
Predicate Nominative	Do you know *who that **player** **is**?* (That player is who.)
Direct Object	The outfielder *whom **we** **cheered*** tipped his cap. (We cheered whom.)
Object of Preposition	The rookie *to whom **he** **hit** the ball* made a spectacular catch against the outfield wall. (Hit the ball to whom.)

Practice Your Skills

CONCEPT CHECK

Who* and *Whom   Write the pronoun that correctly completes each of the following sentences.

1. Scientists have long wondered (<u>who</u>, whom) the builders of England's mysterious Stonehenge were.
2. For years, the Druids were the people to (who, <u>whom</u>) the feat was credited.
3. Recently, however, a controversy has been stirred by archaeologists (<u>who</u>, whom) have a different opinion.
4. These archaeologists believe that the Druids, (<u>who</u>, whom) were sun-worshipers, came to the area at least a thousand years after Stonehenge was constructed.
5. According to the new theories, the first builders were probably a Neolithic, or New Stone Age, people (<u>who</u>, whom) arrived in Britain about 3000 B.C.
6. This is a group about (who, <u>whom</u>) little is known.

Stonehenge,
Salisbury, England

7. Scholars do know that later contributors to Stonehenge were farmers for (who, <u>whom</u>) the movements of sun and moon were very important.
8. That knowledge led Gerald Hawkins, (<u>who</u>, whom) is an American professor, to uncover the possible purpose of Stonehenge.
9. It was he (<u>who</u>, whom) determined that it probably served as a sort of primitive computer.
10. These early farmers, (who, <u>whom</u>) historians once called primitive, used Stonehenge to predict weather cycles and the best times to plant crops.

CHECK POINT
PAGES 736–745

A. Identify each sentence as *Simple, Compound, Complex,* or *Compound-Complex.*

1. Nearly four thousand years ago, the Chinese invented something that could be called ice cream, and vendors sold it on the street.
2. It was a sort of pasty ice milk that was made from rice and spices.
3. In A.D. 132 Chang Heng invented a forerunner of today's seismograph.
4. When an earth tremor occurred, a pendulum inside an eight-foot-tall urn moved.
5. It swung in the direction of the tremor and tilted one of eight horizontal arms.
6. On the outside of the urn were representations of eight dragons.

Writing Theme
Inventions

Clauses and
Sentence Structure **745**

CHECK POINT
PAGES 736–745

You may wish to use the following Check-point exercises as an informal evaluation of student mastery of the rules of sentence structure covered in this handbook.

WRITING THEME Inventions

You might want to encourage students to do additional research on this theme and use it as the subject of a Writer's Workshop assignment or of an oral report.

A.
1. Compound-Complex
2. Complex
3. Simple
4. Complex
5. Simple
6. Simple

7. Complex
8. Simple
9. Compound
10. Compound-Complex
11. Complex
12. Simple
13. Simple
14. Compound
15. Complex
16. Compound
17. Compound-Complex
18. Complex

7. Each dragon's mouth held a ball that was released as the urn tilted.
8. The ball fell into the mouth of a brass frog beneath it.
9. The dragons and frogs were aligned with the points of a compass, so the released ball roughly indicated the earthquake area.
10. Paper as we know it was made first in China, and then it found its way to the rest of the world.
11. Ts'ai Lun, who served in the court of Emperor Ho Ti, first used the inner bark of the mulberry tree for paper fiber.
12. The Chinese also made paper pulp from rags, rope, and old fishing nets.
13. Printing probably also started in China.
14. Printers carved characters on wood and then inked the raised images; later they transferred the ink to paper.
15. The compass, which greatly aided navigation, is another Chinese contribution.
16. A piece of magnetized metal was attached to a straw or a cork, and the device was floated in a bowl of water.
17. Historians are not sure of when or where the weaving of silk was invented, but they do know silk was first used in China.
18. Today, China produces more raw silk than any other country in the world does.

B. Decide if each word group below is a sentence fragment or an incorrect sentence. If the word group is a fragment, add your own words to make it a sentence. If the word group is a sentence, correct the misplaced clause or the incorrect use of *who* or *whom*.

1. A machine was invented by an ancient Greek that could be coin-operated.
2. Hero, a scientist whom lived in Alexandria in the first century A.D., was a very productive inventor.
3. That he was credited with designing a forerunner of the calculator.
4. This mileage meter was mounted on a carriage which had a wheel and gears inside a box.
5. A combination level and angle-measuring device for surveyors.
6. Hero had many friends for who he invented ingenious toys and amusements.
7. Puppet shows with curtains that rose and fell amazed his guests when a string was pulled.
8. Who used steam or hot air to operate some of his creations.
9. He developed a device handy in the kitchen that extracted olive oil and grape juice.
10. Throughout history there have been few people whom have demonstrated such genius.

B.

Errors are underlined on page. Answers will vary. See typical answers below.

1. An ancient Greek invented a machine that could be coin-operated.
2. Hero, a scientist who lived in Alexandria in the first century A.D., was a very productive inventor.
3. Did you know that he was credited with designing a forerunner of the calculator?
4. This mileage meter, which had a wheel and gears inside a box, was mounted on a carriage.
5. He also designed for surveyors an instrument that was a combination level and angle-measuring device.
6. Hero had many friends for whom he invented ingenious toys and amusements.
7. Puppet shows with curtains that rose and fell when a string was pulled amazed his guests.
8. He was an inventor who used steam or hot air to operate some of his creations.
9. He developed a device that extracted olive oil and grape juice and was handy in the kitchen.
10. Throughout history there have been few people who have demonstrated such genius.

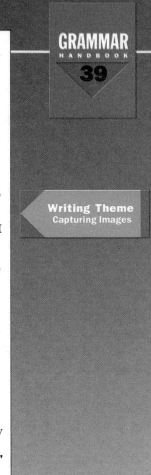

GRAMMAR
H A N D B O O K
39

Writing Theme
Capturing Images

A. Recognizing Types of Sentences Identify each sentence below as *Simple, Compound, Complex,* or *Compound-Complex.*

(1) Today, photography is a national hobby, and we owe it all to George Eastman, a shy man who rarely allowed his picture to be taken. (2) The work of Eastman and others led to greatly improved cameras. (3) Now, if you can push a button, you can take a picture. (4) Cameras have also become much smaller, and they are inexpensive. (5) In fact, you can even buy a camera that you use once and then discard!

B. Application in Literature Write *Adjective, Adverb,* or *Noun* to identify each italicized clause.

(1) *When I think of the hometown of my youth,* all that I seem to remember is dust—the brown, crumbly dust of late summer—arid, sterile dust (2) *that gets into the eyes and makes them water, gets into the throat and between the toes of bare brown feet.* I don't know (3) *why I should remember only the dust.* Surely there must have been lush green lawns and paved streets under leafy shade trees somewhere in town; but memory is an abstract painting—it does not present things (4) *as they are,* but rather (5) *as they feel.* And so, (6) *when I think of that time and that place,* I remember only the dry September of the dirt roads and grassless yards of the shantytown (7) *where I lived.*

(8) *Whenever the memory of those marigolds flashes across my mind,* a strange nostalgia comes with it and remains long (9) *after the picture has faded.* . . . I think of those marigolds at the strangest times. I remember them vividly now as I desperately pass away the time waiting for you, (10) *who will not come.*   **Eugenia Collier, "Marigolds"**

C. Using Different Kinds of Clauses Write each sentence. Add a subordinate clause, following the instructions in parentheses.

1. Photography, _____ , is similar to some kinds of painting. (an adjective clause beginning with *which*)
2. _____ , a photographer may spend days looking for good subjects. (an adverb clause beginning with *Before*)
3. _____ is the way light affects the subjects, as well as composition, color, and value. (a noun clause beginning with *What*)
4. _____ , they are not the only subjects for a good photographer. (an adverb clause beginning with *although*)
5. Landscapes, city buildings, animals, and everyday objects are all subjects _____ . (an adjective clause beginning with *that*)

Clauses and
Sentence Structure   **747**

Application and Review

These activities have been designed to allow students to apply concepts presented in this handbook. Exercise A requires students to identify and classify types of sentences. Exercise B requires students to identify types of clauses. For Exercise C, students must demonstrate an understanding of the use of various types of subordinate clauses. Exercise D requires students to correct sentence fragments, misplaced clauses, and incorrect uses of *who* and *whom.*

Additional Resources
- Tests and Assessment, Mastery Tests, pp. 95–100
- Elaboration, Revision, and Proofreading Worksheets, p. 30

WRITING THEME   Capturing Images

A. Recognizing Types of Sentences
1. Compound-Complex
2. Simple
3. Complex
4. Compound
5. Complex

B. Application in Literature
1. Adverb
2. Adjective
3. Noun
4. Adverb
5. Adverb
6. Adverb
7. Adjective
8. Adverb
9. Adverb
10. Adjective

C. Using Different Kinds of Clauses
Answers will vary. See typical answers below.
1. Photography, which is done with a camera instead of a brush, is similar to some kinds of painting.
2. Before he or she takes a picture, a photographer may spend days looking for good subjects.
3. What the photographer looks for is the way light affects the subjects, as well as composition, color, and value.
4. Although people are interesting, they are not the only subjects for a good photographer.
5. Landscapes, city buildings, animals, and everyday objects are all subjects that have merit.

6. Perceptive photographers know that almost any subject can make a prize-winning shot.

7. Everyday subject matter, which most beginners sometimes overlook, can often be as interesting as exotic or very elaborate scenes.

8. A common vegetable can be photographed so that it seems astonishingly beautiful.

9. Images that both catch the eye and appeal to the senses are rarely hard to find.

10. For most photographers, the trouble is deciding how to present each subject in a thought-provoking way.

D. Writing Sentences Correctly

Errors are underlined on page. Answers will vary. See suggested answers below.

1. Before there were movies with sound, filmmakers faced special challenges.

2. Filmmakers who wanted to tell a story used striking visual images.

3. Over their popcorn boxes, moviegoers watched silent black-and-white films that expressed everything by action alone.

4. These early films, which had very simple plot developments, delighted audiences.

5. *The Great Train Robbery,* which was the first complete-story movie, was produced in 1902.

6. Often no more than rooms with folding chairs and a white wall, nickelodeons were theaters that charged a nickel to see a moving picture.

7. The film comedians whom people seemed to like most relied heavily on physical humor, such as flying falls, and clumsy accidents.

8. Although the silent screen was not devoted entirely to high adventure and wild slapstick humor, those kinds of films were extremely popular.

9. One of the classic silent dramas, *Potemkin,* which portrayed the class struggles in Europe in the early part of the century, was made by a Russian director.

10. There are many film historians today for whom this movie is a masterpiece of the silent screen.

---

6. Perceptive photographers know _____ . (a noun clause beginning with *that*)

7. Everyday subject matter, _____ , can often be as interesting as exotic or very elaborate scenes. (an adjective clause beginning with *which*)

8. A common vegetable can be photographed _____ . (adverb clause beginning with *so that*)

9. Images _____ are rarely hard to find. (an adjective clause beginning with *that*)

10. For most photographers, the trouble is deciding _____ . (a noun clause beginning with *how*)

D. Writing Sentences Correctly Each item below contains an error: a sentence fragment, a misplaced clause, or an incorrect use of *who* or *whom*. Rewrite each sentence correctly, adding words as needed.

1. Before there were movies with sound.
2. Filmmakers whom wanted to tell a story used striking visual images.
3. Moviegoers watched silent black-and-white films over their popcorn boxes that expressed everything by action alone.
4. Which had very simple plot developments.
5. *The Great Train Robbery* was produced in 1902, which was the first complete-story movie.
6. Nickelodeons were theaters, often no more than rooms, with folding chairs and a white wall that charged a nickel to see a moving picture.
7. The film comedians who people seemed to like most relied heavily on slapstick, physical humor, such as flying falls and clumsy accidents.
8. Although the silent screen was not devoted entirely to high adventure and wild slapstick humor.
9. One of the classic silent dramas, *Potemkin,* was made by a Russian director, which portrayed the class struggles in Europe in the early part of the century.
10. There are many film historians today for who this movie is a masterpiece of the silent screen.

Capitalization

PROPER NOUNS AND PROPER ADJECTIVES

Capitalize proper nouns and adjectives.

A **proper noun** is the name of a particular person, place, thing, or idea. A common noun, on the other hand, names a general class. Proper nouns are capitalized. Common nouns are not.

Proper Noun	Common Noun
Shakespeare	writer
India	country
Elizabeth	queen

A **proper adjective** is an adjective formed from a proper noun.

Proper Noun	Proper Adjective
Shakespeare	Shakespearean
India	Indian
Elizabeth	Elizabethan

There are many different kinds of proper nouns. The following rules will help you to identify them and capitalize them correctly.

Names of People and Personal Titles

Capitalize people's names. Also capitalize the initials that stand for people's names.

John Lennon   H.G. Wells   Susan B. Anthony

Capitalize titles used before people's names. Also capitalize abbreviations for those titles.

Justice Sandra Day O'Connor   Dr. Elizabeth Blackwell
Dame Kiri Te Kanawa   Father Jacques Marquette

The titles *Miss, Ms., Mrs.,* and *Mr.* are always capitalized. The abbreviations *Jr.* and *Sr.,* which follow names, are also capitalized.

Mrs. Bennett   Mr. Ralph Bouquard, Jr.

In general, do not capitalize a title when it follows a person's name or when it is used without a proper name.

Barb Sloan, president of Lake Bank, is on the school board.
The judge has given the jury instructions.

Capitalization

Proper Nouns and Proper Adjectives

Objectives

- To capitalize proper nouns and adjectives
- To capitalize correctly the names of people, personal titles, and words referring to family relationships, the Supreme Being, and sacred writings
- To identify and correct errors in capitalization

Teaching Strategies

Teaching Tip: Proper Adjectives

Point out to students that most proper adjectives are derived from the names of persons and from geographical names, especially countries: Spanish settlement, French design, Japanese industry.

Linking Grammar and Writing

Point out that capitalization of personal titles often helps to avoid confusion. For example, *Ms.* is a personal title, whereas *ms.* is the standard abbreviation for "manuscript." Also, point out that a personal title, whether it is abbreviated or spelled out, always requires capitalization when used before a name: for example, *Dr. Blackwell, Doctor Blackwell.*

 Individualizing Instruction

ESL Students Languages utilizing other writing systems, such as Hindi, Chinese, and Arabic, do not distinguish between small and capital letters. Therefore, all capitalization rules will be new concepts for students who speak these languages.

In German, all nouns are capitalized. German-speaking students will have to distinguish between common and proper nouns in order to follow English rules.

Evaluating To help students appreciate the category of "uniquely important positions," give some contrasting examples of titles that would not be capitalized if used without a person's name: for instance, senator, bishop, pastor, judge.

Stumbling Block

Students may have difficulty remembering the rules for capitalizing titles indicating family relationships. Give them additional sentences to clarify these rules.

Additional Resources

- Tests and Assessment
  Pretests, pp. 31–32
- Grammar and Usage Practice
  Book, pp. 167–168

WRITING THEME Ballooning

You might want to encourage students to do additional research on this theme and use it as the subject of a Writer's Workshop assignment.

A. Concept Check

Proper Nouns and Adjectives

Words to be capitalized are underlined on page.

Ancient scroll of the
Pentateuch

Writing Theme
Ballooning

750 Grammar Handbook

Capitalize a title used without a person's name if it refers to a head of state or anyone in a uniquely important position.

the **P**resident of the United States
the **V**ice-**P**resident of the United States
the **S**ecretary of **S**tate (and other Cabinet members)
the **C**hief **J**ustice of the Supreme Court
the **P**ope

Family Relationships

Capitalize the titles indicating family relationships when such titles are used as names or as parts of names.

What was **D**ad like when he was sixteen, **G**randma?
The person who just called was **A**unt Allison.

If the title is preceded by a possessive adjective or by _a, an,_ or _the,_ it is not capitalized.

Our uncle works as a scientist overseas.
My mom's car needs a new battery.

The Supreme Being and Sacred Writings

Capitalize all words referring to God, to the Holy Family, and to religious scriptures.

the **A**lmighty   the **B**ible   **A**llah
the **L**ord   the **T**almud   the **N**ew **T**estament

Capitalize personal pronouns referring to God.

They asked the Lord for **H**is blessing.

Do not capitalize the words _god_ and _goddess_ when they refer to mythological deities.

Practice Your Skills

A. CONCEPT CHECK

Proper Nouns and Adjectives Write the following sentences, using capital letters where necessary.

1. The <u>bible</u> and other creation stories, such as tales of the <u>buddha</u>, separated creatures of the air from those of the earth, but the development of hot-air balloons sent people and animals into the sky.
2. In the late 1700's, <u>joseph montgolfier</u> of <u>france</u> sent a rooster, a duck, and a sheep into space in a smoke-filled bag.

3. Montgolfier, assisted by his brother, <u>jacques étienne</u>, had earlier launched an unmanned balloon which traveled a little more than a mile.

4. According to <u>aunt ruth</u>, who writes about ballooning, later that year two <u>frenchmen</u>, burning wood and straw to heat the air, flew over <u>paris</u> for 23 minutes in a <u>montgolfier</u> balloon.

5. Two years later an <u>american</u> doctor, <u>john jeffries</u>, and a <u>frenchman</u>, <u>Jean-pierre blanchard</u>, crossed the channel between <u>england</u> and <u>france</u> in a balloon filled with hydrogen.

6. Blanchard's wife, <u>madeleine-sophie</u>, was also a balloonist.

7. In 1793, <u>president george washington</u> watched <u>blanchard</u> make the first balloon ascent in the <u>united states</u>.

8. In the 1950's, with the approval of the <u>president</u>, the <u>united states</u> launched a series of balloon flights designed to explore the stratosphere.

9. An altitude record of 102,800 feet was set by <u>commander malcolm ross</u> and <u>lieutenant commander victor a. prather, jr.</u>, of the <u>united states</u> in 1961.

10. In 1984, two centuries after the first ascent, <u>air force captain joseph w. kittinger, jr.</u>, made the first solo balloon flight from the <u>united states</u> to <u>europe</u>.

Mexican balloon race

B. PROOFREADING SKILL

Correct Capitalization The following paragraphs contain errors in capitalization. On your paper, write the <u>incorrectly</u> capitalized <u>words</u> correctly after the number of the sentence in which they appear. Write *Correct* for the one sentence that is correctly capitalized.

(1) The hot-air balloon *Children's Moon* is a flying sculpture created by an artist from <u>vienna</u>, <u>austria</u>. (2) The artist, <u>andré heller</u>, considers the sky an "incredible stage" that most other artists have overlooked. (3) As a child, Heller dreamed about a moon with six eyes. (4) The <u>viennese</u> artist used this dream as the inspiration for *<u>children's moon</u>*. (5) This and two other flying sculptures, *Kiki* and *The Dream Lab,* were given to <u>america</u> by the people of <u>vienna</u>. (6) Flying high over large <u>american</u> cities such as <u>philadelphia</u>, these sculptures have often been reported to the police as UFOs. (7) The flying <u>Sculptures,</u> which range in height from 69 to 123 feet, are flown by licensed <u>Pilots</u> with the help of computers.

Capitalization **751**

Geographical Names

Objectives

- To understand and use the rules for capitalizing geographical names correctly
- To capitalize correctly words referring to directions, geographical sections, and bodies of the universe
- To identify and correct errors in capitalization, spelling, and punctuation

Teaching Strategies

Stumbling Block

Students may be confused about the rules for capitalizing directions and sections. You might use the following activity to encourage the class to generate additional examples. Have small groups prepare promotional advertisements to visit your city or state. Locate the area in sentences like the following: "Sacramento is one of the most beautiful cities in the West" or "Sacramento is northeast of San Francisco and almost due north of Stockton."

(8) The art of <u>mr. heller</u> has also extended in other directions. (9) In the summer of 1987, he created a show that included a carousel by <u>keith haring</u>, a glass labyrinth by <u>roy lichtenstein</u>, an "enchanted" tree by <u>david hockney</u>, and works by twenty other artists. (10) The show was planned to spread <u>heller's</u> reputation throughout <u>europe</u> and <u>north america</u>.

GEOGRAPHICAL NAMES

In a geographical name, capitalize the first letter of each word except articles and prepositions.

If the article *the* appears before a place name, it is not part of the name and is therefore not capitalized.

Continents	**A**frica, **N**orth **A**merica, **E**urope, **A**sia, **A**ustralia, **A**ntarctica
Bodies of Water	the **I**ndian **O**cean, the **O**hio **R**iver, the **G**ulf of **M**exico, the **S**outh **C**hina **S**ea, **H**udson **B**ay, the **P**anama **C**anal, **L**ake **M**ichigan, **Y**osemite **F**alls
Landforms	**M**ount **C**ook, the **A**leutian **I**slands, **D**eath **V**alley, the **A**llegheny **M**ountains, the **B**lack **H**ills, **C**ape **H**orn, the **A**tacama **D**esert
World Regions	the **O**rient, the **F**ar **E**ast, the **M**iddle **E**ast, **C**entral **A**merica, **O**ceania

Landsat image of Kansas shows aerial view of land and water.

752 Grammar Handbook

Special Terms	the **S**outhern **H**emisphere, the **E**quator, the **T**ropic of **C**apricorn, the **S**outh **P**ole
Political Units	**F**lorida, **D**enver, the **P**rovince of **O**ntario, the **R**epublic of **K**enya, the **S**tate of **I**srael, the **T**hirteenth **C**ongressional **D**istrict
Public Areas	**G**lacier **N**ational **P**ark, **F**ort **L**ee, **B**adlands **N**ational **M**onument, **C**entral **P**ark, **S**tokes **S**tate **F**orest
Roads and Highways	**R**oute 66, **I**nterstate **H**ighway 610, the **S**anta **F**e **T**rail, **H**ampton **R**oad, **F**ifth **A**venue, **M**agnolia **S**treet

When a word that names a geographical feature is not used as part of a proper noun, it is not capitalized.

The highest falls in the world are in Venezuela.
We visited the historic town of Marshall, Michigan.

Directions and Sections

Capitalize names of sections of the country or the world.

The **W**est has many old ghost towns.
The Sorensons moved from **N**ew **E**ngland to the **W**est **C**oast.
Japan has close economic connections with the **W**est.

Capitalize proper adjectives that come from names of sections of the country or the world.

a **M**idwestern town	the **S**outhern states
an **E**ast **C**oast company	**E**astern religions

Do not capitalize directions of the compass.

Fairbanks, Alaska, is north of Anchorage.
Drive east on Interstate 80 to New York.

Do not capitalize adjectives that merely indicate direction or a general location.

The parking lot is on the north side of the main building.
The hurricane hit the southern coast of Florida.

Bodies of the Universe

Capitalize the names of planets and other objects in the universe. Do not capitalize the words *sun* and *moon*.

Pluto	the **M**ilky **W**ay	an eclipse of the sun
Mars	**H**alley's **C**omet	rocks from the moon

Capitalization　　**753**

Individualizing Instruction

ESL Students Adjectives of nationality are not capitalized in French and German. Remind these students to capitalize them in English.

Writing Theme
Geographical Oddities

Capitalize the word *earth* only when it is used with the names of other planets. Do not capitalize *earth* after the article *the*.

> On Mercury the average daytime temperature is 625 degrees Fahrenheit; on Earth it is only 60 degrees Fahrenheit.
> Many communication satellites circle the earth.

Practice Your Skills

A. CONCEPT CHECK

Geographical Names Write the following sentences, using capital letters where necessary.

1. An interesting example of a misleading geographical name is the canary islands.
2. These islands, including tenerife, hierro, and lanzarote, belong to spain.
3. They are located about one hundred miles west of morocco, off the coast of north africa.
4. The name of these islands in the atlantic ocean has nothing to do with canaries.
5. Their spanish name, *islas canarias,* means "dog islands."
6. They got this name in ancient times, when the ruler of mauritania in africa reported that he had found the islands inhabited by packs of wild dogs.
7. Another example of an odd name is an area in the city of london known as rotten row.
8. The name of this royal bridle path in hyde park comes from a french phrase meaning "road of the king."
9. In this country, one of alaska's best-known cities, nome, is named for cape nome on the bering sea, where it is located.
10. Cape nome's name may have originated when a mapmaker drew alaska and wrote "name?" next to this unnamed landmass.

B. PROOFREADING SKILL

Focus on Capitalization On your paper rewrite the following paragraphs about Australia. Correct all errors in capitalization, spelling, and punctuation.

> Australia is a land of oddities. In addition to the Continent's unusual animals, such as koalas and kangaroos, there are several geographical features that make it unique. One of the strangest lakes in the world is lake George, which is near Australias capitol city of Canberra. The Lake keeps appearing and disappearing, its disappearances apparently due to a combination of evaporation and low rainfall.

Another geographic curiosity lies below the Oceans surface. The largest coral structure in the world extends for 1,250 miles along the northwestern coast of Austrailia and is called the great barrier reef it is home to at least 350 species of coral and teams with marine life. Another feature that looks almost as if it came straight from the Moon is Ayers rock, which towers 1,000 feet over the flat desert floor of northern Australia. Australia's Landscape has vast stretches of dry, open spaces. A visitor can fly 1,900 miles Northeast across Australia and see only a few signs of human habitation.

C. APPLICATION IN WRITING

Report of a Discovery You have just discovered gold. Write a paragraph describing the location of the find. You may choose to place your discovery in a realistic location, or you may wish to make up geographical names. Be sure to capitalize all locations correctly.

ORGANIZATIONS, EVENTS, AND OTHER SUBJECTS

Capital letters are needed to distinguish names of organizations, nationalities, and events.

Organizations and Institutions

Capitalize the names of organizations and institutions.

Use capital letters in the names of political parties, governmental bodies or agencies, schools, colleges, churches, hospitals, clubs, and businesses. Also capitalize abbreviations of these names.

Republican Party	Federal Aviation Administration
Federal Trade Commission	Children's Memorial Hospital
Stevenson High School	Universal Motor Corporation
University of Georgia	Numismatic Club
St. Joseph's Church	**AFL-CIO**

Do not capitalize such words as *school, company, church,* and *hospital* when they are not used as parts of names.

Several people from our church do volunteer work at the hospital.
The stamp collecting club meets at the university.

Another geographic curiosity lies below the ocean's surface. The largest coral structure in the world extends for 1,250 miles along the northwestern coast of Australia and is called the Great Barrier Reef. It is home to at least 350 species of coral and teems with marine life. Another feature that looks almost as if it came straight from the moon is Ayers Rock, which towers 1,000 feet over the flat desert floor of northern Australia. Australia's landscape has vast stretches of dry, open spaces. A visitor can fly 1,900 miles northeast across Australia and see only a few signs of human habitation.

C. Application in Writing
Report of a Discovery
Answers will vary.

Organization, Events, and Other Subjects

Objectives

- To use capital letters correctly in a variety of categories
- **Writing** To identify and correct errors in capitalization, spelling, and punctuation in sentences and paragraphs

Linking Grammar and Writing

Because some students may be overwhelmed by the number of different categories for the rules on this page, encourage them to become more familiar with the categories by making up their own sentences and using different combinations of items. Start students off with an example such as the following: "Who would have thought that a Thai restaurant would celebrate the American heritage by serving a delicious Thanksgiving Day dinner at 6:00 P.M.?"

Additional Resources
- Grammar and Usage Practice Book, pp. 171–172

Writing TIP

Using capital letters to distinguish proper nouns helps you to avoid confusion and convey your meaning more precisely.

Races, Languages, Nationalities, and Religions

Capitalize the names of all races, languages, nationalities, and religions.

Greek	Polish	English	Hinduism
Oriental	German	Catholicism	Judaism

Also capitalize any adjectives that come from these names.

the Italian heritage   Native-American cultures
a Thai restaurant   Polish sausage

Events, Documents, and Periods of Time

Capitalize the names of historical events, documents, and periods of time.

Battle of Concord   Panama Canal Treaty
the Hundred Years' War   the Middle Ages

Months, Days, and Holidays

Capitalize months, days, and holidays, but not seasons.

July   Thursday   Thanksgiving Day   winter

Abbreviation for Time

Capitalize the abbreviations B.C., A.D., A.M., and P.M.

The Pyramids of Egypt were begun about 3000 B.C.
Mohammed was born in A.D. 570.
The flight takes off at 10:25 A.M.
The practice ended at 2:15 P.M.

School Subjects

Do not capitalize the general names of school subjects. Do capitalize titles of specific courses that are followed by a number. Always capitalize the title of language courses.

history   Math 300   Woodworking I   Spanish

Ships, Trains, Airplanes, and Spacecraft

Capitalize the names of specific ships, trains, airplanes, and spacecraft.

U.S.S. Constellation   *Spirit of St. Louis*
Orient Express   *Voyager II*

Monuments, Bridges, and Buildings

Capitalize the names of monuments, bridges, and buildings.

Vietnam Memorial   Gateway Arch   Sears Tower

Awards and Special Events

Capitalize the names of awards and special events.

Pulitzer Prize   World Series   Mardi Gras

Brand Names

Capitalize the brand names of products. Do not capitalize a common noun that follows a brand name.

Dazzle detergent   White Teeth toothpaste

Practice Your Skills

A. CONCEPT CHECK

Organizations, Events, and Other Subjects Write the following sentences, using capital letters where necessary. If a sentence requires no added capitalization, write *Correct.*

1. The land that is now california has been inhabited since about 20,000 b.c.
2. The first native americans reached the area by crossing what was then a land bridge between asia and alaska.
3. In a.d. 1542, european explorers arrived to search for wealth.
4. They were followed by missionaries of the roman catholic church and mexican farmers.
5. In the 1840's, thousands of americans moved west during the historic period known as the gold rush.

Writing Theme
California

Managing the Paper Load

You might wish to organize a game show format for Exercise A. Have student teams work together against the clock to identify words that need to be capitalized. Award points instead of grades for Exercise A. Then have students write answers to Exercises B and C. Remind them that Exercise B contains improperly capitalized words and that Exercise C also contains errors in spelling and punctuation.

WRITING THEME   California

Suggest that students do additional research on this theme or on their own state history and use it as the subject of a Writer's Workshop assignment.

A. Concept Check
Organizations, Events, and Other Subjects
Words to be capitalized are underlined on page. Sentences 12 and 14 are correct.

6. They were followed by <u>chinese</u> workers hired by the <u>central</u> <u>pacific</u> <u>railroad</u>.
7. Immigration continued, bringing <u>italians</u>, <u>central</u> <u>americans</u>, <u>japanese</u>, and people from almost every foreign land.
8. This cultural diversity explains why a traditional <u>christmas day</u> dinner in <u>california</u> may well include tacos, lasagna, or fried rice instead of turkey.
9. California still draws people, from tourists longing for a sight of the <u>golden gate bridge</u> to actors hoping for an <u>academy award</u>.
10. Life in California is not all glamour; dockworkers are more in demand than are crew members for the starship *enterprise*.
11. Therefore, taking only the course <u>filmmaking II</u> will not prepare you for life in <u>california</u>.
12. Courses in electronics and business would be more helpful.
13. For example, there is so much manufacturing in <u>california</u> that one would not be surprised to see racks in a clothing store loaded with brands such as <u>california classic, west coast weaves, and san diego duds</u>.
14. Agriculture is also big business, since spring and summer seem to last forever in this sunny state.
15. Although the <u>gold rush</u> is over, <u>california</u> still offers golden opportunities for newcomers, whether they want to make a splash at <u>columbia</u> pictures or at one of the beaches.

B. REVISION SKILL

Correcting Capitalization Errors On your paper, write the following sentences, using capital letters where necessary and correcting improperly capitalized words.

1. In <u>a.d.</u> 1542, Juan Rodriguez Cabrillo became the first <u>european</u> to <u>sail</u> into what is now San Diego Bay.
2. Cabrillo was a <u>portuguese</u> navigator exploring for <u>spain</u>.
3. Cabrillo <u>national monument</u> commemorates his exploration.
4. His landing is re-created at the <u>september cabrillo festival</u>.
5. Junipero Serra, a <u>franciscan</u> missionary, established the first mission in San Diego in 1769.
6. The <u>serra museum</u> in Presidio Park bears <u>His</u> name.
7. Another historic date, <u>july</u> 29, 1846, marked the landing of the U.S. sloop *cyane* in San Diego bearing troops to fight in the <u>mexican war</u>.
8. Today, the city is known for its warm <u>Winters</u> and mild <u>Summers</u>.
9. Tourists flock to the <u>san diego zoo</u> and the <u>salk institute</u>, a famous research center.
10. The <u>university of california</u> at <u>san diego</u> draws students in search of challenging <u>Science</u> courses.

B. Revision Skill
Correcting Capitalization Errors
Words to be capitalized and words incorrectly capitalized are underlined on page.

C. PROOFREADING SKILL

Capitalizing Correctly Carefully proofread and then rewrite the following paragraphs. Correct all errors in spelling, punctuation, and capitalization.

One of california's most famous native sons was the writer jack London. He was always a wild boy, but he began his real adventures when, at the age of sixteen, he signed on as a sailor on the *sophia sutherland* and headed for the japanese Coast. After a year; he returned home to california. He soon became bored working at a local Cannery and for the oakland street railway, however, so he hopped a freight, and went to the world's fair in Chicago.

Jack returned home at the age of nineteen and started High School, where he took english, History, and other classes with much younger students. At the age of twentey, he passed the exams to enter the university of california. Adventure beckoned again, however, and In 1897, Jack headed to the yukon territory of northwestern canada to join the klondike gold rush. He may have left his books to head North, but it was there in the Klondike that Jack London really became a Writer.

CHECK POINT
PAGES 749–759

A. Write the following sentences, adding capital letters where necessary. If a sentence requires no added capitalization, write *Correct*.

1. Marco Polo, named after saint mark, was born in a.d. 1254.
2. He did not have the kind of formal education now available to most americans, who can take such courses as world history I.
3. He learned from life in the city of venice, italy.
4. As a boy, marco spent hours wandering among the city's wharves, marveling at the ships from europe, india, asia minor, and north africa.
5. Before Marco was born, his father and uncle had set sail to visit foreign lands.
6. Guided by the north star, they sailed past greece and into the sea of marmara.
7. They stopped first in constantinople long enough to increase their wealth and then sailed on toward the volga river and on to the land of the mongols.
8. The mongols honored the provisions of a document called the "pax tartarica," which guaranteed the safety of travelers.

Writing Theme
Marco Polo

Capitalization **759**

9. Kublai Khan ruled the mongol lands, which stretched from hungary east to the pacific ocean and from the indian border north to the arctic ocean.

10. Kublai khan had been crowned emperor of china after much dispute and bloodshed.

11. Interested in the teachings of the bible, kublai khan asked the polos to take a letter to the pope.

12. The letter requested that the pope send china one hundred scholars who knew about christianity.

13. The khan also requested that some oil from the lamp burning at the holy sepulchre in jerusalem be brought back.

14. As a highly favored servant of kublai khan, Marco spent seventeen years in the east and wrote a detailed journal.

15. His experiences formed the body of Polo's book *description of the world*.

16. He died on january 8, 1324, at the age of seventy.

17. Although there is no marco polo day to honor him, he greatly expanded people's knowledge of the world.

B. Rewrite the following passage on your paper. Correct all errors in capitalization, spelling, and punctuation.

> One misconception about marco polo involves spagetti. For years, it was thought that marco polo had brought pasta to europe. However, the Truth is that the greeks had dined on pasta since before the middle ages and the italians had been eating it for Centuries before polo's time. No one knows for sure in what Country and century it originated.
>
> Some Historians believe that the very first forms of pasta emerged about 5000 b.c. It is true that the chinese were almost certainly eating it by 1700 b.c. In fact, Marco polo reported that he dined on noodles at the Palace of the emperor of china.
>
> Whatever the history of pasta may be, it has become a popular dish all over america, from new york city to los angeles, from the great lakes to the rio grande.
>
> There are over one hundred kinds of pasta and nearly as many Brands, such as little pony macaroni and sunshine harvest spaghetti, From Linguini in Cream served at the Captain's table on the *queen elizabeth II* to Spaghetti with Meatballs eaten from a tray in the caffeteria of the world trade Center, pasta is always a hit!

FIRST WORDS AND THE PRONOUN *I*

Capitalize the first word of every sentence.

The system of writing called Braille was devised for the blind.

Poetry

Capitalize the first word of every line of poetry.

By the rude bridge that arched the flood,
    Their flag to April's breeze unfurled,
Here once the embattled farmers stood,
    And fired the shot heard round the world.

Ralph Waldo Emerson, "Concord Hymn"

Sometimes, as in the poem below or in some modern poetry, the lines of a poem do not begin with capital letters.

the sun pours down gold
fountains pour out green water
colors touch us like fingers
of green quetzal wings.

Aztec Indian, "A Song of Nezahualcoyotl"

Quotations

Capitalize the first word of a direct quotation.

A **direct quotation** tells the exact words of a speaker or writer.

Emerson said, "The only way to have a friend is to be one."

A **divided quotation** occurs when a direct quotation is broken into two parts by words such as *he said*. Do not capitalize the first word of the second part unless it starts a new sentence.

"I believe," Tina said, "that a good friend is rare. Don't you?"

Letter Parts

Capitalize the first word in the greeting of a letter. Also capitalize the name or title of the person addressed.

Dear Ms. Valdez: Dear Mr. Nash: Dear Sir or Madam:

In the complimentary close, capitalize only the first word.

Very truly yours,   Sincerely yours,

Modern poet e.e. cummings disregarded grammar and punctuation in his search for a new form of expression.

Capitalization   **761**

Objectives

- To capitalize the first words of sentences and the first words of most lines of poetry
- To use capital letters correctly in direct quotations, letter parts, outlines, and titles
- To capitalize the pronoun *I*
- **Writing** To use capital letters correctly in personal and assigned writing

Teaching Strategies

Stumbling Block

Students may be confused about the rules for capitalization in direct quotations. Provide additional examples such as the following to illustrate these rules:
Emerson once wrote, "To speak truly, few adult persons can see nature."
"Most persons," Emerson continued, "do not see the sun. At least they have a very superficial seeing."

Linking Grammar and Literature

Some modern poets have experimented with capitalization, punctuation, and spacing on the page for special effects, as in these famous lines by e. e. cummings:

in Just-
spring   when the world is mud-
luscious the little
lame balloonman

whistles   far   and wee

Point out that this poem is a visual representation; discuss the effect achieved by its arrangement on the page and the use of capitalization.

Have students orally identify all the conjunctions, articles, and prepositions in these titles. Remind them that most prepositions consist of fewer than five letters. (See Grammar Handbook 34, pages 620–621, and Grammar Handbook 35, pages 652–654 and 664.)

 Individualizing Instruction

ESL Students Pronoun capitalization differs from language to language. For example, in Spanish and French, the words for *I*—*yo* and *je*—are not capitalized unless they occur at the beginning of a sentence. Point out this difference between English and students' native languages.

Outlines

Capitalize the first word of each item in an outline. Also capitalize letters that introduce major subsections of the outline.

    I. **H**olidays
        A. **C**hief legal holidays
            1. **N**ational
            2. **S**tate or local
        B. **R**eligious holidays

Titles

Capitalize the first word, the last word, and all other important words in titles. Do not capitalize conjunctions, articles, or prepositions with fewer than five letters.

Book Title	*The Other Side of the Mountain*
Newspaper	*Los Angeles Times*
Magazine	*Ebony*
Play	*You Can't Take It with You*
Movie	*The Sound of Music*
Television Series	*Wide World of Sports*
Work of Art	*The Sunflowers*
Musical Composition	*Carmen*
Ballet or Dance	*Jacob's Pillow*
Short Story	"To Build a Fire"
Poem	"A Word Is Dead"
Song	"I Want to Hold Your Hand"
Chapter	Chapter 3, "The Mediterranean World"
Magazine Article	"Today's Changing Family"

The word *the* at the beginning of a title is capitalized only when it is part of the formal name. Similarly, the word *magazine* is capitalized only when it is part of the formal name.

The Times	the *Chicago Tribune*
Audubon Magazine	*Newsweek* magazine

When you write titles, underline them or put them in quotation marks. Rules for punctuating titles are given in Grammar Handbook 41, page 800.

The Pronoun *I*

Capitalize the pronoun *I*.

Stanley and **I** rented *2001: A Space Odyssey.*

Practice Your Skills

A. CONCEPT CHECK

Capitalization of Words and Titles   Rewrite each of the following items, correcting all errors in capitalization.

1. A report outline on sports figures might start like this:
   I. sports figures
      a. coaches
         1. Vince lombardi
         2. Casey Jones
2. The part of the report about Lombardi could have a subtitle such as "invincible Vince."
3. that would not be an overstatement, because Vince Lombardi was one of the greatest football coaches of all time.
4. lombardi grew up in brooklyn, new York, The oldest son of Italian Immigrant parents.
5. After doing well in grade school and High School, he enrolled at fordham university in New york city.
6. He received a Business Degree but went on to teach Physics, Algebra, and Chemistry at a high school in new Jersey, while also coaching the football team.
7. He then held coaching jobs that led from fordham university to the U. S. military academy and on to the new York giants.
8. in 1958 lombardi became Head Coach of the green bay packers, a position he held until 1968.
9. As a reporter for *The New York times* once said, "there is no more famous football man anywhere."
10. known for his hot temper, Lombardi once commented, "I coach with everything that is within me, and i employ that temper for a purpose."
11. he preached humility to his players, and when a day was set aside to honor him, the organizers received only one letter of complaint.
12. "I don't think Vince Lombardi is important enough," it said, "To have a day set aside for him."
13. The letter was signed, "Sincerely Yours, Vince Lombardi."
14. To explain why he wore a jacket and tie for most games, he said, "a game day is a business day."
15. To remind his players to be humble and dignified during interviews, he posted this poem in the locker room:
      what you see here
      what you say here
      what you hear here
      let it stay here
      when you leave here

Writing Theme
Famous Sports Figures

Additional Resources
• Grammar and Usage Practice Book, pp. 173–174

WRITING THEME   Famous Sports Figures

Encourage students to list famous sports figures whom they admire as possible subjects for future writing.

A. Concept Check
Capitalization of Words and Titles
Words to be capitalized and words incorrectly capitalized are underlined on page.

16. in addition to being a coach, Lombardi was an author.
17. He wrote a book titled *Run to daylight*.
18. People think that Lombardi said, "winning isn't everything; it's the only thing."
19. According to *Bartlett's familiar quotations,* however, he actually said, "winning isn't everything; wanting to win is."
20. A journalist for the *press gazette* explained why Lombardi was a popular speaker by writing, "something that sounded trite or mundane if said by anyone else, he made sound as if it was chiseled in stone."

B. REVISION SKILL

Focus on Capital Letters On your paper, write the words that should be capitalized after the number of the sentence in which they appear.

(1) i am one of the few people i know who hate sports. (2) i can confess to never having watched the super bowl. (3) further, it baffles me how anyone can remember which baseball teams are in the national league and which are in the american league. (4) i do, however, enjoy humorous stories and anecdotes about sports, particularly ones about baseball, and most particularly those about yogi berra, the former catcher for the new york yankees. (5) once a reporter asked yogi, "how did you like school when you were growing up, yogi?" (6) yogi replied, "closed." (7) another time yogi commented, "you can't think and hit at the same time." (8) i also like humorous books about baseball, especially joe garagiola's *baseball is a funny game* and the two-volume *baseball hall of shame* by bruce mash and alan zullo. (9) nothing, however, has made me want to go to see a baseball game in person, and i can only agree with yogi once again. (10) "if the people don't want to come to the park," yogi once observed, "nobody's going to stop 'em."

C. APPLICATION IN WRITING

Letter to the Editor Imagine that you are a serious sports fan and that sports influences every part of your life. You are one of ten students being interviewed by your school paper for a feature article. To complete the article, the paper needs to know the titles of your favorite song, book, and movie. Write the information in a letter to Alice Evans, the paper's editor. Your answers should reflect your intense interest in sports. Use correct capitalization throughout your letter.

A. Rewrite each sentence, adding capitalization where necessary. If a sentence requires no added capitalization, write *Correct*.

Writing Theme
Maine

1. Margaret chase Smith, one of maine's most famous citizens, was the first woman to serve in both houses of the united states congress and the first woman to seek a major political party's nomination for the presidency.
2. Born margaret madeline chase in skowhegan, maine, she met her husband, Clyde Smith, while working at the *independent reporter,* a newspaper in skowhegan.
3. He was a member of the house of representatives; after his death, his wife was appointed to replace him.
4. During campaigns she would say, "this is what i think about things, and this is what i've done."
5. Her job in that famous building, the u.s. capitol, was very important to her.
6. She served her country for a period that included world war II, the infamous McCarthy "witch trials," the cuban missile crisis, and John Glenn's orbit of the earth in *friendship* 7.
7. About herself she had little to say; her entry in the *congressional directory* read only, "Margaret Chase Smith, republican."
8. When she became one of the first senators to speak out against joseph McCarthy and the unamerican activities committee, however, she was eloquent in her opposition to McCarthy's tactics.
9. "It is a victory of a cause," she said after one successful campaign for the u.s. senate, "rather than of a candidate."
10. Her life and career are well covered in a book by alice fleming, *the Senator from maine: Margaret chase Smith.*

B. APPLICATION IN LITERATURE

Capitalization   Rewrite the following passage. Correct the capitalization errors.

> (1) One Summer, along about 1904, my father rented a camp on a Lake in maine and took us all there for the Month of august. (2) We all got ringworm from some Kittens and had to rub pond's extract on our arms and legs night and morning, and my Father rolled over in a canoe with all his clothes on; but outside of that the Vacation was a success, and from then on none of us ever thought there was any place in the World like that Lake in Maine.
>
> **E. B. White, "Once More to the Lake"**

Capitalization **765**

CHECK POINT
PAGES 761–764

You may wish to use the following Checkpoint exercises as an informal evaluation of student mastery of capitalization rules.

Managing the Paper Load

To limit the number of exercises to correct, you may wish to model the first five items of Exercise A. Then have students complete the exercise. Prepare answer key material for Exercise A and make it available to students for self-check. In Exercise B, pair LEP students with partners to make sure that errors are corrected.

WRITING THEME   Maine

A.
Words to be capitalized are underlined on page.

B. Application in Literature
Capitalization
Words to be capitalized and words incorrectly capitalized are underlined on page.

(1) One summer, along about 1904, my father rented a camp on a lake in Maine and took us all there for the month of August. (2) We all got ringworm from some kittens and had to rub Pond's extract on our arms and legs night and morning, and my father rolled over in a canoe with all his clothes on; but outside of that the vacation was a success, and from then on none of us ever thought there was any place in the world like that lake in Maine.

Application and Review

These activities have been designed to allow students to apply concepts presented in this handbook. Exercises A and B require students to capitalize words as necessary. Exercise C challenges students to supply capitals where they are required and to correct improperly capitalized words.

Additional Resources

- Tests and Assessment, Mastery Tests, pp. 101–104
- Elaboration, Revision, and Proof-reading Worksheets, p. 31

WRITING THEME   The Southwest and Mexico

A. Capitalizing Correctly

Words to be capitalized are underlined on page. Numbers 3, 7, and 20 are correct.

GRAMMAR
HANDBOOK
40

Writing Theme
The Southwest and Mexico

A. Capitalizing Correctly   Capitalize words as necessary in each of the following sentences. If no additional capitals are needed, write *Correct.*

1. Georgia o'keeffe, best known for her portrayal of the american southwest, was born on november 15, 1887, in sun prairie, Wisconsin.
2. Both of her grandmothers lived near this little midwestern town, as did a number of aunts and uncles.
3. Despite a close family relationship, independence was always important to her.
4. "I decided that the only thing i could do that was nobody else's business was to paint," she said.
5. She went on to say, "i could do as i chose because no one would care."
6. her first contact with the culture and beauty of the west came when she went to texas.
7. She was invited there to teach drawing and penmanship.
8. "It had always seemed to me that the west must be wonderful," she said. "so when I had a chance to teach, off i went."
9. She later moved to new mexico and, during her first summer there, created one of her best paintings, *the lawrence tree.*
10. In 1934, the Metropolitan museum of Art purchased one of her paintings, which helped to expand her reputation.
11. In 1938, the n. w. ayer advertising agency flew her to hawaii to make two paintings for ads by the dole company.
12. In 1942, both she and general Douglas MacArthur, the head of the u.s. armed forces in the pacific, received honorary Ph.D. degrees from the university of Wisconsin.
13. At the age of sixty-six, she made her first visit to europe, where she visited the louvre in france and the prado in spain.
14. she was not interested in meeting Pablo picasso when she had the chance because she could not speak french.
15. "I didn't care very much about looking at him. We couldn't talk," she said. "so what's the point?"
16. She preferred the far east to europe and the simplicity of oriental art to the elaborate religious art she saw in rome.
17. Marcia Winn of the *chicago tribune* once observed, "if you like her work, you love it; if you don't, you can't forget it."
18. In 1946, O'Keeffe was elected to the National institute of arts and letters, a prestigious organization.
19. Her largest painting, *sky above clouds* IV, was inspired by a view from an airplane.
20. She has become one of the most popular contemporary painters.

B. Correcting Capitalization Errors Rewrite the following sentences, capitalizing words where necessary.

1. everywhere in mexico, the past is preserved in great monuments, such as the one known as the pyramid of the sun.
2. Along the yucatán coastline, the temples of the ruined cities of the mayan indians look out over the caribbean sea.
3. One of the oldest mexican cultures was that of the olmecs.
4. In 1869, a bulletin of the mexican geographic society revealed the discovery of olmec artifacts.
5. The olmec culture developed around 1200 b.c.
6. It reached from the gulf of mexico to the tuxtla mountains.
7. The olmecs were the first astronomers of ancient america.
8. They used their observations of the sun to create a calendar.
9. The chief olmec deity was named jaguar-man.
10. The olmec civilization lasted until around 400 b.c.

C. Correcting Mistakes in Capitalization Rewrite the following letter, correcting all mistakes in capitalization.

```
                          624 Washtenaw avenue
                     Ypsilanti, michigan 48109

                          july 4, 19—

dear Lynn,
     I received your letter this afternoon, and i'll be
happy to accept your invitation! I've always wanted to
see the unique land and Civilizations of the south-
west, and traveling with you and aunt Pat sounds like
the perfect way to do it. When I asked mom if I could
go, she said, "only if I can go too!" She was just teas-
ing, of course!
     My summer classes, chemistry 2 and the math
class I told you about, will be over thursday.
     Please send me the details of our trip. I have a res-
ervation on east airlines leaving detroit on saturday,
july 30, at 10 a.m. and arriving in phoenix at
12:45 p.m.
                     your cousin,
                     Anita
```

B. Correcting Capitalization Errors
Words to be capitalized are underlined on page.

C. Correcting Mistakes in Capitalization
Words to be capitalized and words incorrectly capitalized are underlined.

624 Washtenaw Avenue
Ypsilanti, Michigan 48109
July 4, 19—

Dear Lynn,
     I received your letter this afternoon, and I'll be happy to accept your invitation! I've always wanted to see the unique land and civilizations of the Southwest, and traveling with you and Aunt Pat sounds like the perfect way to do it. When I asked Mom if I could go, she said, "Only if I can go too!" She was just teasing, of course!
     My summer classes, Chemistry 2 and the math class I told you about, will be over Thursday.
     Please send me the details of our trip. I have a reservation on East Airlines leaving Detroit on Saturday, July 30, at 10 A.M. and arriving in Phoenix at 12:45 P.M.

                     Your cousin,

                     Anita

After discussing the feature on page 768, your students may be interested in further researching the origin of the expression *O.K.* In *The American Language*, H. L. Mencken presents these other possible etymologies: the initials of Old Keokuk, the Indian chief who was "all right"; schoolmasters marking examination papers with *omnis korrecta;* shipbuilders marking boards to indicate that they will start with the *outer keel No. 1;* or the Choctaw word *okey* for "It is so."

You may also wish to have your students research the etymologies of these words: *malapropism, frankfurter,* and *watt.* In addition to Mencken's work, these sources may also be helpful or interesting:

Dictionary of American English, William Craigie;

A Dictionary of Americanisms on Historical Principles, Mitford Mathews, editor;

A Dictionary of Slang and Unconventional English, Eric Partridge;

I Hear America Talking, Stuart Flexner;

Morris Dictionary of Word and Phrase Origins, William and Mary Morris; and

Webster's Unabridged Dictionary.

On the Lightside

OK

American presidents are remembered for many contributions to world history, but President Martin Van Buren was responsible for what is surely one of the most unusual contributions—he popularized the expression *OK.*

No one is exactly sure when *OK* was used for the first time. Some

scholars claim it can be traced to a West African expression in use before the American Revolution. Others think it came from a port in Haiti called "Aux Cayes." Still others link it to an expression in the early nineteenth century, "Orl Kerrect." In any case, it came to prominence during President Van Buren's reelection campaign in 1840.

Van Buren, who was elected President in 1836, was a native of Kinderhook, New York. He was known by the nickname of "Old Kinderhook," or "O.K." His supporters formed the O.K. Democratic Club, and "O.K." became a familiar cry of approval for the candidate. People chanted "O.K." at rallies, and the letters appeared frequently on placards and in political cartoons. Foreign coverage of the campaign even carried the expression to Europe and Latin America. Since then, OK has traveled all around the world. It has become a term of approval that is understood and used in almost every language. Unfortunately for President Van Buren, its popularity did not mean Old Kinderhook was *OK* with the voters. Van Buren was defeated in his reelection bid by William Henry Harrison.

Punctuation

END MARKS

End marks are the punctuation marks that indicate the end of a sentence. The three kinds of end marks are the **period,** the **question mark,** and the **exclamation point.**

The Period

Use a period at the end of a declarative sentence.

A **declarative sentence** is a sentence that makes a statement.

> The American artist Grandma Moses began painting full time in her seventies.

Use a period at the end of most imperative sentences.

An **imperative sentence** is a sentence that gives a command or makes a request.

> Please clean your brushes before the end of class.

When an imperative sentence expresses strong emotion, an exclamation point, not a period, is used at the end of the sentence.

> Get away!   Hurry up!   Help!

Use a period at the end of an indirect question.

An **indirect question** indicates that someone has asked a question.

> Captain Ahab asked whether the ship was on course.

A **direct question** shows the speaker's exact words.

> Captain Ahab asked, "Is the ship on course?"

A direct question shows the exact words of the person asking the question. A direct question ends with a question mark.

Use a period at the end of an abbreviation or an initial.

An **abbreviation** is a shortened form of a word. An **initial** is a first letter that stands for a word.

> Gov. James R. Thomas   4:00 P.M. on Aug. 4
> Lt. Margaret B. Hill   5 lb. 12 oz.
> Mr. Don Ibarra, Jr.   3 hr. 42 min.

Writing
— **TIP** —

With the exception of titles, years, and times, avoid the use of abbreviations in formal papers.

End Marks

Objectives

- To use periods correctly at the ends of sentences and in abbreviations, initials, outlines, and decimals
- To use question marks and exclamation points correctly

Individualizing Instruction

ESL Students Not all languages use the period as an end mark. For example, Hindi and related Indian languages use a vertical bar to denote the end of a declarative sentence.

Point out that acronyms are special kinds of abbreviations with which periods are seldom used: for example, NASA or UNESCO. Challenge students to name as many acronyms as they can.

Individualizing Instruction

ESL Students In Spanish, in addition to the question mark and exclamation point at the end of interrogative and exclamatory sentences, there is also an inverted question mark or exclamation point at the beginning of the sentence. Remind these students to omit the beginning punctuation mark in English.

For certain abbreviations, periods are optional. Use your dictionary to check whether periods are required.

USA, U.S.A. (United States of America)
UN, U.N. (United Nations)

Use a period after each number or letter in an outline or a list.

Outline	List
I. Sports	1. nails
A. Team	2. hammer
1. Football	3. putty
2. Baseball	
B. Individual	
II. Hobbies	

Use a period between dollars and cents and also to indicate a decimal.

$13.64 $2.98   3.14   .007

The Question Mark

Use a question mark at the end of an interrogative sentence.

An **interrogative sentence** is a sentence that asks a question.

Why does the tail of a comet point away from the sun?
You've finished that novel already?

The Exclamation Point

Use an exclamation point to end an exclamatory sentence.

An **exclamatory sentence** shows strong emotion.

That's terrific!
You look great!
What a great game!

Use an exclamation point after a strong interjection.

An **interjection** is one or more words that show strong feeling. Sometimes the interjection is a sound, as in the first example below.

Whoops!   Not again!   Super!   Hurray!   Zoom!

When an interjection is followed by a sentence, the sentence end mark may be a period, a question mark, or an exclamation point.

Oh, oh! I forgot to call her.
Great! When do we leave?
Wow! That was the best concert ever!

Holy Cow!

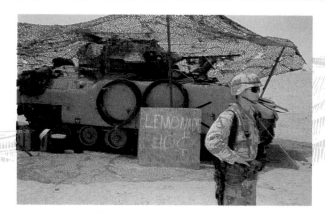

American soldier in
Saudi Arabia

Practice Your Skills

A. CONCEPT CHECK

End Marks Write the following sentences, adding the correct
punctuation. In punctuating abbreviations, consult a dictionary if
necessary.

1. The first morning at the camp, Sgt Williams offered to show me
   some of the mysteries of the desert
2. It was about 7:00 AM when we pulled out
3. I asked whether Sgt Williams liked the desert in this part of the
   USA He said it was fascinating
4. Boy Was he right
5. It was cool when we left our car on US95
6. Two hours later, the temperature had reached 118 degrees F in the
   shade I thought I was going to roast
7. I asked, "Why are we wearing these heavy J Boone hiking boots in
   such hot weather"
8. They must have weighed over five lbs each
9. Sgt Williams pulled out the list of instructions we'd received before coming to the camp and pointed about halfway down
   III Hiking boots
       A Insulation against heat
       B Protection from snakebite
10. "Don't argue if you haven't done your homework"
11. I decided to check my other supplies:
    1 An 8–oz bottle of sunscreen, SPF 44
    2 A 2–qt canteen
    3 A first-aid kit

Writing Theme
Hiking

Additional Resources

- Tests and Assessment,
  Pretests, pp. 33–34
- Grammar and Usage Practice
  Book, pp. 175–176

WRITING THEME   Hiking

A. Concept Check
End Marks
Answers will vary. See suggested answers
below.
   1. The first morning at the camp, Sgt. Williams offered to show me some of the mysteries
of the desert.
   2. It was about 7:00 A.M. when we pulled
out.
   3. I asked whether Sgt. Williams liked the
desert in this part of the U.S.A. He said it was
fascinating.
   4. Boy! Was he right!
   5. It was cool when we left our car on U.S.
95.
   6. Two hours later, the temperature had
reached 118 degrees F in the shade. I thought I
was going to roast!
   7. I asked, "Why are we wearing these
heavy J. Boone hiking boots in such hot
weather?"
   8. They must have weighed over five lbs.
each.
   9. Sgt. Williams pulled out the list of instructions we'd received before coming to the camp
and pointed about halfway down.
III. Hiking boots
   A. Insulation against heat
   B. Protection from snakebite
   10. "Don't argue if you haven't done your
homework."
   11. I decided to check my other supplies:
1. An 8-oz. bottle of sunscreen, SPF 44
2. A 2-qt. canteen
3. A first-aid kit

12. Suddenly, Sgt. Williams shouted, "Don't move!"
13. My heart stopped! I was afraid to breathe.
14. "You were about to step on a young *cardón* cactus. All vegetation in the desert has a fragile hold on life."
15. I asked if he knew how fragile my hold was just then.

B. Revision Skill
Punctuating Correctly
(1) Imagine that you are on a hiking trip in the mountains and you become separated from your party. (2) You are alone in the wilderness. (3) It is already 6:00 P.M., and the temperature is far too cold for your thin jacket. (4) Uppermost in your mind is how to survive until morning. (5) How can you overcome fear and win your struggle with nature?

The Comma

Objectives

- To use commas correctly in a variety of grammatical constructions
- To understand the use of commas to set off nonessential elements
- To use conventional commas correctly

---

12. Suddenly, Sgt Williams shouted, "Don't move"
13. My heart stopped I was afraid to breathe
14. "You were about to step on a young *cardón* cactus All vegetation in the desert has a fragile hold on life"
15. I asked if he knew how fragile my hold was just then

B. REVISION SKILL

Punctuating Correctly   Write the following sentences, adding the correct punctuation.

(1) Imagine that you are on a hiking trip in the mountains and you become separated from your party (2) You are alone in the wilderness (3) It is already 6:00 PM, and the temperature is far too cold for your thin jacket (4) Uppermost in your mind is how to survive until morning (5) How can you overcome fear and win your struggle with nature

THE COMMA

Commas can help you express your ideas clearly when you write. They can slow down the rhythm of a sentence, show a shift in thought, or add clarity. The following rules will help you understand when commas should be used.

Commas in a Series

Use a comma after every item in a series except the last one.

A series consists of three or more items of the same kind. Your writing may contain a series of words, phrases, or clauses.

Words	Woody Allen is a writer, an actor, and a director of popular movies.
Phrases	We searched under beds, inside drawers, and in closets for the lost ring.
Clauses	The doctor explained how the blood test is done, what it reveals, and why it is necessary.

Use commas after words like *first*, *second*, and *third* when they introduce a series.

Note also the use of semicolons (;) in the following example. For more about semicolons, see pages 785–786.

There are four steps to any painting job: first, scraping; second, sanding; third, priming; and fourth, painting.

Writing
TIP

Omitting any essential commas leads to confusion in meaning.

Use commas between two or more adjectives of equal rank that modify the same noun.

Kristen applied a blue, shiny glaze to the vase.

To determine whether the adjectives are of equal rank, try placing *and* between them. If *and* sounds natural and if you can reverse the order of the adjectives without changing the meaning, use a comma between them.

Dr. McFadden treated the cold *and* wet *and* sick dog. (The *and*'s sound natural. Changing the order of the adjectives does not change the meaning. Commas are needed.)
Dr. McFadden treated the cold, wet, sick dog.

Mom bought Dad a brown *and* easy chair for Father's Day. (The *and* sounds awkward, and the order of the adjectives cannot be reversed. No comma is necessary.)
Mom bought Dad a brown easy chair for Father's Day.

Practice Your Skills

A. CONCEPT CHECK

Commas   Write the following sentences, adding necessary commas. If a sentence requires no added punctuation, write *Correct*.

1. Throughout history there have always been fads in music clothing hairstyles and diets.
2. Fads catch on for a number of reasons: first they are fun; and second they make people feel as though they belong to the popular culture.
3. Some of the most enjoyable harmless fads include dances toys games and jewelry.
4. However, fads such as diets skateboards and freestyle bicycles can be dangerous.
5. In the 1920's, college students started swallowing small live goldfish; it was a rather cruel, foolish thing to do.
6. On the other hand, the brightly colored hula hoops of the 1960's provided good physical exercise.
7. Of course, many silly costly fads and fashions are often promoted by ambitious designers manufacturers and advertisers.
8. They make fortunes persuading consumers what to eat how to dress and whom to watch on television.
9. These promoters actively shape how people think act and speak.
10. When a fad appears on the horizon, take the time to decide whether it is harmful examine what it costs and then try it out.

Punctuation   **773**

Additional Resources
• Grammar and Usage Practice Book, pp. 177–178

WRITING THEME   Fads, Fashions, and Crazes

A. Concept Check
Commas
   1. Throughout history there have always been fads in music, clothing, hairstyles, and diets.
   2. Fads catch on for a number of reasons: first, they are fun; and second, they make people feel as though they belong to the popular culture.
   3. Some of the most enjoyable, harmless fads include dances, toys, games, and jewelry.
   4. However, fads such as diets, skateboards, and freestyle bicycles can be dangerous.
   5. Correct
   6. Correct
   7. Of course, many silly, costly fads and fashions are often promoted by ambitious designers, manufacturers, and advertisers.
   8. They make fortunes persuading consumers what to eat, how to dress, and whom to watch on television.
   9. These promoters actively shape how people think, act, and speak.
   10. When a fad appears on the horizon, take the time to decide whether it is harmful, examine what it costs, and then try it out.

B. Revision Skill

Achieving Clarity

1. Correct
2. One of these fads had its origins when the government commissioned James Wright to create an all-purpose rubber compound for making jeep tires, gas masks, and airplane tires.
3. Wright produced a material that bounced higher, stretched farther, and resisted mold, decay, heat, and cold better than rubber.
4. The government couldn't use Wright's curious, impractical compound, but a man named Paul Hodgson could.
5. Three things made Hodgson the perfect person to take advantage of Wright's invention: first, his understanding of people; second, his experience as an advertising copywriter; and third, his toy store.
6. In 1949, Hodgson sold more of Wright's Silly Putty than red wagons, popguns, or any other toy in his store.
7. Correct
8. When Richard James knocked one off a shelf, he saw it "walking" down lower shelves, over stacks of books, and onto the tabletop.
9. Correct
10. Betty James named the toy, co-founded a sales company, and directed the marketing that gave the world the sensational Slinky.

B. REVISION SKILL

Achieving Clarity Making sure that commas are correctly placed is an important step in revising your work. Write the following sentences, adding commas to make the meaning clear. If a sentence requires no added punctuation, write *Correct*.

1. Two inventions that failed became major fads during the 1940's.
2. One of these fads had its origins when the government commissioned James Wright to create an all-purpose rubber compound for making jeep tires gas masks and airplane tires.
3. Wright produced a material that bounced higher stretched farther and resisted mold decay heat and cold better than rubber.
4. The government couldn't use Wright's curious impractical compound, but a man named Paul Hodgson could.
5. Three things made Hodgson the perfect person to take advantage of Wright's invention: first his understanding of people; second his experience as an advertising copywriter; and third his toy store.
6. In 1949, Hodgson sold more of Wright's Silly Putty than red wagons popguns or any other toy in his store.
7. Another fad, intended to be a new counterbalancing nautical device, began as a spring.
8. When Richard James knocked one off a shelf, he saw it "walking" down lower shelves over stacks of books and onto the tabletop.
9. Richard's wife quickly realized that the delicate metal spring could be sold as a toy.
10. Betty James named the toy co-founded a sales company and directed the marketing that gave the world the sensational Slinky.

Commas with Introductory Elements

Use a comma after introductory words or mild interjections such as *oh, yes, no,* and *well.*

> No, we didn't see any rattlesnakes while we were hiking in the mountain.
>
> Oh, I thought your appointment with the dentist was scheduled for tomorrow.

Use a comma after two or more prepositional phrases at the beginning of a sentence.

> After four rounds with the champ, Diaz was ready to call it a day.

A single prepositional phrase that begins a sentence may be set off by a comma if it is followed by a natural pause when read.

> Because of a sore throat, Janna was unable to sing her solo.

When there would be almost no pause in speaking, or the phrase is very short, a comma is not necessary.

At noon the farm auction will begin.

Use a comma after verbal phrases and adverb clauses that are used as introductory elements.

Spinning wildly, the folk dancers left the stage. (verbal phrase)
When the party ended, we left. (adverb clause)

Commas with Interrupters

Use commas to set off one or more words that interrupt the flow of thought in a sentence.

The judge, after long deliberation, sentenced the prisoners.
William, moreover, made the all-state hockey team.
The tire has a slow leak, by the way.

The following words and phrases are commonly used as interrupters. Set them off with commas when you write.

Words and Phrases Often Used as Interrupters			
however	I suppose	by the way	of course
therefore	moreover	in fact	furthermore
for example	I believe	after all	nevertheless

Use commas to set off nouns of direct address.

The name of someone who is spoken to directly is a **noun of direct address.** Nouns of direct address may also be common nouns, as shown in the last example.

Marsha, call a timeout!
In the hallway, Mark, is a package for you.
Will you assemble the telescope for me, Cindy?
When you leave, girls, lock the garage.

Use commas to set off most appositives.

As you know, an appositive is a word or phrase that explains or identifies another word. Usually the appositive comes directly after the word it explains. There are two types of appositives—nonessential and essential. In order to punctuate them correctly, you must understand the differences between them.

Punctuation **775**

Teaching Tip: Interrupters

Remind students that interrupting words and phrases may add information to a sentence but that these words can be omitted without harm to the basic thought. Have students test this for themselves by using the interrupters listed in the chart in the sample sentences. Tell them that the same principle applies to nonessential appositives and clauses, discussed below.

 Individualizing Instruction

LD Students You may wish to limit the number of exercise items assigned to LD students and allow them to refer to the rules and examples in the text as needed.

Most appositives are **nonessential.** These appositives merely add extra information to an already clear and complete sentence. Nonessential appositives must be set off by commas. Abbreviations such as *Jr.* and *Sr.* are nonessential appositives.

> Timmy, the smallest of the boys, was teasing my sister.
> The Super Bowl, the biggest game of the year, is held late in January.
> Alonzo Rawson, Jr., won the swimming medal.

Essential appositives, however, are needed to make the meaning of the sentence clear. Do not use commas with essential appositives.

> The author Ernest Hemingway is known for his simple, unadorned writing style.
> The musical *Les Misérables* is based on a novel written by Victor Hugo in 1862.

For more information about appositives, see pages 693–694.

Practice Your Skills

A. CONCEPT CHECK

Commas with Introductory Elements and Interrupters Commas have been left out of the following sentences. Write the word that comes before each missing comma, and add the comma.

1. Alice Walker the famous writer was born in Georgia.
2. At the age of twelve she lost the sight in one eye in a shooting accident.
3. This young girl nevertheless did not let her partial loss of sight hold her back.
4. Inspired and driven by determination to succeed she eventually won a scholarship to Spelman College.
5. From Spelman with more goals in mind she went to Sarah Lawrence College in the state of New York.
6. An African American herself Walker studied the history of Africa and became involved in the civil rights movement.
7. Talented and hard-working she soon wrote a book of poems that was accepted for publication.
8. That book her first was titled *Once*.
9. During this period in her life she met and married Melvyn Leventhal.
10. Over the next few years she taught, lectured, and continued to write.
11. In 1982 her eighth book *The Color Purple* was published.

Additional Resources
• Grammar and Usage Practice Book, pp. 179–180.

WRITING THEME Writers

A. Concept Check
Commas with Introductory Elements and Interrupters
1. Walker, writer,
2. twelve,
3. girl, nevertheless,
4. succeed,
5. Spelman, mind,
6. herself,
7. hard-working,
8. book, first,
9. life,
10. years,
11. book, *Purple*,

Writing
—**TIP**—

You can explain or define special names or terms by using appositives.

Writing Theme
Writers

Pulitzer Prize winner
Alice Walker, author of
The Color Purple

12. Achieving popularity almost immediately it became a bestseller.
13. Yes the critics praised the book highly; within a year it won the Pulitzer Prize a major honor.
14. Later made into a movie *The Color Purple* stayed on the bestseller list for twenty-five weeks.
15. In fact this book established Alice Walker once and for all as a major American writer.

B. REVISION SKILL

Achieving Clarity   Ten commas have been left out of the following paragraph. Write the word that comes before each missing comma. Then place the comma correctly.

> (1) Almost unknown in her own time Emily Dickinson has become one of America's most widely read poets. (2) Dickinson born in 1830 lived a very quiet life in Amherst, Massachusetts. (3) Her father Edward Dickinson was a prominent local attorney. (4) Although she was encouraged as a poet by important writers and editors only ten of Dickinson's poems were published during her lifetime. (5) Nevertheless her poetry is considered among the best in American literature. (6) Common themes in Dickinson's poems are love death and eternity. (7) For most of her poems Dickinson did not provide a title.

C. Application in Literature
Punctuation

Answers will vary.

Across the river and ahead, small herbaceous flowers of white, yellow, and purple, blending into the half-grown grass bright green with new life, extended to the horizon. But the child had no eyes for the fleeting spring beauty of the steppes. Weakness and hunger were making her delirious. She started hallucinating.

"I said I'd be careful, Mother. I only swam a little ways, but where did you go?" she muttered. "Mother, when are we going to eat? I'm so hungry, and it's hot. Why didn't you come when I called you? I called and called, but you never came. Where have you been? Mother? Mother! Don't go away again! Stay here! Mother, wait for me! Don't leave me!"

She ran in the direction of the mirage as the vision faded . . . , but the cliff was pulling back from the water's edge, veering away from the river. She was leaving her source of water. Running blindly, she stubbed her toe on a rock and fell hard.

C. APPLICATION IN LITERATURE

Punctuation Some end marks and commas have been left out of the following excerpt. Copy the paragraphs and add the correct punctuation.

> Across the river and ahead small herbaceous flowers of white yellow and purple blending into the half-grown grass bright green with new life extended to the horizon But the child had no eyes for the fleeting spring beauty of the steppes Weakness and hunger were making her delirious She started hallucinating
>
> "I said I'd be careful Mother I only swam a little ways, but where did you go?" she muttered "Mother when are we going to eat I'm so hungry, and it's hot Why didn't you come when I called you I called and called, but you never came Where have you been? Mother? Mother! Don't go away again! Stay here! Mother wait for me Don't leave me!"
>
> She ran in the direction of the mirage as the vision faded . . . , but the cliff was pulling back from the water's edge, veering away from the river She was leaving her source of water Running blindly she stubbed her toe on a rock and fell hard.
>
> **Jean M. Auel, *The Clan of the Cave Bear***

Commas with Quotations

Use commas to set off the explanatory words that precede or follow a direct quotation.

Explanatory words are statements such as *he said, Greg replied,* and *Sheila asked.* They are not part of the quotation. Use a comma after explanatory words when they precede the quotation. When the explanatory words come after the quotation, the comma belongs at the end of the quotation, inside the quotation marks.

> Rich said, "Take the expressway to the third exit."
> "Take the expressway to the third exit," Rich said.

Sometimes a quotation is broken into two parts. The explanatory words separate the two parts. In a divided quotation, use a comma within the quotation marks at the end of the first part of the quotation. Also use a comma after the explanatory words.

> "Take the expressway," Rich said, "to the third exit."

An **indirect quotation** does not include the speaker's exact words. Do not use a comma before an indirect quotation.

> Rich said that we should take the expressway to the third exit.

Commas in Compound Sentences

Use a comma before the conjunction that joins the two main clauses of a compound sentence.

> The Dodgers won the pennant, but they lost in the seventh game of the World Series.
> Lewis seems to be unhappy, or maybe he's just concentrating.

The comma is not necessary when the main clauses joined by *and* are very short.

> We walked in and the telephone rang.

Do not confuse compound sentences with sentences that have compound predicates. There is no comma before the *and* that joins the parts of a compound predicate.

> Elizabeth jumped into the swimming pool *and* rescued the struggling child.
> The movie starts at six *and* ends at eight.

Practice Your Skills

A. CONCEPT CHECK

Commas with Quotations and Compound Sentences Commas have been left out of the following sentences. Write the word that comes before each missing comma. Then add the comma. If no commas are needed in a sentence, write *Correct*.

1. "Whoever wants to know the heart and mind of America" one historian said "had better learn baseball."
2. Most young Americans learn about this game and they delight in stories about legendary players such as Babe Ruth.
3. A mighty home-run hitter, "The Babe" once daringly pointed to center field and then smashed the next ball over the center-field fence.
4. "If I'd missed that homer after calling it" Ruth later told a sportswriter "I'd have looked like an awful fool."
5. Tension mounted as another great player, "Jolting Joe" DiMaggio, hit safely in his fiftieth straight game and fans jammed ballparks to witness baseball history.
6. "His nerves are steady as his bat" the sportswriters declared.
7. DiMaggio's streak ended at an incredible fifty-six games and his batting average during the streak climbed to .408.
8. "Go get a shoebox," manager Casey Stengel once told sixteen-year-old Phil Rizzuto.

Additional Resources
- Grammar and Usage Practice Book, pp. 181–182

WRITING THEME Baseball

Encourage students interested in baseball and sports to consider this theme as a possible topic in the Writer's Workshops. Since Exercise C requires students to punctuate dialogue, you might want to encourage students to find examples of conversations or interviews about sports in newspapers and magazines.

A. Concept Check
Commas with Quotations and Compound Sentences
1. America, said,
2. game,
3. Correct
4. it, sportswriter,
5. game,
6. bat,
7. games,
8. Correct

9. DiMaggio,
10. said, game,

B. **Application in Literature**
Using Commas for Clarification
  1. Correct
  2. right,
  3. Correct
  4. be,
  5. Correct
  6. Correct
  7. kid,
  8. ball,
  9. soon,
 10. Pete,
 11. Correct
 12. right, said,
 13. Pete, said,
 14. me, said,
 15. right,

C. **Application in Writing**
Dialogue
Answers will vary.

9. At 5 feet, 6 inches, and 150 pounds, Rizzuto did not have Ruth's power or the quiet grace of DiMaggio but he proved that baseball dynamite can come in a small package.
10. Sportswriters said "He is one of the finest shortstops ever to play the game" as Rizzuto led the league in putouts, assists, and double plays.

B. APPLICATION IN LITERATURE

Using Commas for Clarification   For each numbered item, write the word that comes before a missing comma. Then add the comma. If no commas are needed, write *Correct*. Notice how commas clarify and separate ideas.

> (1) I asked him if this wasn't the town where that kid named Maneri played ball. (2) "That's right" the guy said. (3) "He's a pretty good ballplayer."
>
> (4) "He should be" I said. (5) "I read that he was the new Phil Rizzuto. . . ."
>
> (6) "What kind of a kid is he?"
>
> (7) "He's a nice kid" the guy said. (8) "He plays good ball but I feel sorry for him. (9) He thought he'd be playing for the Yankees soon and here he is in this town. . . ."
>
> (10) "Hello, Pete" the guy at the desk said. (11) "How goes it today?"
>
> (12) "All right" the kid said but you could see he was exaggerating.
>
> (13) "I'm sorry, Pete" the guy at the desk said "but no mail today."
>
> (14) "Excuse me" I said "but you're Pete Maneri?"
>
> (15) "That's right" the kid said, turning and looking at me.
>
> **W.C. Heinz, "One Throw"**

C. APPLICATION IN WRITING

Dialogue   Three people are discussing their favorite baseball or softball players. Write their conversation. Have each speaker describe a special player and tell why he or she is a favorite. Place commas correctly and include at least one divided quotation.

> *Example*   "I think André Dawson is great," said Kelly, "because he hits so many home runs."
>
> "Yes, but did you know that Dave Winfield has one of the league's best batting averages?" asked Joe.
>
> "I'd rather see Ryne Sandberg play," Jane stated.

Commas with Nonessential Clauses

Use commas to set off nonessential clauses.

Clauses, like appositives or appositive phrases, may be nonessential or essential. A **nonessential clause** merely adds extra information to a sentence. The sentence would be complete without the clause.

An **essential clause** is necessary for the meaning of a sentence. If an essential clause is dropped from a sentence, the meaning changes.

To see if a clause is essential or nonessential, read the sentence without it. If the meaning doesn't change, the clause is nonessential. Use commas before and after it.

Nonessential Clause	Babe Ruth, *who had a lifetime total of 714 home runs,* began his career in the major leagues as a pitcher. Babe Ruth began his career in the major leagues as a pitcher. (The adjective clause is nonessential; it can be dropped.)
Essential Clause	Babe Ruth was the legendary hitter *who began his career in the major leagues as a pitcher.* Babe Ruth was the legendary hitter. (The adjective clause is essential; it cannot be dropped.)

For more information on essential and nonessential clauses, see Grammar Handbook 39, pages 727–728.

Practice Your Skills

CONCEPT CHECK

Commas with Nonessential Clauses   Write each of the following sentences, adding commas where they are needed. If a sentence does not need commas, write *Correct.*

1. Hugh Herr who is from Pennsylvania is an enthusiastic mountain climber.
2. People who don't understand him may even say he's obsessed.
3. Hugh first started rock climbing which became his life's passion at the age of nine.
4. At the age of thirteen, he was making climbs that were too difficult for much older, more experienced climbers.
5. In 1982, Hugh who was then seventeen went with a friend on a climb in New Hampshire and met tragedy.
6. The terror began with a blizzard that struck suddenly and brought winds of up to seventy-three miles per hour.

Writing Theme
Perseverance

Stumbling Block

Some students may have difficulty distinguishing between essential and nonessential clauses. Have students read each sentence aloud, omitting the clause. Then have them determine whether the clause is essential to the meaning of the sentence. This strategy is also useful for distinguishing essential from nonessential appositives.

Additional Resources
• Grammar and Usage Practice Book, pp. 183–184

WRITING THEME   Perseverance

Concept Check
Commas with Nonessential Clauses
1. Hugh Herr, who is from Pennsylvania, is an enthusiastic mountain climber.
2. Correct
3. Hugh first started rock climbing, which became his life's passion, at the age of nine.
4. Correct
5. In 1982, Hugh, who was then seventeen, went with a friend on a climb in New Hampshire and met tragedy.
6. Correct

7. Hugh and his friend, who searched constantly for a trail, survived four days of subzero weather.

8. Correct

9. In March, Hugh's legs, which had been damaged by loss of circulation, were amputated six inches below his knees.

10. Herr, who has two artificial limbs, still climbs mountains.

Linking Grammar and Writing

Encourage students to review letters that they have recently written or received to check the punctuation of dates, place names, salutations, and complimentary closes.

Individualizing Instruction

ESL Students Since the rules for punctuation and capitalization of these items tend to be very different in foreign languages, urge these students to study this section with particular care. Encourage them to give examples of usage in their native language and then to compare these with the English equivalents.

Teaching Tip: Commas

You might want to encourage students to find examples in literature, in newspapers, or in magazines of the uses of commas described in this section.

7. Hugh and his friend who searched constantly for a trail survived four days of subzero weather.
8. Shocked rescuers found two climbers who were suffering from hypothermia, exhaustion, and frostbite.
9. In March, Hugh's legs which had been damaged by loss of circulation were amputated six inches below his knees.
10. Herr who has two artificial limbs still climbs mountains.

Commas in Dates, Place Names, and Letters

In dates, use a comma between the day of the month and the year. When only the month and the year are given, the comma is not necessary.

February 22, 1989   May 8, 1945   October 1966

When a date is part of a sentence, a comma also follows the year.

A talking picture was shown on July 6, 1928, in New York.

Use a comma between the name of a city or town and the name of its state or country.

Houston, Texas   Athens, Greece

When an address is part of a sentence, use a comma after each item. Do not put a comma between the state and the ZIP code.

Jackson lived in Yuma, Arizona, until his death in 1951.
For more information, write to the American Library Association, 50 East Huron Street, Chicago, IL 60611.

Use a comma after the salutation of a friendly letter. Use a comma after the complimentary close of a friendly letter or a business letter.

Dear Gretchen,   Yours truly,

Commas to Avoid Confusion

Without commas, these sentences could be misunderstood:

On the river boats drifted lazily with the current.
Inside everything was a mess.

With commas, the sentences are clearer.

On the river, boats drifted lazily with the current.
Inside, everything was a mess.

Practice Your Skills

A. CONCEPT CHECK

Commas in Dates and Place Names; Commas to Avoid Confusion
Write each sentence, adding necessary commas. If no commas are needed, write *Correct*.

1. Toward a distant star watchers gaze from hills, back porches, and observatories.
2. Whenever there is a clear night all over the earth people adjust telescopes and binoculars.
3. These are the stargazers—from Chicago Illinois to Aberdeen Washington to Greenwich England.
4. Whether amateur or professional stargazers add to this world's knowledge of other worlds.
5. Until now, those who observed watched with their feet planted firmly on the earth.
6. The August 1989 issue of *Omni* magazine, however, described a move that might provide as much information as traveling among the stars.
7. The cover of the issue featured robots; but inside an article described how a space shuttle would carry the Hubble space telescope into orbit.
8. Cape Canaveral Florida was the site of the launch of the space shuttle *Discovery* on April 24 1990.
9. Within it it held the Hubble ninety-four-inch telescope, two cameras, a photometer, and two spectrometers.
10. Unfortunately, as astronomers eagerly awaited the first images the telescope developed problems; and down on the ground scientists worked frantically to find solutions.

B. REVISION SKILL

Adding Commas Commas have been left out of the following items. Number your paper 1 to 15. For each item, copy the word or number that comes before each missing comma. Then add the comma. If no commas are needed, write *Correct*.

1. Dear Alonzo
2. In the letter you wrote last week you asked what I had been studying in science.
3. I can't imagine why you want to know but here goes.
4. On second thought however I think you might find it fascinating—or interesting, at least.
5. On June 30 1908 a ball of fire blazed across the sky of Siberia.
6. It touched the earth causing a tremendous explosion.

Punctuation **783**

Additional Resources
• Grammar and Usage Practice Book, pp. 185–186

WRITING THEME   Stargazers

A. Concept Check
Commas in Dates and Place Names; Commas to Avoid Confusion
1. Toward a distant star, watchers gaze from hills, back porches, and observatories.
2. Whenever there is a clear night, all over the earth, people adjust telescopes and binoculars.
3. These are the stargazers—from Chicago, Illinois, to Aberdeen, Washington, to Greenwich, England.
4. Whether amateur or professional, stargazers add to this world's knowledge of other worlds.
5. Correct
6. Correct
7. The cover of the issue featured robots; but inside, an article described how a space shuttle would carry the Hubble space telescope into orbit.
8. Cape Canaveral, Florida, was the site of the launch of the space shuttle *Discovery* on April 24, 1990.
9. Within it, it held the Hubble ninety-four-inch telescope, two cameras, a photometer, and two spectrometers.
10. Unfortunately, as astronomers eagerly awaited the first images, the telescope developed problems; and down on the ground, scientists worked frantically to find solutions.

B. Revision Skill
Adding Commas
1. Alonzo,
2. week,
3. know,
4. thought, however,
5. June 30, 1908,
6. earth,

7. fact,
8. Correct
9. phenomenon,
10. hole, meteor,
11. However,
12. is, Siberia,
13. Correct
14. friend,
15. Correct

CHECK POINT
PAGES 769–782

You may wish to use the following Checkpoint exercise as an informal evaluation of student mastery of rules for the use of periods, question marks, exclamation points, and commas covered in this handbook.

WRITING THEME The Sun

1. For more than thirty-five billion years, the sun has been a constant source of light for the earth.
2. However, there are occasionally great changes called maximums in its normal light-giving patterns.
3. During the maximums, sunflares shoot tens of thousands of miles above the sun's surface.
4. What causes these flares?
5. They are produced by exploding sunspots, and they occur in twenty-two-year cycles.
6. Besides these flares, great blobs of the sun's corona sometimes break free, traveling at speeds of up to two million miles per hour.
7. A recent maximum began on March 9, 1989.
8. What a spectacular phenomenon it was!
9. For a period of three days, the blasts of X-ray and ultraviolet radiation seared through the earth's upper atmosphere.
10. A dedicated scientist who works at Sunspot, New Mexico, recorded data.
11. He considered it, at one point, a record-breaker.
12. Can you imagine the tremendous power generated by these solar hiccups?
13. A maximum, according to one expert, can produce enough energy to supply a major city with power for 200 million years. Astonishing!
14. A poet, George Meredith, once wrote, ''The sun is coming down to earth. . . .''

7. In fact it destroyed about 2,000 square kilometers of forest.
8. Yet the interesting part of the story is that there was no impact crater left on the site where the fireball hit.
9. Scientists have suggested many theories for this phenomenon which is called the Tunguska Event.
10. It might have been caused by a black hole a meteor or even the crash of an extraterrestrial vessel.
11. However most scientists believe that a comet was involved.
12. That is in 1908 a piece of comet struck the earth in Central Siberia Russia.
13. What's your theory?
14. Your friend
15. Amy

CHECK POINT
PAGES 769–784

Write the following sentences, adding periods, question marks, exclamation points, and commas where they are needed.

1. For more than thirty-five billion years the sun has been a constant source of light for the earth
2. However there are occasionally great changes called maximums in its normal light-giving patterns
3. During the maximums sunflares shoot tens of thousands of miles above the sun's surface
4. What causes these flares
5. They are produced by exploding sunspots and they occur in twenty-two-year cycles
6. Besides these flares great blobs of the sun's corona sometimes break free traveling at speeds of up to two million miles per hour
7. A recent maximum began on March 9 1989
8. What a spectacular phenomenon it was
9. For a period of three days the blasts of X-ray and ultraviolet radiation seared through the earth's upper atmosphere
10. A dedicated scientist who works at Sunspot New Mexico recorded data
11. He considered it at one point a record-breaker
12. Can you imagine the tremendous power generated by these solar hiccups
13. A maximum according to one expert can produce enough energy to supply a major city with power for 200 million years Astonishing
14. A poet George Meredith once wrote "The sun is coming down to earth. . . ."

Northwest Coast Indian Bella Coola mask, representing the sun.

784 Grammar Handbook

Humanities Connection

Art Note *Bella Coola Mask* is a wood carving done by a Native American artist of the Northwest Coast tribes in British Columbia. The coastal tribes of the northwestern United States and Canada created very symbolic, intricately carved masks and totem poles. Often, the owner did not reveal the true meaning of the mask or the story behind its creation. Ask: What type of masks are popular in our culture at Halloween, for example? What do these masks say about our culture?

15. During the three-day period in March the sun did indeed seem to be coming down to earth
16. Low-orbiting satellites that encountered the force were slowed
17. Shortwave transmissions were interrupted for twenty-four hours or more
18. Automatic garage doors opened on their own mystifying owners
19. There was a huge devastating power outage throughout the city of Montreal Canada
20. The famous northern lights which are amazing at any time became so spectacular that they were seen as far south as Brownsville Texas

THE SEMICOLON AND COLON

Like commas, semicolons separate elements in a sentence. The semicolon, however, signals a more emphatic break than a comma. Colons are generally used to point out what comes next. A colon causes an abrupt break in the rhythm of the sentence.

Use a semicolon to join the parts of a compound sentence if no coordinating conjunction is used.

The overseas operator interrupted the call; our time was up.

When there are several commas in the parts of a compound sentence, separate the clauses with a semicolon.

On this plan I can eat whole-grain bread, fruits, and vegetables; but candy, soft drinks, and desserts are forbidden.

When commas occur within parts of a series, use semicolons to separate the parts.

In the Olympics the first-place winner gets a gold medal; second-place, a silver medal; and third-place, a bronze medal.

Use a semicolon before a conjunctive adverb that joins the clauses of a compound sentence.

You know that the parts of a compound sentence are sometimes joined by such words as *therefore, however, otherwise, consequently, besides, nevertheless,* and *moreover.* These words, called **conjunctive adverbs,** are preceded by a semicolon and followed by a comma.

Tamika is good at batting; however, her pitching is weak.

Punctuation   **785**

15. During the three-day period in March, the sun did, indeed, seem to be coming down to earth.
16. Low-orbiting satellites that encountered the force were slowed.
17. Shortwave transmissions were interrupted for twenty-four hrs. or more.
18. Automatic garage doors opened on their own, mystifying owners.
19. There was a huge, devastating power outage throughout the city of Montreal, Canada.
20. The famous northern lights, which are amazing at any time, became so spectacular that they were seen as far south as Brownsville, Texas.

The Semicolon and Colon

Objectives

- To use semicolons correctly in compound sentences, series, and before a conjunctive adverb
- To use colons correctly in lists, business letters, expressions of time, and biblical references, between sentences, and before long or formal quotations
- **Writing** To use proofreading and revision skills to correct and add punctuation

Teaching Tip: Colons

Students will improve their mastery of these rules for the uses of colons by making up their own sentences combining two or more uses. Start them off with an example such as the following:

"Dear Ms. Briggs:

Please ship the following items for delivery no later than 4:30 P.M. next Wednesday: the two lamps, the pair of side chairs, and the carpet."

Spot Check

Use the quotation as an opportunity for students to review some of the rules they have studied so far. For example: commas with introductory elements ("When at table,"); semicolons joining compound sentences in the absence of a conjunction ("the business of the moment; his look seemed riveted"); commas with nonessential clauses ("appetite, which was so fierce"); and commas in compound sentences ("his forehead swelled, and generally a strong perspiration was visible").

Linking Grammar and Writing

You might want to have students analyze James Boswell's use of commas in his quotation about Samuel Johnson. Point out that his punctuation, which was accepted style in the eighteenth century, is not acceptable today. Challenge students to rewrite the passage using the conventions of modern punctuation.

Usage Note Many of the words listed on the preceding page can also be used as interrupters. In this case, use commas to set off the word.

> Tony turned in his paper a day late; however, he got a high grade. (conjunctive adverb)
> Mr. Becker, however, gave Tony a high grade. (interrupter)

The Colon

Use a colon to introduce a list of items.

Use a colon when it might have the meaning "and here it is" or "and here they are." A colon often follows a word or phrase such as *these* or *the following items*.

> The FBI investigates the following federal crimes: spying, treason, kidnapping, and counterfeiting.

Never use a colon after a verb or a preposition.

> The term *mass media* refers to television, radio, newspapers, magazines, and books.

Use a colon after the greeting of a business letter.

> Dear Ms. Nolan: Dear Sir or Madam:

Use a colon between numerals indicating hours and minutes.

> 4:30 P.M.   8:15 A.M.

Use a colon between chapter and verse in a biblical reference.

> Genesis 2:4–7   Job 3:2–4

Use a colon between two sentences when the second explains or summarizes the first.

> It's obvious why you're tired: you've been staying up too late.

Use a colon to introduce a long or formal quotation.

> James Boswell once had the following to say about Samuel Johnson: "I never knew any man who relished good eating more than he did. When at table, he was totally absorbed in the business of the moment; his looks seemed riveted to his plate; nor would he say one word, or even pay the least attention to what was said by others, till he had satisfied his appetite, which was so fierce, and indulged with such intenseness, that while in the act of eating, the veins of his forehead swelled, and generally a strong perspiration was visible."

Broadway Boogie Woogie, by Piet Mondrian, 1942–43

Practice Your Skills

A. CONCEPT CHECK

Semicolons and Colons   Write the following sentences, adding the necessary semicolons, colons, and commas.

1. Great composers didn't just hear music they saw it—in color.
2. Scientists do not know the causes of "colored hearing," or chromesthesia therefore they cannot explain how it works.
3. The *Encyclopaedia Britannica* states "Sounds, physically considered, consist of rapid variations in the density of a medium, usually the air."
4. These sound waves may be translated by some brains into waves of the color spectrum we just don't know.
5. Among the composers who "saw" colors however are the following Beethoven, Rimsky-Korsakov, Liszt, and Scriabin.
6. To Rimsky-Korsakov, F-sharp major was green to Alexander Scriabin, violet to Serge Koussevitzky, strawberry red.
7. Franz Liszt's commands to his orchestra, when he conducted, often confused them he asked for more pink, less blue.
8. Besides musicians, people with chromesthesia may include the following writers, plumbers, bank tellers, or anyone at all.
9. Nonmusicians may simply not talk about the phenomenon besides they may not pay a great deal of attention to it.
10. Who knows moreover how many people see colors of the rainbow as music flows from their radios at 715 every morning?

Writing Theme
Musicians

Additional Resources
- Grammar and Usage Practice Book, pp. 187–188

WRITING THEME   Musicians

You might want to encourage students to do additional research on this theme and use it as the subject of an expository Writer's Workshop assignment.

A. Concept Check
Semicolons and Colons
1. Great composers didn't just hear music; they saw it—in color.
2. Scientists do not know the causes of "colored hearing," or chromesthesia; therefore, they cannot explain how it works.
3. The *Encyclopaedia Britannica* states: "Sounds, physically considered, consist of rapid variations in the density of a medium, usually the air."
4. These sound waves may be translated by some brains into waves of the color spectrum; we just don't know.
5. Among the composers who "saw" colors, however, are the following: Beethoven, Rimsky-Korsakov, Liszt, and Scriabin.
6. To Rimsky-Korsakov, F-sharp major was green; to Alexander Scriabin, violet; to Serge Koussevitzky, strawberry red.
7. Franz Liszt's commands to his orchestra, when he conducted, often confused them: he asked for more pink, less blue.
8. Besides musicians, people with chromesthesia may include the following: writers, plumbers, bank tellers, or anyone at all.
9. Nonmusicians may simply not talk about the phenomenon; besides, they may not pay a great deal of attention to it.
10. Who knows, moreover, how many people see colors of the rainbow as music flows from their radios at 7:15 every morning?

Humanities Connection

Art Note   Pictured is a typical, non-objective painting by the Dutch artist, Piet Mondrian (b. 1872, the Netherlands, d. 1944). Mondrian painted non-objective or totally abstract canvases during his last period in the United States. These paintings were inspired by the colors he sensed in musical compositions, especially jazz. Mondrian believed that line, geometric shapes, and brilliant primary colors best conveyed his "colored music." Ask: What song or songs do you visualize when viewing this painting?

B. Revision Skill

Eliminating Confusion

(1) Teresa Carreño was an inspired pianist, a successful opera singer, and a fascinating woman. (2) Carreño showed musical talent by the age of three; at six, she began piano lessons. (3) In 1862, when Teresa was nine, her life changed dramatically: her family moved from Venezuela to New York. (4) Her first public appearance occurred a few months later; she was a success. (5) During her teens, Carreño was given help and advice by the following great musicians: Rossini, Liszt, Bazin, and Rubinstein.

(6) Unlike many child prodigies, Carreño continued to grow musically; consequently, she became one of the greatest pianists in the world. (7) Her playing was colorful; it was exaggerated, rapid, individual, and full of fire. (8) Only one pianist could be considered her equal; his name was Eugen d'Albert. (9) Inevitably, the two great musicians met; moreover, they married. (10) The marriage did not last; however, Carreño's career did, until she died at sixty-three.

C. Proofreading Skill

Adding Punctuation

Dear Mr. Velez:

Here are the scheduled departure times for flights to London, England: 8:05 A.M., 12:30 P.M., and 9:15 P.M.

As for bringing your guitar aboard, I've checked; you surely may. The rule is as follows: bring the instrument as carry-on baggage if you have a first-class ticket. There are additional requirements: first, you must be at the gate twenty minutes before flight time; second, the guitar must be in a case; and third, it must be insured. We cannot guarantee that you can fly incognito; however, we will do everything within our power to protect your privacy.

Sincerely yours,

Rebecca T. Emerson

B. REVISION SKILL

Eliminating Confusion   When you revise, you can use punctuation to correct problems, such as run-on sentences, that can confuse a reader. Rewrite the following paragraphs, using semicolons, colons, and commas correctly.

(1) Teresa Carreño was an inspired pianist a successful opera singer and a fascinating woman. (2) Carreño showed musical talent by the age of three at six, she began piano lessons. (3) In 1862, when Teresa was nine, her life changed dramatically her family moved from Venezuela to New York. (4) Her first public appearance occurred a few months later she was a success. (5) During her teens, Carreño was given help and advice by the following great musicians Rossini, Liszt, Bazin, and Rubinstein.

(6) Unlike many child prodigies, Carreño continued to grow musically consequently she became one of the greatest pianists in the world. (7) Her playing was colorful it was exaggerated, rapid, individual, and full of fire. (8) Only one pianist could be considered her equal his name was Eugen d'Albert. (9) Inevitably, the two great musicians met moreover they married. (10) The marriage did not last however Carreño's career did, until she died at sixty-three.

C. PROOFREADING SKILL

Adding Punctuation   On your paper, copy the following letter. Add each missing punctuation mark.

Dear Mr Velez

Here are the scheduled departure times for flights to London England 805 A.M., 1230 P.M., and 915 P.M.

As for bringing your guitar aboard, I've checked you surely may. The rule is as follows bring the instrument as carry-on baggage if you have a first-class ticket. There are additional requirements first you must be at the gate twenty minutes before flight time second the guitar must be in a case and third it must be insured. We cannot guarantee that you can fly incognito however we will do everything within our power to protect your privacy.

Sincerely yours
Rebecca T Emerson

THE DASH AND PARENTHESES

Like commas, dashes and parentheses are used to set off words that break into the main idea of a sentence. Use commas for material closely connected to the main idea. Use dashes to show a looser connection, and parentheses to set off material with only a slight connection.

Dashes with Interrupters

Commas set off words and short phrases, such as *however* and *by the way,* that interrupt a sentence. With an abrupt change of thought, or an idea that breaks into the flow of a sentence, use dashes to set off the words.

> People grew impatient—the parade was already thirty minutes behind schedule—and began to leave.

The Dash Before a Summary

Use a dash after a series to indicate that a summary statement will follow.

> Edsels, Packards, and Hudsons—these cars are no longer made.

Do not use dashes to replace semicolons or periods.

Parentheses

Except for enclosing source documentation in reports, parentheses are rarely needed by student writers. Since parentheses are used to separate material that is only vaguely connected to the main idea of a sentence, it is usually better to put this material in a separate sentence. Use commas or dashes for more closely related ideas.
The following examples show the use of parentheses:

> It was a black suit with a formal Mao jacket (what the Chinese call a Sun Yat-sen suit), and black cloth shoes to match.
> If anything is not "quite right" with your order (fit, style, or even color), please return it for a full refund or exchange.
> Even the old shell game (which shell covers the pea?) goes back to the beginnings of recorded history.
> After a pause, which my appearance seemed to produce (for he eyed me closely as I approached), he gave a whoop, and swore that he could out-swap any man that ever walked the hills.

The Dash and Parentheses

Objectives

- To use dashes correctly with interrupters and before a summary
- To use parentheses correctly

Teaching Strategies

Linking Grammar and Writing

Point out to students that they should be careful not to overuse dashes since this practice may result in choppy, disjointed writing.

WRITING THEME   Herbs and Flowers

A. Concept Check

Dashes

Answers will vary. See suggested answers
below.

    1. Cooking, decorating, healing—all these
are uses for herbs.

    2. Parsley and mint, which are fragrant
herbs, can repel insects.

    3. Chamomile—perhaps your grandmother
uses it—is popular as a hot, soothing beverage.

    4. Herbs are used in many products—
soaps, cosmetics, toothpaste—that are sold in
health-food stores.

    5. During the Middle Ages, people were less
systematic, or maybe they simply used different
concepts about classifying herbs, flowers, and
vegetables.

    6. Mint, lettuce, and roses—all these were
considered herbs during the fifteenth century.

    7. Flowers, besides being used as decora-
tive items, were used in salads and as flavoring
in desserts.

    8. Shakespeare's *Hamlet*, a sixteenth-cen-
tury play, refers to rosemary as "for remembrance."

    9. Victorians used flowers to send mes-
sages—daisies for love, violets for faithfulness,
and pansies for thoughts.

    10. Regret, purity, flattery, love—these are
only a few of the symbolic meanings herbs have
had.

The Hyphen

Objective

• To use hyphens correctly

Writing Theme
Herbs and Flowers

Practice Your Skills

CONCEPT CHECK

Dashes   Write the following sentences, adding commas or dashes
where they are needed.

1. Cooking, decorating, healing all these are uses for herbs.
2. Parsley and mint which are fragrant herbs can repel insects.
3. Chamomile perhaps your grandmother uses it is popular as a hot
   soothing beverage.
4. Herbs are used in many products soaps, cosmetics, toothpaste that
   are sold in health-food stores.
5. During the Middle Ages, people were less systematic or maybe they
   simply used different concepts about classifying herbs, flowers, and
   vegetables.
6. Mint, lettuce, and roses all these were considered herbs during the
   fifteenth century.
7. Flowers besides being used as decorative items were used in salads
   and as flavoring in desserts.
8. Shakespeare's *Hamlet* a sixteenth-century play refers to rosemary
   as "for remembrance."
9. Victorians used flowers to send messages daisies for love, violets
   for faithfulness, and pansies for thoughts.
10. Regret, purity, flattery, love these are only a few of the symbolic
    meanings herbs have had.

▪HE HYPHEN

    **Use a hyphen if part of a word must be carried over from one
line to the next.**

      The FBI reported that it had about 169,000,000 finger-
         prints on file.

    Only words having two or more syllables can be broken by a
hyphen. Never divide one-syllable words like *growl* or *weight*. A
single letter should not be put at the end or beginning of a line. For
instance, these divisions would be wrong: *e-lection, cloud-y.*

    **Use hyphens in compound numbers from twenty-one to
ninety-nine.**

      seventy-six trombones   fifty-five glass marbles

    Use hyphens in fractions.

      a two-thirds majority   one-fourth of the votes

Use hyphens in certain compound nouns.

Words like *brother-in-law, drive-in, great-grandmother,* and *self-control* are hyphenated.

The *editor in chief* of the local paper is my *sister-in-law.*

Use a dictionary to determine whether a compound noun needs a hyphen.

Use a hyphen or hyphens between words that make up a compound adjective used before a noun.

Stephen King's latest thriller is a well-written book.

Compound adjectives after a noun are not usually hyphenated.

Stephen King's latest thriller is well written.

Practice Your Skills

CONCEPT CHECK

Hyphens Copy the word or words that should be hyphenated in each sentence. Then add the necessary hyphens. Use a dictionary if necessary.

1. Historically, honey has always been a much valued product.
2. Ancient Greeks considered it an all purpose remedy.
3. They even used it as a hair restoring preparation!
4. Athletes depended on it as a long lasting energy source.
5. It was also an easy to obtain antiseptic.
6. Actually, honey contains hydrogen peroxide, a well known, dependable germ killer.
7. Besides, honey is used in many tried and true recipes.
8. An old recipe for Roman dates calls for one half cup of honey.
9. An orange flavored rice dish from North Africa also contains some honey.
10. Your great grandmother probably knew ninety nine different ways of using honey herself!

Writing Theme
Honey

Punctuation **791**

You may wish to use the following Checkpoint exercise as an informal evaluation of student mastery of the rules for using semicolons, colons, dashes, and hyphens covered in this handbook.

WRITING THEME Ancient Greece

1. A typical day for a male citizen in ancient Athens—it was much different for women and slaves—began with a leisurely meal.

2. An Athenian breakfast was a piece of wine-soaked bread, sometimes accompanied by a handful of olives; this was usually followed by a visit to the market.

3. The ancient Greek market—it was called the *agora*—was a place for people to shop and to visit.

4. Greengrocers' stalls, bakers' stalls, and trays of just-caught fish—all of these were set up at dawn.

5. People gathered ordinarily for one of the following activities: to sell, to buy, to gossip, or to discuss serious topics, such as philosophy or politics.

6. Lunch was light; it was followed by a nap.

7. An afternoon of exercise—public gymnasiums were available to all men—was followed by a bath.

8. Dinner was eaten around 5:00 P.M. and usually consisted of these foods: eggs, fish, and cheese.

9. The ancient Greeks also had a taste for garlic-flavored foods.

10. ''Fingers only'' was the rule; no forks, knives, or spoons were used.

11. The beverage, Greek wine, was syrup-like, so water was used to dilute it—one-third wine to two-thirds water.

Banquet scene from a Greek krater (mixing bowl)

Greek serving vessel

Write the following sentences, adding any semicolons, colons, dashes, and hyphens that have been left out.

1. A typical day for a male citizen in ancient Athens it was much different for women and slaves began with a leisurely meal.

2. An Athenian breakfast was a piece of wine soaked bread, sometimes accompanied by a handful of olives this was usually followed by a visit to the market.

3. The ancient Greek market it was called the *agora* was a place for people to shop and to visit.

4. Greengrocers' stalls, bakers' stalls, and trays of just caught fish all of these were set up at dawn.

5. People gathered ordinarily for one of the following activities to sell, to buy, to gossip, or to discuss serious topics such as philosophy or politics.

6. Lunch was light it was followed by a nap.

7. An afternoon of exercise public gymnasiums were available to all men was followed by a bath.

8. Dinner was eaten around 500 P.M. and usually consisted of these foods eggs, fish, and cheese.

9. The ancient Greeks also had a taste for garlic flavored foods.

10. "Fingers only" was the rule no forks, knives, or spoons were used.

11. The beverage, Greek wine, was syruplike, so water was used to dilute it one third wine to two thirds water.

12. Nuts, olives, figs these accompanied after dinner conversation.
13. After the meal, the men enjoyed singing however, serious discussion was considered another form of entertainment.
14. Life was slow, civilized, and this was true only if you were wealthy very pleasant.
15. The following activities were considered proper for women managing the large, busy households supervising servants, especially the females spinning and weaving.

THE APOSTROPHE

Use the apostrophe to form the possessive of nouns.

To use the apostrophe correctly, you must know whether a noun is singular or plural. To form the possessive of a singular noun, add an apostrophe and *s* even if the singular noun ends in *s: student's, Les's*. To form the possessive of a plural noun ending in *s*, add only the apostrophe: *racers', Smiths', boys'*. Plural nouns that do not end in *s* take an apostrophe and *s: women's, children's*. For a complete discussion of forming possessive nouns, see Grammar Handbook 31, pages 541–542.

To form the possessive of an indefinite pronoun, use an apostrophe and *s*.

> everybody + 's = everybody's   someone + 's = someone's

Do not use an apostrophe with a possessive personal pronoun.

> hers   ours   yours   its   theirs

Use an apostrophe in a contraction.

In contractions, words are joined and letters are left out. An apostrophe replaces the letter or letters that are missing.

> she's = she is *or* has   hasn't = has not
> they're = they are   won't = will not
> it's = it is *or* has   shouldn't = should not

Use an apostrophe to show the omission of numbers in a date.

> the spring of '89 (the spring of 1989)

Use an apostrophe and *s* to form the plurals of letters, numerals, and words used as words.

> ABC's   two *n*'s   three 4's   *yes*'s and *no*'s

Greek serving vessel

Humanities Connection

Art Note Shown in pages 792 and 793 are two examples of ancient Greek pottery, *Oinokoe a testa femminile* and *Coppa a testa d'arie*. Oinokoe means *jug* in Greek. Coppa is derived from the Latin word for *cup*. Testa is Italian for *head*. *Aries* means *ram* in Latin. Ask: How would you translate each descriptive phrase?

12. Nuts, olives, figs—these accompanied after-dinner conversation.
13. After the meal, the men enjoyed singing; however, serious discussion was considered another form of entertainment.
14. Life was slow, civilized, and—this was true only if you were wealthy—very pleasant.
15. The following activities were considered proper for women: managing the large, busy households; supervising servants, especially the females; spinning; and weaving.

The Apostrophe

Objectives

- To use apostrophes correctly to form the possessive of nouns and indefinite pronouns
- To use apostrophes correctly in contractions, omissions of numbers, and certain plurals and other expressions
- **Writing** To use revision skills to correct errors in the use of apostrophes

Teaching Strategies

Individualizing Instruction

Basic Students Draw special attention in this section to the importance of apostrophes for clarity in writing. Remind students that omitting a necessary apostrophe can lead to confusion of two words: for example, *she'll* and *shell*, ''*we'll* and *well*, or *it's* and *its*. The last example is an especially common error. If students are confused by the fact that personal pronouns such as *ours* do not take apostrophes, point out that such pronouns are *already* possessive in form; they do not need an apostrophe to indicate possession.

ESL Students Because the apostrophe does not exist in most other languages, it might be necessary to stress to these students the difference in form and function between the apostrophe and the comma.

Practice Your Skills

A. CONCEPT CHECK

Apostrophes   Find the words with errors in the use or omission of apostrophes. Write each word correctly on your paper.

1. An orangutans weight can be up to two hundred kilo's.
2. Many orangutans skeletons' reveal broken bones, suggesting that they were too heavy for the trees they inhabited.
3. Acrobatic skills are among some species notable traits.
4. Gibbon apes abilities include leaping great distances in trees.
5. A chimpanzee is curious and it's temperament is lively.
6. Chimpanzees diet's include termites and ants.
7. Its clear that grooming is important in chimps' lives.
8. Combing each others hair is a sign of friendship.
9. That some chimps learn sign language cant be denied.
10. Indeed, their's is an interesting story.

Squirrel monkey, Baker, being prepared for 1959 NASA space flight.

B. PROOFREADING SKILL

Using Apostrophes Correctly   In the following passage, find the words with errors and write them correctly.

(1) The guenons' are a genus of monkey found throughout sub-Saharan Africa. (2) They've all got long tails. (3) The smallest of all guenon monkey's is the Allen swamp monkey. (4) Its the size of a large squirrel. (5) It's face is black with gray circles around the eyes. (6) It has dark whisker's and a yellow throat. (7) A swamp monkeys home is the damp jungle.

(8) Another guenon monkey is the talapoin, a native of the Congo River region. (9) One of the talapoins favorite foods is green nuts that are so bitter humans cant eat them. (10) The talapoin sports a yellow mustache and whiskers'.

QUOTATION MARKS

Use quotation marks at the beginning and at the end of a direct quotation.

Quotation marks are used to show that a speaker's exact words are being stated.

Linda said, "Someone is following me."

Quotation marks are not used with indirect quotations. The word *that* often signals an indirect quotation.

Linda said *that* someone was following her.

When explanatory words come at the beginning of a sentence, use a comma directly after them. Begin the quotation with quotation marks. Place the period at the end of a sentence inside the quotation marks.

The flight attendant announced, "Fasten your seat belts."

Sometimes explanatory words end the sentence. In such cases, the quoted statement at the beginning of the sentence is followed by a comma. The comma belongs inside the quotation marks.

"Fasten your seat belts," the pilot directed the passengers.

To write a quote within a quote, use single quotation marks to enclose the inside quotation. In these instances a double quotation mark follows the single quotation mark.

"Patrick Henry gave his famous speech in which he said, 'Give me liberty or give me death!' before the Virginia Provincial Convention on March 23, 1775," Mr. Gomez told us.

Divided Quotations

Sometimes a quotation is divided by explanatory words. Then each part of the quotation is enclosed by quotation marks.

"A healthful snack," Pam said, "is granola with yogurt."

When the divided quotation is a single sentence, begin the second part with a small letter, as in the example above. When the second part begins a new sentence, use a capital letter.

"There is entertainment at half time," Toby noted. "The marching band will perform."

Objectives

- To use quotation marks correctly
- To combine quotation marks with other punctuation marks correctly
- To punctuate titles correctly

Teaching Strategies

Linking Grammar and Writing

Point out that newspaper, magazine, and research writers have a special responsibility to identify accurately the exact words of direct quotations and to distinguish them from indirect quotations or paraphrases. Encourage students to review articles in the local newspaper for examples of direct and indirect quotations.

Individualizing Instruction

ESL Students   Languages such as Spanish and Russian use inverted opening quotation marks. Stress the difference in English for these students.

WRITING THEME Limericks

Drafting Skill

Using Direct Quotations

Answers will vary. See typical answers below.

1a. "If you have never written a limerick,"
Sue said, "you really should try your hand at it."

b. Sue said, "If you have never written a limerick, you really should try your hand at it."

c. "If you have never written a limerick, you really should try your hand at it," Sue said.

2a. "A limerick is a brief, humorous poem with five lines and regular patterns of rhyme and rhythm," she continued.

b. She continued, "A limerick is a brief, humorous poem with five lines and regular patterns of rhyme and rhythm."

c. "A limerick," she continued, "is a brief, humorous poem with five lines and regular patterns of rhyme and rhythm."

3a. "Yes," Sue noted, "the first and second lines rhyme with the fifth, and the third and fourth lines rhyme."

b. "Yes, the first and second lines rhyme with the fifth," Sue noted, "and the third and fourth lines rhyme."

c. Sue noted, "Yes, the first and second lines rhyme with the fifth, and the third and fourth lines rhyme."

4a. I interrupted, "I hear that some people call limericks the lowest form of verse."

b. "I hear that some people," I interrupted, "call limericks the lowest form of verse."

c. "I hear that some people call limericks the lowest form of verse," I interrupted.

5a. "It would be a great deal of fun," my older sister said, "to write a limerick that begins 'There once was a student of English . . .'"

b. "It would be a great deal of fun to write a limerick that begins 'There once was a student of English . . . ,'" my older sister said.

c. My older sister said, "It would be a great deal of fun to write a limerick that begins 'There once was a student of English . . .'"

The first part of a divided quotation is followed by a comma. Commas always appear inside closing quotation marks.

> "By the way," Mario said innocently, "there is an ant on your arm."

The explanatory words in the middle of a divided quotation are followed by either a period or a comma. Use a period if the first part completes a sentence. Use a comma if the sentence continues.

> "Before you set up camp," Eric cautioned, "check for rattlesnakes."
>
> "First, we spread paste on the wallpaper," Ginger said. "Then we hang the paper and trim the excess."

Practice Your Skills

DRAFTING SKILL

Using Direct Quotations Write each of the following sentences as a direct quotation in three different ways. Add or subtract words or change punctuation if necessary. Use explanatory words other than *said* in some of the sentences.

1. If you have never written a limerick, you really should try your hand at it.
2. A limerick is a brief, humorous poem with five lines and regular patterns of rhyme and rhythm.
3. Yes, the first and second lines rhyme with the fifth, and the third and fourth lines rhyme.
4. I hear that some people call limericks the lowest form of verse.
5. My older sister said it would be a great deal of fun to write a limerick that begins "There once was a student of English. . . ."

Other Punctuation with Quotation Marks

Place question marks and exclamation points inside the quotation marks if they belong to the quotation itself.

> Jacob asked, "Have you met my dog Brutus?"
>
> Reuben exclaimed, "What a beautiful animal!"

Place question marks and exclamation points outside the quotation marks if they do not belong to the quotation.

> Did you hear Ray Washington say, "I can't possibly come to class next week"?
>
> How nice to hear Adam say, "I'll lend you my notes"!

Practice Your Skills

A. CONCEPT CHECK

Quotation Marks Punctuate the following sentences correctly, using quotation marks, end marks, and commas. Remember that indirect quotations need only end punctuation.

1. This way called the guide Your tour down the world-famous Rhine River is about to begin
2. Martha asked Will we pass the cliff where Lorelei lived
3. Yes, we will answered the guide In fact, it's just outside Mainz which is around the next bend
4. Who inquired Blake is Lorelei
5. The guide explained that, according to legend, she was a water nymph who lured sailors to their deaths
6. Did she say Lorelei was a water nymph
7. Be quiet and listen exclaimed Martha
8. Look! That cliff must be hundreds of feet high! marveled Blake
9. I don't believe that stuff scoffed Jeff It's impossible
10. Don't be too sure the guide replied Remember that the Roman scholar Tertullian said I believe it because it is impossible

B. DRAFTING SKILL

Using Quotations Write each of the following sentences as a quotation. Add explanatory words such as *Della stated*. In some of your sentences, put the quotation first. In others, put it at the end or divide the quotation with explanatory words.

1. Honestly! Through the ages, some of the tales that travelers have spun have been wild.
2. You mean like the story of the Loch Ness monster?
3. Yes, but there are other alleged encounters with odd beings that are just as strange.
4. Have you heard the tale of the Gulo of northern Sweden?
5. It's a creature that's supposed to look like a large dog with a cat's face.
6. The local people used its brown hair to make caps. They used its hoofs to cure earaches.
7. Not all travelers' tales are ancient. Some are modern.
8. The story of the Yeti in the Himalayas is an example of a contemporary tale, isn't it?
9. That's right. People in every mountain range in the world seem to tell similar stories of a "Bigfoot."
10. In the Gobi it's called the Meti; in Assam, Kang Mi; and in the Canadian Rockies, Sasquatch.

Punctuation   **797**

A. Concept Check

Quotation Marks

Answers will vary. See suggested answers below.

1. "This way!" called the guide. "Your tour down the world-famous Rhine River is about to begin."
2. Martha asked, "Will we pass the cliff where Lorelei lived?"
3. "Yes, we will," answered the guide. "In fact, it's just outside Mainz, which is around the next bend."
4. "Who," inquired Blake, "is Lorelei?"
5. The guide explained that, according to legend, she was a water nymph who lured sailors to their deaths.
6. "Did she say Lorelei was a water nymph"?
7. "Be quiet and listen!" exclaimed Martha.
8. "Look! That cliff must be hundreds of feet high!" marveled Blake.
9. "I don't believe that stuff," scoffed Jeff. "It's impossible!"
10. "Don't be too sure," the guide replied. "Remember that the Roman scholar Tertullian said, 'I believe it because it is impossible.'"

B. Drafting Skill

Using Quotations

Answers will vary. See typical answers below.

1. "Honestly!" Alan laughed. "Through the ages, some of the tales that travelers have spun have been wild."
2. "You mean like the story of the Loch Ness monster?" Sandy asked.
3. "Yes," Alan replied, "but there are other alleged encounters with odd beings that are just as strange."
4. "Have you heard," added José, "the tale of the Gulo of northern Sweden?"
5. Kim explained, "It's a creature that's supposed to look like a large dog with a cat's face."
6. "The local people used its brown hair to make caps," she continued. "They used its hoofs to cure earaches."
7. Dean added, "Not all travelers' tales are ancient. Some are modern."
8. "The story of the Yeti in the Himalayas is an example of a contemporary tale," Jenna volunteered, "isn't it?"
9. "That's right," Dean answered. "People in every mountain range in the world seem to tell similar stories of a 'Bigfoot.'"
10. "In the Gobi," Jenna elaborated, "it's called the Meti; in Assam, Kang Mi; and in the Canadian Rockies, Sasquatch."

Linking Grammar and Literature

On the board write the following passage from W. W. Jacobs's "The Monkey's Paw."

"I should like to see those old temples and fakirs and jugglers," said the old man. "What was that you started telling me the other day about a monkey's paw or something, Morris?"

"Nothing," said the soldier, hastily. "Leastways nothing worth hearing."

"Monkey's paw?" said Mrs. White, curiously.

"Well, it's just a bit of what you might call magic, perhaps," said the sergeant major, off-handedly.

Ask students to read the passage carefully, noticing the punctuation of the dialogue. Then challenge them to identify the rules of punctuation covered in this chapter that are exemplified in the passage.

Using Long Quotations

When two or more sentences are spoken by the same person, do not use an end quotation mark until after the final sentence.

> "I'll be up early to get your breakfast, boys. Your father says you can go to the show." As she handed the money to the eldest, she felt a sudden throb of allegiance to her husband and said sharply, "And you be careful of that, and don't waste it. Your father worked hard for his money."
>
> **Willa Cather, "The Sentimentality of William Tavener"**

Punctuating Dialogue

Dialogue is conversation between two or more people. Begin a new paragraph each time the speaker changes.

> The boy was probably twelve years old, but undersized. He wore overalls and a torn shirt. . . .
>
> He said, "I can chop some wood today."
>
> I said, "But I have a boy coming from the orphanage."
>
> "I'm the boy."
>
> "You? But you're small."
>
> "Size don't matter, chopping wood," he said. "Some of the big boys don't chop good. I've been chopping wood at the orphanage a long time."
>
> . . . . I was well into my work and not inclined to conversation. I was a little blunt. "Very well. Go ahead and see what you can do."
>
> **Marjorie Kinnan Rawlings, "A Mother in Mannville"**

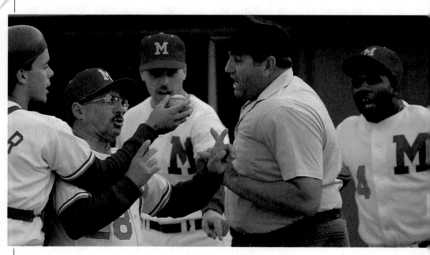

If one speaker's words continue for more than a paragraph, each paragraph begins with a quotation mark. However, the closing quotation mark is not used until the end of the entire quotation.

> Tony said, "Katharine Hepburn was nominated twelve times for an Academy Award and won four times.
>
> "Bette Davis was the next most-nominated star. She was nominated ten times and won two Oscars."

Practice Your Skills

A. CONCEPT CHECK

Dialogue Punctuation   Rewrite the following dialogue, adding the correct punctuation and paragraph divisions.

> The teacher opened the class saying Let's discuss some reasons why Europeans settled in Kenya The climate was good for crops Elena answered and tea was popular in England. Lions, elephants, cheetahs, and zebras flourished there, and Europeans loved exotic animals said Clark Don't forget, though said Gina that many settlers did not *choose* to go there. Sometimes people convicted of crimes were sentenced to move to the colonies.

B. APPLICATION IN LITERATURE

Punctuating Dialogue   Rewrite the following passage, adding the correct punctuation and paragraph divisions.

> (1) Perhaps said General Zaroff you were surprised that I recognized your name (2) You see I read all books on hunting published in English French and Russian (3) I have but one passion in my life Mr. Rainsford and it is the hunt (4) You have some wonderful heads here said Rainsford as he ate a particularly well-cooked filet mignon (5) That Cape buffalo is the largest I ever saw (6) Oh that fellow (7) Yes he was a real monster (8) Did he charge you (9) Hurled me against a tree said the general (10) Fractured my skull (11) But I got the brute (12) I've always thought said Rainsford that the Cape buffalo is the most dangerous of all big game (13) For a moment the general did not reply (14) He was smiling his curious red-lipped smile (15) Then he said slowly No (16) You are wrong sir (17) The Cape buffalo is not the most dangerous big game (18) He sipped his wine (19) Here in my preserve on the island he said in the same slow tone I hunt more dangerous game

Richard Connell, "The Most Dangerous Game"

Additional Resources
- Grammar and Usage Practice Book, pp. 197–198

WRITING THEME   The Call of the Wild

A. Concept Check

Dialogue Punctuation

The teacher opened the class, saying, "Let's discuss some reasons why Europeans settled in Kenya."

"The climate was good for crops," Elena answered, "and tea was popular in England."

"Lions, elephants, cheetahs, and zebras flourished there, and Europeans loved exotic animals," said Clark.

"Don't forget, though," said Gina, "that many settlers did not *choose* to go there. Sometimes people convicted of crimes were sentenced to move to the colonies."

B. Application in Literature

Punctuating Dialogue

(1) "Perhaps," said General Zaroff, "you were surprised that I recognized your name. (2) You see, I read all books on hunting published in English, French, and Russian. (3) I have but one passion in my life, Mr. Rainsford, and it is the hunt."

(4) "You have some wonderful heads here," said Rainsford, as he ate a particularly well-cooked filet mignon. (5) "That Cape buffalo is the largest I ever saw."

(6) "Oh, that fellow. (7) Yes, he was a real monster."

(8) "Did he charge you?"

(9) "Hurled me against a tree," said the general. (10) "Fractured my skull. (11) But I got the brute."

(12) "I've always thought," said Rainsford, "that the Cape buffalo is the most dangerous of all big game."

(13) For a moment the general did not reply. (14) He was smiling his curious, red-lipped smile. (15) Then he said slowly, "No. (16) You are wrong, sir. (17) The Cape buffalo is not the most dangerous big game." (18) He sipped his wine. (19) "Here in my preserve on the island," he said in the same slow tone, "I hunt more dangerous game."

Additional Resources
- Grammar and Usage Practice Book, pp. 199–200

 Individualizing Instruction

LD Students/LEP Students You may wish to limit the number of exercises assigned to LD and LEP students and allow them to complete exercises orally when appropriate.

WRITING THEME Biography and Autobiography

A. Concept Check
Punctuation of Titles
   1. People have captured the experiences of their lives in many artistic media: the string quartet *From My Life* by Czech composer Bedřich Smetana is one example.
   2. American tennis player Althea Gibson wrote an autobiographical article, "I Always Wanted to Be Someone."
   3. Dutch artist Vincent van Gogh chose to do a series of self-portraits; my favorite is *Self-Portrait in Front of an Easel.*
   4. Film director Bob Fosse recorded the events of his life in the movie *All That Jazz.*

Writing TIP

Use quotation marks to set off slang words or words with special emphasis. Use underlining to set off foreign words or words used as words.

Writing Theme
Biography and Autobiography

Punctuating Titles

Use quotation marks to enclose the titles of magazine articles, chapters, short stories, TV episodes, essays, poems, and songs.

Magazine Article	"Fads of the Eighties"
Chapter Title	Chapter 2, "The New World"
Short Story	"Clothes Make the Man"
TV Episode	"Lucy and Desi in London"
Essay	"The Dog That Bit People"
Poem	"The Raven"
Song	"The Star-Spangled Banner"

Underline the titles of books, newspapers, magazines, plays, movies, TV series, works of art, epic poems, and long musical compositions.

In writing or typing, such titles are underlined, like this: <u>Old Yeller</u>. In print, these titles appear in *italics*. Note that the word *the* is not underlined unless it is actually part of the title: <u>The Columbus Dispatch</u>, but the <u>Chicago Tribune</u>.

Book Title	<u>All Creatures Great and Small</u>
Newspaper	<u>New Haven Register</u>
Magazine	<u>Field and Stream</u>
Play	<u>The Miracle Worker</u>
Movie	<u>The Pink Panther Strikes Again</u>
TV Series	<u>I Love Lucy</u>
Work of Art	<u>Mona Lisa</u>
Epic Poem	<u>The Odyssey</u>
Long Musical Composition	<u>The Pirates of Penzance</u>

Practice Your Skills

A. CONCEPT CHECK

Punctuation of Titles Copy the following sentences, enclosing titles in quotation marks or underlining titles where necessary.

1. People have captured the experiences of their lives in many artistic media: the string quartet From My Life by Czech composer Bedrich Smetana is one example.
2. American tennis player Althea Gibson wrote an autobiographical article, I Always Wanted to Be Someone.
3. Dutch artist Vincent van Gogh chose to do a series of self-portraits; my favorite is Self-Portrait in Front of an Easel.
4. Film director Bob Fosse recorded the events of his life in the movie All That Jazz.

5. Some biographical films, such as The Jolson Story, were highly romanticized.

6. Helen Reddy, an Australian singer and composer, asserted her identity in the song I Am Woman.

7. Steve Goodman sang If Jethro Were Here to honor a friend.

8. Harold Krents, a blind lawyer, wrote an autobiographical article, Darkness at Noon, that appeared in The New York Times.

9. Krents's life was also the inspiration for the play and film Butterflies Are Free.

10. I Remember Mama, a television series popular in the 1950's, was based on Kathryn Forbes's book Mama's Bank Account.

11. The PBS series The American Experience devoted an episode to the life of former President Richard Nixon.

12. The poet Ben Jonson wrote of the death of his child in the poem On My First Son.

13. The story of Marie Curie was told by her daughter in the book Madame Curie.

14. Playwright Moss Hart's autobiography, Act One, became a best-seller.

15. Then there were social activist Margaret Sanger and composer Igor Stravinsky, who wrote books titled simply Autobiography.

B. PROOFREADING SKILL

Punctuating Titles Correctly   Find ten titles in the following paragraphs. Rewrite them on your paper, using correct style.

(1) In her autobiographical book I Know Why the Caged Bird Sings, Maya Angelou tells about the problems she experienced as an African-American girl in America. (2) There were many obstacles to overcome—racism, sexism, poverty, family crises—but Angelou overcame them all. (3) She was named "Woman of the Year" in communications in 1976 by the Ladies Home Journal, a popular magazine. (4) Maya Angelou has enjoyed great success as a writer, an actor, a director, a singer, a dancer, a teacher, and an activist for civil rights. (5) She has written numerous short stories, magazine articles, songs, and poems, including Still I Rise and My Arkansas.

(6) During the 1960's she lived in Africa, where she wrote for two newspapers, the Arab Observer and the Ghanian Times. (7) She has written screenplays, and she directed the film All Day Long. (8) For the television series Black African Heritage, she narrated the episode entitled The Slave Coast. (9) In addition, she toured twenty-two countries in a production of the opera Porgy and Bess. (10) She has taught at several universities.

Maya Angelou, author of *I Know Why the Caged Bird Sings*

Punctuation   **801**

5. Some biographical films, such as The Jolson Story, were highly romanticized.

6. Helen Reddy, an Australian singer and composer, asserted her identity in the song "I Am Woman."

7. Steve Goodman sang "If Jethro Were Here" to honor a friend.

8. Harold Krents, a blind lawyer, wrote an autobiographical article, "Darkness at Noon," that appeared in The New York Times.

9. Krents's life was also the inspiration for the play and film Butterflies Are Free.

10. I Remember Mama, a television series popular in the 1950's, was based on Kathryn Forbes's book Mama's Bank Account.

11. The PBS series The American Experience devoted an episode to the life of former President Richard Nixon.

12. The poet Ben Jonson wrote of the death of his child in the poem "On My First Son."

13. The story of Marie Curie was told by her daughter in the book Madame Curie.

14. Playwright Moss Hart's autobiography, Act One, became a best-seller.

15. Then there were social activist Margaret Sanger and composer Igor Stravinsky, who wrote books titled simply Autobiography.

B. Proofreading Skill

Punctuating Titles Correctly
Titles are underlined on the page.

1. I Know Why the Caged Bird Sings (1)
2. Ladies Home Journal (3)
3. "Still I Rise" (5)
4. "My Arkansas" (5)
5. Arab Observer (6)
6. Ghanian Times (6)
7. All Day Long (7)
8. Black African Heritage (8)
9. "The Slave Coast" (8)
10. Porgy and Bess (9)

You may wish to use the following Checkpoint exercise as an informal evaluation of student mastery of the rules for apostrophes, quotation marks, commas, and underlining covered in this handbook.

WRITING THEME   Popular Culture

1. Everybody's an expert when it comes to popular culture; that's what Ms. Fenster's English class seemed to think.

2. Nora described how Shakespeare's plays drew crowds in sixteenth-century England.

3. "*A Midsummer Night's Dream,*" commented Ms. Fenster, "was as popular as a good movie would be today."

4. "Did they slurp jumbo soft drinks and eat popcorn in the theater?" joked Melvin.

5. "Worse," said Ms. Fenster. "They ate whole meals of bread and cheese and washed them down with ale."

6. "What about Dickens and the Victorians?" asked Juana. "Didn't his novels *Great Expectations* and *Oliver Twist* first appear in magazines?"

7. "Yes," said Ms. Fenster, "and when Little Nell, in his novel *The Old Curiosity Shop,* was on her deathbed, people waited for the next installment the way film fans have waited for the latest *Star Wars* movie."

8. "Some of Mark Twain's books ran as serials in a magazine called *Harper's Monthly,*" said George.

9. "Oh, yes," said Ms. Fenster. "Mark Twain was a very popular writer."

10. "Like Stephen King?" asked Maria, skeptically.

11. "If you check the sales figures," said Nora, "he definitely was."

12. The class went on to talk about an article Ms. Fenster had assigned, titled "Is There Any Culture Left in Pop Culture?"

13. They discussed whether *Oklahoma!* was a serious work of art.

14. Then Ms. Fenster asked, "Have any other works created just for entertainment become classics?"

15. Someone quickly answered, "The movie *Night of the Living Dead* became a creepy classic!"

16. "Because of Superman," said George, "1938 *Action Comics* magazines are collectors' items today."

17. "But does that make them classics?" asked Nora.

18. Ms. Fenster's next question was, "What is a classic?"

19. "Sometimes the opposite occurs," Maria stated, "and serious works of art and literature become popular."

20. "Sure," said Melvin. "They're using the painting *American Gothic* to advertise overalls. If that isn't popular culture, what is?"

Writing Theme
Popular Culture

Write the following sentences, punctuating each correctly. Add apostrophes, quotation marks, commas, and underlining where necessary.

1. Everybodys an expert when it comes to popular culture; thats what Ms. Fensters English class seemed to think.

2. Nora described how Shakespeares plays drew crowds in sixteenth-century England.

3. A Midsummer Nights Dream commented Ms. Fenster was as popular as a good movie would be today.

4. Did they slurp jumbo soft drinks and eat popcorn in the theater joked Melvin

5. Worse said Ms. Fenster They ate whole meals of bread and cheese and washed them down with ale.

6. What about Dickens and the Victorians? asked Juana Didn't his novels Great Expectations and Oliver Twist first appear in magazines?

7. Yes said Ms. Fenster and when Little Nell in his novel The Old Curiosity Shop was on her deathbed, people waited for the next installment the way film fans have waited for the latest Star Wars movie.

8. Some of Mark Twains books ran as serials in a magazine called Harper's Monthly said George.

9. Oh, yes said Ms. Fenster Mark Twain was a very popular writer.

10. Like Stephen King asked Maria, skeptically

11. If you check the sales figures said Nora he definitely was.

12. The class went on to talk about an article Ms. Fenster had assigned titled Is There Any Culture Left in Pop Culture?

13. They discussed whether Oklahoma! was a serious work of art.

14. Then Ms. Fenster asked Have any other works created just for entertainment become classics?

15. Someone quickly answered The movie Night of the Living Dead became a creepy classic!

16. Because of Superman said George 1938 Action Comics magazines are collectors items today.

17. But does that make them classics asked Nora

18. Ms. Fensters next question was What is a classic?

19. Sometimes the opposite occurs Maria stated and serious works of art and literature become popular.

20. Sure said Melvin Theyre using the painting American Gothic to advertise overalls. If that isnt popular culture, what is?

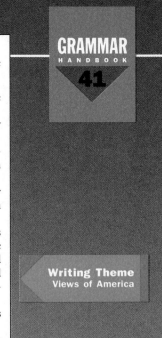

GRAMMAR
HANDBOOK
41

A. Punctuating Correctly Write the following sentences, adding the correct punctuation.

1. In the early years of this nation a Frenchman named Alexis de Tocqueville wrote a book called Democracy in America
2. He was one of the first but certainly not the last of the many foreigners who have chosen to write about this nation
3. Do you know for example about Frances Trollopes profitable writing career which began with the book Domestic Manners in America
4. Mrs. Trollope who was the mother of English novelist Anthony Trollope didn't especially want to be a writer or to comment on America she simply had a family to support
5. Both Tocqueville and Trollope made many enemies with their books however their writings also brought both of them fame and fortune
6. Although Oscar Wilde the amusing writer or perhaps witty would be a better word was already famous when he toured the United States in 1882, his article Personal Impressions of America increased his celebrity status.
7. While visiting Leadville Colorado Wilde noted a sign that read as follows Please do not shoot the pianist He is doing his best
8. More recently Alistair Cooke who is probably best known as the host of Masterpiece Theatre gave the world another European's view in his book America
9. Tocqueville Trollope Wilde and Cooke all of these writers have something in common
10. They may have experienced any of a hundred other emotions about America but they also felt fascinated curious and perhaps even a little overwhelmed.

B. Semicolons, Colons, Dashes, and Hyphens Add semicolons, colons, dashes, and hyphens to the following sentences. If none are needed, write *Correct*.

1. They were five Canadian musicians who loved all kinds of American music blues, country, rockabilly, and gospel.
2. They were young and ambitious they were also eager to create their own musical sound and to sing about America as they saw it.
3. The group included the following Rick Danko, Levon Helm, Garth Hudson, Richard Manuel, and Robbie Robertson.
4. For years they toured the East Coast as a little known rock-and-roll band however, they were not unknown to Bob Dylan.
5. Dylan needed a new group for his tours in 1965 and 1966 therefore, he signed them for the job.
6. They began the two year tour as a group of talented rookies and ended it as a well known group of skilled veterans.

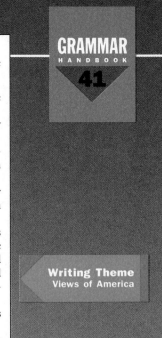
Writing Theme
Views of America

Application and Review

These activities have been designed to allow students to apply concepts presented in this handbook. Exercise A requires students to add correct punctuation. Exercise B focuses on semicolons, colons, dashes, and hyphens. Exercise C challenges students to restore the missing punctuation in a literary excerpt. Exercise D focuses on apostrophes, quotation marks, and underlining. Exercise E challenges students to add necessary punctuation and to correct punctuation errors in a letter.

Additional Resources

- Tests and Assessment, Mastery Tests, pp. 105–108
- Elaboration, Revision, and Proofreading Worksheets, p. 32

WRITING THEME Views of America

A. Punctuating Correctly

1. In the early years of this nation, a Frenchman named Alexis de Tocqueville wrote a book called Democracy in America.
2. He was one of the first—but certainly not the last—of the many foreigners who have chosen to write about this nation.
3. Do you know, for example, about Frances Trollope's profitable writing career, which began with the book Domestic Manners in America?
4. Mrs. Trollope, who was the mother of English novelist Anthony Trollope, didn't especially want to be a writer or to comment on America; she simply had a family to support.
5. Both Tocqueville and Trollope made many enemies with their books; however, their writings also brought both of them fame and fortune.
6. Although Oscar Wilde, the amusing writer—or perhaps witty would be a better word—was already famous when he toured the United States in 1882, his article "Personal Impressions of America" increased his celebrity status.
7. While visiting Leadville, Colorado, Wilde noted a sign that read as follows: "Please do not shoot the pianist. He is doing his best."
8. More recently, Alistair Cooke—who is probably best known as the host of Masterpiece Theatre—gave the world another European's view in his book America. (commas are also acceptable)
9. Tocqueville, Trollope, Wilde, and Cooke—all of these writers have something in common.
10. They may have experienced any of a hundred other emotions about America, but they also felt fascinated, curious, and perhaps even a little overwhelmed.

B. Semicolons, Colons, Dashes, and Hyphens

1. They were five Canadian musicians who loved all kinds of American music: blues, country, rockabilly, and gospel.
2. They were young and ambitious; they were also eager to create their own musical sound and to sing about America as they saw it.
3. The group included the following: Rick Danko, Levon Helm, Garth Hudson, Richard Manuel, and Robbie Robertson.
4. For years they toured the East Coast as a little-known rock-and-roll band; however, they were not unknown to Bob Dylan.
5. Dylan needed a new group for his tours in 1965 and 1966; therefore, he signed them for the job.
6. They began the two-year tour as a group of talented rookies and ended it as a well-known group of skilled veterans.

7. They had performed under many names over the years—The Hawks, The Crackers, The Canadian Squires—but finally become known simply as The Band.

8. The Band, in 1968, recorded their now-famous album "Music from Big Pink."

9. Suddenly, The Band was no longer an anonymous group of Canadians; it was a group of professional musicians offering insights about American life.

10. Music critic Greil Marcus identified the magic of The Band: "They have a spirit of excitement, humor, history, and a determination to find plurality and drama in America."

C. Application in Literature

Errors are underlined on the page.

We found the Americans as strange in their customs as they probably found us. The grocers did not give children a *pilón;* they did not stand at the door and coax you to buy, as they had in Mazatlan. . . . Neither was there a plaza, only parks that had no bandstands, no concerts every Thursday, no Judases exploding on Holy Week, and no promenades with boys going one way and girls the other. There were no parks in the *barrio;* the ones uptown were cold and rainy in the winter, and in summer there was nowhere to sit. . . . When there were celebrations, nobody set off rockets in front of your house to announce to the neighborhood that a wedding or baptism was taking place. . . . The Americans paid no attention to the Sixteenth of September, but they made a great commotion about the Fourth of July. . . .

In Tucson, when I had asked my mother again if the Americans were having a revolution, the answer was, "No, but they have good schools, and you are going to one of them."

D. Apostrophes, Quotation Marks, and Underlining

1. "Do you know the difference between immigrants and emigrants?" asked Natalie.

2. Millie answered, "Emigrants are people who leave their native country for another; they're immigrants in the new country."

3. "Much of our country's literature concerns immigrants," said Emil.

4. The group recalled that Willa Cather's novel *My Ántonia* concerns immigrant settlers of Nebraska.

---

7. They had performed under many names over the years The Hawks, The Crackers, The Canadian Squires but finally became known simply as The Band.

8. The Band in 1968 recorded their now-famous album "Music from Big Pink."

9. Suddenly, The Band was no longer an anonymous group of Canadians it was a group of professional musicians offering insights about American life.

10. Music critic Greil Marcus identified the magic of The Band they have a spirit of excitement, humor, history, and a determination to find plurality and drama in America.

C. Application in Literature Restore the missing punctuation in the excerpt below.

> We found the Americans as strange in their customs as they probably found us The grocers did not give children a *pilón* they did not stand at the door and coax you to buy, as they had in Mazatlan. . . . Neither was there a plaza, only parks that had no bandstands no concerts every Thursday no Judases exploding on Holy Week and no promenades with boys going one way and girls the other There were no parks in the *barrio* the ones uptown were cold and rainy in the winter and in summer there was nowhere to sit. . . . When there were celebrations nobody set off rockets in front of your house to announce to the neighborhood that a wedding or baptism was taking place. . . . The Americans paid no attention to the Sixteenth of September but they made a great commotion about the Fourth of July. . . .
>
> In Tucson, when I had asked my mother again if the Americans were having a revolution, the answer was No but they have good schools, and you are going to one of them.
>
> **Ernesto Galarza,** *Barrio Boy*

D. Apostrophes, Quotation Marks, and Underlining Add apostrophes, quotation marks, underlining, and any other necessary punctuation marks.

1. Do you know the difference between immigrants and emigrants asked Natalie.

2. Millie answered Emigrants are people who leave their native country for another; theyre immigrants in the new country.

3. Much of our countrys literature concerns immigrants said Emil.

4. The group recalled that Willa Cathers novel My Ántonia concerns immigrant settlers of Nebraska.

5. And Harry Golden wrote about New York immigrants in column after column of The Carolina Israelite Natalie added.
6. Millie mentioned that John Montagues poem The Rough Field describes his familys emigration and his return to Ireland.
7. Isnt Ernesto Galarzas book Barrio Boy a unique look at life in America commented Healy.
8. Yes I really enjoyed it said Natalie Didn't you?
9. Well, Franklin Roosevelt was right put in Charlie when he said All of our people all over the country—except the pure-blooded Indians—are immigrants or descendants of immigrants.
10. You can call us the Melting Pot said Millie or the Salad Bowl, but were certainly a remarkably multicultural population!

E. Proofreading   Proofread the following letter for incorrect or missing punctuation and other errors. Rewrite the letter correctly.

3006 Merton Road
Palo Alto California, 94306
May 23 19—

Sales Manager
Elite Records
680 broadway
New York New York 10006

Dear Sir or Madam
   On april 26 I ordered a record album containing the song The night They Drove Old Dixie Down by The band. The album I received contained songs like Wheels on Fire and I shall be Released but it didnt have the song I want. Will you please send me the correct album?
   Also can you tell me how I can get a copy of The Bands movie called The Last Waltz directed by Martin scorsese? The latest movie and video guide says This is a truly wonderful documentary.

Sincerely

Martin E Green

5. "And Harry Golden wrote about New York immigrants in column after column of *The Carolina Israelite*," Natalie added.
6. Millie mentioned that John Montague's poem "The Rough Field" describes his family's emigration and his return to Ireland.
7. "Isn't Ernesto Galarza's book *Barrio Boy* a unique look at life in America?" commented Healy.
8. "Yes, I really enjoyed it," said Natalie. "Didn't you?"
9. "Well, Franklin Roosevelt was right," put in Charlie, "when he said, 'All of our people all over the country—except the pure-blooded Indians—are immigrants or descendants of immigrants.'"
10. "You can call us the Melting Pot," said Millie, "or the Salad Bowl, but we're certainly a remarkably multicultural population!"

E. Proofreading
Errors are underlined on page.

3006 Merton Road
Palo Alto, California 94306
May 23, 19—

Sales Manager
Elite Records
680 Broadway
New York, New York 10006

Dear Sir or Madam:

   On April 26 I ordered a record album containing the song "The Night They Drove Old Dixie Down" by The Band. The album I received contained songs like "Wheels on Fire" and "I Shall be Released," but it didn't have the song I want. Will you please send me the correct album?
   Also, can you tell me how I can get a copy of The Band's movie called *The Last Waltz*, directed by Martin Scorsese? The latest movie and video guide says, "This is a truly wonderful documentary."

Sincerely,
Martin E. Green

These exercises allow your students to practice skills acquired in Handbooks 39–41. You may wish to use the exercises to provide a thorough review of the material in these chapters or to evaluate student mastery of the concepts.

Additional Resources

- Grammar and Usage Practice Book, pp. 201–203
- Standardized Test Practice

Skills Assessment Test 4
1. B—, especially egg white and gelatin,
2. A—rubber, and
   B—feathers—all (dash between *feathers* and *all*)
3. C—on a field, hockey players
4. B—were
   D—law of gravity
5. C—your
   D—exception."
6. A—, who was the daughter of a Piute chief,
   D—people
7. E

ASSESSMENT

Directions   One or more of the underlined sections in the following sentences may contain errors of grammar, usage, punctuation, spelling, or capitalization. Write the letter of each incorrect item, then rewrite the item correctly. If there is no error in an item, write E.

> **Example**   African elephants <u>are associated</u> with <u>hannibal the great,</u>
> A   B
> <u>who</u> took them across the <u>Alps. When</u> he invaded Italy <u>in 218</u> B.C.
>   C   D
> <u>No error</u>
> E
>
> **Answer**   B—Hannibal the Great; C—Alps when

1. <u>Some</u> paint ingredients <u>especially egg white and gelatin</u> could <u>just as easily</u> be used
   A   B   C
   <u>to make dinner.</u> <u>No error</u>
   D   E

2. Stone, wood, <u>rubber and</u> leather stuffed with <u>feathers; all</u> of <u>these</u> materials <u>were used</u>
                 A   B   C   D
   by ancient civilizations to make balls for sports and games. <u>No error</u>
                                                                 E

3. <u>On the ice, hockey pucks</u> are <u>dense, cylindrical</u> disks made of rubber or plastic; <u>on a field</u>
   A   B   C
   <u>hockey players</u> use <u>softball-sized</u> balls made of wood or plastic. <u>No error</u>
                         D   E

4. A number of <u>Isaac Newton's</u> original manuscripts <u>was</u> <u>scorch marked</u>; thus, the discoverer
                A   B   C
   of <u>the Law of Gravity</u> is sometimes called the first absent-minded professor. <u>No error</u>
      D   E

5. "I never forget a <u>face,"</u> said Groucho <u>Marx,</u> "but <u>in you're case</u> I'll make <u>an exception"</u>.
                      A   B   C   D
   <u>No error</u>
   E

6. Sarah Winnemucca <u>who was daughter of a Piute chief</u> once <u>served</u> as a military <u>scout</u>
                      A   B   C
   and later became a spokeswoman for <u>the rights of her poeple.</u> <u>No error</u>
                                        D   E

7. "I was gratified <u>to be able</u> to answer promptly, and I <u>did,"</u> said Mark Twain <u>in his book</u>
                     A   B   C
   <u>*Life on the Mississippi.* "I</u> said I didn't know." <u>No error</u>
   D   E

---

8. Bob Zimmerman <u>left</u> his hometown of <u>Hibbing Minnesota in</u> <u>september of 1959,</u>
   A B C
   became a folk <u>singer, and</u> changed his name to Bob Dylan. <u>No error</u>
   D E

9. <u>*The Adventures of Huckleberry Finn* follow</u> a young boy on a raft trip down the
   A B
   <u>Mississippi river</u> and is one of <u>Mark Twain's</u> most famous books. <u>No error</u>
   C D E

10. Mary Austin spent <u>much of her life</u> studying Indian <u>legends</u> and poetic <u>rhythms and</u> her
    A B C
    book <u>*The Basket Woman* reveals</u> her dedication. <u>No error</u>
    D E

11. The <u>person who helped write</u> former President Gerald Ford's <u>memoirs was</u> not credited
    A B
    on the title page of the <u>book because</u> the publisher considered it <u>inapropriate</u>. <u>No error</u>
    C D E

12. <u>When asked what</u> jazz <u>was, Louis Armstrong</u> answered, <u>"man,</u> if you gotta ask,
    A B C
    <u>you'll never know." No error</u>
    D E

13. After being turned down by every <u>medical school</u> in <u>new york and philadelphia,</u>
    A B
    Elizabeth Blackwell studied <u>anatomie</u> in a private school and began applying to <u>rural</u>
    C D
    <u>colleges. No error</u>
    E

14. Scholars <u>have asked</u> whether <u>Samuel Richardson's</u> <u>"Pamela"</u> was the first English <u>novel?</u>
    A B C D
    <u>No error</u>
    E

15. <u>Some</u> talented football players who <u>have become</u> even more famous in other fields
    A B
    <u>are: Kris</u> Kristofferson, Paul <u>Robeson, and</u> Byron "Whizzer" White. <u>No error</u>
    C D E

16. The <u>heaviest snowfall</u> on record <u>took place</u> on April 14–15, <u>1921, in</u> <u>Silver Lake,</u>
    A B C D
    Colorado, when 76 inches fell in 24 hours. <u>No error</u>
    E

17. The <u>word "nonannouncement"</u> is one of <u>the few words</u> in the <u>English language</u> that have
    A B C
    six <u>ns</u> in them. <u>No error</u>
    D E

18. Charles Dodgson <u>better known as Lewis Carroll</u> wrote <u>*Alice's Adventures in*</u>
    A B
    <u>*Wonderland*</u> <u>when he was</u> <u>thirty three</u> years old in order to amuse Alice Liddell, the
    C D
    daughter of a friend. <u>No error</u>
    E

19. <u>Tchaikovsky,</u> <u>who</u> wrote the *1812 Overture,* died when he <u>had drunk</u> unboiled water
    A B C
    <u>during a cholera</u> epidemic. <u>No error</u>
    D E

20. Aspirin, perhaps the <u>most common</u> pain remedy in the world, was introduced by
    A
    Hermann <u>Dresser, a German</u>, and the <u>bayer</u> company <u>proceded</u> to market it in 1899.
    B C D
    <u>No error</u>
    E

21. Though his impersonators may say he <u>did James Cagney</u> never said, <u>"You</u> dirty <u>rat.</u>
    A B C D
    <u>No error</u>
    E

22. <u>Yes, it</u> was <u>Leif Ericson,</u> according to many archaeologists and historians, <u>who</u> discovered
    A B C
    <u>America.</u> <u>No error</u>
    D E

23. Stevie <u>Wonder in</u> <u>the recording studio</u>, often takes on the <u>vocal instrumental and</u>
    A B C
    production responsibilities <u>himself.</u> <u>No error</u>
    D E

24. <u>Handsome dangerous</u> gangster Joseph Doto adopted the name <u>Joe Adonis</u> because he
    A B
    thought <u>himself</u> as good-looking as the Adonis of <u>greek mythology</u>. <u>No error</u>
    C D E

25. Sargent Shriver may be <u>well known</u> for being <u>John F. Kennedy's</u> <u>brother in law</u>, but he is
    A B C
    also the <u>father-in-law</u> of Arnold Schwarzenegger. <u>No error</u>
    D E

Directions One or more of the underlined sections in the following sentences may contain errors of grammar, usage, punctuation, spelling, or capitalization. Write the letter of each incorrect item, then rewrite the item correctly. If there is no error in an item, write E.

> **Example** After <u>giving up</u> <u>England's throne,</u> <u>king Edward VIII</u>
>   A   B   C
> became known as the <u>Duke of Windsor.</u> <u>No error</u>
>   D   E
>
> **Answer** C—King Edward VIII

1. <u>Actor Will Geer</u> was <u>best known</u> for his portrayal of the <u>Grandfather</u> on <u>the television</u>
   A   B   C   D
series *The Waltons*. <u>No error</u>
            E

2. Robert Louis Stevenson and <u>his wife, Fanny,</u> reportedly disagreed <u>among themselves</u> <u>as</u>
                A   B   C
<u>to how</u> *The Strange Case of Dr. Jekyll and Mr. Hyde* <u>should be writen</u>. <u>No error</u>
                                          D   E

3. <u>As a competor</u> in the <u>1988 Olympics</u>, Florence Griffith-Joyner <u>earned gold medals</u> for
   A   B   C
running <u>faster than any woman athlete</u>. <u>No error</u>
            D   E

4. Pekinese make <u>good pets</u> for apartment <u>dwellers, since they are</u> protective and <u>need</u> little
              A   B   C
exercise. <u>No error</u>
  D   E

5. <u>Andy Warhol's film</u> *Four Stars* is one of the <u>most longest</u> films <u>ever made; it</u> is
   A   B   C
<u>twenty-five hours long</u>. <u>No error</u>
      D   E

6. <u>The Grimm brothers'</u> collection of fairy tales <u>were</u> published <u>in 1823</u> under <u>the title</u>
   A   B   C   D
German Popular Stories. <u>No error</u>
                   E

7. If you read <u>this here book</u> by <u>Maya Angelou, *I Know Why the Caged Bird Sings*,</u> you
          A   B
<u>will realize</u> that <u>its</u> autobiographical. <u>No error</u>
  C   D   E

These exercises allow your students to practice skills acquired in the Grammar and Usage Handbook. You may wish to use the exercises as a thorough review of the material or as a summative test for the grammar and usage portion of this text.

> *Additional Resources*
> • Standardized Test Practice

Skills Assessment Post-Test
1. C—grandfather
2. B—between themselves
   D—written
3. A—competitor
   D—any other woman athlete
4. E
5. B—longest
6. B—was
7. A—this book
   D—it's

8. The plays of <u>Montana writer William S. Yellowrobe</u> describe <u>life in the American west</u>
    A   **B**
   <u>more better</u> than do <u>the novels of Louis L'Amour</u>. <u>No error</u>
   C   **D**   **E**

9. <u>Nineteenth-century</u> social reformer<u>, Dorothea Dix,</u> was born in <u>Hampden, Maine,</u> where
   A   **B**   **C**
   her <u>father</u> was a fundamentalist minister. <u>No error</u>
   D   **E**

10. <u>Spanish cellist Pablo Casals</u> was one of the <u>worlds'</u> premier concert musicians, who also
    A   **B**
    devoted part of his time to <u>learning young musicians</u> <u>how to play</u> the cello. <u>No error</u>
    C   **D**   **E**

11. Leo Tolstoy, the <u>great Russian author</u> of the <u>Nineteenth Century</u>, <u>writes</u> <u>such novels as</u>
    A   **B**   **C**   **D**
    War and Peace and *Anna Karenina*. <u>No error</u>
    E

12. Mabel Normand, <u>a popular star of the silent screen</u>, never <u>speaked</u> in <u>her many movies</u>
    A   **B**   **C**
    made <u>from 1911 to 1923</u>. <u>No error</u>
    D   **E**

13. <u>Film director Francis Ford Coppola</u> got <u>the idea for</u> his movie <u>"Apocalypse Now"</u> from
    A   **B**   **C**
    Joseph <u>Conrad's novel</u> *Heart of Darkness*. <u>No error</u>
    D   **E**

14. Animal rights <u>activist's</u> protest against the <u>raising of veal calves</u> <u>inside of</u> small, confining
    A   **B**   **C**
    pens because of the discomfort the animals are forced <u>to endure</u>. <u>No error</u>
    D   **E**

15. It was a surprise when fifteen-year-old <u>sharpshooter Annie Oakley</u> <u>beat</u> professional
    A   **B**
    marksman Frank Butler <u>in a shooting match</u> because Butler had never been beaten by
    C
    <u>no</u> woman before. <u>No error</u>
    D   **E**

16. Devil's <u>Island, a</u> prison that <u>lays</u> off the coast of <u>french Guiana, got</u> its name not from
    A   **B**   **C**
    the conditions in the prison but from the fierce <u>wind and water</u> surrounding it.
    D
    <u>No error</u>
    E

17. The first railroad in the U.S. <u>was</u> the Baltimore and Ohio, which began <u>service in</u> 1830;
    A   **B**
    <u>beside</u> freight, it took a small number of passengers for a <u>9-cent</u> charge. <u>No error</u>
    C   **D**   **E**

18. Bette Davis <u>chose</u> not to play <u>Scarlett O'Hara</u> in <u>***Gone With The Wind***</u> because she
    A   B   C
    thought that her costar would be Errol Flynn, <u>with whom</u> she refused to work.
    D

    <u>No error</u>
    E

19. On October 2, <u>1925, John</u> Logie Baird persuaded a frightened boy to sit under bright
    A
    lights in <u>his</u> laboratory; the <u>boy's</u> picture <u>is</u> the first living image transmitted by
    B   C   D
    television. <u>No error</u>
    E

20. While <u>earth</u> is the only planet known to support <u>life, it</u> seems <u>possibly</u> that <u>planets</u> in
    A   B   C   D
    other systems may have life-forms as well. <u>No error</u>
    E

21. The word <u>*farce,*</u> referring to a wild comedy filled with <u>jokes, sight gags, and wild</u>
    A   B
    goings-on, comes from a <u>Latin</u> word meaning <u>"to stuff."</u> <u>No error</u>
    C   D   E

22. Alfred Nobel, <u>who</u> we know as the <u>founder</u> of the <u>Nobel Prize, invented</u> <u>Dynamite</u> in
    A   B   C   D
    1866. <u>No error</u>
    E

23. The names of at least <u>one-half</u> of the fifty states were <u>derived</u> <u>of</u> Native-American words
    A   B C
    such as <u>Kansas. Which</u> means "a breeze near the ground." <u>No error</u>
    D   E

24. <u>Him publishing</u> the song <u>by singing</u> it on radio surprised <u>everyone, we</u> did not know that
    A   B   C
    a song does not have to be printed <u>to be considered</u> published. <u>No error</u>
    D   E

25. <u>Neither common words</u> nor even proper nouns <u>were spelled</u> consistently in <u>Shakespeare's</u>
    A   B   C
    time; the playwright <u>himself</u> signed his own name with many different spellings.
    D

    <u>No error</u>
    E

18. C—*Gone with the Wind*
19. B—Baird's
 D—was
20. A—Earth
 C—possible
21. E
22. A—whom
 D—dynamite
23. C—from
 D—Kansas, which
24. A—His publishing
 C—everyone. We *or* everyone; we
25. E

Appendix

This appendix provides some of the material most commonly needed by student writers.

813

IDEAS FOR WRITING

Ideas for writing are everywhere. You need only to recognize them and build upon them. To help get your mental wheels rolling, read the following sections and use your thinking skills to generate topics. The first section lists ideas according to types of writing. The second provides ideas for writing in the subject areas.

Narrative
a vacation adventure
a time when you learned
    something important
a sports experience
an incident involving your
    favorite person
a childhood event
a science-fiction story
an encounter with a
    famous person
a turning point in your life
a wedding
an event at school
a visit to a famous place

Descriptive
a secret hideaway
unusual hairstyles
a building in the future
a train station at midnight
big-city streets at noon
a stream in the woods
a national landmark
a shopping mall
an abandoned place
a dream rocm
a place you have always
    wanted to see
a place you are seeing from
    a distance
an attic
an unusual playground
a person you know well

special clothes
your pet
people waiting in line
a group of skateboarders
a special painting

Informative Exposition

Process
how TV ratings work
how to repair a bike
how a neon sign glows
how to clean up oil spills
how a telephone answering
    machine works
how to apply stage makeup
how atoms are split
how to train a parakeet to talk

Definition
lasers	nutrition
rap music	life-style
free speech	journalist
censorship	progress
public health	comedy

Advice
how to deal with peer pressure
how to make lunch hours
    productive
how to be a friend
how to stop procrastinating
how to deal with criticism
how to reduce TV viewing
how to find a summer job
ways to get more exercise

Persuasive
Should school run year round?
Should professional athletes
    be so highly paid?
Should song lyrics be censored?
Should smoking be banned?
Should animal research be
    prohibited?
Should violence on TV be
    restricted?
Should high-school libraries
    restrict certain books?
Should your community have
    a curfew?
Should journalists refuse to
    cover negative political
    campaigning?

Reports
search for the *Titanic*
Loch Ness monster
a historic site in your community
the history of video games
a place you would like to live
teenage alcoholism
diet fads
effects of smoking
women in colonial America
dreams
robotics
civil rights movement
rain forests
endangered species
advances in photography

Ideas for Writing in Subject Areas

Art

how to weld metal
how to make a clay sculpture
compare/contrast modern and
   classical art
folk art
public sculpture
life of Picasso
the drawings of Escher
fashion design
computer art
how color affects mood
art deco
the influence of Frank
   Lloyd Wright
the art of Ed Pashke
the Louvre
free-form furniture

Consumerism

how to budget your money
style fads
cost of automobile pollution
discount shopping
effects of advertising
how to estimate tax deduc-
   tions from your paycheck
weekly/yearly cost of
   smoking
costs of medical care
food labeling
drug testing
borrowing money
automatic teller machines
the credit-card industry
fast-food meals vs. home-
   cooked meals
how to balance a checkbook
24-hour automobile production plants
earning money from collecting baseball cards

Health

healthy weight loss
effects of lost sleep
compare/contrast jogging
   and walking
reducing cholesterol
exercise programs to avoid
how to reduce air pollution in
   your community
cosmetics and allergies
new ways to treat stress

Mathematics

careers for mathematicians
my experiences learning
   math
how geometry is useful in
   everyday life
mathematics and video
   games
how to figure baseball
   batting averages
compare/contrast two summer
   jobs with different rates of
   pay and transportation
   costs
how public opinion polls
   work

Music

compare/contrast two popular
   singers
the life of a famous musician
how music alters your moods
careers in music
the origins of jazz
the history of rock music
controversies about song
   lyrics
the music of the future
the career of Quincy Jones
computer music

Science

What causes acid rain?
What is the ozone effect?
Why explore space?
How are newspapers
   recycled?
how an organ is
   transplanted
the chemical waste
   problem
how a tornado forms
What causes earthquakes?
saving endangered animals
understanding medically
   valuable plants
global warming
designing interactive
   computer software

Social Studies

American Indians and the
   U.S. government
civil rights in the '90's
democracy movements in
   Eastern Europe
the Iron Curtain
population growth in
   the U.S.
a global economy
Should a President serve
   more than two terms?
Should public service be
   compulsory?
the beginning of U.S.
   labor unions
the Great Wall of China
the origins of Machu Picchu
building the trans-
   continental railroad in
   the U.S.
the British East India
   Company

Ideas for
Writing   **815**

OUTLINE FORM

Outlines are an efficient way of organizing ideas for writing, and they are also useful for taking notes. By helping you organize information in a concise and logical way, outlines can make both writing and note taking easier.

Types of Outlines

A **formal outline** gives detailed information and indicates relationships between ideas. Use a formal outline to organize a formal composition or speech or a chapter for study purposes.

Formal outlines can be either **sentence outlines** or **topic outlines.** In a sentence outline, each main topic and subtopic is written as a complete sentence. Here is a portion of a sentence outline.

Walt Disney and the Animated Film

Introduction—Walter Elias Disney was an important pioneer in the field of animated film.

I. Walt Disney was interested in cartooning as a youth.
  A. He was born in Chicago in 1901.
  B. At the age of 16, he studied art in Chicago.
  C. At 19, he worked for the Kansas City Film Company, creating crude cartoon advertisements.

II. Disney started his own film business.
  A. In 1923, he moved to Los Angeles to draw cartoons for movies.
  B. He started a film studio in his garage.
  C. His first successful character was Mickey Mouse.
  D. Disney achieved several movie-making firsts.
    1. *Steamboat Willie* was the first sound cartoon.
    2. *Flowers and Trees* was the first cartoon to be made in full Technicolor.

III. Disney produced the first full-length cartoon features.
  A. In 1937, he introduced *Snow White and the Seven Dwarfs*, which was an immediate artistic and commercial success.
  B. He created a number of childhood classics in succeeding years, including *Pinocchio* (1940), *Dumbo* (1941), *Alice in Wonderland* (1951), and *Peter Pan* (1953).

In a **topic outline,** words or phrases are used for each main topic and subtopic. Below is a portion of a topic outline.

The Arctic

Introduction—to describe the little-known arctic world
  I. Arctic lands
   A. The true Arctic
   B. Subarctic regions
     1. Not part of the true Arctic
     2. Warmer summers than the Arctic
  II. Natural resources
   A. Minerals
     1. Coal
     2. Radioactive ores
       a. Thorium
       b. Uranium
     3. Petroleum
   B. Animals

Decide whether a sentence outline or a topic outline better suits your purpose and personal style. Once you begin your outline, do not mix forms.

Correct Outline Form

1. Center the title at the top of the page. Below it, write your thesis statement, or a shortened version of it.
2. To label main points and subpoints, use the arrangement of numerals and letters that you see in the two models.
3. When a heading is a subpoint of a previous heading, indent its letter or numeral, placing it directly underneath the first letter in the first word of the previous heading.
4. Do not use a single subheading. Use two or more subheadings under a heading, or don't use any. For every *A* there should be a *B*; and for every 1, a 2.
5. In a topic outline, keep items of the same rank in parallel form. For instance, if A is a noun, then B and C should also be nouns. Subtopics need not be parallel with main topics.
6. Begin each item with a capital letter. Do not use end punctuation in a topic outline.

Outline
Form

BUSINESS LETTERS

When you use the correct form for your business letter, you make a positive impression on your reader. Following are explanations of the parts of a business letter and examples of two correct business letter forms.

Block Form and Modified Block Form

Use plain, white, 8″ × 11″ paper for all business letters, whether you handwrite or type them. In **block form,** all parts begin at the left margin. Use this form only when you type the letter. In **modified block form,** the heading, closing, and signature are aligned near the right margin; the other parts begin at the left margin.

Block Form

```
_____     Heading
_____
_____

_____     Inside
_____     Address
_____

_____ :   Salutation

_____
_____
_____     Body
_____
_____

_____ ,   Closing
~~~~~~~~~~       Signature
_____
```

Modified Block Form

```
           Heading  _____
                     _____
           Date      _____

_____     Inside
_____     Address
_____

_____ :   Salutation

_____
_____
_____     Body
_____

           Closing   _____ ,
           Signature ~~~~~~~~~~
                     _____
```

Heading   The heading is written at the top of the page. The first line contains your street address; the second line contains your town or city, state, and ZIP code. Separate the city and state with a comma and write out the name of the state. The third line gives the date of the letter. Place the heading at the left or the right margin, depending on whether you use the block form or the modified block form.

Inside Address The inside address tells to whom the letter is being sent. Place the inside address at the left margin at least four lines below the heading. On the first line you should place the name of the receiver. If there is room, place the person's title on the same line, separated from the name by a comma. Otherwise, place the title on the next line. If you do not know the name of the person who will receive your letter, use the person's title or the name of the department. On the succeeding lines, place the company name and address, including the city, state, and ZIP code.

The inside address is important because occasionally a letter is opened by someone other than the addressee, and the envelope is discarded. If this happens, the name and address of the receiver can still be found. The following are two typical inside addresses.

Ms. Janet McPherson, Personnel Director
Lakeland Craft Cooperative
3701 Bloom Street
Rochester, New York 14619

Recreation Department
City of New Orleans
121 Canal Street
New Orleans, Louisiana 70130

Salutation Position the salutation two lines below the inside address. Begin with the word *Dear,* follow it by the name of the person to whom you are writing, and end with a colon. Use only the person's last name, preceded by a title such as *Mr., Mrs., Ms., Dr.,* or *Professor.* The following forms are acceptable.

Dear Mr. Allen: Dear Sir or Madam:
Dear Ms. Kreutzer: Dear Customer Service Department:
Dear Mrs. Jackson: Dear Editor:

Body The body, the main part of the letter in which you write your message, begins two spaces below the salutation. The body may contain a single paragraph or several paragraphs. Leave a space between each paragraph.

Closing The closing is placed two lines below the body, in line with the heading. Closings commonly used for business letters include *Sincerely yours* and *Very truly yours.* Note that only the first word is capitalized and that the closing ends with a comma.

Signature Type or print your name four spaces below the closing, and sign your name in the space between.

USING A WORD PROCESSOR

A word processor can help you write freely and revise effectively. Here are some word-processing techniques to help you get started.

Goal	Technique	Comment
Find a fresh writing topic.	Freewrite without stopping for ten minutes with the screen light dimmed. Print. Circle ideas you like.	With the screen dimmed, you can write freely without worrying about errors.
Add, replace, or reorder text.	Use the insert, delete, replace, move, cut, and paste commands to change text as often as you wish.	Making changes easily is one of the most compelling reasons to use a word processor. Using insert and delete together replaces text; cutting and pasting moves text.
Make handy notes to yourself.	Type notes to yourself in all capital letters. Place the notes at any point in your paper.	During revision you can insert new text to expand on a note and then delete the note itself.
Find the best way to express an idea.	Experiment. Write a number of alternatives separated by slashes (/). At a later stage, use the search command to find the slashes— places where you will make choices.	Write as many alternatives as you like, then delete or move the ones you don't wish to use.

Goal	Technique	Comment
Spell every word correctly.	Use a "spell-checker" program, if you have one, to find and correct misspelled words. Or scroll through your document, proofreading and correcting errors.	Spellcheckers identify misspellings and query the spellings of most proper nouns. You must also proofread to catch words that may be used incorrectly.
Make the organization clear.	Use underlining, italics, and boldface type to highlight the various headings and subheadings in your paper. You can also add extra space between sections.	Various type sizes and styles are offered by many word-processing programs. Boldface type and underlining are almost always available.
Create an attractive page.	Create a *header* or a *footer;* include the command to number pages automatically. Set margins and line spacing. Insert page breaks at natural divisions. Print a clean copy after you have made all necessary revisions.	A *header* is text printed at the top of each page; a *footer* prints at the bottom. Either can include automatic page numbering. A *page break* is a command to start a new page at whatever point you choose.

TECHNIQUES FOR PEER RESPONSE

The following response techniques can help you give and receive useful responses as you share your writing with others. These techniques can also help you as the writer to be in charge of the feedback process and to find out what kinds of responses are most useful to you.

How to Use	When to Use
Sharing	
Read your words out loud to a peer. Your purpose is simply to share and to hear how your words sound. Your listeners may ask you to slow down or to read your piece again, but they offer no feedback of any kind.	Do this when you are just exploring and you don't want criticism. Reading to a peer is also useful when your writing is finished and you want to celebrate by sharing it with another person.
Saying Back or Restating	
Ask readers, "What do you hear me saying?" As readers say back what they hear, they are inviting you to figure out better what you really want to say.	Use this type of feedback when you are still exploring and when you want to change and develop your ideas.
Pointing	
Ask readers to tell you what they like best in your writing. Tell them to be specific and to avoid simply saying, "I liked it."	Use this technique when you want to know what is getting through or when you want some encouragement and support.

How to Use	*When to Use*
Summarizing	
Ask readers to tell you what they hear as the main meaning or message in your writing. Make clear that you don't want evaluation of the writing at this time.	Use this technique when you want to know what is getting through to readers.
Responding to Specific Features	
Ask for feedback on specific features of the writing, such as the organization, or the persuasive power, or the spelling and punctuation. Ask readers to respond to specific questions, such as, "Are the ideas supported with enough examples?" "Did I persuade you?" "Is the organization clear enough that you could follow the ideas easily?"	Use when you want a quick overview of the strengths and weaknesses of your piece.
Replying	
Discuss the ideas in your writing with your readers. Ask readers to give you their ideas on the topic. Be sure to talk with your peer readers about *what* you have said, not *how* you have said it.	Use this strategy when you want to make your writing richer by using new ideas.
Playing Movies of the Reader's Mind	
Invite readers to tell you what happens inside their heads as they read your writing. Interrupt the reading and ask readers to tell you what they are thinking at the moment of interruption.	This technique is useful at any stage of the writing. Because it can lead to blunt criticism, use this peer response method only when you have a relationship of trust and support with your reader.

Techniques for
Peer Response   **823**

USING THE RIGHT WORD

The words in this section are often used incorrectly. Study them so that you can learn to use the right word at the right time.

accept, except   *Accept* means "to agree to or willingly receive something." *Except* usually means "not including."

> Todd was willing to *accept* the new rules.
> Everyone *except* Todd denied being late.

affect, effect   *Affect* means "to influence." *Effect* means "the result of an action."

> The teacher's excellent reputation *affected* Sue's choice.
> Lack of rainfall had a devastating *effect* on the crops.

all ready, already   *All ready* means "all are ready' or "completely prepared." *Already* means "by the given time" or "even now."

> Pablo was *all ready* for his trip.
> We are *all ready* to begin.
> The other group has *already* begun.

all right   *All right* is the correct spelling. *Alright* is nonstandard English and should not be used.

> Frank was very upset, but now he is *all right*.

a lot   is informal and should not be used in formal writing. *Alot* is always incorrect.

among, between   are prepositions. *Between* refers to two people or things. The object of *between* is never singular. *Among* refers to a group of three or more.

> I'll see you *between* classes.
> I had a hard time choosing *among* the four colors.

beside, besides   *Beside* means "at the side of." *Besides* means "in addition to."

> He rode *beside* me on the train.
> There are other kinds of books *besides* mysteries.

borrow, lend   *Borrow* means "to receive something on loan." *Lend* means "to give out temporarily" and is often used with an indirect object.

> May I *borrow* your pen?   Could you *lend* me that book?

Borrow is used with *from,* not *off.*

I can't lend you the book because I *borrowed* it *from* Sam.

bring, take *Bring* refers to movement toward or with. *Take* refers to movement away from.

I'll *bring* you a sandwich.   Please *take* him a sandwich.

different from is used to compare things that are unlike. *Different than* is nonstandard.

My image of Brooklyn was *different from* his.

farther, further *Farther* means "more distant." *Further* means "additional."

We had ridden much *farther* than I realized.
I think my story needs *further* rewriting.

fewer, less *Fewer* refers to numbers of things that can be counted. *Less* refers to amount or quantity.

Today the baker used *less* dough and baked *fewer* loaves.

in, into *In* refers to an unchanging position—where a person or thing is now. *Into* indicates movement or a change of position.

The paints are *in* the box.
I'll be going *into* my sophomore year.

it's, they're, who's, and you're All are contractions, not possessives. The possessive forms are *its, their, whose,* and *your.*

They're not my favorite authors.
Kipling gives an unusual explanation of how the elephant got
its trunk.

kind of, sort of Neither of these two expressions should be followed by the word *a.*

What *kind of* radio do you have?

The use of these two expressions as adverbs, as in "I'm kind of thirsty" and "It's sort of warm today," is informal.

lay, lie *Lay* is a transitive verb that means "to place." It takes a direct object. *Lay* is also the past tense of *lie.* *Lie* is an intransitive verb that means "to rest in a flat position" or "to be in a certain place." It never takes a direct object.

Lay the records on the table.   The cat is *lying* on the sofa.

Using the
Right Word   **825**

learn, teach *Learn* means "to gain knowledge or acquire a skill." *Teach* means "to instruct."

> We are *learning* Spanish.
> He is *teaching* us to sing in Spanish.

leave, let *Leave* means "to go away from." *Leave* can be transitive or intransitive. *Let* is usually used with another verb. It means "to allow to."

> Don't *leave* without your keys.
> Did someone *leave* a lunch on the table?
> Don't *let* their wide receiver get around you!

like is a preposition. Do not use it as a conjunction before a clause. Use *as* or *as if* instead.

> It looks *like* a bad year for farmers.
> Ramon talked *as if* he had a cold.

of is incorrectly used in a phrase such as *could of.* Examples of correct wordings are *could have, should have,* and *must have.*

> Darryl *should have* locked his bike.

raise, rise *Raise* is a transitive verb that means "to lift" or "to make something go up." It takes a direct object. *Rise* is an intransitive verb that means "to go upward." It does not take a direct object.

> The play *raises* issues of loyalty.
> Near the lake is a mountain that *rises* into the clouds.

real, really *Real* is an adjective meaning "actual; true." *Really* is an adverb meaning "in reality; in fact."

> Marcia explained her *real* reasons.   Does she *really* mean it?

set, sit *Set* usually is a transitive verb that means "to place." It can take a direct object. *Sit* is an intransitive verb that means "to occupy a seat or a specific place." It never takes a direct object.

> *Set* the oven to 350 degrees.   Shall we *sit* at this table?

than, then *Than* is used to introduce the second part of a comparison. *Then* means "next in order."

> Miguel is taller *than* Henry.   Wash the car and *then* wax it.

way refers to distance; *ways* is nonstandard and should not be used in writing.

> We walked all the *way* to Battery Park City.

Good spelling is important in all writing, from personal notes to formal business communications. You can take various steps to become a better speller. One of the best ways is to become familiar with many words by writing frequently. Keep a notebook for recording words you aren't sure how to spell. Look those words up in a dictionary. Use memory helps, called mnemonic devices, for words that give you trouble. For example, you might remember that *license* contains *lice*. Always proofread your writing carefully and learn the basic spelling rules that are listed here until their use becomes automatic.

The Final Silent *e*

When a suffix beginning with a vowel is added to a word ending in a silent *e*, the *e* is usually dropped.

approve + al = approval	desire + able = desirable
write + er = writer	pore + ous = porous

When the final silent *e* is preceded by *c* or *g*, the *e* is usually retained before a suffix beginning with *a* or *o*.

outrage + ous = outrageous	change + able = changeable
manage + able = manageable	notice + able = noticeable

When a suffix beginning with a consonant is added to a word ending in a silent *e*, the *e* is usually retained.

base + ment = basement	care + ful = careful
blame + less = blameless	lone + ly = lonely

The following words are exceptions: *truly, argument, judgment, wholly, awful.*

Words Ending in *y*

When a suffix is added to a word ending in *y* preceded by a consonant, the *y* is usually changed to *i*.

Two exceptions are: (1) When *-ing* is added, the *y* does not change. (2) Some one-syllable words do not change the *y*: *dryness, shyness.*

funny + er = funnier	luxury + ous = luxurious
party + es = parties	fuzzy + ness = fuzziness
carry + ed = carried	carry + ing = carrying

Improving Your
Spelling

827

When a suffix is added to a word ending in _y_ preceded by a vowel, the _y_ usually does not change.

enjoy + ing = enjoying   delay + ed = delayed
pay + able = payable   play + ful = playful

Exceptions: day + ly = daily, gay + ly = gaily

The Suffixes -_ness_ and -_ly_

When the suffix -_ly_ is added to a word ending in _l_, both _l_'s are retained. When -_ness_ is added to a word ending in _n_, both _n_'s are retained.

occasional + ly = occasionally
stubborn + ness = stubbornness

The Addition of Prefixes

When a prefix is added to a word, the spelling of the word remains the same.

dis + satisfied = dissatisfied   mis + spell = misspell
il + legible = illegible   trans + plant = transplant
im + movable = immovable   co + author = coauthor

Words with the "Seed" Sound

Only one English word ends in _sede: supersede_
Three words end in _ceed: exceed, proceed, succeed_
All other words ending in the sound of "seed" are spelled _cede: secede, accede, recede, concede, precede_

Words with _ie_ and _ei_

When the sound is long _e_ (ē), the word is spelled _ie_ except after _c_.

I _before_ E

thief   grief   niece
chief   achieve   relieve
yield   brief   piece

except after C

ceiling   receive   deceit
conceive   perceive   receipt

Exceptions: _either, neither, financier, weird, species, seize, leisure._

Doubling the Final Consonant

Words of one syllable ending in one consonant preceded by one vowel double the final consonant before adding a suffix beginning with a vowel.

1. The words below are the kind to which the rule applies.

   plan   sit   shun   red

These words double the final consonant if the suffix begins with a vowel.

   plan + ing = planning   shun + ed = shunned
   sit + er = sitter   red + est = reddest

2. The rule does not apply to the following one-syllable words because *two* vowels precede the final consonant.

   clear   speak   coat   shoot

With these words, the final consonant is *not* doubled before the suffix is added.

   clear + est = clearest   coat + ed = coated
   speak + er = speaker   shoot + ing = shooting

3. The final consonant is doubled in words of *more* than one syllable when these conditions are met.

   • When they end in one consonant preceded by one vowel.
   • When they are accented on the last syllable.

   oc cur'   com pel'   sub mit'   pa trol'

   • When the same syllable is accented in the new word formed by adding the suffix.

   oc cur' + rence = oc cur' rence
   com pel' + ing = com pel' ling
   sub mit' + ed = sub mit' ted
   pa trol' + er = pa trol' ler

Note   If the newly formed word is accented on a different syllable, the final consonant is not doubled.

   con fer' + ence = con' fer ence
   de fer' + ence = def' er ence
   re fer' + ence = ref' er ence
   re fer' + ee = ref er ee'

Improving Your
Spelling   **829**

A sentence diagram is a drawing that helps you understand how the parts of a sentence are related. In addition, diagraming sharpens your critical thinking skills by requiring you to analyze sentences, classify their parts, and determine relationships among those parts. The base for a sentence diagram is made up of a horizontal main line crossed by a short vertical line.

Subjects and Verbs

Place the simple subject on the horizontal main line to the left of the vertical line. Place the simple predicate, or verb, to the right. Capitalize only those words that are capitalized in the sentence. Do not use punctuation except for abbreviations.

Adam spoke.   Dogs were barking.

| Adam | spoke | | Dogs | were barking |

Interrogative Sentences

In an interrogative sentence, the subject often comes after the verb or after part of the verb phrase. In diagraming, remember to place the subject to the left of the vertical line and the verb to the right.

Do geese migrate?   Did something spill?

| geese | Do migrate | | something | Did spill |

Imperative Sentences

In an imperative sentence, the subject is usually not stated. Since commands are given to the person spoken to, the subject is understood to be *you*. To diagram an imperative sentence, place the understood subject *you* to the left of the vertical line. Then enclose *you* in parentheses. Place the verb to the right of the vertical line.

Listen!   Try!

| (you) | Listen | | (you) | Try |

Modifiers

Diagram adjectives and adverbs on slanted lines below the words they modify. If an adverb modifies an adjective or another adverb, write the adverb on an L-shaped line connected to the adjective or adverb that it modifies. Keep in mind that words like *not* and *never* are adverbs.

A small child anxiously joined the line.

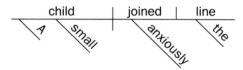

When two or more modifiers are connected by a conjunction, place the modifiers on slanted lines below the words they modify. Connect the slanted lines with a broken line and write the conjunction on it.

The warm but wet wind blew strongly.

Direct and Indirect Objects

In a diagram, place the direct object on the main line after the verb. Separate the direct object from the verb with a vertical line that does not extend below the main line. Place indirect objects below the verb on lines parallel to the main lines and connected to the main line by slanted lines, as you see here.

Lana bought a cassette. (*Direct Object*)

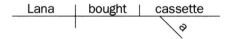

Lana bought her brother a cassette. (*Direct and Indirect Objects*)

Sentence
Diagraming **831**

Subject Complements

Place a predicate nominative or a predicate adjective on the main line after the verb. Separate the subject complement from the verb with a slanted line that extends in the direction of the subject.

Mr. Freed is our advisor. (*Advisor* is a predicate nominative.)

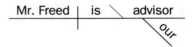

That tire looks flat. (*Flat* is a predicate adjective.)

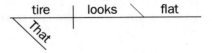

Sentences with Compound Parts

To diagram compound parts, place the parts on parallel horizontal lines as shown below. Then connect the parallel lines with a broken line. On the broken line, write the conjunction that connects the compound parts. Attach the compound parts to the main line using solid diagonal lines. The sentence below has a compound subject and a compound verb.

Sheep and goats roam the mountains and graze freely.

Compound Direct Objects and Indirect Objects   To diagram compound direct objects or indirect objects, place the objects on parallel horizontal lines connected with a broken line. Write the conjunction on the line. Attach the compound parts to the main line as shown in the sentence at the top of the next page.

Their mother gave Brendan and Sandra new guitar strings and picks. (*Compound indirect and direct objects.*)

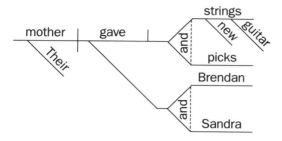

Prepositional Phrases

Draw a slanted line below the word the phrase modifies. From the slanted line, draw a line parallel to the main line. Place the preposition on the slanted line and the object of the preposition on the parallel line. Words that modify the object of the preposition are placed on slanted lines below the object.

The guests on the show talked about their new movies.

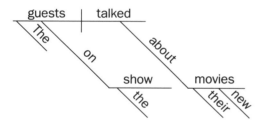

If a preposition has a compound object, place the objects on parallel lines as shown below.

We fished for trout and bass.

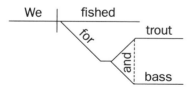

Sentence
Diagraming   **833**

Gerunds and Gerund Phrases

To diagram a gerund, place it on a line drawn as a step (⌐╚). Put the step on a forked line (人) that stands on the main line. The placement of the forked line varies and is determined by whether the gerund or gerund phrase is used as a subject, a direct object, a predicate nominative, or the object of a preposition. If the gerund phrase includes a direct object or modifiers, place those on lines as shown below.

Telling jokes will cheer us up. (*Gerund phrase used as subject*)

We thanked Valerie for helping us.
(*Gerund phrase used as object of a preposition*)

Participles and Participial Phrases

To diagram a participle, place the participle on an angled line below the word it modifies. If the participial phrase includes a direct object, separate the object and the participle with a vertical line. Place modifiers on slanted lines below words they modify.

Diving dramatically, the right-fielder made the catch.

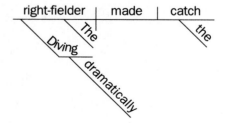

Infinitives and Infinitive Phrases

To diagram an infinitive, place the infinitive on an angled line. Write the word *to* on the slanted part and write the verb on the horizontal part of the angled line. Put the angled line on a forked line that stands on the main line. The placement shows how the infinitive or infinitive phrase is used in the sentence. In the following sentence the infinitive is a direct object.

Alexander liked to swim.

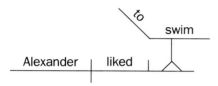

Appositives and Appositive Phrases

To diagram an appositive, place the appositive in parentheses after the word it identifies or explains. Place modifiers on slanted lines below the appositive.

Our neighbor, Ms. Frazer, writes historical novels.

Adjective Clauses

To diagram an adjective clause, place the clause on its own horizontal line below the main line and diagram it as if it were a sentence. Use a broken line to connect the relative pronoun in the adjective clause to the word that the clause modifies.

The people who run the space program are in Houston.

Sentence
Diagraming   **835**

Adverb Clauses

To diagram an adverb clause, place the clause on its own horizontal line below the main line and diagram the clause as if it were a sentence. Use a broken line to connect the adverb clause to the word it modifies. Write the subordinating conjunction on the broken line.

When Carlos was twelve, he moved to New York.

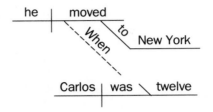

Noun Clauses

To diagram a noun clause, place the clause on a separate line that is attached to the main line with a forked line. The placement of the forked line in the diagram shows how the noun clause is used in the sentence. Diagram the word introducing the noun clause according to its function in the clause.

What you need is a sense of humor.
(*Noun clause used as subject*)

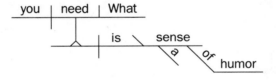

Many people say that good times are coming.
(*Noun clause used as object of verb*)

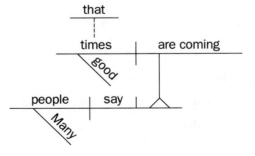

Compound Sentences

To diagram a compound sentence, place the independent clauses on parallel horizontal lines. Leave enough room to attach modifiers where they belong. Then use a broken line with a step to connect the verb in one clause to the verb in the other clause. Write the conjunction on the step. If the clauses are joined by a semicolon, leave the step blank.

The wait was a long one, but we had a great conversation.

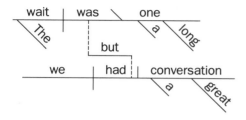

Complex Sentences

To diagram a complex sentence, decide whether the subordinate clause is an adjective clause, an adverb clause, or a noun clause. Then follow the rule for diagraming that kind of clause.

Compound-Complex Sentences

To diagram a compound-complex sentence, diagram the independent clauses first. Then attach the subordinate clause or clauses to the words they modify. Leave enough room to attach a subordinate clause where it belongs.

I would have bought the book that you recommended, but the clerk could not find it anywhere.

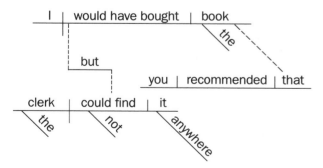

Sentence
Diagraming   **837**

ANALOGY a comparison usually used to explain an idea or support an argument. For example, an analogy for how a government works might be created by comparing government to a family.

ANALYSIS a way of thinking that involves taking apart, examining, and explaining a subject or idea.

ANECDOTE a brief story, usually told as an example to illustrate a point.

ARGUMENT speaking or writing that expresses a position or states an opinion and provides the evidence or reasons to support it—often presented in the context of opposing points of view.

AUDIENCE the readers or listeners to whom any discourse is directed.

AUTOBIOGRAPHY a biography (life story) told by the person whose life it is.

BIBLIOGRAPHY a list of sources used or recommended (articles, books, encyclopedia) in a research paper or report.

BRAINSTORMING a way of gathering many ideas by quickly listing them as they occur, without judging their usefulness.

CAUSE AND EFFECT a strategy for analyzing a subject by examining the reasons for specific actions or events or the consequences or results of certain causes.

CHRONOLOGICAL organized according to time sequence.

CLARITY the quality of being clear or as easy to understand as possible.

CLASSIFICATION a type of writing that involves systematically grouping items by some system or principle; frequently involves defining or comparing and contrasting items or groups of items.

CLICHÉ a phrase, figure of speech, or idea used so often that it is predictable, showing little imagination or thought, as in "pretty as a picture."

CLUSTERING a brainstorming technique that shows how ideas are connected to one another; gives a quick map of thoughts about a topic.

COHERENCE connectedness; a sense that parts hold together; an essay is coherent when its parts fit together logically and are linked by connecting words and phrases.

COLLABORATION working with other people; giving others support and advice; helping others solve problems.

COLLOQUIAL conversational; linguistically informal; the way people ordinarily speak in conversation.

COMPARISON AND CONTRAST a strategy for thinking or writing that involves explaining, defining, or evaluating subjects by showing how they resemble and differ from each other or from some standard for evaluation.

CONNOTATION the attitudes and feelings associated with a word or idea as opposed to its dictionary definition. The word "cheap" differs from "inexpensive" in its connotations.

CONTEXT the setting or situation in which something happens; the parts of a statement that occur just before and just after a specific word and help determine its meaning.

CONTROVERSY a disagreement, often one that has attracted public interest.

COUNTERARGUMENT a refutation; an argument made to oppose (counter) another argument.

CRITICISM discourse (usually an essay) that analyzes something (usually a literary or artistic work) in order to evaluate how it does or does not succeed in communicating its meaning or achieving its purposes.

CUBING a method for discovering ideas about a topic by using six strategies (in any order) to investigate it: describe it, compare it, associate it, analyze it, apply it, argue for or against it.

DEDUCTIVE REASONING deriving a specific conclusion by reasoning from a general premise.

DENOTATION the literal meaning of a word, without its connotations.

DESCRIPTION an account, usually giving a dominant impression and emphasizing sensory detail, of what it is like to experience some object, scene, or person.

DIALECT a form of language (usually regional) differing from the standard language in pronunciation, word choice, and syntax. Southern American English or New England English or Australian English are dialects of English.

DIALOGUE the spoken conversation of fictional characters or actual persons as it is presented in a novel, story, poem, play, or essay.

DOCUMENTATION naming the documents or other sources used to provide the information reported in an essay or other discourse; usually cited in footnotes or in parentheses.

ELABORATION the development of an argument, description, narration, or explanation with facts, statistics, sensory details, evidence, and other support.

EXPOSITION writing that explains an idea or teaches a process.

EXPRESSIVE characterized by expression; describing discourse full of meaning or feeling; often personal writing used by writers to explore ideas.

FICTION made-up or imaginary happenings, as opposed to statements of fact or nonfiction. Short stories and novels are fiction, even though they may be based on real events. Essays, scientific articles, biographies, news stories are nonfiction.

FIGURATIVE LANGUAGE language that uses such figures of speech as similes, metaphors, and personification to show one thing as if it were something else.

FORMAL LANGUAGE language in which rules of grammar and vocabulary standards are carefully observed; used in textbooks, reports, and other formal communications.

FREEWRITING way of discovering what you know or think or feel by writing rapidly, without stopping, without editing, and without looking back (until you finish) at what you've written.

GENERALIZATION a statement expressing a principle or drawing a conclusion based on examples or instances.

GLEANING a method of picking up ideas by observing events and by scanning through newspapers, magazines, and books and talking to others in order to find material to write about or to use in writing.

GRAPHIC ORGANIZER   a method for visually organizing a complex body of information; includes charts, graphs, outlines, clusters, and tree diagrams.

IMAGERY   figurative language and descriptions used to produce mental images.

INFERENCE   a logically valid conclusion derived by reasoning from facts.

INTERPRETATION   to explain the meaning of any text, set of facts, object, gesture, or event. To *interpret* something is to try to make sense of it.

INVISIBLE WRITING   writing done with a dimmed computer screen or an empty ball point pen on two sheets of paper with carbon paper between them.

JARGON   the special language and terminology used by people in the same profession or who share specialized interests; for example, sportswriters, computer programmers, musicians.

JOURNAL   a record of thoughts and impressions mainly for personal use.

KNOWLEDGE INVENTORY   a list of statements or phrases representing what a writer knows about a topic, including questions to direct further research.

LEARNING LOG   a journal or notebook in which a student records questions, problems, and state of understanding about a particular subject as it is studied and learned.

LOOPING   a process for discovering ideas by freewriting on a topic, stopping to find promising ideas, then producing another freewrite on that subject, repeating the loop several times.

MAPPING   See Clustering.

MEMOIR   an account of true events told by a narrator who witnessed or participated in the events; usually focusing on the personalities and actions of persons other than the writer.

METAPHOR   a figure of speech describing something by speaking of it as if it were something else, without using such terms as "like" or "as" to signal the relationship. To say "the meeting was a circus" is to speak *metaphorically*.

MONOLOGUE a speech by one person without interruption by other voices. A *dramatic monologue* reveals the personality and experience of a person through a long speech.

MOOD feeling about a scene or subject created for a reader by a writer's selection of words and details; the mood of a piece of writing may be suspenseful, mysterious, peaceful, fearful, and so on.

NARRATION discourse that tells a story—either made up or true. Some common types of narrative are biographies, short stories, and novels.

NONSEXIST LANGUAGE language free from gender bias, representing men and women as equals and showing both sexes in traditional and nontraditional roles.

PARAPHRASING rewording the meaning expressed in something spoken or written, but retaining all of the original ideas.

PARENTHETICAL DOCUMENTATION the placement of citations or other documentation within the text and in parentheses.

PEER RESPONSE response to one's writing provided by other writers who are peers or classmates rather than teachers or other editors.

PERSONIFICATION a figure of speech in which objects, events, abstract ideas, or animals are given human characteristics. "Water hates fire" or "the evening wind whispered gently" are examples of personification.

PERSUASION discourse focused on influencing a listener or reader to support a point of view or take an action. Examples of persuasive discourse would include political speeches, advertisements, position papers, editorials, and courtroom speeches by lawyers.

PLAGIARISM presenting the ideas or words of another as if they were one's own. Writers who use the ideas of others will avoid plagiarism by acknowledging their sources.

POINT OF VIEW the perspective from which the reader views the events in a story; determines what the narrator can know and tell about.

PORTFOLIO a holder (usually a large folder) in which writing is stored for future reference and review and can be presented for evaluation.

PRECIS a short summary of an essay, story, or speech, capturing only the essential elements.

PROOFREADING usually the last stage of the revising or editing process, when a writer checks work to discover typographical and other errors.

PROPAGANDA discourse aimed entirely at persuading an audience, often containing distortions of truth. Usually refers to manipulative political discourse.

PROSE the usual language of speech and writing, lacking the special properties of meter and form that define poetry; any language use that isn't poetry.

SENSORY DETAIL descriptive detail based on sensory experience—experiences associated with touch, smells, tastes, sights, and sounds.

SIMILE a figure of speech comparing two things that are essentially unlike, signaling the comparison with such words as "like" or "as."

SPATIAL ORDER a pattern of organization based on space or position, used in descriptive writing; for example, a scene may be described from foreground to background, from left to right, from top to bottom.

STYLE the distinctive features of a literary or artistic work that characterize a particular individual, group, period, or school.

SUMMARY the theme or central idea of a larger work presented in brief form.

SYMBOL a word, object, or action that suggests something else by association, resemblance, or convention. For example, a flag can stand for a nation; a withered plant may suggest a failing relationship.

SYNTHESIS the putting together of separate elements to form a coherent whole.

THEME the underlying idea or central concern of a work of art or literature.

THESIS the main point of an essay or other discourse.

TONE the writer's attitude toward a subject—detached, ironic, serious, angry, and so on.

TOPIC SENTENCE a statement expressing the main point of a paragraph; the idea (stated or unstated) around which a paragraph is organized.

TRANSITION in discourse, passage from one subject to another, usually marked by transitional words or phrases such as "next," "furthermore," or "on the other hand."

TREE DIAGRAM (also known as an idea tree or spider map) a graphic way of showing the relationships among ideas; particularly useful in generating ideas.

TRITE PHRASE a phrase used so commonly that it lacks precise meaning and suggests a lack of imagination, thought, or originality.

UNITY oneness; the concept that in a written work all the parts must form a single whole, held together by a central theme or idea.

VOICE the "sound" of a writer's work; determined by stylistic choices such as sentence structure, diction, and tone.

Imagery, 841
Imperative sentence, 499
  diagraming, 830
  end marks and, 769
  subject in, 509
Implied main idea, 362
Implied topic sentence, 349
Importance, organization by order of, 65,
  166, 332
Improper appeals to emotion, 454–55
in, 659
Incidents
  for elaboration of ideas, 353
  for introductions, 342
Incomplete thoughts, and sentence
  fragments, 524
in contrast to, 142, 334
Indefinite articles, 620–21
Indefinite pronouns, 561, 706–7
  agreement with, 566, 706–7
  as antecedents, 566–67
  subject-verb agreement and, 706–7
Independent clauses, 721–22
  in complex sentences, 738
  in compound-complex sentences, 739
  in compound sentences, 737
  in simple sentences, 736
Index cards
  for note cards, 274
  for source cards, 273
Indexes, 271, 272
Indirect objects, 513–14
  diagraming, 831, 832–33
  nouns as, 536
  noun clauses as, 733
  pronouns as, 553
Indirect question, punctuation of, 769
Indirect quotations, 795
Inferences, 462–63, 841
Inferring word meanings from context,
  438–41
Infinitive phrases, 203–5, 687
  diagraming, 835
Infinitives, 686–87
  defined, 686
  diagraming, 835
  split, 687
Informal diction, 407
Informal English, 409–10

Information; *See also* Library resources
  dialogue to reveal, 434
  gathering and developing, 17–18
  organizing, 275–76
  sources of, 271–72, 476–77
  transitions that signal more, 367
Informative/Classificatory writing
  comparison and contrast, 138–42
Informative/Descriptive writing
  description, 58–71
  field notes, 72–75
Informative Exposition
  analysis, 147–71
  assessment essays, 304–5
  cause-effect writing, 162–67
  classification, 117–42
  comparison and contrast, 138–42
  consumer report, 192–96
  definition, 118–28
  describing a process, 148–61
  essay of advice, 178–91
  extended metaphor, 132–36
  flowchart, 168–71
  problems and solutions, 198–202
  research report, 266–86
  short answer essays, 296–303
  synthesis, 177–202
Informative Exposition, ideas for writing,
  814
Informative/Narrative writing
  describing a process, 148–61, 313
  flowchart, 168–71
Initials, punctuating, 769
Inside address, 819
Inspiration, and writing haiku, 78
instead, 142
Institutions, capitalization of, 755
Integrated writing and language concepts
  and skills. *See* Prewriting; Drafting;
  Revising; Publishing and presenting
Intensifiers, 626
Intensive pronouns, 556
Interest inventory, 318
Interjections, 669, 674, 676, 770
  exclamation points with, 669
Interpretation, 841
  as a test prompt, 299
Interrogative pronouns, 562
Interrogative sentences, 499, 508–9
  diagraming, 830

S

Sacred writings, capitalization of, 750
Salutation, for business letters, 819
Saying back, 822
Scanning, 463
School subjects, capitalization of, 756
Science, ideas for writing about, 815
Scotch-Irish influence on music, 255
Second-person point of view, 430
Second-person pronouns, 549
Sections, capitalization of, 753
"Seed" sound, spelling rules and, 828
Self-assessment, 36, 40, 66, 71, 94, 126, 155,
    184, 190–91, 216, 245, 279, 378
Semicolons, 772, 785
    in compound sentences, 737
    and conjunctive adverbs, 187
    and correcting run-on sentences, 528
    in series, 785
Senses, using, 75, 78, 122, 384
Sensory details, 62–64, 843
    and elaboration of ideas, 352
Sensory language, 65
Sentence completion, on tests, 488
Sentence composing
    analyzing sentences, 53–55
    author expansions, 306–7
    delayed modifiers, 113–15
    infinitive phrases, 203–5
    introductory modifiers, 81–83
    introductory prepositional phrases, 173–75
    inverted word order, 143–45
    relative clauses, 261–63
    skill review, 290–93
    See also Combining sentences
Sentence diagraming, 830–37
Sentence fragments, 38, 524–25, 526, 742
Sentence outline, 816
Sentences
    adding words and information to,
        421, 693
    analyzing, 53–55
    capitalization of first word in, 761
    combining, 419–20, 421, 425, 427–28
    complete, 497, 502
    complex, 416, 738
    compound, 416, 737
    compound-complex, 416, 739
    compound sentence parts, 517–18
    correcting problem, 38, 391–92, 394–95,
        396–97
    declarative, 499
    diagraming, 830–37
    empty, 391–92
    exclamatory, 499
    imperative, 499
    interrogative, 499
    inverted, 508, 709
    objects of verbs, 512–14
    overloaded and padded, 396–97
    predicates, 503–4
    run-on, 528
    simple sentences, 416, 736–37
    simple subjects and predicates, 503
    stringy sentences, 394–95
    subject complements, 515–17
    with subjects in unusual order, 508–9
    types of, 416
    varying, 416–18, 510
    and voice, 405–6
    See also Sentence composing; Sentence
        structure
Sequence
    and cause-and-effect, 166
    relationships, 462
Series
    commas in, 772
    semicolons in, 785
set, sit, 614, 826
Setting, in a personal narrative, 92
Sharing, 241, 401–2, 822. *See also*
    Publishing and presenting; Sharing
    techniques
Sharing techniques
    brainstorming, 60, 121, 135, 150, 211,
        323–24, 329, 457, 838
    discussion, 324–25
Ships, capitalization of, 756
Short answer tests, taking, 486
Short research paper, 266–86
    drafting strategies, 277–79
    prewriting and exploring, 268–71
    researching a topic, 271–76
    revising, 279–82
Short stories
    capitalization of titles, 762
    punctuation of titles, 800
Short stories, responding to. *See*
    Literary/Narrative writing

Acknowledgments for Teacher's Edition

34, 280: Universal Press Syndicate, Inc: For CALVIN AND HOBBES cartoons by Bill Watterson. Reprinted by permission of Universal Press Syndicate, Inc. All rights reserved. **61**: Curtis Brown Ltd.: For an excerpt from "You Need to be Upstairs" from *Gone: A Thread of Stories* by Rumor Godden. Copyright 1940, 1944, 1947, 1949, 1953, 1954 ,©1959, 1968 by Rumor Godden. Reprinted by permission of Curtis Brown Ltd. **128, 189, 286**: Cartoons reprinted by permission of Frank Cotham. **220**: Cartoon reprinted by permission of Randy Jay Glasbergen. **301**: Cartoon by Peter Steiner. **584**: Wesleyan University Press: For "The Base Stealer" reprinted from *The Orb Weaver*, Wesleyan University Press. By permission of University Press of New England. Copyright © 1948 by Robert Francis. **761**: Liveright Publishing Corporation: For an excerpt from "in Just-" from *Tulips and Chimneys* by E. E. Cummings, edited by George James Firmage. Copyright 1923, 1925, renewed 1951, 1953 by E. E. Cummings. Copyright© 1973, 1976 by Trustees for the E. E. Cummings Trust. Copyright © 1973, 1976 by George James Firmage. Reprinted by permission of Liveright Publishing Corporation. The authors and editors have made every effort to trace the ownership of all copyrighted materials found in this book and to make full acknowledgment for their use.

ACKNOWLEDGMENTS

Sources of Quoted Materials

28: Macmillan Publishing Company: For an excerpt from *Be True to Your School* by Bob Greene; copyright © 1987 by John Deadline Enterprises, Inc.; reprinted by permission of Atheneum Publishers, an imprint of Macmillan Publishing Company. **76:** Charles E. Tuttle Co., Inc.: For "Angry, I came home" by Ryota, and "Living in the town" by Issa, from *The Japanese Haiku;* copyright © 1957 by Charles E. Tuttle Co., Inc.; reprinted by permission of Charles E. Tuttle Co., Inc. City Lights Books: For "Nodding against the wall, the flowers sneeze," from *Scattered Poems* by Jack Kerouac; copyright © 1970, 1971 by The Estate of Jack Kerouac; reprinted by permission of City Lights Books. Macmillan Publishing Company: For "The Peacock" by José Juan Tablada, from *The Yellow Canary Whose Eye Is So Black,* edited and translated by Cheli Durán; copyright © 1977 by Cheli Durán Ryan; reprinted by permission of Macmillan Publishing Company. Sally Stolte: For "Fall" by Sally Andresen. **86:** St. Martin's Press, Inc.: For an excerpt from *Act One: An Autobiography* by Moss Hart; copyright © 1959 by Catherine Carlisle Hart and Joseph M. Hyman, Trustees; copyright renewed © 1987; reprinted by permission of St. Martin's Press, Inc. **132:** Alfred A. Knopf, Inc.: For "Mother to Son," from *Selected Poems of Langston Hughes* by Langston Hughes; copyright 1926 by Alfred A. Knopf, Inc., renewed 1954 by Langston Hughes; reprinted by permission of Alfred A. Knopf, Inc. **148:** The New York Times: For "Slice of Life" by Russell Baker, as appeared in *The New York Times,* November 24, 1974; copyright © 1974 by The New York Times Company; reprinted by permission. **178:** International Paper: For "How to Read Faster" by Bill Cosby, adapted from the advertisement "Power of the Printed Word"; reprinted by permission of International Paper. **192:** Consumers Union: For an adaptation of "The Nuttiest Peanut Butter," from *Consumer Reports,* September 1990; copyright © 1990 by Consumers Union of United States, Inc., Mount Vernon, NY 10553; adapted by permission from Consumer Reports, September 1990. **198:** Harold Matson Company, Inc.: For an excerpt from *The Torn Invitation* by Norman Katkov; copyright 1952, © 1980 by Norman Katkov. Reprinted by permission of Harold Matson Company, Inc. **205:** Alan S. Honig: For an excerpt from *Man of La Mancha* by Joe Darion; copyright © 1965, words Joe Darion, music Mitch Leigh, Andrew Scott, Inc., Helena Music; reprinted by permission of Alan S. Honig, Administrator, *Man of La Mancha.* **208:** Susan Swartz: For "Non-Jocks Deserve a Chance" by Susan Swartz, as appeared in the *Santa Barbara News-Press,* September 20, 1988; reprinted by permission of Susan Swartz. **222:** Aurie A. Pennick: For "Letter to the Editor" by Aurie A. Pennick, as appeared in the *Chicago Tribune,* February 1990; reprinted by permission of Aurie A. Pennick. **228:** Chicago Tribune: For an excerpt from *"The Piano Lesson* hits a powerful chord on racial justice" by Richard Christiansen, as appeared in the *Chicago Tribune,* January 17, 1989; copyright © 1989 Chicago Tribune Company; all rights reserved; used with permission. **235:** HarperCollins Publishers: For an excerpt from *Why We Can't Wait* by Martin Luther King, Jr.; copyright © 1963, 1964 by Martin Luther King, Jr.; reprinted by permission of HarperCollins Publishers. **238:** William Stafford: For "Traveling Through the Dark," from *Stories That Could Be True: New and Collected Poems* by William Stafford; copyright © 1973 by William Stafford; reprinted by permission of William Stafford. **250:** Random House, Inc.: For an excerpt from "Raymond's Run," from *Gorilla, My Love* by Toni Cade Bambara; copyright © 1972 by Toni Cade Bambara; reprinted by permission of Random House, Inc. **256:** USA TODAY: For "Oil potential spawns fears in Alaska tribe" by Bill Nichols, as appeared in *USA TODAY,* August 29, 1990; copyright © 1990 by *USA TODAY;* reprinted with permission. **266:** Beacon Press: For an excerpt from *The Broken Spears* by Miguel Leon-Portilla; copyright © 1962 by Beacon Press; reprinted by permission of Beacon Press. **289:** Farrar, Straus & Giroux, Inc. For an excerpt from *Miss Thistlebottom's Hobgoblins* by Theodore M. Bernstein; copyright © 1971 by Theodore M. Bernstein. Reprinted by permission of Farrar, Straus & Giroux, Inc. **412:** Henry Holt and Company, Inc.: For excerpt from "Fire and Ice" by Robert Frost, from *The Poetry of Robert Frost,* edited by Edward Connery Lathem; copyright 1923, © 1969 by Holt, Rinehart and Winston; copyright 1951 by Robert Frost; reprinted by permission of Henry Holt and Company, Inc. **523:** Omni Publications International, Ltd.: For "Writer's Rules" by Scot Morris, from *Omni Magazine,* Vol. 9, No. 8, May 1987; copyright © 1987 by Scot Morris; reprinted by permission of Omni Publications International, Ltd. The authors and editors have made every effort to trace the ownership of all copyrighted selections found in this book and to make full acknowledgment for their use.

Illustration and Photography Credits:

Commissioned Illustrations: Robert Bergin: **791;** YoungSook Cho: **350, 514, 699;** Bradley H. Clark: **342;** Mark DaGrossa: **752;** Mark DaGrossa, Gary Sanders: **178/179;** Brenda DeNoyer: **108/109;** Terri Melia Hamlin: **415, 601, 760;** Christopher Herrfurth: **56, 236, 310, 739;** James Higgins: **viii, 58/59, 148/149, 255, 385, 559, 619, 680;** Pinnacle Design Group: **275, 557, 566;** Gary Sanders: **266/267;** Leslie Staub Shattuck: **12, 24, 46, 47, 95, 172, 196, 226, 227, 232,**

250/251, 254, 288, 302, 343, 374, 402, 513, 527, 538, 544, 551, 554, 560, 571, 627, 655, 663, 701, 709, 768, 770, 771, 798; Christopher Vallo: 26, 69, 151, 176, 181, 294, 429, 579, 661, 668, 685, 717; Rachel L. Witt: 33. **Assignment Photography:** France Photography: **xiii,** *l & r* 27, 28/29, 42/43, 48, *r & b* 85, 102/103, 108/109, 132/133, *t* 162, *tr & br* 177, 192/193, 198/199, 207, 208/209, 222/223, 296/297; Patterson Graphics, Inc.: **vii, xiii, 31, 45, 95, 130, 279, 323, 335, 355, 385, 403, 471, 671. Photos and Illustrations: vi:** © The Phillips Collection, Washington, D.C. (detail); **x:** Orion, FPG; **xi:** Lee Christiansen; **ix:** © Joe Viesti, Viesti Associates, Inc.; **xii:** Bonnie Timmons, The Image Bank; **xiv:** Art Resource; **xv:** Philippe Weisbecker; **1:** © The Phillips Collection, Washington, D.C.; **9:** © Breton Littlehale, National Geographic Society; **12:** National Air and Space Museum; **15:** *l* AP/Wide World Photos; *r* Culver Pictures, Inc.; **20:** Jim Koernick, Experimental Aircraft Association; **24:** Peter de Seve; **27:** *br* Painting by John Dawson, © National Geographic Society; **33:** *l* Jim Whitmer Photography; *r* Stuart Cohen, Comstock **35:** Superstock; **37:** J. Myers, H. Armstrong Roberts; **40:** Robin Feld; **41:** Don Smetzer, TSW-Click; **45:** *b* © Universal Press Syndicate; **46:** Jan Baker; **47:** Michael Philip Manheim, The Stock Solution; **49:** Painting by John Dawson, © National Geographic Society; **52:** Anita Kunz; **57:** *tr* H. Armstrong Roberts; *br* Kimbell Art Museum, Fort Worth, Texas; **61:** William H. Blahd; **63:** Worcester Art Museum, Worcester, Massachusetts; **65:** © Joe Viesti, Viesti Associates, Inc.; **68:** Clint Clemens; **72/73:** H. Armstrong Roberts; **76/77:** Kimbell Art Museum, Fort Worth, Texas; **79:** Hans-Peter Dimke, The Image Bank; **80:** Frank D. Denman, Courtesy of the Isamu Noguchi Foundation, Inc.; **84:** © James Thurber; **85:** *l* The Granger Collection; **87:** The Granger Collection; **88:** Nelson C. McClary; **90:** © Joe Viesti, Viesti Associates, Inc.; **97:** Globus Brothers, The Stock Market; **99:** Anthony Russo; **100:** Dugald Stermer; **105:** Ann Leslie, FPG; **106:** Jim Whitmer Photography; **111:** David Lui; **116:** Chuck Kuhn, Nike and Jump; **117:** *l* Scala, Art Resource; *tr* The Library of Congress; *br* Don Hamilton Photography; **118/119:** Ulf Sjostedt, FPG; **119:** Scala, Art Resource; **123:** Orion Press, FPG; **124:** Ulf Sjostedt, FPG; **127:** John Zielinski; **131:** Vivienne Flesher; **133:** The Library of Congress; **136:** Floyd Holdman, The Stock Solution; **137:** Sam Opee, FPG; **138/139:** *l* The Metropolitan Museum of Art, Sansbury/Mills Fund, 1973; *r* Don Hamilton Photography; **141:** Comstock; **146:** © 1960 Loew's Inc. & Galaxy Films, Inc. 1988 Turner Entertainment Co. & Galaxy Films, Inc.; **147:** *tr* Movie Still Archives, FPG; *br* Sal Maimon, Superstock; **155:** Reprinted with special permission of King Features Syndicate; **156:** William E. Whitehurst, The Stock Market; **160:** Lee Christiansen; **162:** Ray Shaw, Globe Photos; **163:** Movie Still Archives, FPG; **166:** UPI, Bettmann; **167:** *t* Millard Sharp, TSW-Click; *b* Raymond G. Barns, TSW-Click; *c* TSW-Click; **168/169:** Sal Maimone, Superstock; **172:** Mike & Carol Warner, Comstock; **176:** © Will & Deni McIntyre, Science Source, Photo Researchers; **183:** Ron Sherman, TSW-Click; **185:** *c* Melissa Grimes; **190:** Bonnie Timmons, The Image Bank; **191:** Reprinted by permission of UFS, Inc.; **196:** Mercedes McDonald; **201:** John Cuneo; **206:** © Al Hirschfeld; **207:** *br* courtesy The Goodman Theatre; **213:** Kobal Collection, Superstock; **215:** HarperCollins Publishers; **218:** Hubertus Kanus, Superstock; **226:** M.R. Tingley, London Free Press; **227:** *t* Reagan Bradshaw, The Image Bank; **228/229:** Jeffrey Sylvester, FPG; **228:** courtesy The Goodman Theatre; **229:** courtesy The Goodman Theatre; **232:** *t* Melissa Grimes; **236:** Superstock; **237:** *l* Joseph Povereskin, TSW-Click; *br* H. Darr Beiser, USA Today; **238/239:** Joseph Povereskin, TSW-Click; **241:** Victoria & Albert Museum, Art Resource; **247:** Steve Bjorkman; **253:** Marc Rosenthal; **257:** *all* H. Darr Beiser, USA Today; **260:** Phil Marco Productions, Inc; **264:** Peter Tengler; **265:** *l* Anthropology Museum, Comstock; *r* The Phillips Collection, Washington, D.C.; **267:** *t* Anthropology Museum, Comstock; *b* Kenneth Garrett, FPG; **271:** Robert Brosch Archival Photography; **275:** T. Tracy, FPG; **277:** Philippe Weisbecker; **285:** Aaron Jones; **287:** The Phillips Collection, Washington, D.C.; **288:** Mick Wiggins, Jacqueline Dedell, Inc.; **295:** Ron Thomas, FPG; **298:** Superstock; **300:** Springer, Bettmann Film Archive; **302:** The Bettmann Archive; **304:** Doris De Witt, TSW-Click; **305:** Ron Thomas, FPG; **308:** © 1990 ARS N.Y./ SPADEM, Scala, Art Resource; **310:** Drawing by Booth: © 1976 The New Yorker Magazine; **314:** The Museum of Modern Art, New York; **317:** Andy Zito, The Image Bank; **318:** Jim Whitmer Photography; **321:** Chris Mooney, FPG; **324:** Julius Ciss, The Image Bank; **326:** Superstock; **327:** *l* Finley Holiday Films; *c* Comstock; *r* The Bettmann Archive: **337:** Billy Morrow Jackson, National Gallery of Art, Washington, Gift of the artist (Date: 1967; Hardboard; 1.221 × 1.829 (48 × 72 in.)); **344:** Jean/Francois Podeuin, The Image Bank; **347:** Ansel Adams Publishing Rights Trust; **362:** Superstock; **365:** © Chronicle Features; **367:** National Gallery of Art, Washington (Date: c. 1872/1883; Millboard; 0.300 × 0.350 (11 3/4 × 13 3/4 in.)); **369:** D. Degnan, H. Armstrong Roberts; **374:** *t* Jeannie Meeds Wilson; **378:** © 1990 ARS N.Y./SPADEM; **381:** Kevin D. MacPherson, The Image Bank; **383:** © Universal Press Syndicate; **387:** *r* The Pace Gallery, New York; *l* Sue Cunningham, TSW-Click; **388:** UPI, The Bettmann Archive; **391:** The Telegraph Colour Library, FPG; **394:** Brad Holland; **400:** The Granger Collection; **402:** *r* © 1990 Gary Brod; **404:** *all* © Universal Press Syndicate; **407:** Marie Cosindas; **408:** Whitney Museum of American Art; **410:** Kobal Collection, Superstock; **418:** Scala, Art Resource; **422:** Paula Court; **426:** Museum of American Folk Art; **429:** Barbara Kraus, TSW-Click; **433:** Superstock; **437:** Hearst Publications; **441:** Mary Ellen Mark/Library; **443:** *l* UPI, Bettmann Newsphotos; *r* The White House; **445:** © Universal Press Syndicate; **448:** © 1990 ARS N.Y./SPADEM, Scala, Art Resource; **454:** Joe Munroe, Life